Politics and Statecraft
in the Kingdom of Greece
1833-1843

POLITICS
AND STATECRAFT
IN THE
KINGDOM OF GREECE
1833-1843

John Anthony Petropulos

PRINCETON, NEW JERSEY
PRINCETON UNIVERSITY PRESS
1968

In Memory of my Mother
and
For my Father

Preface

THIS BOOK, originally a doctoral dissertation, is an exploratory study of
political groups during the first decade of the kingdom of Greece. The
reader may question the application of the term "party" to these political
groupings. To be sure, they do not accord with the models derived from
Western European political experience, and, because of this, some Greek
scholars have refused to consider them as parties in any sense. But the
term is shorter and more convenient than "political group" and it was
regularly used by contemporaries. So long as one defines what "party"
means in this early context (as the Introduction and Chapter II do), the
use of the term seems justifiable as well as convenient.

The mass of Greek government papers for the early Othonian period
(1833-44), located in the General State Archives of Greece, were unavailable when I was doing the research for this book and are only now in the
process of being catalogued. Until this time-consuming process is completed and specialized monographs are written, a definitive study of
neither the early Othonian period nor the early political parties can be
written. Nor can a definitive study of the early Othonian period be
written without full research on the parties and their role in events. With
regard to the parties during the early Othonian period, this book is an
attempt to raise questions which may lead to further specialized research
and to provide tentative answers for further testing. It is also intended to
open new paths for research on the antecedents of the parties in the
1820s and even back in the Ottoman period, while at the same time
pointing the way to the next clearing operation—a study of the subsequent career and eventual demise of these particular parties after 1844.
With regard to the Othonian period as a whole, this book is intended to
demonstrate how the illumination of one facet of the period necessitates
a revised overview of the entire period. Although no attempt is made in
the book to compare the political experience of what was then a newly
independent state with that of more recent ones or to treat the subject
as a case study of political modernization, it is hoped that the book will
have some value for those interested in comparative politics and the
politics of modernization.

In the Appendix, I have included, besides a critical bibliography, a
selected prosopography, so that the reader may easily identify the large
number of Greeks mentioned in the book, and a translation, in its entirety,
of a very illuminating and hitherto unknown document with special
relevance to the parties. I wish to thank the directorate of the General
State Archives of Greece for permission to publish this document for the
first time. The translation of this document and the translations elsewhere
in the text and notes, unless otherwise specified, are mine.

Since the book deals with a society using a different calendar and alphabet from the West, a few remarks are necessary on citation of dates and transliteration of titles and names. In the nineteenth century, there was a twelve-day difference between the old-style (Julian) calendar, which the Greeks used, and the new-style (Gregorian) calendar of the West. In the text of the book, I have rendered all dates according to the new-style system, which the Greeks have since adopted. In the footnote references, I have cited dates just as they appear in the sources. When dates are rendered old-style, I have indicated this by having *o.s.* follow the cited date; when rendered according to both calendars, I have cited both dates, separating them with a virgule. Dates cited without any special notation should be assumed to be new-style.

Non-Greek titles have been cited in their respective languages and without English translation. Both in footnotes and bibliography, Greek titles have been cited first in transliteration, then in bracketed English translation. Abbreviated Greek titles, after first citations, have been rendered in English but with the continued use of brackets to indicate that the citation is in translation. The names of newspapers, which are cited in transliteration in both text and footnotes, are translated only in the bibliography.

I have transliterated Greek titles according to the system employed by the Library of Congress, which has become pretty much standard, but, with the exception of newspaper titles in text and footnotes, I have not included the *macron* sign over the long *e* standing for η (*eta*) or over the long *o* standing for ω (*omega*). I have attempted to employ the same system for Greek surnames (except in the Prosopography, where the *macron* is used). But I have made some modifications, primarily where strict adherence to the system would prevent the reader from approximating the Greek pronunciation of the names. I have, in the first place, exercised the option of rendering β (*beta*) with a *v* rather than a *b*. Other modifications are: *b* rather than *mp* for μπ (but only when μπ are initial letters of a name); *av* rather than *au* for the diphthong αυ; and *ev* or *ef* rather than *eu* for the diphthong ευ. In the early period of Greek independence, even the Greek spelling of some surnames was not standardized; for instance, one encounters both Palamides and Palamedes, Loidorikes and Lidorikes, Tzavelas and Tsavelas. In such cases, I have simply chosen arbitrarily. In the Prosopography of the Appendix, though nowhere else, I have included the *macron* sign over the long *e* (η) and the long *o* (ω), both to facilitate pronunciation and to assist those wishing to check such names in Greek reference works. My slightly modified system of transliteration has not been applied to the names of Greeks who chose to transliterate their names differently, e.g. Rangabe; and in the case of books written in the various languages of the West by Greek authors, the published rendering of their names has been left intact. Because he was a Russian subject, though of Greek origin, I have used *Catacazy*, a Westernized form of the Greek name Katakazes (other

Westernized forms frequently seen are Katakazi and Katakazy). Finally, in the case of Greek personal names familiar to the Western reader, I have retained the familiar form, e.g. Pericles rather than Perikles, Alexander rather than Alexandros, but Theokletos. I have deviated most from the Library of Congress system of transliteration in rendering Greek place names and terms. In the former case I have used, as much as possible, the spellings enjoying widest currency in general atlases and encyclopedias. In the latter case, especially Greek words of Turkish origin or, more precisely, Greek renderings of Turkish words, I have conformed to conventional, phonetic spellings. With respect to pure Greek words, I have adhered more closely to the Library of Congress system, but, with such words as *anaktovoulion* and *vouleuterion,* I have exercised the option of rendering β (*beta*) with a *v,* and I have used *enosis* instead of *henosis* because the former rendering has become common since the Cyprus question attracted world attention.

In this study, two distinct revolutions receive frequent mention—the great one of 1821-27, and the much briefer one of 1843. To distinguish between the two, without having to mention their dates on each occasion, I have capitalized all references—both noun and adjective—to the Revolution of 1821-27.

The major research for this book (in Greece and England) was made possible by a Rotary Foundation Fellowship, awarded and financed by Rotary International. In addition to all the Rotarians who contribute to this fund and all the officials in Evanston, Illinois, who assist Rotary Fellows, I wish to thank the Rotary Club of Lewiston-Auburn, Maine, which sponsored me for this fellowship, and Rotary District 285, which selected me for it. Their kindness and interest has continued ever since. Of course, the views expressed in the book are solely my own and in no way reflect on any of the individuals or institutions which helped me in its preparation.

The book is based largely on extensive research in the archival collections of a number of institutions—the Otho, Mavrokordatos, and Palamides Archives of the General State Archives of Greece, the Lontos Archive of the Benaki Museum, the Archives of the Greek Foreign Ministry, the Finlay Papers of the British School of Archeology, all in Athens, and the diplomatic correspondence of British envoys in Greece, located in the Public Record Office in London. To the governing authorities of these institutions I am grateful for permission to use the collections and to quote extensively in this book from them. More especially, I must acknowledge Constantine Diamantes, then assistant-director, now acting-director of the General State Archives, Angelos Papakostas, custodian of the archives of the Greek Foreign Ministry, and Eugenia Chadzidakis, wife of the director of the Benaki Museum—all three serious scholars who are thoroughly familiar with their respective collections and zealous in their efforts to advance scholarship. They were helpful beyond all expectation, not only in familiarizing me with their materials but also in helping decipher some of the almost unintelligible documents that came up from time to time. For their courteous attention I also thank Emmanuel Protopsaltes, then director of the General State Archives, and Hans Rall, director of the Bavarian Geheimes Hausarchiv in Munich.

Without access to the treasure-house of published material in the Gennadius Library, Athens, with its ideal working conditions, the research for this book would have been far more difficult and much less pleasant. Its greatest asset was its staff. Peter Topping, then director, was always eager to help and was able to do so because of his impressive knowledge of Greek history, his familiarity with the vast collection in his library, and his long experience in the Greek academic world. I am deeply grateful to him, as I am to Eurydice Demetracopoulou, assistant-director of the Library, who familiarized me with much valuable material and gave continuous assistance.

Librarians elsewhere deserve recognition as well. Theodore Alevizos, librarian in the Harvard Library system, assisted me there. Porter Dickinson, Floyd Merritt, and Lena Page, all in the reference department of the Amherst College Library, were unsparing with their help in locating references and securing books through interlibrary loan. I also wish to express my gratitude to Harriet Dorman, secretary of the History Department at Harvard University, for technical advice and moral support; Rosa White and Laura Williams for painstakingly typing final portions of the manuscript; the late Evelyn Cooley, whose patience, endurance, and typing proficiency saw the manuscript through a number of revisions; and Roy E. Thomas of Princeton University Press for thorough and painstaking editing. Thanks are also due the History Department of Amherst College for help and cooperation in a number of ways.

Finally, I reserve for special mention and thanks William Langer, who made valuable suggestions and criticisms after reading the manuscript in dissertation form, and Robert Lee Wolff, who as thesis advisor gave valuable advice and rigorous criticism, combined with needed encouragement and kind consideration at moments when they counted most. The debt I owe my wife for tolerance, encouragement and help during my long courtship with the book is beyond measure. Loving thanks go to Ansia for zealous sorting and to Stephanie for not doing any damage. But, ultimately, I owe my greatest debt of gratitude to my mother, who made the Greek tradition a living and vital thing, and to my father, who put it in broad perspective. The book is in memory of her and in honor of him.

J. A. P.

Amherst, Massachusetts
March 1967

Contents

Glossary

The English terms below have been included because they have a special connotation in the text beyond their accepted meaning.

Achaikon "party"—one of the two chief contending Peloponnesian Greek factions during Ottoman rule

agoyates, -es—muleteer

alliance—a horizontal association of equals

anaktovoulion—an unofficial body of palace officials, a nonstatutory royal cabinet as distinct from the statutory cabinet of government ministry heads

archchancellor (archikangellarios)—the highest governmental officer in Greece from June 1835–February 1837, namely Armansperg

archsecretary (archigrammateus)—(see archchancellor)

archon—an elected headman of a commune (see demogeron)

Areopagos—the highest court of appeal in Greece

armatolik—the position of armatolos; also the region officially policed and effectively controlled by an armatolos

armatolos, -oi—a military chieftain and mountaineer, often a former klepht-brigand, employed by the Ottoman authorities to guard important mountain passes and to fight brigands

autochthon—an indigenous Greek inhabitant of independent Greece, as distinct from an immigrant Greek (heterochthon)

Bavarianism—the policy and practice of employing Bavarian nationals in Greek state service

bey—a Turkish title signifying in this book a rich and influential notable of a district

beyship—a term applied to the governorship of Mane under Ottoman rule, especially between 1770-1821

boulouxides—the plural of a term applied to the chief military chieftains of Mane, who constituted a sort of provincial aristocracy

caloyer—monk

capitan-pasha—the commander of the Ottoman navy and governor-general of the Aegean Islands

captanlik—the position of captain or military chieftain, more especially of an armatolos; also the region policed and controlled by such a functionary

chef d'armes—the head of a privately recruited, local or district military force

chiliarchy—a military unit of a thousand soldiers commanded by a chiliarch civilian "party"—one of the two major political divisions during the early part of the Greek Revolution, identified with the interests of the civilian notables

clientele—a hierarchical relationship of dependency

Constitutionalist—an opponent of the Governmentalists (Kapodistrians or Napists) avowedly in favor of a constitutional, parliamentary form of government; a term covering members of both the "English" and "French" parties in Greece

control board—the highest organ of fiscal control and administration in early modern Greece, an autonomous body acting independently of all ministries

Council of State—a consultative, royally appointed body of politically prominent Greeks in early modern Greece

demarch—the head of a deme

demarchal—pertaining to the deme

deme—the smallest administrative unit of independent Greece

demogeron—an elected headman of a commune, usually a landed gentleman whose influence was limited to his locale; a synonym for archon or elder

demotic—pertaining to the deme

dotation law—the law offering the sale of national land to Greek citizens who had contributed to the War of Independence

dragoman—an interpreter, often a Greek, who often functioned in fact as executive deputy in the office to which he was assigned

enosis—the union of Greek-inhabited lands with Greece

eparch—the head of an eparchy, a district or canton governor

eparchal—pertaining to the eparchy

eparchy—the intermediate administrative unit of independent Greece, a district or canton

ephor—the highest tax official and inspector of a province or district, directly under the jurisdiction of the ministry of economic affairs

faction—a term used in this book to denote a political grouping *limited to* a region of the state and united around a single family or person rather than by a set of ideas

first regency—the Bavarian regency during the minority of King Otho, consisting of Armansperg, Maurer, and Heideck, functioning from February 1833 to July 1834

fusionism (synchoneusis)—an unsuccessful attempt to achieve the fusion of all parties into a single national movement

gendarmerie (chorophyake)—a national police force

Governmentalist—a political follower of Kapodistrias, governor of Greece (1828-31) or an adherent of the "Russian" party; a synonym for Kapodistrian and (later) for Napist

Great Idea (Megale Idea)—the Greek irredentist ideal of liberating all Greeks from foreign rule and incorporating them into a greater Greece with Constantinople as its capital

heterochthon (neelys, neelydes)—a Greek, born outside of independent Greece, who settled there after the outbreak of the War of Independence (1821)

hospodar—either of the two princes appointed by the Ottoman government to rule over the Danubian (Rumanian) principalities of Wallachia and Moldavia respectively

Kapodistrian—a political follower of Kapodistrias or an adherent of the "Russian" party; a synonym for Governmentalist and (later) for Napist

kapos, -oi—the private policeman or guard of a local notable or community during Ottoman rule

Karytaino-Messenian "party"—one of the two chief contending Peloponnesian Greek factions during Ottoman rule

klepht—a Greek brigand and outlaw who became a kind of Greek Robin Hood and folk hero during the Ottoman period

kodza-bashi—a notable (see primate)

koumpariá—a ritual relationship between the families of a married couple and their best man *or* between the families of a godfather and his godchild

"major" plot—the Napist Greek intrigue to end the regency prematurely

military "party"—one of the two major political divisions during the early part of the Greek Revolution, identified with the interests of the irregular chieftains

"minor" plot—the intrigue of Franz, a Bavarian, to have Armansperg become sole regent of Greece

moirarch—a captain of the gendarmerie

morayannes—either of the two Peloponnesian Greek notables elected annually during the pre-Revolutionary period to serve on the pasha's advisory council in Tripolis, the capital of Peloponnesos

Morea—the Peloponnesos

Napist—an adherent of the "Russian" party in Greece

nomarch—the head of a nomarchy, provincial governor

nomarchal—pertaining to the nomarchy

nomarchy—the largest administrative unit of independent Greece, a province otzak—hearth, meaning by extension the head (armatolos) of an important military house or family

palikar—a brave young man or hero, a term applied to klephts and armatoloi and more generally referring to irregular soldiers

party—a term used in this book to denote a political grouping extending beyond a single district and identified in some way with an ideological position

pasha—a title signifying in this book the Ottoman Muslim governor of a province during Turkish rule

pashalik—an Ottoman provincial governorship or province

phalanx—a reserve corps of army officers devised as reward for and recognition of distinguished military service during the War of Independence

Phanariot—a member of an unofficial Greek aristocracy, originating in the Phanar district of Constantinople and exercising great influence in the Ottoman empire during the eighteenth century

phara—a term denoting in Albania and Souli a small clan

Philike Hetairia—the extensive Greek secret society organized in 1814 for revolt against Ottoman rule and contributing to the outbreak of the Greek Revolution in 1821

Philorthodox—a term denoting the fervent loyalty of Greek religious conservatives to traditional Orthodoxy and applicable to the majority of Napists and adherents of the "Russian" party; more especially, the name of a secret society and plot in 1838-39

Phoenix society—a pro-Kapodistrias secret society

primate (proestos, -oi; prokritos, -oi; prouchon, prouchontes; kodzabashi)—a civilian notable and large landowner exercising local *and* regional influence

référendaire (eisegetes, -ai)—a palace official, usually Bavarian but sometimes heterochthon Greek, acting as a liaison between government bodies (ministries and Council of State) and the king, and probably intended as agents of royal control in those bodies; members of the anaktovoulion

regency majority—a grouping, within the first regency, of Maurer and Heideck, two of its three members, and Abel, an alternate regent

second regency—the Bavarian regency during the minority of King Otho, consisting of Armansperg, Kobell, and Heideck, functioning from July 1834 through May 1835

Sharia—the sacred law of Islam

streme (strema, stremmata)—a unit of land the approximate equivalent of one-fourth acre

synod—the highest ecclesiastical body of Greece

third series—the third installment of a 60,000,000 franc loan to the Greek state, guaranteed by Britain, France, and Russia

vekiles—either of the two Peloponnesian Greek notable officials sent to reside in Constantinople as spokesmen of Greek Peloponnesian interests

Vlach—a nomad or seminomad of Rumanian ethnic affinity in the Balkans, especially in Macedonia

voivode—the Ottoman Muslim head of an administrative district or canton during Turkish rule

vouleuterion—(see anaktovoulion)

Politics and Statecraft
in the Kingdom of Greece
1833-1843

Introduction

THIS BOOK is a study of both political parties and statecraft during the first decade of the modern Greek kingdom (1833-43). As a study of parties, it is an attempt to treat them for the first time as an object of serious research—to locate and classify them, to determine their membership, and to analyze their institutional structure and societal function. As a study in statecraft, it seeks to determine the role of the parties in the process of statecraft and politics during the period 1833-43, when a newly established monarchy attempted to lay the foundations of a new state. It attempts to substantiate the hypothesis, suggested by my early research, that the parties, either as conditioning factors or as active agents, influenced the nature of more or less permanent state institutions in genesis and development, and hence helped determine the fundamental structure of the modern Greek state. In contrast with the parties, which have been grossly neglected, these institutions have received from historians factual elaboration and analysis as to structure and function. But such accounts have suffered from the failure to consider the parties as an influence in their genesis and development.

For reasons stated below, of the many groupings called "parties" or "factions" in the sources, only three—those most easily identifiable by their foreign affiliations—have been considered to merit this label and these will constitute the main subjects of this study. The first generation of political parties in independent Greece enjoyed a life-span of something like thirty years. They were conceived about halfway through the great War of Greek Independence (1821-27). They took definite form during the first period of settled government under President John Kapodistrias (1828-31). They lived out the rest of their existence under King Otho, first king of modern Greece (1833-62), losing their identity sometime after the Crimean War (1854-56).

Because of limited time for research abroad, I have excluded from consideration the constitutional period starting in 1844, even though party activity was brisk, and coverage of the period 1825-32 has been restricted to a merely exploratory and analytical account based largely on secondary and some published primary sources. Intensive research has been done on only the middle period—the period of absolutism, starting in 1833, when royal government got under way, and ending in 1843, when a successful revolution resulted in the establishment of a constitution. There are two reasons for selecting the middle period. Least is known about the parties during this time, their activities being less apparent under a nonconstitutional regime. Then, too, it was during this period that the basic structure of the Greek state was created. This period seemed to offer the best chances for testing and substantiating the hypothesis mentioned above.

Within the period of absolutism, five subperiods emerge, according to

3

the succession of governments and the shift of political primacy from one party to another: (1) the period of the first regency (1833-34); (2) the period of rule by Armansperg, first as regent, then as archchancellor (1834-36); (3) the first part of Otho's personal rule, which was characterized by the political primacy of the "Russian" party (1838-39); (4) the brief interlude of attempted political reform under the aegis of the "English" party (1841); and (5) the latter part of Otho's personal absolutism, this time with the "French" party in the ascendant (1841-43). These subperiods, each considered in a separate chapter, constitute the core of the book (Part Two).

But in order to understand the character and activities of the parties in the period of absolutism, it is necessary to delineate the major factors in Revolutionary Greece which make the character and activities of the parties intelligible (Chapter I), to trace the emergence of embryonic parties (1821-27) out of a situation of fluid political groupings and persistent social forms (Chapter II), and to describe the birth and consolidation of three parties between 1828 and 1832 under the Kapodistrian and post-Kapodistrian regimes (Chapter III). Finally, a kind of epilogue (Chapter IX) deals with the period of the constituent assembly (1843-44), first, because the positions taken on major constitutional issues make it possible to examine the relation of the parties to ideas and principles; second, because the temporary collapse of the three-party system, in conjunction with the temporary absence of certain previously operative factors, sheds indirect light on the reasons for the survival of the three parties between 1833-43 and dramatically illustrates the divisive intra-party factors which were less immediately apparent during the absolutist period.

The two following sections of this introduction will enumerate more specifically some of the major questions and problems with which this book is concerned and will explain the basic conceptualization employed. The first section will do so with respect to the parties' nature and function, the second with regard to their role in the process of statecraft and in the unfolding of political events.

The constant reference to parties (*kommata*) or factions (*phatriai*) in contemporary documents, Greek and non-Greek, indicates that they constituted a regular feature of the political picture. So persistently are they mentioned that one is all the more impressed with the lack of precision in the use of the terms. It is never obvious, or immediately apparent, what the accepted generic meaning of the terms was, how many parties there actually were, or whom and what, if anything, they represented. Later historians have not helped matters any. They have persisted in using these terms in their manifold contexts without ever clarifying the distinct meanings and their connections to each other.[1]

[1] Often the sources use the terms interchangeably, with no apparent difference in

The contemporary sources show a consensus on two points only—(1) that at the very least, parties were groups designed to secure public office for their members;[2] and (2) that the existence of parties was a misfortune for the nation, incompatible with public interest.[3] Beyond this primary

---

meaning. In some cases, though, they casually imply a contrast, either in respect to size (a "faction" having smaller membership) or purpose (a "faction" devoid of all patriotic sentiment). Deliberate attempts to define or distinguish these terms are rare and seldom fruitful. For instance, *Athēna* (11 July 1837*o.s.*) defined a faction as "an understanding among men which didn't limit its machinations to the acquiring of offices and honors, as did the parties, but also cast its glance on the national government itself, trying either to conquer it or make it odious to the public." In short, a party made reasonable demands for place and position, while a faction wanted to monopolize or destroy power.

Concerning the lack of consistency in categorizing specific parties, I will cite only three examples, each a work of distinction and erudition: (1) George K. Aspreas, *Politike Historia tes Neoteras Hellados 1821-1921* [*Political History of Modern Greece*], 2nd edn. (Athens, 1924), 3 vols.; (2) George Finlay, *A History of Greece from its Conquest by the Romans to the Present Time, B.C. 146 to A.D. 1864*, ed. H. F. Tozer (Oxford, 1877), 7 vols.; and (3) Edouard Driault and Michel Lhéritier, *Histoire Diplomatique de la Grèce de 1821 à nos Jours* (Paris, 1925), 5 vols.

Aspreas talks about "foreign" and "indigenous" parties in one section (i, 29-30); three foreign-oriented parties ("English," "French," "Russian") in another (i, 74-79); and personal coteries in still another context (i, 193).

Finlay pretty consistently uses the categories of "Kapodistrian" and "Constitutionalist" parties (see for instance, vi, 72-106 passim); yet he has to lapse into talk about "English," "French," and "Russian" parties when he arrives at the years 1842-44 (vii, 171, 185). He refers to them as "the old parties under Mavrokordatos, Kolettes, and Metaxas," which makes us wonder why he has not mentioned them over so many pages or, if we are to assume they disappeared for a time, why he does not then explain why they suddenly reappeared.

Driault and Lhéritier (*Histoire*) generally talk about a Napist ("Russian") and a National party (ii, 130, 194-95, 225), which they label "conservative" and "liberal" in another section (ii, 227); yet they find themselves sometimes forced to talk about three foreign-oriented parties (i, 298, and ii, 140), even though they don't feel that one of these ("English") merits the name "party" (ii, 227). Significantly, however, they are not clear on why they don't feel that it qualifies for the name; or for that matter, why the others do.

[2] See, for instance, the Greek newspapers *Athēna*, 3 July and 11 July 1837*o.s.*; *Triptolemos*, 16 Sept. 1833*o.s.*; and *Ethnikē*, 1/13 Oct. 1834.

[3] The newspaper press almost unanimously declared itself against the existence of parties; for instance, *Triptolemos*, 16 Sept. 1833*o.s.*; *Ethnikē*, 11/23 Oct. 1834; *Sōtēr*, 25 Oct. 1834*o.s.*; *Anagennētheisa Hellas*, 25 Aug. 1836*o.s.*; *Athēna*, 4 Dec. 1837*o.s.*; and *Aiōn*, 25 June 1839*o.s.* Two quotations from these sources will give some idea why men believed, or at least said, that the existence of parties went counter to national interest:

"If the party heads restricted themselves to fighting the cabinet, the evil would probably not be too great. But worse yet, they fight, insult, slander, and rival each other so as to inherit the direction of affairs. . . . This war between them is the more frightening because it has the most frightful consequences. Party men, in order to increase and strengthen their parties, rouse some of the people against other segments of the people. They instigate the masses, they predict the worst prophecies,

definition and this negative evaluation, the sources diverge, even on the ostensibly simple matter of identifying particular parties by name.

The ostensibly simple matter of merely identifying and enumerating particular parties turns out to be anything but simple. How many parties were there? What were their names? Depending on context and concern, contemporaries tended to think and speak in terms of at least three distinct classifications. Sometimes they talked about an almost endless number of personal cliques, each as the personal projection of an individual leader.[4] At other times they saw politics as a three-way struggle between the "English," "French," and "Russian" parties, which they identified as the followings acquired by the three European powers with special influence in Greek affairs.[5] On still other occasions, talk went on

---

they attribute the worst schemes to the government and other parties. Thus they precipitate the division of the nation, mistrust, disobedience, and reprehensible movements of the simple or the adventurous. . . ." (*Triptolemos*)

". . . if parties had not existed in Greece, not only would the nation have thrown off the yoke [of the Turks] much sooner, but the bases of our political community would have been broader and sounder. Parties everywhere and always become the obstacles of any nation's prosperity. But the time that they become most harmful . . . is certainly when the nation is occupied in setting the foundation of its governmental forms." (*Anagennētheisa Hellas*)

For similar sentiments, see a public talk by Regas Palamides, which was published with the title [*Speech of Regas Palamides, Deputy from Mantineia*] in reply to the speech of A. Metaxas, retiring minister of economic affairs, in the Chamber session of 23 Aug. 1845 (n.p., n.d.), p. 2; and a private letter from Philip Ioannou to A. Mavrokordatos, Athens, 1 Oct. 1837*o.s.*, no. 5423, Vol. 20 (1837-40), Mavrokordatos Archive, General State Archives, Athens. The latter, after reviewing the party situation, expressed his wish that he were back in "peaceful Germany."

On the other hand, there were a few exceptions to the general clamor against parties during the decade 1833-43: the newspaper *Hēlios*, 8 Aug. 1833*o.s.*; and *Athēna*, 11 July 1837*o.s.* In going against the tide, these articles offer two types of argument: (1) that parties existed automatically in any society and were hence inevitable, (2) that they were valuable as watchdogs, keeping an eye both on the government and each other. The reader should notice that both *Triptolemos* and *Athēna* were also cited above as participants in the antiparty campaign, which shows that they did not remain consistent.

[4] The newspaper *Hēlios* (4 July 1833*o.s.*), in a lead article, cited seven such personal coteries; and Philip Ioannou writes about "so many parties" (same citation as that of previous footnote). See also J. A. Buchon, *La Grèce Continentale et la Morée* (Paris, 1843), pp. 107-108; Theobald Piscatory to M. Guizot, Athens, 6 Sept. 1841 [7th report], in "Textes et Documents, La Grèce d'Othon," ed. Jean Poulos, in *L'Hellénisme Contemporain*, 2nd ser., IX (1955), 427; and Friedrich Thiersch, *De l'état actuel de la Grèce* (Leipzig, 1833), I, 182.

[5] *Hēlios*, 25 Aug. 1833*o.s.*; *Ethnikē*, 16/28 Oct. 1834; *Athēna*, 3 July 1837*o.s.*; and *Aiōn*, 6 Dec. 1839*o.s.* In addition to these newspapers, see the following items of personal correspondence: M. Argyropoulos to P. Argyropoulos, Pera, 26 Mar./7 Apr. 1841, no. 5857, Vol. 21 (1841), and Kolettes to Mavrokordatos, Nov. 1842, no. 6512, Vol. 22 (1842), both from Mavrokordatos Archive; Guizot's instructions to Piscatory, Paris, 16 May 1841, *L'Hellénisme Contemporain*, IX, 334; and J. Eynard to D. Chrestides, 17 Feb. 1843, published in *La Restauration Hellénique*

as if only two parties occupied the political arena—the *Constitutionalists*, ostensibly the advocates of constitutional government, and the *Kapodistrians* or *Governmentalists*, those faithful to the authoritarian system of John Kapodistrias, governor of Greece from 1828-31.[6] One person was likely to use the vocabulary of more than one classification scheme, even on the same occasion.[7]

To add to the complication, primary and secondary sources tended to speak of politics in terms of broader social groups, classified according to three deep-rooted divisions in Greek society involving differing ways of life. The first classification, a socio-economic one, distinguished between the *military* and *civilian* elements, or more precisely between military chieftains and landed primates. The second classification was regional, involving a three-way division between major geographical divisions of insurgent Greece (Peloponnesos, Rumely, and the Islands). The third classification rested on a cultural split between those distinguished for their allegiance to the secular, liberal West and those faithful to the other-worldly, authoritarian tradition of Byzantium.

Contemporaries did not usually go so far as to call these social groups "parties." Only in the case of the military-civilian elements did they make an exception, and even then, only for the early period of the Revolution when politics momentarily assumed class lines.[8] But they tended to think

---

d'après la correspondance de Jean-Gabriel Eynard, ed. Edouard Chapuisat (Paris, Geneva, 1924), p. 154.

[6] In the first years of Otho's reign especially, this classification was used. The newspapers *Triptolemos* (2 Aug. 1830*o.s.*), *Sōtēr* (16 Aug. 1834*o.s.*), *Ethnikē* (14/26 Oct. 1834), and *Ho Hellēnikos Tachydromos* (nos. 42-43 and 59, 1837) made reference to the parties in these terms. In the later 1830s and early 1840s, probably to avoid the impression that only a part of the nation desired a constitution, most newspapers, excepting the anticonstitutionalist *Hellas* and *Ho Hellēnikos Tachydromos*, dropped this terminology. See also, in private correspondence, Philip Ioannou to Mavrokordatos, Athens, 15 Aug. 1838*o.s.*, no. 5520, Vol. 20 (1837-40), and S. Valetas to Mavrokordatos, Athens, 26 May 1842*o.s.*, no. 6355, Vol. 22 (1842), both in Mavrokordatos Archive.

[7] For instance, *Triptolemos* used the two-fold system in its issue of 2 Aug. 1833*o.s. Hēlios* wrote about seven personal coteries (4 July 1833*o.s.*) and wrote about their merger into three (25 Aug. 1833*o.s.*). Philip Ioannou (to Mavrokordatos, Athens, Vol. 20 [1837-40], Mavrokordatos Archive) referred to "many parties" (1 Oct. 1837*o.s.*), then to the Constitutionalist and Napist (15 Aug. 1838*o.s.*). Or see a reference to the effect that ". . . one was a Governmentalist, one a Constitutionalist, another English, another French, another Russian and so forth" in John Makrygiannes, *Apomnemoneumata* [*Memoirs*], ed. John Vlachogiannes, 2nd edn. (Athens, 1947), II, 120.

[8] For a historical account of the early years of the Revolution in terms of the "military" and "civilian" parties, see Spyridon Trikoupes, *Historia tes Hellenikes Epanastaseos* [*History of the Greek Revolution*], 3rd edn. (Athens, 1888), III passim. Concerning the marked tension between these two social groups, and its political implications, see Nicholas Dragoumes, *Historikai Anamneseis* [*Historical Reminiscences*] 2nd edn. (Athens, 1879), I, 20-21; and Antoine Grénier, *La Grèce en*

of these social groups in primarily political terms and to link up political parties with these social categories. In 1838 the newspaper *Aiōn* went as far as to interpret party rivalries, from the outbreak of the Revolution till the moment of publication, as an expression, through various phases, of a struggle between military and civilian oligarchies.[9] Some attempted to set up a correspondence between the three foreign-oriented parties and the three-way sectionalist feeling—the "English" as the party of the Islanders, the "French" as the party of Rumely, and the "Russian" as the party of the Peloponnesos.[10] In *L'Histoire Diplomatique de la Grèce*, Driault and Lhéritier attempted to make such a correspondence between the two-fold political classification on the one hand and regional and cultural factors on the other:

> There was in Greece, as everywhere, a conservative party and a progressive party; the one associated with the "Russian" party, offspring of the presidency of Capodistrias, powerful in the Peloponnesos through the influence of the Kolokotrones'; the other, a liberal and national party, powerful in Rumely and in most of the islands which were the cradle of liberty. It recognized John Kolettes as chief.[11]

George Aspreas, the Greek historian, described the "first parties" as an expression of conflict between the European and the indigenously Greek ethos. He cited two parties, the foreign (*xenikon*) and the indigenous (*enchōrion*), the former representing Westernized Greeks and the latter consisting of the traditionalists or vast mass of Greeks. According to him, this division continued throughout the reign of Greece's first

---

1863 (Paris, 1863), p. 105. For an excellent secondary source, see Douglas Dakin, *British and American Philhellenes during the War of Greek Independence 1821-1833* (Thessaloniki, 1955), p. 163.

[9] In two consecutive lead articles of a historical nature (12 Oct. and 28 Oct. 1838 *o.s.*), *Aiōn* based its whole analysis of the political past on the fact of tension between military and civilian elements. Indeed, the early rivalry between Prince Demetrios Ypsilantes and Alexander Mavrokordatos it interpreted along these class lines. "The primates were suspicious of Ypsilantes' inclination toward the soldiery," it wrote. "From this stems the first division of spirits and it continues through various phases until our present epoch. . . . The first element was essentially the military, and the second the political civilian oligarchy." The Constitutionalists it identified as descendants of the Mavrokordatists; the Governmentalists as heirs of the Ypsilantists with the Kolokotronists representing an intermediate stage.

[10] See, for instance, Thiersch, *État actuel*, II, 217. This correspondence, however, is more frequently made by the secondary sources, such as Karl Mendelssohn-Bartholdy (*Geschichte Griechenlands von der Eroberung Konstantinopels durch die Türken im Jahre 1453 bis auf unsere Tage* [Leipzig, 1870-74], I, 439-40), who identified the "English" party primarily with insular Greece, the "French" with mainland Greece, and the "Russian" with the Peloponnesos. See also Dakin, *Philhellenes*, pp. 89-90, and Nicholas Kaltchas, *Introduction to the Constitutional History of Modern Greece* (New York, 1940), p. 49.

[11] Driault and Lhéritier, *Histoire*, II, 227.

monarch (1833-62). And each party, as a matter of practical politics, sought as close an identification with indigenous culture as possible.[12]

This kaleidescopic perception of the parties, capricious in its shifting images, is obviously no basis for a systematic analysis of parties or for a synthetic description of party politics. Any such study must give primacy to one of the three classifications as *the* standard one. For three reasons, I have chosen to treat the "English," "French," and "Russian" parties as the basic political groupings. In the first place, this classification was the most universally held of the three and more consistently in use through-out the 1830s and the early 1840s than either of the other two. Second, the special status of England, France, and Russia in Greek affairs and the active exercise of patronage by their respective legations in Athens gave these groupings an influence and prominence unknown to the others. Third, other groupings tended to converge into these three. Personal coteries tended to merge into alliances roughly equivalent to the three foreign-oriented parties. On all but a few rare occasions the so-called Constitutionalist party tended to dissolve into its two constituent parts— the "English" and "French" parties.

Though for the sake of analysis and clarity it is necessary to give primacy to one of the classifications, it is also necessary to avoid over-simplification and to utilize the other classifications when they render an event or situation more intelligible. Once one has chosen a particular classification of political parties, one must relate it to the three deep-seated societal divisions cited above. Indeed, this book will attempt to analyze the socio-economic basis as well.

Since multiplicity of classifications reflects an objective fact—the fluidity of political groupings—this book will also attempt to clarify the relation between the various political groupings and hence the objective grounds for the validity of each classification: (1) Did the type of political division (multiple, three-fold, and dual) bear any relation to the levels of political activity (local, provincial, and national)? (2) With which of the three types (personal, foreign-oriented, Constitutionalist-Governmentalist) did the average individual identify himself most closely? (3) Speaking of national politics, in response to what kinds of stimuli did political divisions follow dual rather than three-fold lines?

A few words, then, about the nomenclature of these three parties. Generally the newspaper sources referred to them as "so-called English," "so-called French," and "so-called Russian." These names were descriptive in the sense that they indicated the foreign sympathies of each group.

---

[12] But what Aspreas observed was a cultural division which affected political alignments rather than a political division itself. As he himself admitted, the in-digenous body of opinion could not be characterized, in the strict sense of the word, as a party, because it lacked both organization and a focal point. The same applies, however, to the other group as well. See Aspreas [*Political History*], i, 28-32. See also Grénier, *Grèce*, pp. 32, 96-97.

But they were also polemical terms, designed to suggest betrayal of national interests in return for foreign patronage and reserved for rival parties. Even when engaged in polemics, the press used these terms guardedly ("so-called French" rather than "French").[13]

A second set of labels, likewise originating as terms of abuse during the bitter civil war of 1831-32, derived from the names of individuals important only for their partisan fanaticism. Moschos, a turbulent military captain from Rumely, commanded a unit (*manga*) of irregulars within the army of Theodore Grivas, a disreputable though influential military figure in the Constitutionalist camp. This particular unit was called *moschomanga* (unit of Moschos). So irresponsible and cruelly did it behave when Grivas entered Nauplion in 1832 that its name became a byword for wanton brutality and a nasty name for the "French" party, to which Moschos so vociferously expressed his loyalty. Members of the "English" party came to be known as *Parlaioi* (adherents of Parlas) by association with Basil Parlas, a fanatical Anglophile who led an armed attack on the Governmentalist gendarmes of Nauplion in 1832. Napas, a large-framed and fanatical Russophile, who clashed with French forces in Nauplion in 1833, lent his name to the "Russian" party which came to be known as the *Napist* party. Of this set, only the term Napist stuck and even gained a measure of respectability, although the Russophiles preferred to call themselves Governmentalists. The terms "parlaioi" and "moschomangites" were almost never used in newspapers or private correspondence during the royal period.[14]

Throughout the decade of the 1830s the press engaged in a running debate on whether parties actually existed in Greece.[15] In this debate the

[13] For instances of the widespread journalistic practice of prefacing the foreign party names with "so-called" (*legomenon*), see *Athēna*, 3 July 1837 and 26 July 1841*o.s.*, and *Aiōn*, 6 Dec. 1839*o.s.* In the polemics of the press, other descriptive labels of a deprecatory kind were also used. The "French" newspaper *Sōtēr* constantly called the "English" party the "party of intrigue" (*radiourgikon*), trying to identify it with a Greek élite group called the Phanariots, who had a reputation for intrigue, and the "Russian" the "antinational party," because of its alleged efforts in behalf of a foreign power (5 Aug. 1834 and 25 Oct. 1834*o.s.*). The pro-"English" *Ethnikē* called the "French" party the "party of turbulence," referring to its heavy representation of military elements, or the "party of Ali-Pasha-ism," referring to the earlier association of its leader, Kolettes, with the intrigue-ridden court of Ali Pasha of Janina (10/22 Mar. 1835 and 24 Mar./6 Apr. 1835).

[14] See "Moschos," "Parlas," and "Napas" in *Megale Hellenike Enkyklopaideia* [*Grand Hellenic Encyclopedia*], 24 vols. (Athens, 1926-34).

[15] For instances of the thesis that parties did exist, see *Triptolemos*, 29 July 1833*o.s.*; *Sōtēr*, 11 Oct. and 18 Oct. 1834*o.s.*; *Ethnikē*, 7/19 Mar. 1835; and *Aiōn*, 6 Dec. 1839*o.s.* Representing the other side of the debate were *Anagennētheisa Hellas*, 25 Aug. 1836*o.s.*; *Aiōn*, 28 Oct. 1838*o.s.*; and *Athēna*, 8 Jan. 1836, 3 July 1837, 15 Jan. 1838, and 20 Apr. 1838*o.s.* The reader will notice that *Aiōn* shifted its position; within issues of each other (nos. 63 and 65, 1837), *Sōtēr* did too. This was characteristic. Indeed, the former position was usually that of progovernment newspapers that were attempting to justify the presence of Bavarians in the administra-

existence of groups in search of public favors and political power was never in question. The issue was whether these groups merited the name of "parties"; that is, whether they fulfilled the terms of the definition implied by current educated usage. No one attempted any systematic formulation of the concept, but the generic meaning of the term, as used by Westernized intellectuals at least, becomes apparent from scattered references. A survey of the language of four contemporary observers will permit a formulation of the concept, which in turn will provide us with important questions to ask about the nature of the political groups with which we are concerned.

A more or less formal approach to the question was provided by Michael Petrokokkinos, a secondary school teacher, in a speech which he delivered in 1833.[16] He started with a definition.

> Politically a thing is called a stand [*stasis*] or faction [*phatria*] when some individuals wish a certain element to prevail in the nation instead of another, or want the government to take the form of a despotism, aristocracy, or democracy. All the individuals comprising the party know what they want and what purpose they strive for. Inhabiting various cities of the realm, unacquainted with each other personally, they share nevertheless a common set of objectives.

Groups in England and France, he asserted, met the terms of his definition. Even the most insignificant person believed that the prosperity of the nation depended on the supremacy of his party.

Petrokokkinos then proceeded to his main point—Greece had no "parties." Ask a soldier why he belonged to the so-called party of Theodore Kolokotrones, a military hero of the Greek Revolution and an influential party figure, and he would reply, "Because he drew pay from Kolokotrones as a soldier in his private army." Take away the leader of a so-called party and nothing remained but a mere collection of individuals. No fundamental political differences divided the Greeks. Now that independence had been won, they merely wanted peace, order, and law.

Early in 1838, the liberal Greek newspaper *Athēna* devoted a lead article to the question of parties:

> Systematic factions [*phatriai*] or parties [*kommata*] exist and sustain themselves on a foundation of political principles. Only such entities can be called parties. By itself, competition for political office makes neither a faction nor a party. Only this competition exists in Greece today and it will always exist by the very nature of things. But whoever

---

tion or the Crown's denial of a constitution; the latter was the position of those who argued that partisan strife had subsided enough to allow the Greeks control of their own affairs.

[16] Published in *Hēlios*, 11 July 1833o.s.

considers this competition evidence of the existence of parties does not know the real meaning of the term in any language.

On another occasion, it defined parties as "unions of men, having the same interests and beliefs, which conflicted with the interests and beliefs of other similar unions."[17]

Unlike these two statements, the third and fourth references to parties came from correspondence of a confidential nature. Constantine Zographos, a prominent political figure with long experience in party politics, was foreign minister of Greece when he wrote his remarks to a friend early in 1839.[18] He made essentially the same point as Petrokokkinos and *Athēna*. The division into these parties, he wrote, was based upon differences of material interests and personal relations rather than upon differences of political principles and beliefs. A body of public opinion, reflecting the interests and needs of different classes of Greek society, he said, had not yet formed because classes themselves had not yet issued as distinct entities from the chaos of the Revolutionary decade (1821-32). In short, he was adding that the parties *could not* reflect differing political ideas because social fluidity had not permitted the formation of distinct interest groups and the consequent articulation of group differences on substantive political issues.

The fourth reference comes from the correspondence of Theobald Piscatory,[19] a French diplomat who, albeit not Greek, knew Greek conditions intimately and at first hand as a result of his Revolutionary services as a philhellene. Returning to Greece in 1841 on an official mission this time, he denied the existence of "real" parties because he could discover no differences among the so-called parties on questions most vitally affecting the country. All displayed loyalty to the king, ardently sought the liberation of their brethren still under Ottoman domination, and urgently desired an end to administrative breakdown. In the one case where he was willing to admit the possible existence of a "real" party, he cited as characteristics "cohesiveness, a common interest centered about an ecclesiastical issue, and strong organization," but he also pointed out, in qualification, that the party was small in numbers.

From these four statements there emerges a conception of "party," obviously drawn from contemporary conditions of Western Europe (England and France), in terms of which to discuss the Greek political groups whose existence all acknowledged. By inference if not by open assertion, all four observers judged the so-called parties as groupings resting upon the personality of an influential leader and the personal relations existing among the members. But all four also shared a concep-

[17] *Athēna*, 15 Jan. 1838 o.s. The other occasion was its issue of 11 July 1837 o.s.

[18] Zographos to Mavrokordatos, Athens, 19 Feb./3 Mar. 1839, no. 5579, Vol. 20 (1837-40), Mavrokordatos Archive.

[19] Piscatory, Athens, 20 June 1841 (1st report) and Athens, 30 July 1841 (4th report), *L'Hellénisme Contemporain*, IX, 339-40, 410.

tion which required of "real" parties three characteristics: first and primarily, representation of ideas; second, structure or organization; third, command of a popular following. All four observers stated these characteristics only to point out their absence in the case of Greek groupings. But the question of whether these characteristics were totally absent is an open one which was disputed even then. For that reason, I will write about the parties with these questions in mind and address myself explicitly to them again in the conclusion. Since they are important, they deserve at this point separate attention.

Did parties represent ideas? Those who answered negatively[20] could argue in two ways. They might, like the four observers cited, insist that there were no important differences of opinion which the so-called parties might reflect. Or they might point to the frequent defections and changes of party allegiance as evidence that expediency rather than conviction determined party membership.[21] But such a negative reply was challenged, though by no means refuted, by the persistence of such party classifications as Constitutionalist-Governmentalist, liberal-conservative, or European-traditional, and also by apparent motivation behind some of the sources.[22]

As a basis for some sort of judgment, the following questions must be considered: Were there issues which divided segments of Greek society? If so, to what extent did the parties reflect such divisions of opinion? If so, on what level did the differences of opinion take place—on the level of cultural allegiance or way of life, which went beyond the category of strictly political ideas; on the intermediate level of political principles,

[20] For negative opinions, besides that of Piscatory (Athens, 20 June 1841 [1st report], *ibid.*, IX, 340), see *Hēlios*, 11 July 1833*o.s.*; *Philos tou Laou*, 3 June 1838*o.s.*; and *Athēna*, 15 Jan. and 20 Apr. 1838*o.s.*

[21] Speaking in this case specifically about a Napist but with the implication that the point applied to a man of any party, Piscatory wrote (Athens, 30 July 1841 [4th report], *L'Hellénisme Contemporain*, IX, 410): ". . . a personal interest makes one quit the [Napist] party to enter the national party. To do this one does not have to change one's principles or language. One quarrels with some to accommodate himself with the others. This is what just occurred to one of the members of the Kolokotrones family and to his friends." In another instance (Athens, 20 Aug. 1841 [5th report], IX, 413) he wrote: ". . . clients often seek two protectors at the same time or desert one to try for another."

[22] Respectable as these authorities are, one must treat their judgments critically. All disapproved of parties, whether in principle or by interest. The French, like any other foreign mission, did not wish to antagonize differing segments of Greek opinion by becoming associated exclusively with the ideological position of any particular group. Petrokokkinos and Zographos could not admit the ideological basis of parties without implying their permanence and justifying their existence as genuine expressions of public opinion. Moreover, basing their observations of party differences on the example of England and France, where such basic questions as the merits of aristocracy and democracy were vital and where conflicting dynastic claims had arisen, they considered whatever differences might exist among the Greeks as trivial by comparison.

13

such as forms of government, relations between church and state; or on the level of public policy or substantive issues of immediate concern, such as proposals for a national bank, ways and means to curb brigandage, trade with the Ottoman empire?

Were the parties organized into a system so as to unite men from various parts of the country, men who might not know each other personally? This question never attracted any real debate. But Petrokokkinos implied a negative answer by his observation that, without its leader, a party would not hold together, whereas Piscatory made an exception for at least one party.[23] The crucial question, on this issue, is whether organization was absent or whether it was often considered absent because it did not conform with the expected European pattern.

This question is crucial to an understanding of the period. A major contention of this book is that the persistence of parties, in spite of royal efforts to undermine and destroy them, is intelligible only in terms of a positive answer to this question.

To what extent did the parties enjoy popular support and command the loyalties of the average individual? This question came up for repeated debate in the press, as people felt it expedient to argue for the seriousness or for the negligibility of factionalism throughout the body politic. As a result, there exists much conflicting testimony. For instance, the newspaper *Ethnikē* expressed this view in 1834:

> Fortunately, the whole nation was never divided—among the four or five party leaders—as many have often said. Most of the Greeks always remained neutral to them in their passions and wars. Only a few friends and acquaintances were the faithful and firm followers of the party leaders. . . .

Yet a few months later that same newspaper, in order to justify the presence of so many non-Greeks in public service, asserted the rareness of qualified Greeks without the stigma of party affiliations. If *Ethnikē* partially contradicted its previous assertion, others went further. Maurer, one of the three regents during the minority of the king, asserted that in 1831-32 the whole Greek nation had split up into parties, and the newspaper *Sōtēr* claimed ". . . there is no one in Greece who, even involuntarily, does not belong to one of the various political parties which divide Greece." It is the view of this book that this question is intimately related

[23] Petrokokkinos, in *Hēlios*, 11 July 1833*o.s.* Piscatory's exception was the following (Athens, 6 Sept. 1841 [7th report], *L'Hellénisme Contemporain*, IX, 436): "The difference which exists therefore in Peloponnesos between the Russian and English parties, on the one hand, and the French party, on the other, is that men who, in the various provinces, constitute the force of the first two parties, are nothing without the chief who has great influence, while the man who would put himself at the head of the French party could guide the chiefs but could not destroy their influence."

to an evaluation of the function of parties in Greek society as well as an understanding of their socio-economic foundation.[24]

For the period of absolute rule (1833-43), one should not expect to encounter the features characteristic of political parties in modern parliamentary democracies, such as open campaigning for office on a party platform with a party list of candidates, the formation of a homogeneous government of one party, the formal recognition of an opposition constituted by the party or parties temporarily removed from power, or a clearly delineated group of voting blocs by party in the legislative assembly that finally appeared in 1844. But if they did none of these things, what role did they play in the political and social spheres?

Secondary accounts fail to treat the parties as a structural part of their political analysis. It is one thing to devote a few paragraphs to a discussion of the parties and quite another to describe state policy, institutional development, social conflict, and political opposition in terms of party behavior. A few examples of what such failure means will suffice. The refusal of the king to grant a constitution has so often been explained in terms of mere personal inclination, parental influence, and official Russian opposition. The exclusion of influential Greeks from high office, which in the case of party leaders took the form of appointment as ministers plenipotentiary to foreign courts, and the employment of Bavarians and philhellenes so often look like a mere case of Bavarian ethnocentrism and lack of Western appreciation for indigenous talent. The creation of a centralized administration which ignored traditional privileges of local self-government and a caesaropapist system which transformed the church into an arm of the government too often seem like the work of doctrinaire Bavarians. Valid as such assertions may be, they are only half truths. They ignore the basic fact that the Greek Revolution had failed to produce a sufficient concentration of power to prevail over the centrifugal forces which the parties reflected and strengthened in a markedly unhomogeneous society.

Even a recent history, which acknowledged this fact and underlined the connection of the ruling oligarchies to the party complex, failed to draw the full implications of its insights when evaluating both particular acts and general opportunities of royal policy. Just because the Crown did not suffer the limitations of representative government and formally enjoyed absolute power, the author of this history ignored the informal but none the less real power of social and political groups to seriously limit the area of effective royal authority. Consequently, he seems not to

[24] *Ethnikē*, 1/13 Oct. 1834 and 7/19 Mar. 1835. George Ludwig von Maurer, *Das griechische Volk in öffentlicher, kirchlicher und privatrechtlicher Beziehung vor und nach dem Freiheitskampfe bis zum 31. Juli 1834* (Heidelberg, 1835), II, 19-21. *Sōtēr*, 11 Oct. 1834*o.s.* See also Makrygiannes [*Memoirs*], II, 120.

have understood the motivation behind several royal attempts to remove such curbs. For instance, he believed royal authority sufficiently secure to permit the existence of potential, if not actual, instruments of party rivalry, such as an autonomous church and decentralized administration. Indeed, with regard to the regency which exercised royal power from January 1833 to June 1835, he wrote: "They, perceiving whatever they believed good and useful for the land, had their hands free to do it. They were unchecked and not worn down by myriads of party demands."[25]

Only the historian George Aspreas, in his [*Political History of Greece*], has consistently analyzed and described political developments in terms of the parties. He clearly perceived the role of the parties as a political opposition. He understood that the parties, by their very existence as a source of disorder and insubordination, conditioned royal policy in a variety of ways intended to destroy them or nullify their influence. His brief treatment of this period did not permit more than the more obvious illustrations of these points. But it sufficed to inspire the attempt in this book at analyzing statecraft and policy of the Crown as a partial function of an existing party situation.[26]

[25] T. N. Pipineles, *He Monarchia en Helladi 1833-1843* [*The Monarchy in Greece 1833-1843*] (Athens, 1932), p. 109. For other instances of the same shortcoming, see the two following quotations from the same source:

"Permanent in its destiny and essence, powerful because free from all dependence on political bodies, free from the need to use electoral machinery to mobilize the masses, the monarchy, supporting its power on other bases, had no need to fear an organized and autonomous church, and if it had reason not to allow the church to interfere in secular matters, it had no need to exploit its [the church's] influence on the faithful" (p. 82).

"On the other hand, the existence of a strong and permanent monarchical power, not forced to exploit public and local influences during elections for the mobilization of popular support, ought to have, without fear of disintegration, granted broad decentralization and local self-government" (p. 88).

[26] For instance, Aspreas [*Political History*], I, 129-30, 139, 143, 146.

Part One
Before 1833

CHAPTER ONE

The Setting: Bases for Political Divisions

1. SECTIONALISM AND NATIONALISM

THE TERRITORY finally incorporated within the borders of independent Greece in 1832[1] consisted of three basic geographical units: (1) the *Morea* or *Peloponnesos*, the large southern peninsula; (2) *Rumely* or *mainland Greece*, separated from the northern territory of Epirus and Thessaly by a lateral frontier running from Arta in the West to Volos in the East and including Euboea, an island usually considered more continental than insular because of its accessibility from the mainland; and (3) numerous *Aegean Islands*, including the Northern Sporades (Skiathos, Skopelos, and Skyros), the Cyclades (Syros, Andros, Tenos, and Naxos), and the so-called maritime islands of Hydra and Spezza lying immediately off the northeastern coast of the Peloponnesos.

Geography largely determined the type of contributions made by each section to the Revolution. Blessed with several fertile valleys and coastal plains, the Morea was the breadbasket of insurgent Greece and the greatest source of its tax revenue. Thanks to a highly developed system of local autonomy under Ottoman rule, its native leaders provided considerable political experience and skill. Because less exposed to the enemy than either the islands or the mainland, it became and remained the center of the Revolution.

Rumely, where the mountains were higher and more formidable than in the Peloponnesos, was divided by the southern spurs of the Pindus range into two distinct and separate parts—East and West Rumely, each facing away from the other. The chopped up terrain and the difficult communications had made this the home of brigands and the setting for guerrilla warfare. With a long tradition of heroism, the Rumeliots lent their martial skills to the cause. Because their provinces lay athwart the overland routes from the sources of supply to the center of the revolt in the Peloponnesos, they bore the brunt of the annual Turkish campaigns. Early in the Revolution, they learned what devastation meant.

Of the Aegean Islands, only three contributed significantly to the war effort—Hydra, Spezza, and Psara, the last lying southeast of the Northern Sporades toward Asia Minor. Without their naval and financial contribution, the Revolution could not have succeeded. Unable to support any significant vegetation, these three barren rocks had long served as refuge

[1] The convention of Constantinople (21 July 1832), to which Britain, France, Russia and the Ottoman empire were signatories, conceded definitively to the new Greek state a northern boundary running from Volos in the East to Arta in the West. See Edouard Driault and Michel Lhéritier, *Histoire Diplomatique de la Grèce de 1821 à nos Jours* (Paris, 1925), II, 87-93.

from the Turks and as pirates' nests. During the Napoleonic wars, when naval blockades placed a premium on the services of privateers and smugglers, the inhabitants of these islands had gained virtual control of the carrying trade in the Mediterranean and had made vast profits. Later their privately owned ships, supported by their own capital, made up the bulk of the Revolutionary navy. Such captains as Constantine Kanares of Psara and Andrew Miaoules of Hydra became heroes in spectacular victories over the much larger Turkish navy. By maintaining control of the seas most of the time, these islands protected insurgent Greece from the sea.[2]

In view of the geographical barriers of sea and mountains, it is not surprising that localism and sectionalism should have been strong. The force of nationalism in 1821 was still new, and town, village, or district still commanded primary loyalty. Traditionally, administration had conformed to geography and had intensified sectionalism. What became independent Greece had never constituted a single unit within the Ottoman empire. Not even each of its acknowledged geographical divisions had enjoyed administrative unity. Moreover, Ottoman rule had favored sectionalism in two ways—by allowing communities and regions a large degree of autonomy and by never attempting to introduce any widespread uniformity of administration.[3]

The strength of this heritage became apparent at the outbreak of the Revolution. Within six months, three areas of political authority appeared: a Peloponnesian senate, made up of native magnates who announced themselves the supreme authority of the peninsula; an assembly of Western Rumely, sitting at the strategically placed coastal town of Mesolongi; and the Areopagus, a similar assembly for Eastern Rumely.[4] The members of the first national assembly, held in December 1821 at Epidaurus, came as delegates of their regional governments, not as representatives of constituent parts of a unified state. They managed to have the assembly recognize the regional governments which they represented

[2] For an excellent brief account of the geographical factors in the Greek Revolution and the distinctive contribution of each major region of insurgent Greece, see C. M. Woodhouse, *The Greek War of Independence* (London, 1952), pp. 58-65.

[3] On the weakness of nationalism in general, even during the Revolution, see George Finlay, *A History of Greece from its Conquest by the Romans to the Present Time, B.C. 146 to A.D. 1864*, ed. H. F. Tozer (Oxford, 1877), VI, 231. For a vivid —because it is extreme—case of localism among Peloponnesian mountaineers, see Thomas Gordon, *History of the Greek Revolution* (Edinburgh, 1832), II, 189. On the character of Ottoman administration, see H.A.R. Gibb and Harold Bowen, *Islamic Society and the West*, Vol. I, Part I (Oxford, 1950), 159-61, 208-16.

[4] For the latest account of the organization of three regional authorities, see George D. Demakopoulos, *He Dioiketike Organosis kata ten Helleniken Epanastasin 1821-1827* [*The Administrative Organization during the Greek Revolution*] (Athens, 1966), pp. 62-85.

and set up national organs of government too weak to exercise any real control.[5]

The existence of regional authorities per se need not have aroused any misgivings, had they not been accompanied by two other products of sectionalism: suspicion of any nationwide authority and interregional jealousy. Suspicion of centralized power, a legacy from Turkish days when that power was alien, accounts for the initial preference for a strong legislature, where each region could defend its rights, combined with a weak executive unable to encroach upon sectional rights. Some, usually foreigners, accepted sectionalism as a justifiable concern for one's region and recommended a federal system as a way of encouraging local initiative and fostering voluntary cooperation. Most Greek leaders, however, regarded sectional sentiment with disfavor and feared lest federalism and decentralization doom the Revolution by leaving them disunited before a mighty foe. A situation of crisis, they believed, required a strong executive. At least in theory and when things were going badly against the Turks, most Greeks favored centralization and integral unity.[6]

Sectional jealousies played an important role in politics. Rumeliots and Peloponnesians came heartily to dislike each other. The Rumeliots looked on the more prosperous and peaceable Peloponnesians as untrustworthy and effete. The Peloponnesians regarded their northern brothers as backward and boorish. The Islanders displayed an insular contempt for all mainlanders. There were also intraregional jealousies, the one most damaging to the war effort being that between Hydriots and Spezziots.[7]

Intersectional jealousies reached such a peak at the end of 1824 as to cause the second civil war of the Greek Revolution, when Rumeliots and Islanders combined to put down the Peloponnesians.[8] This Rumeliot occupation of the Peloponnesos left bitter memories there and intensified ill feelings between the two sections even more. Sectional strife diminished rapidly thereafter, under the impact of a new and more serious Turkish threat, and it never assumed such proportions again. Nevertheless, to keep sectional jealousies from flaring up, the central government

[5] Nicholas Kaltchas, *Introduction to the Constitutional History of Modern Greece* (New York, 1940), p. 53; Finlay, *History*, vi, 236-47; and Woodhouse, *Greek War*, pp. 74-78.

[6] For an example of one foreigner who favored a federal system for Greece, see John Comstock, *History of the Greek Revolution* (New York, 1825). On the Greek attitude, even among those most bound by sectional loyalties, see Kaltchas, *Constitutional History*, pp. 41, 46-48.

[7] On intersectional jealousies and suspicions, see Woodhouse, *Greek War*, p. 82; and W. H. Humphreys, "Journal of a Visit to Greece," *A Picture of Greece in 1825; as Exhibited in the Personal Narratives of James Emerson, Count Pecchio, W. H. Humphreys* (New York, 1826), ii, 193-94. On Hydra-Spezza difficulties, see James Emerson, "Journal of a Residence among the Greeks in 1825," *ibid.*, i, 123-24.

[8] Humphreys, *ibid.*, ii, 193-94. For more information and documentation on the second civil war, see pp. 87-88 below.

21

had constantly to exercise care in making job appointments, to see that each section had a satisfactory quota.[9]

The great influx of Greeks not native to the insurgent provinces gave rise to sectional jealousies of another sort—between natives or *autochthons* and immigrants or *heterochthons*. The latter came from any of the three general regions which Greeks then inhabited: (1) the Balkans and Asia Minor, under Ottoman rule; (2) the Ionian Islands, lying off the western coast of the lower Balkans, under British rule since the treaty of Vienna (1815); and (3) the colonies of the Greek diaspora throughout Western Europe. The influx during the Revolution came in three waves. The first wave consisted of idealistic and patriotic volunteers who came from places where Ottoman power was too great to permit revolt or from the merchant communities of the Greek diaspora where there was no Turkish overlord against whom to rebel. A second wave (1822-26) came as refugees from places where the Ottomans had snuffed out revolt. Many were civilians who had survived Turkish massacres, such as merchants from the islands of Chios and Psara or princely families from the Danubian principalities. Others were fighters who came in groups to offer their services once their own attempts at home had proved unsuccessful. Such were the warlike Souliots of Epirus, who were expelled from their homeland by the Turks in 1822, the Cretans, whose revolt was temporarily suppressed in 1824, Thessalians and Macedonians, and even Bulgarians. A third wave came during the administration of President John Kapodistrias, a native of the Ionian Islands (1828-31). Many Ionian Islanders were attracted by him, not only because of his high regard for them and their trust in him, but also because the Islanders, continuously under Venetian rule from Byzantine times until 1797 and never under Ottoman domination, were more Westernized than the authochthons and better qualified for the functions necessitated by the establishment of a new Greek state.[10]

Antiheterochthon prejudice became apparent in the opening months of the Revolution, when such heterochthons as Demetrios Ypsilantes, Alexander Mavrokordatos, and Theodore Negres first made contact with the indigenous elements. Autochthons attempted to establish legal disabilities against the newcomers. For instance, in 1825-26, some of the warriors of Western Greece organized an autochthon movement to curb

[9] Kaltchas, *Constitutional History*, p. 74; and George Ludwig von Maurer, *Das Griechische Volk in öffentlicher, kirchlicher und privatrechtlicher Beziehung vor und nach dem Freiheitskampfe bis zum 31. Juli 1834* (Heidelberg, 1835), I, 451-52.

[10] Concerning the first category, see Maurer, *Griechische Volk*, II, 31-38, 41-42. On the second, see *ibid.*, I, 50; Humphreys, *Picture of Greece*, II, 215; and F. Thiersch, *De l'état actuel de la Grèce* (Leipzig, 1833), I, 225-27, who estimates Souliot survivors in Greece at 1,200, armed Cretan refugees at 4,000 (without families) and fighting men from the Olympus region of Greece at 2,500. On the third category, see Maurer, *op.cit.*, II, 42-43.

the growing influence of the Souliots in their native provinces.[11] The problem was to assume greater dimensions in the royal period.

One ought not exaggerate the extent of sectionalism. The Greeks soon abolished the initial regional authorities. Moreover, nationalism, though relatively a new sentiment compared with age-old sectionalism, was clearly in the ascendant and infectious. Time was with it. The longer the Revolution continued, the greater the sense of participation in a common enterprise and the sense of belonging to something bigger—the nation. As far as the authochthon-heterochthon controversy was concerned, it was mitigated to a large extent by considerations for the Great Idea (*Megale Idea*). This ideological expression of nationalism envisaged the liberation of all Greeks from Ottoman rule and their incorporation into a nation-state with its capital in Constantinople or merely the restoration of the Byzantine empire on the ruins of the Ottoman state. This ideal had been the inspiration of the *Philike Hetairia*, the secret society which was organized in 1814 by Greek merchants in Odessa and which planned the Greek Revolution. By 1821 the society, with all the paraphernalia of oaths, initiations, and hierarchical ranks, had branches among Greeks throughout the Ottoman empire and had used its extensive organizational apparatus to propagate the Great Idea.[12]

The population of the new Greek state came to about 800,000, only about one-fourth the total Greek population in the Near East living under Ottoman rule or on the British-dominated Ionian Islands. The new Greek state was therefore considered only a rump state. Many authochthons realized that, unless they overcame their prejudices and treated heterochthons fairly, they would so alienate the Ottoman and Ionian Greeks that the Great Idea would become totally impracticable.[13]

[11] Thiersch, *État actuel*, I, 229-30.

[12] Concerning the Great Idea, Thiersch (*ibid.*, I, 198-99) wrote that even the "last class" in Greece claimed Constantinople as the real capital of the Greeks. On the Philike Hetairia, its vast organization and its role in planning the Revolution, the major works are: John Philemon, *Dokimion Historikon peri tes Philikes Hetairias* [*Historical Essay concerning the Philike Hetairia*] (Nauplion, 1834); (2) Takes Kandeloros, *He Philike Hetereia* [*The Philike Hetairia*] (Athens, 1926); (3) *He Philike Hetairia. Anamnestikon teuchos epi te 150eteridi* [*The Philike Hetairia. Memorial Volume on the 150th Anniversary*], ed. Emmanuel G. Protopsaltes (Athens, 1964); and (4) *Philike Hetairia. A. Paranoma Ntokoumenta. B. Apomnemoneumata Agoniston (E. Xanthos–G. Leventes)* [*Philike Hetairia. A. Illegal Documents. B. Memoirs of Contestants. . . .*], ed. Tasos Vournas (Athens [1965]).

[13] Leften Stavrianos (*The Balkans since 1453* [New York, 1959], p. 281) estimates that the total Greek population at the beginning of the nineteenth century was 3,000,000. Finlay (*History*, VI, 2) estimated it at 3,500,000 at the outbreak of the Revolution: 1,000,000 in the Balkans, 1,000,000 scattered in Crete, Cyclades, Ionian Islands, and Constantinople, and 1,500,000 in Asia Minor, Cyprus, the trans-Danubian principalities, Russia, and other countries. Driault and Lhéritier (*Histoire*, II, 110) estimated the total population of Greece at independence at 509,061, and at the following population figures for the three major sections of Greece: 247,804 (Peloponnesos); 98,744 (Continental Greece); and 162,513 (Islands).

2. Social Structure and Social Groups

Under Ottoman domination, the primary social divisions among Greeks were the same as those that characterized Ottoman society as a whole—the horizontal division between rulers and ruled. To be sure, all Greeks theoretically fell into the second category so far as Muslims were concerned. But thanks to the Ottoman practice of allowing religious and local autonomy, Greek-ruling élites did exist vis-à-vis Greeks and other Orthodox Christians. One's status, first and foremost, had depended on one's relationship to the Ottoman administration—whether one held a position recognized by the Ottoman overlord or whether one simply worked and paid taxes. It depended, in other words, on the power which state recognition allowed one to exercise over other Greeks. A second criterion of status, vis-à-vis other Greeks, was the loyalty or respect one commanded by virtue of either real or imagined embodiment of accepted cultural values.

Of the Greek élite groups based on the first criterion, there were those who functioned as part of the central administration: the ecclesiastical leaders (bishops) and secular leaders (Phanariots). The provincial élites were basically three, each dominant in a particular region of what eventually became liberated Greece: (1) primates or landed gentlemen, dominant in the Peloponnesos; (2) *armatoloi* or military commanders, characteristic of Rumely; and (3) shipowners and capitalists, primarily in the Islands. As an élite, the ecclesiastical hierarchy had its official status reinforced by its acknowledged position as cultural and spiritual leaders. But the *klephts*, those brigand and outlaw rebels against constituted authority, whether that authority was Greek or Turkish, held an élite or at least semi-élite position solely because of the respect which they commanded among the folk and the values which they shared with the people.[14]

Ecclesiastical Leaders

To understand the importance of the upper clergy in the Ottoman empire, it is essential to understand what type of state the Ottoman empire was and the special role of the Orthodox church in it. In the political tradition of the Near East, the Osmanlis preferred to deal with communities rather than with individuals. As Muslims they believed that the distinctive feature of a people was its religion rather than its nationality. Their Sacred Law (*Sharia*) elaborated rules of behavior for Muslims but said nothing about the internal governance of non-Muslim communities. Hence the Osmanlis had organized their state into a series of parallel religious communities called *millets*. One of these was the Ortho-

[14] On the extent of social differentiation among the Greeks, see Finlay, *History*, vi, 9.

dox millet ruled by the traditional religious leader of Byzantine Greeks, the patriarch of Constantinople.[15]

As Muslims did not distinguish between religious and secular, the Osmanlis allowed the patriarch and his hierarchy powers which went beyond the merely religious. As an agent of the Turkish power, the patriarch became what he had never been so long as a Byzantine emperor existed—a political chief vested with far-reaching judicial, fiscal, and administrative powers, which he delegated to his bishops, archbishops, and metropolitans. As responsible heads of their flock, he and his hierarchy were liable to execution in the event of insurgency. In 1821, there were forty-one bishops, archbishops, and metropolitans in the territory that became insurgent Greece. Since the power of the church was normally exercised at their level of administration, the type of authority which they exercised is worth examination.[16]

In judicial matters the bishop was the counterpart of the Muslim judge or *kadi*. As the kadi heard cases between Muslims or between Muslims and non-Muslims, according to the Sharia, the bishop listened to cases between the Orthodox according to the canon law of the church or the civil Byzantine law as recorded in the manual of Armenopoulos, a fourteenth-century jurist of Thessaloniki. Nowhere were the bishops permitted to judge criminal cases. Everywhere cases of marriage, divorce, and wills between Orthodox adherents fell within their exclusive jurisdiction. Otherwise their judicial powers differed from place to place. Usually they acted as mere arbitrators among people who preferred their judgment to that of anyone else. In short, the unofficial authority of the bishops extended beyond their acknowledged duties. The notaries, to whom people went for the preparation of official documents such as deeds or wills, were usually ecclesiastical officials under the bishops' control. The bishops were often asked to act as guardians of minors, to sign documents in order to give the documents greater authority, and to intervene with the Turkish or Greek secular leaders in order to seek redress of individual grievances. As unofficial advisers and defenders, they were in many ways the real rulers of the people, but only so long as the Turks sanctioned their authority from above and the people gave their confidence from below. When these two conditions were no longer present during the Revolution, the power of the church hierarchy collapsed.[17]

Phanariots

"Phanariot" means resident of *Phanar* (lighthouse), the name of a district in Constantinople where the patriarchate has been located since

[15] *Ibid.*, pp. 8, 10; or more comprehensively though generally, Gibb and Bowen, *Islamic Society*, Vol. i, Part ii, 212-16.

[16] Driault and Lhéritier, *Histoire*, i, 102; Finlay, *History*, vi, 7-8; and Kaltchas, *Constitutional History*, pp. 27-28.

[17] Maurer, *Griechische Volk*, i, 89-91, 93-97, 104f.

1601. Gradually the term came to apply to a few select families, wealthy, well-bred and proud, a type of unofficial aristocracy which came in the eighteenth century to fill important posts in the Ottoman administration. They rose to such power because of what they had to offer—their European cultivation and their knowledge of languages, European and oriental. Since Turkish officials usually knew only Turkish, Arabic, and Persian, the Phanariots were indispensable to these Turkish officials in their dealings either with Greek subjects or European powers. They occupied four offices of great importance: two as interpreters or *dragomans* and two as princes or *hospodars*. The Dragoman of the Fleet was the executive deputy of the *capitan-pasha*, commander of the Ottoman navy and governor-general of the Aegean Islands. Representing his superior in the latter capacity, the Dragoman was the real governor of those Islands. The Dragoman of the Porte, chief interpreter, actually became a type of foreign minister for European affairs. After 1711, when the native Rumanian princes cooperated with the Russians against their Turkish overlord, Phanariots occupied as hospodars the separate thrones of the Danubian principalities of Wallachia and Moldavia. Their influence there explains why the first bid for Greek independence in 1821, an unsuccessful one, took place in the Danubian principalities.[18]

With the exception of the Islands, the Phanariot class had never exercised any direct influence over what became insurgent Greece. There they became important only after the outbreak of the Revolution when, as eager volunteers or care-worn refugees, they migrated to the liberated provinces. Among the immigrant Phanariot families were the Ypsilantes', Mavrokordatos', Argyropoulos', Soutsos', Karatzas', and Katakouzenos'. One was Michael Soutsos himself, the hospodar or virtually independent governor of Wallachia in 1821, when the revolt broke out. They were a distinguished group, many of them related to each other, all trying to make the best of their primitive surroundings by reviving a bit of the elegant social life they once had known. The memoirs of Alexander Rangabe, scion of one of these families and talented *littérateur*, give an intimate picture of this group. But they were resented in free Greece. Their way of life seemed frivolous, their titles violated the egalitarian

[18] For excellent general accounts of this group, see any of the following: Robert Lee Wolff, *The Balkans in Our Time* (Cambridge, Mass., 1956), pp. 61-63; Stavrianos, *Balkans*, pp. 270-72; Driault and Lhéritier, *Histoire*, ɪ, 102-103. For a closer though less comprehensive look, see Maurer, *Griechische Volk*, ɪ, 9-10, 22-24, 91-93. Older standard studies are M. P. Zallony, *Essai sur les Fanariots* (Marseilles, 1824); P. E. Giannopoulos, *Hoi phanariotai* [*The Phanariots*] (Athens, 1929); and N. Iorga, "Le despotisme éclairé dans les pays roumains au XVIIIᵉ siècle," *Bulletin of the International Committee of Historical Sciences*, ɪx (1937), 100-15; supplemented by an unpublished dissertation by H. W. Held, "Die Phanarioten, ihre allmähliche Entwicklung zur fürstlichen Aristokratie bis zu deren Untergang 1821" (Bern, 1920), and a more recent article by J. Gottwald, "Phanariotische Studien," *Leipsiger Vierteljahresschrift für Südosteuropa*, v (1941), 1-58.

sentiments of the people, and their European manners seemed alien. Being a Phanariot was a great drawback politically, as Alexander Mavrokordatos soon found out, and in the press "Phanariot" became a term of reproach.[19]

Primates

Ottoman provincial administration functioned on three levels: that of the province or *pashalik*, that of the district or *eparchy*, and that of the commune (either a town or a collection of villages). In differing proportions on each level, two parallel authorities functioned: that of the Turks as agents of the ruling race and appointees of the central government; and that of the Greeks, in areas inhabited exclusively (Islands) or predominantly (Rumely and Morea) by Greeks, as chosen representatives of the local population. A pasha, appointed by the sultan, ruled over the province, and a *voivode*, appointed by the pasha, over the district. Ostensibly, the administration of the Aegean Islands would seem to present an exception, but not really. Each island was the equivalent of an eparchy, and the whole complex of islands a type of pashalik under the capitan-pasha, commander of the Ottoman fleet.

Exercising an autonomy going back to pre-Ottoman days, the communes elected their own officials, who were known variously as elders, *demogerons*, and archons. These men did not simply administer the affairs of their respective communes. From each commune at least once a year they met before the voivode as an advisory district assembly. Among other things, this assembly elected one or two of its members for the voivode's executive council, a standing body subject to reelection annually. Those who served on the voivode's council were therefore eparchal leaders and were distinguished from elders of mere local importance by such names as primates or notables (*proestoi, prokritoi, prouchontes,* or *kodza-bashis*).

This system was designed primarily to serve the fiscal needs of the empire. The imperial government would specify in advance the contribution of each province. The pasha would estimate the province's expenses for the coming year, add this sum to the amount specified by the imperial government, and allot the quota among the districts. In each district the voivode would confer with his council and call the assembly in order to determine the eparchal budget and distribute the tax burden among the communes. Finally, the communal elders would assess each family according to its ability. With the ecclesiastical officials, the primates and elders also enjoyed some judicial duties, whose extent depended on local custom.

[19] On the difficulties of adjustment of, and the popular resentment against, the Phanariots, see Alexander R. Rangabe, *Apomnemoneumata* [*Memoirs*] (Athens, 1894), I, 1-19 and passim; Maurer, *Griechische Volk*, II, 31-32; and Thiersch, *État actuel*, I, 229.

The system worked to the mutual advantage of the Ottoman authorities and the Greek taxpayers. For the former, the system had the merit of locating a select few who could prevail upon the mass and who could serve as virtual hostages for the good behavior of that mass. For the latter, it lessened contact with Turkish officials and permitted local autonomy. The intermediaries, that is, the primates and elders, carried the heavy burden of mediating between demands from above and complaints from below. Their lives were often in danger, especially when Turkey's foreign wars encouraged internal revolts, but they were rewarded for their risks by possessing power and the means of enrichment.

The primates were strongest and most prominent in the Peloponnesos where the system of regional autonomy found its greatest elaboration. The primates did not simply sit in a voivode's council. From all over the Peloponnesos they met annually as a provincial assembly to advise the pasha. Two of them, elected by this assembly, sat permanently in Tripolis, the centrally located Peloponnesos capital, on the pasha's advisory council for one or more annual terms. Each official was called a *morayannes*. Two others, each named a *vekiles*, served as virtual ambassadors of the Peloponnesos in Constantinople, where they could often exercise influence to obtain a new pasha or correct some injustices.[20]

In Peloponnesos, the primates constituted a distinct economic group among their fellow-Greeks. In the first place, they were large landowners. With the monasteries, they owned one and a half million *stremes* (*stremmata*) (four stremes to an acre) or one-third of the land estimated as the Greek portion of arable land in Peloponnesos. Since the other three million belonged to Turkish magnates, the mass of Peloponnesian Greeks were mere landless tenants on the property of their Greek or Turkish masters. Second, they engaged in tax-farming, the lucrative business of paying the imperial treasury a fixed sum in advance and then in practice taking for oneself all that one could collect. Since the tax-farming contracts usually applied to whole districts and sold at a great price, only the primates among the Greeks could afford to pay for them. Third, toward the close of the Turkish period they engaged more and more in commerce. As tax-farmers, who collected from the peasants in kind, they held a virtual monopoly over the saleable material. Only they had the means to get the produce to the market ports, to store it there, and to sell

[20] The most complete and authoritative work on Ottoman provincial administration in the Peloponnesos and the role of the primates in it is that of Michael B. Sakellariou, *He Peloponnesos kata ten Deuteran Tourkokratian 1715-1821* [*Peloponnesos during the Second Period of Turkish Rule*] (Athens, 1939), pp. 84-96. For an unfavorable and unfair treatment of the primates, see Takes A. Stamatopoulos, *Ho Esoterikos Agonas kata ten Epanastase tou 1821* [*The Internal Struggle during the Revolution of 1821*] (Athens, 1957), I, 79ff. Maurer (*Griechische Volk*, I, 59-89) gives a fairly detailed account of primate administration in the Peloponnesos as well as in the other two major sections of Greece. See also Finlay, *History*, VI, 14, 25, and Kaltchas, *Constitutional History*, pp. 28-31.

to the foreign merchants in the bulk desired. Their monopoly allowed them to control prices and hence multiply the cash value of the taxes collected. Thanks to the French Revolution and its foreign wars, they were able to drive out foreign competition, especially that of French merchants who had formerly dominated Peloponnesian commerce.[21]

The Peloponnesian primates were very much a social class—self-perpetuating, cohesive, and alike in their style of life. Though they were theoretically elected to office, only a fraction of the population in a commune possessed the franchise and that fraction voted by acclamation rather than by secret ballot. The system itself favored their continuance in office, because only men of affluence and experience could carry out the duties of a primate. Power tended therefore to become hereditary. Only some extraordinary event, like the revolt of 1770, could dislodge a family from its position.[22]

As in most traditional societies, marriage served as a means of cementing bonds between families. Virtually all the primates were related to each other by blood. Their mobility and the experience of acting collectively added to the cohesiveness of blood. Like pashas, each of the primates maintained a type of court consisting of a secretary, who handled all correspondence, a doctor, a priest, sometimes a police guard, and a large number of servants. This style of life set them off from other Greeks as superior. But the abject servility demanded by the Turk and the pasha's power of life and death, frequently exercised, served as painful reminders of their inferior status vis-à-vis the Turks. Such isolation, from both fellow-Greeks and Turks, must have bred greater social solidarity among them.[23]

Social unity could not prevent bitter factional strife among the Peloponnesian primates. The prize of political supremacy was too valuable not to excite competition among them. Their factionalism was too important a source of Greek weakness for the jealous Turkish magnates not to exploit it. Very often blood was shed in factional strife, leaving bitter memories which neither common social interests nor the challenge of a new class of captains could efface.[24]

---

[21] Maurer (*Griechische Volk*, II, 24) defines the primate class, everywhere except in the islands, as that group "basing their power on immoveable property." He is also aware of their tax-farming activities (I, 523) as is Finlay (*History*, VI, 24-25), who has a clearer understanding of their mercantile activities as well. But the most exhaustive account, thus far, of the primates' economic role in the Peloponnesos is that of Sakellariou [*Peloponnesos*], pp. 48-49, 217-20. See also Stavrianos, *Balkans*, p. 280.

[22] Kaltchas, *Constitutional History*, p. 32; Maurer, *Griechische Volk*, I, 54-55; and Sakellariou [*Peloponnesos*], p. 94.

[23] On kinship ties, see Sakellariou [*Peloponnesos*], p. 220; and Thiersch, *État actuel*, I, 222. On their style of life, see Finlay, *History*, VI, 26, and Maurer, *Griechische Volk*, I, 47.

[24] Gordon, *Greek Revolution*, I, 143-44.

Kodza-bashi, like Phanariot, became a term of contempt during the Revolution, when the people were free to express their antipathy toward their former masters, who had often oppressed them more than the Turks had.[25] They were commonly known as "Turk-worshippers" or "uncircumcised Turks," not merely because of their long association with the Turks in the administration but because of their outward cultural affinity to the Turks. The memoirs of Chrysanthopoulos Photakos, an opponent of the primates, reflects the popular judgment:

> The khoja-bashi imitated the Turk in everything, including dress, manners, the household. His notion of living in style was the same as the Turk's, and the only difference between them was one of names: for instance, instead of being called Hasan the Khoja-Bashi, he would be called Yianni, and instead of going to mosque he would go to church. This was the only distinction between the two.[26]

Independently, George Finlay, the English philhellene and historian, describes the haughty bearing of George Sisines during the Revolution. The pomp of his household, the title of *bey* assumed by his sons, the insistence on having the peasants kneel when addressing him—all these things reveal that what the primates found wrong with the Ottoman empire was not its institutions but the Turks' domination of those institutions.[27] Regardless of what the people felt, however, the primates had borne the brunt of Turkish rule and had probably suffered its insecurities more than the people.

Captains (Klephts, Armatoloi, and Kapoi)

The practice of carrying arms served as the basis for a separate social group. Its members might be property-owners or not, officials or outlaws, separated by geography, but they all enjoyed military power and shared an ethos which exalted the military virtues and despised work on the soil. Such people found their natural abode in the mountains, secure from encroachment by any of the usual enemies (central authority, alien race,

[25] Gennaios Kolokotrones, *Apomnemoneumata* [*Memoirs*], ed. Emmanuel G. Protopsaltes (Athens, 1955), p. 49; and Thiersch, *État actuel*, I, 218.

[26] Leicester Stanhope, "Report on the State of Greece," *Greece in 1823 and 1824: Series of Letters and other Documents on the Greek Revolution*, new edn. (London, 1825), p. 237; Edward Blaquière, *The Greek Revolution, its Origin and Progress* (London, 1824), p. 290: "The primates are more prone to Turkish customs of every kind than any other class of Greeks"; and Sakellariou [*Peloponnesos*], p. 135. The quotation, translated by Arnold Toynbee and cited in his *A Study of History* (London, 1954), VIII, 683, is taken from Photios Chrysanthopoulos Photakos, *Apomnemoneumata peri tes Hellenikes Epanastaseos* [*Memoirs of the Greek Revolution*], ed. Stavros Andropoulos (Athens, 1899), I, 33-34.

[27] The affluence and Ottomanization of the Sisines family seems to have been sufficiently pronounced to attract widespread attention, as witnessed by the following specific references to it: Finlay, *History*, VI, 336; Stanhope to Bentham, 11 May 1824, in *Greece in 1823-24*, p. 204; and Thiersch, *État actuel*, I, 14-15.

settled population) and free to ignore the solemn prohibition by the Sharia against the bearing of arms by non-Muslims. The many mountains of Greece bred these people, especially the precipitous Pindus range running from Rumely northwest into Epirus and Albania, but also the formidable mountain country of Mane in southeast Peloponnesos.[28]

There were roughly three distinct military types: klephts or brigands, armatoloi or militia men acknowledged by the empire, and kapoi or a type of police force hired by local or provincial authorities. The élite of any one of the three types were the captains. The rank and file were called *palikars*, meaning brave young men.

Klephts were outlaws who formed into bands and lived on plunder. Criminals, debtors, misfits, adventurers, victims of tyrannical officials— from generation to generation these types fled to the mountains. They sometimes robbed, tortured, even murdered fellow-Greeks—affluent ones, however, rather than simple peasants. More often they raided the Turks, from whom they were divorced by religion and nationality as well as by social class. They enjoyed the support of the generally oppressed common folk, from whose ranks they came, because they represented opposition to established authority. A whole oral tradition of folk poetry testifies to the sympathy they evoked and the reputation for patriotism they acquired.[29]

The geography of Rumely favored brigandage, and there it was perennial. In the Peloponnesos, where brigands could more easily be suppressed by the authorities, they usually clustered in a few select regions, such as Kalavryta, Karytaina, and southeast Laconia on the fringes of Mane. Mane and the Ionian Islands offered safer refuge in case of emergency.[30]

The armatoloi differed from the klephts in having their habit of bearing arms officially acknowledged, and so made lawful, by the Ottoman authorities, who employed them to guard passes, keep communications open, and maintain general order. The system of armatoloi was in part a concession to the demands of the mountain population for the right to maintain their own means of self-defense, and in part a Turkish device for curbing brigandage, either by suppression or by recruitment of brigands into armatoloi ranks. Indeed, the line between klephts and armatoloi was in practice not always clear. Armatolism became a disguised form of thievery when landlords in the plains had to buy immunity from the pillaging with which the armatoloi threatened them. On the other hand, brigands changed status overnight by enlisting in the ranks of the armatoloi or the mercenary troops of a pasha. The action of the imperial

[28] On klephts and armatoloi, see Tasos Vournas, *Harmatoloi kai Klephtes* [*Armatoloi and Klephts*] (Athens, 1958). Finlay (*History*, vi, 163) cites Aetolia and the Pindus region of Rumely especially as "the land of armatoloi."

[29] Driault and Lhéritier, *Histoire*, i, 104-05; Finlay, *History*, vi, 22-24; Maurer, *Griechische Volk*, i, 44-46, 497-500, ii, 24-26; and Sakellariou [*Peloponnesos*], p. 136.

[30] Finlay, *History*, vi, 22; and Sakellariou [*Peloponnesos*], p. 141.

government in the eighteenth century blurred the distinction even further. It encroached upon the traditional privileges of the armatoloi by employing brigands against them, and the pursued armatoloi often took to the mountains as brigands.[31]

Unlike klephtism, armatolism involved communities of people, not just bands under individual leaders. The region policed by a group of armatoloi was known as an *armatolik* or *captanlik*. Each was a complex of so-called head-villages (*kephalochoria*) or free villages, enjoying complete autonomy, which meant being spared any resident Ottoman officials or Turkish settlers. The leader of the band was called a *boulouk-pasha* or an *otzak*. He ruled as well as protected his village or group of villages. Like his counterpart the elder of a peasant commune or the voivode of a province, he was responsible for the collection of the taxes, which he farmed out at a profit to himself, and he was elected by the residents, though "election" usually meant acknowledgement of the person able to provide for, and command the respect of, most retainers.[32]

The two most famous aggregations of such captanliks were Souli, whose inaccessible peaks overlooked the Acheron River in southern Albania, and the Peloponnesian district of Mane. Both these virtually independent republics, which paid only a token tribute, supported native military aristocracies. In Souli, only a few families enjoyed the right to carry arms. These families provided the captains of clans and ruled like feudal superiors over the peasants, whose sons often found social advancement by joining the ranks of a Souliot captain. When the Revolution proved unsuccessful there, Souliot captains such as the Botsares' (Markos and Notes) and Kitsos Tzavelas migrated to Western Rumely, where they and their contingents became an important political factor. The traditional feud between the Botsares' and the Tzavelas' was to play a role in the rise of the "English" and "Russian" parties in West Rumely.[33]

In Mane there was also a sharp social cleavage between the aristocracy of captains or *boulouxides*, who inhabited the characteristic stone fortresses which dotted Mane, and the *phamelis*, followers of the boulouxides who were allowed to carry arms but lived in hovels and held inferior status. By 1821 the two chief boulouxis families were the Mavromichales', who dominated Western Mane, and the Tzanetakes', who controlled Eastern Mane. Traditionally, the families rivaled each other for the leadership or beyship of Mane. The last bey before the Revolution was Petros Mavromichales (1781-1821), leader of a huge family. At the outbreak of the Revolution, Mavromichales, better known as Petrobey, assumed the

[31] Finlay, *History*, vi, 19-22; Maurer, *Griechische Volk*, i, 5-8, 497-98; and John Vlachogiannes, *Klephtes tou Moria* . . . [*Klephts of the Morea, Historical Study based on New Sources 1715-1820*] (Athens, 1935), p. 13.

[32] Maurer, *Griechische Volk*, i, 44-47, 83-84.

[33] Driault and Lhéritier, *Histoire*, i, 105-06; and Finlay, *History*, vi, 36-52, 79-91.

commanding role in the liberation of the southern Peloponnesos. The move in this direction was no coincidence. The Maniats had always looked longingly down at the rich lands of Messenia from their peaks, and now they simply filled part of the power vacuum left there by the many departed Turkish magnates. From even before the Revolution, Petrobey enjoyed an alliance with Panagiotes Benakes, a rich primate of Kalamata, through the marriage of Benakes' sister to Petrobey's brother.[34]

Smaller armatoliks, without the cohesion of Souli or Mane, characterized the provinces of West Rumely, especially the region of Agrapha. Everywhere in West Rumely, alliances between virtually independent captains formed and reformed, each time establishing some sort of balance of power between them. The region therefore had many captains to offer the Greek Revolution. The most prominent were Andrew Iskos, the Stratos' (John and Nicholas), and the Grivas' (Phloros, Stavros, Theodore, and Gardikiotes) in the westernmost and wildest province of Acarnania; George Varnakiotes and Staïkos Staïkopoulos of Aetolia; Papakostas and Mitsos Kontogiannes of Phthiotis. Here, as among captains generally, the idea of a nation had only begun to penetrate their consciousness. Their main political objective was simply that of expanding the boundaries of their captanliks and consolidating their own power within them. What was better than to become a pasha and how did one go about doing so but by the traditional manner of bargaining, either with Muslims or Christians, Turks or Albanians? That is why Finlay could report occasional desertions to the Turks of such captains as Varnakiotes, Iskos, Rangos, and Valtinos.[35]

In East Rumely, Greek primates were stronger than in West Rumely, and Turkish magnates were present, at least in Attica and Boeotia. Here the authority of the Turks fell more heavily on the Greeks, and local autonomy was not so well developed. As a result, at the outbreak of the Revolution few captains existed to take over. Those who ultimately became influential in this region were military parvenus—men who obtained wealth and power through the military profession opened up to them by the Revolution. The four chief ones merit attention. Nicholas Kriezotes, the chief force in Euboea by the end of the Revolution, had been a shepherd in Asia Minor. Vasos Mavrovouniotes, a Montenegrin, had started out as a brigand in Asia Minor and established an influence which extended throughout East Rumely. John Mamoures, who dominated the central Rumelian region of Phocis, owed his power to his adoption by

---

[34] Finlay, *History*, vi, 26-27; Maurer, *Griechische Volk*, i, 70-76 (administration), and i, 179-82 (social system).

[35] On Agrapha, where the armatoloi were hired by the Turkish authorities to guard the strategic passes of Mt. Pindus, see Finlay, *History*, vi, 18-19, 22. On desertions, see *ibid.*, p. 274. For descriptions of the various captains cited, see Chap. III below in sections on the "French," "English," and "Russian" parties.

John Gouras, the revolutionary captain who died in battle in 1826. John Makrygiannes, one of the finest figures of the Revolution and the author of splendid memoirs, was born into a peasant-shepherd family of central Rumely.[36]

After much debate among Greek scholars, it seems quite certain now that those Peloponnesian chieftains who distinguished themselves during the Revolution had been mere kapoi in spite of their contrary assertions. A *kapos* was anyone who served as a member of a primate's personal armed force. He differed from the armatolos with respect to his employers, his duties, and the extent of his power. His employer was a primate rather than the Turkish authorities. He policed the lands of the primate and asserted the primate's authority. He only sometimes took on the chief duty of an armatolos, namely pursuit of brigands. Unlike the armatolos chieftain, a kapos chief was in no sense a ruler.[37]

That the leading Peloponnesian chieftains of the Revolution had been kapoi rather than armatoloi is important for two reasons. It explains the bitterness of the struggle between captains and primates during the Revolution—the captains smarting under the humiliation of having served them, the primates indignant that these upstarts should wish to challenge their own power. It also means that kapoi were not members of a ruling group in their capacity as kapoi. Insofar as they were also brigands, and distinguished ones at that, they wielded some influence over the peasants. Otherwise they are mentioned here because they became a very important class during and after the Revolution.

Among the Revolutionary leaders who had served as kapoi were none other than Theodore Kolokotrones himself, scion of a famous klepht family and leader of the military "party" in the Peloponnesos during the Revolution; Demetrios Koliopoulos, better known as Plapoutas; Niketas Stamatellopoulos, otherwise known as Niketaras; and Basil Petimezas. The first three served the Delegiannes', primates of their native Karytaina; the last, the Zaïmes' of Kalavryta. After they had risen on the social ladder, they tried to draw a curtain over their humble past by referring to themselves by the proud name of armatolos. These men, however, were only part-time kapoi, temporarily abandoning brigandage, perhaps to escape repression, perhaps to make a little money. In 1806, the Turks undertook an all-out campaign to suppress brigandage. The above persons had to flee. In the Ionian Islands, a traditional place of refuge from the Turks, they enrolled in light regiments, designed by the British rulers for the Greeks and commanded by Richard Church, the English philhellene who was to serve with distinction in the Greek Revolution and then settle permanently in Greece. During their long exile, they learned much about the outside world, came into contact with Souliots and

[36] See Chap. III below in sections cited in n. 35 above.
[37] Finlay, *History*, vi, 26; Sakellariou [*Peloponnesos*], p. 142; and Vlachogiannes [*Klephts*], pp. 26-33.

Rumeliots who, like themselves, were refugees, and probably shed some of their provincialism.[38]

Merchant Capitalists

The only two places in insurgent Greece where a merchant capitalist group, clearly distinguishable from a landed proprietor class, constituted a ruling group were Hydra and Spezza. Like many of the other Aegean Islands, Hydra and Spezza enjoyed complete autonomy, that is, they merely paid an annual fixed tribute and never allowed the Turks to settle among them. They also practiced municipal self-government, which means that they elected their own notables or primates to conduct their affairs. But in Hydra and Spezza, where everyone depended on commerce for his livelihood because agriculture was unprofitable, the primates were capitalists. The inhabitants belonged to three categories: notables, skippers or captains, and sailors. A notable enjoyed his title by virtue of being wealthy enough to build himself a large home and retire from the actual sailing of his own ships. The title was not hereditary. Until the end of the Napoleonic wars, classes were fluid because fortunes were easily made and lost. Thereafter, when commerce became stagnant, the number of notables became almost stationary and relative incomes remained fixed. The wealthiest Hydriot family by far were the Kountouriotes', Lazaros and George; the wealthiest Spezziot probably Nicholas Botases, whose ships had played such an important role in Black Sea commerce.[39]

The People

There was little social diversification among the ruled in any one region. They did the work, and the type of work available was usually a matter of geography. In the Peloponnesos, the peasants were most prominent because the land was fertile, and best off because the population was thin. Though they may have cultivated the same plot of land for generations, they usually had no title to the land. Thus they depended on their Greek or Turkish landlord, though legally they were free. Peasants in the mountain regions, which meant most of the Rumeliot ones, were small freeholders, getting less from the land than their Moreot brothers but exercising greater independence. Since his plot was small and grazing was standard, the Rumeliot usually combined shepherding with his culti-

[38] On Kolokotrones, et al., see the section on the Kolokotrones faction in Chap. II below. For an account of the Ionian regiments, see "Introduction," John Makrygiannes, *Apomnemoneumata* [*Memoirs*], ed. John Vlachogiannes, 2nd edn. (Athens, 1947), I, 2: "The Greek troops serving in the Ionian Islands were military schools for whole phalanxes of men, among whom were Kolokotrones, Niketaras, Petimezas, many Rumeliots and Epirots."
[39] For a summary of the Greek commercial revival of the eighteenth century, see Stavrianos, *Balkans*, pp. 274-79; or Maurer, *Griechische Volk*, I, 49-53. On the merchant classes of Hydra and Spezza more especially, see Finlay, *History*, VI, 30-33, 166; Stavrianos, p. 275; and Woodhouse, *Greek War*, p. 59.

vating duties. Those who were primarily or solely shepherds were more mobile than peasants. Indeed, the Vlachs, those people of Rumanian origin, were nomads. Shepherds were familiar with remote and brigand-infested regions and were thus important either in protecting brigands or assisting the authorities to pursue them. Usually they did the former.[40]

In the Islands, the working people were the common sailors. Under the system of Hydra and Spezza, where everyone who participated in a voyage shared the profit, the sailors prospered until the peace of 1815, which caused a fall in the price of grain in Europe and freight in the Mediterranean. In 1820 the harvest in Western Europe reduced gains even more and left a large number of sailors in both islands unemployed and a great source of unrest.[41]

Petty merchants and artisans, an urban class or people of the bazar, played no significant part in the Revolution, nor were they very different in mores and mentality from their rural brothers. A much more important group connected with overland trade were the muleteers or *agoyates*. Since everything in those days was transported by pack-horse or mule, these men were very numerous and somewhat cosmopolitan, some knowing smatterings of various languages. Every class, dependent on them, considered it good to conciliate them. They were important most of all as conveyers of information and new ideas as well as goods.[42]

Members of the lower clergy usually had more in common with their fellow villagers than with their ecclesiastical superiors. Most were men with no schooling, natives of their parish, married men who plowed their fields during the week. During the Revolution, they often fought beside their brothers. The monks, though equally illiterate and socially inferior, were more influential than the priests because they were often more mobile and hence, like the agoyates, valuable go-betweens for conspirators or mere political allies.[43]

What did the ruled expect from the Revolution and why did they take up arms? For many, of course, there was no choice. Primates as well as captains often forced reluctant peasants to fight who were tied to the land and could not yet make much practical sense out of nationalism. In Rumely, captains sometimes pursued a scorched earth policy against their own peasants so that, uprooted, the peasant would have to join the ranks. But other peasants took up the sword willingly, at least in their own districts, and so long as it was not harvest season. They wanted land and believed that the fertile land left by the Turks would become theirs as their reward for fighting. Among the more ambitious, the Revolution was

[40] Finlay, *History*, VI, 12-13, 119; and Thiersch, *État actuel*, I, 220-25.
[41] Finlay, *History*, VI, 168-69.
[42] *Ibid.*, p. 19; and Thiersch, *État actuel*, I, 222-24.
[43] Stanhope to J. Bowring, Argos, 14 Apr. 1824, in *Greece in 1823-24*, p. 179: "Almost every captain has some priests among his soldiers. . . ." See also Stavrianos, *Balkans*, p. 281; and Thiersch, *État actuel*, II, 184-85.

a chance to win wealth, power, and social advancement by joining up with some captain and eventually advancing to the command of a force oneself. In the Islands, where the depression caused widespread unemployment, the sailors were enthusiastic supporters of the Revolution, partly because fighting was a form of employment and might bring in valuable spoils.[44]

3. WESTERNIZATION AND CULTURAL SCHISM

Virtually all Western sources attest to the striking cultural contrasts among Greeks during and even after the Revolution. In matters of dress and style of life the contrasts were most noticeable. Some, in the manner of Europe, wore the black redingote, slept on beds and sat in chairs, and took their meals with their wives. They spoke at least one European language. Others, the vast majority, slept on mats or out-of-doors and squatted on pillows. They kept their wives well covered and lived socially apart from them. Of these, the mainlanders wore white kilts (*fustanelles*) in the manner of the Albanians, while the Islanders generally wore the baggy trousers (*vrakes*). Differences in the realm of ideas were harder to define but no less real. For instance, those who enjoyed any contact with Europe thought of statehood in terms of nationalism, centralization, bureaucracy, perhaps constitutionalism. For the indigenous elements, the machinery of the Ottoman state—pashaliks, captanliks, maybe theocracy —was quite satisfactory if possessed exclusively by Greeks in general or by a particular class of Greeks.[45]

However varied and complex the cultural contrasts, they tended to run along East-West or indigenous-European lines. Since the age of exploration at least, European society had been radiating its culture. It assumed, and convinced others, that its culture was synonymous with civilization and that the degree of civilization achieved by any other society de-

[44] Finlay, *History*, vi, 169-72, 200; Maurer, *Griechische Volk*, i, 499-500; and Stavrianos, *Balkans*, p. 280.

[45] "No people is composed of such different levels of civilization, customs, and interest as those which inhabit the kingdom of Greece" (Thiersch, *État actuel*, i, 217). Compare this with the statement written by an equally acute French observer a decade later, concerning Athens, the most Westernized city in Greece: "The customs of the Orient have not yet contracted a marriage with the customs of the Occident; they co-exist separately, without being either blended or erased" (Jean Alexandre Buchon, *La Grèce Continentale et la Morée* [Paris, 1843], p. 62). See also Maurer, *Griechische Volk*, ii, 22-23; Henry M. Baird, *Modern Greece* (New York, 1856), pp. 71-72, 88, 190-91; and Antoine Grénier, *La Grèce en 1863* (Paris, 1863), p. 32. On the indigenous political dream of a restored Byzantine empire, see Finlay, *History*, vi, 7; on the more limited political goals of the primates, see Woodhouse, *Greek War*, p. 133, and Kaltchas, *Constitutional History*, pp. 42-43. On the two ideological currents of Byzantine oecumenism (Greek domination of the Ottoman empire) and liberal nationalism (the formation of a National State), see Dionysios Zakythenos, *He Tourkokratia* [*Turkish Rule*] (Athens, 1957).

pended on how closely that society approached European standards.[46] At the time, the Greeks themselves acknowledged the East-West character of the contrast. Among later historians, George Aspreas has treated the early history of independent Greece as a conflict between an indigenous (enchorion) and foreign (xenikon) "party"; and W. Alison Phillips has cited this cultural difference as a basis for the rise of civilian and military "parties" in the early years of the Revolution.[47]

Generally speaking, Westernizers were drawn from three distinct though overlapping groups: (1) the mercantile elements, including those living in commercial centers of the Near East, such as Constantinople, Smyrna, and Chios, as well as those of the Greek diaspora settled in European cities such as Venice, Marseilles, London, Vienna, and Odessa; (2) the Phanariots, who started out as merchants and owed their important positions in the Ottoman state to their familiarity with Europe; and (3) graduates of European universities, professional men (mainly doctors, lawyers, secretaries, writers, and journalists), usually sons of merchants, but in some cases sons of captains and primates as well. Besides the mass of the people, the captains, primates, and most of the upper clergy were traditionalists. The peasants, at least, were traditionalists because they knew no culture but their own indigenous one. Many of the captains, primates, and clerics, however, had had some contact with the West, though usually through Westernized Greeks or Russians rather than directly.[48] Theirs was therefore a conservatism in the literal sense of wishing to conserve a way of life which presumably was being challenged. Their experience pointed up a simple though important truth—that contact with the West did not necessarily evoke approval of the West. Indeed, centuries of contact between Greeks and Westerners had resulted in a strong tradition of xenophobism. The background of this tradition merits attention.

The schism between Western and Eastern Christianity in 1054 and the Latin conquest of Constantinople in 1204 did irreparable damage to relations between Europe and Byzantium. "It is better to see in the city [Constantinople] the power of the Turkish turban than that of the Latin

[46] For instance, "Politically speaking the Greeks were Asiatics, and all their oriental ideas, whether social or political, required to be corrected or eradicated, before they could be expected to form a civilized people upon civilized European principles" (William Mure, *Journal of a Tour in Greece and the Ionian Islands* [Edinburgh and London, 1842], II, 216). See also Baird, *Modern Greece*, pp. 85, 88, passim.

[47] George K. Aspreas, *Politike Historia tes Neoteras Hellados 1821-1921* [*Political History of Modern Greece*], 2nd edn. (Athens, 1924), I, 29-30; and W. Alison Phillips, *The War of Greek Independence 1821 to 1833* (New York, 1897), p. 118. John Comstock, (*History*, pp. 171-73) sees the nation in 1821 as divided between *Hetairists*, Europeanized members of the Philike Hetairia, and ephors or primates, the indigenous ruling groups.

[48] For example, Thiersch (*État actuel*, II, 217) writes: ". . . one finds European profusion in the homes of the archons. . . ."

tiara." These famous words, uttered by Lukas Notaras, a prominent Byzantine, dramatize the sentiment of at least an important segment of the Greek population in the fifteenth century, as they faced the alternatives of conquest by the Muslim Turks or submission to the Papacy in return for military aid. After conquering Constantinople in 1453, Sultan Mohammed II capitalized on this sentiment by giving the Greeks autonomy under their patriarch in Constantinople. The legacy of hatred toward the West was kept alive during the Ottoman period by the militant missionary activity of Catholics and the ostensible sympathy of some few clerics for Protestant ideas.[49] Ultimately the European Enlightenment strengthened that legacy, but only because it, unlike either Catholicism or Protestantism, captivated the most influential segment of Greek society.

The Enlightenment coincided with the Greek economic revival, which brought Greek merchants in contact with Europe and weaned them from the other-worldly spirit of traditional Greek society. The works of Locke, Descartes, Leibnitz, Rousseau, and Voltaire were translated into Greek not long after their appearance in Europe. In the religiously oriented curricula of the Greek schools, mathematics, science, and secular literature were being introduced, and Greek students were travelling to Europe to continue their studies. Even the church was becoming humanized. Though there were always conservatives around to object, the patriarchate, largely in the hands of the Phanariots, became one of the chief propagators of the new learning. It maintained a distinguished school, organized a publishing house, and set up grants to enable the clergymen to study in Europe. The traditional anti-Western feeling was giving way to admiration for the West.[50]

As it did elsewhere, the French Revolution caused a serious rift in Greek society. Following the lead of Russia's Catherine II, the patriarchate of Constantinople now became a center of reaction. The conservative clerics gained the upper hand, and often those who had started out as liberals turned conservative. Two aspects of this reaction were the revival of anti-Western sentiment and an accompanying defense of Ottoman rule. Both attitudes found classic expression in an anonymous pamphlet entitled *Paternal Instructions* (1798). It justified the Ottoman empire as a divinely sanctioned instrument for the protection of Orthodoxy from Western

[49] Michael Dukas, *Historia Byzantina*, ed. I. Bekker (Bonn, 1834), xxxvii, 264, as quoted by A. A. Vasiliev, *History of Byzantine Empire 324-1453* (Madison, 1952), p. 647. Arnold Toynbee (*A Study of History* [London, 1934-54], vi) gives an excellent account of the intrigues centered about the figure of Patriarch Cyril Loukares, revealing because of its description of Catholic missionary activity in the Ottoman Empire, Protestant attempts to maintain relations with the patriarch of Constantinople, and indigenous Greek hostility to both Western enterprises.

[50] Maurer, *Griechische Volk*, i, 18-28; and Stavrianos, *Balkans*, pp. 146-49; but a much fuller account of the eighteenth-century Greek enlightenment appears in Constantine Th. Demaras, *Historia tes Neohellenikes Logotechnias* [*History of Modern Greek Literature*], 2nd edn. (n.p., n.d.), pp. 103-92.

39

heresies. Because of its new attitude, the church forfeited its cultural leadership among the Westernizers and broke its alliance with the Phanariots, most of whom remained loyal to the new doctrines, especially that of nationalism.[51]

Leadership of Greek liberalism fell appropriately to Adamantios Koraes, son of a Chiot merchant and product of a European education. Though trained to become a doctor, Koraes settled permanently in Paris to assume no less a task than the cultural regeneration of his people by reforming the language, translating the ancient classics into modern Greek, and prefacing each translation with a long didactic introduction. He preached the virtues of individual liberty, constitutionalism, republicanism, and nationalism. An ardent admirer of Europe, his hopes for Greece did not end with mere liberation from the Turks. He sought for the Greeks entry into the European family of nations and participation in European culture. Like other liberals he turned his back on the medieval period of Greek history as one of superstition and ignorance. His influence, both during and after his lifetime, was tremendous, precisely because he articulated the aspirations of an important segment of the Greek community. So it was altogether fitting that he should reply to the patriarchal pamphlet in his own tract entitled *Brotherly Instructions* (1798). He denounced Ottoman rule as barbaric and castigated the clergy for supporting the status quo.[52]

By the beginning of the nineteenth century, then, a cultural conflict, which had begun as a clash between two societies, had become a cultural schism within the bosom of Greek society because one segment, small but influential, had adopted as its own the dominant cultural values of the West. Knowing the West personally, as so many of them did, impressed as they were with its large and wealthy cities, its technical and scientific progress, its rule of law and efficient administration, they were ashamed and disgusted by conditions at home. Bad roads, unsanitary conditions, extortion and confiscation, ignorance and superstition—all these they blamed on four centuries of Ottoman rule. They were intolerant of conservatives and looked upon everything defended by conservatives as barbaric, backward, and medieval.[53]

[51] Demaras [*History of Literature*], p. 142; and Stavrianos, *Balkans*, pp. 151-52.

[52] The finest biography of Koraes is a separate work devoted exclusively to him by Constantine T. Demaras, *Ho Koraes kai he epoche tou* [*Koraes and his Age*] (Athens [1953]) and the standard one in English is by S. G. Chaconas, *Adamantios Korais: A Study in Greek Nationalism* (New York, 1942). For brief portraits and biographical sketches, see also Demaras [*Greek Literature*], pp. 195-214; Kaltchas, *Constitutional History*, pp. 10-18; and Stavrianos, *Balkans*, pp. 148-49, 152, and 278.

[53] Contemporary Greek newspapers, edited largely by such Westernizers, reflect this adulation of the West combined with shame of indigenous conditions; for instance *Hēlios*, 7 July 1833*o.s.* ("Wretched Greece! without the faintest notion of the perfections of wise Europe"), *Triptolemos*, 29 July 1833*o.s.* (on the superior state of European agriculture), and *Sōtēr*, 18 Jan. 1834*o.s.* See also Stavrianos, *Balkans*, pp. 277-79.

During the decade preceding the outbreak of the Revolution, as plans for liberation got underway and revolutionary sentiment gathered momentum, the cultural conflict subsided. Virtually no one argued for Ottoman rule. Opinions differed only on matters of timing and planning. But once Turkish rule was overthrown, the question of what should take its place excited dissension, dissension growing out of the cultural schism.[54]

The revolutionary situation gave the Westernizers the upper hand. The success of the Revolution depended ultimately on Europe—on official Europe for diplomatic recognition if not outright diplomatic support, on unofficial opinion for money and moral support. Westernizers could therefore argue for their objectives on strictly utilitarian grounds, namely that Europe must be favorably impressed. Conversely, the church, logical leader of any conservative program, suffered serious disruption. Since their office carried responsibility for the good conduct of the Greeks, eighty bishops, including the patriarch of Constantinople, Gregory V, were executed by the Turks. The rest fled to insurgent Greece as humble petitioners for placement and sustenance rather than as potential leaders. Bishops like Germanos of Patras gave counsel, and priests, like Gregory Dikaios, better known as Papaphlessas, took up arms, but they acted as individuals, not as a corporate body that knew what type of society it wanted. Moreover, since the Revolution was successful only in a part of the Ottoman empire, the church became divided between two separate political authorities. Because the patriarch was an appointee of the sultan, who forced him to excommunicate the rebels, the office lost all moral authority over the free Greeks.

What, in particular, did Westernizers like Mavrokordatos or Negres want for Greece? No one ever issued any program, but, inferring from statements and judging from the Revolutionary constitutions, one can detect at least four objectives: (1) a constitutional state, in which a constitution would guarantee individual liberty as well as public good and in which a popularly elected assembly would register the will of the nation; (2) a secular state, in which the church would merely minister to the spiritual needs of the nation and simply constitute one of several state institutions; (3) a legal-bureaucratic state, in which justice would be rendered according to Western law codes and administration conducted along Western lines; and (4) a state with a regular army, that is, an army armed, dressed, drilled, and organized according to Western practice. All but the first objective, which seemed to offer protection to sectional and corporate bodies, clearly encroached upon the established rights of powerful groups. The second objective would deprive the clergy of its judicial powers and reduce it to political impotence. The third would render useless the political experience of the primates because their

---

[54] For a good statement on this conflict between those who wished to preserve the Ottoman empire intact in order to inherit it gradually and those who advocated immediate resort to arms, see Woodhouse, *Greek War*, p. 41.

experience applied only to the traditional system. The fourth would reduce the captains, private military entrepreneurs possessed of private armies which they hired out to the state as integral units under their command, to mere salaried servants of a bureaucratic state military establishment, appointed on a purely individual basis, operating within a centralized chain of command, and because transferable from one assignment to another, no longer enjoying either personal or permanent ties with the men under their command.[55]

These issues did not engage much debate during the Revolution because everything was so provisional. They were bequeathed to the new king and his regency. But hints of these issues and symptoms of the cultural schism did appear. In the first place, very suddenly and in a relatively small area, the extremes met and reacted. There were parts of the Ottoman empire where Westernization among the Greeks had gone much farther than in what became insurgent Greece. There was bound to be a reaction among the autochthon elements. For instance, Makrygiannes' memoirs are full of tirades against the "man-eating" Westernized Greeks: "Behold the great learning possessed by all those who went to Europe and came to govern us—[they wanted] the Rumeliots to become their helots."[56] Second, the many philhellenes who came to Greece did not receive the hearty welcome they had a right to expect. Especially the captains, who resented their suggestions for the creation of a regular army, viewed them with suspicion as opportunists who had come "to eat our bread."[57] Finally, in 1828 came the first of the American and English Protestant missionaries. Even though they came ostensibly to contribute to the educational system by opening schools and publishing books, many Greeks suspected them of wishing to proselytize and to undermine Orthodoxy. Their presence was bound to reopen the cultural conflict. Even the slightest departure in religious observance was likely to arouse the prejudice of the masses, a consideration which did not escape the notice of the demagogues. The religious spirit was still so deeply engrained in Greek society that in this realm a Western innovation was likely to evoke a reaction from the ambivalent or semi-Westernized Greek. Moreover, Orthodoxy and nationality were so closely associated in the minds of even the religious skeptics that the weakening of the former was considered a blow against the latter.[58]

[55] For instance, see Kaltchas, *Constitutional History*, pp. 34-57.

[56] Makrygiannes [*Memoirs*], II, 13.

[57] Humphreys (*Picture of Greece*, II, 184-85) in 1825 accuses only the government of resentment against the philhellenes; Maurer ([*Greek People*], II, 33-35) perceives it as a more widespread national phenomenon based upon the intense competition for public place and position.

[58] On the identification of Orthodoxy and nationalism, see Finlay, *History*, VI, 7; on the missionaries in Greece, see Theodore Saloutos, "American Missionaries in Greece: 1820-1869," *Church History*, XXIV (1955), 152-94, and unpublished article by John Petropulos, "American Missionary Activity in Greece."

4. European Intervention and Domination

The rulers of Europe responded to the news of the Greek Revolution with marked disfavor. Like the revolts in Spain and Naples, which had broken out in 1820, it smelled of radicalism and violated the principle of legitimacy. Even worse, it reopened the nightmarish "Eastern Question": what to do with the rapidly declining Ottoman empire. This problem of European diplomacy posed two dreadful possibilities: either an upset in the European balance of power, if one state unilaterally conquered a part or the whole of the empire; or hopeless complications probably leading to a European war, if the interested states attempted a negotiated partition. A third solution—the creation of small, independent successor states—was still new in 1821 and too radical for serious consideration. To support the territorial integrity of the Ottoman empire was the fourth and safest option, particularly appealing because it accorded well with the general dedication of European diplomats to the status quo. In 1821 Russia, for over a century the traditional enemy of Turkey, was feared in Europe as the state most likely to exploit the Greek situation for her own advantage, but Tsar Alexander I had no taste for the European entanglements that such an adventure might entail. So the Concert of Europe, consisting of Britain, France, Russia, Prussia, and Austria, tried to ignore the Greeks and hoped that the sultan could snuff out the revolt.[59]

From the very beginning it was clear to the Greek leaders that the success of their cause depended on the support of at least some European powers. Money and arms they might obtain privately, but only official Europe could secure the eventual acquiescence of the sultan and admit an independent Greece into the European family of nations. Greek words and acts were calculated to impress Europe. Greek leaders insisted repeatedly that theirs was no ordinary revolution, inspired by demagoguery or Jacobinism. It was rather a crusade of Christians against Muslims, the attempt of a Greek nation to remove the barbaric Turkish yoke and revive the culture of its famed ancestors. The Greek constitutions, at least in part, were calculated to impress liberal European opinion. For official Europe the Greeks devised more special methods: one, the offer of a crown to the scion of some distinguished family, preferably royal; and the other, the more intricate game of exploiting the mutual jealousies of the powers in an attempt to secure their assistance. A major objective in this game was to excite Russian-British competition for popularity among the Greeks. Owing to a century of intermittent Russian propaganda and the sharing of a common Orthodoxy with the Russians, Russia started out with a virtual monopoly of Greek good will. Alexander Mavrokordatos, one of the Revolutionary political leaders, shrewdly and persistently broke that monopoly by building up a reputation for England as a potential

[59] Driault and Lhéritier, *Histoire*, i, 143-67, or more briefly, Stavrianos, *Balkans*, pp. 286-88.

benefactor, and so let Russia know that it would have to make a renewed bid for continued popularity.[60]

Eventually it even became habitual for the Greek leaders to consider the impact of their words and acts on Europe. It became natural for Greeks to pick their favorites among the European powers and to be categorized according to their choice. Such groupings eventually became a basis of emerging political parties.[61]

Many factors contributed to the eventual intervention of Europe in the Greek Revolution. Aside from stimulating private donations of money and supplies for the Greeks, philhellenism mobilized so strong a public sentiment that even the diplomats could not entirely ignore it. Turkish atrocities, such as the massacre of Chios (1822), had a way of getting publicized in Europe, whereas equally savage acts committed by the Greeks got scanty attention. In Russia, where philhellenism was absent, the feeling of sympathy for coreligionists took its place and, through members of his court, exercised a strong influence on the tsar. Commercial considerations could not be ignored either. Greco-Turkish naval hostilities disrupted trade in the eastern Mediterranean and thereby affected the British, French, Austrians, and Russians. The most important factor, however, was a military one, namely the tenacity of the Greeks in thwarting repeated Turkish attempts to crush the revolt. Thanks largely to terrain, they were even able to survive the almost fatal intervention of Egyptian forces in behalf of the sultan.[62]

In February 1825, Mohammed Ali, vassal of the sultan though virtually independent ruler of Egypt, broke the Greco-Turkish stalemate. With 10,000 infantry and 1,000 cavalry, his son Ibrahim invaded the southwestern Peloponnesos from the sea. Before this well disciplined, Westernized army which had been trained by Colonel Sèves, a veteran of Napoleon's expedition to Egypt (1798-1801), the Greek irregulars fled in battle after battle. Ibrahim conducted a devastating campaign, which did not spare even the civilian population. In no time he captured the key fortresses of the peninsula, but without destroying the Greek army. It simply fled to the many mountain fastnesses, where regular troops were virtually useless and where the dispossessed civilians swelled its ranks.

[60] For a good account of this maneuvering of the Greeks for European support, see Kaltchas, *Constitutional History*, pp. 35-41.

[61] In the first year of the Revolution, Kolokotrones dispersed an armed mob ready to commit violence against the assembled primates with a warning that such action would create in Europe the impression that the Greeks were Carbonari (Karl Mendelssohn-Bartholdy, *Geschichte Griechenlands von der Eroberung Konstantinopels durch die Türken im Jahre 1453 bis auf unsere Tage* [Leipzig, 1870-74], I, 225). Or to take another example, Makrygiannes ([*Memoirs*], I, 230) writes: ". . . there were foreigners here [in Greece], Europeans who were observing us, and I wanted them to see that we really thirst for liberty and laws, that we are not plunderers."

[62] Woodhouse, *Greek War*, pp. 85-94.

With the exception of the coastal cities, Ibrahim was at any given time master of only the spot occupied by his army.[63]

European intervention, when it came in 1826, took place under the aegis of Britain, in part because George Canning headed its government (1822-27), in part because the Greek government appealed to Britain for mediation in August 1824 and again in 1825, in part because Russia had lost its chance after antagonizing the Greeks in 1824 by proposing the establishment of three autonomous principalities rather than a united and independent Greek state. Already Canning had shown the Greeks favor. In 1823 he had recognized them as belligerents and in 1824 he had deigned to reply to their appeal. He was not a philhellene. He simply feared that Russia might take unilateral action against the Ottoman empire. By 1825 he believed a settlement absolutely necessary and considered the time ripe for negotiation with Russia when Tsar Nicholas I ascended the throne at the end of 1825. The conservative Russian sovereign felt for the Greeks the same antipathy that he felt for all rebels, but he was shrewd enough to realize that Russia could not afford to let England, already its great rival in the Near East, win the popularity and hence the influence which it had traditionally exercised among the Greeks. Mavrokordatos' policy was bearing fruit. This mutual jealousy between Britain and Russia produced the so-called St. Petersburg Protocol of 4 April 1826, by which the two powers agreed that Britain was to offer its mediation between Greeks and sultan on the basis of Greek autonomy under Ottoman suzerainty.[64]

The Protocol provided for its submission to the other three major European powers for either approval or adherence. Without qualms, Austria and Prussia refused their assent and hence deprived themselves of any real influence in Greece for decades thereafter. France, on the other hand, was jealous of English and Russian interference in the Near East, where it had traditionally played an active role, and so decided to associate itself with its two rivals in order to deprive them of the sole direction of affairs. Thus the St. Petersburg Protocol got transformed into the Treaty of London (6 July 1827). In recognition of British leadership, the treaty was negotiated in London by the British foreign secretary and the ambassadors of Russia and France. This so-called Conference of London was to function off and on during the royal period.[65]

[63] Douglas Dakin, *British and American Philhellenes during the War of Greek Independence, 1821-1833* (Thessaloniki, 1955), pp. 132-33; Finlay, *History*, vi, 349-72; and Woodhouse, *Greek War*, pp. 106-15.

[64] On the British official attitude toward the Greek Revolution and events leading up to the Protocol of 4 Apr. 1826, see C. W. Crawley, *The Question of Greek Independence. A Study of British Policy in the Near East, 1821-1833* (Cambridge, Eng., 1930), pp. 30-62; also Driault and Lhéritier, *Histoire*, i, 259-74, 303-21; Finlay, *History*, vii, 6-11; and Phillips, *War*, pp. 237-48.

[65] For the only satisfactory account of French involvement and its motives, as well

In accordance with the treaty, the three powers offered the belligerents their mediation in August 1827. Because of a military situation now favorable to the Turks, who had reconquered Mesolongi in April 1826 and Athens in June 1827, the Greeks willingly accepted the proffered mediation and the Turks did not.[66] In the meantime, the three powers instructed the admirals commanding their respective fleets in the Mediterranean to impose an armistice. Since their instructions were not clear, Sir Edward Codrington, the British admiral, took matters in hand to suit his own philhellenic sentiments. As senior admiral and commander of the largest fleet, he took the lead and his Russian and French colleagues followed. After establishing a blockade of insurgent Greece, he hunted down the combined Egyptian-Turkish fleet in the bay of Navarino. Ostensibly, at any rate, the great naval battle of Navarino, which took place on 20 October 1827, began by accident. By the end of the day, the Egyptian-Turkish fleet lay at the bottom of the sea. The Treaty of London and the battle of Navarino together constituted a major turning point in the history of the Greek Revolution. The former served notice that the European powers would not allow the reduction of the Greeks to their former subjection and the latter committed them inextricably to autonomy for the Greeks as a bare minimum at least.[67]

Thanks to the three European powers, the fortunes of the Greeks changed overnight. Turkish troops left Rumely to strengthen the Danubian provinces against an imminent Russian invasion. The London Conference authorized a French expedition to the Morea, the prospect of which induced Mohammed Ali to agree to evacuate his troops peaceably. Through the direct action of the powers, insurgent Greece was reliberated and enabled to take the offensive in Rumely, which it did on the correct assumption that the powers would not exclude from the new state territory in insurgent military possession.[68]

But Allied intervention was not an unmixed blessing. It involved domination as well as liberation. From the autumn of 1828, when London, Paris, and St. Petersburg respectively despatched representatives to insurgent Greece, the three powers kept permanent residents in the Greek capital, men who willy-nilly became centers of intrigue and patrons of respective Greek factions. The Allied admirals also exercised their influence in Greek internal affairs, and of course, the London Conference,

---

as a good account of the events leading up to the Treaty of London, see Driault and Lhéritier, *Histoire*, I, 241-58, 365-79. See also Crawley, *Greek Independence*, pp. 34, 63-78.

[66] Woodhouse, *Greek War*, pp. 122-23.

[67] On the battle of Navarino and its consequences, see Crawley, *Greek Independence*, pp. 79-97; Driault and Lhéritier, *Histoire*, I, 379-95; Finlay, *History*, VII, 16-20; Phillips, *War*, pp. 268-80; and Woodhouse, *Greek War*, pp. 123-28.

[68] Crawley, *Greek Independence*, pp. 105, 107-108, 112, 116; and Woodhouse, *Greek War*, pp. 131-32.

consisting of the British foreign minister and the French and Russian ambassadors to England, meeting periodically, became the arbiter of Greek destiny. In the meantime, to the great resentment of most Greeks, French troops occupied the Morea. The 14,000 troops which disembarked on 30 August 1828 were sent as Allied forces, under the authorization of the London Conference, "to supervise the withdrawal of the Egyptian army." France had offered them primarily because it wished to establish a base from which it might prevent Russia from swallowing up too much of the Ottoman Empire during the Russo-Turkish war, which took place in 1828-29.

Even though Ibrahim had withdrawn by early 1829 and the ostensible objective had been accomplished, a token force of French troops stayed on Greek soil and did not withdraw until Russia insisted (1833). During most of the occupation, the French troops remained located in southwestern Morea and offered valuable services, such as road-building, retilling devastated land, and draining marshes, but as the sequel reveals, they became involved in Greek politics before their tenure was over.[69]

The Russo-Turkish war of 1828-29 raised the expectations of the Greeks, who expected to benefit greatly by it, but the treaty of Adrianople (14 September 1829), which brought that war to an end, was moderate and conciliatory in its terms, and left the Greeks bitter and disappointed. With respect to Greece, the treaty registered the sultan's willingness to accept the mediation of the powers on the basis of the latest London protocol (22 March 1829). On several counts the Greeks rejected the protocol. It gave them merely tributary status under Ottoman suzerainty rather than full independence. It deprived them of all voice in the selection of the hereditary prince who should rule over them. It excluded the islands of Samos and Crete from the proposed principality.[70]

Indirectly, however, the Russo-Turkish war did contribute to Greek independence. Strengthened by the peace of Adrianople in other parts of the Near East, and then adopting a new Russian policy based on the preservation of the Ottoman empire, Russia became a much more formidable rival of Britain than it had been before the war as a declared enemy of the sultan. Alarmed at the new turn of affairs, Britain decided that complete independence for the Greeks would offer greater security against Russian influence than tributary status which, in the case of the Rumanian principalities at least, had permitted constant Russian interference. Unable to oppose this British proposal of Greek independence

[69] On the despatch of residents, see Kaltchas, *Constitutional History*, p. 40. On the French occupation, see Crawley, *Greek Independence*, pp. 116-18, 157-58; Driault and Lhéritier, *Histoire*, I, 408-19; and Finlay, *History*, VII, 27-28.

[70] On the Russo-Turkish war, the London protocol of 22 Mar. 1829, and the Treaty of Adrianople, see Crawley, *Greek Independence*, pp. 103-105, 153-54, 168-70; Driault and Lhéritier, *Histoire*, I, 396-419, 433-53; Finlay, *History*, VII, 51-52; Phillips, *War*, p. 312; and Woodhouse, *Greek War*, pp. 138-41.

without further loss of popularity in Greece, Russia agreed. On 3 February 1830, the London Conference issued *the* protocol which established an independent Greek state under the guarantee of the three powers. A sovereign still had to be elected and the boundaries of Free Greece decided. The fact that the London Conference made both decisions, without consulting the Greeks, shows how real Allied domination had become.[71]

European involvement in Greek affairs during the Greek Revolution left results of lasting consequence. It confirmed Greek suspicions that Europe could and would play a decisive role in Greek affairs and established the insidious Greek habit of appealing to one or more of the powers for help, even on partisan or personal matters. Worse still, it became self-perpetuating. Collective intervention, a device of the powers for moderating the acts of each other, had grown out of mutual suspicion between them and the fear of each lest the others intervene separately in Greece and establish exclusive influence there. But collective involvement, as practiced by competing Allied residents, competing Mediterranean admirals, and competing diplomats in London, nourished even greater mutual suspicion, which made continued involvement seem urgent. Thus Britain, France, and Russia established a special international status for Greece, a type of European suzerainty exercised by themselves and disguised in the more palatable phrase, "under the guarantee of the three powers." As we shall see below, the treaty of 7 May 1832, which registered the election of a Greek monarch, also spelled out the machinery for the exercise of this suzerainty. "Independence," in the diplomatic dictionary of the Allies, meant independence from Turkey and from the exclusive control of any one of them. It did not mean independence from the joint control of all three. Ironically, the Greeks had themselves erected this foreign tutelage.[72]

5. Constitutionalism and Monarchy

One of the most important products of the Revolutionary decade was the strong tradition of constitutionalism. In 1821, each of the three sectional authorities enacted a regional constitution. By conventional calculations, which mercifully ignore the chronic mushrooming of rival assemblies, six national assemblies met between 1821 and 1832: (1) Epidaurus (December 1821–January 1822); (2) Astros (December 1822); (3) Troezene (April 1827); (4) Argos (July–August 1829); (5) Argos (December 1831–March 1832); (6) Pronoia (July–September 1832). Three constitutions were enacted: that of Epidaurus in January 1822, that

---

[71] On the protocol of 3 Feb. 1830, see Crawley, *Greek Independence*, pp. 166-75; Dakin, *Philhellenes*, pp. 194, 197; Driault and Lhéritier, *Histoire*, I, 454-65; Finlay, *History*, VII, 53-55; and Phillips, *War*, p. 333.
[72] Kaltchas, *Constitutional History*, pp. 91-92.

of Troezene in May 1827, and a less well-known one of Nauplion in 1832. A legislative body of some sort figured almost continuously in the governmental machinery.

It was perfectly natural that the Greeks in 1821 should adopt representative and constitutional government. Under the system of administrative autonomy allowed them by the Turks, the Peloponnesian primates had habitually assembled from time to time to confer about the affairs of the peninsula. When they met in June 1821 to declare themselves the ruling authority, they were simply adapting an existing institution to the new revolutionary situation. In the two sections of Rumely, where regional assemblies were not as customary, the convening of representatives was the work of two outsiders, Mavrokordatos and Theodore Negres, who had to resort to some such device to get their authority recognized. How else, but in a national assembly such as the one at Epidaurus in December 1821, could the will of the nation be expressed, when there was no single group or individual universally acknowledged as the mouthpiece of the nation? How else could the leadership effectively obtain and retain the cooperation of diverse social elements, but by offering the guarantee of periodic assemblies through which the respective interests would receive consideration from their own representatives?[73]

For the actual adoption of a constitution, however, there was no indigenous precedent. Westernized Greeks, such as Mavrokordatos, were most responsible for this Western innovation. To Greeks conversant with Western ideas and practices, a constitution was the social contract, a natural and enlightened step among free men. It was also, of course, good advertisement of the Greek cause in Europe. Because it spelled things out, it was intended to signify the beginning of the end of the traditional arbitrariness of government. Even some common people, to whom the West was totally unfamiliar, understood the essential function of a constitution, as Kapodistrias discovered when a peasant remarked that a constitution indicated what the government owed its citizens as well as what they owed it.[74]

If the Greek leaders understood the function of constitutions generally, they also had definite ideas about the basic objectives of their particular constitutions. One was a unitary state to weld together the diverse elements into a nation and a central government strong enough to carry through the difficult ordeal of revolution. Another was a set of safeguards for the freedom of the individual citizen from domestic autocracy. A third was the separation of powers and the primacy of the legislative over the executive to guarantee each social and regional group its continued existence as well as to prevent dictatorship. Government, in

[73] Kaltchas, *ibid.*, p. 33; and Woodhouse, *Greek War*, p. 81.
[74] On the motives of those who drew up the constitution of Epidaurus, see Woodhouse, *Greek War*, p. 82. On the common man's understanding of a constitution, see Kaltchas, *Constitutional History*, p. 40.

principle at least, was conducted during the Revolution on the assumption that sovereignty resides in the nation and that the nation consists of the people who act through their duly elected representatives.[75]

So successfully did the tradition of constitutionalism take hold in insurgent Greece that no one, publicly at least, dared challenge representative government as an ideal. Desirability of a constitution was never at issue. Feasibility was and it continued in the royal period to be a very real issue on which parties took their stand.[76] A constitution understandably restricted the executive authority and established the tradition of a strong legislature in order to secure the nation against the possibility of autocracy. But a restricted executive, it was felt in many quarters, could not perform its essential tasks, such as winning a favorable peace settlement and undertaking the work of reconstruction.[77] Moreover, constitutionalism came to be identified with the partisan strife and civil anarchy which too often accompanied electioneering and the convening of assemblies. So it could be argued that conditions in Greece were not ripe for parliamentary government.[78]

Yet the sure prospect of monarchy, a foreign one at that, impressed on all Greek leaders the necessity of convoking an assembly which should show that the constituent power still resided in the nation, rather than in the London Conference or in the new king. An assembly would enact a constitution to provide the guarantees for a continual limitation of the monarchy by a representative body. For the Greeks, constitutionalism and monarchism were inseparable issues.[79]

Neither republicanism nor royalism commanded widespread loyalty among them as political tenets, either before or during the Revolution. Monarchy secured general preference only because the exigencies of the Greek situation, foreign and internal, seemed to dictate it.[80] The Greeks were quick to realize the value of monarchy as an instrument of diplomacy. They understood that monarchy might be necessary as a concession to the conservative temper of the Concert of Europe. The voluntary espousal of monarchy, they hoped, would dissociate the Revolution from Jacobinism. More important still, if a member of some European royal house could be induced to accept the Greek crown, to secure his own future he would certainly try to obtain from the Concert of Europe the best possible settlement for Greece, in terms of international status, territorial boundaries, and monetary loans, and his dynastic connections would give him a tremendous advantage over any Greek in such an enterprise.[81]

[75] *Ibid.*, pp. 34, 45-46, 56, 67.
[76] *Ibid.*, pp. 73-74.   [77] *Ibid.*, p. 51.
[78] Leonard Bower and Gordon Bolitho, *Otho I: King of Greece* (London, 1939), pp. 53-54.
[79] Kaltchas, *Constitutional History*, p. 39.
[80] *Ibid.*, p. 37.   [81] *Loc.cit.*

The Greek crown was no great prize and many of the individuals considered by the Greeks showed that they knew this by promptly refusing to consider a definite offer. But the classical associations of a *Hellenic* nation and the exciting challenge of presiding over the creation of a new state excited the fancy of a person as prosaic and calculating as Leopold of Saxe-Coburg, son-in-law of King George IV of England and later to become first king of Belgium. Indeed, in 1828 Kapodistrias suggested Leopold to the powers because he believed that the Duke of Wellington might be induced to accept larger boundaries for a Greece ruled by a man with English connections. Faithful to the expectations of the Greeks, Leopold, who accepted the throne in February 1830, demanded of the powers a loan, troops, and larger boundaries. Since the powers would not meet such demands, Leopold resigned the following May.[82]

Monarchy possessed a second advantage, which received greater consideration by the Greeks as civil strife assumed greater dimensions. It seemed the best guarantee of internal unity and stability, a neutral factor to serve as referee between the hostile factions. And neutrality seemed best assured in a foreigner with no connections in Greece. During Turkish times, the Turks had served such a function. The civil war, which broke out after the assassination of Kapodistrias in October 1831 and assumed such tremendous proportions, dispelled any lingering doubts (if there were any) about the urgency of a foreign monarchy. When Otho, prince of Bavaria, was selected by the powers in May 1832, the jubilation in Greece had virtually nothing to do with sentiment for his person or the institution which he embodied. The Greeks hailed the event as deliverance from civil war, anarchy, and devastation.[83]

The external and internal factors which explain the rise of monarchy in Greece also account for the difficulties confronting it. A foreigner's rootlessness might render him neutral so that he could moderate between domestic rivals, but it would also leave him politically ineffective unless he came well endowed with money, troops, and great political talent. The guarantee of his kingdom by the powers might seem like a valuable prop for his regime, but it meant that he would have to keep them satisfied, individually and collectively. What would happen if they made conflicting demands on him, as they were likely to do? Even though he probably would enjoy the "love" of his adopted people, a love conditional on his ability to maintain domestic peace and the support of Europe, his people were divided into at least three parties whose rivalry was already intense and likely to become more intense as they competed for his favor. Necessary and difficult as it was for the monarch to moderate between rivalry within each threesome (powers and Greeks), the

---

[82] On the nomination and resignation of Leopold, see Crawley, *Greek Independence*, pp. 174-88; Dakin, *Philhellenes*, pp. 192-97; Driault and Lhéritier, *Histoire*, II, 10-31; and Kaltchas, *Constitutional History*, pp. 69-71.

[83] Finlay, *History*, VI, 32; and Kaltchas, *Constitutional History*, p. 37.

system of foreign-supported parties committed the future monarch to the equally necessary and even more difficult task of moderating between three separate alliances of a domestic party and a protecting power.

As far as the powers collectively were concerned, the king, in his role as a stabilizing factor, must prevent the Greeks from embarking on any adventure against Turkey and must see that Greece meticulously met its financial obligations abroad. As for the Greeks, however much they appreciated the advantages of monarchy, they also understood its possible disadvantages. It seemed unlikely that the monarch would belong to the Orthodox faith, because the Russian ruling house was the only Orthodox one and the powers had agreed among themselves that members of their respective houses should be disqualified for candidacy. In that case, the Greeks desired that the king convert to their faith, but would be satisfied if his heir at least were brought up an Orthodox. It seemed probable that the new sovereign might be a minor, in which case a regency would have to rule for him temporarily. Since the regency could not be Greek for the same reason that a king could not, a period of foreign rule would paradoxically have to initiate independence. It was possible that the king might become an autocrat. The traditional fear of one-man rule or of a strong executive, as well as misgiving about a possible regency, was allayed only by the prospect of a constitution. Thus the issues of monarchy and constitutionalism converged. As it turned out, with the election of Otho all three disadvantages were realized.

CHAPTER TWO

The Revolutionary Period, 1821-27:
The Origins of the Parties

1. THE PRE-REVOLUTIONARY POLITICAL TRADITION

MOST SOURCES treat the three parties as if they were the artificial creations of foreign legations and Westernized Greeks bearing no organic relation to Greek social and political life. Because of the public disrepute of parties, especially parties with foreign labels, no one at the time wanted to bear the responsibility for their existence nor acknowledge them as the outgrowth of a national tradition. Parties, virtually everyone said *in public*, were three clienteles, limited largely to the capital, organized by the foreign legations, consisting of self-seeking individuals representing no one but themselves, and receiving favors from their respective legations in return for bits of intelligence and some semblance of support for the power in question.[1] Clienteles indeed, but nothing new among the Greeks nor peculiar to foreign legations. Clienteles belonged to the corporate tradition of the Ottoman empire[2] and existed in even the most remote regions among the Greeks. The system of clientage in general— not the particular clienteles of three legations—is the starting point of any study of the Greek political parties, whether these or any others.

The System of Clientage

Since the Greeks took the system for granted, Greek sources seldom say anything explicit about it, although passing remarks in political correspondence betray its existence. Only those foreigners informed by longer stays and more intimate contacts than the usual visitor became aware of the system. Of these few, Friedrich Thiersch, the Bavarian

---

[1] Among foreigners, see George Ludwig von Maurer, *Das Griechische Volk in öffentlicher, kirchlicher und privatrechtlicher Beziehung vor und nach dem Freiheitskampfe bis zum 31. Juli 1834* (Heidelberg, 1835), II, 19-20; and Casimir Leconte, *Étude économique de la Grèce* . . . (Paris, 1847), pp. 410-11. Among Greeks, see Nichols Dragoumes, *Historikai Anamneseis* [*Historical Reminiscences*] 2nd edn. (Athens, 1879), I, 292, who attributes the existence of the parties to the "intervention of foreigners," and John Makrygiannes, *Apomnemoneumata* [*Memoirs*], ed. John Vlachogiannes, 2nd edn. (Athens, 1947), II, 51, who addresses the Europeans rhetorically in the following terms: "Later you filled us up with factions—Dawkins wants us English, Rouen wants us French, Catacazy Russian, and you left no Greek alone. Each of you took his portion and turned us into your ballerinas. . . ."

[2] On the corporative structure of Ottoman society in general, see H.A.R. Gibb and Harold Bowen, *Islamic Society and the West*, Vol. I, Part I (Oxford, 1950), 158-60, 209-13.

scholar who came into close contact with Greek political groups in 1832, has left the classic description of clientage:

> To understand the nature of this clientage and the obligations which it imposed on the patrons, one must understand the state in which centuries, perhaps thousands of years, had left society in Greece. As there was no central authority, capable of controlling and defending the inhabitants, each was forced to look elsewhere for support and protection. The most natural and surest support was found in the family, whose members and even relatives to the second degree were nowhere so closely connected and ready to aid each other as they were in Greece. In the second place, the isolated man had to take his position in the midst of others. According as he felt himself weak or strong, he made himself the partisan of some influential man or collected partisans about himself. In this manner each distinguished man has a more or less considerable number of subordinate persons who associate with him, listen to him, ask his advice, execute his wishes, and defend his interests, always careful to merit his respect and win his confidence. This is the origin and nature of the innumerable coteries with which Greece is covered. Their chiefs, when they do not feel powerful enough to be self-sufficient by themselves and their followers, range themselves with the latter under a stronger chief and augment by this accession his power and influence. They therefore combine the role of patron toward their clients with that of client toward the patron placed on a higher level. It is by this grouping of coteries that the parties are formed. . . . In the time of which we talk [1831-32], there were in appearance only two large parties with their recognized heads, but in looking closer, one saw that there were as many as there were influential men. None the less these parties were all stratified in such a manner as to support and augment the power of certain eminent men whom one saw at the head of the general movements.[3]

Theobald Piscatory, a French philhellene and diplomat in equally close touch with Greek affairs, shared this view. According to him also, the system of protection and clientage constituted "the true character of the parties," which owed their existence to indigenous custom, not merely to the existence of diverse foreign legations. George Finlay, the English philhellene who wrote a major history of medieval and modern Greece, nowhere analyzed this system in any detail nor elaborated upon its tremendous importance for the structure of Greek politics, but he gave it passing recognition when he referred to "the personal followers and bands of armed men" of the primates.[4] As late as 1863, Antoine Grénier, a

---

[3] F. Thiersch, *De l'état actuel de la Grèce* (Leipzig, 1833), I, 181-82.

[4] Piscatory to Guizot, Athens, 20 Aug. 1841 (5th report), in "Textes et Documents, La Grèce d'Othon," ed. Jean Poulos, in *L'Hellénisme Contemporain*, 2nd ser., IX

French traveler in Greece, noted the still persisting legacy of this system:

Under the Turkish domination the Greeks had two sorts of protectors against their tyrants: 1st their primates or captains, 2nd foreign consuls. Hence, the habits, the traditions, virtually the necessities, which still subsist.[5]

Another Western source in describing the case of a single captain, demonstrates how deeply embedded a political clientele often was in the military system and economic conditions of Greek society:

The *Capitani* being the most powerful and influential men in Greece, I will give you a short account of one of them named Stonaris. This chief lives at a village called Kutchino, near the river Aspropotamos, in Thrace. A portion of his property lies in the plain, and the rest in the mountains. He possesses about one hundred and twenty villages, and each of these contains, upon an average, about seventy families. The people of the mountains are chiefly occupied with their herds. Stonaris himself has about 7 or 8,000 head of cattle, and his family altogether own about 500,000. They consist of horses, oxen, cows, sheep, and goats, but chiefly of the two latter. The flocks remain seven months in the mountains, and the rest of the year in the plains. The *Capitano* lets out his cattle to herdsmen, who are bound to give him yearly, for each sheep, two pounds of butter, two pounds of cheese, two pounds of wool, and one piastre. Each family has from fifty to one hundred and fifty head of cattle, and they generally clear a small tract of ground and cultivate it. The plains are tolerably well cultivated. They do not belong to Stonaris, but are held by the cultivators, who pay one-third of their rent to the Turks, one-third to the *Capitano*, and one-third for the maintenance of the soldiers. . . .

The inferior *Capitani*, under Stonaris, each receive the dues of three or four families, and each command a certain number of men.

The regular soldiers under Stonaris amount to 400. He could muster 3000 more from among his peasantry. They are paid only during three months of the year: the first class receive twenty piastres per month; the second, fifteen; and the third, twelve. They live well, and eat twice a day bread and meat. They receive their rations from the owners of the houses where they dwell. They are furnished with ammunition and hides to make shoes of from the *Capitano*, but they find their own arms and clothes. They are subjected to no military discipline or punishment, and can quit their chief at pleasure. . . .

(1955), 413; and George Finlay, A History of Greece from its Conquest by the Romans to the Present Time, B.C. 146 to A.D. 1864, ed. H. F. Tozer (Oxford, 1877), VI, 232.

[5] Antoine Grénier, La Grèce en 1863 (Paris, 1863), p. 99.

There is a Primate in each village. These Primates are under the control of the Capitani, who are the princes of the country.[6]

The Role of Kinship in the Formation of Clienteles and Alliances

Though its role varied from place to place according to custom, the family constituted not merely the basic social unit, but the fundamental economic and political unit as well. Economic and political activity was organized on a family basis. The husband usually administered his wife's dowry. His sons, even when adult, enjoyed no individual claims to part of the family property until they married. The eldest *or* youngest son, depending on the region, lived with the father as "heir apparent." Even though the rest of the sons often, but not always, set up separate households, they had little to do in determining the size of the portion of land allotted to them. This decision was rather a product of intricate family arrangements directed by the family patriarch. Even after the formal establishment of a new household, its lands would most likely continue to be administered and cultivated in common as the family holdings had been before partition. Indeed, family property, whether in land, houses, or water sources, was often divided in such a way as to make inevitable economic dependence between the individual recipients.[7]

As the land was cultivated in common under the direction of the father, so too commercial undertakings in the Islands were family enterprises. A primate, even if in personal command of his best ship, would entrust other ships to his sons and close relatives. The poorer relations took employment with him as sailors, so that his ships' crews consisted largely and even exclusively of relatives. According to Ludwig von Maurer, one of the regents of Greece during part of the royal minority (1833-34), in the Islands primate families constituted a kind of Scottish aristocracy, each jealous of its independence. Of course, in places like Mane and Souli, family solidarity was classic. In the former region each important family occupied a "fortress-castle" and family federations were extensive.[8]

If the family was organized in such a way as to provide a livelihood for its members, it also assumed what by modern standards are public functions. It would place select members in official positions in order to exploit public office for the protection or the advancement of family interests. It would assume police powers by which to guard its possessions

[6] Stanhope to Bowring, Mesolongi, 27 Jan. 1824 in Leicester Stanhope, *Greece in 1823 and 1824: Series of Letters, and other Documents on the Greek Revolution,* new edn. (London, 1825), pp. 93-94.

[7] Maurer, *Griechische Volk,* I, 143-47; II, 431-33.

[8] On the family basis of commercial enterprises, see James Emerson, "Journal of a Residence among the Greeks in 1825," *A Picture of Greece in 1825: as Exhibited in the Personal Narratives of James Emerson, Count Pecchio, W. H. Humphreys* (New York, 1826), I, 121-27. On kinship ties in the Islands and Mane, see Maurer, *Griechische Volk,* I, 52-53; II, 24, 29-30.

and even go on the offensive against local foes. It would even perform welfare measures in behalf of its members, such as care for the indigent, guidance of orphans and widows, and perhaps formal education for the most promising among the young. As Thiersch thoroughly understood, the importance of the family is understandable in terms of a society where central political rule—either because weak or arbitrary and oppressive—bred insecurity and peril. Only the members of one's own family were considered trustworthy and capable of withstanding by their joint efforts the threats and assaults of a hostile world. This trust generally remained inviolate, not merely because of the holy aura attributed to blood ties but also because the interests of family members were so organically intertwined—economically, politically, and socially—that group interest amounted to self-interest as well.[9]

In order to fulfill its manifold functions as effectively as possible, the family had to extend beyond the simple biological unit of parents and unmarried children. "Family" was not synonymous with "household." "Family" denoted many households, extending even to those of distant cousins, bound together by ties of blood. Physical proximity of residence, frequent intercourse in the same locale, and cultivation of the same land by generations of the same extended family tended to compound the importance of kinship ties.

If kinship and material interests bound as many as a hundred individuals or more into an extensive group which regarded itself a family, there were wider institutionalized ties, supported by very strong sanctions, which united families either into a horizontal association of equals (alliance) or in a hierarchic relationship of dependency (clientage), or both. These institutionalized ties were primarily four: marriage, adoption, *koumpariá*, and fraternal friendship. The first was clearly an alliance (except when it was an elopement based on passion or abduction, calculated to establish some connection with social superiors, rather than the product of carefully conducted family negotiations); and the second was a special form of clientage. The third and fourth might be either—an association of equals or the establishment of dependency.

Marriages were often disguised political alliances between prominent families, sometimes involving the merging of economic resources. Through marriages, families brought together all kinds of distinct assets. For instance, the marriage of the sister of Panagiotes Benakes, a rich primate of Kalamata, to the brother of Petrobey, the ruler of Mane, combined mercantile wealth with military might, the Benakes' being able to lend Petrobey valuable assistance in his commercial enterprises, Petrobey

---

[9] Numerous examples of these family functions appear in the extensive account of customary law in various regions of Greece in Maurer, *Griechische Volk*, I, 122-379, and II, 298-468. Christian A. Brandis (*Mittheilungen über Griechenland* [Leipzig, 1842], III, 239) realized the fundamental connection between extended families and parties during the absolutist period.

being able to protect the Benakes' interests in the Messenian lowlands from the predatory Maniats who traditionally marauded from their mountain strongholds. Marriage sometimes cemented the regional branches of a party, as was the case when Kolokotrones' eldest son married the daughter of Kitsos Tzavelas. Once marriage was contracted, all the members of one family automatically became *sympetheroi* (sing., *sympetheros*, literally meaning co-fathers-in-law) of all the members of the other family.[10]

Adoption involved not merely orphans, but sometimes indigent children whose parents, still alive, could not afford to bring them up. In either case, the adoptee came from an indigent family, because an affluent family would as a matter of obligation look after its own orphans. The factor of indigence is important because it highlights the importance of adoption as a type of clientage, not merely between the foster parent and the adopted child but quite possibly between the foster parent and the parents or relatives of the adopted child. The adoption was usually legalized by a written agreement between the adopter and the extended family which had inherited the guardianship of the child on the death of its parent. Adoption was the formal method by which captains often bound their young palikar recruits in absolute dependence upon themselves. A noteworthy example of an adoption with important political consequences was that of John Mamoures who, from lowly origins in the Parnassos region of Rumely, became the servant boy of a powerful captain named John Gouras, then his adopted son, then heir to a large part of his political and financial fortune.[11]

The institution of *koumpariá* extended the family even further and contributed toward the ultimate goal of group protection and advancement. Koumpariá was the relationship contracted between the families of a bridegroom and his best man *or* a man and his child's godfather. Confirmed by the church, it was regarded as binding as blood relationship. A member of one family, very often the patron looking for clients, would act as sponsor at a marriage or baptism of a member of the other family. There is on record the case (1833) of a Rumeliot captain successfully soliciting, as his newborn's godfather, Christopher Neezer, a Bavarian officer of assumed importance who had in transit briefly taken up lodgings with the captain as he passed through. A more clear-cut case of the political use of baptism is that of King Otho's sponsorship, through proxy of

[10] Piscatory, Athens, 6 Sept. 1841 (7th report), *L'Hellénisme Contemporain*, IX, 438-39.

[11] On the frequency of adoption, types of adoptees, and various regional legal traditions for adoption, see Maurer, *Griechische Volk*, I, 133, and II, 435-36. Concerning Gouras, see Piscatory, Athens, 6 Sept. 1841 (7th report), *L'Hellénisme Contemporain*, IX, 432-33. On the institution in relation to recruitment into the irregulars, see Thiersch, *État actuel*, I, 221.

one of his regents, of Makrygiannes' son Otho. The institution of koumpariá might involve social equals or blood relatives, but more often it served to initiate and formalize a relationship of clientage between families enjoying no previous kinship.[12]

A special institution, apparently very old and with no such sacramental Christian basis as marriage or koumpariá, was that of "fraternal friendship." Most characteristic of relationships between men of valor and prowess, this convention, unknown in some parts of Greece, was common among the captains in Rumely. Two individuals, filled with respect and admiration for each other, would swear to defend each other for life and unto death. In a formal ceremony which usually took place before a church altar though apparently without benefit of clergy, they would repeat such vows as "Your life is my life" or "Your soul is my soul." Apparently the obligations of such vows were carried out religiously and selflessly. So strong was the bond between such brothers that the institution was often utilized in the formation of such secret societies as the Philike Hetairia (the widespread revolutionary organization leading to the outbreak in 1821), which were by their very nature and for their success dependent on the type of devotion induced by such a relationship. The tie also had the virtue of overriding regional, even religious, differences. During the Revolution, for instance, the mainlander Makrygiannes became the "brother" of the Peloponnesian Niketaras. Before the war, Greek Christians had often become "brothers" of Albanian Muslims.[13]

The Role of Politics in Pre-Revolutionary Greek Society

An account of kinship only explains the mechanism by which clienteles and alliances were formed and cemented. It does not explain the dynamics of the political process or the functions performed by these political groupings. To be sure, fierce family rivalries provided much of the dynamism of Greek politics. Such rivalries often went back generations and acquired a bitterness of epic proportions. Outstanding cases were those between the Plapoutas' and Delegiannes' in Arcadia, the Mavromichales' and Giatrakos' in Mane, the Bountoures' and Kountouriotes' in Hydra, and the Botsares' and Tzavelas' among the Souliots. Very often the rivalry could be traced back to personal quarrels involving questions of family honor and prestige, such as the deadly Kountouriotes-Tsamados feud which was set off by a broken engagement of marriage between a

---

[12] Christopher Neezer, *Apomnemoneumata . . . [Memoirs concerning the First Years of the Establishment of the Greek Kingdom]*, trans. (from German) J. C. Neezer, ed. D. Kampouroglou, 2nd edn. (Athens, 1936), p. 112; and Makrygiannes [*Memoirs*], II, 58.

[13] Maurer (*Griechische Volk*, II, 436-38) sees a direct correlation between the extent of this practice and the degree of political chaos, and believes it an important basis for secret societies and political formations. Concerning Makrygiannes and Niketas, see Vlachogiannes' introduction to Makrygiannes [*Memoirs*], I, 13.

59

member of each house.[14] But there were more fundamental bases for these family feuds. They were often struggles for economic, political, and military power.

To understand the situation, one must realize an important fact. Politics was, partially at least, an economic activity, a means of securing a livelihood. The accumulation of booty from raids, successful litigation over land boundaries, and tax-farming with its sizeable profits were ordinary forms of economic enterprise in a society which was both administratively too primitive to prevent illicit sources of profit and economically too restricted to afford more productive economic enterprise. For the first type of activity, military power was necessary; for the second and third, political control over those who rendered court decisions and awarded tax-farming contracts. Even the bribe to secure public office, so notorious in the Near East by this time, was a type of investment which could bring ample returns, if not through the usual perquisites of office, then by subsequent extortion and peculation.[15]

The traditional attitude toward a specific post, as a source of private profit to its holder rather than as an instrument of public benefit to all, became transferred to the entire state apparatus when the success of the Revolution made the state an object of contention among the Greeks. Out of loyalty to the family, which as a group still took precedence over the nation, as well as because of self-interest, the individual normally intended to exploit the state apparatus in the interest of his relatives and friends and at the expense of his enemies. Out of office, he expected the same type of maltreatment which he had intended for enemies, regarded with suspicion the state in the hands of others, and mobilized all resources to obstruct state measures. The behavior resulting from the conception of the state as an instrument of exploitation could only serve to confirm these attitudes. The state was without threat only when one controlled it. One's own behavior, while in office, proved this. The stakes in this political struggle were sometimes gigantic, involving loss of life as well as loss of fortune as a result of exclusion from power. Permanent compromise between factions rather than momentary truce proved virtually impossible.[16]

In view of this situation, politics in Greece was not merely an avocation of the rich and powerful or the full-time profession of a specially trained

[14] John Vlachogiannes, *Klephtes tou Moria* . . . [*Klephts of the Morea, Historical Study based on New Sources 1715-1820*] (Athens, 1935), p. 33. See also Maurer, *Griechische Volk*, II, 423.

[15] On the causes for the attractiveness of local office, see pp. 381-85 below. For a case of raids committed by state troops, see n. 106, Chap. V below.

[16] "In Greece all power is considered a source of profit," writes (even later than this period) Nassau W. Senior (*A Journal kept in Turkey and Greece in the Autumn of 1857 and the Beginning of 1858* [London, 1859], p. 272). In more general terms, concerning the basic Near Eastern idea that authority confers privilege, see Gibb and Bowen, *Islamic Society*, Vol. I, Part I, 205.

select few, as it tended to be in the well-administered, economically dynamic countries of the West. Most Greeks were vitally interested in politics. For them it was not a mere pastime which offered pleasure in return for time and money. It was a constant preoccupation of the aspiring and ambitious, to be sure; but it was even more a vital means of self-protection, a necessary activity to keep what little one had. Under such conditions, even the most ignorant and humble peasant, however unconscious of national political issues, could not conduct his everyday activities without some consciousness of, if not some participation in, local politics. He, more than anybody else, needed a client.[17]

The clienteles and alliances which existed in Greece at the outbreak of the Revolution were family associations designed to protect and advance private corporate interests. They and the factions that developed during the early part of the Revolution were not organizations of individuals bound together by common ideas rather than by kinship, nor were they groups dedicated to the formulation and execution of a political program. They were not groups seeking the good of all. This fundamental character of such clienteles and alliances explains both their public disrepute and their flourishing condition. In terms of new nationalist sentiment, which placed loyalty to the nation above all other loyalties and judged all activity in terms of the public good, the factions looked antisocial, antination, exclusive and selfish. Yet, in spite of possible pangs of conscience, attachment to a clientele or alliance remained strong in the absence of a central authority strong, efficient, and impartial enough to offer protection, render justice, and provide new opportunities for improvement. They, rather than the state, commanded allegiance because they performed these functions for their members more effectively than the state for its citizens.

The role of politics in pre-Revolutionary Greek society points up another characteristic of clienteles and alliances—the absence, by and large, of ideological differences on issues of public policy. The major issues of public policy had been debated and settled by the Turkish overlord or his regional representatives. The Greek clienteles and alliances had operated on the administrative level. When in control of the limited offices available to Greeks, the clienteles and alliances had executed rather than formulated major policy decisions. Out of office, their chief function of warding off abuses had placed them in the role of thwarting established policy as well as its abuses and had given them no incentive to propose alternative policies of their own.

The Terms "Faction" and "Party"

Within a province an extensive alliance of families (social equals), each with its own dependencies or clienteles, might place itself under the

[17] Thiersch (*État actuel*, II, 25) shows this is true when he points out, in 1832, the penetration of party divisions into villages, even families.

patronage of a single family (powerful by virtue of wealth, prestige, or temporary possession of an important public post). This type of alliance, restricted in membership to a particular province or even more extensively to an entire region, I shall hereafter refer to as a *faction*. In pre-Revolutionary Greece, factions had tended to grow to the limits of the largest administrative unit or region. Since regional autonomy had characterized Ottoman administration, the self-contained administrative units had ranged in size from the large Peloponnesos to small places like Mane and Hydra. With the Revolution, however, the Greek state, consisting of all of insurgent Greece, became *the* self-contained unit, a combination of all the smaller pre-Revolutionary administrative regions. Understandably, the same process of political formation would operate to create great national combinations of factions. It is this process which Part I of this book will attempt to describe. I will reserve the term *party* for this type of national combination, which acquired a national membership, membership drawn from all three regions of Greece.

But the terms "faction" and "party" will also be based on another distinction. What I call factions were by and large devoid of any public identification with any particular set of principles or ideas. Parties, on the other hand, developed a reputation for some sort of position, however vague, on national issues, such as the proper social composition of government—popular ("military") or aristocratic ("civilian"); the orientation of foreign policy—toward England, France, or Russia; or the most appropriate form of government—representative or authoritarian.

Since a party grew out of a faction or a combination of factions, and since one type of grouping faded almost imperceptibly into the other, it is sometimes difficult to maintain the distinction. But it is a distinction that is valid as well as useful for the sake of analysis. By these two criteria, national membership and ideological identification, no stable party formations are discernible until the end of the 1820s and the beginning of the 1830s.

2. FAMILY FACTIONS

In 1833, after a study of the political situation, the newly founded newspaper *Hēlios* published an article in which it enumerated seven "parties," each bearing the name of its leader: the Mavrokordatist, Kolokotronist, Kolettist, Zaïmist, Delegiannist, Mavromichalist, and Kountouriotist. This article described the so-called parties as the personal following of these seven political figures, whose thirty or forty political lieutenants enjoyed the support of a number of local leaders (demogerons or elders), each of whom in turn controlled a small segment of the people.[18]

Certainly this observation was not an isolated one. Thiersch commented at approximately the same time that, although a broad look might reveal two or three large parties, closer observation betrayed as many

[18] *Hēlios*, 4 July 1833 *o.s.*

parties as there were influential men in Greece. Nine years later, two Frenchmen, Theobald Piscatory and Jean Buchon, noted the same phenomenon. The former, a diplomat on an official mission for his government, referred to Greece as "a country where individual influences, though diminishing, had profound origins in the past" and the latter, an independent traveler and historian, noted "heads of clans behind whom marched their whole families." Moreover, Nicholas Dragoumes, a contemporary Greek official, in discussing the parties, merely gave a detailed biography of the acknowledged leaders, as if that was all the subject required. His [*Memoirs*] leave the distinct impression that the leader *was* the party.[19]

The analysis of the political situation as a configuration of *personal* factions, held together by a strong personality, seems untenable in view of the description contained in section one, where parties were represented as family associations based on kinship. Actually, both analyses are correct—that which stresses kinship for the pre-Revolutionary factions which persisted into the Revolutionary period, and that which highlights the personal element for the new factions which arose in the new Revolutionary setting.

Moreover, each faction partook of both types. A faction run like a family enterprise still relied heavily on a strong leader; a faction created by an individual personality utilized family resources as much as possible. In short, categorizing factions depends on emphasis, and no faction falls easily into either ideal type. None the less, the clienteles and alliances of the pre-Revolutionary period fall into the category of *family factions*, which included the last four listed by *Hēlios*—the Lontos-Zaïmist (what *Hēlios* called simply "Zaïmist"), Delegiannist, Mavromichalist, and Kountouriotist. The first three groups on its list belong to the category of *personal factions*. In this category one could also cite the short-lived faction of Odysseus Androutsos in Eastern Rumely or the far less important Makrygiannes faction which persisted into the royal period. Since personal factions came into being during the Revolution, they will be dealt with in a later section.

This section will deal with the family factions—already present before the Revolution—which managed to survive the outbreak of the Revolution and play important roles in the national politics which developed. All owed their pre-Revolutionary influence to participation in the Ottoman regional administration. As a result, all had to readjust to the new institutional and social arrangements of the Revolution. All contributed large parts of their sizeable family fortunes to the Revolutionary cause and emerged from the Revolution relatively less wealthy than before, Lontos and Zaïmes even impoverished. All represented strong sectional

---

[19] Thiersch, *État actuel*, I, 182; Piscatory, Athens, 6 Sept. 1841 (7th report), *L'Hellénisme Contemporain*, IX, 427; Jean Alexandre Buchon, *La Grèce Continentale et la Morée* (Paris, 1843), p. 107; and Dragoumes [*Reminiscences*], II, 301ff.

interests, an advantage in local politics but, as it turned out, an insuperable barrier to the creation of a national following, which was a prerequisite for an independent party. All participated in the deliberations of the national government by virtue of their possession of local strongholds.

The territorial base of each faction was located in areas where they, rather than the Turks, had controlled the land; that is, in regions relatively isolated and protected by mountains or seas. Such regions were Kalavryta, a district in the north-central Peloponnesos around Mt. Kyllene; Vostitsa or ancient Aigion, a coastal region facing the gulf of Corinth in the north but separated from the interior by an arc of mountains; Karytaina, the central Peloponnesian district around Mt. Lyceus; Mane, the southern tip of Mt. Taygetus which extended into the central promontory of the southern Peloponnesos; and Hydra, that naked rock lying off the northeastern promontory of the Peloponnesos. In the first reigned the Zaïmes'. The second was the seat of the Lontos', the third that of the Papagianopoulos family, better known in modern Greek history as the Delegiannes'; the fourth that of the Mavromichales clan; and the last that of the Kountouriotes'.

Of these, the first three were landed primate families. The first belonged to the older group of primate families which had risen to importance since at least the Turkish reconquest of the Peloponnesos in 1715. The second and third were parvenus. Like other such families, they had risen to power as a result of the Peloponnesian revolt of 1770, implication in which had compromised or destroyed older and more influential families.[20] The Mavromichales' were a leading military clan, and the Kountouriotes' a mercantile primate family.

The Zaïmes-Lontos and the Delegiannes Factions

The sources reveal the existence of two factions in the Peloponnesos in the decades preceding the Revolution, important because of their participation in the provincial administration which covered most of the Peloponnesos and because of their rivalry for predominance in that administration. These pre-Revolutionary political divisions merit special attention because they roughly correspond, in membership, to the later Peloponnesian branches of the "English" and "French" parties during the royal period. One was the Achaikon party, deriving its name from the region (Achaia) of its leader, Soterios Lontos. Its membership included Asemakes Zaïmes of Kalavryta and George Sisines of Gastouni. The competing faction, called Karytaino-Messenian, received the first part of its name from the region inhabited by its leader John Delegiannes from Langadia in Karytaina. His allies included Soterios Charalampes,

[20] John Vlachogiannes [Klephts], pp. 183-95; and Michael B. Sakellariou, *He Peloponnesos kata ten Deuteran Tourkokratian 1715-1821* [*Peloponnesos during the Second Period of Turkish Rule*] (Athens, 1939), pp. 96, n. 2, 139-40.

competitor of the Zaïmes' in Kalavryta, Thanos Kanakares of Patras, and Panoutsos Notaras of Corinth.

In the decade before the Revolution, factionalism assumed alarming proportions. In order to exercise his authority, a new Turkish pasha would ally himself with one of the factions. His successor, in order to establish his authority, would ordinarily call on the assistance of the rival faction which had suffered eclipse during the previous administration. In 1812, the Turkish magnates of the Peloponnesos threw their weight behind the Achaikon party, which thus forced Lontos on the new pasha. According to the ordinary rules of the game, Delegiannes accused Lontos before the pasha of corruption. The pasha executed Lontos and struck terror in the hearts of his adherents, then advanced Delegiannes to the position of morayannes. In 1816 the Achaikon party staged a comeback and avenged itself on its rivals by winning the support of a subsequent pasha and securing the execution of John Delegiannes.[21]

The Zaïmes family, headed by Androutsos Zaïmes, had participated in the Peloponnesian revolt of 1770 and had fled to neighboring Zante after its failure. Panagiotes, brother of Androutsos, joined the Russian navy, traveled to Petersburg where he received the honors reserved for such Balkan clients of Russia, and would have settled his family permanently in Russia had his death not intervened. In the meantime, Androutsos returned to the family seat (Kerpine) in Kalavryta and through his resourcefulness reestablished the family influence, first becoming a primate of his province, then a primate of the entire Peloponnesos. In the 1770s he went to Constantinople to plead with the Ottoman government for a policy of moderation toward the defeated Peloponnesian rebels. So successful was he in his dealings with the Ottoman authorities that he returned to the Peloponnesos to assume the position of morayannes. But in 1789, he suffered the frequent fate reserved for Greeks in his position— Ottoman disfavor and strangulation. His successor was his nephew Asemakes, eldest son of Panagiotes, whom Androutsos had sent to Pisa for education after his father's death. Asemakes played an important part in Peloponnesian affairs until his death in 1826 and left the mantle of his authority to his son Andrew, one of the leading political figures in Revolutionary and Othonian Greece.[22]

<hr/>

[21] Thomas Gordon (History of the Greek Revolution [Edinburgh, 1832], i, 143-44) points out the intimate connection between factionalism among the Greeks and that among the Turks: "The principal Mussulmans of that province [Peloponnesos] were split into two factions, headed by Kyamil-bey of Corinth, and Sheyk Nejib Effendi, each having in its train a party among the primates; in the latter class, the families of Londos of Vostizza, and Papayani (now called Delhiyani) of Karitena, made a very conspicuous figure." More importantly, see Sakellariou [Peloponnesos], pp. 95-96, especially p. 96, n. 2, for a listing of important names in each faction; and Vlachogiannes [Klephts], pp. 183-95, based largely on a manuscript from the papers of the klephtic Petimezas family.

[22] On the history of the Zaïmes family, see Anastasios N. Goudas, Bioi Paralleloi ton

In manner, appearance, and sectional loyalty, Andrew Zaïmes epitomized the average kodza-bashi. Like so many of his class, he seems originally to have envisaged an independent Greece as little more than the
traditional system run by Greek primates rather than Turkish pashas. His
disposition was generous, his private conduct upright, his patriotism
unquestionable, but his education and energy were quite limited. Like
other primates, he tried to play the role of statesman and military chief,
but his contemporary, George Finlay, was not far from the mark when he
wrote that Zaïmes "was too weak for a political leader, and utterly unfit
for a soldier." Born into great wealth, he died a poor man, in part
because he had served the Revolutionary cause so generously. Though a
very controversial figure during the Revolution, by the time he died
(1840) he had established a firm hold on the esteem of the nation.[23]

In the eighteenth century, the Lontos family settled in Vostitsa in the
district of Aigion, where it prospered greatly from the increasing foreign
demand for currants, the chief crop of the region. As a producer of a
commercial crop, the family acquired large landholdings and the political
authority which traditionally accompanied wealth. By mid-century, it was
the leading family in Vostitsa and, as a result of the temporary eclipse
of the Zaïmes' after the revolt of 1770, rose to a dominant position in the
northern Peloponnesos. Soterakes (b. 1750), its head, served frequently
as vekiles in Constantinople and was that very morayannes whose execution in 1813 was described above. Soterakes left three sons who attained
positions of prominence during the Revolutionary and royal periods.
Luke, the youngest, settled in Patras where he managed the export of
products from his land. Anastasios, educated in Italy, entered politics and
served several times during the Revolution as member of successive
legislative commissions. But Andrew (1784-1846) attained the greatest
prominence.[24]

An ugly midget addicted to riotous living, his openheartedness, energy,
and bravery won him many friends. In 1809 he entertained Byron on one
of the latter's visits to Greece. After his father's downfall in 1813, he fled
to Constantinople where he used his talents to win over important
Ottoman officials. In 1818 he returned to Vostitsa as the adviser of an
incoming Turkish official. Once at home, he quickly restored the old
family influence and used the family fortune to organize, equip, and
personally lead a private army under the family standard in behalf of

---

epi tes Anagenneseos tes Hellados Diaprepsanton Andron [*Parallel Lives of Distinguished Men in the Rebirth of Greece*] (Athens, 1874), v, 341-78; and *Megale
Hellenike Enkyklopaideia* [*Grand Hellenic Encyclopedia*], 24 vols. (Athens, 1926-34).

[23] On Andrew Zaïmes' character and career, *loc.cit.*; also Finlay, *History*, vɪ, 334,
but more especially the funeral oration of George Ainian, published under the title
To Kata ten Kedeian tou Makaritou A. Zaïme [*At the Funeral of the deceased A.
Zaïmes*] (Athens, 1840), pp. 3-27.

[24] On the history of the Lontos family, see [*Grand Encyclopedia*].

the Greek Revolution. He was as brave on the battlefield as he was skilful in politics. Though he concentrated on the military aspects of the Revolution, he represented his province at the second and third national assemblies. Cousins as well as personal friends, he and Zaïmes (both Andrews) most always worked in harmony with each other. This partnership preserved the old Achaian faction in the Revolutionary period as the Lontos-Zaïmes faction, and as with the older grouping, the Lontos element at first held primacy.[25]

The John Delegiannes executed in 1816 was the father of eight sons and two daughters, a tremendous asset for a rich and influential family seeking even greater wealth and influence.[26] One of his daughters became the wife of Andrew Zaïmes in spite of the rivalry between the two families, perhaps as a bond of conciliation between them. His eldest son Anagnostes he sent to Constantinople as vekiles during his own term of office as morayannes. Theodore, his second son, became rich in his own right as a result of support from Soterakes Kougeas, the all-powerful dragoman in Tripolis whose daughter he married. In the early days, his father used him on two important missions—one to Napoleon Bonaparte, the other to Ali Pasha of Janina in 1807. During his father's tenure as morayannes, he served as chief assistant and adviser. After his father's death, he became morayannes but died as a hostage of the Turks shortly after the outbreak of the Greek Revolution. As a result, headship of the Delegiannes faction passed to Anagnostes (b. 1771).

Anagnostes married the daughter of a rich banker (Tampakopoulos) of Tripolis. From 1800 until 1821, he resided in Constantinople. Together with his brothers Kanellos and Nicholas, who joined him there after the father's downfall, he joined the Philike Hetairia, the secret organization which planned the Greek Revolution. During the Revolution he followed the political career so typical of influential primates—as a member of the Peloponnesian senate, as an appointee to successive governing executive bodies from 1821 to 1827, as representative of his province in all the national assemblies. Piscatory characterized him in 1841 as "very old, timid, very religious, preoccupied with church affairs." Very much a kodza-bashi in his aristocratic bearing, he held rigidly to the old values until his death in 1856 and never forgave the captains for their defiance of primate influence during the Revolution. Yet the fortunes of his two

25 On Andrew Lontos' character, career, and close relation to Zaïmes, loc.cit.; see also Finlay, History, vi, 334-35; Piscatory, Athens, 6 Sept. 1841 (7th report), L'Hellénisme Contemporain, ix, 440; and Takes Stamatopoulos, [Andreas Lontos] (Athens, n.d.).

26 On the Delegiannes', see Goudas [Parallel Lives], vii, 203-44; [Grand Encyclopedia]; and Piscatory, Athens, 6 Sept. 1841 (7th report), L'Hellénisme Contemporain, ix, 437-38. On the role of the Delegiannes' before and during the Revolution, see Kanellos Delegiannes, Apomnemoneumata [Memoirs] in Apomnemoneumata Agoniston tou 21 [Memoirs of Fighters of (18)21], ed. Emmanuel G. Protopsaltes (Athens, 1957), xvi-xviii.

sons, each in a different way, reflected the family's adaptation to the newer trends. Petros studied law in Paris during the Revolution and returned to Greece in 1832 to become director in the ministry of foreign affairs. Charalampos followed the family tradition of marrying into money, but in this case the woman was the daughter of Karaïskakes, a fallen revolutionary hero to be sure, but a captain nevertheless, and her dowry took the form of a grant of rich currant land from the state in acknowledgment of her father's Revolutionary valor.

Of the other six sons of John the morayannes, one died before the Revolution. All the rest served the state in a military or political capacity. The only one that requires special mention is Kanellos, because he became one of the leading generals of the Revolution and wrote his personal memoirs which constitute an important source of information on the Greek Revolution. Unlike his brother, he was much more conciliatory in his attitude toward the rival Kolokotrones family and, in the grandest gesture of conciliation, gave his daughter in marriage to Panos, Kolokotrones' eldest son.

Though the Lontos-Zaïmes and the Delegiannes factions were family enterprises in the sense that one or related families dominated them, since pre-Revolutionary days they had also another aspect—an alliance of families of equal *social* prominence, each with its own clientele, though the hegemony in each alliance fell to the Lontos-Zaïmes combination or the Delegiannes' respectively. During the Revolutionary and royal periods, the Lontos-Zaïmes faction consisted of the following rich and important primate families: the Dariotes' of Nisi, the Venizelos-Rouphos' of Patras, and the Meletopoulos' of Vostitsa, the first by its attachment to Zaïmes and the last by its marriage connection with the Lontos'. The Delegiannes faction consisted of the Palamides' and Christakopoulos' from Tripolis, the Kanellopoulos' of Andritsaina, and the Poneropoulos' of Arcadia, all rich and influential families in their respective provinces. A major difference between the pre-Revolutionary factions and their Revolutionary and post-Revolutionary successors was the loss of a major family and area in each case. Owing apparently to tremendous losses incurred during the civil strife which accompanied the Revolution, the Sisines' of Elis and the Notaras' of Corinth, each of whose members played prominent military or political roles in the 1820s, seem to have acquired a distaste for national politics and thereafter confined their attention to the consolidation of their regional influence. Hence, by the royal period, the Sisines' and the Notaras' were no longer allied with the Lontos-Zaïmes and Delegiannes factions respectively.[27]

[27] On these parties' character as alliances of social equals, see Piscatory, Athens, 6 Sept. 1841 (7th report), *L'Hellénisme Contemporain*, IX, 436; also 437 (Palamides and Christakopoulos), 438 (Kanelopoulos and Poneropoulos), 439 (Dariotes and Meletopoulos), 440 (Rouphos), 441 (Notaras). Also see Goudas [*Parallel Lives*]: VI, 311-40 (Rouphos-Kanakares family); VII, 277-301 (Sisines family). On Sisines, see also Finlay, *History*, VI, 335. Also see [*Grand Encyclopedia*] for all of these.

The Mavromichales Faction

Since Mane enjoyed complete autonomy during the pre-Revolutionary period and hence remained administratively separate from the rest of the Peloponnesos, it is understandable that the Mavromichales faction[28] developed quite apart from the other two or that its concerns remained focused on the southern Peloponnesos. A faction, almost by definition, presupposes the existence of another against which the first is organized. That other, in the case of Mane, was the Tzanetakes family, which dominated the eastern part of Mane while the Mavromichales lorded it over the western part. For a century at least, these two families competed with each other for the supreme position of bey of Mane. The Tzanetakes' had held the post on three different occasions, the Mavromichales only once, though on that one occasion the tenure was a long one, lasting from 1781 to 1821. The holder of that office was Petros Mavromichales, called Petrobey (1765-1848), who owed his great influence in part to his very large family of sons, brothers, and nephews, all daring and energetic men. Of him, Finlay wrote:

> He was a restless, vain, bold, and ambitious man, lavish in expenditure, and urged to seek change by a constant want of money. He was deficient in ability, but more prompt to form courageous resolutions than most of his countrymen in high station.

His constant need for money was not merely the result of personal cupidity, as so many of his critics have maintained, but rather the outcome of having to provide largesse in order to maintain extensive political influence. Family, courage, and largesse, therefore, in combination with a frank and gay disposition, secured him widespread authority, even after the office of bey came to an end as a result of the Revolution. But even in pre-Revolutionary times, his influence extended beyond Mane proper into the Messenian lowlands around Kalamata. Touching each other, Western Mane and the rich lowlands had depended on each other during Turkish times. The lowlands, held largely by wealthy Turkish landowners, offered the relatively poor Maniats plunder; the mountains offered lowland Greeks a place of refuge from the Turks, as well as military assistance in time of need. In Messenia, the richest and most distinguished primate family was that of Panagiotes Benakes. The symbiotic relationship between Western Mane and Messenia is reflected in the symbiotic relationship created by the marriage of Benakes' sister to one of Petrobey's brothers. Her dowry brought the Mavromichales' wealth and her family relations extended their influence. On the other hand, their support was useful to the Benakes' both before and after the Revolution. This equal

[28] On the Mavromichales family, especially Petrobey's character and career, see Goudas [*Parallel Lives*], VII, 117-52; [*Grand Encyclopedia*]; Finlay, *History*, VI, 148, VII, 68-69; and Piscatory, Athens, 6 Sept. 1841 (7th report), *L'Hellénisme Contemporain*, IX, 441-42 (which deals also with the Tzanetakes').

alliance between landed wealth and military power presents a marked contrast to the situation in the rest of the Peloponnesos.

Petrobey was the chief instigator of the Revolution in the southern Peloponnesos. At the beginning, his leadership there was unchallenged. His forces liberated the southwestern part of the Peloponnesos from the Turks and, owing to his military successes, he played a major part in the organization of the Peloponnesian senate, over which he presided. Both the size of his family and the magnitude of its contribution to the Revolutionary cause can be estimated by the fact that, over the entire period, he saw forty-nine members of his family fall in battle. Indeed, two of these—Kyriakoules and Elias, both sons—secured a high place among Greece's fallen heroes, both for their distinguished valor and their unusual selflessness. All of this thrust him onto the national political scene. He served as delegate from Mane at all the national assemblies. The convocation of the second national assembly at Astros (December 1822) marked the peak of his political fortunes. The assembly elected him its presiding officer and then appointed him president of the national executive commission. Although his national influence suffered a rapid eclipse as the Revolution progressed, his hold over Mane remained secure until challenged by the president of Greece at the end of the 1820s.

The Kountouriotes Faction

The Kountouriotes',[29] one of the oldest and most distinguished families of Hydra and by all odds the richest in all of independent Greece, descended from the younger son of an Albanian peasant, who settled as a boatman on the barren rock after the expulsion of the Venetians from the Morea (1715) but before the island became colonized into a permanent community. During the Revolutionary and post-Revolutionary periods, the leadership of this family was shared by two brothers. Lazaros, the elder (1769-1852), confined his attention to local politics. He was one of the finest figures of the Revolution and one of the most unusual in his lack of concern for national fame. Without his energy and generosity, the large merchant marine of Hydra could not have contributed to Greek independence as mightily as it did. George, his brother (1782?-1858), was altogether a different type—far less distinguished and much more ambitious. He represented Hydra at all the national assemblies and was, as president of the executive commission, nominal head of the Greek government in 1824-25, but it was evident to all, except possibly himself, that he lacked both the education and the acumen to rule effectively.

In Hydra, where status and position depended solely on moneyed wealth, the Kountouriotes' were bound to be the first family. But this does not mean that they monopolized power. There were many primate fam-

[29] On the Kountouriotes family, see Goudas [Parallel Lives], IV, 223-50; [Grand Encyclopedia]; Finlay, History, VI, 32; and Piscatory, Athens, 6 Sept. 1841 (7th report), L'Hellénisme Contemporain, IX, 442.

ilies, jealous of their liberties and rich enough to defend them, and the island was notorious for its factionalism. It becomes necessary to single out the Kountouriotes faction from among Hydra's other factions because, during and after the Revolution, it managed to play a relatively independent role on the national scene, whereas other Hydriot families, as we shall see later, simply became adjuncts to the national parties. Moreover, the Kountouriotes' managed to gain some clients on the mainland, such as George Tisamenos from Epirus and Andronikos Païkos from Salonika.[30]

3. New Aspirants for Power, 1821

The Revolution removed the Turkish overlords, who had served as the main props of a family faction's influence by relying on its political skills and allowing it to exercise patronage. Rather than sultan or patriarch, the sources of legitimate political authority were now either the Philike Hetairia, which had organized the Revolution and now spoke for the ill-defined Revolutionary élite, or the representative assemblies ostensibly speaking in behalf of the region or the nation. And the new situation introduced new aspirants for state power—captains and Phanariots, each serving a social function with greatly enhanced value as a result of Revolutionary needs. The captains' function of fighting was indispensable in this society engaged in a war for survival. Phanariots, like Demetrios Ypsilantes, Alexander Mavrokordatos, Theodore Negres, and Constantine Karatzas, were lettered men of more than provincial experience, men with important contacts abroad, men with skill in manipulating representative assemblies.[31]

The Rise of the Military Element

In the early years of the Revolution, class struggle played almost as important a part as a nationalist bid for independence. So long as the Turks ruled, the social antagonism between Greeks was overridden by religious and nationalist antipathy toward the Turks. The collapse of Turkish rule, however, meant the removal of all restraint and frantic competition among Greeks for the wealth and power wrested from the Turks. The class conflict took a different form in each of the major sections of insurgent Greece.[32]

[30] Piscatory, Athens, 6 Sept. 1841 (7th report), L'Hellénisme Contemporain, ix, 445-46 (Tisamenos and Païkos). On Tisamenos, see also N. Patseles, Hoi politikoi Andres tes Epeirou [The Political Men of Epirus] (Janina, 1959).

[31] On the Philike Hetairia, see Chap. I, n. 12; on the captains and Phanariots, see Chap. I, section 2 above.

[32] The most prominent interpretation of the Greek Revolution as a class struggle is that of the Marxist historian Gianni Kordatos, Politike Historia tes Neoteres Hellados [Political History of Modern Greece] (Athens, 1925), i, but the royalist work by T. Pipineles, Politike Historia tes Hellenikes Epanastaseos [Political History of the Greek

In the Islands, the only serious case of open conflict occurred in Hydra, where class lines were clearly drawn and where oligarchical government was untempered by any democratic features. As in Spezza, unemployment had resulted from the recession of trade since 1815, but the population of Hydra was larger (20,000) and the distress more widespread. As in Spezza, the sailors clamored for the island to join the Revolution, which would give them employment, pay, and booty, as well as offer the satisfaction of serving a patriotic cause, but in Hydra the capitalist oligarchs hesitated until the choice was wrested from them by rebels. Unemployed sailors, led by Anthony Oikonomou, an unemployed captain, exacted from the frightened oligarchy through negotiations a sum of money equivalent perhaps to $30,000, which they divided among themselves. Fearing that the sailors would seize their idle ships and commit the island to the Revolutionary cause anyway, the oligarchs fitted out the ships themselves and took credit for joining the Revolution. By making the necessary concessions, therefore, the notables ended the revolt and reestablished their authority. After seeing to the assassination of Oikonomos, the oligarchs encountered no further challenge to their authority, but their brief experience with insurgents at home seems to have made them ready to support the primates of Peloponnesos and Phanariot newcomers to Rumely against any stirrings from below.[33]

Unlike Hydra, where the ruled rose against their rulers, Rumely witnessed a bitter struggle between two distinct ruling classes: the captains and the primates. The violence of the captains was swift and terrible. In Eastern Rumely, the Kontogiannes' slaughtered the Chatziskos primates. In Western Rumely, the Grivas' of Vonitsa destroyed the Chasapes'. At Agrapha in 1822, Karaïskakes drove out the Tsolakoglou's from their seat of authority in Rentina, and the feud between Odysseus Androutsos and the primates of Livadia was deadly.[34] The primates in Rumely had been generally more oppressive than those in Peloponnesos, perhaps because the land was poorer and the peasants less able to pay all required of them, perhaps because the Rumeliot regions where primates usually functioned enjoyed less autonomy than the mountain regions and suffered from the

---

Revolution] (Athens, 1928) also uses the concept of class as an analytical tool. The fullest and most detailed account of social conflict, especially in the early years of the Revolution and primarily between the primate and military groups, is the two-volume antiprimate work of Takes A. Stamatopoulos, *Ho Esoterikos Agonas kata ten Epanastase tou 1821* [*The Internal Struggle during the Revolution of 1821*], i (Athens, 1957) and ii (Athens, 1964). On class antagonisms in the Peloponnesos before the Revolution, see Sakellariou [*Peloponnesos*], p. 135. On the social conflict during the first years of the Revolution, see also Nicholas Kaltchas, *Introduction to the Constitutional History of Modern Greece* (New York, 1940), p. 41 and Vlachogiannes [*Klephts*], passim.

[33] Finlay, *History*, vi, 170-72, 174-76, and Stamatopoulos [*Internal Struggle*], i, 229-31.

[34] Vlachogiannes [*Klephts*], p. 31.

more direct rule of the Turks. But such brutal acts of class hatred were not unconnected with the social revolution wrought by Ali Pasha, the Albanian governor of Epirus, in his long and persistent attempt to uproot the influential and concentrate power in his own hands. He had undermined the established armatolik to such an extent that many armatoloi had had their authority reduced to that of mere local policemen. Others had resorted to brigandage rather than suffer such loss of status. To weaken the armatoloi, Ali Pasha of Janina had deliberately given much greater power to the primates because they were rivals of the armatoloi and not influential enough to constitute a real threat to his centralizing tendencies. The captains settled old scores with the primates in the opening months of the Revolution, and the recently increased authority of the primates collapsed.[35]

Though waged by primates and captains also, class struggle in the Peloponnesos during the early years of the Revolution was a conflict between rulers and ruled. As in Rumely, the common people became for the first time an important political factor, because the success of the Revolution depended on their willingness to fight the Turks and their possession of weapons gave them the chance to turn them against whomever they would. The established power of the primates, as large landholders, masters, and associates of the Turks, rendered them especially odious to the people, who gave spontaneous demonstration of their feelings when they tried to murder some primates in Vervena in the summer of 1821. They would have succeeded if their captain leaders had not held them back. But in the Peloponnesos, where the captains as kapoi had not constituted an official ruling group, as had some armatoloi of Rumely, they acted initially as leaders of the people in their bid to curb the oligarchs rather than as a partially dispossessed class trying to regain its former power.[36]

The outbreak of the Revolution offered military elements much more than a mere chance to wreak vengeance on the primates. It initiated a process of social mobility through the carrying of arms, both because the function of fighting was indispensable to a society engaged in war and because of the military system of irregular warfare which prevailed. This system requires special attention because it reveals how already estab-

[35] On Ali Pasha's policy and its effects, see *ibid.*, 31, and Stamatopoulos [*Internal Struggle*], ı, 43f. That its effects were erased by the Revolution is attested to by a letter of A. Mavrokordatos to D. Ypsilantes in 1824 (as quoted by Vlachogiannes [*Klephts*], p. 20): "Here in Rumely, the captains are everything. They always had first place and the entire administration of the eparchies, without the primates being consulted at all."

[36] On the popular outburst at Vervena, see Karl Mendelssohn Bartholdy, *Geschichte Griechenlands von der Eroberung Konstantinopels durch die Türken im Jahre 1453 bis auf unsere Tage* (Leipzig, 1870-74), ı, 222-25, and Stamatopoulos [*Internal Struggle*], ı, 209f. On military leadership of the people in several parts of Greece, see Kaltchas, *Constitutional History*, p. 43; also Pipineles [*Political History*], p. 164.

lished captains were able to build up great influence and enterprising individuals of humble peasant stock were able to become captains.

In many ways the military system was like the factions in structure. It was decentralized, with the strongest units the local ones. A military system of clientage, it was hierarchically organized. The individual captain recruited his men, determined the amount of their remuneration, and led them as his private company of soldiers. The ties between a captain and his men, at the lowest level, were based on more than the cash nexus. They might be blood ties; if not, then the types of ritual kinship mentioned in section one. Such captains, in turn, hired out their troops to wealthier, more powerful, and better known captains, and so on up the military pyramid. In organizing its military forces, the state did not recruit and pay directly the mass of soldiers. It hired the private, already established armies of the most influential captains and commanded their loyalty only so long as it could pay. These captains in turn paid their subordinate captains, who then paid their soldiers. As a result, soldiers were men of their chiefs rather than those of the government.[37]

How did an ambitious peasant or shepherd become a captain? As one source graphically puts the matter, one hung a flag outside one's door as advertisement that one would hire. One's success in obtaining recruits depended primarily on three factors: (1) kinship, (2) reputation for bravery, and (3) money to pay. The third factor placed a premium on having friends in the government or belonging to a faction which could obtain control of the state, because the state was the ultimate paymaster and hirer.[38]

The case of John Makrygiannes (1797-1864), born of peasant and shepherd stock, is illustrative of the career open to talent provided by the military system. Born in a small village in Lidoriki (west-central Rumely), he migrated at an early age to Arta in southern Epirus where he engaged in petty trade. When the Revolution broke out, he recruited eighteen Ionian Greeks living in Arta and formed them into his own personal company. Ismail Bey, his Albanian protector whose friendship with Ali Pasha automatically made him the opponent of Turkish administration in Arta, provided Makrygiannes with arms and a letter of introduction to Gogos Bakolas. First with this chieftain, later with Gouras, Makrygiannes contracted to provide the services of his troops in return for some kind of remuneration. Eventually Makrygiannes became Gouras' sublieutenant, then a supreme chieftain hired directly by the state to provide the services of his troops.[39]

[37] "Extracts of Letters to Colonel Stanhope from a Gentleman lately returned from Greece, on the State of the Country . . ." in *Greece in 1823-24*, p. 368; Humphreys, *Picture of Greece*, II, 166, 182-84; and Maurer, *Griechische Volk*, II, 26, 28.

[38] *Ibid.*, pp. 24-26. On methods of recruitment, also see F.C.H.L. Pouqueville, *Histoire de la Régénération de la Grèce*, 2nd edn. (Paris, 1925), II, 599f.

[39] Concerning this phenomenon in general, see Finlay, *History*, VI, 36. For the concrete example of Makrygiannes, see Vlachogiannes' introduction to Makrygiannes [*Memoirs*], I, 9, as well as the text itself, passim.

In a sense, the influential captain at the top of the pyramid of captains, each in turn with his private company, commanded not merely an army but a faction as well—a faction that was armed. The two men who rose to such exalted heights were Odysseus Androutsos in Rumely and Theodore Kolokotrones in the Peloponnesos, the first only temporarily, the second permanently. In Eastern Rumely, where armatolism was weak, the primates not strong, and the vacuum left by the collapse of a more centralized Turkish administration great, undivided authority was easily monopolized by the ambitious, able, and popular Odysseus, an already established armatolos. In 1822 he became commander of the garrison on the Acropolis and by virtue of this, governor of Athens. As virtual ruler of East Rumely until discredited by treasonable dealings with the Turks, he nullified all attempts by the national government to extend its authority over that region. The career of Kolokotrones requires more extended treatment because of his very important role in the Revolution and his success in creating a faction that lasted beyond his death in 1841.[40]

Theodore Kolokotrones (1770-1843) was fifty when the Revolution started. Still vigorous and ambitious, he jumped at this unique chance simultaneously to serve his nation and advance his own interests. His fifty years fitted him for military leadership. Born into a distinguished klepht family which had never acknowledged Turkish sovereignty, he had at an early age mastered the skills of guerrilla warfare and learned to defy the Turks—indeed all authority. His irregular life involved the usual hardships—the early death of his father and uncles at the hands of the Turks; then exile, first among the Maniats (1779-86), later in Zante, one of the Ionian Islands (1806-21). During the interval between these two exiles he sometimes robbed, sometimes took service as a kapos. While in Zante he served in one of the irregular regiments of the British (1810-17) and made contacts which proved valuable during the Revolution. A cattle dealer the rest of the time, his work kept him in close connection with the Morea, whence most of the cattle came.[41]

[40] On Odysseus, his character and career, see Takes Lappas [*Odysseas Androutsos*] (Athens, 1960), and Stamatopoulos [*Internal Struggle*], ii, 11-196 passim. See also Finlay, *History*, vi, 249-50; Gordon, *Greek Revolution*, i, 403-404; Samuel G. Howe, *An Historical Sketch of the Greek Revolution* (New York, 1828), pp. 150-53; and Stanhope to J. Bowring, Athens, 11 Mar. 1824, in *Greece in 1823-24*, p. 134.

[41] For an account of Kolokotrones' pre-Revolutionary career, see his memoirs in the original Greek: *Diegesis sympanton tes Hellenikes phyles apo ta 1770 heos ta 1836* [*Narration of Events of the Greek Race from 1770 to 1836*] (Athens, 1846), or in English translation under the title *Kolokotrones, Klepht and Warrior*, trans. Elizabeth M. Edmonds (London, 1892). See also the controversial work of Vlachogiannes ([*Klephts*], pp. 45-51), which proposes the interesting thesis that the Kolokotrones' had been mere klephts and kapoi and that Theodore made a deliberate attempt, after achieving fame, to construct a more distinguished family past. For briefer contemporary accounts, see Finlay, *History*, vi, 154-57; Gordon, *Greek Revolution*, i, 221-22; and Humphreys, *Picture of Greece*, ii, 152-55. For a general biography, see Spyridon Melas, *Ho Geros tou Moria* [*The Old Man of the Morea*] (Athens, 1931); C. Stasinopoulos, *Ho alethinos Kolokotrones* [*The Real Kolokotrones*] (Athens, 1958); and Goudas [*Parallel Lives*], viii, 81-120.

Kolokotrones returned to the Peloponnesos from exile early in 1821 with little else than his distinguished brigand name and a readiness to initiate the Revolution. Neither he, nor lesser captains like Basil Petimezas, Nicholas Plapoutas, or Niketas Stamatellopoulos, possessed the personal wealth or the political experience of their former lords, but they commanded military skills unknown to those lords. At the outset, they sought the hospitality of Petrobey in Mane and then joined him in initiating the Revolution in southern Peloponnesos.[42]

Within six months of the outbreak of the Revolution, Kolokotrones had an impressive army recruited mostly from Leondari, his wife's native district, and Karytaina, his own—those two provinces of the central Peloponnesos which soon became known as "Kolokotrones District." In this region, then, Kolokotrones had extensive family relations and his social origins, well-known to everyone, became a twofold asset. The people felt a sense of social kinship with him, and the Delegiannes', former employers of Kolokotrones and *the* ruling family of Karytaina, were prevented by his humble past from imagining him an eventual challenger of their own power. So they strongly supported him and secured for him the command of the Karytaina troops whom only the Maniats, of all Peloponnesians, surpassed in numbers and prowess.[43]

Even deprecators marveled at the confidence which Kolokotrones inspired in his men. Their loyalty to him seems to have gone beyond love, fear, or personal interest. That remarkable quality, then as always, defied explanation. One could only suggest certain elements of his dynamism—physical features, such as his powerful frame, bold face, and booming voice, or less tangible characteristics, such as keen intelligence, disarming frankness, and good nature. He skilfully used vivid fables and pungent aphorisms, which the humble folk liked and understood. The people may even have admired those qualities which his critics found so objectionable—cunning, avarice, and violent temper. Personality, then, as well as age and the personal wealth accumulated in plunder, explain why Kolokotrones rather than Plapoutas or Niketaras won such leadership.[44]

The Arrival of Phanariots

The year 1821 brought four distinguished Phanariot princes onto the

[42] Finlay, *History*, vi, 148, 157-58.

[43] "Extracts of Letters to Colonel Stanhope from a Gentleman lately returned from Greece, on the State of the Country . . ." in *Greece in 1823-24*, p. 352; Gordon, *Greek Revolution*, i, 222; and Makrygiannes [*Memoirs*], i, 212.

[44] For accounts of his character and appearance, see Finlay, *History*, vi, 153-54; and Gordon, *Greek Revolution*, i, 222-23. Stanhope (*Greece in 1823-24*, p. 27) estimated Kolokotrones' worth at a million dollars. This is obviously an exaggeration, but Makrygiannes ([*Memoirs*], i, 220) comments on his personal enrichment, and Piscatory (Athens, 6 Sept. 1841 [7th report], *L'Hellénisme Contemporain*, ix, 437) later mentioned the great fortune acquired by Kolokotrones in taking Tripolis and imposing contributions on the provinces.

Revolutionary scene—Demetrius Ypsilantes, Alexander Mavrokordatos, Theodore Negres, and Constantine Karatzas. Though conscious of their class, they did not act as a class or in behalf of class interests. Only the last two came and acted together, Karatzas as a junior partner of Negres. It is convenient, therefore, to deal primarily with the first three. Each brought with him a separate following. In his own way each was an ardent patriot. Because of rivalry between them, each established himself in a different part of Greece—Ypsilantes in the Peloponnesos, Mavrokordatos in Western Rumely, and Negres in Eastern Rumely.

Demetrios Ypsilantes was the son of the Wallachian hospodar (prince), whose deposition by the Ottoman government in 1806 had touched off a Russian declaration of war on Turkey, and the brother of Alexander, supreme head of the Philike Hetairia and leader of its unsuccessful attempt to establish the Greek Revolution in the Rumanian principalities. He arrived in the Peloponnesos in June 1821. Unlike his Phanariot rivals, who came as private individuals, he entered the scene in an official capacity—as the envoy of his brother, as the appointee of the Philike Hetairia—and thus had a legal basis for his claim to the leadership of insurgent Greece. His claim provoked the determined opposition of the primates, who had already attempted to constitute themselves the authoritative spokesmen of the Revolution in the Peloponnesos by organizing themselves into the so-called Peloponnesian senate. But the same claim received the enthusiastic acceptance of the people. This tiny, awkward, sickly man became the idol of the people. As Finlay wrote, "The supreme authority of the Hetairia still exercised a magic influence over men's minds." Finlay might have added that the people transferred some of their warm love for Russia on the man whose family had maintained such close connections with that power. But even more, the people embraced Ypsilantes as the benevolent "master" they had been longing for, the "master" who would give them land, a just administration (what they called a "system"), and most of all, liberation from the rule of the primates. Reflecting popular sentiment, the military element rallied to his cause and acknowledged his authority as the only effective political curb on the power of the primates.[45]

Ypsilantes proved himself one of the finest characters of the Greek Revolution. His tremendous courage, his fervent patriotism, his great integrity impressed even his enemies. But he was not cut out to lead. He lacked the qualities necessary to deal successfully with the primates—

[45] On the Ypsilantes family, see Goudas [*Parallel Lives*], VI, 1-49; and [*Grand Encyclopedia*]. On Demetrios Ypsilantes and his early career in Greece, see Finlay, *History*, VI, 234-37, 239-40. On the aspirations of the people, see Kaltchas, *Constitutional History*, pp. 43-44. On Ypsilantes' negotiations with the Peloponnesian primates at Kaltezon and Vervena, and the mass demonstration in the latter case, see George D. Demakopoulos, *He Dioiketike Organosis kata ten Helleniken Epanastasin 1821-1827* [*The Administrative Organization during the Greek Revolution*] (Athens, 1966), pp. 45-54, and n. 36 above.

experience, judgment, tact, and capacity to compromise. Nor was he better equipped to act as tribune of the people. With too much of the aristocrat and too little of the demagogue in him, with too high a sense of purpose to risk precipitating a civil war, he refused the advice of Papaphlessas, the warrior-priest, to head a popular movement backed by military force. And so he committed a series of fatal blunders that compromised his chances for a promising political future. He doomed to failure his negotiations with the primates by insisting on the formal abolition of the Peloponnesian senate, a demand which they could not accept. By a sudden withdrawal from the conference table and a dramatic announcement that the primates' selfishness was forcing him to leave Greece—all of this as a gesture to win his ascendancy over the primates—he unwittingly precipitated at the beginning of July 1821 a mass demonstration at Vervena which almost led to the wholesale slaughter of the assembled primates. This demonstration secured his victory over the primates, but he alienated his following by reprimanding the demonstrators, and he lost his momentary ascendancy over the primates by failing to follow up his victory.[46]

Alexander Mavrokordatos (1791-1865) belonged to one of the oldest and most distinguished Phanariot families. As a descendant of hospodars, he carried the title of "Prince." Like those of his class, his manners were polished, his dress and cultural orientation Western, and his learning extensive. Because of his natural talents, he excelled even in this distinguished company. He knew seven languages, European and Oriental. He had charm and tact. His enemies insisted on his slippery character and his deceitfulness. From 1812-18 he served as secretary to Prince Karatzas, hospodar of Wallachia, whom he followed into exile. In Pisa when the Revolution broke out, he proceeded to Marseilles, where he loaded a ship with arms and ammunition purchased at his own and Karatzas' expense. Together with some young Greeks, as well as French and Italian officers, he sailed for Greece on 10 July 1821.[47]

[46] Finlay, *History*, vi, 234-35; Mendelssohn Bartholdy, *Geschichte Griechenlands*, i, 222-25.

[47] For thumbnail sketches of Mavrokordatos' personality and accounts of his political role in the early years of the Revolution, see Douglas Dakin, *British and American Philhellenes during the War of Greek Independence 1821-1833* (Thessaloniki, 1955), p. 33; Finlay, *History*, vi, 236-37, 245-46, 321, 333-34; Gordon, *Greek Revolution*, i, 231-33, 267; Howe, *Historical Sketch*, pp. 49-52; and Giuseppe Pecchio, "A Visit to Greece in the Spring of 1825," *Picture of Greece*, ii, 48-49. Kaltchas (*Constitutional History*, pp. 36-39) gives a skilful analysis and summary of Mavrokordatos' ideas and policies.

A definitive biography of Mavrokordatos has yet to be written; but the best is probably Anastasios N. Goudas [*Parallel Lives*], vi, 185-242. Other biographical essays are E. Yemeniz, *Alexandre Mavrocordato d'Après des documents inédits* (Paris, 1866); Jules Blancard, *Études sur la Grèce contemporaine* (Montpellier, 1886), pp. 1-49; an offprint from *Galérie des Contemporains Illustres*, Gennadius Library, pp. 1-36; and a collection of three funeral orations published in a pamphlet entitled *Hoi* . . .

Mavrokordatos embarked on his political career with the odds against him. He had virtually no money after his initial expenditure for military supplies, and he was too honest to enrich himself at the expense of the state. Thus he had no chance to buy himself into the influential position of a landed proprietor. His experience had prepared him for drawing-room politics, where politeness, persuasiveness, and shrewd bargaining carried the day. Now he found himself in a revolutionary situation which demanded that its leaders court the masses and win military victories. The strategy and tactics which he had studied in Italy only invited contempt in this new society which was alien even if Greek. The rough, relatively backward regions of West Rumely only accentuated his cultivated ways. There and elsewhere in liberated Greece he encountered undying resentment of his Phanariot background and his Western ways. He quickly dropped his title, but he never endeared himself to his new countrymen. He was too much the aristocrat even to try. Again and again he tried to play the part of a general, not because of personal vanity or misplaced patriotism, as some said, but because military distinction invited respect if not popularity and meant political influence. His attempts, however daring and admirable in their perseverance, turned into political liabilities because he only demonstrated his military incompetence.[48]

Nevertheless, he quickly analyzed the mainsprings of power in Greece and then applied what talents he had toward its acquisition. Without further elaboration, George Finlay, English philhellene and historian, attributed his success to "prudence." Careful calculation, diplomatic skill, and deceitfulness were more precisely the qualities which permitted Mavrokordatos to overcome his disadvantages. He demonstrated these in the first delicate operation of his career in Greece—coming to terms with Ypsilantes, who was already established there. On his arrival at Trikorphois (Peloponnesos) for his meeting with Ypsilantes, the conflict between Ypsilantes and the primates was already apparent to him. He quickly perceived that his stay in the Peloponnesos would only involve him in the dispute and that such involvement could only do him harm. In his usual manner, he played the friend of both sides. But since Ypsilantes still held the upper hand in the conflict and claimed authority over all of insurgent Greece, Mavrokordatos meticulously avoided giving any encouragement to the primates and employed all his talents on Ypsilantes, so as to pave the way for his own establishment of a bailiwick elsewhere. From Ypsilantes he secured formal authority to organize mainland Greece and got letters of introduction to primates and captains there. In short,

---

Logoi . . . [Funeral Orations in memory of the great Greek statesman Alexander Mavrokordatos, who died in Aegina on the 6th and was buried in Athens on the 7th of August 1865, by university professors N. I. Saripolos, P. Rompotos, and Diomedes Kyriakos . . .] (Athens, 1865).

[48] Concerning his misplaced military ventures, see Dakin, *Philhellenes*, pp. 33-34; Finlay, *History*, vi, 245-46; and Howe, *Historical Sketch*, pp. 224, 230.

though he had come to Trikorphois as a private individual, he left there the official delegate of the Peloponnesian ruler and ultimately of the. Philike Hetairia. Equipped with a vague mandate which would permit him to go far beyond what Ypsilantes intended, Mavrokordatos proceeded from Trikorphois to Vytina in the north central Peloponnesos for a conference with Theodore Negres and Constantine Karatzas.[49]

Scion of one of the leading Phanariot families, Theodore Negres had just been appointed a secretary in the Turkish embassy at Paris when the Revolution broke out. At the news, he tore up his credentials and proceeded in April to insurgent Greece. The first incident of his career in Greece, though due to a misunderstanding, is indicative of the popular antipathy toward the Phanariot way of life and the obstacles which faced a Phanariot ambitious for political influence in Greece. On arrival at the island of Spezza, the masses, unaccustomed to his dress and manner, mistook him for a Turkish spy and almost lynched him. With Constantine Karatzas, son of the hospodar whom Mavrokordatos served as secretary, he proceeded to Vytina for the conference with Mavrokordatos.[50]

Relations between Ypsilantes, on the one hand, and Negres and Karatzas, on the other, had been strained since their dealings in the Rumanian principalities. Negres and Karatzas both resented Ypsilantes, the former because Ypsilantes had denied him the mandate to organize Crete, the latter because Ypsilantes had acquired the leadership which he felt his father should have. Ypsilantes regarded Negres as an incorrigible intriguer and Karatzas as an incompetent. In his conference with Mavrokordatos, Ypsilantes had refused to consider an appointment for Negres but had acquiesced in Mavrokordatos' pretended intention of employing Negres for the execution of "minor duties."[51]

The negotiations at Vytina took place between two parties (Mavrokordatos on the one hand, Negres and Karatzas on the other), even though three men were present. They came to a decision to partition Rumely. Mavrokordatos would establish his seat at Mesolongi and organize West Rumely; Negres, assisted by Karatzas, would do the same at Salona for East Rumely. From Vytina, they issued an encyclical to all the inhabitants of Rumely, announcing the convocation of two assemblies, one in each town, and instructing them to send delegates to the closest town. On receiving news of this action, Ypsilantes formally denounced Negres and Karatzas and instructed the primates and captains of East Rumely not to cooperate with them. Nevertheless, Negres carried out the decision of Vytina, convoked what was called the Areopagus of East

---

[49] Finlay, *History*, vi, 238; and Mendelssohn Bartholdy, *Geschichte Griechenlands*, i, 242-43.

[50] On Negres, see Goudas [*Parallel Lives*], vi, 1-49; on both him and Karatzas, see [*Grand Encyclopedia*]. On the incident at Spezza, see Mendelssohn Bartholdy, *Geschichte Griechenlands*, i, 241.

[51] Mendelssohn Bartholdy, *Geschichte Griechenlands*, i, 242-43.

Rumely, and established a separate regional authority. His action, a challenge to the predominance of the military chieftains there, enjoyed only temporary success. Deprived of the moral authority which a mandate of Ypsilantes would have given him, vigorously opposed by the rival military administration of Odysseus at Athens, his weak administration collapsed by 1822.[52]

In West Rumely, Mavrokordatos enjoyed permanent success, in part because of his greater skill in dealing with men, in part because of his prudence in choosing West Rumely as his "political headquarters." Though undoubtedly a difficult region to manage because of the rivalries among the captains, West Rumely offered several advantages: the political vacuum created by the lack of native political talent and the reluctance of potential heterochthon rivals to enter this backward region; an excellent geographical position, giving access to both Epirus in the north and the Peloponnesos in the south, away from the Turkish centers of power and close to any assistance which might come from Europe or the Ionian Islands. Even the apparent difficulties were advantages. The feuding of captains left a wedge for some outsider to come in as moderator. As happened with the Souliot troops which immigrated to this region in 1822, captains preferred to subordinate themselves to a total stranger rather than to each other. And however much the mountaineers might resent the cultivation of Mavrokordatos, respect and envy undoubtedly nourished the resentment.[53]

Mavrokordatos found a hearty welcome in West Rumely. His first arrival with a ship full of arms and foreign officers created an ineffaceable impression of widespread influence and personal affluence. Who could refuse his summons to attend a regional assembly on his return in September? Vexed by military oppression, the primates wanted an efficient civil administration which would equalize the public burden and give them greater power. Mavrokordatos understood administrative procedure and its importance. Now that the Turks were gone, the captains looked for a new authority to legalize their commands. What better way than through a popular assembly?[54]

By the winter of 1821, therefore, three immigrant Phanariots, without wealth, family connections, or local strongholds in insurgent Greece, had

---

[52] On the negotiations at Vytina, *ibid.*, I, 341-42. On the civilian administration of Negres in East Rumely, see Finlay, *History*, VI, 237-38, and Demakopoulos [*Administrative Organization*], pp. 67-74.

[53] Finlay, *History*, VI, 238. Gordon (*Greek Revolution*, I, 267-68) attributes his success with the feuding captains to "patience and address." Spyridon Trikoupes (*Historia tes Hellenikes Epanastaseos* [*History of the Greek Revolution*] (London, 1853-57), III, 111) describes the difficult situation into which he entered and cites especially the conflicts between captains and primates.

[54] C. M. Woodhouse, *The Greek War of Independence* (London, 1952), p. 84; and Finlay, *History*, VI, 237-38. On Mavrokordatos' assembly of Western Rumely, see Demakopoulos [*Administrative Organization*], pp. 62-67.

performed the impressive feat of establishing their individual leadership, one in each of the three major regions of Greece. The leadership of each differed in two major respects: (1) the social basis of its support, and (2) the legal source of its authority. Ypsilantes became the leader of the military element in a bitter conflict with the primates; Negres became the focus of organization for the weak primates against the military power of Odysseus; and Mavrokordatos, in organizing a civilian administration backed by a group of important captains, managed to win both types of support. Ypsilantes owed his success primarily to the authority derived from the Philike Hetairia; Negres legalized his authority by convoking a regional assembly, an action dependent on his knowledge of Western parliamentary skills; and Mavrokordatos, again owing to his political acumen, utilized both sources. Of the three men, Mavrokordatos achieved the strongest position and the only one which was to last.

4. The Military and Civilian "Parties," 1821-24

The Revolution was likely to lead to some sort of embryonic formations which had the two identifying characteristics of a party—transregional extent and ideological overtones. The framework of a nation-state, the holding of national assemblies, the formation of a national government, and the influence of heterochthons who thought in terms of a unitary Greece rather than Greece as a composite of regions—all these products of the Revolution tended toward the eventual formation of coalitions directed to national problems. Undetermined, though, was the character that these embryonic formations would take and whether any particular set would develop or remain stillborn.

By the end of 1821, two coalitions were beginning to form in reflection of the isolated and widespread clashes between the military and primate elements. Indeed, they were recognized at the time and actually called "parties": one civilian "party" and the other military "party." Of these, only the former was a party in the sense of a national coalition, which in this case consisted of the Peloponnesian primates, the Island notables, and the Phanariot leaders in Rumely. The military elements in Rumely failed to ally themselves with Ypsilantes, perhaps because the war kept them pinned down to their respective fronts, perhaps because sectionalist sentiment overrode national cooperation, perhaps because they lacked skill in organizing politically. The so-called military "party" was therefore largely restricted to the Peloponnesian group of captains who rallied first around Ypsilantes, then around Kolokotrones.[55]

---

[55] The military and civilian "parties" were parties only in the loosest sense of the word. They were rather loose socio-political divisions. Though loose, they were nonetheless real, real enough for virtual unanimity among the sources in drawing attention to these as an important factor in the early years of the Revolution. Among the primary sources, see for instance Trikoupes [*History*], iii, 34-35; *Aiōn*, 21 Oct. 1838 *o.s.*, which labels the military and civilian groups Mavrokordatism and Ypsilan-

Whatever issues there were, to say nothing of positions toward them, were never clearly articulated. Sometimes they seem altogether absent. One can effectively argue that politics was merely a reflection of class conflict and personal rivalries. But certainly these may have ideological overtones. Two issues seem vaguely discernible, both concerned with the form which government ought to take. Sometimes it seemed basically a matter of whether government ought to be aristocratic (that is, under primate and Phanariot control) or popular (that is, in the hands of chieftains, who more closely represented the sentiments of the people). Sometimes it seemed a question of whether government ought to be oligarchical (that is, run collectively by a group of men together representing a composite of diverse local interests) or dictatorial (that is, concentrated in the hands of one man, such as Ypsilantes, who by his popularity seemed to embody the general will).

The formation and subsequent dissolution of these two "parties" is reflected in a series of important political events: (1) the first national assembly of Epidaurus (December 1821–January 1822), (2) the second national assembly of Astros (December 1822), (3) the first civil war (November 1823–June 1824), and (4) the second civil war (November–December 1824).

The First National Assembly (Epidaurus)

The first national assembly of Epidaurus (December 1821–January 1822) marked the first round in the struggle between the two parties. Ypsilantes had proposed the assembly in order to obtain national recognition of a unitary state with a supreme ruler. He sought the establishment of a centralized national government and the election of himself as its head.

Since the delegates to the assembly were mostly appointees of the three existing regional authorities, membership derived almost exclusively from the civilian element which opposed Ypsilantes. It was at Epidaurus that these civilian elements—Peloponnesian primates, Mavrokordatos, Negres, and Islanders like Kountouriotes—formed themselves into the civilian "party," which consequently dominated the assembly. The leader of this group was Mavrokordatos who, in the domain of constitution-making and parliamentary maneuver, came into his own. Owing to his position as head of a regional government and his skilful domination of the assembly, Ypsilantes' program suffered complete defeat.

The regional authorities were recognized and their autonomy acknowledged; hence, the creation of a federal state, its federal character to last

tism respectively; Maurer, *Griechische Volk*, I, 47, 442-43; and Stanhope to Bowring, Athens, 21 Mar. 1824, in *Greece in 1823-24*, pp. 146-47. Among secondary sources, see W. Alison Phillips, *The War of Greek Independence 1821 to 1833* (New York, 1897), p. 117; Mendelssohn Bartholdy, *Geschichte Griechenlands*, I, 238-40; and Pipineles [*Political History*], p. 130.

only until the next national assembly. The national government was to consist of a legislative committee and an executive directorate of five; that is, collegiate government was instituted and remained a constant feature of Greek statehood until 1826. Whatever little power the assembly allowed the national government after reserving each region its autonomy, it vested in the directorate. Mavrokordatos became president of the executive directorate; Ypsilantes was excluded from membership. It is a tribute to Mavrokordatos' realism that he did not remain in Corinth, the first national capital, where as president he really belonged. He knew that the office gave him no actual power and that its value lay simply in the enhanced prestige it would give him back in Mesolongi.[56]

Outmaneuvered by his opponents at Epidaurus, Ypsilantes lost his influence over the military "party" to Kolokotrones. By winning victories over the Turks, Kolokotrones won prestige as a liberator, enriched himself and rewarded his followers with booty, acquired strategic fortresses which gave him control of liberated regions, and then farmed out the taxes of the regions in order to benefit his closest followers and secure funds for his cause. So influential did he become that the Peloponnesian senate was forced to acknowledge him as commander-in-chief of the Peloponnesian forces. In this capacity, he won credit for destroying in August 1822 the large Turkish army of Mohammed Ali Pasha, better known as Dramali, and hence preventing a Turkish invasion of the Peloponnesos for that year. As a result of that triumph, the city of Nauplion, with its virtually impregnable fortresses, capitulated to him in December 1822. In the meantime, the national government had dispersed on the advance of Dramali and discredited itself completely. A propaganda campaign, organized by Kolokotrones, Petrobey, and Ypsilantes, attempted to exploit the class sentiment of the captains and their soldiers by accusing the primates of plans to assassinate the former and enslave the latter.[57]

The Second National Assembly (Astros)

At Astros, the second national assembly convened in December 1822. This time captains came as delegates. The division into two "parties" was dramatically apparent with the military "party" encamped in one village, the civilian in another. The main target of the civilians was Kolokotrones. Taking advantage of their political skill, they excluded Kolokotrones from

[56] Dragoumes [Reminiscences], I, 10-19; Finlay, History, VI, 239-44; Mendelssohn Bartholdy, Geschichte Griechenlands, I, 244-48; and Pipineles [Political History], p. 161.

[57] On the prestige and actual political control growing out of military victories, see Pipineles [Political History], p. 164; and Woodhouse, Greek War, p. 94. A letter from the Mavrokordatos Archives, assumed to be written by G. Kountouriotes to A. Mavrokordatos in 1822 and giving an illuminating account of the propaganda activities of the Kolokotrones group, is published in Demetrios A. Petrakakos, Koinobouleutike Historia tes Hellados [Parliamentary History of Greece] (Athens, 1935), I, 310-12.

membership on the executive committee. With threats of violence, Kolokotrones took over the vacant place intended for a representative from the Islands. In April, the civilians abolished the office of supreme military commander, an act which amounted to the dismissal of Kolokotrones, who held the office, and vested military affairs in a committee of three. This time Kolokotrones openly defied the assembly. He seized the members of the executive committee and carried them off bodily to his stronghold at Nauplion. Of these, Zaïmes, a Peloponnesian primate, escaped to join the civilian legislative committee, a part of which had settled in Argos. Petrobey, president of the executive, and Andrew Metaxas, a heterochthon member, remained with Kolokotrones. Greece had two rival governments.[58]

The First Civil War

The two rival bodies remained at peace long enough to get through the Turkish campaign season. The first civil war (November 1823–June 1824) broke out when, after provocation from the civilian group, Petrobey drove the legislative committee out of Argos. It settled in Kranidi, a Peloponnesian coastal village easily protected by nearby Hydra and Spezza. The new site of government chosen by the civilians made them financially as well as geographically dependent on the Islands. This fact was reflected in the political predominance of the Island primates in the new civilian executive directorate, which the legislative committee appointed. It named George Kountouriotes president and Nicholas Botases, a rich Spezziot, vice-president. Andrew Zaïmes represented the Peloponnesian primates and John Kolettes the Rumeliot element. Because the latter was the moving spirit in this government, which eventually triumphed over Kolokotrones' rival government, and because he eventually created the "French" party, he deserves more extended consideration.[59]

Born into a primate Vlach family, John Kolettes (1774-1847) grew up in the prosperous Vlach village of Syrako in the Arta valley of Epirus. Thanks to the patronage of George Tourtoures, a rich Janina merchant distantly related to him, Kolettes studied medicine at Pisa and became personal physician to Muhtar Pasha, son of Ali Pasha of Janina. In the ruthless and intrigue-ridden court of Ali, he learned his brand of politics and made many of the friends and enemies who played such an important part in his later political career. In the fall of 1821, after the Turks had suppressed the uprising in his village and his own attempts to spread the revolt in Epirus had failed, he migrated to the center of the Revolution in the Peloponnesos, a heterochthon refugee with practically no private funds. His political career began at the assembly of Epidaurus, when his

[58] Dragoumes [Reminiscences], I, 19f; Theodore Kolokotrones [Memoirs], p. 198; Pipineles [Political History], p. 165; and Trikoupes [History], III, 34-35.

[59] On the first civil war, see Finlay, History, VI, 329-33; Mendelssohn Bartholdy, Geschichte Griechenlands, I, 325-29, and Stamatopoulos [Internal Struggle], I, 300ff.

maiden speech endeared him to the influential Papaphlessas. In January 1822, he became minister of the interior and temporary minister of war in the national government.[60]

Like Kolokotrones he possessed great native intelligence and a charismatic personality. As Samuel Gridley Howe, the American philhellene, said of him, ". . . the stranger who sees him in a crowd, turns to look upon him again, and marks him for an extraordinary man." On closer contact, Kolettes revealed a fascinating combination of coarse manners and personal charm, ruthless ambition and fervent patriotism, shrewd realism and naive sentimentalism. Many of the contradictions in his personality reflected his mixed cultural orientation, which proved a distinct political asset. His oriental qualities, which he publicized by his dress in the native kilts, appealed to the people. Yet his partial familiarity with Western ways permitted him to hold his own against Westernized Greeks and even to charm Europeans. Other traits, prized by the Greeks because unusual among them, were absence of boastfulness or pretentiousness, gravity, reserve, and silence. These he perhaps owed to his Vlach ancestry.[61]

The government at Kranidi had elements of strength which were to prove decisive. It had the prestige of legitimacy. By virtue of his European reputation, Mavrokordatos, president of the legislative committee, was the philhellenes' choice as the recipient of the loans being negotiated on the London money market. Indeed, in the spring of 1824, the news of the imminent arrival of some of the money made all the difference. It permitted Kolettes to secure an army, made up of Rumeliot captains and their men, in order to wrest military control of the Peloponnesos from Kolokotrones. It prompted Kolokotrones, who was losing battles against the Rumeliots anyway, to negotiate a settlement in order to share some of the loan. Zaïmes and Lontos, proud Peloponnesians who were beginning to have second thoughts about an alliance that brought Rumeliot troops into the Peloponnese as invaders, acted as mediators of such a settlement. On 5 June 1824, Kolokotrones surrendered Nauplion in return

[60] For a full biography of Kolettes, see Gianni G. Benekes [Koletes . . .] (Athens, 1961). Five shorter biographical studies bear mention: (1) Goudas [Parallel Lives], VI, 243-88, the earliest; (2) Blancard, Études, pp. 83-118, based largely on Goudas; (3) Demetrios Eliopoulos [John Kolettes: Study read before the Parnassos Society on 10 March] (Athens, 1890); (4) Elias P. Georgiou [Th. Piscatory concerning John Kolettes] (Athens, 1952); and (5) "Kolettes" in Patseles [Political Men]. See also Finlay, History, VI, 199, for a brief resumé of the pre-Revolutionary career of Kolettes.

[61] For character sketches of Kolettes, see Emerson, Picture of Greece, I, 65; Finlay, History, VI, 332-33; and Howe, Historical Sketch, pp. 221-22. A. Prokesch-Osten (Geschichte des Abfalls der Griechen vom Türkischen Reich im Jahre 1821 und des Grundung des hellenischen Königreiches, aus diplomatischen standpunkte [Vienna, 1867], I, 274) calls Kolettes "the only one of the Greek chiefs who could combine the spirit of the old barbarism with that of the new culture. . . ."

for a sum of money. The Kranidi government now became the undisputed national government of Greece.[62]

The first civil war marked both the climax of the conflict between the civilian and military "parties" and the beginning of the end of political formations along these lines. Even at the second national assembly the chiefs had not been completely united. The civilian "party" had included such captains as Petimezas of Kalavryta and Giatrakos of Laconia, and more significantly, Anagnostaras, the former arch foe of the primates. On the other hand, Kolokotrones, at the price of almost losing his leadership over the military group, had formed an alliance with Kanellos Delegiannes and had sealed it with the marriage of his eldest son, Panos, to Delegiannes' daughter.[63]

Several factors account for the breakdown of the military-civilian division and for the subsequent political realignments along different lines. The chieftains' need for allies with political skill and the primates' need for armed support led to cross-alliances. In the meantime, each group had lost its peculiar character. The captains had taken to acting more like would-be primates than tribunes of the people. The primates, realizing the importance of popular support and military power, had taken the field themselves as *chefs d'armes* and recruited their own forces with their private funds. The masses became less and less important as a factor in the Revolution as they stopped offering their support along class lines. Finally, regional sentiment proved stronger than class antagonism, as the second civil war (November–December 1824) demonstrated.[64]

The Second Civil War

This clash had its origins within the Kountouriotes government itself. From the very beginning, the influence of the Peloponnesian element in that coalition had been subordinate to that of the Islanders and Rumeliots, because Zaïmes, Lontos, and Sisines, the chief Peloponnesians in that coalition, were operating away from their local strongholds and without strong military support. But that influence declined even further when the arrival of the English loan freed the government from its normal dependence on the taxes collected in the Peloponnesos, which had for-

[62] Finlay, *History*, vi, 329; Mendelssohn Bartholdy, *Geschichte Griechenlands*, i, 327-28; and Trikoupes [*History*], iii, 105-11.

[63] Gennaios Kolokotrones, *Apomnemoneumata* [*Memoirs*], ed. Emmanuel G. Protopsaltes (Athens, 1955), p. 90; and Trikoupes [*History*], iii, 34.

[64] Pipineles ([*Political History*], p. 170) asserts that by 1824 the clearly popular element was confused and lost; Finlay ("On the conditions and prospects of Greece," pp. 13-14, Miscellaneous [MSS], Finlay Papers, The British School of Archeology, Athens) speaks of the military leaders of various provinces as gradually assuming the power of "petty despotic sovereigns." For some account of *chef d'armes*, see Piscatory, Athens, 6 Sept. 1841 (7th report), *L'Hellénisme Contemporain*, ix, 437.

merly constituted the chief source of revenue. Zaïmes, Lontos, and Sisines resented their subordinate role. In addition, they resented the favoritism shown by Kountouriotes toward the Islanders and by Kolettes toward Rumeliot and Bulgarian captains. The withdrawal of these primates from the coalition was precipitated when the mandate of the government ran out. The legislative committee reappointed all members of the government but Zaïmes for a second term. Photelas, the appointee named as Zaïmes' successor, was also a Peloponnesian but he too withdrew in protest with the other Peloponnesian primates. The withdrawal led to the formation, for the first time, of a Peloponnesian regional alliance.[65]

This combination of the Lontos-Zaïmes and Delegiannes factions with the newly formed faction of Kolokotrones marked the beginning of the second civil war. Owing largely to Kolettes' creation of a powerful coalition of Rumeliot captains, the government swiftly defeated its challengers on their own home soil. The Rumeliot invaders pillaged the primate estates mercilessly and treated the Peloponnesians as if they had been Turks. Lontos and Zaïmes fled for refuge to West Rumely. Kolokotrones and Delegiannes were captured and imprisoned in Hydra. Sisines fled to Corfu, only to be turned over by the British authorities to the Hydriots. Besides causing the primates severe economic losses, from which Lontos and Zaïmes never recovered, the Rumeliot invasion of the Peloponnesos raised sectional feeling to a fever pitch and left bitter memories which damaged sectional relations for a long time thereafter.[66]

But sectionalism was not to serve as the basis for permanent party formations, as some might have predicted at the end of 1824, any more than class antagonisms were. The search for foreign diplomatic support in 1825 was to lay the basis for the permanent party formations. But in the meantime, personal factions, which had already served as the raw material for the civilian-military groupings and were to constitute the core of all subsequent groupings, had crystallized.

5. PERSONAL FACTIONS

Personal factions, held together by loyalty to an individual rather than to a family, were products of opportunities provided by the Revolution, the work of parvenus—outsiders, like Mavrokordatos and Kolettes, or upstarts, like Kolokotrones, Makrygiannes, and a host of other captains. Three such factions demand attention here because each became the core of the three permanent parties: the Kolokotrones faction, the Mavrokordatos faction, and the Kolettes faction. By the beginning of 1825 they were formed. The personalities and careers of these men have already

[65] Finlay, *History*, VI, 333-34; and Mendelssohn Bartholdy, *Geschichte Griechenlands*, I, 329-31.

[66] Phillips, *War*, p. 148; Makrygiannes [*Memoirs*], I, 222-24; Mendelssohn Bartholdy, *Geschichte Griechenlands*, I, 328-33; Trikoupes [*History*], III, 168-79; and Stamatopoulos [*Internal Struggle*], I, 371ff.

been described. The task here is to describe the character of the faction which each created and methods by which it was done.

The Kolokotrones Faction

Of the three personal factions, this one was very much a family enterprise, inspired and led by its most dynamic member. Kolokotrones' closest associates were all relatives—his brother-in-law Nicholas Plapoutas, his nephew Niketas Stamatellopoulos, better known as Niketaras, and his son John, nicknamed Gennaios ("the brave") because of his exploits on the battlefield. According to Friedrich Thiersch, the Bavarian philhellene, Kolokotrones' "men" were only peasants momentarily dragged from the plow against their wills. In this respect, his organization was a single clientele which had never become an alliance.[67]

Kolokotrones tried unsuccessfully to make some Peloponnesian alliances. Petrobey joined political forces with him in 1823, but vacillated too much to be a dependable or permanent ally. To bring their families and factions together, the conciliatory Kanellos Delegiannes gave his daughter in marriage to Panos Kolokotrones, the eldest son, who fell during the second civil war, but Plapoutas, Kolokotrones' subordinate, refused to make peace with Delegiannes, his former employer, while proud Anagnostes Delegiannes, elder brother of Kanellos, refused to treat his former kapos as an equal and used his position as head of the extended family to counteract the intended effect of the marriage alliance.[68]

Kolokotrones did establish one outside contact which lasted. Count Andrew Metaxas (1790-1860), an Ionian Greek from Cephalonia, had come to the Peloponnesos in 1821 at the head of a band of Ionian Greek enthusiasts. Although he had commanded on the battlefield, his forte was politics, and to be an effective politician he required some military support. Kolokotrones, on the other hand, sought political counseling. Mutual need thus formed the basis of their political ties, which look less like an alliance than the employment of Metaxas as Kolokotrones' political counselor.[69]

---

[67] Makrygiannes [*Memoirs*], I, 212; and Thiersch, *État actuel*, I, 219. On both Plapoutas, born with the surname Koliopoulos, and Niketas Stamatellopoulos, see [*Grand Encyclopedia*]; on the former, also E. Th. Gregoriou, *Ho Niketaras* (Athens, 1942), and K. A. Konomos, *Bios Niketa Stamatopoulou, e Niketara. Katagraphe Georgiou Tertsete ek tessaron neon cheirographon* [*The Life of Niketas Stamatopoulos, or Niketaras. Recording of George Tertsetes from four new Manuscripts*]. (Athens, 1953). Concerning Gennaios Kolokotrones, see introduction by Emmanuel Protopsaltes in his edition of Gennaios' memoirs: *Apomnemoneumata* [*Memoirs*] (Athens, 1955).

[68] Takes Kandeloros, *He Dike tou Kolokotrone kai he epanastasis tes Peloponnesou* [*The Trial of Kolokotrones and the Revolution of the Peloponnesos*] (Athens, 1906), pp. 34-35; and Gennaios Kolokotrones [*Memoirs*], p. 90.

[69] For more biographical information on Metaxas, see Francis Lenormant, *Le comte André Metaxa et le parti napiste en Grèce* (Paris, 1861), and Pericles Mazarakes

But Kolokotrones' faction differed markedly from the family factions in commanding widespread popular support throughout the Peloponnesos. Some of this he acquired by the same means as had the primates traditionally—buying up land and becoming the patron of the peasants on the land, or in the territory under his military control, becoming the chief tax farmer and parcelling out tax-farming contracts. Though traditional, these means were acquired suddenly by military exploits on the battlefield rather than gradually through the economic or political process, as had been the case with the primate families. In short, Kolokotrones won his popular following by virtue of his exploits on the battlefield. Besides wealth, these exploits won him the love of some, the admiration and fear of others. They cast him in the role of that "master" whom the people longed for and who Ypsilantes turned out not to be. Most important of all in terms of political reality, they secured him widespread control over local administration, such control as in wartime only a military commander could enjoy. It was a tremendous asset when it came time to elect delegates to a national assembly, it was always a great boon in securing funds and dispensing patronage, and it was much more absolute, secure, and lasting than the control exercised by Mavrokordatos and Kolettes on the provincial and national levels of administration. He picked up additional popular support throughout the Peloponnesos in 1824-25, first because the primates patched up their quarrel with him, second because Ibrahim's direct invasion of the Peloponnesos from the south seemed to demand a strong military figure. Owing to foreign intervention, from the south this time, and because the Peloponnesians would not fight without him, the government in 1825 released Kolokotrones from confinement in Hydra and restored him to his former position as commander-in-chief of the Peloponnesian forces.[70]

The Mavrokordatos Faction

The Mavrokordatos faction had its base in West Rumely. Although a national figure by virtue of his election as first president of Greece, Mavrokordatos concentrated his main efforts on the political organization of that region and employed his national reputation to establish his personal influence there. Of the three factions, his was the only one to draw its membership from the three main social groups of Revolutionary Greek society—Westernized intellectuals (whether Phanariots or otherwise), primates, and captains.

[Andreas Metaxas] (Athens, 1931); for a family study, Epaminondas K. Metaxas, Historia tes Oikogeneias Metaxa apo tou 1081 mechri tou 1864 etous [History of the Metaxas Family from 1081 to 1864] (Athens, 1878). See also Blancard, Études, pp. 49-82; Howe, Historical Sketch, p. 360; and Piscatory, Athens, 6 Sept. 1841 (7th report), L'Hellénisme Contemporain, IX, 444. On Metaxas' desire for some alliance with a military figure, see Gennaios Kolokotrones [Memoirs], p. 202.

[70] Finlay, History, VI, 337, 366.

The Westernized intellectuals he attracted because of his own social and intellectual eminence. The most important among these were George Praïdes, a Thracian heterochthon who served him as personal secretary, John Soutsos, a Phanariot who acted as a civil governor in West Rumely, and Spyridon Trikoupes (1788-1873), an ardent Anglophile educated in England through the patronage of Lord Guilford, British philhellene and former high commissioner of the Ionian Islands.[71]

The Trikoupes' were a family of primates from Mesolongi allied to Mavrokordatos through the marriage of his sister to Spyridon Trikoupes. This connection played an important role in securing Mavrokordatos primate support, though his social origins and his civilian administration also won him primate friends. Chief among these was Tatzes Manginas of the Xeromeros district of Acarnania, an able though unscrupulous man who had long served Ali Pasha.[72]

The chief members of Mavrokordatos' captain clientele were Andrew Iskos of Lepenou, George Tsongas of Vonitsa, Staïkos Staïkopoulos of Vrachori, and the Botsares' (Markos, Kostas, and Notes), the distinguished Souliot family which settled in Lepanto and Vrachori. His opportunity to secure this support stemmed largely from the political condition of this region, where power was distributed among its various parts and contended for by rival captains in each part. Though beneficial because it provided him with captains in search of a strong patron, such local rivalry had the disadvantage of creating—each time he won a client—an enemy in the person of his client's traditional rival. George Varnakiotes, the rival of Tsongas, Nicholas Vlachopoulos, the competitor of Staïkopoulos, and Kitsos Tzavelas, the deadly foe of the Botsares', were such enemies.[73]

Mavrokordatos' personal rule over West Rumely went through two phases. The first extended from his arrival there in 1821 until the end of 1822, when the second national assembly of Astros dissolved the three autonomous governments of East Rumely, West Rumely, and Peloponnesos. The second started at the end of 1823, when Mavrokordatos returned to Mesolongi as governor-general in behalf of a new centralized national government and continued until early 1825. This administration

[71] For biographical sketches of Trikoupes, see Dragoumes [Reminiscences], I, 25f.; Emerson, Picture of Greece, I, 66; Howe, Historical Sketch, p. 234; and Piscatory, Athens, 6 Sept. 1841 (7th report), L'Hellénisme Contemporain, IX, 434-35. On Praïdes, see Piscatory, Athens (7th report), IX, 444, and Stanhope, Greece in 1823-24, p. 399. On J. Soutsos, see Finlay, History, VI, 333-34.

[72] Piscatory, Athens, 6 Sept. 1841 (7th report), L'Hellénisme Contemporain, IX, 434.

[73] Piscatory, Athens, 6 Sept. 1841 (7th report), ibid., IX, 434 (Iskos) and 435 (Botsares'). On Mark Botsares, see Patseles [Political Men]. On the Varnakiotes-Tsongas feud, see Makrygiannes [Memoirs], I, 156; Gennaios Kolokotrones [Memoirs], p. 67 and Gordon, Greek Revolution, I, 455. On the Staïkos-Vlachopoulos struggle for power in the province of Vlochos, see Finlay, History, VI, 273.

was not as popular as his first. He had to call an assembly of primates and captains to restore his waning authority. To the disgust of Finlay, who lacked political realism, Mavrokordatos acquiesced in the existing system of captanliks and thus enhanced the local power of each military chief. But his second administration benefited him in two respects. He became host of Lord Byron in Mesolongi and hence the receiver of foreign funds, whose use allowed him to provide employment for his captain supporters. He refrained from participating in either civil war and spared himself the enmity of the defeated.[74]

These two advantages—his intimacy with Byron, who administered the English loans, and his lack of involvement in bitter civil strife—cemented even further two important alliances which he had made in 1823, during the lull between the stormy sessions of Astros and the outbreak of the first civil war. One alliance was with the Kountouriotes faction and other Island primates, the other with the Lontos-Zaïmes faction. Kolettes, as we have already seen, was a party to this civilian combination, but as yet did not command a significant following. This combination, part of the larger civilian "party," was important. Geographically, it created a band of territory which ran from Hydra northwestward to Rumely and cut Kolokotrones off from his potential ally, Odysseus, in East Rumely. Politically, it was the later "English" party in embryo.[75]

At the end of the second civil war, Lontos and Zaïmes were allowed by Mavrokordatos to take refuge in West Rumely and receive succour from G. Tsongas, a supporter of Mavrokordatos. Kountouriotes, whose political incompetence rendered him a mere figurehead for Kolettes, secured Mavrokordatos' appointment early in 1825 as secretary to the executive body, so that Mavrokordatos might curb Kolettes. The price that Kountouriotes paid was growing dependence on Mavrokordatos.[76]

By exploiting, therefore, a number of resources—public office, local rivalries, foreign connections (with Byron and others), family ties (with the Trikoupes')—Mavrokordatos had, by 1825, created a regional political stronghold and a faction based on diverse social groups. Moreover, of the three personal factions, his was the only one, as a result of the alliances it had contracted, to look like a party in embryo. But the alliance with Kountouriotes, which became closer in 1825, was not continuous and did not extend into the royal period. As for most of the other Hydriot primates and the Lontos-Zaïmes faction, they remained permanent allies.[77]

[74] Dakin, *Philhellenes*, p. 82; and Finlay, *History*, VI, 333-34.

[75] Dakin, *Philhellenes*, p. 49. *Hēlios* (4 July 1833 o.s.) attests to the alliance between the Lontos-Zaïmes and Mavrokordatos factions.

[76] On refuge given Lontos and Zaïmes, see Finlay, *History*, VI, 336. Concerning Kountouriotes' animosity toward Kolettes and Mavrokordatos' tactful domination of Kountouriotes, see Howe, *Historical Sketch*, p. 221.

[77] Piscatory, Athens, 6 Sept. 1841 (7th report), *L'Hellénisme Contemporain*, IX, 442.

The Kolettes Faction

Kolettes was late in creating a faction. By the time he took national office in 1822, all the power vacuums had been filled—by Kolokotrones and the primates in the Peloponnese, by Mavrokordatos in West Rumely, by Odysseus in East Rumely, and by Kountouriotes in the Islands. To become more than a secondary figure, he had to establish his personal influence somewhere and dislodge someone. Rumely, which he knew best and where he had the greatest contacts, was the logical place. Odysseus was the most vulnerable leader.

At odds with Areopagus, the provincial government of East Rumely now acting as executive agent of the central government, Odysseus had resigned his official post as a military officer (*chiliarch*) and was exercising power on a personal basis as an independent chieftain. Already people suspected him of secret dealings with the Turks. Kolettes knew the man well, from the days when both had been members of Ali Pasha's court, and had good reason to expect that Odysseus, paranoic and reckless, might commit some fatal act. In over two years of struggle with Odysseus, Kolettes employed two devices which subsequently proved effective against other rivals as well. He utilized public office on the national level to undermine Odysseus' authority and build up his own. Once having put Odysseus on the defensive, he waited patiently for Odysseus to commit some blunder on which to capitalize.[78]

In 1822, acting in his capacity as minister of war and minister of the interior, Kolettes sent Alexis Noutsos, a wealthy and influential primate of Zagori (Epirus) and Christos Palaskas, a Souliot captain, to East Rumely, the first to serve as civil governor and the second to head the military. These appointments threatened Odysseus who, by virtue of his personal control over most chieftains, had amassed both military and political authority. Fearing assassination, Odysseus had both Kolettes appointees murdered in their sleep. The government then put a price on Odysseus' head. Makrygiannes believed this incident a carefully laid plot, by which Kolettes hoped to rid himself of two rivals, one actual (Odysseus) and one potential (Noutsos). Such allegations, of course, cannot be proved. In any case, Kolettes did not then succeed in unseating Odysseus, whose services were needed by the government in the summer of 1822 to fight off that season's Turkish invasion.[79]

Kolettes bided his time and showed that he knew how to make long tenure in the national executive body (1823-25) serve personal political ends. Though himself a civilian, Kolettes assumed the role of advocate of the chieftains' interests. A keen analyst of power and a pragmatist, he

[78] On Odysseus, see above, p. 74, and n. 40. See Finlay, *History*, VI, 332-33, on Kolettes' skilful use of these devices.

[79] Finlay, *History*, VI, 281-82; Gordon, *Greek Revolution*, I, 406-408; Makrygiannes [*Memoirs*], I, 157-59; and Nicholas Speliades, *Apomnemoneumata* [*Memoirs*] (Athens, 1851-57), I, 346.

knew that in Rumely, the chief military front of the Revolution, the chieftains were, by virtue of their military indispensability, the key to political power. It was they who, as supporters, were responsible for Odysseus' political strength, and it was they who—if they could be successfully wooed away from him—could make it possible to dislodge him. Through past association with the court of Ali Pasha and through family connections in Rumely, Kolettes knew many of the captains personally. Now Kolettes used public office to disassociate them from Odysseus and bind them by interest to himself.

After the Turkish military campaign of 1822, the Kountouriotes government, owing to the counsel of Kolettes, its most influential member, ceased employing Odysseus' services, which is to say that it cut off the pay and rations of Odysseus and his men. It lured away his lieutenants and their dependents by appointing them to *captanliks*, thereby establishing their local independence and offering them alternate means of enrichment. In spite of all its abuses, Kolettes supported the captanlik form of provincial administration, and he had no scruples about helping his own military supporters cheat the state of funds. As self-appointed agent for the chieftains within the government, he bargained with his colleagues in the national executive for their appointment to desirable districts, as well as for liberal pay and rations. He used his influence to secure them tax-farming contracts in regions which they commanded, and he advised them on the number of imaginary soldiers for whom they could safely charge the state.[80]

Until the second half of 1824, Kolettes still had no faction. The outbreak of the second civil war and the arrival of the English loan provided him with a golden opportunity. The civil war gave Kolettes control of the government because only he had formulated a policy, one of absolute repression, which he had the will to carry out. It is characteristic that he did not openly challenge the nominal leadership of Kountouriotes. He cared nothing for honors so long as he wielded real power and he knew that second place excited less envy. Invasion of the Peloponnesos offered all the Rumeliot chieftains employment at pay made possible by the arrival of the foreign loan, and it had the added attraction of providing booty from affluent primate homes in the Peloponnese. Through John Makrygiannes, Kolettes secured the services of John Gouras and Tzames Karatasos, the chief competitors of Odysseus. Among the captains who participated in the invasion, there were many, such as Nakos Panourgias of Salona, John Velentzas of Phthiotis, and Nicholas Kriezotes of Euboea, who became mainstays of the Kolettes faction. But adherents of Mavrokordatos, such as Kostas Botsares, as well as future "Russian" adherents, like Kitsos Tzavelas, also took part in the Rumeliot invasion of the Peloponnese.[81]

[80] Finlay, *History*, vi, 332, 381-83.

[81] Phillips, *War*, p. 148; Makrygiannes [*Memoirs*], i, 222-24; Mendelssohn Bartholdy, *Geschichte Griechenlands*, i, 328-33; and Trikoupes [*History*], iii, 168-79.

Kolettes emerged from the second civil war at the head of what seemed like a pan-Rumeliot military faction. But the basis of his success—identification with the military class and with Rumeliot sectionalism—threatened to keep his following restricted geographically and socially. Nor was his following as extensive as it appeared, because the acquiescence of Mavrokordatos in the Peloponnesian campaign had permitted Mavrokordatist captains to join it. The quick rise of Kolettes' political fortunes precipitated an equally quick though furtive alliance between Mavrokordatos and Kountouriotes against him.[82]

Meanwhile Odysseus, seeing his power undermined and fearing for his own safety, made peace with the Turks. By the new Revolutionary standards of nationalism, such acts looked like gross treason. To the captains, several of whom did the same both before and after Odysseus, such pacts were not intended to be permanent. They were simply accepted as part of the political game, meant as security against possible victory by the Turks or as support against their Greek rivals. But Odysseus clearly put himself in the wrong and he did not get the chance to redeem himself by later changing sides. After Kolettes had courted John Gouras with all sorts of favors, Gouras betrayed Odysseus, his former patron and commander. Odysseus, who had given himself up to Gouras for protection, was found murdered in July 1825.[83]

Victory over Odysseus did not give Kolettes undisputed leadership in East Rumely. Other aspiring chieftains, some of them former dependents of Odysseus whom Kolettes had wooed away and strengthened, sought to amass power for themselves and assert their own personal control over the region. John Gouras wrested most of Odysseus' power for himself. On his death in 1826, Karaïskakes succeeded to some of that power until he too was killed in battle the following year. In short, the destruction of Odysseus simply opened the way for other chieftains to challenge the effective, if not the moral, leadership of Kolettes. It was only after a chance set of deaths that no one captain in East Rumely was strong enough to stand over the others and all had to look outside the region to some national figure like Kolettes for support.

Kolettes' chief political weakness was that he did not build his faction from the ground up, piece by piece, and that, much more than Mavrokordatos, he depended on holding national office in order to maintain his hold over his following. In 1826, a year of Turkish military successes on all fronts, the critical situation led to the adoption of a more unified control over both the governmental and military systems. Kolettes and Kountouriotes were turned out of office. Zaïmes became head of the government and Karaïskakes head of the troops. Out of office, Kolettes had neither the money nor the local stronghold to keep his dependents entirely loyal and united. It seems no mere coincidence that the Kolettes faction remained divided and in relative political eclipse until another

[82] Howe, *Historical Sketch*, p. 240.
[83] Finlay, *History*, vi, 381-83.

critical situation in 1831 brought Kolettes again to an important public office. Nevertheless, the fragmentation of power in East Rumely after the death of Karaïskakes made him the rallying point of lesser military figures. So successfully had Kolettes cultivated his reputation as an effective advocate of Rumeliot military interests that captains thereafter looked forward to his appointment as an opportunity for them.[84]

6. THE FOREIGN-ORIENTED FACTIONS, 1825-27

It has been said that the "English," "French," and "Russian" parties had their origins in three intrigues which took place between 1824-26.[85] The statement is correct if all one means by it is that each of the dominant personal factions became associated with one of the three European powers. No source before 1825 gives the factions foreign labels. But the personal factions, which received the foreign labels, were already in existence by early 1825 and, with the possible exception of the Mavrokordatos group, were not parties according to my usage of the term. At this point an additional fact needs consideration—this was not the first time in modern Greek history that foreign clienteles had characterized the Greek political scene.

Since the days of Catherine the Great's oriental projects, the Greeks had grown accustomed to the arrival and departure of foreign agents encouraging revolt and promising assistance. During the Napoleonic wars, especially between 1807 and 1814 when Britain was struggling to wrest the nearby Ionian Islands from France, Russia had to share the field with these two powers, whose agents traveled throughout the Peloponnesos and Rumely to pick up recruits on the spot and to rally support against the day when they might wish to appropriate these lands. In 1810 there was even some question of a British protectorate over the Peloponnesos. Foreign consuls, of whom there were many in Greek lands, gathered round them types of clienteles.[86]

---

[84] In 1831, Rumeliot soldiers still regarded Kolettes their patron and advocate (Finlay, *History*, VII, 74).

[85] Dakin, *Philhellenes*, pp. 97-98; Nicholas Vlachos, "He Genesis tou Anglikou, tou Gallikou, kai tou Rosikou Kommatos en Helladi" ["The Genesis of the English, French, and Russian Parties in Greece"], *Archeion Oikonomikon kai Koinonikon Epistemon* [*Archive of Economic and Social Sciences*], XIX (1939), 25-44. For an alternate view that the parties had their rise under Kapodistrias and in 1832, see Dragoumes ([*Reminiscences*], I, 296), who, though he identifies the rise of parties with foreign intervention, nevertheless dates their rise at the "epoch of the governor."

[86] On Russian influence among the Greeks before 1821, see B. H. Sumner, *Peter the Great and the Ottoman Empire* (Oxford, 1949); L. S. Stavrianos, *Balkan Federation, A History of the Movement toward Balkan Unity in Modern Times*, Smith College Studies in History, XXVII (October 1941–July 1942), 6-11, 30-31. On French influence during the Napoleonic age, see E. Driault, *Napoleon et la resurrection de la Grèce* (Paris, 1924); C. Kerofilas, "Napoleon et la Grèce," *Les études franco-grecques*, II (1919), 145-55, 202-11, 273-81, and 324-33; Constantine Rados, *Napoleon I et la*

There were even then divisions among the Greeks, depending on which power's interference they most favored or expected. Mane, for instance, was split between the Anglophiles and the Francophiles. On the whole, the Peloponnesian primates still looked to Russia for liberation, even though Russia had let them down in their revolt of 1770, but they respected the might of Napoleon enough to place some hope in France. On the whole, the Greek primates did not consider Britain dependable, whereas, the Turkish beys of the Peloponnesos, dissatisfied with the imperial regime, looked to Britain because they had heard about British subsidies. Nevertheless, the Lontos', according to a French functionary who toured the Peloponnesos on an intelligence mission in 1811, passed for warm partisans of Britain. Enough research has been done to prove that foreign "parties" of sorts existed long before the Revolution, when revolt was only contemplated. Were more known, one might find a striking correlation between the foreign loyalties of families before and during the Revolution. As seems likely in the case of the Lontos', one might even find that a family was not making a fresh foreign commitment during the Revolution but renewing an old one.[87]

The Three Intrigues

Neither the Russian government nor individual Russians organized the so-called *"Russian" intrigue*, which was organized to promote the election of John Kapodistrias as president of Greece. But because Kapodistrias, a Greek from Corfu, had risen in Russian service to the post of foreign minister, his opponents believed, or at least charged, that Russian officialdom stood behind the move to get him elected. In 1822 Kapodistrias had obtained leave of absence from the tsar and had taken up residence in Geneva to help the Greek cause. A group of European philhellenes, European and Ionian Greeks, as well as Greeks from the revolted provinces, interpreted his retirement to Geneva as an expression of his willingness to head the Greek state. To these so-called Kapodistrians, united by their fear of the rising power of the captains in insurgent Greece, Kapodistrias seemed the man most capable of curbing them and saving Greece from militarism. Later their opposition to Mavrokordatos made them all the more enthusiastic for Kapodistrias. By April 1825, the inner

---

Grèce (Athens, 1921); E. Rodocanachi, *Bonaparte et les îles Ioniennes* (Paris, 1899); and Jean Savant, "Napoleon et la liberation de la Grèce," *L'Hellénisme Contemporain*, 2nd ser., iv (1950), 320-41, 474-85, v (1951), 66-76, 389-413, vi (1952), 103-21. The last work cites French correspondence reporting an agreement between British individuals and Anagnostaras in 1810 by which the former promised to provide material assistance for a Peloponnesian revolt in return for a British protectorate over the Peloponnesos (iv [1950], 482-84, and v [1951], 67-71). On the clienteles which formed about foreign consuls, see Howe, *Historical Sketch*, 337; and Piscatory, Athens, 20 Aug. 1841 (5th report), *L'Hellénisme Contemporain*, ix, 413.

[87] Jean Savant, "Napoleon," *L'Hellénisme Contemporain*, iv (1950), 482-84, and v (1951), 67-71.

circle of the Kapodistrias movement sought to bring their nominee to Greece, but he refused to go without formal invitation by a national assembly. In the meantime, Kapodistrian activities had stimulated other intrigues.[88]

In inception, objective, and strategy the *"French"* and *"English"* *intrigues* were both quite similar. Foreign philhellenes and heterochthon Greeks organized both. Each had its own candidate for the Greek throne. Each sought to organize a following in Greece which could prevail upon the Revolutionary government or a national assembly to invite its candidate officially.

Candidate of the "French" intrigue was the young Duke of Nemours, second son of the man who eventually became king of France in 1830, Louis Phillipe, Duke of Orléans. Count Jourdain, a French philhellene serving in Greece, had originated the idea which won the enthusiastic response of the three brothers Vitales, his Westernized Greek friends. In May 1824, Spyros Vitales went to Mavrokordatos in Mesolongi with a letter from Laisné Villévéque, an Orleanist, suggesting that Mavrokordatos organize a party in behalf of Nemours. That same year George Vitales visited the Duke of Orléans, who promised his approval should the Greeks express themselves. Subsequently, Orléans and Villévéque agreed that General Roche, an Orleanist, should go to Greece to form a party, while the Orleanist members of the newly formed Paris Greek Committee of French philhellenes should round up the necessary financial support in France.[89]

The "English" intrigue was a response to the "French" one.[90] It originated in the Ionian Islands with Lord Guilford, the English philhellene, and his protégé, Trikoupes. Guilford had selected as alternative candidates for the Greek throne Leopold of Saxe-Coburg and the English Duke of Sussex. Sir Frederick Adam, high commissioner of the Ionian Islands, believed that the Kapodistrians and Orleanists were respectively front groups for the Russian and French governments. Since he wished to

[88] Dakin, *Philhellenes*, pp. 97-98. Thiersch (*État actuel*, I, 7) refers to a secret society, of which the most noteworthy members were the brothers Metaxas, D. Perroukas, and Theodore Kolokotrones.

[89] Dakin (*Philhellenes*, especially pp. 98-99) has utilized Ionian Island correspondence of the British Colonial Office, Public Records Office, London, and so unearthed much that is unavailable elsewhere. Vlachos ("Genesis," *Archive*, XIX, especially p. 28) has utilized published collections of private Greek correspondence (e.g. *Roma Archive* or *Archives of Hydra*). See also Edouard Driault and Michel Lhéritier, *Histoire Diplomatique de la Grèce de 1821 à nos Jours* (Paris, 1925), I, 287-302; and an article devoted exclusively to the subject by Constantine Rados, "Peri to Stemma tes Hellados, He Apopeira ton Orleanidon (1825-1826)" ["Concerning the Crown of Greece, The Orleanist Attempt"], *Epeteris* [*Annual*], 2nd period, XIII (1918), 35-116.

[90] Maurer (*Griechische Volk*, I, 444) would have it the other way round—a French intrigue in response to Mavrokordatos' liaison with Commander Hamilton for British protection.

remove an imagined threat of a Franco-Russian alliance in Greece, he acquiesced, without the approval of his government, in the counter-intrigue. The Zante Committee of wealthy and influential Ionian Greeks, led by Count Dionysios Roma, Constantine Dragonas, and Dr. Stephanos, served very much the same function as the Paris Greek Committee.[91]

Roche arrived at Nauplion on 12 April 1825. Though merely an agent of the Paris Greek Committee, he passed himself off as a representative of the French government. He reputedly bribed the captains to agitate for Nemours. With the Vitales', he approached Mavrokordatos, Kolettes, Kountouriotes, and Kolokotrones, all of whom listened politely. The Zante Committee worked zealously to thwart Roche's attempts. Count Roma kept an agent planted by Kolokotrones' side during the crucial days of this rivalry. In May, while Kountouriotes and Mavrokordatos were absent from the capital, the Kountouriotes-Kolettes executive government promised Roche to convene a national assembly in September to elect Nemours king. Only a month later, when Kountouriotes and Mavrokordatos had returned, that same government sent George Spaniolakes on a mission to London, there to ask the British government to select someone to occupy the Greek throne and to propose the name of Leopold. On his way Spaniolakes was to stop in Paris to determine the official French attitude toward the Orleanist plan.[92]

In the meantime, the Zante Committee had formulated a new objective—to put Greece under the sole protection of Britain. Roma and his friends had drawn up a petition and sent copies to various parts of insurgent Greece for the collection of signatures. Four copies of this so-called Act of Submission have been accounted for. Kolokotrones, Zaïmes, Delegiannes (all three allies since the second civil war), and some hundred Moreot officers signed one dated 6 or 7 July 1825, after some hesitation, and transmitted it through Roma to Adam for transmission to London. Though basically a Russophile, Kolokotrones affixed his signature to this document for at least three reasons. He realized that the invasion of the Peloponnesos by Ibrahim in 1825 critically endangered the Revolution and necessitated the acquisition of aid from any quarter; he wished to be in good standing with the British in case they did decide to play a major role in Greece; and he was, since the second civil war, cooperating with the pro-British Zaïmes. Andrew Miaoules, a Hydriot captain who had distinguished himself as a Revolutionary naval commander, and the principal Hydriots affixed their signatures to a second dated 22 July. A third (26 July) was circulated at Athens and a fourth (8 August) at

[91] Dakin, *Philhellenes*, pp. 99-100. Gennaios Kolokotrones ([*Memoirs*], p. 127) cites the same three figures and their agent Christos Zachariades.

[92] Dakin, *Philhellenes*, pp. 105-107; Driault and Lhéritier, *Histoire*, I, 287-302; Howe, *Historical Sketch*, pp. 270-71; Gennaios Kolokotrones, *Hellenika Syngrammata* [*Greek Notes*] (Athens, 1856), p. 198; Theodore Kolokotrones, *Klepht and Warrior*, p. 217; Rados, ["Crown of Greece," *Annual*], XIII, 43-52; and Vlachos ["Genesis," *Archive*], XIX, 31.

Mesolongi. On 1 August, the Greek legislative committee approved the petition and commissioned, Anthony, the eldest son of Miaoules, to sail to England with the act. Indeed, the partisan assembly of Piada (April 1826) confirmed this act by passing a resolution asking Stratford Canning, English ambassador to Turkey, to mediate between the Greeks and Turks and defining for him the terms on which Greece would negotiate.[93]

Not to be outdone, Roche called a meeting of his followers in Athens early in October. On 20 November, they passed an "act" in behalf of Nemours. George Vitales set out for France the following February with an address for the Duke of Orléans, signed by Petrobey, Kolettes, Zaïmes, Ainian, and others. It was a very discreetly written letter, sounding out the duke through four general questions: Can Greece choose a prince from one of the illustrious European families without antagonizing other kings? Can Greece be assured that a prince-designate would accept the throne? What kind of a constitution would best suit Greece? Can Greece count on the support of the state from which she chooses her king? A third "act," offering submission to Russia, was signed by Kolokotrones, Ypsilantes, Niketas, and their partisans in November 1825. This time, acting as the head of his own faction, Kolokotrones could give vent to his Russophilism and adhere to his rule of keeping all irons in the fire. Taken first to Geneva, where Kapodistrias would not give it open approval, the petition then went to St. Petersburg in December.[94]

The Relation of the Intrigues to the Personal Factions

We must now examine more closely the relation of the three dominant factions to these intrigues. What role did each faction play? How did each leader, with his following, become identified with one of the three powers?

In his personal sympathies Kolettes leaned toward France, the nation of culture and the state of the great Napoleon. Keenly aware of the continuing duel for power between Britain and Russia in the Near East, he mistrusted both giants and believed their imperialist ambitions incompatible with Greek national aspirations. Because he deemed Britain more powerful, he feared it more. He suspected it of wishing to set up, under its control, several small Mediterranean Greek states on the pattern of the Ionian Islands. Like most Greeks he considered such a solution of the Eastern Question worse than Ottoman domination, which at least had the virtue of being decrepit and promised to be short-lived. France seemed like the most disinterested power. As early as 1801, Kolettes was

[93] Dakin, *Philhellenes*, pp. 107-108; Driault and Lhéritier, *Histoire*, I, 287-302; Gennaios Kolokotrones [*Memoirs*], pp. 127-30, and [*Greek Notes*], p. 198; Theodore Kolokotrones, *Klepht and Warrior*, p. 216 ("We were all in despair in this conjunction of affairs, and therefore we signed it. . . ."); Rados ["Crown of Greece," *Annual*], XIII, 54-58; and Vlachos ["Genesis," *Archive*], XIX, 28-29.

[94] Dakin, *Philhellenes*, pp. 110-111; Driault and Lhéritier, *Histoire*, I, 287-302; and Rados ["Crown of Greece," *Annual*], XIII, 62-63.

telling his friends to expect the most effective help from France. But the Orleanist plot presented serious problems. There was small probability that official France, headed by a Bourbon, would approve, and even less chance that Russia or Britain would permit a Frenchman to accept the Greek crown.[95]

Viscount Rumigny, the aide-de-camp of the Duke of Orléans, approached Kolettes. With his customary caution toward anything uncertain and risky, Kolettes ostensibly held aloof from the Orleanist intrigue. Others, less circumspect than he, actively promoted the idea: John Soutsos, a Mavrokordatist until then, and George Ainian—both eventually "Russian"—as well as close associates of Kolettes such as Demetrios Chrestides, a school teacher from Constantinople who eventually became a leading figure in the "French" party; Adam Doukas, a native of Epirus; John Theotokes, a native of Cephalonia who served Kolettes as private secretary; and John Gouras. More independent elements, such as Demetrios Ypsilantes and Constantine Mavromichales, became associated with this group, the first primarily because he opposed the English petition. Ainian, an intellectual to whom the Duke of Nemours appealed for romantic reasons, carried on an active correspondence with Villévéque. Chrestides indiscreetly exhorted the crowds in the square of Nauplion to back France. Eventually Soutsos, Ainian, and Theotokes got clapped into prison for campaigning in Rumely against the English petition. A rumor was perpetrated throughout Rumely at this time that England favored the return of Rumely to Ottoman sovereignty. Indeed, the "French" displayed themselves more anti-British than pro-French.[96]

For Mavrokordatos, personal tastes had no place in matters of state. Neither dogmatic nor naive in his search for foreign support, he acted on the realistic premise that powers acted exclusively for their own national self-interest. By 1825 he believed the greatest hope for Greece lay in stimulating rivalry between Britain and France. That is why he encouraged both the "English" and the "French" intrigues, while really favoring neither per se. It also seemed clear that England would play a major role in the eventual Greek settlement. Since he wanted to take a decisive part in the eventual negotiations, Mavrokordatos gave Britain primacy over France in his attention. Besides, he stood the best chance of winning British approval.[97] Already in 1824 official Britain favored him as the best bulwark against the possible rule of Kapodistrias, which it equated with Russian domination.[98] Moreover, Mavrokordatos' brother-in-law, Trikoupes, was an ardent Anglophile.

[95] On Kolettes' pro-Revolutionary sentiments, see J. M. Apostolakes, "He Hellenike Epanastasis kai he Europaike Politike ["The Greek Revolution and European Policy"], Messeniaka Grammata [Messenian Letters] (1956), p. 73.

[96] Rados ["Crown of Greece," Annual], XIII, 39, 57-58, 61; and Vlachos ["Genesis," Archive], XIX, 28.

[97] Dakin, Philhellenes, pp. 106-107; and Kaltchas, Constitutional History, pp. 38-39.

[98] Dakin, Philhellenes, p. 74.

The "English" intrigue involved friends and allies of Mavrokordatos. The Hydriots, under Andrew Miaoules and the brothers Tompazes (Manuel and Iakomakes), always looked on England with favor. George Spaniolakes, who went to London to ask for a king, was a Mavrokordatist, as was Trikoupes. Then, too, Andrew Lontos and Andrew Zaïmes controlled the assembly (Piada) which passed the resolution asking Stratford Canning's mediation.[99]

Sentiment played a significant role among Greek Russophiles. The fact of a common Orthodoxy was extremely important in a society where religion had traditionally defined the chief divisions in the state and dictated the culture of each division. To a marked degree, common orthodoxy meant common culture. The wandering monk, such a familiar figure and such a valuable source of information about the outside world to the immobile peasant, had often traveled to Russia or at least known Russian monks. Many Ottoman Greeks had relatives in Russia, where all found excellent economic opportunities and some the patronage of the tsar. Monks and relatives, as well as a long succession of Russian agents since the days of Peter the Great, had taught the common people to look upon Russia as the ultimate liberator and the great benefactor.[100]

A second important determinant of Russophilism was the memory of Russia's brief rule in the Ionian Islands (1799-1807). So close were the Ionian Islands ethnically and geographically that Ottoman Greeks kept informed about them through personal contacts. France had ruled there just before and just after Russia. England had taken over from France and ruled on a permanent basis since 1815. The Greeks thus felt that they had some comparative basis for evaluating the attitude of each country toward Greek national aspirations. Most Greeks formulated their image of Russian intentions from this episode, which was one of the most felicitous and enlightened instances of Russian imperialism.

The Russian occupation of the Ionian Islands coincided with the liberal phase of Tsar Alexander I's reign. During their first occupation (1797-99) the French had introduced democratic government and sweeping social reforms. The Russians did even better. In a grandiose gesture which impressed republicans and nationalists alike, they united the Islands into the so-called Heptanesian republic, the first autonomous Greek state in modern times. Under this Russian protectorate the Ionian Greeks enjoyed constitutional government of a moderate kind.[101] When the French returned in 1807, the strategic value of the islands and the threat of their loss to the British induced Napoleon to dissolve the re-

---

[99] *Ibid.*, pp. 106, 133.

[100] Sumner, *Peter the Great and the Ottoman Empire*; also Stavrianos, *Balkan Federation*, pp. 6-11.

[101] On the Russian record in the Ionian Islands and one instance of its favorable impression on an Ionian family (Metaxas'), see Lenormant, *Metaxa*, pp. 8-16. See also Dakin, *Philhellenes*, pp. 14-15, and Kaltchas, *Constitutional History*, pp. 22-27.

public and organize a military regime which governed absolutely. In 1815 the islands again became an independent republic, this time under a British protectorate, but the British established an illiberal constitution which placed all power in their hands. Throughout the reign of Greece's first king, nothing was to do the British cause in Greece more harm than their rule in the Ionian Islands, where they looked like tyrants thwarting nationalist aspirations. Indeed the Ionian problem would be the Cyprus question of that period.[102] In contrast, Russia, on the basis of her record in the Ionian Islands, looked like the power which respected nationalism and constitutionalism.

This explains the Russophilism of such Ionian Greeks as John Kapodistrias, who in 1827 became president of Greece, and Andrew Metaxas, whose two paternal uncles had been living in Russia since participating in the Peloponnesian revolt of 1770.[103] Kolokotrones, Plapoutas, and Niketas had served in the Ionian Islands long enough to participate in the dissatisfaction with British rule and the consequent idealizing of the former Russian protectorate. If their attachment to Russia was a matter of sentiment and belief in Russian respect for Greek aspirations, their espousal of Russia was also possibly influenced by the consideration that they might win more of the common folk to their cause. Russophilism in the islands, especially Spezza, is largely explained by the fact that, since the Russo-Turkish treaty of Kutchuk Kainarji (1774), many Greek merchants had sailed their ships under the Russian flag and enjoyed immunity from Turkish extortion.[104]

By March 1826, a "Russian" party was coming into being. Spyridon Metaxas, brother of Andrew, visited Nauplion and Epidaurus to recruit members. In that same month Kolokotrones wrote to Zante that agents were organizing a "Russian" following in Rumely with the help of money and grandiose promises. And by the time Kapodistrias arrived in Greece in January 1828, the Kapodistrian party enjoyed considerable support, particularly from secondary figures.[105]

The Increase of Foreign Influence

None of the leaders wished to have their names permanently identified with a particular power.[106] Each protected himself, during 1825-26, by

---

[102] On the reactionary British arrangements after taking over in 1815 and the bad international reputation earned by Britain for this protectorate, see William Miller, *The Ottoman Empire and its Successors 1801-1927*, 4th edn. (Cambridge, Eng., 1936), pp. 44-45, 58-61. On the calumnious attacks by the Greek press on British rule in the Ionian Islands, see Finlay, *History*, VII, 304.

[103] Lenormant, *Metaxa*, pp. 8-10.

[104] On the Greek regiments organized in the Ionian Islands, see Dakin, *Philhellenes*, pp. 12-17. On Russophilism in Spezza, see Piscatory, Athens, 6 Sept. 1841 (7th report), *L'Hellénisme Contemporain*, IX, 443.

[105] Dakin, *Philhellenes*, p. 143; and Vlachos ["Genesis," *Archive*], XIX, 39.

[106] Prokesch-Osten (*Geschichte*, I, 413) says that Kolettes did not want to be called the head of a party.

temporizing, remaining outwardly noncommittal toward the intrigue he supposedly favored and giving some hope of support to the agents of other intrigues. Mavrokordatos listened politely when approached by Vitales. Kolokotrones signed the Act of Submission and favored the assembly's appeal to England in 1826. So deftly did each play his hand that the agents to each intrigue often thought they enjoyed the support of all the leaders.[107] But each man owed his permanent identification with a particular power to his enemies. Could one more effectively discredit a rival than by branding him the agent of a foreign power and the betrayer of national interests?[108] Once the reputation caught hold, a man could hardly shake it off. As foreign influence became more pronounced, the leader was tempted to exploit his reputation even though he continued to disclaim it publicly. And indeed, the years 1826-27 witnessed a marked increase in foreign influence.

The ravages of Ibrahim throughout the Peloponnesos, the loss of Mesolongi and Athens on the mainland—all these military reserves prevented the government from collecting any sizeable revenue and resulted in an empty treasury. From mid-1826 the Greek government became dependent on private foreign donations made possible by the great wave of philhellenism which had swept through Europe in 1825. Even the factions were receiving financial support from such sources—Kolettes from the French *and* the Kapodistrians, Kolokotrones from a French philhellene, Dr. Bailly, who believed he was supporting an anti-British group.[109]

The powers, first Russia and Britain (protocol of 4 April 1826), then France too by the treaty of 6 July 1827, intervened officially. Their representatives on the spot, first the admirals of the individual Mediterranean fleets, then the ministers assigned to Greece in 1828, began to act as patrons of the existing factions. For instance, in 1826 Rowan Hamilton, a captain in the English fleet, intervened in Hydriot politics to support the anti-Kountouriotes faction headed by Miaoules and the brothers Tompazes. In the course of the Revolution, the Kountouriotes' had placed themselves at the head of the "democratic party" or the lower classes, which had rallied to Oikonomou in 1821 and which were now agitating against Miaoules and Tompazes. The Kountouriotes rivals had escaped with their ships to Poros, and George Kountouriotes was on the verge of pursuing them when Captain Hamilton heard the news. Recognizing Miaoules and the Tompazes' as staunch Anglophiles and suspecting Kountouriotes of wishing to punish them for their Anglophilism, Hamilton rushed to Hydra. He sternly warned the community against touching the

[107] Dakin, *Philhellenes*, p. 99.

[108] Theodore Kolokotrones (*Klepht and Warrior*, p. 217) writes that Mavrokordatos alleged that the body of chiefs to which Kolokotrones belonged was in opposition to England and devoted to Russia. Blancard (*Études*, p. 38) speaks of "calumnious accusations that Mavrokordatos belonged to the English party."

[109] Dakin, *Philhellenes*, pp. 134, 139, 140.

property of either family, forbad it to attack the ships at Poros, and to put some fear in the sailors, severely punished a Kountouriotist for committing an act of piracy. As a result, Hamilton unwittingly created Anglophobes in order to protect some Anglophiles. Kountouriotes became anti-English and made a pact with Kolokotrones.[110]

The political events of early 1827 illustrate how much the existence of an affiliate foreign power, even when not yet actively intriguing, could enhance the internal weight of a faction. At the end of 1826, the following political groupings prevailed: (1) the "English" alliance of the Mavro-kordatos, Lontos-Zaïmes, and Miaoules-Tompazes (anti-Kountouriotes) factions; (2) the "Russian" Kolokotrones faction; (3) the "French" Kolettes faction; and (4) the Kountouriotes faction. But only two powers —Britain and Russia—had yet associated themselves officially in the Greek question. Is it merely coincidental that the "English" and "Russian" factions played the decisive parts in Greek politics during the first half of 1827? Kolokotrones set up his "Russian" assembly at Kastri (Hermione) in February, and Zaïmes, at the head of the government since mid-1826, called an "English" assembly at Aegina. The Kolettes and Kountouriotes factions remained relatively passive. When these two assemblies merged at Troezene they voted measures realizing the objectives of the "Russian" and "English" factions. The "Russian" faction wanted to elect Kapodistrias president of Greece. The "English" faction wanted the appointment of Sir Richard Church and Alexander Cochrane, both English philhellenes, as respective commanders of the Greek army and navy. Chiefly because they wanted England to acquiesce in the presidency of Kapodistrias, the "Russians" supported the appointment of Church and Cochrane. Fearing that Kapodistrias would turn Greece into a Russian dependency, the "English" and Kountouriotist factions continued to oppose his election until Church and Cochrane recommended it and thereby revealed that England would not support them in their obduracy. Others must have realized that, although Kapodistrias would not let his sympathy for Russia take precedence over his patriotism, he was best qualified to win Russian friendship for the new Greek state, a friendship which was necessary in view of Russia's official involvement in the Greek question.[111]

In this settlement of the Troezene assembly, however, nothing was done to appease France or to please the "French" party. It must have become clear to Kolettes that, unless France associated itself in the Greek question, his hold over his own faction would diminish and his faction's influence would wane before that of the others. As things stood after the assembly of Troezene, the "English" party had their two candidates in charge of the entire military establishment and the "Russian" party would soon have its candidate at the head of the state. The "French" and Koun-

[110] *Ibid.,* pp. 140-41.
[111] On the assembly of Troezene and the election of Kapodistrias, see *ibid.,* pp. 140-41, 145-48; and Finlay, *History,* vi, 420-21.

touriotes were left without this means of influence at a time when it had become clear that no Revolutionary Greek leader could prevail politically and that his only hope of further influence lay in winning the favor of outsiders. In short, by 1827 the mainsprings of central or national power had changed from the internal ones, such as popular support and military control, to external ones, such as the diplomatic support of the powers or the financial support of philhellenes.

The Revolutionary period (1821-27) produced all the ingredients for the formation of parties but no parties as such. Four family factions managed to survive the Revolution and to play, at one time or another, a significant role in national politics. Three personal factions rose to national prominence. There were issues as well, even though they were not clearly defined—one set, pressing in the early part of the period, concerning the nature of government; the other set, prominent from 1825, concerning foreign policy. The national grouping of existing factions went through three phases. For the first three years (1821-23) the grouping of factions developed along class lines. During the next (1824), the factions realigned themselves according to sectional lines. Finally, in 1825, the three personal factions, dominant among all the others, became identified according to their support of one of the three powers (England, France, or Russia) and eventually came under their protection. Of these three factions, only that of Mavrokordatos looked like a real party by the end of 1827, in view of its alliance with the Lontos-Zaïmes and Miaoules-Tompazes factions. But at that point there was no certainty that this alliance would prove any more permanent than previous alliances. As it turned out, the "English" party did not develop much beyond this in scope, although momentarily, during the next period, it looked as if it might combine with the "French." For an account of the rise of parties and their crystallization into three permanent ones, we must now move to the Kapodistrian period.

CHAPTER THREE

The Kapodistrian Period (1828-31) and Interregnum (1831-32): The Crystallization of the Three Parties

1. THE POLICY OF KAPODISTRIAS

JOHN KAPODISTRIAS (Capo d'Istria) was fifty-one years old when he arrived in Greece in January 1828, a diplomat of international reputation. Born at Corfu into a noble family of modest means, he pursued his higher education in Italy, as was the frequent practice of members of his class during Venetian rule. While studying medicine at the University of Padua (1794-98), he witnessed Napoleon's Italian campaign. His return to the Ionian Islands coincided with the Russian occupation (1799-1807), which resulted in the establishment of the Heptanesian republic. This period of Ionian independence, under the tutelage of Russia, marked his entry into political affairs, first as provisional governor of Cephalonia, then as secretary of state of the republic. When the French returned in 1807, he preferred to migrate to Russia rather than live under Napoleonic rule. While in Russia he attracted the favorable notice of Tsar Alexander I, who was at the height of his liberal phase. As Russian minister, Kapodistrias rose rapidly and represented the tsar at the congresses of Vienna, Paris, and Aix-la-Chapelle. With the outbreak of the Revolution (1821) he had taken leave of absence from the imperial service and retired to Switzerland to help his fellow Greeks in a private capacity. Only after obtaining the consent of the new tsar, Nicholas I, did he accept the presidency of Greece.[1]

[1] The major published works on Kapodistrias are: André Papadopoulos-Vretos, *Mémoires biographiques-historiques sur le Président de la Grèce, le Comte Jean Capo d'Istria* (Paris, 1837), 2 vols.; P. Kalevras, *Politikos Bios tou Aoidimou Ioanne Kapodistria, Kybernetou tes Hellados* [*The Political Life of the late John Kapodistrias, Governor of Greece*] (Athens, 1873); Spyridon M. Theotokes, *Ioannes Kapodistrias en Kephallenia kai hai staseis autes en etesi 1800, 1801, kai 1802* [*John Kapodistrias in Cephalonia and its Revolts in the Years 1800, 1801, and 1802*] (Corfu, 1889); Tryphon E. Evangelides, *Historia tou Ioannou Kapodistriou, Kybernetou tes Hellados, 1828-1831* [*History of John Kapodistrias, Governor of Greece . . .*] (Athens, 1894); A. M. Idromenos, *Ioannes Kapodistrias, Kybernetes ton Hellenon* [*John Kapodistrias, Ruler of the Greeks*] (Athens, 1900); S. T. Lascaris, *Capodistrias avant la Révolution grecque, sa carrière politique jusqu'en 1822 . . .* (Lausanne, 1918); Lysimaque Oeconomos, *Essai sur la vie du Comte Capodistrias* (Paris, 1926); E. K. Mavrakes, *Ho Kapodistrias kai he Epoche tou* [*Kapodistrias and his Epoch*] (Athens, 1926); D. Gatopoulos, *Ioannes Kapodistrias, ho protos Kybernetes tes Hellados* [*John Kapodistrias, the first Governor of Greece*] (Athens, 1932); Alexander I. Despotopoulos, *Ho Kybernetes Kapodistrias kai he Apeleutherosis tes Hellados* [*Governor Kapodistrias and the Liberation of Greece*] (Athens, 1954), and *He Hellas epi Kapodistria* [*Greece*

Political Creed and Governmental System

For the purposes of this account, three features of Kapodistrias' political creed bear special mention: (1) Russophilism, (2) moderate liberalism, and (3) Westernism. His Russophilism requires no elaboration, only the qualification that it remained secondary to his Greek patriotism, and the observation that it prejudiced Western diplomacy and Greek Russophobes against him. His brand of liberalism combined hostility to revolution with opposition to the *ancien régime* and led him to advocate the gradual enfranchisement of the middle classes under the auspices of a paternalistic state. His Westernism was a product of his Western European education and his association with Russian liberalism. A child of the Enlightenment (its humanitarianism though not its radicalism), he had a keen sense of responsibility for the welfare of the community and the protection of the common man. The political ideal arising from his creed was a unitary, bureaucratic state on the Western model, administering an enlightened law code with the concurrence of the propertied classes in the interests of all the people. This creed accounts for much of the president's behavior in Greece, but it underwent some modification during his Greek experience. Indeed, he prided himself on formulating a policy designed to meet specific Greek needs rather than to accord with abstract principles of no relevance to the Greek situation.[2]

What did he believe the Greek situation called for? In order to answer this question adequately one must remember what was implied by his election to the presidency. It revealed a recognized need for someone of sufficient weight and skill to obtain for Greece the best international settlement. It betrayed a failure of leadership in Greece; that is, both some shortcoming in each of the pretenders to power (such as Ypsilantes, Kountouriotes, Mavrokordatos, Kolokotrones, and Kolettes) and an extremely unhealthy balance of power among the various factions which led to interminable civil strife and permitted no one the power necessary to rule and establish order.[3] It demonstrated the necessity of qualifications

---

under Kapodistrias] (Athens, 1957); and William P. Kaldis, *John Capodistrias and the Modern Greek State* (Madison, 1963). For briefer accounts of Kapodistrias' pre-presidential career, see George Finlay, *A History of Greece from its Conquest by the Romans to the Present Time, B.C. 146 to A.D. 1864*, ed. H. F. Tozer (Oxford, 1877), vii, 30-32; Nicholas Kaltchas, *Introduction to the Constitutional History of Modern Greece* (New York, 1940), pp. 58-64; Anastasios N. Goudas, *Bioi paralleloi ton epi tes anagenneseos tes Hellados diaprepsanton andron* [*Parallel Lives of Distinguished Men during the Regeneration of Greece*] (Athens, 1869-76), vii, 1-48.

[2] Kaltchas, *Constitutional History*, pp. 58-65.

[3] George Finlay ("Copy of a Memorial I presented to H. M. the King of Greece," p. 34. Miscellaneous [MSS], Finlay Papers, The British School of Archeology, Athens) wrote: "No possibility existed of producing any combination, from the materials in the country, powerful enough to enforce order and obedience to the general system of government." See also Douglas Dakin, *British and American Philhellenes during the War of Greek Independence 1821-1833* (Thessaloniki, 1955), p. 143; and Kaltchas, *Constitutional History*, p. 83.

which a king was later expected to bring with him—influence among the powers (in the case of Kapodistrias by virtue of his great diplomatic experience rather than through the dynastic ties of a king), and freedom from the domestic quarrels of the parties and the taint of partisanship which would make him unacceptable to the nation as a whole. In short, the situation seemed to demand an influential outsider to rule, one with *power* enough to stamp out internal dissensions and conduct a strong foreign policy, one with *impartiality* enough to escape identity with any party.[4] An account of how Kapodistrias tried to meet these requirements is important because it prefigures the same basic problem which faced the later royal regime, as well as many similar measures undertaken by it.

Kapodistrias' policy as president was determined most of all by his attitude toward the Revolutionary ruling classes whom he found already established. His brand of impartiality toward them and the parties into which they organized was one of equally apportioned hostility. Primates, military chieftains, and Phanariots—he considered them all oppressors of the people, perpetrators of internecine strife, instigators of foreign interference, and potential traitors to any ruler who placed national above factional or sectional interests.[5] He gave them all office in a bid for universal support and as proof of impartiality, but he had no intention of associating them in the actual exercise of political power. On the contrary, he sought every means of destroying their power and replacing what he considered a system of selfish oligarchical rule by a provisional dictatorship legally sanctioned by a popular mandate and morally justified in terms of an emergency and transitional situation.[6] If perhaps too doc-

---

[4] Dakin, *Philhellenes*, p. 143; Finlay, *History*, vii, 29-30; and Kaltchas, *Constitutional History*, p. 37.

[5] Concerning Kapodistrias' low opinion of the existing ruling groups, see Finlay, *History*, vii, 33; Kaltchas, *Constitutional History*, pp. 66-67; *The Portfolio: or a Collection of State Papers and other Documents and Correspondence, Historical, Diplomatic, and Commercial* . . . First ser., iii, 248, which ethnocentrically suggests that Kapodistrias disliked the primates because "these were attached to England"; and Friedrich Thiersch, *De l'état actuel de la Grèce* (Leipzig, 1833), i, 13, who speaks of Kapodistrias' general contempt for anyone who rose above the rank of laborer or worker. See also Gennaios Kolokotrones, *Apomnemoneumata [Memoirs]*, ed. Emmanuel G. Protopsaltes (Athens, 1955), p. 206: "The Governor feared the Phanariots because of their education . . . but he wanted to have a few of them as friends and so took as secretary of the senate Panagiotes Soutsos. . . ."

[6] *Hēlios*, 4 July 1833 o.s.; Lyons to Palmerston, Nauplion, 8 Feb. 1834, no. 6, Archives of the British Foreign Office, Public Record Office, London, ser. 32, vol. 43 [hereafter to be cited as FO 32.43 and so on]: "Kapodistrias tried to take from primates and captains the great authority which fell to them during the Revolution, by implication through his provincial administrative system in part"; George Ludwig von Maurer, *Das griechische Volk in öffentlicher, kirchlicher und privatrechtlicher Beziehung vor und nach dem Freiheitskampfe bis zum 31, Juli 1834* (Heidelberg, 1835), i, 446: "To break the power of the kodza-bashis and the otzaks, the court supported agriculture and commerce especially, as well as those living off it"; and Thiersch, *État actuel*, i, 14-16.

trinaire in his attitude toward the ruling classes, he was probably too naive in his faith in "the brave and good people" for whose needs (as judged by himself) he displayed such solicitude. Indeed, his concern for them partially accounts for his antipathy toward those whom he believed their oppressors. As he assured the king of France in a letter, the people were anxious to be rid of "the tyranny of the primates and the military chieftains." Once Greece had been recognized internationally, with independence and boundaries secure, Kapodistrias hoped through the distribution of public lands to the mass of landless peasants to create a constitutional state of small proprietors.[7] In brief, Kapodistrias made a distinction between the immediate, transitional regime (based on the urgency of overcoming great evils and meeting difficult problems) and the ultimate polity of constitutionalism and paternalism (in accord with his general political creed).[8]

In order to set up the provisional regime and pave the way for the ultimate state of affairs, he first secured the suspension of the Constitution of Troezene by which the third national assembly had intended him to govern. Yet he meticulously respected the principle of constitutionalism, as witnessed by the means he devised to establish a temporary dictatorship. The national assembly voted to suspend the constitution, and by an enabling act of 30 January 1828 it transferred its power to the president and a consultative body of twenty-seven members, then called the *Panhellenion* and later reconstituted as a more pliable *Senate*. As one authority has rightly observed, "But it was a dictatorship of delegated powers, limited in duration and accountable to a national assembly on the expiration of its mandate."[9] Kapodistrias also attacked the parties, the instruments of the ruling groups, by withholding recognition from them, denying them the exercise of any state patronage, and actively attempting to wean the people from their loyalty to the parties.[10] Third, he sought to establish an efficient, impartial, and just bureaucracy of Western-trained outsiders like himself to replace the partisan oligarchs as administrators. By means of a paternalistic regime he hoped to identify the state, rather than the parties, with the role of protecting and advancing individual and family interests.

[7] Thiersch, *État actuel*, II, 58: "To secure control of Greece, the president wished to base himself on the most passive and tranquil class of people and he succeeded in fact in procuring for the laborers the possibility of delivering themselves in peace to useful occupations. He did not wish any competitors for his authority and instead of containing independent men, he tried to ruin or destroy them." See also Finlay, *History*, VII, 33; Kaltchas, *Constitutional History*, pp. 65-66; and Maurer, *Griechische Volk*, I, 445-46.

[8] Kaltchas, *Constitutional History*, p. 75.

[9] *Ibid.*, p. 73.

[10] According to *Hēlios* (4 July 1833 o.s.), he first used the second rung of party leaders against the first rung, and thereby prevailed at the Argos assembly through this "middle class."

Creation of the Kapodistrian Party

It soon became clear that "the brave and good people" were too dis-united to serve as an adequate weapon against the local power of the oligarchy which controlled the factions. Either Kapodistrias had to woo the support of all the factions and maintain a delicate balance between them, or he had to unite with some of the factions in an attempt to overpower the others. Either course posed serious difficulties. Given the exaggerated demands of each faction and the general unwillingness of factions to compromise with each other, it was impossible to keep them all satisfied. To maintain a policy of neutrality toward all would probably tend to alienate them all into a united front against the government. Moreover, maintaining a delicate balance meant allowing the parties to continue their rivalry and thereby to perpetuate the paralysis of the administration. On the other hand, to associate the government with some factions would only intensify party strife and win for the government undying enemies. In spite of the basic dilemma, Kapodistrias took the latter course. Perhaps the open opposition of some factions forced him into the arms of others. Perhaps he needed faithful lieutenants to ad-minister the state and organize the masses; men who, in the state political affairs at the time, were bound to constitute simply one more faction. Perhaps he hoped that the ascendancy of one party over the others would produce the needed political stability. If a government party could be-come sufficiently broad in its foundations and mobilize the support of the peasant masses, it might become associated with the nation. The transi-tional period seemed to warrant the creation of a strong party to end all parties and become the voice of the nation.[11]

Internal Structure of the Kapodistrian Party

Playing the role of patron—the only role open to an outsider—and using the bureaucratic machinery of the state as an institutional frame-work for a political grouping, Kapodistrias put together a nationwide party out of already existing regional factions and local clienteles. The nucleus of the so-called Kapodistrian, or Napist, or Governmentalist party was the "Russian" faction which had successfully managed to bring Kapodistrias to Greece. The *Phoenix society*, apparently in existence before his arrival, continued to exist as the unofficial organization acting in behalf of the government.[12] But with almost four full years of almost

[11] *Loc.cit.*

[12] No one has really studied the Phoenix society, and references to it are only passing ones. Thiersch (*État actuel*, I, 25) refers to *Phoenix* as the secret society (consisting of the Metaxas', Theodore Kolokotrones, Niketas, Rangos, Perroukas, Kanares) which called him to Greece, the nucleus of the Kapodistrian movement and "la pouvoir compacte et formidable." He adds (I, 25-26) that the original nucleus, during the presidency of Kapodistrias, was surrounded by a corps of subalterns and spared neither promises, money, nor distinctions to attract as large a following as

absolute power, Kapodistrias utilized the reorganization of fiscal, administrative, and judicial organs to expand his following. Heterochthon Greeks, hitherto politically and socially insignificant, owed their power and position to him alone and therefore gave their loyalty to him by interest. He converted demogerons, local heads formerly chosen by the municipalities, into government-appointed agents of the executive authority, and hence undermined the traditional system of local autonomy. He increased the influence of the loyal chieftains by allowing them to farm large districts in the collection of taxes. Likewise he appointed judges in accordance with their professed loyalty to the regime. In short, by virtue of the state power which he wielded, Kapodistrias planted his partisans throughout the state, on the local as well as on the provincial level.[13]

The regional strongholds, based on the loyalty of regional factions, were three: central Peloponnesos, the Phocis region of East Rumely, and Spezza. The Peloponnesian branch of the party he found ready-made—the Kolokotrones faction. Initially Kapodistrias had feared its independent power and had mistrusted its palikar origins, but then he wooed it successfully with great advantage to his cause. Though the single source of support in Peloponnesos, this faction was so extensive in its influence, so popular among the people, and so loyal to the president, that it was regarded as the keystone of the entire party and Napist or pro-Russian sentiment became identified with Peloponnesos.[14]

Phocis, political stronghold of John Gouras Mamoures, developed into

possible. Its members, to be accepted, had to give proof of their attachment to Kapodistrias and swear an oath to maintain him in authority. A third reference (I, 65) says that the society of Phoenix persisted and remained active, with "her legion disseminated by cohorts on the continent and isles," even after the president's death. See also T. Pipineles, *Politike Historia tes Neoteras Hellados* [*Political History of the Greek Revolution*] (Athens, 1928), p. 125, who says that Phoenix changed into the association of "True Orthodox."

[13] On the military, civil, financial, and judicial administration of Kapodistrias, see Finlay, *History*, vii, 34-48; Karl Mendelssohn Bartholdy, *Geschichte Griechenlands von der Eroberung Konstantinopels durch die Türken im Jahre 1453 bis auf unsere Tage* (Leipzig, 1870-74), ii, 22-46, 51-60, 74-79; and Thiersch, *État actuel*, i, 16.

[14] On the initial mistrust of Kapodistrias, see the memoirs of Theodore Kolokotrones, *Diegesis sympanton tes Hellenikes phyles apo ta 1770 heos ta 1836* [*Narration of Events of the Greek Race from 1770 to 1836*] (Athens, 1846), or in its English translation under the title *Kolokotrones, Klepht and Warrior*, trans. Elizabeth M. Edmonds (London, 1892), pp. 275-76. Gennaios Kolokotrones ([*Memoirs*], pp. 197-200, 202) asserts that Kapodistrias overcame his antipathy toward the Kolokotronists, who had fifty deputies in the Argos assembly, and espoused them, largely because virtually all the primates were against him and because he wanted a political nucleus of power. He also mentions lingering suspicions of Kapodistrias toward Kolokotrones after this (p. 204). According to John Makrygiannes (*Apomnemoneumata* [*Memoirs*], ed. John Vlachogiannes, 2nd edn. [Athens, 1947], ii, 11), Metaxas acted as mediator for this alliance between Kolokotrones and Kapodistrias. See also Takes Kandeloros, *He Dike tou Kolokotrone kai he epanastasis tes Peloponnesou* [*The Trial of Kolokotrones and the Revolution of the Peloponnesos*], (Athens, 1906), p. 37.

the center of the Napist ("Russian") party in mainland Greece as a result of a close alliance between Kapodistrias and Mamoures. This alliance benefited both men. Through it Kapodistrias penetrated into the alien stronghold of Kolettes. Mamoures' attachment to the Napist party became so close that it persisted into the post-Kapodistrian period when he staunchly defended the town of Salona against the Constitutionalists (1831-32). Mamoures, the adopted son and heir of John Gouras, derived two main advantages from his alliance with Kapodistrias. Practically the sole military figure of real importance in the Rumeliot branch of the Kapodistrian party, he enjoyed an independence from other leading Rumeliot chieftains with whom he would have had to share political influence in either of the other two parties. Furthermore, he managed to retain the loyalty of his father's clientele by using his friendship with Kapodistrias to secure them positions in the state military establishment.[15]

Elsewhere in Rumely, where Kolettes and Mavrokordatos had long established political strongholds, continued local rivalries and feuds provided Kapodistrias with a chance to secure a following. His typical recruit was the traditional rival of a Kolettist or a Mavrokordatist. For instance, John Rangos, a West Rumeliot rival of the Kolettist Karaïskakes, became an able but timid devotee of Kapodistrias. But in Rumely, Kapodistrias' late entry into the political game proved a permanent handicap to his cause. Some of his recruits were men of questionable patriotism, such as George Varnakiotes and Mitsos Kontogiannes, captains of Aetolia and Valtos respectively. Each had remained on the Turkish side through most of the Revolution, Varnakiotes (it seems) because his rival Tsongas had won over him for the patronage of Mavrokordatos, Kontogiannes apparently in order to destroy his rivals, the Zotos' and Chatziskos', who had joined the Revolution. Kapodistrias also recruited primates, such as Panagiotes Loidorikes of Doris, an honest and capable administrator, and Lampros Nakos of Livadia, whose pre-Revolutionary influence had vastly diminished with the Revolutionary resurgence of the military element. Unlike Mamoures, all these other men had little to offer Kapodistrias in return for his patronage. Indeed, their sunken fortunes and damaged prestige probably hurt his cause. Their weakness became painfully apparent when the protecting hand of Kapodistrias no longer existed. Nakos and Varnakiotes were reduced to permanent political impotence, and the rest had to find new local alliances for political survival.[16]

The attachment of Spezza to Kapodistrias stemmed partly from the

[15] Piscatory, Athens, 6 Sept. 1841 (7th report), in "Textes et Documents, La Grèce d'Othon," ed. Jean Poulos, in *L'Hellénisme Contemporain*, 2nd ser., IX (1955), 432-33. See also *La Grèce du Roi Othon. Correspondance de M. Thouvenel avec sa famille et ses amis 1845-50*, ed Edouard A. Thouvenel (Paris, 1890), p. 429.

[16] Piscatory, Athens, 6 Sept. 1841 (7th report), *L'Hellénisme Contemporain*, IX, 434 (Rangos and Varnakiotes), 431 (Kontogiannes), 433 (Loidorikes), and 430 (Nakos). On the struggle between Rangos and Karaïskakes in Agrapha, see Finlay, *History*, VI, 273.

strong sentimental and commercial attachment of the inhabitants to Russia, which in pre-Revolutionary days had allowed Spezziot ships to enjoy all the advantages of sailing under its flag; and even more perhaps from the intense rivalry of Spezziots with the largely Anglophile Hydriots. John Mexes, the patriarchal leader of the island, and the influential Kolandroutsos family became the chief adherents of the "Russian" party on the island.[17]

The heterochthon branch of the party was unusually large, in part because the heterochthons more often possessed the Western skills desired by Kapodistrias for statecraft, in part because he preferred not to rule through the indigenous ruling groups. But it was a heterogeneous group which, for the sake of convenience, might be divided into four categories, according to the original or adopted domicile of individuals before coming to liberated Greece: (1) Ionian Islanders, (2) mainlanders, especially from Epirus, (3) Greeks of the Eastern Mediterranean (Aegean Islands and Asia Minor), and (4) those who had spent considerable time in Russia.

A large number of Ionian Islanders had settled in liberated Greece before the arrival of Kapodistrias. Mostly Cephalonians, they had put troops into the field at their own expense and had personally commanded them. Most prominent were the Metaxas brothers (Andrew and Constantine), the Panas cousins (Daniel and Elias), Demetrios Valsamakes, and Theodore Vallianos. Though less prominent than Andrew, Constantine Metaxas took part in the Revolution and remained in Greece until 1835, when he returned permanently to Cephalonia as a result of the anti-Napist attitude of the government of Greece. Daniel Panas had studied law at the University of Padua and in Paris before he became military commander of his own troops. Like Andrew Metaxas, he attached himself to Kolokotrones, but in a military rather than political capacity. Like Andrew Metaxas, Elias Panas commanded his own group of some 300 Cephalonians and Zantiots at the battle of Lala (Elis province) in June 1821. Demetrios Valsamakes, who first fought in the Rumanian principalities, served as director of artillery and public building in Nauplion during the middle years of the Revolution. Theodore Vallianos financed a body of Cephalonian recruits and led them into the field in the spring of 1822, but because of his special connection with Russia will be dealt with in the fourth category below. Already established in Greece by 1828, all six of these Cephalonians rallied to the government of Kapodistrias.[18]

The arrival of Kapodistrias precipitated a new influx of Ionian Islanders, this time mostly Corfiots like himself. Most prominent were his two brothers, Viaro and Augustine, on whom he relied most heavily, probably

[17] Piscatory, Athens, 6 Sept. 1841 (7th report), *L'Hellénisme Contemporain*, IX, 443.

[18] "Panas" and "Valsamakes," in *Megale Hellenike Enkyklopaideia* [*Grand Hellenic Encyclopedia*], 24 vols. (Athens, 1926-34).

because of their personal attachment to him. He placed each in control of critical areas where the "English" party held sway. His elder brother Viaro he entrusted with absolute control over the Western Sporades (Hydra, Spezza, Poros, and Aegina), and his younger brother Augustine he appointed plenipotentiary to West Rumely, where the Mavrokordatos interest prevailed and Richard Church commanded. Unfortunately, neither brother possessed much talent for governing and both provoked much hatred through their overbearing manner. Hardly less influential were two other Corfiots who followed Kapodistrias to Greece: Andrew Mustoxides, a talented literary figure, and John Gennatas, a lawyer whose subsequent organization of the secret police made him the most hated man of the Kapodistrian administration. However, these four close associates of Kapodistrias played no direct part in Greek politics during the royal period because they left Greece after the death of John Kapodistrias. In the Ionian Islands they became determined opponents of the British protectorate, in large part because they believed Britain responsible for the failure of the Kapodistrian cause in Greece. On the other hand, opposition to the British protectorate and fanatical Russophilism forced Andrew Papadopoulos-Vretos to migrate to Greece shortly before his compatriots left it. A doctor by profession, former director of the library of the Ionios Akademia (Ionian Academy), condemned by an Ionian court for his opposition to the British, Papadopoulos-Vretos arrived in Greece from Constantinople in April 1831 and became the editor of *Miroir Grec* [*The Greek Mirror*], the Napist journal, in 1832.[19]

The three most important Napist heterochthons from mainland Greece were Epirots: Kitsos Tzavelas, Michael Spyromelios, and Constantine Rados. Scion of a distinguished Souliot family, Tzavelas grew up in exile in Corfu. In 1822, after his return to Greece, he became the head of his family. Since his family traditionally held first place in his particular *phara*, an Albanian equivalent of a small clan, his headship of the family placed him in control of an entire phara, which he settled in Mesolongi. He first obtained the patronage of Karaïskakes, then switched his allegiance to Mavrokordatos when Karaïskakes became implicated in secret negotiations with the Turks (1824). But membership in the Mavrokordatos faction brought him no support in his traditional rivalry with the equally distinguished Botsares family because the Botsares' also belonged to the Mavrokordatos faction and took precedence through prior membership. In Kapodistrias he found a strong patron who wished to under-

---

[19] According to Thiersch (*État actuel*, I, 26-27), he called many Ionians to Greece "because he didn't have confidence in native Greeks." On Kapodistrias' brothers and other Ionian confidants, see Finlay, *History*, VII, 41-44, 48, 127; and General Pellion, *La Grèce et les Capodistrias pendant l'occupation française de 1828 à 1834* (Paris, 1855). On Papadopoulos-Vretos, see Andrew Papadopoulos-Vretos, *Historike Ekthesis tes ephemeridos Ho Hellenikos Kathreptes; Le Compte-Rendu du Miroir Grec* [in Greek and French] (Athens, 1839), and *Politika Symmikta; Mélanges de Politique* [in Greek and French] (Athens, 1840).

mine the political power of Mavrokordatos in West Rumely. Tzavelas' Napism, however, went beyond personal loyalty to Kapodistrias. He cultivated close relations with Andrew Metaxas, and in 1829 he gave his sister Photine in marriage to John Kolokotrones.[20] Spyromelios of Chimara came from a part of Greece (Epirus) which for centuries had provided Italy with mercenary soldiers. Thanks to his grandfather, who served the kingdom of Naples in this capacity, he studied military science in Naples and returned to Epirus in 1819 for service with Ali Pasha. At the out-break of the Revolution, he and his brothers placed themselves at the head of 250 Chimariots. One of those besieged by the Turks at Meso-longi, he escaped and subsequently wrote a valuable account of the historic siege. Under Kapodistrias he received the important task of organizing the irregular troops into chiliarchies.[21] Rados, who studied in Pisa and joined the Italian carbonari before the outbreak of the Revolu-tion, served as extraordinary commissioner (provincial governor) to important provinces (Argolis, then West Rumely) under Kapodistrias. Through these three men the Napists penetrated to some extent into West Rumely.[22]

Most notable among the East Mediterranean heterochthons were: Con-stantine Kanares of Psara; Aristides Moraïtines of Smyrna; George Ralles, Andrew Mamoukas, and George Glarakes, all three of Chios; and Pana-giotes Rodios of Rhodes. In Kanares, distinguished naval hero of the Revolution, Kapodistrias sought a political counterpart to Kolokotrones and Mamoures in the Islands. He showered many gifts on Kanares and, in so doing, created a loyal political lieutenant. But the protecting powers did not include Psara in the new Greek state. As a result, Kanares, himself a refugee of modest means, commanded only a limited following among his fellow refugees who settled in Greece and, in a political sense, had "no worth but his name."[23]

Unlike Kanares, the remaining five enjoyed the favor of Kapodistrias because of their qualifications as officials. Indeed, Moraïtines and Ralles, both young men who had studied law in Paris, came to Greece at the

[20] "Kitsos Tzavelas" in Niketas Patseles, *Hoi politikoi andres tes Epeirou* [*The Po-litical Men of Epirus*] (Janina, 1959); *Thouvenel Correspondance*, pp. 456-57; and Thiersch, *État actuel*, I, 127-28. Strangely, Piscatory makes no mention of him in his catalogue. For a full-length study of the Tzavelas', see Demetrios Botsares, *To Souli kai hoi Tzavelaioi* [*Souli and the Tzavelas'*] (Athens, 1941).

[21] Editor's ["Biographical Introduction"] in Spyromelios, *Apomnemoneumata tes Deuteras Poliorkias tou Mesolongiou . . .* [*Memoirs of the Second Siege of Meso-longi 1825-1826*], ed. John Vlachogiannes (Athens, 1926), pp. iii-xxv; and "Spyro-melios" in Patseles [*Political Men*] and in [*Grand Encyclopedia*].

[22] "Constantine Rados," [*Grand Encyclopedia*].

[23] Dionysios P. Kalogeropoulos, *Ho Kanares* (Athens, 1947); S. Malaphoures [*Kanares*] (Athens, 1959); and D. Photiades [*Kanares*] (Athens, 1960); Piscatory, Athens, 6 Sept. 1841 (7th report), *L'Hellénisme Contemporain*, IX, 443; *Thouvenel Correspondance*, pp. 400-401; and [*Grand Encyclopedia*].

special invitation of Kapodistrias, who sorely needed judges familiar with Western law. The rest, established in Greece, served Kapodistrias in posts akin to those which they had already filled. Mamoukas, who had served as secretary on various Hydriot and Spezziot ships, became one of the president's most trusted officials. A poor boy who had studied medicine in Göttingen through the support of his fellow Chiots, Glarakes served as secretary of state to two consecutive executive commissions (April 1826–February 1828). In this post he became actual head of the national administration, invested it with some system, and distinguished himself for efficiency and integrity. In the latter part of Kapodistrian rule he served as minister of the interior. Rodios, who first studied medicine in Padua and then enjoyed the patronage of Koraes in Paris, went to Greece in 1822 and served as aide-de-camp to Mavrokordatos, with whom he organized the regular army destroyed at the battle of Peta. In 1824 he commanded a new regular army under Fabvier. As minister of the army (1828-31) under Kapodistrias, he established the army officers' school of Evelpides, which still exists, and, from personal animosity against the French, encouraged Kapodistrias in his resentment of the French occupation.[24]

Two types of Greeks left Russia to participate in the Greek Revolution: private members of Greek commercial colonies in Russia and students or clergymen enjoying official Russian patronage. To the first group belonged Panagiotes Anagnostopoulos and Nicholas Speliades, both natives of the Peloponnesos; to the latter, Demetrios Kallerges of Crete, Theodore Vallianos of Cephalonia, and Constantine Paparregopoulos of Constantinople. Before the Revolution, both Anagnostopoulos and Speliades served as clerks in large Greek commercial establishments of Odessa. Their ostensibly humble social origins, which may account for their families' emigration from the Peloponnesos, may have induced their apparent antipathy toward the Peloponnesian primate class and their consequent sympathy with the policies of Kapodistrias. Anagnostopoulos, one of the leaders of the Philike Hetairia, accompanied Ypsilantes to Greece as political advisor because of his Peloponnesian background. Kapodistrias used him as a provincial governor in Elis. Originally from Tripolis, Speliades had received enough education to find employment as a clerk, and learned French and Italian in Odessa. During the Revolution he had served as secretary to several officials or bodies, among them the Peloponnesian senate, the ministry of religion, the Mavromichales execu-

---

[24] "Moraïtines," "Mamoukas," "Rodios" [Grand Encyclopedia]; A. Kalvokoreses [Andreas Zane Mamoukas] (Athens, 1958). On Ralles, see Piscatory, Athens, 6 Sept. 1841 (7th report), L'Hellénisme Contemporain, IX, 444-45, and Papadopoulos-Vretos, Compte-Rendu, p. 12. On Glarakes, see Piscatory (7th report), 444; and Thouvenel Correspondance, pp. 418-19. On Rodios, see also Gennaios Kolokotrones [Memoirs], p. 211.

tive committee (1823), the assembly of Troezene (1827). Under Kapodistrias he succeeded Trikoupes as secretary of state.[25]

Demetrios Kallerges, scion of one of Crete's most distinguished families, was the orphaned nephew of Count Karl Nesselrode, Russian foreign minister. He studied in a St. Petersburg school for noble children after the death of his father. From there he went to Vienna, where he began to study medicine. At the outbreak of the war he returned to Greece and led a body of Cretans. He joined Fabvier's regular army, became his aide-de-camp, and then served Kapodistrias in this capacity. After Kapodistrias' assassination he became cavalry commander in Argos. Though a heterochthon, he established considerable influence, not simply because of his money, his position as cavalry commander, and his influence over the many Cretan refugees in independent Greece, but also through his marriage to Sophia Rentes, beautiful daughter of a Corinthian primate, whose distinguished family had at one time occupied the dominant provincial position later usurped by the Notaras'.[26]

After studying at the military academy in St. Petersburg and becoming known to Tsar Alexander I, Vallianos had become a captain in the Russian engineer corps until 1821. In 1822 he went to Greece with the permission of the Russian government and with enough money to fit out his own body of Cephalonians. He organized a body of 300 artillerymen; Kapodistrias named him highest staff officer of the Greek engineer corps.[27]

Constantine Paparregopoulos was born in Constantinople where his father, a Peloponnesian, had settled as a banker and vekiles. When the Turks massacred the adult male Paparregopoulos' in the first days of the Greek Revolution, Constantine escaped to Odessa with his mother. There he attended the Lyceum of Richelieu, a distinguished school under the patronage of the tsar. He did not go to Greece until 1830. It was through the generosity of official Russia that he was able to buy up vast estates in Euboea and Attica.[28]

Owing to his decisiveness, energy, and determination, Kapodistrias built up a large following, gave it cohesion, and made as many devoted friends as he made undying enemies. He welded existing factions into a party with an overlay of educated heterochthons. As Piscatory remarked some time later, "It was he who, very ably, created this party by his enticing manners and his ability to handle men."[29] This was significant not merely because the party gained cohesion in four years, but also

---

[25] "Anagnostopoulos" and "Speliades" [Grand Encyclopedia]; on the former, see also Piscatory, Athens, 6 Sept. 1841 (7th report), L'Hellénisme Contemporain, ix, 429.

[26] "Kallerges" [Grand Encyclopedia]; Alexander R. Rangabe, Apomnemoneumata [Memoirs] (Athens, 1894), i, 268; and Thouvenel Correspondance, pp. 424-25.

[27] "Vallianos" [Grand Encyclopedia].

[28] "Paparregopoulos" [Grand Encyclopedia]; Piscatory, Athens, 6 Sept. 1841 (7th report), L'Hellénisme Contemporain, ix, 445.

[29] Piscatory, Athens, 30 July 1841 (4th report), L'Hellénisme Contemporain, ix, 410.

because the party became national to an unprecedented extent, covering the entire state geographically and penetrating into the remotest villages. The success of this penetration, especially in the Peloponnesos, was to become evident during the first years of Otho's reign when the discredited Kapodistrians were to display so much tenacity. As a matter of fact, as late as 1841 Piscatory was to point to the Kapodistrian party as the only one worthy of the name, with an organization and ethos which no doubt owed much to this four-year period of growth and consolidation. Moreover, this party had won itself an extensive popular following among the peasantry because of their devotion to Kapodistrias. Even his most deadly opponents admitted the mass popularity of the man, whose restoration of order in the countryside—by curbing the excesses of primates and captains—and whose numerous tours through the provinces endeared him to the people. In 1833, Thiersch, a Bavarian critic of Kapodistrias, reluctantly admitted, "The people cried and still cry for him as their father and benefactor." But the same characteristic which secured the party a popular following constituted its chief weakness—it consisted primarily of humble people, "vagabonds and men without a future," as Thiersch contemptuously put it, men who amounted to little politically without strong leaders.[30]

2. THE OPPOSITION TO KAPODISTRIAS: MANE, HYDRA, AND KARATASOS REVOLTS

Even though the sources often treat the Constitutionalists as a single party, embracing all the anti-Kapodistrian factions, no such party ever existed. During the presidency of Kapodistrias (January 1828–October 1831) and the succeeding interregnum (October 1831–January 1832), four distinct Constitutional groups were distinguishable: the "English," the Kountouriotes, the Mavromichales, and the "French" factions. At no time were they all united either under an acknowledged leader, in a definite organization, or in behalf of a common policy. Their common bond was opposition to the Kapodistrias regime but even this could not unite them. During the lifetime of Kapodistrias, the active opposition consisted of an alliance between the first three groups and a small segment of the fourth, an alliance dominated by the first. After his death, the fourth group emerged as the leader of a new alliance consisting of the last three groups, an alliance to which the first group would not adhere.[31]

[30] Thiersch, *État actuel*, I, 58; he also admits that Kapodistrias benefited the poor (I, 56-57) and comments on the social composition of the party (I, 65).

[31] On the Constitutionalists as a single party, see p. 6-7 of Introduction above. According to *Hēlios* (4 July 1833o.s.), three factions (Zaïmes', Mavrokordatos', and Delegiannes') formed a political opposition in the Panhellenion and at the Argos Assembly. A year later, the Mavromichalist faction joined, three months later the Kountouriotist, and last of all the Kolettist.

During the same period, there were four armed revolts against Kapo-distrian rule, each organized on a sectional basis: (1) the revolt of Mane, led by the Mavromichales family, deadly opponents of Kapodistrias; (2) the Hydra revolt, organized by the "English" party in conjunction with the Kountouriotes faction; (3) the revolt of minor Rumeliot chieftains under the command of Tzames Karatasos; and (4) the Rumeliot invasion of the Peloponnesos, under the command of John Kolettes, in order to depose Augustine Kapodistrias, brother and successor of the assassinated president. The last will be dealt with in a later analysis of the interregnum period. This section will deal with the first three because they coincided in time, acted upon each other, and together brought the regime of John Kapodistrias to a dismal end.

Local Grievances

The earliest outbreak occurred during the Easter celebration of 1830 in Tsimova, one of the main towns of Mane. This revolt continued inter-mittently until it reached its culmination in the far-off capital of Greece (Nauplion) with the assassination of Kapodistrias on 9 October 1831. The flight of Mavrokordatos, Trikoupes, and Miaoules in August 1830 marked the beginning of the Hydra revolt, which flickered out only after Augustine Kapodistrias gave up his claim to the presidency of Greece in the spring of 1832. The third and least important started in Talanti (Rumely) in May 1831 as an insurrection of irregular army officers of "French" complexion and after swift government suppression continued as a succession of raids from across the Turkish border.

In each case, fundamental local grievances, peculiar to each section, sparked the revolt. Under the Turks, Mane had enjoyed virtual inde-pendence, maintained its militaristic social system, and preserved its customary law in which the practice of vendetta figured so prominently. All of this was incompatible with the centralizing policy of Kapodistrias, which sought to incorporate Mane into the regular administration and erase customary practices which seemed barbarous. Since the Mavro-michales', headed by Petrobey (the so-called "King of Mane"), were the leading family of Mane, and perhaps because of growing personal estrangement between himself and Petrobey, Kapodistrias seems mis-takenly to have believed that the shortest road to success, in pursuit of this policy, was destruction of the Mavromichales' influence. To do so, he removed members of the Mavromichales family from the offices which they had occupied on his arrival. He proceeded to exploit the traditional rivalries for local influence between the Mavromichales' and other leading Maniat families. He showed favoritism toward the Mourzinos' and en-couraged the ambitions of the Koutouphares', Troumpianes', and Tzane-takes'. Playing up his and the state's role as protector of the Maniat populace against arbitrary acts of its native oppressors, he seized upon numerous complaints laid before the Greek government against Petrobey for misdeeds. But this device backfired. Petrobey pronounced himself champion of Maniat autonomy and shifted attention away from his own misdeeds. The issue, as he presented it on the local level at least, was not that of individual liberation from local tyranny but rather that of collective local autonomy against centralized tyranny from the outside. In view of the corporate nature of Maniat society, it is no wonder that Petrobey induced the Maniats to make his cause their own. It was Petrobey's brother John, together with one of Petrobey's sons, who incited the people of Tsimova to revolt on Easter day of 1830. It was Petrobey's brother Constantine, at the end of that same year, who revived the revolt with the express purpose of marching on Nauplion to free Petrobey and several other members of his family who had either been imprisoned by Kapodistrias or kept under surveillance in the capital.[32]

Like Mane, Hydra had also enjoyed almost complete autonomy under the Turks and now resented the centralizing tendency of Kapodistrias. But the Hydriot problem had an added dimension—the economic decline of the island which had started prior to the Revolution but whose consequences were only now becoming acute. Trade had contracted and unemployment among the sailor population had grown to frightening proportions. All this was basically due to the shifting pattern of international trade in the Mediterranean, but it was intensified by the imposition of customs duties by the Greek government and the establishment of a quarantine system which slowed up trade. In response to this trade depression, the Hydriot primates sought economic relief from the Greek state for their sizeable financial contribution to the Revolutionary struggle. The better part of 1830 was spent in negotiations between Kapodistrias and the Hydriot leaders to determine the exact sum of such compensation. Though Kapodistrias made some concessions, the Hydriots not only persisted in their original demand of 18,000,000 phoenixes—three times the sum which Kapodistrias eventually offered—but insisted on charging the state interest on this sum, which amounted to an additional one and one-half million.[33]

Although the revolt took place after the breakdown of negotiations over money, it was formally waged as a sectionalist movement against the centralizing and absolutist tendencies of Kapodistrias. The rebels established a seven-man "constitutional committee" consisting exclusively of Hydriots, even though such prominent non-Hydriots as Mavrokordatos, Trikoupes, and Zaïmes were in their midst. In July 1831 they convoked

[32] Finlay, *History*, vii, 68-70; and Mendelssohn Bartholdy, *Geschichte Griechenlands*, ii, 264-70. According to Thiersch, (*État actuel*, i, 40), the Mane revolt was restricted by the presence of Rumeliot battalions in Messenia and Laconia. See also Edouard Driault and Michel Lhéritier, *Histoire Diplomatique de la Grèce de 1821 à nos Jours* (Paris, 1925), ii, 54.

[33] Mendelssohn Bartholdy, *Geschichte Griechenlands*, ii, 224-25.

a general assembly which issued a manifesto framed in sectionalist terms. It attacked the "tyranny" of Kapodistrias for depriving the island of its former autonomy, invited the powers to assist the Hydriots against the president, and threatened to find asylum with the Turks if left helpless against superior force.[34]

The grievances of the rebel army officers, which Tzames Karatasos exploited, were much simpler. They complained against arrears in their pay and against abuses of the government's tax farmers. It seems reasonable to assume, from the existence of the second category of complaints, that officers no longer served as tax farmers, as so many of them had during the Revolution. If this inference is correct, then they were probably rebelling against the government's policy of keeping fiscal and military duties separate, a policy which deprived them of an added source of income.[35]

Coordination into a Constitutionalist Opposition

Even though each revolt fed on grievances which grew out of local conditions affected by government policy, all were undoubtedly precipitated by two events which took place in Europe during 1830: (1) the unexpected announcement by Leopold of Saxe-Coburg on 17 May that he had reversed his former decision to accept the Greek crown, and (2) the outbreak of the July Revolution in France. So long as the arrival of a new king seemed imminent, dissatisfied Greeks could put up with the Kapodistrias regime as something only temporary. Once that expectation vanished, patience ran out. News of events in France stimulated revolutionary sentiments among dissatisfied educated Greeks, who began to preach that France had again shown the world how to deal with tyranny.[36]

Though each revolt involved local issues and grievances, the first two at least were also waged in terms of the national issue of constitutionalism. If Mavromichalists posed on the local scene as champions of Maniat privileges and autonomy, Petrobey in Nauplion called for the convocation of a national assembly and the restoration of the constitution which Kapodistrias had temporarily suspended. On 31 March 1831, Athanasios Polyzoïdes, a Thessalian intellectual fresh from Paris, began to publish the *Apollōn* in Hydra after the authorities had prevented him from setting up his press in Nauplion. The motto of the newspaper revealed its program: "national assembly, constitution," and everyone regarded *Apollōn*

[34] Finlay, *History*, VII, 63; Mendelssohn Bartholdy, *Geschichte Griechenlands*, II, 230-31; and Thiersch, *État actuel*, I, 42. The members of the Hydra committee were: G. Kountouriotes, A. Miaoules, B. Bountoures, M. Tompazes, D. Voulgares, A. Kriezes, N. Oikonomou.

[35] Mendelssohn Bartholdy, *Geschichte Griechenlands*, II, 222-23.

[36] Gennaios Kolokotrones ([*Memoirs*], p. 208) suggests a connection between the revolt and the July Revolution in France, which curtailed French financial assistance to Kapodistrias and hence his ability to pay his Rumeliot troops. See also Mendelssohn Bartholdy, *Geschichte Griechenlands*, II, 209-15, 221-22; and *The Portfolio*, III, 301.

as the mouthpiece of *the* nationwide Constitutionalist opposition rather than as a mere organ of sectionalist interests. To some extent, armed opposition had taken on a national character. Hydra served as a place of refuge for the important political figures opposed to Kapodistrias—Zaïmes, Zographos, Klonares and others, in addition to Mavrokordatos and Trikoupes. Thanks to the Hydriot fleet and the sympathy of refugee Psariot and Chiot merchants there, the rebels got control of Syros, the Aegean entrepôt so important for its customs revenues, and extended their sway over neighboring Aegean islands. Elections were taking place during the summer of 1831 in anticipation of a forthcoming national assembly called by Kapodistrias. The rebels influenced elections in some coastal regions of the Peloponnesos and harbored the deputies elected. Thus, an opposition movement, though sectional in origin and name, spoke and acted unofficially in the name of a national opposition.[37]

Moreover, the leaders of each rebellion began to respond to each other's successes and even to establish contact with each other. In February 1831, the Maniat rebels appointed a seven-man committee to establish contact with the Hydriot committee and work out a plan of concerted action. Since the Hydriots controlled the seas, it was easier for them to establish contact with the Maniats and they were not slow to take the initiative. In September, for instance, Hydriot ships appeared in the gulf of Coron (Messenia) and negotiated revolt with the Maniats. Around that same time, Tzames Karatasos suddenly appeared on a Hydriot ship sent to the Peloponnesos to raise a revolt.[38]

By October 1831, affairs had reached a kind of stalemate. The Karatasos revolt was the only one which Kapodistrias had been able to snuff out, but even then, Karatasos kept coming back, either on his own resources or in conjunction with the Hydriots. Favored by geography, the rebels in Hydra and Mane were strong enough to withstand government attempts to restore its authority, but in no position to march on Nauplion and topple the government. Early that year Kapodistrias had managed, with great dispatch, to have Petrobey arrested at Katakolo where he had fled from Nauplion and to have Constantine, the leader of the revolt in Mane, decoyed on board a government ship. Once returned to Nauplion, Petrobey was accused of high treason and imprisoned at Itch-Kalé, while

[37] A secret society of Hercules was formed during this time by the opposition; for the alleged text of its catechism, see the supplement to *Ephemeris tes Kyberneseos tou Basileiou tes Hellados* [*Government Gazette, Kingdom of Greece*], no. 65, 26 Aug. 1831*o.s.*; see also Makrygiannes [*Memoirs*], II, 27. Concerning the retirement of Mavrokordatos, Trikoupes, and Miaoules to Hydra, see Driault and Lhéritier, *Histoire*, II, 54. On *Apollōn*, see Finlay, *History*, VII, 60-61, and Mendelssohn Bartholdy, *Geschichte Griechenlands*, II, 226-30. For quotations from *Apollōn* between 21 Mar. and the last issue of 7 Oct. 1831*o.s.*, see Demetrios A. Petrakakos, *Koinobouleutike Historia tes Hellados* [*Parliamentary History of Greece*] (Athens, 1935), I, 431-32, n. 19. On Syros, see Finlay, *History*, VII, 63, and Thiersch, *État actuel*, I, 39-40.

[38] Mendelssohn Bartholdy, *Geschichte Griechenlands*, II, 258, 270.

Constantine and George, Petrobey's son, were confined in another place. Although these arrests deprived the revolt of its leadership, the long detainment of these men in prison—for lack of sufficient evidence against them—only fortified the determination of the Maniat rebels to resist the government. With regard to Hydra, the government's last chance of suppressing the revolt suddenly vanished when Miaoules, supported by Kriezes and Mavrokordatos as advisers and a crew of 150 Hydriot sailors, boldly seized the government naval arsenal at Poros on 27 July 1831 and dramatically destroyed the government's fleet (13 August) rather than give it up to the Russian admiral acting in behalf of Kapodistrias.[39]

The Assassination of Kapodistrias

Those failures, together with the now open hostility of the French and British governments towards Kapodistrias, whom they regarded as a pawn of Russia, provoked in Kapodistrias an uncompromising attitude which precipitated his unfortunate destruction. Seeing the necessity of quelling at least one of the two remaining revolts, Ricord, the Russian admiral, attempted to mediate a conciliation between Mavromichales and Kapodistrias. Before considering conciliation, Kapodistrias insisted on the humiliating condition that Mavromichales admit himself guilty of treason. Mavromichales reluctantly agreed. Kapodistrias then gave permission for Petrobey to dine on board the Russian flagship of Admiral Ricord, thus giving the impression of a presidential pardon for past offenses. In the meantime, the government received news that Kapodistrias had become the object of a scathing criticism in the English press. This news seems to have been responsible for suddenly making Kapodistrias less conciliatory. Petrobey's meeting with Ricord came to nothing and Petrobey was returned to prison.[40]

Constantine and George Mavromichales seem to have interpreted these recent events as a nefarious scheme to humiliate Petrobey. Revenge in this case was a duty imposed by the Maniat code of honor. In the early morning of 9 October, only three days after Petrobey's unsuccessful visit to Ricord, Constantine the brother and George the son placed themselves on either side of the door leading into the church of St. Spyridon where Kapodistrias worshipped regularly. On the appearance of Kapodistrias, one shot, the other stabbed him to death. Constantine was immediately caught and slain, and his body exposed to the insults of an infuriated crowd. George found asylum in the home of the French resident, Baron Rouen, who subsequently turned him over to the authorities for trial and execution. An act of personal vengeance had toppled the Kapodistrian

[39] On the continuation of the Mane revolt, see Finlay, History, vii, 70-71, and Mendelssohn Bartholdy, Geschichte Griechenlands, ii, 270-73. On the Poros Affair, see Finlay, vii, 63-68; Mendelssohn Bartholdy, op.cit., ii, 234-50; and Thiersch, État actuel, i, 42f.

[40] Finlay, History, vii, 71; and Mendelssohn Bartholdy, Geschichte Griechenlands, ii, 273-75.

regime, which could not last without its leader, but the act of vengeance is only understandable in terms of the hardening attitude which characterized Kapodistrias as the result of increasing opposition to his rule, an opposition consisting of the "English" party, the Kountouriotes and Mavromichales factions, and a dissident group of Rumeliot chieftains. Up to the moment of assassination, Kolettes and his following had remained aloof and thus deprived the opposition of a truly national character.[41]

3. Interregnum and Civil War, October 1831–January 1833

The New Anti-Kapodistrian Alliance

After the assassination of Kapodistrias, the senate, largely Kapodistrian in composition and the sole remaining repository of state authority, appointed a three-man commission, consisting of Augustine Kapodistrias, Kolokotrones, and Kolettes, to rule temporarily in place of the president. Though no friend of Kapodistrias, Kolettes had remained quiet up to the assassination. He had probably respected too much the power of the man, nor was it his method to rebel without at least a thin disguise of legitimacy. His appointment was regarded as an attempt by the senate to compromise him with his following, but even more important, it was probably an attempt to keep him from joining the Hydriot opposition in what then would have become a nationwide constitutionalist opposition. In view of his political methods of quiet subversion, the post was more an advantage than a disadvantage to him. Through it, he might be able to monopolize power. Failing that, he could at least organize an opposition from a position of legitimacy or at least use such legitimacy to assume leadership of the already existing opposition.[42]

Before his death Kapodistrias had authorized elections for a new assembly. His assassination led to postponement of its opening until December but enhanced the urgency of its meeting to decide on a new regime. As had happened so many times before, the convening of a national assembly widened rather than closed the political breach. It soon became apparent that the Kapodistrians would have a decided majority in the coming assembly, from which the rebel opposition would be excluded. They would certainly use their majority to elect Augustine as his brother's successor in an attempt to maintain their political mo-

---

[41] Finlay, *History*, vii, 71-72; and Mendelssohn Bartholdy, *Geschichte Griechenlands*, ii, 276-79.

[42] Finlay (*History*, vii, 73) describes the appointments as a device by which the senate could retain the power of government in its own hands, because of the incapacity of Augustine and the irreconcilable hostility between Kolettes and Kolokotrones. Makrygiannes ([*Memoirs*], ii, 35) claims that Augustine obtained Kolettes' acceptance by promising him everything, and that Kolettes fraternized with the Napists rather than Rumeliot delegates and promised Augustine not to let the representatives from Hydra come.

nopoly.[43] Kolettes, who stood to lose both his official position and his own following unless he blocked the Kapodistrian maneuvers, now assumed the leadership of a parliamentary opposition within the assembly. Tatzes Manginas rallied the Rumeliot captains (among whom were Theodore Grivas and Nicholas Zervas), long tied to Kolettes by sentiment and interest, and united them with deputies from the Islands, Rumely, even Morea. In the meantime, Kolettes managed to win over some of the important Peloponnesian primates, who had escaped from Kapodistrias to Lepanto in Rumely. Finally, he assumed the role of spokesman for the Hydriot and Maniat opposition by demanding the admittance of their deputies to the assembly, only to have his demand voted down by his colleagues in the provisional commission.[44]

The Rumeliot and Kapodistrian parliamentary groups, each with its armed guard, appeared in Argos in mid-December to convene the so-called fifth national assembly. They never met as one body. The Kapodistrians equipped themselves with ample military protection, which consisted of Augustine's guard, the corps of Tzavelas, the cavalry of Kallerges, and the private troops of Kolokotrones, Rangos, and A. Metaxas. The artillery and regular infantry corps stood ready for action in nearby Nauplion. On 19 December, the Kapodistrians united in a schoolhouse, declared themselves the national assembly, and by acclamation elected Augustine second president of Greece. The Rumeliot deputies, some eighty or ninety in number, convened at the home of Zervas, only to be attacked by the forces of Kallerges, who had received an order from Augustine to disperse them as rebels while the Kapodistrians still had the military advantage. After resisting for three days, the Rumeliots retreated along the Isthmus of Corinth to Megara, enjoying the moral advantage of being victims rather than aggressors.[45] Their deputies resumed their sittings at the town of Perachora, where they gained strength from the arrival of deputies from Hydra and Mane. There a new three-man committee was appointed, consisting of Kolettes, Zaïmes, and Kountouriotes, with Mavrokordatos made secretary of state. The appointment was a gesture by Kolettes to represent the three sections of Greece and to give the movement as comprehensive a political base as possible by including the Hydriot opposition. It remained to be seen whether the Hydriot opposition would accept the invitation.[46]

[43] Finlay (History, vii, 74-75) describes the way in which Kapodistrias, through the open support of Russian Admiral Ricord, was able to secure a majority.

[44] Finlay, History, vii, 75-77; Gennaios Kolokotrones [Memoirs], p. 215; and Thiersch, État actuel, i, 68-70.

[45] Finlay, History, vii, 77-78; Makrygiannes [Memoirs], ii, 37-38; and Thiersch, État actuel, i, 71-72.

[46] Gennaios Kolokotrones ([Memoirs], pp. 215-16) cites the following as supporters of the Perachora movement: Botsares, Iskos, Stratos, Kontogiannes, Kriezotes, Vasos, Grivas, Chatzepetros, Zervas. For the text of Kolettes' revolutionary proclamation from Megara, dated Feb. 1832o.s., see Petrakakos [Parliamentary History], i, 442. See also Finlay, History, vii, 80-81; Makrygiannes [Memoirs], ii, 39-40; and Thiersch, État actuel, i, 73.

Anti-Kapodistrian Polarization into "French" and "English" Parties

Kolettes' appointment of himself, Zaïmes, and Kountouriotes as a three-man governing commission provided the one and only opportunity for the opposition to achieve real unity, even cohesion into one Constitutionalist party. But at that point it would have been a unity dependent on the military power of the Rumeliot captains and subservient to the leadership of Kolettes. By January 1832, it was virtually certain that military force would decide the contest between Augustine and Kolettes, and the odds were in favor of Kolettes. The threat of Kolettes' renewed political ascendancy began to overshadow the hostility of the Hydriot coalition toward Augustine, and past animosity against Kolettes revived. The threat of a new Rumeliot occupation of the Peloponnesos, designed to crush the nucleus of Kapodistrian power, aroused Peloponnesian sectionalist feeling and alarmed politicians lest the captains once again exploit their military power for political purposes.[47]

As a result, several important members of the Hydriot opposition sought reconciliation with Augustine in an attempt to thwart Kolettes, the Rumeliots, and the military element. Zaïmes, the first of these "Hydriots," wrote Kolokotrones as early as October 1831 offering reconciliation, now that John Kapodistrias was no longer an obstacle, and in order to avoid civil war. A bitter enemy of Kolettes since 1825, Zaïmes remembered the Rumeliot ravages committed in the Peloponnesos and sought to avoid a similar recurrence. His reconciliation with Kolokotrones was therefore based on a common hostility toward Kolettes, even more on their common Peloponnesian sentiment. Along with Trikoupes he made his peace with Augustine, through the mediation of Plapoutas and Gennaios Kolokotrones, and left Hydra for Nauplion. Even though he did not go to Perachora where Kolettes had made a place for him on the three-man commission, he tried unsuccessfully to reconcile the Nauplion and Megara camps.[48]

Others followed Zaïmes' course, not without encouragement from Sir Edward Dawkins, the British resident. Up to the death of Kapodistrias, Dawkins had acted in concert with Baron Rouen, the French resident, because both men believed that Kapodistrias was working for Russian preponderance in Greece. Now the growing threat of Kolettes alarmed Dawkins into uniting with Baron Rückman, the Russian resident, against what he feared presaged French preponderance. In a very real sense, then, Kolettes' identification with French interests was to prevent him from organizing a united anti-Kapodistrian party. According to Thiersch, Dawkins influenced Trikoupes to reach an accord with Zaïmes and Au-

---

[47] Gennaios Kolokotrones ([*Memoirs*], pp. 216-17) cites both factors—jealousy of Kolettes and sectionalist feeling.

[48] Concerning Zaïmes' reconciliation with the Napists, *loc.cit.* See also Mendelssohn Bartholdy, *Geschichte Griechenlands*, II, 310, 374, and Thiersch, *État actuel*, I, 107f., 110, 116-18.

gustine, and found another willing person in the Hydriot Bountoures, whose long-standing hostility toward Kountouriotes, now a Hydriot supporter of the Rumeliot interest, made him ready for a break with the Hydriot opposition. The nucleus of these three men, supported by Dawkins, was bound to attract others too, as actually happened when Mavrokordatos, Klonares, and Zographos joined that group.[49]

In some secondary accounts of that period, these defectors from the anti-Kapodistrian opposition are represented as having acted as individuals. But the newspapers of 1833 show quite clearly that this group was regarded as one of three parties, called the "Kapodistrian-Constitutionalist" party by its enemies (*Hēlios*) and the "moderate" party by its friends (*Triptolemos*), midway between the Kapodistrians on the right and the Constitutionalists (Kolettists) on the left.[50] The formation of this group or party was, in effect, the continuation of the old "British" faction in the sense that the persons who composed it were considered British partisans, and their formation into a separate group was partially attributable to the deliberate intentions of Dawkins. The remainder of the old Hydriot opposition was associated loosely with the Kolettist Constitutionalists who, in large part, were the old "French" faction.

The political dispute between Kolettes and Augustine ended, as it had begun, with a resort to force. Only this time the victory went to Kolettes. During the winter of 1831-32, Perachora became a refuge for anti-Kapodistrians and just plain soldiers who were not being paid by Augustine's bankrupt government. In the spring, Kolettes decided to invade the Peloponnesos, as he had done in 1824. The Kapodistrian army of Kallerges fled before his Rumeliot troops at Corinth and so left open the road to Nauplion. In this crisis, the residents of the three protecting powers virtually compelled Augustine to resign, once Kolettes insisted that no reconciliation was possible between opposing sides so long as Augustine remained in Greece. Shortly after his resignation Augustine

[49] Concerning Trikoupes' reconciliation with Nauplion, see Gennaios Kolokotrones [*Memoirs*], p. 216, and Mendelssohn Bartholdy, *Geschichte Griechenlands*, II, 374. According to Finlay (*History*, VII, 89), Mavrokordatos, Trikoupes, Klonares, and Zographos "abandoned the cause of civil liberty." Maurer (*Griechische Volk*, I, 449) writes, "Thus, once he [Dawkins] thought that the French party under Kolettes was becoming too strong, he induced men of the English party, such as Zaïmes, Trikoupes, Zographos, etc. to give their hands to the Russian party, and on the contrary, not only to grasp the offered hand of the Russophiles, such as Andrew and Constantine Metaxas, Ainian, etc. but to pretend friendship as well." See also Thiersch, *État actuel*, I, 107f., 110, 112.

[50] As an instance of analysis in terms of two parties only, see Finlay, *History*, VII, Chap. 3, in which he deals with the interregnum, p. 89 especially; or *The Portfolio*, III, 343, to the extent that it considers them members of the "Russian" party when they defect from the Constitutionalists, as if there were only two alternatives. For contemporary accounts in terms of three parties, see anonymous letter to the editor dated 30 Aug. 1833*o.s.*, in *Hēlios*, 25 Aug. 1833*o.s.* and *Triptolemos*, 6 Sept. 1833*o.s.*

left Greece forever with the body of his murdered brother. On 10 April Kolettes rode into Nauplion triumphantly.[51]

From 6 April to 21 April Kolettes, now triumphant militarily, negotiated with the three residents, the senate, and the third party in an attempt to decide on the seven persons who would constitute the governing commission. He refused to accept either Bountoures, Trikoupes, or Zographos, regarding them as betrayers. Finally, the following were agreed upon: Kolettes, Kountouriotes, Botsares, Ypsilantes, Zaïmes, Metaxas, and Plapoutas. The first four represented his "French" party, which called itself "the Constitutional party," the last two the Kapodistrians, and Zaïmes the "English" party which were styled "moderates." But the latter was likely to vote with the Kapodistrians on all important matters. The provision which required the assent of five members to give the force of law to any of the commission's acts meant, in effect, that the Constitutionalists could not utilize their majority. Clearly then, Kolettes' military victory did not result in a clear-cut political triumph. The cabinet consisted of Mavrokordatos, Trikoupes, Zographos, Klonares, and Voulgares, men who belonged to the "English" moderate party. This compromise was not, therefore, one between merely two parties (Constitutionalists and Kapodistrians), as it often is represented, but rather between three, with proportional representation given each in the government.[52]

Constitutionalism: Policy Differences among the Three Parties

Something needs be said about the constitutional question, especially because party labels at this time suggested an ideological basis for the political division. Ostensibly the Constitutionalists favored a constitution and some form of representative government, while the Kapodistrians were political absolutists, and the third group political opportunists who "betrayed the fight for civil liberties" when expedient. Whatever the private opinion of the people concerned—and there were many who felt, like Kapodistrias, that the country was not ready for Western parliamentary government—each group took a distinct position during this period.

The first group to do so was the Kapodistrians in their assembly, which ran from December 1831 to March 1832. This same assembly which elected Augustine president and excluded both the Kolettists and the other opposition deputies, finished its work by voting a constitution. This may seem paradoxical in view of the previous position of Kapodistrias. But Kapodistrias had never disclaimed the constitution as such, and now his adherents, no longer enjoying a monopoly of power, saw the constitution as a way of legally ensuring themselves some say in the govern-

---

[51] Finlay, *History*, vii, 81-85; Makrygiannes [*Memoirs*], ii, 41-42; and Thiersch, *État actuel*, i, 93.

[52] See Finlay's account (*History*, vii, 85-86) which bases its analysis on this misleading assumption of a two-way struggle.

ment. Its most characteristic provision was the establishment of a two-chamber legislature, one to consist of a senate appointed by the king for life. This provision left them open to the charge that they favored the establishment of some sort of aristocracy and that they intended to continue their influence by forcing the king to legalize the existing Kapodistrian senate. The most one can say is that this was a conservative constitution. In view of their enemies' attempts to brand the Kapodistrians political absolutists, it is important to note, however, that the Kapodistrian assembly actually *did* vote for a constitution.[53]

The position of the other two parties on the constitutional question became dramatically clear during the assembly of Pronoia, which sat from 26 July to 1 September 1832. This was predominantly an "English"-"French" body. The conflict which arose reflects, therefore, the split of the opposition into its two component parts. The assembly began its work by declaring a general political amnesty and sanctioning the powers' recent election of Otho, the second son of the Bavarian king Ludwig, as Greek monarch. But the majority of the assembly intended to go much further. They dissolved the existing Kapodistrian senate, they intended to appoint a new government, and they planned to turn themselves into a constituent assembly which would proceed to draw up a constitution. The dissolution of the senate and the assembly majority's self-transformation into a constituent assembly immediately drew the official protest (dated 10 August 1832) of the three residents, who defended the continued existence of the senate as a means of continuing a policy of conciliation between all parties. According to Karl Mendelssohn Bartholdy, however, it was only with the greatest reluctance that the French resident associated himself with this protest. Kolettes, unwilling to thwart the opinion of the three residents, went along with them, but he maintained official silence, most probably because it was his own partisans in the assembly who had been responsible for the dissolution.[54]

Inspired by the three residents, a group of some twenty-one deputies, including Mavrokordatos, Trikoupes, and Zographos, issued a declaration that the formulation of a constitution should be put off until the king could actually participate. The president of the assembly, Panoutsos Notaras, determined to go ahead with the assembly majority's plans, replied to the residents and the twenty-one deputies by insisting that the assembly did not mean to present the king with a *fait-accompli*, that they

[53] Indeed, the Kapodistrians, early in September 1832, started publishing the Franco-Greek newspaper *Miroir Grec* with the motto "Constitutional Monarchy" (Papadopoulos-Vretos, *Compte-Rendu*, p. 12). For a summary of the constitution and text of the assembly bill approving the election of the king, see Petrakakos [*Parliamentary History*], I, 440-41. Thiersch does not deal with the assembly or the constitution at all.

[54] For a partial text of the protest and text of the reply see Petrakakos [*Parliamentary History*], I, 447-49. See also Finlay, *History*, VII, 93-95; Papadopoulos-Vretos, *Compte-Rendu*, p. 18; and Thiersch, *État actuel*, II, 169.

would be expecting him to make his modifications later.[55] The means subsequently employed to prevent the promulgation of a constitution were dubious in the extreme. The Rumeliots, dissatisfied because they had received no pay, dissolved the assembly by force, and kidnapped some twenty-seven deputies, who had to pay a handsome ransom for their release. There is evidence that Dawkins had hinted at some such resolution of the problem to the dissatisfied Rumeliot troops and that even Kolettes had gone along with this.[56] None the less, sixty-three deputies protested bitterly against this act. The "French" Constitutionalists intended to revive something like the Troezene constitution, making the necessary modifications for the existence of a monarchy, and they considered the formulation of a constitution as essentially the work of the nation, with the king only assenting and modifying. The "English" party never denied the need for a constitution, they merely argued that it must be postponed until the arrival of the king. By their assertions they implied that sovereignty now adhered in the king as well as in the nation.[57]

Constitutionalists vs. Kapodistrians

Although the "French" and "English" parties remained at odds with each other and exchanged bitter accusations against one another, the resurgence of the Kapodistrian party during the interregnum brought them temporarily together in an effort to deal with the common foe. To this extent it is permissible to speak of the contestants in the civil war of 1832 as Constitutionalists and Kapodistrians. But this two-fold division applies in yet another way to the civil war of 1832, which took place largely in the provinces. On the local scene, factional rivalry seems to have been a two-way affair only, and even if three or even more factions were involved, they were not necessarily affiliated with the "French" and "English" parties because the latter were insufficiently developed to have penetrated into all the nooks and crannies of Greece.[58] Those who had

[55] The Portfolio, III, 450.

[56] Finlay, History, VII, 95; Makrygiannes [Memoirs], II, 47 (who says that Thiersch approached him to fight Pronoia intentions); Papadopoulos-Vretos, Compte-Rendu, p. 78; and Thiersch, État actuel, I, 170.

[57] An anonymous letter, dated 30 Aug. 1833o.s., in Triptolemos, 6 Sept. 1833o.s., represents Trikoupes as the defender of the royal prerogative for his share in this case.

[58] This is a safe guess, but the evidence is really insufficient. The guess is based on the following additional observations: (1) the influence of the diplomatic foreign missions did not penetrate to any extent into the provinces, except possibly in the few places where consulates existed, such as Patras, Nauplion, Syros, and Mesolongi; (2) very often, though not always in the provinces, the struggle was a two-way rather than a triangular one, both because the system of clientage tended to unite families into the smallest number of groupings, and also because party subgroups, where they existed, tended to unite, at least momentarily, against those who held office; (3) the terms "British," "Russian," and "French," for the average man, did not have the ideological content or distinctness that did such pairs as Orthodoxy (including Russia) and non-Orthodoxy (applying to the West as an undifferentiated entity).

been associated in the local administration during the Kapodistrian period were Kapodistrians. The rest were, by virtue of their exclusion from local power, anti-Kapodistrians and adopted the convenient label "Constitutionalists." As a result, we shall write in this section in terms of "Constitutionalists" and "Kapodistrians."

Though recognized by the residents and the senate, the governing commission, appointed after Kolettes' triumph in April 1832, lacked the power to enforce its authority. The only available troops were Rumeliot, but their insubordination made them extremely unreliable. Its very existence threatened, the commission invited French troops to occupy Nauplion and Patras. Already occupying southwestern Morea in the name of the three powers, these troops, because French, excited the jealousy of the British and Russian residents and aroused Kapodistrian fears lest the pro-French Kolettes exploit them for partisan purposes. On 19 May 1832, Colonel Courbet entered Nauplion, but before the French could arrive at Patras, where the many Ionian merchant residents had implored the protection of the British minister,[59] the strong Kapodistrian party in that city had instigated a mutiny among the regular Greek troops and invited Tzavelas to assume the command. Tzavelas refused to admit the French, who had to withdraw when the British and Russian residents would not associate themselves in any allied order to take the place by force.[60] The authority of the commission therefore went no further than Nauplion. Elsewhere they had to rely on the good will of the inhabitants. By virtue of securing Patras, the Kapodistrians controlled the province of Achaia in the northern Peloponnesos, the fortresses of Rhion and Antirhion, which commanded the entrance to the gulf of Corinth, and so were able to maintain communications with mainland Greece.[61]

As the incident at Patras reveals, the Kapodistrian party benefited from its defeat at Corinth and the departure of Augustine from Greece. Augustine's general unpopularity had always made him a liability to the party. The entrance of some 8,000 Rumeliot troops into the Peloponnesos revived the drama of 1824-25—soldiers living at free quarters in various parts of the peninsula and very often spreading terror by their exactions and cruelty. As a result, the greater part of the Morea adhered to the Kapodistrians as their surest defenders against the Rumeliot soldiery. Several Moreot primates, hitherto Constitutionalists, now abandoned the cause, as had Zaïmes already. Most of the demogerons of the provincial cities and villages, appointees of Kapodistrias, undertook the management of local affairs in the absence of a dependable central authority and appealed to the military leaders of the Kapodistrian party. Under these circumstances, Kolokotrones again united his cause with the cause of the people, assumed the role of defender of the local authorities, and, to use

[59] *The Portfolio*, III, 440.
[60] Gennaios Kolokotrones [*Memoirs*], p. 220, and Thiersch, *État actuel*, I, 134.
[61] Finlay, *History*, VII, 89-91, and Makrygiannes [*Memoirs*], II, 44.

the phrase of Finlay, became "the champion of the people's rights." He became the leader of the Kapodistrian party, as his popularity became even greater than it had been before.[62] Roughly speaking, Arcadia and Achaia remained staunchly Kapodistrian, thanks to the power of Kolokotrones and Tzavelas respectively. Argolis, Corinth, and Laconia remained loyal to the governing commission. Messenia and Elis, where the Kapodistrians and Constitutionalists were more evenly matched, became the scenes of bitter civil strife. In mainland Greece, the Kapodistrians had a stronghold at Salona, where Mamoures held a strong garrison. In the Archipelago, Tenos remained loyal to the Kapodistrians, while Androutsos and Miaoules employed their ships to keep Spezza and Aegina for the Constitutionalists.[63]

However strong the Kapodistrians in the provinces, their political future in the new kingdom seemed to depend on their strength in the central authority. No provincial organ would be able to exercise the same influence over the regency that the central government could. The governing commission would, of course, be dissolved on the arrival of the king. It was rumored that the regency intended to retain the existing cabinet, which included no Kapodistrians. The senate, already formally dissolved by the Pronoia assembly, remained under surveillance of French troops in Nauplion. These considerations probably explain the reckless actions of the Kapodistrians on the eve of the king's arrival.

In mid-November, seven Kapodistrian senators secretly left Nauplion to be joined on 21 November by the president Tsamados and two more senators. Kolokotrones and a body of Moreot troops met them at Astros. With the government printing press, which they had sneaked out of Nauplion, they issued a proclamation annulling the recent decree which invested Kolettes, Zaïmes, and Metaxas with the executive authority.[64] Trusting in the military support of the Kapodistrian party and the help of Russian Admiral Ricord, an acknowledged party to their intrigues, these senators probably intended to pull off a coup similar to that of Kolettes the previous April, although they argued that restrictive surveillance by French troops in Nauplion precipitated their fight. They appointed a military commission to govern Greece, consisting of several powerful captains, both Moreots and Rumeliots—Kolokotrones, Tzavelas, Nicholas Kriezotes, A. Chatzechrestos. Some of these, like Tzavelas and Chatzechrestos, were not traditionally associated with the Kapodistrians. This military league was significant because it represented a reconciliation of a large body of the military class and a type of resurgence of the

---

[62] On Kolokotrones' popularity, see Finlay, *History*, vII, 91-92, 98-99. Concerning his administrative control, see Thiersch, *État actuel*, I, 177-88. See also Gennaios Kolokotrones [*Memoirs*], pp. 218-19, 221.

[63] Finlay, *History*, vII, 88, 91.

[64] Theodore Kolokotrones, *Klepht and Warrior*, p. 303, and Papadopoulos-Vretos, *Compte-Rendu*, pp. 26-30.

old military "party."[65] Finally, the senate elected Ricord president of Greece, hoping thereby to receive effective support from Russia.[66]

Reacting to the possibility of their forceful exclusion from power before the king's arrival, the three-man commission in Nauplion appealed to the residents for French troops to garrison Argos, where Kriezotes and Tsokres were in nominal command. The French troops arrived on 15 January 1833. On the following day Greek irregulars attacked them. After considerable street fighting, the French troops prevailed and the Greek troops were ousted. Two weeks later the king and regency arrived in Greece.[67]

These last-minute efforts of the Kapodistrians ended in dismal failure. Clearly, they had attempted unilaterally to change the status quo and they had utterly discredited themselves on many counts—for appointing a Russian as president when a new king's arrival was imminent, for uniting most of the military chieftains identified with the prevalence of anarchy, and for attacking French troops acting in the name of the three powers. They had, in other words, given their enemies the chance to discredit them with the new king and regency by charging them with disloyalty.

4. The Crystallization of Three Parties

Major Contributing Factors

By the end of 1832, three parties were in existence, each with branches extending through the major regions of the state, each with its particular orientation regarding foreign policy and constitutionalism, each dominated by one of the three personal factions, each encouraged and sustained by one of the three foreign residents. Three major factors had contributed to their formation and crystallization. First, the relatively long and vigorous rule of Kapodistrias had enabled him to employ his widespread mass popularity and the state bureaucratic machinery to construct a well-organized party commanding broad popular support. His and his brother's rule had contributed indirectly to the growth of counteralliances designed to give protection against the Kapodistrians and oust them from power. Second, the presence of the three foreign residents and the three foreign admirals, representing powerful outside influence, offered an institutional source of central direction and hence gave these parties permanence. Indeed, this system of foreign interference

[65] Makrygiannes ([*Memoirs*], II, 48) claims his side (Rumeliot) took the initiative in behalf of the military league, with the object of preventing pillaging by opposing forces. See also Papadopoulos-Vretos, *Compte-Rendu*, p. 20, and Thiersch, *État actuel*, I, 236.

[66] Finlay, *History*, VII, 97-98.

[67] *Ibid.*, VII, 103-104; Theodore Kolokotrones, *Klepht and Warrior*, p. 302; and Mendelssohn Bartholdy, *Geschichte Griechenlands*, II, 421-25.

was a major factor in the failure of the Constitutionalist opposition to coalesce into a party. But for the residents of England and France, the "English" and "French" parties would probably not have been able to retain their separate existence *as parties*. One would probably have become a part of the other, or as actually happened with the Kountouriotes or Mavromichales groupings, preserved its freedom of action by falling back to the position of a faction with only limited influence. Finally, the assassination of Kapodistrias and the civil war of 1832, the longest and most damaging of any yet known in Greece, created intense bitterness, especially between the "English" and "French" parties, and in reaction, fanatic devotion to one's own group. As a result, the internal cohesion of each party and the mutual exclusiveness between them had a firm psychological basis. The internal structure of the Kapodistrian party has already been discussed. We must now do the same for the "English" and "French" parties.

The "English" Party

Essentially, the "English" party had three component parts: the Mavrokordatos following, the Lontos-Zaïmes faction, and the Miaoules-Tompazes interest in Hydra. The Mavrokordatos following consisted of two groups: the military and civilian elements of West Rumely, where Mavrokordatos had his geographical base, and the corps of Westernized intellectuals concentrated in the capital where they filled important posts. His military followers remained largely the same as they had been in 1825. Richard Church commanded campaigns in West Rumely from the end of 1827 until the spring of 1829. Perhaps his activities there and his self-styled role as defender of palikar interests made these captains Anglophiles as well as Mavrokordatos clients.[68] Of the primates, two deserve mention: Tatzos Manginas, an early client (already mentioned) who by now acted as a type of political lieutenant for Mavrokordatos in West Rumely, second only to him; and Athanasios Loidorikes of Doris, an elderly man who had once served Ali Pasha as secretary and keeper of the seal.[69]

The Mavrokordatos circle of intellectuals and bureaucrats, which had grown since 1825, merits special attention because its public image explains the party's reputation for great administrative talent as well as alien ways. To be sure, these men were all Westernizers with professional skills and mostly heterochthons. Christodoulos Klonares of Epirus, George Praïdes of Adrianople, and Anastasios Polyzoïdes were lawyers who later

---

[68] On Sir Richard Church, see E. M. Church, *Sir Richard Church in Italy and Greece* (Edinburgh, 1895), and Stanley Lane-Poole, *Sir Richard Church . . . commander-in-chief of the Greeks in the war of independence* (London, 1890); Dakin, *Philhellenes,* pp. 5-8, 12-18, 26-28, 144-56, 160-61, 174-89, 214-20; and Piscatory, Athens, 6 Sept. 1841 (7th report), *L'Hellénisme Contemporain,* IX, 447.

[69] *Ibid.,* pp. 434 (Manginas) and 443 (Ath. Loidorikes).

became judges, and Pericles Argyropoulos, the Phanariot brother-in-law of Mavrokordatos, had studied jurisprudence and administration in Europe enough to be considered an expert in these fields in Greece. Theocletos Pharmakides, Neophytos Vamvas, and Misael Apostolides, monks educated in the West and influenced by Western theology, all represented the extreme liberal wing of the clergy. Nicholas Theochares, who grew up in Germany, and George Spaniolakes, an Anglophile, knew more than most Greeks about finance. Polyzoïdes, the poet Alexander Soutsos, and the Cretan Manuel Antoniades all took up journalism, the former two momentarily, the latter permanently. Although George Psyllas, son of a drunken Athenian cobbler, and Trikoupes, native of Mesolongi, were both autochthons, their years of education abroad rendered them as alien to the ways of the provincials as any heterochthons. Anagnostes Monarchides, a Psariot heterochthon, was the least Westernized intellectual of the group. As a result, he was also the most influential politically and owed his influence least to Mavrokordatos. The group and, as a result, Mavrokordatos, suffered from one great handicap. They excited the jealousy and antipathy of indigenous elements and so, instead of bringing support to Mavrokordatos, he had to risk his own reputation to defend them. Moreover, many had not fought in the Revolution, either because of youth or their studies abroad, and therefore forfeited the prestige which such service brought. For reasons not entirely clear, the party also attracted or gave quarter to the extreme liberals, republicans at heart such as the poet Alexander Soutsos or Antoniades.[70]

As a result of his political prominence during the Revolutionary and Kapodistrian periods, Zaïmes emerged head of the Lontos-Zaïmes faction. Andrew Lontos had concentrated on a military career, important in building up the military power of the faction and controlling a mass following for it. But Zaïmes seems to have commanded the personal loyalty of the most prominent Peloponnesian adherents: the wealthy and distinguished primate Venizelos Rouphos of Patras; the Dariotes brothers of Nisi, one of the richest families in the rich province of Messenia; and Constantine Zographos, able and well-educated but in need of such an ally (or perhaps patron) as Zaïmes because he lacked local influence.[71] Andrew Miaoules and the brothers Tompazes headed an alliance of vir-

[70] *Ibid.*, pp. 428 (Psyllas), 434-35 (Trikoupes), 443 (Monarchides), 444 (Klonares, Praïdes, Pharmakides), 446 (Apostolides, Antoniades); Finlay, *History*, vi, 173 (Vamvas), and vii, 60-61 (Polyzoïdes); Mendelssohn Bartholdy, *Geschichte Griechenlands*, ii, 148 (Psyllas) and 226; (Polyzoïdes); Rangabe [*Memoirs*], i, 246 (Polyzoïdes) and 291 (Klonares); and Leicester Stanhope, *Greece in 1823 and 1824: Series of Letters and other Documents on the Greek Revolution*, new edn. (London, 1825), p. 400 (Praïdes). On Klonares, see also Patseles [*Political Men*].

[71] Piscatory, Athens, 6 Sept. 1841 (7th report), *L'Hellénisme Contemporain*, ix, 439 (Dariotes), 440 (Andrew and Anastasios Lontos, Rouphos, Zographos). *Hēlios* (4 July 1833o.s.) attests to the alliance between the Lontos-Zaïmes and Mavrokordatos factions.

136

tually all the Hydriot primates against the tremendous wealth and popular control of the Kountouriotes family. Most probably their adhesion to the "English" party stemmed partially from their need for outside help against the Kountouriotes', but by sentiment they were pro-"English." The most ardent Anglophiles were Anthony Kriezes, a poor Hydriot captain with a large family, and Basil Bountoures, whose family had been feuding with the Kountouriotes' since the sudden breaking off of an engagement between a member of each family. In Spezza the Anargyros family represented the "English" party.[72]

The "French" Party

Between October 1831 and April 1832, Kolettes created a party. His original faction of Rumeliot palikars, modified internally by the deaths of Gouras and Karaïskakes and the adhesion of more Rumeliot primates, constituted the core of the new party. To this core, however, adhered groups from other sections of Greece, especially an important branch of the Peloponnesian primates. A few political lieutenants, mostly Westernized intellectuals without local followings but with bureaucratic skills, gave a certain cohesion to the sectional groupings. Finally, the whole enjoyed the occasional support of the French resident, the French troops in the Peloponnesos, and the Bavarian philhellene Thiersch, whose great influence derived from the Greek assumption that he was the unofficial spokesman for King Ludwig of Bavaria.[73]

After Gouras died, the authority he had usurped from Odysseus became fragmented. Mamoures, his legal heir, managed to hold on to the large district of Phocis in the west only. In the eastern districts of East Rumely (Boeotia, Attica, and Euboea), three men emerged supreme: Nicholas Kriezotes and Vasos Mavrovouniotes, both captains, and Adam Doukas, a rich primate. All three befriended each other, supported Kolettes, and constituted the solid core of the "French" party in its political stronghold of East Rumely. According to a common pattern of often close collaboration between shepherd and brigand, Kriezotes, a Euboean shepherd from Caristo, and Vasos, a Montenegrin brigand and soldier of fortune, had become friends. Under Gouras they had shared the command of an irregular body of troops during the Revolution. Contact with Colonel Fabvier, former officer of Napoleon and French philhellene whose regular army defended the Acropolis in 1825-27, may have inspired their sympathy for France. Into the royal period Kriezotes exercised "almost absolute authority over the whole Euboean population" while Vasos, "the most important man of eastern Greece," enjoyed an influence extending over Attica, Livadia, Talanti, Boudounitsa, and Phthiotis, and

---

[72] Piscatory, Athens, 6 Sept. 1841 (7th report), *L'Hellénisme Contemporain*, IX, 442 (Kriezes, Bountoures), 443 (Anargyros); Thiersch, *État actuel*, II, 187 (Kriezes); and Finlay, *History*, VI, 172 (Iakomaki Tompazes).

[73] Mendelssohn Bartholdy, *Geschichte Griechenlands*, II, 341-42.

would have equaled the authority of Kriezotes in Euboea if the two men had not been in such perfect accord.[74]

Adam Doukas, scion of one of the first families of Epirus, had married into a Euboean family and was in Livadia when the Revolution broke out. His own family connections made him influential in what became the frontier provinces, while the influence of his wife's family, his own long residence and large landholdings, and his patronage of captains during the Revolution, made him an important political factor in Euboea and East Rumely. Indeed, he served as an important liaison-officer between Kolettes and the captains, whose confidence he enjoyed.[75]

There were "French" persons of secondary importance in East Rumely as well, both military and civilian. Among the captains, John Makrygiannes of Attica maintained close relations with Kriezotes. Klemakas and Skourtaniates strengthened the influence of Vasos in Boeotia, as did John Velentzas of Armyro in Phthiotis. Nakos Panourgias of Salona (Amphissa) and Papakostas represented the "French" interest in the overwhelmingly Napist district of Phocis in East Rumely. Through family connections, Panourgias had influence in the Doris district of Lidoriki in East Rumely as well as the Aetolian district of Kravari in West Rumely. Papakostas' influence coincided with that of Panourgias and extended even further into the Phthiotis frontier districts of Eurytania and Agrapha.[76]

On the whole, the primates of East Rumely did not adhere to the "French" party on an individual basis. Instead, a primate family would previously attach itself to a local captain, from whom it derived military protection in exchange for political advice, and these local allies would then "join" the party jointly. For instance, Manolakes Ierolimos, a rich proprietor of Karpenisi in Phthiotis, enjoyed the protection of Papakostas, while Constantine Logothetopoulos of Galaxidi allied himself locally with Panourgias. The Zotos family of Phourna in Phthiotis had ties with practically all the petty captains of Agrapha. A few primates enjoyed greater independence, however—Anastasios Loidorikes because of the family strength in Phocis and his own participation in national politics, Demetrios Chatziskos of Lamia (also called Zeitouni) because his membership in an old primate family gave him considerable influence over the peasants in his district.[77]

Even though the "English" party predominated in West Rumely, the

[74] On Kriezotes, see Piscatory, Athens, 6 Sept. 1841 (7th report), L'Hellénisme Contemporain, IX, 429-30; on Mavrovouniotes, see ibid., pp. 431-32; Rangabe [Memoirs], I, 298; and Thiersch, État actuel, I, 91.

[75] Piscatory, Athens, 6 Sept. 1841 (7th report), L'Hellénisme Contemporain, IX, 429.

[76] Ibid., pp. 428 (Makrygiannes), 430 (Klemakas, Skourtaniates), 432 (Velentzas, Papakostas), 433 (Panourgias). For an excellent biographical essay on Makrygiannes, see Vlachogiannes' introduction to Makrygiannes' [Memoirs].

[77] Piscatory, Athens, 6 Sept. 1841 (7th report), L'Hellénisme Contemporain, IX, 431 (Chatziskos), 432 (Ierolimos, Zotos), 433 (Logothetopoulos, An. Loidorikes).

"French" party found representation in two important military families. The one, headed by the capable John Stratos, inherited the support of practically all the captains who had marched under the banner of Karaïskakes, his relative. The other consisted of the four Grivas brothers (Phloros, Stavros, Theodore, and Gardikiotes) and had its local seat in Acarnania (Vonitsa). Theodore, its most prominent and powerful member, supported Kolettes in 1832. But his cruelty and avidity discredited the Constitutional movement wherever his troops penetrated and made him undependable in his party engagements.[78]

The "French" party in the Peloponnesos developed around the Delegiannes faction and embraced one branch of the Peloponnesian primate class. These two facts suggest some identification between it and the pre-Revolutionary *Karytaino-Messenian* primate "party." Unlike the "Russian" party in the Peloponnesos, a more or less stratified arrangement of a few powerful leaders and a mass of social subordinates, insignificant without their leaders, this party was something like an alliance of many local magnates, each with his own following, each recognizing the party leader or leaders as first among equals only. Though similar in composition to the Peloponnesian branch of the "English" party, itself a party of primates too, it differed in structure; that is, power was diffused among many more primates, the acknowledged leaders enjoyed less authority, and the geographical representation of the party in the Peloponnesos was much more extensive.[79]

In the province of Arcadia, the principal figures were the Delegiannes' with their family seat at Langadia, Regas Palamides and Basil Christakopoulos of Tripolis, and Kanellopoulos of Andritsaina. By his close cooperation with the older Anagnostes Delegiannes, Regas Palamides, young, vigorous, and able descendant of an equally distinguished primate family and son of a morayannes, came to share the leadership of the faction with Anagnostes. The rich Christakopoulos, a relative of Anagnostes and close friend of Palamides, associated himself with both Kanellopoulos, a *parvenu* among primates, had purchased several villages from the Turks before the Revolution.[80]

The most prominent "French" adherents elsewhere were: in Messenia, Nicholas Poneropoulos of the coastal town of Arcadia (otherwise known as Kyparissia), a merchant by profession, military and political chief of his province during the Revolution, and George Bastas of Coron; in Elis, Lycurgus Christenites of Pyrgos; in Achaia, Demetrios Meletopoulos of Vostitsa and Andrew Kalamogdartes of Patras; in Corinth, the Notaras

---

[78] *Ibid.*, pp. 435 (Stratos), 435-36 (Grivas). On the latter, see also Rangabe [*Memoirs*], I, 294, and Thiersch, *État actuel*, I, 149, as well as the full-length biography by D. Kampouroglou [*Theodoros Grivas*] (Athens, 1896).

[79] Piscatory, Athens, 6 Sept. 1841 (7th report), *L'Hellénisme Contemporain*, IX, 436-42.

[80] *Ibid.*, pp. 437 (Palamides, Christakopoulos), 437-38 (Delegiannes), 438 (Kanellopoulos).

family which, though it tried to remain independent of all party alignments, joined the Constitutionalist cause in 1832; in Laconia, Meletopoulos of Mistra; and in Mane, the Tzanetakes' of Marathonesi, the other
leading Maniat family which contended traditionally with the Mavromichales' for the beylik. Only two members of this group were not primates: the Petimezas' of Calavryta and the Giatrakos' of Mistra, both
captain families of more humble origins.[81]

The above men attached themselves to the "French" party as an already established group with an internal cohesion based upon ho-
mogeneity of social background and Peloponnesian sectionalist feeling.
When they attached themselves is uncertain. The most one can say is
that such an alliance did not exist at the end of 1824, when the Rumeliot
invasion of the Peloponnesos started, and that it did exist by 1832. In his
account of the civil war of 1832, Rangabe cites three individuals as supporters of the Kolettes movement—Anagnostes Delegiannes, Regas Palamides, and Basil Christakopoulos. He also reveals that none of these three
joined the political opposition until after the death of Kapodistrias, a
political stance corresponding to that of Kolettes. The "how" of the alliance is hardly clearer than the "when." One can say with certainty that
it was not based on any personal allegiance to Kolettes or any individual
attachments to Rumeliot adherents of the party. Indeed, the association
of the Kolettes faction with the dreadful Rumeliot invasion of the Peloponnesos in 1824-25 must have given the "French" primates second
thoughts about allying themselves with such objects of Peloponnesian
resentment.[82]

What made this alliance desirable and feasible? It is possible that some
of the primates negotiated some sort of pact with Kolettes during the
first civil war in order to spare themselves total destruction. It is known,
for instance, that the Notaras' made a financial settlement with the invaders in 1825 and thus escaped the wanton plundering suffered by
Lontos and Zaïmes. On the whole, the alliance took place for negative
reasons it seems: in the case of the Delegiannes' because of bitter rivalry
against Kolokotrones and an even older rivalry against Lontos and
Zaïmes; in the case of Tzanetakes because of hostility toward the Mavromichales'; in the case of the Petimezas' because they felt the characteristic aversion of former kapoi toward their former master Zaïmes.[83] On

[81] *Ibid.*, pp. 438 (Poneropoulos, Christenites), 439 (Bastas, Meletopoulos, Giatrakos), 439-40 (Kalamogdartes); 440 (D. Meletopoulos), 440-41 (Petimezas), 441
(Notaras'), 442 (Tzanetakes).

[82] Rangabe [*Memoirs*], I, 295. *Hēlios* (4 July 1833o.s.) says that four factions got
together—Kolettes', Kountouriotes', Mavromichales', and Delegiannes'. Thiersch (*État
actuel,* I, 116-17) says most, having sought refuge from the president in Lepanto,
were behind the government of Perachora and united with Kolettes only after the
president's assassination.

[83] J. Vlachogiannes, *Klephtes tou Moria* . . . [*Klephts of the Morea, Historical Study
based on New Sources, 1715-1820*] (Athens, 1935), pp. 29, 32 (Delegiannes-Ko-

the positive side, however, the presence of a French resident in Greece and French forces in the Peloponnesos (since 1828) must have impressed all those who became "French" with the efficacy of French protection. The only unpleasant requirement of such French patronage was forming an alliance with the Kolettes faction. Yet such an alliance must have been rendered easier, first by the opportunity to become client to the French resident rather than Kolettes, second, by the identification of the Kolettes movement in 1831 with the broad causes of Constitutionalism *and* autochthonism (against such outsiders as Augustine Kapodistrias and other hated Ionian Islanders).

In the Islands, the "French" party was weaker than either of the other two parties. It enjoyed the support of the Zachines family in Hydra, but Nicholas Botases and Ghikas Karakatsanes, both of Spezza, constituted the chief props. Botases, an unlettered man, owned a large fleet of merchant ships which had brought him great wealth through participation in the Black Sea carrying trade. Karakatsanes, "one of the few Greeks who know anything about finance," became an intimate friend of Kolettes during the Revolution in his role as member of successive legislative committees.[84]

The "French" party did not acquire a very large corps of intellectuals with bureaucratic skills until the beginning of the royal period. During the Perachora days, Kolettes' "cabinet" consisted of one man only— Demetrios Chrestides of Constantinople. Sometime teacher, a bureaucrat in the Wallachian court at the outbreak of the Revolution, Chrestides arrived in Greece in 1822. He became closely associated with Kolettes and served as secretary of the executive committee in which Kolettes played such an influential role (1823-26). A man of spirit, a hard worker and an opportunist, he acquired many friends during the Revolution and through them extended his contacts in the provinces. But he never secured the local influence characteristic of a native landowner or captain. Another associate of Kolettes, like Chrestides a Westernized heterochthon who arrived early in Greece, was Drosos Mansolas, a native of Thessaly, who spoke French, German, and Italian. A third, of greater interest than importance, was Panagiotes Sophianopoulos, a native of Calavryta who became personal secretary and political adviser to Gouras. Before the Revolution he studied medicine in Italy and then became an instructor at Patras. A passionate enemy of the kodza-bashis, he helped instigate the invasion of the Peloponnesos in 1824. After the death of Gouras he went to Paris to continue the study of medicine and became an impassioned devotee of France. Reckless and with no judgment, he often proved

---

lokotrones rivalry), 28 (Petimezas vs. Zaïmes). Piscatory, Athens, 6 Sept. 1841 (7th report), *L'Hellénisme Contemporain*, IX, 441 (Petimezas vs. Zaïmes) and 442 (Tzanetakes vs. Mavromichales).

[84] *Ibid.*, 443 (Zachines, Botases, Karakatsanes).

an inconvenient friend. Other intellectual adherents were Nicholas Skouphos, a native of Smyrna, who arrived in Greece in 1826 looking for a place but remained politically inactive until 1832, and Alexander Rangabe, a young Phanariot litterateur who studied in Munich and became a clerk to his old schoolmaster Chrestides at Perachora in 1832. Besides these men, Kolettes had as political lieutenants or mediators between himself and the sectional branches of the party: Adam Doukas in Rumely, Regas Palamides in the Peloponnesos, and Karakatsanes in the Islands.[85]

General Weaknesses of the Parties

Although this chapter's account of the Kapodistrian period reveals the emergence of parties, it also contains evidence of their incompleteness. One cannot help but be impressed with the frequent shifting of alliances. In spite of all its commitments to the anti-Kapodistrians, the Lontos-Zaïmes group easily made its peace with Augustine Kapodistrias. The Kountouriotes faction abandoned the "English" party to join the "French," though even then only temporarily. The Mavromichales' and the Notaras' withdrew into relative isolation, the former after October 1831 and the latter after the forced dissolution of the Pronoia assembly in the fall of 1832. The captains of both the "French" and "Russian" parties seemed to be merging into a class party at the end of 1832, or to state the matter differently, such captains as Kriezotes and Chatzechrestos momentarily abandoned Kolettes to join Kolokotrones. Although the historian can discern the general outline of distinct party positions on the constitutionalist issue, there was much confusion at the time. The Kapodistrians often looked like absolutists, even though their assembly drew up a constitution at Nauplion. Kolettes, most probably because of pressure from the French resident, stood with the "English" party against his own in opposing the attempt of the Pronoia assembly to vote a constitution into existence without the participation of the new king. Moreover, the local politics of the provinces did not often seem to manifest an "English"-"French" division between the Constitutionalists.

The analysis of party origins in Chapter II makes understandable several general weaknesses of the parties which had emerged—the weakness and vagueness of the principles which they represented, the relative absence of institutions and organizations peculiarly their own, the more than frequent disunity and ineffectiveness of action at the national level, the paradox of often fierce party loyalties on the local level and flagrant opportunism on the national level. The first was a carry-over from the factions, which were never devised to represent principles. The second was largely due to the fact that factions had their institutional basis in

[85] *Ibid.*, pp. 431 (Mansolas), 445 (Chrestides), 446 (Sophianopoulos), 446-47 (Skouphos); and Rangabe [*Memoirs*], ɪ, 280 (Chrestides) and 289 (Skouphos). For an excellent account of Sophianopoulos, a Utopian Socialist, see John Kordatos, *Historia tes Neoteres Helladas* [*History of Modern Greece*] (Athens, 1957), ɪɪɪ, 213, n.

the family and thus required no special organization to serve their function. The third and fourth require further discussion.

The constituent parts of a party—its local clienteles—enjoyed all the cohesion and tenacity given by face-to-face contacts, ties of family, and mutual economic interests. They gained a certain permanence from the relatively stable power developed by local patrons after the early fluid years of the Revolution. But such sanctions proved effective only for relatively small regional groupings. The average person seems to have given his primary loyalty to his immediate patron and offered support to the acknowledged head of a political alliance only because or so long as his immediate patron did. In turn, any favors rendered by that head were mediated through the hierarchy of patrons. Loyalty to party as a central organization was undoubtedly weak, among large numbers probably nonexistent.[86]

The higher up the party pyramid a patron got and the broader the national base of that pyramid, the more regionally diverse his clients became, the more tenuous the ties of sentiment uniting them to each other and to him, and the greater his own inability to use whatever wealth and local power he commanded to control clients who at that level possessed as much as or more than he. His chance to maintain his leadership would depend largely on the possession of high public office (and the power of patronage which went with it) or close association with an influential foreign power (and the power of protection it afforded). The instability of internal politics rendered tenure too short and uncertain for a leader to fully exploit public office in behalf of his clients. For the short time that he remained in office, the poverty of state resources rendered him unable to grant all the favors demanded of him by his clients. Close association with a foreign power could benefit only a select few at the top because foreign powers by and large stayed out of local politics.

As a result, there was a tendency for local clienteles to fall back on their own resources, to support their distant patrons at the national level when they could get something from them and to withhold support when dissatisfied, even more to make their peace with any regime, of whatever complexion, so as to serve their primary function of protecting their clients from exploitation. So, on the national level, where the cohesive power of sentiment was weakest, interest (the chief operative factor) was least satisfied and, when it was, satisfaction was channelized through local patrons whose command of personal allegiance rested on the solid props of both interest and sentiment.

If one would understand the behavior of the parties in the royal pe-

[86] For instance, Constantine Zographos, a contemporary Greek political figure of note, makes this observation in a letter to Mavrokordatos, dated 19 Feb./3 Mar. 1839, no. 5579, Vol. 20 (1837-40), Mavrokordatos Archive, General State Archives, Athens.

riod, one must conceptualize their internal structure as a relatively loose affiliation of factions, dominated at the top by a party leader and a foreign resident, mushrooming at the base into a multitude of local clienteles. The unity of each party was always being threatened by the centrifugal forces of sectionalism, class antagonism, and personal rivalry. One must view the total party situation as one in which a number of relatively independent factions (such as that of Mavromichales and Kountouriotes) or semi-independent factions loosely affiliated to a party (such as that of Makrygiannes) moved between the orbits of the three parties or looked for a supreme patron (like the king) so as to advance themselves to the position of a fourth party.

5. The Condition of the New Kingdom

International Settlement

The international position and internal polity of the already independent Greek state received final legal articulation in the treaty of 7 May 1832. This document was the culmination of a long series of changing protocols by which Britain, France, and Russia sought to end the Greek Revolution and reestablish peace and stability in the Near East. These powers, acting as trustees of the Greek nation, had offered the Crown to Otho, seventeen-year-old second son of Ludwig I, the ardently philhellenic king of Bavaria who had actively supported the Greek Revolution.[87] Ludwig had accepted in behalf of his minor son. But the appointment of Otho and the conditions of his acceptance, in order to have a firm and lasting juridical basis in the international sphere, required a formal treaty between internationally recognized sovereign states. As a result, Bavaria, rather than Ludwig as head of a ruling house or Otho as recipient of the Crown, became the fourth party to the treaty and the only other one besides the three powers. The Greek state, still without general international recognition as a constituted sovereign entity and without a government enjoying undisputed recognition in Greece, had no part in the signing of the treaty or in the negotiations leading up to it. The absence of the Greek state as a party to the treaty needs empha-

[87] For a full-length biography of Ludwig, which gives considerable attention to his philhellenism and his relationship to Greek affairs after his son became king of Greece, see Egon Caesar Corti, *Ludwig I. von Bayern, Ein Ringen um Freiheit, Schönheit und Liebe* (Munich, 1937), trans. into English Evelyn B. Graham Stamper (London, 1938). See also Johann Sepp, *Ludwig Augustus, König von Bayern und das Zeitalter der Wiedergeburt der Künste* (Schaffhausen, 1869, Regensburg, 1903); Karl T. Heigel, *Ludwig I. König von Bayern* (Leipzig, 1872, 2nd edn., 1888); Otto Riedl, *Ludwig Augustus, König von Bayern* (Herder, 1888); and Z. L. Papantoniou, *Othon kai he Romantike Dynasteia* [*Otho and the Romantic Dynasty*] (Athens, 1934), which deals with him as well as Otho. For a brief biography, see *Allgemeine Deutsche Biographie*, 56 vols. (Leipzig, 1875-1912).

sis because it meant that neither Otho nor a duly constituted Greek representative body, as spokesmen for the Greek state, had thereafter any internationally recognized legal basis for altering or rejecting provisions of the treaty. And it should be added that the treaty itself contained no provision for its ratification by Otho or any other duly authorized spokesman for the Greek state.

The provisions of the treaty may be summarized in four chief categories. First, the document designated Prince Otho of Bavaria as hereditary monarch with the title of king (Arts. 1-3). It established the rule of hereditary succession by primogeniture, placing Otho's younger brother and heirs next in line for the throne so long as Otho should remain childless, and making his youngest brother and heirs eligible if the younger brother should also be without progeny (Art. 8). Second, the treaty authorized Ludwig to appoint a three-man regency to exercise the royal authority until Otho attained his majority, set at his twentieth birthday on 1 June 1835 (Arts. 9-10). Third, it provided for the recruitment of as many as 3,500 to take the place of the existing French army in Greece and sanctioned the employment of some Bavarian officers to assist in the organization of a Greek army (Arts. 14-15). Last, it placed the Greek independent monarchical state under the guarantee of the three powers (Art. 4) and promised a three-power guarantee of foreign loans whose total maximum was set at 60,000,000 francs (Art. 12).[88]

These major provisions, which the text described as terms under which Ludwig accepted the throne on behalf of his son, were obviously intended to provide the new Greek state with the security necessary for advancement, and Otho with the necessities for establishing a solid hold in a land with neither strong monarchical sentiment nor personal loyalty to Otho—money, an army, and the "guarantee of the powers." But the very provisions which secured these assets implicitly established a Bavarian protectorate over Greece as well as the suzerainty of the three powers. As Nicholas Kaltchas, an eminent authority on the constitutional history of Greece, asserted,[89] by virtue of the treaty of 7 May 1832 Greece became "a Bavarian protectorate under the suzerain control implicit in the ambiguous 'guarantee' of the three powers." To state the obvious first, not one iota of the treaty, which placed limitations on the state's sovereign right to determine its own polity, could be changed either by the king or a future representative assembly without the consent of the four powers which were the sole signatories. And presumably they had the right to nullify any domestic law which *they* interpreted as out of

[88] For the text of the treaty, see Tryphon Evangelides, *Historia tou Othonos Basileos tes Hellados 1832-1862* [*History of Otho King of Greece*] (Athens, 1893), pp. 7-13; for a resumé of its essentials, see Driault and Lhéritier, *Histoire*, II, 85-86.
[89] Dakin, *Philhellenes*, p. 202, and Kaltchas, *Constitutional History*, p. 92.

harmony with the treaty provisions. But Kaltchas' assertion needs further elaboration in order to understand the later Greek outburst against what they called "Bavarianism" and the machinery by which the three powers exercised their tutelage and interference continuously.

What conditions made possible a Bavarian protectorate? The rule of Bavarian regents for two and a half years, the establishment of a Bavarian army 3,500 strong, as well as Bavarian army officers to supervise the organization of a Greek army. Up till 1835, at any rate, the ultimate source of authority would be Ludwig, who, since he had been given the power to appoint the regents, had by implication the power to instruct and dismiss them. Even after the regency, Bavarian influence would remain considerable through Ludwig's hold on his son and the continuance of many Bavarians in Greek service.

"Guarantee of the three powers" was simply mentioned in passing and was not defined. For the powers, the ambiguity of the phrase possessed the dual advantage of sounding like benevolent protection rather than selfish meddling and of placing no maximum limit on their right to interfere. Article 12, which provided for three-power guarantee of the loan, did however provide permanent opportunities for three-power intervention, either unilaterally or collectively, in Greek internal affairs. The opportunities consisted of two types: one in connection with securing the rest of the loan, the other with respect to satisfying the financial obligations of the loan.

The loan, which the three courts were to guarantee up to 60,000,000 francs, was to be contracted in three installments (series) of 20,000,000 francs each. For the present only the first installment would receive a guarantee. The treaty made no definite promise regarding the second and third installments. It simply stated that they would be contracted "according to the needs of the Greek state, with the previous understanding of the three powers and the king of Greece." Since guarantee of the remainder of the loan was not automatic, each power could and did (separately) make its guarantee conditional on royal adoption of recommendations which amounted to the demand for a privileged position both for its minister in Athens and for the Greek party which it patronized.

The treaty required the Greek state to set aside annually the first receipts of the Greek treasury for payment of interest and amortization charges on the loan. Income could be used for no other purpose until the obligations of the loan had been met for that year. By charging the ministers of the three powers in Athens with the task of overseeing the execution of this provision, the treaty opened the road to all manner of interference in Greek fiscal matters. Indeed, the continuous indigence of the state left the king dependent on loans to meet the debt charges. Since the powers largely controlled the availability of new loans, they could cut them off, which was equivalent to forcing the state to default in its international fiscal obligations, and then use any form of coercion to enforce Article 12 *and* realize their own political objectives.[90]

Two important issues of the period from 1833 to 1844—constitutionalism and the succession question—stemmed from what the treaty left unsaid. The treaty failed to specify that: (1) Otho ought to rule under a constitution; (2) Otho ought to espouse the eastern Orthodox faith or at least a non-Orthodox person ought to be barred from the succession; and (3) Otho's election ought to be formally ratified by some legally constituted organ of the Greek nation.[91] These omissions, on points over which the king and the bulk of articulate Greek opinion differed, precipitated the salient political issues of the future: the constitutionalist issue, the question of the succession (once it looked as if Otho would be childless and his brothers would refuse conversion), and the fundamental problem of where sovereignty was ultimately located—in the king or in the nation. Differing shades of opinion on these issues were to characterize the parties in the 1830s.

The Legacy of Civil War

W. Alison Phillips epitomized the last civil war of the Greek Revolution as follows:

> The year 1832 had been the most miserable of all the war; the Greeks had suffered more from the cruelty and rapine of their own countrymen than in all the Ottoman invasions, more even than they had endured at the hands of the armies of Ibrahim; and now, at the end of the year, the country was utterly exhausted. . . .[92]

These adversities, which all Greeks suffered, left a lasting impression and set the tone for the work of the new administration. For convenience, the consequences of 1832 may be considered as administrative, economic, and political.

Administratively, the year 1832 witnessed the complete breakdown of central authority. Paralyzed by its coalition makeup, the mixed commission had virtually no authority outside Nauplion, and even there its authority depended on the protection of foreign bayonets. The activities of the cabinet (ministerial heads) had no administrative meaning, only a symbolic one of bearing shadowy witness to the feeble existence of a Greek state. By December, for instance, Zographos, minister of war, confessed to Mavrokordatos, minister of finance, his total ignorance of the number of men under arms. Indicative of the confusion in national affairs, the national assembly of Pronoia had abolished the senate only to suffer

[90] Finlay, "On the condition and prospects of Greece," pp. 7-8, Miscellaneous (MSS.), on finance as a means of political interference, Finlay Papers.

[91] These were the points on which Kapodistrias had insisted in connection with the candidacy of Leopold. See W. Alison Phillips, *The War of Greek Independence 1821 to 1833* (New York, 1897), p. 337, and Kaltchas, *Constitutional History*, pp. 85-87.

[92] Phillips, *War*, p. 394.

dissolution by the frustrated soldiery. In October, the national courts closed their doors, an act which dramatically indicated naked force as the sole means of survival.[93]

The irregulars, whose discipline always degenerated with the government's inability to pay for their upkeep, responded to state bankruptcy by leaving their officers and plundering mercilessly in bands. The plundered, in an attempt to stay alive, only swelled the ranks of the plunderers as irregulars. To quote Maurer, "Each [political] party seized arms and found open protection and support from the navy of its protecting power." Kolokotrones, the new leader of the Kapodistrian party, had to assume direction of tax-collection in the areas under his control in order to support and consequently hold together an army.[94]

So thoroughly had central government broken down, however, that the communes, reduced to virtual impotence by Kapodistrias' centralizing tendencies, now assumed new life as they were forced, for survival, to curb fratricidal strife within their midst and to mobilize the peasants into local defense battalions. Government had become minimal and local because this was the only type of government possible. The elaborate administrative edifice erected by Kapodistrias crumbled into ruin—a fact which by itself indicates the overwhelming extent of the chaos. The year's administrative legacy to the regency was a task both easier and more difficult: easier by giving the regency virtual carte blanche in its operations (only scrap to clear away), more difficult by challenging the unifying efforts of the regency with the resurgence of localism and the renewed strength of the indigenous ruling classes whom localism favored.[95]

It is hard to separate the devastation wrought by 1832 from the total devastation produced by the whole Revolution. The deserted towns and devastated villages, the attrition of livestock, the destruction of vineyards, the burning of olive trees it would take years to replace, even the absence of seed for planting and men for plowing (so many peasants having resorted to arms)—who can tell what part of this wartime destruction was attributable to the civil war of 1832? The best one can do is cite such imprecise statements as this one by Maurer: "Plundered fields and villages transformed into heaps of ruins are to this moment [1835] the eloquent testimony of the achievements of those days." Suffice it to say that 1832 compounded the already overwhelming task of economic reconstruction facing any new regime and wiped out the gains made by Kapodistrias.[96]

[93] Driault and Lhéritier, *Histoire*, II, 94ff.; Finlay, *History*, VII, 96-97; Maurer, *Griechische Volk*, I, 448-50; and Mendelssohn Bartholdy, *Geschichte Griechenlands*, II, 419.

[94] Finlay, *History*, VII, 98, and Maurer, *Griechische Volk*, I, 450-51.

[95] Concerning the resurgence of the Kapodistrians and localism in the Peloponnesos, see Finlay, *History*, VII, 91-92.

[96] Maurer, *Griechische Volk*, I, 450-51, and II, 21-22.

The immediate problem was a social one—namely, the hungry and disorderly soldiery and its swelling ranks. But a more basic problem was the financial one. By destroying such capital or productive agricultural goods as trees and orchards, mills and tools, even manpower, national income suffered a contraction which would take years to overcome. In an attempt to obtain funds, the government had alienated public land at only a fraction of its worth, thus reducing state income permanently. Until the new regime could reestablish an administration able to collect customs duties and agricultural taxes, even the reduced sources of state income would not meet their full potential. It seems probable that the state was inheriting responsibilities which even the most frugal government could not support from its own sources of wealth alone. In the light of the state's international financial obligations and the possibility of foreign interference in the event of their nonfulfillment, this economic picture assumed frightening proportions.[97]

The political consequences of 1832 were varied and even worked at cross purposes. On the one hand, as the repeated newspaper pleas for unity and an end to past animosities indicate, bitterness, resentment, vengefulness over past injuries and insults were not easy to efface. These emotions nourished factionalism. The atmosphere of tension and suspicion which they produced made it impossible for men of different camps really to work together or even to respect a permanent truce. Candidates for office in a new administration had by their party activities become so controversial that their availability stirred up the fears of their enemies and the ambitions of their friends.[98]

On the whole, however, the political consequences of 1832 gave cause for hope. For one thing, the public had come to identify the terrible chaos and disorder of 1832 with the existence of parties. One might comfortably say that a legacy of 1832—indeed of the Revolutionary period in general —was an almost universal antipathy toward all parties, which was no less real even if people violated their own moral sentiments by indulging in partisan behavior.[99] Second, the inferno of 1832 left little doubt, even among convinced Greek republicans, that only foreign monarchy stood between the Greeks and national self-annihilation through fratricidal strife. Even the Conference of London participated in this belief when it met in an atmosphere of emergency in February 1832 to select a king, once and for all. As Finlay rightly pointed out, "The people welcomed

[97] The treasury was found, on Augustine's departure, to contain a sum equivalent to £4 15s. 7d. and bills amounting to nearly £17,000 (Woodhouse, *Greek War*, p. 149).

[98] For instance, *Sōtēr*, 29 July 1834o.s. ("only harmony constitutes power"); or *Triptolemos*, 29 July 1833o.s. ("don't animosities still exist in the hearts of some . . . ?" "unfortunately there still exist division and disharmony. . . .")

[99] *Triptolemos*, 29 July 1833o.s.; *Sōtēr*, 25 Oct. 1834o.s.; and *Ethnikē*, 1/13 Oct. 1834.

the king as their savior from anarchy" even if the imminence of the royal arrival set the parties frantically jockeying for the best position.[100] Third, so sobered had serious political figures become by the conviction that Greece, through her own internal strife, had come dangerously close to dissolution, that they now were willing to suffer much irregularity in administration, too much rather than too little government, even absolutism, rather than resort again to violence or revolt against the established government. In short, they became satisfied with something far short of their ideals and expectations because they had painfully learned that the remedy could be far worse than the disease.

The internal political situation produced by 1832 seemed on the whole auspicious for the new royal government. The king came with a tremendous reservoir of goodwill, the public disdain for parties provided ready moral backing for the regency's projected campaign against all parties, and the politicians had been intimidated into subservience by the memory of past chaos. Yet in ten years the parties showed irresistible tenacity. In spite of all factors against them, they managed to survive. The king, in spite of all his initial advantages at the beginning of 1833, barely managed to retain his throne in 1843. It is this book's primary purpose to describe this process of party survival and royal enervation and to account, as much as possible, for how it happened.

[100] Driault and Lhéritier, *Histoire*, II, 82; Finlay, *History*, VII, 106; and Rangabe [*Memoirs*], I, 298.

Part Two

The Royal Period of Absolutism, 1833-43

CHAPTER FOUR

The First Regency,
February 1833–July 1834

TRAVELING as guests on board the English frigate *Madagascar*, the seventeen-year-old Otho, his three regents, and the royal entourage arrived at Nauplion harbor on 30 January 1833. This seaport and garrison town, hastily transformed into the national capital by Kapodistrias, offered none of the amenities to which the king was accustomed, but it was endowed with plenty of sunshine and easy access to most parts of the kingdom. The royal disembarkation and entry into the city was fixed for 6 February, the allowance of a full week for preparations indicating the importance of this event both as a "festival of national regeneration," as Finlay put it, and as a dazzling demonstration of monarchical splendor and power. When the day finally arrived, throngs of people had assembled from all parts of Greece to participate in the festivities and satisfy their curiosity.

The festivities started early in the morning with twenty-one rounds of cannon fire. Bavarian troops at attention smartly lined the shore. In the harbor, the naval squadrons of the three protecting powers fired salutes as the king descended from the *Madagascar*. Kountouriotes, as president of the now defunct governing commission, greeted the king in a brief speech, and then the king mounted his horse to start the jubilant procession. At the entrance of the city the demogerons greeted him but it was the French commandant, not they, who conferred the keys of the city on him. The procession then turned toward the church of St. George, the site of Kapodistrias' assassination, and this time the archbishop of Corinth spoke in behalf of the clergy. After a *Te Deum*, punctuated throughout by 101 shots from both the citadels above the town and the squadrons in the harbor, the king received the oath of fidelity from the public officials, then proceeded to the "palace" where he appeared on the balcony symbolically between the French Colonel Courbet and the Bavarian Colonel Stöffel. On the forts even more symbolically waved the flags of the protecting powers as well as those of Bavaria and Greece. Then the king delivered his proclamation, a short composition full of references to past anarchy, vibrant with royal determination to make the Crown the guarantor of public order and personal security, imploring in its call for brotherly love and obedience to the Crown, mildly threatening in its pronouncement of severity against disturbers of the peace.

The whole scene was as telling as it was vivid. The jubilation demonstrated the vast gulf between belief and reality, and explains the intensity of later disillusionment when reality closed in on the people. Independence and a return to peace posed the gigantic task of reconstruction and development under an untried king, an even greater challenge than that of national liberation. The national struggle had simply taken a new and more difficult form. Yet, on that day, there was no mistaking the feelings of the crowds—the national struggle was now over and the Crown would end past miseries. Nothing in their behavior suggested an awareness of the hints of reality contained in the scene. The presence of the allied squadrons in the harbor and the waving of their flags on the forts indicated the foreign tutelage which had replaced Turkish sovereignty. The Bavarian troops suggested how the regency meant to impose order, if order did not come voluntarily. Even the youthfulness of the king boded ill in the face of difficulties which would have taxed the powers of a more experienced man. Yet, on that sunny day, with cannon firing and brass bands playing, all seemed rosy, and what, in retrospect, looked like omens of a gray future, then appeared as happy signs—the allied squadrons to protect little Greece in an international world of giants, the Bavarian troops to add lustre to the throne and to offer internal protection, veiled regency threats to serve as deterrents to disorder, and a teenager whose youth would permit him to grow into a real Greek.[1]

A reality that the ceremonies of that day did not indicate was that the real power for the next two and a half years would be in the hands of the three regents. In written regulations of 23 July 1832 issued before the regents had been actually appointed, Ludwig had spelled out the internal organization of the regency. It was to arrive at all its decisions by majority vote and to signify its previous collaboration on all matters by affixing all three signatures to its documents. One of the three regents was to serve as president, apparently only as first among equals. To preside over regency deliberations, to hold the state seal, to represent the regency in its dealings with the representatives of foreign courts, even to make oral agreements with them subject to the approval of his colleagues—these were the special rights of the regency president.[2]

[1] For accounts of the royal arrival and all that it meant, see the following sources: George Finlay, *A History of Greece from its Conquest by the Romans to the Present Time, B.C. 146 to A.D. 1864*, ed. H. F. Tozer (Oxford, 1877), vii, 107-109; John Makrygiannes, *Apomnemoneumata* [*Memoirs*], ed. John Vlachogiannes, 2nd edn. (Athens, 1947), ii, 57-58; Alexander R. Rangabe, *Apomnemoneumata* [*Memoirs*] (Athens, 1894), i, 356; Edouard Driault and Michel Lhéritier, *Histoire Diplomatique de la Grèce de 1821 à nos Jours* (Paris, 1925), ii, 99-101; and Karl Mendelssohn Bartholdy, *Geschichte Griechenlands von der Eroberung Konstantinopels durch die Türken im Jahre 1453 bis auf unsere Tage* (Leipzig, 1870-74), ii, 426f.

[2] For some directly quoted provisions of the written regulations, see George Ludwig von Maurer, *Das griechische Volk in öffentlicher, kirchlicher und privatrechtlicher Beziehung vor und nach dem Freiheitskampfe* (Heidelberg, 1835) ii, 89-91, and Mendelssohn Bartholdy, *Geschichte Griechenlands*, ii, 434-35. More general accounts of the relatively equal status of the three regents appear in Driault and Lhéritier, *Histoire*, ii, 119, and Finlay, *History*, vii, 110.

By a decree of 5 October 1832, Ludwig had formally appointed the three regents—Count Joseph von Armansperg, president, Professor Ludwig von Maurer, and Major-general Karl Wilhelm von Heideck. Karl von Abel, a councilor in the Bavarian Foreign Office, was named secretary and alternate regent, while Johann Baptist Greiner, a Bavarian bureaucrat, became a type of liaison-officer between regency and ministries. In Munich, the three regents decided to include Abel and Greiner at their meetings, each with an advisory vote, and to parcel out the labor among the five of them. Maurer was to concentrate on judicial, ecclesiastical, and educational affairs, Heideck on military and naval matters, Abel on internal administration and foreign affairs, and Greiner on economic affairs. Armansperg was to act as general overseer and master of ceremonies. Only after Greiner left Greece prematurely did Armansperg take over economic matters. Each regent was to collect the necessary information in his field and draw up legislation for presentation to the regency as a whole.[3]

However disappointing they proved themselves in Greece, the appointees were unquestionably men of political reputation and prominence who had filled important posts in Bavaria. Armansperg had headed the so-called constitutional party in Bavaria and had lost his portfolio of economic affairs in the Bavarian cabinet as a result of Ludwig's disapproval of the July revolution in France (1830). His reputation for liberalism had made him the candidate of England and France, when the question of regency appointments came up, whereas Count Wrède, head of the absolutist party in Bavaria, had been the choice of Russia. Ludwig had felt many doubts about Armansperg on personal grounds and had tried to bind him by specific conditions of subordination to Ludwig on Greek affairs. Armansperg had argued that the regency, by its very nature endowed with the exercise of royal sovereignty in an independent state, had to be completely independent of all foreign interference, including that of Bavaria. Supported by Maurer on this point, he had departed for Greece free of the specific commitments that Ludwig had hoped to obtain. Even if ambitious, unscrupulous, and scheming, Armansperg seemed like a good choice for Greece, not merely because of his reputation for liberalism, but because of his experience in economic affairs as well as his political tact and charming manners. Besides, Ludwig probably thought, his colleagues would serve to hold him in check.[4]

[3] Driault and Lhéritier, *Histoire*, II, 96; Maurer, *Griechische Volk*, II, 91-93; Mendelssohn Bartholdy, *Geschichte Griechenlands*, II, 431-32; and Finlay, *History*, VII, 110.

[4] On the character and reputation of Armansperg, see Leonard Bower and Gordon Bolitho, *Otho I, King of Greece, A Biography* (London, 1939), pp. 30, 45; Driault and Lhéritier, *Histoire*, II, 95-96; Finlay, *History*, VII, 110, 112-13; Maurer, *Griechische Volk*, II, 49-55; Mendelssohn Bartholdy, *Geschichte Griechenlands*, II, 432-33; and Rangabe [*Memoirs*], I, 383. The only book on Armansperg is J. M. von Söltl, *Ludwig I. König von Bayern und Graf von Armansperg* (Nördlingen, 1886). Essentially a compilation of selected correspondence in a sketchy narrative framework, it is not a

Maurer, trained in Paris and Heidelberg, was one of Bavaria's outstanding jurists, a distinguished professor of law and former minister of justice in Bavaria. Although pedantic, irritable, niggardly, and overbearing, he brought industriousness, diligence, and integrity to his tasks. Unlike Armansperg, he was a man of principle. Heideck had a way of letting painting and shellfish collecting—his passionate hobbies—get in the way of his duties, but he enjoyed a qualification lacked by his colleagues—long first-hand familiarity with Greek affairs. A Bavarian philhellene sent by Ludwig at the end of 1826 to serve as an observer of events, he had fought diligently with the Greeks against the Turks and had later shown such ability and integrity in building up the administration of the army and customs system as to win the praise of Greeks. But familiarity with Greece also led to entanglement in party politics, a drawback of which his colleagues were originally, but not for long, free. By the time of his appointment as regent, Heideck was irretrievably identified with the Napists. Indeed, the Russian government had urged Ludwig to appoint him regent. Abel, like Maurer, was able and hard-working as well as rude and aloof. His practical experience, his familiarity with the actual everyday routine of administration, and his meticulousness promised much needed skills for the organization of the state. But like men of his type, his performance suffered from the narrowness of a bureaucratic orientation.[5]

---

full-length study of the man. There exists, however, an unpublished dissertation (not consulted) by R. von Armansperg, "Joseph Ludwig Graf v. Armansperg" (Munich, 1949).

On the powers' positions concerning regency appointments, see Mortier, French minister in Bavaria, to Sebastiani, French foreign minister, Munich, 26 May 1832, in *Gesandschaftsberichte aus München 1814-1848*, Abteilung I: *Die Berichte der französischen Gesandten*, ed. Anton Chroust, Vol. III (Munich, 1936), 35.

On Ludwig's suspicion of Armansperg and the conflict over the terms of Armansperg's appointment, see for instance Sercey, French minister in Bavaria, to Argout, French foreign minister, Munich, 14 Sept. 1832, *Gesandschaftsberichte*, ed. Chroust, Abt. I, Vol. III, 82-83; and Friedrich Engel-Janosi, "Austria and the Beginnings of the Kingdom of Greece," *Journal of Central European Affairs*, I (1941), 30. See also "Armansperg," in *Allgemeine Deutsche Biographie*, 56 vols. (Leipzig, 1875-1912).

[5] On the other two regents and Abel, see George Finlay, Journal (MSS) entry for 28 [May] 1833, Finlay Papers, The British School of Archeology, Athens; Finlay, *History*, VII, 111-13, 135; Bower and Bolitho, *Otho I*, pp. 30, 46; Mendelssohn Bartholdy, *Geschichte Griechenlands*, II, 433-34; and Rangabe [*Memoirs*], I, 383-84. For a full biography of Maurer and his role as legist in the context of nineteenth-century German legal study, especially for his part in definitively laying the foundations of the Greek legal system (pp. 50-82), see Karl Dickopf, *George Ludwig von Maurer 1790-1872* (Kallmunz, 1960). There is also an unpublished dissertation (not consulted) by Heinz Gollwitzer, "Karl v. Abel und seine Politik 1837-1847" (Munich, 1944), dealing with Abel's later political career in Munich as head of the Bavarian government. The copy deposited in the University of Munich Library was destroyed during World War II. See also Maurer, "Heideck," and "Abel," in *Allgemeine Deutsche Biographie*.

The collegiate character of the regency, though apparently intended to prevent any one man from acquiring too much power, opened the road to factionalism at the very place where unity was essential in order to end the internecine strife of the Greeks. Paradoxically, those features of the regency which built into its structure mutual checks and versatility— the mutual familiarity of the men, their divergent personalities and talents, their conflicting ambitions—all those things contributed to its division into two camps which inevitably meshed with the rivalry of the powers and the conflict of the parties.[6]

Within the regency itself, Maurer and Heideck soon found themselves in conflict with Armansperg. With the added weight, knowledge, and work of Abel, they managed to prevail against Armansperg in the day-to-day work of government and came to be known as the "regency majority."[7] Armansperg may have intrigued more successfully, but he did not govern until (through his skill at intrigue) he succeeded in securing the recall of Maurer and Abel at the end of July 1834. This marked the end of the first regency. Ägid von Kobell, the pliable successor of Maurer in the second regency, always went along with the wishes of Armansperg, while Heideck withdrew into the background. In the second regency, therefore, Armansperg was the real ruler and policy-maker. This chapter will deal with the period of the first regency (February 1833–July 1834). Chapter V will cover the period of the second regency (August 1834–May 1835) as a part of Armansperg's more extended rule from August 1834 to January 1837.

For both the regency and the king the undesirability of the parties was axiomatic.[8] Official approach toward the party system was twofold: (1) the long-term approach, involving nothing less than the removal of the conditions on which parties thrived through the creation of efficient and beneficent institutions; and (2) the short-term approach of undermining, curbing, and neutralizing party activities, chiefly through a careful and calculated system of appointments together with an obdurate stance against the slightest indication of resistance. The first approach attacked the causes of party existence and depended on institution-building. The second approach sought to treat the symptoms and involved everyday political decisions. Each of these approaches will receive separate attention in the first two sections of this chapter. In the third and final section,

[6] On the basis of the regency quarrels, which started from Munich, see *The Portfolio; or a Collection of State Papers and other Documents and Correspondence, Historical, Diplomatic, and Commercial, Illustrative of the History of our Times,* 1st ser. (London, 1836-37), III, 464-68; Finlay, Journal (MSS), 4 Aug. 1834, and History, VII, 112-13; Maurer, *Griechische Volk,* II, 49-62; and Mendelssohn Bartholdy, *Geschichte Griechenlands,* II, 434.

[7] For instance, Driault and Lhéritier, *Histoire,* II, 121.

[8] Maurer, *Griechische Volk,* II, 8-9, 19-21; and report of Prokesch-Osten, Austrian Minister to Greece, to his government, 5 May 1835, quoted by Mendelssohn Bartholdy, *Geschichte Griechenlands,* II, 507.

an analysis of political developments over the year and a half of the first regency's tenure will show the extent to which the regency got sucked into the vortex of party politics.

1. STATECRAFT

It is not my intention in this section either to give a full description of the institutional structure of the state or to attribute the character of those institutions entirely to considerations of factionalism. Other factors operated in the plans of the regency as well—the precedent of the past, the anticipation of a greater Greece for which, it was felt, these institutions had to be adaptable, and the adoption of Western models as those ensuring the greatest progress. Yet it is my view that many regency acts, together with the resultant governmental system, were inspired by the objective of nullifying party activities. This hypothesis is made all the more plausible by the fact that Thiersch, who was influential in advising Ludwig on royal policy, had recognized that the system of clienteles, on which the party situation rested, grew out of conditions in which the central government was weak and unable to provide security and chances of advancement.[9] In short, a study of statecraft requires consideration of the party situation and the problems which it posed.

Absolutism

In their attempts to forestall any Greek attempts to promulgate a constitution before the arrival of Otho, both the protecting powers and Bavaria gave the Greeks cause to expect that the king would convoke an assembly to draw up a constitution acceptable to both Crown and nation. The proclamation of the London Conference (26 April 1832), announcing the election of Otho, called on the Greeks to assist the king "in the task of giving the state a definitive constitution." Even more, Gise, Bavarian foreign minister, in a letter of 31 July 1832 to Trikoupes, Greek foreign secretary, pledged that the regency would convoke a general assembly to receive the monarch and collaborate with it in the preparation of the definitive form of government.[10] On its arrival, however, the regency ignored the constitutional issue, at least in public. The royal proclamation made no mention of it, indeed implied a nonpopular source of royal power by the phrase "Otho, by the grace of God, King of Greece." Pri-

[9] See the long Thiersch quotation in Chap. II, p. 54 above.

[10] The important passages of the London proclamation are quoted in several places: Driault and Lhéritier, *Histoire*, II, 85, from the Archives of the Greek Foreign Ministry, Athens; Finlay, *History*, VII, 116, from Parliamentary Papers, Annex D to Protocol of 26 Apr. 1832; and Demetrios A. Petrakakos, *Koinobouleutike Historia tes Hellados* [*Parliamentary History of Greece*] (Athens, 1935), I, 457. The letter of Gise to Sp. Trikoupes, Munich, 31 July 1832, is printed in *Recueil des traités, actes et pièces concernants la fondation de la royauté en Grèce et le tracé de ses limites* (Nauplie, 1833), p. 62, and is quoted by Finlay, *op.cit.*, p. 115, n. 2.

vately, in response to demands of the existing Greek government that the pledge of Gise be fulfilled, the regency alleged the existence of instructions from Ludwig against any action in favor of a constitution. Without coming out categorically against constitutionalism, Ludwig had argued, in his instructions to the regency, that the granting of a constitution was a royal prerogative that no one but the king could exercise when he came of age. The regents were bound by an oath, before their departure for Greece, to preserve the rights of the king and to alienate none of these.[11]

Ludwig's opposition to a constitution was undoubtedly based on personal conviction. Pressure from the Russian court for a royal power "in its full plenitude" fed his personal convictions. But circumstances in Greece undoubtedly influenced his position. At the Conference of London, at the meeting of 26 April 1832, his envoy stated that Otho would govern "by the laws," but that:

> . . . in the state in which the nation finds itself, it is desirable that the government be strong and monarchical, and that it be reserved to the prince to satisfy the national wish through the forms which experience will demonstrate the most favorable to the development of its prosperity.[12]

Baron Gise, in conversation with the French ambassador in Munich shortly after, expressed fear that a Greek constitution drawn up before the arrival and concurrence of the Crown would probably be so democratic that the sovereign could not maintain his authority and would probably be "ein Parteiwerk." So long as Otho remained a minor, the royal policy toward a constitution was controlled by Ludwig.

None the less, Maurer at least, and most probably the rest of the

---

[11] For the Greek text of the proclamation dated 25 Jan. 1833o.s., see Tryphon E. Evangelides, *Historia tou Othonos Basileos tes Hellados (1832-1862)* [*History of Otho King of Greece*] (Athens, 1893), pp. 38-41. Maurer, in his unpublished memoirs, quotes from Ludwig's instructions of 23 July 1832 to the regency and describes the acute embarrassment suffered by the regency when it discovered the contradiction between Ludwig's instructions to them against permitting a constitution and his promise to the Greeks through Gise. The pertinent passage from these unpublished memoirs was published by K. T. von Heigel, "Denkwürdigkeiten des bayerischen Staatsrats Georg L. v. Maurer," Sitzungsberichten . . . der Kgl. Bayer. Akademie der Wissenschaften (Munich, 1903), IV, 482f, as quoted by Petrakakos [*Parliamentary History*], I, 455-56.

[12] On Russian pressure, see for instance "Instruction to Catacazy, Jan. 1833, enclosed in Nesselrode to Gagarin, St. Petersburg," in Barbara Jelavich, *Russia and Greece during the Regency of King Otho 1832-1835* (Thessaloniki, 1962), p. 57. On Ludwig's and Gise's statements, see Archives of the British Foreign Office, Public Record Office, London, Ser. 97, Vol. 234 (hereafter cited as FO 97.234 and so on), as quoted by Driault and Lhéritier, *Histoire*, II, 84, who serve as the source of other information in this paragraph (II, 81, 84); also Mortier, French minister in Bavaria to Casimir-Perier, French foreign minister, Munich, 9 Mar. 1832, in *Gesandschaftsberichte*, ed. Chroust, Abt. I, Vol. III, 31-32.

regents, agreed with Ludwig. In his published account of the first regency period, Maurer asserts his belief that conditions were not ripe:

> The chaos which then prevailed, from the material and spiritual point of view, had reached such large proportions that no calm and objective observer could expect anything good from the convocation of the national assembly.[13]

Under such conditions, he continued, the regency could expect no help, only hindrances, from an assembly in its primary objective to organize a state able to ensure stability. Public peace, an efficient administrative system, and "order among the native leaders" were his estimated prerequisites for the constitutional enterprise. To the objection that the regency, like Kapodistrias, could have called an assembly for the sole purpose of ratifying the king's authority, Maurer replied that the king as monarch needed no such authorization, implying thereby that the nation did not constitute the source of sovereignty.

In the available sources, at any rate, no one ever elaborated a defense of absolutism, but by inference a justification, indeed a motivation, for absolutism emerges—a justification based squarely on the party situation in Greece. Early in the Revolution it became apparent that only a foreign monarch would be sufficiently free from party prejudice to fulfill his function of impartiality and justice in the treatment of his subjects. As Maurer asserted:

> The threatening position of the parties made necessary the presence of one foreign mediating factor. . . . The parties were then in such lively opposition to each other that the members of the regency often heard Greeks . . . asking to be given, preferably, a foreigner as leader, rather than to have to submit to their irreconcilable foes.[14]

The most effective means of breaking down the parties was to make inroads into the system of clientage, whether that of the foreign ambassadors or that of influential Greeks. In order to do so, one had to abolish the social and economic necessity for attaching oneself to an important patron. A system of complete fairness was needed in the distribution of local justice, in the allotment and collection of taxes, in the determination of past services and personal merits for government appointments, and in the sale of government land to the landless. Complete fairness, in itself already impossible to attain, was made less likely by the fact that most Greeks were too tied up by party allegiances to allow the government a sufficient number of impartial administrators.

---

[13] Maurer, *Griechische Volk*, II, 71. The source for the remaining statements of this paragraph is the same (II, 71-74).

[14] *Ibid.*, II, 9-10.

Hence, absolutism was considered indispensable to preclude any party from exploiting public authority for partisan purposes.[15]

The treaty of 7 May 1832 bestowed upon the regency the full exercise of the sovereign rights of the king. Since Ludwig kept these rights free from the limitations of any public body in Greece, the regency's power was unrestricted. In actual practice, of course, its freedom of action was circumscribed by the will of Ludwig, whose right of appointment by treaty implied a similar right of dismissal which he actually exercised in July 1834. But the regency nevertheless constituted the institutional expression of royal absolutism until the king's majority.[16] The division of power among the regents and alternates, already described above, suggests the regency's self-assigned role as a type of supercabinet enjoying the powers and initiative of cabinets in constitutional states.

The ministerial council or cabinet, consisting of the heads of the seven existing ministries, was an established institution which the Crown inherited in 1833. Its powers received elaboration in a royal decree of 15 March 1833. Although a president was to be appointed by the Crown from one of the seven, his position in no sense made him prime minister or head of the government, the decree explicitly stating the equal rank of all ministers. All state matters, legislation, and tax laws and budgets were to be presented to the council for discussion. Decisions were to be registered and communicated to the king, but there was nothing in the decree to indicate that their decisions were to be binding on the king or regency. The decree in no way defined the cabinet as a check on the royal power or as the seat of popular sovereignty.[17] Maurer betrayed the regency's attitude toward the cabinet's function when he wrote, "The regency possessed the highest state authority, but for the exercise [of such authority] it needed organs." The chief organ was the cabinet, a mere executive body.[18] To be sure, the Revolutionary cabinets had been little more, but they had been executive organs of higher bodies ultimately responsible to the popular will. Although the regency might have mitigated royal absolutism by enlarging the powers of the cabinet and giving it greater autonomy, it did not.

[15] Ibid., II, 10-11.

[16] Finlay, History, VII, 110. See also p. 145 above.

[17] Decree of 3/15 Mar. 1833 concerning the formation of secretaryships, Ephemeris tes Kyberneseos tou Basileiou tes Hellados [Government Gazette, Kingdom of Greece], no. 13, 10/22 Apr. 1833.

[18] Maurer, Griechische Volk, II, 97-98; Gennaios Kolokotrones, Apomnemoneumata (Cheirographon Deuteron 1821-1862) [Memoirs (Second Manuscript 1821-1862)], ed. Emmanuel Protopsaltes (Athens, 1961), p. 74 (hereafter cited as [Memoirs II]). See also George K. Aspreas, Politike Historia tes Neoteras Hellados 1821-1921 [Political History of Modern Greece], 2nd edn. (Athens, 1924), I, 129-30, who saw the connection between the reduction of the ministers "to mere civil servants" and the aim to assuage partisan strife.

161

Bavarianism

Bavarianism—the policy of employing Bavarian nationals in the Greek state service—was justified by the regency on the grounds that the Greeks needed Western administrative and technical assistance to create a state. This was so, if you conceived of a state in Western terms, as did the regency. In the fashion of the nineteenth century, it believed that being civilized was being European. It interpreted the Greek Revolution as an attempt to adopt European forms and customs—which in fact it was for a small but important segment of the Greek people. Since European ways were desirable and desired, Europeans were obviously the best, indeed the only, suitable teachers. Maurer wrote:

> Only foreigners can teach civilization in its fullness. . . . Just as the Greeks in the fourteenth and fifteenth centuries brought Greek wisdom to the rest of Europe, so now Europeans, especially the Germans, must return the light to its homeland from which it has long since vanished.[19]

But why the Germans or Bavarians especially? Maurer never answered this question, although he suggested an answer in another connection. He justified the regency's preference for Swedish, rather than Russian or British or French, technical naval assistance on the grounds that help from one of the protecting powers would only excite the jealousy of the others and interfere with the impartiality and independence which Greece wanted to maintain. The same justification would of course hold for Bavaria, too small a power to have its influence in Greece provoke serious jealously among the major states of Europe.[20]

There was another reason for the desirability of foreigners, particularly Bavarians—the same reason which justified absolutism. The Greeks were, on the whole, too partisan not to exploit political power for partisan ends. Absolutism meant keeping any significant power from them. But it also concentrated tremendous power in the hands of one man who could not possibly bear the full burden. The question then became: To whom could this one man delegate power with least risk of disobedience to himself or of favoritism to a particular party? By this criterion, foreigners took priority over Greeks. Of the foreigners, the Bavarians best filled the bill because of presumed loyalty to, or actual fear of, Ludwig, who remained their sovereign. Besides Bavarians, a number of Frenchmen were employed in the Greek administration, probably because France was considered less selfish in her concern for Greece than either Russia or England, who were considered the real rivals in Greece.[21] Because they

[19] Maurer, *Griechische Volk,* ii, 39-40.
[20] *Ibid.,* ii, 278.
[21] On the employment of Frenchmen in the Greek administration, see Maurer's account of Regny's appointment (*Griechische Volk,* ii, 307-308) in conjunction with his remarks about the disinterestedness of French policy in Greece (i, 40-41). On

were less likely to have the strong party connections bred by local roots, and so were more dependent on the Crown, heterochthons were considered preferable to autochthons among the Greeks. In short, we must view Bavarianism in its twofold aspect: as part of the regency's attempt to Westernize, and as part of its drive to curb partisan strife and the influence of the three protecting powers.[22]

The two centers of Bavarianism were the army and the court (royal household, regency, and clerical staff). In the army, the Bavarians overwhelmingly outnumbered the Greeks. By the end of 1834, some 5,000 Bavarian volunteers had come to Greece while only a handful of Greeks had joined the regular army.[23] But Bavarian control rested on more than mere numerical superiority. In the first place, a regiment was to consist of three Greek and three Bavarian companies. Such mingling, according to Maurer, was intended for the edification of the Greeks, but it also meant that the Bavarian companies could serve as watchdogs over the Greek ones if need be. More important still, the Bavarians held most of the key positions in the army. Lesuire became minister of war, Christian Schmaltz inspector general of the army, Fuchs director general of forts and arsenals, Zech director of the engineer corps, and Lüders director of artillery. Thomas Gordon, the British philhellene, was appointed head of the general staff, and Francis Graillard, the French philhellene, chief of the gendarmerie. Such appointments, however, were not inconsistent with the regency's policy of withholding such important posts from Greeks.[24]

---

some few of the Frenchmen still employed by the Greek government in 1843, see also Piscatory to Guizot, Athens, 19 Sept. 1843, published in the monograph by John Ch. Poulos ["The Revolution of 3 September 1843 on the Basis of the French Archives"] *Deltion tes Historikes kai Ethnologikes Hetaireias tes Hellados* [*Bulletin of the Historical and Ethnological Society of Greece*], xi (1956), 259.

[22] The assertions in the above paragraph I have derived mostly by inference from the sources rather than by direct statement of primary or secondary sources. For instance, the disqualification of most influential Greeks for positions of importance because of partisan behavior and party loyalties is asserted outrightly by F. Thiersch, *De l'État actuel de la Grèce* (Leipzig, 1833), I, 236-64, esp. 243: "There are many men so compromised that their reappearance in important affairs would be inconvenient and would even prejudice the respect which the royal government ought to inspire." See what amounts to the same thing, in inarticulate and less generous terms, by Finlay (*History*, vii, 146), who, however much he disliked Bavarian rule, contended for its superiority over that of the Greeks because "Kolokotrones, Mavrocordatos, Konduriottes, and Kolettes had all proved themselves more *unprincipled*" [italics mine to indicate the key word which is Finlay's moralistic interpretation of traditional party behavior]. What virtually no source ventures to say, perhaps dares not say, was that Bavarians first, then heterochthon Greeks, were more dependable in their loyalty to the Crown and their neutrality to all sides than the Greeks; instead, sources stated the necessity of Bavarian and heterochthon employment in terms of technical qualifications. An exception is *Ethnikē*, the semiofficial newspaper (9/21 May 1835), which justifies the continued use of foreigners in terms of the partisan taint of most qualified Greeks.

[23] Finlay, *History*, vii, 116.

[24] Maurer, *Griechische Volk*, ii, 125, 244-50, 266.

On the surface, the civil service was relatively free of Bavarians. As ministerial councilors, positions just below that of cabinet minister, only two Bavarians were appointed: Dr. Wibmer, court physician, as medical councilor of the ministry of the interior, and Dr. Gustav Geib in the ministry of justice, though on his forswearing Bavarian citizenship. The architect Schaubert was commissioned to plan the capital of Athens. Weissenburg, a distinguished architect, became director of antiquities, while Ludwig Ross was appointed one of the three curators (for the Peloponnesos), both attached by their positions to the ministry of education and religious affairs. Owing to the absolutist system and the impotence of the cabinet as an independent body however, actual appointment of Bavarians to office was unnecessary. The regency itself was a type of supercabinet with a large staff of its own, some to serve as interpreters (Herold, Heymann, and Franz), others to draw up legislation (such as Berg on the stamp tax and Zwierlein on the customs system).[25]

In these two aspects of Bavarianism, one can discern the twofold purpose of the regency. To utilize Western skills was the primary aim in such cases as the introduction of engineers and technicians, even perhaps in the employment of Bavarian army officers. Indeed, of the 5,000 Bavarian recruits, more than 1,000 were mechanics or skilled workmen engaged in road-building, gardening and husbandry, the establishment of brick factories, and the construction of public and private buildings. The importation of such individuals is perfectly understandable in terms of the Westernization process because such skills were generally unknown to Greek laborers.[26]

But in other respects the Westernization motive was secondary. The concentration of key army posts in Bavarian hands was clearly inspired by a desire to control the army completely. Of the more than twenty forts and arsenals in Greece, the regency assigned Greeks to command all but the seven which it considered strategically crucial for military control of the country.[27] More revealing was the disparity between the regency's reorganization of the army and navy. In the navy, all the top commands were placed in Greek hands. Technical help from Sweden was arranged, but on a much smaller scale than the comparable military help from

---

[25] *Ibid.*, II, 16, 197 (Herold, Heumann, and Franz); 69, 322 (Geib); 123 (Schaubert); 223-24 (Weissenburg and Ross); 294 (Zwierlein); 301 (Berg). See also Nicholas Dragoumes, *Historikai Anamneseis* [*Historical Reminiscences*] 2nd edn. (Athens, 1879), I, 341-42: "Like Kapodistrias believing us inexperienced, the regency drew up in German most of the documents, which were then translated in the bureau consisting of three Germans—the well-known Hellenist Franz, Heymann, and Herold, who knew very little of our language."

[26] Maurer, *Griechische Volk*, II, 243-49.

[27] *Ibid.*, II, 271-72.

Bavaria and with no foreign recruitment for the ranks.[28] What made the difference? Certainly the navy needed Western discipline and equipment as well as the army, but the navy had never played the same role in national politics as had the army, and it could not seriously challenge the authority of the Crown without some help of land forces.

Military Reorganization

The continued existence of Revolutionary armies constituted one of the regency's thorniest problems. Since 1829 all fighting against the Turks had ceased, yet the soldiers had not laid down their arms. Indeed the parties, by their indiscriminate awarding of officer rank, had made new recruits during the fratricidal strife of 1832.[29] At the time of the arrival of the regency, some 5,000 irregulars and 700 regulars remained at arms, unpaid by the government and quartered in the countryside at the expense of the peasants. The bulk of these were from Rumely where they had either been born into the coveted military life or had "risen" into it during the Revolution. Most of them, if not all, considered civilian life—which in Greece meant following the plow—ignoble. Return home they might, as had the Peloponnesians, though not actually to cultivate the land. A large number of the veterans could not return home, however, because home had not been incorporated within the borders of the new kingdom. Such Cretans, Souliots, Thessalians, Epirots, Macedonians, and Albanians were landless and homeless. In view of their distaste for civilian life and their landlessness, these veterans needed and expected some assistance from the government—employment, pensioning, or distribution of land.[30]

By 1832, when Ludwig was negotiating for the Greek throne with the powers, the faults of the palikar system were glaringly obvious against the backdrop of renewed and ever worsening civil strife attendant on Kapodistrias' assassination. Heideck, now back in Bavaria, remembered the frequent tumult and peculation which he had witnessed in Greece, and Friedrich Thiersch, the learned Bavarian professor, tutor of Otho, and philhellene, had been commissioned by Ludwig to survey the Greek situation and was now caught in the middle.[31] Warned by the experience

---

[28] *Ibid.*, II, 274-81. Even in this area, however, the regency took the step of inviting Duplat of Hanover, a German, to become director of the naval workers and naval artillery (II, 277).

[29] *Ibid.*, I, 505-506, and II, 81.

[30] *Ibid.*, II, 28-29, and Mendelssohn Bartholdy, *Geschichte Griechenlands*, II, 447.

[31] Under the system of fighting and politics in insurgent Greece, palikars gave their prime loyalty to their captains, not to the state. In turn the captains, invariably enroled in some politician's clientele, supported party first, then central government. During the Revolution, chieftains directly or party leaders with the support of irregular forces had defied state authority. Successive Revolutionary governments had lacked the military strength to punish such defiance or protect the people against the

of both men and with the sympathetic understanding of the powers, Ludwig wanted the royal government militarily strong, strong enough to withstand the demands or to punish the abuses of any party. For absolute loyalty, non-Greek troops, free from rival local and party allegiances, were considered a better bet than the Greeks. For iron discipline and central control, the Western military system seemed unquestionably superior to the loose, autonomous guerrilla organization of the Greeks. As a temporary device, Ludwig negotiated with the powers for the recruitment of 3,500 men in the German states, and concluded with the Greek government a treaty (1 November 1832)[32] regulating the terms of service and payment of these men. Maurer explains the purpose of these foreign forces in the following terms:

> The foreign forces were not intended to be used—as partisan people today contend—for the oppression of the Greek nationality, the support of a foreign rule, or the establishment of despotic power, etc. . . . The very threatening position of the parties had rendered necessary the presence of a mediating foreign factor.[33]

While still in Munich the regency decided to disband the irregulars. As Maurer well realized, such an act was bound ultimately to constitute an attack on the parties. It would deprive them of their military backing and hence weaken their bargaining position vis-à-vis the royal government. It could therefore be expected to arouse strong opposition. The regency was determined to assert its authority by the use of force if necessary. To provide such force, Ludwig loaned Bavarian troops to the regency until the German recruits had been assembled. Thiersch had recommended such severity in the event of refractoriness. So aware was the regency of the wider implications of the projected dissolution that it regarded the measure as absolutely essential and as the first crucial test of its effective authority.[34]

---

frequent lawlessness and arbitrariness of the troops. Further, see p. 74 above. As an example of Bavarian awareness of this situation and of hindrance to the establishment of an effective central authority, see Ludwig Ross, *Erinnerungen und Mitteilungen aus Griechenland* (Berlin, 1863), pp. 62-63. Concerning Heideck's adverse opinion of the Greek irregulars, see Finlay, *History*, VII, 116; concerning Thiersch's, see Thiersch, *État actuel*, I, 251, which speaks of the absolute necessity of purging the country of the irregular system in order to maintain political stability and domestic order.

[32] The text of this treaty between Bavaria and Greece on recruitment appears in both Greek and German in [*Government Gazette*], no. 20, 29 May/10 June 1833. See also Maurer, *Griechische Volk*, II, 12, and Mendelssohn Bartholdy, *Geschichte Griechenlands*, II, 451.

[33] Maurer, *Griechische Volk*, II, 9.

[34] Concerning the regency's decision to disband the irregulars, see Finlay, *History*, VII, 118. In his awareness of the connection between the irregular system and the party system, Maurer was not wholly consistent. Sometimes he considered the ir-

By the time the regency arrived in Greece, it seems to have assumed that force would be necessary and a showdown inevitable. Certainly the palikar attack on French troops at Argos just before the king's arrival made such an assumption plausible. That the event made a deep impression on the regents and was interpreted as a party maneuver is evidenced by a later statement of Maurer:

> It seems that the secret purpose of many party heads was—as many affirm—to establish themselves firmly in Argos, and then, with arms in hand, to impose terms on the arriving king and regency.[35]

When it came time to implement their decision, the regency took every precaution against impending resistance. As recommended by Thiersch, the chief fortresses of the state were taken over by Bavarian troops.[36]

The initial decrees of the regency were three: (1) dissolution of the meagre remnants of the Greek regular army, and a wholesale reorganization of the regular army, to consist of infantry, cavalry, artillery, and engineers, and to be trained in the weapons, tactics, and discipline of a western army; (2) the disbanding of the remaining irregular troops; and (3) the creation of ten battalions of skirmishers, a body designed to absorb some 2,000 former irregulars, intended to make some allowances for the palikar aversion to Western dress, weapons, and tactics, but regulated by the same general canons of discipline and centralized control as the regular army.[37]

Even ostensibly the regency intended the body of skirmishers only as a modest and temporary concession. Since its size was set at some 2,000 (Art. 2), it would absorb only two-fifths of the existing veterans. Because no veteran younger than thirty and no new recruit would be accepted, the body could last only for a generation. There is even reason to believe that the regency preferred to have fewer skirmishers than the statutory maximum or none at all. After all, this body could not possibly differ markedly enough in discipline and centralized control to offer much improvement over the traditional system of irregulars. The regents set the

---

regulars disunited, divided by their support of different political parties (*Griechische Volk*, I, 450, and II, 81); sometimes he believed them a separate military "party" united against other parties (II, 9). On Thiersch's recommendations for the use of force if necessary, see Thiersch, *État actuel*, I, 242; and on the regency's sense of urgency about these measures, see Maurer, *op.cit.*, II, 86.

[35] *Ibid.*, II, 20.

[36] *Ibid.*, II, 84-85.

[37] Text of the decree for the organization, 25 Feb./9 Mar. 1833, appears in [*Government Gazette*], no. 5, 8/20 Mar. 1833; commentary on it and its implementation appears in Maurer, *Griechische Volk*, II, 85-86, 243-57, and T. N. Pipineles, *He Monarchia en Helladi 1833-1843* [*The Monarchy in Greece*] (Athens, 1932), p. 35. Decree for the dissolution of the irregular forces, 2/14 Mar. 1833 [*GG*], no. 6, 8/20 Mar. 1833; Maurer, *op.cit.*, II, 81-82, and Pipineles, *op.cit.*, p. 31. Decree for the formation of battalions of skirmishers, 2/14 Mar. 1833 [*GG*], no. 6, 8/20 Mar. 1833; Maurer, *op.cit.*, II, 83-84, and Pipineles, *op.cit.*, p. 32.

pay surprisingly low (Art. 5), prescribed as the standard weapon the scorned bayonet (Art. 4), and imposed the same general canons of military discipline as those applying to the regulars (Art. 7). In any case, three-fifths of the existing irregulars would have to become civilians or members of the regular army. Those who were refugees were promised a suitable portion of national land, though when and how was not specified (Art. 4). Those chieftains who volunteered as skirmishers and were turned away (because of full quota) would have their military record reviewed by a special committee to determine what type of reward they merited. In the meantime the law ordered the irregulars to register themselves at once at appointed places, and then to go home or to a recruiting office (Arts. 7-9). Failure to do so would invite punishment or exile.[38]

The bulk of palikars was encamped outside Argos when the military decrees appeared. By law each individual should have registered himself within forty-eight hours, then taken to the road within another twenty-four. Whether because of inadequate administrative machinery or from willful refusal to disperse, the Argos camp seems to have been still intact when a delegation of 300, representing it, appeared before the fortress of Nauplion. The petitioners came unarmed and ostensibly merely to ask a little bread, although their appearance testified dramatically to their wretchedness. The garrison commander invited them to return to Argos after he had promised them some help, and cautioned them against any further demonstrations of this sort. The government sent flour for distribution. Two weeks after the first appearance, a second delegation arrived before Nauplion, probably not as submissive this time. According to Maurer, these palikars shouted threats after announcing their determination not to submit to the announced measures. "Then," said Maurer, "we decided it [the regency] must intervene energetically." The form of such energetic intervention was the appearance of infantry and artillery contingents, the outcome the dispersal of the demonstrators.[39]

It is a moot point whether a show of force against the palikars was really necessary to bring compliance or whether the regency merely interpreted these demonstrations according to its preconceived expectations

[38] See Mendelssohn Bartholdy, *Geschichte Griechenlands*, II, 448, on some of the reasons why many of the provisions were unacceptable to the irregulars; also Makrygiannes [*Memoirs*], II, 66, on the low pay (12 groschen per month), "barely enough for one man to live on," not enough to support a family.

[39] Makrygiannes [*Memoirs*], II, 64-66; Maurer, *Griechische Volk*, II, 84-85; and Mendelssohn Bartholdy, *Geschichte Griechenlands*, II, 448-49. In the account of Maurer, the sequence of events is the same as that of Mendelssohn Bartholdy, but there are some discrepancies on the amount of time intervening between events. Maurer's account tends to telescope the set of events. He also presents the demonstrations as more strident, inspired by attempts to intimidate the government rather than as manifestations of despair. Typically and perhaps correctly, Makrygiannes, himself an irregular captain, suspects the politicians of instigating and exploiting these demonstrations for their own purposes, hence using the military men as their dupes.

of resistance. In any case, the regency had apparently taken due precautions against any possible response among all palikars to the news of forced dispersal. It had assigned Bavarian auxiliary contingents to key spots throughout the kingdom and had instructed provincial authorities to call on the nearest contingent for help if anyone refused to comply with the decrees. Such precautionary measures, according to Maurer, prevented the palikars throughout the kingdom from translating their indignation at the Nauplion incident into violent opposition. Reluctantly they began to disband.[40]

Where did they go? Only some thirty-five enlisted for the skirmisher battalions. Needless to say, they would not consider the regular army where Western dress, discipline, and Bavarian command were completely anathema to them. An undetermined number, sizeable enough to make an impression, crossed the northern frontier into Turkish territory where they either took service with Taphil Bouzé of Domokos, a Turkish captain of some importance, or took up the wild life of brigandage in the mountains separating Greece from the Ottoman domains. The rest, unemployed and without honor from the government, went home or moved in with relatives.[41]

In the meantime, the public was aroused as it confronted daily evidence of the contrast between the relative prosperity of foreign recruits and the penury of its Revolutionary heroes. According to Gennaios Kolokotrones, a Bavarian captain received the salary of a Greek colonel. Even the alarming outbreak of brigandage was excused as the inevitable consequence of dissolution. As a result, the regency won only a partial victory. It had eliminated large concentrations of potential armed opposition, but at the cost of spreading dissatisfaction, which entered the hamlets along with the returning palikars. By refusing to join the new military forces or to do anything more than merely reside on the land, the veterans nullified the regency's plan of giving the palikar problem a permanent solution. Indeed, the unsettled state of the northern frontier obliged the regents to concentrate nearly all the Bavarian troops there and to leave garrison towns elsewhere largely unprotected.[42]

[40] Maurer, *Griechische Volk,* ii, 85.

[41] Makrygiannes [*Memoirs*], ii, 66; Maurer, *Griechische Volk,* ii, 339; Mendelssohn Bartholdy, *Geschichte Griechenlands,* ii, 450-51; and Pipineles [*Monarchy*], p. 34.

[42] Gennaios Kolokotrones [*Memoirs II*], p. 47. A number of important consequences of the regency majority's military settlement are reported in the correspondence of Dawkins, British minister to Greece, for his government (FO 32.37 and 32.38 passim). From Nauplion, Dawkins suggested to Palmerston, British foreign minister, a connection between palikar unemployment and brigandage in the province of Livadia (27 Sept. 1833, no. 57, FO 32.37), reported the concentration of Bavarian troops on the northern frontier (31 May 1833, no. 30, FO 32.37). Even in the newly organized army, Greek officers complained bitterly of preferential treatment toward the Bavarians (22 Dec. 1833, no. 78, FO 32.38). Dawkins' translation of a regency report to the foreign powers on the "major" and "minor" plots (to be discussed later in this chap-

The regency had acted swiftly and severely in order to accomplish its unpopular acts. From then on, it pursued a policy intended to allay widespread discontent and to absorb the unemployed into useful occupations. This policy was initiated on the king's birthday (1 June 1833), an occasion intended then and thereafter to identify the Crown with clemency and statesmanship. One measure amnestied those palikars who had crossed the frontier and hence failed to comply with the regulations for disbandment. Although intended as an act of grace, the law offered the pardoned the meagre choice of remaining unemployed or joining the regular army. The prospect of a corps of skirmishers had been quickly abandoned by the regency.[43]

A second measure proved more felicitous, both in providing a substantial number of dissatisfied palikars with gainful and honorable employment, and in creating an institution which was to become one of the props of the dynasty and monarchy. The gendarmerie (*chorophylake*)—a supplementary branch of the regular army created ultimately for the maintenance of civic order throughout the kingdom, but more immediately to garrison towns for which there were insufficient Bavarian troops—offered some 1,200 posts. To be sure, dress and weapons were to be Western, but the pay was much better and the uniforms much flashier than in the regular army. With a few exceptions, the officers were appointed from among the distinguished irregular captains. None the less, so strong was the intractability of the palikar groups that enlistments proceeded very slowly at first, and even after a full year had elapsed the enrolment had reached only 800, or two-thirds of the intended size. Even so, these 800 consisted almost exclusively of palikars.[44]

On the same occasion of the king's birthday a year later, two further decrees revealed the continuing urgency of the problem. The first provided that all veterans be awarded commemorative medals which conferred, besides honor of possession, such privileges as precedence of place in official ceremonies of the deme, the restored right to carry weapons without special permission (an easing up of a previous ban), and exemp-

---

ter) betrays regency awareness of the widespread discontent excited by the dissolution of the irregulars (28 Nov. 1833, no. 74, FO 32.38). See also Makrygiannes [*Memoirs*], II, 66, on the brigand behavior of the irregulars who crossed the border, and Mendelssohn Bartholdy, *Geschichte Griechenlands*, II, 451: "The regency . . . managed to transform loyal subjects into brigands. . . ."

[43] Decree concerning the amnesty of returning irregulars . . . , 20 May/1 June 1833 [*Government Gazette*], no. 19, 20 May/1 June 1833; also Maurer, *Griechische Volk*, II, 258-59.

[44] Decree concerning the organization of the gendarmerie, 20 May/1 June 1833 [*Government Gazette*], no. 21, 3/15 June 1833. Dawkins to Palmerston, Nauplion, 31 May 1833, no. 30, and 22 Dec. 1833, no. 78, FO 32.37. Makrygiannes ([*Memoirs*], II, 67) is a good example of a captain who refused to serve under Graillard or give up his palikar clothing, even if the salary was good. Maurer, *Griechische Volk*, II, 264-69; Mendelssohn Bartholdy, *Geschichte Griechenlands*, II, 452; and Pipineles [*Monarchy*], p. 32.

tion from the obligation of performing any physical labor on public projects. Intended to satisfy the self-esteem of the palikars and to appeal to their vanity, it did nothing to solve their economic plight. The second measure addressed itself to this issue and proferred the solution of land cultivation by offering plots of state land as gifts, but it applied only to the indigent and provided for careful and humiliating tests of indigence. In neither case did the decrees go into practice because Maurer and Abel received their summons to Bavaria shortly after. Even if the decrees had been implemented, however, they were insufficient to cope with the greater problem.[45]

Many Greeks and foreigners who did not suffer personally from the first regency's military policy condemned it. So convincing did the criticism become by constant repetition that later historians accepted the condemnation unquestionably. Mendelssohn Bartholdy's history was the most systematic and emphatic in its criticism of these measures. To create a Westernized regular army, he maintained, was expensive and unnecessary—expensive because a regular army required the employment of so many Bavarians and philhellenes (as irregulars refused to serve in it), and unnecessary because the mountainous warfare so characteristic of Greece rendered it militarily ineffective. The disbanding of the irregulars deprived the state of those troops trained in mountain warfare, invited palikar jealousy of the well-paid Bavarians, and precipitated a serious social problem by creating a mass of unemployed, poverty-stricken men.[46]

Mendelssohn Bartholdy and subsequent Greek historians are right in asserting that the regency did not meet the problem adequately and only aggravated the situation. But they fail to offer any satisfactory explanation for the regency's behavior, right or wrong, good or bad. They leave the distinct impression that the regency ignored the advice of its Greek advisors and acted merely from a doctrinaire belief that the Greek military system had to be Westernized at all costs. These assumptions are untenable if scrutinized in the context of the party situation. Many Greeks recognized the disruptive behavior of the irregular forces and advised

[45] Decree for the distribution of medals . . . , 20 May/1 June 1834 [*Government Gazette*], no. 20, 3/15 June 1834; Maurer, *Griechische Volk*, II, 261. Decree concerning officers, subofficers, soldiers and sailors not in active service, 20 May/1 June 1834 [*GG*], no. 22, 16/28 June 1834; Maurer, *op.cit.*, II, 261-64.

[46] Mendelssohn Bartholdy bases his own evaluation of the situation on extensive quotation from two primary sources: (1) *Begebenheiten in Griechenland seit 1833*, written by an unidentified Bavarian critic (*Geschichte Griechenlands*, II, 449-51), and (2) Report of Prokesch-Osten, Austrian minister to Greece, 4 Feb. 1835, Austrian Archives (*op.cit.*, II, 453). Among later historians, see Evangelides ([*History*], pp. 45-46) who characterizes the reorganization of the military establishment and its implementation with such phrases as "the immense fault," "such a barbarous and unjust manner," and "inappropriate decrees." Indeed, almost word for word, he follows Mendelssohn Bartholdy's account, only leaving out the latter's saving qualifications.

their disbandment. Some Greek political figures often had only the lowest opinion of the irregulars and readily conveyed their feelings to the regency. Often one military clique would defame another to gain preferential treatment from the regency and hence gave the regency good cause to entertain the cumulative impression that the military groups were a dangerous and anarchical element.[47]

As the preceding account attempts to demonstrate, the problem of the irregulars was political as well as social, military, and cultural, and the regency was keenly aware of its political aspects. It believed a regular organization preferable to an irregular one in large part because the former was more susceptible to its control. In its eyes, Bavarians and disbanded regulars—consisting of philhellenes from all parts of Europe and Anatolian (heterochthon) Greeks "with absolutely no influence"— were more dependable than irregulars precisely because they owed everything to the Crown, nothing to the local patron. It is no exaggeration to say that, in dissolving the irregulars, the regency was attempting to deprive the parties of their military strength.[48]

Administration Centralization

During the Revolutionary period three levels of provincial administration had been established. Following this precedent, the regency divided the kingdom into ten provinces or *nomarchies*, which in turn were subdivided into counties or *eparchies*, some forty-seven in all. The local unit was the *deme*. The chief official was the *nomarch, eparch,* and *demarch* (mayor) respectively, each with a council elected by the people of the administrative unit. This scheme was intended to represent a compromise

[47] The Greeks who complained about the irregulars and even approved their disbandment belonged to different social groups, among them some Westernizers, those whom the German author of *Begebenheiten* somewhat unfairly calls "the superficially educated office-seekers" who rested quietly in Europe while the irregulars fought (quoted by Mendelssohn Bartholdy, *Geschichte Griechenlands*, II, 449-50) as well as oppressed peasants, who sometimes petitioned the government for protection against the irregulars (Makrygiannes [*Memoirs*], II, 63). The act of dissolving the irregulars was one of the few regency acts of which Finlay approved (*History*, VII, 116-19); he regarded them as "measures which were necessary in order to put an end to anarchy" (also Journal [MSS], 28 [May] 1833); this point of view is also expressed by the Bavarian Christian A. Brandis, *Mittheilungen über Griechenland* (Leipzig, 1843), III, 263-65. *Triptolemos* (13 Sept. 1833o.s.), a pro-regency majority newspaper to be sure, contains a letter to the editor expressing satisfaction with the military reorganization and its Westernizing forms and criticizing the disbanded irregulars for not joining the regular army. On civilian antipathy toward the military captains as a class or those supporting an opposing political party, see Makrygiannes, *op.cit.*, II, 60, 64, 71.

[48] Maurer as much as says so when he explains, in terms of Greek domestic politics, the *raison d'être* of the French expedition to Greece of 1828-33 (*Griechische Volk*, II, 8-12). And, as Makrygiannes points out ([*Memoirs*], II, 64), each political party had its military arm in a part of the irregular troops.

between the principle of centralization, which had reached its fullest elaboration under Kapodistrias, and that of local autonomy, which had served the Greeks so well under Turkish rule. In actuality, it established a highly centralized system. The nomarchs and eparchs, by statute nothing more than executive organs of the capital, were appointed by the Crown and subject to dismissal or transfer at any time. Since the regency took no steps to bring the nomarchal or eparchal councils into being and refrained as a matter of policy from appointing a native as head of any given district, local opinion could find virtually no expression through nomarchal or eparchal government.[49]

On the local level, the regency was sincere about establishing demarchal councils, and provided for some popular control over the choice of mayor, yet without nullifying the principle of centralization. Members of the demarchal council were directly elected but not by all the citizens, not even by all those paying direct taxes. Presumably the incumbent mayor and his council designated a certain proportion of the taxpaying electors for each election. Once elected, the council, together with an equal number of electors, selected three persons as candidates for mayor. Of the three nominees, the Crown chose and appointed one in the large demes, the minister of the interior made the selection in each of the smaller demes. In brief, selection of the mayor was by an intricate process of limited suffrage, indirect election, and central appointment. He was a native of the deme, represented local interest, and served a three-year term. But the jurisdiction of the mayor and council was carefully circumscribed by statute, and all were subject to suspension or dismissal from office by the Crown without benefit of judicial decision.[50]

Checks and balances were another feature of the royal provincial system. The regency divided administrative authority into a large number of limited jurisdictions, apparently so defined as to check and balance each other and thus avert an overconcentration of power or abuse. Horizontally, on the nomarchy level, seven major officials shared authority in 1834: nomarch, bishop, *ephor*, treasurer, *moirarch* of the gendarmerie,

---

[49] See the text of the decree for the division of the kingdom, 3/15 Apr. 1833 [*Government Gazette*], no. 12, 6/18 Apr. 1833, and Maurer's characterization of the system as a compromise between two extremes (*Griechische Volk*, II, 101-11). Finlay undoubtedly came closer to the truth when he cited the principle of centralization as the distinguishing feature of the regency's organization ([*History*], VII, 119); for thus "virtually abolish[ing] the old popular municipal system" he condemned the regency.

[50] Law concerning the establishment of demes, 27 Dec./8 Jan. 1834 [*Government Gazette*], no. 3, 10/22 Jan. 1834; the supplementary decree concerning the election of demotic authorities, 24 Apr./6 May 1834 [*GG*], no. 17, 16/28 May 1834; and decree concerning the instructions for demotic elections, 8/20 June 1834 [*GG*], no. 26, 25 July/6 Aug. 1834. See also P. Argyropoulos, *Demotike Dioikesis en Helladi* [*Public Administration in Greece*], 2nd edn. (Athens, 1859); Maurer, *Griechische Volk*, II, 112-19; and Finlay, *History*, VII, 120-21.

public health officer, officer of the engineer corps. Eventually the capital of each nomarchy also became the seat of a court of first instance.[51] Unlike other functions of government, military and naval affairs remained quite separate from the ordinary provincial administration and rested completely outside the competence of the nomarch (Art. 5). The decree defining his responsibilities instructed him to refrain from intervention in court affairs, but to prevent the "independence" of courts from gaining administrative mastery (Art. 4), judges could not decide the legality of administrative measures or try a nomarch in his role as public official. In principle, all other officials of the nomarchy were under the jurisdiction of the nomarch, subject to the proviso "so long as such officials are not subject by explicit decrees to the direct supervision of the ministries" (Art. 17). But the fact that each official had a superior, ministerial or otherwise, in the capital signified a real limitation on the nomarch's control. Indeed, in the case of the bishop and ephors, who usually received positive instructions from their respective ministries, the nomarch in effect served as the watchdog of the ministries to see that neither official overstepped the bounds of his authority. Entrusted with jobs which allowed, almost invited, them to keep watch over the nomarch were the director or the secretary of the nomarchy. Ostensibly intended to lighten the load of the nomarch, they were officially responsible to him, yet they were unlikely to be his mere puppets since the capital rather than he appointed them. On the local level, the chief—but by no means the only—instance of checks and balances was that between the mayor and his demotic council.[52]

Vertically, the checks and balances were just as prominent. On the local level, where a bit of local influence was permitted, the provision for intervention by the three higher levels of administration was paramount. Certain types of demotic decisions, mostly concerning the administration of demotic public property, remained null and void without ratification by the nomarch. Still others, relating to the levy of new demotic taxes, needed royal consent. All other demotic measures acquired the force of law only if they had not been vetoed within fifteen days of presentation to the eparch and nomarch. On the other hand, any such veto or change was subject to appeal by the demotic authorities to "the chief authority," presumably the Crown or ministry of interior. Lower officials in the nomarchy were instructed by decree to report their grievances to the nomarch, presumably over the head of the eparch. On the other hand, the law placed the nomarchs under the jurisdiction of four ministries (economic, ecclesiastical-educational, foreign, and internal affairs).[53]

[51] See Maurer, *Griechische Volk*, II, 147, 169-70, 269-70, 308-309, on these various offices.

[52] Decree concerning the jurisdiction of nomarchs . . . , 26 Apr./8 May 1833 [*Government Gazette*], no. 17, 4/16 May 1833. Also Maurer, *Griechische Volk*, II, 101-11.

[53] See n. 50 above.

Many like Finlay, then and subsequently, regretted the disappearance of the pre-Revolutionary system of local autonomy "which enabled the people to employ their whole strength against the Turks and . . . contained within itself the germs of improvement and reform." According to Finlay, Kapodistrias had struck a mortal blow at the traditional system because of "its close connection with the actions and wants of the people," and the regency continued his centralizing reforms for lack of imagination. But Finlay, even though he implies the contrary elsewhere in the same volume, missed the mark here.[54]

The principle of centralization had already been established during the Revolution as a counterweight to the excessive localism and vast differences in customs between provinces. It was also in keeping with the ends of absolutism—to curb public abuses against the state as well as official abuses against the public. But an additional factor is important too. Local autonomy had not often meant democracy, even in Turkish times, and though it had made the Turkish yoke lighter, it had often made heavier the yoke of the local Greek oligarchy. Kapodistrias, as Maurer well realized, centralized the provincial administration in order to crush the political power of the primates and chieftains. According to Maurer, there had always been a tendency toward arbitrariness under the old system, and this tendency had become more pronounced since the Revolution when the Greek oligarchy captured the system. In short, the new system was intended not as a blow against the people, but rather as the instrument for their liberation from local oligarchy.[55] Although this basic intention was identical with that of Kapodistrias, his system had depended less on checks and balances and concentrated more authority in provincial governors responsible directly to him, possibly because he tended to rule through his own carefully created party.

Fiscal and Tax System

The regency walked into a depressing fiscal situation. Here the chaos reached staggering proportions. The always inadequate fiscal machinery had completely broken down during the confusion of 1832. Many vital records were nonexistent, either because they had never been kept or

---

[54] Finlay, *History*, vII, 40-41, 420. Or see the criticism of Dragoumes ([*Reminiscences*], II, 4-5) who, it seems to me, was wrong in accusing the Bavarians of transplanting the Bavarian administrative system into Greece with no attempt at accommodating it to local conditions. For regency concern with and adherence to the Greek Revolutionary, though not pre-Revolutionary, tradition, see next paragraph in the text.

[55] "In Greece . . . the communal administration had quickly lost its originally simple social and political character, so firmly had it been tied to and completely absorbed by the agrarian oligarchy of the provinces and the civil oligarchy of the cities. The big landowners and the capitalists of the commercial centers, economically omnipotent in the countryside, were almost of necessity the demotic leaders as well. Appropriating as they did both economic and political power, they always tended, by the fatal connection of things, to rise up against the central monarchical authority" (T. Pipineles [*Monarchy*], p. 90). See also Maurer, *Griechische Volk*, I, 446, and II, 112-13.

because interested parties had found it expedient to destroy them. As a result, the state lacked essential information. No one knew the precise extent of public land or could do more than guess at the annual state revenue. If the lack of administrative machinery made fact-finding virtually impossible, it rendered the state helpless against the flagrant abuses of both its tax-farmers, who took all they could get, and its taxpayers, who paid only what they were forced to.[56]

On the regency's arrival, the treasury was empty, public land had been illegally sold or illegally occupied, and there were foreign debts to pay and native claims to meet. By July 1833, two-thirds of the 60,000,000 franc loan, which the powers had promised to guarantee, had been contracted. But the Greek treasury enjoyed almost none of this for its current needs. To begin with, discounts and commissions on the loan about halved its proceeds. Of what the regency did get, it had to return the 60,000 francs lent Kapodistrias by the protecting powers, indemnify the Turkish government 12,000,000 francs for the national territory not won by conquest (Euboea and parts of Attica), and redeem the short-term loans made by Ludwig and the philhellenic banking house of Eichtal to tide the regency over in its early days. Moreover, it seemed probable that an annual budget deficit would gradually absorb the remaining 20,000,000 francs due on the loan.[57]

The financial objectives of the regency were patently clear: (1) to maintain the strictest economy, (2) to provide the order and security necessary for land cultivation, revival of trade, and increased national production, (3) to obtain the remainder of the 60,000,000 franc loan, and (4) to secure the state against the dishonesty of its officials and the tax evasion of the public.[58] The party situation threatened to thwart the realization of all four objectives. With respect to the first two objectives, parties could stir up internecine strife at any time (brigandage or revolt), and the suppression of such strife cost money for troops, investigations, and court proceedings. Regarding the third objective, each party could encourage its protecting power to withhold its guarantee on the third series as a way of securing from the state concessions benefiting both party and power.[59] This feature of party activity became important later, when the government was in dire need of money. The parties' relationship to the fourth objective requires some elaboration of the traditional system of tax-farming and how it worked.

All levels of activity in this system involved organization into factions

[56] *Ibid.*, I, 535, and II, 286.

[57] On the difficulties of obtaining favorable loans and on the outstanding expenses—many the fault of the regency (Maurer said the fault of the second regency)—for which most of the money was used, see *ibid.*, II, 301-305. See also Pipineles [*Monarchy*], p. 20, and Aspreas [*Political History*], I, 154f.

[58] Maurer, *Griechische Volk*, II, 304-305. By the end of 1833, Greece had already opened negotiations with the powers for the third portion of the loan (Dawkins to Palmerston, Nauplion, 21 Dec. 1833, no. 76, FO 32.38).

[59] See, for instance, n. 4 in Conclusion below.

or parties. Who were the affluent who could afford to secure the contracts but primates or captains, individually or in combination, the very ruling classes who formed the backbone of the parties? Who were the sublessees but their dependents? Who were the overtaxed but their rivals, who had to unite in self-defense and devise methods of tax evasion? Party cooperation was most pronounced in efforts to obtain the lease at the lowest possible price. When the day of auction approached, brigandage was often organized to reduce the value of the lease on the grounds that disorder would make collection difficult for the tax-farmer. There sometimes were indications of collusion among bidders to keep the price of the leases down. When the day of payment for the lease came, the lessees, pleading poverty and insufficient collections, would ask for a reduction of the original price or petition for indefinite postponement of payment.[60] Success in the satisfaction of such requests depended, of course, on having friends in the administration. All such underhanded activities, then, presupposed the type of cooperation and collusion for which the parties were so well adapted. As a result, the regency's general attack on the parties and the ruling classes had a fiscal dimension, and conversely, its reorganization of the fiscal and tax system probably took shape with an eye toward the political situation.

What action did the regency take? In this area, perhaps because of inadequate administrative machinery, perhaps because of vigorous obstructionism on the part of those who had so much to lose by wholesale reorganization, the reform was minimal.[61] We may treat the reform in three parts: (1) the establishment of a control board, (2) the attempt to press unfulfilled state claims originating in the preroyal period, and (3) the modification of the tax-farming system.

Finance was an area in which few Greeks were skilled. Moreover, it was for obvious reasons the area in which parties would most intensively compete for control, often committing the most reckless abuses. This probably explains why the fiscal system was so tightly organized, so centrally controlled, and under such careful foreign tutelage. A board of control, performing its functions independently of all ministries, was established in October 1833 as the highest administrative watchdog. Its most important duties were to examine the financial accounts of all administrative organs, checking to see that each organ spent its allotted allowance as intended, and to guard against administrative violation of laws, decrees, and instructions. It also served as the highest administrative court for the entire fiscal administration of the kingdom, the only permissible organ of appeal against its decisions being the council of state. In brief, this institution was virtually all-pervasive and second only to the regency in power.[62]

[60] Maurer, *Griechische Volk*, I, 522-25.

[61] Maurer offered, as an additional reason, Armansperg's lethargy (*ibid.*, II, 313).

[62] Decree concerning the establishment of a board of control, 27 Sept./9 Oct. 1833 [*Government Gazette*], no. 32, 7/19 Oct. 1833; and Maurer, *Griechische Volk*, II, 305-308.

It consisted of a president, vice-president, royal commissioner, and four auditors. The system was a collegiate one, but the real control lay in the hands of the president, who, during most of the absolutist period, was a Frenchman named Artémonis Jean-François de Regny. Jean Gabriel Eynard, the staunch philhellene and Swiss banker, recommended this appointment. Although appointed in his private capacity rather than as an official representative of France, Regny was the object of persistent public criticism as a reminder of foreign influence. To facilitate the work of the control board and at the insistence of Regny, the regency established treasuries—a central one in the capital and several provincial ones to collect and dispense the public monies. They were to take their orders from the ministry of economic affairs, but were subject to the ultimate authority of the control board.[63]

The attempt to press the state's unfulfilled financial claims continued throughout the period of absolutism and even grew more intense as the threat of state bankruptcy increased. Its importance lies not in its success, which was dubious, but in the demonstration of obstructionism toward it and its stimulation of party activity. One of the regency's first acts was an investigation designed to expose all illegal sales of or unwarranted claims to public lands. Maurer explained the regency's repeated failure to obtain such information in the following terms: "The order was repeated and again nothing was done . . . because the primates and other speculators had the greatest interest that it not be done."[64]

Moreover, the government attempted, through the control board, to press the financial claims of the state against tax farmers who, during the Revolution or the civil war of 1832, had never paid for any or all of their contracts. Such a campaign, sound enough fiscally, violated the regency's own policy of letting bygones be bygones, and stimulated party activity as partners in crime worked together to exonerate themselves, to pin the blame on somebody else, or to secure the immunity provided by somebody's patronage. In 1835, while on tour of the provinces in Rumely, George Finlay discovered that much of the political unrest derived from the near panic of men whom the state was prosecuting or threatening to prosecute for tax debts originating during the Revolution. Some surviving correspondence, now located in the Palamides Archive of the Greek National Archives, shows even more specifically what was happening. Sometime in 1834, Ghikas Karakatsanes, an official of the control board and member of the "French" party, privately informed Regas Palamides and Basil Christakopoulos, his friends and party associates, that the board was planning to call them to account for failure to submit full payment

[63] Decree for the organization of treasuries, 6/18 Feb. 1834 [*Government Gazette*], no. 14, 13/25 Apr. 1834; and Maurer, *Griechische Volk*, II, 308-309.

[64] Decree of 6/18 Feb. 1833 announced by the minister of the economy on 11/23 Feb. 1833 in [*Government Gazette*], no. 3, 28 Feb./12 Mar. 1833, and Maurer's commentary on it, *Griechische Volk*, II, 286.

on a tax-farming contract for 1832. It seems apparent, from the correspondence, that Palamides was nervously trying to fabricate a story to exonerate himself and Christakopoulos, one which placed the blame for nonpayment on their political enemy Kolokotrones who, they alleged, prevented them from collecting in their tax-farms. It seems equally obvious that Karakatsanes was drawing on his own intimate knowledge of the board's intentions and procedure, in order to help them make as strong a case as possible. There is no further correspondence to indicate how the problem was resolved, but enough exists to show that a threat of government persecution could lead to two types of partisanship—the making of false accusations against political enemies and the exploitation of public office so as to protect party members.[65]

The regency continued the system of tax-farming into the royal period, attempting only to mitigate its abuses. Its decree stated that the leases be issued for smaller fiscal units (by communities rather than provinces), that the cost of the lease be paid in installments (presumably to assist the small tax-farmer without the entire capital immediately at hand), and that the annual public auction be held in as many towns and with as much publicity as possible so as to attract all aspirant tax-farmers. These provisions clearly indicated the regency's intention to eliminate the middlemen in the tax-farming procedure so as to share the middlemen's profits with the peasantry; that is, its intention to increase the price of the lease while reducing the tax burden on the peasantry. But political motives as well actuated the regency, for these provisions would tend to weaken the primate class and foster a yeoman class by giving the latter a chance to compete against the former or to obtain the small lease directly from the state rather than through the primate-protector. At the auctions eparchs and ephors, presumably men with no local connections, would be present to ensure that the proceedings were conducted fairly. Each official would act as a check on the fairness of the other. Both would assist tax-farmers to collect their due and peasants to resist excessive demands.[66] Moreover, the regency announced and at least partially car-

[65] Finlay, Journal 1835 (MSS), 20 July 1835, Finlay Papers. The correspondence in question consists of six letters, all in folder 257 (1833-39), the first dated 12 Sept. 1834*o.s.*, unnumbered, and the last 29[?] Nov. 1834, from B. Christakopoulos to Regas Palamides, from Nauplion, then Sparta, in the Palamides Archive, Vlachogiannes Collection, General State Archives, Athens. Concerning a commission to examine public accounts from 1822 until the arrival of the regency, see Dawkins to Palmerston, Nauplion, 22 Dec. 1833, no. 78, FO 32.38.

[66] The above summary of the system for collecting the tenths is based upon: (1) the decree concerning the collection of revenue for the year 1833, 15/27 Apr. [*Government Gazette*], no. 15, 19/28 Apr. 1833; (2) a similar decree for 1834, 10/22 Apr. 1834 [*GG*], no. 13, 10/22 Apr. 1834; (3) instructions of the Ministry of Economics to the general and royal ephors, 10/22 Apr., Supplement B [*GG*], no. 13, 10/22 Apr. 1834; and Maurer, *Griechische Volk*, II, 294-98. None the less, the system in favor of the middling classes was not always observed, as Finlay pointed out

ried out its intention to hire some tax officials to undertake direct collection for the government in case bids for tax farms fell below a statutory minimum. The object of this announcement was, of course, to prevent collusion among bidders at an auction.[67]

The Church Settlement: Caesaropapism

By the beginning of 1833, chaos in the church had probably gone farther than in any other institution. In many ways the Revolution had shattered the institutional strength of the church. By cutting the church in Greece off from Constantinople, the Revolution deprived it of its two traditional props (the support of Ottoman authority and the leadership of the patriarch) at the very moment that independence created a new Greek state to challenge its traditional authority. Of thirty-three archbishoprics and twenty-three bishoprics in what became Greece, ten of the former and nine of the latter were vacant in 1833. Refugee bishops and monks from all parts of the Ottoman empire, fleeing the wrath of the Turkish authorities, poured into independent Greece. Because of their desperate economic condition and their lack of employment, they wielded little authority. They thus found it difficult to refuse the offers of support from demagogues and to resist the lure of office as a tacit exchange for their docility. Their presence in Greece also undermined the independence of the autochthonous clerics, who recognized the necessity of courting favor with the secular authorities in order to avoid replacement by the refugee bishops. Separated by conflicting material interests and divergent sectional loyalties, the bishops could not speak or act as a united corporation.[68] Monasticism also suffered a severe decline because the Revolution, by its promise of adventure, its opportunities for enrichment, and the removal of traditional restraints, encouraged what seems to have been a mass exodus from the monasteries.[69] Clearly then, state action was necessary to regularize church affairs once again.

The regency majority decided to revamp the entire structure of the

---

(Journal 1835 [MSS], 21 July 1835) in citing the case of Patradjick, where the tenths were sold en masse in 1835 for 97,000 drachmas and then privately resold in the villages with a profit of 8,000 drachmas to the original tax-farmers.

[67] Ministry of the economy on hiring collectors if necessary, 10/22 Apr. 1834 [*Government Gazette*], no. 13, 10/22 Apr. 1834; and Dawkins to Palmerston, Nauplion, 22 Dec. 1833, no. 78, FO 32.38.

[68] According to Maurer, (*Griechische Volk*, II, 170), there were fifty-three "unemployed" bishops in Greece in 1833. According to the minutes of the fourth meeting of the ecclesiastical commission, dated 20 Apr. 1833o.s., published in Constantine Oikonomos, *Ta Sozomena Ekklesiastika Syngrammata* [*Collected Ecclesiastical Writings*], ed. Sophocles Oikonomos (Athens, 1864-66), II, 103, of fifty-two ecclesiastical primates only twenty-two were bishops established in Greece before the Revolution; the rest were refugees. See also Dawkins to Palmerston, Nauplion, 20 Aug. 1833, no. 49, FO 32.37.

[69] Finlay, *History*, VII, 130-31, and Thiersch, *État actuel*, II, 184.

church. Its definitive settlement consisted of three fundamental parts: (1) the establishment of an autocephalous church, (2) the creation of a caesaropapist system, and (3) the partial dissolution of the monasteries. The first two parts were embodied in the act of 4 August 1833. That act declared the church in Greece independent of the mother church in Constantinople, of which it had been a part until the outbreak of the Revolution. In effect, the regency was only formalizing a *de facto* division precipitated early in the Revolution when the patriarch of Constantinople, under duress from the Ottoman authorities, excommunicated the rebel Greeks. It limited the separation to administration and stipulated the continued doctrinal unity of the church in Greece with all Orthodox churches. But the regency's decision to act unilaterally, rather than to negotiate some sort of settlement with the patriarch, in effect served notice that Constantinople should keep its nose out of Greek ecclesiastical affairs.[70]

The second part of this settlement dealt with the issue of church-state relations and resolved it in favor of the state. The king was declared head of the church and its governance was put in the hands of a royally appointed synod of five clerics. To be sure, the charter made a distinction between the external and internal affairs of the church. Over the former, which included the demarcation of bishoprics and the supervision of monasteries, the state, through the minister of educational and ecclesiastical affairs, should have direct control. Over the latter (dogmatic-liturgical), the church, as embodied in the synod, was to enjoy full autonomy. But even in this limited area a series of provisions nullified autonomy. The king was to make synodal appointments annually, a royal commissioner (Theokletos Pharmakides until 1840) was to be present at all meetings of the synod, and synodal decisions required royal approval for validation. The synod could communicate with no one outside the kingdom—a provision directed against the tsar of Russia and the patriarch of Constantinople—and could deal with its own clergy only through the ministry of educational and ecclesiastical affairs. Constantine Oikonomos, the most vocal exponent of church rights and champion of the conservative position, was correct in his assertion that the church lay completely under the thumb of the secular power.[71]

The third part of these ecclesiastical measures came considerably later

---

[70] Proclamation concerning the independence of the Greek church, 23 July/4 Aug. 1833 [*Government Gazette*], no. 23, 1/13 Aug. 1833. The text also appears in Oikonomos [*Collected Writings*], II, 177-84. See also Maurer, *Griechische Volk*, II, 160-66.

[71] That the effect and objective of the law was not just independence from Constantinople but freedom from any internal clerical interference is cogently argued by Oikonomos [*Collected Writings*], II, 198-200, III, 55-56, 81, 201-10. This is confirmed, with a deep sense of satisfaction, by Dawkins to Palmerston (Nauplion, 20 Aug. 1833, no. 49, FO 32.37) in the following words: ". . . the authority of the King is limited to its civil administration, but . . . on the other hand the synod is so restricted as to be in fact dependent on His Majesty."

in three installments. The first decree (7 October 1833) ordered the suppression of all monasteries with not more than six monks residing in them. The second (9 March 1834) dissolved all but three nunneries, leaving only one for each major geographical section of Greece. All nuns under forty years of age were instructed to return to lay life unless they insisted upon remaining. Those above forty years were permitted to cast aside the veil if they could find some means of support, otherwise they were to proceed to one of the three remaining monasteries. A third measure (8 May 1834) forbade any further donations of property by private individuals to the church. All the confiscated monastic property—the proceeds from the sale of moveables as fixed capital and the produce of the land as annual revenue—was to support a separate treasury of ecclesiastical and educational affairs intended primarily for the support of a state educational system (teachers' salaries, renting of schools, student scholarships, financing of archeological studies) but was also intended for the material and educational improvement of the lower clergy. The surviving monasteries were expected to pay the state a double tenth on their annual income.[72]

Of a total 524 monasteries, 146 survived—83 because they fell within the legitimate category of houses with more than six monks, 63 because they lay in Mane where the government dared not touch them for fear of prolonging a revolt partly precipitated by the dissolution decrees. About 900 monks in all were dispossessed. Of the existing 16 or 18 nunneries, only 1 legally survived, the Peloponnesian and Rumeliot nunneries projected in the original decree being abandoned when the statutory quota was not filled by subscription of the existing nuns. Popular opposition, however, forced the government to leave the law in abeyance in three cases.[73]

[72] On the dissolution of the monasteries in general, see Constantine Dyovouniotes, "He kata to 1834 dialysis ton monasterion en te Eleuthera Helladi ["The 1834 Dissolution of the Monasteries in Independent Greece"], Hieros Syndesmos [Sacred Association], XII (1908). Strangely, though perhaps to avoid publicity for an unpopular measure, the major decree of dissolution, under the misleading name of decree "for the taxing and farming-out of monasteries," dated 25 Sept./7 Oct. 1833, does not appear in [Government Gazette] for 1833. The text is published in Oikonomos [Collected Writings], II, 234-35, and summarized and evaluated by Maurer, Griechische Volk, II, 181-83. For the decree concerning convents, dated 25 Feb./9 Mar. 1834, see [GG], no. 15, 23 Apr./5 May 1834, and Oikonomos, op.cit., II, 252-65, who includes in addition the text of the memorandum from the minister of ecclesiastical affairs to the synod; also Maurer, op.cit., II, 183-86. On the decree concerning private monasteries and churches, dated 26 Apr./8 May 1834, see [GG], no. 30, 22 Aug./3 Sept. 1834; Oikonomos, op.cit., II, 265-66; Maurer, op.cit., II, 186-87. On a separate ecclesiastical treasury, see ibid., II, 181; Oikonomos, op.cit., II, 268-70; and Pipineles [Monarchy], pp. 84-85.

[73] The above figures are taken from Oikonomos [Collected Writings], II, 264-65, because they seem most accurate. Finlay (History, VIII, 130-31) estimates the number of dissolved monasteries at 412 rather than Oikonomos' 378, and calculates the number of monks remaining at 2,000. Maurer (Griechische Volk, II, 178-80, 182)

As for the method of dispossession, the disposal of church property (hastily carried out by the provincial administration) became a public scandal, not merely because the sale of holy objects seemed sacrilegious to the public but also because of all the patent dishonesty of the transactions. The result was regrettable. Politically it entailed a widespread public outcry against the dissolution as a part of the entire ecclesiastical settlement and probably did more than anything else to discredit the regency majority. Financially, it meant that the annual income of the new treasury met less than half the cost of the educational establishment and offered nothing in behalf of the lower clergy.[74]

The regency's church settlement was essentially the work of Maurer, the regent responsible for ecclesiastical and educational matters as well as judicial affairs. He himself was a Protestant. Undoubtedly, his settlement was inspired by his own secular values and the example of Bavaria, where the secular power dominated both the Catholic and Protestant churches. But Dawkins, the British minister, was quite right when he wrote his government that "higher considerations of a political nature" determined this settlement. In political terms, the church settlement was merely another facet of an overall enterprise governed by the following objectives: national independence, royal absolutism, state centralization, and curbing the native ruling classes. Autocephaly was intended as a barricade against Russian influence and thus as a safeguard to independence. Caesaropapism was a guarantee of royal absolutism vis-à-vis the national church, a means of maintaining central control over provincial bishoprics, and an institutional safeguard against insubordination or disloyalty on the part of a traditional ruling class (bishops). Maurer, the chief architect of the ecclesiastical settlement, frankly expressed his view that the bishops were the ecclesiastical counterpart of the primate class, no worthier in their exercise of power and possibly more dangerous as a more cohesive group. In short, the ecclesiastical settlement stood on a par with the new military system and the revised administrative setup, each devised to break the power of one of the existing ruling classes. Otho, while still in Bavaria, wrote his father on 13 May 1832:

. . . the spiritual authority of the clergy in the country could become

---

estimates the existing number of monasteries before the decrees at 400, the number of convents between 30 and 40, the number of monks at less than 8,000, and 100 nuns. He asserts that only 82 monasteries remained.

[74] On the execution of the monastic dissolution and its abuses, see Oikonomos [*Collected Writings*], II, 268-78; on the popular dissatisfaction and the text of an apologia which the synod circulated, see *ibid.*, II, 287-92. See the attitude of Makrygiannes ([*Memoirs*], II, 75-76), who deplored the act and expressed sympathy for the monks, whom he had sometimes criticized before this. Finlay, who sympathized with the church settlement, attributed the outcry, in part at least, to the method of tax collection, the tax-farmers being more severe than the monks (*History*, VII, 130-31). On the financial consequences for the state income, see Oikonomos, *op.cit.*, II, 267.

dangerous to the secular ruler if the upper clergy attached themselves to a party, since then the whole clergy might bring over the people to their side and against him. I think that one could overcome all these difficulties if one set up a synod under the direction of a metropolitan who would function like the president of our chambers and not actually possess power. The ruler could choose the members of this synod at certain times.

Most likely, when he wrote that the upper clergy might attach themselves to a party, Otho was referring to the "Russian" party, which was noted for its strong support among the clergy.[75]

Maurer also stressed the importance of political considerations in the regency's enactment of the settlement. The whole operation, its swiftness of action and its steamrolling methods, represented a determined attempt to head off the political opposition of which there were ominous signs during the spring of 1833. By that time the intentions of the regency were clear. On 27 March a seven-man ecclesiastical commission was established to look into the problems of the church. Its membership was such as to indicate the direction that a settlement would take. In connection with the ministry of educational and ecclesiastical affairs, a decree of 15 April, defining the duties of the new ministries, referred to a holy synod even though the commission had not yet finished its deliberations. According to Maurer, "Intriguers of all kinds, of whom there is unfortunately an abundance in Greece, set about to render suspect the good intentions of the government." Of these so-called intriguers, monks were especially prominent. Around July 1833, one from Mount Athos, named Procopius Dendrinos, agitated against autocephaly and other objectives of the regents under their very noses in Nauplion. Before some he charged the regency with intentions of Catholicizing the Greeks, before others he cited the spectre of Protestantism. At the same time the ex-bishop of Adrianople concentrated his efforts on organizing the bishops into an effective resistance. His position as Russian pensioner and his personal intercourse with Gabriel Catacazy, the Russian minister, who arrived in Greece in late April, as well as "some communications" addressed by Catacazy to the bishops, seemed to implicate Russian diplomacy in these maneuvers. Ultimately the newspapers took up the issue. *Chronos*, the Kapodistrian organ, encouraged resistance to the impending measures. On the other hand, liberal newspapers recommended that the prospective convocation of bishops, summoned to confirm an ecclesiastical settlement, should include lower clergy as well, should exercise full freedom of de-

[75] Dawkins to Palmerston, Nauplion, 20 Aug. 1833, no. 49, FO 32.37; Maurer, *Griechische Volk*, I, 53-54; and Pipineles [*Monarchy*], 81-82. The quotation is taken from Hans Rall, "Die Anfänge des Konfessionspolitischen Ringens um den Wittelsbacher Thron in Athen," in *Bayern: Staat und Kirche, Land und Reich*, ed. Wilhelm Winkler (Munich, 1961), p. 193.

cision, and should open its deliberations to the public. These proposals, wrote Maurer, threatened to turn an ecclesiastical convocation into a Polish diet. Actually he feared the agitation that extended public debate of such an explosive issue might precipitate. He suspected the stirrings of opposition as merely a smoke screen of the Kapodistrian party for its political campaign against the regency and a device of Russian diplomacy for keeping its foot in the door. "All this agitation and activity was not intended for the good of state and religion, but derived exclusively from clearly partisan objectives," he wrote.

It was the patriarch of Constantinople who finally forced a showdown. For the first time since the schism began, he made an appointment to a bishopric in Greece, probably as a test case. When the appointee arrived at his assigned episcopal seat at Zeitouni, the regency took immediate action.[76] To strengthen its settlement, which the ecclesiastical commission had formally drawn up, the regency wanted it officially confirmed by a vote of the bishops. It summoned them all to meet on 27 July 1833, refugees without sees as well as autochthonous bishops, and all gave their formal assent. Yet a number of circumstances rendered this show of unanimity suspect. The impending appointments of the state to the newly delineated bishoprics made opportunists willing to suppress their genuine opinions in order to court favor. Moreover, the procedure of the regency in securing assent was questionable. It gave the bishops such short notice to appear in the capital that many could not complete the trip from their dioceses by the appointed date. It called upon them to register their assent in smaller groups as they arrived. Hence they had no time to organize any opposition nor did they ever meet as a whole body. And finally, it failed to incorporate most of the revisions proposed by some of the bishops when they arrived in Nauplion.[77]

These revisions indicate what many, perhaps a majority, of the bishops really felt. To the statement acknowledging the Crown's right of administration over the church, the revisionists proposed the addition

[76] The members of the commission were Spyridon Trikoupes, president; Ignatios, bishop of Ardamerios; Païsios, bishop of Elaia and vicar of Messenia; Panoutsos Notaras; Skarlatos Vyzantios; Constantine Schinas; and Theokletos Pharmakides. For the decree of 3/15 Apr. 1833, see [Government Gazette], no. 14, 30 Mar./10 Apr. 1833. On the events leading up to regency action, see Maurer, Griechische Volk, II, 154-58, and I, 480: "Unfortunately, in their resistance to the secular authority, the bishops were supported secretly or openly by many primates." Concerning Prokopios, see Pipineles [Monarchy], pp. 77-78, and Takes Kandeloros, He Dike tou Kolokotrone kai he Epanastasis tes Peloponnesou [The Trial of Kolokotrones and the Peloponnesian Revolution] (Athens, 1906), p. 44.

[77] On the assembling of the hierarchs, see Dawkins to Palmerston, Nauplion, 20 Aug. 1833, no. 49, FO 32.37, which ignores evidence of clerical opposition; Hēlios, 18 July 1833 o.s.; Maurer, Griechische Volk, II, 158-60; Oikonomos [Collected Writings], II, 98, 163-77, and III, 168-90; Pipineles [Monarchy], pp. 75-76, and Charles A. Frazee, "The Orthodox Church of Greece from the Revolution of 1821 to 1852" [unpubl. doct. diss.] (Indiana University, 1965), pp. 213-15.

"without, however, running contrary to the holy canons." In the section specifying the duties of the holy synod, they specified that the synod should "direct ecclesiastical affairs according to the ecclesiastical canons." In short, they meant canon law to serve both as the standard of synodal activity and as a limit on the secular power. Unlike the primates and chieftains, the bishops enjoyed in support of their claims a written law code (canon law) and a very old and respectable religious tradition. For the next decade "adherence to the holy canons" was to serve as a short-hand slogan summing up such manifold demands as reconciliation with the patriarch, autonomy for the ecclesiastical authorities, and restoration of the clergy's traditional jurisdiction in such matters as education and marriage.[78]

Two succeeding events reveal the crux of the dispute between church and state. The first took place just after the government promulgated the charter without incorporating any of the proposed revisions. When the first synod again proposed them, in a formal letter dated 23 September 1833, the minister of religion, in a reply of 11 October 1833, not only reprimanded it for insubordination but also betrayed the government's extreme caesaropapist position by referring to the bishops as govern-mental officials and interpreting their proposed revisions as an unwar-ranted limitation of royal sovereignty. In 1837, to anticipate for a moment, the same Neophytos pronounced an excommunication without obtaining the previous consent of the governor of Attica, as required by royal decree. When asked to account for his act, he replied:

that canon law never required civil consent for the act of excommuni-cation and that the king, as successor of the Byzantine emperors, would surely not expect a royal decree in church matters to take precedence over canon law.[79]

The jurisdictional issue in church-state relations thus took two forms: (1) who should have the ultimate say, in social and ecclesiastical as well as strictly religious matters, the king and his political advisers or the bishops? (2) which should take precedence, secular or canon law?

Prejudice as well as financial considerations lay behind the monastic settlement. Monasticism was regarded as an outworn and backward institution. Furthermore the regency wanted to exploit this vast store of wealth—producing an estimated annual income the equivalent of $200,000—in behalf of the public, the theory being that the state rather than the church should dispense the benefits of education and charity. But there was probably a political dimension to the dissolution as well—fear of the monks' political role as liaison agents in the organization of

[78] Oikonomos [Collected Writings], II, 170-71.
[79] Ibid., II, 198-213, including texts of communications between the synod and the minister of ecclesiastical affairs. Lyons to Palmerston, Nauplion, 27 Sept. 1837, no. 105, FO 32.71.

plots, as leaders of the people, and as adherents of Russia. The monks, more than any other group, were opposed to the church settlement and were the most vigorous partisans of Russia. Moreover, they were extremely mobile and in close contact with the public. There is ample evidence that they acted as agents of communication between political groups and stirred up the people on politically sensitive issues. Surveillance over such potentially dangerous groups was more manageable if they were concentrated in fewer places. It is telling that the very first encyclical issued by the new synod in 1834 concerned controlling the journeys of monks outside their monasteries, and at the end of the same year, new directives went out to the same effect. Indeed, the phenomenon of wandering monks, so difficult to curb and control, occupied the synod during the succeeding years.[80]

Although the ecclesiastical settlement was, in its inspiration and implementation, ultimately the work of the Bavarian regency, it also reflected the Western secular values of a Greek Westernized minority who assisted in its actual formulation and implementation. The ecclesiastical settlement reflected already existing issues arising out of the long-standing Greek cultural schism described in Chapter I. Adamantious Koraes, the great liberal publicist operating from Paris, had advocated an independent church as early as 1821 and had singled out "title-bearing monks" as the greatest evil besetting the church. Theokletos Pharmakides, one of the prominent Greek theologians of his day, was, along with Maurer, the moving spirit behind the church settlement. As a student of theology at Göttingen (1819-21), he had come in contact with Protestant thought and had become familiar with Koraes' writings. By the end of the Revolution, he had become a member of the "English" party and believed Russia to be an enemy of Hellenism. On the recommendation of the famous savant George Gennadios, Maurer had invited Pharmakides to Nauplion to advise on ecclesiastical matters. After a month's work,

---

[80] Concerning the financial motive for dissolution, see Dawkins to Palmerston, Nauplion, 20 Aug. 1833, no. 49, FO 32.37, and Finlay, History, vii, 130-31. The best source for attitudes toward monasticism is the report of the ecclesiastical commission, dated 7/19 July 1833 and published in its entirety in Oikonomos [Collected Writings], ii, 125-62. Concerning innate prejudice for instance, see the expression of preference for the secular clergy on the grounds that marriage has made them think and act in terms of public interest whereas lack of marriage has allegedly made monks conscious only of their individual interests (ii, 135). Even though the report claims not to enter into the question of the usefulness or uselessness of monasticism, it raises the question in such a way as to intimate that its uselessness is a foregone conclusion (ii, 159). See also the charge that church lands were not well administered (ii, 139).

For the encyclical letter, dated 16 Jan. 1834, see Hai anangaioterai Enkyklioi, Epistolai, Diataxeis, kai Odegiai tes Hieras Synodou tes Ekklesias tes Hellados 1834-1854 [The Most Important Encyclicals, Letters, Decrees, and Directives of the Holy Synod of the Church of Greece] (Athens, 1854), pp. 1-4. See also Frazee, "The Orthodox Church" [unpubl. doct. diss.], pp. 232-34.

Pharmakides produced a draft ecclesiastical constitution, which was translated into German. This draft served as the basis for Maurer's own draft. All of this took place before the appointment of the ecclesiastical commission at the end of March.[81]

The truth is that the religious settlement, though ardently encouraged by Maurer, reflected the Westernizing sentiments of Spyridon Trikoupes, minister of educational and ecclesiastical affairs, of Constantine Schinas and Skarlatos Vyzantios, his assistants in the same ministry, as well as those of the "protestantizing" Pharmakides. These four constituted a majority in the seven-man ecclesiastical commission. The report of this commission is a very revealing document containing many laudatory remarks about the West and mostly condemnatory comments on the Eastern clergy. These men reflected the sentiments of a small but very influential segment of the Greek population, as the liberal newspapers *Athēna* and *Sōtēr* reveal, and in their sheer anticlericalism perhaps a broader part of the masses.[82] For the sake of contrast, the two extreme positions in this cultural schism—the liberal and the conservative—must be delineated, though many Greeks belonged somewhere in between.

The conflict with regard to autocephaly entailed differences on the interpretation of Revolutionary aims, on the basis of legitimate separation from the mother church, on the implementation of the Great Idea, on the conception of the church, and on questions of ultimate values and goals stemming from a clash between secular nationalism and a theocratic world-view. Concerning Revolutionary aims, the liberals argued that the Greeks had waged the Revolution against the tyranny of the patriarch as well as that of the sultan, and that the separation from the patriarchate was a product of the Revolution. Moreover, they believed that a politically independent nation had the right to ecclesiastical independence as well. The conservatives denounced this view, asserting that the Greeks had fought the Revolution exclusively against the Turks and

[81] On Koraes, see D. S. Balanos, "Hai threskeutikae ideai tou Adamantiou Korae" ["The Religious Ideas of Adamantios Koraes"] (Athens, 1920), 82ff. On Pharmakides' role, see D. S. Balanos, *Theokletos Pharmakides 1784-1860* [*Theokletos Pharmakides*] (Athens, 1933); Theokletos Pharmakides, *Apologia* [*Apology*] (Athens, 1840), pp. 6-9; and T. Charalambides, "Die Kirchenpolitik Griechenlands," *Zeitschrift für Kirchengeschichte*, vi (1935), 162.

[82] Such "Westerners" as the four on the commission Makrygiannes ([*Memoirs*], ii, 75-76) refers to as "cursed politicians" and "corrupt leaders"; the views of such men are reflected by such newspapers as *Hēlios*, edited by Alexander Soutsos, the Westernizing liberal poet, e.g. 14 July 1833*o.s.* Exaggeratedly, Dawkins (to Palmerston, Nauplion, 21 Apr. 1834, no. 31, FO 32.44) takes credit for planning the ecclesiastical reform with Trikoupes before the arrival of the regency and for pressing the regent Armansperg for its adoption. For the text of the minutes of the Commission's meetings, its draft law, and its report of 7/19 July 1833, see Oikonomos [*Collected Writings*], ii, 99-162, especially 126-27 on the alleged abuses of the Greek clerics and an unfavorable comparison between them and European clergymen.

maintaining that the separation had been an unintentional and deplorable by-product of the Revolution requiring correction.[83]

No one contended that administrative separation *per se* was illegitimate. The issues revolved around the proper procedure for separation. The liberals asserted the inalienable right of a fully sovereign state to sever unilaterally the connection with a "foreign potentate" (patriarch). The conservatives argued the necessity of consent by both parties to the relationship (mother and daughter churches) according to a formula spelled out by canon law.[84]

Concerning the implementation of the Great Idea, the dream of a Greater Greece, the liberals firmly believed that only the king, as head of the vanguard state, could be the leader of Greater Greece and organizer of the struggle to realize it. The conservatives pointed out that schism caused a breach of unity in the greater Greek nation and so impaired the realization of the Great Idea. Implicit in the argument of some was the notion that the patriarch was potential leader of the irredentist movement.[85]

Each group also differed on its view of the church. For the liberals, it was a national institution in the narrow sense, coextensive with the territorial limits of the state, only one aspect of society and one branch of the administration. For the conservatives, it was a national institution in the broadest sense, coextensive with Greeks everywhere, the constitutive principle of society and pervader of all administration. For some, the church was supranational Orthodoxy, defined by dogma rather than by mere nationality or ecclesiastical division.[86]

But the crux of the dispute lay in the divergence in basic values and goals involving the issue of secularism. For liberals, the main problem was maintaining political sovereignty because they considered the state as an emblem of national self-respect, as the embodiment of national power, and as the road to material advancement. Zealous for national sovereignty, the liberals feared that the sultan—or even worse Russia— would use patriarchal influence to interfere in the internal affairs of Greece. The ultimate concern of the conservatives was ecclesiastical communion because only this would preserve the unity of the dogma, main-

[83] Maurer, *Griechische Volk*, ii, 154. Oikonomos [*Collected Writings*], ii, 148 (text of commission report), 188-89 (quotation from *Athēna*, no. 137), and iii, 1-17, 21 (quotation of liberals that the state had a right to an autocephalous church).

[84] Maurer (*Griechische Volk*, ii, 160) put forth the view that the regency fell heir to the sovereignty and full prerogatives of the sultan. See *Hēlios*, 18 July 1833o.s., for the position of some conservative bishops.

[85] Oikonomos [*Collected Writings*], iii, 46. For a fuller explanation of the Great Idea, see p. 23, Chap. I above, and pp. 345-48 of Chap. VII below.

[86] See *ibid.*, ii, 60-63, for the ecumenical view of the church and clericalism. See Maurer, *Griechische Volk*, ii, 167, for the expression of national pride over a church bearing the same name as the state.

tain the ascendancy of religion as an organizing principle of society, and secure defenses against Western cultural penetration. Anxious lest a divided Orthodoxy rent by schism succumb to the undermining pressures of Western missionaries and diplomats, the conservatives regarded close association between patriarch, Russia, and the church in Greece as absolutely necessary for mutual defense.[87]

In the domestic matter of church-state relations, the liberals backed unlimited state sovereignty because of their anticlericalism, which considered the bulk of bishops too uneducated (which meant educated in the oriental tradition), too bigoted, and even too dishonest to meet the universally acknowledged need for church reform. A letter published in *Athēna*, no less than a bitter tirade against the bishops, reflected this attitude:

> Let us bear in mind what our bishops were in the time of Turkish tyranny. With a few exceptions, they were all despots, tyrants over Christians. They were chosen, not on account of their virtue or learning, but on account of their slavish flattery, their bountiful gifts of money, and having thus fraudulently seized the pastoral staff, they levied unmerciful tributes upon their wretched flocks, fraudulently sold out the office of deacons and priests, dedications, consecrations, liturgies, and all the ordinances which are performed for Christians; gave out for heavy sums of money those harsh and inhuman excommunications. . . . They despised education, and persecuted those who were educated, whenever they did not find them to be flatterers of the Bishops' tables and advocates of their arbitrary tyrannical deeds. . . .[88]

For men who felt this way, church reform had to come through a government of enlightened men with the assistance of the few enlightened clerics, i.e., men trained in Western Europe. Clearly, if the clergy could not put their own house in order, they were in no position to act as leaders in society, either as judges or as educators. Thus the financial resources of the church, in the form of monastic wealth primarily, should be appropriated by the state because the only justification of such holdings was the satisfactory performance of such social functions as education, and care for the sick, indigent, and aged. Moreover, the liberals could have no faith in clerics who seemed to owe their primary allegiance to the patriarch or the tsar rather than to the Greek king.[89]

[87] On liberal concerns, see *ibid.*, II, 160-61, and *Hēlios*, 14 July 1833 and 18 July 1833o.s. On conservative views, see Oikonomos [*Collected Writings*], III, 217, 234, and 249-59 (which contains part of the text of a letter of 20 Sept. 1833o.s. by the patriarch of Constantinople criticizing the Greek promulgation of an independent church).

[88] *Athēna*, 16 May 1836o.s.

[89] For statements of the view that a church independent of Constantinople and dominated by the secular power was the only basis for improving the quality of the clergy, see Dawkins to Palmerston, Nauplion, 22 Aug. 1833, no. 49, FO 32.37;

The bishops, on the other hand, not only insisted on putting their own house in order, through the utilization of the church's material resources and the full application of canon law, but refused to forego the important role they had formerly played in Greek society or their traditional prerogatives in areas that the liberals considered strictly secular, such as marriage and education.[90] Conservative suspicion of secular power was as intense as liberal suspicion of clerical influence. In the first place, the king and regency were non-Orthodox. Second, those in influential political and educational positions were often Westernizing liberals. Third, the secular power, merely by virtue of being secular, would place nonreligious considerations above religious ones.[91]

Oikonomos, writing later, thought he saw ample evidence to confirm conservative fears of secular influence. According to him, many of the professors at the law school, teaching the bulk of students at the university, had been educated in France and Germany, and were instilling in "the gentle souls of the students the materialistic and democratic theories of modern jurisprudence. . . ." Even in the theological section of the university, the impact of the Reformation had affected some of the faculty, thus influencing a whole new generation of prospective bishops. Take a look at the schools and the army, he urged. Religious instruction took place only once a week, and even then, consisted merely of a short catechism and a summary of church history, taught in such a way as to blur the distinctive character of Orthodoxy. In the army barracks there was little evidence of piety. Only on Sundays were the soldiers taken to church. For the secular authority, Orthodoxy was merely a matter of Christian morals. It minimized the distinctiveness of Orthodox dogma and Orthodox custom so that the state could make the Greeks more receptive to Western beliefs, render them more tolerant toward other Christian sects, and induce better political relations with such non-Orthodox powers as France and England. In short, Oikonomos opposed the whole trend to secularism taking place in Greek society. It was precisely such opposition that made the conservatives such staunch defenders of clerical rights, expanded clerical jurisdiction, and "adherence to the holy canons."[92]

These issues were manifestations of the basic cultural conflict in Greece between secularism and spiritualism, Westernism and Easternism, modernity and medievalism. An excellent example of the conflict between the other-worldly tradition and the rising secular nationalism is revealed by the French traveler Buchon in his brief description of an encounter

---

Maurer, *Griechische Volk*, ii, 168; and a synodal encyclical, dated 4 May 1834*o.s.*, to all dioceses in justification of the church settlement, published by Oikonomos [*Collected Writings*], ii, 288.

[90] *Ibid.*, ii, 199.
[91] *Ibid.*, ii, 250; and iii, 58, 251.
[92] *Ibid.*, iii, 294-300.

with a Greek peasant. The liberals deplored the tremendous number of religious feast days as a severe economic drawback in an underpopulated country. Buchon expressed this sentiment to the peasant, who replied that if the government felt there were too many feast days, it should not create new political ones like the anniversary of the king's arrival or his entry into Athens. He liked both the king and queen, he continued, "but he also esteemed very much St. Athanasius and was not going to refuse the homage that his family had always accorded the saint."[93] Apparently anti-Westernism, in some form or other, was such a potent propaganda weapon that the ultraliberal pro-Western *Athēna* sought to discredit the conservatives by identifying them in the public mind with one facet of the West, accusing the conservatives of mimicking the Papacy, of wishing to convert the church into a state within a state, of trying to transform the patriarch into an eastern pope, and of denouncing the public's right to read and interpret the Bible for itself.[94]

The regency's ecclesiastical settlement remained, throughout the absolutist period, one of the greatest sources of public protest. In every revolt which broke out during the absolutist period, the rebels gave religious grievances a prominent place in their proclamations. To understand the widespread dissatisfaction which it provoked, one must realize, as the handful of Westernized Greek leaders did not or would not admit, that the mass of Greek people were still very much non-Western in culture and that the most basic element in their non-Western cultural orientation was their religion. That is why, even though they could accept so many Western innovations with relative equanimity, their receptivity stopped short on matters of religion. Moreover, no aspect of the inherited culture had as articulate a tradition to sustain it or as determined a body of spokesmen. However weak the clergy might be as a corporate body in political affairs, it was the strongest conservative group, both in its control over the people's minds and in its support from Russia.

2. ANTIPARTY PROGRAM

Political Objectives

The regency majority understood its mission primarily in terms of two political objectives: to unite all the parties behind the Crown and to secure the independence of Greece from all foreign interference. Since the regency did not believe that the parties could ever tolerate each other and develop a sincere loyalty to the Crown as parties, Maurer's phrase "uniting all parties behind the Crown" in effect meant the dissolution of parties. Though distinct, these two goals bore a close relationship to each other because of the connection already established between domestic

[93] Jean Alexandre Buchon, *La Grèce Continentale et la Morée* (Paris, 1843), p. 367.
[94] *Athēna*, 5 Apr. 1839 o.s.

parties and foreign powers. A major reason why parties were anathema was their habit of appealing to outside powers or giving them a pretext to intervene. As a matter of established practice, the powers encouraged party resistance to the government from below in order to press their demands more effectively from above. Parties and powers, therefore, were regarded as equal threats to state authority. Each was believed to pursue selfish goals which prejudiced the national interests.[95]

The official program, formulated by the regency majority in order to secure these ends, must be distinguished in some respects from the program actually put into practice. The latter, though it contained many elements of the official program, developed both as a pragmatic response to actual circumstances and as the outcome of underlying suspicions and prejudices. In the following, therefore, I will distinguish between what may be called the *official* and the *actual* program and try to explain the reasons for the divergence.

Official Program

The Bavarian philhellene Friedrich Thiersch, who observed Greek politics on the spot in 1831-32, published a two-volume work on Greece in 1833. In it he recommended measures for a campaign against the parties. On his return to Bavaria he must also have made these recommendations personally to Ludwig and the regency. His personal antipathy toward the Kapodistrians and his identification in Greece with the Constitutionalist cause disqualified him for a position as regent, which he obviously wanted, and may have lessened the force of some of his advice. But these recommendations were nonpartisan in their purpose. Whether the regency adopted them from him or arrived at them separately, five of these measures were constituted into an "official" regency program: (1) withholding official recognition of the parties, (2) removing influential party figures from their political strongholds, (3) representing all three parties in the administration, (4) pursuing a policy of severity and force against resistance from any quarter, and (5) maintaining a stance of impartiality toward all foreign powers. These measures were never proclaimed publicly as a program, but those connected in any way with the regency in public affairs or anyone who later took the trouble to read Maurer's memoirs was in the position to reconstruct for himself the essentials of this program.[96]

Thiersch wrote in 1833:

The most essential thing will be not to recognize the parties as such, not to enter into an arrangement with any faction, but to demand an

---

[95] Maurer, *Griechische Volk*, I, 31-35: "The union of all these parties and their turning toward the new royal throne constituted naturally the primary mission of the regency."

[96] Thiersch, *État actuel*, I, 236-64, and Maurer, *Griechische Volk*, II, 45-86, for instance.

equal submission from all . . . for if one once makes deals, one will never finish, everyone will wish to be compensated for his adhesion and obedience.[97]

That this was initially the approach of the regency is evidenced by its response when delegations from the surviving senate and the rump of the Pronoia assembly presented themselves. The regency received neither, for the reasons stated by Maurer:

> It was proved to us, moreover, that those two bodies represented only different parties, hostile toward one another, the Senate indeed the resurrected Russian party, the assembly the other two [parties], namely the English and the French. The recognition of the Senate, therefore, would, in a way, mean orientation toward the Russian party. On the other hand, to recognize the assembly would mean demonstration that we were in favor of the English and French parties as against the Russian. But because we believed it unworthy of a royal government to demonstrate itself immediately in favor of any party, neither the delegation of the Senate nor that of the assembly was received. . . .[98]

By the total absence of any royal acknowledgment, the regency forced each body to disappear. At no time during the decade of absolutism were the parties accorded any official recognition. This implied their proscription.

Undoubtedly, the belief that personalities played a major role in party formations induced the regency to adopt the practice of disassociating itself from influential party figures or removing them from their centers of political influence. "Rather than associate itself with the hatred and suspicion attaching to some men," Thiersch had asserted, "the Crown ought to keep them at a distance." He suggested two concrete measures: (1) the appointment of prominent politicians, especially the Peloponnesian primates whose influence he felt needed curbing, to gubernatorial or judicial posts far away from their provinces so that "they would lose contact with their center of power and find themselves among strangers and possible competitors in other sections of Greece," and (2) the exclusion from the cabinet of men with special party influence. The first proposal received immediate adoption by the regency, which appointed secondary party figures as provincial governors far away from their native provinces with the intention that periodic transfers would prevent them from establishing any personal influence through their official posts.[99]

[97] Thiersch, État actuel, I, 240-41.

[98] Maurer, Griechische Volk, II, 70-71.

[99] Thiersch, État actuel, I, 246-48. For an instance of the implementation of this advice, see the announcement of appointments of nomarchs, 23 Apr./5 May 1833 [Government Gazette], no. 16, 28 Apr./10 May 1833. Most of the appointees were heterochthons. Only one man (Zographos) was appointed to a nomarchy (Arcadia) anywhere close to his native province (Kalavryta), and he was soon replaced by Monarchides, a Psariot (29 July/10 Aug. 1833), and Zaïmes, a native of Kalavryta,

The regency did not immediately adopt the second suggestion. But as the cabinet members Trikoupes, Mavrokordatos, and Kolettes, in that order, came into conflict with regency policy and provoked the opposition of other parties, the second policy came gradually into force. Since mere exclusion of such party leaders would not nullify their influence and might indeed provoke them to lead their respective parties into clandestine opposition, the regency devised the clever expedient of what was virtually honorable exile, namely the appointment of these men as ministers to the foreign capitals of Europe. In 1834 Trikoupes was sent to London, Mavrokordatos to Munich and Vienna, and Metaxas, first to Cairo, then to Madrid. Kolettes suffered the same fate at the hands of Armansperg, when he was named Greek minister to France in 1835.

It was argued that such appointments offered these men generous recognition of their past services to their country and provided them with the chance to serve their country once again in its crucial dealings with the great powers. This contention carried some force, except in the case of Metaxas, whose presence in Madrid no one could justify on grounds of national necessity. The chief motive, however, was undoubtedly to remove these men from the Greek scene. Since this practice by the early 1840s was almost universally condemned as opportunistic, it should not be forgotten that the practice had originally been popular precisely among partisan persons, when it applied to the leaders of opposing parties, and acceptable to the less partisan citizens as an evil rendered necessary to calm the partisan strife provoked by the mere presence of such controversial figures.[100]

---

was appointed to replace Monarchides in Aetolia-Acarnania (21 Aug./2 Sept. 1833) [GG], no. 29, 14/26 Sept. 1833.

[100] For an instance of the rationalization of this policy, take the case of Trikoupes. *Triptolemos* (18 Oct. 1833o.s.) explained his appointment as the result of his eminent qualifications, which were quite real (his familiarity with English language and culture, his Anglophilism, and the respect he commanded among Englishmen). In his despatch of 23 Oct. 1833 to Palmerston (no. 74, FO 32.38), Dawkins wrote concerning Trikoupes' appointment, "motive is principally to send the fittest person to London." The more fundamental motive is substantiated by many documents. Finlay (in his Journal [MSS], 20 June 1834) explains Mavrokordatos' appointment to the Bavarian and Austrian courts as follows: "He is considered too much under Dawkins' influence." Dawkins (to Palmerston, Nauplion, 20 June 1834, no. 41, FO 32.44) writes: ". . . it is the policy of the regency to remove gradually all the party leaders whose rivalry has hitherto impeded the public service, whose personal influence has been at times too strong for the central government. . . ." He strongly implies (28 Nov. 1833, no. 74, FO 32.37) that Metaxas' despatch to Cairo, then Madrid, was motivated by suspicions of his implication in the Kolokotrones plot. *The Portfolio* (III, 518) asserts that Metaxas was confronted by the government with the choice of standing trial for alleged implication in the Kolokotrones plot (see below) or to retire to Cairo as consul, and that he delayed his departure from Nauplion for months on the pretext of ill-health. Or, in connection with the appointment of Kolettes as minister to Paris, semiofficial *Ethnikē* (6/18 June 1835) wrote: "Our king decided, it seems, to temporarily remove from affairs all those representing parties. . . ."

"The Crown ought then to unite around itself capable and respectable men of all political complexions," wrote Thiersch, "and this party of the king, extending little by little to all of Greece, will end up re-uniting the whole nation." Though the regency did not give official recognition to the parties, its formal policy of giving so-called equal representation in the administration to all three parties forced it to examine the party affiliations of any candidate for office. What advantages was this policy intended to serve? It would hopefully avoid antagonizing the parties themselves or the foreign powers that sponsored them and in the meantime would serve notice to both the parties and the protecting powers that they should not seek exclusive influence. It would use the three parties, as represented by their members in the administration, to serve as checks upon each other and hence prevent partisan abuses. It would demonstrate that membership in no one party offered any special advantages to the office-seeker. Finally, by such nonpartisan behavior, the regency probably hoped that most party members would transfer their primary allegiance from party to Crown.[101]

Thiersch also recommended the use of force "if any should resist the efforts of the government," the premise being that any signs of government indecision or lack of nerve would invite all kinds of pressure and intimidation. Ostensibly, strong-armed methods were to be used conditionally, but a Thiersch statement about party tactics implied that resistance from some quarter was inevitable:

> Demonstrations of good will, zeal, and devotion will be made but each [party] will calculate its submission and obedience according to the satisfaction it receives and the influence it obtains, or even worse, each will try to create difficulties, obstacles, and embarrassments, retaining the means to make them cease the moment it obtains what it wants.

If Thiersch was correct in his assertion that the dissatisfied would resort to some form of resistance, then resistance was inevitable because, as Maurer himself asserted independently, the regency could not hope to satisfy the exaggerated demands of everyone.[102]

This type of reasoning was dangerous because it bred suspicion in the regency and might encourage it to imagine the existence of opposition in all sorts of unlikely places and by its response to breed it where it had not existed before. In any case, this type of reasoning transformed the question of using force from one of "if" to one of "when."

This policy must have been adopted in general terms as early as the

---

[101] Thiersch, *État actuel*, I, 244, and Maurer, *Griechische Volk*, II, 319, 495.

[102] Thiersch, *État actuel*, II, 240, 243, and Maurer, *Griechische Volk*, II, 44-45. As Makrygiannes points out ([*Memoirs*], II, 60), the regency's expression of its determination was often crude, even allowing for the exaggeration of the narrator, as in the case of Heideck's threat to Makrygiannes: "You [military men] will do whatever you are told. Your opinions are not being solicited. Bavaria has 30,000 bayonets which she can use to invite submission."

negotiations of the treaty of 7 May 1832, which stipulated the necessity of Bavarian troops for the Crown. Its affirmation came in the first royal proclamation, on that occasion as a pointed threat intended as a deterrent:

> Forgetting the political passions of the past, I confidently expect that each of you will submit to the nation by rendering proper obedience to its laws and the officials assigned to execute the laws, and [I expect each citizen] to return quietly to his home. In this way, I certainly hope to be released from the frightful necessity of having to prosecute, with the full severity of the laws, rebels and disturbers of the public peace.[103]

In all fairness it must be said that the essentially negative policy of severity was intended only as a part of a much wider program reserved, after completion of the positive acts designed to win over the majority, for the remaining dissatisfied few. Moreover, the enunciation and partial implementation of the policy was intended as a deterrent meant to paralyze through intimidation the stratagems of the dissatisfied. For instance, it was undoubtedly hoped that the show of force before Nauplion would suffice not only to disperse the irregulars on that occasion, but to discourage any similar attempts as well. But the regency was not merely bluffing. It was determined to do the unpleasant when it was challenged.

Finally, the regency believed that for Greece to be free and independent it must pursue a policy of impartiality toward all the powers. "Impartiality" had both a positive and a negative meaning. Positively, it meant the maintenance of friendly relations with all the powers. Negatively, it signified vigilance against attempted interference from any quarter. A first step in this negative sense was the regency's request that each of the protecting powers replace its existing residents—Dawkins for England, Rouen for France, and Rückman for Russia. It reasoned that these men, habituated by the extraordinary events between 1828-32 to a mediating role with powers far beyond those of normal diplomatic representatives in a foreign capital, could not easily acclimate themselves to the restricted functions necessitated by the changed circumstances of an independent regime. It demonstrated its impartiality by making the same request of all three powers, but received a positive response only from Russia, which in 1833 replaced Rückman with Gabriel Catacazy, a man who ironically proved even less palatable to the regency majority.[104]

Actual Program

The actual program deviated markedly from the official program in

[103] I have translated this passage from the published text which appears in Evangelides [*History*], pp. 38-41, this particular passage being from p. 40.

[104] Maurer, *Griechische Volk*, II, 46-47, 63-66, and Driault and Lhéritier, *Histoire*, II, 106-107.

what were probably the two most crucial planks—equal representation in the administration for each party and impartiality toward the powers. Even in its first months before its members started quarreling among themselves, the regency violated its own good intentions of not becoming identified with any one party. Events of 1832—the "election" of Ricord as president and the attack on the French forces at Argos—roused its suspicions that the "Russian" party, perpetrator of these events, was opposed to the Bavarians and would only submit to intimidation. Nesselrode, Russian foreign minister, was probably right in his later charge that the regency arrived in Greece with the conviction that Russia would try to dominate the new state and with determination to resist such domination. The Russian government had already lent credence to such suspicions by the demands it began to press on Ludwig and the regency during 1832—that the king convert to Orthodoxy and that the regency give "adequate" representation to the Napist party in the Greek administration.[105]

As a result, the military command of Kolokotrones was not recognized, and no representation was given the Napists in the cabinet. Some Kapodistrians received official employment, but more were excluded. To balance the scales and in an apparent attempt this time to appease the Russian government, which had complained about the influence of what it called the "ultra-liberal" (essentially "French") party, the regency scorned prominent Constitutionalist chieftains and gave no one of the Pronoia group a cabinet post. It studiously withheld medals of honor from Kolokotrones, Tzavelas, and Theodore Grivas, this gesture being considered no doubt a slap at both Napists and Constitutionalists.[106]

Greeks, however, took the composition of the cabinet as an indication of a regime's party orientation. On its arrival, the regency had retained the existing cabinet, but on 15 April 1833 it appointed a new cabinet consisting of Trikoupes, Mavrokordatos, Psyllas, Praïdes, and Kolettes. Of these only the last belonged to the "French" party, and he received the politically unimportant ministry of the navy. As far as most Greeks were concerned, the cabinet was largely that of the "English" party, which had probably won the good will of the regency by betraying the Constitutionalist cause at Pronoia.[107]

[105] On Nesselrode's view, see his Memorandum to Michael Soutsos, special Greek emissary to Russia [Nov. 1833], in Jelavich, *Russia and Greece*, pp. 77-78. On Russia's pressure for Otho's conversion, see Nesselrode to Liven, St. Petersburg, 17 Feb. 1832; Nesselrode to Heideck [n.p., n.d.]; Nesselrode to Potemkin, St. Petersburg, 16/28 July 1832, in Jelavich, *op.cit.*, pp. 40, 47, 48. For a more extensive treatment of the subject, see Hans Rall, "Anfänge des Konfessionspolitischen Ringens" in *Bayern*, pp. 181-215. On pressure for inclusion of the "Russian" party, see Nesselrode to Potemkin, St. Petersburg, 19/31 Oct. 1832, and Nesselrode to Heideck, St. Petersburg, 19 Oct./1 Nov. 1832, in Jelavich, *op.cit.*, pp. 52, 53.

[106] Maurer, *Griechische Volk*, II, 70-72, 84-85, 502-504.

[107] *The Portfolio* (III, 515) says in this regard: "It is to be remarked that the

The regency probably believed that by striking out at both Napists and Pronoians, then opting for the cabinet members it chose, it was attacking the two extreme fringe groups while inviting the support of the moderates. Indeed, if one thought only in terms of two parties—Napists and Constitutionalists—then a case could be made that the cabinet was largely nonpartisan. Though the regency might have interpreted its own acts as an attack on parties in general, such behavior could be interpreted by the parties as nothing less than discrimination—in policies of appointment and otherwise—against the "Russian" and "French" parties and favoritism toward the "English." Indeed, the obvious discrimination against the "Russian" party was one of the major factors in the alienation of Russian diplomacy.[108]

The alienation of Russian as well as British diplomacy also stemmed from demonstrated signs of favoritism toward France. The regency maintained the closest contacts with Rouen. During the first Egyptian crisis (1833) it formally petitioned the London Conference for the prolongation of the French occupation beyond the agreed date and hence supported France in its insistence on keeping its troops in Greece against vociferous protests from Russia and the more quiet opposition of England. The regency majority even went as far as to suggest to Rouen the marriage of Otho to Louis Philippe's daughter as a way of cementing Greco-French friendship. If we may trust Maurer's account as a trustworthy description of regency motives rather than as a *post hoc* attempt to rationalize a policy of drift, favoritism toward France was the result of a carefully reasoned analysis of each European power's real sentiments toward Greece.[109]

Regency on their first arrival in Greece allowed themselves to be directed by the English representative in most of the appointments, being desirous of availing themselves of his local information and long experience of the country, and also of showing their attachment to England."

[108] Such diverse sources as the following concurred in attributing a strong regency bias in favor of the "Constitutionalist party": (1) Dawkins to Palmerston, Nauplion, 28 Nov. 1833, no. 74, FO 32.38, and (2) the Russophile Andrew Papadopoulos-Vretos, *Historike Ekthesis tes ephemeridos Ho Hellenikos Kathreptes: Le Compte-Rendu du Miroir Grec* (in Greek and French) (Athens, 1839), p. 42. But *Hēlios* (25 Aug. 1833*o.s.*), representing the "French" portion of the so-called Constitutionalist party, was more precise in locating the object of regency favoritism—the "English" party. On the regency majority's aversion to the "Russian" party and the "Russian" party's just cause for complaint, see Mendelssohn Bartholdy, *Geschichte Griechenlands*, II, 473, 474-75.

[109] Driault and Lhéritier, *Histoire*, II, 120-21. Apparently the regency, jittery over the restlessness of the dissolved palikars and without enough Bavarians to fill all the crucial posts in the kingdom, anxiously sought the retention of French troops already in the Peloponnesos until it obtained all its recruits from Bavaria (Dawkins to Palmerston, Nauplion, 31 May 1833, no. 30, FO 32.37). For confirmation that Rouen, the French minister in Athens, lent support to the regency majority, see Bower and Bolitho, *Otho I*, p. 65.

Two premises lay at the basis of this analysis. The first premise went something like this: If Greece was a battleground for European diplomacy, the participants were essentially only England and Russia. Maurer referred only to England and Russia when he wrote about the attempts of outside powers to dominate Greek internal affairs. To put the matter a little differently, only English and Russian interests really conflicted over Greece, hence each sought desperately for the exclusion of the other's influence in Greece. Austria and France, on the other hand, were neutral in their attitude toward Greece and were its only real friends. This being the case, it was to Russia and England that Greece should avoid making any concessions or showing any favoritism, because conceding to one would antagonize the other and vice versa. Absolute impartiality toward the two was essential because they were jealous of each other. Intimacy with France or Austria, on the other hand, was not dangerous because they wanted nothing for themselves and so did not arouse the jealousy of England or Russia in Greece.[110]

The regency majority held a second premise that the vital interests of Russia and England clashed with those of Greece, Greek interests in this case understood in the grandiose context of the Great Idea. Greece and Russia were potential rivals for possession of the heart of the Ottoman Empire, namely Constantinople and the Straits. In fact, since the Treaty of Adrianople in 1829, Russia had warmed up to the Turks and had adopted an unprecedented policy of support for the Ottoman Empire. Such an about-face demonstrated growing Russian awareness of a potential Greek threat to her ambitions. At present the British navy controlled the Mediterranean, and British merchants dominated the Near Eastern economy by virtue of Ottoman weakness. British diplomacy could not countenance the replacement of this "sick man" by a strong, independent, commercial state with developed European ways. Such a state—the probable Greek state of the future—would exercise a magnetic pull on the Near Eastern economy and might eventually extend its economic activities toward the East Indies, seriously undermining British commercial hegemony throughout South Asia. So, to the far-sighted British, the present small Greek kingdom appeared to be a new rival. Of the major powers, only France and Austria would accept Greek resurgence because, unlike the exclusive British, they were used to sharing with others in the Near East. In such terms did Maurer diagnose the international picture vis-à-vis Greece.[111]

This whole analysis, a mixture of truth and error, implied, even if it did not explicitly conclude, that Russia and Britain, separately and for different reasons, would pursue a policy deliberately devised to keep Greece weak and hence unable to achieve its ambitions. This being the case, it is no wonder that the regency majority should feel quite justified

[110] Maurer, *Griechische Volk*, I, 35-41, and II, 46-48.
[111] *Ibid.*, I, 35-41.

in seeking the protection of France and Austria. Maurer only regretted that a minister from Austria was late in coming and did not arrive until the end of 1834 after his own departure from Greece. This reasoning led ultimately to an apparent paradox that justified the regency's violation of its own professions of impartiality, namely, that immunity from the influence of Russia and England necessitated the influence of France and Austria. But the same word changed its meaning. The "influence" of Russia and England was interference; that of France and Austria legitimate support.

3. POLITICAL DEVELOPMENTS

The "Major" and "Minor" Plots

The regency miscalculated if it thought that intimidation would invite easy submission. Kolettes was willing to bide his time until circumstances favored the return of his party to the ascendancy it had enjoyed in 1832. The Napists were more reckless and less wise. Despairing of any chance to win the good will of the regency, they sought the only other immediate alternative for ameliorating their political position—working toward the downfall of the regency.

Through the newspaper *Chronos*, financed by Kolokotrones and Vlassopoulos, they sought to arouse the public by criticizing the regency's unpopular measures, such as dissolution of the irregular troops and dissolution of the monasteries. Through a series of brigand outbreaks they hoped to prove the regency ineffective.[112] On 3 February 1833, while on board the flagship of the Russian Admiral Ricord, Kolokotrones had sent a letter to Count Nesselrode expressing his anxiety over the regency's ecclesiastical policy. The Russian foreign minister had replied on 11 July in a nonpartisan fashion, advising on behalf of the tsar that the Greeks rally round the throne and remain faithful to their religion. Catacazy, receiving it from the Asiatic department of the Russian foreign ministry, delivered it to Kolokotrones. Copies of this letter allegedly circulated among the discontented, who looked upon it as proof of Russian support and as indication of Kolokotrones' close connections with Petersburg.[113]

[112] Dawkins to Blackhouse, Nauplion, 20 Aug. 1833, no number, FO 32.37; Maurer, *Griechische Volk*, II, 498-99; and Mendelssohn Bartholdy, *Geschichte Griechenlands*, II, 475.

[113] On Kolokotrones' letter, no copy of which could then be found, and Nesselrode's reply, see Dawkins to Palmerston, Nauplion, 25 May 1834, no. 36, FO 32.44, and Catacazy to Nesselrode, Nauplion, 17/29 June 1834, in Jelavich, *Russia and Greece*, p. 102. For the published text of Count Nesselrode's letter, dated 11/23 July 1833, see Kandeloros [*Trial*], 69f.; Henry Parish, *The Diplomatic History of the Monarchy of Greece* (London, 1838), pp. 274-76; Jelavich, *op.cit.*, pp. 104-105; or the Greek translation of Maurer's work (George Ludwig von Maurer, *Ho Hellenikos Laos . . . [The Greek People . . .]*, trans. Christos Pratsikas and Eustathios Karastathes [Athens, 1943-47], II, 435-36, n.).

Simultaneously, the Napists circulated for signatures a petition to the tsar. It requested that Petersburg use its influence to obtain the recall of the regency and allow Otho's immediate assumption of power. These illicit activities constituted the so-called "major plot."[114]

A concurrent "minor plot," designed to make Armansperg sole regent, was hatched by Dr. Franz, a Bavarian scholar of ancient Greek, who was serving as one of the regency's interpreters. He circulated a petition addressed to Ludwig, calling for the dismissal of Maurer and Heideck.[115] Most probably Armansperg, ambitious and calculating, knew about the petition and gave his tacit approval. When later pressed, he admitted that Franz had proposed to him the idea of a sole regent and that he had expressed his approval of a change without specifying any one of the three regents as a more suitable choice than the others. Indeed, Armansperg had objected to a collegiate regency, as a source of discord, before he had ever left Munich.[116]

On the surface the connection between the "major" and "minor" plots may seem dubious because their objectives differed, the former petitioning for the recall of the entire regency, the latter for only two of its members. Most likely the Napists organized the "major" plot when they thought the entire regency responsible for the anti-Kapodistrian policy. Later, however, Armansperg shrewdly dropped hints here and there that the acts of the regency reflected the policy of his colleagues who constantly overruled his opposition. Count Dionysios Roma, the Greek Zantiot, assured Kolokotrones in Tripolis and Plapoutas in Argos that Armansperg sympathized with the Kapodistrians. From the point of view of the Napists, this information rendered the maintenance of a sole regent (Armansperg) preferable to the rule of a young boy-king whose sentiments were yet uncertain and over whom they had no control. But before

114 It has been assumed, from these facts, that Kolokotrones was concerting measures for a revolution. Maurer is inconsistent on this point. On the one hand, he asserts (*Griechische Volk*, II, 499-500, II, 435-37) that a revolt was envisaged "if the petitions did not lead to the intended results"; on the other, he alleges (II, 500) that the date for the outbreak had been set for September 16. If the former statement is true—and it must be, otherwise why bother with petitions at all—then why did the plotters decide to revolt before the effectiveness of the petitions was tested? On the circulation of the petition, see Dawkins to Palmerston, Nauplion, 25 May 1834, no. 36, FO 32.44. More generally, and extensively on the "major plot" see Finlay, *History*, VII, 136-37; Kandeloros [*Trial*], pp. 68-105; and Mendelssohn Bartholdy, *Geschichte Griechenlands*, II, 476-78.

115 For the text of both versions of the petition, see for instance the Greek translation of Maurer's book, where the editors have included them ([*The Greek People*], II, 447-50).

116 On Armansperg's involvement and feelings and response, with regard to the uncovered plot and its objective, see Dawkins to Palmerston, Nauplion, 26 May 1834, no. 38, FO 32.44; Maurer, *Griechische Volk*, II, 511-16; and Mendelssohn Bartholdy, *Geschichte Griechenlands*, II, 477-78. On the "minor" plot see also Finlay, *History*, VII, 137-38; Pipineles [*Monarchy*], p. 129; and Kandeloros [*Trial*], passim.

the Napists could revise their own petitions (assuming of course that they wanted to), the regency majority cracked down on them.[117]

Recognizing the dangerous consequences of appeals to foreign powers against the legally constituted rulers of Greece, suspecting Napist plans for an armed rebellion, and probably anxious to deprive Armansperg of potential allies, the regency majority first arrested Franz and ousted him from the country.[118] On 18 September, three weeks later, Kolokotrones, his son Gennaios, Plapoutas, Tzavelas, and several others, either Kapodistrians or military captains associated with Kolokotrones since the end of 1832, suffered arrest and imprisonment.[119] On 23 September 1833, the promulgation of three press laws represented an attempt to silence the opposition newspapers, or as Maurer put it, "to render all similar intrigues and uprisings, if not impossible, at least very difficult, in the future."[120] When Psyllas, minister of the interior, objected that the arrests had taken

[117] Mendelssohn Bartholdy (*Geschichte Griechenlands*, II, 472) uses the terminology of "major" and "minor" plots and considers them intertwined. He points out that the "Russians" began to consider Armansperg their friend (II, 477); he believes them both a product of the disaffection caused by the regency's reorganizing acts (II, 472). Maurer (*Griechische Volk*, II, 498-500) treats the two plots as one and the same affair. Dawkins (to Palmerston, Nauplion, 28 Nov. 1833, no. 74, FO 32.38) translates a regency report to the powers which reiterates this view; and speaking for himself (to Palmerston, Nauplion, 27 Sept. 1833, no. 57, FO 32.37), he treats them as one, with the farfetched interpretation that the Napists instituted the "minor" plot.

[118] Announcement of a plot to change the regency and instructions to provincial authorities, issued by the palace, Nauplion, 19/31 Aug. 1833, folder 131 (Palace Documents), Otho Archive, Vlachogiannes Collection, General State Archives, Athens. *Hēlios*, 15 Aug. 1833o.s.; Maurer, *Griechische Volk*, II, 511-15; and Mendelssohn Bartholdy, *Geschichte Griechenlands*, II, 480.

[119] Among others arrested were Karatasos, Mamoures, Roukes, Kriezotes, Vagias, Spyromelios, Apostolaras, Demetrakopoulos, Alonistiotes, (Mendelssohn Bartholdy, *Geschichte Griechenlands*, II, 482, and Gennaios Kolokotrones [*Memoirs II*], p. 74), and Prince Gustavus de Wrede, a German who had left the service of Austria for that of Greece in 1826, married a Greek, attached himself to the Napist party, and was in 1833 director of the nomarchy of Arcadia (Dawkins to Palmerston, Nauplion, 28 Nov. 1833, no. 74, FO 32.38). On the arrests in general, see Maurer, *Griechische Volk*, II, 500-502; Pipineles [*Monarchy*], p. 132; and Ross, *Erinnerungen*, pp. 66-67. On public response to these arrests, see the newspapers *Chronos*, 11 Sept. 1833o.s., *Hēlios*, 12 Sept. 1833o.s., and *Triptolemos*, 9 Sept. 1833 and 13 Sept. 1833o.s.; as well as Makrygiannes ([*Memoirs*], II, 69-70), who was also approached by someone who claimed to be carrying instructions for a conspiracy from Kolettes and Mavrokordatos.

[120] The three measures ([*Government Gazette*], no. 29, 14/26 Sept. 1833) were as follows: (1) decree concerning the right to practice printing, lithography, or bookselling; (2) law concerning the policing of the press; (3) law concerning the crimes arising from the abuse of the press, the first two dated 11/23 Sept. and the last 6/18 Sept. 1833. As a result of these laws, *Hēlios* and *Triptolemos* had to limit themselves to literary and scientific articles, and shortly after the change in the character of their coverage they discontinued publication altogether. See also Maurer, *Griechische Volk*, II, 501-502; Mendelssohn Bartholdy, *Geschichte Griechenlands*, II, 482; and Pipineles [*Monarchy*], pp. 138-39.

place without previous knowledge of the cabinet, Maurer threatened to arrest him for not having discovered the plots. Psyllas, Praïdes, and Trikoupes were all removed from the cabinet. Mavrokordatos, the only remaining member of the "British" party, became minister of foreign affairs and lost the valuable patronage he had enjoyed as minister of the economy.[121]

These events gave Kolettes the opportunity he desired and drove the regency majority into the hands of the "French" party, which now captured two key ministries. The "robust hands of Kolettes," to use the phrase of Maurer, took over the ministry of the interior, while the "energetic" Constantine Schinas became minister of justice.[122] These men, both enemies of Kolokotrones, were obviously the most dependable persons for the task of overseeing the necessary investigations and preparations for an unfavorable trial, but for the same reasons one could hardly expect them to conciliate the opposing parties. The Napists hated Schinas as one of the authors of the ecclesiastical settlement, and Kolettes was too partisan a figure to inspire anything but dread among the rank and file Napists and "British," lest they now suffer expulsion from coveted provincial posts and discrimination from Kolettes' appointees. The identification of the regency majority with Kolettes and the "French" party became certain when Sōtēr, the Kolettes newspaper organ, achieved semiofficial status, marked by its publication at the royal printing office at half rate. Maurer justified this pro-French orientation by declaring that the "French" party was the national party representing the interests of the people and enjoying the leadership of "the most popular man in all Greece." His remarks show how far he and his colleagues, caught in the vortex of party conflict, had departed from their original policy of remaining above all parties. In order to free itself from the suspected attempt at domination by one party, it was becoming the organ of another.[123]

The Regency Crisis

During the interval of almost eight months that elapsed between the arrest of Kolokotrones and Plapoutas in September and their trial during May, the Napist party, according to Maurer, recovered from the demoralization dealt by the arrests of September and gained confidence:

from the position taken in the meantime by the president of the regency and Dawkins. Because honorable men had, at the indication of ruptured relations, drawn away from these two, so much the more did

[121] Bower and Bolitho, *Otho I*, p. 60; Maurer, *Griechische Volk*, II, 501; and Mendelssohn Bartholdy, *Geschichte Griechenlands*, II, 483.

[122] Maurer, *Griechische Volk*, II, 501, 509, and Mendelssohn Bartholdy, *Geschichte Griechenlands*, II, 483. According to Gennaios Kolokotrones ([*Memoirs II*], p. 74), Kolettes fabricated this nonexistent plot.

[123] Maurer, *Griechische Volk*, II, 46. See pp. 197-98 above.

they [the Napists] feel the need to associate with intriguers and especially with Phanariots.[124]

The "intriguers" and Phanariots referred to were probably members of the "English" party and what this statement actually reflects is the growing connection of the Napist with the "English" party under the auspices of Dawkins and Armansperg.[125]

What specifically *was* the position of these two men? Both men became engaged in a whispering campaign about the dissension within the regency, attributing unpopular acts to the regency majority and intimating that if Armansperg should come to exercise exclusive control of affairs, he would redress all grievances. By registering his disapproval of regency acts in this offhand manner and by frequenting Armansperg's house on every possible occasion, Dawkins gave the impression that London supported Armansperg. Though temporarily in doubt, this support later materialized.[126]

Dawkins also entered into a temporary alliance with Catacazy, the new Russian minister, who opposed the regency majority because of its ecclesiastical settlement and its treatment of Kolokotrones. Their common objective was apparently to secure a favorable court decision for Kolokotrones. British newspapers in London began predicting the favorable outcome of the trial.[127] Mavrokordatos began taking private action toward this goal, and Klonares, an adherent of Mavrokordatos, decided to defend Kolokotrones in court as his legal counsel. As the common position of the newspapers *Chronos* and *Athēna à propos* the trial indicated, the "Russian" and "English" parties had come together in opposition to the government.[128]

Immediately after the discovery of the two intrigues, the regency unanimously decided to petition London for the recall of Dawkins. It

[124] *Ibid.*, II, 448.

[125] Makrygiannes ([*Memoirs*], II, 64) asserts a close connection between the two parties in general terms during this time, though not specifically in this connection. Finlay wrote, ". . . all the Napists are in Dawkins' interests now," in his Journal (MSS), 20 June 1834. On the intrigues in Nauplion during the winter of 1833-34, see Ross, *Erinnerungen*, pp. 68-70.

[126] For instance, Finlay (Journal [MSS], 19 Apr. 1834) quotes Dawkins as criticizing the government to him personally for being so slow: "I saw that for some intrigue of his own he wanted one to re-echo what he said. . . ." See also Maurer, *Griechische Volk*, II, 511-20. By March, when defending himself to Palmerston against personal accusations made by Henry Headley Parish, secretary of the British legation in Nauplion, Dawkins admitted to his government his preference for Armansperg (Dawkins to Palmerston, Nauplion, 31 Mar. 1833, no. 24, FO 32.43). See Parish's *apologia* of his own behavior before recall to Britain and his continued criticism of British policy in Greece in *Diplomatic History*.

[127] *The Portfolio*, III, 536.

[128] *Ibid.*, III, 509, reports the existence of a letter from Count Roma to a Greek, stating that General Church was a party to the "minor" plot. Kandeloros [*Trial*], p. 157.

accused him of attempting to disturb the unanimity of the regents. In reality the regency majority wanted to deprive Armansperg of a valuable ally. Three successive legates (M. Schinas, Trikoupes, and Karatzas) went to London to implore the British government. Fully informed by Armansperg on the secret proceedings of the regency meetings, Dawkins wrote to London denying the charges against him and offering the countercharge that the hostile regents were catering to the interests of Russian diplomacy in seeking to be rid of him.[129] At the end of April 1834, after a long period of uncertainty, Palmerston broke the suspense with his first note, characterized by what Maurer called "expressions which diplomatic custom never knew until now." The note emphatically refused to recall Dawkins. The failure of the regency majority dramatized its blundering methods. By asking for the recall of Dawkins, the hostile regents had only provoked the wrath of Palmerston and given him the opportunity to intervene against them in Munich. They had only forced Armansperg and Dawkins into closer alliance.[130]

Once the recall of Dawkins appeared unlikely at the end of April, the regency majority turned their attention to Munich where they decided to appeal against Armansperg. In the meantime, they voted, along with other acts against him, to withdraw the special fund for state entertainments assigned Armansperg as president of the regency. They hoped thus to remove any semblance of his primacy and to withhold any money which might be used for partisan purposes. They also broke the news of the regency crisis to Otho and persuaded him to discontinue his visits to Armansperg's home, so as to convey to the public royal disapproval of the regency president. In response, Armansperg wrote Ludwig asking for his own dismissal on the grounds that he was no longer able to work with his regent colleagues. In effect he was forcing Ludwig to choose between them.[131]

[129] On the request, see Dawkins' four letters of self-defense, sent to Palmerston, Nauplion: (1) 31 Mar. 1834, no. 24, FO 32.43; (2) 1 Apr. 1834, no. 25; (3) 21 Apr. 1834, no. 31; and (4) 26 May 1834, no. 38, the last three in FO 32.44. See also Maurer, *Griechische Volk*, II, 521-24, and *The Portfolio*, III, 531-32.

[130] Dawkins had recommended to Palmerston a strong statement so as to admit no further doubt of British support for Armansperg, indeed so as to influence the public, but even more the king, by such British support (Dawkins to Palmerston, Nauplion, 21 Apr. 1834, no. 31, FO 32.44). On the whole affair of petitions to London for the recall of Dawkins, see Maurer, *Griechische Volk*, II, 521-26, and Mendelssohn Bartholdy, *Geschichte Griechenlands*, II, 491-94.

[131] For a summary of these acts against Armansperg, see Dawkins to Palmerston, Nauplion, 6 May 1834, no. 32, FO 32.44; Maurer, *Griechische Volk*, II, 524-35; and Mendelssohn Bartholdy, *Geschichte Griechenlands*, II, 494-95. On Armansperg's response, see Vaudreuil, French minister to Bavaria, to Count Regny, French foreign minister, Munich, 16 June 1834, in *Gesandtschaftsberichte*, ed. Chroust, Abt. I, Vol. III, 188-90.

For detailed though pro-regency majority accounts of the differences between Armansperg and the regency majority, see (1) the private memoir of Maurer and

The Kolokotrones Trial

Under these circumstances, the trial of Kolokotrones assumed even greater political importance. A favorable court decision would constitute a moral defeat for the regency majority and make the arrests of the previous September seem like unjust and arbitrary acts. Catacazy observed that a condemnation was "a political necessity which had to be achieved at all costs."[132]

The long and elaborate preparations that went into the state's holding of the trial attests to its importance for the regency majority. Edward Masson, the Scottish philhellenic public prosecutor, conducted the investigations with the assistance of Kanellos Delegiannes, a personal enemy of Plapoutas as a result of a long family feud. Both Masson and Delegiannes were adherents of the "French" party. Both encountered great obstacles in obtaining information and in rounding up witnesses because of the widespread loyalty to, and fear of, Kolokotrones in the provinces concerned, and because of the secret opposition of some Napist officials. They obtained as witnesses for the prosecution mostly personal enemies of the accused, men of little or no property or importance in their communities—a fact that rendered their testimony questionable.[133]

Before the trial, the state replaced two of the five judges in the court empowered to try the case. It substituted two men ill-disposed toward the accused for two judges rendered unfit by their Napist affiliations.[134] The indictment dated 7 March 1834—"more like a party statement than a legal document," to quote Finlay—accused Kolokotrones and Plapoutas of:

> organizing and directing together, during May, June, July, August and the beginning of September of the past year, a conspiracy with the

---

Abel, dated Munich, 31 Oct. 1834, and addressed to Ludwig as an *apologia*, and (2) a report from von Gasser, Bavarian minister to Greece and partisan of the regency majority, to Ludwig, Nauplion, 27 Oct. 1833, about regency dissensions. Both these manuscripts, located in the Geheimes Staatsarchiv, Munich, have been published by Apostolos Vakalopoulos, "Germanika Engrapha apo to Geheimes Archiv tou Monachou schetika me ten prote Periodo tes Antibasileias sten Hellada (1833-1834)" ["German Documents from the Geheimes Archiv of Munich concerning the first Period of the Regency in Greece"], *Epistemonike Epeteris Philosophikes Scholes* [*Scholarly Annual of the Philosophical School*], University of Thessaloniki, VIII (1960), 49-97. Neither report, however, relates these differences in any detail to the parties and the domestic politics of Greece.

[132] Catacazy to Nesselrode, Nauplion, 17/29 June 1834, in Jelavich, *Russia and Greece*, p. 98.

[133] Kandeloros [*Trial*], pp. 147-57; Theodore Kolokotrones, *Diegesis sympanton tes Hellenikes phyles apo ta 1700 heos ta 1836* [*Narration of Events of the Greek Race from 1770 to 1836*] (Athens, 1846), p. 258; Gennaios Kolokotrones [*Memoirs II*], p. 75; and Mendelssohn Bartholdy, *Geschichte Griechenlands*, II, 484. For a study of Edward Masson, see K. Vardoniotes, "Edouardos Masson" ["Edward Masson"], *Parnassos*, XI (1915).

[134] Dawkins to Palmerston, Nauplion, 22 June 1834, no. 43, FO 32.44. Also Gennaios Kolokotrones, [*Memoirs II*], p. 75.

object of disturbing the public peace, of drawing the subjects of His Majesty into brigandage and civil war, and of dissolving the established polity.

It mentioned two petitions to foreign powers and accused the two men of originating the one and supporting the other. It pressed the charge of treason against both and recommended the death penalty.[135]

There seems hardly any doubt that Kolokotrones and Plapoutas were implicated in the outbreak of brigandage and the appeal to foreign powers, but the prosecution could offer nothing more than circumstantial evidence of a questionable sort. Nor could it, strictly speaking, make its set of accusations meet the popular conception of treason.[136] Public opinion, agitated by the struggle between Armansperg and his colleagues, regarded more than the strictly legal aspects of the case. It looked upon Kolokotrones and Plapoutas, however controversial politically, as heroes of the Revolution who deserved a better fate. In addition, all the so-called acts of treason—brigandage, appeal to foreign powers, secret societies— were established practices in Greek political life, indulged in by all political oppositions, and even hallowed by the patriotic purposes toward which Greeks had employed them in the past. Furthermore, Kolokotrones' activities were extenuated in public opinion by their connection with regency dissensions and possible Armansperg intrigue. The accused seemed to be the victims of their political opponents and foreign regents. The demand for the death penalty only aroused the patriotism and xenophobia of the public and gained for the accused the strong sympathy invited by imminent martyrdom.[137]

At this juncture, the acts of the "English" party made the ultimate victory of the regency majority a hollow one. Mavrokordatos openly condemned the proceedings, and the regency retaliated by dismissing him from office, leaving Kolettes in undisputed control. *Athēna*, loud in its protests, had to defend itself in court against state charges of violating the press laws of the previous year. Finally, the three-man majority opinion of the court condemned the accused and handed down the death penalty with recommendation of royal clemency, but the two-man minority, Polyzoïdes and Tertsetes, who had recently been showing greater

[135] Finlay, *History*, vi, 139, n. 1; Kandeloros [*Trial*], pp. 21-22; Mendelssohn Bartholdy, *Geschichte Griechenlands*, ii, 484-85; *Sōtēr*, 18 Mar. 1833 *o.s.* (copy of the accusation). Besides the thorough account of the trial by Kandeloros ([*Trial*]), for published installments of *proces*, see *Sōtēr*, 18 Mar. 1834, 3 May 1834, 6 May–7 June 1834, all *o.s.* Also Finlay, *op.cit.*, vii, 139-40; Maurer, *Griechische Volk*, ii, 505-506; Mendelssohn Bartholdy, *op.cit.*, ii, 482-87; and Pipineles [*Monarchy*], pp. 136-37. Parish (*Diplomatic History*, pp. 270-73) published in English the act of accusation as well as the sentence of the court.

[136] Dawkins to Palmerston, Nauplion, 25 May 1834, no. 36 FO 32.44.

[137] *Loc.cit.* Also Finlay, *History*, vii, 138-39, and Rangabe [*Memoirs*], i, 375, who responded to the accused as Revolutionary heroes rather than as rebels or traitors.

friendliness to Armansperg, dissented. The law required dissenting judges to sign the majority condemnation, but these two men boldly refused their signatures and would have withdrawn from the court had not gendarmes physically held them in their places in court. The regency dismissed them from their judicial posts and brought state legal action against them.[138]

Thus the regency majority achieved its goal only by violating the liberty of the press and the irremoveability of judges. Its acts looked as despotic and arbitrary as anything that Kapodistrias had done. At the insistence of the king and over the protests of Kolettes, the Crown (regency) commuted the penalty first to life imprisonment, then to twenty-five years (the equivalent of life imprisonment for Kolokotrones who was then in his sixty-fifth year). The public attributed such clemency to the king, or possibly to Armansperg, certainly not to the regency majority.[139]

The Mane Insurrection[140]

A direct consequence of the trial was the outbreak of an insurrection in Mane.[141] The basic cause of the revolt was the regency's attempt to integrate all parts of Greece into a single, unified state, and the specific measure that Mane resisted was one being applied to all of Greece—the dismantling of towers, which were the private homes traditionally fortified for self-defense under conditions of lawlessness, anarchy, and blood feuds. In most parts of Greece, such towers were rare, remnants of a vanishing past. In Mane, they represented the traditional way of life for the ruling warrior class and in 1834 some 800 of them existed. The Maniats zealously maintained them, as much against outside government interference as against incursions of local enemies. Six months before the outbreak, the regency had decided to take action. Realizing that the decree might encounter resistance, they had sent Maximilian Feder, a Bavarian officer, to Mane with money and troops, the former to "indemnify" or bribe the landlords into acquiescence, the latter to impose the decree on the in-

[138] Dawkins to Palmerston, Nauplion, 20 June 1834, no. 41 (on Mavrokordatos' behavior), and 22 June 1834, no. 43 (on Polyzoïdes and Tertsetes), FO 32.44. Also see George Tertsetes, *Apologia* [*Apology*] (Athens, 1835), and Gennaios Kolokotrones [*Memoirs II*], p. 75.

[139] Mendelssohn Bartholdy, *Geschichte Griechenlands*, II, 486-87, and Gennaios Kolokotrones, [*Memoirs II*], p. 75.

[140] See generally Finlay, *History*, VII, 151-53; Kandeloros [*Trial*], pp. 312-13; Maurer, *Griechische Volk*, II, 506-11; Mendelssohn Bartholdy, *Geschichte Griechenlands*, II, 487-91; and Andrew S. Skandames, *Selides Politikes Historias kai Kritikes*, Tomos I: *He Triakontaetia tes Basileias tou Othonos 1832-1862* [*Pages of Political History and Criticism*, Vol. I: *The Thirty-year Period of the Kingship of Otho 1832-1862*] (Athens, 1961), 340-47. In more detail on the Mane revolt of 1833-34 and the Messenian revolt of 1834 are unpublished documents, some twenty-four despatches, either from eparchs in Mane to the nomarch of Laconia or nomarch to ministry of the interior, collected in a separate folder (folder 143) entitled "Undated (1834)," Otho Archive.

[141] Bower and Bolitho, *Otho I*, p. 64, and *Sôter*, 14 June 1833 and 22 July 1833 o.s.

transigent. Until the Kolokotrones trial Feder was slowly succeeding in his mission without meeting any forceful opposition.[142]

According to Maurer, the revolt originated in Nauplion to divert the regency from pursuing the condemnation of Kolokotrones, but he did not specify who the alleged instigators in Nauplion were. He made a specific charge against Mavrokordatos, whom he accused of purposely failing to carry out the regency's instructions to send the fleet as a threat against Maniat resistance. Other documents reveal another type of connection between the rebels and the Kolokotrones trial. Present among the rebellious Maniats were Metropetrovas and Kritsales, partisans of Kolokotrones, who were shortly to emerge as leaders of the Messenian revolt. It seems, therefore, that such Napists from other parts of the Peloponnesos—whether at the instigation of others in Nauplion or not—deliberately incited already dissatisfied Maniats into rebellion.[143] Priests and monks allied with Maniat landlords in arousing the people by announcing that the "Jewish" regency intended to destroy their religion and imprison the monks (a reference to the decree for the dissolution of the monasteries), that dismantling of the towers was only a prelude to the imposition of a "head tax" (from which Maniats had remained free even in Turkish times), and that Maniat autonomy was being threatened.[144]

Luckily for the regency, the two most important families of Mane, Tzanetakes and Mavromichales, used their influence to make the Maniats acquiesce, and clergymen appointed by the holy synod reassured the Maniats that no one would violate their religion.[145] But pacification came only through a negotiated settlement which conceded to the Maniats guarantees of their autonomy, monetary grants, the nonexecution of the monastic laws, and the organization of Maniats into their own specially organized military corps in return for the partial dismantling of towers. But the regency's willingness to negotiate came only after Bavarian

[142] Maurer, *Griechische Volk*, II, 506-507, and Mendelssohn Bartholdy, *Geschichte Griechenlands*, II, 488.

[143] Maurer, *Griechische Volk*, II, 507, and Mendelssohn Bartholdy, *Geschichte Griechenlands*, II, 487. *The Portfolio* (III, 539) accuses Metaxas of sending agents to Mane from Nauplion. An official document refers to 2,000 inhabitants of Mane "*irrités par de fausses renommées adressées éxprés [sic] de Messenie. . . .*" (report of Praïdes, nomarch of Laconia, to the ministry of the interior [n.p., n.d.], folder 134, Otho Archive).

[144] The same document cited in n. 143 above. Also the report of P. Monasteriotes, eparch of Itilou, to nomarch Praïdes (n.p., Apr. 1834, folder 134, Otho Archive) states the Maniat rebel demands as follows: no demolition of towers, no Maniat payment of tribute, no conscription into the regular army, no implementation of the state laws on the dissolution of the monasteries and convents. See also Maurer, *Griechische Volk*, II, 507-509; Mendelssohn Bartholdy, *Geschichte Griechenlands*, II, 487-88; and Pipineles [*Monarchy*], p. 102.

[145] Holy synod to protosyngelos of Kalamata, instructing him to proceed to Sparta where a special commission of the Holy Synod would meet him, Nauplion, 22 May 1834*o.s.*, folder 132 (ministry of ecclesiastical affairs, 1833-62), Otho Archive.

troops—some 2,500 sent under the command of Christian Schmaltz, a Bavarian officer, to suppress the revolt by force—had suffered humiliating defeats in the treacherous and unfamiliar mountain terrain of Mane.[146] The most important consequence of the revolt was that it dispelled the belief that the Bavarian troops were invincible and damaged the moral authority of the regency. Revolt had proved a useful way to extract concessions from an apparently weak government. This observation lent encouragement to potential rebels elsewhere.[147]

In the meantime, the regency crisis was forcing Ludwig to take action. In spite of the regency majority's pro-French policy, at least Vaudreuil, the French minister in Munich, joined England in support of Armansperg. In April 1834, Vaudreuil wrote his government that Armansperg's "political tendency is constantly favorable to us." By June, Ludwig, as father of Otho and original designator of regency membership, decided on the recall of Maurer and Abel. By pointing to Russia's lack of satisfaction with the decision and by identifying Kobell, Maurer's replacement, as a liberal "attached to France," Vaudreuil seemed intent on convincing his government that the decision presaged no setback for French diplomacy in Greece. But during July, D'Hailly, the secretary of the French legation in Munich, took issue with that view. Noting that the Bavarian government wanted to keep France ignorant of the decision, he interpreted the change as making the regency exclusively dependent upon England. Russia, desiring the recall of Armansperg as well, was even less pleased. To reassure Russia, Gise attributed to the regency majority those features of regency policy displeasing to Russia and indicated that Armansperg would move toward a policy more in keeping with Russia's desires. In fact, Gise falsely accused Maurer and Abel of wishing to grant Greece an ultraliberal constitution, like the French Jacobin constitution of 1793, and gave this as a primary reason for their recall. Obviously the Bavarian government was willing to risk French alienation to secure Russian support. Yet France joined England in approving the change. The Russian government responded to Gise's statements with frank skepticism and acquiesced only provisionally by announcing that it would suspend judgment until the new regency proved itself through its future acts. In the meantime, the Russian government urged Catacazy to press the new

146 Eparch of Gytheon to nomarch Praïdes (n.p., n.d.), on the dismantling of some towers; Praïdes to minister of the interior (n.p., n.d.), recommending force for dismantling; Monasteriotes to Praïdes (n.p., n.d.), on people pleading for mercy on the grounds that they have been duped; the minister of the interior to the minister of war (n.p., n.d.), quoting the recommendation of the eparch of Itilou that Maniats be organized into light corps, that the Mavromichales' help gain acquiescence for the dismantling of towers—all from folder 143, Otho Archive. See also Bower and Bolitho, *Otho I*, pp. 64-65; Makrygiannes [*Memoirs*], II, 73; Mendelssohn Bartholdy, *Geschichte Griechenlands*, II, 488-91; and Pipineles [*Monarchy*], p. 102.

147 Mendelssohn Bartholdy, *Geschichte Griechenlands*, II, 491.

regency in the right direction. In effect, it was asking for change in policy as the price of its support.[148]

News of the Maurer–Abel recall arrived in Greece at the beginning of August. This unexpected regency shakeup, rendered even more extraordinary by the limited time remaining until the royal majority (eleven months), represented a resounding victory for Armansperg and English diplomacy. The manner of its occurrence betrayed the real arbiters of Greek destiny—not the domestic parties or the young king, but rather Ludwig in Munich responding to pressure from London and St. Petersburg. Even though the parties did not play a decisive role in these events, they contributed to the outcome and, even more, demonstrated their ability to resist and thwart the most determined efforts to overwhelm them.

4. Political Opposition and Government Response

Patterns of Party Behavior

One might attribute the failure of the regency majority to their egregious tactical blunders against slippery foes or to their uncompromising and perhaps visionary commitment to the total and immediate eradication of publicly recognized evils (foreign influence, party pressures, and disguised political resistance). One might contend that their strong-arm policy of repression did not receive a fair trial because it was attempted by a regency divided against itself. But when all this is admitted, the first regency's experiences during this period are significant, from our standpoint, because of the light they shed on three subjects: (1) the tenacity of the parties when challenged to a struggle for survival, (2) the pitfalls of a faulty understanding of the party situation, and (3) the dilemmas facing any government determined to govern.

The circumstances in 1833 invited the parties to fulfill the functions to which they were best suited—the positive function of serving as channels to positions of importance in the new regime and the negative function of acting as defensive organizations against unwelcome state actions, such as the measures to eradicate the parties.

Since the regency would countenance no public debate of issues and would not delegate to its highest officials the power necessary to enact a program, the main focus of party activity was the securing and main-

[148] For the French side and its information about Gise's justification of the decision and Russia's displeasure, see Vaudreuil to Regny, Munich, 16 Apr. 1834, 24 June 1834, and D'Hailly to Regny, Munich, 5 July 1834, 10 July 1834, 25 Sept. 1834, in *Gesandschaftsberichte*, ed. Chroust, Abt. i, Vol. iii, 181-82, 192-93, 195, 196-98. For the Russian side and Gise's justification to the Russian government, see Nesselrode to Gagarin, Russian Minister to Bavaria, St. Petersburg, 29 Aug./10 Sept. 1834; Gise to Bray, Bavarian minister to Russia, Munich, 27 June 1834; and Nesselrode to Catacazy, St. Petersburg, 17/29 Aug. 1834, in Jelavich, *Russia and Greece*, pp. 83-88, 88-92, 92-98.

taining of public office. One of the outstanding phenomena of the first regency period, when a new and permanent administration created many posts with prospects of secure tenure, was the widespread aspiration to public office. Thiersch, writing on the eve of the regency's arrival in Greece, said, "Among the various parties, plans of government and administration have already been made; places in the cabinet down through the police bureaus have already been assigned." According to the newspaper *Sōtēr*, numerous office-seekers invaded the capital and stayed on, waiting to win themselves some coveted post. Many not only spent what money they possessed in order to remain in the capital near the distributors of patronage, but they even borrowed. So great a prize did a man consider public office that he would gamble away his small means to obtain it instead of investing in the purchase and cultivation of land.[149]

Public office was coveted for three reasons: as a means of livelihood, as a source of prestige, and as the only real guarantee against oppression by one's enemies. The first factor dominated in the case of the socially and politically prominent, such as Mavrokordatos, Metaxas, and Zaïmes, who emerged from the Revolution penniless and in debt, as well as in the case of indigent veterans whose aversion to cultivating the soil left them a meagre choice between brigandage or some petty post such as postman, policeman, or office boy in a government office. So great was the prestige of public office—maybe because of Greek exclusion from the central administration during the days of Ottoman rule—that a private profession acquired its value primarily as a means of entering state service. Lawyers sought judicial and professorial posts (the latter being by government appointment in a state which enjoyed few private educational institutions). Kapodistrias, Kolettes, and Glarakes were only three of the many examples of doctors who preferred the political to the medical life.[150]

An extant letter reveals the importance of political office to people who had reason to fear the vengeance and discrimination of their political enemies. As Christos Vlases wrote to Regas Palamides, when urging great care in the appointment of personnel to the new courts and requesting a court appointment for himself and his brother:

> . . . the chief desire on our part for that post is not dictated so much by a need for the salary, as from wanting to establish relations with that important branch, because unfortunately . . . [those men], appointed by the Kapodistrian will, have roasted our hearts. . . . So, if

---

[149] Thiersch, *État actuel*, I, 240. See also Gennaios Kolokotrones ([*Memoirs II*], p. 80), who observes that a new appointee to office, dispensing patronage, was hounded by place-seekers.

[150] "In Greece the high class of the community does not have independent means, but practically all, suffering from the effects of war and anarchy, assemble around the state and ask to live through the public service" (*Hēlios*, 7 July 1833 o.s.).

you can place us, then we shall at least have men of our confidence, such as Papalexopoulos, Tariotes, and such others.[151]

The parties, reflecting their origins in the system of clientage, served as the clearinghouse for office-seekers, as numerous documents reveal. Panagiotes Mothonios, a soldier who had fought under the command of Andrew Lontos throughout the Revolution, asked for his former commander's intervention in Nauplion (then the nation's capital) to secure him a place in the local contingent being sent to fight some rebels. "Please forgive me for my boldness [in asking this favor]," he concluded, "but I . . . have nowhere else to turn for assistance . . . and hope that you will protect me as usual. . . ." Christakopoulos, apparently a client of Regas Palamides, wrote requesting him to appeal to Kolettes, then minister of the interior and the highest party official, for the appointment of at least one Tripolis native to the gendarmerie—and Christakopoulos gave five names—"because they have bedevilled me with their letters." The second of the two illustrations is a fine example of the rather elaborate mediating procedure of the clientage system for getting a local petition relayed to the highest party official. On the highest level the patron who intervened to find a place for his client was the minister of one of the three protecting powers.[152]

It is ironic that merely by carrying out the necessary task of appointing the bureaucracy, the Crown stimulated the very party activity it was attempting to discourage. Unwittingly, the government contributed to the mania for office by adopting an appointment policy imposed upon it by public opinion and by its own fair-minded sentiments, namely that public office should be a reward for Revolutionary services. Such official acknowledgment implicitly confirmed the traditional image of public office as a chance for private gain and security rather than as a burden assumed by a reluctant citizen for the nation's good. The relatively high salary scale, probably designed to discourage the acceptance of bribes by officials, only made public office more attractive. Inevitably, the regency's own cabinet ministers were allowed to exercise some patronage, hence making it apparent to office-seekers that adherence to a party was the surest way of securing and holding office.[153]

A party performed its negative role when out of power and in disfavor. Its opportunity to exercise patronage and benefit its members depended on a change of regime. To secure such a change, it resorted to every device to discredit the government in power (such as perpetrating dis-

[151] Chr. Vlases to Regas Palamides, n.p., 6 June 1834 *o.s.*, 7 June 1834 *o.s.*, folder 257 (1833-39), Palamides Archive.

[152] P. Mothonios to A. Lontos, Nauplion, 9 Aug. 1834 *o.s.*, no. 32, folder 18/1059, Lontos Archive, Benaki Museum, Athens; and B. Christakopoulos to Regas Palamides, Nauplion, 25 Oct. 1834 *o.s.*, folder 257 (1833-39), Palamides Archive.

[153] Makrygiannes ([*Memoirs*], II, 58, 61) is representative of this view and urged it on the regency.

orders, provoking the government to acts of tyranny, and circulating reports of government instability), or contributed positively to its downfall (soliciting the intervention of foreign powers or obtaining the good will of the regents). It became the practice for each party to maintain a newspaper, which defended itself when in power or, when out of office, concentrated on exposing all the abuses of the existing regime as well as circulating rumors of its impending collapse.[154] Brigandage became a way of exhausting the regime's resources and convincing the public in a dramatic way that the regime could not perform even the most elementary functions of maintaining order and offering protection.[155] An appeal to foreign powers might take the form of a petition addressed directly to a foreign capital (such as Kolokotrones' letter to Nesselrode) or of quiet gentlemen's agreements with the ministers of those powers in Athens.[156] The way to influence the Crown, or those exercising its prerogatives, was to discredit one's foes in office by legitimately uncovering administrative abuses, by placing the worst possible interpretations on official acts, or even by resorting to frameups.[157] Finally, parties threatened by discrimination or repression would enter into temporary alliance in order to fight the government, only to part company when one or the other had obtained government favor. As the regency majority's experience shows, the parties skillfully employed devices which rendered the consequences of state acts just the opposite of those intended by the regents.

Misunderstandings and Dilemmas

In reviewing with the benefit of hindsight the intentions and behavior of the regency, we find a number of misunderstandings, miscalculations, and false assumptions in the record, all of them showing how difficult an understanding of Greek politics actually was. Perhaps the regency majority's least justifiable mistake, because it concerned European diplomacy, was the false assumption that power rivalry in Greece was simply a two-way affair. In actuality, England and Russia, though most jealous of each other, also feared French influence in Greece and feared it enough to call a temporary truce to cooperate in fighting French diplomatic ascendancy there. In their eyes, France was neither neutral nor disinterested in its Greek policy.

A second mistake involved essentially the failure to recognize parties as parties, though what the regency majority said may have been mere public rationalization. If indeed a real mistake, it took two forms—either the misinterpretation of a party as a mere collection of moderate, qualified individuals (as in the case of the "English" party at first) or its identi-

---

[154] Dawkins to Blackhouse, Nauplion, 20 Aug. 1833, no number, FO 32.37.

[155] *Loc.cit.* Even if not true in the case of the "major" plot, to which the remark refers, it reflects the type of practice in which parties engaged.

[156] Maurer, *Griechische Volk*, I, 31-32.   [157] See pp. 374-76, Chap. VII below.

fication of a party with the nation or the people (as in the subsequent belief that the "French" party was *the* national party). This type of error discredited the regency as being the patron first of the "English" party, then of the "French," rather than an impartial mediator between the parties.

A third error was the failure to recognize the deep roots of the parties and their extensive connections. This led, on the one hand, to the facile belief that, by a series of appointments, men could be weaned from long-established party connections. This bred unwarranted optimism. On the other hand, that same error concealed the dangerous consequences of acts of severity. For instance, even though the regency considered its tough policy toward the "Russian" and subsequently the "English" parties as a fight against two small cliques (Phanariots and remnants of the Kapodistrians, as Maurer called them respectively), the public at large interpreted its behavior as an attack by one-third of the nation (the "French" party with the blessing of the regency) against two-thirds of the nation as represented by the two remaining parties. The regency also failed to realize that its prosecution of Kolokotrones and Plapoutas for what by Western standards it considered illegitimate practices was interpreted as the trial of an entire party for acts which constituted normal party behavior.

A fourth mistake, crucial because its policy of severity depended on military effectiveness, concerned the regency's military establishment. Foreign recruitment and Western organization—the conditions which it believed indispensable for a politically loyal and militarily obedient army—were the very causes which made this army militarily ineffective because foreigners did not know the terrain and were not familiar with the irregular tactics most effective for such mountain warfare. As a result, when the regency put its power to the test against the Maniats, it exposed its weakness to the public, or perhaps it is more accurate to say, discovered its own weakness.

Finally, the regency probably underestimated the close connection between foreign policy and party policy, at least in practice. By discriminating against the Napists from the start, it antagonized Russian diplomacy (which was also angered by the church settlement). This case shows how a government's party policy would prejudice its foreign policy. The converse became obvious from the fact that, by favoring French diplomacy, the regency majority came ultimately to court the "French" party. Hence, favoritism toward France (which alienated Britain) and discrimination against the Napists (which alienated Russia) forced these powers and their affiliate parties into an alliance which ultimately toppled the regency.

The above includes only the most important misunderstandings and relates to a complex situation made even more so by the regency's understandably faulty analysis of the party situation. The experiences of the first regency are important because they reveal dilemmas that were to plague subsequent governments even though these governments had the example of the regency majority. In brief, these dilemmas were built into the situation. For easy subsequent reference, I refer to these as: (1) the dilemma of neutrality, (2) the dilemma of plot response, and (3) the dilemma of administrative deterrence.

Attempted neutrality, with respect to the three powers, tended to unite them in opposition to the neutral regime. To avoid such common opposition, a regime had to court at least one power, and such courtship simply intensified the pressure from at least one of the others. The same situation applied to the party rivalries. Each party sought the ascendancy. To fight down one party's bid for power a regime fell dependent on another party for help.

If a regime dealt severely with a discovered plot in order to deter any future attempts from other quarters, it might also provoke a defensive reaction leading, out of desperation, to further subversion. On the other hand, if the state treated such plotters leniently, or even negotiated with them (as in the case of the Mane revolt), such leniency might be interpreted as a sign of weakness and hence encourage any dissatisfied group to adopt the same means. This was the dilemma of plot response.

The dilemma of administrative deterrence involved the fundamental premise that the basic condition for undermining the parties was an efficient and fair administration capable of outdoing the parties in providing security and opportunity for advancement. For successful operation, such an administration required nothing less than a Western-trained, nonpartisan officialdom, which is to say that major appointments would go to foreigners and recently arrived heterochthons, men with the least claim on the state for past services. Because of lesser education and party affiliations, autochthons and long-established heterochthons, frequently men with records of distinguished Revolutionary service, would be offered inferior or merely honorary positions involving loss of prestige, influence, and sometimes income. This latter group was likely to fight such a policy by falling back upon the parties, which had already proved effective in paralyzing the administration until accommodated with official appointments for adherents. Through patronage of the protecting powers, the parties could harass the Crown. Through attacks in the press, they could rob the existing regime of public confidence. If necessary, they could go as far as to disrupt administration through organized brigandage. All of this would in turn perpetuate the administrative chaos on which the parties thrived. And if all three parties were simultaneously excluded from sufficient participation in the administration, they were capable of rising above their rivalries in common alliance against the existing regime. Hence, the very policy designed to establish the basic condition for the demise of the parties tended rather to mobilize them into action and thereby preclude the possibility of establishing that condition.

CHAPTER FIVE

The Armansperg Regime
July 1834–February 1837

IT IS CONVENTIONAL to treat this time span as two periods rather than one. With respect to the formal locus of power, this conventional treatment is justified. On 1 June 1835 the second regency came to an end by provision of the treaty of 7 May 1832 and the king, now of age, took over. In actual fact, Armansperg exercised the real power in Greece, before 1 June as chief regent, thereafter as chancellor. To be sure, he had to pay greater deference to the wishes of the king after 1 June, but the king was still young and inexperienced. Moreover, the king was absent from Greece between 10 May 1836 and 14 February 1837, visiting his parents in Bavaria, trying to restore his weak health, and looking for a suitable bride. Regardless of his changed formal status and variations in the actual amount of power delegated to him, Armansperg ruled throughout the two and a half years indicated above.

1. THE SECOND REGENCY PERIOD, JULY 1834–MAY 1835

The ten months of the second regency were marked by more than the curious duality of actual political power which resulted from Armansperg's dependence on Kolettes as minister of the interior. The lame-duck nature of the existing regime left it unfit for any constructive statecraft. Growing anticipation of the king's accession and increasing uncertainty about the control of the new royal regime led to active intrigue and feverish jockeying for power. The two chief political struggles of the period involved Armansperg, first against Kolettes, later against the king himself. This ten-month period may be regarded as Armansperg's concerted and successful attempt to stay in power.

Armansperg had not won a total victory in July 1834. Political strength acquired by Kolettes in the ministry of the interior placed a serious limitation on Armansperg's actual authority. The political fate of Armansperg would depend on the decision, ten months hence, of Otho, who was already ill-disposed toward him. One cannot understand the nature of the chancellorship or Armansperg's later policy toward the party or the reasons for his ultimate dismissal in February 1837 apart from the politics of the second regency period.

The Messenian Revolt

The power struggle between Armansperg and Kolettes reached its peak in the months immediately following the Messenian revolt. In mid-August

1834, special messengers rocked Nauplion with news of a Peloponnesian revolt[1] which had broken out on 11 August. Although known as the "Messenian revolt," it covered the west-central section of Peloponnesos (parts of Arcadia) as well as Messenia in the south. The leaders were

[1] The Messenian revolt has received rather thorough treatment, at least compared with most other revolts during the reign of Otho, in the extensive monograph of Takes Kandeloros, *He Dike tou Kolokotrone kai he Epanastasis tes Peloponnesou* [*The Trial of Kolokotrones and the Peloponnesian Revolution*] (Athens, 1906), which makes extensive use of valuable newspaper sources. The subject has also had a monograph devoted exclusively to it in a military journal which I have not been able to consult—N. Kteniades, "He Messeniake Epanastasis" ["The Messenian Revolt"], *Stratiotike Echo* [*Military Echo*], I (1932). Primary accounts appear in George Finlay, *A History of Greece from its Conquest by the Romans to the Present Time, B.C. 146 to A.D. 1864*, ed. H. F. Tozer (Oxford, 1877), VII, 153-56; Ludwig Ross, *Erinnerungen und Mittheilungen aus Griechenland* (Berlin, 1863), pp. 75-76, and Gennaios Kolokotrones, *Apomnemoneumata (Cheirographon Deuteron 1821-1862)* [*Memoirs (Second Manuscript 1821-1862)*], ed. Emmanuel Protopsaltes (Athens, 1961), p. 76 (hereafter cited as [*Memoirs II*]). Brief secondary accounts appear in Tryphon Evangelides, *Historia tou Othonos Basileos tes Hellados 1832-1862* [*History of Otho King of Greece*] (Athens, 1893), p. 57; Gianni Kordatos, *Historia tes Neoteres Hellados* [*History of Modern Greece*] (Athens, 1957), III, 51-52, and Andrew S. Skandames, *Selides Politikes Historias kai Kritikes. Tomos I: He Triakontaetia tes Basileias tou Othonos 1832-1862* [*Pages of Political History and Criticism. Vol. I: The Thirty-year Period of the Kingship of Otho 1832-1862*] (Athens, 1961), 347-49. Other general works (Karolides, Mendelssohn Bartholdy, Driault and Lhéritier) mention it barely or not at all.

Like Kandeloros, I have utilized the contemporary newspaper accounts. On the other hand, I have had access to two sets of documents unavailable to him. The first is a set of twelve documents in a special envelope labeled "Undated 1834," in folder 134 (Ministry of Interior 1833-37), Otho Archive, Vlachogiannes Collection, General State Archives, Athens. These are despatches between civil and military officials, at all levels of administration (from the regional eparch to the minister of interior, for instance) as well as a few private letters which they acquired in the course of their investigation. For this subject, their primary value is the revelation of a conflict between "English" and "French" parties and between rival provincial authorities (military and civil) in suppressing and investigating the revolt. There is one particularly good example of the way in which one civil official attempted to obtain the release of a friend, arrested on suspicion. His particular method was that of alleging that he (the civil official) had planted the suspected party as a spy (no. 7 below). An itemized list of the twelve documents follows: (1) Nengas, eparch of Gortynia, to Delegiannes, colonel in the gendarmerie (one side); Delegiannes to Nengas (other side), (2) Nengas to Delegiannes, (3) Nengas to nomarch of Arcadia (Silivergos), (4) *Proces verbal* of Delegiannes' interrogation of Sergopoulos (a suspect), (5) Adam Doukas, director of the nomarchy in the absence of the nomarch, to John Kolettes, minister of the interior, (6) John Kolettes to Lesuire, minister of war, (7) Panagiotes Delegiannes, eparch of Elis, to Vronikorsky, submoirarch of Achaia and Elis, (8) Vronikorsky to P. Delegiannes, (9) John D. Kritsales, one of the rebel leaders, to captains at Andritsaina, (10) Athanasios Gregoriades to Constantine Oikonomopoulos (both individual conspirators), (11) Mavromichales, moirarch of Messene, to the commandant of the gendarmerie, and (12) Mavromichales' report of 3 Aug. 1834*o.s.*

The second is a set of four letters from Dawkins, British minister to Greece, to the foreign office, which deal exclusively with the revolt and the subsequent investiga-

Napist captains of secondary importance, dependents of the imprisoned Kolokotrones, hitherto implicated with him in the "major" plot.[2]

According to Dawkins, this outbreak was the product of large plans organized jointly by members of the Napist and "English" parties for a general uprising to overturn the regency majority. Driven to the opposition by the dismissal of Mavrokordatos, some of his adherents had allegedly assented to a plan whereby an outbreak in the Morea would set off a series of simultaneous uprisings—in Hydra and Spezza and in Rumely, among the ill-affected palikars in conjunction with 200 to 300 men who had emigrated to Thessaly after the dissolution of the irregular troops in 1833. News of the recall of Maurer and Abel nine days before the actual outbreak in Messenia allegedly satisfied the "English" party and the pro-Armansperg palikars sufficiently for them to cancel their revolutionary intentions. Such may have been the case with more prominent Napists as well. Hence the revolt never passed beyond its original stage as a localized Napist affair.[3]

Dawkins' report is important in establishing the revolt—in its inception at least—as a joint undertaking of both the "Russian" *and* the "English" parties, and hence corrects the general belief, deliberately propagated by *Sōtēr* and the "French" party, that the revolt was exclusively "Russian." But it fails to point out an additional fact, which emerges from "French" criticisms of the way in which the investigation of the revolt took place. George Gregoriades, brother of a friend of the "English" Zaïmes and hence probably "English" himself, participated in the revolt. This fact

---

tions, located in Archives of the British Foreign Office, Public Record Office, London. They are as follows: (1) 25 Aug. 1834, no. 62, Foreign Office, Ser. 32, Vol. 45 (hereafter cited as FO 32.45 and so on), (2) 26 Sept. 1834, no. 68, FO 32.46, including a translation of a rebel proclamation, (3) 21 Oct. 1834, no. 74, FO 32.46, and (4) 21 Nov. 1834, no. 79, FO 32.46.

[2] There were five acknowledged leaders, all Napists: Metros Plapoutas and Petros Plapoutas, both from Gortynia and both nephews of the imprisoned Demetrios Plapoutas; J. Gritsales of Psari; Metros Petrovas, an octogenarian from Karatzes; and Niketas Zermpines, nephew of Kolokotrones. In addition, Asemakes Sergopoulos seems to have played a prominent role as a liaison between Nauplion and local conspirators (Dawkins to Foreign Office, Nauplion, 25 Aug. 1834, no. 62, FO 32.45; Kandeloros [*Trial*], p. 326); and *Sōtēr*, 2 Aug. 1834 and 5 Aug. 1834*o.s.*

[3] Dawkins to Palmerston, Nauplion, 25 Aug. 1834, no. 62, FO 32.45. For information on Dawkins' observation about the dampening effect of the news of a regency change on rebel ardor, see a letter (in French) from Athanasios Gregoriades to Constantine Oikonomopoulos, n.d., folder 134 (Ministry of the Interior, 1833-37), Otho Archive: "Finally his majesty the king of Bavaria . . . replaced the two members of the regency Messrs. Maurer and Abel by a certain Mr. Kobbell [*sic*], a man who enjoys French respect and is full of spirit. So it is hoped that everything will take a different turn and justice will reign. You must go to Arcadia to the field [*champ*] and there you will learn more about everything, but I counsel you to be patient, wise and faithful to the throne since we now have a king. We hope tomorrow or the day after to be released and after that the old man [Kolokotrones] and Kolipoulos [Plapoutas]. Patience and you will see good things. . . ."

suggests that the plot, in its execution as well as its inception, was a joint "English"–"Russian" undertaking of secondary or even tertiary party figures.[4]

Kandeloros mentions and cites partial evidence to substantiate rumors that Armansperg had some time before joined in plans for the conspiracy in order to precipitate the recall of Maurer. He allegedly approved the goal of the conspirators (dissolution of the regency) on the assurance that he would become chancellor of the new royal government. If true, this simply further suggests at least the initial involvement of the "English" party, which favored Armansperg.[5]

Especially in view of Dawkins' remark about the effect of the Maurer–Abel recall on "English" participation, it seems odd that even some of the rebels would proceed to revolt. Armansperg's triumph over his rivals in the regency satisfied one of the alternate Napist aims of 1833 and gave hope of a more conciliatory policy than that of the regency majority. That some rebels may not yet have heard about the Maurer–Abel recall is a distinct possibility but only a partial explanation.[6] Perhaps the rebels belonged to a branch of the Napist party which placed no more faith in Armansperg than in the other regents. Or perhaps, by the time they received the news of the Maurer–Abel recall, leakage of their intentions left the rebels no alternative but to strike immediately.

The sources concur in attributing two goals to the rebel leadership— first, dissolution of the regency and immediate accession of the king; also the release of Kolokotrones and Plapoutas from prison. A rebel proclamation, a copy of which Dawkins sent to his government, enunciates neither as an objective. It states the purpose of the revolt as "deliverance of the fatherland from the evils which oppress it and vengeance in behalf of the sacred religion." This does not disprove the sources. It merely shows that the rebels had to appeal to the people on other grounds.[7]

The same document complains about the lack of a constitution, rule by men who did not fight in the Revolution (Phanariots, according to the proclamation, but probably heterochthons and Bavarians in fact), and oppressive taxation. Gennaios Kolokotrones, in his memoirs on this period, attributes the revolt to the new tax-collection system, whereby the tax on

---

[4] For a statement of Sōtēr's position, see its issue of 2 Aug. 1843o.s. Concerning the participation of Gregoriades in the conspiracy, see Sōtēr, 6 Sept. 1843o.s.

[5] Kandeloros [Trial], p. 325.

[6] See the Gregoriades letter cited in n. 3 above. Since it is undated, one cannot tell if it was written before or after the outbreak. It is quite possible that it was written after, in which case some of the rebels did not know.

[7] On the dual aim of rebel leaders, see Kandeloros [Trial], p. 326, and Finlay, History, vii, 153-54, who also declares as an aim "to secure for themselves concessions similar to those accorded to the Maniates." The Dawkins copy of the proclamation, dated 3/15 July 1834, addressed "to the Christians and Primates of Phanari, Arcadia, and the Mountains of Caritaina" and signed by Kolias Plapoutas, was translated into French and enclosed in the despatch of 26 Sept. 1834, no. 68, FO 32.46. Finlay refers to it (History, vii, 154).

grain was calculated in terms of one sheaf measured, and to the success of the Maniat revolt in exacting concessions from the government. Dawkins cited a number of discontented groups that were susceptible to rebel propaganda—the "English" who resented the removal of Mavrokordatos, the clergy who deplored the new ecclesiastical settlement, and the peasants who reacted against the new method of collecting tenths. He went on to write:

> The peasantry had been persuaded by their priests that the Regency and all Bavarians were Jews, and told that the King was kept a prisoner at Argos by the regency, and that it was the duty of every good subject to deliver him.[8]

The government betrayed its own belief in the importance of the religious issue as a factor in the popular support of the rebels when it had the holy synod issue an encyclical as one of many measures to put down the revolt. In it, the synod alleged the educational benefits to be derived from monastic wealth and gave assurance that no one would ever tamper with the faith. It comes as no surprise, then, that the rebels at first rounded up considerable popular support and won some immediate military successes.[9]

To the men who took up arms, the timing of the revolt must have seemed propitious. The transition from the old to the newly composed regency was bound to weaken the central government temporarily, and all available government troops were engaged in Mane. The revolt took the government and provincial authorities completely by surprise.[10] But Kolettes, as minister of the interior, acted swiftly and the government soon rallied to turn the tide. Aside from the encyclical issued by the holy synod, the government issued a proclamation dated 16 August. It declared martial law in the revolted provinces (Messenia and Gortynia). It sent out a special investigating committee headed by Andrew Zaïmes and established an *ad hoc* military tribunal to try the rebels. Armansperg dismissed Constantine Schinas from the ministry of religion-education. Unpopular because he was a Phanariot and identified with the religious settlement, Schinas had been chosen as the object of special mention in

[8] Gennaios Kolokotrones [*Memoirs II*], p. 76; Dawkins to Foreign Office, Nauplion, 25 Aug. 1834, no. 62, FO 32.45.

[9] On the synodal encyclical, see Kandeloros [*Trial*], p. 334, and *Athēna*, 11 Aug. 1834 *o.s.* Dawkins estimated rebel forces at 1,200 (25 Aug. 1834, no. 62, FO 32.45). On military movements of the rebels, see *Sōtēr*, 2 Aug., 5 Aug., 9 Aug. 1834 *o.s.*; also Finlay, *History*, vii, 154.

[10] "When intelligence reached Armansperg, he found not a man could be spared from the garrison of Nauplia, whence the revolt received its direction, and that at Argos there were scarcely troops enough to protect the King's person, but most fortunately he had already taken measures to suspend hostilities in Maina and conciliate the inhabitants, so the force shut up there under Schmaltz was free and a large body of Mainates volunteered to serve under him against the rebels" (Finlay, *History*, vii, 154).

the rebel proclamation. To prevent the revolt from spreading, the government amnestied the Maniats and promoted several of the Rumeliot captains.[11]

With Mane now partially conciliated, Christian Schmaltz was able to take 1,000 of his regulars and some 500 Maniats to Aslanaga in Messenia where he fought and routed the chief body of insurgents. Unemployed palikars, seeing their chance to obtain both plunder and government favor, volunteered for a campaign against the insurgents and a needy government responded with fervor. Under Theodore Grivas and Chatzechrestos, and with the assistance of some Moreot irregulars organized by Lontos, Delegiannes, and Sisines, they attacked the northern branch of rebels.[12] In six weeks government forces had reestablished tranquility and an *ad hoc* court sentenced the principal rebels to either death or long imprisonment.[13]

So much did Kolettes benefit politically from this revolt that many believed—at least his enemies could plausibly argue—that he had known about the plans for it and had contributed to its outbreak; if not positively, then by taking no action to prevent it.[14] Finlay accurately, if

[11] The proclamation, issued by Kolettes and dated 3 Aug. 1834*o.s.*, was published in *Sōtēr*, 5 Aug. 1834*o.s.* but did not get published in the *Government Gazette*. The same issue of *Sōtēr* published a proclamation issued by the entire cabinet as well. The decree "concerning disorders in Arcadia and Messenia," dated 9/21 Aug. 1834 (*Ephemeris tes Kyberneseos tou Basileiou tes Hellados* [*Government Gazette, Kingdom of Greece*], no. 28, 10/22 Aug. 1834) includes provisions for martial law, the military tribunal, and the special investigating committee. Thomas Gordon was appointed president of the court with the following as judges: Panagiotes Giatrakos, Anastasios Lontos, and Spyromelios; and D. Soutsos as prosecutor. As members of the investigating committee, the decree appointed, besides Zaïmes, George Valtinos and Demetrios Meletopoulos. On the decree dismissing C. Schinas and replacing him with Praïdes, dated 8/20 Aug. 1834, see [*GG*], no. 27, 10/22 Aug. 1834. On the amnesty for the Maniats, dated 13/25 Aug. 1834, see [*GG*], no. 30, 22 Aug./3 Sept. 1834. On all these measures in general, see Kandeloros [*Trial*], pp. 334, 338, 340, and Dawkins, Nauplion, 25 Aug. 1834, no. 62, FO 32.45, and 26 Sept. 1834, no. 68, FO 32.46.

[12] On military operations in general, see Kandeloros [*Trial*], pp. 333-34, 340-43; *Sōtēr*, 5 Aug. 1834, 9 Aug. 1834, 12 Aug. 1834*o.s.*; also Finlay, *History*, VII, 155. Concerning the palikars, see Dawkins, 25 Aug. 1834, no. 62, FO 32.45: ". . . a great many palicari were apprized no doubt of what was going on and were ready to take advantage. They knew Armansperg had always wanted to enroll and discipline a large portion of them, while his colleagues had denounced them as 'incorrigible' and had chosen to depend entirely on their Bavarian Troops."

[13] Kritsales, An. Tsamales, and Metros Petrovas were sentenced to death; the first two were shot and the third had his sentence commuted to life imprisonment because of his age and his services during the Revolution. Three got fifteen-year sentences and two got five-year sentences (*Ethnikē*, 18/30 Nov. 1834).

[14] Prokesch-Osten, Austrian minister in Athens, wrote his government that Russian diplomacy regarded the revolt as the work exclusively of Kolettes (see Karl Mendelssohn Bartholdy, *Geschichte Griechenlands von der Eroberung Konstantinopels durch die Türken im Jahre 1453 bis auf unsere Tage* [Leipzig, 1870-74], II, 501-502). According to Dawkins, Kolettes' friends accused Armansperg of insinuating that

scornfully, judged the effect of this event on the balance of power between Kolettes and Armansperg:

> His [Armansperg's] own feebleness of character compelled him to trust everything to Coletti at the time the rebellion in Messenia broke out, and unless by good fortune [General Thomas] Gordon had stopped the career of vengeance which Coletti wished to wreak on the opposite party, the Count would have become the slave of Coletti.[15]

To be sure, Kolettes initiated an angry pursuit of Napists. Niketas and Kollinos Plapoutas appeared before Armansperg asking to go alone and unarmed to pacify Messenia, but instead suffered imprisonment in Nauplion, together with many prominent Napists and others. Similar arrests took place in Tripolis and Kalamata, the total number of those seized reaching seventy. If John Speliotopoulos had not intervened in their behalf, it was said, Kolokotrones and Plapoutas would have suffered the worst. For a moment it looked as if Kolettes, through judicial murders, might succeed in crippling the Napist party permanently. By persuading Armansperg to call in the irregular bands of Grivas and Chatzechrestos for the suppression of the revolt, Kolettes was reestablishing his traditional popularity among the Rumeliot chieftains and his military control of the Peloponnesos.[16]

Circumstances forced Armansperg into the position that Finlay deplored. Armansperg had no reason to believe that the Bavarian regulars would prove any more effective in putting down this revolt than they had against the Maniats, nor could he assume that the revolt would not

---

Kolettes "encouraged or at least permitted it [the revolt] to break out in the Southern Provinces, in order to make himself indispensable to Armansperg and to have a pretext to employ Rumeliot Palicari" (26 Sept. 1834, no. 68, FO 32.46). See also Kandeloros [*Trial*], p. 325, and John Makrygiannes, *Apomnemoneumata* [*Memoirs*], ed. John Vlachogiannes, 2nd edn. (Athens, 1947), II, 73.

[15] George Finlay, Journal (MSS), 3 June 1835, Finlay Papers, The British School of Archeology, Athens; also Finlay, *History*, VII, 153.

[16] Among those arrested were D. Kallerges, P. Valsamakes, D. Tsokres, Rangos, Vallianos, Zacharias, Metaxas, Razes, Antonopoulos, Speliades, Alonistiotes, Vagias, Gennaios and Kollinos Kolokotrones, Niketas Stamatellopoulos, Th. Zacharopoulos, Typaldos. On the attempts of Plapoutas to mediate, see Kandeloros [*Trial*], p. 334. On the arrests, see, in addition to Kandeloros, Gennaios Kolokotrones [*Memoirs II*], p. 76; *Sōtēr*, 3 Aug., 9 Aug., 6 Sept. and 9 Sept. 1834*o.s.*; Dawkins to the Foreign Office, Nauplion, 25 Aug. 1834, no. 62, FO 32.45, and Nauplion, 26 Sept. 1834, no. 68, FO 32.46. *Sōtēr* estimated the number of arrested at forty-three; Dawkins at seventy. On Kolettes' aims, see Finlay, *History*, VII, 154-55: "Kolettes . . . even though he had been the staunch partisan of Maurer, resolved to use his power in such a way as to have little to fear from the count's enmity when the insurrection was suppressed. He determined, therefore, to restore some of his old political allies, the chiefs of the irregular bands of Northern Greece, again to power. . . . On this occasion, therefore, he repeated, as far as lay in his power, the measures by which he had overpowered the Moreot primates and the Moreot klephts under Kolokotrones in 1824."

spread to Rumely unless some of the dissatisfied Rumeliots received immediate employment.[17] He had reason to suspect the most prominent Napists of implication in the plot and could count on Kolettes' reliability in suppressing the revolt because Kolettes had a personal and partisan interest in doing so.

If Finlay failed to see the necessity of Armansperg's momentary dependence on Kolettes, he also failed to mention the measures which Armansperg shrewdly devised to reduce that dependence. The investigation of the revolt, which rightly lay within the jurisdiction of Kolettes as minister of the interior, he assigned to an *ad hoc* committee under the chairmanship of Zaïmes. As might have been expected, this defender of Peloponnesian interests and arch foe of Kolettes returned from the scene of the revolt with the verdict that the revolt stemmed solely from local grievances and had no connection with the previous "Russian plot." He was obviously trying to dissociate the revolt from identification with any party and to keep the number of condemned to the barest minimum.[18] Armansperg was responsible for the appointment of Gordon as president of the military court, who displayed great moderation in trying the accused and handed down sentences condemning only the few ostensible rebel leaders. The release of all prominent Napists, with the sole exception of Gennaios Kolokotrones, placed them under some obligation to Armansperg for protecting them against the vengeance of Kolettes.[19]

[17] Dawkins reported (Nauplion, 25 Aug. 1834, no. 63, FO 32.45) that Armansperg had proof that Bavarian troops alone could not cope with the situation, whereas Finlay maintained (*History*, vii, 154), that Bavarian troops and Greek regulars could have suppressed the revolt without difficulty. According to Dawkins (Nauplion, 26 Sept. 1834, no. 68, FO 32.46), there was evidence of prior plans in Rumely to support the revolt: "Private accounts from H M Consul General in Albania confirm those received by the Greek government as to preparations which were making for a general revolt in Continental Greece, when change of Regency took place. Mr. Meyer indeed states that this change was not considered sufficient by the Rumeliots and that combinations were still going on at the latter end of last month. . . ."

[18] See complaints against Zaïmes in a letter of Moirarch Mavromichales to the commandant of the gendarmerie (n.p., n.d., folder 134, Ministry of the Interior, 1833-37), Otho Archive. *Sōtēr* (6 Sept. 1834o.s.) published, practically verbatim, the same complaints against Zaïmes. Also Dawkins to Palmerston, Nauplion, 26 Sept. 1834, no. 68, FO 32.37: "Zaïmes' reports, I understand, represent the whole province of Messenia (the only one he has hitherto visited) to have been in arms, and the Revolt to have had no connexion with last year's conspiracy. He recommends the whole population be indiscriminately disarmed and shall be made to pay the expenses incurred by the government." See also Gennaios Kolokotrones [*Memoirs II*], p. 76.

[19] On release of prisoners, see *Sōtēr*, 16 Sept., 13 Oct., 11 Nov., 18 Nov., 1834o.s.; *Ethnikē*, 15/17 Nov., 22 Nov./4 Dec., and 25 Nov./7 Dec. 1834. Finlay (*History*, vii, 155) explains Armansperg's policy of leniency as follows: "He knew that they were more likely to join his party than the Kolettists by whom they had been defeated. Perhaps he also feared that a close examination of their conduct might throw more light than was desirable on the connection that had grown up between the Capodistrian conspiracy and the Armansperg intrigue." According to Gennaios

Armansperg vs. Kolettes

With the revolt and its dangers passed, an open breach between Kolettes and Armansperg took place. *Sōtēr* offered the first indications by its public attack on Armansperg for his policy of leniency toward the Napists. In retaliation, Armansperg withdrew *Sōtēr's* semiofficial status and established a new newspaper, *Ethnikē*, to serve as his mouthpiece. Stepping up its attacks on Armansperg, *Sōtēr*, Kolettes' paper, complained that the regency did not consult the cabinet on important matters. *Ethnikē* recklessly replied that, since the cabinet was not a constitutional assembly, the regency had the right to consult it only when it saw fit. Three days later, *Ethnikē* retracted this bald statement of absolutism, but remarked provocatively that a cabinet which disapproved of the regency's actions had the obligation to resign.[20] Commenting much later (1836) on the breach between Armansperg and Kolettes, Lyons quoted Armansperg as saying:

> Mons. Colettis, you complain of want of confidence! how can I give my confidence to a man whose only associates are my personal adversaries and the opponents of our government: I am told that the leading articles of the Opposition paper [*Sōtēr*] are submitted to your approval, and as I know that the Editor [Skouphos] is the person with whom you spend the principal part of your time, how can I doubt it?[21]

At any rate, a stalemate occurred because Kolettes would not resign and Armansperg would not fire him. Anton von Prokesch-Osten, the Austrian minister, wrote Vienna that Armansperg and Kobell retained Kolettes because of his valuable advice on technical matters requiring knowledge of local conditions. They intended, the letter went on, to dispense with him at the opportune moment because they believed him dangerous. Lyons stated a more cogent reason for Kolettes' retention:

> Armansperg felt it expedient to keep him [Kolettes] in office till the king's majority, lest he should rouse all Rumeliots, of whom he is champion, in opposition to the government.

Kolokotrones ([*Memoirs II*], pp. 76-77), Armansperg, pressed by Masson, did not extend his lenient policy to Gennaios, who, after Gordon refused to try him, was tried on two subsequent occasions and acquitted both times.

[20] Ross (*Erinnerungen*, pp. 85-86) discusses the Armansperg–Kolettes conflict; also Chr. Aug. Brandis, *Mittheilungen über Griechenland* (Leipsig, 1843), III, 270-73. *Sōtēr* (2 Aug. 1834o.s.) implied Russian involvement in the plot and (9 Aug. 1834 o.s.) announced the regency's disapproval of any newspaper statements alleging foreign participation in the plot. In the latter issue it criticized the policy of leniency, but did not openly attack the regency until it published its 13 Sept. and 16 Sept.o.s. issues. On Armansperg's withdrawal of support from the newspaper, see Kandeloros [*Trial*], p. 338. *Ethnikē*, 4/16 Oct. and 7/19 Oct. 1834.

[21] Lyons to Palmerston, Athens, 3 Jan. 1836, no. 2, FO 32.58.

Moreover, Armansperg, with an eye toward his own retention after the expiration of the regency, probably wished to allay Otho's doubts about his popularity among the Greeks, not just by conciliating the Napist party but by refusing to antagonize the "French" party as well.[22]

Kolettes and his supporters, aware of this situation, were ready to exploit it. Of his friends, some portrayed him as the great pillar of royal support in Greece, while others more boldly warned that, owing to his great influence, his dismissal from office would precipitate a revolution. When brigandage assumed serious proportions in Rumely in the spring of 1835, Kolettists openly pointed to it as proof of the continued necessity for Kolettes' vigorous leadership and intimated some connection between the brigand outbreak and public dissatisfaction over rumors of Kolettes' imminent dismissal. In short, they interpreted Rumeliot brigandage as a warning of worse to come in Kolettes' stronghold if the king did not retain him as first minister. Indeed, many suspected that Kolettes or his followers had instigated these outbreaks of brigandage to make their point.[23]

During Kolettes' tenure as minister of the interior in 1834-35, local elections took place. His failure to win most of them may be attributed to the opposition of Armansperg. None the less, he used his office to influence the elections in his party's favor. He tried to build up a party in Athens when it became certain that the capital would be moved there, first by allying himself with one of the Athenian factions, and second, by giving first option to potential supporters for the purchase of commercially valuable land in what the government projected as the new business district of Piraeus.[24] An interesting case of his party's vigorous campaigning is revealed by a letter of John Petrokopes to Regas Palamides concerning Tripolis, the native deme of both men:

> Recently, through a secretary of mine, I pointed out the diligence I had displayed so that our demarch [mayor] should be one of our friends and of our persuasion. This resulted favorably, because I came to an agreement with those here [in Tripolis], who responded with joy to my proposal, and as a result I can inform you positively that the mayor will be of our choice. Mr. Anagnostes Rontopoulos apostolically toured those villages that will become part of the deme, and instructed the inhabitants, the individuals of their party [probably Napist], to vote, but here it is certain that the struggle is in vain [for them].

[22] Prokesch-Osten, 2 Feb. 1835, as quoted by Mendelssohn Bartholdy, *Geschichte Griechenlands*, II, 501-502; Lyons to Palmerston, Athens, 2 June 1835, FO 32.52.

[23] On warnings concerning Kolettes' dismissal from office, see *Ethnikē*, 6/18 June 1835. On the Kolettist interpretations of the outbreak of brigandage in 1835, see Finlay, Journal 1835 (MSS), 19 July 1835, Finlay Papers: "A few of the party of Coletti try to give the disorders that appearance [organized insurrection of Kolettes party] to make their party appear strong and intimidate the Gov't at Athens. . . ."

[24] On the poor showing of his party in the elections, see *Ethnikē*, 16/28 May 1835, and Makrygiannes [*Memoirs*], II, 77-78. On his attempts to build up a party in Athens, see *ibid.*, II, 74-77.

Regas Palamides forwarded the letter to Kolettes with the following note attached:

> From Petrokopes' [letter] you again see the mayoralty activities of Rontopoulos, whom the nomarch roused to the organization of those villages.[25]

Of the Greeks, Kolettes was the only serious contender for the leadership of the royal government and the Kolettists the only ones to intrigue actively so as to influence the king's selection of a first minister on the expiration of the regency. According to Catacazy, a chief opponent, Kolettes pursued a strategy of leading the regency from mistake to mistake in order to discredit Armansperg completely. Finlay reveals a more positive strategy as well. Realizing that the king intended to entrust affairs to a Bavarian, Kolettes decided to back the ambitious Bavarian Lesuire, minister of war in the Greek cabinet at the time, who wanted to replace Armansperg as head of affairs. He and Kolettes contracted "an unholy alliance based on mutual deceit." Lesuire, a lone wolf among the Bavarians, sought to utilize Kolettes' political influence to secure his elevation. Kolettes, certain that Lesuire's narrow policy of Bavarianism would make him odious to the Greeks, apparently calculated that Lesuire could not last in Greece for more than six months and that he himself would be the next logical choice of the king. Hence Kolettes supported him in order to rid Greece of Armansperg, the stronger and more formidable rival. Surprisingly enough, Dawkins, who disliked Armansperg's courtship of the Napists and Catacazy, supported Kolettes against Armansperg because Kolettes' undying suspicions of Russian policy and the Napists rendered him a surer bulwark against Russian influence in Greece. This scheme did not enjoy much chance of success. In spite of Dawkins' personal action, British diplomacy was committed to Armansperg; Lesuire enjoyed no backing in the royal court or in Munich; and Kolettes' aversion to Lesuire's anti-Greek spirit finally prevailed over his personal antipathy toward Armansperg.[26]

Armansperg vs. Otho

As the day of the king's majority approached, it became virtually certain that Otho would not entrust affairs directly to the Greeks because of their party affiliations, that he would not rule personally because of

[25] Petrokopes to Palamides, Tripolis, 11 July 1834o.s., folder 257 (1833-39), Palamides Archive, Vlachogiannes Collection, General Archives of Greece, Athens.

[26] On Catacazy's views, see Prokesch-Osten to Metternich, 2 Feb. 1835, as quoted by Mendelssohn Bartholdy, Geschichte Griechenlands, II, 501. On the abortive Lesuire-Kolettes alliance and the role of Dawkins, see Finlay, Journal (MSS), 3 June and 11 July 1835, Finlay Papers. On Dawkins' espousal of Kolettes, see The Portfolio; or a Collection of State Papers and other Documents and Correspondence, Historical, Diplomatic, and Commercial, Illustrative of the History of our Times, 1st ser. (London, 1836-37), v, 179-80; and George K. Aspreas, Politike Historia tes Neoteras Hellados 1821-1921 [Political History of Modern Greece], 2nd edn. (Athens, 1924), I, 135.

his youth and inexperience, and that he would delegate authority to only one Bavarian because the sad experience of the regency had revealed only too clearly the pitfalls of collective rule.[27]

Otho's known antipathy toward Armansperg raised the possibility that the choice of a single head of affairs might go to some other Bavarian and provoked feverish maneuvering among Bavarians in the court. On 5 May 1835, Prokesch-Osten noted with dismay the intense factionalism among the Bavarians in the king's household, stemming directly from divided opinion in Munich. Even the servants were involved, he wrote Vienna. The lowest Bavarian official was presumptuous enough to hope for a high place in the new political arrangements. Meanwhile, with the exception of Kolettes and his adherents, the Greeks remained relatively passive.[28]

Bavarian intrigue over this question comprised the last chapter of the rivalry between Maurer–Abel–Heideck, on the one hand, and Armansperg on the other. Though absent from Greece, Maurer and Abel still had personal allies in the royal household, the chief of whom was Heideck. Otho, in whose hands lay the ultimate decision to retain or replace Armansperg, had sympathized with the regency majority during the regency crisis of 1833-34 and had regretted the recall of Maurer and Abel. Since then, he had been on intimate terms with Heideck, who encouraged him to get rid of Armansperg. At first, he contemplated the recall of Abel to Greece, but Abel was too closely identified in the public mind with some still controversial acts of the regency majority, such as the disbanding of the irregulars and the dissolution of the monasteries. Moreover, Otho had made the tactical mistake of confiding his thoughts to Sir Edmund Lyons, successor to Dawkins as British minister to Greece, and had thereby given British diplomacy the opportunity to express in advance its unqualified opposition to Abel. Then Maurer and Abel, through Heideck, recommended to Otho an altogether new name, that of Ignaz von Rudhart, who eventually became Armansperg's successor early in February 1837.[29]

[27] On the general decision to entrust affairs to a single Bavarian, see Prokesch-Osten to Metternich, 19 Mar. 1835, as quoted by Mendelssohn Bartholdy, *Geschichte Griechenlands*, II, 505-506. On partisanship as the reason for not appointing a Greek, Prokesch-Osten, in an earlier report to Metternich (9 Mar. 1835, as quoted in Mendelssohn Bartholdy, *op.cit.*, II, 504) wrote: "The natives [Greeks] all have emerged out of a revolution which destroyed their prestige, and they are unable to cast aside their partisan hatreds or unlearn their partisan behavior." Of the secondary sources, Aspreas ([*Political History*], I, 143) understood why Otho would not delegate power to the Greeks. It was not, he wrote, "a result of scorn for the Greek political leaders, but the result of care to prevent the strengthening of one of the existing parties to the detriment and wrath of the other two."

[28] Prokesch-Osten to Metternich, 5 May 1835, as quoted by Mendelssohn Bartholdy, *Geschichte Griechenlands*, II, 508.

[29] On Otho's aversion to Armansperg and his determination to be rid of him, see report of D'Hailly, French minister to Bavaria, to Regny, French foreign minister,

Otho's lack of confidence in Armansperg probably lay at the bottom of the most deplorable intrigue at this time—an intrigue against the king himself, a virtually helpless, homesick boy. With the apparent intention of taking the choice out of Otho's hands and reducing him to a figurehead even after coming of age, Wibmer, one of Otho's physicians, represented his illness and melancholia as a physical and mental inability to rule. Ludwig received reports to this effect, one in 1834, two more in the spring of 1835, and a fourth even after Otho's accession. The list of signatures on each successive report grew longer.[30]

Munich, 23 Feb. 1835, in *Gesandtschaftsberichte aus München 1814-1848*, Abt. i: *Die Berichte der französischen Gesandten*, ed. Anton Chroust, iii (Munich, 1936), 206-207. On Lyons' interview with Otho and his declaration of British opposition to Abel's appointment, see Lyons to Dawkins, Nauplion, 7 Nov. 1834, FO 32.52: "Mention of Abel astonishes and embarrasses Otho, who seems to have been under the delusion like Abel himself, that since not a regent he was not responsible and so could be brought back as Otho's minister after his majority." For the rest of the information in this paragraph, see Prokesch-Osten to Metternich, 2 Feb. and 9 Mar. 1835, as quoted by Mendelssohn Bartholdy, *Geschichte Griechenlands*, ii, 503-505.

[30] The fullest enumeration of these reports is contained in a despatch of Lyons to Palmerston, marked "Separate and confidential," 1 Oct. 1835, FO 32.53. Prior to the recall of Maurer and Abel, Wibmer, one of the king's two physicians, drew up and sent to Munich the first such report. Saporta, marshal of the court, and Lehmaier, the king's private secretary, affixed their signatures to that of Wibmer in the second report, which was dated 9 Mar. 1835. The third, dated May 1835, contained the signatures of Baron Hunoltstein and Roeser, Otho's other physicians, "who however did not go all the lengths of his colleague Wibmer." The fourth was sent after the king's accession. Lyons presumably received this information during an interview with Saporta, who conveyed to Lyons "his conviction of the King's utter incapacity for business of any sort. . . ." Lyons reported, in the same despatch, that Jenison, Bavarian minister to Greece and friend of Armansperg, confirmed Saporta's judgment.

Leonard Bower and Gordon Bolitho (*Otho I. King of Greece, A Biography* [London, 1939], pp. 77-78) quote at some length courtier Hunoltstein's version of one of these reports (n.d. but probably written before Otho's accession) over the signature of Jenison, the Bavarian minister to Greece. It deserves full inclusion here:

"The undersigned, referring to his respectful deposition on the 13th instant, finds himself compelled to declare that the mental condition of His Majesty King Otho is not only the same as at that time, but has, on the contrary, been aggravated. The grounds, which were expressed in his last report, for his temporary inability to take up the reins of government are, as at that time, due to considerable lack of positive knowledge, an unconquerable lack of concentration, a latent desire for independence, a passion for detail which has increased to nervous pettiness, a lack of confidence in the ability of others, and a conviction of having sufficient knowledge to reign alone. This lack of concentration is why His Majesty is unable to read for any length of time, and is also the cause of his lack of apprehension.

"The undersigned is also of the opinion that he owes it to His Majesty to state that the King's present condition of mind makes it all the more difficult for him, even with the support, guidance, and counsel of one or more reliable statesmen, to take over the reins of government, and that this is partly on account of his petty, timorous detailing of every problem before he considers himself able to reach a decision—a tendency which cannot be prevented even by the most urgent representations of danger to his personal honour, to the public weal and individual persons, not even by

Armansperg's signature never appeared on any of these reports, but his implication in this affair, as in the "minor" plot of 1833, seems virtually certain. The authors of these reports belonged to his clique within the royal court. His refusal to question their unfavorable judgment of Otho, once expressed, was interpreted by Lyons and undoubtedly others as amounting to tacit concurrence. Through oblique and casual remarks, carefully circulated by Lyons, he spread the same opinion among the Greeks. Most telling of all, he had the most to gain from such a "professional" certification of Otho's incapacity. If Otho had not really come of age mentally, then he, Armansperg, was absolutely indispensable, not merely as the king's first minister but as the actual wielder of full royal sovereignty, as the actual if no longer the formal regent.[31]

---

sympathy. All this makes the King (intent on the insistent pursuit of the smallest detail as he is) overlook the principal object involved. This is the impression given by His Majesty King Otho when in his study and, of course, it differs vastly from the impression he makes in public. It is the innermost conviction of the undersigned that this is as accurate and true a description as his honour and conscience demand."

See also a reference to one of the reports in a letter from Prokesch-Osten to Metternich, Athens, 29 Dec. 1835, in *Aus dem Nachlasse des Grafen Prokesch-Osten*, ed. Anton von Prokesch-Osten [the younger] (Vienna, 1881), II, 159.

The incident had an embarrassing and painful sequel—articles in the British newspaper *Morning Chronicle* in 1839, revealing the existence of "a certificate that had been signed by several Bavarian members of King Otho's household, declaring that his majesty was incapable of governing his little kingdom" (Finlay, *History*, VII, 169-71). In its issue of 6 Mar. 1839, *Morning Chronicle* wrote slanderously: "King Otho's address, the contortions of his countenance, his stuttering, his deafness, his silly remarks, his outrageous obstinacy, his preference shown to the low hangers-on about his person, his unbounded conceit, and his indifference to his pretty wife are unequivocal signs of his incompetency and imbecility." On 22 May 1839, the same newspaper published a letter which read as follows: "Not only was one certificate signed on this lamentable subject, but three certificates appeared within a very short time of each other, all declaring King Otho to be a born idiot. The first was signed at Nauplia by Dr. Wibmer alone: but not being considered of sufficient force, the King of Bavaria, whose object was to continue to govern Greece by a Bavarian Regency, ordered other certificates to be drawn up, and accordingly, in March previous to King Otho's reaching his majority, this document, to which I and others have so frequently alluded, was produced."

Until the public announcement in 1839, Otho had apparently not known that his mental condition had ever been the subject of reports to Munich. In a public statement dated 11/23 July 1839, which *Athēna* published (15 July 1839*o.s.*), Wibmer, Lehmaier, and Stengel, still members of Otho's court, denied having ever expressed "that we feel the King incapable of ruling; on the contrary, we declare a liar anyone who expresses such a thought about the king." But shortly after, these men "resigned" their posts and returned to Bavaria.

The only secondary account to give this subject any adequate treatment is Bower and Bolitho, *op.cit.*, pp. 77-78, 109-12; see also Finlay, *op.cit.*, VII, 169-71, for an account of the sequel in 1839.

[31] According to Lyons (Athens, 1 Oct. 1835, "Separate and confidential," FO 32.53), Armansperg did not associate himself with these gentlemen in testifying to Otho's incapacity but his silence signified agreement with them. "I have however

Though intrigue and counterintrigue went on while Otho persisted in his reluctance to retain Armansperg, Ludwig had long since made up his mind. As early as February 1835 he is reported to have urged Armansperg to stay on in Greece and in a letter dated 8 April 1835 he wrote Armansperg, "I think you are the best choice and I have written my son so." Ludwig's problem was to convince Otho. In April he sent Count Jenison on a personal mission to Greece to do just that.[32]

Ludwig apparently shared some of Otho's mistrust of Armansperg. Echoing rumors in Munich, the French minister to Bavaria maliciously suggested that Ludwig supported Armansperg in Greece to remain free of him in Bavaria. In a letter to Otho on the eve of his accession, Ludwig gave three reasons why he felt that Armansperg was the only suitable man: (1) he was the only Bavarian to enjoy "the trust of Europe," (2) he enjoyed a firsthand acquaintance with Greece, and (3) he possessed administrative talent, especially in the crucial field of finance.[33]

Most likely, the main factor determining Ludwig's support of Armansperg was the diplomatic one. The British made it quite clear that they would be satisfied with no one else. Austria strongly supported Armansperg, and France was not yet hostile to him. Russia, though not favorable, seemed as if it would acquiesce, and Ludwig sought to secure such acquiescence by offering the prospect of a new Greek policy more in keeping with Russian desires. At least it was rumored that he had instructed Jenison to advise that Kolokotrones be amnestied and the patriarch of Constantinople be appeased in some way. In short, Armansperg seemed like the only available Bavarian who could satisfy Britain without irrevocably antagonizing Russia and, by virtue of this, the one most likely to conciliate all parties in Greece.[34]

---

said enough to give him [Armansperg] the opportunity of setting me right if he had thought me misinformed, but he was quite silent."

In his private journals (Journal [MSS] 7 Sept. 1835, 19 Oct. 1835, and 9 Nov. 1835), Finlay repeatedly deplored the "shameless way" in which Armansperg and Lyons both tried to defame and discredit Otho so as to give the impression that he was incapable of ruling without Armansperg: "Vlachopoulo spoke to me concerning the general opinion entertained of the King's incapacity. Armansperg spreads all kind of reports on this subject in the most unjustifiable way. Gordon told me that Lyons had told him the King sometimes throws himself back in his chair in a flood of tears when Armansperg presses him to sign any paper."

[32] For the contents of Ludwig's letter, see J. M. von Söltl, Ludwig I von Bayern und Graf von Armansperg (Nördlingen, 1886), pp. 58-59. On the Jenison mission and Ludwig's action as early as February, see the reports of D'Hailly to Regny, Munich, 23 Feb. 1835, and 16 Apr. 1835, in Gesandtschaftsberichte, ed. Chroust, Abt. I, Vol. III, 206-207 and 210.

[33] Bourgoing, French minister in Munich, to De Broglie, French foreign minister, Munich, 20 July 1835, in Gesandtschaftsberichte, ed. Chroust, Abt. I, Vol. III, 218. For Ludwig's enumeration of reasons, see Söltl, Ludwig I, pp. 63-67.

[34] On Armansperg's command of support from Britain, Austria, and Bavaria, see Lyons, 2 June and 28 June 1835, FO 32.52, and Friedrich Engel-Janosi, "Austria and

With Ludwig's mind made up, Otho's hands were effectively tied, since it was highly unlikely that any Bavarian would remain in Otho's service against the wishes of his own sovereign. A week before the expiration of the regency, after a long and painful period of indecision and procrastination until the last possible moment, Otho finally made up his mind to retain Armansperg.[35]

2. THE OFFICE OF ARCHSECRETARY OR ARCHCHANCELLOR, JUNE 1835–FEBRUARY 1837

Obviously a new office for Armansperg had to be instituted and defined. The office eventually created was, in official documents, called that of archsecretary (*archigrammateus*) but in common parlance and in the press, especially the opposition press, the German equivalent archchancellor (*archikangellarios*) was used. One suspects that usage depended on whether or not one wished to suggest overtones of absolutism identified with "archchancellor." The decision to retain Armansperg still left open the question of what the actual powers of the office would be. Since Otho had waited so long to finally make up his mind, the office was defined in last-minute and mutually antagonistic negotiations between Otho and Armansperg against a background of personal tension dating back to the earlier regency quarrels.

Significantly, while urging Otho to retain Armansperg, Ludwig freely made broad recommendations about future royal policy and advised Otho to consult with Prokesch-Osten, the Austrian minister to Greece, in defining the essential features of such policy. Obviously the intention was that Otho, in conjunction with his father and Prokesch-Osten, should be the one to determine policy, that he should do so *before* appointing Armansperg, and that Armansperg should work within the limits of that policy. On 17 March, during private consultation lasting seven hours, Prokesch-Osten advised Otho to limit Armansperg's role to a consultative rather than a governing one. Ludwig concurred, "so that you can be in-

---

the Beginnings of the Kingdom of Greece," *Journal of Central European Affairs*, I (1941), 37. The latter, basing his assertion on the private papers and diplomatic reports of Prokesch-Osten, states that Prokesch-Osten, along with most members of the diplomatic corps in the Greek capital, felt that Armansperg was the only suitable man to head the government. T. N. Pipineles (*He Monarchia en Helladi 1833-1843* [*The Monarchy in Greece 1833-1843*] [Athens, 1932], p. 183) attributes Armansperg's retention to British influence.

On the Jenison mission and Ludwig's desire for a partial reorientation of policy in favor of Russia, see Bourgoing to De Broglie, Munich, 16 Apr. 1835, in *Gesandtschaftsberichte*, ed. Chroust, Abt. I, Vol. III, 210.

George Aspreas ([*Political History*], I, 143) attributed Armansperg's advantage to the domestic support he enjoyed among two of the three parties in Greece (the "English" and the "Russian").

[35] Concerning Otho's failure to appoint Armansperg until the last moment, see Lyons to Palmerston, Athens, 2 June 1835, FO 32.52.

dependent." Armansperg's role, then, was seen as that of merely administering and implementing policy already determined by others, advising only when his advice was solicited. Obviously there was lingering suspicion about Armansperg's ambitions, and some determination was made to keep him from securing mastery over the king.[36]

Armansperg, on the other hand, sought a role giving him broad powers and full initiative. Characteristically, Otho tried to avoid a showdown with Armansperg by informing him through a third party of his appointment and by refusing to grant him an audience to determine his new powers. But Armansperg stood his ground after Lyons confided to him "that if he [Armansperg] stood firm the King must yield, for I was convinced His Majesty had made no other arrangement [for the appointment of a chancellor]."[37]

The available sources give no full enumeration of Armansperg's terms but Lyons' correspondence reveals some of them: to remove Kolettes from the ministry of the interior, to discontinue the office of prime minister and to preside himself over the Greek cabinet. The king most objected to Armansperg's demand for the right to sign all state papers and control the appointments to the king's household. In his latter demand Armansperg obviously sought to destroy the Maurer–Abel influence over the king and, more specifically, to expel Heideck and Lesuire, as well as Kolettes, from Greece. The unyielding attitude of both sides led to lengthy negotiations, which explain the delay of an entire month (June 1-29) before official publication of the decree defining Armansperg's duties and the character of the new office.[38]

Both Armansperg's demands as well as the compromise nature of the settlement become apparent from a reading of the decree which established the office.[39] Though it declared the archsecretary president of the cabinet, it gave him the right to preside only when the king did not choose to. Though it entrusted him with the royal seal, it restricted its

[36] Prokesch-Osten to Metternich, 19 Mar. 1835, as quoted by Mendelssohn Bartholdy, *Geschichte Griechenlands*, II, 505, and Söltl, *Ludwig I*, p. 63. On Ludwig's advice that Otho consult Prokesch-Osten, see Engel-Janosi, "Austria," *JCEA*, I, 31.

[37] Lyons to Palmerston, Athens, 2 June 1835, FO 32.52.

[38] "At six o'clock in the morning of 1st June, Armansperg told me he had carried all his points as to his own powers, even those to which the King had most objected, i.e., that he should sign all state papers and have the nomination of the King's household, and that in order to settle that point he had on the spot made six nominations, four of whom were Greeks, and that His Majesty was quite satisfied with them.

"Armansperg arranged with him to have a deliberative senate introduced. Armansperg proposed and the King had no opposition to name a Minister of the Interior instead of Coletti, who will probably be offered a seat in the Senate. Armansperg intends to discontinue the office of President of the Ministry and to preside himself" (*loc.cit.*).

[39] Decree concerning the duties and the rank of the archsecretary of state, 20 May 1835*o.s.* [*Government Gazette*], no. 1, 17 June 1835*o.s.*

exclusive use to those documents which the king had already signed. Though Armansperg had obviously insisted on countersigning every decree as a means of requiring the king to consult him on all affairs, the decree explained the provision for this countersignature as a guarantee that a third party would not use the royal seal. The decree granted the archsecretary the right to issue decrees, but only upon special approval of the king.

In terms of the strict letter of the decree, Otho won out. It qualified practically every right of office assigned Armansperg by the phrase "according to Our decrees." It explicitly stated the direct responsibility of each cabinet minister to the king rather than to the archsecretary. It required that the ministers submit all proposals for administrative appointments directly to the king. And it did not put in writing the king's reluctant concession to give Armansperg control over the appointment of the royal household.

Yet, in a political sense, the odds lay with Armansperg. The language of the decree was sufficiently loose to allow the archsecretary broad powers, if political conditions permitted. And the concessions which Armansperg secured, though seemingly unimpressive because political rather than constitutional, created such conditions. By virtue of his success in getting rid of Kolettes, Lesuire, and Heideck, Armansperg virtually forced the king into a position of political dependence.

3. STATECRAFT

The basic framework of the new state edifice was constructed in two main stages. The first stage, covering the period of the first regency, has already been described. The second, initiated by the king's ascension to the throne, covered the last six months of 1835. In this stage, four basic institutions were created—the office of archsecretary, the system of small private landholdings, the council of state, and the royal phalanx, in that order. The first, dealt with in the section immediately preceding, lasted only until the fall of Armansperg in mid-February 1837. Although the second got off to a slow start, it eventually became a basic feature of the Greek social system. The third, in its initial form and with its original functions, lasted until the promulgation of a constitution in March 1844. Owing to growing financial difficulties, the last was progressively reduced in size from 1838 until its virtual dissolution during the grave financial crisis of 1843.

Of these four institutions, only the first came into being as a last-minute, makeshift response to the immediate question of what to substitute for the regency as the highest organ of the Crown. The other three accorded with the general blueprint devised much earlier by the first regency to meet the general recommendations of King Ludwig with the help of his advisor Friedrich Thiersch. Their construction had intentionally been delayed to coincide with Otho's majority, so that the Crown might take credit for them and hence benefit from the popularity which they were expected to enjoy.[40] This section, in dealing with the three institutions yet to be described, will attempt to show how much the purpose and form of these institutions owed to the royal objective of curbing and ultimately destroying the political parties.

The Dotation Law

Before the Greek Revolution, a small minority of Turkish landed magnates had held approximately two-thirds of all arable land, by far the most fertile, in what became independent Greece. The Greek primate class had held most of the rest, most Greek peasants working as tenants on the estates of their Greek or Turkish masters. Land hunger had consequently constituted one of the major causes of the Greek Revolution.[41]

The Revolutionary assemblies had declared all lands of the dispossessed Turks as national property and had adopted the principle that each Greek would eventually receive as his private property a portion of the national domains as reward for service to the national cause. In 1833 Thiersch had estimated that only one-sixth of the peasants in Greece owned their own plots of land, the rest cultivating national land at a rental of 25 per cent of their annual produce in contrast to the 10 per cent tax-rate of the free-holders. The royal government therefore fell heir to the obligation of redeeming a long-standing promise. It accepted its obligation with enthusiasm, not only in order to allay social and political unrest, but as a major step in the advancement of its apparent dream of creating a nation of small, enterprising, independent landholders who would be the mainstay of a strong paternalistic Crown and its loyal ally against the primate and captain classes.[42] The dotation law of 1835 was the most comprehensive attempt to realize this dream.

[40] F. Thiersch, *De l'État actuel de la Grèce* (Leipsig, 1833), I, 245-49; George Ludwig von Maurer, *Das Griechische Volk in öffentlicher, kirchlicher und privatrechtlicher Beziehung vor und nach dem Freiheitskampfe bis zum 31 Juli 1834* (Heidelberg, 1835), II, 97-100. The Council of State is presupposed and mentioned in Art. 15 of the decree of 3/15 Apr. 1833 [*Government Gazette*], no. 12, 6/18 Apr. 1833.

On correspondence between Ludwig and Otho, see for instance a letter from Ludwig to Otho, on the eve of Otho's accession, which mentions a "senate, whose members you name; only consultative, without pay" (Söltl, *Ludwig I*, p. 65).

[41] On the phenomenon of land hunger, see Finlay to "My dear Sir" [probably Trikoupes], 1836, Letter Book 1827-1836 (MSS), Finlay Papers: "all desire to be proprietors"; also Thiersch, *État actuel*, I, 105-107, and Pipineles [*Monarchy*], p. 155.

[42] Thiersch, *État actuel*, I, 105-107. That the Crown sought, through the dotation law, to lessen the influence of the large landowners, see Brandis, *Mittheilungen*, III, 277. Pipineles ([*Monarchy*], p. 156) writes: "On the other hand, the monarchical authority of Greece would find in this organization, and development of this class of small agricultural landowners, its natural, and one might say, its historical support against the agrarian oligarchy. . . ."

236

Unlike the abortive law of June 1834, which made indigence and past *military* service the criteria of eligibility, the dotation law of 7 June 1835[43] covered all residents of the Greek kingdom: autochthons, heterochthons, and philhellenes, whether property-owners or not, employed or unemployed, so long as they had contributed to the Revolutionary struggle in a military or civilian capacity. Demotic councils, with the confirmation of the ministry of interior, would determine eligibility. The ministry of economic affairs would then issue a note valued at 2,000 drachmas to each eligible family head, who at public auction could bid for plots of land varying in size and quality. Each man could purchase as much as his note would buy him, so long as the amount did not exceed the statutory maximum of forty stremes. Each year for thirty-six years thereafter he would pay the government in cash 9 per cent of the value of his land, or 180 drachmas, if he had purchased up to the maximum value of his note. Of the 9 per cent, two-thirds was for interest and amortization, one-third to take the place of the usual land tax in kind. To the dissatisfaction of many, this law also differed from its prototype in not giving the land gratis.

Certain features rendered the law fiscally and economically beneficial to the state. By taxing land value, fixed by auction price, rather than land yield, which fluctuated according to weather and peasant work habits, the government could be sure of a fixed income and its treasury more nearly calculate its income in advance. Fixed payments would serve as a stimulus to greater productivity and as a curb on tax evasion. A cultivator would no longer be able to relax his efforts and cut down his productivity without bearing the full loss himself, whereas any increase in productivity would remain entirely his own. In addition, concealing the full amount of his harvest from the tax-collector would no longer be advantageous. The law also constituted a first step in the abolition of the tax-farming system. Requiring taxes in money rather than in kind would eliminate all the complications of weighing, transporting, and disposing of taxes in bulk. Collecting would thus become simple enough for the state to undertake it directly and the profit of the defunct tax-farmer would go either to the taxed person or to the treasury.[44]

Political factors also inspired the law. In a long note written to clarify its objectives and provisions,[45] the minister of economic affairs went as far as to say that political considerations had prevailed over economic ones in drawing up the law. What were these political considerations?

---

[43] Law concerning the dotation of Greek families, 26 May 1835*o.s.* [*Government Gazette*], no. 2, 19 June 1835*o.s.* For a summary of the provisions, see Pipineles [*Monarchy*], pp. 160-61, and Aspreas [*Political History*], ɪ, 143.

[44] But Pipineles ([*Monarchy*], p. 160) also points out a major financial sacrifice in the fact that the government was now collecting only 3 per cent tax instead of the regular 25 per cent on national land.

[45] "Clarification of the law of dotation . . . ," 27 Nov. 1835*o.s.* [*Government Gazette*], supplement, no. 20, 16 Dec. 1835*o.s.*

First, the principle "attested by universal history" that private property is the only sound basis of a nation's political economy and of a well-organized state. Second, that by raising so many men of tenant status to the dignity of property-owners, and by presumably satisfying a long-standing Revolutionary aspiration, a contented populace would be thus created. The note said as much as it could say publicly. In all probability a third and possibly more important political objective existed. If executed to its full extent, the law would produce that large independent yeoman class on which the Crown seems to have wished to bank its future and at the same time weaken the landed oligarchy by depriving it of its traditional role as tax-farmer, a role which brought it wealth and power. At first the royal government had refused to abolish tax-farming once and for all, lest it invite the determined resistance of all those benefiting from the system. Instead, it seems as if it chose to take the first step in this direction by incorporating partial abolition into a measure popular enough to silence any particular protests.[46]

Public response, so necessary for the successful execution of the law, was disappointing. The government's explanatory note, itself an attempt six months later to stir up some enthusiasm, reveals the public's misgivings by the arguments to which it addressed itself. No, land could not be given gratis. No, this was not a disguised attempt to raise taxes, but rather a temporary sacrifice of some public income in return for the immediate good of each Greek family and the ultimate good of the treasury. If those eligible did not take advantage of their opportunity, foreign colonists would eventually appear to buy some land and they would not be turned away. Finally the note declared it a matter of patriotic duty to commend the law to the people and exhorted public officials in such a tone as to accuse them of insufficient enthusiasm. If evidence were available, it is quite possible that one would find that the deliberate obstructionism and encouragement of the peasant's suspicious nature by large landholders was as important a factor in the snail-pace execution of the law as the inadequate administrative machinery.[47]

The Council of State

The Council of State was established by decree of 30 September 1835.[48]

[46] Pipineles [Monarchy], p. 156.

[47] "Clarification of the law of dotation," 27 Nov. 1835o.s. [Government Gazette], supplement, no. 20, 16 Dec. 1835o.s. According to Pipineles ([Monarchy], p. 162), the chief cause for delay in implementation was the lack of adequate administrative machinery.

[48] Decree for the introduction of a Council of State, 18/30 Sept. 1835 [Government Gazette], no. 8, 18 Sept. 1835o.s. A monograph, presented as a doctor's thesis in law at the University of Paris, has been published by C. L. Chaniotes, Le Consul d'État en Grèce de 1830 à 1930 (Paris, 1930), but he does not deal with the politics of its establishment. A valuable primary source on its establishment is Brandis, Mittheilungen, III, 273-75. For general accounts, see Aspreas [Political History], I, 144-45;

The first regency had envisaged such an institution and had in fact already defined some of its duties in various statutes establishing the state administration.[49] It was both a consultative assembly and the highest administrative court of the kingdom. As consultative assembly, it could discuss and pass judgment on the budget, new tax laws, and new legislation. It could interpret already existing laws as well. As a court, it could review decisions of the control board, judge conflicts of jurisdiction between judicial and administrative authorities, evaluate complaints in connection with demotic and eparchal elections, and judge charges against cabinet ministers which the king might bring to its attention. On all matters, the Council, consisting of at least twenty members, would vote as a body after legislation or administrative cases had been discussed by the four committees into which its members were divided (on civil and penal legislation, on economic matters, on remaining administration, and on cases of administrative conflicts). The king had the right to commission individual councilors to examine the functioning of a ministry or visit the provincial authorities to investigate public complaints against them.

The founding charter placed many curbs on the initiative of the body. Membership was by royal appointment for an unlimited period, but councilors were subject to outright dismissal or removal from the activities of the Council by concurrent appointment to a post away from the capital. Although the founding charter virtually required the king to submit all proposed legislation for judgment, the qualifying phrase "with the special exception of pressing circumstances which permit no delay" provided a loophole, and the statute nowhere made the judgment binding on the king. Moreover, it offered the Council no opportunities to formulate or initiate its own legislation. Even in matters of its internal organization the decree restricted the Council by preventing it from electing its own officers (who were to be appointed by the king) or by deciding when or how often it should meet. Indeed, the actual functioning of the Council later revealed its weakness vis-à-vis the royal authority. On the occasions when it disapproved or expressed reservations about measures in proposed legislation, the king commonly promulgated them anyway.[50]

The preamble of the founding charter stated the two-fold purpose of the establishment of this institution:

Kordatos [*History of Modern Greece*], III, 83; Pipineles [*Monarchy*], pp. 188-91; and Epaminondas Kyriakides, *Historia tou Neoterou Hellenismou* [*History of Modern Hellenism*] (Athens, 1892), I, 297-98.

[49] See Art. 15, decree for the division of the kingdom, 3/15 Apr. 1833 [*Government Gazette*], no. 12, 6/18 Apr. 1833.

[50] For instance, the new press law of 1837 rejected most of the modifications recommended by the Council of State (Lyons to Palmerston, Athens, 3 Dec. 1837, no. 138, and 12 Dec. 1837, no. 144, FO 32.72; 19 July 1838, no. 121, FO 32.77).

having the aim of surrounding Our throne with eminent men and of making their knowledge and experience useful to the state, and wishing, moreover, to give Our subjects a new token of Our love and trust toward them. . . .

In short, this institution was ostensibly intended to utilize the knowledge and experience of Revolutionary political leaders or, as time went on, the administrative knowledge gained by retired civil servants. It was intended as a substitute for an elective legislative assembly and initiated as a gesture toward appeasing public opinion, which resented the lack of royal trust implied by the employment of so many Bavarian and heterochthon Greeks in political posts.[51] As a palliative, the Council of State was the counterpart on the political level of the phalanx on the military level (see below). Though each institution sometimes offered the state valuable service, each was essentially a body of well-paid and profusely honored pensioners deprived of any real power.

A third motive never expressed in the statute was undoubtedly that expressed by Thiersch in 1833 when he recommended the establishment of such an institution of "the most important men" to be *placed under the eyes of the regency,* allowing the government to know them, appreciate their abilities, and *penetrate their designs*" (italics mine). Art. 56, which stated "No councilor of state is permitted to leave the capital without permission of the king," suggests the intention of keeping these men under surveillance in Athens and the desire, stated by Thiersch in another connection, to uproot them from the provincial centers of their political influence.[52]

The Royal Phalanx

The royal phalanx, an inactive reserve corps of army officers, was established by a decree of 30 September 1835 to honor unemployed irregular chieftains for distinguished Revolutionary service and to provide them with economic support. To allay dissatisfaction and render financial aid, the regency had already created two small reserve companies—one for Peloponnesian officers, the other for Epirot and Souliot officers—and had pensioned off a few chieftains on an individual basis. These small-scale measures now served as precedents for this major attempt to absorb the vast number of dissatisfied chieftains who had forcibly been dissolved

[51] See the text of the founding charter, as cited in n. 48 above. According to Maurer (*Griechische Volk,* II, 97), the Council of State was intended to substitute for the senate, to discuss important matters of state, and to find a solution for administrative problems. For its role as substitute for a legislative assembly, see Alexandre P. Couclelis, *Les Régimes Gouvernmentaux de la Grèce de 1821 à nos Jours* (Paris, 1921), p. 31: the Council of State was instituted "to give satisfaction to the partisans of a constitution."

[52] Thiersch, *État actuel,* I, 245. For the text of the decree establishing the Council of State, see reference in n. 48 above.

in 1833. The founding decree created an *ad hoc* tripartisan committee to select and rank all those deemed eligible. In the spring of 1836, the state announced the appointment of 800 men, organized into thirteen so-called tetrarchies. Although the original decree pronounced the state's right to use these tetrarchies in time of war or civil disturbance, it invited those wishing active service to join the gendarmerie, militia, or light battalions and thus betrayed the fact that the phalanx would be little more than a glorified pension system. The 400,000 drachmas spent by the state on it annually was the price necessary to appease a dispossessed military class deemed politically dangerous. Quite clearly, then, the establishment of the phalanx was motivated by political rather than military considerations.[53]

4. POLICY TOWARD THE PARTIES

Armansperg initiated his administration with a series of moves designed to appease the "Russian" party, avert a Kolettist counterattack, and prevent an alliance of the two parties against him. Through royal clemency he released Kolokotrones and Plapoutas from prison, amidst much public rejoicing, and pardoned or reduced the prison terms of those incarcerated for their role in the Messenian revolt. The Napist Kitsos Tzavelas was one of the five newly appointed royal aides-de-camp.[54]

Armansperg experienced great anxiety over the possible political repercussions of Kolettes' dismissal and proceeded warily. He held up the dismissal for two weeks and hence:

arranged matters so that Colettis' resignation be announced at the same time as a plan for the employment of the Palicari chiefs, which will considerably neutralize this person's power.

On 11 July, General Gordon left his post as head of the Peloponnesian forces to conduct an expedition through Rumely, the Kolettes stronghold, where continued brigandage might have turned into a Kolettist revolt. To the Peloponnesos, in the meantime, Armansperg sent Lüders, newly appointed Bavarian aide-de-camp, because of reported movements of both Kolettists and Napists there. Kolettes' continued presence in Greece during

[53] Decree for the formation of a Greek phalanx, 18/30 Sept. 1835 [*Government Gazette*], no. 6, 18 Sept. 1835*o.s.*; decree concerning the Greek phalanx, 18/30 Sept. 1835 [*GG*], no. 12, 11 Oct. 1835*o.s.*; decree of appointments, 25 Apr./7 May 1836 [*GG*], no. 26, 10 June 1836*o.s.* Pipineles ([*Monarchy*], p. 221) estimated the cost at 400,000 drachmas. Thiersch (*État actuel*, I, 249) also suggested the idea of some such institution when he wrote: "In Rumely and the Peloponnesos, about thirty captains, who because of reputation and influence, should be attached immediately to the king . . . and assured an honorable position in the new order of things." See also Aspreas [*Political History*], I, 144, and Brandis, *Mittheilungen*, III, 275-77.

[54] For the proclamations pardoning Kolokotrones and Plapoutas and appointing Tzavelas, see *Ethnikē*, 20 May/1 June 1835.

the summer, on the plea of illness, only contributed to suspicions that a Kolettist plot was afoot. But no revolt occurred and on 10 August Kolettes left to take up his post in Paris.[55]

On the surface Armansperg's policy toward the parties looks like a continuation of that during the first regency period. The parties received no official acknowledgment, the process of removing party leaders was completed with the departure of Kolettes, and the attempt to create a large body of small yeomen as a counterweight to the primates and captains found expression in the dotation law. And indeed, the Crown remained committed to its original aim—the weakening of the parties and their ultimate destruction.

In actuality Armansperg's policy differed radically from that of the first regency, if only because Armansperg, a shrewd political realist, knew enough to profit from the first regency's errors. No one can accuse him of repeating those same errors. In his foreign policy, he did not misread the power rivalry over Greece. On the contrary, he seems to have rightly recognized Britain as the strongest and most aggressive factor in the Near East. In his domestic calculations, he did not fail to identify and locate the parties. The realism which rescued him from the misunderstandings to which the first regency fell prey encouraged him to make bold responses to the same three dilemmas that had plagued the regency—the dilemmas of (1) neutrality, (2) plot response, and (3) administrative deterrence (as described at the end of Chapter IV).

In response to the first, Armansperg seems to have accepted the fact that neutrality was impracticable and to have decided to line up with the strongest elements on the foreign and domestic scenes. Betting on British supremacy in the Near East, he readily accepted dependence on Britain. By the unwritten rules of such practice, he should have based his regime on the "English" party, and this he did to some extent. But he must have realized that too close an identification with the "English" party would constitute a serious domestic weakness, in part because the "English" party enjoyed nowhere near the natural predominance in Greek politics that Britain enjoyed in European politics, in part because the fairly even power balance between the three parties in Greece prevented any government from surviving without the support of at least two of the three parties. In avoiding exclusive dependence on the "English" party, he risked alienating Britain by not sufficiently patronizing

[55] Concerning Armansperg's arrangements prior to the dismissal of Kolettes, see Lyons to Palmerston, Athens, 2 June 1835, FO 32.52. On 30 May/11 June 1835, *Ethnikē* announced Kolettes' dismissal and his appointment as Greek minister to France. Concerning the Gordon mission, see Finlay, Journal (MSS), 1 July 1835; concerning the Lüders mission, see *ibid.*, 7 Sept. 1835 and 9 Nov. 1835: ". . . it was deemed necessary for the movements of the Koletti [*sic*] and Napist parties to despatch Lüder [*sic*] immediately to the command." On Kolettes' delay in leaving Greece, see Edouard Driault and Michel Lhéritier, *Histoire Diplomatique de la Grèce de 1821 à nos Jours* (Paris, 1925), II, 139.

Britain's client party. So successfully did he convince Palmerston and Lyons of his loyalty, however, and hence demonstrate that Britain could exercise its influence directly instead of through its client party, that Palmerston and Lyons seem to have acquiesced in his giving the "English" party less influence than it desired.

With regard to the dilemma of plot response, Armansperg practiced a policy of leniency. As he demonstrated during the Messenian revolt and was again to demonstrate during the Acarnanian revolt of 1836, he was willing to deal lightly with the rebels and avoided making martyrs of them by meting out heavy penalties. Moreover, he used the occasion to win the support of irregular chieftains, by employing them to suppress the rebellion and tolerating the abuses which they committed in its suppression. Since he had never assumed the pose of severity, as the first regency had, his lenient practice during a crisis was less likely to be interpreted as a sign of weakness.

Finally, Armansperg seems to have been willing to live with the parties, even to wink at some of their abuses and allow them some freedom of action, so long as they would help him control the country and at least shoot most of their arrows at each other rather than at him. Since he virtually abandoned the policy of trying to destroy the party system, the dilemma of administrative deterrence was no longer a real one for him. He would forego administrative efficiency since he was no longer opposed to the party activities that administrative efficiency might deter.

The reconstruction of Armansperg's policy, which includes intentions and goals, rests entirely on inference from deeds of his administration since, to our knowledge, neither he nor anyone associated in administration with him ever articulated the policy or a rationale for it. This section will describe Armansperg's policy toward the parties in four different phases and will, in the process, show how for political purposes Armansperg created and modified, and used and abused the new institutions discussed in the previous section.

Exclusive Dependence on Britain

To some extent Armansperg became dependent on Britain in his power struggle with Maurer and Abel and could not very well extricate himself after the service which Palmerston had rendered his cause. But there is no reason to believe that Armansperg did not freely choose to ally himself with Britain. When Dawkins turned against Armansperg just before his return to England in mid-1835, Armansperg could have used the rupture as a pretext for loosening his ties with Britain had he wished. But he seems to have leaned toward Britain not, as Maurer had in the case of France and Austria, because he believed Britain to have the fewest ulterior motives. On the contrary, he apparently befriended Britain because of its eagerness to oppose Russian influence everywhere in the Near East and its consequent willingness and power to support with

243

vigor, even interfere in behalf of, any local exponent of British interests. Armansperg wanted an interested rather than a disinterested power, one tied to its friends by self-interest. He displayed a willingness to risk the combined hostility of all the other powers, so great was his faith in Britain's strength to sustain him in power.[56]

When Sir Edmund Lyons replaced Dawkins as British minister in Athens, Armansperg's connection with Britain became even stronger. According to Driault, Lyons supported him with all his influence. As Lyons' correspondence shows, he represented Armansperg to the British government as a liberal, a skilful leader, and a popular figure among most Greeks. He took every opportunity to demonstrate to the Greeks that Armansperg enjoyed British confidence.[57]

The greatest demonstration of British support came from Palmerston at the Conference of London, which deliberated during 1835-36 over a three-power guarantee of the third series of the loan envisioned in the treaty of 7 May 1832. As early as the end of 1833, the Greek government had placed its request for the third series, which it sorely needed to meet what became by 1836 recurring budget deficits. Palmerston vigorously urged three-power guarantee for a loan, which was bound to strengthen the Armansperg government. By the fall of 1836, after deliberations had dragged and broken down and the prospects of French and Russian cooperation seemed worse than ever, Palmerston secured Parliamentary assent to a unilateral British advance of 1,000,000 francs. Ironically, the money got to Greece too late to benefit Armansperg, whom Otho had by this time dismissed.[58]

[56] Concerning Dawkins' rupture with Armansperg, which none of the secondary sources mention, see Finlay, Journal (MSS), 11 July 1835: "Dawkins . . . doubted Armansperg as a Russian." Driault and Lhéritier, (Histoire, ii, 139) do mention a letter of Dawkins to Rouen, in which Dawkins recommends that, after the royal accession, Kolettes form a ministry to which Armansperg should accord entire confidence. Of course, such a recommendation, running counter to Armansperg's determination to be rid of Kolettes, reflects the break between Dawkins and Armansperg. On Armansperg's decision to rely almost exclusively on Britain, see ibid., ii, 139-40: "Count Armansperg decided that he needed only the support of the British government."

[57] Ibid., ii, 140; or Finlay, Journal (MSS), 1 Mar. 1836: "Lyons has only one idea—keeping Armansperg in place"; or Finlay, History, viii, 143. For some samples of Lyons' expressed evaluation of Armansperg, see Lyons to Palmerston, Athens, 2 June 1835, FO 32.52: "The King is decidedly popular but the hopes of the nation are fixed upon Count d'Armansperg and his hopes are in general measure fixed on the countenance and support of England"; or Lyons to Palmerston, Athens, 28 Aug. 1835, no. 35, FO 32.52: "I believe that Durham [English statesman who had just visited Greece] is impressed with the conviction that Armansperg is a statesman of enlightened and liberal views and that he is heart and soul engaged in the regeneration of Greece, but it has not escaped him that there exists an impediment to his good intentions, and that the difficulty lies in the Royal Mind."

[58] For the best account of this phase of the financial deliberations of the Conference of London, see Driault and Lhéritier, Histoire, ii, 157-63.

Armansperg did not, indeed could not, always comply with British requests or recommendations, such as taking steps toward the establishment of constitutional government. Nevertheless, he frequently deferred to the suggestions of Lyons, especially those concerning patronage. He went as far as to conclude an agreement, strongly backed by Lyons, with a private British investor for the establishment of a bank in Greece.[59]

Creation of a Political Following

Armansperg's efforts to establish a solid core of political support for his regime differed in three major respects from those of the regency majority. He saw the problem as one of wooing to his standard segments of the existing parties rather than assembling individuals. He selected as objects of special favor or appointees to the most coveted positions the politically influential rather than those with professional qualifications or no party connections. Nor does he seem to have been naive enough to believe that any one party could be designated as *the* national party. Just as his realism in the analysis of the international situation made him bold enough to risk identification with one power, his realism dictated against his basing himself on any one party.

Inevitably the creation of a following involved making inroads into the strongholds of the existing parties. Armansperg employed three primary means: (1) keeping party leaders outside the country, (2) wooing secondary political figures from all three parties, and (3) winning over the military element as a body, hence cutting across all party lines and splitting the military segment of each party from its political leaders.

It is noteworthy that Armansperg recalled from abroad neither Trikoupes nor Mavrokordatos, both acknowledged leaders of the "English" party. The government needed Trikoupes' services in London, and Mavrokordatos had made himself so unpopular as minister of finance in 1833-34 that his recall would only prejudice the popularity of the "English" party and the Armansperg regime. So Lyons explained Armansperg's failure to recall these men. More likely Armansperg remembered the mistake of the regency majority in becoming identified with a single party by its reliance on Kolettes and wished to avoid similar identification of himself with the "English" party.[60]

[59] Armansperg often resisted British pressure for internal reform; he once had with Lyons a small quarrel lasting some twenty-four hours (*ibid.*, II, 163). Concerning Lyons' influence, see Finlay (Journal [MSS], 9 Nov. 1835), who, in spite of his many reservations concerning Lyons, gives him the credit for what he considers the excellent appointments to the Council of State. Lyons himself (1 Jan. 1836, no. 1, FO 32.58) speaks about "my official and private influence with the King and the Chancellor." On the abortive agreement for a bank, see Pipineles [*Monarchy*], pp. 201-203, and Evangelides [*History*], p. 115f. and 144f.

[60] Indeed, Makrygiannes identified Armansperg with the "English" party, probably because of his close association with Lyons (see [*Memoirs*], II, 81-82). Lyons to Palmerston, Athens, 3 Jan. 1836, no. 2, FO 32.58.

In spite of his bids for Napist support, he would only go so far. Russian diplomacy was attempting to place Michael Soutsos and Andrew Metaxas, its most prominent Napists, in the cabinet. Armansperg assured Lyons:

> he'd never permit it. He remarked that as Soutso would be wholly without influence if not in office, he should not object to his spending his leave of absence from Petersburg [where he was Greek minister to Russia] with his relations in Athens, but that he considered Metaxa a dangerous man and would find some employment for him out of the country, and he is going to Madrid. . . .[61]

As a study of the internal structure of the parties will later show, the policy of honorary exile for party leaders, though it by no means led to a dissolution of the party, precipitated a series of adjustments among members which involved intraparty dissensions. The vacancy in party leadership enhanced the power of party lieutenants and gave them a vested interest in the exile of the original leader. Hence, in effect this policy contributed to the aim of courting secondary political figures.

The establishment of the Council of State gave Armansperg an excellent opportunity to exploit his power of patronage to woo away secondary party figures from their acknowledged leaders or allies. Of the twenty regular appointees, ten, according to Lyons' exaggerated estimate, seven according to mine, belonged to the "English" party, in either case a large proportion of the total membership. Armansperg undoubtedly intended to please both Lyons, who took credit for suggesting most of the appointments, and the party which enjoyed Lyons' protection. The "Russian" appointees were Theodore Kolokotrones, George Ainian, and Andrew Metaxas, whose mission to Madrid rendered his appointment honorific. Andrew Zaïmes, another appointee, and Ainian became extremely susceptible to Armansperg's courting, perhaps because of their personal antipathy toward Kolettes. More significant appointments were those of close associates of Kolettes (John Mexes, Nicholas Botases, Drosos Mansolas, Nicholas Zacharitsas) or men who had formerly cooperated with him (Petros Mavromichales, Anagnostes Delegiannes, Panoutsos Notaras, George Kountouriotes). Indeed, the relative balance of party representation in the Council of State is an accurate reflection of the status enjoyed by each party under the Armansperg administration. Mere appointment to the Council of State did not bring wholehearted support to Armansperg, but as the sequel significantly reveals, this body as an institution remained faithful to him to the bitter end.[62]

[61] *Ibid.*, 1 Oct. 1835, "Separate and Confidential," FO 32.53.

[62] Lyons, in a letter to Palmerston (Athens, 2 Nov. 1835, no. 2, FO 32.53), enclosed the following list of regular appointees (in "service ordinary" as distinct from supplementary members in "service extraordinary"), together with his own classification of these men by party affiliation:

P. Mavromichalis—English   *Anag. Delyanni—uncertain

Armansperg employed the establishment of a phalanx to make a serious dent in the "French" party, which commanded the support of so many chieftains, but he also permitted a broad appointment policy which would cut across all party lines. The six-man committee, which he appointed to determine eligibility and to recommend the rank of each veteran captain, gave representation to all three parties. Although the committee betrayed some favoritism in its recommendations, the favoritism did not run primarily along party lines. One may judge the success of this policy, at least in part, by the farewell banquet in behalf of Armansperg just after his dismissal in February 1837. Prominent chieftains of both the "French" and "Russian" parties, such as Nicholas Kriezotes, the Grivas', John Mamoures, John Roukes, Demetrios Plapoutas, Gennaios Kolokotrones, and Demetrios Tsokres, were present and—to the indignation of Makrygiannes—wept over the impending departure of the fallen chancellor.[63]

Even though Armansperg made continual bids for some Napist support, his regime represented only a relaxation of the previous discrimination against the Napist party rather than full parity with the other parties. To have gone any further would undoubtedly have alienated British diplomacy which, after all, supported Armansperg as the best guarantee against Russian penetration into Greek affairs. But Armansperg did flirt with the "French" party. He surely realized what Finlay privately observed—that if he did not attach to himself the Kolettist party, he would fall completely into the hands of the "British." Moreover, a type of alliance between the "English" and "French" parties seemed feasible on

---

*Panoutsos Notaras—English
Andre Metaxas—*Russian*
Noti Botzari—English
*G. Condouriotti—English
*Andre Zaimi—Russian
Richard Church—English
Jean Mexi—Coletti
Th. Kolokotroni—*Russian*
Athanase Lidoriki—English

Basili Boudouri—English
Emmanuel Xeno—English
A. Monarchides—English
Tatzi Manghina—English
Nic. Botassi—Coletti
*Georges Valtino—uncertain
Georges Ainian—*Russian*
*Drosso Mansolas—uncertain
*Nic. Zacharitza—uncertain

"Zaimi is opposed to Constitutional Government but not attached to Russia in any other way." [Hence, Lyons does not italicize "Russian" in his case.]

I have starred those whom I have classified differently (see Prosopography in Appendix below). I can only account for Lyons' mistakes in terms of his desire to have the body look more "English" and less "French" than it actually was. Concerning close ties between Zaïmes and Ainian on the one hand and Armansperg on the other, see *Athēna*, 24 May 1836 o.s. On continued loyalty of the Council of State, see n. 116 below.

63 The six-man committee, appointed 15 Dec. 1835 o.s., consisted of Church as president, Kriezotes, Niketaras, Tzavelas, Omorphopoulos, and Makrygiannes (Makrygiannes [*Memoirs*], II, 81, including n. 4 of editor). Concerning favoritism, see *ibid.*, II, 82-83. For a list of the appointments, see the decree of 25 Apr./7 May 1836 [*Government Gazette*], no. 26, 10 June 1836 o.s., and for an account of the farewell party, see Makrygiannes, *op.cit.*, II, 89-90.

the basis of their common espousal of constitutionalism. His own reputation for liberalism would tend to attract constitutionalists to his cause.[64]

Lyons fell in with this strategy—perhaps even inspired or encouraged
it. During this period, Lyons' correspondence is full of remarks illustrating
his official contention that there were no separate "English" and "French"
parties in Greece, rather a single "Constitutional party" looking to both
France and England for joint patronage. He probably realized that the
"English" party did not command sufficiently broad support in Greece to
constitute by itself a sufficient political base for the regime. He may have
welcomed leaning toward the "French" as a way of keeping Armansperg
from veering toward the "Russians," and certainly he was trying to win
the French minister over by convincing him that Armansperg's regime
represented the Constitutional rather than simply the "English" party.
Moreover, Armansperg's domestic policy complemented Palmerston's
desire to associate France in a Western alliance against Russian influence
in the Middle East, with France as junior partner.[65]

Momentarily, English diplomacy won its objective. The new govern-
ment of Thiers in France in 1836 instructed Theodose de Lagrené, the
French minister in Athens, to work in harmony with his English colleague.
To demonstrate to the Greeks and Russia this "Western alliance," the
British and French fleets appeared before Phaleron harbor (outside
Athens) in August. But the cooperation proved only momentary because
Lagrené would not follow Lyons' lead. Under conditions of nineteenth-
century diplomacy, representatives in foreign capitals could often deviate
with impunity from the instructions of their government, but one suspects
that, in the case of Lagrené, his government was content to have him
disregard its pious platitudes so as to score a French advantage.[66]

[64] Indeed, continuation of discrimination against the Napists was pronounced
enough for *Athēna* to remark about Armansperg's policy of "keeping one segment of
men from affairs" (15 Jan. 1838*o.s.*) or even speak more specifically about Armansperg's removal of men "from the public service simply because they were adherents
of the so-called Napist or Kapodistrian party" (25 June 1835*o.s.*). See also Finlay,
Journal (MSS), 3 June 1835.

[65] "There are but two parties in Greece, the Constitutional party and the Russian
party: the great desire of the Constitutionalists is to see the connexion between the
French Governments and Mons. Coletti dissolved, and to look with equal confidence
to France and England for support" (Lyons to Palmerston, Athens, 27 Jan. 1836, no.
7, FO 32.58). For an example of Lyons' habit of using "Constitutionalists" as synonymous with adherents of the "English" and "French" parties, see his following remark:
"Rudhart tried to separate the English and French parties, but the Constitutionalists
are more numerous and united than ever" (Athens, 29 Dec. 1837, no. 153, FO 32.72).
Concerning Palmerston's desire for a common Anglo-French policy in Greece, see
Lyons to Palmerston, Athens, 27 Jan. 1836, no. 7, FO 32.58, writing about "the great
object of England and France in preserving Greece from dependence on Russia."

[66] Concerning Lagrené's instructions, see Driault and Lhéritier, *Histoire*, ɪɪ, 155;
also reference to them in Lyons to Palmerston, Athens, 11 Apr. 1836, no. 22, FO
32.59. In that same letter, Lyons complains that Lagrené told the Spanish consul that
he and Lyons agreed "in principle but not in personnel"; in another (Athens, 29

In any case, Lyons secured the sudden conversion of the formerly Kolettist *Sōtēr* into an exponent of the new regime. "It seems," said Finlay, "when Lyons bought Scouffo [*Sōtēr's* editor] for Armansperg he [Skouphos] was promised a place in the Council of State or a portfolio." He may also have played some part in winning Armansperg the support of the Grivas', who maintained close connections with the British legation in Athens. Winning over such former Kolettists as Skouphos and Grivas may have looked like a great gain for Armansperg, but it proved a liability. Opportunism was to make Skouphos as ready to desert Armansperg as he had been to desert the fallen Kolettes. Owing to their turbulence, the Grivas' were to bring discredit on Armansperg himself.[67]

Working Through the Parties

"Absolute inaction reigned in the Gov't [*sic*] since Count Armansperg became sole minister," wrote Finlay in his private journal a few months after Otho's accession. In retrospect years later, as he looked back on Armansperg's regime as a whole, his verdict remained unchanged:

> He wasted his time in manoeuvres to conceal his ignorance and in talking to foreign ministers concerning his financial schemes and his projects of improvement. On looking back at his administration, it presents a succession of temporary expedients carried into execution in a very imperfect manner. He had no permanent plan and no consistent policy.

In 1841, Pericles Argyropoulos, brother-in-law of Mavrokordatos and member of the "English" party, expressed the opinion that Armansperg had undermined almost everything of real value in the administrative system created by the first regency.[68]

Except for the first three months of the royal majority, when the Crown promulgated major legislation, and the last two months of his regime, when a spate of hastily drawn up decrees betrayed a frantic attempt to revive his political fortunes,[69] Armansperg's regime manifested not even

---

Sept. 1836, "Private," FO 32.60) that the Lagrené's visited the Catacazy's for a week in Aegina; in another (Athens, 20 Sept. 1836, no. 96, FO 32.71) that Lagrené warmly supported Rudhart and hence refused to fall in with British policy.

[67] Finlay, Journal (MSS), 1 Mar. 1836.

[68] Finlay, "Observations," p. 19, Journal 1835 (MSS), and Finlay, *History*, VII, 142. P. Argyropoulos to Mavrokordatos, Report on the Ministry of the Interior, undated [1841], no. 5865, Vol. 21 (1841), Mavrokordatos Archive, General State Archives, Athens.

[69] Most notable of the many decrees, most of which remained inapplicable because inadequately drawn up and intended only to impress, were: (1) decree for eparchal councils, 18/30 Dec. 1836 [*Government Gazette*], no. 77, 24 Dec. 1836*o.s.*; (2) decree for a corrective prison [*GG*], no. 81; (3) decree for a demotic police force [*GG*], no. 85; (4) decree for the introduction of a university [*GG*], no. 86; (5) decree for the regulation of Greek schools and gymnasiums [*GG*], no. 87. The last four of the

the outward signs of constructive statecraft. Throughout his stay in Greece, Armansperg rationalized his inactivity and the great gap between his lavish promises and his meagre achievements by resorting to a device which began as merely immoral though effective and ended up as extremely dangerous and finally fatal to his career in Greece. He created a succession of scapegoats whom he portrayed as the great obstacles to his liberal program. The blame fell first on the regency majority, then on Kolettes, and finally, when no one else remained, on the king himself, whose competence, even sanity, Armansperg skilfully called into question. Besides its failure to maintain order, balance the budget, grant a constitution or even approximate these objectives, the Armansperg administration earned quick notoriety for its corruption and its toleration of abuses.[70]

Finlay attributed this state of affairs to Armansperg's personal failing— incompetence and laziness—and as the above quotation suggests, to the lack of any consistent policy.[71] He was only half right. If Armansperg's misrule suffered from personal failings, they were failings of another order, moral rather than mental or physical. If he had no policy, the policy he lacked concerned statecraft, not politics. To my mind, Armansperg did formulate a policy for governing Greece. Indeed, he adhered to it consistently and skilfully. It was the policy of a politician rather

---

five mentioned were all dated 31 Dec. 1836/12 Jan. 1837 and the issues of [*GG*] in which they appeared were all dated 31 Dec. 1837*o.s.* In addition, another notable feature of [*GG*], during December 1836 was its publication, for the first time, of the budgets of each ministry for the three-year period 1833-35. This was obviously intended to satisfy the Conference of London's requirement for granting the third series and to restore Armansperg's waning reputation as an expert in financial administration.

[70] "During the existence of the Regency, their quarrels served as an excuse for doing nothing or going wrong at first and latterly when Count Armansperg had the administration in his own hands—the rebellion in Messenia—the change of the capital to Athens and the intrigues of or against Coletti served one after another for his either doing nothing or signing decrees drawn up by others of which his friends say he does not approve. All the hopes of the people therefore were directed to the majority of the King—that took place, Coletti was dismissed & Count Armansperg declared sole minister—months elapsed & nothing was done—his friends said wait until Coletti is gone to France as Minister—to France Coletti is gone and the patience of the people is gone too—" (Finlay, Journal 1835 [MSS], "Observations," p. 7-8). Taking his point a step further, Finlay wrote, in connection with Armansperg's inaction (Journal [MSS], 7 Sept. 1835): "Now Armansperg as an apology for his trifling & imbecility tells all these stories [about Otho's alleged incompetence] against the King to Lyons—is this fair?"

Makrygiannes ([*Memoirs*], II, 89) is typical in his suspicion, even exaggeration, of corruption in the Armansperg administration, from the *head* down, when he writes: "The King gave Armansperg 100,000 dr., he took some million dollars, and he went on his way [after dismissal]. And so he came a louse-infected count and left a real one."

[71] Finlay, Journal (MSS), 10 May 1836, Journal 1835 (MSS), 1 Aug. 1836.

than that of a statesman or administrator—pragmatic, realistic, and administratively unambitious. And without realizing it, Finlay put his finger on the reasoning behind this policy when he quoted Armansperg as saying:

My notion is you can only govern Greece by the instruments existing— these instruments are the leading statesmen, soldiers & landed proprietors of the country good or bad. They alone make the machine move.[72]

Armansperg realized that only "the instruments existing" could provide him with effective political support and that the price for such support was the enjoyment of some privileges which, from the point of view of state administration and peasant interests, amounted to abuses. Since "the existing instruments" acted often through their respective political parties, which they controlled, and the oppressed often resorted to patrons and parties when the state failed to offer protection, Armansperg's policy meant, on the provincial level, government through parties.

In a comparison between the "systems" of Armansperg and the first regency, Prokesch-Osten showed his awareness of Armansperg's policy. The first regency had based itself on "outside pressure." By this he meant Bavarian troops and administrators, perhaps heterochthon Greeks, too. Armansperg relied on "the indigenous energies of the Greeks themselves, and this has as its result the dependence of the government on the parties and its exploitation by them."[73] Or, as Mendelssohn Bartholdy pointed out, "neutrality toward the parties" took a radically different form under Armansperg. Instead of equal subversion of all parties, the formula meant equal freedom of abuse for all. To support his assertion concerning the absence of a consistent policy, Finlay stated a fact which really demonstrates the political policy described above:

In one district the Capodistrians were allowed to persecute the constitutionalists, and in another the Kolettists domineered over the Capodistrians.[74]

In the sense used here, the policy of administration through the parties had three chief aspects: (1) special favor for and acquiescence in corruption by political supporters, (2) revival of the irregular or palikar military system, and (3) revision or altered administration of land and tax policies.

Armansperg's lavish expenditures represented more than sheer vanity or self-indulgence. He spent to bestow favors and to pay the expense of

[72] Finlay to "My dear Sir" [probably Trikoupes], 1836, Letter Book 1827-1836 (MSS).

[73] Prokesch-Osten to Metternich, 2 Feb. 1835, as quoted by Mendelssohn Bartholdy, *Geschichte Griechenlands*, II, 500-501.

[74] Finlay, *History*, VII, 142. Mendelssohn Bartholdy (*Geschichte Griechenlands*, II, 497) paraphrases Finlay's quotation to make his own point.

the peculation which he permitted, all in an attempt to keep himself in place. "Every abuse is attempted by the Count to serve his partisans," wrote Finlay. The dotation law offered an excellent opportunity for corruption, especially when administered by as dishonest a head of the ministry of economic affairs as Lassanes, friend and appointee of Armansperg. Allegedly, Lassanes parceled out to friends of the regime valuable national land, especially in the fertile and valuable regions of the northern Peloponnesos which produced currants, a cash crop sold abroad. Indeed, the animosity between him and Regny, a previous appointee of the first regency to head the control board, stemmed from Regny's power and determination to curb financial abuses. Eventually, because of their differences, Regny resigned and hence gave Armansperg free rein. According to Makrygiannes, those chieftains who gave Armansperg a farewell party were such ardent supporters because of both land and money which they had received. In fact, toleration of abuses and rendering of special favors proved far more effective in rounding up a following than the mere exercise of patronage.[75]

Although the Armansperg regime persisted in the original policy of establishing a Westernized regular army under Bavarian tutelage, it permitted the gradual reinstatement of the older system of palikarism. The resurgence of the system, which the first regency had abolished with such damage to its popularity, took place as a series of expedients to meet crises and enjoyed no statutory justification, except for passing references in legislation concerned with the regular army. To meet both the Messenian revolt of 1834 and the Acarnanian revolt of 1836, Armansperg commissioned some of the old captains to recruit their old military clienteles for the campaign against the rebels. This policy made sense because of irregulars' fighting superiority over the regulars in Greek terrain. It also proved an effective way of allaying palikar discontent by giving them employment. Many suspected that the palikars had encouraged these revolts as a way of forcing the government into dependence on them. In a way Armansperg was committed to some such policy by virtue of his criticism of the first regency's military policy.[76]

[75] For the Finlay quotation and notice of the cotton monopoly of Livadia, see Finlay, Journal (MSS), 17 July 1836; see also the entry under 16 December 1836 of the same journal: "His lavish expenditure has been to keep himself in place and when his interests have allowed it, he has been economical." On Lassanes and his association with the scandals of administering the dotation law, see *Athēna,* 17 June 1836 o.s. *Athēna* (11 Apr. 1836o.s.) covered the story of Regny's resignation and his replacement by N. Silivergos. On Armansperg's showering favors on the chieftains, see Makrygiannes [*Memoirs*], II, 89-90.

[76] On Armansperg's general restoration of palikarism, see Finlay, *History,* VII, 118, and Finlay to "My dear Sir" [probably Trikoupes], 1836, Letter Book 1827-1836 (MSS). On the recruitment of 3,000 irregulars to put down the Messenian revolt, see Bower and Bolitho, *Otho I,* p. 68. On the recruitment of 2,000 palikars for the suppression of the Acarnanian revolt, see the notice of *Athēna,* 18 Feb. 1835o.s.

Actually, nonstatutory supplementation of regular troops took two forms: light infantry battalions and a national guard (*ethnophylake*). The former originated as a part of the negotiated settlement between the state and the Maniats when the latter agreed to serve against the Messenian rebels in return for their organization into exclusively Maniat battalions enjoying some of their traditional military habits. So effective a prop did the Maniat expedient prove that the government subsequently extended it to non-Maniats. The arrangement, similar to the first regency's abortive scheme for battalions of skirmishers, represented a compromise between a strictly Western system and traditional palikarism.[77]

The national guard reflected the old palikar system in so far as the state commissioned captains to recruit, pay, and maintain a stipulated number of soldiers at the expense of the villages or demes, which negotiated pay rates with the captains. This system revived all the old abuses. Captains charged the public purse for nonexistent soldiers and often forced villages to pay exorbitant rates. And as Finlay keenly understood, a revived palikar system bore close connection with the administration of tax-farming because the strong men could monopolize the purchase and dictate the price of the contracts. As the next section will show, irregular troops commissioned to put down rebels or seek out brigands often proved a worse scourge to the peasantry.[78] The dilemma is obvious: an improvement in the condition of the military élite, through revival of the palikar system, destroyed even the few traces of regularized administration and public order, rendered the peasants discontented, and defrauded the state of revenue.

The same sort of benevolence toward the ruling élite appears in the administration of the dotation law, the renting of national land for cultivation, and the awarding of tax-farming contracts. In all three cases perhaps, this reorientation of state policy from that of coddling the "middling classes" was the only feasible course, thanks to the obstruc-

[77] Finlay, Journal (MSS), 7 May 1836, and "Observations," p. 17, Journal 1835 (MSS).

[78] "These national guards are enrolled by the civil authorities & paid by the villages according to a certain agreed on rate of pay during 3 months of this year and in some cases for six months these troops were regularly paid but the villages were in most cases unwilling & in many unable to continue their payment & accordingly the force has been completely dissolved. It is to be remarked also that in many cases the leaders of the national guard having collected a certain force compelled the villages to pay for a very great number of men & many of the leaders of national guards never have the number of men they were paid to maintain. As the provisioning & paying these forces was of necessity entrusted to their leaders, a door was opened to every species of peculation again flourishing which had reigned during the revolution & which had finished by furnishing Greece with an army of officers & not a soldier to command" (Finlay, "Observations," p. 12, Journal 1835 [MSS]). On the connection between palikarism and the purchase of tenths, see Finlay to "My dear Sir" [probably Trikoupes], 1836, Letter Book 1827-1836 (MSS).

253

tionism of the ruling *élite* and the unwillingness or inability of the peasant to respond to the dotation law or to take on a tax-farming contract.

The trend away from stated policy, again through a series of specific administrative measures rather than a statutory reformulation of policy, is evidenced in a number of cases. At Patradjick, instead of selling small contracts directly to the villages, the government sold the collection of the tenths in 1835 in a large unit. The purchaser then parceled out and resold at a profit of 8,000 drachmas. Or take the case of an affluent man in Mesolongi, who leased from the state the villages of Bochori and Galata at 12,000 drachmas a year. Finlay commented as follows:

> The contract is considered a very favorable one for the lessee and every body was surprised to see Gov't break through their pretended rule of striving to do every thing for the middling classes. They could easily have raised the same sum by apportioning the land out in small portions & by selling it in small lots they would have benefitted the country more.[79]

A similar departure from stated policy relates to the appointment of a financial official in his native province, a departure from the stated policy of making appointments to areas where a man had no local roots or personal influence. After asserting the official's proneness to cheat both government and peasantry, Finlay comments:

> I think this is to be feared when a man of the country is named to a place in the administration of the revenues. A stranger . . . may perhaps defraud the Gov't but he will find some difficulty in cheating the inhabitants.[80]

The dilemma is apparent. Even though a man could bring to his post in his own locale invaluable knowledge of local conditions, his partisanship and involvement with a local faction would disqualify him on grounds of partiality.

An explicit modification of past policy came in the modification of the unsuccessful dotation law. In November 1836, about six months after the bulk of the land was supposed by statute to have been distributed, a decree offered to sell as many as eighty additional stremes to whoever had bought an allotted forty and to charge only 6 per cent interest on any indebtedness between 2,000-6,000 drachmas, 8 per cent on anything over. This decree, in its actual encouragement of large private landholdings, ran counter to the spirit of the original law and the more general objective of creating an extensive yeoman class.[81]

[79] Finlay, Journal 1835 (MSS), 21 July 1836 (Patradjick case) and 4 Aug. 1836 (Mesolongi case). For another instance, cited during the Acarnanian revolt as a possible contributing factor, see *Athēna*, 11 Mar. 1836o.s.

[80] Finlay, Journal 1835 (MSS), 11 Aug. 1836.

[81] Decree concerning dotation, 13/25 Nov. 1836 [*Government Gazette*], no. 67, 22 Nov. 1836o.s.

This system, a departure from the regency majority's policy of cracking down severely on administrative abuses and favoring the poor against the large landholders, had the advantages of attracting those who actually wielded political influence (chieftains and primates) and freeing the regime of the necessity of using punitive means against corruption. But, since there was not enough to go around, Armansperg's system made as many deadly enemies among those who did not receive as it did ardent supporters among those who took. Moreover, it aggravated popular restlessness against increasing abuses.

Absolutism and Bavarianism

Armansperg could afford to allow his Greek following greater freedom of abuse and more petty administrative initiative because its real power remained only minimal. The continued system of absolutism allowed effective and controlling power to be concentrated elsewhere. At the level of central government his Greek following only seemingly ruled. Neither the phalanx nor the Council of State exercised any real political power, and an ineffective cabinet became even more ineffective through Armansperg's policy of often not filling the vacancies in the cabinet. Besides, Iakovakes Rizos-Neroulos, George Praïdes, and Nicholas Theochares, the three Greek cabinet members until early 1836, hardly showed any initiative of their own.[82]

The real power lay in a small and informal camarilla, consisting of Sir Edmund Lyons, Maximilian Frey, Sir Richard Church, Panagiotes Soutsos, and Ägid von Kobell. So influential did Lyons become, on appointments as well as policy, that Finlay expressed what many believed when he wrote that Armansperg and Lyons ruled Greece. Maximilian Frey, a Bavarian army officer, officially just a member of the king's private cabinet, served in many capacities: as economic advisor in charge of the dotation law, as Armansperg's brake against Otho's exclusive control over his own royal cabinet, and as a sort of acting archchancellor when Armansperg was ill. "Mr. Frey seems to be king and nation," wrote Finlay scornfully during one of Armansperg's illnesses. Sir Richard Church, military commander of Rumely and councilor of state, owed his important role to his personal influence with the irregular chieftains and his friendship with Lyons. Panagiotes Soutsos, secretary of the Council of State,

---

[82] "Rizzo, the Minister of Foreign Affairs, is a cypher; he consults a young frenchman who paid 5 fr. once to go to a ball at Marseilles on points of etiquette. Praides of Justice is a good honest, timid, incapable man, a Mavrocordatist. Theochari of Finance, a German Greek, has all the slowness of a German & the indecision of a Greek. He takes to bed when things go wrong & he is as ignorant of Finance as possible—how he has kept his place is inconceivable except that he understands German & has no idea of his own" (Finlay Journal [MSS], 3 June 1835). *Athēna* (22 Jan. 1836*o.s.*) complains about paralysis of the ministries and inadequacy in general of the ministers.

served as Armansperg's instrument for controlling that body. Kobell, an outgoing member of the second regency, returned in October 1835 as Bavarian minister and served as Armansperg's mediator with Ludwig.[83]

The composition of this camarilla reflects a modified form of Bavarianism at the top—limited to the select few Bavarians of the royal household whose personal loyalty Armansperg commanded, balanced by the official British interest, and penetrated somewhat by the presence of two nonautochthon Greek citizens (the Phanariot Soutsos and the philhellene Church), both members of the "English" party. Actually, Armansperg owed his power ultimately to the three factors represented by those groups—to Bavarian influence wielded by Ludwig through Otho, to official British interest, and only last to Greek support.

5. CHARACTER OF THE OPPOSITION

Grounds for Complaint

The first six months of Armansperg's administration as chancellor shattered many hopes or confirmed many suspicions. Most Greek politicians believed a constitution premature for the country, but many of them complained that Armansperg had taken no steps in the direction of constitutionalism by giving the ministries greater initiative or setting up the expected eparchal and nomarchal elective councils. Indeed, his new designation, which the Greek press termed archchancellor (*archikangelarios*), carried overtones of absolutism and seemed to belie his professed liberalism.[84] A larger segment of the articulate public grew impatient at the terribly slow implementation of the phalanx law, which had produced no concrete result by the end of 1835, and feared that the dotation law, through abuse of implementation, would serve as a legal device for a small group to seize national land and constitute themselves a landed oligarchy.[85] Perhaps the most characteristic and pronounced feature of public sentiment was anti-Bavarianism, which grew stronger and more embittered daily. However much Armansperg tried to dissociate himself

[83] Finlay, Journal (MSS), 1 Mar. 1836 (Lyons) and 16 Mar. 1836 (Frey). *Athēna* (4 Jan. 1836*o.s.*) announced Frey's take-over during Armansperg's illness and prayed that Greece would be liberated from him. On Frey, see also Ross, *Erinnerungen*, pp. 101-102. On the rest, see Makrygiannes [*Memoirs*], II, 85 (Church), and II, 86 (P. Soutsos as "Armansperg's advisor in all matters"); and Finlay, Journal (MSS), 16 Mar. 1836 (Kobell).

[84] In a lead article, *Athēna* (8 Jan. 1836*o.s.*) criticized Armansperg on three counts: (1) for instituting a Council of State "when we were awaiting a national assembly," (2) his failure to institute eparchal and nomarchal councils, and (3) his adoption of the title "archchancellor," which "made the worst impression on us, and we began to wonder if this man was the proclaimed liberal Armansperg."

[85] On the fears connected with abuses in the implementation of the dotation law, see *Athēna*, 17 June 1836*o.s.*

from the policy of Bavarianism, his popularity suffered from identification with foreign domination.[86]

But disappointment turned into active mistrust and resentment among the conservative and popular elements when a personal event in Armansperg's life suggested his contempt for Orthodox tradition and his perfidy toward Otho. The event was the marriage of his two older daughters to the Katakouzenos brothers, Phanariot princes whose alleged descent from the Byzantine emperors gave them some vague claim to a restored Greek imperial throne. Insignificant as the event may appear on the surface, it compromised Armansperg on many counts. Already closely associated with P. Soutsos and Rizos-Neroulos, he became even further identified with the Phanariot element, which as a group aroused popular antipathy. By violating a church canon forbidding two brothers to marry two sisters, it left Armansperg open to the charge of flaunting holy Orthodox tradition and hence of contributing to ultimate subversion of the faith. Third, it rendered him susceptible to the serious charge of preparing a member of his own family, rather than Otho, as crowned head of an eventually revived Byzantine empire. Even though the charge may seem absurd, the Greeks had cause to suspect Armansperg of placing personal above royal interests.[87]

It was a public secret that Armansperg had all too frequently expressed a low opinion of Otho's abilities. The politically informed knew that his relations with the king continued to be chilly and difficult. In September 1835, Armansperg permitted a fourth report, bound for Munich, to issue from the royal household. It reiterated the verdict that Otho was unfit to govern. In his private conversations and his official correspondence with London, Lyons was hopefully contemplating the possibility of Otho's resignation and the establishment of a new regency. There seems to be no question that Armansperg deliberately contrived the image of an incompetent Otho so as to prove, both to the Greeks and to Ludwig, his own indispensability.[88]

The dissatisfaction issuing from various quarters did not immediately crystallize into an organized opposition before 1836. Armansperg's policy had not become sufficiently clear to antagonize permanently any groups, but the formation of an opposition was bound to come. Armansperg's

[86] For instance, Finlay to "My dear Sir" [probably Trikoupes], 1836, Letter Book 1827-1836 (MSS): "The Bavarians are losing all moral energy from seeing the hatred which the Greeks show to them & the best are all gone—."

[87] Driault and Lhéritier, *Histoire*, ii, 138-39, and Makrygiannes [*Memoirs*], ii, 82. The Greeks were also irritated because Armansperg secured royal recognition of the Phanariot titles of his sons-in-law, even though Revolutionary constitutions had abolished all titles of nobility. For a typical reaction to this event on religious grounds, see Makrygiannes' remark (ii, 82), "And so they interfered with our religion so as to convert us to their dogma, little by little."

[88] See n. 30 above. Also Lyons to Palmerston, Athens, 3 Jan. 1836, "Separate and confidential," FO 32.58, on the possibility of Otho's abdication.

apparent popularity before June 1835 had stemmed largely from his silent patronage of the opposition, first against the regency majority, then against Kolettes. Once he had eliminated all rivals for political control, he himself became the next logical target of the almost universal Greek desire for greater control of their own affairs.[89] All other things being equal, patriotism would incline virtually all Greeks toward the opposition, so long as Armansperg, a foreigner, ruled absolutely. But organizing or joining the political opposition involved risks—risks which only the man of principle or the personally dissatisfied man would take. Though one could not count on heroism, one could make a safe bet that the limited resources of Greece would leave a host of discontented persons. A political opposition was inevitable; its character, however, depended on Armansperg's political adroitness in satisfying personal demands and the lead given by European capitals and their ministers in Greece.

Role and Methods of the Powers

Four European powers played an active role in Greek affairs during the absolutist decade: Britain, France, Russia, and Austria—the first three by virtue of their status as protecting powers, the last because of its defense of the dynastic principle and Otho's consequent trust in it. Presumably, fear of Russian aspirations in Greece united France and England, and Austria's self-appointed role was one of helping the king steer a neutral path between Russia and the West.[90]

In actual fact, by the beginning of 1836, France, Russia, Austria, and Prussia (which echoed Austria's support of the dynastic principle), manifested a common antipathy toward Armansperg. Although their capitals did not pursue a concerted policy against Armansperg, they were all ultimately trying to put down England's ascendancy in Greece. By the end of 1835, Prokesch-Osten, the Austrian minister, had gotten from Armansperg the Austro-Greek commercial treaty that he wanted, and it had become apparent to Catacazy that neither Soutsos nor Metaxas would receive cabinet appointments. Shortly after the arrival of Kolettes in Paris, French policy showed marked signs of hostility toward Armansperg, a hostility reflected in the reports of the French minister in Munich to his

[89] See n. 70 above. As early as September 1835, Finlay wrote of the Livadiots (Journal 1835 [MSS], 4 Sept. 1835): "Count Armansperg is now accused of rapacity for power as well as incapacity & is no longer considered the friend of Greece he formerly was supposed to be."

[90] Evidence of Otho's trust in Austria is offered by: (1) the long audiences granted Prokesch-Osten for his advice on the formation of royal policy after the accession (Mendelssohn Bartholdy, Geschichte Griechenlands, II, 505-508), (2) the correspondence of Prokesch-Osten in Aus dem Nachlasse, ed. A. Prokesch-Osten, II, 152-279, passim, and (3) the exchange of warm letters between Otho and the King of Austria on the occasion of Otho's accession (Otho to the Austrian King, 20 May/1 June 1835; and the Austrian King to Otho, 9 Aug. 1836, text of both appearing in Demetrios A. Petrakakos, Koinobouleutike Historia tes Hellados [Parliamentary History of Greece] [Athens, 1946], II, 253-56).

government.[91] Lyons' increasing influence and suspicions that both Armansperg and Lyons were attempting to undermine Otho's position aroused Russian and French, but even more, Austrian and Prussian hostility toward Armansperg.[92] In addition, the conclusion of a written agreement for the establishment of an English-financed bank in Greece alerted everyone to the possibility that England might obtain exclusive financial control of Greece and use such control to perpetuate her political preponderance.[93]

At the top level, conflicting interests tended to receive clearest expression in the Conference of London, where the antigovernment powers tried to alter or topple the existing regime by withholding their guarantee of the third series of the loan or by demanding impossible conditions for such a guarantee. In 1836, France and Russia were the opposition powers. Perhaps because it saw no immediate prospect of expanding its influence, Russia took a hard and fast position of noncooperation. France, on the other hand, seemed more willing to cooperate and hence made specific political as well as financial demands.[94]

At the end of 1835, the Duke de Broglie, still foreign minister of France, privately communicated to London a set of political demands

[91] Lyons to Palmerston, Athens, 29 Feb. 1836, no. 12, FO 32.58. For evidence of the French reversal of attitude toward Armansperg, see Bourgoing to De Broglie, Munich, 17 Nov. 1835, in *Gesandschaftsberichte*, ed. Chroust, Abt. I, Vol. III, 233-35.

[92] Lyons to Palmerston, Athens, 3 Jan. 1836, "Separate and confidential," FO 32.58: "A few days before the arrival of King Ludwig, the Prussian minister Count Luisi called on me and told me in confidence that he was shocked at the last attempts that were in the making to overthrow Armansperg, and that he had determined on withdrawing, in this point at least, from our Austrian and Russian Colleagues, provided I should authorize him to say to his government that I didn't believe Armansperg, in jealousy of the development of the King's promising talents, kept him in the background, and prevented him from transacting business with the Greek ministers; in short that he was not sacrificing the King's interests to his own ambitious views." Also Prokesch-Osten (to Metternich, 29 Dec. 1835, *Aus dem Nachlasse*, ed. A. Prokesch-Osten, II, 159) shows that he, Prokesch-Osten, went as far as to advise the abolition of the archchancellorship.

[93] Lyons to Palmerston, Athens, 1 Jan. 1836, no. 1, FO 32.58: "No other administrative measure since the arrival of the King in Greece has met so much opposition from the Diplomatic Corps—representatives of each government appeared to feel that Great Britain is acquiring an influence in the Levant which it might by timely foresight have secured to his own country; they wish to make it appear that the whole weight of the British Government was thrown into the Scale; the most violent protests were made against my official and private influence with the King and the Chancellor, and attempts even made to produce an impression that Count d'Armansperg was selling Greece to England." Finlay, who forfeited Lyons' friendship as a result, published and circulated a tract condemning the agreement as sacrificing Greek interests (Finlay, Journal [MSS], 1 Mar. 1836). He also circulated a letter briefly stating his reasons for opposing the agreement. A copy appears in Finlay to "My dear Sir," 1836, Letter Book 1827-36 (MSS). Ultimately, the agreement failed to receive the authorization of the Greek government.

[94] Driault and Lhéritier, *Histoire*, II, 161 (on the Russian position), and II, 161-62 (on the French stand).

which went beyond the usual French and Russian demand for Greek budgetary, financial, and administrative improvement. As a minimum he demanded greater representation in the Greek administration for the "national party," which he equated with the "French" party. But he also demanded the convocation of a constituent assembly and the appointment of Kolettes to head an interim government. The conditions stipulated by the successor French government of Thiers on 22 November 1836 were less patently political: the dismissal of all Bavarians from the army of Greece, reduction of the central administrative expenses by limiting the number of ministries, and dissolution of the Greek legations abroad. The third condition was a diplomatic method of condemning the system of honorary exile and demanding the return of Kolettes to Greece. And anti-Bavarianism now took the place of constitutionalism as France's propaganda weapon against the Greek regime.[95] One wonders what, if any, role Kolettes as Greek minister in Paris played in the formulation of these French demands. Certainly his prestige with the French and his skill in manipulating people suggest some influence. The system of honorary exile involved the risk that a party leader might continue to wage his opposition from abroad through the government to which he was accredited.[96]

The Russian and French refusal to offer guarantees for a loan procured no such political concessions as France demanded, but it did lead to a series of money-saving devices, urged by England on Armansperg in an attempt to win over at least France. Some of these devices Armansperg turned to his political advantage. He abolished the nomarchies as administrative units and amalgamated the forty-two existing eparchies into thirty directorates or governorships. He replaced the system of ephors with a system of economic commissioners. He left vacant the cabinet post of minister of economic affairs and allowed the director, second in command, to direct the ministry. Each decree justified the change in terms of cutting administrative costs. Actually the first two decrees provided a convenient occasion for making wholesale changes in personnel.[97]

[95] On Broglie's demands, see *ibid.*, II, 151-52. Lyons, in despatches to Palmerston, replied to them, one by one (Athens, 27 Jan. 1836, no. 7, and 24 Feb. 1836, no. 11, both FO 32.58). For an account of Thiers' demands, see Driault and Lhéritier, *Histoire*, II, 161-62, and for Louis Philippe's advice, *ibid.*, II, 153-54.

[96] Lyons to Blackhouse, Athens, 27 Jan. 1836, FO 32.58: "We have been trying to maintain the prestige of France in Greece, but so long as the French government continues to get its impressions from Bois le Comte and Coletti, it is to no avail." Lyons to Palmerston, Athens, 24 Feb. 1836, no. 11, FO 32.58: "Rouen says it [French official attitude] is due to the way his government is 'induit en erreur' by Coletti, Roujeux [Kolettes' secretary], and others on the real state of the country [Greece]."

[97] Decree on administrative organization, 20 June/2 July 1836 [*Government Gazette*], no. 28, 21 June 1836*o.s.*; decree on the duties of governors, 26 June/8 July 1836 [*GG*], no. 32, 3 July 1836*o.s.*; decree for the abolition of ephors and the

Russian and French refusal decidedly undermined Armansperg's position on two fronts, the domestic and the royal. From lack of funds Armansperg had to introduce new taxes—an income tax of 5 per cent for the trading, commercial, and professional classes, a 2 per cent increase in the existing tax levied on rented houses, and a stamp tax. Only the last tax might affect the peasant, but not nearly so hard as it did the urban and educated classes, on whom the other two taxes exclusively fell. These taxes pinched precisely those groups best able to articulate their grievances and organize an opposition. And their very promulgation provided these groups with a rationale for their opposition; that is, that only a national assembly, popularly elected, could authorize new taxes.[98] But Russian and French refusal must have also worked as well on Otho's antipathy toward Armansperg. It served notice that they could lend no assistance so long as Britain and Lyons dominated Greece through Armansperg.

Excluded from the Conference of London and without the mechanism of finance as a means of interference, Austria and Prussia resorted to dynastic ties in order to fight Armansperg. Together with Russia, they sought to influence Otho through Ludwig. While Ludwig visited Greece early in 1836 (December 1835–March 1836), Austrian and Prussian representatives in Athens tried to convince Ludwig that Armansperg was deliberately undermining Otho's interests, and that he was keeping Otho in the background and barring him from direct contact with the Greek ministers. Ludwig must have needed little convincing, since he undertook the trip in large part to investigate personally the unfavorable health reports emanating from Otho's household.[99]

The Acarnanian Revolt[100]

Ludwig's visit also set in motion all sorts of domestic attempts to cast

---

establishment of commissioners, 19/31 Mar. 1836 [GG], no. 11, 28 Mar. 1836 o.s.; and decree for the appointment of an economic director and his duties, 1/13 Apr. 1836 [GG], no. 13, 13 Apr. 1836 o.s.

[98] For a listing of the new taxes and criticism on the grounds of no taxation without representation, see Finlay, Journal (MSS), 29 Aug. 1836.

[99] Lyons to Palmerston, Athens, 3 Jan. 1836, no. 2, FO 32.58: "Judging from what I see in Athens and accounts from European capitals, it seems King Ludwig's arrival is a signal for attacks on Armansperg." Lyons to Palmerston, Athens, 3 Jan. 1836, "Separate and confidential," FO 32.58: "I have seen the letter from Gise, which removes all doubt of Ludwig's visit to this country having been undertaken in consequence of reports respecting Otho's incapacity, which had been sent to Munich by Jenison, Saporta, and the royal physician."

[100] The three richest primary sources on the Acarnanian revolt of 1836 are: (1) Lyons' correspondence to his government, Athens, 29 Feb. 1836, no. 12, FO 32.58; 6 Apr. 1836 and 28 Apr. 1836, no. 27, FO 32.59; (2) regular despatches from correspondents in Mesolongi and Lamia, rich with information on military movements of the insurgents and government forces, in every issue of the bi-weekly *Athēna* from 8 Feb. 1836 to 25 Apr. 1836 o.s.; and (3) a long letter from Porphyrios, bishop of

doubt on Armansperg's popularity and capacity to rule. Armansperg's enemies obviously believed Ludwig an important, if not decisive, factor in determining the archchancellor's future in Greece.[101]

The most dramatic anti-Armansperg demonstration took the form of a revolt, which broke out in Acarnania-Aetolia (West Rumely) on 3 February 1836. The partisan affiliations of the rebel leaders and the character of the rebel proclamations suggest that the revolt was a joint enterprise of local Napist and "French" captains, many of whom had not yet received notice of their appointment to the newly organized phalanx. One group, headed by Nicholas Zervas, a partisan of Kolettes, and the Stratos', members of the "French" party, adopted the motto "Constitution" and demanded the convocation of a national assembly. A second group, headed by Malamos, former aide-de-camp of Augustine Kapodistrias, used the phoenix as its symbol and appealed to the people on behalf of an allegedly threatened Orthodoxy. A third group, led by Demos Tselios, a disappointed captain, declared itself against Armansperg and the Bavarians, and professed itself loyal to the king ruling under a constitution. Among those who rallied to the support of the rebels were "Albanian freebooters," "the lowest caloyers of the suppressed monasteries" and remnants of the dissolved irregular bands. The government was still feeling the effects of a policy dating back to 1833.[102]

Acarnania [probably to the government], Mesolongi, 22 Feb. 1838*o.s.*, no. 4367, folio 132, Otho Archive, and published by Constantine Rados ["The Revolt of Aetolia-Acarnania in 1836 under Otho"], *Deltion tes Historikes kai Ethnologikes Hetaireias tes Hellados* [*Bulletin of the Historical and Ethnological Society of Greece*], ix (1926), 539-41. In addition see Karl G. Fiedler, *Reise durch alle Theile des Königreiches Griechenland* . . . (Leipzig, 1840-41), i, 150-57, for a day-by-day account of insurgent movements around Mesolongi; and "Postscript, July 20," and a letter dated 1 Nov. 1836, Athens, in *The Portfolio*, iii, 606-11, and v, 169-76, respectively. See also Finlay, *History*, vii, 162, and Makrygiannes [*Memoirs*], ii, 84.

Finlay's Journal 1835 (MSS) deals almost totally with a tour of the mainland provinces by Thomas Gordon and troops, commissioned by the government for the investigation and suppression of brigandage, which had assumed alarming proportions in 1835. Finlay accompanied Gordon. His journal contains both a day-by-day account of the excursion (11 July–4 Sept. 1835 [pp. 1-190]) and a long report of general conditions and causes of brigandage called "Observations on the State of Northern Greece" (pp. 193-216). It contains excellent information which serves as background for the revolt of 1836 because the grievances of the rebels and rebel supporters were undoubtedly the same in 1836 as they had been in 1835. For a brief secondary account, see Skandames, i [*Kingship of Otho*], 349-53.

[101] Lyons (Athens, 3 Jan. 1836, no. 2, FO 32.58) remarks that Ludwig's arrival was the "signal for attacks on Armansperg."

[102] Finlay (*History*, vii, 162-63) cites all three groups; Lyons (to Palmerston, Athens, 29 Feb. 1836, no. 12, FO 32.58) cites only the second and third. In a subsequent despatch to his government (6 Apr. 1836, no. 20, FO 32.59), he mentions an additional leader, "Balasca, an officer in the Gendarmerie, a relation of Mons. Coletti's mistress and always treated as one of the family." In both despatches, he discusses the composition of the rebel following.

In this revolt, as in others, many suspected that influential party leaders had organized the revolt from Athens. Rumors circulated that Rumeliot chieftains, among them the Grivas', Tzavelas, Rangos, and Mamoures, at least had encouraged the revolt so as to earn the gratitude of the Armansperg regime in helping to suppress it. The evidence would seem to implicate Russian agents acting from the nearby Ionian Islands. Glarakes, the Napist nomarch of Achaia-Elis, started interfering with the passage of troops from Patras to the scene of the revolt. Priests in Peloponnesos and the islands tried to induce shepherds to resist the sheep tax and sought to instigate popular uprisings by circulating the rumor that Rumeliot soldiers were invincibly marching on Athens.[103]

The refusal of France and Russia to grant their portion of the loan and the social intimacy of the French and Russian ministers in Athens must have served as encouragement to the rebels and inspired them with hopes that the French and Russian ministers would not assist Armansperg in suppressing the revolt. Indeed, when Lyons asked Lagrené to send a French ship to the scene of the revolt to silence any rumors that the French secretly sympathized with the rebels, Lagrené delayed.[104]

Armansperg handled the Acarnanian revolt with political adroitness. Instead of using Bavarian or Peloponnesian troops, he commissioned the leading Rumeliot chieftains of both the "Russian" and "French" parties (Kitsos Tzavelas, Theodore Grivas, Vasos Mavrovouniotes, John Gouras, Mamoures, and Tsongas) to recruit a total of 2,000 troops for the suppression of the revolt. He thus won them to his cause more effectively than by merely including them in the phalanx and weakened any further joint "French–Russian" action against him. His appointment of Mansolas as minister of the interior was obviously intended as a gesture to appease France and the "French" party. His advancement of Lassanes as director of the finance ministry gave him a lieutenant able and unscrupulous enough to manipulate the implementation of the dotation law in such a way as to win him the support of politically influential people.[105]

[103] Makrygiannes ([*Memoirs*], II, 84) writes: ". . . my conscience wouldn't let me [go to] suppress the rebels, when others were the cause. And so the government appointed Vasio [*sic*], Mamoures, Tzavelas, and the instigator [Theodore] Grivas and his brother Gardikiotes. And they set out against the rebels, whom they had instigated to revolt and had promised 'and we are with you.'"

Lyons (to Palmerston, Athens, 29 Feb. 1836, no. 12, FO 32.58) alleges that Demos Tselios was worked upon by Sikelianos, "a native of the Ionian Islands and a Russian emissary," that the leaders circulated rumors about the imminent expectation of money and ammunition from the "Russian Party" in the Ionian Islands. On Glarakes, see Lyons to Palmerston, Athens, 24 Mar. 1836, no. 15, FO 32.58, and 19 Dec. 1837, no. 46, FO 32.72; on the efforts of monks, see *ibid.*, 6 Apr. 1836, no. 20, FO 32.59.

[104] Lyons (to Palmerston, Athens, 24 Feb. 1836, no. 11, FO 32.59) remarks about "the extreme intimacy which Mons. Catacazy has had the address to draw on between the Russian and French missions." On the poor cooperation of Lagrené, see Lyons to Palmerston, Athens, 29 Feb. 1836, no. 12, FO 32.58.

[105] On the commissioning of irregulars, see Lyons to Palmerston, Athens, 6 Apr.

The revolt became a turning point. Its quick suppression left Armansperg stronger than he had been before. It provoked him to cut across party lines in bidding for political support. So successful was his creation of a following that the opposition had to re-form. To be sure, at the end of June 1836, Lyons was still writing about "the combined efforts of the Russian agents and the Kolettist faction to create disorder," a clear reference to some sort of alliance between "Russian" and "French" parties, but Armansperg had effectively nullified those efforts.[106] In part because France was now partially satisfied with greater "French" representation in the administration, in part because of a change of government in France, Lagrené received instructions to cooperate with Lyons.[107]

Armansperg's increased power also derived from the absence of King Otho, who left early in May 1836 for an extended trip to Bavaria in search of a wife. Until the king's return at the end of January 1837, Armansperg's actual power remained unchecked, even though by statutory provision Otho had delegated some royal powers to "the ministerial council under the presidency of the first-secretary" (not to the first-secretary alone), even though the same statute specifically withheld certain measures from the competence of anyone (such as making any changes in the personnel of the Council of State, the holy synod, the control board, or the high military posts). A majority of the cabinet could not overrule a decision of the archchancellor, though it could create a deadlock, since statute required explicit royal decision on any matter in which the archchancellor was outvoted. But the archchancellor was by statute given control over

---

1836, no. 20, FO 32.59; the decree for the defense of the northern frontier, 16/28 Feb. 1836 [*Government Gazette*], no. 5, 17 Feb. 1836o.s.; and *Athēna*, 18 Feb. 1836 o.s. Lyons, who was very close to Armansperg, wrote (to Palmerston, Athens, 29 Feb. 1836, no. 12, FO 32.58): "he [Mansolas] is a Rumeliot and has considerable influence on the frontier Provinces [where the danger of disaffection was greatest and where the rebels could get aid or withdraw to safety]." According to Finlay (Journal [MSS], 29 Aug. 1836), Dr. Röser, a member of the royal court, recommended Mansolas, who was himself a doctor by profession. On Lassanes, see the same entry in Finlay's Journal, where he refers to the new appointee as "a man of capacity but of known dishonesty and villainy."

There were also the usual measures, all dated 16/28 Feb. 1836: (1) a proclamation addressed to the Rumeliots and exhorting them to rally to the defense of the royal government; (2) a decree for the despatch of A. Monarchides as special emissary (investigator) to Achaia and Elis; (3) the dismissal of G. Glarakes as nomarch of Achaia and Elis [because of his presumed support of the insurgents—see n. 103 above] and his replacement by Venizelos Rouphos, a Constitutionalist; and (4) the despatch of Venizelos Rouphos as special emissary (investigator) to the scene of the revolt ([*GG*], no. 5, 17 Feb. 1836o.s.). See also notices about these in *Athēna*, 18 and 22 Feb. 1836o.s.

There was eventually a decree offering amnesty to all but specifically mentioned leaders (28 Apr./10 May 1836 [*GG*], no. 19, 12 May 1836o.s.).

[106] Lyons to Palmerston, Athens, 28 June 1836, no. 40, FO 32.59.
[107] Lyons to Palmerston, Athens, 11 Apr. 1836, no. 22, FO 32.59.

the *anaktovoulion* through his right to handle all correspondence directed to it; he had handpicked the very cabinet which had a legal right to curb him; and he could, through his influence over this cabinet and the Council of State, legislate on virtually any matter, subject only to the approval of the king within three months of his return. But his greater power left him exposed to the full brunt of political opposition.[108]

The Re-Formation of an Opposition

The new opposition had its origins in the revolt crisis. Dissatisfied over Armansperg's failure to give him a cabinet appointment, George Skouphos, the pro-French newspaper publisher, joined the opposition. John Makrygiannes, now active in Athenian municipal politics, became an irreconcilable foe of the regime because of the ravages of Theodore Grivas in putting down the revolt and Armansperg's inclusion of former brigands in the phalanx at Grivas' recommendation. Though not in conjunction, both Skouphos and Makrygiannes, the former as editor of *Sōtēr* and the latter as a prominent military leader, figured importantly in an opposition concentrated primarily in Athens among politicians of lesser importance. To the rather restrained opposition of *Athēna* came the more vociferous criticism of the newly established *Elpis*, a newspaper edited by the "French" Constantine Levides and printed on a press sent by Kolettes from Paris.[109]

[108] Decree concerning the governmental functions during the period of the King His Majesty's absence, 23 Apr./5 May 1835, no. 18, 4 May 1836*o.s.* Also see Finlay, Journal (MSS), 29 Aug. 1836; and letter from Finlay to Hancock, 30 May 1836, Letter Book 1827-36 (MSS): "Count Armansperg retains his distinct powers as Chancellor somewhat increased indeed. . . ." On the extent of Armansperg's power during Otho's absence, see also Ross, *Erinnerungen*, p. 96.

[109] Finlay, Journal (MSS), 1 Mar. 1836: "It seems when Lyons bought Scouffo fur Armansperg he was promised a place in the Council of State or a portfolio . . ."

In order to suppress the revolt and curb brigandage, Armansperg, through Grivas, recruited many former brigands to serve in the government's irregular forces. Makrygiannes and four other members of the six-man committee (to recommend on military appointments), in defiance of Church, the committee chairman, refused to comply with Armansperg's request for confirmation of those appointments, "to let veterans walk about in need and make the brigands officers." But such recruits were made and Grivas brought some hundred to Athens with him after the suppression of the revolt. "And Athens became a nest of brigands; and no one dared to go outside" (Makrygiannes [*Memoirs*], II, 84-85).

"Government seem to be in difficulties with Griva; not content with the 3 battalions of 200 men which he was ordered to form like the other four Cols., he has taken 300 of the insurgents into his service and many others and has written to the Minister of War and to the Chancellor to send him money and diplomas for his officers. The Count had the folly to answer him and he shews the letter to all the world and says he will soon be named Commander-in-Chief in Roumely instead of Church. He has levied contributions of provisions and money on the country where he passed—imposing 6 drachmas on every house and seizing the silver ornaments of the male and female Albanian dresses under threat of accusing the possessors of being in correspondence with the robbers; evidence of which he says he has in abundance and

The opposition sought nothing less than royal dismissal of Armansperg. The strategy consisted of provoking Armansperg into behavior that would seem arbitrary and high-handed to the Greeks, proving to Europe that Armansperg was incapable of maintaining even the essentials of security and order, and convincing the king that growing constitutionalist sentiment stemmed from increasing dissatisfaction with Armansperg. Makrygiannes developed two new weapons for this campaign: the private banquet as a demonstration of political opposition and the demotic council of Athens, of which he was a member, as the official means by which to criticize the Count.

Skouphos launched his attack on Armansperg in July 1836. So scathing was the *Sōtēr* article that for the first time the chancellor invoked the press laws of 1833 to institute legal proceedings against Skouphos. When *Sōtēr* continued publishing the same type of article, the regime suppressed it. Both these government attacks on the liberty of the press constituted a sharp departure from the chancellor's previous practice. Although a lower court condemned Skouphos, the trial revealed considerable public sympathy for the accused. On appeal, a higher court (the Areopagus) dismissed the case on a legal technicality.[110]

To Armansperg's misfortune, some thugs attacked Skouphos in the streets of Athens and subsequently escaped to the house of Grivas. This event provoked Makrygiannes and Kalliphronas to secure a vote from the Athens demotic council, of which they were both members, for the establishment of a municipal police to provide security for the Athenians. The act boldly asserted that Athens was no longer a safe place to live— a clear reference to what Makrygiannes called the stationing of Grivas' brigands in Athens as members of the phalanx. The act constituted a se-

---

truely as false evidence can be procured in any quantity amongst his 300 robbers. He is accused of seizing a Justice of the Peace with the intention of rendering himself master of his seal in order to falsify some papers. Numerous reclamations are said to have arrived here against him and General Church has done nothing in his journey but shew his weakness and destroy two squadrons of cavalry. The inhabitants say they must fly to Turkey from the disorders of the Troops which attend Church and Griva and several villages have fled bag and baggage" (Finlay, Journal [MSS], June 1836).

Lyons (to Palmerston, Athens, 8 Aug. 1836, no. 45, FO 32.60) refers to Levides as "a person to whom Mons. Coletti has recently sent a Press from Paris. . . ."

[110] "Yesterday [Sunday] the newspaper the *Sōtēr*—already under prosecution was seized, there was an article in which it was stated that Gov't intended to destroy the periodical press by demanding a deposit for each newspaper of 15,000 drachmas. There was another article in which it was stated that the Bavarian troops are regularly paid, but that the Greeks are two months in arrear. This is incorrect tho' it is certain there has been some delay in paying some of the troops" (Finlay, Journal [MSS], 8 Aug. 1836).

On the trial itself, see Finlay to Robinson, 25 Aug. 1836, Letter Book of 1827-1836 (MSS); Lyons to Palmerston, Athens, 27 Aug. 1836, no. 48, and 29 Oct. 1836, no. 59, FO 32.60; and *Athēna*, 15 Aug. 1836*o.s.*

vere criticism of Armansperg's administration by implying that Armansperg's government could not provide security even in the capital itself. Armansperg refused his sanction, which was necessary to validate the act, but he quietly sent Grivas and his retainers away from Athens.[111]

At this juncture Catacazy stepped in to take advantage of the open collision between Skouphos and Armansperg. With his financial backing Sōtēr started publication again, this time in behalf of a constitution. This new connection was Catacazy's way of suggesting Russia's espousal of constitutionalism for Greece. Toward the end of October 1836, the "Russian" party was arguing that the imminent death of the Crown prince of Bavaria would place Otho in line for the Bavarian throne and that only a constitution could prevent another Bavarian regency.[112]

Armansperg's initial forbearance toward Makrygiannes reveals his initially tolerant approach toward political opposition. He tried unsuccessfully to court the favor of Makrygiannes by inviting him to dinner on numerous occasions. Then he threatened to prosecute Makrygiannes for allegedly plotting against the state. Then he employed Botsares and Valtinos to mediate a reconciliation and finally he simply let the matter pass.[113]

Makrygiannes then took a more threatening step against Armansperg. He sent a letter directly to Otho in Bavaria, telling him of all the abuses in the administration and asking him to come and govern his kingdom. Then he invited the anti-Armansperg Bavarians to his home for dinner and encouraged them to send a similar petition to Bavaria. Armansperg shortly found out about these petitions from Katakouzenos, his son-in-law, who had undertaken a government mission to Bavaria. Then, said Makrygiannes, without specifying the particulars, "Armansperg began to take action so as to suppress me."[114]

At the end of November, first reports of Armansperg's possible dismissal began to filter back to Greece. These rumors coincided with— perhaps owed their circulation to—a stepped-up campaign intended apparently to demonstrate the national character of the antipathy toward Armansperg and to convince the king that he must go. Makrygiannes again acted through the demotic council of Athens, which voted to petition Otho against the current abuses and for a constitution. Before publication of the petition, Makrygiannes held another banquet to which he

[111] On the attack on Skouphos, see Finlay, Journal (MSS), entry dated 17 July 1836, and Makrygiannes [Memoirs], II, 85-86.

The municipal police act of the demotic council of Athens was reported by Sōtēr (5 July 1836o.s.) and published in Athēna (11 July 1836o.s.). Regarding the two municipal councilors who voted against the act (Gennadios and Kokkides), see Anagennētheisa Hellas, 1 Aug. 1836, 11 Oct. 1836o.s.

[112] On Sōtēr's new connection with Catacazy and the propaganda of the "Russian" party, see Lyons to Palmerston, Athens, 29 Oct. 1836, no. 59, FO 32.60.

[113] Makrygiannes [Memoirs], II, 86.

[114] Loc.cit.

invited about sixty political leaders, among them Kountouriotes, Botases, Kolokotrones, Botsares, Valtinos, and Mavrovouniotes. When the meal was finished, Makrygiannes proposed a toast to the king and his new queen and prayed that they should govern through constitutional laws. Although nothing more extreme was said or done, the banquet obviously served as a demonstration against Armansperg and Armansperg himself so interpreted it.[115]

Armansperg responded swiftly and drastically. He had the Council of State, where he enjoyed a majority, vote a message to the king praising his work. Only Kountouriotes, T. Kolokotrones, Botases, and Valtinos dissented. A decree of 15 January 1837 dismissed the mayor of Athens and dissolved the council for allegedly exceeding its jurisdiction. The commandant of Athens' garrison ordered Makrygiannes to prepare at once for transferral from Athens. When Makrygiannes pleaded illness, doctors arrived to examine him, and he wrathfully resigned from the phalanx. Armansperg kept his house under guard. All these acts looked as arbitrary as those of Kapodistrias and the regency majority before him. Moreover, a number of "liberal" acts, promulgated by Armansperg to restore his ebbing popularity, came too late to impress anyone and looked like nothing more than the desperate acts of a doomed man.[116]

Armansperg's Dismissal

During his stay in Bavaria, Otho had married Amalia of Oldenburg, a Protestant princess whose choice allayed prior European anxieties that he might marry a French or Russian princess and thereby give one of those powers a special advantage in Greece.[117] With a new queen and renewed self-confidence, Otho arrived in Greece on the eve of 2 February 1837, resolved to dismiss Armansperg. The efforts of Lyons to dissuade the king met with no success. On the next day the king issued the decree dismissing Armansperg and announced the dissolution of the of-

[115] *Athēna* reported the rumor in its issue of 19 Dec. 1836*o.s.* The act, in the form of a petition to the king, was passed on 5 Jan. 1836*o.s.* and published in *Elpis* on 22 Jan. 1836*o.s.* See also Lyons to Palmerston, Athens, 7 Feb. 1837, no. 13, FO 32.69, and Makrygiannes [*Memoirs*], II, 87.

[116] For the text of the measure passed by the Council of State, see *Elpis*, 16 Jan. 1837*o.s.*, and for a lead article on the same measure, see *Elpis*, 28 Jan. 1837*o.s.* For the decree dismissing the Athens mayor and municipal council, dated 15 Jan. 1837*o.s.*, see [*Government Gazette*], no. 2, 10 Jan. 1837*o.s.* On Makrygiannes' orders for transfer and subsequent house arrest, see Makrygiannes [*Memoirs*], II, 87-88.

[117] On the relation of the marriage question to diplomacy and the religious confession of the Greek Crown, see Hans Rall, "Die Anfänge des Konfessionspolitischen Ringens um den Wittelsbacher Thron in Athen," in *Bayern: Staat und Kirche, Land und Reich*, ed. Wilhelm Winkler (Munich, 1961), 181-215. For biographies of Amalia, see G. Tsokopoulos, *He Basilissa Amalia* [*Queen Amalia*] (Athens, 1904); Soteria Alimpertes, *Amalia, he Basilissa tes Hellados* [*Amalia, Queen of Greece*] (Athens, 1916); and M. Channouses [*Amalia*] (Athens, 1958). See also Chap. VI, n. 29, for books dealing with both Otho and her.

fice of first minister. Ignaz von Rudhart, the proposed candidate of Maurer and Abel back in 1835, became head of the king's household and president of the cabinet. The substitution of Rudhart for Armansperg as chief political official of the king involved four separate decrees, all dated 14 February 1837: (1) "accepting" Armansperg's repeated resignations, (2) abolishing the office of archchancellor entirely, (3) appointing Rudhart minister of foreign affairs and the royal household, and (4) enlisting Rudhart into the Greek service, appointing him president of the ministerial council and associating him in the affairs of the anaktovoulion.[118]

Most probably the ultimate cause of Armansperg's dismissal was Otho's persistent coolness toward him and his own involvement in the delicate question of Otho's competence. The decisive factor was the king himself in conjunction with his father. The fatal weakness of Armansperg's strategy, therefore, was its failure to court the king's favor rather than intrigue against him, or even more, insufficient appreciation that Otho could and would risk alienation of Britain to be rid of somebody personally distasteful to him. It is impossible to tell exactly how much the decision of Otho and his father owed to direct pressure or indirect warning from the powers or how much to the maneuvers of the Greek opposition. But a few summary remarks about these two factors and their relation to Armansperg's regime can be made.

First, the political opposition, after the revolt of 1836, accorded with traditional party lines no more than did Armansperg's political following. The fact demonstrates both the strength (skill and success in crossing party lines) and weakness (sharing the odium of supporters' abuses) of his political strategy. There is no evidence that longer tenure would have destroyed the parties as such. The evidence is all the other way. But Armansperg might very well have caused a permanent realignment of parties or their constituent parts—though at the price paid by Kapodistrias, garnering bitter enemies as well as loyal friends. Second, the opposition succeeded in provoking even as tolerant and deliberately lenient a ruler as Armansperg into drastic acts which destroyed his reputation for liberalism. And last, the domestic and international oppositions complemented and reflected each other, if not by common plan and deliberation, then by independently responding to the acts of each other.

[118] On Lyons' attempt to dissuade Otho, see Driault and Lhéritier, *Histoire*, ii, 164-65; Lyons to Palmerston, Athens, 15 Feb. 1837, no. 16, and 2 Mar. 1837, no. 18, FO 32.69; and Finlay, Journal (MSS), 1 Jan. 1837: Lyons "told the King a rebellion would follow Armansperg's dismissal." For confirmation that Rudhart had been proposed as early as 1835, see Prokesch-Osten to Metternich, 9 Mar. 1835, as quoted by Mendelssohn Bartholdy, *Geschichte Griechenlands*, ii, 505. See also [*Government Gazette*], no. 4, 3 Feb. 1837o.s., and Ross, *Erinnerungen*, pp. 103-104.

CHAPTER SIX

The Early Period of Othonian Absolutism and "Russian" Ascendancy, 1837-40

THE PERIOD between the fall of Armansperg early in 1837 and the initiation of serious efforts to conciliate Britain in 1840 owes its distinctness to two salient characteristics—the personal rule of the king and the political ascendancy of the "Russian" party. In these terms, the period did not begin until the very end of 1837, when Otho dismissed Rudhart and became in effect his own prime minister, and appointed as minister of the interior George Glarakes, the ardent Russophil. But the short tenure of Rudhart (February–December 1837) was the gestation period of these trends. Otho established his personal rule only after a prolonged struggle with Rudhart. Though not yet dominant, the "Russian" party no longer suffered discrimination under Rudhart.

Although "Russian" ascendancy gradually diminished during 1840, the personal rule of Otho extended beyond this period to the revolution of September 1843. But the recall of Mavrokordatos to Greece early in 1841 and the formation of his government posed a serious challenge to Otho's personal absolutism and divided this period of his personal rule from the later one.

1. SYSTEM OF PERSONAL ABSOLUTISM

The Triumph of the System: Otho vs. Rudhart

By the end of 1837, it was apparent that Otho opposed constitutionalism by free and considered choice, not because others were making his decisions for him. When Lyons in 1837 reminded Otho of constitutional promises held out to the Greeks by Bavaria and the powers in 1832, he replied:

> that it might be true that the Allied Powers and His Father had held out such hopes [for a constitution] but that no time had been specified, and that if He thought it for the ultimate good of the People that they should be governed for some years . . . without a Constitution, that He would be ashamed to yield His right to the demands of the People.

To be sure, Otho's education and upbringing predisposed him toward absolutism as a political ideal. His father's advice of 1835 must have fallen on willing ears: "A constitution is a lion's den from which no footsteps emerge." His close association with Prokesch-Osten was undoubtedly effect rather than cause of anticonstitutionalism.[1]

[1] Lyons to Palmerston, 2 Mar. 1837, no. 18, Archives of the British Foreign Office, Public Record Office, London, Ser. 32, Vol. 69 [hereafter cited as FO 32.69 and so

Otho's preference for absolutism also owed something to his analysis of Greek political conditions. The mutual recriminations exchanged by segments of the ruling élite, the tendency of party members to compromise their loyalty to the king by close connections with foreign legations, the turbulence which had attended electioneering during the Revolution —these and many more factors gave him no cause to have a very high opinion of the Greek ruling classes. Like Kapodistrias, he probably considered them the enemies of both people and state and believed that a constitutional system would benefit only them.[2]

Particularly when their opinions conflicted with his own, Otho refused to acknowledge the Greek political leaders as anything more than spokesmen for an oligarchical minority. Conscious of his popularity with the people, he considered himself both the best judge of popular interests and the best interpreter of popular wishes. His frequent royal tours, which brought him into direct contact with the people and gave them a chance to express their grievances, must have seemed to him a far better mirror of public opinion than either representative assemblies that would fall under the control of these oligarchies or the press, which already had. Precisely because he believed in government *for* the people, he disregarded government *of* and *by* the people as legal fictions by which a selfish oligarchy could, in the name of the people, depose as well as enthrone monarchs, and use as well as abuse the people. The monarchy, rather than a constitution, would educate the people to exercise their political duties and would guarantee their liberation from the tyranny of their former Greek masters.[3]

---

on]. Ludwig to Otho, 5 Apr. 1835, as published in *König Ludwig I von Bayern in seinen Briefen an seinen Sohn den könig Otto von Griechenland*, ed. Ludwig Trost (Bamberg, 1891), p. 47, or as quoted by Leonard Bower and Gordon Bolitho, *Otho I, King of Greece* (London, 1939), p. 77.

[2] The only secondary source to suggest this as a factor in explaining Otho's anticonstitutionalism is George K. Aspreas, *Politike Historia tes Neoteras Hellados 1821-1921 [Political History of Modern Greece]*, 2nd edn. (Athens, 1924), I, 145-46. He wrote that the government did not want an elective assembly because it wanted to turn the attention of Greeks away from party rivalries. One contemporary source (Gregory A. Perdicaris, *The Greece of the Greeks* [New York, 1845], I, 59) vaguely suggests this when he writes: "every event and every circumstance combined to destroy his confidence in and his love for his subjects"; another (Nicholas Dragoumes, *Historikai Anamneseis [Historical Reminiscences]* 2nd edn. [Athens, 1879], II, 259) cites the judgment of J. Speliotakes, editor of *Krisis*, that Otho's suspiciousness probably stemmed from the Greeks and their mutual recriminations. Dragoumes heartily concurs in this judgment and is more explicit when he attributes Otho's suspicion largely "to the actions of Greeks, who made him that way."

[3] On Otho's marked sense of his popularity among the people, see Finlay, Journal (MSS), 7 Sept. 1835, Finlay Papers, The British School of Archeology, Athens. In a despatch to Palmerston (Athens, 24 May 1838, no. 89, FO 32.77), Lyons wrote: "Otho feels he is Lord and Master, sent by providence to govern according to the dictates of his own judgment and conscience." According to Lyons, in another

Ignatz von Rudhart, when he arrived in Greece to succeed Armansperg, was forty-eight years of age, a mature man with an established reputation in Bavaria as an able scholar and public servant. With a doctorate of law from the University of Munich, he had concentrated his scholarship on economic affairs and had already published two well-received books, one of them a statistical survey of the Bavarian kingdom and the best of its kind. By preference a private scholar, he had been drawn into public life out of a sense of duty and had served as a successful provincial governor, earning for himself a reputation for administrative ability. When he accepted his Greek assignment, he was serving as a member of the Bavarian Council of State. The French ambassador in Munich reacted favorably toward his appointment, describing him as a man of proved ability and initiative, a philhellene, and a liberal. But he tempered his praise with the observation that Rudhart was totally unfamiliar with the ways of the world. Indeed, for all his good intentions, his integrity, and his lack of self-seeking, Rudhart was stuffy, inflexible, and unable to handle men.[4]

From the outset, Rudhart's mission in Greece was beclouded by the attitude of the powers. The mere fact that he was replacing Armansperg, whom England had so vigorously supported, predisposed English diplomacy against him. English disapproval turned into vigorous and continual opposition when, on his appointment, Austria expressed its wholehearted approval. Willy-nilly therefore he acquired the reputation of being the candidate of the Holy Alliance, a reputation which aroused serious opposition to him among the Greeks.[5]

But the factor which brought his term of service in Greece to such a rapid end was his clash not with English diplomacy, but with Otho himself. The tension that developed between Rudhart and Otho never touched the basic principle of monarchical absolutism, which both men

despatch to Palmerston (Athens, 26 Mar. 1840, no. 42, FO 32.97), Zaïmes observed Otho's belief that he (the King) was "better able than any statesman to contend with the difficulties around him. . . ."

[4] For further information on Rudhart, see Ferdinand Koeppel, *Die griechische Ministerpräsidentschaft J. v. Rudharts unter König Otto. Teildruck aus Ignaz von Rudhart. Eine politische Biographie* (Kallmünz, 1931); Andrew S. Skandames, *Selides Politikes Historias kai Kritikes. Tomos* i: *He Triakontaetia tes Basileias tou Othonos 1832-1862* [*Pages of Political History and Criticism.* Vol. i. *The thirty-year Period of the Kingship of Otho 1832-1862*] (Athens, 1961), 156-70; and letters of Bourgoing, French minister to Bavaria, to Molé, French foreign minister, Munich, 15 Nov. 1836, 18 Nov. 1836, 29 Dec. 1836, and 11 Jan. 1837, in *Gesandtschaftsberichte aus München 1814-1848.* Abt. i: *Die Berichte der französischen Gesandten,* ed. Anton Chroust, iii (Munich, 1936), 291, 293, 303, 305. See also "Rudhart," in *Allgemeine Deutsche Biographie,* 56 vols. (Leipzig, 1875-1912).

[5] See for instance Edouard Driault and Michel Lhéritier, *Histoire Diplomatique de la Grèce de 1821 à nos Jours* (Paris, 1925), ii, 165-69; also Bourgoing to Molé, Munich, 22 May and 24 July 1837, in *Gesandtschaftsberichte,* ed. Chroust, Abt. i, Vol. iii, 328, 339.

upheld. Nor did either man differ in his commitment to create a national administration, an administration staffed largely by the Greeks themselves. Disagreement developed over the issue of personal absolutism and what a national administration, in the context of monarchical absolutism, really involved. How much of the royal power ought the king to exercise personally and how much ought he to delegate? Ought his prime minister be a mere bureaucrat or a responsible leader? Ought the ministerial council be a council of execution kept in motion by the active intervention of the king or a council of delegated powers freely exercising broad powers of initiative within the limits of general royal policy?

Otho's position on these questions is not hard to divine. He had not relieved himself of Armansperg to submit in turn to Rudhart's domination. He had no intention of letting the office of prime minister develop into a disguised chancellorship. He wanted to rule as well as reign and he diligently reviewed Rudhart's acts and intentions, either personally or through royal clerks. It is no wonder that he trusted no one when one considers how flagrantly Armansperg had betrayed royal interests. With regard to the ministerial council, Otho decided in advance of his accession that he would work with it only at such times as he considered advisable.[6]

On the other hand, Rudhart felt that royal interference slowed up the administrative process and threatened to leave real power in the hands of household clerks. He sought for himself, as president of the ministerial council, a position as actual head of the government, accountable to the king for a total record, but not for every step he took. He also tried to increase the jurisdiction of the ministerial council and the ministries so as to give them greater initiative and hence free them from the paralysis imposed by all sorts of controls. He obtained some concessions from Otho but not enough to transform this body into a healthy institution. He undoubtedly inspired the promise, embodied in the decree for the abolition of the chancellorship, to extend cabinet prerogatives.[7]

The decree of 20 March 1837,[8] which fulfilled this promise, probably

[6] Lyons to Palmerston, Athens, 11 Sept. 1837, no. 92, FO 32.71: ". . . the King gives Rudhart's *projets d'ordonnances* to young aides-de-camp to be revised. Rudhart remonstrated and His Majesty said He would modify whenever and however he pleased." See also Karl Mendelssohn Bartholdy, *Geschichte Griechenlands von der Eroberung Konstantinopels durch die Türken im Jahre 1453 bis auf unsere Tage* (Leipzig, 1870-74) II, 506-507.

[7] For firsthand information on Rudhart's attempts to govern and the objectives he pursued, see a series of ten letters from him to Thiersch, written between 18 Feb. 1837 and 12 Mar. 1838, in *Friedrich Thiersch's Leben*, ed. Heinrich W. J. Thiersch (Leipzig, 1866), pp. 448-520 passim. That Rudhart interpreted Otho's interference as a lack of confidence in him, see Lyons to Palmerston, 11 Sept. 1837, no. 92, FO 32.71. Otho wrote his father (19 Apr. 1837, as quoted by Koeppel, *Ministerpräsidentschaft*, p. 32), "Rudhart thinks that I place more trust in Frey than in him. . . ."

[8] Decree concerning the jurisdiction of the ministries, 11/23 Mar. 1837, *Ephemeris tes Kyberneseos tou Basileiou tes Hellados* [Government Gazette, Kingdom of Greece], no. 11, 17 Mar. 1837*o.s.*

fell short of what he wanted. It specified that ministers could act without previous royal authorization in such matters as (1) the discharge of the expenses provided for the ministry in the annual budget (although the ministries ought to continue to send expense accounts regularly to the royal court), (2) grants of three-month leave or permits for visiting the capital to subordinate officials in the ministry, and (3) appointment, transfer, or dismissal of such minor ministry officials as purveyors, bailiffs, or prison guards. This decree startlingly reveals how restricted the powers and initiative of ministerial heads had been and continued to be, because presumably anything more than such trivial matters *did* require prior royal consent. Even at that, the decree qualified its list of exemptions with such phrases as "reserving our right to oversee their acts, and if need be, to modify them," and "but they must be careful not to overstep the bounds of their jurisdiction."

When not plagued by the hostility of British diplomacy, Rudhart spent most of his time in a tug of war with Otho. As his first move, he successfully gained control over the royal household. Frey, Armansperg's protégé and Lyons' continued ally, resigned in May after Rudhart asked Ludwig by mail for his recall. Otho branded Rudhart's conduct in this case as infamous. Baron Weichs, master of ceremonies, deserted Lyons and went over to Prokesch-Osten and Rudhart. Count Saporta, a court official, and Major Karl Purkhardt, a Bavarian army officer, both became Rudhart's close associates. This triumph proved decisive in the first open clash with the king, when he submitted his first resignation (11 September 1837) on the grounds of not enjoying royal confidence. Because of pressure from pro-Rudhart members of his own household, Otho could not accept the resignation.[9]

[9] Aspreas ([*Political History*], I, 152-54), in his commendable concern for the internal opposition to Rudhart and its role in his eventual downfall, ignores the far more significant factor of Rudhart's conflict with Otho. This omission may very well be a result of Aspreas' lack of access to the material which gives evidence of the conflict.

On the conflict between Frey and Rudhart and the eventual triumph of the latter by appealing to Munich, see Koeppel, *Ministerpräsidentschaft*, pp. 32-33; Bower and Bolitho, *Otho I*, p. 98; and Lyons to Palmerston, 26 Mar. 1837, no. 30, and 31 May 1837, no. 60, FO 32.70.

On Baron Weichs, master of ceremonies of the court, see Finlay, Journal (MSS), 18 Apr. 1837: "*Rough & cringing*, useful as Lyons' creature about the palace but apparently a great fool," and 30 Nov. 1837: "Weichs after intriguing with England joined Prokesch & insulted Sir EL [Edmund Lyons] by having him standing during the whole of a royal comedy." See also Koeppel, *Ministerpräsidentschaft*, p. 43.

On Saporta, Purkhardt, and Rudhart as a "council of government of Greece according to Ludwig's instructions," see Lyons to Palmerston, Athens, 26 Mar. 1837, no. 31, and 15 July 1837, no. 70, FO 32.70. On Saporta individually, see Finlay, Journal (MSS), 18 Apr. 1837: "He keeps the accounts, seems a sincere friend of the King—is rude, vulgar, ill educated, but honest & sincere"; and Lyons to Palmerston, Athens, 2 Mar. 1837, no. 18, FO 32.69: "Saporta had been the prime mover in all the intrigues against Armansperg." On Purkhardt individually, see Finlay, Journal

Influenced by the queen's dislike for Rudhart as well as his own difference of political opinion, Otho started to undermine Rudhart's influence in the court. Thanks to a personal slight to Lyons, who made it a *cause célèbre* and the source of much complaint, Weichs was dismissed (11 October 1837). Saporta and Purkhardt resigned by the beginning of November, and Charles Soutsos, the successor of Saporta as a court official, slowly usurped Rudhart's place in the royal cabinet.[10] These royal acts provoked Rudhart's second resignation on 28 November. This time Rudhart secured the king's refusal of the resignation not by the support of Bavarians, but by reminding the king that Russian support depended on his retention.[11]

The conflict continued, however, and came to a head when Rudhart made his continued stay contingent on his freedom to make major changes in administrative and judicial personnel. In control of the Bavarians in his household at last, Otho accepted the third resignation (27 December 1837). To avoid alienating Russian diplomacy, he appointed as minister of both internal and educational-ecclesiastical affairs George Glarakes, who had been recommended by Rudhart and Gennaios Kolokotrones,

---

(MSS), 18 Apr. 1837: "abused by Lyons as a spy—conceited & as presumptuous in the affairs of Greece as [he is] ignorant"; and Lyons to Palmerston, Athens, 5 Mar. 1837, no. 24, FO 32.69: "has long been reputed a spy of King Ludwig," and 26 Mar. 1837, no. 31, FO 32.70.

Lyons (to Palmerston, Athens, 17 Sept. 1837, no. 94, FO 32.71) reported that Rudhart cited loss of royal confidence as the cause of his resignation: "Rudhart's resignation was followed by those of Bavarians attached to the court. His Majesty received many of them with firmness, but when a Secretary on whom He thought He could most depend, tendered his, the King affected to tears and asked him with beseeching look and voice if he too would abandon Him. And so the King gave way and asked Rudhart to remain." See also Lyons to Palmerston, Athens, 11 Sept. 1837, no. 92, and 12 Sept. 1837, no. 93, FO 32.71; and Koeppel, *Ministerpräsidentschaft*, pp. 40-41: "The King said he could not do without him because he had no one to substitute for him."

[10] On the Queen's dislike of Rudhart, see Driault and Lhéritier, *Histoire*, II, 169. On the celebrated Lyons-Weichs incident (6 Oct. 1837), in which Weichs slighted Lyons and his wife by leaving them standing for three hours at a theatrical performance at the palace, see Lyons to Palmerston, Athens, 26 Oct. 1837, no. 116 (with enclosure of Lyons' long correspondence in demand of an apology), and 10 Nov. 1837, no. 131, FO 32.72. See also Bower and Bolitho, *Otho I*, p. 99. On the resignation of Saporta and Purkhardt, see Lyons to Palmerston, Athens, 10 Nov. 1837, no. 132, FO 32.72. On the rise of C. Soutsos, see Lyons to Palmerston, Athens, 10 Nov. 1837, no. 132, and 28 Nov. 1837, no. 137, FO 32.72.

[11] In his despatch of 28 Nov. 1837 (no. 137, FO 32.72), Lyons writes that Rudhart felt it his duty "to state that Russia has consented to the advance of a million of francs upon the Loan because he was Prime Minister, that she would not feel bound to pay it, or be disposed to fulfill the hopes held out of further advances unless he remained, or a minister of his selection should succeed him. He suggested either Perroucas or Glarakes." Apparently this observation proved decisive in inducing Otho not to accept the second resignation. See Koeppel, *Ministerpräsidentschaft*, p. 45, for confirmation of this point.

one of Otho's aides-de-camp.[12] By a decree dated 20 December 1837, it was announced that the king would thereafter preside over the meetings of the ministerial council when in the capital and that in his absence Kountouriotes or Zaïmes, as vice presidents of the Council of State, would substitute for him. The office of prime minister was in effect abolished, or to put it differently, the king became his own prime minister. This decree marks the formal beginning of Otho's personal absolutism.[13]

Greek hostility toward Rudhart is ironic in view of later developments. Actually his attempts to broaden the jurisdiction of the ministries, to make the prime minister actual head of the government, and to limit administrative interference by the king anticipated similar efforts of Mavrokordatos in 1841. If Rudhart had succeeded in restricting the king's personal cabinet and transforming the state cabinet into a strong and responsible institution, the Greeks would not have needed to resort eventually to force to achieve such an objective.

But the issue of personal absolutism was not yet apparent to the public in 1837 because that system had not yet come into being. Greek antipathy concentrated itself on Bavarianism, which had existed long enough to enflame Greek resentment. Writing retrospectively, Nicholas Dragoumes remarked:

The Bavarian officers conducted themselves in the same manner [arrogantly as did the Bavarian civil servants] toward ours [Greek army officers], even if for the most part they possessed no importance in

[12] "Yesterday Mr. Rudhart is said to have proposed to the King to change a number of the Judges & dismiss several persons in the service of Government who are considered as too strongly tinctured with liberal principles. Common reports say the number of the prescribed amounted to 32. I cannot believe that a man of Rudhart's timidity would have ventured such a sweeping proposition. However it is evident, that he had prepared himself with the advice & consent of Mr. Katacazi & primed & pushed forward by that desperate agitator Prokesch to make a decisive attempt & risk everything to secure a despotic gov't" (Finlay, Journal [MSS], 20 Dec. 1837).

"On 20 December, he issued the king a veritable ultimatum: he demanded the actual presidency of the council—which the young sovereign had often reserved for himself—and carte blanche for the administration of the country, the dismissal and replacement, on his indication, of thirty-eight functionaries notoriously hostile to the Austro-Russian influences" (Driault and Lhéritier, Histoire, II, 171, based on despatches of Lagrené, dated 19 and 27 Dec. 1837, nos. 188 and 191, Affaires Étrangères de la France, Correspondance politique, Grèce, Vol. 25). For corroborative evidence, see Lyons to Palmerston, Athens, 1 Jan. 1838, no. 2, FO 32.76, and Koeppel, Ministerpräsidentschaft, p. 46.

Rudhart recommended Glarakes as a person enjoying the favor of Russia (Lyons to Palmerston, Athens, 28 Nov. 1837, no. 137, FO 32.72), as did Gennaios Kolokotrones, as he states in his Apomnemoneumata (Cheirographon Deuteron 1821-1862) [Memoirs (Second Manuscript 1821-1862)], ed. Emmanuel Protopsaltes (Athens, 1961), p. 83 (hereafter cited as [Memoirs II]).

[13] Decree on the presidency of the ministerial council, 8/20 Dec. 1837 [Government Gazette], no. 40, 8 Dec. 1837o.s.

their own country, even if with the exception of a few, Armansperg would hardly deign receive them.[14]

This mutual antipathy between Greeks and Bavarians came to a dramatic head in the fall of 1837, when the term of service of the German recruits was about to expire and the government of Rudhart was trying to induce them to reenlist for another term of service. It was fanned to a fever pitch by the press warfare that took place between *Elpis*, newspaper of bold and vocal Levides, and *Ho Hellēnikos Tachydromos*, the semi-official mouthpiece of Rudhart. The former had already criticized Bavarians in Greek service and the latter had already attacked the personal character of Levides, when the government issued an "order of the day," dated 30 September 1837, to its armed forces. The order was full of statements which were bound to arouse anti-Bavarian sentiment and wound Greek national sentiment. It praised the Bavarian volunteers for "undergoing the greatest privations and hardships with persistent zeal." It declared the government's intention to maintain the existing Bavarian forces at their current strength, "so long as their presence is demanded for tutoring of Our national troops." It expressed its great disapproval of the "slanders and insults of some newspapers against men of Our selection, enjoying Our confidence. . . ."

Elpis criticized the order extravagantly, and the government initiated court proceedings against the newspaper. Levides allowed the judgment to go by default in the lower court and then exercised his right of appeal. In the meantime, his newspaper published a violent philippic against the Bavarians. So violent was the language that even Lyons admitted the government's right to prosecute the newspaper and its legal editor, a straw man for Levides. But instead of doing this, the palace attempted to strike directly at Levides and so issued a royal ordinance for his arrest on alleged suspicion of treason. He was arrested and subjected to a severe investigation, but no evidence of treason was discovered. So bitter was the Greek response, in the capital at least, that Païkos, a man seldom willing to place principle above interest, refused to carry out the royal ordinance as minister of justice. Feeling ran even higher in behalf of Levides and against the Bavarians because of a dramatic incident which took place shortly before Levides' arrest.

On 13 November 1837, Major Feder and six to eight other Bavarian

---

[14] Dragoumes [*Reminiscences*], ii, 67. See Philip Ioannou, Athens, 1 Oct. 1837*o.s.*, who wrote to Mavrokordatos as follows: "What should I say about the irreconcilable hatred which I have painfully observed since my arrival between the Bavarians and our own [Greeks]. It is true that the latter have good cause, but they ought to distinguish between persons and to remain moderate" (no. 5423, Vol. 20 [1837-40], Mavrokordatos Archive, General State Archives, Athens). Rudhart had only been in Greece a few months when he informed a German friend of Lyons that "the Greeks detest us . . ." (Lyons to Palmerston, Athens, 8 May 1837, no. 52, FO 32.70). See also Chap. VII, n. 38, below.

officers attacked Levides in the coffeehouse of *Bella Graecia*, where Levides had been peacefully reading. Thanks to the intervention of the gendarmerie, Levides was rushed to safety. To avenge him, some friends of his a few days later forcefully attacked Purkhardt, a member of the royal household whom his attackers suspected to be the author of the "order of the day." A court-martial tried Feder and sentenced him to a fifteen-day house arrest for assaulting a Greek, but many Greeks accused the government of favoritism toward the Bavarians when it compared, not entirely fairly, Feder's treatment with that of Levides. In any case, the court of appeal released Levides for the first charge against him, and the government dropped its treason proceedings. Undoubtedly, this whole chain of events did much to discredit Rudhart's government and created an embittered atmosphere that only a change of government could dispel.[15]

To be sure, Greek liberals reserved special censure for Rudhart because of his identification with the Metternichian system and his promulgation of more severe press laws at the insistence of Ludwig. But practically all Greeks hated him as a symbol of Bavarian domination.[16] So, in an attempt to rid Greece of him, the Greeks implicitly and unknowingly contributed to the triumph of what would become successive targets of Greek opposition—first the anaktovoulion and then personal absolutism itself.

[15] For a copy of the "order of the day," see [*Government Gazette*], no. 32, 22 Sept. 1837*o.s.*, and *Ho Hellēnikos Tachydromos*, 30 Sept. 1837*o.s.* For Levides' philippic, see *Elpis*, 30 Oct./11 Nov. 1837. Sources for this chain of events are: Finlay, Journal (MSS), 30 Nov. 1837; Lyons to Palmerston, Athens, 20 Nov. 1837, no. 133, and 22 Nov. 1837, no. 135, FO 32.72; *Athēna*, 3 Nov. 1837*o.s.*; and Bower and Bolitho, *Otho I*, p. 100.

[16] *Athēna* wrote in a lead article in its issue of 30 Jan. 1837*o.s.*: "According to a newspaper of Frankfurt, Rudhart was to go to Vienna. Such a visit by a man who is to come to Greece does not seem innocent to us. . . . So we advise Rudhart to abandon the polity of the north before he sets foot on Greek soil, if indeed he comes to Greece initiated into its mysteries. . . . Absolutism means Turkism. . . ." See also Aspreas [*Political History*], I, 152-53.

Concerning the tendency to identify Rudhart with Austrian policy because of the Greek government's behavior, especially in connection with a celebrated case called the Usiglio incident, see p. 301 below.

On the "law on slander in general and on the press," 23 Nov./5 Dec. 1837, see [*Government Gazette*], no. 37, 23 Nov. 1837*o.s.* On the genesis of this law and its eventual promulgation, see Lyons to Palmerston, Athens, 22 July 1837, no. 73, 11 Sept. 1837, no. 92, and 17 Sept. 1837, no. 94, FO 32.71; 3 Dec. 1837, no. 138, and 12 Dec. 1837, FO 32.72; also Bower to Bolitho, *Otho I*, pp. 100-101. The inspiration of this law came from Ludwig, himself the victim of abuse by the Greek press, and its chief impulse from the Austrian minister in Athens (Prokesch-Osten).

Athēna (8 Sept. 1837*o.s.*), commenting on Rudhart's first resignation, wrote: "Rudhart is the last representative of foreign rule [*xenokratia*]; that is why we are so happy over his resignation."

In their blissful ignorance they hailed the departure of Rudhart as the end of Bavarian domination and the beginning of "national" government. A few hopeful signs only deceived the more. Most of the Bavarian recruits had left Greece as their term of service expired, in spite of government bids for their reenlistment, and the rest were going.[17] No longer was a Bavarian subject, such as Armansperg or Rudhart, to head the government, and Greeks seemed to be moving into positions of authority. Charles Soutsos, a Phanariot Greek, was replacing Count Saporta as marshal of the court, and Constantine Zographos was returning from his post as Greek minister to the Porte to become minister of foreign affairs. The recall of Spyridon Trikoupes from London and Michael Soutsos from Petersburg seemed to presage the reversal of the policy of honorary exile for the party leaders and their return to positions of power within the central government. Even Mavrokordatos, seldom guilty of overoptimism, believed that Zographos would exercise the actual power of prime minister even though he did not enjoy the title.[18]

Structure and Characteristics of the System

Otho rejoiced for different reasons. Elatedly he wrote his father early in 1838:

> In my position, without State Chancellor, without Prime Minister, I feel a new incentive to devote myself with greater activity to my calling, for the success of the good cause depends more on me now than formerly.[19]

Under this new system of Othonian absolutism, what evolution did the following take—ministerial council, Bavarianism, and anaktovoulion?

Zographos received his formal appointment to the foreign ministry as a complete surprise, without any previous notification by or understanding with the king. His initial surprise turned into dismay and suspicion when he arrived in Athens to find the king absent from the capital. Quite justifiably, as shown by the later repetition of this practice, Zographos interpreted the absence as the king's way of avoiding the necessity of

[17] On the expiration of the enlisted Bavarians' period of service, the government raised their pay a half penny per day to induce them to reenlist. But of 800 whose term was expiring in the first quarter of 1837, only 37 decided to stay (Lyons to Palmerston, Athens, 24 Apr. 1837, no. 47, FO 32.70). By fall of the same year, Lyons reported that only 2,000 of the original 3,500 volunteers remained (20 Sept. 1837, no. 96, FO 32.71), and early in 1838, he predicted that many of the 1,400 remaining privates would have gone by the following August (18 Jan. 1838, no. 17, FO 32.76). See also Bower and Bolitho, Otho I, p. 97.

[18] Zographos was recommended by Rudhart, apparently after he had first and unsuccessfully suggested Michael Soutsos (Koeppel, Ministerpräsidentschaft, p. 46; and Lyons to Palmerston, Athens, 1 Feb. 1838, no. 23, FO 32.76). Trikoupes arrived in April 1838 (Lyons to Palmerston, Athens, 19 Apr. 1838, no. 72, FO 32.76).

[19] Otho to Ludwig, 27 Jan. 1838, as quoted by Bower and Bolitho, Otho I, p. 103.

talking terms with him before his assumption of official duties. As a result, he was forced to take office unconditionally.[20]

Consequently, he served as little more than a clerk, so little authority did the king give him or any other ministerial head. In a letter to Mavrokordatos, Zographos revealed the incredible fact that his chief source of information about other branches of government, sometimes even his own, was the newspapers. More than ever, it seems, the ministerial council was a mere collection of men largely ignorant of each other's governmental affairs, rather than a team working together. The council's increasing atrophy may have been the price exacted for its achievement of a "national" character and freedom from direct oversight by a Bavarian chancellor or prime minister.[21]

The chief institution of absolutism, after the dissolution of the chancellorship, was the royal cabinet, sometimes called *vouleuterion* but more often known as anaktovoulion. It originated chiefly as the remnants of the regency's secretarial staff to which the king fell heir on his accession. As in the case of all other state institutions, no statute established the anaktovoulion or defined its role *in toto*. Occasionally, [*Government Gazette*] published appointments to the royal cabinet, though only offhandedly as an adjunct to some other office. The extra-legal status of this institution becomes apparent from the fact that its members received their salaries from the royal budget rather than from the state treasury.[22]

[20] "It seems, he [Zographos] says, that you [Mavrokordatos] construed the change [of government] a basic one and believed him the full heir of his predecessor [Rudhart]. On the basis of what he had observed up to that time, isn't this conclusion too comforting, in comparison with the one we came to in our [Zographos' and M. Argyropoulos'] deliberations here? In full knowledge he was doomed to become a victim because he was being forced to assume his duties, in all likelihood without prior agreement, etc. [from the king to his conditions for taking office]. You know that he sees everything in the darkest terms and I take comfort from this, but I am anxious until I find out the degree to which he will enjoy the [royal] confidence, what he will be able and what he will want to do" (M. Argyropoulos to A. Mavrokordatos, Pera, 2/14 Feb. 1838, no. 5482, Vol. 20 [1837-40], Mavrokordatos Archive) [MA]. ". . . Up to the moment, he [Zographos] had not seen the King, he doesn't know the degree to which he will win His confidence and get Him to listen to his advice"; indeed, Zographos didn't want the job at all (M. Argyropoulos to A. Mavrokordatos, Pera, 4/16 Feb. 1838, no. 5482, Vol. 20 [1837-40], MA). Spaniolakes was also appointed "without his wishes being consulted" (Lyons to Palmerston, Athens, 1 Feb. 1937, no. 23, FO 32.76).

[21] Zographos to Mavrokordatos, Athens, 24 July/5 Aug. 1839, no. 5608, Vol. 20 (1837-40), Mavrokordatos Archive. See also M. Argyropoulos to Mavrokordatos, Bucharest, 20 May/1 June 1838, no. 5512, Vol. 20 (1837-40), MA, who refers to the "disharmony and perhaps suspicion [of the cabinet members] to each other, or at least the absence of agreement."

[22] Concerning the origins of the anaktovoulion, Dragoumes ([*Reminiscences*] ii, 67) wrote: "Under the regency a special bureau existed, but it occupied itself exclusively with the copying and expediting of affairs [decrees] drawn up in German by its members. Often Stademann, its director and a modest gentleman, repeated that

Some decrees gave indirect legal sanction to the royal cabinet by making passing reference to it. The founding charter of the Council of State distinguishes between petitions to the royal cabinet and petitions to the king, reveals the existence of an anaktovoulion seal (apparently distinct from the royal seal), and stipulates that the royal cabinet, not the king, convey complaints about demotic and eparchal elections from minister of interior to the secretary of the Council of State. It also refers to *référendaires* (*eisēgētai*) in the various ministries or *référendaires* charged by the king with the task of introducing bills before the Council of State.[23]

In 1835, the year of the decree, ministerial *référendaires* existed only on paper or remained too insignificant to attract widespread attention. Available documents do not mention such officials until 1837, when Lyons reported the assignment of one for each ministry. Since [*Government Gazette*] never announced the appointment of *référendaires* as such, the exact function of this office is unclear and the length of time it continued to exist is unknown. Perhaps the king intended *référendaires* to serve as a check on the "increased" jurisdiction and initiative allowed the ministries in 1837.[24]

---

he was incapable of anything else and that, in Bavaria, the place of [clerical] expediters was reserved as a sinecure for old functionaries who were incompetent, either because of imperfect education or because of their inexperience in a service which demanded more knowledge than they had. On his departure, Stademann was replaced by a writer named Graf, a man entirely devoid of instruction and cultivation, who nevertheless succeeded in transforming the simple bureau into a royal cabinet and in raising himself to the position of director. He treated the [Greek] ministers as inferiors and gave them orders."

See Mendelssohn Bartholdy's *Geschichte Griechenlands*, II, 507. This account of Prokesch-Osten's discussions with Otho, on the eve of the royal accession, shows that the establishment of an anaktovoulion with broad responsibilities was envisaged and intended: "The highest administration would be carried out by an anaktovoulion, the Council of State, and the council of ministers. In the anaktovoulion would work specialists to whom the Count [Armansperg] would distribute the work."

For an example of such an appointment, which took the form of an "announcement" rather than that of the usual "decree," see the "announcement concerning the appointment and uniform of the councilor of the anaktovoulion Mr. Frey," 24 Nov./6 Dec. 1835 [*Government Gazette*], no. 20, 16 Dec. 1835o.s. or announcement of the appointment of Skarlatos Soutsos for use in the King's vouleuterion and the ministry of the army [*GG*], no. 1, 17 June 1835o.s. On the funds for salaries, see *Hellas*, 11 Oct. 1839o.s.

[23] See Arts. 41, 46, 47, and 65 of the "organic decree for the introduction of a Council of State," 18/30 Sept. 1835 [*Government Gazette*], no. 8, 18 Sept. 1835o.s. For other such decrees making passing reference to this institution, see decree concerning the presentation of petitions and acting upon them, 21 July 1835o.s. [*GG*], no. 3, 9 July 1835o.s., Art. 3; and decree concerning governmental functions during the period of the King His Majesty's absence, 23 April/5 May 1836 [*GG*], no. 18, 4 May 1836o.s., Art. 8.

[24] In a despatch to Palmerston (Athens, 4 Mar. 1837, no. 20, FO 32.69), Lyons announced that a Bavarian "référendaire" would be introduced in each ministry as

Someone had to assume the work formerly done by Armansperg and Rudhart. There was too much for the slow, inexperienced, and meticulous Otho. Consequently, the anaktovoulion increased in size to handle the mass of documents coming into and going out of the royal office. No longer held in check by Rudhart and completely unwatched during royal tours of the kingdom, its powers grew and attracted public notice. The Greek press opened fire at the end of 1838. Although perhaps exaggerated, its attacks give some idea how powerful the anaktovoulion had become. "We knew," wrote *Athēna*, "that the camarilla [royal cabinet] had advisory power but not that it also had executive power. We learn that it dismisses and appoints at will." A month later, *Athēna* announced that the camarilla had dismissed economic commissioners, treasurers, and mayors, while the king toured the provinces, and replaced them with others. And again, "The cabinet is inert and the camarilla still controls."[25]

Even though the last Bavarian foot soldier left Greece in 1838, Bavarianism survived. The king retained a small group of Bavarian officers, well-paid and highly ranked in order to seal their loyalty to the royal cause, and carefully placed so as to control the key fortresses of the kingdom and the main branches of the army. Christian Schmaltz, a Bavarian, continued to serve as minister of the army, the only Bavarian in the cabinet, until 1841. Although some Greeks eventually gained entrance to the anaktovoulion, they were heterochthons without any independent political influence, and the Bavarian element always prevailed. Mane, ever difficult to manage, became a type of bailiwick of Maximilian Feder, who in return prevented it from instigating such sedition as that which ultimately led to Kapodistrias' downfall. Quite clearly a contracted Bavarianism still controlled the two instruments of political power—military (army) and administrative (anaktovoulion). Otho apparently saw no other way to secure his personal absolutism and keep the monarchy effective, that is, able to prevent the parties from capturing political power and from resorting to military insurrection.[26]

follows: interior—Captain of the infantry Lehmaier; war and marine—Major Purkhardt; finance—Frey; religion—"officer whose name I don't know but Greeks say he is a Jew" (identifiable as Salome from a subsequent despatch of Lyons, dated 31 Jan. 1838, "Separate & Confidential," FO 32.76). On 13 Jan. 1840 (no. 10, FO 32.96), Lyons mentioned that Theochares, a German-educated Greek, had been secretary and "référendaire" for the past two years.

[25] *Athēna*, 29 Apr. 1839, 20 May 1839, and 9 Aug. 1839, all *o.s.* See also *Aiōn*, 6 Dec. 1839*o.s.*; and M. Argyropoulos (to Mavrokordatos, Bucharest, 20 May/1 June 1838, no. 5512, Vol. 20 [1837-40], Mavrokordatos Archive) in an obvious reference to the anaktovoulion: "But there exists within the cabinet an invisible power which hinders progress, both generally and with respect to each individual [member]."

[26] In a letter to Trikoupes (Piraeus, 17/29 Sept. 1841, quoted by Dragoumes [*Reminiscences*], II, 59), Mavrokordatos wrote concerning Bernard Hess, a Bavarian adviser to the king until 1843: "He wished to imply that there were only fourteen

By its very nature the system of personal absolutism bore the stamp of Otho's personality, which therefore becomes crucial to an understanding of this and subsequent periods of his reign. Elements of his childhood prefigure the man—seclusion from the rough-and-tumble of life because of delicate health, long periods of depression and exhaustion following on temper tantrums, and an education designed to prepare him for the priesthood or a minor state post. Otho never learned to manipulate people, and so he easily offended them or remained ineffective with them. Although tall and good-looking and anxious to please the Greeks by wearing native dress and quickly learning the language, he lacked the robustness, charm, even cunning and cruelty which Greeks generally identified with leadership. His childhood moodiness developed into a neurosis; he became suspicious, procrastinating, compulsively concerned with administrative details, and he found making decisions excruciatingly difficult. Since he would leave nothing alone, he wore himself out, slowed everything and everybody down, and contributed markedly to the paralysis of the administration.

Although he wrote the following a few years later, Piscatory has left a very telling sketch of Otho, all the more significant because his remarks were a frank and reluctant avowal of weaknesses in a man with whom French diplomacy was sympathetic:

Defiance of everyone and confidence in himself—the King has these to a degree which is rare. I believe that he is honest and just, but a bad action or an injustice does not make him indignant, does not impel him to punish or repair. He merely remembers it with an incredible memory, which stores up grievances against every proper name. It would be going too far to say that the king completely lacks intelligence. He has a remarkable memory. He can argue with infinite resources on the smallest question. But his mind is uncultivated and perfectly narrow. It cannot examine anything but the smallest facts, taken one by one; he cannot draw a conclusion or take a position. Certainly a character and mind were never less suited to the demands on a king of a new country, especially Greece.[27]

Bavarians [officers] in the army, whereas I had a list of 154 officers, without counting the forest guards and others." See also Lyons to Palmerston, Athens, 18 Jan. 1838, no. 17, FO 32.76: "The [Bavarian] officers are anxious to stay and the government will keep them." Schmaltz was appointed minister of the army by decree of 10/22 June 1835 ([*Government Gazette*], no. 3, 9 July 1835*o.s.*), and retained his post for the unprecedented length of six years, until Mavrokordatos insisted on an entirely Greek cabinet in 1841. Two of the Greeks in the anaktovoulion were Theochares (see n. 24 above) and Provelengios (*Athēna*, 20 Sept. 1841*o.s.*, and 10 Dec. 1841*o.s.*). Concerning Feder and his special position of control in Mane, formally as head of the light battalions of Mainats but also as the final arbiter of all administrative and judicial matters in the province, see *Athēna*, 26 Apr. 1839*o.s.*

[27] Theobald Piscatory to M. Guizot, Athens, 27 Aug. 1841 [6th report], in "Textes

Like a good man and bad king, he placed principle above *raison d'état*. He could have avoided many misunderstandings with Russia and endeared himself to his people if he had embraced the Orthodox faith, but he placed personal piety above political considerations. He found it difficult to separate personal matters from matters of state. His state policy toward England became closely bound up with his great personal antipathy toward Lyons and with the grave humiliation caused by intimations in the English press that he was impotent and even uninterested in the opposite sex. Ill-health, childlessness, and the perfidy of his personal physicians laid him open to such charges. In short, except for love of his people and great dedication to his royal mission, he had little to commend him as a king and much to commend him as a man—honesty, piety, hard work, thrift, and perseverance. But nothing could have been more unfortunate for Greece and himself than the combination in his person of meagre talents and personal dedication. It meant that he would let no one else do what he was unable to do.[28]

---

et Documents, La Grèce d'Othon," ed. Jean Poulos, in *L'Hellénisme Contemporain*, 2nd ser., IX (1955), 422.

On Otho's early life, see Bower and Bolitho, *Otho I*, pp. 23-28; on his assumption of the native Greek costume on his return to Greece in 1837, see Lyons to Palmerston, Athens, 15 Feb. 1837, no. 15, FO 32.69; on his suspicious and indecisive nature, see Lyons to Palmerston, Athens, 2/28 June [*sic*] 1835, "Copy/private," FO 32.52, and Piscatory, Athens, 20 June 1841 [1st report], *L'Hellénisme Contemporain*, IX, 340: "It is the king who wishes to see everything, do everything, decide everything. He does not cease taking part in even the smallest questions. Everyone accuses him [Otho], even those closest to him, his ministers offer no other response to complaints but the impossibility, in which they find themselves, of obtaining from the King a decision or his signature. . . ." *Athēna* (20 Aug. 1841*o.s.*) says virtually the same thing. On the same point, see also Bower and Bolitho, *Otho I*, p. 105, and Gennaios Kolokotrones [*Memoirs II*], p. 78.

[28] On Otho's insistence that his religious affiliation was a personal matter of conscience, see his letter to Ludwig, 13 May 1832, as quoted by Bower and Bolitho, *Otho I*, p. 32; and more generally, Hans Rall, "Die Anfänge des Konfessionspolitischen Ringens um den Wittelsbacher Thron in Athen," in *Bayern: Staat und Kirche, Land und Reich*, ed. Wilhelm Winkler (Munich, 1961), 181-215. Concerning the implied slanders of the English press, see Chap. V, n. 30, above. A fair estimate of the king's character is offered by Perdicaris (*Greece of Greeks*, I, 57-60): "Otho is an upright and religious man: no stain and immoral intrigues can be said to sully his character or disgrace his household. His court is a model of good order. . . ." Otho's honesty and good intentions are pointed out by Piscatory, Athens, 20 June 1841 (1st report), *L'Hellénisme Contemporain*, IX, 340.

For unfavorable accounts of Otho with respect to his public character, see Anastasios N. Goudas, *Bioi Paralleloi ton epi tes Anagenneseos tes Hellados Diaprepsanton Andron [Parallel Lives of Distinguished Men in the Rebirth of Greece]* (Athens, 1875), VII, 49-96, and George Finlay, *A History of Greece from its Conquest by the Romans to the Present Time 146 B.C. to 1864*, ed. H. F. Tozer (Oxford, 1877), VII, 168; also Bourgoing, French minister in Munich, to Thiers, French foreign minister, Munich, 16 June 1836, in *Gesandtschaftsberichte*, ed. Chroust, Abt. I, Vol. III, 270-74.

For biographies on Otho, see, besides Bower and Bolitho (*Otho I*), Marinos Papa-

Royal Policy toward the Parties

Otho apparently sought to forge a policy lying somewhere between that of the first regency and that of Armansperg. He neither set his goals so high (respecting the destruction of the parties or the construction of a streamlined administration) nor did he brandish the sword as much as the first regency. His policy was not unprincipled like Armansperg's nor did it wink at abuses. Like the first regency, he sought to uphold a just, impartial, and paternal administration carefully supervised from above against partisan abuses. Like Armansperg, he recognized the necessity of coexisting with the parties and even tried to utilize them for his antiparty purposes. In one of his interviews with Prokesch-Osten before his accession, he declared that the Crown could neither destroy the parties nor act as if they did not exist. It had to live with them. At best it could only undermine them gradually.[29]

The continuity which characterized all previous regimes, including his own, derived from the fact that either he or his father had from the beginning elaborated and reviewed the general objectives of Crown policy. With regard to the parties, royal policy involved essentially (1) the attempt to create a royal following as a substitute for the party system, and (2) the attempt to balance existing parties and their patron powers in such a way as to avert incipient civil war, to prevent their coming together against the throne, and, simply, to keep the administration going.

Friedrich Thiersch wrote in 1833:

The royal cause must be based on a gathering of capable and respectable men of all political complexions, and this royal party, expanded little by little throughout Greece, will finally reunite the entire nation.

And Maurer reiterated:

The union of all the parties and their turning toward the new throne constituted naturally the chief mission of the regency.

---

dopoulos-Vretos, "Othon, Ho Protos Basileus tes Hellados" ["Otho I King of Greece"], *Ethnikon Hemerologion* [*National Almanac*] (1869), pp. 242-351; G. Thomaïdes, *Historia tou Othonos* [*History of Otho*] (Athens, 1895); G. Sophroniades [*Othon-Amalia*] (Athens, 1895); Agis Kleomenos, *Dialexis peri ton Proton Monarchon tes Hellados Othonos kai Amalias* [*Lecture on the First Monarchs of Greece Otho and Amalia*] (Athens, 1904); [anon.], *Ho Basileus Othon. Historikon Eranisma* [*King Otho. Historical Compilation*] (Athens, 1917); Z. L. Papantoniou, *Othon kai he Romantike Dynasteia* [*Otho and the Romantic Dynasty*] (Athens, 1934); K. N. Loures, *Anekdota engrapha schetikos me ten ateknian ton Basileon Othonos kai Amalias* [*Unpublished Documents relating to the Childlessness of Otho and Amalia*] (Athens, 1958); and E. Weis, "Otto, König der Hellenen," in *Bayern in Europa*, Unbekanntes Bayern, no. 10 (Munich, 1965). See also "Otho, King of Greece," in *Allgemeine Deutsche Biographie*.

29 Mendelssohn Bartholdy, *Geschichte Griechenlands*, II, 507.

But even before either of these men, the seventeen-year-old Otho, still in Bavaria, answered his brother's misgivings about his acceptance of the Greek throne, "I will become the center of one and only national Greek party." These words summed up in advance what was to be the basic objective of his policy toward the parties.[30]

Many sources attest to Otho's immense popularity with the Greeks. He owed virtually none of it to his personal traits, and most of it to his royal office, which became the object of all hopes—a guarantee against anarchy, a source of national unity, a means of national aggrandizement. Thanks to the succession of regimes which had kept Otho in the background, all the odium of bad administration—severity or peculation, slow economic progress, extensive poverty, absence of a constitution—had left the royal office untouched. So great was its lustre that it remained free from direct attacks of the press until the Mavrokordatos episode in 1841—a rather long time for a ruler to escape the antipathy which his personal absolutism invited. Yet practical experience showed that, if the sovereign wished to rule as well as reign, or even if he simply wanted to maintain a delegated absolutism, he needed more than amorphous public loyalty which well-wishers euphemistically called a "national party."[31]

The question was not whether his subjects wished him well but whether, if forced to choose between party patron and him, they would choose him. He soon realized that concerted action was necessary to meet this test successfully. He adopted three main lines of action: (1) he supported and expanded a large class of small landholders to serve as the chief prop of his regime, (2) he undertook frequent royal tours throughout the kingdom, and (3) he formed a royal following of Greeks. The first course, initiated during the first regency period, suffered a severe setback because of the poor popular response to the dotation law. Otho's attempt to foster this objective will receive attention later in

[30] F. Thiersch, *De l'État actuel de la Grèce* (Leipzig, 1833), I, 244; George Ludwig von Maurer, *Das griechische Volk in öffentlicher, kirchlicher und privatrechtlicher Beziehung vor und nach dem Freiheitskampfe bis zum 31 Juli 1834* (Heidelberg, 1835), I, 34; and Christopher Neezer, *Apomnemoneumata . . . [Memoirs. The First Years of the Establishment of the Greek Kingdom]*, trans. [from German] D. Kampouroglou, 2nd ed. (Athens, 1936), p. 7. In addition, Driault and Lhéritier (*Histoire*, II, 169) write as follows: ". . . she [Queen Amalia] encouraged her husband to form around him a national party, to quickly be able to rule without obstacles and without limitations."

[31] The most notable exception is Lyons, who early in the reign began to cast doubt on the popularity of Otho (for instance, Lyons to Palmerston, Athens, 3 Mar. 1837, no. 19 [reporting no cheers for the king and queen when they appeared in public], and 8 May 1837, no. 53 [reporting criticism of the king among the inhabitants of an Attic village], both FO 32.70). But these criticisms and any others that were made were related to Otho's personal shortcomings. The monarchy, and Otho as the person embodying that institution, remained popular (see Piscatory, Athens, 20 June 1841 [1st report], *L'Hellénisme Contemporain*, IX, 5, 340) because most Greeks continued to regard it the surest guarantee against anarchy, etc. (see Finlay, *History*, VII, 106, and Chap. III, n. 100, above).

connection with the activities of the "Russian" administration. Here I will consider only the last two.

On the eve of Otho's accession to the throne, Prokesch-Osten and he agreed that the Crown only ". . . nourishes them [the parties] by making difficult the king's contact with his people." This remark explains the *raison d'être* of the numerous royal tours in the provinces. The king expected to stimulate loyalty to his person by face-to-face contact. By hearing petitions and grievances from even the most humble, the Crown, rather than the local party leaders or primates, presumably would become the great patron and defender against oppression.[32]

Otho slowly developed a personal following among two types of Greeks: the educated heterochthons, such as Rizos-Neroulos, Andronikos Païkos, Constantine Schinas, Constantine Provelengios, N. Silivergos, and George Tisamenos, and the autochthons of tremendous revolutionary prestige and great local influence, such as the Kolokotrones', the Mavromichales', the Kountouriotes', Andrew Zaïmes, Kitsos Tzavelas, Notes Botsares, and Anthony Miaoules. The first group enjoyed professional qualifications for government service. They became loyal adherents of the royal cause, presumably because they owed their influence to royal patronage.[33]

[32] Mendelssohn Bartholdy, *Geschichte Griechenlands*, II, 507. Gennaios Kolokotrones ([*Memoirs II*], pp. 80-81) asserts that the object of such tours was successfully thwarted by provincial officialdom who, by prior arrangement, sealed Otho off from those with grievances. For vivid and detailed accounts of such royal progresses, which were very numerous, see the accounts of Ludwig Ross, a Bavarian archeologist who accompanied the royal couple on them: *Reisen des Königs Otto und der Königinn Amalie in Griechenland* (Halle, 1848) and *Wanderungen in Griechenland in Gefolge des Königs Otto und der Königinn Amalie* (Halle, 1851).

[33] Perdicaris (*Greece of Greeks*, I, 75) wrote: "Since the establishment of the present state of things, there has arisen a fourth party. This is the government, or rather the court party, and consists partly of Bavarians, and partly of Greeks, who have been bought over by court favors and royal smiles." Aspreas ([*Political History*], I, 146) saw what the king was trying to do when he wrote that the king was trying to find substitutes for the Bavarian personnel among Greeks who were not tied up with the traditional parties. See also *Sōtēr*, 18/30 Oct. 1834, for an acknowledgment of this policy.

With regard to the first group, see Piscatory, Athens, 6 Sept. 1841 (7th report), *L'Hellénisme Contemporain*, IX, 445 (Rizos and Tisamenos), 445-46 (Païkos), and 446 (C. Schinas); *Athēna*, 20 Sept. and 10 Dec. 1841*o.s.* (Provelengios), and 11 June 1841*o.s.* (Silivergos). For further information on Rizos, see Finlay's not too favorable opinion (Journal [MSS], 3 June 1835 and 10 Dec. 1835); on C. Schinas, see Alexander R. Rangabe, *Apomnemoneumata* [*Memoirs*] (Athens, 1894), I, 357; on Provelengios as the chief of the Greek portion of the camarilla (anaktovoulion), see Lyons to Palmerston, Athens, 10 July 1841, no. 103, FO 32.106. Of this group, Païkos was reserved for legal affairs, Schinas for court matters, and Provelengios, Silivergos, and Tisamenos for financial matters.

With regard to the second group, see especially Piscatory, Athens, 6 Sept. 1841 (7th report), *op.cit.*, IX, 436-37 (Kolokotrones), 441-42 (Mavromichales—"He [Petrobey] is uniquely devoted to the King who has always treated him very well,

The second group went over to the king for different reasons. They had all learned from experience the dangers and disappointments of finding themselves opposed to the existing regime, and they now sought the comfort and security that accompanied their association with the royal government. The acceptance of royal rather than foreign legation patronage coincided with patriotic duty. All enjoyed the social respectability that royal favor imparted to them and the great deference with which the royal court received them. The king appointed Gennaios Kolokotrones, Katsakos Mavromichales (son of Petrobey), Kitsos Tzavelas, Kostas Botsares, and Anthony Miaoules his aides-de-camp. He named Petros Mavromichales (Petrobey), George Kountouriotes, and Andrew Zaïmes vice-presidents of the Council of State, where they usually rounded up a majority of votes for the Crown.[34]

In spite of its distinction for professional skills or patriotic service, this twofold royal following remained relatively small and brought little practical benefit to the Crown. The king could count on the first group, the educated heterochthons, but derived no popular support through it. The men in the second, or autochthon, group commanded sizeable followings, but they continued to play politics and could withhold their support from the king at pleasure. The king more and more found himself in the same dilemma as Kapodistrias before him. To organize a solid backing, the king would have had to step down from his lofty position of presumed neutrality and act the role of a party leader, which would surely alienate a sizeable segment of the nation. To remain arbiter between the parties, he had to exercise restraint and could employ few of the means necessary to create anything more than an unsubstantial or undependable following. Unlike Kapodistrias, he chose the latter course.

Even if the king recognized the necessity to coexist with the parties, he felt it equally necessary to keep them within bounds. From the very beginning, the Crown adopted the official policy of giving representation in the administration to all three parties. By so doing it sought to give partial satisfaction to the demands of the parties and more important, to their sponsoring powers. It apparently sought to make statutory checks and balances effective by selecting men of different parties or groupings to occupy counterbalancing offices, on the grounds that an official of one party would willingly detect and report abuses of officials belonging to other parties. In short, it attempted to make partisan jealousy serve the

---

often come to his aid, and given office to his sons who tend to be only mediocre"), and 442 (G. Kountouriotes—"The King courts Mr. Kountouriotes, who assures him a majority in the Council of State").

[34] The decree for the appointment of all but Kolokotrones, who was appointed later, and Miaoules, who had been appointed already, as the king's aides-de-camp, dated 20 May/1 June 1835, appeared in [Government Gazette], no. 1, 17 June 1835 o.s. For the appointment of the three vice-presidents of the Council of State, see decree of 15/27 Oct. 1835 [GG], no. 15, 26 Oct. 1835 o.s.

needs of impartial administration. Zographos described the system quite clearly when he wrote Mavrokordatos in 1839:

> The parties on the one hand and foreign diplomats on the other accepted these canons of logic and [the] method of equal representation or shared participation, this way to defend the interests and demands of the parties, the prestige of European courts and their political influence in Greece. Both factors demand to be represented in the formation of the ministries, and when this does not happen, everything is in grave danger. . . .[35]

This policy was most obvious in the composition of the successive cabinets, where the Crown made it a point to include a representative of each party as well as a Bavarian and a heterochthon Greek. As Zographos pointed out in 1838, the Crown carefully maintained a balance of party representation in the cabinet so as not to antagonize the parties themselves or the foreign powers supporting them.[36] Throughout the absolutist period the desirability of a homogeneous cabinet, temporarily representing one party and made up of men whose mutual affability rendered them capable of acting in concert, was constantly being argued. The argument carried force, but it was equally true that a homogeneous cabinet would provoke the united opposition of the two opposing parties and their sponsoring foreign powers. Such a dilemma, posed by the conflict between government efficiency and political considerations, characterized the difficult situation in which the Crown found itself.[37]

The experience of the regency and Armansperg regimes showed that equal representation was neither possible in practice nor even desirable. Each party sought more than equal treatment. To satisfy one, consequently, one had to discriminate against the others. Not to discriminate

[35] Zographos to Mavrokordatos, Athens, 19 Feb./3 Mar. 1839, no. 5579, Vol. 20 (1837-40), Mavrokordatos Archive. One clear instance of this is the simultaneous appointment, to the Council of State in 1839, of S. Trikoupes, favorite of English diplomacy, and M. Soutsos, favorite of Russian diplomacy (*Athēna*, 4 Oct. 1839o.s.).

Concerning checks and balances in practice and their paralytic effect on administration, see an unsigned, undated memorandum (probably drawn up by Mavrokordatos in 1841), no. 5793, Vol. 21 (1841), MA. There is no positive evidence that the government deliberately selected men along these lines or that the rivalry among officials was along party lines, but it seems probable.

[36] Zographos to Mavrokordatos, Athens, 19 Feb./3 Mar. 1839, no. 5579, Vol. 20 (1837-40), Mavrokordatos Archive.

[37] For instance, in 1834, *Sōtēr* and *Chronos* engaged in a debate over this issue. *Sōtēr*, organ of Kolettes, who was then minister of the interior and desiring a complete "French" cabinet, argued for a homogeneous cabinet: "It is preferable to have five men of similar views, even if middle-of-the-roaders and of limited knowledge, than fifteen geniuses and philosophers of varied principles, systems and ideas." *Chronos* (Oct. 1834o.s.), wishing to see the "Russian" party represented in the cabinet, argued with equal force of logic that every Greek government hoping to consolidate its position must include the chiefs of all factions.

against one meant the virtual alienation of all. Armansperg found that a rough balance, tipped in favor of one party or alliance of parties, seemed a more workable scheme. Otho favored this scheme and sought to adopt a procedure in which the dominance of any given party was only temporary, ultimately giving way to some other party so that eventually all would get their chance. By giving one party preponderance, he provided for some modicum of effective administration and gained that party's effective support by appealing to its self-interest. By rearranging the balance between parties periodically and constantly shifting personnel, the Crown probably hoped to ward off the permanent hostility or utter desperation of any one party or its sponsoring power. There was even more to the scheme than this. Otho wanted apparently to shift his favor from one protecting power to another until he had induced each in turn to guarantee its share of the third series.[38]

But this scheme, pragmatic and sensible, was like walking a tightrope and demanded of Otho such political acumen and skillful handling of men as he did not possess. Also, as will be seen, in this attempt to be administratively fair to the parties, Otho risked dissatisfying the dominant party, with the result that he successively alienated rather than satisfied each preponderant party. Besides, the constant changing of personnel proved administratively disruptive.

Consciously but necessarily the Crown fell into the pattern of allowing its own cabinet ministers and the foreign ambassadors the exercise of some patronage. In the case of the latter, Otho would in some cases comply with their recommendations in order to avoid having to give way to their pressure on some matter of policy. In the case of the former, he would allow them some, though not complete, leeway in order to compensate for their lack of any real power and so that they should have subordinates on whom they could rely to execute royal commands. But in each case he was making it apparent to office-seekers that adherence to a party was the surest way of securing and holding office.[39]

[38] No one ever stated this as a policy, but looking at the overall record from 1834-43, it is obvious that the political preponderance in the Greek government passed in succession from the "English" to the "Russian" to the "French" parties, and that Otho secured a major portion of the third series of the loan from the patronizing power before he changed the political balance in his government. The closest thing to a description of the practice as a policy is in Perdicaris (*Greece of Greeks*, I, 75): "In the meantime, his [Otho's] interests require the cooperation of one or the other of these three parties, and he has been obliged to call to his aid men with whom he can have but little sympathy. In so doing, however, he has in no degree sacrificed his policy, and has succeeded to flatter or foil in turn, Mons. Lagrene [sic], Katekazi [sic], and Sir Edmond Lyons."

[39] For instance, in 1837 the Crown appointed Karatzas to the Council of State and Botases to head the ministry of economic affairs, so as to secure French support for Rudhart (Lyons to Palmerston, Athens, 20 Sept. 1837, no. 96, FO 32.71, and 24 Apr. 1837, no. 47, FO 32.70). Or in 1841, after Otho had triumphed over Mavrokordatos and hence defeated his reform program, which Britain had supported, Otho

2. "RUSSIAN" ASCENDANCY

The "Russian" Party (1833–38)

Before considering in detail this initial implementation of royal policy, which during this period took the form of state Russophilism, both foreign and domestic, it is first necessary to take a look at the internal evolution of the "Russian" party since 1833 under conditions of state disfavor and the effect of its new position in 1838 on its internal structure. From 1833 until the beginning of 1837, the "Russian" party faced a serious crisis. The rabidly anti-Napist first regency drove some Napists underground and others into retirement or exile. The more tolerant but by no means really friendly Armansperg attracted many into his camp. But under both regimes membership in or identification with the party became a distinct liability. In 1836 demoralized Napists were lamenting their lack of a recognized leader. Theodore Kolokotrones, imprisoned from 1833-35, had retired from active politics and Andrew Metaxas had gone into honorable exile. The absence of strong leadership was especially damaging to this party because of its social composition (men who amounted to little politically without strong leaders) and its descent from the personal faction of Kolokotrones.[40]

To understand how the party survived and why it escaped permanent damage, one must consider the basic structure of the party, which Piscatory has happily described. The metaphor of the pyramid best applies. At the top, the Russian legation in Athens served as the supreme patron. The "Russian" faction constituted the second echelon of party leaders:

. . . small in number, but strongly united and tightly organized; . . . a type of orthodox free-masonry which conducts, to my mind, the unofficial policy of Russia and prepares her future in return for money, favor, and protection.

As an auxiliary to the "Russian faction," the so-called "Napist party" comprised the rank-and-file who were:

Napist because they belonged to such and such a faction or such and

---

tried to pacify British diplomacy by consulting Lyons on the nomination of a minister of war and minister of public instruction (Lyons to Palmerston, Athens, 6 Sept. 1841, no. 103, FO 32.107). The best example of the kind of patronage that a Greek minister was allowed to exercise is offered by Glarakes, who undoubtedly enjoyed enough (although not absolute) control over personnel to give the Napist party a majority of the governorships (see below in section on Otho's Russophil policy).

[40] Concerning the government's anti-Napist policy and its effect on party leadership, see [Anon.], "Apomnemoneumata peri tes eis ten Hellada systetheises philorthodoxos hetairias" ["Memoirs concerning the Philorthodox Society introduced in Greece"], n.d., no. 5794, Vol. 21 (1841), p. 3, Mavrokordatos Archive (hereafter to be cited as ["Anonymous Memo"]), since it is really a memorandum rather than memoirs). For the full text, see Appendix I below.

such a national assembly, or because they served under Kapodistrias who included them in the administration.

At the base stood "the inferior classes, who recall the zeal of the President in behalf of their interests and material needs." Taking each constituent in reverse order, we will examine some factors that explain how the party survived during this crisis.[41]

The same regimes which challenged the existence, or at least integrity, of the "Russian" party strengthened its hold over the masses, whose religiosity now made them responsive to Napist propaganda about the threat to Orthodoxy. In his everyday life, the peasant felt the effects of dissolving the monasteries, to which he had resorted on pilgrimages for spiritual uplifting and festive recreation. If the peasants were silent in their opposition to the dissolution, the lower clergy, their representatives, were vocal in theirs. Indeed, if the truth were known, one might find that the Napists actually expanded their popular base at the same time that the fortunes of the party seemed most grim.[42]

But there is also evidence of antimonasticism, even among some popular elements, which indicates that the religious settlement may not have been as overwhelmingly unpopular as generally supposed. William Mure, an English traveler, described a conversation which took place in his presence in a Peloponnesian village called Ali Tschelepi during his visit to Greece in 1838:

> Radical principles were in the ascendant, and most of the arguments against monastic establishments, which for the last two or three centuries have become stale and hackneyed commonplaces in western Europe, were here urged as ingenious novelties, with all the pomp and pride of intellectual ultra-liberalism, by the majority of the assembly, headed, as was to be expected, by Nicóla [Mure's guide], and seconded by the Chorophylax [gendarme]. Monasteries in general were pro-

[41] Piscatory, Athens, 30 July 1841 (4th report), *L'Hellénisme Contemporain*, IX, 410.

[42] In *Turkey, Greece, and Malta* (London, 1837), Augustus Slade wrote (I, 249) about the dissolution of the monasteries as ". . . a true way of increasing the attachment of the people to the brotherhoods, and of disposing the latter toward the power friendly to their interests." On the creation of an autocephalous church, he commented (I, 247): ". . . the government did not represent the people on this point—if on any; and that, although certain capitani, merchants, and Philhellenists, might be indifferent about religion, the mass of the population clung zealously to old usages, and revered the patriarch as the head of their national church. In supporting the rights of the metropolitan, M. Catacazi canvassed the goodwill of the people." Piscatory (Athens, 20 June 1841 [1st report], *L'Hellénisme Contemporain*, IX, 338) made the connection between the religious question and the popular strength of the Napist party: ". . . the religious question gave it [Napist party] a tie and a common interest, especially when the government misread the profound sentiments of the nation in this respect." See also Aspreas [*Political History*], I, 133; Driault and Lhéritier, *Histoire*, II, 225; and Perdicaris, *Greece of Greeks*, I, 72.

nounced to be mere hives of useless drones; the government was commended for what had been already done towards their suppression, and hopes were expressed that the country would soon be rid of them altogether. The monks of Alí-tschelepi were denounced in their individual capacity, as traitors to the only useful duty they had to perform—that of affording hospitality to the traveller. From all this, an elderly substantial-looking merchant, who sat by me, and who seemed to be the only staunch Conservative of the party, scarcely ventured to dissent by an occasional shake of the head, or an expression or two of simple disapprobation.[43]

The second constituent part, what Piscatory called the "Napist party," remains elusive precisely because of the party's social composition, largely that of anonymous clerics (practically the entire regular and monastic clergy), unnamed local officials whom one hostile source refers to as "those with the smell of Napism," and the middling groups of small landholders whom Thiersch contemptuously labeled "men without a future" and whom Piscatory called "men who are nothing without a leader of great influence." In conjunction with the Napist party's membership of anonymous small men, one must also consider the converse— the virtual absence of large landed primates and Phanariots. This peculiar social composition we may attribute to Kapodistrias' policy of favoring the landless peasants and small landholders against their traditional Greek masters.[44]

By passion and policy, the "French" and "English" rank and file seem to have fostered the Napist sense of identity and discouraged Napist defections. To a large extent, the local officials who replaced their Napist rivals and oppressors wreaked vengeance for their former disabilities and hence offered the Napists the cohesion of common desperation. Other officials may have deliberately discouraged potential defectors, for whom the state was looking, so as to keep down the competition for their jobs and to avoid having to share the limited spoils of office.[45]

If many of the Napist rank and file had no choice but to remain Napists,

---

[43] William Mure, *Journal of a Tour in Greece and the Ionian Islands* (Edinburgh and London, 1842), II, 297.

[44] Chr. Vlases to Palamides, 6 June 1834, folder 257, Palamides Archive, Vlachogiannes Collection, General State Archives, Athens. See also Henry M. Baird (*Modern Greece* [New York, 1856], p. 112), who contends that almost the entire clergy were among the Napist party's adherents; Thiersch, *État actuel*, I, 58; and Piscatory, Athens, 6 Sept. 1841 (7th report), *L'Hellénisme Contemporain*, IX, 436. See also Chap. III, pp. 109-110 and 118-19.

[45] On oppression of Napists by Constitutionalists, where the latter were in control, see Mendelssohn Bartholdy, *Geschichte Griechenlands*, II, 497. The converse was equally true (II, 497), but during this period of Napist eclipse there were more local areas under the control of Constitutionalists. For an instance of the way in which the Napist leadership exploited the memory of former anti-Napist discrimination to stimulate present Napist solidarity, see *Aiōn*, 16 Nov. 1838o.s.

they probably utilized the secret societies to maintain a collective existence. Since the Phoenix society continued to exist throughout possibly the whole of the absolutist decade, we may assume that these men were in some way bound to each other and to the party leaders by all the sentimental bonds and institutional ties that characterized these underground organizations. At this level of their operation they remained beyond the reach of the state, which lacked the administrative and police weapons to locate and suppress them.[46]

The gravest disruption of the Napist party took place at the level of the party élite, which suffered from the loss of its former leaders (Kapodistrias, Kolokotrones, Metaxas). After confusion and demoralization, it acknowledged two new leaders, one arriving from Russia, the other rising from its own midst. Constantine Oikonomos and Gennaios Kolokotrones gradually rewove the torn fibers of the party fabric.

Constantine Oikonomos,[47] the learned and distinguished Thessalian cleric, began his career as a liberal disciple of Koraes. Like so many others, he grew conservative with age and found honors and employment in Russia, the haven of Orthodox conservatives since the end of the Napoleonic wars. From Russia, he watched the regency enact its ecclesiastical settlement. In 1834 he arrived in Greece with a strong sense of mission. He obviously wanted to organize the conservative bishops into a strong force and mobilize public opinion so that the church might reassert its former rights and renew its relations with Constantinople.

His tremendous energy, sincerity, and moral fervor put some verve into the clerical opposition. He stood behind the publication of [Evangelical Trumpet], a periodical designed for the religious education of the people and edited by Germanos, a monk with views similar to his own. There are indications that Oikonomos also coached and encouraged the conservative group within the holy synod and drew up many of the synodal acts which displeased Greek liberals.[48]

[46] On the continued existence of the Phoenix society throughout the absolutist decade, see Thiersch, État actuel, I, 65; ["Anonymous Memo"], n.d., no. 5794, Vol. 21 (1841), Mavrokordatos Archive.

On his return to Greece in 1841, Mavrokordatos told Lyons (to Palmerston, Athens, 9 Aug. 1841, no. 113, FO 32.106) that he was "surprised and alarmed since his return to find proofs of its being a powerful engine, of which Russia holds the lever for the overthrow of the Ottoman Empire in Europe." Then this secret society became a part of the movement of 3 September 1843.

[47] On the life of Oikonomos, see D. S. Balanos, "Konstantinos Oikonomos ho ex Oikonomon" ["Constantine Oikonomos"], Ekklesia [Church], xxxiv (1953), 491-98, as well as the biographies in Megale Hellenike Enkyklopaideia [Grand Hellenic Encyclopedia], 24 vols. (Athens, 1926-34); Threskeutike kai Christianike Enkyklopaideia [Religious and Christian Encyclopedia], and Goudas [Parallel Lives], I, 169-206; also Charles A. Frazee, "The Orthodox Church of Greece from the Revolution of 1821 to 1852" [unpubl. doct. diss.] (Indiana University, 1965), pp. 242-44.

[48] For instance, according to Lyons (to Palmerston, Athens, 27 Sept. 1837, no.

According to Makrygiannes, this "child of Russia" did not limit his activities to the clergy alone. He and an archimandrite named Anatolios sought to organize laymen too. The former took responsibility for recruiting the politicians, the latter worked among the military men. In 1837, Lyons privately denounced "Economos and his satellites" and "the pecuniary means at their disposal." This brief reference suggests Oikonomos' success in consolidating some sort of following. By that time at least, he enjoyed undisputed leadership of the party's ideological warfare and ecclesiastical membership.[49]

In 1836 Gennaios Kolokotrones came to the fore by virtue of the prestige attached to his name and the influence derived from his official position. On retirement from politics, his father designated him to be his successor and privately announced to adherents that they should take instructions from him thereafter. That same year he became one of Otho's aides-de-camp, a position which brought him into intimate contact with the Bavarian councilors and the king himself. The extent of his influence in this position in 1841 impressed Piscatory, who considered him dangerous in that post because "whether consulted by the king or not, he always had an opinion which the cabinet ministers encountered as an obstacle to anything which they proposed." What Piscatory was not aware of was the counteracting influence of Schmaltz, minister of war, Rosmer, and other Bavarians in court, who were antipathetic toward Kolokotrones.[50]

Without the leadership, protection, and support of the Russian legation in Athens, the Napist party élite might not have survived. The conduct of its activities rested in the hands of Gabriel Catacazy, Russian minister to Greece from 1833-43. "By the admission of everyone," wrote Piscatory, he was "a spirited individual of remarkable ability, who has known how to exploit all influence for the object he pursued and how to distribute the money and favors at his disposal." His selection for this post reveals the astuteness of Russian diplomacy.[51]

105, FO 32.72), the draft of a bold letter ostensibly written by the Bishop of Attica to justify his excommunication of a communicant without prior consent of the state was Oikonomos' handwriting.

[49] John Makrygiannes, *Apomnemoneumata* [*Memoirs*], ed. John Vlachogiannes, 2nd edn. (Athens, 1947), II, 112; Lyons to Palmerston, Athens, 30 Aug. 1837, no. 85, FO 32.71; also Lyons to Palmerston, Athens, 25 Aug. 1837, no. 81, FO 32.71, referring to Oikonomos as "the intriguing Priest and Russian Pensioner."

[50] ["Anonymous Memo"], n.d., no. 5794, Vol. 21 (1841), Mavrokordatos Archive; and Piscatory, Athens, 6 Sept. 1841 (7th report), *L'Hellénisme Contemporain*, IX, 437. Gennaios ([*Memoirs II*], p. 83) attests to Otho's confidence in him and his free access to Otho, as well as to the antipathy of Schmaltz and the court Bavarians towards him.

[51] Piscatory, Athens, 20 Aug. 1841 (5th report), *L'Hellénisme Contemporain*, IX, 415-16. See also Perdicaris (*Greece of Greeks*, I, 72), who writes of "the ability of her representative who, being a Greek by birth, language, and religion, has been enabled to maintain her position in so masterly a manner as to be admired and respected even by those who are opposed to the policy of his government."

He descended from a Russianized Greek family that had migrated to Russia from Mane after the unsuccessful Peloponnesian revolt of 1770 and had since distinguished itself in the Russian diplomatic service. As a lower official in the Russian embassy at Constantinople, he had assisted many Greeks in 1821 to escape the vengeance of the Turkish authorities there. He had participated in the famous naval battle of Navarino (1827) as diplomatic assistant to Admiral Heyden, commander of the Russian fleet. Consequently, when he arrived in Nauplion in April 1833, many Greeks considered him an intimate friend and all respected him as a well-informed diplomat on Greek affairs. In an attempt to win more friends, retain old ones, and pick up information, he made his large home one of the chief centers of Athenian social life.[52]

Unlike the other legations, Greeks occupied the two immediately subordinate posts in the Russian legation. Constantine Paparregopoulos, a consul-general, served as chief liaison between the legation and Napist party leaders and interpreted official Russian policy to them. Brother-in-law of Rados and Moraïtines, both outstanding Napists, he established such extensive contacts that Piscatory estimated his reputation within the party as on a par with Kolokotrones'. Leles, second secretary of the legation, was the son of a Peloponnesian Greek who had served as an admiral in the Russian fleet. He too took part in party activities. In 1836 he accompanied the fanatical Germanos into the Peloponnesos for a storming propaganda tour against Protestant missionary activities and other alleged threats to Orthodoxy.[53]

Like the English and French missions, the Russian sought the predominance of its client party in the Greek government and administration. To be sure, on his appointment as minister to Greece, Catacazy was instructed by his government to advise partisans of Russia, like Kolokotrones, to rally round the regency regime, offer their devotion with no strings attached, and abstain from any activity disturbing public order. In effect, the Russian government was serving notice that its partisans were no longer to operate as a party. And Nesselrode's subsequent reply to the letter of Kolokotrones offered the same kind of advice. But in the same instructions received by Catacazy, it is apparent that such an ostensibly antiparty position was intended to assuage regency suspicions,

[52] For a biographical sketch, see [*Grand Encyclopedia*]. See also Rangabe [*Memoirs*], II, 8: "The biggest house in the capital [Athens] was that of Paparregopoulos, reshaped and expanded from Turkish times, occupied by Katakazes (a relative of my mother), who was then the most hospitable of all in Athens."

[53] On the personnel of the Russian legation (Persiany and Leles), see Lyons to Palmerston, Athens, 8 Mar. 1838, no. 44, FO 32.76; also Piscatory, Athens, 6 Sept. 1841 (7th report), *L'Hellénisme Contemporain*, IX, 433 (Rados) and 455 (Paparregopoulos). On Moraïtines and his relationship to Paparregopoulos, see P. Argyropoulos to Mavrokordatos, 8/20 April 1840, no. 5860, Vol. 20 (1840), Mavrokordatos Archive. On Leles' accompanying Germanos, see Lyons to Palmerston, Athens, 29 Oct. 1836, no. 59, and 31 Dec. 1836, no. 69, FO 32.60.

fanned by the English and French missions, that Russia was intriguing to get the "Russian" party in power. Moreover, Catacazy was to point out to members of the "Russian" party that "submission and good order" would win them the good will of the regency and offer the best chance "of coming to power and prevailing over their liberal adversaries." In short, non-partisan behavior was advocated as a tactical device to bring the party to power.[54]

During the regency period, the Russian government's frequent complaints about the ascendancy of the "ultraliberal" party and discrimination against the "Russian" party constituted an implicit demand for its representation in the administration. Russia used the regency's announced policy of uniting all parties as an argument for including a large proportion of Napists in the administration. Like the missions of the other two protecting powers, the Russian also sought office for specific individuals within its client party. Russian influence, for instance, got George Ainian into the Council of State in 1835 and placed Mamoures as commanding colonel of the second frontier regiment. On other occasions Catacazy failed. For a year he tried to secure the appointment of Michael Soutsos as minister of foreign affairs, only to have Soutsos sent to Russia as Greek minister instead.[55] But the Russian mission did not limit its activities to merely unofficial intervention in behalf of Napists. As Piscatory asserted, "the constant policy of the Russian legation was to conserve, fortify, protect, and recruit this [Napist] party." In 1836 Lyons was so impressed with the speed with which "Russian agents" spread rumors that he cited this as proof of "how numerous and how well paid their hirelings must be."[56]

Because the Russian mission represented an Orthodox state which had long distinguished itself as protector of the Greek church in the Ottoman Empire, it was able to court an already sympathetic clergy as a special means of influence closed to the other missions. In a memorandum attached to Catacazy's initial instructions, the Russian government outlined a plan for sending a Russian ecclesiastic into the provinces of Greece to survey the most pressing needs of the churches and clergy and then, on

[54] Instructions to Catacazy, Jan. 1833, enclosed in a despatch of Nesselrode to Gagarin, St. Petersburg (8/20 May 1833) in *Russia and Greece during the Regency of King Othon 1832-1835*, ed. Barbara Jelavich (Thessaloniki, 1962), pp. 62-63.

[55] On Russia's general demand for the inclusion of Napists in the administration, see Nesselrode to Potemkin, St. Petersburg, 19/31 Oct. 1832; Nesselrode to Heideck, St. Petersburg, 19 Oct./1 Nov. 1832; "Memorandum [Nov. 1833]," from Nesselrode to Michael Soutsos, special emissary of Greece to Russia; Nesselrode to Catacazy, St. Petersburg, 17/29 Aug. 1834; all in *Russia and Greece*, ed. Jelavich, pp. 52, 54, 81, 94-95. On the placement of Ainian and Mamoures, see Piscatory, Athens, 6 Sept. 1841 (7th report), *L'Hellénisme Contemporain*, IX, 431, 433. On efforts in behalf of M. Soutsos, see Lyons to Palmerston, Athens, 29 July 1836, no. 44, FO 32.59. Lagrené believed Païkos and Glarakes his nominees (Lyons to Palmerston, Athens, 17 Jan. 1838, no. 13, FO 32.76).

[56] Piscatory, Athens, 20 Aug. 1841 (5th report), *L'Hellénisme Contemporain*, IX, 416; Lyons to Palmerston, Athens, 29 Oct. 1836, no. 59, FO 32.60.

the basis of such a survey, having Catacazy distribute "to the poorest communities, to the neediest clergy" both money and religious articles. Such a practice would demonstrate to the people that "in preserving the faith of their fathers and rejecting dangerous innovations, they would always enjoy the powerful support of the Tsar and a protection rich in benefits." This statement of intentions lends weight to later allegations concerning such behavior. Some priests were reputedly in Russian pay. Some, like Oikonomos, might have been Russian pensioners. Russian generosity took the more usual form of bestowing "with great solemnity splendid presents from the Emperor consisting of Pontificals and Communion Plate." In 1837 bishops and clergy assembled in great pomp at the Russian chapel of Athens for just such a display. According to Lyons, in 1839 the Russian legation gave $2,000 to the Napist party in Mane and Sparta, but this information he received secondhand. Piscatory also spoke of "the money and favors at his [Catacazy's] disposal."[57]

"Russian" political ascendancy, beginning at the end of 1837, did not end the internal problems or dissensions of the party. It only posed a new set. Now there were too many potential leaders rather than too few. Differences concerned the objectives of power rather than the strategy of survival. George Glarakes, highest "Russian" official in the government, did not really weld together the constituent parts of the party. He simply created a vigorous faction of subordinate officials, who exercised a type of hegemony among other constituents of the party.

The king's Russophil policy, as well as attempts to economize, produced the recall of Andrew Metaxas from Spain and of Michael Soutsos from Russia. Perhaps because of his eclipse by other rising stars, perhaps because he had tired of politics and its risks, Metaxas remained passive after his return and recaptured the reins of party leadership only when the success of the revolution of 1843 brought him to the fore as one of its organizers. When he returned to Greece in 1839, he was a moderate as compared to Glarakes. As Piscatory stated in 1841, "he would certainly not yield to the demands of his friends if he had confidence in the future of the government." This type of leader seemed like a bit of an anachronism in a party imbued with the aggressive spirit of Glarakes, but by his presence, if not by actual deliberation, he provided an alternative locus for Napist party loyalties.[58]

According to Makrygiannes, Michael Soutsos came to an understanding with the Russians before returning to Greece. He promised to work for

[57] Instructions to Catacazy, Jan. 1833, in *Russia and Greece*, ed. Jelavich, pp. 66-67. Lyons to Palmerston, Athens, 24 Apr. 1837, no. 47, FO 32.70 (on ecclesiastical articles), and 9 Feb. 1840, no. 25, FO 32.96 (on the $2,000). See also Piscatory, Athens, 20 Aug. 1841 [5th report], *L'Hellénisme Contemporain*, IX, 416.

[58] Piscatory, Athens, 6 Sept. 1841 (7th report), *ibid.*, IX, 444. For a notice of Metaxas' return in 1839, see *Aiōn*, 1 Oct. 1839o.s.

the liberation of Thessaly and Macedonia, over which he would become reigning prince under Russian suzerainty. Back in Greece, he sponsored a secret society dedicated to this scheme. His personal secretary, Formanos, worked with Anatolios, the associate of Oikonomos. Anatolios held Russian money for this organization and his home became its center. Because of his Phanariot background, Soutsos never enjoyed any popularity among the Greek masses and, apart from Russia's patronage, he was nothing more than the impoverished head of a large Phanariot family which had immigrated to Greece. Nevertheless, Soutsos became the center of a new "Russian" faction and hence contributed to the pluralism which frustrated Glarakes' efforts to build a monolithic party structure.[59]

In that same year (1838) a third figure arrived in Greece to complicate party structure even more—George Kapodistrias, youngest brother of the deceased president. Ostensibly he came to settle his brother's estate and advance financial claims against the state. An anonymous source says that some Napists had invited his brother Viaro to Greece in 1836 when the party was looking for a head. It asserts that George's arrival precipitated some embarrassment and alarm among the leaders, who intended him as a front for their subversive activities and then found him determined to actually direct the party. Certainly his name, which might serve as a rallying point for the masses, made him a potential threat to the established party leadership.[60]

Otho's Russophil Policy

It is useful and correct to consider 1838-39 as the Napist period of the Crown's first decade. But this way of thinking will prove misleading unless one understands the meaning of such descriptive phrases as " 'Russian' ascendancy" or " 'Russian' preponderance." The composition of the ministerial council certainly did not reflect government by one party. Of six members, five of whom were Greek, only two were Napists—George Glarakes (interior and education–church affairs) and A. Païkos (justice). Spaniolakes (economy) and Kriezes (navy) both belonged to the "English" party as had Zographos (foreign affairs) before he became the

[59] Makrygiannes [Memoirs], II, 112. Athēna (29 Apr. 1839o.s.), wrote: "Some meetings were held recently in the house of M. Soutsos, where there also appeared some foreign officials personally and by representation, and where Regny directed the talks. At the very least the meeting decided on the downfall of the cabinet."

For a biographical sketch of M. Soutsos, see [Grand Encyclopedia], and Goudas [Parallel Lives], VI, 158-84.

[60] So dimly has the memory of the Philorthodox plot been preserved by historians that this figure is not dealt with in the standard Greek encyclopedias. Lyons (to Palmerston) says a bit about him in his despatch of 10 Jan. 1840, no. 6, FO 32.96. The richest information on him, with respect to his role in Greek politics, is found in ["Anonymous Memo"], n.d., no. 5794, Vol. 21 (1841), Mavrokordatos Archive (see Appendix I).

special target of British hostility.[61] Nor did any Napist sit in the anakto-voulion. Although Gennaios Kolokotrones and Kitsos Tzavelas enjoyed access to the king as aides-de-camp, other aides belonged to other parties. In short, Otho remained true to his policy of mixed administration carefully supervised by his anaktovoulion.

But his policy also provided for balance in favor of one party—during this period the "Russian." Although they made up only one-third of the cabinet, Glarakes and Païkos exercised the patronage covering the administrative, educational, ecclesiastical, and judicial systems. *Athēna* probably exaggerated when it asserted that only five or six out of forty-seven provincial governors were non-Napists, but Piscatory reiterated the general point about achieved Napist control of provincial governorships when he wrote in 1841; "It is incredible to what extent the governors belong to the 'Russian' party."[62] In the ministry of education-religion, Glarakes delegated most of his responsibility to Andrew Mamoukas (religion) and Kokkones (education), his loyal and ardent Napist subordinates. During this period, the Napist bishops controlled the holy synod by possession of its chairmanship and a majority of three out of five.[63]

[61] For instance, Lyons (to Palmerston, Athens, 11 Jan. 1840, no. 8, FO 32.96) talks about the "Russian" party still being "in power." Also Rangabe (*[Memoirs]*, ii, 90) states that the cabinet of 1838-39 was considered "Russian."

Glarakes, Spaniolakes, and Zographos rose to cabinet rank at the end of 1837 (by decrees of 29 Nov./11 Dec. 1837 [*Government Gazette*], no. 39, 1 Dec. 1837*o.s.*; 23 Dec./4 Jan. 1838 [*GG*], no. 43, 28 Dec. 1837*o.s.*; and 8/20 Dec. 1837 [*GG*], no. 40, 8 Dec. 1837*o.s.*, respectively) and enjoyed a tenure of about two years, Spaniolakes until the end of 1839 when the ministry of economic affairs was turned into a directorate, Glarakes and Zographos until the beginning of 1840. Païkos came to office by decree of 12/24 April 1837 [*GG*], no. 15, 13 Apr. 1837*o.s.*, and remained until Mavrokordatos formed a new cabinet in 1841. Krieres enjoyed the longest tenure—from early 1836 (by decree of 13/25 Feb. 1836 [*GG*], no. 4, 14 Feb. 1836*o.s.*) until the revolution of Sept. 1843.

[62] *Athēna*, 25 June 1838*o.s.*, and Piscatory, Athens, 20 Aug. 1841 (5th report), *L'Hellénisme Contemporain*, ix, 415. See also Lyons to Palmerston, Athens, 11 Jan. 1840, no. 8, FO 32.96 ("the important governments of Nauplia, Messolongi, and Patras, are assigned to them . . ."), and 26 Mar. 1840, no. 42, FO 32.97.

[63] Kokkones and Mamoukas, "Glarakes' creatures, still have charge of public instruction," wrote Lyons to Palmerston, Athens, 19 Jan. 1840, no. 13, FO 32.96; see also *Athēna*, 29 Jan. 1838*o.s.*

The synod of 1838-39 (summer to summer) consisted of: *Dionysios, Bishop of Kynouria*, president (names that are italicized indicate those with conservative-Napist leanings); *Theodoretos of Sellasia*, Jonas of Damala (Elis), Gerasimos of Hydra, and *Neophytos of Phocis*; with *Neophytos of Attica* and Anthimos of Cyclades as alternates (*Athēna*, 23 July 1838*o.s.*). The synod of 1839-40 consisted of *Dionysios of Kynouria*, president; Gerasimos of Hydra, *Theodoretos of Sellasia, Joseph of Messenia*, and *Ignatios of Gortynos*; with *Neophytos of Attica* and Jonas of Damala as alternates (decree of 23 July/4 Aug. 1839 [*Government Gazette*], no. 15, 29 July 1839*o.s.*, or Lyons to Palmerston, Athens, 8 Aug. 1839, no. 16, FO 32.69, or *Athēna*, 26 July 1839 *o.s.*). As *Athēna* (26 July 1839*o.s.*) was quick to point out, Dionysios of Kynouria had signed the patriarchal excommunication decree of 1821 against anyone supporting the Greek Revolution.

Athēna also complained about the widespread replacement of Constitutionalist judges. Even though Piscatory wrote when the balance had already begun to shift away from the Napist party, he marveled at existing Napist control of many palace positions and high military posts.[64] Such partial, though not exclusive, infiltration into all branches of government warrants the assertion that the Napists were in the ascendancy.

The period of "Russian" ascendancy also involved a marked reorientation of Greek foreign policy away from Britain toward Russia. A desire to extricate Greece from exclusive British domination partially inspired the dismissal of Armansperg. Britain responded to Rudhart accordingly and did its utmost to portray him publicly as the creature of Russian-Austrian diplomacy. Lyons cited as evidence Rudhart's visit to Metternich while enroute to Greece and his expulsion—at Austrian insistence —of Usiglio, an Italian revolutionary traveling in Greece with a British passport. As an apparent gesture of goodwill, Rudhart appointed an "Englishman" (Polyzoïdes) as minister of the interior, but Lyons remained unimpressed.[65]

Progressively, relations between Lyons and Otho degenerated into personal enmity. Lyons resented Otho's attempt to have him recalled. Otho resented Lyons' quarterdeck manner, which denied him the deference he expected as king. As the personal factor intruded itself in the relations between the two countries, reconciliation became ever more difficult, indeed impossible. Even before he had assumed personal power, Otho wrote:

> To remain on good terms with England is absolutely out of the question as long as Lyons is her envoy here. . . . Only by patience can this irk-

---

[64] *Athēna*, 29 Jan. 1838*o.s.*; Piscatory, Athens, 20 Aug. 1841 (5th report), *L'Hellénisme Contemporain*, ix, 415.

[65] Lyons wrote Palmerston (Athens, 3 July 1838, no. 112, FO 32.77) that Otho believed "Armansperg had governed the country entirely under sinister instructions from you [Palmerston]. . . ." For Lyons' statements about Rudhart as the representative of Austrian diplomacy, see his despatch to Palmerston, Athens, 11 Sept. 1837, no. 92, FO 32.71, and 31 Oct. 1837, no. 123, FO 32.72; as the representative of Russian diplomacy, see 29 Dec. 1837, no. 153, FO 32.72.

Concerning Rudhart's four-hour interview with Metternich on his way to Greece, see Koeppel, *Ministerpräsidentschaft*, p. 11; Gianni Kordatos, *Historia tes Neoteres Helladas* [*History of Modern Greece*] (Athens, 1957), iii, 109; and Epaminondas K. Kyriakides, *Historia tou Synchronou Hellenismou . . .* [*History of Contemporary Hellenism from the Establishment of the Kingdom of Greece until our own Days*] (Athens, 1892), i, 325.

Concerning the celebrated Usiglio case, see *Athēna's* lead article, 28 July 1837*o.s.*; Lyons to Palmerston, Athens, 8 Aug. 1837, no. 76, FO 32.71, with numerous enclosures of Lyons' official protest; Driault and Lhéritier, *Histoire*, ii, 167-70; and Bower and Bolitho, *Otho I*, p. 98.

According to Lyons (19 Dec. 1837, no. 146, FO 32.72), Armansperg had suspected the "honesty and soundness of his [Polyzoïdes'] political principles." As early as 22 May 1837, Lyons wrote (no. 55, FO 32.70): "Polyzoïdes is not equal with three

some guest be shaken off. Only when the present distrust on the part of the English government is removed and its irritation soothed, can we renew measures to that end.[66]

But why, aside from British support of Armansperg, did Otho try in the first place to reduce England from a privileged status to an equal or subordinate one among the protecting powers? The answer is largely because Russia and France, during the deliberations of the London Conference in 1836, had both served notice that they would offer Greece no financial help so long as things remained as they were. Although they did not say so outright, one of those things was the extent of British domination. By the end of 1837, Greece had received some of the British portion of the third series as a result of Armansperg's pro-British policy and could expect no more from that quarter.[67]

Now the king had to work on Russia and France to secure their share. Of the two, Russia seemed the more willing to use the promise of a loan as inducement for the establishment of a pro-Russian government. Before Otho returned to Greece in 1837, Nesselrode had indicated that the future type of government in Greece would determine Russia's policy on the loan, and when resigning, Rudhart reminded Otho that Greece would get the Russian loan only if a Napist succeeded him. Otho's new policy bore fruit in 1838 with the Russian award of 1,000,000 francs toward her portion of the third series.[68]

Faced with the dilemma of winning the friendship of one power at the price of alienating the other two (the dilemma of neutrality), Otho fol-

---

portfolios to the task of counteracting the national [*sic*, but antinational?] system." By executing the royal ordinance for Levides' arrest in Nov. 1837 (see n. 15 above), Polyzoïdes discredited himself completely with Lyons (20 Nov. 1837, no. 133, FO 32.72).

[66] Concerning Otho's attempt to have Lyons recalled, see Lyons to Palmerston, Athens, 31 Jan. 1838, "Separate and Confidential," FO 32.76. Concerning the conflict between Otho and Lyons, Bower and Bolitho wrote (*Otho I*, p. 81): "The King was slow and hesitating, whereas Lyons was hasty and impetuous. Added to this was the difference in age and tradition. Otho was a German surrounded by German advisers. Lyons was a British Naval officer brought up to command. He was unaccustomed to opposition, and he was a fervent admirer of Palmerston's policy of British domination in Europe. This he was prepared to support to the utmost of his ability. Otho's education had given him a distaste for Constitutional Government." See also Otho to Ludwig, 13 Nov. 1837, as quoted by Bower and Bolitho, *op.cit.*, p. 102.

[67] Concerning the deliberations and Russian and French warnings, see Driault and Lhéritier, *Histoire*, II, 159-62. The English loan, sanctioned by the British government to strengthen Armansperg's position in Greece, did not arrive until the end of October 1837 (Lyons to Palmerston, Athens, 26 Oct. 1837, no. 115, FO 32.72).

[68] On Nesselrode's statement, see Lyons to Palmerston, Athens, 2 Mar. 1837, FO 32.58. On Rudhart's reminder to Otho, see Lyons to Palmerston, Athens, 7 Dec. 1837, no. 142, FO 32.72. On the Russian loan, see Driault and Lhéritier, *Histoire*, II, 177, and T. N. Pipineles, *He Monarchia en Helladi 1833-1843* [*The Monarchy in Greece 1833-1843*] (Athens, 1942), p. 270.

lowed Rudhart's previous strategy—to isolate Lyons by winning over France as junior partner of Russia in support of his regime. Rudhart would have liked to recall Kolettes from Paris, but Otho adamantly refused. Instead, Rudhart enticed Lagrené by appointing the "French" Karatzas to the Council of State, then the "French" Botases as minister of the economy and the "French" Karakatsanes as second in command there. Otho satisfied the French legation by inviting Regny back to Greece as head of the control board. Momentarily at least, France remained hopeful that Regny would bring some order into Greek finances. During most of the period 1838-39, the government remained stable because it enjoyed the joint support of Lagrené and Catacazy.[69]

Otho's reasons for giving preponderance in administration to the Napist party were not based entirely on considerations of foreign policy. The domestic situation, especially the role of the "Russian" party in it, suggests other motives which seem highly probable but for which there is no direct evidence. By 1837 Otho probably realized that the popular support of the "Russian" party exceeded all calculations of previous regimes. By courting it, he might enhance his own popularity and secure the support of the "middling classes" which, though small, seemed concentrated in the "Russian" party. He also wished to relax, without repudiating or abandoning, the unpopular ecclesiastical settlement of the first regency. No administration would more gladly introduce such relaxation than a "Russian" one. Moreover, it only accorded with the policy of successive rather than simultaneous balance of parties to reverse the scales now in favor of the "Russian" party and compensate it for its past oppression. Finally, the "Russian" party was least identified with constitutionalism.[70]

3. THE POLICIES AND POLITICS OF ROYAL ADMINISTRATION

The "Russian" administration of 1838-39 was second only to that of the first regency in its vigor and determination. Like the first regency, it was hailed by the public as a new possibility for healing public ills. Like the first regency, too, it enjoyed dedicated and determined leadership—that of Otho and his minister of interior Glarakes. Otho momentarily possessed

[69] On Rudhart's strategy, see Lyons to Palmerston, Athens, 29 Dec. 1837, no. 153, FO 32.72, and 24 May 1838, no. 86, FO 32.77. On Rudhart's preference for Kolettes, see Lyons to Palmerston, Athens, 24 July 1837, no. 66, FO 32.70, and Driault and Lhéritier, *Histoire*, II, 166. On the securing of French support through the appointment of Karatzas, see Lyons to Palmerston, Athens, 20 Sept. 1837, no. 96, FO 32.71; through the appointment of Botases and Karakatsanes, see 25 Sept. 1837, no. 99, FO 32.71. Concerning the appointment of Regny, see n. 103 below.

[70] On the popular support of the "Russian" party and its representation of the "middling classes," see n. 44 above. On the Crown's desire to relax the previous ecclesiastical policy, see n. 90 below. As indication of the Russian party's temporary espousal of absolutism, see the opening issues (e.g. 25 Sept. and 2 Oct. 1838*o.s.*) of *Aiōn*, which took as its motto, "Religion, Fatherland, and King."

the confidence that came from having triumphed over both Lyons and Rudhart and having won full powers to carry out his program. Glarakes was especially noted for his energy.

But the task now was different from and harder than that of the first regency. At the beginning of 1833, conditions had been so bad that they could only get better. Now, at the beginning of 1838, much had been accomplished even though much remained to be done, and the rate of improvement had naturally slowed down. The dramatic work of establishing institutions was over and the credit had gone to others. The task now was the much more routine one of making the institutions work more effectively. This task was essentially one of administration, where the increment of improvement was likely to be too small to impress an impatient public.

This new government addressed itself to four major objectives: (1) ending the annual budget deficits, (2) promoting public security, (3) maintaining a balance between liberals and conservatives on religious matters, and (4) further consolidating the throne. The first objective was clearly the most urgent because budget deficits made Greece dependent on the powers for additional loans and hence subject to foreign interference. Toward this end, the government tried simplifying the administration to cut down expenses and improving tax-collecting to increase revenue.[71] The second goal involved a concerted drive to end brigandage; the third, acquiescence in greater ecclesiastical conservatism; and the fourth, continued efforts to increase the "middling classes" and to weaken the parties.

There are two significant features about the implementation of this program, one concerning the king and one concerning Glarakes. Glarakes implemented the program in such a way as to promote his party's advantage. The king's acquiescence in the partisan implementation of his program reflects his willingness to use the party system in order to realize his objectives. In short, Glarakes made politics out of policy, and Otho resorted to politics in order to effect policy. But the price for such utilization of a party or for giving it some freedom of action was the outbreak of renewed party strife, which in some provinces looked more like incipient civil war. In 1840 Lyons reported, "The provinces are torn asunder by party spirit engendered by Glarakes and kept alive by his creatures."[72]

Policy and politics can best be considered in terms of: (1) provincial affairs, (2) ecclesiastical affairs, and (3) financial affairs. The balance

[71] Lyons to Palmerston, Athens, 19 July 1838, no. 121, FO 32.77. See also n. 103 below.

[72] Lyons to Palmerston, 12 June 1840, no. 77, FO 32.97; also 2 July 1841, no. 81, FO 32.98: ". . . Messenia, where the Constitutionalists had been driven almost to desperation by the governor, Yanco Soutzo, creature of Glarakes. . . ." Gennaios Kolokotrones ([Memoirs II], p. 83) reports that party strife became intensified by Glarakes' appointment to the cabinet and his own closeness to the king.

between policy and politics was different for each area. The "Russian" party exercised widespread influence in the first, some in the second, and virtually none in the third. The king allowed the "Russian" party considerable leeway in the first, overruled it at several points in the second, and excluded it completely from the third.

Provincial Affairs

George Glarakes came to his new responsibilities at the end of 1837 with four years' experience in provincial administration. His partisan activities as nomarch of Patras (1833-36) had provoked Armansperg into dismissing him. In his subsequent post as governor of Messenia, he had galvanized what *Athēna* called a dead party. Although the liberal pro-British *Athēna* became his severest critic, it expressed respect for his devotion to principle above personal advantage, and for his sincerity and vigor. But it condemned "his fanatical devotion to his system and his exclusive behavior." On his assumption of office, there was every reason to expect that he would press the advantage of his party, and that is exactly what happened.[73] Enjoying two full years in power and the confidence of the king, he and his party came to dominate the provincial administration. He did this (1) by securing a majority of gubernatorial posts for his followers and by manipulating local elections through them; (2) by artificially attempting to create a "popular movement" called fusionism; and (3) by organizing a drive against brigandage which increased administrative at the expense of judicial action.

As minister of the interior, Glarakes had the right to invalidate mayoralty elections in the large demes. In conjunction with the Crown he could pass over the mayoralty candidate with the most votes for one of the other two who might be of his party. He could influence mayoralty elections in his party's favor negatively by refusing to heed the complaints of local persons concerning the way that elections were run. In the case of the smaller demes, the governor exercised the same powers, and since the majority of governors was appointed by the minister of the interior from his own party, they usually supported the minister of the interior in his partisan objectives. It was not mere coincidence, therefore, that during the tenure of Glarakes the majority of governors and local authorities belonged to the Napist party.[74]

[73] Lyons to Palmerston, Athens, 24 Mar. 1836, no. 15, FO 32.58 (dismissal from Patras nomarchy). *Athēna*, 24 Aug. 1838o.s., and 25 June 1838o.s. See also Lyons to Palmerston, Athens, 19 Dec. 1837, no. 146, FO 32.76.

[74] See the law concerning the establishment of demes, 27 Dec./8 Jan. 1834 [*Government Gazette*], no. 3, 10/22 Jan. 1834, or *Athēna*, 14 Apr. 1841o.s., reiterating the point that the minister of interior had the right to validate or invalidate elections. Lyons (to Palmerston, Athens, 24 Aug. 1837, no. 77, FO 32.71) cites a case where a Napist (Antonopoulos) with seventeen votes was appointed mayor of Nauplion by the ministry of interior, rather than a Constitutionalist with twenty-seven. Piscatory, Athens, 20 Aug. 1841 (5th report), *L'Hellénisme Contemporain*, IX, 415.

The reorganization of provincial administration, ostensibly for economic reasons, gave Glarakes a chance to place his dependents into key gubernatorial posts. In general he seems to have concentrated his greatest efforts on areas where Napism languished or had never taken hold. He named Tompakakes as governor of Vonitsa and Constantine Rados as governor of Mesolongi to give weight to Napist opinion in these "English" strongholds. To cut into the overwhelming influence of the Notaras primate family in Corinth, Glarakes named a Napist governor who supported "unknown" men and employed all means to get them elected in the demes. Through Panagiotes Anagnostopoulos, governor of Euboea, Glarakes tried to form a party by backing his "creatures" in demotic elections against the prevailing influence of the "French" Adam Doukas and Nicholas Kriezotes.[75]

Most probably the "unknown men" of Corinth and the "creatures" of Anagnostopoulos were small landholders whose interests conflicted with such landed magnates as Notaras and Kriezotes. If so, Glarakes was exploiting the social conflict between economic groups, a conflict cited by Piscatory for Euboea at least, in order to further his party's interests. The king certainly knew what was going on. That he permitted Glarakes to support small landholders against the primate-captain groups probably reflects a decision to rely on party channels in order to accomplish what neither statutory provision nor electoral machinery had been able to do—strengthen the middling classes against the primates and captains. Like Armansperg in a different connection, the king was capitulating to the parties to the extent that he was partially working through them for the realization of his program.[76]

Yet the interesting feature of these attempts to build up the party from above is how few were successful and how ephemeral was the success of these few. Local organizations and family influences were often too strong for governors and ministers of the interior, as was the case in Euboea, Western Rumely, and Corinth. For instance, in Patras, although the "French" Kalamogdartes was transferred away from his native province in 1836, by 1841 his son Antonaki Kalamogdartes had taken over the

[75] According to Lyons (to Palmerston, Athens, 19 July 1838, no. 121, FO 32.77), "The ostensible object of the new distribution of provinces is saving of not quite £3,000 a year; but the real object obtained by the Napist ministry is the removal of some of Tricoupes' friends to insignificant places and the dismissal of others." *Athēna* (25 June 1838*o.s.*) also complained that the reorganization gave Glarakes a chance to plant "men of his system" in all but five or six of the gubernatorial posts. See the decree of 22 June/4 July 1838 [*Government Gazette*]. See also Piscatory, Athens, 6 Sept. 1841 (7th report), *L'Hellénisme Contemporain*, ix, 429 (Anagnostopoulos), 433 (Tompakakes and Rados), 441 (Notaras); also Patras, 12 July 1841 (3rd report), ix, 347 (Anagnostopoulos).

[76] On large vs. small landholders, see Piscatory, Chalcis, 25 June 1841 (2nd report), *L'Hellénisme Contemporain*, ix, 346.

reins of the local party and "created" (Piscatory should probably have said "reestablished and expanded") a serious influence over the peasants, the old military men, and a part of the primates.[77]

In June 1837, the recently revived *Sōtēr* announced and hailed the "rise" of a "movement" which it called *fusionism* (*synchōneusis*). Fusionism derived its name from its objective of fusing all parties into a single movement that acknowledged no other leader but the king and dedicated itself to the goal of national unity. It was a kind of party to end all parties by incorporating them all.[78]

For the rest of the year 1837 and most of 1838, *Sōtēr* and the semiofficial *Ho Hellēnikos Tachydromos*, which favored fusionism, gave the "movement" all the publicity they could. They represented it as a grassroots movement which had originated in the provinces. They published eulogizing letters allegedly written by individuals from all parts of Greece. They published a series of manifestos in behalf of fusionism, officially drawn up by the demotic councils from various provinces. They reported the despatch of occasional delegations to attest to the king personally their dedication to fusionism. Without clarifying whether they meant the principle or the actual movement, they declared that the king had espoused fusionism as the only way for the nation and the throne to prosper. From an exclusive reading of these two newspapers, one would think that Greece was undergoing a popular groundswell of proabsolutist, antiparty, monarchical sentiment—the kind of spontaneous union between people and king against selfish oligarchy that the king had privately expressed as his ardent hope.[79]

Athēna responded to this press campaign with vigorous and persistent denunciations. At the beginning, it treated fusionism as a kind of movement and limited its criticism to questions of its necessity and desirability. It denied that the nation was still torn and endangered by partisan strife. It insisted that parties were necessary so long as man's nature prompted him to disagree with others. It warned that, since movements tended to split up eventually, the king would end up as the head of a party instead of the undisputed national leader, as he now was. It intimated that *Ho Hellēnikos Tachydromos'* support of the movement did not necessarily reflect official approval.[80] By 1838 *Athēna* was writing differently. Fusionism, it alleged, was nothing more than a fiction by means of which a few unprincipled Napists and renegade Constitutionalists were trying to work

[77] Piscatory, Athens, 6 Sept. 1841 (7th report), *ibid.*, ix, 439-40.

[78] *Sōtēr*, 17/29 June 1837. Also *Athēna*'s coverage of news in *Sōtēr*, 28 June, 7 July 1837*o.s.*

[79] *Sōtēr*, 17/29 July, 8/20 July, 18/30 July 1838; 20 Jan./1 Feb., 3/15 Feb., 12/24 May, 21 July/2 Aug. 1838. Also *Ho Hellēnikos Tachydromos*, 6/18 Jan., 13/25 Jan. 1838, and *Athēna*, 2 Mar. 1838*o.s.*

[80] *Athēna*, 7 July 1837, 11 July 1837, 15 Jan. 1838, all *o.s.*

their way into office. "Napo-fusionism" was merely a faction—antinational, laughable, unimportant, completely without popular support.[81]

The phenomenon of fusionism is still shrouded in mystery. No history of the period has ever treated it. Besides the current newspapers, only scanty references in the correspondence of Piscatory and Manoles Argyropoulos give any information. According to Piscatory, a French philhellene named Graillard originated the idea. Skouphos and Schinas spearheaded the drive through *Sōtēr*, which the former edited. Apparently the renegade Constitutionalists, to whom *Athēna* referred, were these former members of the "French" party. In February 1838, Argyropoulos mentioned fusionism only to ask a question about it. What was the purpose of digging up the explosive subject of parties? he asked. To prevent the return of the party leaders from honorary exile (one of them, Trikoupes, was at that very moment on his way back to Greece)? Two months later Argyropoulos wrote that the center of fusionism was the Russian embassy. Its ostensible director, he said, was Skouphos, but its real director was Lehmaier, the Bavarian editor of *Ho Hellēnikos Tachydromos* who had close contact with the court.[82]

It seems safe to assume that both Otho and Glarakes gave their support to the "movement." The succession of manifestos drawn up individually by demotic councils in behalf of fusionism necessitated some sort of organized activity, which could not have taken place without the cooperation of the minister of the interior and the acquiescence of the king. Most probably, fusionism was a front organization for the Napist party, designed during 1837 to gain access to office by winning royal favor and intended thereafter to consolidate both royal and Napist strength in the provinces. Apparently, fusionism's prominent "French" members simply defected, as individuals, from the "French" to the Napist party and used their "French" past to make the "movement" look like a partial fusion of the "French" and the "Russian" parties.

In spite of what *Athēna* wrote, fusionism probably did enjoy some popular support—from Napists if from nobody else. Its rather well-organized activities reflected the vigor and thoroughness which characterized Glarakes. The "movement" is significant as an attempt to use paternalism or even absolutism as a political slogan or an instrument of popular appeal. It shows how conservatives attempted to use "liberal" institutions like the municipal councils for illiberal purposes, and how for party purposes they tried to turn mere administrative organs into mouthpieces of "public opinion." It also suggests that, once more, the king was acquiescing in a party maneuver that advanced his ultimate objective to unite all groups around the throne.

[81] *Athēna*, 2 Mar. 1838, 7 June 1838, 29 Oct. 1838, all *o.s.*

[82] Piscatory, Athens, 6 Sept. 1841 (7th report), *L'Hellénisme Contemporain*, IX, 446 (Schinas), 446-47 (Skouphos), and 447 (Graillard). M. Argyropoulos to Mavrokordatos, Pera, 2/14 Feb. 1838, no. 5482, and 29 Mar./10 Apr. 1838, no. 5500, Vol. 20 (1837-40), Mavrokordatos Archive.

Another area in which Glarakes' administration manifested alarming vigor was the government program to curb and suppress brigandage. The last section of this chapter will deal with the way in which a political opposition organized and utilized this brigandage to undermine the existing government. What is of concern here is the way that Glarakes' anti-brigand program strengthened his party and intensified party strife in the provinces.

The fundamental decree regulating the state's attempt to end brigandage belonged to the end of the Armansperg period.[83] It displayed no lack of understanding of what gave tenacity to the system. The government knew that—in Rumely at any rate—the large nomadic population of shepherds often served as accomplices or protectors of the brigands. It understood that helpless peasants often aided the brigand only to escape his wrath and that local authorities seldom exercised the vigilance necessary to protect all their citizens.[84]

As a result, this decree, by adopting the principle of collective responsibility, sought to stimulate local initiative in order to meet the brigand problem. All citizens were required to go in pursuit of the brigands as a type of unpaid militia whenever the call went out. The entire deme had to compensate the victim of brigandage or his survivors, in case of murder, by levying each time a direct tax on each citizen. In turn the deme enjoyed the right of confiscating the property of the guilty party, his family, or the guarantor (with annual income of at least 200 drachmas). The decree limited the chances for abuse by requiring three-fourths of a demotic council's voting membership to approve a list of persons suspected as potential brigands and permitting appeal by a suspected party to the provincial governor. It separated executive from judicial authority by letting the courts, through due process of law, decide claims for financial satisfaction and questions of guilt.

[83] Decree concerning the responsibility of the demes for acts of brigandage committed within their jurisdictional limits, 10/22 Nov. 1836 [Government Gazette], no. 64, 13 Nov. 1836o.s.

[84] After all, Armansperg commissioned Gordon in the summer of 1835 to march against the brigands of Rumely and report back on conditions there, and certainly Gordon reported back to the government the findings which Finlay records in his Journal 1835 (MSS), Finlay Papers: "It seems clear that the shepherds are too often connected with robbers—this arises in part from that opposition of interests & consequent hatred which may be observed in Greece between the peasant & the shepherd. Also from the circumstances of most of the shepherds of this part of Greece being from the Turkish provinces & having therefore frequent relationship with the robbers or else being afraid of the vengeance of the robbers not only now but when they return to their native villages" (21 July 1835).

"These National guards responsible for guarding against brigandage are enrolled by the civil authorities & paid by the villages according to a certain agreed on rate of pay during 3 months of this year & in some cases for six months these troops were regularly paid but the villages were in most cases unwilling & in many unable to continue their payment & accordingly the force has been completely dissolved" ("Observations on the state of northern Greece," p. 15).

The decree received a trial run until the end of 1838. It burdened the demes beyond their resources, it was unable to amass sufficient evidence to satisfy the requirements of law, and hence it diminished the incidence of brigandage little if at all. Still, the government renewed it for another year (1839).[85]

In the meantime, the government experimented with other methods to handle the problem. In August 1838, Païkos, minister of justice, proposed the establishment of special military courts to handle cases of brigandage. The proposal stemmed from the fact that the requirements of the regular judicial process seldom permitted a conviction. Even though the Council of State refused to sanction the proposal, on 17 November 1838 a royal decree authorized the establishment of special military courts in certain Peloponnesian provinces (Gortynia, Kynaithe, Elis, Messenia, and Lacedemonia). In addition, the government tried to use a series of mobile military units (metavatika) for preventive action, but dissolved them in 1839 because their abuses constituted a source of oppression to the peasants.[86]

Glarakes began to toy with the idea of reinstituting something like the pre-Revolutionary system of kapoi or armatoloi as a substitute for mobile units. Demes would hire brigands to pursue other brigands. This method would partially eliminate one of the causes of brigandage—insufficient means of livelihood—and would benefit by the hired brigand's inside knowledge of the system. Presumably for the purpose of discussing this experimental measure and its enactment, Glarakes authorized a few regional meetings of governors, mayors, and demotic councilors, and Gennaios Kolokotrones made a tour during which he attended some of them. Such meetings as those at Gortynia in Arcadia and Pedema in Messenia ostensibly reflected some attempt at real deliberation and collaboration among officials at all levels of the provincial administration. But at the time and a little later, in the light of the Philorthodox plot, some saw these meetings as conspiratorial sessions of the Napist party.[87]

[85] Decree for the prolongation of the validity of the decree concerning the responsibility of demes for the commission of brigand acts, 31 Dec. 1838/12 Jan. 1839 [Government Gazette], no. 1, 4 Jan. 1839o.s.

[86] Athēna, 31 Aug. 1838o.s. (Païkos' proposal and Council of State's rejection); 23 Nov. 1838o.s. (institution of some ad hoc courts by decree of 17 Nov. 1838o.s.); Aiōn, 26 Feb. 1839o.s., 23 Aug. 1839o.s. (on mobile units and their abuses).

[87] Aiōn (20 Aug. 1839o.s.) reported the Gortynia meeting: "The governor of Gortynia invited all the mayors and some demotic councilors to appear in the provincial capital on 15 August. The purpose of this assembly is undisclosed, but on that day Colonel John Kolokotrones is awaited." In the following issue (23 Aug. 1839o.s.), Aiōn described the purpose of the Gortynia meeting as that of implementing Glarakes' new program of curbing brigandage. Athēna (30 Aug. 1839o.s.) suspiciously reported the Pedema meeting: "They wrote us from Messenia that Gennaios Kolokotrones reached Pedema and was immediately met by Governor Soutsos, attorney general Typaldos, and Colonel of the fortress Giannouses, Nicholas Pierakos, and Judge Perotes. All mayors are invited to convene; the purpose of such an assemblage is unknown."

Glarakes introduced another innovation through an encyclical, dated 27 September 1839, to all his governors. This one provided for the removal of family heads suspected of harboring brigands. Glarakes apparently wished to employ administrative measures, through his governors, rather than the judicial process over whose officials he enjoyed no personal control.[88]

Aiōn, which by this time had joined the political opposition, pointed up the partisan purposes for which these devices might be used. The proposed kapoi system, it said, would give demotic authorities a chance to give succor to their clients by offering them employment. The encyclical of 27 September put tremendous powers in the hands of the governors who could punish without authorization of the courts.[89]

These criticisms reveal the dilemma in which the king found himself. An administration which provided checks against abuses failed miserably to curb or end brigandage, whereas an administration unchecked either by statutory limits on its jurisdiction or the balance of equal representation for all parties acquired alarmingly great powers that it could use for partisan purposes against its foes. To secure the order that went with the suppression of brigandage, the king had to devise methods which precipitated the disorder of party strife.

Ecclesiastical Affairs

On his assumption of power, the king fell heir to four religious issues: (1) monasticism, (2) autocephaly, (3) caesaropapism, and (4) toleration. He dispensed with the first by quietly allowing the statutory provisions of dissolution, after the initial phase, to go unenforced. As early as 1835, Ludwig, perhaps under Russian pressure, advised Otho to allow the remaining monasteries to regain some of their alienated goods and start receiving novices again. "Let the existing monasteries take novices and regain their property. Do it, in spite of Armansperg. You are the ruler, not he," wrote Ludwig to Otho on the eve of Otho's accession. *Aiōn* announced in March 1839 that 149 monasteries still remained, with a total of 1,230 monks and 1,161 servants residing in them.[90]

[88] Instruction of the minister of interior to the governors for the removal of heads of families suspected of harboring brigands, published by *Aiōn*, 1 Oct. 1839*o.s.* It was not published in [*Government Gazette*]. See lead article in *Athēna*, 7 Oct. 1839*o.s.*, in criticism of it.

[89] *Aiōn's* criticisms appear in its issues of 23 Aug. 1839*o.s.* (on kapoi system), and 5 Oct. 1839*o.s.* (on the encyclical of 27 September). Lyons (Athens, 12 June 1840, no. 77, FO 32.97) wrote Palmerston about these measures as "the system by which Glarakes endeavoured to wield political power by means of apparently administrative measures" and cited political persecution as "an effect of the Royal Ordinance for the deportation of families of robbers."

[90] As quoted by J. M. von Söltl, *Ludwig I König von Bayern und Graf von Armansperg* (Nordlingen, 1886), p. 67. According to *Aiōn* (1 Mar. 1839*o.s.*), 72 were in the Peloponnesos, 32 in Rumely, and 45 in Mane. It added that the statutory minimum of six months, for the continued existence of a monastery, was beginning to lapse.

311

The issue of religious toleration arose first in connection with the unsolicited presence of American and British Protestant missionaries in Greece since 1829. The activities of these missionaries fell into three categories—teaching in their own missionary schools, circulating books translated and published by missionary societies, and preaching as much as popular prejudice would permit. As a part of their enterprise in Greece, the missionaries commissioned Neophytos Vamvas, a well-educated disciple of Koraes, to translate the Bible into modern Greek for the religious enlightenment of the average Greek, who could not understand the Septuagint and Koine Greek.

In principle, both liberals and conservatives supported religious toleration and denounced attempts at proselytism. Yet the conservatives denounced the missionaries, while the liberals staunchly defended them. The liberals argued that the missionaries had come as educators, not as proselytizers. So long as the kingdom could not meet all of its educational needs, only folly would stand in the way of utilizing missionary schools and books. For the more doctrinaire liberals, defense of the missionaries was a duty imposed by the precepts of the liberal creed; for the more pragmatic, a necessary act to impress enlightened Europe.

The conservatives believed in toleration to the extent of recognizing the right of private worship in Greece by non-Orthodox foreigners, but they would countenance no Western attempts at proselytism. For them, missionary schools and books were disguised means of undermining the Orthodox faith. To the assertions of missionaries that they were trying to reform Orthodoxy in some of its "externals," such as "icon-worship," veneration of the Virgin and saints, the clergy replied that externals and internals, form and essence, were inseparable, that to change one iota was to damage the whole. Moreover, they condemned translations of scripture as unwarranted tampering with holy writ.[91]

Even if the missionaries had never come to Greece, however, the question of religious toleration would probably have arisen because of the more basic cultural conflict that the Westernization process had precipitated. With the influx of foreigners during and after the Revolution, mixed marriages were bound to take place. A source of great scandal were the several cases of marriages contracted within the canonically forbidden degrees of kinship (siblings of one family marrying siblings of another). Some heresy was bound to occur among the Western-

[91] See the unpublished monograph by John Petropulos, "American Missionary Activity in Greece, 1830-69"; also P. E. Shaw, *American Contacts with the Eastern Churches 1820-1870* (Chicago, 1937), passim.; *Aiōn*, 30 Oct. 1838o.s., on the occasion of the establishment of two missionary schools in Laconia, warning the missionaries to teach only; and Tryphon E. Evangelides, *Historia tou Othonos, Basileos tes Hellados (1832-1862)* [*History of Otho, King of Greece*] (Athens, 1893), p. 174. Concerning the polemical tract warfare engaged in by Vamvas and Oikonomos on the issue of translated scriptures, see Frazee, "Orthodox Church" [unpubl. doct. diss.], pp. 247-51.

educated. On the other hand, the conservatives were not willing to countenance religious deviation on the part of the Greeks. They believed the clergy responsible for detecting such deviation and the state bound to assist the clergy with punitive means if necessary.[92]

The issues of autocephaly and caesaropapism, already dealt with in Chapter IV, were not only inseparable from each other, but tied up with the issue of religious toleration as well. For instance, the efforts of clergymen to dissuade parents from sending their children to missionary schools by refusing to grant them communion roused the wrath of liberals. *Athēna* used the occasion to charge some of the clergy with wishing "to put church above state, and king under the church." The government's toleration of missionary schools and publications, however, merely confirmed conservative suspicions about the incapability of the secular arm to rule an Orthodox state. The patriarch of Constantinople in 1836 issued an encyclical forbidding the Orthodox believer to attend missionary schools or read missionary literature. Conservatives welcomed the act as a necessary bit of assistance and read the encyclical in church in Greece, even though without the requisite governmental permission. Liberals, on the other hand, cited this as unauthorized interference by a foreign potentate and a thrust at the system of autocephaly.[93]

As one might expect, the various aspects of the religious problem became entangled with party and power rivalries. Pharmakides, the author of the original church charter and acknowledged leader of the liberal clergymen, belonged to the "English" party, while Oikonomos, the chief exponent of religious conservatism, was clearly a member of the "Russian" party. The pro-English *Athēna* and the pro-Russian *Aiōn*, by keeping the various issues before the public, identified the opposing positions with the "English" and "Russian" parties. Moreover, the protecting powers took sides for political reasons. On the question of religious tolera-

[92] As a kind of epilogue to his account of the uncanonical marriages of Armansperg's two daughters to the two Katakouzenos brothers, Makrygiannes ([*Memoirs*], II, 82) wrote: "And that example was followed by other Greeks, who married in the same fashion." He was not simply being rhetorical. In 1837 (Lyons to Palmerston, Athens, 20 Sept. 1837, no. 96, FO 32.71) the Bishop of Attica excommunicated a young man for marrying the sister of his brother's wife.

The frequence of simple intermarriages between Greek Orthodox and non-Orthodox is evident from the promulgation of a synodal decree forbidding such Greek intermarriages with Catholics and Protestants (Lyons to Palmerston, Athens, 7 Dec. 1837, no. 140, FO 32.72).

A celebrated case of a marriage that was both uncanonical and mixed was that of Alexander Rangabe, the young poet, to Caroline Skene, a Scottish young lady whose brother had already married Rangabe's sister. As a result of the marriage, Rangabe was dismissed from his post in the ministry of religion-education (see Alexander Rangabe [*Memoirs*], II, 103-106).

[93] *Athēna*, 7 June 1838*o.s.*, and a lead article, entitled "Germanos and the intrigues of some of our clergy," 5 Apr. 1839*o.s.*; Lyons to Palmerston, Athens, 29 May 1836, no. 34, and 28 July 1836, no. 43, FO 32.59.

tion, the English legation supported the missionaries, while the Russian legation supported the conservative Greek clergy. On the issue of auto-cephaly, both England and France firmly supported the separation of churches, lest Russia, through its influence with the patriarchate, exercise a special influence in Greece. In 1839 the French government expressed its staunch espousal of autocephaly in Greece to the Greek government through the following despatch to Lagrené:

> Perhaps in 1833 we feared that the separation of the two churches was imprudent and immature; but the attempt has succeeded; the Greek national church has existed for six years, perfectly independent of the patriarch of Constantinople, without schism, without religious discords; and now we will consider all modification of this independence as re-lated to projects of political influence which it is within our right and interest to combat as well as within the right and interest of Greece to reject.

Russia, on the other hand, remained opposed to the settlement of 1833 from the very beginning.[94]

In the midst of this embittered religious conflict stood the Crown, faced with one of its thorniest problems. Bitter experience had shown how explosive the issues were. Dissolution of the monasteries was one of the causes behind the Mane and Messenian revolts of 1834 and the Acar-nanian revolt of 1836. Apparently spontaneous popular outbursts against English and American missionaries stationed in Syros (1836) raised the spectre of public disorders if too liberal a course were followed.[95]

Since the king was non-Orthodox, there was always reason to be anxious lest the desire to replace Otho with an Orthodox king spread from the extremist group of Napists to others as well. The vulnerability of the king as a Catholic is revealed by the incident of the antimissionary Peloponnesian tour in 1836 of Germanos who, "finding he could not stir up the people by denouncing the Protestants, went a step further and declared that the King wishes to make them Catholics. At last his lan-guage became so violent that the provincial authorities arrested him and

[94] As quoted by Driault and Lhéritier, *Histoire*, ɪɪ, 193-94. On Pharmakides, see Piscatory, Athens, 6 Sept. 1841 (7th report), *L'Hellénisme Contemporain*, ɪx, 444; on Oikonomos, see for instance Makrygiannes [*Memoirs*], ɪɪ, 112.

Russia and Britain actually intervened unofficially. The second secretary of the Russian legation (Leles) actually accompanied Germanos on a tour of the Pelopon-nesos and preached against Protestant heretics (see Lyons to Palmerston, Athens, 29 Oct. 1836, no. 59, FO 32.60, and n. 53 above). Because of the intervention of Griffiths, secretary of the British legation, the government refused its sanction for a synodal circular condemning the English and American missionary schools and for-bidding parents to let their children attend (see Lyons to Palmerston, Athens, 17 Jan. 1838, no. 13, FO 32.76).

[95] On the religious issue as a contributing factor in revolts, see Chap. IV, p. 210, and Chap. V, pp. 221-22 and 262, above. On the Syros riots, see Lyons to Palmerston, Athens, 29 May 1836, no. 34, and 28 July 1836, no. 43, FO 32.59.

he was escorted by the gendarmes to Athens" and subsequently ordered to confinement in a monastery in the island of Skiathos.[96]

On the other hand, the king could not allow the conservatives so much leeway as to provoke the Greek liberal press, discredit the country in Western Europe, or alarm France and Britain about the possibility of renouncing autocephaly. To steer clear of both Scylla and Charybdis, the Crown devised the method of allowing the Napist party to control both the ministry of religious affairs and the holy synod, while reserving to itself, through the caesaropapist system, veto power on all synodal acts. For instance, Otho admitted in 1839 that he had reappointed a Napist bishop (Dionysios of Kynouria) as president of the holy synod in order to please Russia but promised that he "would be suspicious of all synodal proposals and not sanction any without consulting the Council of State or the cabinet." He thus hoped to curb any conservative excesses.[97]

From July 1837, when the conservatives gained a majority, the holy synod began to take aggressive measures in behalf of conservatism. Many of these were constructive attempts to foster religious education, such as the appointment of special preachers to various parts of Greece. But many were prescriptive. Late in 1837 Otho gave his consent to a synodal decision forbidding intermarriages between Orthodox and non-Orthodox. Only a firm protest from Griffiths, secretary of the British legation, prevented Otho early in 1838 from confirming a synodal circular condemning the missionary schools.[98]

In 1839, two acts of the holy synod raised the issue of autocephaly again. It requested Holy Chrism from the patriarch of Constantinople for the anointment of new bishops. It also secured the removal of Pharmakides as secretary general of the holy synod and his appointment as professor of literature, not theology, at the recently established national university. Although the first act accorded with canonical procedure,

[96] Lyons to Palmerston, Athens, 31 Dec. 1836, no. 69, FO 32.60. See also an apologia by Germanos in *Athēna*, 9 Dec. 1836 o.s. A second incident revealing the king's vulnerability relates to Otho's assembling of the holy synod, on 15/27 Feb. 1837, and promising that he would raise his children in the Greek faith (Lyons to Palmerston, Athens, 4 Mar. 1837, no. 22, FO 32.69).

[97] Lyons to Palmerston, Athens, 9 Jan. 1839, no. 4, FO 32.85.

[98] *Athēna* (20 July 1838 o.s.) reported a decree of 19 July 1838, which appointed five—two for the Peloponnesos, two for Rumely, and one for the Islands. Glarakes reputedly got his candidates appointed: Joseph Vyzantios, Kallinikos Kastorches, Daniel Georgopoulos, Kallinikos Iasos, and the monk Elias. On the decree forbidding intermarriages, see Lyons to Palmerston, Athens, 7 Dec. 1837, no. 140, FO 32.72, and Driault and Lhéritier, *Histoire*, ii, 194. On Griffith's intervention, see Lyons to Palmerston, Athens, 17 Jan. 1838, no. 13, FO 32.76.

The shift of church policy, marked by its more conservative orientation, was interpreted in some quarters as Rudhart's attempt to increase the powers of the clergy (Lyons to Palmerston, Athens, 22 May 1837, no. 55, FO 32.70) or as his attempts to make the church subservient to the patriarch of Constantinople (Lyons to Palmerston, Athens, 30 Aug. 1837, no. 85, FO 32.71).

liberals interpreted it as an informal recognition of the primacy of the patriarchate. The second act was interpreted as a disavowal of the settlement of 1833 because Pharmakides had been one of the authors of separation. It was also considered a further recognition of patriarchal authority because the patriarch had previously urged the dismissal of Pharmakides. One need only check the official correspondence of the British and French to appreciate the alarm which these acts caused.[99]

A third incident in 1839 only highlighted the religious issue even more. Learned, educated, humane, morally upright, and courageous, the cleric Kaïres refused the perquisites of public office for the quiet life of teaching at an orphanage which he himself established from private subscriptions in his native island of Andros in 1835. As Oikonomos represented the Koraes disciple who had turned conservative with age, Kaïres represented the other extreme—the Western-educated disciple whose liberalism had passed beyond Orthodoxy into a kind of theosophy. As he himself admitted privately, he had his own esoteric cult, complete with special ceremonies, hymns, and prayers. And most probably he was teaching his pupils many of his non-Orthodox doctrines. Like Oikonomos, he lacked his master's sense of measure and practicality. But he used his dedication or fanaticism in behalf of the liberal principle of a free conscience and was unyielding in its defense.[100]

On 10 July 1839 the holy synod invited him to make his confession of faith. After he refused this invitation and ignored a second one, the government commissioned Constantine Kanares, celebrated naval hero and Napist, to sail to Andros, arrest Kaïres, and bring him to Athens for questioning. By now the case had gained notoriety through the press. The arrest precipitated much public commotion, especially in Andros, where Kaïres had many sympathizers. The conservatives pressed for a quick condemnation. They sounded the alarm that Orthodoxy was being betrayed from within, and the masses responded with fear and excitement to evidence of heresy within the clergy itself. By implication the conservatives attributed such "undermining" of Orthodoxy to the caesaropapist system and the lack of government vigilance. The liberals, on the

[99] Lyons to Palmerston, Athens, 9 Jan. 1839, no. 4, FO 32.85; Driault and Lhéritier, *Histoire*, II, 194-95; *Athēna*, 22 Nov. 1839*o.s.*; and Evangelides [*History*], pp. 176, 179.

[100] On the Kaïres incident, see Evangelides [*History*], pp. 174-76; K. D. Demaras, *Historia tes Neohellenikes Logotechnias* [*History of Modern Greek Literature*] (Athens, n.d.), 2nd edn., pp. 209, 211-13; Constantine Oikonomos, *Ta Sozomena Ekklesiastika Syngrammata* [*Collected Ecclesiastical Writings*], ed. Sophocles Oikonomos (Athens, 1864-66), II, 459-65; and Demetrios Paschales, [*Theophilos Kaïres*] (Athens, 1928). See also the contemporary writings: G. Athanasiou, *Ta kata Kaïren . . .* [*Acts against Kaïres, or the declaration of the truth*] (Athens, 1840); D. Gregoriades, *Hieros thriamvos . . .* [*Holy Triumph*] (Constantinople, 1840); Th. Kaïres, *Logos* [*Speech*] (Andros, 1839); *Ta Kaïreia . . .* [*Concerning the Kaïres Episode* from 'Aiōn'] (Syros, 1839); and *Ta Kata ton Th. Kaïren* [*Acts against Th. Kaïres, from 'Ho Hellēnikos Tachydromos'* (Athens, 1839). See also Frazee, "Orthodox Church" [unpubl. doct. diss.], 262-64.

other hand, thought the manner of Kaïres' arrest unduly harsh and un-warranted, in violation of the liberal creed, and damaging to Greek prestige in Europe. So enflamed did the situation become that the govern-ment postponed Kaïres' appearance before the synod until tempers cooled.[101]

At a meeting of the synod of 21 October 1839, Kaïres formally refused in principle to make the confession of faith. He accused that body of setting itself up as a medieval inquisition and objected to any violation of his freedom of conscience. Two days later the synod excommunicated him. Again the situation became so enflamed that the government inter-vened with a compromise solution which satisfied no one. It forced the synod to "postpone" the excommunication and persuaded it to send Kaïres to a monastery in Skiathos for repentance. So badly did the fanatical monks treat him that the government transferred him to Thera until 30 March 1842, when it granted his wish to go to England in exile. In a sense, the dismissal of Pharmakides represented a government con-cession to the conservatives, who accused him of being in league with Kaïres.[102]

Financial Affairs

Financial affairs posed the most urgent political problem of the royal government because the constant annual deficits exposed the Greek state to the persistent threat of foreign intervention in its internal affairs. Since the fall of Armansperg, Palmerston had continually pressed home his point that only constitutional government could remedy the Greek financial problem. France, on the other hand, contended that the Greeks needed an improved financial administration to facilitate tax-collecting and make the most of limited resources.

In 1837 the French government had proposed that the three powers each send a financial expert to examine the Greek situation and make recommendations for reform to the Greek government.[103] To ward off this collective intervention and to isolate Britain from France, the king acquiesced in a face-saving form of limited foreign interference, which is probably all that France expected to gain from its proposal anyway. At the recommendation of Jean-Gabriel Eynard, the Swiss philhellenic banker, Otho rehired Regny, the French financial expert who had re-signed because of his differences with the Armansperg administration.

[101] See, for instance, *Aiōn*'s lead "Theismos," 6 Aug. 1839*o.s.* and "Kaïreia," 12 Nov. 1839*o.s.*; *Athēna*'s lead, 15 Nov. 1839*o.s.*; and Evangelides [*History*], p. 175.

[102] *Ibid.*, p. 176; and decree for the confinement of Th. Kaïres to the Skiathos monastery, 28 Oct./9 Nov. 1839 [*Government Gazette*], no. 24, 18 Nov. 1839*o.s.*

[103] For instance, at the Conference of London, which met on 14 May 1838, Palmerston contended that representative institutions were "the only way to serious-ly control the finances of the Greek state" (Driault and Lhéritier, *Histoire*, II, 174-76). On the French proposal to send commissioners to Greece to survey finances, see Lyons to Palmerston, Athens, 26 Mar. 1837, no. 37, FO 32.70, and 24 June 1838, no. 66, FO 32.70 (Eynard suggested the proposal and recommended Regny for the job).

In May 1838, Regny returned to Greece. Even though hired in a private capacity, his presence in Greece required leave of absence from his post in the French foreign office and clearly gave official France a special influence. That is essentially why Lyons opposed his return so strongly, even though he justified his objection on the grounds that Regny was a Napist.[104]

The overwhelming portion of articulate Greek public opinion objected to the return of Regny for largely the same reasons as it objected to the presence of Bavarians. As *Athēna* complained, it constituted foreign interference in Greek domestic concerns and registered lack of confidence in Greek ability (the newspaper might have added, honesty) to control this crucial area of public administration. Just as the military establishment remained outside the sphere of politics, lodged in Bavarian control, so too the changes effected by Regny gave him and the king exclusive control. It was logical for the king to withhold such a tempting object of peculation from the politician and equally natural for the politician to resent his exclusion. It is as mistaken to speak about Napism in financial matters as it is to speak of it in military matters.[105]

The first major reform came with the creation of a reserve treasury, established by the controversial law of 6 August 1839.[106] Its capital, as distinct from that of the regular treasury, was to consist of judicial and extrajudicial deposits (apparently money given as bail pending trial, fines, or bonds for occupying office), as well as any reserve capital (acquired as a part of the third series of the guaranteed loan, although the statute did not say so). In the event that the general treasury faced a deficit, it could borrow from the reserve treasury, which would issue government notes carrying a maximum of 8 per cent interest against the guarantee of certain anticipated government revenue. A three-man governing board, consisting of a nominee of the Council of State from its

---

[104] For a copy of the ordinance defining Regny's powers as intendant general, see Lyons to Palmerston, Athens, 21 June 1838, no. 103, FO 32.77. According to Lyons (Athens, 24 May 1838, no. 86, and 2 June 1838, no. 95, FO 32.77), Lagrené was delighted with the appointment of Regny, which changed his attitude toward the Greek government to one of favor and support. On Lyons' continued objections to Regny as a Napist and his resentment that he had been kept completely in the dark during the nine months of negotiations prior to Regny's reappointment, see Lyons to Palmerston, Athens, 8 May 1838, no. 81, and 2 June 1838, no. 94, FO 32.77, and 9 May 1840, no. 62, and a second one of the same date marked "Private and Confidential," FO 32.97.

[105] *Athēna*, 12 June 1838*o.s.* (referring to Regny as "a foreigner, a kind of archchancellor for economic affairs") and 12 Nov. 1838*o.s.* See also *Aiōn*'s remark (26 July 1839*o.s.*): "What an insult when we are told that it is due to Regny that our income increased and our expenses diminished; as if without him we could not have been saved."

[106] Law for the introduction of a reserve (deposit) treasury, 25 July/6 Aug. 1839 [*Government Gazette*], no. 15, 29 July 1839*o.s. Aiōn* (2 Aug. 1839*o.s.*) also published the text of the law.

membership, a comptroller from the control board, and a royal delegate, would direct the affairs of the treasury independent from all authority save that of the control board.

As opponents of this bill pointed out,[107] the operations assigned to the reserve treasury technically involved nothing that the general treasury could not do, such as to issue itself the notes against its anticipated income. Ostensibly, this new institution was intended to provide a permanent fund for temporary relief from budget deficits, but it did not solve the problem of how the regular treasury, while continuing to meet the ordinary expenses of administration, would repay the loans it contracted. Actually, the reform gave Regny the opportunity to act the part of a financier. It allowed him to press economy measures on the regular administration by making it meet its payments on its loans from the reserve treasury. It also allowed him to provide some sort of security to any of the powers that the money they guaranteed would not be squandered. The reform, in short, was intended to encourage loans from abroad and press economy measures on the administration, but at the risk and even humiliation of leaving the office of intendant general free from all restraint, save what little a royal delegate and councilor of state might offer within the statutory terms of their commission.

The second major reform, effected by a decree of 28 October 1839, reorganized the ministry of economy so as to give it a collegiate character.[108] Instead of a single minister, its governing head consisted of a director and two commissioners, one a legal and one a financial specialist. The director was to head the ministry as its chief administrator, but on policy-making he was required to consult his commissioners. For the director's ministerial decision to become valid it required the assent of at least one commissioner. The king appointed George Tisamenos, an educated heterochthon from Epirus and member of the Kountouriotes faction, as director, John Soutsos and John Vizoulas as commissioners.

The reform curtailed the power of any one man to commit abuses or exercise influence. It extended the Crown's policy of built-in institutional checks and Regny's policy of transferring financial affairs from the politician to the specialist. It kept this important ministry out of the control of any one party—apparently the source of great disappointment to the Napists who had been working for the appointment of Ainian, a prominent Napist, as minister of the economy. By the king's appointment of Tisamenos, the ministry was placed under the direct control of the

---

[107] See for instance *Athēna*, 3 May and 27 May 1839*o.s.*, and *Aiōn*, 10 June 1839*o.s.*

[108] Decree for the direction of the ministry of economic affairs and for the introduction of a special economic council, 16/28 Oct. 1839 [*Government Gazette*], no. 22, 18 Oct. 1839*o.s. Athēna* (4 Oct. 1839*o.s.*) attributed the measure to foreign intrigue, namely Regny's direct influence and the indirect influence of the Swiss philhellenic banker Eynard. *Aiōn* (8 Oct. 1839*o.s.*) saw it as turning this ministry over to foreign domination, such as had been characteristic of the ministry of military affairs from the beginning. See also *Athēna*, 28 Oct. 1839*o.s.*

anaktovoulion. The collegiate principle tended to disperse authority at this level when Regny had consolidated his own, further up, through the reserve treasury law.

These two reforms are of added significance because, as proposals, they went before the Council of State for deliberation. So strong was the opposition to these bills, probably as a result of some organized effort by the opposition parties, that the king and his personal following had to resort to a series of pressure tactics. The bill for the reserve treasury met with greater difficulty. The committee of the Council, to which it was first submitted, rejected it. In spite of this, the king sent it for confirmation to the body as a whole, where a clear majority opposed it. In the meantime, Zaïmes, who spearheaded the king's campaign to secure its passage, held private conferences with the less steadfast councilors. The king issued dinner invitations to some councilors. Finally, it was announced that the king would be present at the debate. Through these means the king won over enough councilors to win confirmation for the bill, but the opposition had clearly won a moral victory. Remaining steadfast to the last were leaders of the "French" party—Palamides, Rizos-Neroulos and Delegiannes. The second bill passed more easily, but only after the announcement went out that the king would insist on its promulgation in any case.[109]

In general, the return of Regny intensified the increasing severity with which the government attempted to deal with tax evasion and furthered attempts to simplify the administration so as to cut down expenses. Though sound economically, both trends had adverse political effects. Abuses were bound to accompany investigations and punishments of tax evasion. Reduction of public posts left many unemployed or pensioned off at an inadequate income.[110]

4. THE POLITICAL OPPOSITIONS

There were three levels of political opposition during the period of Napist ascendancy—the foreign, represented by Britain; the "English" and "French" parties loosely combined in a Constitutionalist opposition;

[109] Concerning pressure on the Council of State in behalf of the treasury bill, see *Athēna*, 3 May 1839*o.s.*, and *Aiōn*, 18 June 1839*o.s.* On similar pressure in behalf of the collegiate ministry, see *Athēna* and *Aiōn*, the 7 Oct. 1839*o.s.* issue in both cases.

[110] For instance, Lyons reported to Palmerston (Athens, 19 July 1838, no. 121, FO 32.77): "We are assured that the reduction of 1,200,000 dr. will be effected in the War department, the same in the Navy, and about 1 million in the other branches of service."

For an example of the government attempts to make good old financial claims and the dire effects they produced, see Finlay, "Observations on the State of Northern Greece," pp. 17-18, Journal 1835 (MSS): ". . . all prosecutions for debts and claims originating during the revolution and not founded on a written obligation must be annulled or these provinces will one scene [*sic*] of intrigue, & confusion & soon of civil war." On the concerted campaign to collect taxes and wipe out tax evasion as a factor in the Messenian disturbances of 1838, see n. 116 below.

and startlingly enough, the Napist leadership itself. On the first level, British diplomacy criticized virtually everything about the regime of personal absolutism, even the figure of the king. On the second, the king remained untouched, but critics concentrated their attacks on two objects—the anaktovoulion as an embodiment of Bavarianism and absolutism, and the Napist party as the party in power. They demanded "national government." The third level poses a seeming paradox—the party in power also in opposition, not just a dissident faction of that party but apparently some of the leaders themselves, including Glarakes. Each level bears further examination, especially the third, which involved the abortive Philorthodox plot.

The Opposition of British Diplomacy

On the level of the London Conference, Britain and Russia now reversed roles with respect to Greek requests for the third series. France continued noncommittal but friendly after the Greek government had rehired Regny. With his help the Greek government had formulated a financial scheme and an economy drive which the French ambassador to London introduced for deliberation at the conference. In March 1838, Palmerston made two demands—that Greece use none of the prospective loan to repay Ludwig for a short-term loan which he had made in 1836 to carry the state over temporarily, and that Greece balance its budget at once by drastically reducing its military and naval establishment. Compliance with the second demand would, of course, have thrown many Greeks out of employment and precipitated a serious wave of social discontent. That is what actually happened in 1843.[111]

A month later, when France and Russia approved Regny's program, Palmerston added his third condition—demand for representative institutions which he claimed necessary as a way of exercising serious control over Greek finances. As he put it, "The French government proposes administrative control over Greek finances; I have the right to prefer another sort of control." On 4 August 1838, Palmerston gave a definite "no" to Regny's program, insisting, as had the Russian representative two years before, that Greece devote its first revenues to the service of the loan.[112]

In Greece, Lyons boldly made known British demands for a constitution and gave impetus to the official opposition, which used "constitution" as a slogan calling for change. In a campaign to discredit and harass the existing regime, he magnified a series of petty incidents into causes for major complaints involving long and complicated correspondence. For instance, the overnight arrest of his Maltese groom he interpreted as a deliberate attempt to offend the dignity of the British government and damage the honor of his Queen. He protested in behalf of Greeks claim-

[111] Driault and Lhéritier, *Histoire*, ɪɪ, 174-75.
[112] *Ibid.*, ɪɪ, 175-76.

ing Ionian (hence British) citizenship, once against conscription of two Ionians, another time against alleged mistreatment by Greek police of an innocent victim. In September 1838, he took up the Finlay affair, which involved the historian's financial claims for expropriated land and continued until the Don Pacifico affair in 1850. The king also suspected that Lyons stood behind the slanderous articles concerning the king in the English newspaper *Morning Chronicle*.[113] This strategy made virtually no use of the "English" party, perhaps a sign that the party was not an important enough factor in Greek politics or an indication that the "English" disapproved of such personal attacks on the king or such crude threats as Palmerston's:

> ... if ... we are obliged to recall Sir Edmund Lyons, it would certainly be Admiral Stopford, and not a diplomatic agent, who would come to Greece to replace our recalled minister.[114]

The Constitutionalist Opposition

The resignation of Rudhart removed the Constitutionalist opposition's most vulnerable target. Initially at least, it could not openly attack a regime which was ostensibly "national." Nor could it fulminate too freely against a regime of personal absolutism because the prestige of the king was still too great to permit the personal criticisms that such fulminations would involve.

During the earlier part of the Napist period, then, when the public was hopeful of improvement, the Constitutionalist opposition, never clearly discernible, had to exercise restraint and find pretexts for criticism of Napist rule. It exploited all kinds of discontent stemming from the regime's attempt to maintain order and to achieve a balanced budget. Minor revolts in Hydra (April 1838), Messenia (July-August 1838), and Mane (April 1839) demonstrated the effect of these measures. Although some accused Lyons of instigating the Hydra revolt and Otho himself believed this to be the case, it was generally agreed that clumsy handling of the conscription law precipitated it. The military conscription law, dated 10 December 1837, had been intended to make possible a national army which could take the place of the Bavarian recruits who were currently leaving Greece as their terms of duty expired. This was one of the most unpopular pieces of legislation enacted during this period. Mure,

[113] Bower and Bolitho, *Otho I*, pp. 104-109, and Driault and Lhéritier, *Histoire*, II, 173-74, 180-84. On the articles in the *Morning Chronicle*, see Chap. V, n. 30, above, and more especially Bower and Bolitho (*op.cit.*, p. 109), who write: "Lyons was further accused, not without some justification, of writing defamatory articles against Otho's regime," and (p. 110): "Lyons openly declared that he possessed transcripts of the reports and, on this account, Otho decided not to reply through the Press because he thought the matter would develop into a vulgar scandal."

[114] Quoted from a despatch in French, dated 11 Sept. 1838, from the archives of the Greek foreign ministry by Driault and Lhéritier, *Histoire*, II, 174.

who happened to be in Greece during the initial period of the law's implementation, emphasized the great aversion to service in the regular army, largely because of "a strong repugnance to French discipline and dress," and emphasized the increase of lawlessness and brigandage as effects of this law, since some draftees preferred the life of outlaw to that of regular military service.[115] Messenia rose up against the severity with which the authorities punished tax evasion. It appears that Yanko Soutsos, "creature of Glarakes," had driven the Constitutionalists in Messenia to desperation and turned Messenia into a faction-ridden province. Mane revolted against renewed attempts to collect taxes. If not actually organized by the parties, these outbreaks surely served the parties' allegations of misgovernment. The opposition increasingly employed the strategy of trying to discredit the existing regime so completely that it would have to give way to a new system and new officials.[116]

Brigandage by its very nature served this purpose well. So deeply rooted was brigandage in the existing social situation, that no government could uproot it under present technological conditions. It was always there for the asking, a tempting weapon in the hands of both the ruthless and the desperate. During the absolutist decade, the state itself provoked individuals to take up the brigand life, by dissolving the irregulars in 1834, by pressing financial claims going back to the Revolutionary era, and, from 1838 on, by persisting in its attempt to introduce a system of military conscription. The peculiar political value of brigandage stemmed from its elusiveness, its ability to serve the politician without incriminating him. Brigands seldom got caught. Even if they did, there was never any legally valid proof that they had been acting in behalf of some political group.

The description of brigandage that follows in the paragraphs below could apply to almost any part of the absolutist period because instances of brigandage occurred continuously and because the subject itself is so

[115] On the Hydra revolt, see Lyons to Palmerston, Athens, 27 Apr. 1838, no. 78, FO 32.76; 8 May 1838, no. 81, 24 May 1838, no. 89, 3 July 1838, no. 89, 3 July 1838, no. 113, all FO 32.77; *Athēna*, 13 Apr., 23 Apr., 27 Apr. 1838*o.s.* For the view that Lyons and the Constitutionalists were involved in provoking the revolt, see a report by Wallenburg, secretary of the Austrian legation in Athens, to Metternich, Athens, 13 Jan. 1840, edited under the title "The Philorthodox Conspiracy of 1839" by Barbara Jelavich, *Balkan Studies*, vii (1966), 96-97. The best concise and comprehensive account appears in Skandames, i [*Kingship of Otho*], 354-56. See *Athēna*, 22 Jan. 1838*o.s.*, for publication of the official instructions for the execution of the conscription law; and 26 Jan. 1838*o.s.* for the published text of the law itself; also Lyons to Palmerston, Athens, 18 Jan. 1838, no. 17, FO 32.76, and Mure, *Journal*, i, 131, 136, 198, and ii, 286.

[116] On the Messenian disturbances, see *Athēna*, 30 July, 20 Aug., 24 Aug. 1838*o.s.* On the Mane revolt, see *ibid.*, 12 Apr., 15 Apr., 26 Apr., 19 July, and 20 Sept. 1839*o.s.*; *Aiōn*, 5 Apr., 16 Apr., 19 Apr., and 23 Apr., 1839*o.s.*; and Lyons to Palmerston, Athens, 8 May 1838, no. 81, FO 32.77. On both revolts, see Skandames, i, [*Kingship of Otho*], 356, 357-58.

steeped in mystery that one can only generalize about it. Nevertheless, at some points brigandage became more pronounced than at others and some governments took more vigorous measures against it. The "Russian" period was such a time.

William Mure, an educated British gentleman who traveled in Greece in the spring of 1838, wrote a description of the brigand system which merits extensive quotation:

> Their system of organization is very complete. Each band is distributed into three, or at the most, four classes. The first comprehends the chief alone—the second his officers, or more accomplished marauders—the third the remainder of the gang. The booty is distributed into a corresponding number of shares. The chief is entitled to one for himself, and each subdivision of his force to another respectively. . . . When acting in detached parties, for the more ready communication with each other, or with head-quarters, they have a system of signals. . . . When on the march, and anxious to observe secrecy in their movements, they are careful never to follow the beaten track for more than a certain distance at a time, but every two or three miles the whole party strike off at separate tangents into the mountains, and remuster at a preconcerted point on a more advanced stage of their journey. While on the road, they travel in single file, one in front of the other, and the last two or three of each party drag a bush behind them to efface the mark of their footsteps in the dust. . . .
>
> In laying their ambush, their tactic is to entrap their victims into the very centre of their body. . . . The art they possess of concealing their persons, on such occasions, is said to be most extraordinary. . . .
>
> They have also an organized system of espionage, and their means of obtaining intelligence as to the plans of their enemies, in the cabinet or the field, are very wonderful. . . . and each corps of outlaws, fighting under such colours, is seldom without a sufficient body of partisans among the peaceful inhabitants of the district it haunts, who furnish a medium of access to the secrets of the police or military. . . . The leaders of these bands in more turbulent times, it must also be remembered, unlike the Italian Capi di Comitiva, who are usually base-born dissolute knaves, or renegade monks, frequently belonged to the leading feudal nobility of the district, who took the field at the head of their followers. . . .[117]

This quotation is invaluable for a number of reasons. It reveals how well organized and yet flexible the system was, far more efficient, one might say, and suited to local conditions, than the administrative system of the government. It suggests an organization practically identical with the irregular military system of Revolutionary times and demonstrates

[117] Mure, *Journal*, II, 149-52.

that the only difference was that one served and one opposed the state. It makes a point of the popular support which brigands enjoyed.

In the late 1850s, Nassau Senior, a distinguished traveler, quoted a foreign resident in Greece as follows:

> . . . in Greece the robber is a political element. Some of our principal persons have belonged to this profession. Through them a communication has been kept up with the chiefs, and they have been used as they were wanted. . . . During the occupation [of Athens-Piraeus by Anglo-French forces in 1854-56], when the court wished to make it appear that the allies could not govern better than they did themselves, bands were encouraged to come almost into Athens.[118]

What applied in that improved decade certainly was true for the earlier two decades. The accusations of connection between brigand acts and political schemes, in any exposure of revolutionary plots, would not have been so persistently made or entertained as plausible if experience had not already provided enough instances of such a connection. Moreover, the connection is not hard to understand. A captain, whether retired or in government service, could easily turn brigand simply by calling his "men" together. Through the hierarchical system of clientage, a political patron could very quickly and effectively precipitate a series of brigand incidents.

The motives for encouraging brigandage might be any one of many. One might want to demonstrate the weakness and inefficiency of the government. One might want to provoke it into cruel and arbitrary acts. One might hope to give it the jitters. One might try to arouse peasant resentment against the government for not providing sufficient protection against brigandage. In any of these cases, the object was to discredit the government and the party that dominated it.

A patron might want to demonstrate to the government his influence in a particular region in order to gain concessions from it. He might want to create the need for a military campaign, by which some of his clients might obtain state employment, and hence demonstrate the efficacy of party patronage to his clients. Sometimes brigandage was probably merely local; that is, a part of the raids and counterraids which accompanied family and clan rivalries in the countryside.[119]

As paternalism became increasingly synonymous with Otho's refusal to delegate authority and with foreign Bavarian rule, the anaktovoulion bore the brunt of growing criticism. The demand for "national" government increased, although its exponents were divided by the question of what form such "national" government ought to take—tempered absolut-

[118] Nassau W. Senior, *A Journal kept in Turkey and Greece in the autumn of 1857 and the beginning of 1858* (London, 1859), p. 262.

[119] On some of the motives behind brigandage, see Finlay, "Observations on the State of Northern Greece," pp. 1-17, Journal 1835 (MSS), and Senior, *Journal*, pp. 262-65, 281-82. On brigandage, see also Aspreas [*Political History*], I, 146-47.

ism or representative government.[120] The moderates advocated a government of delegated powers exercised by acknowledged Greek leaders, and the radicals favored representative government guaranteed by a constitution.

In the former camp belonged most of the political leaders, whether former Constitutionalists like Zaïmes, Kountouriotes, and Kolettes, or Napists like Kolokotrones and Metaxas. In principle the moderates accepted the desirability of constitutional government, but they did not feel the time was ripe. Some argued that the king's intransigence would necessitate resorting to revolution. Others insisted that Greece still lacked the institutions and experience necessary to make constitutional government work. Virtually all agreed with the judgment of Kolokotrones, who said with his usual acumen:

> A constitution means that you educated ones will sit on the sidelines, scorned and impotent, while I and such boors as myself take the center. But do we know anything about administration?

In actual fact, the moderates placed little faith in the ability of the people to rule themselves. They were just as paternalistic as the king, but wanted a paternalism exercised by themselves in the name of the king. They believed in government of and for the people rather than government by the people. They would favor any constitution which guaranteed this type of élitist government, but they felt that, under existing conditions, a constitution would only breed chaos and possibly a worse form of despotism.[121]

---

[120] See for instance *Athēna*, 8 Apr., 27 May, 9 Aug., and 25 Nov. 1839*o.s.*, and *Aiōn*, 6 Dec. 1839*o.s.*

[121] On the conservative position in general, and its espousal by such men as Mavrokordatos, Zaïmes, and Kolettes, see Dragoumes [*Reminiscences*], ɪɪ, 18f. The conservative views which he elaborates are those of Mavrokordatos and he does so by quoting at some length two of Mavrokordatos' letters (no date specified but probably written around the beginning of 1837). In the first, Mavrokordatos specified the following six prerequisites for constitutional government: (1) improvement of the deme system, (2) demotic and eparchal councils, (3) complete independence of the judiciary, (4) extension of jury jurisdiction, (5) freedom of the press, (6) extension of the rights of the Council of State and creation of a national army.

For a more academic presentation of the conservative position, see the pamphlet Sibi (pseud. for Spyridon Valetas), *Ho Geron Limperes* [*Old Man Limperes*] (Athens, 1836), where the young man's position is an epitome of the conservative views (pp. 77-88).

For Kolokotrones' statement, see Dragoumes, *op.cit.*, ɪɪ, 30-31.

Lyons (Athens, 5 July 1838, no. 119, FO 32.77) quotes Kountouriotes as saying: "a Constitution we shall have, if Foreign bayonets should not be sent to stifle the wishes of the nation; but will the King and men of property have their due weight in it? I fear not, if it be delayed much longer." Even though Lyons may not have represented his or Zaïmes' views accurately, he *was* stating the view of some conservatives, who by 1838 were beginning to advocate a conservative constitution granted from above as a way of preventing a radical constitution established by lower elements through revolt.

Radicalism drew its recruits from among both the unlettered captains and the intellectually sophisticated. Makrygiannes, a member of the former group, simply equated constitutional government with efficient and fair government. In view of the palikars' prejudice against the politicians and their own self-regard as spokesmen of the people, radical military men must have considered the observation of Kolokotrones an argument for, rather than against, constitutional government.[122]

The faith of the latter group in a constitution was more complicated. Men like Spyridon Trikoupes, Emmanuel Antoniades, editor of *Athēna*, and Alexander Soutsos, poet of liberalism, owed their ideal of government to their Western liberal education. Trikoupes had learned to admire the English system. Antoniades and Soutsos were republicans in principle but conceded the necessity of monarchy for Greece.[123] But the Western education of this group inspired their radicalism in more subtle ways. It taught them to judge themselves by Western liberal standards, according to which nations "unripe" for constitutional government were culturally backward. The undercurrent of national inferiority flared up when moderates argued that Greece was unprepared for a constitution. Radicals denounced such arguments as unpatriotic, even traitorous, disparagement of the nation. Even *Aiōn*, when it joined the radical camp in 1839, betrayed the same feeling when it asked: Were Greeks either black barbarians of Santa Domingo or backward Slavs of Serbia to be denied a constitution? In his *Memoirs*, Dragoumes actually says that Trikoupes desired a constitution as a symbol of Greek cultural maturity.[124]

Connected with this sense of national inferiority was the set of inferences which radicals drew from the observed correlation, among European nations, between prosperity and "civilization" on the one hand and constitutional forms on the other. While the moderates asked, "Is Greece ready yet for a constitution?" the radicals formulated their own question, "Can Greece scale the economic and cultural heights of civilization without a constitution?" By mechanically adopting European political forms Greece could cultivate the spirit of Europe. This line of thinking reflected

[122] Makrygiannes ([*Memoirs*], II, 42) wrote, concerning the year 1832: "I wanted a constitution for my country, so that it would be governed by laws and not by [the attitude] 'that's the way *I* want it.'"

[123] On Trikoupes' liberalism, see Goudas, "Spyridon Trikoupes" [*Parallel Lives*], VII, 165-202, but more especially a letter of 1 May 1837, which he wrote Mavrokordatos, chiding him for his recent conservatism, and Dragoumes' commentary in his [*Reminiscences*], II, 18f. On Antoniades, see [*Grand Encyclopedia*] and a most typical one of the many constitutionalist articles which appeared in his newspaper *Athēna* (4 Oct. 1839o.s.). In this lead article, he refers to representative democracy of the American type as the "freest and most just government," "a product of providence"; and he accepts constitutional monarchy as only a second best alternative imposed on Greece by a variety of conditions. On A. Soutsos, see [*Grand Encyclopedia*]. For the liberal position in general, see the old man's long defense of immediate constitutionalism for Greece in [*Old Man Limperes*], pp. 89-103.

[124] *Aiōn*, 4 June 1839o.s., and Dragoumes [*Reminiscences*], II, 18f.

the optimistic faith common to European liberal thought, but it was also analogous in spirit with the belief of Greek purists that restoration of the ancient Greek language would revive the ancient Greek genius or with the rigid formalism of the Orthodox church which feared that any change in outward form would corrupt the essence of the inner faith.[125]

Kolettes and Mavrokordatos did not often find cordial support among their partisans in behalf of their moderate stand. Both leaders from abroad had to urge their followers to abandon calls for a constitution. The "French" party also had to acquiesce for lack of official French support. On the sole occasion (1836) when the French government, under the Duke de Broglie, openly called for a constitution, Mansolas, then minister of the interior, boldly submitted to the Crown a memorandum making the same suggestion. This incident suggests that when given the backing of a strong source, the real "French" party feelings would arise. On the other hand, the constitutionalist "English" partisans, finding more than ample support from Lyons and Palmerston, could afford to challenge the position of Mavrokordatos and offer strong encouragement to the radical forces in Greece.[126]

The Napist newspaper *Aiōn*, founded in 1838 as a continuation of *Chronos*, took up the support of absolute monarchy and attempted to sanctify the institution by giving it a high place in the national vocabulary alongside "fatherland" and "religion." In the spring of 1839, however, it changed its color and openly called for the granting of a constitution.[127] According to Lyons and *Athēna*, this about-face was a tactical maneuver induced by a realization that the "Russian" party was losing credit with the people because of its anticonstitutional stand. Catacazy, in a private conversation, which could not have remained private very long in the gossip-ridden atmosphere of Athens, asserted that Russia could have no

---

[125] See, for instance, a lead article in A. Soutsos' newspaper *Hēlios* (1 Aug. 1833*o.s.*) which actually draws up lists of "despotisms" and "constitutional monarchies," correlates the frequency of the latter with that of prosperity, and then infers a causal relationship, with the political form (constitutionalism) the imputed cause of prosperity.

See also the remark of the constitutionalist old man ([*Old Man Limperes*], p. 89): "Why do you make an end out of the means? You want Greece to be enlightened so as to quickly develop toward constitutional freedom. I want her to become constitutionalized so that the nation can proceed more quickly to civilization, its chief goal."

[126] On the anticonstitutionalist exhortations of Kolettes to his followers, see Lyons to Palmerston, Athens, 24 June 1837, no. 66, FO 32.70. On Mansolas' report to the king, in which as minister of the interior he insisted that "only through a constitutional system could the nation prosper and the throne be consolidated," see *Aiōn*, 10 Sept. 1839*o.s.*

[127] For samples of *Aiōn*'s early position, see lead articles of the 2 Oct. and 29 Oct. 1838*o.s.* issues. The issue which proclaimed *Aiōn*'s new proconstitutional policy was that of 25 Mar. 1839*o.s.*, followed up by a lengthy lead article in the issue of 4 June 1839*o.s.*, although a prelude was an article on the history of Athens, appearing in the issue of 19 Feb. 1839*o.s.*

objections to the king's sharing of sovereignty with an assembly of some thirty or forty men. Espousal of a constitution, openly by an acknowledged Napist organ and unofficially by the Russian minister, meant that a major part of the Napist party had moved into the political opposition.[128]

The Philorthodox Plot[129]

The startling phenomenon of this period, for one unfamiliar with the prevailing absolutist system and existing Greek politics, is the paradoxical

---

[128] *Athēna*, 22 Feb. 1839*o.s.* (lead called "*Aiōn* and the Constitution"). Lyons to Palmerston, 14 Mar. 1839, no. 32, FO 32.85.

[129] The published primary material on the Philorthodox plot, its discovery and the immediate aftermath, is slight. The memoirs of Makrygiannes ([*Memoirs*], II, 102-103, 112-13), and Gennaios Kolokotrones ([*Memoirs II*], pp. 83-85), deal briefly with it, the first from a Constitutionalist, the second from a Napist point of view. The latter position is also taken by Andrew Papadopoulos-Vretos, *Un Grec très dévoué à la Russie victime du chancelier de cet empire le Prince Gortchacoff* (Paris, 1873). Second, there are the contemporary newspaper accounts and accusations (*Aiōn*, *Athēna*, etc.), as well as an anonymously published article entitled "He Philorthodoxos Hetairia . . ." ["The Philorthodox Society, or the Fanaticism of the Kapodistrians"] in *He Proodos tou 1840 . . .* [*The Progress of 1840 . . .*] (Athens, 1840). Finally, there are a few published diplomatic reports—a report about it from Wallenburg, secretary of the Austrian legation in Athens, to his government, ed. B. Jelavich, in *Balkan Studies*, VII (1966), 95-102, and reports of Baron de Bourgoing, French ambassador to Bavaria, to his foreign office, dated 1 Feb. and 24 Feb. 1840, published as items no. 860 and 864 in *Gesandtschaftsberichte*, ed. Chroust, Abt. I, Vol. III, 144-46 and 153-54.

The secondary literature on the Philorthodox plot is also very thin. Some major works (Aspreas [*Political History*], and Finlay, *History*) make no mention of it at all. Others (Evangelides [*History*], p. 160) dismiss it in a sentence or two. Evangelides, a victim of the contemporary Napist press apologies, actually explains the plot away as a phantom creation of the "English" party in order to discredit the "Russian" party. Of those who do treat it as a subject of importance (Driault and Lhéritier, *Histoire*, II, 195-96; P. Karólides, *Synchronos Historia tōn Hellenōn . . .* [*Contemporary History of the Greeks . . .*] [Athens, 1922-29], II, 383-85; and Kordatos [*History*], III, 133-34, 137-39), Driault and Lhéritier, who base their brief account on the material of the French foreign archives, do not elaborate enough, and the other two base their accounts on the contemporary press reports and what little information Makrygiannes ([*Memoirs*], II, 102-103, 112-13) gives.

This book's account of the Philorthodox plot is based on a number of valuable unpublished primary sources, hitherto unexploited. They are of four kinds. The first consists of documents found by government officials in the archives of the society's leader George Kapodistrias. It served as evidence in the trial which followed. The particular copies which I have used were sent by Lyons to his government, after he had obtained them from the Greek foreign office. They are as follows:

(1) What Lyons called "a catechism" and "diplomas for members of the society," a rambling document intersected by the following rubrics: "System of Arch-presidency," "Dread Oath," "Oath of Presidents," "Attributes and Rights of Representatives, Commissioners, Presidents, Assessors, and Missionaries," "Circular Letter" (a letter of identification of the recently delegated agent for Epirus), "Instructions" (attached to the letter of identification), "To the Chief President of the Orthodox Society" (in Epirus), "Form of Diploma," "Oath of Representatives," "Certificate," "Second Examination of Presidents" (both

fact that the most aggressive and subversive opposition to the Napist-dominated government came from the Napist party itself. The paradox turns out to be no paradox at all, if one recognizes that the target of this opposition was the king himself, probably because of his failure to delegate more of his power to his Napist-dominated government. By the

---

the Greek text and English translation enclosed in Lyons to Palmerston, Athens, 10 Jan. 1840, no. 7, with them a better copy in 19 Jan. 1840, no. 14, FO 32.96).

(2) Form letter addressed to the patriarch of Constantinople, respecting the Philorthodox society (enclosed in Lyons to Palmerston, Athens, 30 Jan. 1840, no. 18, FO 32.96).

(3) Two letters from Charalampes N. Soliotes to his uncle Anag. Kanellopoulos, mayor of Locris, Athens, dated 15 Apr. and 9 May 1838o.s. [with no proved connection to this plot, though of an intriguing nature] (enclosed in Lyons to Palmerston, Athens, 7 Mar. 1840, no. 36, FO 32.97).

The second consists of legal documents, products of the investigation and the trial that followed. Again, these are copies, in English translation, sent by Lyons to his government. They include:

(1) The indictment of the council of the tribunal of first instance in Athens, dated 15 May 1840o.s., against Kapodistrias, Niketaras, and Renieres (enclosed in Lyons to Palmerston, Athens, 18 June 1840, no. 78, FO 32.97).

(2) Text of the deposition by Renieres (undated).

(3) Text of the verdict of the correctional tribunal of Athens, dated 12 July 1840o.s.

(4) Text of the verdict of the court of Areopagus, dated 29 July 1840o.s. (items [2], [3], and [4] enclosed in Lyons to Palmerston, Athens, 27 Aug. 1840, no. 98, FO 32.98).

The third category consists of correspondence from various archival sources:

(1) The correspondence of Lyons to Palmerston, reporting information from oral sources about the plot, in FO 32.96 and 97 (covering Jan. through June 1840) but also FO 32.98.

(2) Two letters of Mavrokordatos discussing the plot and its discovery at length, one by D. Papiolakes, Trieste, 9/21 Jan. 1840, no. 5679, and one by Zographos, Piraeus, 3/15 Mar. 1840, no. 5695, both in Vol. 20 (1837-40), Mavrokordatos Archive.

(3) Also five official items in Vol. 18.1 (1840: London Embassy), the Archives of the Greek Foreign Ministry, Athens.

(a) Païkos to Mavrokordatos, Athens, 6/18 Jan. 1840, envelope 54 (as acting foreign minister, announcing the plot to the Greek minister in London for conveyance to the British government of this information).

(b) Païkos to Mavrokordatos, Athens, 26 Feb. 1840o.s., envelope 60 (information minimizing the plot).

(c) Païkos to Mavrokordatos, Athens, 8/20 Mar. 1840, envelope 61 (information minimizing the plot).

(d) Païkos to Mavrokordatos, Athens, 5/17 June 1840, envelope 69 (information minimizing the plot).

(e) Greek government to Mousouros, Turkish minister to Greece, 17/29 July 1840, envelope 75 (on the trial and subsequent executive action).

The fourth and final item is also the most important. It belongs to a category by itself because it is a report, written by an anonymous source who was himself not a party to the plot but who purported to be conveying information given him by

beginning of 1839, it became clear that the king had no intention of abandoning his habit of diligent watch over every branch of government. French influence, through Regny, kept the Napists from the financial branch of the government, and the continued stay of the Bavarians excluded Napist control of the military arm of government. As a result, the Napists probably despaired of ever persuading the king to delegate sufficient power to them. Nothing is so revealing of the political weakness of the Othonian system as this situation.

The abortive Philorthodox plot came to light at the end of 1839. Around 22 December, Emmanuel Papas, a Macedonian Greek, voluntarily gave himself up as a member of a self-styled Philorthodox society. Through Tzames Karatasos, a frequenter of court circles, he presented Otho with documents implicating as leaders of the organization the Revolutionary hero Niketas Stamatellopoulos and George Kapodistrias, youngest brother of the assassinated president. This betrayal merely confirmed previous reports received by the government. On 23 December, the police searched the houses of Kapodistrias and Niketas and seized papers from each. Two days later the authorities arrested both men in Athens, and the agent Nicholas Renieres, a Westernized Peloponnesian Greek, in Spezza on his way back to the Ionian Islands.[130]

The stated purpose of this organization was the liberation of the Ottoman provinces of Macedonia, Epirus, and Thessaly, and the support of an allegedly threatened Orthodoxy.[131] From the testimony of Papas or some discovered documents, the government suspected that the members of this society intended to seize the king at church services on New Year's day, 1840, and confront him with the choice of accepting the Orthodox faith or abdicating. On New Year's day, the king and queen attended church services as planned. Guards watched to prevent any armed per-

---

Kapodistrias and Renieres themselves. If so, this is inside information mediated through a second person. It is ["Anonymous Memo"] (full title cited in n. 40 above), n.d., 38 pp. (14" x 6½"), in a good hand (obviously a copy), no. 5794, deposited in a folder entitled "undated" in Vol. 21 (1841), Mavrokordatos Archive. See also n. 137 below.

Additional unpublished material, dealing with the plot but not used for this book, is cited by Barbara Jelavich in her short introduction to her published edition of the Wallenburg report of the Philorthodox plot (see her "The Philorthodox Conspiracy of 1839," *Balkan Studies*, vii [1966], 94-95, nn. 8-12). This material consists of diplomatic reports deposited in the Geheimes Staatsarchiv, Munich.

[130] Makrygiannes ([*Memoirs*], ii, 103) mentions Karatasos as the go-between. Gennaios Kolokotrones ([*Memoirs II*], p. 83) makes no mention of Papas and, alleging Karatasos a member of the Society, simply calls him the informer. Lyons (to Palmerston, Athens, 10 Jan. 1841, no. 6, FO 32.96) attributes the discovery not to Papas' betrayal, but rather to the chance discovery by a servant in a Piraeus house of a letter addressed by Renieres to Kapodistrias. Finding it contained evidence of a conspiracy, Lyons wrote, the servant had it put into Otho's hands. For a general account of this discovery and arrests, see *Athēna*, 27 Dec. 1839o.s.

[131] Driault and Lhéritier, *Histoire*, ii, 195.

sons from entering the church. The royal couple received more than the usual acclamation of their subjects, who by this time had heard of the plot and wished to express their continued allegiance.[132]

Meanwhile, the palace, primarily at the initiative of Bavarians like Schmaltz and Rosmer, employed the gendarmerie to investigate for evidence of the conspiracy in the provinces. It also kept under surveillance such "Russian" party figures as Gennaios Kolokotrones, Tzavelas, Mamoures, and Glarakes himself. An investigation was made in Kalavryta, among Napist officials there, but nothing turned up. The gendarmerie intercepted a mason on his way to Kalavryta, with money on his person and a letter from Kolokotrones to officials there, but again the letter was not incriminating and the object of the money was allegedly personal.[133]

The revelation of some sort of conspiracy threw the country into a turmoil of party strife unparalleled since 1833. When conservative members of the synod set out for the palace one day, university students jeered at them. Students built a bonfire outside the home of Glarakes on the night of 30 December and kept shouting, "Long live the constitution. Down with Glarakes and the Napist party."[134]

The "English" and "French" opposition grabbed at the chance to discredit their rivals, as they had in 1833, and hence work their way back into greater influence. On 27 December, *Athēna* took the offensive. It alleged the plot widespread, in preparation for some time, organized by a segment of the Napist party for the overthrow of the status quo. It delved into the past and implied that a tour of the Peloponnesos by Gennaios Kolokotrones and certain meetings of eparchs and mayors in 1838-39 all had constituted a part of the conspiracy. Vague religious prognostications about drastic and happy changes in the year 1840 seemed like Napists' efforts to alert the public in advance of their coup. More serious still, *Athēna* raised the question of the Russian mission's implication in the plot. According to Wallenburg, secretary of the Austrian legation in Athens, the Constitutionalist opposition was also alleging the overthrow of English rule in the Ionian Islands as an additional objective of the conspiracy.[135]

---

[132] *Ibid.*, ɪɪ, 195-96. See also Lyons to Palmerston, Athens, 31 Jan. 1840, no. 21, FO 32.96 (according to whom accomplices in the provinces expected to hear news of the king's assassination on 1 Jan. 1840); Wallenburg to Metternich, Athens, 13 Jan. 1840, ed. Jelavich, in *Balkan Studies*, ᴠɪɪ (1966), 100; and Makrygiannes [*Memoirs*], ɪɪ, 103 (according to whom "all the inhabitants [of Athens] gathered together at church and gave one 'Long live the King' to give him courage because he had been terrified").

[133] Gennaios Kolokotrones ([*Memoirs II*], pp. 84-85), who relates the incident, claims that he was, in the message, simply carrying out the king's request that Kolokotrones inform these officials of the king's belief in their innocence and that, when the king saw the contents of the message, his confidence in Kolokotrones was restored.

[134] *Aiōn*, 3 Jan. 1840*o.s.*

[135] *Athēna*, 27 Dec. 1839*o.s.* ("The Napist Conspiracy"), and 30 Dec. 1839*o.s.*

After remaining silent for several days, *Aiōn* reported the plot as an insignificant undertaking of Renieres and Papas, agents of a dethroned bishop by the name of Agathangelos, who had planned the whole thing from Trieste. The society's sole purpose, it reported, was the liberation of subject Greeks. Niketas and Kapodistrias had been the mere dupes of these two agents. In subsequent articles, however, *Aiōn* began to develop the idea that Renieres and Papas were the instruments of the "English" party, which allegedly sought to implicate Kapodistrias and Niketas in order to bring the Napist party into disrepute. According to Wallenburg, the Napists alleged that the "English" party thereby hoped to stage a *coup de main* against the ultranationalist opposition (Napist) in the Ionian parliament and stage a political comeback in Greece. In short, *Aiōn*, spokesman of the Napist party, answered the charge of "Napist plot" with as serious a charge of "English frame-up." No one, then or after, really took *Aiōn's* charges seriously. They seemed merely a clever contrivance to clear the Napists of guilt and put the opposition on the defensive.[136]

An anonymous manuscript in the Mavrokordatos Archive[137] gives a lengthy account of the origins, organization, and purpose of the conspiracy. Its author was an inmate at the Medresa prison in Athens, where Kapodistrias and Renieres were taken after arrest. Much of what it says bears no confirmation elsewhere and its author may have written it primarily to discredit certain prominent Napists. Essentially it is an elaboration of the position taken by *Athēna*. In my description of the event and its aftermath below, I rely heavily on it when its information is confirmed by other sources or when it provides plausible information going beyond other sources. Unless indicated by footnote citations, the

("The Delusion of Prophecies for the year 1840; and again the discovered plot"). In his memoirs ([*Memoirs II*], p. 83) Gennaios Kolokotrones asserts that he undertook his tour to help the government, through his personal and family influence, get families to submit to the unpopular draft law and to cooperate to curb brigandage. See also Wallenburg to Metternich, Athens, 13 Jan. 1840, ed. Jelavich, in *Balkan Studies*, VII (1966), 98.

[136] *Aiōn*, 1 Jan. 1840*o.s.* ("The Philorthodox Plot"), 3 Jan. 1840*o.s.* ("Passions and Slanders"), 3 Jan. 1840*o.s.* [*sic*, no. 124, and published separately from the issue of the same date, numbered 123] ("What is the source of the Philorthodox Society?"), 10 Jan. 1840*o.s.* ("Parallels"—referring to a plot of 1839 in France), 4 Feb. 1840*o.s.* ("The hindering of the Theme of 22 December"). See also Wallenburg to Metternich, Athens, 13 Jan. 1840, ed. Jelavich, in *Balkan Studies*, VII (1966), 99.

[137] ["Anonymous Memo"], n.d., no. 5794, Vol. 21 (1841), Mavrokordatos Archive. Internal evidence shows that the author was a prison inmate. Makrygiannes ([*Memoirs*], II, 113) possibly identifies this man in the following remark: ". . . in the prison to which he [Kapodistrias] was committed was also someone named Kampouroglos, and the brother of Kapodistrias catechized him and confided in him; and he gave him the catechism and the documents. Then Kampouroglos asked me to go to the prison to get the documents and give them to the king. I told him that I don't get mixed up in such affairs; so he gave them to Pharmakides who gave them." For the full text, see Appendix I below.

following details are drawn from this invaluable and revealing memorandum.

According to this account, after failing to obtain Viaro Kapodistrias, the Napists invited George Kapodistrias to Greece in 1836 in the belief that his name would revive flagging spirits and lend an air of sanctity to their program. The main features of that program were the establishment of a hereditary and exclusively autochthon senate; the limitation of public office to autochthons, heterochthons who had held office before the Argos assembly of 1829, and Ionian Greeks whose families had contributed in some way to Greek independence; reunion of the church in Greece with the patriarchate of Constantinople, expulsion of all missionaries, and banning of all missionary publications; the king's recognition of eastern Orthodoxy as the religion of the state and of his successors; imposing political disabilities on the Mavromichales family, its heirs, and all others implicated in the assassination of Kapodistrias; and state satisfaction of all the financial claims put forth by the Kapodistrias family and the appointment of Viaro Kapodistrias as president of the senate. Glarakes would work out basic laws for the internal governance of the realm. Finally, a national assembly would meet, apparently as a constituent body, to institute this program, rather than as a continuing legislative assembly renewing itself through periodic elections.

Aiōn declared publicly for a constitution in the spring of 1839 in order to prepare public opinion for this Napist reversal on constitutionalism. So as not to prejudice himself with the king, Glarakes pretended to break with *Aiōn*, which had been regarded as his newspaper organ, and established a new newspaper named *Hellas*.[138] But party members received secret instructions not to cancel their subscriptions to *Aiōn*. Glarakes was to feel the king out on the possibility of a constitution. If the king seemed adamantly opposed, then Kolokotrones, Rangos, and Mamoures would call out the brigands to agitate, and if need be, to precipitate a revolution. In the meantime, the Napists catechized army officers and frequently sponsored meetings of demotic authorities, confided their ideas to some thirteen Napist governors, and sent prominent chieftains and politicians to tour the provinces.

Then came the Anatolian crisis of 1839. The dissolution of the Ottoman empire seemed imminent and the Russian troops might march on Constantinople. Consequently the Napists decided that the time seemed ripe for force. They apportioned among themselves the various sections of the kingdom: Western Rumely to Rangos, Eastern Rumely to Ainian and Loidorikes, Kalavryta to Speliotes, Elis and Achaia to Petimezas and Plapoutas, Tripolis and Karytaina to Kolokotrones, Argolis to Tsokres and

---

[138] The first issue of *Hellas* appeared 28 June 1839*o.s.*; the last (the twenty-sixth) was published on 3 Jan. 1840*o.s.* Throughout its short career it was strongly Governmentalist and engaged in a press debate with *Aiōn*, its chief target. On the reversal of *Aiōn*'s position on a constitution, see n. 127 above.

Heliotes, and Laconia to Giatrakos. John Kolokotrones, Leles, Glarakes, and Valsamakes exercised the central leadership. They usually held meetings at about 2:00 A.M. at the home of Leles, where documents were deposited. Only the highest ranking party figures were admitted to these high-level meetings.[139] Glarakes presided, Valsamakes served as secretary.

Founded in June 1839, the Philorthodox society itself was essentially a front organization, modeled in organization and ritual on the Philike Hetairia, the secret revolutionary society which had organized the Revolution of 1821. The Philorthodox society was designed to make recruits, organize cell groups throughout the provinces, disguise the real intentions of the conspirators, and protect the real leadership from legal accountability in the event of premature exposure. A supreme three-man committee, consisting of a political figure, a chieftain, and a cleric, was envisaged as the ostensibly supreme authority of the society, but only two individuals could be induced to accept the serious risks of office—Kapodistrias out of vanity and Niketas from levity.[140] Neither Oikonomos nor the president of the holy synod could prevail upon the bishop of Damala, so the third seat remained vacant.

The membership of the society was organized hierarchically, according to three progressive orders. The "simple" or low order consisted of untried individuals, usually non-Napists, to whom the society was represented as merely irredentist. Mostly clergymen constituted the "grand" or middle order, dedicated to the "restoration" of Orthodoxy. The "awesome" or high rank fell on influential chieftains, higher clergymen, and distinguished Napist politicians, who were the only ones to learn the ultimate purpose of the society—the acquisition, through force, of special privileges, Napist party supremacy, and an Orthodox kingdom, implying an

[139] *Athēna*, as early as 29 June 1838*o.s.*, had referred obliquely to meetings over which Glarakes presided, some publicly acknowledged and at his home, the others "somewhere else which is secret and only receives initiates." Whether there is any connection between these and the accusation of the memorandum is unknown. Also Wallenburg (to Metternich, Athens, 13 Jan. 1840, ed. Jelavich, in *Balkan Studies*, VII [1966], 96) states that the home of Leles served as a regular meeting-place for the ultraorthodox elements who, under the direction of Oikonomos, staged a concerted attack on the caesaropapist settlement in Greece. He adds that such meetings, allegedly for staging propaganda campaigns, were an object of public knowledge.

[140] As stated in one of the society's papers (entitled "The System of Arch-Presidency"), discovered in a search of Kapodistrias' home and a copy of which Lyons included in his despatch of 7 May 1840, no. 36, FO 32.97: "Of the first chief presidency: 1a. Chief presidency composed of three members: ecclesiastical, military, civil; all of equal rank and empowered as the supreme authority to act independently, according to its own views and opinions, for the benefit of the society. . . . 2b. If within six months there is not found an ecclesiastical chief worthy of confidence for oath, then the chief presidency may be composed of the two other members only, reserving to themselves the right to select one afterwards." Wallenburg (to Metternich, Athens, 13 Jan. 1840, ed. Jelavich, in *Balkan Studies*, VII [1966], 101) writes that some of the instructions and certificates of the Philorthodox society were copies of those used by the Philike Hetairia in 1819-20.

Orthodox king without specifying if Otho would be converted or replaced by an Orthodox adherent.

Membership in the middle order entitled one to act as recruiter or "apostle" and possession of the highest rank allowed one to appoint apostles. In each town, apostles appointed a president as well as a variable number of assessors, according to the size of the town, to supervise the local cells and to take over the local administration when the revolution broke out. On appointment, the apostles expected the president of a town to write two letters, one to the patriarch of Constantinople and the other to Kapodistrias, asking both to petition the Tsar to help and protect them.[141] The size of membership, calculated according to the number of certificates of membership or "diplomas" issued, was very large, exceeding the large number of recruits made by Kolettes (in 1831, presumably through a similar system) and amounting to over 1,000 for Athens alone.

By taking his nominal leadership seriously and believing himself actual leader, Kapodistrias antagonized the Napist heads. They considered it presumptuous for him to admit new members into the higher circles without their consent. The presence of the young and untried Renieres and Papas, who closely collaborated with Kapodistrias and learned important secrets from Niketas, disturbed them most. Glarakes and his associates agreed to accept the membership of the two men, provided that Kapodistrias get them out of the kingdom at once. Kapodistrias commissioned them to serve abroad as agents of the society, Papas in Thessaly and Macedonia, Renieres in the Ionian Islands.[142]

Renieres and Papas actually proved the undoing of the conspiracy, the former through carelessness, the latter through deliberate betrayal. Renieres received instructions to go through Aegina, Poros, and Spezza in order to convey messages to local Napists,[143] but he exceeded his instruc-

[141] Lyons to Palmerston, Athens, 7 May 1840, no. 36, FO 32.97. All these enclosures by Lyons constitute the constitution of the society (describing its organization, the formal oaths to be administered, the "attributes and rights of the representatives, commissioners, presidents, assessors, and missionaries"), the official credentials (letter of introduction) of the society's representative in Epirus, and his official instructions, etc. For instance, one bit confirms the memorandum's discussion of the intended local cells of the society: "1. Representatives . . . will elect presidents in every place where they can find honorable and worthy men capable of executing the duties of [local] presidency with which they will be charged. . . . 3. Presidents have the right of electing as assessors honorable, worthy, and capable men, from five to nine: The assessors will also each elect nine missionaries, and every missionary has the right to elect nine others to the tenth degree. . . . 4. Every President will support one of the nine assessors as Treasurer and one as controller."

[142] This is confirmed by the indictment of the tribunal of first instance in Athens (dated 15 May 1840 o.s.), a text of which indictment Lyons enclosed in his despatch of 18 June 1840, no. 78, FO 32.97. For instance, Art. 2 of the evidence reads as follows: "There exists in the dossier of the procès two of these brevets presented by Michael Papas, representative of the arch-presidency in Macedonia and Thessaly, ..."

[143] Loc.cit. Proposal no. 11 reads: ". . . Reniere had a part in the redaction of the

tions. So careless was he in making recruits that news leaked out and ultimately reached Schmaltz, minister of war, through Kolokouvaros, an anti-Napist inhabitant of Spezza.

In the meantime, Papas continued to stay in Athens on various pretexts, angry that the leadership had appointed someone else secretary of the supreme committee instead of him. At last he demanded 1,500 drachmas to leave, quarreled with Kapodistrias, who refused his demand, then decided to betray the plot to the government, when he realized that Kapodistrias was making false promises in an attempt to get damaging documents out of Papas' possession.

In November, when the government began to suspect something, the Napist leadership decided on immediate action, but they had worked out no actual strategy. They hurriedly considered several plans. The most detailed proposed to instigate simultaneous uprisings in both Rumely and Peloponnesos, to capture Mesolongi and Nauplion, to garrison the cities of each region, and finally to make a combined attack on an isolated Athens. They abandoned the plan as impracticable. Nauplion was too strongly fortified to take by assault and those in control—Almeida, the Portuguese philhellene in command of the garrison, and Hitz, the Bavarian commander of the artillery—were incorruptible and loyal to the regime. The Rumeliot troops in Athens would undoubtedly rise to a royal summons for the defense of the city. Besides, Mamoures was unwilling to initiate the uprising in Rumely.

Kapodistrias then proposed that some 600-800 troops secretly assemble in Athens and capture the royal mint, where the public monies were deposited, so as to paralyze the government financially. All agreed to the scheme but no one would take the responsibility for its execution. Such indecision, lack of nerve, and procrastination left the conspirators totally unprepared when the government proceeded to act.

Glarakes had put the king off once by saying that he could discover no signs of a conspiracy, but the second time Otho proved more insistent, revealing that he possessed documents proving the existence of a society, and ordered Païkos, the minister of justice, to make investigations as well. Glarakes persuaded Païkos to wait a few days on the pretext that he, as minister of interior, should first place the governors and gendarmerie on the alert. In the meantime, Glarakes called a secret meeting of the leaders, who abandoned their revolutionary plans in order to escape incrimination. The incriminating evidence had to be destroyed or hidden.

Kapodistrias blamed himself for having introduced the betrayer Papas into the conspiracy. He now nobly offered to leave in his own files, for the discovery of the authorities, a document in Renieres' handwriting

---

book of regulations of the society and he was especially charged in name and for the purpose of the society with special functions, as for example to travel to Poros, Egina, Spetza where he tried to make proselytes, to initiate and give oaths and receive their contributions. . . ."

337

giving an incomplete description of the society.[144] This evidence implicated only himself, Niketas, and Renieres. He could, on its discovery, argue that the document merely expressed his own unexecuted ideas for an irredentist movement. The rest accepted the idea. They calculated that no evidence at all would lead to extensive and possibly fatal investigations, whereas the bit of evidence left undestroyed or unhidden would satisfy the government into assuming that nothing more was involved. After five days Païkos dared wait no longer and instituted the house-to-house investigations which led to the above-mentioned arrests.

Officially the government acted as if the plot was a trivial affair. In his official communiqué to the powers, Païkos, acting foreign minister in the absence of Zographos in Constantinople, characterized the whole affair as purely a "foolish enterprise of a very limited number of misled men."[145] Yet, in private, the king expressed his growing conviction that Russia stood behind the conspiracy, that it had been directed against his throne, and that his life had been endangered. Lyons accounted for this contradiction between public declaration and private belief by alleging that the king did not dare antagonize Russia by prosecuting the whole Napist leadership or admit his own unpopularity by bringing the whole affair into the open.[146]

But there are indications that royal prestige and Greek international relations played no greater role as factors in this behavior than the internal situation, where party strife had been rekindled by anti-Napist

[144] The documents described in n. 140 above.

[145] Païkos to Mavrokordatos, Athens, 15/17 June 1840, no. 36 "touchant l'association philorthodoxe," envelope 69, Vol. 18.1 (1840: London Embassy), Archives of the Greek Foreign Ministry, Athens. In two previous official despatches, Païkos had complained to Mavrokordatos about what he alleged were misconceptions about the plot. In the first, dated 26 Feb. 1840*o.s.*, no. 11, envelope 60, Vol. 18.1 (1840: London Embassy), he wrote: "I never imagined that lying would reach such a degree of shamelessness, that it would offend His Hellenic Majesty, by alleging that the main purpose of the society was an attack on the Holy Person of the King, enforced baptism, and in the event of refusal, assassination. As if this weren't enough, the lying attempted to incriminate a foreign protecting power. . . ." The second, dated 8/20 Mar. 1840, no. 12, envelope 61, Vol. 18.1 (1840: London Embassy), stated: "Since I informed you about the government's discovery of a society called philorthodox, the newspapers of Europe have not ceased to publish news different from that which I gave you, whether true or false." The correspondence shows Païkos' concern, lest Otho's command of his subjects' allegiance be doubted in Europe, also lest Russian implication involve Greece in a feud with Russia. According to Lyons (Athens, 28 Feb. 1840, no. 34, FO 32.96), Païkos was delighted by an article in the *Austrian Observer,* which presented Metternich's view as that of discounting the Philorthodox plot as an insignificant conspiracy.

[146] According to Lyons (Athens, 28 Feb. 1840, no. 34, FO 32.96), many of Catacazy's friends no longer denied complicity of the Russian mission in the plot. According to Driault and Lhéritier (*Histoire,* II, 196), the Greek government didn't dare get to the bottom of the affairs, as Palmerston wished, because "it feared that it would find itself in conflict with the Russia that one felt behind the Philorthodox."

attempts to work their way back into power by discrediting the Napists and by Napist fears of open persecution or expulsion from the administration. The semiofficial *Ho Hellēnikos Tachydromos* reflected the king's uneasiness about the tense internal situation. Emphatically it stated the government's irrevocable decision to remain impartial toward all parties to avoid falling under the exclusive sway of any one, and to punish and reward individuals rather than parties. This newspaper was obliquely reassuring frightened Napists that they need not fear wholesale persecution and warning anti-Napists that they must not exploit the situation to advance themselves to exclusive power.[147]

The king undoubtedly realized now, even better than the regency had in 1833-34, that this policy of maintaining a curb on all parties precluded a thorough investigation of the plot or legal prosecution of all suspects. A thorough investigation would require the removal of all those Napists who, by their official position, were able to thwart the unearthing of incriminating evidence. If the information in the secret memorandum is true, meting out justice would mean virtually rounding up all the prominent Napist leaders. Such purging of the administration and legal prosecution would involve open warfare with the entire Napist party and might drive it to desperate acts such as the Messenian revolt in 1834. Even if the Napist party could be paralyzed, such suppression of the Napists would upset too suddenly the party balance and irrevocably make the king reliant upon the Constitutionalists. As the new ruling party, they might prove as disloyal in their attempt to obtain a constitution as the ruling Napists had been in trying to realize their own aims. The king actually expressed his fears of alienating the Napist party when he refused requests for an immediate appointment of a pro-British cabinet. In brief, the king was confronted by the dilemma of plot response (discussed at the end of Chapter IV).[148]

In his account of events immediately after the discovery of the plot, Gennaios Kolokotrones represents the king as being gradually convinced that the society had had only irredentist aims and that no conspiracy against the throne had existed. Kolokotrones certainly tried to bring Otho round to this view and apparently Otho eventually spoke to Kolokotrones as if he agreed with him. But Lyons' contrary assertion of Otho's increasing belief in the plot and its Russian inspiration is probably closer to the truth, if one considers such acts as the dismissal of Glarakes. Most likely, Otho wanted Kolokotrones and other Napists to believe himself duped so as not to alarm them or drive them into taking defensive action.[149]

[147] *Ho Hellēnikos Tachydromos*, 14/26 Jan. 1840.

[148] Lyons to Palmerston, Athens, 30 Mar. 1840, no. 40, FO 32.97. See also Pipineles [*Monarchy*], p. 297: "As long as the matter was squelched at its genesis, the government thought it better to let it be forgotten, since otherwise the elements of guilt seemed confused and fears existed of involving Russia if all was brought to light." Pipineles failed to recognize Otho's apparent concern for the internal party balance.

[149] Gennaios Kolokotrones [*Memoirs II*], pp. 84-85.

Otho's acts seem to suggest a desire to dismiss the Napists gradually and accept anti-Napists only partially. The king first dismissed Glarakes and Axiotes, governor of Attica. The decrees simply announced their retirement from office, but they did not contain the usual acknowledgment of past services and they received no substitute employment, according to established practice. All evidence indicated royal disapproval and raised suspicions about their guilt, but the state brought no legal action against them.[150]

The king gave direction of the investigations, which rightfully belonged to the Napist Typaldos, prosecutor of the Athens court of first instance, to the Constitutionalist C. Pitsipios, prosecutor of the court of appeal, who later twice complained that Païkos was obstructing the investigations. The replacement of Glarakes and Axiotes by Constitutionalists, the appointment of a predominantly liberal holy synod in July, the repeal of past Napist-sponsored acts for the curbing of brigandage, and the implementation of the unexecuted Armansperg law of 1836 for the establishment of provincial councils, all reflected a royal shift, however moderate and restricted, toward the Constitutionalists. As Barbara Jelavich, in a recent article on the Philorthodox plot has pointed out, the Constitutionalists, in conjunction with the British legation, had used the incident to advance their own interests against those of Russia and the "Russians," but owing to the shrewdness of Otho, not to the degree they desired.[151]

Leniency characterized the investigations and indictment. The prolonged investigations led only to three further arrests—those of Anastasios Androutsos, Constantine Mavrogiannes, and Peter Valves. In May the

[150] On the dismissal of Glarakes, see decree of 30 Dec./11 Jan. 1840 [*Government Gazette*], no. 2, 18 Jan. 1840*o.s.*; Lyons to Palmerston, Athens, 13 Jan. 1840, no. 10, and 16 Jan. 1840, no. 12, FO 32.96; and A. Païkos to Mavrokordatos, Athens, 6/13 Jan. 1840, envelope 54, Vol. 18.1 (1840: London Embassy), Archives of the Greek Foreign Ministry: ". . . Glarakes, for the little ability which he showed on this occasion, has been deprived of his functions. . . ." On Axiotes' dismissal, see Lyons to Palmerston, Athens, 11 Jan. 1840, no. 8, FO 32.96.

[151] On the complaints of Pitsipios, see Lyons to Palmerston, Athens, 1 June 1840, no. 70, FO 32.97. By decree of 23 July/4 Aug. 1840 ([*Government Gazette*], no. 17, 26 Aug. 1840*o.s.*) the synod of 1840-41 consisted of Cyril of Argolis, president; Gerasimos of Hydra, Zacharias of Thera, Theodoretos of Sellasia (who had some conservative-Napist leanings), Neophytos of Phocis, with Neophytos of Attica and Jonah of Elis as alternates; see also Lyons' comments, Athens, 8 Aug. 1840, no. 93, FO 32.98. On the repeal of antibrigand acts, see decree of 8/20 Jan. 1840 [*GG*], no. 1, 9 Jan. 1840*o.s.* The convocation of the provincial councils, which had been elected in 1837 but never convoked, was required to give effect to the original Armansperg law of late 1836 which had abortively remained on the statute books; the convocation was effected by three separate decrees: 9/21 Apr. 1840 [*GG*], no. 7, 10 Apr. 1840*o.s.*; 13/25 May 1840 [*GG*], no. 9, 17 May 1840*o.s.*; 2/14 July 1840 [*GG*], no. 13, 9 July 1840*o.s.* See also Lyons to Palmerston, Athens, 23 Apr. 1840, no. 53, FO 32.97, and ed. Barbara Jelavich, "The Philorthodox Conspiracy of 1839," *Balkan Studies*, vii, (1966), 94.

indictment, recommended by Typaldos and accepted by the court of first instance in Athens, dismissed charges against those three on grounds of insufficient evidence. It cited only Niketas, Kapodistrias, and Renieres for trial. It accused the former two of organizing, the latter of serving as agent of, a secret society whose primary aim was irredentist. It charged them with misdemeanor, rather than treason, and cited Arts. 212, 214, and 217 of the penal code which proscribed secret societies. Niketas, whose alleged prison sufferings *Aiōn* publicized with vigor, obtained release from prison pending trial without bail. Kapodistrias and Renieres each paid bail of 600 drachmas. According to Lyons, the king's advisors recommended such mildness and the public expected it. Indeed, it was generally believed that the government wanted to hush up the whole affair. Certainly the government's attitude toward this plot contrasted sharply with that of the regency with regard to the Napist plot of 1833.[152]

The trial took place on 11 July. Curiously, it turned into another battle in the warfare of charges and countercharges exchanged by *Aiōn* and *Athēna* since the previous January, fought out this time between the lawyers for the defense. In the morning the prosecution presented its documentary evidence—a rough draft of the organization of the society, three diplomas, a letter addressed by Kapodistrias to the patriarch of Constantinople—and called its three witnesses—Papas, Venthylos, and Kolokouvaros.

After the noon recess, just before the defense was ready to present its case, Stroumpos and Masson, lawyers of Renieres, rose unexpectedly to make startling charges—that a plan was underway to exculpate Niketas and Kapodistrias by making Renieres bear the full blame, that persons had approached Renieres in prison, with threats and bribes, to make him charge that Klonares, Manouses, Pharmakides, and Praïdes, all members of the "English" party, had feigned the existence of a society and commissioned him to implicate Niketas and Kapodistrias. In order to prove their allegations, Renieres' lawyers asked the court to allow a reexamination of the three morning witnesses and to permit the introduction of new witnesses, namely prison inmates, among them perhaps the author of the anonymous memorandum, who supposedly could testify to the pressure Renieres had suffered. The court granted the first request but refused the

---

[152] For instance, Lyons complained that a Lasgaris had been allowed to leave Greece with important incriminating evidence (Athens, 13 Feb. 1840, no. 28, FO 32.96); and that Typaldos had allowed three suspects to escape (30 May 1840, no. 68, FO 32.97).

For the text of indictment, dated 15 May 1840*o.s.*, and drawn up by the court of first instance in Athens, see the enclosure in Lyons' despatch of 18 June 1840, no. 78, FO 32.97. For comments on the indictment and charges, see Lyons to Palmerston, Athens, 30 May 1840, no. 68, and 1 June 1840, no. 70, FO 32.97; *Aiōn*, 2 June 1840*o.s.*; and *Athēna*, 5 June 1840*o.s.*

On *Aiōn*'s press campaign in criticism of official treatment of Niketas, see issues of 18 Feb., 5 May, and 19 May 1840*o.s.*

second. Without new witnesses the Renieres charge could not be proved —but no need. Renieres' lawyers had simply acted to prevent the lawyers of Kapodistrias and Niketas from introducing trumped-up charges against their client or from bringing accusations against members of the "English" party.[153]

That the lawyers of Kapodistrias and Niketas actually intended on that afternoon to adopt this strategy is uncertain. According to the anonymous memorandum, the lawyers of Niketas, one of whom was Paparregopoulos, the Russian consul in Greece, had intended to take this approach. Niketas and Kapodistrias would deny their signatures on the documents, their lawyers would then ask the court to order the arrest of Papas and Renieres for forgery, and request the dismissal of the present case on the grounds that the Philorthodox society was the invention of prominent members of the "English" party. But, said the memorandum, when Kapodistrias refused to perjure himself and threatened to go to the king with information that would incriminate prominent Napists, the lawyers decided to abandon this scheme. None the less, Renieres' lawyers, of whom Masson at least was strongly anti-Napist, probably did not know that the scheme had been abandoned and hence moved swiftly to thwart it.[154]

Whether because of Renieres' coup in court or Kapodistrias' previous failure to cooperate, the lawyers of Niketas simply based their defense on a legal point, namely that the society was planned by only two self-appointed leaders and two agents, not actually established by the accession of members, and that consequently the articles of the penal code forbidding secret societies did not apply. Since no one provided evidence to prove the actual existence of membership, the five judges returned a verdict of not guilty for all three defendants.[155]

The verdict angered and disappointed the king. He dismissed Typaldos, the prosecutor, on the day following the trial. The state appealed the case and brought charges against the judges of the lower court for neglect of duty. Although the Athens court of appeal declared the decision of the lower court a false interpretation of the pertinent articles in the penal code, it declared itself legally unable to impose penalties on the acquitted or to prosecute the judges. As a result, the king reverted to administrative action. He ordered Kapodistrias out of the Greek kingdom and placed

---

[153] On the proceedings of the trial, see *Aiōn*, 14, 17, 21, 28 July 1840*o.s.*; *Athēna*, 13 July 1840*o.s.*, and its publication of a long letter of 26 July 1840*o.s.* by P. Stroumpos, describing his defense of his client Renieres at the trial, in the issue of 31 July 1840*o.s.*

[154] ["Anonymous Memo"], n.d., no. 5794, pp. 35-37, Vol. 21 (1841), Mavrokordatos Archive.

[155] For the text of the verdict, dated 12 July 1840*o.s.*, see the enclosure in the despatch of Lyons to Palmerston, Athens, 27 Aug. 1841, no. 98, FO 32.98.

Niketas in confinement at Aegina. Small wonder, then, that the king, who was unable to secure legal action against the three, had not tried to secure a conviction against others whom he may have suspected privately.[156]

[156] On the appeal, see Lyons to Palmerston, Athens, 30 July 1840, no. 91, FO 32.98; for the text of the ruling of the court of Areopagus, see the enclosure in Lyons to Palmerston, Athens, 27 Aug. 1840, no. 98, FO 32.98. On the dismissal of Typaldos, confinement of Niketas, and exile of Kapodistrias, see Lyons to Palmerston, Athens, 30 July 1840, no. 91, and 13 Aug. 1840, no. 96, FO 32.98, and *Athēna*, 17 July 1840*o.s.* Most revealing is the official letter of explanation (of the verdict and subsequent administrative action) to Mousouros, the Turkish ambassador to Greece who had an interest in the punishment of men ostensibly involved in a plot against his state. It is dated Athens, 17/29 July 1840, no. 51, envelope 75, Vol. 18.1 (1840: London Embassy), Archives of the Greek Foreign Ministry. A part of it reads as follows: ". . . these individuals [the three accused] were unfortunately acquitted by the tribunal, because the magistrates were unable to find in facts of the accusation all the collection of circumstances whose support the law demands, so that it can give a condemnation. Nevertheless, the government, which already had the moral conviction of the guilt of the accused, has been confirmed in this opinion by the incidents in the course of the *procès* during which the accused made confessions which incriminated them. While respecting the judicial sentence, the government of the King has wished to do all in its power to show to the Porte the good faith and sincerity with which it has always acted . . . and it has taken the following measures. The King's procurator, who did not act in the exercise of his functions with all the vigor one could expect on this occasion, has been dismissed. Count George Kapodistrias, one of the two chief accused persons and an Ionian subject, has been expelled from the kingdom. Several other analogous measures will be taken with respect to the other accused within the limits of the law."

CHAPTER SEVEN

The Mavrokordatos Episode and the
Near Eastern Crisis of 1839-41

FOR a brief period during 1841, it looked as if Greece might, through peaceful transition, get a national government within the framework of a modified absolutism. The drive in this direction was episodal and it proved abortive. On the other hand, it constituted a landmark in Greek political evolution by momentarily uniting all currents of opposition behind a moderate set of reforms which might at one and the same time have strengthened the Crown and weakened constitutionalism. The failure of the moderate reform effort merits careful consideration, because it reveals the dynamics of party politics during a critical period and serves as background for the revolutionary events which took place two years later.

Strictly speaking, the episode began on 22 February 1841, when Otho recalled Mavrokordatos from London to become foreign minister, and ended on 20 August of the same year, when Mavrokordatos submitted his resignation. But the episode was really a part of the general Near Eastern crisis of 1839-41 which, together with the progressive deterioration of administration in Greece, precipitated an internal crisis.

The Near Eastern crisis of 1839-41 lasted just over two years.[1] It began in June 1839 when the superior military power of Mohammed Ali, insubordinate viceroy of Egypt, for a second time brought the Ottoman empire to the brink of collapse. It ended at the end of August 1841 with the suppression of a Cretan revolt by the Ottoman empire, which had secured the humiliation of Mohammed Ali and had gotten a new lease on life through the intervention of the European concert. In terms of European diplomacy, this crisis went through four phases.

On 27 July 1839, the five major European powers issued a collective note announcing their intention to intervene in the Turkish-Egyptian conflict as a matter of vital European concern. This act marked the rebirth of the European concert in Near Eastern affairs and ushered in the first phase of the near Eastern crisis (July 1839–July 1840)—European cooperation in behalf of Ottoman integrity.

Behind France's back the other four powers of the European concert negotiated the Treaty of London (15 July 1840) by which they agreed to force on Mohammed Ali a settlement in behalf of the Ottoman empire.

---

[1] For the best treatment of the second Egyptian crisis as it relates to Greece, see Edouard Driault and Michel Lhéritier, *Histoire Diplomatique de la Grèce de 1821 à nos Jours* (Paris, 1925), II, 179-220. For an authoritative treatment of the same phenomenon from the European point of view, see Harold Temperley, *The Crimea, England and the Near East* (London, 1936), Chaps. 3-5.

Such deliberate exclusion of France from the European concert brought Europe to the verge of war, as an infuriated French public sought to avenge what one French politician called "a diplomatic Waterloo." The Straits Convention of 13 July 1841, by which the five European powers agreed to close the Straits to all warships in time of peace, formalized the French return to the European concert. But the second phase of the Near Eastern crisis—the alienation of France from her European associates and the threat of a European war—actually ended with the fall of the Thiers government in France (October 1840) or the Convention of Alexandria (27 November 1840) by which England forced terms on Mohammed Ali.

Within the European concert once again, between November 1840 and July 1841, France emerged from isolation and humiliation to close association with Russia, Prussia, and Austria against the recently won dominance of Britain in Near Eastern affairs. The third phase (November 1840–February 1841) therefore marked the reentry of France into a European concert dominated by Britain. The fourth phase (February–August 1841) represented the resurgence of France within the European concert and her bid for a comeback in the Near East.

So responsive was the Greek domestic situation to international occurrences that Greek policy, with some variations due to local circumstances, went through four parallel phases: (1) from a pro-Russian orientation to equally solicitous treatment of all European powers in an attempt to wrest Crete through diplomatic measures from both Egyptian control and Ottoman suzerainty; (2) contemplation of war against the Ottoman empire and the courtship of France as a powerful ally against the possibility of a general European war; (3) a complete reorientation of foreign and domestic policy to appease and satisfy all-powerful England; and (4) a return to intimacy with France once France emerged from British dominance within the European concert. The Mavrokordatos episode coincides with the third and fourth phases. His recall is understandable only in terms of the third; his downfall only in terms of the fourth.

1. International Crisis and Internal Turmoil

The Great Idea

The Great Idea,[2] the inspiration of the Greek Revolution, electrified Greece during the Near Eastern crisis of 1839-41. It had never lost its hold over the Greek heart and mind, sustained as it was by persistent evidence of Ottoman weakness and consequent belief, even in Europe, that "the sick man" would soon expire. The Near Eastern crisis of 1831-33, during

---

[2] "At a single word 'Great Idea,' the most sane heads become incontinent and unreasonable," wrote Antoine Grénier, *La Grèce en 1863* (Paris, 1863), p. 230. On the Great Idea, see also T. N. Pipineles, *He Monarchia en Helladi 1833-1843* [*The Monarchy in Greece 1833-1843*] (Athens, 1932), p. 288; and Lefton Stavrianos, *The Balkans since 1453* (New York, 1959), pp. 467-68.

which Mohammed Ali first challenged his Ottoman overlord, evoked no special ardor in behalf of the Great Idea among a people utterly exhausted by civil war and completely taken up with the arrival of its king. Between 1833-39, energies in Greece focused primarily on the task of reconstruction and state-building, and Near Eastern affairs remained relatively stable. By 1839, however, neither condition any longer held. Finding the task of state-building frustratingly difficult, many Greeks turned wishfully to what looked like a more exciting, more patriotic, and more direct path to viable statehood. Religious prophecies, a medium of expression which the peasants could understand, gained widespread circulation and predicted 1840 as the year in which a cataclysmic change would restore Greek fortunes.[3] By providing what looked like a concrete opportunity, the Near Eastern crisis of 1839-41 intensified this feeling of restlessness and hopefulness. It also posed the practical question of how the Greek state could exploit this opportunity to liberate the majority of Greeks who still remained under Ottoman domination.

Not the validity of the Great Idea but its translation into actual policy precipitated profound differences of opinion among the Greeks. These differences took articulate form during the Near Eastern crisis of 1839-41 and deepened the ideological orientation with which each party emerged from the Greek Revolution. Disagreement centered over four basic questions during these years and, owing to lack of any progress toward the Great Idea, posed a fifth one for longer-range considerations.

First, should Greece rely primarily on European diplomacy or on a new Greek war of liberation to achieve its irredentist objectives? Second, which of the European powers could and would assist Greece most effectively, whether diplomatically or militarily? Next, if *enosis* or union of Greek-inhabited lands with Greece were impossible at that time, what course was preferable as the short-term foreign policy of Greece—support of continued Ottoman domination, which at least provided corporate unity for most unliberated Greeks and offered the hope of eventual collapse, or acquiescence in the fragmentation of Greek-inhabited lands into a number of nominally independent or autonomous states (such as the Ionian Islands and Samos, respectively), which were actually English

---

[3] According to Driault and Lhéritier, (*Histoire*, II, 185-87), a book of prophecies circulated in the provinces, announcing 1840 as the year of complete regeneration of Greece: "The formulas remained imprecise and enveloped in smoke-screens like those of Python, and they gave flight to imaginations. Some saw in it the regime of the Ionian Islands extended to all of Greece; the others, the Napists . . . interpreted in more grandiose terms . . . Greece reunited to the Turkish empire under the government of a Greek, that is to say Orthodox, prince, for example one of the sons of Tsar Nicholas."

The particular book in question went through several editions, all in Greek; for instance [*The Prophecies of Agathangelos*] (Athens, 1837), [*The Vision of Agathangelos, a Collection of Varied Prophecies*] (Athens, 1838), and [*Prophecies, or Prophetic Role of the Monk Agathangelos of Blessed Memory*] (Bucharest, 1838).

protectorates of longer life-expectancy than Ottoman domination? Fourth, if Greece were to decide on military action against the Ottoman empire, ought it to await a European war as an opportune moment or to under- take a war singlehandedly with the hope of drawing Europe in after it, as had been the case with the Greek Revolution? Finally, ought Greece to concentrate its limited resources on internal development so as to cre- ate a model state that would retain the loyalty of unredeemed Greeks and attract the support of Europe, or to build up a war machine for early war against the Ottoman empire on the grounds that the existing limits of the Greek kingdom rendered the development of a viable state geograph- ically impossible? Rather than enumerate answers to each question, one by one, we shall treat the subject of implementing the Great Idea as a succession of policies which embodied various combinations of answers to these questions.[4]

Any Greek government faced a conflicting set of demands because of the tension between two totally different conceptions of statehood held simultaneously by most Greeks. On the one hand, the Greek kingdom was visualized as an instrument for the well-being of its citizens and a member of the European family of nations. As such, its task consisted of regularizing relations with its neighbors, settling down to peaceful pur- suits, and concentrating on internal development. On the other hand, the Greek kingdom was conceived of as a kind of temporary and makeshift military base from which the already redeemed Greeks must carry on the national crusade in behalf of their unredeemed brethren. This view committed the government to the task of exploiting national resources for the benefit of those outside the kingdom, addressing itself to warlike preparations, and creating all state institutions to fit the size of the en- visioned future empire centering on Constantinople rather than the actual needs of a few liberated provinces [5]

Owing to its limited resources, no Greek government could carry out both tasks at the same time. Yet most of its citizens expected it to. As a result, it was bound to disappoint its own populace on one or the other count and certain to alienate the European powers by threatening to open up at any time the explosive Eastern question. Up to 1839 the royal government was able to pursue the objectives of internal development with only token gestures in behalf of the Great Idea. The Near Eastern crisis of 1839-41 made all that impossible. It stimulated all kinds of reck- less irredentist schemes in Greece, which the government could not countenance without offending at least some of the European powers. All Greeks, even those not prone to wishful thinking, saw the crisis as a

---

[4] For a discussion of these issues and the positions taken, see Conclusion.

[5] For presentations of the latter irredentist conception, see Grénier, *La Grèce*, p. 246; and Nicholas Kaltchas, *Introduction to the Constitutional History of Modern Greece* (New York, 1940), p. 4.

chance to advance toward at least partial realization of the Great Idea.[6]

The First Phase, June 1839–April 1840

By presenting a united front in behalf of the Ottoman empire early in the game, the five European powers virtually spelled out the only practicable course open to the king. Greece was militarily and financially in no shape to defy all of Europe in an overt or covert attack on the Ottoman empire. Her only recourse was diplomacy. She must appeal to the European concert for some compensation in a Near Eastern settlement or request at least some support in Constantinople for the satisfaction of limited objectives. Such objectives must not violate the principle of Ottoman integrity which the powers were defending. Within the framework of this diplomatic approach, only two objectives seemed practicable: the acquisition of Crete and a commercial treaty with Turkey.

The island of Crete had taken up arms twice during the Greek Revolution—once from the Revolution's outbreak until Mohammed Ali reconquered the island for the sultan in 1824 and added it to his pashalik as reward, and again in 1828 at the instigation of Kapodistrias. That distinguished Revolutionary record, the strategic position of the island, and its repeated consideration by the protecting powers at the end of the Revolution for inclusion in the Greek state, placed it in competition with Thessaly and Epirus for first place on the priority list of Greek irredenta.

In 1839 the character of the international picture made it top choice of Greek policy. Enosis for Crete would contribute to the European policy of containment for Mohammed Ali without taking away from direct Ottoman rule anything that had not been given up already. Privately, a group of Greek Cretan notables addressed a moving appeal for enosis to all three protecting powers on 10 August 1839. Through normal diplomatic channels, the Greek government petitioned the powers for the same kind of diplomatic intervention in Constantinople that in 1832 had ob-

---

[6] "The moment is come for our diplomacy to put itself in a position to profit from the great events which are preparing themselves in the Orient. I find here all the spirits in the best dispositions and all are ready to act. My despatches to my government are very pressing," wrote M. Argyropoulos in Constantinople to Chrestides, as quoted by Driault and Lhéritier, *Histoire*, II, 187. Mavrokordatos hoped that the Egyptian victories and the death of Mahmud II might lead to the union of Crete and Greece (*ibid.*, II, 193).

For a dramatic example of the frenzied enthusiasm of the youthful idealist, see Alexander R. Rangabe, *Apomnemoneumata* [*Memoirs*] (Athens, 1894), pp. 89-94. Unwilling to pass up any chance "to see their most cherished dreams [Great Idea] realized," he and his friends drew up military plans, proclamations, and governmental schemes for a revolt of the "still enslaved brethren in Turkey." Indeed he even sold his furniture to collect necessary funds. All came to nought when Veïkos, son of a Revolutionary hero, refused to lead the revolt as he had promised, and when Karatzas, whose financial support P. Argyropoulos had promised, failed to come through with funds.

tained Boeotia and Attica for Greece in return for financial compensation to the sultan.[7]

Before the Greek Revolution, the lands that became independent Greece had conducted the bulk of their trade with other parts of the Ottoman empire. It was only natural that the disruption of this trade during the Revolution should have caused great hardship and should have prompted a desire for its resumption, at least until it could be re-directed toward Europe. Widespread smuggling attested to the extent of the necessity and the desire for trade with the Ottoman provinces. But though smuggling tended to moderate some of the economic dislocations, it was not a permanent basis for sound and secure business, and it robbed the state of sorely needed customs revenues. Obviously, then, economic and fiscal considerations demanded the resumption of normal trade with the Ottoman empire. Such resumption necessitated the regularization of relations between Greece and the Ottoman empire in the form of a commercial treaty.[8]

To the very end of his life Sultan Mahmud II had ruled out the possibility of such a treaty by absolutely refusing to deal with former subjects whom he despised as rebels. His death in mid-1839 and the attendant crisis offered hope that the Porte might now be willing to negotiate a reasonable treaty. Since Greece depended more on Ottoman trade than vice versa, her bargaining position was weaker, and she obviously needed the support of at least some European powers both to initiate negotiations and to get reasonable terms. There was good cause for optimism about European support because regularization of Greco-Turkish relations through a treaty would reduce the threat to peace in the Near East and stabilize the status quo. At the advice of Zographos, Otho decided to initiate negotiations. The importance he attached to this objective is

[7] On 27 Aug. 1839, Otho wrote Ludwig: "How important the union of Crete with Greece is, I need scarcely enlarge on: it is a necessity for Greece from a financial and geographical (strategic) standpoint. . . . The present moment is a very valuable one for negotiations since it may easily be that the Porte (and other Great Powers interested), having regard to Mahemet Ali's desire for the negotiation of his claim, might now agree to transfer it to me, but not later . . . ," as quoted by Leonard Bower and Gordon Bolitho, *Otho I, King of Greece. A Biography* (London, 1939), p. 112. From the tone of a letter written by Zographos to Mavrokordatos on 23 July 1839 *o.s.* (as quoted by Driault and Lhéritier, *Histoire*, II, 188-90), it is clear that the government had decided to remain neutral, that it was pleading the virtue of such neutrality to establish some claim on the gratitude and good opinion of Europe.

Mavrokordatos argued, in his discussions with the British government, that *enosis* with Crete did not involve a violation of Ottoman integrity (*ibid.*, II, 192). On the petition of the Cretan notables, see *ibid.*, II, 189-90.

[8] Pipineles [*Monarchy*], pp. 262-64, based on an official analysis of Zographos' treaty, dated March 1843, by Mavrokordatos as Greek minister to the Porte after he had faced the same difficulties in his negotiations for a new treaty that Zographos had before him.

demonstrated by his decision to send Zographos to negotiate personally.[9]

Although adoption of the diplomatic approach to the irredentist problem formally committed Greece to a position of complete impartiality toward all three powers, it initiated a reorientation of foreign policy away from Russia toward the two Western powers. In part the moves away from Russia simply redressed the balance previously upset in Russia's favor. But other factors operated as well. Perhaps the Greek government interpreted as a sign of weakness Russia's willingness to associate itself with other European powers instead of invoking its exclusive right of intervention under the terms of the Treaty of Hunkiar Iskelesi. Certainly Greece took heed when Palmerston, who in 1830—albeit out of power— had favored inclusion of Crete in Greece, now expressed his reluctance to strengthen "a state which appeared to serve Russian interests in the Near East." Moreover, Greece had no minister in Petersburg, whereas in Paris and London Kolettes and Mavrokordatos, respectively, did their utmost to win the sympathy of the Western powers. Like Kolettes and Mavrokordatos, Zographos, foreign minister, was convinced at the outset that the government's policy of moderation depended on England and France for success. Yet he soon lost confidence in Britain and veered toward Russia when he found the Russian ambassador most helpful to him in his negotiations in Constantinople.[10]

Among the Greek populace, three distinct positions are discernible during the first phase of the crisis. The Philorthodox plot, already treated in Chapter VI, rejected the official approach of moderation, favored a war policy, and looked to Russia for realization of the Great Idea. That was the extremist position, identified at this stage with Napism. Supporters of official policy represented the other two positions, according to their advocacy of one or the other Western power as the major source of hope.

The French vice-consul in Athens visited Nauplion, where Cretan refu-

[9] Driault and Lhéritier, *Histoire*, II, 197. Zographos arrived in Constantinople on Dec. 1839, signed the Greco-Turkish commercial treaty on 3 Mar. 1840, and returned to Greece on 20 Mar. 1840.

[10] On Palmerston's reluctance, see *ibid.*, II, 192. On Kolettes' and Mavrokordatos' belief in the necessity of accord between the two Western powers, see Kolettes to Mavrokordatos, Paris, 13 Mar. 1840, Vol. 20 (1837-40), Mavrokordatos Archive, General State Archives, Athens, and as quoted also by Demetrios A. Petrakakos, *Koinobouleutike Historia tes Hellados* [*Parliamentary History of Greece*] (Athens, 1946), II, 260-62. On Zographos' concurrence, see Pipineles [*Monarchy*], p. 291. In a despatch to Mavrokordatos, M. Argyropoulos, Greek chargé d'affaires in Constantinople, wrote on 4/20 Mar. 1840 (no. 5696, Vol. 20 [1837-40], Mavrokordatos Archive) that Zographos got much help in his negotiations from the Austrian and Russian ambassadors. Lord Ponsonby, the British ambassador in Constantinople, notorious for his extreme suspicion of Russia, would neither help nor harm. He frankly stated, wrote Argyropoulos, that Greek commercial and naval development was not in the British interest, that the Greeks were inevitably pro-Russian because of their religion.

gees were settled, and confirmed rumors that a petition in behalf of a British protectorate for Crete was circulating. Obviously such individuals were reviving the precedent of appeal to England in 1825 and opting for a type of Heptanesian settlement rather than the return of Crete to Turkey. In Constantinople, meanwhile, the British were privately proposing for Crete a regime like that of Samos—autonomy within the Ottoman empire under a Christian chief. Because of British naval supremacy and Britain's good chances of influencing the choice of a Christian candidate (as it had in Samos), such a regime would have amounted to a British protectorate. The strategy of the Anglophiles was basically sound —that Britain might moderate its espousal of Ottoman integrity out of self-interest if it could get away with it.[11]

But many Greeks became alarmed at what looked like a conflict between British imperialism and Greek nationalism. Kolettes became the chief exponent of this position. Taking umbrage from the direct British control of the Ionian Islands and strong British influence in Samos, he suspected Britain of casting covetous glances at other Greek lands such as Crete and Chios. Carving up Greek lands into a number of states, whether independent, autonomous, or under the protection of a European power, became a new possibility. For him and those like him, this possibility constituted the greatest obstacle to Greek irredentism, which aimed at unity as well as independence. He also realized very well that while liberation from the Ottoman empire was only a matter of time, freedom from European tutelage would pose a problem of infinitely greater magnitude.[12]

His tendency to bet on France may have stemmed from predisposition, but the same could not be said for Zographos or Mavrokordatos who also counted heavily on France. As early as September 1839, the former decided that Britain would insist on returning Crete to Turkey so that

[11] On the findings of the French vice-consul and the maneuverings of the British in Constantinople, see Driault and Lhéritier, *Histoire*, II, 190-91. See also John Makrygiannes, *Apomnemoneumata* [*Memoirs*], ed. John Vlachogiannes, 2nd edn. (Athens, 1947), II, 116; he refers to the members of the Cretan Committee as "becoming English,"trying to give Crete the status of the Ionian Islands, once they failed in securing *enosis*. See also a letter from the members of the Cretan Committee (M. Apostolides, N. Renieres, Emm. Antoniades, and S. Antoniades) to Mavrokordatos, dated 23 Aug. 1839*o.s.*, in which they refer to Great Britain as the one "from whom results all for our country" (no. 5618, Vol. 20 [1837-40], Mavrokordatos Archive).

[12] "Just as the Greeks ought to work toward the unity of the Christians of European Turkey, so it seems to be unfortunate when some of them seek to persuade the inhabitants of some provinces to place themselves under the protection of the powers. Is it true that our good friend Antoniades is circulating a petition to be signed by Cretans in Greece, by which the protection of another power is asked? . . . I haven't stopped nor will I stop telling those here my opinion and to say it with an axe . . . ," Kolettes to Mavrokordatos, Paris, 13 Mar. 1840, Vol. 20 (1837-40), Mavrokordatos Archive, and as quoted by Petrakakos [*Parliamentary History*], II, 260-62. See also Kolettes to Mavrokordatos, Paris, 29 Apr. 1840, no. 6300, Vol. 22 (1842) [improperly catalogued], Mavrokordatos Archive.

Britain might retain the option of taking it over at some future date. Long before the breach between France and the rest of Europe, therefore, there was a strong tendency in Greece to look toward France as the power most sympathetic toward the Great Idea. Britain and Russia, it was suspected, coveted Greek lands for themselves.[13]

The Second Phase, April–December 1840

On 20 March 1840, Zographos returned triumphantly from Constantinople with the completed Greco-Turkish treaty of commerce in hand. Under the existing political system, ratification of the treaty should have taken place very easily—by a mere act of approval by the king after private consultation with his personal advisers, the cabinet, and the Council of State. Instead, the question of ratification became a widely discussed public issue. For the first time since the foundation of the kingdom, an articulate body of public opinion directly and visibly forced the government to reverse itself on a high matter of state. The great public uproar against ratification of the treaty represented a turning point, both in giving the upper hand to extreme irredentist groups and in forcing the government to consider seriously a war policy in behalf of the Great Idea.

The storm began to brew just as soon as *Aiōn* published, on 30 April, the full text of the treaty. To protect itself from the full force of public opinion, the Crown made it a practice never to release for publication any act or treaty until the royal seal had been finally affixed. This time the boldness of *Aiōn* got the document to the common citizen before the official world had even considered it. As the king was currently absent from Athens touring the provinces, one could be sure that the issue of ratification would get a thorough examination before any decisive official act took place. In a lead article in the next issue, *Aiōn* vigorously denounced the treaty for its alleged betrayal of national interests. *Athēna* and *Philos tou Laou*, reflecting "English" and "French" sentiment respectively, enthusiastically joined what became an intensive press campaign against both the treaty and Zographos, its negotiator.[14]

[13] On Kolettes' persistent faith in France, see his letter of 7 June 1841, no. 5932, Vol. 21 (1841), Mavrokordatos Archive: "We should not, it seems to me, have any further doubts about the desire of France to see Greece well organized in all the branches of her administration, and developed in all things necessary to constitute a strong and wealthy nation, worthy of expanding and enjoying a happy career in the future. I believe their desire unchangeable because I believe it now, as I always have, in harmony with her interests." On Zographos' and Mavrokordatos' hope for French support, see Driault and Lhéritier, *Histoire*, II, 191, 193.

[14] Following its publication of the text of the treaty in its issue of 18 Apr. 1840*o.s.*, *Aiōn* denounced the treaty in a lead article in its issue of 24 Apr. 1840*o.s.* *Athēna* criticized the treaty in a lead article (27 Mar. 1840*o.s.*) even before the full contents of the treaty had been made public. The full text of the treaty was published in *Athēna* (20 Apr. 1840*o.s.*), and has since been published *in toto* in two major secondary works: Tryphon E. Evangelides, *Historia tou Othonos, Basileos tes Hellados*

On 11 May, at a cabinet meeting over which Zaïmes presided, all but Zographos voted to recommend rejection of the treaty. The treaty then went to the Council of State, whose deliberations received exaggerated public attention because the sudden death of Zaïmes two days later was attributed to his excitement in denouncing the treaty before that body. His alleged martyrdom made what he called an "infamous" treaty look even more infamous.[15]

As Zographos bitterly pointed out, the issue of ratification became the topic of conversation in every office, coffee house, and grocery store of the capital. But public excitement went beyond mere conversation or debate. In a ritual act, involving each man's utterance of a curse as he threw a stone into a pile before Zographos' residence, many Athenians anathematized Zographos solemnly. Violence might have ensued if Zographos had not stayed indoors. Excitement reached such a pitch that it was impossible for Otho to ratify the treaty without incurring serious risks. By the end of June, the treaty was definitely dead, and Zographos, forced to resign (16 May 1840), was utterly ruined politically.[16]

In private correspondence, Zographos accused the "English" party of fanning the embers of public dissatisfaction into a conflagration which consumed him. Though he did not use the term " 'English' party," it is clear that this is what he meant by his own term "clique." According to him, the *mot d'ordre* went out from Lyons to Zaïmes, Trikoupes, P. Soutsos, Monarchides, and Antoniades, editor of *Athēna*. They in turn roused the rabble through the press. According to Zographos, the objective was to get him out of the cabinet. "Everyone in Athens is occupied these days in receiving the *mot d'ordre* from *Athēna*, it seems, and in denouncing the treaty. According to them I did nothing less than prove

---

(1832-1862) [*History of Otho, King of Greece*] (Athens, 1893), pp. 164-73; and Glanni Kordatos, *Historia tes Neoteres Helladas* [*History of Modern Greece*] (Athens, 1957), III, 122-28.

[15] On the cabinet meeting, see the *procès verbaux*, dated 29 Apr. 1840*o.s.*, no. 5718, Vol. 20 (1837-40), Mavrokordatos Archive. On the deliberations of the Council of State and Trikoupes' role as leader of the attack on the treaty, see Driault and Lhéritier, *Histoire*, II, 198-99. See also a letter of Zographos to Mavrokordatos, dated 6/18 May 1840, in which he describes P. Soutsos as having said that Zaïmes had died "fighting an infamous treaty insulting to the autonomy of Greece" (no. 5722, Vol. 20 [1837-40], Mavrokordatos Archive).

[16] See Zographos' apology in *Athēna*, 1 June 1840*o.s.* On the public commotion and acts of hostility, see Zographos' personal correspondence with Mavrokordatos during this time, Athens, 17/29 Apr. 1841 (for his observation quoted in the text above), no. 5711, 6/18 May 1840, no. 5722, and 13/25 June 1840, no. 5734, Vol. 20 (1837-40), Mavrokordatos Archive; Lyons to Palmerston, Athens, 30 May 1840, no. 68, Archives of the British Foreign Office, Ser. 32, Vol. 97 (hereafter to be cited as FO 32.97 and so on); and Finlay, Journal (MSS), 27 May 1846, Finlay Papers, The British School of Archeology, Athens (". . . the Treaty which Zographos lately concluded with Turkey almost threatened a popular commotion"). See also the following secondary sources: Driault and Lhéritier, *Histoire*, II, 197-99; and Pipineles [*Monarchy*], p. 260.

myself the modern betrayer of Greece, Pausanias, sacrificing Greek interests and securing Russia's indirectly in the way which Voutaniev [Russian ambassador to Constantinople] dictated to me," he wrote to Mavrokordatos on 29 April 1840.[17]

There is certainly no reason to question Zographos' facts, nor are the motives of those whom he accused hard to discern. Lyons' correspondence betrays his personal animosity toward Zographos, and letters of M. Argyropoulos, Greek chargé d'affaires in Constantinople, attest to the personal jealousy that Zographos aroused in others by his quick success in negotiating the treaty and by his ambition for personal honors. Once a member of the "English" party, Zographos had apparently separated himself from it when he acceded to high office. By the standards of normal party behavior he may even have slighted his old friends. That is probably why Lyons and the rest were obviously using the issue of ratification as a way of toppling him from office, but they were also suspicious of any treaty which received the support this one did from Russia during its negotiation in Constantinople.[18]

It was perfectly natural that Zographos should concentrate on the personal aspects of the press campaign and hence attribute its chief source to the "English" party. But the fact remains that *Aiōn* was the first to act, that *Philos tou Laou* joined in, and that opposition to the treaty became tripartisan even if it did not start out so. Moreover, although some may have exploited the issue of ratification from partisan resentment or for partisan advantage, these were not the reasons for opposition which the press argued nor could they have been the motives which actuated the average citizen.

Opponents of the treaty rested their denunciation on three basic criticisms. First, Greece did not enjoy the full status of most favored nation

---

[17] No. 5711, Vol. 20 (1837-40), Mavrokordatos Archive. From the same volume, see the following letters of Zographos to Mavrokordatos: (1) that of 7/19 Sept. 1840, no. 5767, in which Zographos actually accuses the following of organizing public opinion against him—Zaïmes, Trikoupes, P. Soutsos, Monarchides, and Païkos; and (2) that of 28 Mar. 1841*o.s.*, no. 5703, in which he interprets the purpose of the campaign against the treaty as that of getting him out of office. He also reiterated this same interpretation in his official memorandum to Otho, 20 Apr./2 May 1840, no. 5715, Vol. 20 (1837-40), MA.

[18] As an example of Lyons' early animosity toward Zographos and the possible grounds on which it rested, see Lyons to Palmerston, Athens, 24 May 1838, no. 89, FO 32.77, in which he quoted Zographos as saying that Palmerston's "opinion on the necessity of the economic and political advantages of constitutional government would be very embarrassing to him [Zographos] in his communication with the king. I have before seen signs," continued Lyons, "of Zographos' want of firmness in upholding the principles he professes . . .." M. Argyropoulos to Mavrokordatos, Pera (Constantinople), 3/15 Mar. 1840, no. 5721, and 4/20 Mar. 1840, no. 5696, Vol. 20 (1837-40), Mavrokordatos Archive. P. Soutsos told Lyons that Otho showed him proof that Russia was strongly urging him to ratify Zographos' treaty (Lyons to Palmerston, Athens, 7 May 1840, no. 60, FO 32.97).

in this treaty as it did in commercial treaties already negotiated with other powers. Second, Greek merchants would incur obligations of which the merchants of other countries in Turkey were free. Last, the treaty included "offensive" clauses on citizenship (Arts. XXI and XXIV), especially the one which forbade the renunciation of one's citizenship in either of the two states under any circumstances.[19] Strictly economic considerations might justify the first two criticisms, but the average person probably did not understand such specific considerations nor feel his own interests vitally affected by them. Certainly the third criticism would not stand on strictly legal grounds. Careful consideration of all three criticisms will reveal their source in a strong feeling of nationalism.

The first two criticisms demonstrate the wounded national pride that detected and resented any suggestion of implied Greek inferiority or past rayah status. The third betrayed fears relating to the Great Idea—fears of cutting off certain roads to its realization, fears of calling its very validity into question. The clause against renunciation of citizenship would have permitted the Ottoman government to prevent the much-needed migration of some unredeemed Greeks to underpopulated Greece. It also would have denied Greece the right, enjoyed by the major European powers, to offer citizenship to Ottoman subjects and with it a kind of extraterritoriality which, if extended to Greece, would have given Greeks in the Ottoman empire a privileged status. Indeed, nationalism bred in Greeks the presumption of expecting to enjoy the same prerogatives in the Ottoman empire as the great powers. In addition, besides giving official recognition to the existence of an Ottoman nationality, the citizenship clauses implied a definition of nationality in terms of residence and state sovereignty rather than religious and cultural affiliation. Though impossible to prove, one suspects that for the most ardent Greek nationalists, no treaty, however advantageous materially, would have been acceptable. There was a stigma of immorality to any kind of negotiation with the hated Turks or any sort of recognition of an empire which Greeks felt ensconced on territory that was rightfully theirs.[20]

For the exponents of a military approach to the problem of irredentism —heavily represented in both the "French" and "Russian" parties—opposition to the ratification of the treaty was most probably a veiled attack on the government's policy of moderation. As stated previously, successful completion of a commercial treaty with Turkey was certainly as much an object of government policy as acquisition of Crete. The treaty, pub-

[19] Driault and Lhéritier, *Histoire*, ii, 197-99; Pipineles [*Monarchy*], p. 264; and Evangelides [*History*], pp. 173f.

[20] According to Makrygiannes ([*Memoirs*], ii, 103), "The Turks and other foreigners who want our freedom put it over on him and he made a treaty which for the Greeks was worse than those we had with the Turks before we shouldered our guns." And another comment, ". . . if we can't have a treaty like other powers, the council considers it preferable to maintain the actual state of things," *Procès verbaux* of cabinet meeting, 29 Apr. 1840o.s., no. 5718, Vol. 20 (1837-40), Mavrokordatos Archive.

lished for all to see, was a much more vulnerable target than the general policy, which had no text to be published in the press, analyzed word for word, or presented to the Council of State for deliberation. By attacking the treaty it was possible to convey to the king the prevailing feelings against moderation without openly incriminating Greece in Europe. Moreover, repudiation of the treaty might provoke Turkey into engaging in the kind of retaliation that would serve Greece as a pretext for war.

Otho's behavior at this point seems to indicate some rather clever maneuvering to escape the dilemma of drifting into war with Turkey and alienating Europe, or antagonizing his subjects. His leniency toward those implicated in the Philorthodox plot undoubtedly owed something to the possibility that the Greek public might interpret greater severity as royal repudiation of irredentism. He obviously used Zographos as a scapegoat in order to remove the odium of the treaty from himself. On the other hand, he immediately designated Demetrius Chrestides, member of the "French" party, as Greek minister to Constantinople and instructed him to resume negotiations for a more satisfactory commercial treaty. This act reflects an attempt to forestall any Turkish retaliation which might precipitate a war and indicates Otho's reluctance to abandon completely his policy of moderation.[21]

But this reluctance was greatly weakened by two occurrences—one in Constantinople and the other in Europe. The Porte responded to Greek rejection of the treaty by announcing a series of retaliatory measures which it threatened to make effective on 1 October of that year. These included a ban on the entry of Greek ships into Ottoman harbors, an exclusion of Greeks from Ottoman craft guilds, a surcharge of 20 per cent on the import of oil, olives, or tobacco from Greece, and a sizeable increase in fines on smuggling. In effect, the Porte was bluntly replying to the king's call for resumed negotiations with a "take it or leave it" ultimatum. By taking an uncompromising and threatening stand, it was actually giving the upper hand to extremist elements in Greece. Neither royal nor national honor permitted reconsideration of the treaty under duress or inaction in the face of discriminatory Turkish practices. The Turkish position seemed to make war the only possible course if the Turks decided to make good their threats.[22]

News of the second occurrence—conclusion of the Treaty of London (15 July 1840) as a deliberate act of excluding France from the European

[21] P. Soutsos informed Lyons that Otho told him that "as Zographos had been an obstacle to the settlement of the Ionian Question and a bar to cordial understanding between Great Britain and Greece, he intended to dismiss him immediately" (Lyons to Palmerston, Athens, 10 May 1840, no. 64, FO 32.97). This view reached Lyons again and again. On the decree of Chrestides' appointment, dated 22 May/5 June 1840, see *Ephemeris tes Kyberneseos tou Basileiou tes Hellados* [*Government Gazette, Kingdom of Greece*], no. 11, 4 June 1840*o.s.*

[22] Driault and Lhéritier, *Histoire*, ii, 200; Bower and Bolitho, *Otho I*, p. 116; and Pipineles [*Monarchy*], p. 116.

concert—arrived in Greece on 20 August 1840. "The four power alliance came like a bombshell. The French newspapers have dazzled us, and many among us opened our fantasy up to war, an alliance of Greece, France and Egypt, and the dissolution of the neighboring power," wrote Zographos to Mavrokordatos on 9 September 1840. The war that Turkish behavior might have made necessary now suddenly seemed practicable. The break with Europe allowed the French government to give way to strong domestic pressures and openly support both Greek irredentism and the cause of Mohammed Ali. In the event of a European war, which now seemed a distinct possibility, Greece could rely on France for the money and arms that war against Turkey necessitated.[23]

The class permanently committed to a war policy of irredentism was the palikars. For the first time during the 1830s, they had experienced an agonizing conflict between patriotic duty and professional inclination. With the Turks gone, raiding could only be regarded as theft. With a national rather than alien government at the helm, conspiracy became an unnecessary expense for the state and a form of idleness rendered intolerable by the shortage of labor. Military implementation of the Great Idea provided the only possible justification of their old way of life and offered the only hope of restoring to them the importance and power which they had enjoyed during the Revolution.[24]

Many, perhaps a majority, of the military class had traditionally affiliated themselves with the "French" party. It was only natural that these "French" palikars should renew these affiliations and that others should assume them under the new set of circumstances that seemed to identify Greek and French interests so closely. There is evidence that the "French" party leadership deliberately exploited the situation to strengthen its membership and to expand its popular support. It was during this period especially that the "French" party became identified with the war policy for achieving the Great Idea.[25]

Kolettes contributed to this identification. For the first time since his

[23] No. 5761, Vol. 20 (1837-40), Mavrokordatos Archive. Also Driault and Lhéritier, *Histoire*, II, 201-202.

[24] "So far Greece has managed to keep strictly neutral. But you know how irons scratch the Karatasoi and the endless line of palikars. The great task of the Greek government is to kill, by its negative and moderate behavior, the thrusts and plans of the captains, both in and out of Greece. But for how long?" wrote Zographos to Mavrokordatos from Athens (31 Aug./12 Sept. 1839, no. 5622, Vol. 20 [1837-40], Mavrokordatos Archive). See in the same volume Zographos' reference to "the taste for war of publishers in the capital and palikars" (28 Aug./9 Sept. 1840, no. 5761). According to Lyons (to Palmerston, Athens, 8 Oct. 1840, no. 113, FO 32.98), "The chieftains . . . indulge hopes that Kolettes will head a general Greek uprising throughout the Ottoman Empire." Lagrené also noted the agitation in the adventurous class of palikars; see Driault and Lhéritier, *Histoire*, II, 187.

[25] "Some Greeks of the French party encourage and strengthen these [forceable irredentist] hopes," wrote Lyons to Palmerston (Athens, 8 Oct. 1840, no. 113, FO 32.98).

departure in 1835, he wrote to many of the captains. They and others interpreted this gesture in the most favorable light. Rumor had it that Kolettes had petitioned Otho for a leave of absence to return temporarily to Greece. Many believed that he would return home with the full support of France and place himself at the head of a general uprising within the Ottoman empire.[26]

Concurrently, the government of Thiers encouraged Greek hopes through Sartiges, chargé d'affaires directing the French legation in Athens during the absence of Lagrené in France. In August, Sartiges held a long conversation with Païkos, the successor of Zographos. In this dialogue, which continued until midnight, Sartiges offered discreet encouragement to Greek aggressive aspirations. From Paris, though, Thiers cautioned moderation, probably because his own government had not yet formulated a clear-cut policy.[27]

With popular pressure from below and official encouragement from France, no Greek government could resist the temptation to depart from its position of neutrality. Its relations with France became ever more intimate. On 20 October, the anniversary of Navarino, Otho gave an elaborate dinner in honor of the officers of the French navy who had docked at the Piraeus. This and other such incidents did not pass unnoticed, either by the Greek public which applauded or the foreign diplomats who disapproved.[28]

According to Lyons, the king went much farther. At a cabinet meeting in August 1840, he proposed an invasion of Thessaly. He intended to recall Kolettes to execute the war policy and placed his hopes on French support. After lengthy discussion, Païkos and Tisamenos approved such a policy and Kriezes, Theochares, and Hess (substituting for Schmaltz) disapproved. Because of the division, the king decided to table the question. On the following day, Kriezes appealed privately to the king for restraint until the outcome of British armed intervention in Syria became apparent. Otho promised to abandon the plan if the British met with success, but expressed optimism that King Louis Philippe of France would consent to Thiers' recommendation of war.[29]

Events proved such hopes unfounded. The Egyptian forces were soundly defeated by the British-Austrian intervention in Syria, and the resignation of Thiers on 20 October 1840 reflected Louis Philippe's decision not to risk war. With this severe French diplomatic defeat,

[26] Loc.cit.

[27] Driault and Lhéritier, Histoire, II, 200-201.

[28] Lyons complained to Palmerston, in a letter dated 9 Nov. 1840 (no. 131, FO 32.99), about Otho's alleged determination not to conciliate the Porte and his unaccounted use of some 300,000 drachmas that he borrowed from the treasury and his anticipation of the civil list allowance to the end of the year. See also Driault and Lhéritier, Histoire, II, 202.

[29] Lyons to Palmerston, Athens, 22 Nov. 1840, no. 132, FO 32.99; 4 Jan. 1841, no. 6, and 4 Jan. 1841, no. 7, FO 32.103; and 10 Feb. 1841, no. 28, FO 32.104.

British diplomacy reigned supreme in the Near East as Sir Charles Napier, commander of British land forces in Syria, proved when he single-handedly secured Mohammed Ali's official capitulation in the Convention of Alexandria (27 November 1840).[30]

This dramatic turn of events made the pro-French war policy of the Greek government completely untenable. Yet that policy was not easily reversible. As on the issue of ratification, private initiative again limited the government's freedom of action, but this time through resort to arms. The government had been free to decide whether or not it ought to undertake a war as a signal for Ottoman Greeks to revolt. It could not prevent Ottoman Greeks from making independent bids for liberation, or keep private citizens of Greece from encouraging such bids. By their many friendships and relationships with captains over the border, palikars possessed the means to organize border raids against the Ottoman authorities, apart from anything the Greek government could or dared do to stop them. Likewise, many of the numerous Cretan refugees, who had resided in Greece since the Revolution, maintained contact with the island with an eye to instigating revolt there.[31] Once such revolts took place and Greeks withstood the might of the Ottoman empire, no Greek government could escape the odium of betraying what it considered its sacred mission by remaining inactive.

This is precisely what happened. In Thessaly and parts further north, a pattern of abortive attempts to stir up revolt emerged. Late in October, Major John Velentzas suddenly appeared in Thessaly with a small band that soon swelled as palikars of the mountainous regions joined it. Shortly after, Captain Tzames Karatasos disappeared from Nauplion and appeared near Salonika. Hilarion, monk and friend of Makrygiannes, was arrested by the Turks at Mount Athos and accused of organizing an uprising in the province. All these activities attracted Greek volunteers over the frontiers.[32] But far more important was a sustained Cretan revolt

[30] Temperley, *The Crimea*, pp. 116-36.

[31] On the close relationships between palikars on each side of the border, see Finlay, "Observations on the State of Northern Greece," pp. 9-11, Journal 1835 (MSS), Finlay Papers. On the return of many Cretan colonists in Greece to fight in Crete, see Lyons to Palmerston, Athens, 30 Apr. 1841, no. 68, FO 32.105.

[32] On Velentzas and his exploits, see his own memorandum, dated 14 Dec. 1841o.s., published in the first edition of Makrygiannes' memoirs (*Archeion tou Strategou Makrygianne* [*Archive of General Makrygianne*], ed. John Vlachogiannes [Athens, 1907], I, 289-91). See also Lyons to Palmerston, Athens, 8 Oct. 1840, no. 113, FO 32.98; 22 Nov. 1840, no. 132, and 23 Nov. 1840, no. 133, FO 32.99; and 4 Jan. 1841, no. 7, FO 32.103; the newspaper *Ho Hellēnikos Tachydromos*, 3/15 Nov. 1841; and Driault and Lhéritier, *Histoire*, II, 203. On Karatasos and Hilarion, see *ibid.*, II, 214; and Makrygiannes [*Memoirs*], II, 104. Makrygiannes had talked to Velentzas and Karatasos about Thessaly and Macedonia, but Velentzas left without telling him. According to Lyons, in a despatch to Palmerston dated 30 May 1840 (no. 79, FO 32.97), "Bands of men leave daily for Thessaly and Candia; Prokesch's and my warnings don't seem to take effect."

that broke out in February 1841 and continued until August of that year. The revolt itself belongs to the third phase, but like the attempts in northern regions, its preparation took place in the months of October and November 1840. Like them, it derived its inspiration during the days when French support still seemed a distinct possibility and subsequently proceeded in its plans, hoping to sustain a revolt long enough to force the intervention of both Greece and some European power.[33]

As the discovery of the Philorthodox society showed, the king had good cause to fear private irredentist efforts as a possible threat to his throne. Any such movement, especially when thwarted, could easily turn itself against the government. Theodore Grivas made the government uneasy in October by accusing Makrygiannes of intentions to capture the military garrison in Athens. At the end of December 1840, the government intercepted a letter from Velentzas to a brother officer in Athens, announcing his determination to march on Athens with a large force. Early in 1841, the government sent troops to Acarnania after receiving intelligence about plans for a revolt there.[34]

Obviously Otho had to make some concessions in this prevailing atmosphere of extreme irredentism. There is evidence that although the official *Ho Hellēnikos Tachydromos* condemned private irredentist efforts, the king and his government looked the other way when assistance was being organized in Greece. In addition, Otho continued to hold France in special regard as all observed by the special attention which Lagrené received at a royal ball on 1 January 1841. For conceding to Greek public opinion, however, Otho provoked a sound denunciation from Palmerston, who intimated the possibility of disciplinary action against Greece for disturbing tranquility in the Near East.[35]

By the end of 1840, then, Otho found himself doubly threatened—

[33] For secondary accounts of the Cretan revolt, see George K. Aspreas, *Politike Historia tes Neoteras Hellados 1821-1921* [*Political History of Modern Greece*] (Athens, 1922), I, 157f.; Driault and Lhéritier, *Histoire*, II, 214; and Evangelides [*History*], pp. 186-91. For primary accounts see Makrygiannes [*Memoirs*], II, 115-16, and P. Argyropoulos to Mavrokordatos, Athens, 19 Apr.[?] 1841, no. 5888, Vol. 21 (1841), Mavrokordatos Archive.

[34] Makrygiannes [*Memoirs*], II, 104 (Grivas' accusation); Lyons to Palmerston, 4 Jan. 1841, no. 7, FO 32.103 (interception of Velentzas' letter); *Athēna*, 1 Feb. 1841o.s. (despatch of troops to Acarnania). See Makrygiannes [*Memoirs*], II, 114-15, for one of the irredentist plots in which he was involved. See also P. Argyropoulos to Mavrokordatos, Athens, 19 Apr.[?] 1841, no. 5888, Vol. 21 (1841), Mavrokordatos Archive, where he mentions the government's fear lest the Velentzas bands precipitate an internal revolt, and reports the existence of intelligence, presented by a Delegeorges coming straight from Lamia, to support such fear.

[35] For instance, *Ho Hellēnikos Tachydromos*, 15/27 Aug. 1840. Driault and Lhéritier, *Histoire*, II, 205-206 (warm regard for France and Palmerston's denunciation). As late as May 1841 (Athens, 30 May 1841, no. 79, FO 32.105), Lyons reported to Palmerston a benefit performance of an opera in behalf of the Cretan insurgents. Lyons reported the king's attendance and the presence of Lagrené, alone of all the diplomatic corps. He also alleged that Otho contributed $400 to the Cretan fund.

from within by the possibility of armed revolt and from without by the danger of European intervention. From the viewpoint of many Greeks, he had not met the supreme test of Greek patriotism (full support of the Great Idea). From the standpoint of the powers, especially Britain, he had betrayed the European expectation that the Greek monarchy would serve as a force for moderation in the Near East. So serious did both the internal and international situation appear that Maximilian, crown prince of Bavaria, undertook a special mission to Greece (29 December 1840– August 1841).[36]

2. BACKGROUND OF THE MAVROKORDATOS EPISODE

In entering the third phase, Otho faced two major tasks, each distasteful to him personally. Internally the country had to be restored to some sort of stability. This meant a redirection of national activity to the normal workaday pursuits. It also meant initiating reforms, a task made urgent by the Ottoman reform effort,[37] which posed the prospect of Ottoman revival as a bar to the realization of the Great Idea. Administrative paralysis and dashed irredentist hopes had created a strong wave of reformist sentiment. Its most articulate aspiration was the creation of a "national government," which clearly implied the expulsion of the remaining Bavarians and the limitation of royal power. The anaktovoulion, symbol of both Bavarian control and personal absolutism, became the immediate object of attack. Throughout the country, wherever contact with the Bavarians had taken place over the past eight years, anti-Bavarian sentiment flared up threateningly.[38]

Externally, Greece had to repair its reputation as a potential trouble-

[36] P. Argyropoulos pointed out to Mavrokordatos, Athens, 19 Apr. [?] 1841 (no. 5888, Vol. 21 [1841], Mavrokordatos Archive), two disquieting facts—that the Cretans had not declared a desire to be under Otho's sceptre; that at the Independence day celebrations of March 1841, there were persistent calls for freedom, indeed even insults to the king were heard. He concluded as follows: "Throughout the kingdom, restlessness prevails; everyone is seized by fear of the outbreak of revolts."

On 30 Dec. 1840 (no. 154, FO 32.99), Lyons reported the arrival of Maximilian. It is apparent from Lyons' subsequent correspondence that Maximilian had come to advise Otho and mediate between him and the foreign legations; for instance, see Lyons to Palmerston, Athens, 9 Feb. 1841, no. 23, FO 32.104.

[37] *Tanzimat*, the Ottoman reform effort of the mid-nineteenth century, was initiated by the proclamation called Hatti-Sherif of Gülhané, read in Constantinople at the end of 1839. On 9 Mar. 1840*o.s.*, *Athēna* published a lead article on the Hatti-Sherif and solemnly warned that the future of Greece was problematic, if the Turks advanced on the paths of reform and Greece followed its existing course. See also Driault and Lhéritier, *Histoire*, II, 198.

[38] On anti-Bavarian sentiment in 1841, see Piscatory, Athens, 20 June 1841 (1st report), in "Textes et Documents, La Grèce d'Othon," ed. Jean Poulos, in *L'Hellénisme Contemporain*, 2nd ser., IX (1955), 340; also *Athēna* (21 June 1841*o.s.*), which complained about the large fortunes allegedly acquired by Bavarian officialdom in Greece and about the high ranks they enjoyed, "ranks they never dared dream of in Germany." See Chap. VI, n. 14, above.

maker in the Near East. Since Britain had won the diplomatic ascendancy in the Near East, it was *the* power for the king to appease. In Greece itself, Russia had played a passive role since the exposure of the Philorthodox plot and for the time being was cooperating with England on Near Eastern matters. Catacazy had returned to Russia on leave, and the Russian chargé d'affaires restricted himself to the formal duties of his office. Prokesch-Osten had returned to Athens in 1840 with instructions from Metternich that he should cooperate with Lyons.[39]

Throughout the extremely fluid situation of 1840, Otho had displayed great skill in trying to keep all channels open. He had treated the Napists leniently during the investigations of the Philorthodox plot and had retained for them a fair portion of official positions. He had courted France. He had also made moderate concessions to Britain. An account of Anglo-Greek relations during 1840 will serve as a necessary background for the ultimate appointment of Mavrokordatos.

Anglo-Greek Relations

Longstanding British demands or complaints concerning Greece fell into four general categories. First, Britain complained against specific abuses, real or alleged, such as the practice of quartering troops on the families of conscripts who had deserted the army, the "system of torture" allegedly inspired by Tzenos, moirarch of Athens, the participation of Greek vessels in the clandestine slave trade, and the edict for the deportation of the families of suspected brigands. Such complaints, often based on fact, proved useful in discrediting the Greek government abroad while giving British interference a humane aspect.[40] Second, Britain wished a say in the appointment of government personnel all the way from local administrators to the cabinet itself. It wanted a place for its own partisans, but over and above, urged the removal of Napists from such important places as the governorships, synod, and ministry of education. Lyons kept insisting on a cabinet that could enjoy the confidence of the British government.[41] Third, the British government made

[39] On Catacazy's absence (until Sept. 1841) and the weakening of Russian influence after the discovery of the Philorthodox plot, see Driault and Lhéritier, *Histoire*, II, 197, and Kordatos [*History*], III, 180. "Prokesch has, since his return, shown a desire to cultivate friendly relations with me," wrote Lyons to Palmerston (Athens, 3 June 1841, no. 71, FO 32.97), and such collaboration between the two ministers is confirmed on the Austrian side by Friedrich Engel-Janosi, "Austria and the Beginnings of the Kingdom of Greece," *Journal of Central European Affairs*, I (1941), 208.

[40] For instance, see Lyons to Palmerston, Athens, 9 Nov. 1840, no. 131, FO 32.99, and 9 Feb. 1841, no. 23, FO 32.104; also Piscatory (Athens, 20 June 1841 [1st report], *L'Hellénisme Contemporain*, IX, 339) reported that Lyons "never passed up an opportunity to receive a complaint or support some pretension." See also Driault and Lhéritier, *Histoire*, II, 206. On the slave trade, see Lyons to Palmerston, Athens, 9 Nov. 1840, "Copy private," FO 32.99.

[41] For instance, Lyons suggested the removal of some Napist governors before the

substantive demands which presumably were designed to pave the way to constitutionalism, its ultimate objective. Such demands envisaged the convocation of provincial councils, the establishment of a responsible cabinet that would serve as more than a mere administrative organ of the Crown, and the "reestablishment" of an independent Greek church instead of attempting to reach a *modus vivendi* with the patriarchate of Constantinople.[42] Fourth, Britain demanded the promulgation of a constitution and the institution of representative government.[43] When relations between the two governments grew bad, Britain pressed the first and fourth set of claims, which were nonnegotiable, the first because abuses were an inevitable consequence of an inefficient administration's trying to maintain order, the last because of the king's absolute unwillingness to consider it. Only the second and third could serve as a basis for *rapprochement.*

Between January and August 1840, Anglo-Greek relations improved. But it was only a limited improvement, based on the dubious practice of making tactical concessions in return for a temporary advantage and totally devoid of any genuine sense of common goals. The discovery of the Philorthodox plot gave each side a chance to start anew. Lyons dropped his demand for immediate promulgation of a constitution and asked Palmerston for discretionary power to offer what little remained of the British portion of the loan. As conciliatory gestures, Otho rescinded the edict for the deportation of families, removed actual or alleged Napists from office (Glarakes from the interior, Zographos from the foreign office, Mamoukas from the ministry of education, and Axiotes from the governorship of Attica), convoked the provincial councils, and appointed for 1840-41 a holy synod with a majority of liberal bishops.[44]

---

provincial councils were reinstated (19 Jan. 1840, no. 14, FO 32.96), "a responsible ministry composed of tried ability and of moderate constitutional principles" (31 Jan. 1840, no. 21, FO 32.96), "a cabinet to inspire the confidence of the British" (30 Mar. 1840, no. 44, FO 32.97, and 22 July 1840, no. 88, FO 32.98), and he warned of the "dangers" to be incurred if the new synod were not better composed (19 July 1840, no. 87, FO 32.98).

[42] Lyons to Palmerston, Athens, 19 Jan. 1840, n. 14, and 20 Jan. 1840, no. 16, FO 32.96; and 23 Apr. 1840, no. 54, FO 32.97. In a despatch dated 9 Feb. 1841 (no. 23, FO 32.104), he demanded "a change in system, not just in persons." According to Pipineles ([*Monarchy*], p. 285), Palmerston wanted France to join him in making such demands but France refused (8 June 1839).

[43] For instance, Lyons to Palmerston, Athens, 31 Jan. 1840, no. 21, FO 32.96 ("A Constitution, in which the monarchical principle shall be strong . . ."). "He speaks more or less about a constitution according to whether he is dissatisfied or content with the government," wrote Piscatory (Athens, 20 Aug. 1841 [5th report], *L'Hellénisme Contemporain*, ix, 414).

[44] On Lyons' softening attitude and request for discretionary power, see Lyons to Palmerston, Athens, 30 July 1840, no. 90, FO 32.98. On Otho's concessions, which he communicated in advance to Lyons as virtual concessions, see Lyons to Palmerston, Athens, 19 Jan. 1840, no. 13 (on the edict for deportation and convocation of eparchal

Otho's willingness to exploit the chance for improved relations grew out of two pressing needs—funds to meet the semiannual loan charges on 1 September and postponement of the Turkish deadline of 1 October for the enactment of retaliatory measures. He intimated that Britain might guarantee the loan payment as a part of its portion of the third series and might use its good offices in Constantinople to break down Turkish intransigence. But he made concessions in driblets, perhaps because of a suspicion that Britain would not comply with his requests, more probably in order to concede only so much as was necessary to secure compliance with them. In return, Palmerston congratulated Otho on the "new orientation" of his policy—a diplomatic way of suggesting something not yet accomplished—and promised (though offered no guarantees) that Lord Ponsonby, British ambassador in Constantinople, would support the resumption of Greco-Turkish negotiations for a revised treaty.[45]

Of course, the popular ardor for war between August and December 1840 destroyed what little progress had been made in Anglo-Greek relations. Otho did not get his loan or even effective British support in Constantinople. Lyons did not secure "the responsible cabinet in which Britain could place some confidence."[46]

---

councils), and 31 Jan. 1840, no. 21 (on the removal of Mamoukas, the setting free of Kaïres, the authorization of Trikoupes to take his seat in the Council of State, and the substitution of P. Leventes "a liberal" for Axiotes as governor of Attica), FO 32.96; also 23 Apr. 1840, no. 54 (provincial councils), and 9 May 1840, no. 62 (on the promise to give citizens of the Ionian Islands the same privileges as those accorded British subjects under the terms of the Greco-British commercial treaty), FO 32.97; also 22 July 1840, no. 88, FO 32.98 (on the new holy synod). See the citation of several of these acts as deliberate concessions to the British by Païkos to Mavrokordatos, Athens, 28 Jan./9 Feb. 1841, no. 5811, Vol. 21 (1841), Mavrokordatos Archive.

[45] Soutsos expressed his hope that Palmerston would guarantee the rest of the loan without deducting the sinking fund and interest due 1 September (Lyons to Palmerston, Athens, 12 Aug. 1840, no. 95, FO 32.98). Otho requested British support for Chrestides' negotiations with the Turks (19 July 1840, no. 87) and Païkos appealed to the powers for protection against Turkish retaliation (10 Aug. 1840, no. 94), FO 32.98. On the threat and actuality of Turkish refusals, see *Ho Hellēnikos Tachydromos*, 1/13 Sept. 1840, and 23 Nov./5 Dec. 1840. On Palmerston's congratulations, see Driault and Lhéritier, *Histoire*, ii, 206.

[46] "Otho's assurances increased as the first of October approached for the Porte to decide whether the threats were to be effected. When the Austrian vessel had left on the twenty-third ultimo and it was known that it was too late for me to intercede with Lord Ponsonby, His Majesty withdrew from me and I observed signs of his determination to consolidate his favorite system of absolute power. But in some degrees appearances were observed until His Majesty read Mavrokordatos' private letter of the seventeenth ultimo, stating that you instructed Lord Ponsonby to adhere to the protocols and that you were determined to insist upon Greece providing henceforth for the interest on the loan according to Treaty. Otho re-espoused Glarakis' creatures and principles openly as He could, consistently with his plan of

Otho made no new bid for British friendship until the end of December, when a number of occurrences lent an air of urgency to this objective. The British were again pressing their specific complaints after the embarrassing disclosure that the British navy had captured a Greek vessel engaged in slave traffic. It looked as if Parliament would discuss Greek affairs at its coming session. Otho feared lest Britain "occupy itself seriously with Greece," even more when Lord Londonderry, a Tory passing through Athens at the end of 1840, dispelled any hopes that a change of government in Britain would alter British policy toward Greece.[47]

This time Prince Maximilian, now in Greece, assumed the role of mediator between Otho and Lyons. On 22 February 1841, after having failed in obtaining previous concessions from Lyons, Maximilian announced the appointment of Mavrokordatos as minister of foreign affairs and the removal of Tzenos, target of English diplomacy, from his post as moirarch of Athens. Païkos, the outgoing foreign minister, like Zographos before him, served Otho as a scapegoat for the damaged relations with Britain. Maximilian also informed Lyons that Trikoupes, Britain's first choice for a cabinet appointment, would return to London as Greek minister because the king knew of no one else sufficiently qualified.[48]

These changes, calculated to placate Palmerston and Lyons, actually offended them. Otho had not consulted Lyons before deciding on the changes and, in spite of what Maximilian said, it was obvious that Otho wanted Trikoupes out of the way and had no intentions of giving the

temporizing with France in hopes of obtaining the remainder of Her portion of the Loan" (Lyons to Palmerston, Athens, 22 Oct. 1840, no. 120, FO 32.99). Even before this, Lyons had started in the former fashion bringing charges against Otho's government (24 Sept. 1840, no. 106, and 7 Oct. 1840, no. 110, FO 32.98). And on 22 Dec. 1840, Lyons wrote Palmerston: "I have written Païkos to take measures to provide payment of the interest and sinking fund which will come due next March 1st" (no. 152, FO 32.99).

[47] Concerning the government's general distress over the renewed hostility of British diplomacy, see Païkos to Mavrokordatos, n.d., no. 5813, and 10/22 Jan. 1841, no. 5815, Vol. 21 (1841), Mavrokordatos Archive. Concerning Otho's fears lest Parliament discuss Greek affairs, see Lyons, Athens, 9 Feb. 1841, no. 23, and 10 Feb. 1841, no. 27, FO 32.104. Driault and Lhéritier (*Histoire*, II, 207) intimate a motive of this renewed bid for English friendship was the desire of *enosis* for Crete (it "looked as if the goodwill of England was sufficient since she was then all-powerful in Constantinople") but I find nothing to confirm this. Driault and Lhéritier (*ibid.*, II, 214) admit that Palmerston addressed a remonstrance to Otho on 13 Feb. 1841, and Mavrokordatos in a report of 1/13 Feb. 1841 (no. 5816, Vol. 21 [1841], MA) reiterated the point that the behavior of Lyons was a faithful reflection of British policy which enjoyed bipartisan support in Britain.

[48] On the announcement of Maximilian, see Lyons to Palmerston, Athens, 22 Feb. 1841, no. 35, FO 32.104. For the widespread view that Otho appointed Mavrokordatos because of the deterioration of both the internal and external position of Greece, see *Athēna*, 14 June 1841 *o.s.* On the use of Païkos as a scapegoat, see Lyons to Palmerston, Athens, 18 Jan. 1841, no. 11, FO 32.103.

"English" party a preponderance in the cabinet. In a note which he scribbled on one of Lyons' despatches, Palmerston wrote in April:

> One can't attach value to the professions of the Prince Royal [Maximilian] or King Otho as to the appointment of Mavrocordatos or Tricoupes. Their professions probably, like so many before, are intended for some purpose of the moment and are never to be acted on. The appointments will lead to nothing. Tricoupes will be removed from Greece where his presence is possibly inconvenient to the King, and will be at London where, from the nature of things, he will be able to do no good. Mavrocordatos will probably find, when he enters office, that he has no power to carry any of his own opinions into effect and will most likely be obliged to resign.[49]

The "English" Party

The "English" party had undergone major changes in structure since the days of Kapodistrias, when it consisted of three major coteries (Mavrokordatist, Lontos-Zaïmist, and Miaoules–Tompazist). The departure of Mavrokordatos and Trikoupes in 1834 had left the first coterie rather dormant. The Maioules–Tompazes faction seems to have disappeared as a separate entity after the death of Miaoules in 1835. Only Zaïmes, because of local influence, managed to hold together his coterie of Peloponnesian primates as a distinct element within the party. During the Armansperg period, when the English legation's great influence over the Greek government allowed it to dispense favors with liberality, it became the new center of gravity of the party.[50]

During the leaner days of "Russian" influence, Lyons managed to retain his control over the party. Neither Trikoupes, who returned in 1838, nor Anthony Kriezes, minister of marine and naval affairs since 1835, attracted personal followings, as one might have expected, Trikoupes

[49] For Palmerston's note, see Lyons to Palmerston, Athens, 22 Feb. 1841, no. 35, FO 32.104. On 8 Mar. 1841 (FO 32.104), Lyons wrote Palmerston two despatches. In the first (no. 41) he described his conversation with Maximilian: "although I regretted that King Otho had not decided to avail himself of the services of both men in the ministry here, still I heard with satisfaction that King Otho had adopted an alternative which gave fair prospect of good understanding between the governments [of Britain and Greece]." In the second, marked "private" and unnumbered, he wrote quite differently: "Constitutionalists and Nappists [sic] boast that the King has nothing in view but the ruin of the Constitutional course in the person of Mavrokordatos. Several of the most influential and best-informed Greeks have begged Church [Sir Richard] to tell me that they know that Otho only named Mavrokordatos in hopes of warding off impending attacks in the British Parliament of which Lord Londonderry gave him warnings."

[50] Piscatory (Athens, 6 Sept. 1841 [7th report], L'Hellénisme Contemporain, IX, 439) referred to Zaïmes in 1841 as "chief of the English party in the Peloponnesos." In a letter to Mavrokordatos (Pera, 29 Mar./10 Apr. 1838, no. 5500, Vol. 20 [1837-40], Mavrokordatos Archive), M. Argyropoulos speaks of Zaïmes and company (syntrophia) as something distinct and separate.

because of his former influence, Kriezes because of his high position. Zographos, a possible contender for leadership of the party, ended up outside the party, a victim of Lyons' hostility. Even Zaïmes, during the days of excitement over the treaty, abandoned his previous qualms about Lyons' advocacy of a constitution and moved closer to the British legation.[51] After Zaïmes' death, Dariotes and Rouphos, both Zaïmes adherents, abandoned their "English" affiliations and joined the "French" ranks, perhaps in reaction to what looks like the merger of the Zaïmes faction with the broader party of Lyons. By 1841, Lyons had so completely molded the "English" party into his own faction that Piscatory was able to describe it as a mere congeries of Greeks who:

> to succeed in their ambition or triumph over the slowness of Greek administration, sought the protection of the English legation and its agents.[52]

To achieve this result, Lyons had had to devise new ways to retain his control over the party and to retain, if not expand, its membership. To be sure, Greeks still looked to him for place and position, as Kriezes demonstrated in 1840 when he petitioned Lyons for a midshipman's position in the British navy for Nicholas Miaoules, son of the Revolutionary hero. But the strategy of the English mission changed to meet the needs of a party which had moved into political opposition.[53] Its needs were fundamentally two—first, a vigorous campaign to discredit the existing regime and place itself in power, and second, a rationale that would identify collusion with the British against the king with national, even royal, interest. The aggressive way in which the British legation fulfilled the first need has already been told. The rationale devised by Lyons requires elaboration.

The rationale rested upon a number of premises for which the British legation was constantly trying to win acceptance—that the existing system was intolerable; that its intolerableness derived from the incompetence of the king and his insistence on doing everything himself; and that only a constitutional system would limit the king's power enough to protect Greece from the consequences of his incapacity (anarchy or despotism). In terms of these basic premises, Lyons then justified his practice of loud and persistent complaints against alleged abuses, his advocacy of constitutionalism, and his constant reference to British might as a kind of threat. Britain had the power and courage to protect the

[51] According to Aspreas ([*Political History*], I, 153), since the departure of Mavrokordatos from Greece in 1834, the "English" party had sickened, and then Lyons gave it renewed strength. On Zaïmes, see Lyons to Palmerston, Athens, 18 May 1840, no. 65, and 20 May 1840, no. 66, FO 32.97.

[52] On the Dariotes and Rouphos defection, see Piscatory, Athens, 3 Sept. 1841 (7th report), *L'Hellénisme Contemporain*, IX, 439-40. On how Piscatory characterized the "English" party, see Piscatory, Athens, 20 June 1841 (1st report), *ibid.*, IX, 339.

[53] Lyons to Palmerston, Athens, 22 Jan. 1841, no. 15, FO 32.103.

victims of the existing system, he kept insisting. It advocated the only viable alternative (constitutionalism) to the present system; its obstructionist tactics provided the only way, short of revolution and all its perils, of forcing the king to grant a constitution.[54]

This rationale held a special appeal for conservatives like Zaïmes, for whom the spectre of popular revolt and civil disturbances represented a far greater evil than did British intervention in behalf of constitutional government. For increasingly, as conditions deteriorated, conservatives, who had formerly believed Greece unripe for a constitution, came increasingly to regard it as necessary to appease popular dissatisfaction and curb the king.[55]

This rationale also explains why men who undoubtedly regarded themselves as sincere patriots behaved like virtual spies of Lyons. In a letter to the Austrian representative in London, Prince Metternich attributed the following words to Lyons:

> I know everything that happens in the Palace and in the Government Offices [of Greece]. The King does not say a word without its being reported to me. You will ask how I protect myself against untruth. I never send a despatch to London, unless I have put my informant on oath. . . . I have sworn in more than a dozen Greeks, devoted to England, who dare not approach my house, because the King's police are watching them, and he bears them a grudge.

Lyons' boastfulness was justified. Griffiths, the ubiquitous Greek-speaking secretary of the British legation, maintained extensive social contacts, which in the small community of Athens provided a rich supply of vital information.[56] Lyons' official correspondence confirms the existence of all

54 On the alleged intolerableness, see n. 40 above. On the incompetence of the king, presented always in the form of a statement of fact about the views of the public, see for instance, Lyons to Palmerston, Athens, 24 Sept. 1840, no. 106, FO 32.98: "The nation is unanimous on one point—it considers the King a bar to improvement and feels the sad effects of his assuming responsibility for everything great and small"; also 22 Nov. 1840, no. 132, FO 32.99. On the necessity of a constitution to save Greece from anarchy or despotism, again presented in the form of statement of fact about someone else's alleged view of the matter (in this case Zaïmes' just before his death in the spring of 1840), see Lyons to Palmerston, Athens, 20 May 1840, no. 66, FO 32.97; also 24 May 1838, no. 89, FO 32.77. On Lyons' emphasis on British power, see Piscatory, Athens, 20 Aug. 1841 (5th report), *L'Hellénisme Contemporain*, ix, 414: "he speaks very loudly about the power of the country which he represents; without saying what it [Britain] is able to do *for*, he says voluntarily what it can do *against* Greece."

55 For instance Kountouriotes (Lyons to Palmerston, Athens, 5 July 1838, no. 119, FO 32.77), or Zaïmes (18 May 1840, no. 65, and 20 May 1840, no. 66, FO 32.97).

56 Prince Metternich's words, dated 10 Mar. 1839, are quoted by Bower and Bolitho, *Otho I*, p. 107. ". . . he [Lyons] is in easy contact with men through his secretary of the embassy, who is of marvelous activity and knows Greece very well—a tremendous advantage in a country where conversation plays such an important role and agitates so much," wrote Piscatory of Griffiths, Athens, 20 Aug. 1841 (5th report), *L'Hellénisme Contemporain*, ix, 414.

kinds of informants—out-and-out spies hired and paid for a special job, disgruntled and unsuccessful petitioners of royal favor like Theodore Grivas, and men as distinguished as Sir Richard Church and Spyridon Trikoupes.[57]

Trikoupes conveyed information passed on to him by Zaïmes and Kriezes, whose official capacity gave them access to state secrets. So far as the documents show, information obtained from Zaïmes described royal audiences in which Otho expressed desire for better relations with England. On the other hand, Kriezes provided the compromising news (after the fact, to be sure) of Otho's proposal of a war policy to the cabinet. Whether either Zaïmes or Kriezes knew or intended that Trikoupes would pass on the information to Lyons is uncertain.[58] The case of Theodore Grivas is instructive, not merely because it reveals the persons who would give a hearing to a slanderer of the king, but also because of the persons who supported the allegations of Grivas. Early in 1841, Grivas went to Lyons with the fantastic accusation that Otho had attempted to bribe him into accusing Lyons of distributing money to stir up disturbances. Knowing the unprincipled character of Grivas, Lyons remained doubtful until Church, Trikoupes, and Louriotes (an Anglophile who negotiated the first British loans in 1824-25 and discredited himself by his involvement in the scandal for the order of steamships) expressed their conviction that the assertions were true.[59] That Otho knew generally what was going on is evidenced by his complaint to Lord Londonderry that many of the diplomatic body were encouraging the disaffection of his subjects. Yet Otho shrewdly utilized this system for

---

[57] A letter of 18 Mar. 1840 ("Separate," FO 32.97) sent by Lyons to Palmerston, reported the drawing of a bill for £300 in favor of Messrs Goslings and Sharpe "on account of Her Majesty's Foreign Secret Service" and enclosed with the despatch "the usual receipt for the same." The services paid *for* obviously had some connection with the recently discovered Philorthodox plot in Athens. This is the only such document in Lyons' official correspondence from 1835-43. Most probably Lyons usually obtained his information by other than financial means.

Concerning Church's conveying of information, see Lyons to Palmerston, Athens, 5 Mar. 1837, no. 24, FO 32.69; he would even write up memoranda of his interviews with Otho for Lyons and Palmerston (Lyons to Palmerston, Athens, 1 Feb. 1840, no. 23, FO 32.96 and 10 Feb. 1841, no. 27, FO 32.104).

For Grivas and Trikoupes see nn. 58 and 59 below.

[58] Trikoupes related his own information, derived from an audience with the king (Lyons to Palmerston, Athens, 20 Apr. 1838, no. 74, FO 32.76). But he also conveyed information gained from Zaïmes; for instance (26 Mar. 1840, no. 42, FO 32.97), and from Kriezes, 4 Jan. 1841, nos. 6 and 7, FO 32.103, and 10 Feb. 1841, no. 28, FO 32.104. No. 6 reported the incident about Otho's proposal of a war policy, and no. 7, "most secret and confidential," cited the informant as Trikoupes, who obtained the information from Kriezes, "a person of scrupulous veracity."

[59] Lyons to Palmerston, Athens, 30 Mar. 1841, "Separate, Most Secret and Confidential," FO 32.104, together with two enclosures, the translations of two letters written by Grivas, the first dated 3/15 Jan. 1841 and the second 27 Jan./8 Feb. 1841.

his own purposes, namely as a way of getting information to Lyons of royal friendship for England. Such was obviously Otho's purpose in calling in Church, the English philhellene, for an occasional audience, and perhaps why he emphasized in the audiences which Zaïmes reported to Trikoupes that he intended to follow Palmerston's policy.[60]

In 1841 Piscatory wrote his government that the "English" party was a fiction. The so-called "English" party enjoyed none of the connections (local and provincial, he probably meant) of the "Russian" party nor did it represent national sentiment like the "French" party. An anonymous article in *Galérie des Contemporains Illustres,* inspired perhaps by Piscatory, said the same thing: "This coterie, though able and intelligent, was never able to raise itself to the proportions of a large party."[61] To what extent did the "English" party enjoy the support of the masses (if not the average peasant, then at least articulate local citizens interested in politics)?

To attempt an answer, one must ask the same question about the "French" party because both parties laid claim to the same body of opinion, sometimes referred to as "Constitutional party." The French and its own adherents called the "French" party the "national party," implying that it rested on a broad popular base. Piscatory's correspondence reveals how amorphous and meaningless his use of the term "national party" was. He denoted by it all patriots who wanted Greek independence and a stable administrative system that would protect every individual in the enjoyment of his rights. Almost any Greek fit the terms of this definition, whether "French," "Russian" or "English."[62] Such criteria could not serve as the basis of a meaningful distinction between parties.

The usage was only a rather slipshod propaganda device to enable the

[60] On complaints to the Marquis of Londonderry, see Lyons to Palmerston, Athens, 18 Jan. 1841, no. 11, FO 32.103. On Otho's obviously exploiting this for his own purposes, see Lyons to Palmerston, Athens, 30 Mar. 1840, no. 44, FO 32.97; 24 Sept. 1840, no. 106, FO 32.98. After Pharmakides and Kriezes broke with Lyons, Otho used them to convey to Lyons his continued goodwill toward England. In the case of Pharmakides (21 Dec. 1841, no. 188, FO 32.108), Otho made no secret of his having sent the cleric. In the case of Kriezes (6 Sept. 1841, no. 103, FO 32.107), Lyons reported ". . . though he [Kriezes] did not say so, I don't doubt that he came by command of Otho and that his object was to conciliate the British. . . ."

[61] Piscatory, Athens, 20 June 1841 (1st report), *L'Hellénisme Contemporain,* ix, 339, 341, and Chalcis, 25 June 1841 (2nd report), *ibid.,* ix, 343. Also an offprint from *Galérie des Contemporains Illustres,* Gennadius Library, p. 9; and Jules Blancard, *Études sur la Grèce contemporaine* (Montpellier, 1886), p. 5 (reference to the "English" party as "an innumerous fraction").

[62] On Guizot's equation of "national party" with "French" party, see Guizot's "Instructions to Piscatory," Paris, 16 May 1840, *L'Hellénisme Contemporain,* ix, 334. On Piscatory's usage, see Piscatory, Athens, 20 June 1841 (1st report), *ibid.,* 339-41. See also Blancard, *Études sur la Grèce contemporaine,* p. 5. William Miller (*A History of the Greek People 1821-1921* [New York, n.d., but probably 1922], p. 40) saw that this was "a handy catchword."

"French" party and French policy to represent themselves as a reflection of the vast body of public opinion. One might rather say that the "national party" was that section of public opinion which had suffered either the violation of its civil rights or exclusion from public office under the regime of Kapodistrias, and was therefore characterized by its hostility toward the clearly distinguishable Kapodistrians. It was this following which both the "English" and "French" parties vied with each other to control, monopolize, and represent.[63]

One might concede that the "French" party was more popular than the "English" on several grounds. First, it had a larger following among the military, who reflected the wishes of such a large body of the humble Greek population. Second, the "French" party had come to represent in the public mind Rumely, while the "Russian" was identified with the Peloponnesos. Third, as between Kolettes and Mavrokordatos, the former would certainly be more popular as a personality. But so far as the Mavrokordatos episode was concerned, Mavrokordatos stood a good chance of commanding the support of most of the "Constitutional party" because Kolettes was absent and Mavrokordatos was acting on a program of reform.[64]

The extent to which the "English" party commanded popular support was less a problem for Mavrokordatos than two further questions—was the "English" party loyal to Mavrokordatos or Lyons? to what extent would members of the "English" party assist Mavrokordatos in governing effectively? Most revealing on this point are the letters of Manoles and Pericles Argyropoulos, brothers-in-law and the most devoted political adherents of Mavrokordatos. Neither was politically influential in his own right, but both kept their brother-in-law abreast of Greek affairs during his absence in Munich and London. Their letters to him reveal two outstanding facts—that there was a Mavrokordatos faction, which refrained from too close a connection with Lyons and his faction, and that from among the "English" party there were virtually none endowed with all the necessary qualifications for office, such as administrative skill, political influence, personal loyalty to Mavrokordatos, and sufficient independence of Lyons.

Both Manoles and Pericles Argyropoulos, the center of Mavrokordatos'

[63] So far as I can tell, on the basis of available but really insufficient evidence, popular consciousness of personal affiliation with a national party, where such feeling did exist, went along the lines of Constitutionalist-Governmentalist rather than "English-French-Russian" divisions. Several reasons for this are plausible. First, during the Revolutionary period, Kapodistrias was the only man to hold power long and absolutely enough to create throughout the provinces a well-organized party against which all the others could unite and the protracted period of civil war in 1831-32 crystallized this division. For various additional reasons, see Chap. III, n. 58, above. "I have deprecated the idea of dividing the constitutional party into French and English," wrote Lyons to Palmerston, Athens, 24 Feb. 1836, no. 11, FO 32.58.

[64] See pp. 137-42 on the " 'French' party" in Chap. III above.

personal following, disapproved of too close a connection with Lyons. Manoles characterized Lyons as a monstrous person who ought to be removed from Greece. Pericles, though in contact with Lyons, apparently kept that contact purely formal and infrequent. He criticized Trikoupes for being too servile and polite toward Lyons. He stated his intention of protesting to Lyons against the unfavorable press that Greece received in Britain. In addition, Pericles warned that Mavrokordatos should have no confidence in such men as Roque, a former clerk of Mavrokordatos, or young Bountoures, because the former was an obvious spy for Lyons and the latter a daily frequenter of the minister's home. Clearly, behind Pericles' remarks was the assumption that a client of Lyons was disqualified from becoming a close associate of Mavrokordatos.[65]

According to Piscatory, Mavrokordatos did not consider himself a member of the "English" party although he admitted that most of his friends belonged to it. Mavrokordatos tried deliberately to erase his close identification with Britain in the public mind. He refused a British offer in 1841 of transportation back to Greece in one of its warships. He arrived in a French steamer instead. He emphatically stood his ground against British prodding for his espousal of a constitution, and he managed to extract from Lyons a promise that England would stop antagonizing the king with petty protests. The British preference for Trikoupes until he defected to the king derived from Mavrokordatos' relative independence of Britain.[66]

In advising Mavrokordatos on cabinet appointments, the Argyropouloi disqualified "English" party men one by one. In the extant letters at least, Manoles and Pericles considered only Praïdes, Klonares, John Soutsos, Tisamenos, Spaniolakes, Theochares, and Zographos. Pericles considered Klonares good only for lots of talk. Manoles considered Praïdes and Spaniolakes as the only two loyal enough to Mavrokordatos to qualify for a cabinet post, but thought Praïdes incompetent for such a post and Spaniolakes a political liability since, instead of bringing Mavrokordatos royal and popular support, he would need the shelter of Mavrokordatos against royal and popular disapproval. In fact, one of Mavrokordatos' chief problems, as Manoles and Pericles both agreed, was in finding

[65] M. Argyropoulos to P. Argyropoulos, Pera, 26 Mar./7 Apr. 1841, no. 5857, and P. Argyropoulos to Mavrokordatos, Athens, 18 Apr. 1841*o.s.*; no. 5861, Vol. 21 (1841), Mavrokordatos Archive.

[66] Piscatory, Chalcis, 25 June 1841 (2d report), *L'Hellénisme Contemporain*, IX, 343. On Mavrokordatos' wish to dissociate himself from British diplomacy, see P. A. Argyropoulos, "Ho Alexandros Maurokordatos kai he syntagmatike prospatheia tou 1841" ["Alexander Mavrokordatos and his Constitutional Attempts of 1841"], *Hellenika*, IX (1936), 99. Lyons *said* Britain preferred Trikoupes because circumstances were critical and Trikoupes was already in Greece (Lyons to Palmerston, Athens, 22 Feb. 1841, no. 35, and 8 Mar. 1841, no. 41, FO 32.104).

friends whom he could trust as cabinet colleagues.[67] Indeed, Piscatory was probably right when he asserted that Mavrokordatos possessed friends but no party. Government by coalition was necessary, not merely because each legation and party had to be satisfied, but also because Mavrokordatos did not have enough of a party to staff all important positions.

Administrative Paralysis

By the beginning of 1841, it was painfully evident that the Crown had failed in two of its most persistent efforts over the previous eight years. It had not established an efficient and impartial administration. It had not weakened the political parties. If anything, administration had grown progressively worse and the parties even stronger.[68]

Royal policy had concentrated on the first objective of administration on the ostensible theory that success there would lead automatically to success in achieving the second objective. As described in Chapter IV, the Crown had attempted to secure impartial administration through an administrative structure of built-in checks and balances and through an appointment policy that utilized party rivalry to make the institutional checks effective. In short, it placed members of different parties in mutually dependent offices on the theory that political rivals would willingly police each other, and it transferred its officials frequently.[69]

But the very system that provided mutual checks and balances also prevented cooperation and collaboration because officials of different parties did not work well together. In a private memorandum on the entire state apparatus, Mavrokordatos in 1841 described the acute paralysis that resulted.

. . . but the most general cause of the paralysis is the discord of the various authorities and the loss of the esteem due the central authority of each governorship. In most eparchies, the secretaries are in continual and systematic conflict with their superiors [governors], the economic commissioners in disagreement with the governors, the officers and sub-officers of the gendarmerie exercise police supervision on the one and the other [governors and economic commissioners], and instead of being the executive organs of the superior authority's

[67] P. Argyropoulos to Mavrokordatos, Athens, 8/20 Apr. 1841, no. 5860, and M. Argyropoulos to P. Argyropoulos, Pera, 26 Mar./7 Apr. 1841, no. 5857, Vol. 21 (1841), Mavrokordatos Archive.

[68] On the continued existence of parties and the intensification of party strife in 1838-39, see Gennaios Kolokotrones, *Apomnemoneumata* (*Cheirographon Deuteron 1821-1862*) [*Memoirs* (*Second Manuscript 1821-1862*)], ed. Emmanuel Protopsaltes (Athens 1961), p. 83 (hereafter cited as [*Memoirs II*]). Kolokotrones, though, recognizes just two parties—the Constitutionalists and the Governmentalists.

[69] See Chap. IV, pp. 173-74, above on administrative checks and balances; Chap. VI, pp. 288-89, above on its appointment policy.

[governor's] commands, they simply ignore it [the superior authority]. To these things must be added the lack of punishment of many abuses, which encourage many to copy the bad example, and the resulting grumbling of the people.[70]

Theoretically, impartiality ought to have been the reward for ineffi-ciency. But administrative breakdown rendered the institutional checks unable to prevent the collusion of officials for partisan purposes. Monar-chides, one of the special commissioners sent out periodically to investi-gate provincial administration, reported some of his findings in mainland Greece to Mavrokordatos in 1841. The desperate complaints against rapacious tax-farmers bombarded him wherever he went. Beyond a shadow of doubt, he explained, in the demes where abuses reached extremes, mayors, advisors, and councilors, in some combination, par-ticipated in the corruption. In return for openly supporting the tax-farmers or refraining from preventive action, they went tax free and sometimes even got a cut of the tax-farmer's profits. Judges of administra-tive courts, in return for a bribe from the tax-farmer, ruled against the harassed peasant who sought judicial redress. If the governor of an eparchy happened to be honest, the governor's secretary, who could thwart the corrective measures of his superior, would probably be dis-honest and cooperate with the tax-farmer.[71]

Centralization and absolutism, basic features of the administrative system, had been intended to enforce the checks and curb the collusion. But they too suffered perversion. In large part, the inability of officials to cooperate was probably a mere natural product of party suspicions. But administrative paralysis often resulted from deliberate party action. Parties frequently organized attempts to oust from office adherents of

[70] Private memorandum entitled *General* (n.d., but undoubtedly written in 1841 when Mavrokordatos was in office, probably by Mavrokordatos himself), no. 5793, Vol. 21 (1841), Mavrokordatos Archive [hereafter cited as "Private Memo"].

[71] A. Monarchides to Mavrokordatos, Lamia, 29 June 1841*o.s.*, no. 5919, and 6 July 1841*o.s.*, no. 6028, Vol. 21 (1841), Mavrokordatos Archive. Unfortunately, Monarchides does not specify the exact ways by which a mayor could help the tax-farmer fleece the peasants. One conceivable way was through the mayor's right, with the consent of the council, to appoint the local tax assessor, who would calculate the quantity or value of a peasant's produce (decree concerning the collection of tenths, 8/20 June 1836 [*Government Gazette*], no. 25, 9 June 1836*o.s.*). Most probably, however, the assistance of the mayor and councilors was negative, consisting largely of looking the other way while the tax-farmers did as they pleased. Buchon, though much too general in his remarks to be of help here, does nevertheless echo Mon-archides' main complaint: "The deme law . . . is applied in an onerous and arbitrary manner and produces the most profound discontent in individuals at the same time that it puts into the hands of the tax-farmers the constant means to dominate the government itself" (J. A. Buchon, *La Grèce Continentale et la Morée* [Paris, 1843], p. 455). What he didn't realize, or at least state, was that the tax-farmers could dominate the deme government because the local authorities were their willing ac-complices. On collusion, see also Gennaios Kolokotrones [*Memoirs II*], p. 81.

other parties. They employed the device of petitioning the Crown for a redress of grievances and advancing accusations against the official in question. In its diligence to detect abuses, the Crown fell prey to these frequent slander campaigns of the parties.

In 1834 Kalamogdartes, an ephor at Patras, wrote Lontos alleging that Rouphos, his political rival in Patras, had caused a petition to be circulated there:

condemning me in it to the government as an embezzler of the deme, etc. . . . Now, with this, I stand to be transferred from here or be dismissed completely, so that in this way his lordship Rouphos will be left complete master of the political and economic realms in Patras without anyone's overseeing his acts, and without encountering any further obstacles to his desires.

Indeed, Rouphos soon received an appointment to the Council of State and Kalamogdartes got transferred away from his native province.[72]

In the course of only four years, the government transferred Panagiotes Delegiannes, a "French" governor, from Pyrgos (Elis) to Tripolis (Arcadia) to Corinth (Argolis) at great personal expense to him. At the end of 1837, he faced the prospect of another transfer or complete dismissal as a result of accusations ranging from the acceptance of bribes to unfair behavior in the handling of mayoralty elections. The accusations came from both Elis and Argolis. The government entrusted the investigation to the current governor of Elis, an enemy, who secured the damning evidence from Spyridon Manouses, the very man who had drawn up the petitions against Delegiannes and leader of the party that had circulated them.[73]

This case is a good example of party organization for the purpose of ousting a rival official. Delegiannes' opponents were obviously well enough organized to arrange that complaints come from both Elis and Argolis, that a governor of their persuasion conduct the investigation, and that members of their party serve as the chief source of evidence. Quite possibly Delegiannes was guilty of the alleged abuses, and the rival party had served as a valuable check on venal administration. But the same device could easily serve as a way of falsely discrediting an upright official whose only real "offense" was belonging to another party.

As a result, even the best-intentioned governors hesitated to carry out their duties from fear of antagonizing elements that might then organize a campaign to oust them from office. In general, such partisan charges and countercharges created an atmosphere of suspicion that reinforced

[72] A. Kalamogdartes to A. Lontos, Patras, 7 Mar. 1834o.s., no. 32, folder 18/1057, Lontos Archive, Benaki Museum, Athens.

[73] Panagiotes Delegiannes to Regas Palamides, Corinth, 16 Dec. 1837o.s., and 28 Dec. 1837o.s., folder 257 (1833-39), Palamides Archive, Vlachogiannes Collection, General State Archives, Athens.

the public's lack of respect for public authority and left the king even more hesitant than nature had made him.[74]

Suffering from the same defects as the provincial administration, the central government became a lifeless and inefficient set of ministries, each acting as a separate service having nothing to do with the other. Tripartisan representation in the cabinet was one of the factors that made it unable to act as a corporate and cooperating body.[75]

Much of the paralysis at the top resulted from the overconcentration of royal power in the king and the anaktovoulion. The entire governmental system had been created to derive its motive power and its corrective limits from the Crown. The assumption was that the Crown would be energetic, efficient, and the mediator between conflicting interests. But, by foisting too great a burden on too few men and in its attempts to prevent abuses by checking everything, it acted as a brake on all official initiative, reduced the administrative machine to ineffectiveness, and, in response to problems which could not wait, found itself unprepared to resist unofficial pressures or reverse unauthorized acts. Otho, because of his unwillingness to delegate authority, got bogged down in a mass of administrative detail. His anaktovoulion, because it consisted of Bavarians and heterochthons, became the object of a national prejudice fanned to a peak by the press. Day-to-day royal "policy" became the unpredictable and haphazard product of conflicting pressures from three parties, three affiliate legations, and Bavarian advisors balanced against the resistance of a desperate king. By 1841, Otho had learned that his

[74] In 1841, Otho said to Piscatory (Athens, 27 Aug. 1841 [6th report], *L'Hellénisme Contemporain*, IX, 421): "It is so difficult to know the truth. In Greece they calumniate so much that, in wishing to do justice, I can be so unjust." See also the general remark of a friend of Mavrokordatos (D. Gregoriades to Mavrokordatos, Corinth, 28 Jan. 1841*o.s.*, no. 5812, Vol. 21 [1841], Mavrokordatos Archive): "When the governor doesn't become the organ of anyone, the unsuccessful party becomes angry, shouts, and tears off its clothes, all in opposition to the wretched governor [whom it accuses] as supposedly partial. Then the governor becomes the target for arrows and shouts and petitions, even newspapers."

[75] "Because of the absence of a ministerial council [in the true sense], each ministry is regarded as a separate service having no relation or connection with the rest. From the wretchedness of all the ministers, all the branches within a ministry are alienated from each other," wrote Pericles Argyropoulos to Mavrokordatos in a report on the condition of the ministry of economic affairs (no. 5863, Vol. 21 [1841], Mavrokordatos Archive). For evidence that this situation had long existed, see the following correspondence, addressed to Mavrokordatos (Vol. 20 [1837-40], MA): (1) M. Argyropoulos, Bucharest, 20 May/1 June 1833, no. 5512 ("I can't attribute to the present cabinet members either selfishness or betrayal of public interests. Rather they lack harmony, maybe have no trust in each other; at least they can come to no agreement."); (2) M. Argyropoulos, Pera, 4/20 Mar. 1840, no. 5696 (". . . our master [the King] wants to treat his ministers like Napoleon."); and (3) Kolettes, 11 Feb. 1840*o.s.*, no. 5688 (". . . an administrative system we don't have; only ministers, each going his own way, according to his personal desires or those of foreigners.").

innate tendency to procrastinate was the most effective way of maintaining a negative sort of independence.[76]

To make things worse, the Crown's formal commitment to Western legal procedures and Lyons' harassing tactics of constant complaint made the royal government impotent in the face of flagrant abuses. To quote Monarchides once again:

> The government wants to find some legal proof [of the abuses]. This is impossible, because the briber and the bribed are two, a third never exists. . . . If, as we have proceeded up to now, we proceed again, with legal proofs, alas! to the unfortunate people.

Yet, if the government did not require legal proof, then the possibility of frameups organized by parties against individual officials increased.[77]

This account of administrative paralysis is crucial to an understanding of the conflicting demands made upon a reformer like Mavrokordatos. He could not survive politically unless he adopted a nonpartisan appointment policy. He could not survive administratively unless he appointed men whose loyalty he commanded and whose professional qualifications were beyond question. Faced with this dilemma (the same dilemma of administrative deterrence discussed in Chapter IV), he faltered as others had before him. Even though sincerely interested in administrative efficiency, he had to sacrifice it to the political exigencies of the moment. But since he would not abandon the aim entirely, he had to exclude from his government professionally unqualified members of his own and other parties who could have brought him valuable support.[78]

---

[76] On the seriousness of administrative paralysis and the contemporary tendency to account for it in terms of overconcentration of royal power, see Zographos to Mavrokordatos, Athens, 28 Mar. 1840*o.s.*, no. 5703, Vol. 20 (1837-40), Mavrokordatos Archive, and Pisoatory, Athens, 27 Aug. 1841 (6th report), *L'Hellénisme Contemporain*, IX, 419, 421.

On Otho's preoccupation with detail, see Piscatory, Athens, 20 June 1841 (1st report) and 30 July 1841 (4th report), *ibid.*, IX, 340, 410, and *Athēna*, 23 Nov. 1840*o.s.* On prejudice against the anaktovoulion, see Piscatory's 1st report, *op.cit.*, and *Athēna*, 23 Nov. 1840*o.s.* On Otho's political exploitation of his tendency to procrastinate, see Gregory A. Perdicaris, *The Greece of the Greeks* (New York, 1845), I, 57-58: "The morbid inaction which at present pervades every department of state, is to be sought in the opposition and intrigues of foreign diplomatists, rather than in the disposition of the king, who, encompassed by difficulties, and unable to meet them by open opposition, has been obliged to have recourse to procrastination—to a policy by means of which he has hitherto foiled every opponent and has tired out the most patient of his enemies."

[77] A. Monarchides to Mavrokordatos, Lamia, 29 June 1841*o.s.*, no. 5919, Vol. 21 (1841), Mavrokordatos Archive. See also Gennaios Kolokotrones [*Memoirs II*], p. 79), who makes a big point of Otho's insistence on legal proof of malfeasance in office and by implication shows Otho's dilemma—wanting information on malfeasance to curb it while at the same time wanting to protect his officials from false accusations and encourage public respect for officialdom.

[78] That Mavrokordatos considered politics a prerequisite for good policy, see P.

In a memorandum, presumably drawn up by Mavrokordatos, setting forth comprehensive recommendations for the conduct of governmental policy, lip service was paid to the idea of distinguished military and political service during the Revolution as a standard for admission to the Council of State, but chief emphasis was placed on the "possession of education, knowledge, experience, and specialized ability." Pericles Argyropoulos, in his administrative recommendations to Mavrokordatos in 1841, repeatedly deplored the occupation of posts in all branches of the administration by unqualified persons. He elaborated this principle with striking clarity:

> Care must be taken that only those holding a university degree, or at least a gymnasium diploma, be admitted to public service. When will the ignorance of our administrators end? . . . Where did they learn to administer, even to write? It is essential to declare the principle that, in the future, the educated and qualified are the only ones eligible for public office. For lawyers [to practice], examinations are required. Why should that requirement not be extended to all public officials? In Prussia, this system exists and important and most practiced men ask that it be introduced in France, promising that such a requirement can speed the progress of political and legal science more than all other means.

He further stated that the recently established university at which he was a professor would be graduating that year eighteen young men who qualified for judicial posts. "What will be the advantage of the establishment of a university and of student efforts to learn, if the doors of public service are closed to them and opened only to the knock of ignorance and flattery?" And yet, at the same time, he argued for men politically loyal to Mavrokordatos. Perhaps he thought he could get around this dilemma by building up a party cadre of Westernized bureaucrats.[79]

The Staying Power of the Parties

Not only did administrative inefficiency result in large part from the

Argyropoulos to Mavrokordatos, Athens, 18 Apr. 1841 o.s. (no. 5861, Vol. 21 [1841], Mavrokordatos Archive): "In your last letter of 18/30 March you said that before the preparation of institutions, there must be a change of personnel. I agree."

[79] "Private Memo," n.d., no. 5793, Vol. 21 (1841), Mavrokordatos Archive.

Pericles Argyropoulos has left five reports rich in information on the administration as it existed and in proposed reforms for the future. The first four are each concerned with a ministry and the fifth with the Council of State: (1) ministry of justice, (2) of economic affairs, (3) of education, (4) of the interior, (5) the Council of State (nos. 5862-5866 [n.d.], Vol. 21 [1841], MA). The long quotation by P. Argyropoulos comes from the third report (no. 5864) and the short from the first (no. 5862). In the first he argues for the solemn principle of the irremovability of judges, yet he insists on a change of personnel before the principle goes into effect; in the fourth, he insists that Mavrokordatos cannot improve the provincial administration so long as Glarakes' appointees remain governors.

continued existence of parties. It also perpetuated the need for associations to provide protection against government and private abuses. In the eyes of their adherents, parties proved their usefulness by continuing to satisfy this need. The importance of parties is corroborated in a number of different ways.[80]

For the same period, one finds evidence that the system of clientage continued to exist. Traveling in Greece during 1840-41, Buchon noted that a good number of former military captains and clients came to Athens from the provinces periodically to give proof of their allegiance to their chiefs and to solicit their assistance. They ate and slept at their chief's home. As Vasos Mavrovouniotes, commander of an irregular battalion on the northeastern frontier, pointed out to Piscatory, "We are nothing, we captains, without a political chief"; hence the political pilgrimages to the capital.[81]

On the highest level of clientage, the legations dared not abandon the practice of offering protection because they had no confidence that their rival legations would follow suit, and they knew very well that those seeking protection would go elsewhere if not succored. Indeed, Piscatory found "French" adherents complaining that the French legation had not protected them sufficiently from the rival parties. These complaints represented a solicitation for more effective protection and a veiled threat that they might look elsewhere if insufficiently protected.[82]

There are three characteristics of the central government that especially invited partisan activities. First, the posts that enjoyed the right of any extensive patronage, primarily those of cabinet ministers, usually went to individuals with no local roots (heterochthons), such as Glarakes before Mavrokordatos or Chrestides later. This practice was intended to guaran-

---

[80] Piscatory noted the connection between weak and inefficient government, on the one hand, and the strengthening of parties, on the other; and he recognized the connection because he was aware of the existence of the system of clientage and its role as the basis of the parties. See his 5th report (Athens, 20 Aug. 1841, *L'Hellénisme Contemporain*, IX, 413: "The situation of protection and clientage which *is*, as I have often written, a true character of the parties, is not solely, it must be said, a result of diverse Legations; it is, as you know, Mr. Minister [Guizot, French minister of foreign affairs] in the habits of the country. . . . The establishment of a regular government, the administration of Kapodistrias, the quarrels of the regency have fortified those habits, which the royal government, isolated from the people, without action, without a sense of its power, has not known how, has not wished, has not dared to destroy."

[81] Buchon, *Grèce*, pp. 107-109. Piscatory, Patras, 12 July 1841 (3rd report), *L'Hellénisme Contemporain*, IX, 348.

[82] Piscatory, Athens, 20 June 1841 (1st report), and Athens, 20 Aug. 1841 (5th report), *ibid.*, IX, 341, 413. Perdicaris (*Greece of Greeks*, I, 69-70) wrote: ". . . it must not be forgotten that the interference of the Allied Powers is the cause, and to this must be attributed the existence and continuance of the political parties which are marshalled under foreign colours. In every other country, there is generally the government and opposition parties, but in Greece we find no less than three factions, not one of which has a national cognomen. The presence and the weight of the Allies is seen in the existence of the French, the Russian, and the English parties!"

tee that high officials would be free from the pressure of primates and subordinate party members and entirely dependent on the goodwill of the king. Yet, sole dependence on the king left the appointee uncertain about the length of his tenure and entirely subservient to the royal will. The temptation was to find other sources of support, such as that of Bavarians close to the king or ministers of the foreign powers, in order to bring pressure on the king if necessary. Another source of support—the one which concerns us here—was that of a local clientele, the establishment of which, for a heterochthon who was also poor, was accomplished not through the usual channels of economic and political influence in a home province, but through the right of patronage accruing to the office held. Seekers after such patronage were ready to offer themselves, once a man's appointment was certain. For instance, Mavrokordatos received a multitude of petitions for jobs in 1841 when he was appointed minister of the interior and when it was believed that he would exercise all the powers of prime minister. In return for the support of local clienteles, a patron was expected to use his office as a means of securing them political control of their demes and provinces.[83]

Second, the authority of the cabinet minister was nullified by the paralysis of the administrative channels and by the existence of officials subordinate to him, who were members of a different party and hence disloyal to him. Unless he was willing to remain a passive figurehead, his best means of securing some measure of control over his ministry and rendering it fairly efficient was to rely on men whom he could trust. Such men were usually those of his own party. As Argyropoulos pointed out to Mavrokordatos in 1841, "You cannot administer affairs through the administrative organs of Glarakes." He was perfectly correct, even if the eparchal governors of Glarakes were honest and efficient men, precisely because those governors *were* "organs of Glarakes," faithful to him as a party head rather than as an administrative chief. Such a condition reveals the strength of party ties.[84]

Third, centralization of the government in an effort to curb abuses of parties and primates meant that the parties had to also maintain some degree of centralization and coordination if they were to continue to

[83] Vol. 21 (1841) of the Mavrokordatos Archive is thick with a plethora of such letters from such "friends," with a heavy concentration from Western Rumely, Mavrokordatos' old stronghold. They recalled old connections, expressed their continued loyalty, and petitioned for a position or some favor when he would assume the reins of government. This was in striking contrast to the absence of such letters in the volumes for the years when Mavrokordatos was abroad. See for instance, a letter from K. Petalas, governor of Mantinea, Tripolis, 13 June 1841o.s., no. 5921; Themistocles Trikoupes, brother of Spyridon, Hypate, 6 June 1841, no. 5927; B. Chrysoverges, Mesolongi, 10 June 1841o.s., no. 5948; Oikonomopoulos, Mesolongi, 11 June 1841o.s., no. 5951; etc.

[84] P. Argyropoulos to Mavrokordatos, "Ministry of Interior" (n.d.), no. 5865, Vol. 21 (1841), Mavrokordatos Archive.

exist. In fighting administrative localism the Crown was fighting the localism of parties as well. And even the Crown's policy of strengthening the small landholders politically came eventually to depend on party activities. For wherever such electoral victories of the small landholders over established primate families occurred, it was through the alliance of the small men or through strong central party backing, either condition presupposing the existence of party organization.[85]

Until the establishment of elective eparchal councils, electioneering as an expression of party activity could take place only on the local level, and politics there was intense, not to say turbulent and underhanded. Such elections took place in 1834, 1837, and 1841. On each occasion charges of fraud in the drawing up of electoral lists and in registering of votes were leveled by the losing side, and sometimes elections were invalidated by the provincial and central authorities.[86] In 1841, when the recent amalgamation of most demes increased the importance of remaining mayoralty offices, Piscatory, then touring the country, reported the struggle a lively one and he saw fit to avoid "some cities agitated by the elections."[87]

The causes for the attractiveness of local office merit consideration. Buchon observed that the mayoralty conferred both legal authority and

[85] On an example of how a party became centralized in response to a centralized administration, see a letter from B. Christakopoulos to his apparent patron Regas Palamides, a man of provincial influence, requesting him to appeal to Kolettes, then minister of the interior and highest party official, for the appointment of at least one Tripolis native to the gendarmerie—and Christakopoulos gave five names—"because they have bedevilled me with their letters" (Nauplion, 25 Oct. 1834o.s., folder 257 [1833-39], Palamides Archive). This is a good example of the mediating procedure of the clientage system for getting a local petition relayed to the highest party official.

"Everywhere the middle class is forming," wrote Piscatory, Patras, 12 July 1841 ([3rd report], L'Hellénisme Contemporain, ix, 350), meaning an agrarian middle class. And politically it was becoming more influential, he wrote, citing the case of Vonitsa, where a small proprietor managed to prevail over one of the members of the Grivas family. With the limited sources at hand and for such a short period, too little is known to be able to prove or disprove his observation.

[86] Ethnikē reported that in the elections of 1834-35 at Tripolis, the justice of the peace who was in charge of the election was alleged to have had counterfeit ballots which he registered in place of the real ballots (24 Mar./3 Apr. 1835). Athēna published a letter of 31 Mar. 1837 from Andritsaina, describing alleged irregularities in the Gortynia election in drawing up the catalogue of voters and in the registry of ballots (24 Apr. 1837o.s.). Piscatory reported, concerning the elections of Euboea in 1841, frauds in the formation of electoral lists, the pressing of complaints, and the invalidation of some elections (Piscatory, Chalcis, 25 June 1841 [2nd report], L'Hellénisme Contemporain, ix, 346). The existence of such abuses must have inspired Mavrokordatos to recommend procedural changes in deme elections concerning ballots and the drawing up of electoral lists (["Private Memo," no. 5793], Vol. 21 [1841], Mavrokordatos Archive).

[87] Piscatory, Chalcis, 25 June 1841 (2nd report), and Patras, 12 July 1841 (3rd report), L'Hellénisme Contemporain, ix, 346, 349.

a little revenue and provided easy means to augment both the one and the other. The attractiveness of salary was certainly not lacking, as a law of 1836 reveals. By provision of the original law of 1834, the mayor's salary was to be determined in each case by the demotic council. The amending law of 1837, which fixed a statutory maximum salary, justified itself in the preamble by drawing attention to the previous exorbitance of salaries.[88] Yet the monetary motive, in this restricted sense of actual salary, was certainly not the main one and was actually minor in the case of the many wealthy mayors, some of whom subsequently preferred the unsalaried post of council president to that of the well-paid mayor.[89]

Piscatory asserted that municipal authority was strongly sought after "to conserve an ancient influence or to create a new one." His remark requires further explication, from evidence which he failed to adduce, especially because the statute reduced the mayor to little more than a local executive of the Crown with such limited powers that it is hard to envision him as able "to conserve an ancient influence or to create a new one."[90]

But the statute here is misleading, precisely because the importance of the office derived from extralegal or illegal practices made possible by the collusion mentioned above. This unofficial connection between officials supposedly acting as checks against each other greatly enhanced their power. If a mayor was on good terms with or in control of the demotic council, his authority in the deme was indisputable. This was certainly the case in Hydra, where Lazaros Kountouriotes held the presidency of the council while he "gave" his son-in-law the post of mayor, though there is nothing in their case to indicate that they abused their power. In the same way, if a mayor were on intimate terms with the eparch or some important figure on the provincial level, his informal power was greatly enhanced.[91]

Although local power could be used by its possessor to line his pockets dishonestly, it was more often desired, it seems, to secure one from the attacks of rivals within the province or to defend one's economic interests in the locale from abuses by the central and provincial authorities. It was the large fortune and influence of the Constitutionalist Notaras family in

[88] Buchon, *Grèce*, p. 530. Art. 51, para. 10, law concerning the establishment of demes, 27 Dec./8 Jan. 1834, [*Government Gazette*], no. 3, 10/22 Jan. 1834. Law concerning the regulation of the mayors' recompense, 29 July/10 Aug. 1837, [*GG*], no. 28, 10 Aug. 1837o.s. The maximum ranged from 300-3,000 drachmas per year, depending on the size of the deme, as specified in this law.

[89] For instance, the wealthy Panagiotes Benakes of Kalamata who, though re-elected mayor of Kalamata in 1841, preferred the presidency of the council, as did Lazaros Kountouriotes. See Piscatory, Athens, 6 Sept. 1841 (7th report), *L'Hellénisme Contemporain*, IX, 438-39, 442.

[90] Piscatory, Patras, 12 July 1841 (3rd report), *ibid.*, IX, 350. See deme law as cited in n. 88 above.

[91] Piscatory, Athens, 6 Sept. 1841 (7th report), *ibid.*, IX, 442.

Corinth that made them indifferent to the goodwill or hostility of the national government. If one had aspirations toward political influence on the national level, as the Notaras' did not during the absolutist period, then local power, by virtue of the local following it secured its possessor, helped him command greater attention in his own national party or to invite royal favor in the king's attempt to build up his own "following." The local strength the Kountouriotes' enjoyed permitted them to stand aloof from the national party rivalries and hence remain in the good grace of the king, who sought desperately to join with the least partisan groups.[92]

The best illustration of one who rose to importance in the ranks of the Napist party by virtue of his local influence is that of George Ainian. Ainian was an intellectual who played only a secondary role during the Revolution, when military influence prevailed in his native Rumely. Native of Patradjik in Phthiotis and a professor in Constantinople before 1821, his career really opened up when Kapodistrias, pleased with his cultivation and his pro-Russian sentiments, appointed him to the senate. In 1835, the influence of the Russian legation was responsible for his appointment to the Council of State. But his position always depended on the good will of the central government and the support of foreign interests, and being councilor of state without any strong local influence amounted to nothing much more substantial than enjoyment of prestige. He wished, as Piscatory put it, to create for himself a surer position. So he bought a Turkish village in Phthiotis in order to have direct control over its peasants, and then allied himself with Mitsos Kontogiannes, a veteran captain of that province during the Turkish period, who needed such support as that of Ainian to protect himself against his long-standing enemies (the Zotos' and the Chatziskos'). By virtue of his purchase and his alliance with a captain, Ainian was able by 1841 to select the mayors of his choice in twenty-two communes of Phthiotis.[93]

Ainian's example is instructive because it shows that election to local office depended hardly at all on the independent decision of the electors or on the personal qualifications of the candidate. The decisive factors were one's socioeconomic position and one's control of a local clientele, whether directly or in alliance with other local captains or primates. To own a village or villages gave one control over its electorate; to be in alliance with a captain or primate secured the votes of their dependents. Sometimes one's influence went beyond the home deme, and so he was in a position to virtually designate a political ally or client as mayor of another deme. Conversely, a person might not have sufficient strength to win a mayorship without the support of a more powerful patron of the province. As a result, some elections were virtually assured before the election took place. In fact, there is at least one instance on

[92] *Ibid.*, ix, 441 (Notaras'), 442 (Kountouriotes').
[93] *Ibid.*, pp. 430-31.

record of a party, with their families, going to various villages and establishing mayors without conducting elections at all.[94]

The instances of important men who directed their personal ambition to the local scene almost exclusively are numerous and striking. Phloros Grivas, eldest of the four brothers who distinguished themselves in the Revolution, remained satisfied with the mayoralty of Vonitsa in Acarnania. Meletopoulos, a native of Mistra, formerly a demogeron, resigned his post as president of a court to become mayor of Sparta. George Bastas, of Coron, Messenia, wanted only to be the first in his area and held the post of mayor throughout the period. Similar sentiments characterized Benakes, first mayor, then president of the demotic council of Calamata; Demetrios Meletopoulos, mayor of Vostitsa; and Lazaros Kountouriotes, who held the presidency of the demotic council of Hydra.[95]

Buchon, the French philhellenic observer, was only citing one of many instances when he wrote, in 1840-41, concerning Vostitsa, where the brothers Meletopoulos, having succeeded to the influence of the Delegiannes', were disputing the municipal supremacy with the Lontos family, "The demarch's throne is here a great object of ambition for all the families of the old kodza-bashis." According to him, each party courted the future electors to perpetuate itself in office, and a demarch, not to wound his future electors, became tolerant of their most ridiculous pretensions.[96]

Nor was the demarch's throne sought after by the kodza-bashis alone. It became an object of ambition for the old influential chieftains as well. Just as the importance of the military class had been enhanced by the Revolution, when the function of fighting was so all-important, in a society no longer engaged in open warfare that same function became secondary and its concomitant sources of influence waned. As the chieftain Stratos told Piscatory in 1841:

> We are nothing. It is necessary to have a function to have influence today. What purpose does it serve to have been a good Palikar? It is necessary for him to possess and cultivate land and to *administer his commune* [italics mine]. It is only in that way that one has some friends, some enemies, so that one can serve the former and take vengeance on the others.

Indeed, palikars, such as Chatzepetrakes in Hypata, became mayors in mainland Greece, the traditional seat of their influence, and when unable themselves to be mayor, they allied themselves with the civilian mayor, as

[94] M. Sisines to A. Lontos, Patras, 21 Sept. 1835*o.s.*, no. 32, folder 19/1114, Lontos Archive.

[95] Piscatory, Athens, 6 Sept. 1841 (7th report), *L'Hellénisme Contemporain*, IX, 435 (Grivas), 438-39 (Benakes), 439 (Meletopoulos and Bastas), 440 (D. Meletopoulos), and 442 (Kountouriotes).

[96] Buchon, *Grèce*, p. 530.

in the case of the captain Kontogiannes with Ainian, to the mutual benefit of both.[97] To a large extent therefore, the new local administration, intended to curb the "despotism" of the primates, was falling into the hands of those very primates who had controlled it before or of captains who had already displaced the influence of the primates in their locales during the Revolution.

Nonetheless, elections meant *something* and were hard-fought when the parties of a deme were of relatively equal strength or when a combination of small landholders attempted to unseat the powerful incumbent. But the results of these elections did not depend exclusively or even primarily on the campaigning within the deme. Often provincial or national officials, such as an eparch, nomarch, or minister of the interior, might clandestinely interfere in behalf of their respective parties to tip the scales in their favor.[98]

A further indication of party importance is the changing public attitude toward them. On 8 April 1839*o.s.*, *Athēna* published a lead article entitled "Are Political Parties Harmful or Signs of Social Life?" The form of the question implied the latter alternative. The article pointed to the existence of parties both in the powerful and economically advanced countries of Western Europe and in ancient Athens, which had overthrown its tyrants. The implications were obvious and bold. Political parties brought prosperity and freedom. This was not the first time that newspapers, even *Athēna*, had defended the existence of parties. Such defense was sometimes characteristic of the constitutionalist opposition. But in the early years of the absolutist decade, the guarded language of such defense reflected the public aversion to parties as breeders of intolerable internecine conflict. That language needed no longer to be so moderate may have reflected a changing attitude toward them, either as protection against the full effects of administrative paralysis or as channels for future reform.[99]

The persistence of the parties thus created a second major weakness in the coming position of Mavrokordatos. He had to rule in collaboration with the "French" and "Russian" parties in order to survive.

3. THE MAVROKORDATOS PROGRAM AND ITS FAILURE

The Reform Program

The political views of Mavrokordatos stood somewhere between the typical position of Greek moderates and the more moderate forms of European liberalism. To establish the requisite conditions for a constitution, he envisaged the continued evolution of demotic councils, the establishment of provincial councils, the extension of judicial process by jury,

---

[97] Piscatory, Patras, 12 July 1841 (3rd report), *L'Hellénisme Contemporain*, IX, 350. Buchon (*Grèce*, p. 329) visited Chatzepetrakes in 1840-41.

[98] See n. 85 above.

[99] *Athēna*, 8 Apr. 1839*o.s.*

the consolidation of a free press, and independent courts. In short, the people must be educated to respect the law and to exercise their sovereignty, not by the monarchy, as the king believed, or by a constitution, as the radicals felt, but by these more particular institutions. Without such preparation, a constitution would only invite greater foreign influence through the purchase of votes, lead to the loss of freedoms already possessed, and produce such disruption of the administrative apparatus as to render the king even more antipathetic toward a constitution. How long would it take to create the requisite conditions? Mavrokordatos arbitrarily replied, "Seven years."[100]

Much of this sounds like the Greek moderate talking—the presupposition of popular sovereignty, the conception of step-by-step advance to representative government, the naive estimate of such a short preparatory period. Yet the whole argument also pointed in a different direction— toward a theoretically absolute monarchy limited by the system of ministerial responsibility, the gradual development of stable institutions, the evolution of a respected law and custom, and the entrenchment of an independent judiciary and an efficient bureaucracy. Mavrokordatos declared the Greek form of government a "tempered monarchy." The king could appoint and dismiss his prime minister at will, but he submitted to the limitations incurred in giving his prime minister a mandate to govern and in the recognizing of the Council of State's right to collaborate on fiscal matters.[101]

[100] See the text of Mavrokordatos' reply to a letter of Trikoupes chiding him on his gradualism in Nicholas Dragoumes, *Historikai Anamneseis* [*Historical Reminiscenses*] 2nd edn. (Athens, 1879), II, 35-37.

[101] In "Private Memo" (n.d., no. 5793, Vol. 21 [1841], Mavrokordatos Archive), Mavrokordatos actually used the term "tempered monarchy" as distinct from "absolute monarchy" to refer to the form of government in Greece. This document is largely a set of proposed changes in the constitutive law of the Council of State (pp. 3-11) with additional suggestions on other matters of state (modification of the dotation and deme laws, foreign and internal affairs). The preface to this document (pp. 1-3) contains a general statement of principles, as a definition of "tempered monarchy." The first part of this general statement ends as follows:

"In a tempered monarchy, the rule of law must be complete; no power whatever may violate the laws, because then the monarchy becomes absolute.

"So that the government cannot violate the laws, the actual responsibility of the ministers is required, because the person of the king must always be sacred and unresponsible.

"In order for real responsibility to be bestowed on the ministers, the acts of government must all either arise from the proposals of the ministers *or* be acknowledged and approved by them through their consent and countersignature; in either case, they must be executed by them exclusively.

"From the above it follows that between ministers and king, there can exist no partition [reference is obviously to the anaktovoulion], that the files of the ministry are the files of the king, and the confidence of the king in his ministers must be complete. If the king does not have confidence in the whole of his cabinet, or in some of his ministers, he replaces them with others in whom he can feel confidence.

As a Greek constitutionalist moderate, Mavrokordatos emphasized stage-by-stage *construction* of constitutional monarchy. As a European liberal of the German variety, he talked about evolution toward tempered absolutism, toward what the Germans called the *Staatsrecht*. Essentially, this was one and the same political orientation, conveyed through two different vocabularies—one the vocabulary of the Greek Revolutionary, the tradition of constitutionalism emphasizing political rights and designed for fellow-Greeks, the other the vocabulary of German liberalism, stressing juridical rights and designed for the ears of the king. In 1841 Mavrokordatos had to translate his political philosophy into a number of specific reforms for recommendation to the king. The moderation of these proposals was undoubtedly tactical, in response to anticipated resistance from the king and as a satisfactory code for an inevitable coalition government of all three parties. But his proposals were all informed by his long-standing political orientation.[102]

His proposals, as they emerged in his struggle with the king, were primarily six: (1) dismissal of Bavarian officers from the Greek army, (2) appointment of a Greek as minister of war, (3) abolition of the anaktovoulion, (4) delegation of broad powers to the cabinet, (5) appointment of a permanent cabinet president (prime minister), and (6) granting the Council of State veto power over taxation and budgetary matters. This program was "national" in a dual sense—in its espousal of nationally-held nonpartisan demands (for an end to Bavarian control and a limitation of royal power) and in its positive objective of giving Greeks management of their own affairs (a national government).[103]

If all of the cabinet, or one or more ministers, don't feel they can accept in good conscience the responsibility of acts or deeds of the government, they resign.

"Besides the real responsibility of the ministers, the monarchical authority in Greece is tempered primarily by the following:

"By the actual and complete independence of the courts, and by the jury system.

"By the demotic system and by the laws for demotic and eparchal councils.

"By the Council of State with certain modifications in its fundamental law.

"And finally by the rest of the organic laws and decrees [established basic institutions].

"Respect for the existing laws by the regime, the development and precise application of these laws, the guarantee of individual freedom, life, honor, and property of the citizens are the first components of tempered monarchy."

[102] The former vocabulary characterizes the letter of 1837 to Trikoupes (see n. 100) and the latter the "Private Memo" of 1841 written for Otho (see n. 101). On the Greek constitutional tradition as a heritage of the Revolution, see sec. 5 of Chap. I above. On the juridical emphasis of European liberalism, see Guido de Ruggiero, *The History of European Liberalism*, trans. R. G. Collingwood (London, 1927), pp. 251-64.

[103] On the points of Mavrokordatos' "program," see the four primary sources: *Athēna*, 18 June 1841*o.s.*, Dragoumes [*Reminiscences*], II, 48; Piscatory, Chalcis, 25 June 1841 (2nd report), *L'Hellénisme Contemporain*, IX, 343; and Gennaios Kolokotrones [*Memoirs II*], p. 86; or any one of the following secondary sources: Kordatos

This reform program made no direct advance toward a constitution. The type of government that Mavrokordatos proposed would be representative only in the sense that Greeks reflected public sentiment better than foreigners, only to the extent that the king chose men in tune with public opinion, only to the degree that "public opinion" accurately represented the grievances and vague aspirations of the silent peasants.[104]

[History], III, 163-64; P. Karolides, Synchronos Historia ton Hellenon . . . [Contemporary History of the Greeks . . .] (Athens, 1922-29), II, 308; Petrakakos [Parliamentary History], II, 272-73; and Pipineles [Monarchy], p. 324.

Lyons (to Palmerston, Athens, 10 July 1841, no. 103, FO 32.106) gives more detailed enumeration of Mavrokordatos' terms: "(1) Immediate dissolution of the Bavarian camarilla, and of referendaries. (2) That no person who has not taken the oath of allegiance can be in the cabinet. NB: The immediate consequence of this is that Schmaltz leaves the post of minister of war to make room for a Greek. (3) That all the officers of the Bavarian army shall leave the service of Otho on the expiration of their leave of absence [from the Bavarian state service], and that in the meantime, they are not to expect to retain their present posts, if it should be convenient to replace them by Greeks. NB: There are sixteen of these officers who fill the most influential situations in this country, though they have very inferior rank in Bavaria. Their leave of absence varies from 2-8 months, with the exception of Lieutenant Colonel Rosmer, a Lieutenant in Bavaria, who commands the corps of Gendarmerie, and who has still sixteen months' leave. (4) That the law which defines the powers and the duties of the ministers, and their relative position to the crown, shall be acted up to, and that nothing which has grown into use in consequence of the neglect of that law shall be quoted as a precedent. (5) That the functions of the president of the council of ministers shall be "réelles." (6) That the anomalous administration of the finance department shall cease, and a minister of finance be appointed. NB: The question of the abolition of the office of intendant general of the Finances was not discussed, because Regny is considered to be dying of the effects of a second apoplectic stroke. (7) That the budget shall be submitted to the Council of State three months before the expiration of each year. (8) That the reorganization and enlargement of the powers of the Council of State, and the question whether the members of that body shall hold office for life shall be decided in the council of ministers. (9) That measures shall be taken for rendering the synod and the clergy in general independent of external influence, and for giving freer and more independent action to the provincial councils and to the municipal councils."

Gennaios Kolokotrones, op.cit., p. 86, asserts that Mavrokordatos wanted to establish a senate, consisting of both elected representatives and royal appointees and having more than an advisory function in fiscal and tax affairs.

[104] With the possible exception of the alleged aim of turning the Council of State into more than a mere consultative body in the area of finances and taxation, an aim never prominently asserted, the principle of constitutional or parliamentary government is absent from Mavrokordatos' program. It is important to stress this point for two reasons.

First, P. A. Argyropoulos, the author of ["Alexander Mavrokordatos and his Constitutional Attempts of 1841"] (Hellenika, VIII [1935], 247-67, and IX [1936], 85-102), in an earlier public lecture, probably because of the same mistake made by Blancard (Études, p. 43) as early as 1886, erred in interpreting Mavrokordatos' program as an attempt to promulgate a constitution. In this monograph (Hellenika, VIII, 255) he is forced by more careful research to correct his former error, but he continues to insist on this program as "constitutionalist" in the sense that Mavro-

The Politics of Attempted Reform: The Third Phase, February–August 1841

The attempt at reform involved Mavrokordatos in an embittered duel with the king. From the very outset, Mavrokordatos and Otho mistrusted each other. Each act of one merely confirmed the suspicions of the other until each finally devised a strategy to force compliance by the other. But in his attempt to overcome royal resistance, Mavrokordatos had to descend into the arena of party politics, where he had to bid for the backing of the powers, contend with a split in his own party, and negotiate for the support of the other parties.

When Mavrokordatos learned that Otho was considering him for a cabinet appointment, he expressed his extreme reluctance and announced in private correspondence with Païkos that he could only accept office on certain conditions, which he proceeded to enumerate. The conditions comprised what I have called his reform program. Insistence on their prior acceptance reflected his belief that Otho would otherwise simply try to use him in office as a cipher.[105]

---

kordatos proposed the formulation of a fundamental charter regulating relations between court, cabinet, and bureaucracy. Even this is wrong. Certainly Mavrokordatos was willing to employ written legislation to regulate such relations, but this is different from saying that he wanted to promulgate a *fundamental charter*. There is absolutely no evidence for this.

Second, this point has an important bearing on Lyons' stance toward Mavrokordatos' reform program. In the presence of Piscatory, Mavrokordatos told Lyons bluntly (Chalcis, 25 June 1841 [2nd report], *L'Hellénisme Contemporain*, ix, 344): "Permit me, a constitution such as you expect, would be for Greece, today and for several years, the most complete anarchy. I will not work for it; I will in fact oppose it; and I will no more be a minister for such an enterprise than I would consent to be under present conditions." This may explain why Lyons was only moderately enthusiastic about Mavrokordatos' recall. It even suggests that perhaps Lyons was secretly happy to see Mavrokordatos fail, such failure constituting in his mind a necessary step toward securing a constitution by showing that tempered monarchy was not a workable alternative to constitutional monarchy because the king would not voluntarily limit his own power. See for instance Lyons' reiteration of some remarks which he addressed to Mavrokordatos (22 July 1841, no. 108, FO 32.106): "I reminded him [Mavrokordatos] that I had, the day after his arrival, given him my humble opinion that he was taking upon himself a serious responsibility in adjourning indefinitely the question of representative government, and that I thought he would soon find that to be the case [his impasse with the king], for it was admitted on all hands that Otho was altogether incapable of directing an absolute system of government himself, and as there was no reasonable hope of Otho's really and sincerely delegating power to ministers capable of carrying on a moderate and progressive government, the only chance of avoiding anarchy and danger to the throne, appeared to be to carry into effect, with as little delay as possible, the constitutional principle upon which the monarchy was founded."

[105] On the very day of his appointment, he wrote M. Argyropoulos that he would refuse the post (M. Argyropoulos to Mavrokordatos, Pera, 4/17 Mar. 1841, no. 5842, Vol. 21 [1841], Mavrokordatos Archive). In reply to two earlier despatches, Païkos wrote to him (Athens, 28 Jan./9 Feb. 1841, no. 5811, Vol. 21, MA): "I never expected you to

To one of Otho's despotic bent, the posing of terms must have seemed impudent and their ultimate objective of limiting the royal power deplorable. Unacceptable as these terms might make him, Mavrokordatos, a moderate, was clearly preferable to Trikoupes, a constitutionalist and British favorite. Strategically, in fact, the appointment of Mavrokordatos would constitute a brilliant move against Palmerston, who would have no choice but to support a Greek government headed by the acknowledged leader of the "English" party, even if that government did not meet all British demands. Under persuasion from Maximilian and Prokesch-Osten, Otho finally acquiesced in the recall of Mavrokordatos, but only grudgingly, with reservations, and without any change in political conviction.[106] Sure enough, Mavrokordatos persuaded Palmerston to abandon, for a time at least, his intention to intervene in Greek affairs and to maintain a position of neutrality vis-à-vis the new government.[107]

---

declare so much against your recall." Mavrokordatos proceeded to state his proposed reforms when Païkos (Athens, 10/22 Jan. 1841, no. 5815, Vol. 21, MA) asked him to define what he meant in a previous despatch about the necessity of instituting "a system." In a letter of 10/22 Feb. 1841 (no. 5824, Vol. 21, MA), Otho wrote Mavrokordatos: "I know your principles by your letters, which Païkos has read to me." Since the Mavrokordatos Archive does not, with a few rare exceptions, contain Mavrokordatos' letters to others, the way in which and extent to which he formulated his conditions by mail is unknown. The Archive does contain a copy of a despatch which he addressed to Otho, dated 13/25 Mar. 1841 (no. 5849, Vol. 21, MA). In it he wrote: "After you have heard me [in Athens], if you are sufficiently convinced and think me worthy of your confidence, I will put my energy at your disposal." But Mavrokordatos remained pessimistic about Otho's good intentions and his own chances of success, as Piscatory points out (Chalcis, 25 June 1841 [2nd report], *L'Hellénisme Contemporain*, IX, 344).

[106] Otho was obviously acting under duress of the existing crisis. According to Mavrokordatos, he was just trying to ward off foreign intervention (Mavrokordatos to Trikoupes, 17/29 Sept. 1841, in Dragoumes [*Reminiscences*], II, 53-65). According to Lyons (5 Oct. 1841, no. 154, FO 32.107), Otho said that Mavrokordatos had been imposed on him. See also Kordatos, [*History*], III, 174. On the role of Maximilian and Prokesch-Osten, see Prokesch-Osten to Metternich, Athens, 27 Dec. 1840, *Aus dem Nachlasse des Grafen Prokesch-Osten*, ed. Anton von Prokesch-Osten [the younger] (Vienna, 1881), II, 200; and Zographos to Mavrokordatos, 10/22 Feb. 1841, no. 5826, Vol. 21 (1841), Mavrokordatos Archive (to Maximilian "you owe in large part your recall"). Aspreas ([*Political History*], I, 155) and Kordatos ([*History*], III, 156) put forth the interesting but unsubstantiated view that the French government originated the idea of Mavrokordatos' appointment. The possible motives which they cite are plausible enough—that Palmerston would stop attacking Otho and that Mavrokordatos and the "English" party, which would probably fail, would lose prestige and pave the way for a "French" government.

[107] Mavrokordatos to Trikoupes, 17/29 Sept. 1841, which Dragoumes published in his [*Reminiscences*], II, 53-65; also Pipineles [*Monarchy*], p. 321. Also see an anonymous letter in French in the Mavrokordatos Archive, 4 Apr. 1841, no. 5867: "According to the authorization you gave me, I have communicated to Lyons the contents of your letters. He was pleased and content with the communication. He said he had already so limitless a confidence in you that subsequently he would not interfere directly in the least thing, that he would even mistrust his own judgment in the event that any act of your administration seemed bad to him."

On 22 February 1841, without prior acceptance of Mavrokordatos' conditions, Otho officially appointed him minister of foreign affairs, with a special annual representation fund of 6,000 drachmas added to the regular salary of office. The decree also named him "president of the ministerial council, whenever we are not present." At the same time, Otho appointed Spyridon Trikoupes as Mavrokordatos' successor in London, even though the appointment was not formalized until 31 March 1841. In his personal letter of announcement, the king instructed Mavrokordatos to return home immediately and refrain from discussing proposals with anyone.[108]

These three documents betrayed Otho's attitude and strategy. He assented to nothing, even seemed to deny one condition by making Mavrokordatos only a part-time president of the cabinet. Instead of writing about Mavrokordatos' conditions as if he were giving them serious consideration, he virtually shrugged them off by blandly explaining that he knew what they were and that Mavrokordatos could elaborate them later. By forbidding discussion of terms with others, he was warning Mavrokordatos against soliciting diplomatic support. By sending Trikoupes out of the country, he was depriving Mavrokordatos of important domestic support and creating great dissension within the party.[109] All this suggested that Otho intended to have Mavrokordatos without paying the political price.

Otho's strategy involved both an inducement and a threat, each of a kind to have effect with a man like Mavrokordatos, who depended on state employment for a livelihood. Through the representation fund he was offering Mavrokordatos a good income in his new job, and by send-

[108] Decree for the appointment of Mavrokordatos as foreign minister and president of the ministerial council, 10/22 Feb. 1841 [Government Gazette], no. 2, 14 Feb. 1841o.s. Maximilian and Trikoupes both informed Lyons on 22 February (Lyons to Palmerston, Athens, 22 Feb. 1841, no. 35, FO 32.104) that Otho had decided to send Trikoupes to London, even though the official decree was not issued till 19/31 Mar. 1841 [GG], no. 9, 27 Apr. 1841o.s. The king sent both a formal and a personal announcement to Mavrokordatos, both dated 10/22 Feb. 1841 (nos. 5823 and 5824, Vol. 21 [1841], Mavrokordatos Archive).

[109] Trikoupes' behavior roused great personal animosity toward him, most of all on the part of Lyons, whose favorite he had been since 1838. P. Argyropoulos (Athens, 28 Mar. 1841o.s., no. 5859, Vol. 21 [1841], Mavrokordatos Archive) called him "selfish and grasping"; and M. Argyropoulos commented to P. Argyropoulos (Pera, 26 Mar./7 Apr. 1841, no. 5857, Vol. 21, MA) that Trikoupes would be the first to betray Mavrokordatos.

More important, there was a schism between those who came to the defense of Trikoupes (such as Klonares, Lontos, Manouses, and Pharmakides, the last of whom went over to the king with Trikoupes), and the clientele of Lyons. See Lyons to Palmerston, Athens, 5 Apr. 1841, no. 51, FO 32.105; enclosure of a letter from Finlay on Trikoupes' about-face in a despatch from Lyons to Palmerston, Athens, 22 July 1841, no. 108; Lyons to Blackhouse, 1 Aug. 1841, "Private"; Lyons to Palmerston, Athens, 10 Aug. 1841, no. 115, all FO 32.106.

Worse yet, it was a serious blow to Mavrokordatos' prestige that the first crack in this united front came from members of his own party.

ing Trikoupes to London immediately he was barring the way for Mavrokordatos' return to his old job. In effect, he was saying: take this and you
earn much, turn it down and you earn nothing.[110]

Mavrokordatos responded with a counterstrategy. Violating royal instructions, he held careful discussions with Palmerston, then went to
Paris for consultation with Guizot. Consequently he obtained joint Anglo-
French support for his program. In Paris, Kolettes informed him that the
king wished them both to obstruct French efforts to reach a European
accord on Greece. As Mavrokordatos himself later wrote, from that moment on he was convinced that Otho was using his appointment as a ploy
to gain time and outwit the powers.[111]

From Athens, Pericles Argyropoulos, his brother-in-law, and Daras and
Praïdes, political friends, encouraged these suspicions, as did Manoles
Argyropoulos from Constantinople. Otho, they reported others as saying,
intended to be absent from Athens when Mavrokordatos returned so that
Mavrokordatos would have to take office before talking terms. As a result,
Mavrokordatos violated royal instructions again and delayed his arrival
to coincide with the king's return to the capital.[112] Back in Greece, his
strategy was to force concessions from the king by threatening to resign and
to make this threat effective by persuading other leading Greeks to refuse
office and by getting representatives of the powers to back such a refusal.
If successful, the king would be unable to form a cabinet without him.
Success, however, depended on his securing the support of the other two
parties.[113]

[110] To Païkos, Mavrokordatos stated the difficulty of his financial position in case
of differences with Otho; that was why he did not welcome his recall. See P. A.
Argyropoulos ["Alexander Mavrokordatos"], *Hellenika*, ix (1936), 87.

[111] "We were satisfied with the language and manifest intentions of Mavrokordatos
during his visit to Paris. It seems to me that his manner of seeing the reforms necessary for the Greek administration come much closer to those of the king's government
[probably means French] than the eagerness of the London cabinet to substitute a
constitutional regime," wrote Guizot to Lagrené, 7 June 1841, M. Guizot, *Mémoires
pour servir à l'Histoire de mon Temps* (Paris, n.d.), vi, 455-56; and Guizot assured
him of France's sincere support and tried to pave the way for a *rapprochement* between Kolettes and him (Guizot, *Mémoires*, vi, 262).

Mavrokordatos to Trikoupes, 17/29 Sept. 1841, in Dragoumes [*Reminiscences*],
ii, 53-65. It seems naive as well as irrelevant to say, as does P. A. Argyropoulos in
["Alexander Mavrokordatos"] (*Hellenika*, ix [1936], 87), that Mavrokordatos didn't
leave London till April because his papers of recall were delayed or because London
delayed in accepting his successor.

[112] M. Argyropoulos to Mavrokordatos, Pera, 5/17 Mar. 1841, no. 5842; P.
Argyropoulos to Mavrokordatos, 8/20 Apr. 1841, no. 5860; and Daras to Mavrokordatos, 8/20 Apr. 1840, no. 5878; all Vol. 21 (1841), Mavrokordatos Archive.

[113] As early as 26 Mar./7 Apr. 1841 (no. 5857, Vol. 21 [1841], Mavrokordatos
Archive) M. Argyropoulos recognized the necessity of this strategy, when he said,
"Only a cabinet of one opinion on most important matters, ready to resign as a
body if need be, can overcome difficulties and reach the goal."

Piscatory (Athens, 27 Aug. 1841 [6th report], *L'Hellénisme Contemporain*, ix,

Mavrokordatos started playing party politics in Paris. He promised both Guizot and Kolettes that he would appeal to the king for the recall of Kolettes and that, if the king refused, he would secure some representation for the "French" party in the cabinet. At the same time in Athens, Pericles Argyropoulos was trying to round up support from leading members of the "French" party, who offered their support in return for the inclusion of Chrestides in the cabinet. He also secured assurances of support from such important political figures as Kolokotrones, Metaxas, and Kountouriotes, but only in return for a promise of nonpartisan rule. Yet, without mention of such promises, Gennaios Kolokotrones, in his memoirs, admits without apology that, even though Mavrokordatos' reform proposals were praiseworthy, his identification with the "English" party automatically united most "French" and "Russians" against him and caused Kountouriotes, Delegiannes, and Kolokotrones himself to try to influence Otho against him even at this early date.[114]

Both he and Manoles Argyropoulos recognized what the problem was. Both admitted that the "English" party did not have enough qualified men to constitute a "homogeneous" cabinet, that the resistance of the king could not be overcome nor the support of the public be secured without a united front of all parties. And yet, both realized that administratively the parties tended to work at cross purposes to each other, and that politically their cooperation would last only so long as the emergency lasted or even less if they discerned any partisan advantage. Neither was any more optimistic about the prospects of party cooperation than he was about the good intentions of the king. And with good reason, judging from Gennaios Kolokotrones' later admission. In effect they were expressing fears that the reforms would remain stillborn, even if the king acquiesced in them, precisely because of existing political conditions.[115]

423-24) recognized this as the strategy of Lyons as well, the aim of whose discourse with Piscatory was "to prove the necessity to do all that was necessary so that a cabinet couldn't be formed," or Lyons to Palmerston, Athens, 31 Aug. 1841, no. 126, FO 32.106: ". . . the Prince Royal, Prokesch-Osten, and I, before Mavrokordatos' arrival, came to an understanding that all would probably depend on Mavrokordatos' firmness. . . ."

[114] On Mavrokordatos' bargaining with Guizot and Kolettes, see Piscatory, Athens, 20 June 1841 (1st report), L'Hellénisme Contemporain, IX, 342; M. Argyropoulos (Pera, 4/17 Mar. 1841, no. 5842, Vol. 21 [1841], Mavrokordatos Archive) who said that Otho would not consent to the recall of Kolettes, even though Mavrokordatos had wanted this; Pipineles [Monarchy], p. 323; and Guizot who wrote to Lagrené, (7 June 1841, Guizot, Mémoires, VI, 456): "He [Mavrokordatos] protested loudly against all idea of exclusion in the choice of persons, and recognized that in alienating France and the people who pass as its friends, he was making it impossible to organize a stable and effective administration."

On rounding up support in Athens, see P. Argyropoulos to Mavrokordatos, Athens, 8/20 Apr. 1841, no. 5860, and 19 Apr. [?] 1841, no. 5888, both Vol. 21 (1841), MA. On the real behavior of such avowed supporters, see Gennaios Kolokotrones [Memoirs II], p. 86.

[115] M. Argyropoulos (to P. Argyropoulos, Pera, 26 Mar./7 Apr. 1841, no. 5857,

Yet Mavrokordatos seemed to enjoy striking advantages for his forth-coming struggle with the king—the united support of England, Austria, and France (the absence of Catacazy temporarily nullified Russian in-fluence in Greece), the solid backing of public opinion, and ostensible security from any serious opposition from either the "French" or "Rus-sian" parties, or from the semi-independent following of Kountouriotes.[116]

Mavrokordatos arrived in Greece on 12 June. A week of personal nego-tiations with the king resulted in deadlock. Otho presented two bills for Mavrokordatos' consideration. The first gave legislative initiative in economic matters to the Council of State rather than the cabinet. The second required Mavrokordatos to notify the court three days in advance of calling a cabinet meeting; the king subsequently reduced the limit to two days, then twenty-four hours. Because the first proposal restricted cabinet authority, the second hampered cabinet autonomy, and both together provided opportunity for continued royal interference, Mavro-kordatos rejected both.[117]

For the cabinet Otho proposed men either unfamiliar or unacceptable to Mavrokordatos. Without notifying Mavrokordatos, Otho offered cabi-net appointments to Spyridon Valetas, an "English" constitutionalist, Leon Melas, a young political unknown, and Provelengios, a member of the anaktovoulion. Mavrokordatos' indignation knew no bounds. The act was offensive because it demonstrated the king's persistence in doing just what he pleased. But more important yet, it compromised Mavrokordatos with the "French" and "Russian" leaders, who probably did not know that the king had acted without his approval. It made him seem privy to the ostensible exclusion of the "French" and "Russian" parties from repre-sentation in the cabinet and placed in doubt his professions about non-partisan intentions. It was perhaps only at this point that Kountouriotes, Delegiannes, and Gennaios Kolokotrones concertedly acted against him.

Vol. 21 [1841], Mavrokordatos Archive) summed up the dilemma when he wrote: "Mavrokordatos . . . has two things he can do—either select the somewhat able from various parties and make them associates with the danger of being betrayed in time, or decide to assume all the weight and responsibility of authority and have about him able men. Then he cannot last [politically], but he may do a little in the inter-val." See also P. Argyropoulos to Mavrokordatos, Athens, 8/20 Apr. 1841, no. 5860, Vol. 21, MA.

[116] That Mavrokordatos enjoyed united diplomatic support at the outset, see Lyons to Palmerston, 31 Aug. 1841, no. 126, FO 32.106, and *Athēna*, 18 June 1841o.s. Concerning domestic attitudes toward him, see P. Argyropoulos, Athens, 28 Mar. 1841, no. 5859, Vol. 21 (1841), Mavrokordatos Archive: "Things are getting worse, and every day you are becoming more and more desired as a savior"; M. Argyro-poulos to Mavrokordatos, Pera, 5/17 Mar. 1841, no. 5842, Vol. 21, MA; and Piscatory, Chalcis, 12 July 1841 (2nd report) and Patras, 12 July 1841 (3rd report), *L'Hellén-isme Contemporain*, IX, 343, 350: "His [Mavrokordatos'] arrival at the head of affairs is rendered popular by the removal of Bavarians, well received by all the interests that hope for the benefits of an active and enlightened administration."

[117] Pipineles [*Monarchy*], p. 326.

So the king intended, it seems. In submitting his resignation, Mavrokordatos was attempting as much to dispel "French" and "Russian" suspicions as he was demonstrating against the manifest lack of royal confidence in him.[118]

Insisting that obedience to one's sovereign overruled dissent on principle, Otho exhorted, threatened, and reproached Mavrokordatos. Maximilian, Prokesch-Osten, and Count Bray, Bavarian minister to Greece, all tried to mediate. Mavrokordatos refused to withdraw his resignation. During the next two weeks, Otho tried in vain to form a cabinet without Mavrokordatos. Valetas, Kountouriotes, Rizos-Neroulos, and Metaxas all refused to accept office without prior royal acceptance of the Mavrokordatos terms. This united front, which cut across party lines, proved decisive. The strategy of Mavrokordatos was working.[119]

[118] To kill rumors that Mavrokordatos would advance the "English" party to power (Athēna, 4 June 1841o.s.) and to dispel the impression that the deadlock between Otho and Mavrokordatos involved appointments rather than principle (ibid., 30 Aug. 1841o.s.), Athēna (25 June 1841o.s.) insisted that Mavrokordatos had avoided involvement in the selection of his cabinet colleagues and avoided interfering with the king's choices. Athēna was wrong and probably perpetrated this falsehood to tear down the image of Mavrokordatos as a partisan figure. For the plain fact of the matter is that Mavrokordatos *was* interested in the question of cabinet personnel *because* of his attempt to give all three parties representation and hence both fulfill his promises to them and retain their needed support. As Piscatory pointed out (Athens, 20 June 1841 [1st report], L'Hellénisme Contemporain, IX, 342), "If . . . they [the "French"] believed that Mavrokordatos had failed to meet his [political] promises, they would join together with the Napist party, which without them lacks a chief, and with them could make the most active opposition to the new minister." In his 2nd report (Chalcis, 25 June 1841, ibid., IX, 343), Piscatory wrote that the "French" had demanded "guarantees" for their party and the appointment of some of their party to the cabinet; that Mavrokordatos said he had recommended to the king Kolettes or two of Kolettes' important friends (such as Chrestides, Somaches, Karakatsanes, and Palamides); that on the news of the new appointments, public opinion reacted unfavorably, "the Napists made some advances to the friends of Kolettes, and M. Mavrokordatos saw the danger he was in. . . ."

Concerning the men whom Otho originally proposed to Mavrokordatos, those unfamiliar to him were L. Melas, Provelengios, and Moraïtines, those unacceptable were P. Soutsos and Tisamenos (Mavrokordatos to Trikoupes, 17/29 Sept. 1841, in Dragoumes [Reminiscences], II, 53-65).

For the text of Mavrokordatos' first letter of resignation (dated 7/19 June 1841) in which he cited lack of royal confidence as the cause, see Petrakakos [Parliamentary History], II, 273.

[119] Otho spent some four hours trying to make Mavrokordatos withdraw his resignation; then ordered him to (Pipineles [Monarchy], pp. 326-27). On the attempt of the diplomats to mediate, see Lyons to Palmerston, Athens, 31 Aug. 1841, no. 126, FO 32.106: Maximilian "thought it would be better for Mavrokordatos to make concessions than that the negotiations should be broken off. In that opinion Count Prokesch, Mr. Brassier [minister of Prussia], and Count Bray joined, and certainly Prokesch did all that was in his power to induce Mavrokordatos to meet Otho's wishes. . . ." On the united front, which thwarted the king's attempts to form a cabinet, see Lyons to Palmerston, Athens, 10 July 1841, no. 103, FO 32.106, and Athēna, 14 June, 18 June, and 30 Aug. 1841o.s.

On Mavrokordatos' return to Athens (2 July 1841) after a trip to Nauplion, Lagrené and Heidenstam, the Swedish consul, tried to mediate a settlement. This time the deadlock centered about the questions of dismissing the Bavarian officers, some 150 in number, and substituting a Greek for the Bavarian minister of war, more specifically Metaxas for Schmaltz. Mavrokordatos' insistence upon a Greek minister of war was a matter of principle. His recommendation of Metaxas was a political act to secure Napist support.[120]

Finally, the spectre of possible popular revolt softened the adamancy of both king and minister. About 1,000 armed volunteers for action in Crete had assembled in Athens. There was no telling what they might do during a cabinet crisis sustained by the issue of Bavarian control, a question on which public opinion in Greece was undivided. A fearful Otho assented to most of the demands. On 6 July he announced his decision to appoint Metaxas minister of war, if Mavrokordatos would immediately become minister of interior in order to curb popular agitation. Fearful himself of the impending disorders, Mavrokordatos accepted office, although he had come to no agreement with the king about the appointment of a minister of economy.[121] In addition to Metaxas and

[120] *Athēna* (18 June 1841o.s.) cites these issues as the chief stumbling block; also Pipineles [*Monarchy*], p. 327 (on issues and mediation of diplomats). According to *Athēna* (30 Aug. 1841o.s.), Metaxas was the only person that Mavrokordatos actually recommended. Manoles Argyropoulos wrote P. Argyropoulos on 26 Mar./7 Apr. 1841 (no. 5857, Vol. 21 [1841], Mavrokordatos Archive), "It is necessary to prevent its [the "French" party's] union with the Napist; from the latter some must be included [in the cabinet] but I'm not sure whether it should be Metaxas or someone else. . . ." See also Lyons to Palmerston, Athens, 10 July 1841, no. 103, FO 32.106: ". . . the composition of the ministry came again under discussion. The great difficulty that had arisen on this head was that Otho on the 17th last had, without consulting Mavrokordatos and in contradiction to what Mavrokordatos considered to be the understanding between Otho and him[self], appointed Provelengios, the chief of the Greek portion of the camarilla, to the post of minister of justice. Mavrokordatos again repeated to Otho what he had said to the prince royal of Bavaria, namely that he never could consent to having a colleague appointed without his knowledge, or to the principle of transferring the camarilla to the ministry, and Otho conceded the point, and proposed Melas, *procureur du roi* at Nauplia, to which Mavrokordatos reluctantly assented, after stating his objections, which are that Melas is too young and inexperienced, and cannot in any respect be fairly put in competition with his nominees, Clonares and Mons. D. Soutzo.

"Otho also yielded to Mavrokordatos' objections to the appointment of Silivergo, as minister of finance, but he begged Mavrokordatos not to press the appointment of Spaniolaki, and it was agreed that the nomination of the minister of finances should stand over, but that it should not be delayed beyond thirty days. Otho proposed Andre Metaxas as minister of war, and to this Mavrokordatos gave his full consent" (cf. with *Athēna*'s statement above).

[121] On the spectre of possible revolt, see Lyons to Palmerston, Athens, 10 July 1841, no. 103, and 22 July 1841, no. 108, FO 32.106; Mavrokordatos to Trikoupes, 17/29 Sept. 1841, in Dragoumes [*Reminiscences*], II, 53-65; and Petrakakos [*Parlia-*

Mavrokordatos, who now took the portfolio of the interior, the new cabinet included Melas as minister of justice, Valetas as minister of education, with Kriezes continuing as minister of naval affairs, and the "French" Demetrios Chrestides, recalled from his post in Constantinople, as minister of foreign affairs. Tisamenos was kept on a temporary basis as economic director. The cabinet was clearly tripartisan as Mavrokordatos had intended.[122] This was both an asset and a liability—an asset because the acquiescence of all parties in the leadership of Mavrokordatos was reasonably secure, but a liability because, in the event of another dispute with the king, Mavrokordatos could not be certain, as he might with personally loyal colleagues, that the entire cabinet would resign with him.

The Defeat of Mavrokordatos: The Beginning of the Fourth Phase

The position of Mavrokordatos suffered from other weaknesses as well —weaknesses that became more serious the longer the king held out. First, Mavrokordatos did not possess a corps of followers sufficiently large and cohesive to form a government whose members would work effectively together, stand solidly behind him against palace obstructions, or command a sufficiently large body of popular support. Government by coalition was a necessity.[123]

The second weakness stemmed from the first. Mavrokordatos had to rule in collaboration with the "French" and "Russian" parties in order to secure their needed support. This meant that he always labored under the possibility of betrayal by his collaborators. In spite of his long absence from Greece, his public image still retained some of its partisan character and his return to power aroused envy and suspicion among his former

mentary History], II, 273-74. On Metaxas' replacement of Schmaltz, see decrees of 2/14 July 1841 [*Government Gazette*], no. 13, 5 July 1841o.s., and Pipinelcs [*Monarchy*], p. 327. See also in the same issue the decree on the meetings of the ministerial council, dated 28 June/10 July 1841: "Article 1: all the important subjects, those by nature belonging to the deliberation of the ministerial council, will be discussed in it. For this purpose, we commission the presiding officer of the ministerial council to convoke it, either on his own or at the request of one or more ministers, but he must inform us immediately concerning every forthcoming meeting."

[122] For the decrees of appointment, all dated 24 June/6 July 1841, see [*Government Gazette*], no. 12, 27 June 1841o.s., and Lyons to Palmerston, Athens, 10 July 1841, no. 103, FO 32.106 (who estimated the cabinet as made up of three "English" [Mavrokordatos, Kriezes, Valetas], one "French" [Chrestides], one "Russian" [Metaxas], and one "not claimed by any party" [Melas]). *Athēna* (25 June 1841o.s.) announced the formation of a new cabinet and referred to it as "fusion without any fusionists in it" (see Chap. VI, pp. 307-308, above, on fusionism). Aspreas ([*Political History*], I, 156) recognized the tripartisan character of Mavrokordatos' cabinet, and he cited it as demonstration that Mavrokordatos was not serving the interests of English diplomacy. But he did not mention something far more important—the political necessity of this move.

[123] See pp. 372-73 and 385 above.

foes.[124] Such foes were momentarily able to transcend their envy and suspicion by virtue of the common hostility toward absolutism and Bavarianism. These two major obstacles to any constructive measures constituted the sole basis of cooperation between the parties. Once Mavrokordatos removed them to pave the way for more constructive efforts, he ran the risk of seeing his government disintegrate into dissension and insubordination and of finding his plans without an adequate instrument for their enactment.

Third, the prospect of sustained European cooperation in support of the Mavrokordatos program seemed extremely slight, especially if party dissensions broke out or the king had time enough to lure at least one power into his camp.[125]

The Mavrokordatos government lasted a little over six weeks. According to Mavrokordatos, Otho kept putting off any action to fulfill his promises and then employed devious methods to prevent the cabinet from exercising any initiative. In this phase of the conflict, abolition of the anaktovoulion became the chief issue. A decree of abolition had been prepared, but the king would not issue it. In the meantime, Mavrokordatos learned that Graf, chief of the anaktovoulion, had asked a new lease on the building which housed the anaktovoulion offices. Then news circulated that a "special secretariat" would take the place of the royal cabinet. To Mavrokordatos, this was nothing more than the old anaktovoulion with a new name. He decided to resign.[126]

The circumstances that precipitated Mavrokordatos' resignation tended to obscure the reason for his decision. During the extended negotiations, the abbot and two monks of the Megaspelaion monastery in north-central

---

[124] See pp. 385 and 393, n. 114 above. That Mavrokordatos recognized this necessity, see Guizot, Mémoires, vi, 456, and n. 113 above. On lingering suspicions of Mavrokordatos as a partisan figure and rumors to that effect, see Athēna, 4 June and 30 Aug. 1841o.s.

[125] Guizot (Mémoires, vi, 266) put his finger on one of the major problems. As he rightly pointed out, even when the French and British governments agreed on common action and sincerely cooperated in carrying out a common policy, it was extremely difficult for them to ensure that their respective legations in Athens would display the same willingness and ability to engage in joint and cooperative action.

[126] On the frequent cabinet meetings called for the implementation of Otho's promises and the failure to resolve the differences between king and ministers, see Lyons to Palmerston, Athens, 20 Aug. 1841, no. 120, FO 32.106, and Pipineles [Monarchy], p. 328. On the question of abolishing the anaktovoulion and evidence of its replacement by a new secretariat, see Mavrokordatos to Trikoupes, 17/29 Sept. 1841, in Dragoumes [Reminiscences], ii, 53-65, and Athēna, 2 Aug. 1841o.s. Lyons (22 July 1841, no. 108, FO 32.106) also pointed out another aspect of the same question, which showed Otho's real reservations about allowing cabinet responsibility and about refraining from his or his camarilla's personal supervision on all matters: "Amongst many other causes of dissatisfaction, Mavrokordatos mentioned to me that though the king had been four times reminded of his promise to send immediately from his cabinet [anaktovoulion] to the respective departments the voluminous papers, amounting to many thousands, which are there, his majesty has not yet done so."

Peloponnesos had circulated a manifesto in the nearby provinces. It had accused Mavrokordatos of undermining popular respect for the king and had urged all patriots to rally round the throne. Its implication was clear: Mavrokordatos was encouraging rather than curbing popular unrest. Its objective was equally clear—to drum up some public support for the king. Similar petitions appeared in other parts of Greece as well. The court then drew up a decree awarding medals of honor (cross of the savior) to those very monks. Refusing to sign the decree, Mavrokordatos resigned on 20 August. As he explained later, he did not refuse his signature because he regarded the decree as a personal insult. He refused it because the decree made the first official mention of the special secretariat, which he had no intention of ever acknowledging.

Valetas and Melas resigned immediately. After a week of hesitation, Metaxas withdrew from the government as well.[127] But there were signs that Mavrokordatos no longer enjoyed the strong support he had during the first crisis. When urged by Lyons to resign, Kriezes pleaded poverty and refused. Rizos-Neroulos, who turned down a cabinet post during the first crisis, this time accepted the ministry of the interior. Kountouriotes, never personally well-disposed toward Mavrokordatos, now withheld his support.[128] As for the Napists, they were divided in their support of

[127] On the circulation of petitions near Megaspelaion by monks, in the lowlands of Aigion by Meletopoulos, even in Livadia, see *Athēna*, 6 Aug. and 9 Aug. 1841*o.s.* On the award as a precipitant of his resignation, see primarily Mavrokordatos to Trikoupes, 17/29 Sept. 1841, in Dragoumes [*Reminiscences*], II, 53-65. See also *Athēna*, 13 Aug. 1841*o.s.*; Pipineles [*Monarchy*], p. 329; and Lyons to Palmerston, Athens, 27 Aug. 1841 (no. 122, FO 32.106) in which Lyons writes: "Mavrokordatos would still have persevered if the royal ordinance [making the awards] had not in fact been an answer to the ultimatum [of Mavrokordatos apparently], for it was not countersigned by the minister of religion and consequently showed Otho's persistence on the cardinal points of acting independently of his ministers and of imposing upon them the necessity of blindly countersigning royal ordinances or of resigning."

Piscatory (Athens, 27 Aug. 1841 [6th report], *L'Hellénisme Contemporain*, IX, 422) explained Mavrokordatos' resignation in terms of the party situation, namely the realization that attempts to secure the support of the Napist party had failed. Lyons (to Palmerston, Athens, 31 July 1841, no. 112, FO 32.106) explained Mavrokordatos' willingness to resign at that particular point as his satisfaction that the danger of internal revolt or a reckless irredentist venture had subsided: "Yesterday Mavrokordatos told me that as there was no longer any danger to be apprehended from Valentzas' movement, and as the revolt in Candia had been suppressed, he should resign in two or three days. . . ."

For the decrees accepting the resignations of Mavrokordatos (10/22 Aug. 1841), Melas (10/22 Aug. 1841) and Valetas (11/23 Aug. 1841), see [*Government Gazette*], no. 15, 12 Aug. 1841*o.s.* For that of Metaxas (29 Aug./10 Sept. 1841), see [*GG*], no. 17, 12 Sept. 1841*o.s.*

[128] On Kriezes, see Lyons to Palmerston, Athens, 6 Sept. 1841, no. 103, FO 32.107; on Kountouriotes, see *Athēna* (3 Sept. 1841*o.s.*): "We can thank Kountouriotes, who worked body and soul for this cabinet and opposed the Mavrokordatos cabinet." During the first crisis, Kountouriotes had considered longer than others accepting a post and breaking the united front (*Athēna*, 14 June 1841*o.s.*).

Mavrokordatos. Even though Metaxas remained loyal to him, *Aiōn* withdrew its support. *Athēna* accused the camarilla of bribing Philemon, its editor, and encouraging the monks of Megaspelaion, but it is quite likely that latent hostility toward Mavrokordatos made them more responsive to encouragement.[129] Moreover, like Prokesch-Osten, who had in midstream become lukewarm toward Mavrokordatos, a segment of the Greek public now felt that Mavrokordatos was being perverse, endangering the monarchy, and sustaining rather than correcting the dangerous situation of crisis.[130]

Yet these factors by themselves were not sufficient to secure the king a decisive victory over Mavrokordatos. The formation of a viable cabinet, on which such a victory depended, hinged on two conditions: (1) the acceptance of office by a person with sufficient influence to invite the support of a major party, and (2) the sympathy of at least one protecting power. As it turned out, Chrestides created the first condition and France the second.

Guizot had come to power in October 1840 after France had suffered a severe diplomatic defeat and loss of international prestige. Louis Philippe had chosen him as the most suitable person to bring France back into the European concert and restore good relations with Britain. The price of this task was acquiescence in the primacy of Britain in Near Eastern affairs. But Guizot was not willing to cede all influence to Britain. He wanted to restore French influence in the Near East, perhaps even increase it, but through diplomacy rather than war, and quiet maneuvering

[129] On *Aiōn*'s withdrawal of support and suspicions that there was some connection between this and the court's buying a large volume of Philemon's recent translation of *Plutarch's Lives,* see *Athēna,* 11 June and 3 Sept. 1841*o.s. Athēna* (9 Aug. 1841*o.s.*) also suggested that the instigators of the anti-Mavrokordatos petitions were protagonists and supporters of the Philorthodox society, the equivalent of saying they were Napist extremists. Piscatory reported from Chalcis (25 June 1841 [2nd report], *L'Hellénisme Contemporain,* IX, 343) that some Napists were working against Mavrokordatos; by 30 July 1841, when back in Athens (4th report, *ibid.,* IX, 411) he reported that the "Russian" party, "though it had made some advances [to Mavrokordatos] and received some guarantees [from him], is disposed to attack it [his cabinet]." But in his letter of 27 Aug. 1841 ([6th report], *ibid.,* IX, 420), he admitted that the Napists were divided. See also n. 127 above, which cites Piscatory's explanation of Mavrokordatos' designation in terms of his inability to secure Napist support.

[130] On Prokesch-Osten, see Lyons to Palmerston, Athens, 31 Aug. 1841, FO 32.106; he continues in the same despatch, "since he [Prokesch] has seen that Otho declines to fulfill any, even the most trifling, promises made to Mavrokordatos, he has given that minister all the support in his power." Also Piscatory, Chalcis, 25 June 1841 (2nd report), *L'Hellénisme Contemporain,* IX, 344.

On signs of a turn in public sentiment, see *Athēna,* 30 Aug. 1841*o.s.,* and Piscatory, Athens, 20 Aug. 1841 (5th report), *ibid.,* IX, 418. How real this was it is impossible to say, but there is some reason to doubt. *Athēna* believed this sentiment unrepresentative, fanned by the camarilla; Piscatory may have had ulterior motives for talking as he did because by this time he was critical of Mavrokordatos and obviously trying to sell Guizot on his own change of attitude.

rather than reckless daring. He took a resolute stand against deposing Mohammed Ali. By exploiting Russian and Austrian eagerness to struggle loose from British dominance, he forced the European concert to let Mohammed Ali consolidate his hold in Egypt. He scored a further success in February 1841, when a minor Near Eastern "crisis" occurred. The Ottoman decree, which vested in the family of Mohammed Ali the right of hereditary rule in Egypt, qualified this major concession to Mohammed Ali with so many reservations that it failed to satisfy him. Guizot and Metternich, supported by Nesselrode, forced the Porte to withdraw its reservations. Clearly, by April 1841, France was back in the European concert and had even formed a kind of coalition with Austria and Russia against unlimited British influence.[131]

In Greece, French policy underwent a similar development. Guizot accepted the appointment of Mavrokordatos in good spirit, even though he regarded it as a clear triumph for British diplomacy. He even promised the support of his government for the Mavrokordatos program and instructed Lagrené to do so in Athens. But within the context of formal cooperation with Britain, he also made a bid to wrest the initiative for France and curb British influence by drawing the concert of Europe directly into Greek affairs.[132]

His first move took the form of a circular letter, dated 11 March 1841, addressed to the courts of England, Russia, Austria, and Prussia,[133] to "suggest generally . . . the nature of the advice which the powers could extend to the Greek government in case they felt it necessary, as the cabinet of London seemed to desire, to intervene in order to alert King Otho to the evils" of the Greek administration. The letter was vague, ambiguous, and contradictory. Declaring the French belief that Greece was unripe for a constitution, it made vague suggestions about expand-

[131] Driault and Lhéritier, *Histoire*, II, 207-208.

[132] Concerning Mavrokordatos' appointment and his own response to it, Guizot wrote (*Mémoires*, VI, 260): "For some time, the French government, absorbed in the Orient by more perilous and pressing questions, occupied itself very little with Greece; the English and Russian parties disputed between themselves alone the supremacy, and the English party had recently conquered; Mr. Mavrokordatos, its chief, had just been called to the head of affairs; I judged the moment opportune for France to resume her role there as well. . . ." On his support to Mavrokordatos, see *ibid.*, VI, 262 and 456 (the latter a letter of Guizot to Lagrené, 17 Sept. 1841). According to Driault and Lhéritier (*Histoire*, II, 203-204), Guizot did not want to completely discourage Greek irredentist hopes and so took up with the Greeks the language of his predecessor.

[133] For the complete text of the circular letter of 11 Mar. 1841, see either *L'Hellénisme Contemporain*, 2nd ser., IX (1955), 329-331, or Guizot, *Mémoires*, VI, 261-63. For Guizot's comments on the move, see *ibid.*, VI, 260-63. For an example of unfavorable response in Greece, where many resented it as a case of foreign interference and some because it did not advocate constitutional government, see *Athēna*, 17 Sept. and 27 Sept. 1841o.s. See also Driault and Lhéritier, *Histoire*, II, 207-209, for an account of the king's hostility to this move and Austrian and Russian delight that France had taken an official position against constitutional government in Greece.

ing the competence of the Council of State and "connecting that institution to the provincial and municipal councils" (whatever that meant). It disclaimed the idea of intervening in the affairs of an independent nation, yet claimed the right of Europe to press advice on the king.

On the surface, the letter looked like a mere pious expression of hope that whatever the powers decided to do they do together. But by implication the letter made a number of pronouncements. It announced the return of France to an active interest in Greece, after being "for some time distracted from the Greek situation by more urgent questions." It declared the Greek problem a European, not just a British, concern, and it dissented from Britain on the practicability of a constitution. At the same time, it couched its challenge in language of deference to Britain. It declared French suggestions a follow-up of a British suggestion of intervention. Its suggested reforms amounted to an espousal, in principle, of the Mavrokordatos program of moderate reform.

Concurrently Guizot appointed Piscatory, a staunch supporter of Thiers' more aggressive Near Eastern policy, to undertake a special mission to Greece. Ostensibly, Piscatory was to pick up firsthand information on the situation, as a basis for further elaboration of French policy, to support Mavrokordatos in behalf of reform, and to urge moderation on the "French" with respect to internal and external affairs.[134] Actually he attempted to revive the waning confidence of the "French" party in France and to secure places in the Mavrokordatos administration for French partisans. The Piscatory mission to Greece extended from June to September 1841.[135]

Between November 1840 and June 1841, Otho and Guizot deferred to British supremacy, in part because each thought the other tied to Britain.

[134] On the stated purposes of the Piscatory mission, see (1) Guizot's instructions to Piscatory, in two separate documents, both dated 16 May 1841, *L'Hellénisme Contemporain*, 2nd ser., IX (1955), 332-35, 335-38, (2) Guizot to Lagrené, Paris, 16 May 1841, *ibid.*, IX, 5, 331-32, and (3) Guizot's comments in his *Mémoires*, VI, 260, 263-64. For a favorable evaluation of it, see Driault and Lhéritier, *Histoire*, II, 209. For an unfavorable one, paraphrased by Lyons (6 Sept. 1841, no. 135, FO 32.107), consider the alleged words of Mavrokordatos: "A special mission, ill-advised and ill-executed, unless indeed the object was (and he was unwilling to believe that on the part of Mons. Guizot) to unsettle, dissatisfy, and excite men's minds in this part of the world, and to assist Mons. Chrestides in supplanting him."

[135] Piscatory, indirectly by attributing the view to "French" partisans, intimated to Guizot (20 June 1841 [1st report], *L'Hellénisme Contemporain*, IX, 339, 341) that only a more active French system of patronage and support for the "French" party could win friends for France and compete with the strenuous efforts of the British and Russian legations; in short, that France could only realize her noble ends by playing the party game. In that same letter (p. 342), Piscatory reported that he had both reminded Mavrokordatos of his promises to include "French" in his cabinet and encouraged the "French" to ask of Mavrokordatos the terms they considered necessary for their support. Pipineles ([*Monarchy*], p. 331) is wrong when he says Piscatory urged Mavrokordatos to resign; on the contrary, he urged him not to (Athens, 20 Aug. 1841 [5th report], *op.cit.*, IX, 417-18).

Between June and August, however, it became obvious to each that the other would gladly exercise greater independence of Britain if closer cooperation between France and Greece were possible. The Cretan revolt (March–August 1841) demonstrated a common French-Greek interest in preventing Britain from acquiring a protectorate over Crete, as both sides feared it was trying to do. It also brought each side into strained relations with Britain—Greece because of a renewed outburst of irredentist extremism and royal acquiescence in it, France because it refused to join Britain and Austria in direct naval support of a Turkish reconquest or condemn absolutely Greek irredentist hopes.[136]

Moreover, by August Otho must have realized that the Piscatory mission was intended more as a counterweight to British influence than as a preparation for European intervention, and it became perfectly obvious to Piscatory that the king would be rid of Mavrokordatos if only he could find a way. Both Otho and Guizot must have seen the distinct possibility of discreetly assisting each other to resist Great Britain, Otho by offering a "French" candidate what he refused Mavrokordatos, and Guizot by withdrawing support of Mavrokordatos during the second crisis. The *rapprochement* between France and Greece would then be complete. France would have won Otho's gratitude for being rescued from the grip of Mavrokordatos, and Otho would reward France by giving her a preponderant influence in Greek affairs.[137]

[136] Driault and Lhéritier, *Histoire*, II, 214-20. On Otho's acquiescence in—even encouragement of—the efforts in behalf of the rebels, see Piscatory, Athens, 30 July 1841 [4th report], *L'Hellénisme Contemporain*, IX, 412.

[137] Speaking of one of his later audiences with Otho, Piscatory wrote (Athens, 27 Aug. 1841 [6th report], *L'Hellénisme Contemporain*, IX, 421): "I was received with quite another reception than that which he had extended me when others had persuaded the King that I was going to tour northern Greece to raise it to revolt." But even a month earlier, the king had, giving audience to Piscatory, affirmed his confidence in France and intimated that he was considering the recall of Kolettes to the head of affairs in the future (Athens, 30 July 1841 [4th report], *ibid.*, IX, 411). Also, the king found another inducement in making a bid for French support—France was the only one of the three powers that had not yet guaranteed the bulk of its share of the third series. He raised the question of a loan with Piscatory twice (Chalcis, 25 June 1841 [2nd report], and Athens, 27 Aug. 1841 [6th report], *ibid.*, IX, 345 and 421).

As for Piscatory, by the end of July he was well aware that the king was ever more hostile to Mavrokordatos and would stop at nothing to be rid of him (30 July 1841 [4th report], *ibid.*, IX, 411).

It is impossible to determine whether Guizot was formulating French policy toward Otho and Piscatory carrying it out, or whether Piscatory was presenting Guizot with a *fait accompli* that Guizot could welcome once done. Guizot, in a letter to Lagrené dated 17 Sept. 1841 (*Mémoires*, VI, 456) disclaimed any betrayal of Mavrokordatos, indeed cites a letter in support of Mavrokordatos that arrived in Greece on the day after Mavrokordatos resigned a second time (*ibid.*, VI, 265, and Piscatory, Athens, 27 Aug. 1841 [6th report], *op.cit.*, IX, 422).

It may be that Piscatory's behavior proved most decisive, not because of any influence over Otho or Chrestides, but rather because of a profound influence over

Otho played his hand cleverly. He concentrated all his efforts on Chrestides, who possessed the double merit of being a "French" leader commanding the respect of the French government and of being opportunist enough to sacrifice principle for personal profit. He offered Chrestides the ministry of the interior in place of the less important ministry of foreign affairs. To divorce the issue of reform from his personal conflict with Mavrokordatos, he promised to grant Chrestides all the reforms demanded by Mavrokordatos. All then depended on Chrestides' decision and the willingness of the "French" party to go along with him.[138]

On his arrival, Chrestides accepted office without any previous demand for guarantees. On the evening of his acceptance, he exclaimed proudly, in the midst of his friends:

> What did Mavrokordatos think? That he would rule Greece as he willed? That there were no men to take his place? Yes, gentlemen, I accepted the ministry. It was the will of the king, and to the king we owe obedience.

Lyons urged Piscatory to dissuade Chrestides, but Piscatory refused, saying that a political crisis was a serious matter and that one must give Chrestides a chance.[139] Lyons, Mavrokordatos, and Gennaios Koloko-

---

Guizot (1) through criticism of Mavrokordatos (30 July 1841 [4th report], *ibid.*, IX, 411, and 27 Aug. 1841 [6th report], *ibid.*, IX, 423) for allegedly resorting to partisan behavior, betraying his promises to the "French" on appointments, proving ineffective, damaging the respect for the throne, etc., (2) through portrayal of Mavrokordatos as a virtual puppet of Lyons: "Mr. Lyons described to us the government activity of Mavrokordatos day by day, and I understood why Mr. Mavrokordatos has thrown into his dispute with the king such harshness and haughtiness, which are quite contrary to his character. . . ." (27 Aug. 1841 [6th report], *ibid.*, IX, 423), (3) by telling Guizot early in the game that Chrestides would probably be willing to succeed Mavrokordatos (30 July 1841 [4th report], *ibid.*, IX, 412).

[138] *Athēna*, 13 Aug. 1841*o.s.*; Piscatory, Athens, 20 Aug. 1841 [5th report], and Athens, 27 Aug. 1841 [6th report], *L'Hellénisme Contemporain*, IX, 418 (that Otho intended to use Chrestides so as to get rid of Mavrokordatos), 423 (on the "bombshell" of Otho's getting Rizos to accept the foreign ministry and giving Chrestides Mavrokordatos' portfolio of the interior), 425 (Chrestides told Piscatory, "He [the king] promised me everything; I hope for a little").

[139] Chrestides spoke to Piscatory as follows (Athens, 27 Aug. 1841 [6th report], *ibid.*, IX, 426): "If I don't succeed, no one can reproach me about anything. I did not intrigue against Mr. Mavrokordatos who resigned when I was still absent; I accepted the ministry because I did not wish to be a nobody, because one must not think that in Greece there is only Mr. Mavrokordatos, because I like power. I have accepted without making conditions, on the promise of the king, who is convinced as I am that conditions mean nothing and that a promise can be kept."

The quotation in the text above is from Rangabe, *Memoirs*, II, 114.

On Lyons' demands of Piscatory, see Lyons to Palmerston, Athens, 6 Sept. 1841, no. 133, FO 32.107 and Piscatory, Athens, 27 Aug. 1841 [6th report], *L'Hellénisme Contemporain*, IX, 423-24: ". . . I would not take the responsibility of making Christides refuse and hence leave the country without an administration or inducing the king to return to a cabinet of perfectly incapable men."

trones later intimated that Piscatory had done more than not try to dissuade Chrestides. Lyons alleged that Piscatory had actually urged Chrestides to accept office. To be sure, Piscatory had made a sudden trip to Constantinople and the two men had met on one of the Aegean Islands, but what transpired during the meeting is unknown. Back in France, Piscatory boasted that he had won a victory for French diplomacy in Greece by working for the downfall of the Mavrokordatos government, but even this damaging evidence is partially vitiated by the fact that Piscatory made this boast while campaigning for reelection in the French assembly.[140]

Actually, it had probably been unnecessary for Piscatory to urge Chrestides or anybody else. The "French" party as a whole had never given its wholehearted support to Mavrokordatos. French partisans continued to nurse resentment against Mavrokordatos from Revolutionary days and feared the political supremacy that his reforms would have given him. Regas Palamides, contender against Chrestides for leadership of the "French" party during the absence of Kolettes, hated Mavrokordatos bitterly. Adam Doukas and Vasos Mavrovouniotes placed no confidence in Mavrokordatos' promises to share power with the "French" party. In April before Mavrokordatos arrived, Manoles Argyropoulos wrote that such French partisans as Nicholas Skouphos and Panagiotes Soutsos, men in the court, were involved in an anti-Mavrokordatos intrigue and that Kolettes had had to continually write and scold them and his partisans in Greece for their hostility. Meletopoulos, a "French" partisan influential in the local politics of Achaia, actually circulated petitions similar in sentiment to those of the Megaspelaion monks, and Piscatory had perpetually to argue French partisans into reluctant ac-

---

[140] On Lyons' intimations, see Lyons to Palmerston, 6 Sept. 1841, no. 133, FO 32.107. On Mavrokordatos, see Mavrokordatos to Trikoupes, 17/20 Sept. 1841, in Dragoumes [*Reminiscences*], II, 53-65; on Gennaios Kolokotrones, see his [*Memoirs II*], p. 86; on Piscatory's boasting back in France, Pipineles [*Monarchy*], p. 331. Kordatos ([*History*], III, 183) states that Chrestides decided to accept office because of pressure from "the French minister" and that he "probably also received a letter from Kolettes." He offers no evidence and his assertion seems doubtful because Chrestides hardly seems to have needed prodding. Mavrokordatos (Dragoumes, *op.cit.*) writes that Piscatory left no stone unturned to get Chrestides appointed to the cabinet; there is no reason to doubt this. It is at this point that Piscatory exerted positive pressure for the "French" candidate. After, there was no need to. Piscatory knew how to cover himself very well, by praising Chrestides to Otho at the very moment he expressed Chrestides' alleged desire for the continued existence of the Mavrokordatos cabinet (Athens, 27 Aug. 1841 [6th report], *L'Hellénisme Contemporain*, IX, 422) or ostensibly pointing out the perils of office by telling Chrestides that he would need Lagrené's full support against European diplomacy, a way of telling him he could count on French support (Athens, 27 Aug. 1841 [6th report], *ibid.*, IX, 425). Perhaps the most telling statement about his own behavior is his advice to the "French" partisans in Greece—"that they must act in such a way that no one could hold them responsible for Mavrokordatos' resignation" (Athens, 20 Aug. 1841 [5th report], *ibid.*, IX, 418).

ceptance of Mavrokordatos. So all Piscatory had to do when French policy changed was stop urging support of Mavrokordatos. Chrestides had been anxious to win the king's good graces and other "French" partisans had long been tugging at the leash to take advantage of Mavrokordatos' quarrel with the king.[141]

Significance of the Episode

His own contemporaries and later historians have depicted the Mavrokordatos episode as a case of a united Greek people pitted against the Bavarians, the popular against the royal will.[142] No doubt the recall of Mavrokordatos was genuinely popular insofar as it raised hopes for the end of Bavarian control and a more national government. Quite rightly, as Athēna charged, intrigues against Mavrokordatos originated among the Bavarians and Greeks in the anaktovoulion.[143] But, the image of a prime minister wholeheartedly supported by his people, thwarted by a handful of scheming and self-interested Bavarians, and resigning amid a chorus of universal indignation, is an oversimplification that glosses over the underlying party rivalries and makes unintelligible the king's success during the second cabinet crisis. Indeed this episode revealed the total inability of Kolettes and the partial inability of Metaxas to prevail over their respective party followings for continued support of Mavrokordatos.

It has also been said that the Mavrokordatos episode made revolution

[141] On doubts of Doukas and Vasos, see Piscatory, Patras, 12 July 1841 [3rd report], ibid., ix, 348; on the "French" intrigues and Kolettes' scoldings, M. Argyropoulos to Mavrokordatos, Pera, 15/22 [sic] Apr. 1841, no. 5883, Vol. 21 (1841), Mavrokordatos Archive. M. Argyropoulos (Pera, 26 Mar./7 Apr. 1841, no. 5857, Vol. 21, MA) expressed doubts about the reliability of the "French" as political allies. On Meletopoulos' activities see Athēna, 2 Aug. 1841o.s. On the necessity for Piscatory to constantly urge support for Mavrokordatos, see Piscatory, Athens, 20 June 1841 (1st report); Chalcis, 25 June 1841 (2nd report); Patras, 12 July 1841 (3rd report); and Athens, 20 Aug. 1841 (5th report), all L'Hellénisme Contemporain, ix, 342, 344, 350-51, and 418 respectively. See p. 418 concerning the impatience of the "French": "there is much impatience, and when the king says that all that he refuses Mavrokordatos he will give to his successors, and even more, one has a jubilation with which I think it would be very important for us to associate ourselves."

Piscatory (Athens, 27 Aug. 1841 [6th report], ibid., ix, 423) criticized Mavrokordatos for his "little care for the men of the national party [the "French"], who had a right to expect more"; see also Athens, 20 June 1841 (1st report), and Athens, 30 July 1841 (4th report), ibid., ix, 341, 411, for similar complaints. From the beginning Mavrokordatos had disapproved of a "union with the Kolettist party" (P. Argyropoulos to Mavrokordatos, 8/20 Apr. 1841, no. 5860, Vol. 21, MA). Hence there is good reason to think that the "French" betrayed Mavrokordatos not only because of lingering suspicions and lust for office but also because they felt that theirs was not an important enough role in the coalition government.

[142] See for instance, Athēna, 7 June, 11 June, 9 Aug. 1841o.s.; Dragoumes [Reminiscences], ii, 46, 65-66; and Karolides [Contemporary History], iii, 314.

[143] For instance, Athēna, 7 June and 7 Aug. 1841o.s.; also Dragoumes [Reminiscences], ii, 46.

inevitable.[144] There is a good deal of truth in this assertion. By taking a firm stand, Mavrokordatos had given the public ample proof of the king's unyielding attitude toward even the most moderate reforms. It is indicative of the king's waning popularity that *Athēna*, for the first time, could afford to abandon the polite convention of laying the responsibility for unpopular royal acts to Bavarian advisers.[145] Both the "English" and "Russian" parties, having experienced the frustrations of trying to govern under a system of royal interference, were henceforth willing to cooperate in the attempted use of force to exact concessions from the king. But there still remained the "French" party, which was willing and anxious to try its hand at governing. Not until it too became disillusioned would it be willing to unite with the other two parties against the king. What actually made revolution inevitable was the king's continued unwillingness to yield—even to the one party that remained a potential ally—and the failure of this party to act monolithically.

[144] *Ibid.*, ii, 67; and Petrakakos [*Parliamentary History*], ii, 274.
[145] *Athēna*, 26 July and 20 Aug. 1841o.s.

CHAPTER EIGHT

The Later Period of Othonian Absolutism: "French" Ascendancy (1841–43) and the "Bloodless" Revolution of September 1843

FOR the two years that intervened between the Mavrokordatos episode and the "bloodless" revolution of 3/15 September 1843, the personal absolutism of Otho and the influence of the Bavarians persisted. Two days after Chrestides joined the ministry, Otho issued a decree formally dissolving the anaktovoulion, but the same decree provided for a substitute—a royal secretariat "having no advisory powers." As *Athēna* quickly pointed out, it looked as if the old institution had simply acquired a new name *and* the explicit statutory recognition that it had formerly lacked.[1]

Schmaltz departed from Greece in 1841, but most of the remaining Bavarians in state service were retained. According to *Athēna* early in 1842, 112 continued to serve in the army, 20 in the ministry of military affairs, 35 in the ministry of interior, and an unspecified number in the economic, judicial, and naval branches of the administration. Although a Greek (Vlachopoulos) now headed the ministry of the army, he was an illiterate without the qualifications demanded by the office. Real control allegedly belonged to the Bavarian attached to the ministry as royal councilor. The most influential Bavarians during this period were Graf, head of the new secretariat and councilor in the foreign ministry, Hess, colonel of the artillery, and Spiess, lieutenant-colonel and head of the general staff.[2]

After the Mavrokordatos episode, it became established practice to submit all legislation to the Council of State for consideration before its official promulgation,[3] but nothing was done to increase the power of the Council as France had proposed in Guizot's circular letter of March 1841 or as Mavrokordatos had demanded. Once a united front in support

---

[1] Decree for the abolition of the anaktovoulion, 10/22 Aug. 1841, *Ephemeris tes Kybernoseos tou Basileiou tes Hellados* [*Government Gazette, Kingdom of Greece*], no. 15, 12 Aug. 1841*o.s.*; *Athēna*, 20 Aug. 1841*o.s.*

[2] On the departure of Schmaltz, see *Athēna*, 25 June and 26 Nov. 1841*o.s.*, and Lyons to Aberdeen, Athens, 1 Dec. 1841, no. 176, Ser. 32, Vol. 108, Archives of the British Foreign Office, Public Record Office, London [hereafter to be cited as FO 32.108 and so on]. For the numerical estimates cited above, see *Athēna*, 21 Jan. 1842*o.s.*; for an actual catalogue of Bavarians remaining in state service, see its issue of 9 May 1842*o.s.* On the *real* head of the ministry of the army, see *Athēna*'s allegations of 9 May 1842*o.s.*

[3] T. N. Pipineles, *He Monarchia en Helladi 1833-1843* [*The Monarchy in Greece 1833-1843*] (Athens, 1943), p. 338, and Gianni Kordatos, *Historia tes Neoteres Helladas* [*History of Modern Greece*], (Athens, 1957), III, 185.

of Mavrokordatos had dissolved, the only hope of implementing this basic reform lay in the impetus that might be provided by Chrestides and French diplomacy—the same elements that had won Otho's confidence by helping to dissolve that front. Yet, when questioned by Piscatory about his position on this issue, Chrestides replied:

I am absolutely convinced that there is nothing of value to do there and I regret very much that France has raised the question. . . . I am convinced that nothing would be more unavailing for good administration and that there might be dangers in the immovability, in the veto, or in the election of a body small in numbers, without counterpoise, which would give itself up to the spirit of party or sell out to power.

To this observation, Guizot later responded:

At the distance we stand from the country that he is going to govern, we cannot pretend to judge better than he the route which it is convenient to follow to arrive at our common end, the consolidation of order, the creation of a regular administration which can develop all the resources of Greece.[4]

Guizot was serving notice that France would abide by the judgment of Chrestides on ways and means to realize a "common end" and Chrestides, by his behavior, looked as if he was tailoring his judgment to fit the wishes of the king. In effect both Guizot and Chrestides were announcing that they would not press for reforms which the king did not approve. In the consequent absence of any impetus for reform from those on whom he counted most, Otho stubbornly pursued his former course. The cabinet exercised no greater initiative than it had before and, contrary to the expectations of Guizot, it was the king rather than Chrestides who governed.[5]

The king's policy of associating all parties in the government remained essentially the same. The cabinet, which Kriezes proposed and Kountouriotes approved after refusing office for himself, continued to be mixed and balanced. Rizos-Neroulos (foreign affairs and religion-education) and Kriezes (navy) were both renegades from the "English" party, the former a Phanariot. Tisamenos, heterochthon and client of Kountouriotes, took charge of economic affairs. Alexakes Vlachopoulos, an illiterate military figure of Napist leanings, replaced Metaxas (army). George

---

[4] For the statement of Chrestides, see Piscatory to Guizot, Athens, 27 Aug. 1841 [6th report], in "Textes et Documents, La Grèce d'Othon," ed. Jean Poulos, in *L'Hellénisme Contemporain*, 2nd ser., ix (1955), 425-26. Guizot's response is contained in his letter to Lagrené, 17 Sept. 1841, in M. Guizot, *Mémoires pour servir à l'Histoire de mon Temps* (Paris, n.d.), vi, 457.

[5] On the continued lack of cabinet initiative, see *Athēna*, 23 Sept. 1841 o.s. Lyons (to Aberdeen, Athens, 12 Sept. 1841, no. 143, FO 32.107) summed up as follows: "The Camarilla still exists; the *présidence réelle* of the council of ministers has been put an end to; the king declines to accept the resignation of Bavarian officers."

Ralles, a Napist heterochthon who had performed distinguished government service under Kapodistrias, became minister of justice. He was allowed to exercise wide powers of patronage within the jurisdiction of his office. The king obviously intended to win the partial support of the Napist party and prevent it from following Metaxas *en masse* into the political opposition.[6] But as minister of the interior and the only cabinet member with any major influence in his own party, Chrestides was able to give a "French" complexion to the government. Following the established practice of periodically transferring political primacy from one party to another, during these two years Otho allowed the "French" party to achieve that primacy and pursued a pro-French foreign policy.

In spite of the mixed nature of the cabinet and Otho's design to give the Napist party a vested interest in it, it was the general consensus that the "French" party was "in power." During this period Prokesch-Osten wrote in his diary, "King Otho sees and hears only with the eyes and ears of the French party." The "Russian" Metaxas and the "English" Pharmakides shared the same view, as did the "English" Leon Melas, who wrote Mavrokordatos: ". . . the good old gent Mr. Valetas, with whom I daily think about you, is quite right when he describes all of Greece as one big Moschomanga [nickname for "French" party]." And even more important, the correspondence of Karakatsanes to Palamides in the fall of 1842 shows that these two leading figures in the "French" party considered their party enough in power to discuss in detail and plan for the distribution of posts among party associates.[7]

The Karakatsanes correspondence indicates one of the major reasons for this impression. As minister of the interior, Chrestides was allowed to exercise a certain amount of patronage, which became the subject of intraparty negotiations and discussion. Although only gradually, he secured a preponderance of "French" governors in the administration and hence gave it a "French" complexion. Moreover, he and his party enjoyed the full backing of Lagrené who, in response to Piscatory's oblique criticism of his earlier behavior, now behaved more aggressively in his patronage of the "French" party and in his assertion of French interests.

[6] On the sponsors of the new cabinet, see *Athēna*, 10 Dec. 1841o.s.

Rizos and Ralles were appointed by decrees of 10/22 Aug. 1841 [*Government Gazette*], no. 15, 12 Aug. 1841o.s., and Vlachopoulos by decree of 29 Aug./10 Sept. 1841, [*GG*], no. 17, 12 Sept. 1841o.s. Concerning Ralles, his past and his new office, see two lead articles in *Athēna*, 6 Sept. and 24 Sept. 1841o.s.; concerning his rather broad exercise of patronage, see *Athēna*, 24 Dec. 1841 and 24 Oct. 1842o.s.

[7] Prokesch-Osten's diary entry is quoted by Friedrich Engel-Janosi, "Austria and the Beginnings of the Kingdom of Greece," *Journal of Central European Affairs*, i (1941), 210. Metaxas to Mavrokordatos, Athens, 26 Apr. 1842o.s., no. 6294; Pharmakides to Mavrokordatos, Athens, 18/30 May 1842, no. 6340; and Melas to Mavrokordatos, Athens, 18 Aug. 1842o.s., no. 6430, all in Vol. 22 (1842), Mavrokordatos Archive, General State Archives, Athens. Karakatsanes to Palamides, Athens, 30 Sept., 12 Oct., 13 Oct., 19 Oct., 28 Oct. 1842o.s., folder 258 (1840-49), Palamides Archive, Vlachogiannes Collection, General State Archives, Athens.

But Chrestides never acquired as much authority nor showed as much personal initiative as Glarakes had before him. Nor did his party gain as extensive control over the administration as had the Napist party during Glarakes' tenure of office. The Karakatsanes correspondence, which was cited above, reflects the limitations, difficulties, and slowness encountered by the party in placing its members in office and the consequent dissatisfaction within the party.[8]

This period, then, was no less a period of personal royal absolutism than the "Russian" period had been. The nature and conduct of government remained the same, as did the system of a mixed cabinet and administration in which one party received primacy of representation. In this period it was the "French" rather than the "Russian" party that enjoyed such primacy. But to talk about this period as "the 'French' period" does not reveal its defining characteristic. This period differed from the "Russian" and derived its distinctiveness as a period from a much more important characteristic—for the first time, the political opposition was tripartisan in character and the three protecting powers acted in concert. Like the "Russian" period, this one also witnessed the organization of a conspiracy, but this time it was a triparty rather than a single-party conspiracy and it proved successful, culminating in the revolution of 15 September 1843, which destroyed absolutism and initiated a constitutional regime.

This chapter will therefore focus on this new type of opposition, in which major segments of all three parties rose above their former rivalries in a common effort. But first, in order to explain how major portions of the "French" party, the party of political primacy, went into opposition and joined the conspiracy, I will deal with the internal structure of the "French" party and the shifting balance of power between its constituent parts during the absolutist decade. Then I will take up the formation of an "English"-"Russian" opposition, culminating in the formation of the triparty conspiracy. The final section will cover the revolution itself—the two factors contributing most effectively to its success (the financial crisis

---

[8] On the major changes in the personnel of the governorships, either through new appointments or transfers, see *Athēna*, 3 Oct., 10 Oct., 14 Oct., 24 Oct. 1842*o.s.* Even though *Athēna* cited these changes as evidence of the invisible hand of the camarilla and interpreted them as a sign of revived Napist influence, so far as I can see they also represented an increase of "French" influence, although the "French" did not establish as exclusive a hold as did the Napists under Glarakes.

In connection with Chrestides' relative lack of authority and initiative, see the remarks of Alexander R. Rangabe, *Apomnemoneumata* [*Memoirs*] (Athens, 1894), II, 114-18. Rangabe, who had been called into the ministry of interior by Chrestides to draw up new reform legislation, describes an incident in which Chrestides slept while Rangabe enthusiastically read a draft of some bill which Chrestides had requested. The kind of inertia that Rangabe attempts to illustrate by this vignette was not characteristic of Chrestides' past reputation. Had he simply become older and self-complacent, or had the king's controlling hand robbed him of his zest?

and the behavior of the powers), the events immediately related to its outbreak, and the formation of a provisional regime.

1. THE INTERNAL EVOLUTION OF THE "FRENCH" PARTY

Component Parts of the "French" Party

More than the other two parties, the "French" party seems to have developed a more balanced representation of the well-known interests in Greece. Like the other parties and in spite of its identification with Rumeliot military interests, it included Peloponnesians and Islanders as well as Rumeliots, primates as well as captains, heterochthons as well as autochthons. But it articulated these interests more clearly because each faction in the "French" party retained its own identity, organization, and leader, and bore close association with one or more of the other interests. This situation was advantageous in so far as it made the party more comprehensive, hence national, but it had the disadvantage of causing internal instability and dissension.[9]

There were five readily identifiable constituent parts: (1) the Kolettes faction, consisting of Rumeliot chieftains, primates, and some heterochthons, (2) an East Rumeliot alliance between Kriezotes and Mavrovouniotes, influential captains, and Doukas, an influential primate, (3) a Peloponnesian primate interest, formerly headed by Delegiannes, during the absolutist period by Palamides, (4) the Makrygiannes following, consisting largely of humble captains concentrated mainly in Rumely, and (5) the Kountouriotes Island interest.

The bonds holding these five together in some relationship were the personality of Kolettes, the patronage of the "French" legation in Athens, and the legacy of both a common hostility toward the Napists and a common resentment against the "English" for defecting from the Constitutionalist movement in 1832. But the ties between these five groups were not of equal strength. One might best think of the first three as a closely linked group at the center and the last two as satellites only loosely attached to the center. These two were related this way to the other three largely because Makrygiannes and Kountouriotes refused too close a relationship with either Kolettes or the French legation.[10] The first three have

[9] This may serve as a more acceptable meaning of the term "national," as it applied to the "French" party, than the usage of the "French" and French diplomacy, described in Chap. VII, pp. 370-71, above. But to my knowledge, no one then or since used the word "national" in this sense (as a balanced representation of varied interests). Concerning the frequent identification of the "French" party with the palikar interest, see Antoine Grénier, *La Grèce en 1863* (Paris, 1863), p. 206.

[10] This kind of conceptualization is the only way I can reconcile the ostensibly inconsistent statements about Kountouriotes by Piscatory, to the effect on the one hand that "Kountouriotes is neither of the French nor the English parties, because he has never wanted to unite with Kolettes or Mavrokordatos" (Athens, 6 Sept. 1841 [7th report], *L'Hellénisme Contemporain*, IX, 442), and to the effect on the

already been discussed (Chapter III). The remaining two now demand closer examination.

The faction of Makrygiannes differed from the usual model. To be sure, he had some clients, like any of the captains, but he was not important or rich enough to have many. He lacked either the socio-economic status of Kountouriotes or the high wartime position of Kolo-kotrones or the contact with legations of other men. His faction consisted largely of unknown men, humble but politically conscious veterans, held together largely by the esteem he commanded for disinterestedness and honesty and the plans to which he committed men by administering an oath in the tradition of the Philike Hetairia and as a counterpart of the Napist Philorthodox society. His objective was the creation of a move-ment, not a faction, one which disclaimed personal advantage and pro-fessed its dedication to justice for the veterans and service to the country.[11]

Judging from his repeated attempts to organize this "movement," one would surmise that its organization was extremely loose. He probably exaggerated its numerical strength and geographical extent. Its aims were general and ill-defined, sometimes for the liberation of Greek irredenta, sometimes for the establishment of "just laws" in Greece, some-times for the forcible promulgation of a constitution. Without a specific political program or any clearly defined political strategy, this move-

other that during the Mavrokordatos episode Kountouriotes was closely associated with Kolettes' friends. This same ambivalence toward the central corps of the "French" party, though of different origins, is characteristic of Makrygiannes too. He was "French" enough for Piscatory to include him in the membership of the "French" party (Athens, 6 Sept. 1841 [7th report], ibid., IX, 428) and well at-tached enough to Kolettes for Kolettes to send a French tourist (Malherbe) to enjoy Makrygiannes' hospitality (see John Makrygiannes, Apomnemoneumata [Memoirs], ed. John Vlachogiannes, 2nd edn. [Athens, 1947], II, 124). But Makry-giannes avoided close association with the French legation because of his dislike for all forms of foreign interference (see two such outbursts against this phenomenon in ibid., II, 52, 114) and with Kolettes because he believed him antipathetic to the military interest. In ibid., II, 72, Makrygiannes referred to both Kolettes and Mav-rokordatos as "the grave diggers of the military."

[11] One kind of humble clientele Makrygiannes maintained is revealed in the fol-lowing statement ([Memoirs], II, 93): "And those who fought go from one to an-other person to eat a meal. I have some of these in my house, Mr. minister, whom I support so that they won't resort for bread to bad ways and then you put the laws on them and execute them—we will need them someday." Concerning his administering of an oath or "catechizing," to use the contemporary term, see ibid., II, 110, 114, 119, 120, in which he actually says that he was interested primarily in recruiting men of second rank. One good illustration of his desire to create a movement, rather than a faction, is the following reference in ibid., II, 95, about men who are not "English," "French," or "Russian," but "Greeks, with regard for their fatherland and religion"; another is the oath he began administering at the end of 1841 (II, 120): "Let us not be Constitutionalists or Governmentalists, nor 'English,' 'French,' or 'Russian.' Let us respect all those for their benefactions—and let them leave us and our king alone."

ment was effective only as a potential threat to the existing government or as a potential source of popular support for someone who did have a program.[12]

Suspicious of politicians per se, even more of politicians with foreign dealings such as Kolettes, Mavrokordatos, and Metaxas, he recruited behind their backs and independently of any party. His active collaborators were such military men as Velentzas and Kriezotes, giving his movement the character of a political organization for the military element and linking him with the East Rumeliot interest (group 3 above). None the less, in spite of its attempted independence of any party, Makrygiannes' movement was certainly anti-Napist, and "French" in the sense that most of his adherents and closest allies were identified with the "French" party.[13]

In 1833 *Hēlios* had cited the Kountouriotists as one of the seven "parties" in Greece. Lyons had referred to the two brothers as "the richest, and beyond all comparison the most influential persons in Greece." Three of their followers during the royalist period had been Zacharitsas, the rich Athenian who had always supported George Kountouriotes in the Council of State; Tisamenos the Epirot; Païkos of Salonika, sometime Napist, who owed his appointment as minister of justice in 1837 to George Kountouriotes' influence with prime minister Rudhart. Although their stronghold was in Hydra and their clientele largely humble sailors whom the Kountouriotes' had courted against the Island magnates, this faction also gained adherents from elsewhere, thanks to the presence of George at the center of national affairs in Athens.[14]

---

[12] On both the repeated character of the catechizing and the probably exaggerated description of it ("And I was catechizing the whole nation"), see *ibid.*, ii, 110, 114, 119, 120. On aims, see ii, 107, 114 (irredentism); ii, 119, 122 ("just laws" and good administration); ii, 119, 122 (assembly and constitution). The oath cited in n. 11 above illustrates the conspicuous lack of a program; indeed, so anxious was Makrygiannes for unity that he made his movement everything to everybody. "To one I would say we were concerned with the exterior [irredentism], to another with the interior, so as to make laws and a national assembly. And whoever was interested in the outside, I would encourage him for that. So I continued this way until 1840" (ii, 119).

[13] On his suspicion of the party leaders, see for instance *ibid.*, ii, 95. He described his relationship to Velentzas as follows (ii, 106): "Veletzas [sic] was from those parts and I was tied to him too. Veletzas was a brave palikar. They pursued him so many times and they arrested him in Nauplion and I went through such great pains and expenses so as to save him." Concerning his close relationship to Kriezotes, see Piscatory (Athens, 6 Sept. 1841 [7th report], *L'Hellénisme Contemporain*, ix, 430), who said that Kriezotes consulted Makrygiannes and Adam Doukas on all important matters. Concerning Makrygiannes' anti-Napism, see his remarks about the Philorthodox society, which was irredentist and religiously conservative like himself (ii, 102-103, 112-13).

[14] *Hēlios*, 4 July 1833*o.s.*; Lyons to Palmerston, Athens, 5 July 1838, no. 119, FO 32.77. Piscatory, Athens, 6 Sept. 1841 (7th report), *L'Hellénisme Contemporain*, ix, 428, 445-46 (Zacharitsas, Tisamenos, Païkos).

His hostility toward Russia and the "Russian" party and his feuds with the "English" Hydriot magnates left him only the "French" party to turn to. There his former connection with Kolettes in the government of 1823-25 stood him well. But he was unwilling to attach himself to either Kolettes or Mavrokordatos, although in times of need he found cooperation with the former less distasteful. There are indications that, whenever he did cooperate with another party, it was the "French." In September 1833, Kolettes visited in Hydra with Kountouriotes for two days. They agreed to cooperate against Trikoupes and Mavrokordatos. Then his followers spread rumors against Armansperg.[15]

The Lean Years, 1835–41

Between 1835, when Kolettes departed for Paris, and 1841, when Chrestides became minister of the interior, the "French" party had undergone a number of internal changes precipitated by a set of royal moves and a shift in the strategy of the French government. Of this set, the first and most significant was the removal of Kolettes from the national scene. Because of the esteem he commanded in Paris, he recommended individuals to the French government for the support of the French legation in Athens. He also maintained a steady correspondence with personal friends in Greece. In both ways he managed to retain some control over the party he had largely created, but his absence was bound to weaken the party and diminish his control over it.[16]

The defections from the party, as a result of his fall from power, attest to the importance of personal allegiance in keeping a party together and the considerations of expediency (i.e., need for a client) that motivated many of the party members. From the moment that the fall of Kolettes seemed likely, defections began. In May 1835, Korphiotakes was threatening to desert. After the departure of Kolettes, Rouphos and Dariotes, former associates of Palamides and Christakopoulos, went over exclusively to Zaïmes for protection. Skouphos, notorious for his opportunism and office-seeking, turned his newspaper Sōtēr over to Armansperg's cause and later, even before the fall of Armansperg, allied himself with the resurgent "Russian" party in the fusionist "movement."[17] As Piscatory testified in 1841:

[15] On his suspicion of Russia, see Piscatory, Athens, 6 Sept. 1841 (7th report), ibid., IX, 442. On Kolettes' visit to Hydra, see a letter from Anthony Miaoules, an "English" adherent and Kountouriotes' rival from Hydra, to Mavrokordatos, 11/23 Sept. 1833, no. 5223, Vol. 19 (1833-36), Mavrokordatos Archive.

[16] For instance, Lyons wrote his government (Athens, 25 Sept. 1837, no. 99, FO 32.72) that Lagrené defended the nominations of Botases and Karakatsanes but "assigned no reason beyond their having been recommended to him by Monsieur Coletti." On his correspondence with political friends at home, see Lyons to Palmerston, Athens, 24 May 1838, no. 89, FO 32.77, and 8 Oct. 1840, no. 113, FO 32.98.

[17] "For a long while we see some of the old friends of Kolettes not only leave his flag but ask to work against him," wrote Ethnikē, 30 May/11 June 1835. Con-

His [Kolettes'] long absence has resulted in many of his friends seeking their fortune elsewhere, but he would recover them, and there still remain to him some very devoted ones who command respect.[18]

As time went on, members of his own party gained a vested interest in his continued absence from Greece. According to Zographos in 1837-38, there existed "a group of men, including friends of the two [Mavrokordatos and Kolettes], who, accustomed to act and advance without them, feel their interests and independence will be damaged by their return." Kolettes' expressed disillusionment with his "friends" attests to his awareness of this fact.[19]

But the removal of Kolettes affected the party itself in a more substantial way. The loss of his personal leadership, with its centripetal function, loosened the bond between the constituent parts of the party. His absence must have facilitated the king's attempt to woo the Kountouriotes faction away from its loose association with the "French" party. By appointing Kountouriotes a chairman of the Council of State and calling him in to advise frequently, the king gave him what he had always wanted: the chance to be independent of any one of the major parties. In return, he established a solid source of support for the Crown and weakened the "French" party.[20]

With Kolettes gone, leadership of the party became the object of contention between Regas Palamides and Demetrios Chrestides, the two figures most qualified to succeed him. Sound in his judgment and knowledgeable in local affairs, Palamides stood as the leading exponent of the Peloponnesian interest within the party. He virtually replaced the aged Anagnostes Delegiannes as the leader of the "French" branch of the Peloponnesian primates. According to Piscatory, Chrestides did not possess a party but he enjoyed a good reputation, possessed many friends, and had extensive ties in the provinces. Most of all, he had served as Kolettes' chief political lieutenant during the Constitutionalist movement

cerning the threatened desertion of Korphiotakes, see C. Karakatsanes to Palamides, Athens, 2 May 1835 o.s., folio 257 (1833-39), Palamides Archive. Christakopoulos, in letters to Palamides (Nauplion, 18 Oct. 1834 o.s., and 29 Nov. 1834 o.s., folio 257 [1833-39], PA), wrote as if Rouphos and Dariotes were party intimates and on both occasions sent their personal greetings to Palamides. But we know from Piscatory (Athens, 6 Sept. 1841 [7th report], L'Hellénisme Contemporain, IX, 439, 440) that Rouphos and Dariotes had been clients of Zaïmes until the latter's death in 1840 and had only recently reverted back to the "French" party. Concerning Skouphos' perambulations, see Chap. V, nn. 109 and 112, above.

[18] Piscatory, Athens, 20 June 1841 (1st report), L'Hellénisme Contemporain, IX, 341.

[19] Zographos is quoted by M. Argyropoulos in a letter of Mavrokordatos, Pera, 4/16 Feb. 1838, no. 5483, Vol. 20 (1837-40), Mavrokordatos Archive. "Are there any friends in this world?" asked Kolettes of Mavrokordatos, Paris, 17 May 1842, no. 6337, Vol. 22 (1842), MA.

[20] Piscatory, Athens, 6 Sept. 1841 (7th report), L'Hellénisme Contemporain, IX, 442.

in 1832 and as minister of the interior in the subsequent cabinet. That these two men were the most important in the party, next to Kolettes, is shown by the fact that Pericles Argyropoulos cited them as the natural choices when it looked as if Mavrokordatos would have to include someone from the "French" party in his government.[21]

The king's appointments largely determined the temporary outcome of this rivalry. Whether deliberately or not, he gave Palamides the ascendancy by appointing him to the Council of State and hence placing him in the center of affairs. On the other hand, the king appointed Chrestides governor of Syros (1835-40), then Greek minister to Constantinople (1840-41)—a fate similar to that of Kolettes. In 1837 Chrestides complained to Palamides about members of the party (perhaps a pointed reference to Palamides himself) who sought to dominate everyone in the party, demanding that all see eye to eye with themselves. From Constantinople, he grumbled that Karakatsanes had forgotten him and that all his friends had conspired against him.[22]

Judging from his letters to Palamides, Karakatsanes seems to have become during these years the faithful party lieutenant, mediator of conflicting intraparty interests and a kind of general manager. First, he enjoyed close ties of friendship with Kolettes, Palamides, Chrestides, and Skouphos. Second, owing largely to his knowledge of finance (rare among Greeks of that day), the king appointed him to the control board. This job kept him permanently established in Athens, where the coordinator of a national party would have to reside. By satisfying his ambition, giving him adequate pay, and saving him the anxieties of more political posts, it made him the disinterested person that his function in the party required.[23]

It was Karakatsanes who, in 1835, urged a disaffected and rebellious Korphiotakes to observe party discipline and remain faithful to Kolettes. In 1842 he deplored the threats of Papalexopoulos to defect and defended Chrestides against attacks within the party. He worked patiently to clear the reputation of party members such as Christenites, sought judiciously and tactfully to place the right people of the party in the right places,

[21] Piscatory (Athens, 6 Sept. 1841 [7th report], ibid., IX, 436) observed, after returning from the Peloponnesos, that there was no acknowledged leader of the "French" Peloponnesian interest; "it has in almost every province a man influential by virtue of his personal weight." Concerning Palamides, see Piscatory (7th report), ibid., IX, 437 (see Chap. III, n. 80, above). Concerning Chrestides, see Piscatory, Athens, 30 July 1841 (4th report), and 20 Aug. 1841 (5th report), ibid., IX, 412, 419; Rangabe [Memoirs], I, 280 (see Chap. III, n. 85, above).

P. Argyropoulos to Mavrokordatos, Athens, 8/20 Apr. 1841, no. 5860, Vol. 21 (1841), Mavrokordatos Archive.

[22] Chrestides to Palamides, Hermoupolis (Syros), 20 Nov. 1837o.s., folio 257 (1833-39), Palamides Archive; also Constantinople, 24 Apr./6 May 1840, folio 258 (1840-49), PA.

[23] On Karakatsanes, see Piscatory, Athens, 6 Sept. 1841 (7th report), L'Hellénisme Contemporain, IX, 443; also n. 24 below.

and offered practical advice to party members on how to beat his own control board in its efforts to detect abuses. In a partisan manner, he even sought to take revenge against the Napist George Stavros for having indirectly caused, as he thought, the death of Skouphos. In Athens, he kept together a coterie of second-echelon party lieutenants, including Botases, fellow-Spezziot; Somaches, cousin of Kolettes and counselor to the Areopagus; Zygomalas, a French-bred physician; and Skouphos and Sophianopoulos. These men seldom if ever admitted the military men into their inner deliberations—a fact that explains why the Makrygiannes following and the East Rumeliot interest developed a kind of autonomous alliance with only a partial attachment to the party.[24]

To this loosening of intraparty bonds and rearrangement of intraparty balance, induced by the removal of Kolettes and other royal appointments, the changed strategy of the French government also contributed. Perhaps it felt that, without Kolettes in Greece, utilization of the "French" party to influence Greek state policy was not a safe bet. Most probably it wished to gain the confidence of Otho by complying with his obvious desire to undermine the parties. In any case, the French legation, under Lagrené (1837-43), played a restricted role in Greek domestic politics, both as compared with the contemporaneous behavior of its rival legations or the previous "never ceasing efforts of the French mission to exercise patronage" under Baron Rouen.[25]

When the duke De Broglie controlled the French foreign office and Armansperg reigned supreme in Greece, the French government had pressed for the inclusion of "French" adherents in the Greek cabinet and had urged the promulgation of a constitution on the Crown. By such pressure it had secured the appointment of the Rumeliot Mansolas to the ministry of the interior (1836), then the Spezziot Botases to the ministry of the economy, finally Karatzas to the Council of State. The French government, it seems, then decided to adopt a strategy involving direct influence—through the employment of a number of its nationals in the

[24] G. Karakatsanes to Palamides, Athens, 2 May 1835 o.s., folio 257 (1833-39), Palamides Archive; also five letters of 1842 written to Palamides from Athens, all dated old style: (1) 30 Sept., (2) 12 Oct., (3) 13 Oct., (4) 19 Oct., (5) 28 Oct., folio 258 (1840-49), PA. A typical remark, from item (4), is: "We must all work in harmony. Otherwise we are injured, with no good. . . . The time we lose trying to persuade each other is futile effort. . . . We must have revenge."

[25] "For some time, the Greek government, absorbed in the Orient by questions more perilous and pressing, occupied itself little with Greece; the English and Russian parties disputed between them the supremacy. . . ," wrote Guizot (Mémoires, VI, 259-60), acknowledging the rather passive role of the French legation. See also Gregory A. Perdicaris (The Greece of the Greeks [New York, 1845], I, 71) who wrote: ". . . but in addition to her wavering policy, she [France] has been particularly unfortunate in the choice of her representative. Neither Roane [sic] nor Lagrené were able to manage the Greeks, or cope with their colleagues, the ministers of Russia and England." The quoted phrase about Rouen is from Lyons to Palmerston, Athens, 11 Apr. 1836, no. 22, FO 32.59.

418

Greek administration. The most notable of these was Regny, whose return to Greece the French government negotiated with Otho in 1838. Under the new approach the French government, in effect, agreed to acquiesce in Otho's absolutist system and his antiparty policy in return for its exercise of some direct control over Greek state finances. In this way, it seems to have hoped to gain the sympathy of the king, protect its own bondholders, and avoid dirtying its hands in Greek domestic politics.[26]

It no longer seriously attempted to maintain a regular clientele. In 1838 Lyons cited Constantine Karatzas as "the only Greek who is on any terms of confidence with Mons. Lagrené. . . ." In 1841 Piscatory mentioned only Tzanetakes as "devoted to the French legation." He pointed to the resentment of Zygomalas because of insufficient support from France against political rivals who had the backing of their legations. Indeed, the "French" obviously saw his mission as a chance for them to restore a more active system of French clientship and insisted that to follow the example of other legations was the only way to have a party.[27]

Judging from the accounts of Piscatory, it seems quite evident that the party had suffered in many ways. First, from the lack of support from the French legation such as Vasos Mavrovouniotes felt in his struggle with the Napists, many "French" adherents had to fend for themselves, which led to a diffusion of power within the party, or they had to seek new patrons, which often meant defecting (Skouphos). Mavrovouniotes admitted that, of the three parties, the "French" had, "because of events or faults in the administration, perhaps lost some of the active confidence which had so long sustained it." Second, the relative withdrawal of the French legation deprived the party of another important force to mediate between its conflicting parts and hence partially accounts for the internal dissension that so impressed M. Argyropoulos in 1841. Third, some of the odium the Greeks felt for the sizeable foreign control of Regny got transferred to the French government, which sponsored him.[28]

[26] On France's position under Broglie, see Lyons to Palmerston, Athens, 27 Jan. 1836, no. 7, and 24 Feb. 1836, no. 11, both FO 32.58; also Edouard Driault and Michel Lhéritier, *Histoire Diplomatique de la Grèce de 1821 à nos Jours* (Paris, 1925), II, 151-52. Lyons to Palmerston, 24 Apr. 1837, no. 47, and 25 Sept. 1837, no. 48, both FO 32.70, (Botases); 20 Sept. 1837, no. 96, FO 32.71 (Karatzas). On Regny, see Chap. VI, nn. 103-104, above.

[27] Lyons to Palmerston, Athens, 24 May 1838, no. 88, FO 32.77. Piscatory, Athens, 6 Sept. 1841 (7th report), *L'Hellénisme Contemporain*, IX, 442 (Tzanetakes) and 446 (Zygomalas). See also Piscatory (Athens, 20 June 1841 [1st report], *ibid.*, IX, 341), who claims that the dissatisfied Francophiles told him that the example of the other legations was the only way to have a party. J. A. Buchon (*La Grèce Continentale et la Morée* [Paris, 1843], p. 494) testified that a Napist mayor had commented how unfortunate it was that French policy oscillated so much that one didn't dare risk demonstrating oneself too much France's friend.

[28] Piscatory, Athens, 6 Sept. 1841 (7th report), and Athens, 20 June 1841 (1st report), *L'Hellénisme Contemporain*, IX, 432 (Vasos) and 339 (loss of confidence).

Even though there is no conclusive evidence of a causal connection, it seems as if the passive role of the French legation had an effect on two visible trends within the party—the growing autonomy of an East Rumeliot grouping under the aegis of Makrygiannes, Kriezotes, and Doukas, and the strengthening of the Peloponnesian interest under the leadership of Palamides. Both trends were part of one phenomenon— the self-assertion within the party of the autochthon elements, which enjoyed an obvious advantage when political influence derived from control of the provinces, as it now did, rather than personal contact with and support from the foreign legation. Because the patronage of the French legation lost its value in the political rivalry, the more influential persons allied themselves. Hence, Makrygiannes succeeded in wooing to his "neutral" group some former Kolettes captains, and Palamides succeeded in getting the support of Karakatzanes' directorate in Athens. In this situation the Kolettes clientele lost any clear-cut identity, and Chrestides was too far removed to galvanize his own friends. The foreign-heterochthon complexion of the party temporarily paled.

The Effect of Political Ascendancy, 1841-43

The cabinet appointment of Chrestides could not but affect the internal balance within the "French" party. Chrestides now overshadowed Palamides at the center of political affairs. As a result, the mantle of leadership now fell upon him, and with it went Karakatsanes' "directorate." So far as one can tell, his personal following was largely a heterochthon-Rumeliot mixture. It is quite possible that what he mobilized was in part the eclipsed Kolettes following.[29]

The new balance of forces represented a serious setback for the Peloponnesian interest, itself perhaps the basis of the internal dissatisfaction revealed by limited evidence. Poneropoulos and Papalexopoulos, both Peloponnesians closely associated with Palamides, were prime examples of this discontent. Evidently disappointed with his appointment to the governorship of Syros, the former bitterly accused Chrestides of insufficient concern with the interests of party members. The latter actually threatened to unite with the Napist Tsokres. And Karakatsanes, the great peacemaker in the party, felt compelled to write Palamides and explain Chrestides' admitted slowness in placing more "French." According to him, the other parties delayed royal confirmation of Chrestides' nomina-

---

M. Argyropoulos to P. Argyropoulos, Pera, 26 Mar./7 Apr. 1841, no. 5857, Vol. 21 (1841), Mavrokordatos Archive. Concerning Greek resentment against Regny, see Chap. VI, n. 105, above.

[29] According to Piscatory (Athens, 20 Aug. 1841 [5th report], *L'Hellénisme Contemporain*, IX, 419), "although Mr. Christides does not have what one calls here a party, he has a good reputation and numerous friends"; or again (Athens, 6 Sept. 1841 [7th report], *ibid.*, IX, 445), "he has numerous friends and his relations in the provinces are very extensive."

tions by bringing slanderous charges against the nominees and forcing long royal investigations of such charges.[30]

There is no evidence that Chrestides' primacy gave any greater satisfaction to the military interest than had Palamides'. His faction, too, was a civilian one, and his official position allowed him no influence in military matters.[31] Undoubtedly, the partial eclipse of the Peloponnesian faction and the continued subordination of military interests account for the active involvement of Palamides and Makrygiannes in the conspiratorial plans which culminated in the revolution of 15 September. If more information were available it would probably appear that internal rivalries played as important a role as opposition to royal absolutism in involving part of the "French" party in the conspiracy which toppled the "French" government.

The Chrestides group did, however, enjoy the support of Kountouriotes. During the Mavrokordatos episode of 1841, Kountouriotes had eventually encouraged the king to replace Mavrokordatos with Chrestides. When, in 1842, Chrestides was being attacked from many directions and his group needed strengthening, Karatzas made a special trip to Hydra to secure the immediate return of Kountouriotes to Athens. Many questioned whether the inspiration for the Karatzas mission came from Chrestides or the court. In any case, Kountouriotes complied. By the end of the year, Kountoumas, an influential member of the "French" party, was writing as if Kountouriotes were one of the inner circle.[32]

Chrestides' primacy in the government and in his own party coincided with a more aggressive French policy in Greece. Guizot's desire to restore French fortunes in the Near East took the form of trying to expand French influence in Greece and resulted in the Piscatory mission. Pisca-

[30] On Poneropoulos, see Karakatsanes to Palamides, Athens, 12 Oct., 13 Oct., 19 Oct., and 28 Oct. 1842*o.s.*, folio 258 (1840-49), Palamides Archive; and Piscatory, Athens, 6 Sept. 1841 (7th report), *L'Hellénisme Contemporain*, ix, 438. On Papalexopoulos and on Karakatsanes' apologia for Chrestides, see Karakatsanes to Palamides, Athens, 30 Sept. 1842*o.s.*, folio 258 (1840-49), PA. Concerning the use of slander as a weapon of parties out of power, see Chap. VII, pp. 374-76, above.

[31] On the contrary, Makrygiannes, along with Petros Mantzerakes, responsible editor of *Aiōn*, which published Makrygiannes' remarks, was judged guilty by the magistrate court of Athens on a charge of slandering Chrestides. The article in question was published by *Aiōn*, 15 Mar. 1842*o.s.* and *Athēna*, 20 May 1842*o.s.* See Makrygiannes [*Memoirs*], ii, 121, n. 1 of the editor.

[32] On Kountouriotes' position during the Mavrokordatos episode, see *Athēna*, 3 Sept. 1841*o.s.* (see Chap. VII, n. 128, above); also Piscatory, Athens, 27 Aug. 1841 (6th report) and Athens, 6 Sept. 1841 (7th report), *L'Hellénisme Contemporain*, ix, 426, 442. On the Karatzas mission, see S. Valetas to Mavrokordatos, Athens, 26 May 1842*o.s.*, no. 6355, Vol. 22 (1842), Mavrokordatos Archive. Kountoumas (to Palamides, 21 Oct. 1842*o.s.*, folio 258 [1840-49], Palamides Archive) wrote: "all the friends Kountouriotes, Chrestides, Karakatsanes and the rest asked me in Athens about you. . . ." During the period of the constituent assembly (1843-44), Kolettes and Kountouriotes were again collaborating behind the scenes as they had at the beginning of the absolutist period (Makrygiannes [*Memoirs*], ii, 160-61).

tory, in turn, had played an important role in bringing Chrestides to power and had implicitly criticized Lagrené for the passivity which reflected former French policy.[33] As a result, Lagrené began to act differently and Chrestides "consulted Mons. de Lagrené on every appointment great or small. . . ." The Anglophile Pharmakides described his behavior thereafter in vivid, though perhaps exaggerated, terms:

> French influence . . . becomes daily more audacious and daring. The sillier the French minister becomes, the more he flaunts his influence. Mr. Lagrené is unrestrained. He meddles everywhere; he wishes to participate in all affairs; he intervenes shamelessly in everything. He continually recruits whomever possible into the French or 'national' party. He opened the doors of his house and trumpeted, 'whoever comes to me, I will not reject.' He wanted indirectly to lead us into the company of Sophianopoulos, Skouphos, and the others who constitute his honorable party, but he failed, and that failure he should have foreseen if he were wiser. Night and day at his home, meetings take place, and at them is discussed whatever is happening. So that whatever happens, happens according to his previous knowledge and consent.[34]

There is no information to shed light on the effect of renewed French activity on the conduct of "French" party affairs. It seems safe to assume, however, that though Chrestides gained a valuable source of support, he also lost some of his control to Lagrené. Furthermore, since Kolettes advised the French government on the implementation of its policy in Greece, the stepped-up influence of Lagrené must have served to protect the Kolettes interest within the new party balance. Finally, as the sequel will reveal, it may account for the partial defection of the party to the political opposition when the French government decided to associate itself in three-power intervention in Greek finances.

2. THE POLITICAL OPPOSITION

The Pattern of Complaint

Although Otho managed to preserve his personal absolutism and retain the remaining Bavarians, he found it less easy to restore the public calm on which the survival of his system depended. The Mavrokordatos episode produced alarming signs of defiance and boldness. One was *Athēna's* less veiled attacks on the king himself as the source of the state's ills.

[33] Piscatory's criticism (Athens, 6 Sept. 1841 [7th report], *L'Hellénisme Contemporain*, ix) of Lagrené was implied in suggestions to support Vaso Mavrovouniotes against the Napists (p. 432), show greater solicitude for Poneropoulos in Syros (p. 438), and use influence to have Anastasios Loidorikes placed in the Council of State (p. 433).

[34] Lyons to Palmerston, Athens, 11 Sept. 1841, no. 139, FO 32.107; Pharmakides to Mavrokordatos, Athens, 18/30 May 1842, no. 6340, Vol. 22 (1842), Mavrokordatos Archive.

The press had hitherto maintained the myth of a camarilla victimizing an innocent king. Another was the establishment of a subscription fund for the financial support of Mavrokordatos while he remained out of public office. The widespread and generous response showed as much support of the Mavrokordatos program as it did appreciation for his willingness to place principle above personal advantage.[35] A third sign was the refusal of the Council of State to grant the government's request for release from the statutory obligation to convene eparchal councils that year (1841). The decisiveness of the vote (only four votes for the government's request) gave the refusal the character of a rebuke, directed against both king and Chrestides, for trying to tighten rather than loosen the grip of absolutism.[36]

But the pattern of complaint is best discernible if one examines four incidents that took place in the spring of 1842. The first occurred on the anniversary of the outbreak of the Greek Revolution (25 March/6 April). Each year the government feared its celebration, which aroused the liberal sentiments that one associated with the Revolutionary era. It seems that, during their celebrations, Greek officers of the artillery unit in Nauplion expressed themselves too freely about the continued presence of Bavarians in Greece. It was perfectly natural that anti-Bavarian sentiment should be strongest in the army, which had the largest concentration of remaining Bavarians, and within the army, among those officers whose further promotion the presence of their Bavarian superiors precluded. Hitz, the Bavarian commander, declared them in violation of their military discipline. They, in turn, appealed to the government and accused Hitz of undue severity.

The government did not allow Hitz to carry out the sentence of twenty days' confinement, but without explanation it transferred the condemned

[35] For press attacks on the king, see *Athēna*, 20 July and 20 Aug. 1841o.s. (see Chap. VII, p. 407, above). By the fall of 1842, Kolettes was appalled at the tendency of the Greek press to abuse the King in the fashion of some parts of the European press (Kolettes to Mavrokordatos, Paris, 27 Sept. 1842, no. 6488, Vol. 22 [1842], Mavrokordatos Archive).

On the subscription fund and the government's unsuccessful attempts to bring legal action against the act, see *Athēna* (17 Sept. and 11 Oct. 1841o.s.) which did as much as anyone to organize it. See also the attempts of J. Kleanthes, a Greek architect with close association to the "English" party, to get the king's permission to build Mavrokordatos a home through public subscription (Kleanthes to Mavrokordatos, Athens, 26 Apr. 1842, no. 6295, Vol. 22, MA). Kolettes pointed out another motive behind the subscription fund when he referred to "the collection which the Greeks decided to make for you so as to make you independent and through your independence the defender of national rights [in other words, a free critic of the government]" (Kolettes to Mavrokordatos, Paris, 7 Feb. 1842, Vol. 22, MA).

When Mavrokordatos resigned, the king refused to appoint him to the Council of State, and Mavrokordatos refused the king's offer of a small pension.

[36] The four who voted in favor of the government's proposal were Constantine Karatzas, A. Loidorikes, Francis Mavros, and C. Schinas, all members of the "French" party. On the whole issue and debate, see *Athēna*, 27 Sept., 1 Oct., 4 Oct. 1841o.s.

to garrisons elsewhere. All the while Hitz retained his command. The press exploited this incident in its campaign against Bavarianism. It represented the government action as a clear manifestation of partiality toward Hitz and sure proof that the anaktovoulion was still running affairs.[37]

An incident of an entirely different type revived the ecclesiastical issue of church-state relations. On the incorporation of his bishopric (Sellasia) into the adjoining Lacedemonian one, the government transferred Theodoretos Vresthenios, a prominent conservative primate, to the bishopric of Achaia-Elis. He refused his new post and denounced the transfer of bishops as uncanonical. His denunciation provided the religious conservatives with another complaint against the caesaropapist system. For what it considered his insubordination, the government dismissed Vresthenios from the holy synod, where he was serving a term. He in turn stubbornly refused the small pension offered him by the government. Now a bishop without a bishopric, he seemed to many a martyr in behalf of ecclesiastical autonomy.[38]

The missionary question, an ever-present object of demagogic exploitation and a perennial source of public agitation, regained sudden prominence when *Aiōn* opened fire on the American Protestant mission headed by John Hill. The mission maintained a thriving girls' school in which several prominent Greeks had enrolled their daughters, and it enjoyed some indirect state support in the form of scholarships which the government provided for some of the students at its school. This, like other missions, professed a desire to educate rather than proselytize. *Aiōn* launched its attack by publishing a letter which Mrs. Hill, director of the girls' school, had sent her husband in the summer of 1841 during his visit to the United States. In it she expressed confidence that some of her

[37] See *Athēna*, 25 Apr., 29 Apr., and 25 May 1841*o.s.*; also Metaxas to Mavrokordatos, Athens, 26 Apr. 1842*o.s.*, no. 6294, and S. Valetas to Mavrokordatos, Athens, 26 May 1842*o.s.*, no. 6355, both Vol. 22 (1842), Mavrokordatos Archive. On the effect of the incident on Greco-Bavarian relations in Greece, Metaxas remarked in his letter: "The holiday of 25th March caused unfortunate events in Nauplion. Because of this and because of the mistaken measures taken to correct the evil, the hatred between Greek and Bavarian officers has reached insurpassable and for many reasons frightening proportions."

[38] *Athēna*, 11 Apr. 1842*o.s.* See also the three following letters, all written from Athens, all dated according to old style, all addressed to Mavrokordatos, and all found in Vol. 22 (1842), Mavrokordatos Archive: (1) Rizos, 8/20 Mar. 1842, no. 6239; (2) Metaxas, 26 Apr. 1842, no. 6294; and (3) Valetas, 26 May 1842, no. 6355. Rizos wrote very unfavorably regarding the bishop's conduct: "but to attribute his resignation to his strict adherence to the apostolic and synodal canons and, according to this great commentator [pointed allusion to Theodoretos], to the unlawfulness of the proposal and act of the holy synod, *this* is a wonder, the reduction of holy matters to nonsense and intrigue, and the greatest impudence, that which dares arbitrarily (by one's individual judgment) to interpret the apostolic and synodal canons." See also Lyons to Aberdeen, Athens, 21 Mar. 1842, no. 23, and 20 May 1842, no. 38, FO 32.114.

students had experienced religious conversion. The comment, probably an attempt to round up support at home, seemed to give the lie to all missionary professions about wishing only to educate, because the Hills had been most convincing in these professions. Obviously *Aiōn* was trying to convince the public that the conservatives were right about real missionary intentions. Let the liberals see that one could not accept missionary schooling without risking the loss of one's Orthodox faith. Implicitly, *Aiōn* was also saying, let everyone see the negligence of the government in failing to discern what we have now proved.[39]

The government responded to great public excitement by appointing a committee to investigate the school, its curriculum, and its teachings. Needless to say, the committee found everything satisfactory at the school. But the very fact of government action shows the government's concern to calm public suspicions and exonerate itself of the implied charges. And this concern may be taken as a measure of the public excitement that *Aiōn* had aroused.[40]

To add to the general commotion, a bold and controversial printed pamphlet was circulating in Athens.[41] Published anonymously in Con-

[39] *Aiōn*, 15 Mar. 1842*o.s.* Mrs. Hill's letter had subsequently appeared in the American religious newspaper called *Southern Churchman*, with a comment by the editor and an appended letter written by a Columbia University professor, who ended by indulging "the hope that these schools are to prove the means, under God, of bringing the entire Greek Church into communion with our own." Copies of both letters are enclosed in a letter by Benjamin, a missionary for the American Board of Commissioners for Foreign Missions (ABCFM) in Greece, to Rufus Anderson, secretary of the Board, 20 Apr. 1842, no. 14, Vol. II, "Greece," in the manuscript collection of the ABCFM, deposited in Houghton Library, Harvard University, Cambridge, Mass.

[40] That the report failed to satisfy some portions of the public, see the denunciation of the committee by the newspaper *Anexartētos*, as quoted and translated by Jonas King, chief missionary of ABCFM in Greece, to Anderson, 13 Aug. 1842, no. 69, Vol. II, "Greece" [MSS], ABCFM Collection: "As this committee did not take the trouble to examine what was taught months ago . . . they will never persuade the Greek nation, that the design of Mr. Hill was not proselytism . . . if the object were only the education of the female sex, why does the Society send out in these parts, where it has schools, priests without exception, & never any layman?"

For further accounts of these events, see the American Episcopal missionary periodical, *The Spirit of Missions*, VII (1842), 311-14, and VIII (1843), 284-87, 474; also King to Anderson, 27 July 1842, no. 67, and 6 Aug. 1842, no. 68, and Benjamin to Anderson, 28 Apr. 1842, no. 15, all three in Vol. II, "Greece" [MSS], ABCFM Collection. See also Metaxas to Mavrokordatos, Athens, 26 Apr. 1842, no. 6294, and Pharmakides to Mavrokordatos, Athens, 26 Apr. 1842, no. 6297, Vol. 22 (1842), Mavrokordatos Archive; and *Athēna*, 4 May and 9 May 1841*o.s.*

[41] Anon., *He Baptisis tes Kyrias Aikaterines N. Chantzeres . . .* [*The Baptism of Mrs. Catherine N. Chantzeres. And some historical thoughts on the Greek and Western spirit*] (Hermoupolis, 1842). To my knowledge, I have located the only extant document which reveals the authorship of the tract, although this document obviously refers to a previous edition published in Constantinople rather than Syros, *i.e.*, Rizos to Mavrokordatos, Athens, 8/20 May 1842, Vol. 22 (1842), Mavro-

stantinople, it celebrated the conversion of a Madame Chantzeres, wife of a Russian diplomat, from Roman Catholicism to Greek Orthodoxy. But it reported the event to develop a theme and issue an injunction. The theme was that of a perpetual struggle between East (largely Greece, but including Russia) and West (England, France, Prussia, and the Papacy), two distinct and antagonistic civilizations. Its message was equally simple—Greece must beware of the West.

In developing its theme it turned first to "history." The genius of the ancient Greeks, which had rendered them the benefactors of the West, had aroused Western envy instead of gratitude. Playing the villain, the West had committed crime upon crime in its plot to reduce the Greeks to servitude and keep them there. The Romans had conquered, but they at least had respected the Greek achievement. The barbarian successors, led by the Pope, had ravaged the Byzantine empire during the crusades and had left it helpless against the Turks.

Turning to the contemporary picture, the pamphlet alleged that the West feared eclipse in the face of a regenerated Greek race. The West was now using both political and religious weapons to prevent the universal liberation of the Greeks. Politically, it supported the Ottoman empire and maintained the new Greek state as a puppet. It encouraged internal rivalries and employed a Western monarch to keep the state dependent on it. Religiously, the West sponsored missionary movements to disrupt the unity of the Greek people. The Papacy and France supported Catholic efforts, Britain and Prussia Protestant efforts, but it was all part of one conspiracy. And the object of all this? Not the stated one of warding off Russian influence in the Near East, but fear of the cultural heights that a completely free and united Greek race would scale.

The essay was a dramatic demonstration of Greek ethnocentrism and conservatives' paranoia. In its misreading of history it must have intensified the sense of cultural conflict which everyone increasingly felt in the mixed society of Athens. But its shocking feature was the veiled attack on the king as the hireling of the West and the policeman of Western domination. This feature, more than any other, must have aroused the

---

kordatos Archive. I translate and quote the relevant paragraph in full: "A few days ago a pamphlet, in many copies, was smuggled into the country from Constantinople. The title of the pamphlet is 'The Princess Catherine Chantzeres Baptised.' This pamphlet was published and written in Constantinople. Its author is Gerasimos Panas, a Cephaleniot, perhaps known to your lordship in the period when he defended Mr. Kolokotrones [Theodore, in the celebrated trial of 1834] and when he slapped his lawyer colleague Mr. Klonares. The pamphlet was published on the seventeenth of last January. You certainly did not learn about it and for that reason did not make any reference to it. It is a continuation of the Philorthodox plot. I don't know if Panas, who as I learned, practices law there [Constantinople], is an Ionian citizen or a Greek one. The pamphlet was published at the press of a Cephaleniot called Mousouros, who, going bankrupt, moved his publishing establishment to Kosmetos Siphnios'."

426

government censor and inspired the house searches accompanying attempts at confiscation.[42]

On the surface it looks as if only the first of these four incidents raised an issue (Bavarianism) on which men could agree, in spite of partisan affiliations. The other three raised issues which involved a jealous defense of Orthodoxy, a position that by now the public had come to identify with the "Russian" party and its newspaper organ *Aiōn*. Yet, *Athēna*, which ordinarily attacked the Philorthodox position, this time showed great restraint. Indeed, it sympathized with Vresthenios (and criticized his dismissal from the synod, even if it did not espouse his religious position), agreed on the need for vigilance against attempted proselytism (although it defended the Hills' school), and even went as far as to allow for appeals to Russia in the event that Orthodoxy was threatened in Greece (though it did not espouse the pamphlet's total rejection of the West).[43] The basic complaint underlying all these Philorthodox grievances was one shared by *Athēna* and virtually all other Greeks regardless of partisan affiliation—too much foreign interference. Each party could choose a particular form of foreign interference to attack—Bavarianism, missionaries, the powers, even the king (if one considered him foreign). But they could countenance each other once they recognized that they were working toward a common goal.

In the same way, the "Russians" could accept the favorite objects of *Athēna*'s attacks—camarilla and absolute monarchy. As early as 1834, *Aiōn* was openly attacking Bavarianism and this particular manifestation of it. Likewise, *Aiōn* had shown that it could propose a constitution, not for the doctrinaire reasons which inspired *Athēna*, but from the growing belief that only such a system would guarantee the protection of Orthodoxy, place control of affairs in Greek hands, and provide the means to abolish all forms of foreign interference.[44] A similar concern underlay the considerable dissatisfaction with the long-sought and sorely needed national bank, which the state established at the end of 1841 with the assistance of private capital. The fear, in this case too, concerned too much interference or even financial control by foreign financiers such as Eynard, the Swiss philhellene, Rothschild, and others, or by the new intendant general from France, Lemaître, successor to Regny who had died suddenly in 1841.[45]

[42] *Athēna*, 9 May 1842*o.s.*

[43] *Athēna*, 11 Apr. and 15 Apr. (Vresthenios), 21 Mar. (Hills), 4 May (Chantzeres), 1842*o.s.* On *Athēna*'s moderate support of these Napist pet issues, see Pharmakides to Mavrokordatos, Athens, 26 Apr. 1842*o.s.*, no. 6297, Vol. 22 (1842), Mavrokordatos Archive.

[44] *Aiōn*, 14 Jan. and 25 Mar. 1840*o.s.* See also Chap. VI, n. 128, above.

[45] For instance, see the letter, which *Athēna* published (28 Nov. 1842*o.s.*), deploring the overwhelming influence of George Stavros, director of the new bank, protégé of Eynard and Napist in political complexion, who controlled the meetings of bondholders by distributing the controlling votes of Eynard, Rothschild, and

The "English"-"Russian" Alliance

At the time, the unprecedented truce between *Athēna* and *Aiōn* was reason enough for the public to suspect the existence of an "English"-"Russian" alliance.[46] Now documentary material from private correspondence offers positive proof. In May 1842, Spyridon Valetas, minister of education-religion in Mavrokordatos' short-lived cabinet, wrote a letter which reveals that "English"-"Russian" collaboration had been going on for some time. That same spring Pharmakides, leading protagonist of the ecclesiastical settlement of 1833, was writing Mavrokordatos confidentially about his plans to dedicate a forthcoming publication to the patriarch. For a moment he had even thought of dedicating it to the Russian tsar. His correspondence also reveals that concerted efforts involving Catacazy were being made to reconcile him with Oikonomos, his bitter rival. Presumably the peacemakers were trying to eliminate the religious question as the main stumbling block to cooperation between the "English" and "Russian" parties.[47]

---

many others (Eynard alone held 300 shares; Stavros bought one-fourth the number of shares allotted to the Greek government). Lemaître was accepted by the Greek government as intendant general and government representative in the bank, so as to meet the conditions of the Greek government for its guarantee of a loan of 1,000,000 francs, some to be used by the Greek government to purchase shares in the bank. One of the conditions was that the Greek government accept a banking specialist to guarantee the interests of the French government and foreign bondholders.

On the establishment of the national bank, see the law for the introduction of a national bank, dated 30 Mar./11 Apr. 1841 [*Government Gazette*], no. 6, 30 Mar. 1841*o.s.*, and its modification by decree of 19 Aug. 1841*o.s.*, [*GG*], no. 16, 3 Aug. 1841*o.s.* The charter, dated 31 Dec. 1841, appeared in [*GG*], no. 2, 14 Jan. 1842*o.s.* For related acts, see [*GG*], no. 7, 1 Apr. 1841*o.s.*; no. 8, 11 Apr. 1841*o.s.*; no. 9, 27 Apr. 1841*o.s.*, and no. 2, 14 Jan. 1842*o.s.* See also Pipineles [*Monarchy*], pp. 345-50; I. A. Valaorites, *Ethnike Trapeza tes Hellados, 1842-1902* [*The National Bank of Greece*] (Athens, 1902), and D. L. Zographos, *Historia tes Hidryseos tes Ethnikes Trapezes 1833-45* [*The History of the Establishment of the National Bank . . .*] (Athens, 1925-27), 2 vols.

[46] By March 1842, nasty comments in *Athēna*, about *Aiōn* in particular and Napists in general, disappear. A really telling instance of *Athēna's* change of attitude is provided by a lead article in *Athēna* (17 Oct. 1841*o.s.*) called "Some Observations on Aiōn." The article was a commentary on a series of articles appearing in *Aiōn*, called "East and West," which sometimes called for a constitution, sometimes veered to the other extreme and condemned the spirit of the West. In former days, this kind of thing had roused the ire of *Athēna* and provoked impassioned replies. This time *Athēna*, prefacing its remarks with the observation that it would not condemn things Western wholesale, warned against the renewed attempts of some governments to export their religions and mildly scolded *Aiōn* for being indiscriminate in its criticism of the West.

[47] S. Valetas to Mavrokordatos, Athens, 26 May 1842, no. 6355, Vol. 22 (1842), Mavrokordatos Archive: "the presumed reconciliation of some time ago between the so-called Napists and Constitutionalists."

Pharmakides to Mavrokordatos, Athens, 28 Mar. 1842*o.s.*, no. 6268, Vol. 22 (1842),

Some causes for the alliance are fairly obvious. After all, the political ascendancy of one party tended to provoke the formation of a political opposition among the other two. This was not the first time the "English" and "Russian" parties had cooperated. They had done so in 1833-34 under the first regency. The resignation of Metaxas from the cabinet in 1841 served notice that at least a segment of the "Russian" party was joining the "English" in the opposition camp. But that segment constituted only a minority of the "Russian" party until the beginning of 1842. Aiōn's withdrawal of support from the government was only one element in moving the bulk of the "Russian" party into the opposition.[48]

The other concerned Michael Soutsos, former hospodar of Moldavia and client of Russia. With his son-in-law Zographos, whose political affiliation changed to accord with his marital ties, he headed a coterie of some influence within the "Russian" party. A personal misunderstanding between the queen and Mrs. Soutsos over ladies' fashion provoked the political break between the palace and this "Russian" coterie. Against the king of course, Zographos nursed personal grudges dating back to the days of his service as foreign minister. At the end of January 1842, Michael Soutsos dramatized his break with the king by resigning from

---

MA. Concerning the attempts to reconcile him with Oikonomos and agreement between the "English" and Catacazy, see Pharmakides to Mavrokordatos, Athens, 28 Mar. 1842o.s., no. 6268, Vol. 22, MA: "I have no difficulty in making up with Oikonomos [his archrival in academic and theological as well as political affairs]. But I find it difficult to accept the proposal of Mr. G. Vlachoutses that the reconciliation come from me. Vlachoutses proposed that I go first to visit Oikonomos. I replied that this could never be, because when Oikonomos came to Greece he made the first visit [apparently this was expected of the arriving person] to those he wanted and he did not deign to visit me. He [Vlachoutses] then proposed a third place for the first meeting, but I did not accept precisely because, after the first reconciliation, there would still remain the original difficulty of who should first visit the other. Perhaps my extreme pride will seem strange to you. I am jealous of my honor [philotimos], and if the first step is taken by me, I will suffer in the public mind. Besides, for what purpose this showy reconciliation? We are following surface union with the Russian party, and you read in Athēna more prudent defense of Sellasia. We also reached an understanding with Mr. Catacazy that we would purposely avoid show [of reconciliation] as more harmful than useful, and he approved of this device [oikonomia]. Nevertheless, for this surface union, Oikonomos had the boldness to ascend the pulpit. If that [the union] were lacking, he would never have dared such boldness. Even though he was fearless, he failed completely. . . ."

[48] According to George Finlay (A History of Greece from its Conquest by the Romans to the Present Time, B.C. 146 to A.D. 1864, ed. H. F. Tozer [Oxford, 1877], VII, 173), "The union of the orthodox ["Russian"] and constitutional factions was absolutely necessary in order to give a popular movement any chance of success. This was easily effected, for both desired the immediate expulsion of the Bavarians. . . ."

On the cooperation of the "English" and "Russian" parties during the period of Kolettes' ascendancy in 1834, see Chap. IV, n. 125, above. Certainly by March, with its article of 15 Mar. 1842o.s. against Chrestides, Aiōn had moved into the opposition.

the Council of State. Thereafter his home became one of the main centers for the disaffected.[49]

A further basis for "English"-"Russian" cooperation was the *rapprochement* between the Russian and English governments. The Near Eastern crisis of 1839-41 had precipitated it, and the replacement of Palmerston by Aberdeen in the British foreign office (1841) had secured its continuation. In Athens the increasingly intimate relations between Lyons and Catacazy reflected the changed diplomatic situation and demonstrated the alarm inspired by Lagrené's newly acquired influence in the counsels of the Greek government. Undoubtedly, the "English" and "Russian" parties were responding to the example set by their patron legations.[50]

Opposition Strategy

From a study of *Aiōn* and *Athēna* during the period of "French" ascendancy the general strategy of the opposition press becomes apparent. Positive demands, such as the call for reestablishment of the nomarchal administrative system or constitutional government, played a secondary role. Polite references to the person of the king, as distinct from his advisers, were dropped. Undoubtedly the Mavrokordatos episode had disabused the opposition press of any hope that it might induce the Crown to undertake reform of its own accord. Apparently the opposition

[49] Rangabe ([*Memoirs*], II, 128-29) tells about the misunderstanding in full. *Athēna* (28 Sept. 1842o.s.) announced the resignation: "Michael Soutsos resigns as councilor of state because of discontent with characteristically courtly practices which we think it needless to tell the public." And much later, in a letter to Metternich, Athens, 21 Sept. 1842, Prokesch-Osten pointed to the Soutsoi as active plotters in the Revolution of 3 Sept. 1843. See *Aus dem Nachlasse des Grafen Prokesch-Osten*, ed. Anton von Prokesch-Osten [the younger] (Vienna, 1881), II, 240, and Demetrios A. Petrakakos, *Koinobouleutike Historia tes Hellados* [*Parliamentary History of Greece*] (Athens, 1946), II, 291.

[50] On the period of cordial English-Russian relations, culminating in the celebrated visit of Nicholas I to England in 1844, see Harold Temperley, *The Crimea. England and the Near East* (London, 1936), pp. 251-57. Before 11/23 Jan. 1843, the date of the letter in which Otho makes reference to it, Tsar Nicholas had written to Otho to improve his relations with England (Otho to Nicholas, the text of which appears in Petrakakos [*Parliamentary History*], II, 281-82). According to Kordatos ([*History*], III, 180), it seems that Catacazy, who returned to Greece via England in 1841, had instructions to cooperate with Lyons on the Greek question. Also see Lyons' letter to Aberdeen, which establishes the fact of cooperation even if its explanation of it is debatable (Athens, 21 Sept. 1843, no. 112, FO 32.122): "Russia saw that by continuing to support Otho's antinational system, she was bringing herself into discredit with the Greeks. To recover herself, she found it necessary to join England in manifesting opposition to that system." Or see the remark of Piscatory to his government when he arrived in Greece in June 1843 (Guizot, *Mémoires*, VII, 270): "Mr. Catacazy and he [Lyons] live on perfectly good terms with each other. . . ."

press designed its strategy so as to attract as many as possible into the opposition camp.[51]

It employed a number of tactics in an attempt to win over the public at large. One has already received attention—the attempt to discredit royal policy by identifying it with all manner of foreign interference. In addition, it mercilessly publicized the failings of Chrestides and, by implication, the "French" party. It accused him of inertia and failure to live up to his reform promises. Most of all, it condemned him for failing to institute the nomarchal councils, which all considered a further step toward constitutional government.[52]

In this anti-Chrestides newspaper campaign members of the "English" and "Russian" parties deliberately added to the paralysis of the "French" party. As mentioned previously, Chrestides faced endless delays in securing royal confirmation for his appointments, because members of other parties were so persistent in pressing accusations of past peculation against his appointees. Quite probably the opposition was trying to fan internal rivalries within the "French" party and to deprive Chrestides of the loyal administrators necessary to make his will effective.[53]

But the strategy of the opposition press addressed itself more specifically to the "French" party in an obvious attempt to lure it into the opposition camp. Sometimes it excused the inadequacies of Chrestides by accusing the camarilla of standing in his way. The message was clear. It served notice on Chrestides and his following that the opposition was still willing to receive them and ignore their past mistakes, and to rise above internal differences against a common foreign foe (Bavarianism).[54]

Sometimes the opposition press accused members of the "French" party of using their influence with the Crown to prevent Kolettes' return.

[51] The demand for a restoration of the ten nomarchical divisions of the kingdom, which Armansperg had abolished in 1836, had been a part of Mavrokordatos' plans for reform ("Private Memo," no. 5793, Vol. 21 [1841], Mavrokordatos Archive). *Athēna* published a lead article (26 Dec. 1841*o.s.*) demanding the restoration and subsequently repeated the demand (see the issue of 7 Oct. 1841*o.s.* for instance). Such a demand served as a veiled criticism of Chrestides, a pointed reminder that he had betrayed the unofficial program of reform which he had promised to execute. One of its prominent features had been precisely the restoration of the nomarchies (Piscatory, Athens, 27 Aug. 1841 [6th report], *L'Hellénisme Contemporain*, IX, 425). By March 1842, there is marked silence in *Athēna* about the king (no longer any talk of placing great hopes in him); the former demands for reforms (especially constitutional ones), formerly so prominent, now were only a faint echo. *Athēna* was concentrating all its weapons against foreign interference, cabinet inertia, and bad administration.

[52] For instance, *Athēna*, 1 Oct. and 10 Dec. 1841*o.s.*, 21 Mar. and 23 Sept. 1842*o.s.*; *Aiōn*, 15 Mar. 1842*o.s.*

[53] See n. 30 above.

[54] *Athēna*, 24 Oct. 1841*o.s.*, and 14 Jan. and 30 Dec. 1842*o.s.* In the latter case, it accused the camarilla of standing in the way of his restoring the nomarchies.

Though it mentioned no names, it obviously meant the ruling group within the "French" party, especially Chrestides. Despairing of winning over Chrestides, it seems, the opposition sought to win over the Kolettes faction by talking within the context of intraparty rivalries. It apparently hoped to persuade the Kolettists that the present primacy of the "French" party in the government constituted the gravest threat to the political future of Kolettes and the predominance of their own faction within the party.[55]

Tripartisan Conspiracy

Even though the opposition may have deserved little of the credit, the "French" party eventually did split. Palamides, the chief rival of Chrestides and the one who had suffered most from the new position of the party within the government, went into opposition. Makrygiannes, in alliance with the East Rumeliot faction, did so separately.[56] But two other factors robbed the Chrestides group of its hold on the party as a whole. In the first place, Kolettes continued to express his support for the Mavrokordatos program and his dissatisfaction with development in Greece, and he refused to enter any cabinet which did not include men such as those who had resigned with Mavrokordatos in 1841. His stand constituted an implicit criticism of Chrestides for having accepted office, or at least for having continued in it. Second, by June of 1843, Chrestides had lost the support of the French government.[57]

[55] *Athēna*, 16 May 1842*o.s.* and 4 Aug. 1843*o.s.*

[56] On a split in the "French" party, see Pharmakides to Mavrokordatos, Athens, 18/30 May 1842, no. 6340, Vol. 22 (1842), Mavrokordatos Archive. Concerning Palamides' prominent role, see for instance, Prokesch-Osten to Metternich, Athens, 26 Oct. 1843, in Petrakakos [*Parliamentary History*], II, 295. On Makrygiannes' perhaps more important doings, see Makrygiannes [*Memoirs*], II, 119-32. According to him (II, 126), he initiated a part of his adherents from the "French" party. On "French" participation in the conspiracy, see also George Aspreas, *Politike Historia tes Neoteras Hellados 1821-1921* [*Political History of Modern Greece*], 2nd edn. (Athens, 1924), I, 168.

[57] According to a letter from S. Valetas to Mavrokordatos (Athens, 26 May 1842*o.s.*, no. 6355, Vol. 22 [1842], Mavrokordatos Archive), Kolettes was working in 1842 to secure the king's consent to the Mavrokordatos program. He was at the same time trying to obtain leave to return to Greece for three months (see his letters to Mavrokordatos, Paris, 27 May 1842, no. 6357, 7 June 1842, no. 6374, and 17 June 1842, no. 6381, all Vol. 22 [1842], MA). It may be that he was trying to strengthen Chrestides by securing for him the concessions which Otho refused Mavrokordatos. More likely he wanted to return to Greece in the hope of being invited to power and reassuming the direct leadership of the "French" party. Already in May (Paris, 17 May 1842, no. 6337, Vol. 22 [1842], MA) he was writing to Mavrokordatos expressing the faithlessness of friends, probably a pointed reference to Chrestides and other "French." After the king turned down his request, knowing as he did that Chrestides and other prominent "French" adherents had a vested interest in his continued absence, he must have suspected them of using their influence to secure royal refusal or at least their failure to support his request. Already in 1842 Kolettes was writing Mavrokordatos very critically about the government in Greece, though he did not

Ultimately a part of the political opposition determined on the use of force as the only way to secure needed reform. Conspiracy as such was nothing new in Greek life. In his memoirs, Makrygiannes describes the several secret societies of the 1830s working at cross-purposes and reveals his attempts since 1840 to unite them. But this particular one was uniquely tripartisan. Among its leaders, Metaxas, Zographos, and Michael Soutsos represented the "Russian" party, Lontos the "English," Makrygiannes and Palamides the "French." It drew its membership from among hitherto rival secret societies. The conspiracy came into existence during the fall of 1842.[58]

Owing to the coalition character of the conspiracy, its leaders shared only two common objectives—expulsion of the Bavarians and promulgation of a constitution. Motives underlying the latter objective varied. Some hoped in this way to overcome the hostility of British diplomacy. Others believed Otho incompetent to exercise the powers of absolute monarch. Still others believed that he would abdicate before submitting to constitutional limitations and hoped thereby to secure an Orthodox king, possibly Michael Soutsos. The "Russian" party was most interested in obtaining an Orthodox monarchy, the "French" and "English" in securing a constitutional one.[59]

---

specifically isolate Chrestides for criticism (see for instance his letters of 7 July 1842, no. 6393, and 27 Dec. 1842, no. 6555, Vol. 22 [1842], MA).

See n. 65 below for sources on French participation with Russia and England in a severe policy toward Greece.

[58] On conspiracy and secret societies as regular features of Greek political life, see n. 11 above. By 1842 the progressive worsening, even hopelessness, of the political and administrative situation is reiterated by letter after letter in the Mavrokordatos Archive in letters to Mavrokordatos from men of all political complexions (for instance Metaxas, 26 Apr. 1842, no. 6294; Pharmakides, 26 Apr. 1842, no. 6297; Valetas, 26 May 1842, no. 6355; and Kolettes, 27 Dec. 1842, no. 6555, all Vol. 22 [1842].) One must allow for the factor of exaggeration, even for the fact that such complaint was often an announcement of political opposition, even a kind of code between conspirators. But even if these dark accounts may have served a hidden purpose, they undoubtedly reflect a good bit of truth and indicate the hopelessness which induced cautious men to resort to conspiracy.

Makrygiannes ([Memoirs], II, 122) cites Metaxas, Lontos, and Zographos for special mention as political leaders of the conspiracy. Another source (to be cited hereafter as "Court Memo") mentions Metaxas, Palamides, Zographos, and Psyllas, the latter a member of the "English" party like Lontos. This source is a memorandum on the Revolution of 3 September 1843 o.s., found in the Secret Archive (Geheimes Hausarchiv), Munich, and published in toto in König Ludwig I von Bayern in seinen Briefen an seinen Sohn den könig Otto von Griechenland, ed. Ludwig Trost (Bamberg, 1891), pp. 130-42, and in part in Petrakakos [Parliamentary History], II, 285-90, and in Andrew S. Skandames, Selides Politikes Historias kai Kritikes. Tomos I: He Triakontaetia tes Basileias tou Othonos 1832-1862 [Pages of Political History and Criticism. Vol. I: The Thirty-year Period of the Kingship of Otho 1832-1862] (Athens, 1961), pp. 396-400.

[59] See for instance an extract of a letter written by the British vice-consul in Mesolongi to Lyons, Mesolongi, 17 Sept. 1843 (enclosed in Lyons' despatch of 20

3. THE REVOLUTION OF 1843[60]

There is no sure way of telling whether the conspiracy received direct encouragement from the patron legations in Athens. But the behavior of the powers during the spring and summer of 1843 shows that they possessed indirect weapons for inciting revolt. Their local representatives

---

Sept. 1843, no. 107, FO 32.122): "There is a plan which is very nearly mature . . . to oblige the government to drive out the Bavarians and oblige a certain exalted individual [the king] to grant a constitution. . . . One thing is very certain: the government is as unpopular as it is possible for any government to be and has fallen completely into contempt with all classes of the population, and the *Head* of the Government not less so; and it is the opinion very openly expressed that the only hope of recovery from all of the ills the nation is suffering under, is precisely, nothing more or less than to remove that head, always however without hurting it physically. . . ."

Guizot (*Mémoires*, VII, 271-72) wrote as follows: "The unpopularity of Otho was great, as great among the diplomatic corps of Athens as among the people. . . . Before this attitude and language of the diplomats [Lyons and Catacazy], the Greeks gave free expression to their sentiments. They did not accuse the king of evil designs, contempt of justice, lack of faith, nor acts of violence. They complained of his inertia, his mania for attending to all questions, all affairs, without ever settling any, his sterile taste for absolute power, and his dull and mute opposition to all independent movement, all effective reforms. 'The country is perfectly calm,' Mr. Piscatory wrote me, 'but it has the profound conviction that the king cannot always be there to hinder it from advancing. . . . Greeks or foreigners . . . the remedy that one imagines, whose prospects one discusses, which some demand of the London conference and others of a national assembly, that is a constitution.' "

Makrygiannes ([*Memoirs*], II, 126) wrote: "One wanted to oust the king, another to kill him. I and all who were honorable and good patriots . . . wanted with knowledge and unity to make a national assembly and let good laws be made, with King Otho staying, if he would sign them. . . ."

Rangabe ([*Memoirs*], II, 127) attributed the desire for an Orthodox king to Catacazy as prime motive; Lyons (27 Sept. 1843, no. 113, FO 32.122) spoke about rumors to the effect that some of the conspirators belonged to the Philorthodox party and had planned either to baptize the king or make him abdicate. See Makrygiannes (*op.cit.*, II, 112) on the aspirations of M. Soutsos or others' aspirations for him.

[60] The most valuable source material on events connected with the revolution of 1843 consists of three categories: (1) material drawn from the Secret Archive of Otho (Geheimes Hausarchiv), Munich, (2) published memoirs and firsthand accounts, and (3) diplomatic correspondence.

Secret Archive of Otho. No one has made an exhaustive examination of documents in this category relating to the revolution of 1843 and I have not been allowed access to its materials because of current work being done to publish its major contents. Yet, extremely valuable sources on the revolution have been discovered and published: (1) an invaluable secret memorandum on the revolution, in German and without date or signature, apparently written to apprise Ludwig in detail of events, especially those taking place in and around the palace and those taking place at the extraordinary session of the Council of State; this is the document cited as "Court Memo" in n. 58 above, (2) a letter of Otho to Ludwig, dated 15 Sept. 1843, essentially a condensed version of the "Court Memo," and published for the first time by Skandames [*Kingship of Otho*], pp. 391-93; (3) a private memorandum of 3 Nov. 1843, drawn up by Gennaios Kolokotrones and presented to Ludwig during his visit

did not have to compromise themselves by actually joining the conspiracy.

The Financial Crisis and the Threat of Foreign Control

On 10 January 1843, Rizos-Neroulos, Greek foreign minister, informed the protecting powers that Greece could not meet the regular six-month service charges which came due on 1 March. Consequently, he requested

to Munich at that time, brought to light by Petrakakos [*Parliamentary History*], II, 333-36, and (4) select correspondence between Otho and Ludwig, found primarily in *Ludwig I*, ed. Trost, passim.

Published memoirs and firsthand accounts. (1) In this category, one of the most valuable is an anonymous sixty-page firsthand account, probably by Alexander Heinze, entitled *Der dritte September 1843 in Athen. Von einem Augenzeugen beschrieben und mit den betreffenden Actenstücken begleitet* (Leipzig, 1843). (2) The other firsthand account is a less valuable but sometimes informative work, especially on major actors in these events, by the then celebrated liberal poet Alexander Soutsos, *He Metabole tes Trites Septembriou [The Change of the Third of September]* (Athens, 1844). Of the memoir publications, the two most valuable are (3) Makrygiannes, [*Memoirs*], II, and (4) Nicholas Dragoumes, *Historikai Anamneseis [Historical Reminiscences]*, 2nd edn. (Athens, 1879), II, the former because its author was a principal actor in the events, the latter because of the author's presence before the palace on the night of 14-15 September and his familiarity with the thoughts and behavior of important participants in the events. Especially valuable is Dragoumes' presentation of Kallerges' account of the revolution, an account which conflicts in many ways with Makrygiannes' presentation of events. (5) An especially valuable though short memoir account of the organization of the conspiracy leading up to the revolution is that by A. Georgantas, one of its organizers, "Historika Apomnemoneumata tes Basileias Othonos" [Historical Memoirs of Otho's Kingship], *Parnassos*, I (1881). Less valuable, though sometimes illuminating and vivid accounts, are those of (6) Gennaios Kolokotrones, *Apomnemoneumata (Cheirographon Deuteron 1821-1862) [Memoirs (Second Manuscript 1821-1862)]*, ed. Emmanuel Protopsaltes (Athens, 1961) (hereafter cited as [*Memoirs II*]); (7) Christopher Neezer, *Apomnemoneumata . . . [Memoirs concerning the First Years of the Establishment of the Greek Kingdom]*, trans. [from German] J. C. Neezer, ed. D. Kampouroglou (Athens, 1936); and (8) Rangabe [*Memoirs*], II. For accounts by Kallerges, in addition to that appearing in paraphrase in Dragoumes, see his letter of 8/20 Nov. 1844 which appeared in various Athenian newspapers and his letter of 3 May 1844*o.s.* which appeared in *Athēna*.

Diplomatic correspondence. (1) Because of extensive personal research done in preparation of this book, the Lyons-Aberdeen correspondence in the Public Record Office, London, has been the most valuable source in this category. Though still unpublished, it has served as an important basis for such secondary accounts as Leonard Bower and Gordon Bolith, *Otho I: King of Greece* (London, 1939) and Driault and Lhéritier, *Histoire*, II. (2) Five important documents from the French foreign office have been published by Jean Poulos in "He Epanastasis tes 3es Septembriou 1843 epi te basei ton gallikon archeion ["The Revolution of the Third of September 1843 on the Basis of the French Archives"] *Deltion tes Historikes kai Ethnologikes Hetaireias tes Hellados [Bulletin of the Historical and Ethnological Society of Greece]*, XI (1956), 223-60. Two are Piscatory's reports to Guizot on the revolution of 1843, the first describing the events of the night of 14-15 September, the second dealing with the immediate aftermath of the revolution. The remaining three are the collective report of Lyons, Catacazy, and Piscatory to the Conference of London concerning the guarantee of a new loan so as to meet these payments.[61] A recent Greek historian has attributed the financial plight, which Rizos announced, to the extraordinary state of the Greek economy. He points to the general European depression which had affected a drop in the price of Greek exports, especially currants, on the world market. He cites the bad harvests of 1842. He then explains that the annual state income contracted appreciably.[62]

What he says is true but not especially relevant. Even in better times, Greece had faced budget deficits. Not until 1841 had the state been able to pay the semiannual service charges from its own treasury. On every occasion the state relied on portions of the third series. In 1842 it had to contract a loan which the French government guaranteed.[63] Economic trends did not precipitate the crisis in 1843, *the powers did*—by unanimously refusing, for the first time, to sanction any further loans. That refusal therefore demands concentrated attention.

Russia first responded to the Rizos note by advancing its share of the

---

the revolution; the instructions of Guizot to Piscatory; and Guizot's letter to Piscatory, concerning his conversation with Kolettes before the latter left for Greece and revealing Kolettes' attitude toward and interpretation of the revolution. (3) Of material in the Austrian archives—correspondence between Prokesch-Osten and Metternich—a series of important letters by Prokesch-Osten have been published in *Aus dem Nachlasse*, ed. Prokesch-Osten, II, and many excerpts translated into Greek have been published by Petrakakos [*Parliamentary History*], II, passim. For additional letters by Prokesch-Osten, this time to Duke John of Austria, see *Briefwechsel zwischen Erzherzog Johann Baptist von Österreich und Anton Graf von Prokesch-Osten* . . . , ed. Anton Schlossar (Stuttgart, 1898). (4) In the Greek Ministry of Foreign Affairs Archives, a special envelope entitled "He epibole tou syntagmatikou politeumatos, 1843. Peri ton gegonoton tes 3es Septembrious" ["The Imposing of the Constitutional Polity, 1843. Concerning the events of 3 September"] contains the official communications to the ministers of the foreign powers and their replies. Included in these are the collective note of Lyons, Catacazy, and Piscatory to the Conference of London on the revolution (see the above account of Poulos' collection of French documents) and an official letter of Metaxas, as head of the revolutionary cabinet, to the European powers in justification of the revolution, published in Greek in Skandames [*Kingship of Otho*], pp. 401-402. (5) Finally, for less valuable accounts, once or twice removed, of French, Austrian, and Prussian ministers in Munich, respectively, see *Gesandtschaftsberichte aus München 1814-1848*, Abt. I: *Die Berichte der französischen Gesandten*, v (Munich, 1935-37); Abt. II: *Die Berichte der österr. Gesandten*, III (Munich, 1939-42); and Abt. III: *Die Berichte der Preussen Gesandten*, IV (Munich, 1949-51), ed. Anton Chroust, passim.

[61] Lyons to Aberdeen, Athens, 19 Jan. 1843, no. 44, FO 32.120. See also Driault and Lhéritier, *Histoire*, II, 232; Kordatos [*History*], III, 193; and Pipineles [*Monarchy*], p. 355.

[62] Pipineles [*Monarchy*], pp. 353-54.

[63] On the balance of the budget in 1841, see *ibid.* and Lyons to Aberdeen, Athens, 20 July 1841, no. 105, FO 32.106 (announcing that Mavrokordatos informed him that the Greek government would meet its six-month payments). Concerning Kolettes' success in obtaining the French loan from a reluctant French government, see Kolettes to Mavrokordatos, Paris, 25 Aug. 1842, no. 6449, Vol. 22 (1842), Mavrokordatos Archive.

1 March service charges. Significantly enough, a note from Catacazy provoked a changed attitude in St. Petersburg, which issued an unexpectedly severe reply on 7 March. It demanded repayment of this last loan by 1 June through drastic curtailment of the Greek budget. Greek financial difficulties, it declared, arose from bad government, costly administration, and an unnecessarily large army (consuming one-third the national income). In the meantime, Russia would confer with Britain and France on the adoption of collective measures, involving possibly direct intervention, unless Greece met the 1 June deadline and proved her ability to meet treaty obligations in the future.[64]

In the past Otho had warded off financial crisis by securing a loan from the one protecting power whose party in Greece enjoyed political primacy. According to this pattern, France should have come to Otho's rescue. So England had done during the Armansperg and Russia during the Glarakes period. But Guizot associated himself with the other two powers in withholding any further aid. After all, in 1841 he had recommended the use of outside compulsion, so long as the powers acted in concert and without attempt at separate advantage. In 1842 he had secured the guarantee of a French loan, but had restricted part of its use to some project of permanent economic value. By this time he had probably despaired of seeing necessary administrative and financial improvement within the framework of the existing system. And he discovered that even a favored status did not provide France with the amount of influence he felt necessary to induce reform.[65] The time had finally come when

[64] Driault and Lhéritier, *Histoire*, ii, 232, and Pipineles [*Monarchy*], p. 357. For the text of the Rizos note, dated 23 Feb./7 Mar. 1843, see P. Karolides, *Synchronos Historia ton Hellenon . . . [Contemporary History of the Greeks . . .]* (Athens, 1922-29), ii, 391-95 and n., or Kordatos [*History*], iii, 194-97.

[65] That Otho had the French portion of the loan in mind as he drew closer to France during the Mavrokordatos crisis and that he was using the implied promise of greater French influence (through the appointment of Chrestides) as inducement for the loan is seen from the reports of Piscatory, Chalcis, 25 June 1841 (2nd report), and Athens, 27 Aug. 1841 (6th report), *L'Hellénisme Contemporain*, xi, 345, 421.

According to Valetas (to Mavrokordatos, Athens, 26 May 1842*o.s.*, no. 6355, Vol. 22 [1842], Mavrokordatos Archive), "Kolettes is writing to his friends here that it is impossible for France to give us money [guarantee the loan] unless we accept the reforms demanded by Mavrokordatos. As I see it, Kolettes is pleating ribbons [intriguing], hoping to force us [the king] to accept those reforms, without his appearing on the stage and avoiding the difficulty which the intriguers pointed to—that the king oughtn't have to descend so low as to negotiate a political treaty with one of his subjects." In short, Valetas was suggesting that Kolettes was using the loan as a lever to extract reforms from Otho. If this is so and Guizot was a party to it (as seems most probable in that case), then the failure of the king to make any significant reforms must have convinced both Guizot and Kolettes of the necessity of resorting to more drastic means.

That Guizot and Piscatory were well aware of the need for reform in Greece, see Guizot, *Mémoires*, vii, 271-72. In an address to the French chamber of deputies on 21 July 1843, Guizot reiterated (vii, 273-74) his continued belief in collective European action to deal with Greek problems. To Piscatory, he wrote (vii, 272-73) about

Otho's policy of steering an independent path had alienated all three powers and had contributed to the first real unanimity among them. He suddenly faced a hostile coalition of powers as well as a hostile coalition of parties.[66]

Faced with the threat of foreign intervention, the government drastically curtailed its regular expenses. The king set an example by donating a generous part of the civil list to the public treasury. The government then reduced the salaries of public officials by levying a graduated withholding tax. It forcibly retired some officials at a pension amounting to only a third of their regular salary. It abolished its engineer corps in the ministry of the interior, its forester corps in the ministry of economics, and a large number of its diplomatic-consular posts abroad, including its legations in London and Paris. Many of the clerical pensions it withdrew and it ordered impoverished clerics back to the remaining monasteries for sustenance.[67]

---

the necessity of accepting certain evils (the king and his dislike of a constitution) while pressing for reforms; in short, he was attempting to hold out for a policy of reformism without constitutionalism (his formal position until the revolution of 15 September). And apparently he was willing to use the Conference of London and denial of a further loan as *the* way to bring pressure on the king.

Even more telling than memoirs written long after emotions had subsided, was the confidential despatch of Lyons to Aberdeen (Athens, 1 May 1843, no. 55, FO 32.121): "King Otho is informed that Guizot lately spoke to the Bavarian minister in Paris in regret and disapprobation of the state of affairs at Athens; Otho received a copy of the despatch Guizot addressed to the French minister at Munich on 9 March. The Bavarian chargé had confidentially given me perusal of Guizot's despatch: Guizot laments the deplorable state of Greece and ascribes it in great measure to Otho's having retained *Tisamenos* in Direction of the Finance Department contrary to the advice given Otho; it complains of the artifice by which the Greek government concealed from the French the real state of finances and thereby obtained pecuniary aid; it states King Otho's universal distrustfulness and his undertaking to do everything have produced the feeling of 'impatient irritation' in the Country, dangerous to the State and even to King Otho's person; it concludes with the hope that some benefit may be derived from the paternal counsel of King Ludwig."

[66] As Perdicaris wrote (*Greece of Greeks*, i, 75): "His Majesty will probably find no insurmountable obstacle to his administration so long as he can take advantage of the disunion of others, but should the heads of the parties unite, then 'God Save the King.'" Aspreas ([*Political History*], i, 152) writes: "He combined the many and varied powers against him; and what he did not wish to give the people, these combined forces wrested from him forcefully." But Aspreas did not see, or at least state, that the combination against the king was slowed down for a long time by the king's policy of transferring influence from one power and party to another.

[67] Driault and Lhéritier, *Histoire*, ii, 233, and Pipineles [*Monarchy*], pp. 358-59. The following is a catalogue of the legislation connected with the reduction of expenses (I have omitted the decrees extending the dotation law of 1/13 Jan. 1838, whereby members of the Phalanx could commute their annual pension into the receipt of land from the state). The reference is in each case to [*Government Gazette*], the year is of course 1843, and all dates are old style:

This done, Rizos replied to the Russian note on 9 April. He described the drastic economy drive, promised to investigate further cuts in spending, but insisted that Greece would not be able to pay Russia by 1 June without reducing her civil and military establishment to the point where anarchy would result.[68]

On 1 May, the protecting powers undertook their deliberations through the Conference of London. These sessions and the strong pressure of the legations in Athens culminated in the three power protocol of 5 July. This in turn served as the basis for the financial convention reluctantly signed by Greece on 14 September. It fixed the annual interest and amortization of the loan at 3,635,922 francs and appropriated specified portions of state revenue for its regular payment—proceeds from customs and the stamp tax in any case, income from land tax and patents if need be. The salt tax it appropriated for the gradual repayment of advances made by the powers the previous March. The three ministers in Athens were to oversee these transactions and the firm of Rothschild was to install an agent in Greece to handle the transfer of these funds from the Greek treasury to the foreign creditors. In short, the powers were both depriving Greece of fiscal autonomy and compelling it to reduce its expenditure by three and a half million francs. The already drastic reductions did not even begin to approach the stipulated sum.[69]

The collective action of the protecting powers played a decisive role in precipitating the revolution, as Piscatory, Prokesch-Osten, and Gen-

---

(1) For the appointment of a committee to lessen state expenses, 28 Feb./12 Mar.; no. 7, 17 Mar.

(2) For the necessary balance of the state budget (contribution from civil list), 25 Mar./6 Apr.; no. 10, 29 Mar.

(3) For withholding from salaries of officials (graduated withholding tax monthly), 31 Mar./12 Apr.; no. 11, 8 Apr.

(4) For withholding from salaries of pensioners, 16/28 Apr.; no. 13, 23 Apr.

(5) For withholding from salaries of judicial officials, 26 Apr./8 May; no. 14, 30 Apr.

(6) For the organization of the corps of naval engineers (by 1/3), 7/19 June; no. 20, 28 June.

(7) For the organization of the naval directorate, 12/24 June; no. 20, 28 June.

(8) For the new organization of the infantry and fortress commanders, 9/21 June; no. 21, 29 June.

(9) For the new organization of the infantry and fortress commanders, 21 June/3 July; no. 21, 29 June.

(10) For the new organization of the cavalry, 9/21 June; no. 21, 29 June.

(11) For the new organization of the cavalry, 21 June/3 July; no. 21, 29 June.

[68] For the complete text of the reply, see *Aiōn*, 21 Apr. 1843*o.s.*; Karolides [*Contemporary History*], II, 396-401, n.; Kordatos [*History*], III, 197-202; and Pipineles [*Monarchy*], p. 357. See also Driault and Lhéritier, *Histoire*, II, 232, and Lyons to Aberdeen, Athens, 30 Apr. 1843, no. 54, FO 32.121: "If all the reductions were realized, there would still be a deficit of 2 million drachmas."

[69] Driault and Lhéritier, *Histoire*, II, 232, 233, 236-37; Kordatos [*History*], III, 205; and Pipineles [*Monarchy*], pp. 359-60.

naios Kolokotrones later acknowledged.[70] In the first place, the fact that France agreed to the harsh demands of the London Conference must have weakened Chrestides' position immeasurably and removed the last obstacle to tripartisan cooperation. Even Chrestides began to urge on Otho the promulgation of a constitution. He frankly expressed dissatisfaction with his circumscribed role in the government.[71]

Second, the Crown, valuable in Greek eyes as a source of foreign support, now seemed a national liability, both because of its responsibility in uniting the powers against Greece and in its obvious inability to prevent national humiliation before Europe. Some may even have regarded three-power action as a subtle invitation for Greeks to take matters into their own hands.[72]

Third, at a moment when Greek public opinion—thanks to the efforts of the press—had lost all patience with any form of foreign interference, it looked as if the country was in for more, rather than less, outside control. Revolution appeared to be the only way to ward off a new form of foreign control, more monstrous than anything known thus far. Presumably, Europe would give Greece another chance under a constitutional regime. By September 1843 a constitution, not merely the Mavrokordatos program, seemed to most Greeks the only way to emerge from administrative chaos and save the king from his own perverse folly. Even

[70] ". . . finally appeared the Russian note, which encouraged the conspirators and discouraged the others" (Kolokotrones Memo [Munich], 3 Nov. 1843, in Petrakakos [*Parliamentary History*], II, 333). See also Gennaios Kolokotrones [*Memoirs II*], p. 88.

"It is not a matter of a constitution, but a conspiracy, born of faults of the government and—one must admit it—of the London Conference, whose wretched influence contributed mainly to inflate discontent and disarm completely the king and his followers" (Prokesch to Metternich, 21 Sept. 1843, in *Aus dem Nachlasse*, ed. A. Prokesch-Osten, II, 239, and in Petrakakos, *op.cit.*, II, 291).

[71] Rangabe contradicts himself. On the one hand, he writes ([*Memoirs*], II, 126): "Concerning the constitution, the king always deliberated, but he never would decide and to those who would sometimes remind him he would answer that the matter needed deep consideration. Among those reminding him were neither prime minister [*sic*] Kriezes, who didn't see why he should forge his own chains, nor Chrestides who, as long as he was in the cabinet and prevailed in it, thought any further change useless." Yet he quotes himself (II, 130-31) as saying to M. Schinas on the night of the revolution, " 'And today's ministers want a constitution and are impatient because the king, who also recognizes its need, delays in granting it.' "

[72] From the day that the protocol [of the London Conference, dated 30 July/11 Aug.] arrived from London and the communication delivered by the ministers of the three courts [ambassadors of the protecting powers] created the impression that the king might not yield and the nation not find help from him, it became obvious that sooner or later a direct struggle between king and nation would take place" (Piscatory to Guizot, Athens, 16 Sept. 1843, in [*Bulletin*], XI [1956], 232). On 21 Apr. 1843, Lyons wrote his government (no. 51, FO 32.121): "Every thinking man of the nation, the king's ministers included, sees the impending ruin and ascribes it to one and the same cause."

responsible politicians were willing to incur the risks involved in resort to force, so intolerable had things become.[73]

Finally, the drastic economy drive greatly enhanced the possibility of recruitment to the conspiracy. The reduction of government salaries and the contraction of a bureaucracy is never popular. But when such a sizeable portion of the population is on the government payroll and depends on that salary for its livelihood, as was the case in Greece, then economy measures are bound to cause the same dangerous dissatisfaction which is provoked by unemployment or underemployment. This was especially true in the army, where disaffection was already rife. With three-power demands for further reductions, even those who still remained in their jobs faced an uncertain future. It is probably more than coincidence that the cavalry, which Lyons cited for the uneven way in which salaries were chopped, was to play such an important part during the night and early morning of 14-15 September.[74] Furthermore, the army dismissals and reduction of salaries in 1843 increased the antagonism against the Bavarians. While Greeks were being dismissed, the king retained the Bavarians, upon whom he felt increasingly dependent for loyal service against growing discontent.[75]

Through a periodic shift in the balance of power between the parties, Otho had managed to keep them and their patron powers from uniting

[73] In Aug. 1843, Piscatory, since June the regular French minister to Athens, proposed a plan of reform limited to that of enlarging the powers of the Council of State. According to Lyons, a Revolutionary Greek figure pointed out that the Piscatory plan might have been all right two years before but would no longer do (Lyons to Aberdeen, Athens, 20 Aug. 1843, no. 98, FO 32.122). On 10 June 1843, Lyons wrote (no. 69, FO 32.121): "The Constitution has ceased to be an abstract question. The real question is whether it is possible to go on much longer with the present king under any form of government other than representative. All proclaim this and taking the lead are those who have station and property to lose." Lyons had been saying this for several years, but by now he was probably right in his assertion. See n. 59 above for Guizot's and Piscatory's remarks on the prevailing constitutional sentiment.

[74] "You know, sir, that . . . the largest part of our civil servants depend on their salaries alone . . . ," wrote Rizos to the Russian government (29 Mar./9 Apr. 1843, in Aiōn, 21 Apr. 1843o.s.). See also n. 68 above. Lyons to Aberdeen, Athens, 10 July 1843, no. 78, FO 32.122.

[75] Lyons quickly pointed out the sore spot (loc.cit.): "The Greeks hoped they might have some voice [in the way reductions were made], but arrangements were made by the Bavarians: while about 200 Greek and philhellene officers were placed 'en disponibilité' and receive hardly one-third full pay, many Bavarian officers remain on extravagant full pay and allowances. . . ." On 31 July 1843 (no. 87, FO 32.122), he reiterated: "Favoritism becomes more and more obvious."

See also the remarks of Gennaios Kolokotrones (Kolokotrones Memo in Petrakakos [Parliamentary History], II, 334): "Thus was effected the reduction of the army, and it left in perplexity those who were removed from their posts and deprived of their means of support, and placed the rest in a condition of fear that perhaps the same fate awaited them."

against him. But the very nature of this expedient rendered it effective for only a limited time. Eventually each party, having had a crack at the "ascendancy," came away disaffected because it had directly experienced the king's obstinate refusal to actually delegate power. Each protecting power, realizing how little influence it could wield through Otho, even when "favored," began to consider other modes of action. After ten years, then, the powers began to act in concert against Otho. In response, the three parties followed suit and carried with them the public opinion which they monopolized. In the meantime, Otho had failed to create a new "national" party which could now come to his support. Finally, the reductions imposed upon him by the Conference of London forced him to cut down the size of the army, the very last prop of his regime and the one institution that could meet force with force, and they loosened his grip on what remained. With all the resources of his established policy by now exhausted, Otho fell back on the last remaining expedient. Fifteen days before the revolution broke out, he later told Lyons, he decided to promulgate a constitution. But true to character, Otho came to this decision too late, and he waited too long to implement it.[76]

The Outbreak of the Revolution

Originally the conspirators had set 25 March 1844 as the date to strike. But the unexpectedly swift action of the powers necessitated earlier action. For those who regarded revolution as a way of dissuading Europe from establishing financial control, immediate action seemed vital. Furthermore, the European financial control, once established, would probably strengthen the Crown, at least as a facade for foreign interests, and even give Europe a vested interest in the continuation of absolutism.[77]

Metaxas, Lontos, and Zographos decided to stage an uprising at once, even though they had not secured the prior support of the garrison of Athens, where the revolt was scheduled to take place. Since the conspirators were relying solely on a sublieutenant to rouse the Athenian garrison to revolt, the attempt would have probably turned into a fiasco. But by a touch of irony, the conspirators were saved from bitter failure by what momentarily looked like a stroke of ill-luck. Metaxas discovered that Gennaios Kolokotrones, a loyal royal aide, had learned about the existence of a conspiracy. When asked by Kolokotrones about his own connection with it, Metaxas professed innocence and persuaded Kolo-

[76] For testimony of the nonexistence of a real royal party in 1843, see Piscatory, Athens, 16 Sept. 1843, [*Bulletin*], xi, 237. On Otho's claim that he had decided to grant a constitution, see Lyons to Aberdeen, Athens, 15 Sept. 1843, "Secret and Confidential," FO 32.122.

[77] "We decided on 25 March 1844 as the date for the execution of the change," wrote A. Georgantas, one of the conspirators, in his ["Historical Memoirs"], *Parnassos*, i (1881), 837.

Metaxas told Lyons that the revolution had broken out before they had originally planned (Lyons to Aberdeen, Athens, 21 Sept. 1843, no. 111, FO 32.122).

kotrones, a personal friend, to refrain from informing the court until he, Metaxas, had tried to gather some information.[78]

The conspirators gained time through this deception and were frightened enough to make more adequate arrangements. In August 1843 they initiated Kallerges, head of the Athens cavalry unit, Skarveles, head of the Athens infantry, and Spyromelios, director of the military school at Piraeus, all members of the "Russian" party. When approached, Schinas, head of the artillery unit, remained noncommittal. It was then decided that on the night of 13 September, Makrygiannes and his following should start firing and that Kallerges and Skarveles would then lead their troops to blockade the palace. The latter two lost their nerve, presumably because the court by this time knew about the existence of the plot. They failed to act and the next morning Makrygiannes found his home under the surveillance of the Athens gendarmerie.[79]

By this time the court had gathered information enough to take action. On 14 September, it placed eighty-three names on a list of suspects for arrest and drew up a decree for the establishment of an *ad hoc* military court to start proceedings against the conspirators. It put army officers on twenty-four-hour duty at their barracks, doubled the palace guard, and placed a military detachment in the area of Church of Holy Peace.[80]

---

[78] Makrygiannes [*Memoirs*], II, 129.

[79] *Ibid.*, II, 133-36.

[80] Even though Aspreas ([*Political History*], I, 162) asserts the king's ignorance of the conspiracy, the primary sources agree that the king shared the public secret. According to the "Court Memo" (in *Ludwig I*, ed. Trost, p. 133, Petrakakos [*Parliamentary History*], II, 285-86, and Skandames [*Kingship of Otho*], p. 396), "For some time King Otho had been informed that a public demonstration would take place before the palace, indeed during a time when the head of the garrison would be of one mind with the demonstrators. The evening of 1 September, he received news that during the next two days this plan would be carried out. Subsequently, measures were taken and the officers were instructed to sleep in their barracks. So little, it seems, did the public think of an uprising that all laughed at the exaggerated measures." See also the letter of Otho to Ludwig, Athens, 15 Sept. 1843 in Skandames, *op.cit.*, pp. 391-93, 426; Kolokotrones Memo in Petrakakos, *op.cit.*, II, 334; and Neezer [*Memoirs*], pp. 213-14.

The anonymously published *Der dritte September* (pp. 7, 12, as cited for the first time by Petrakakos, *op.cit.*, II, 302-303, nn. 2 and 3 and subsequently by Skandames *op.cit.*, pp. 400-401), reports the following appointments to the court—Almeïda, Chatzepetros, Pisa, Stavros, Grivas, Feder—and states the intention of proceeding against forty suspects on the morning of 15 Sept. Vlachogiannes (Makrygiannes [*Memoirs*], II, 137, n.), basing his information on an article in the newspaper *Angelos* (8 Sept. 1843*o.s.*), lists the following appointees instead: A. Tzenos, moirarch of the gendarmerie, Karores and Vouros, judges, and N. Valsamakes, state prosecutor.

Piscatory comments as follows (16 Sept. 1843, in [*Bulletin*], XI, 232-33): ". . . the Government was uneasy, it took some measures not even worthy of mention. That night at eight, without asking the opinion of any other minister but the minister of war, the king formed a military court, as all claim. This was great folly, the more so because the secret was not kept, but what gives a true picture of this unfortunate government is the fact that the military court was established without the suspects

Why the king delayed in making the arrests is a mystery. Perhaps the delay simply demonstrated his personal indecisiveness and the inefficiency of his government apparatus. Perhaps the rumors of conspiracy, prevalent throughout his reign, had made him so incredulous that he awaited more decisive evidence against the alleged conspirators. Even the public had learned to treat rumors lightly and in this case made fun of the government for being so jittery.[81] Most likely, however, the king hoped to frighten the would-be conspirators into the abandonment of their plans and hoped to avoid the public unrest that would undoubtedly attend the arrest and trial of prominent figures from all three parties. After all, his position was so precarious that he might precipitate a popular revolt by seeking to crack down on the conspiracy.

Because the court did not act swiftly, its measures triggered the revolt. Feigning sickness, Makrygiannes secured two doctors who informed Metaxas and Kallerges of his confinement. The plight of Makrygiannes probably seemed to confirm the rumors of impending arrests, which leaked out of the palace. With the threat of arrest hanging over their heads, revolt seemed necessary for self-preservation. The conspirators decided to act that very night.[82]

That evening two Spartan battalions came to strengthen the gendarme guard surrounding Makrygiannes' home. For a while Makrygiannes and his family thought themselves doomed, but they gained hope when two small groups of friends managed to elude the guards and get to them. In a similar attempt, a third and larger group of twenty-five proved less successful and provoked the gendarmerie to open fire. The penetrators returned fire and killed one gendarme, the only casualty in the otherwise bloodless revolution. According to Makrygiannes at least, the firing set off the main events of the revolution and transferred the main theater of action to the army barracks where Skarveles and Kallerges responded to the shots by setting out for the palace.[83]

---

being arrested. Whoever in the opposition had a post of some importance thought himself threatened, and an uprising, decided on already but without a time yet set for it, was speeded up." And to quote from the Kolokotrones Memo (in Petrakakos, op.cit., ɪɪ, 34), "The plots were known in part by the king. Only because of his standing superior and his gentle heart, he did not take any measures against the plans. He never dreamed that he would find himself in the position of needing to use the army in this way."

See also Neezer, op.cit., pp. 213-14.

[81] See the letter of Otho to Ludwig, Athens, 15 Sept. 1843, in Skandames [Kingship of Otho], p. 391.

[82] Makrygiannes [Memoirs], ɪɪ, 136. On the court measures as a trigger for the revolt, see also the Piscatory quotation in n. 80 above.

[83] Makrygiannes [Memoirs], ɪɪ, 136-41. See also Finlay (History, vɪɪ, 174-75), who explains the long wait of the gendarmes (and their ostensible ineptitude) by saying that they hoped to surprise several leaders at the same time; he also asserts that the arrest of Makrygiannes was to serve as a signal for the other conspirators. The strengthening of the gendarmerie force in the first place is explained by the

Kallerges later told a different story. After a performance of *Lucretia Borgia*, he went to find Lontos and Metaxas and discovered that neither was spending the night at home. He then went to Makrygiannes' and found him in his nightcap (no mention of the gendarmerie or the shooting incident). Finally he went to the barracks to ready the cavalry and infantry battalions. After a few moments of uncertainty, he stammered a few incoherent words, raised his sword, then shouted, "Long live the constitution." The troops returned the exclamation and proceeded down Aiolou Street, then up Hermes Street to the open square in front of the new palace. He sent orders to open the local prison and free its inmates. "And thus," he concluded, "soldiers, inmates of Medresa [prison], riff-raff from the market-place and a small number of citizens collected [in the square] to call for a constitution."[84]

---

letter of Otho to Ludwig, Athens, 15 Sept. 1843, in Skandames [*Kingship of Otho*], p. 391, and the "Court Memo" in *Ludwig I*, ed. Trost, pp. 133-34, and Petrakakos [*Parliamentary History*], II, 286, the latter stating more specifically that, on the evening of the outbreak, one of the conspirators informed the king that at ten o'clock his comrades would meet at the home of Makrygiannes and that at two in the morning would try to force from the king his signature for a prepared document.

[84] Nicholas Dragoumes ([*Reminiscences*], II, 90-91) quotes Kallerges' story and accepts it as essentially correct, even though by the time Kallerges told it, he and Makrygiannes were no longer friends. Kallerges, in a letter published by *Athēna* (3 May 1844 o.s.), alleged that Makrygiannes deliberately refrained from participation in the revolt because of his preference to stage it in the provinces.

An eyewitness himself and present at the square that night, Dragoumes (*op.cit.*, II, 93) writes about one of his experiences as follows: "A barbarous voice in back of me kept calling, 'Long live the constitution.' 'How long will you be shouting?' I asked angrily of a man with a beastlike face, negroid appearance, and bare to the waist. 'A Constitution is good thing,' cried the monster. 'It got me out of prison.' Hearing this, I shuddered."

For another interesting account of the same scene, see Rangabe [*Memoirs*], II, 129-31: "We had gone to bed late that night, when we heard an unusual commotion of many people passing quickly through the streets. Opening the window, we saw hurrying among them my colleague in the ministry of interior Elias Kalamogdartes and we asked him what was going on. Coming toward us, he told us that the people and the army had assembled outside the palace and were demanding a constitution. . . . And Kalamogdartes immediately left us, anxious to get to the scene of the drama, in which he confessed to me he was not without a role. When my servant, who had gone into the street to learn about happenings, came back, he told me that before the palace thousands of assembled people were shouting, 'Long live the constitution.' Indeed their cries reached as far as our house. The whole army stood there, without attempting anything against the people, limiting its activities to shouting, 'Long live the King.' . . .

"Coming to the square, I found things somewhat different from the way my servant had described them; that is, the army, induced by its leaders to disregard its role as the organ of the executive power, not only did not cry, 'Long live the King,' but was itself the protagonist of this revolutionary drama. But order reigned among all those thousands who filled the square and awaited the decision of the

At midnight the court heard the firing from Makrygiannes' residence and complacently assumed that the house guard had dispersed the conspirators. Shortly after, it received news that both infantry and cavalry units were approaching with demands for a constitution. The king, who was working late as usual, sent orders for Major Schinas, head of the artillery, to disperse the troops with grapeshot. In the meantime, he sent Vlachopoulos, minister of war, and Gardikiotes Grivas, a royal aide, to sway the troops into submission. But both men were seized before they could reach the body of soldiers. Since Schinas had originally refused to commit himself to the conspirators, no one knew exactly which side he would take. On his arrival at the palace he directed a cannon at each entrance. This made military resistance on the part of the king impossible.[85]

The Formation of a Provisional Regime

The king then tried his moral authority. When he appeared on the balcony, Kallerges pronounced "the people's desire for a constitution." Otho promised to consider the "request" but only after the troops had withdrawn and he had had a chance to consult the cabinet, the Council of State, and the protecting powers. The troops were not close enough to hear the king's words, and Kallerges refused to order withdrawal.[86]

Once it became clear that the army would not disperse, the king came to one of the first floor windows so as to be heard better. With him was

---

king, while the military music played and amused the people." See also Neezer, [*Memoirs*], pp. 215-17.

Concerning Kallerges, Finlay (*History*, VII, 175) remarks that "with the prudence which he constantly displayed in great emergencies, and which contrasted with his extreme imprudence on ordinary occasions, he sent out strong patrols to maintain order, and stop the cry of 'Death to the Bavarians!' which the friends of orthodoxy and brigandage attempted to raise."

[85] "Court Memo" in *Ludwig I*, ed. Trost, p. 134, and in Petrakakos [*Parliamentary History*], II, 286. According to it, Schinas' reply to Otho's orders, issued after the outbreak, left the court little confidence in its support. See the collective note of the three ministers (France, England, Russia) addressed to the Conference of London (3/15 Sept. 1843 [*Bulletin*], IX, 243) which refers to "two aides" who, sent to call the army back to obedience, had to flee into the palace for safety; and the letter of Otho (to Ludwig, Athens, 15 Sept. 1843 in Skandames [*Kingship of Otho*], p. 391), which says that Vlachopoulos and Grivas were probably placed under arrest by the conspirators. See also Finlay, *History*, VII, 175, and Neezer [*Memoirs*], p. 215.

[86] "Court Memo" in *Ludwig I*, ed. Trost, p. 134, and in Petrakakos [*Parliamentary History*], II, 286. Another account is that of Neezer ([*Memoirs*], pp. 214-15) and merits quoting: "After a little while, the door of the balcony of the palace opened, the king appeared and addressed himself to Kallerges: 'General Kallerges.' But the latter replied, 'Not general, simply citizen.' After these words there followed the following shout by the army and assembled multitude, 'Long live the constitution. Long live Kallerges.' 'Your Majesty,' shouted Kallerges, 'the people want a constitution.' Then the king withdrew." See also Finlay, *History*, VII, 175, and Piscatory, 16 Sept. 1843 [*Bulletin*], IX, 243.

the hated Major Hess, a Bavarian member of the camarilla. Kallerges handed the king a document containing the terms of the constitution and demanded a quick reply. Hess insisted on the withdrawal of the troops and, according to an eyewitness, Kallerges answered:

> Major Hess, don't interfere. For you the ship is steaming in Piraeus harbor. I will regret it if their Majesties don't also take advantage of that steamship.[87]

In the meantime, the homes of the cabinet ministers were placed under surveillance and the councilors of state were summoned by armed guard to the Council meeting chamber where Metaxas, Zographos, Palamides and Psyllas had already assembled. Outside the building an armed unit kept guard. Inside, Makrygiannes, Spyromelios, and other officers, stood guard, as much to prevent councilors from walking out in protest as to exclude outsiders. The session began at about three in the morning.[88]

Clearly the revolutionaries had not summoned the Council of State to debate freely on the changes to be effected. The revolutionaries wanted primarily to give the stamp of legality to the revolutionary proceedings. The presence of the military attested to the urgency of their desire for a quick and clear consensus. Even under the threat of compulsion, the councilors displayed various shades of opinion. Finlay implies that some councilors still resisted the idea of a constitution, but even if he was right, they were few. Recorded differences of opinion involved other issues. When Zographos proposed the formation of a new cabinet, Anastasios Lontos insisted that only the king enjoyed the prerogative of appointing a cabinet. Apparently dissatisfied with some of the cabinet appointments, Monarchides and Ainian argued for the Council's right to reject some of them. On the other hand, Constantine Veïkos, reflecting the sentiments of some Napists, proposed the baptism into the Orthodox faith as a condition for Otho's retention of the throne. The military guards soon put an end to such dissenting views. Eventually no one dared talk, except for Metaxas, Zographos, Palamides, and Psyllas. The Council approved several decrees for presentation to the king. One provided for the convocation of a national assembly within thirty days, another appointed a provisional cabinet selected initially by Makrygiannes, and a third delegated to the cabinet the right to convene the as-

[87] Neezer [Memoirs], pp. 215-16. See the remarks of Prokesch-Osten to his government (21 Sept. 1843, in Aus dem Nachlasse, ed. A. Prokesch-Osten, II, 274, and in Petrakakos [Parliamentary History], II, 293-94) about Hess, "an honorable but inconceivably thoughtless man. . . . Each Greek considers him a personal enemy. When he dared appear with the king on the balcony at the critical moment, an angry outburst of insults followed. His presence, without any benefit, is the source of danger. As long as he remains with the king, one can barely guarantee the king's life."

[88] "Court Memo" in Ludwig I, ed. Trost, p. 135 and in Petrakakos [Parliamentary History], II, 286-87. See also Finlay, History, VII, 176, and Makrygiannes [Memoirs], II, 141.

sembly. On Zographos' motion, the Council appointed a committee to present the decrees to the king for his signature.[89]

It was early morning by now. Accompanied by an armed guard, the committee proceeded to the palace. Before the king, some of the committeemen excused their presence by pleading compulsion. The king accepted the documents but requested permission to consult the ministers of the protecting powers before coming to a final decision. Instead he was given a time limit for his assent.[90]

In the morning foreign plenipotentiaries met and together tried to gain access to the palace. Fearing the possible influence which some might have, Kallerges refused them admission but promised that the king should suffer no harm. Having no other choice, the ministers withdrew. According to Piscatory, Catacazy was in low spirits (presumably because it looked as if Otho would not abdicate), Lyons justified all, the Prussian minister criticized all, Prokesch-Osten condemned the acts but justified the persons, and the Bavarian minister accepted the event as inevitable.[91]

[89] "Court Memo" in *Ludwig I*, ed. Trost, pp. 135-38, Petrakakos [*Parliamentary History*], II, 287-88, and Skandames [*Kingship of Otho*], pp. 396-98; Soutsos [*Change of September*], p. 87; A. Georgantas ["Historical Memoirs"], *Parnassos*, v (1881), 849. On the committee, see also Finlay (*History*, VII, 176), who states that it consisted of A. Lontos, R. Palamides, and A. Metaxas. But the "Court Memo" implies that there were more, some who went under duress. On Makrygiannes' choosing the cabinet, see in addition to the "Court Memo," Makrygiannes [*Memoirs*], II, 141-42.

The three decrees are dated 3 Sept. 1843 *o.s.* and appear in [*Government Gazette*], no. 31, 3 Sept. 1842 *o.s.*

[90] "Court Memo" in *Ludwig I*, ed. Trost, p. 138, Petrakakos [*Parliamentary History*], II, 288-89, and Skandames [*Kingship of Otho*], pp. 398-99. "The deputation was at last received, but while the king was treating with its members, he was endeavouring to open a communication with his own creatures in the council of state, who, he thought, might now be sufficiently numerous to pass a new resolution in his favour," wrote Finlay (*History*, VII, 176).

According to a letter of Prokesch-Osten to Archduke John of Austria, 21 Sept. 1843 (see *Briefwechsel*, ed. Schlossar, pp. 164-66), "Kallerges, in our presence, communicated to the king that he would bombard the doors of the palace and enter through the windows, if the king did not sign within fifteen minutes." According to the letter of the three ministers in Athens to the Conference of London, 3/15 Sept. 1843 (in [*Bulletin*], IX, 243), the Council of State imposed a time limit of one hour on the king.

[91] "When in the morning my colleagues and I appeared in the palace square, we were informed that there was nothing there for us to do and that the person of the king was in no danger. I sent someone to the countryside to inform the minister of Austria [Prokesch-Osten] and I awaited him impatiently, hoping that he would help me reach agreement with my colleagues of England and Russia for the step which I believed them least disposed to make. I believed it indispensable that we appear at the palace. Both the one and the other feared lest the king ask us for advice. They agreed on the difficulty of replying, but I argued that it was impossible not to display to the whole world, through one such official step, that we were intervening in behalf of the king's interest and that there was a point

The question of whether the ministers of France, England, and Russia were implicated in the conspiracy requires attention because such imputations were later made. Most everyone strongly suspected Catacazy's involvement and many Greeks believed that he had encouraged the conspirators in order to replace Otho with an Orthodox prince. Others suspected Lyons of involvement. According to Dragoumes, himself pro-English, Kallerges refused the ministers admittance to the palace on the recommendation of Griffiths, secretary of the English legation. Even Piscatory, though practically beyond suspicion, suffered charges by Austrian diplomacy.[92] According to Makrygiannes, however, all three

---

beyond which by all means we would prevent them from exceeding. When the minister of Austria arrived, he, the ministers of England and Prussia and I went to the home of the Russian minister, who had again retired, apparently awaiting the evolution of events. Mr. Prokesch agreed with me immediately. But constantly being discussed was what advice should be given the king in case he asked for it. I did not express an opinion, but I did say that if the step was not taken by all of us together I was determined to take it myself. Finally, after we delayed a long time, we set out for the palace. On the road we met many persons, who begged us not to appear and informed us that we should not be allowed entrance. Indeed, we were informed that it was impossible for us to be received. We protested against the force exercised against the king, against the denial of our right, and after painful enough words exchanged between the minister of Prussia and colonel Kallerges . . . we departed." (Piscatory, 16 Sept. 1843, in [Bulletin], IX, 233-34).

"On the morning of the 15th, having been informed, I departed from Kephissia and found the army and people before the palace in relative quiet. Kallerges said to me, 'I guarantee the safety of the king, but no one can go in or come out before the Council of State comes to some agreement with the king.' I then hurried to the house of Catacazy, dean of the diplomatic corps. He was in bed, protesting a headache. 'What have you done thus far?' I asked him. 'Have you tried to enter the palace?' He informed me that Lyons, Piscatory, and he had gone and that Kallerges was personally responsible for the king's safety. . . . In the meantime, the others arrived, demanded that in a body and in uniform we go to the palace. Lyons observed that it was not allowed, and that if it were allowed, we would no longer be able to assume the responsibility to rouse the king against the demands of the Council of State. Catacazy remained quiet. After my persistence, we agreed and went." (Prokesch-Osten to Metternich, 21 Sept. 1843, in Aus dem Nachlasse, ed. A. Prokesch-Osten, II, 241, and in Petrakakos [Parliamentary History], II, 292-93).

[92] On suspicion of Catacazy's involvement, see Piscatory's letter of 16 Sept. 1843 ([Bulletin], IX, 238-39): "Concerning the minister of Russia, I confess that his position is up to now a mystery to me. . . . Was his preference for a national assembly a hope or a forecast, perhaps an announcement? Did he know night before last about what took place last night, or did he simply foresee it? Was his special dejection a weakness, worry over his position, or a desire to cover up the results of an influence which he had exercised? It's still impossible for me to determine the truth. I am tempted to believe there is a bit of truth in all these alternatives. . . . [the day after the revolution] He practically drove Colonel Kallerges from his home. . . . As far as I am concerned the refusal to see Kallerges is one more proof of his former relations with Mr. Catacazy." See also Prokesch-Osten's letter of 21 Sept. 1843 to Metternich (in Aus dem Nachlasse, ed. A. Prokesch-Osten, II, 240, and in Petrakakos [Parliamentary History], II, 292): "Catacazy spent recent times in exceptional dissatisfaction. He repeatedly told me, but always in a painful tone,

knew of the conspiracy. In fact he had represented the objective of the conspiracy differently to each one, so that each would expect the conspiracy to advance the aims of his government.[93] There was no need for these men to offer the conspirators positive encouragement. Their failure to protest was equivalent to moral support.

When the king learned that Kallerges would not give entrance to the ambassadors, and heard the rumblings of the crowd growing more intense, he decided to accept the revolutionary demands. Had he followed his personal inclinations, he later said, he would have abdicated, but he feared that his departure would plunge Greece back into anarchy. Even though Otho had signed the decrees, Kallerges refused to withdraw the army. The new cabinet ministers, he insisted, must first appear before the king.[94]

After the new ministers arrived and took their oath of office, they handed the king two more decrees for his signature. One made the third of September a future national holiday and awarded medals to the conspirators in appreciation for their action; the other expressed thanks to

---

'Things are no longer tolerable; the deluge is coming.' The eve [of the revolution] Kallerges was at his home, where he frequently visited. Catacazy entertained him in the presence of the English and French ministers, and he left without any private conversation. I explain this [visit] as the need of the conspirator to give the public proof of Russia's approval." See also Dragoumes ([Reminiscences], II, 87-88) who alleges that Catacazy advised Otho, through the Bavarian minister, to appoint a regent and leave for Munich, until the consequent anarchy brought the Greeks begging for him to return. He interprets this as proof that Catacazy was trying to get the king out of the country to make way for an Orthodox one.

Concerning Lyons and Griffiths, see ibid., II, 93: "While waiting for the committee [of the Council of State] to come out, Griffiths came running at full speed. He said, 'The ministers are coming in a body. Lyons asks you to persuade Kallerges to refuse them entry before the king signs the decrees. You know why [presumably so that they wouldn't dissuade the king].' He said this [to me] and left. I repeated this immediately to Kallerges and he agreed." See also Perdicaris, Greece of Greeks, II, 75, n.: "There are few who have contributed as largely to the late change in the affairs of Greece as Sir Edmond Lyons, and few who have a better title to her gratitude."

Metternich, in a letter to Prokesch-Osten, dated 13 Oct. 1843 (in Aus dem Nachlasse, II, 251, and in Petrakakos op.cit., II, 295), claimed he had evidence that the revolution was the work of France and Kolettes.

[93] Makrygiannes [Memoirs], II, 136.

[94] "Court Memo," in Ludwig I, ed. Trost, p. 139, Petrakakos [Parliamentary History], II, 288-90, and Skandames [Kingship of Otho], p. 398. See also Dragoumes [Reminiscences], II, 95-96; Finlay History, VII, 177; the letter of Otho to Ludwig, Athens, 15 Sept. 1843, in Skandames, op.cit., p. 392; and the letter of the three ministers to the Conference of London, 3/15 Sept. 1843, in [Bulletin], IX, 245: "I had to ask myself if I should keep my crown or resign. As an individual, I preferred the latter decision, but as king I thought of the anarchy which would inevitably follow my resignation.'"

them for the preservation of order. Regarding these decrees as an intolerable affront, the king refused his approval and again considered abdication. The cabinet justified these decrees as the only way to quiet the people, but some later argued that the authors of the decrees had intended them as a means of forcing Otho's abdication.[95]

In the meantime, the whole diplomatic corps had finally got into the palace. Piscatory found the king agitated, angry, with his eyes full of tears, but not frightened. Otho exclaimed to the diplomatic corps, "I have given up all my privileges; I am no longer king, now that my ministers, the national assembly, and a constitution have been imposed upon me and now that my army has stopped obeying me." According to Lyons, the king also said, "In Greece constitution means nothing more nor less than pillage."[96]

Otho consulted the corps about the two decrees in question, asking whether he should not resign the throne in favor of his brother. The corps first tried to dissuade the cabinet. When the cabinet threatened to resign, the ambassadors convinced the king to make one additional sacrifice and promised that they would help him restore the royal prestige.[97]

By this time the crowd outside threatened to break down the doors of the palace if the king did not appear on the balcony with his ministers. After the king complied, the crowds still remained dissatisfied, demanding now that the king appear to shout "Long live the constitution." But the cabinet ministers declared all the revolutionary demands satisfied. Consequently it ordered the army to disperse the crowd and itself return to the barracks. By three in the afternoon the crowd and the army had left the square. Business resumed for the rest of the day as usual.[98]

News of the revolution was received in the provinces with enthusiasm

[95] For the text of these additional decrees, both dated 3 Sept., see [*Government Gazette*], no. 31, 3 Sept. 1843*o.s.* According to Makrygiannes ([*Memoirs*], II, 142), these decrees were designed to protect the conspirators; according to the "Court Memo" (in *Ludwig I*, ed. Trost, pp. 138-41, Petrakakos [*Parliamentary History*], II, 287-88, and Skandames [*Kingship of Otho*], p. 399), their purpose was allegedly to satisfy the public. See also the letter of the three ministers to the Conference of London, 3/15 Sept. 1843, in [*Bulletin*], IX, 244, and Neezer [*Memoirs*], pp. 216-17.

[96] Piscatory to Guizot, Athens, 16 Sept. 1843, and the letter of the three ministers to the Conference of London, 3/15 Sept. 1843, both in [*Bulletin*], IX, 235, 245. Lyons to Aberdeen, Athens, 21 Sept. 1843, no. 110, FO 32.122.

[97] Piscatory to Guizot, Athens, 16 Sept. 1843, and the letter of the three ministers to the Conference of London, 3/15 Sept. 1843, both in [*Bulletin*], IX, 285, 244-45; and "Court Memo," in *Ludwig I*, ed. Trost, pp. 140-41, Petrakakos [*Parliamentary History*], II, 290, and Skandames [*Kingship of Otho*], pp. 399-400.

[98] "Court Memo," in *Ludwig I*, ed. Trost, p. 141, Petrakakos [*Parliamentary History*], II, 290, and Skandames [*Kingship of Otho*], p. 400. See also Piscatory, Athens, 16 Sept. 1843, and the letter of the three ministers to the Conference of London, 3/15 Sept. 1843, both in [*Bulletin*], IX, 235, 245. See also Makrygiannes [*Memoirs*], II, 143, and Neezer [*Memoirs*], p. 217.

and only a few instances of disorder occurred.[99] A few days later the remaining Bavarians were dismissed from office and sent out of the country immediately.[100]

[99] Piscatory (Athens, 16 Sept. 1843 in [*Bulletin*], ix, 237) reported that in Nauplion and Chalcis the revolt was unanimously accepted without any disruption of order. In a subsequent letter (19 Sept. 1843, *ibid.*, ix, 247, 251), he reported the same reaction in other places, like Patras and Syros, and pointed out that Kriezotes, leaving Chalcis for Athens with 150 palikars, turned back at merely a word from the revolutionary cabinet. Lyons reiterated the same point in his despatch to his government (Athens, 21 Sept. 1843, no. 111, and 27 Sept. 1843, no. 113, both FO 32.122). But he also noted a notable exception at Patras, where feeling broke out against Bavarians on their way home (30 Sept. 1843, no. 114, FO 32.122), and at Mesolongi "where, a few days ago, the subaltern officer in command of a detachment of a Light Infantry Battalion ordered knapsacks to be introduced. The privates considered this an unauthorized innovation and resisted it, and expelled the non-commissioned officers who endeavoured to enforce obedience, and at last refused to receive any orders from their officers, but they guarded the prisons and the Treasury, and scrupulously performed all the ordinary garrison duties, and by the last accounts it appears they were sensible to the gravity of their mutinous offense, and prepared to yield to the summons of the troops which were approaching the City" (16 Nov. 1843, no. 138, FO 32.123).

[100] For the decree for the departure of foreigners, excepting only philhellene veterans, dated 3 Sept., see [*Government Gazette*], no. 31, 3 Sept. 1843*o.s.* The decree spoke of "foreigners" rather than just Bavarians, presumably to secure the removal of Lemaître, intendant general, and other Frenchmen in Greek service. Piscatory wrote his government about these on 19 Sept. 1843 (in [*Bulletin*], ix, 251) and even listed some of them (Guerin, Péretie, Sidager, Dadanrier, and Marlin). Concerning the departure of the Bavarians, especially the chief ones (Hess, Spiess, and Graf), see Lyons to Aberdeen, 21 Sept. 1843, no. 111, FO 32.122.

Part Three

The Making of a Constitution

CHAPTER NINE

The Period of the Constituent Assembly, September 1843–March 1844

DURING the seven months between the bloodless coup of September 1843 and the formal promulgation of a constitution in March 1844, the parties operated in a new and special situation. For the first time they were in formal possession of political power, both by their representation in the cabinet and through their delegations in the constituent assembly. Their acknowledged leaders were once again at the center of the political stage, free from the restraining hand of the king and the competing authority of the Bavarians. Their newspaper organs were free to express themselves openly on all issues. The collapse of royal authority suddenly permitted them to show what they stood for and to what extent they represented public sentiment. Because of its extraordinary character, this short period casts a new light on the parties.

1. THE NEW LOCATION OF POWER

The Internal Situation

Hindsight is likely to obscure the seriousness of the situation created by the revolution of September 3/15. Civil war again became a frighteningly real possibility now that the Crown had become powerless and effective power diffused. The Revolutionary period had shown how precarious and debilitating collective leadership could be. Everyone feared a similar outcome this time—armed struggle between competing groups for power in the state. But one ingredient in this situation had been absent during the Revolution—the painful memory of what horrible consequences civil strife could have. This, above all, seems to have frightened the revolutionary leadership, in spite of conflicting desires, into close cooperation.[1]

The composition of the new cabinet, recommended by Makrygiannes, demonstrated the overriding concern to give virtually equal representation to all three parties. Three of the seven were acknowledged Napists:

[1] According to Piscatory, in a letter to his government dated 16 Sept. 1843, the fear of anarchy was an important factor in preventing the revolutionaries from deposing Otho (published in John Poulos, "He Espanastasis tes trites Septembriou 1843" ["The Revolution of the Third of September 1843"], *Deltion tes Historikes kai Ethnologikes Hetaireias tes Hellados* [*Bulletin of the Historical and Ethnological Society of Greece*], xi [1946], 237, and Prokesch-Osten, in a letter to Archduke John dated 6 Nov. 1843, cites fear of civil war as the chief reason for cooperation between Metaxas, Mavrokordatos, and Kolettes (*Briefwechsel zwischen Erzherzog Johann Baptist von Osterreich und Anton Graf von Prokesch-Osten . . .* , ed. Anton Schlossar [Stuttgart, 1898], pp. 174-77).

Metaxas as prime minister and minister of foreign affairs, Michael Schinas as minister of religion-education, and Constantine Kanares as head of the naval ministry. Two were "French": Palamides—interior, and Drosos Mansolas—economy. Two were "English": Andrew Lontos—army, and Leon Melas—justice.[2] In a spirit of conciliation and nonpartisanship, the cabinet invited the returning Kolettes and Mavrokordatos to participate in its deliberations. Though without portfolio, they gave the cabinet sessions a three/three/three balance. Another sort of balance was also maintained. A Napist headed the cabinet but an "Englishman" and "Frenchman" controlled the key ministries of the army and interior respectively.[3]

[2] Piscatory, on 16 Sept. 1843 ([*Bulletin*], IX, 240), made the following analysis of the new cabinet: "Mr. Metaxas is the most sober individual of the Russian party. He is a capable person and the least pedantic. Messrs Regas and Drosos Mansolas, in the absence of Kolettes, are the most worthy of the French party. Always Constitutionalists and only recently separated from Mr. Christides, the first has a great deal of spirit, the second, who was formerly a minister, is a good choice. They are both sober ministers, especially at this time. Nevertheless, their position is difficult.

"Mr. Lontos is worthy. He is a good and brave officer of the Revolution. He is a stable person, above all a Constitutionalist. He is believed to belong to the English party. I know that he said to someone, 'Yes, I am an anglophile, not because I believe in the good intentions of England toward Greece, but because it has a well-defined policy here, whereas France does not.'

"Mr. Melas resigned from the cabinet along with Mavrokordatos [in 1841] whose friend he is. Mr. Schinas, devoted to Mr. Metaxas, is a shady individual and, I believe, without much worth. Kanares is of the Russian party, and has no other value than his name. It is necessary here, Mr. Minister [Guizot], to mention party tendencies. They are in a position to regain all their former influence and, if they don't follow the good example which we set for them, I would greatly regret that Mr. Kolettes is not here."

A. Georgantas, Rumeliot, Septembrist, a close friend of Makrygiannes (in his "Historikai Apomnemoneumata tes Basileias Othonos" ["Historical Memoirs of Otho's Kingship"] *Parnassos*, V [1881], 833-51), writes about the provisional government as follows: "The revolutionary cabinet, proposed by the council of state . . . was formed from among the three parties, that is, French, English, and Russian. . . . It insured all the parties of Greece and in this way all the citizens, with the exception of a few, accepted it."

[3] Mavrokordatos was returning from Constantinople and Kolettes from Paris. According to John Makrygiannes (*Apomnemoneumata* [*Memoirs*], ed. John Vlachogiannes, 2nd edn. [Athens, 1947], II, 141-42), "Then Metaxas and all the others of our group appointed me to select the new ministers." He also claimed that he persuaded Metaxas "and the others," after great pains, to accept Mavrokordatos and Kolettes "in the government." The latter two, he alleged, were outwardly friends of the revolutionists but secretly working against them; his motive in recommending their inclusion in the government was apparently to prevent them from forming an opposition ([*Memoirs*], II, 148). According to A. Georgantas in his ["Historical Memoirs"] (*Parnassos*, V [1881], 849), when Metaxas proposed to the cabinet the invitation of Mavrokordatos and Kolettes, the "French" members (Palamides and Mansolas) objected on the grounds that the return of these two men would again divide the nation. See text of the letter sent by Mavrokordatos and Kolettes

Yet the breakdown of cooperation between the parties and the paralysis of coalition government seemed to be only a matter of time. Party rivalries from below were likely to intensify latent differences among the cabinet members. Party strife immediately developed in the provinces as conflicting rumors created mutual suspicions. Some individuals believed that their party leaders did not really approve of the revolution. Others regarded the coalition cabinet as a mere front for an opposing party. Office holders under the old regime feared the loss of their jobs.[4]

Differences of opinion arose within the cabinet, though they were hushed up or denied. Metaxas kept insisting that the cabinet was in complete accord, that it did not intend to remove officials, that the revolution was not "French," "English," or Napist, but national and tripartisan. He quietly attempted to prevent the captains from bringing their armed followings to Athens, where they might attempt to gain control of the assembly by force. He and the others rushed elections and hurried to convene the constituent assembly, so as to obtain a constitution and end the crisis before latent dissensions broke out into open dispute.[5]

Though without effective power, the king still enjoyed some influence for two reasons. One, he could threaten to abdicate—a frightening prospect to the moderates. Any interregnum, they realized, possibly would be a long one because suitable persons were unlikely to take on such a risky job, or if they did, to satisfy all three protecting powers. The longer conditions remained unsettled the greater the likelihood of resurgent party rivalries, intensified as they had been in 1825 by conflicting campaigns in behalf of alternate candidates for the throne. The moderates continued to believe Otho an indispensable barrier to civil strife.[6]

---

to Metaxas, dated 25 Oct. 1843o.s., agreeing to participate in cabinet meetings whenever the agenda for discussion concerned the national assembly or the maintenance of order (Demetrios A. Petrakakos, *Koinobouleutike Historia tes Hellados* [*Parliamentary History of Greece*] [Athens, 1946], II, 319). In a petition to the king on 23 Oct./4 Nov. 1843, the cabinet requested that Mavrokordatos and Kolettes attend cabinet meetings with the right to vote. The king assented and the matter was formalized through a decree of 25 Oct. 1843o.s., *Ephemeris tes Kyberneseos tou Basileiou tes Hellados* [*Government Gazette, Kingdom of Greece*], no. 36 (supplement), 16 Oct. 1843o.s. [*sic*].

[4] On the beginnings of party rivalry, see Makrygiannes [*Memoirs*], II, 146. On rumors, see Metaxas to Georgantas, Athens, 9 Sept. 1843o.s., in Georgantas ["Historical Memoirs"] *Parnassos*, v (1881), 845.

[5] *Ibid.*, 845-46. Even in this letter, which insisted on the existence of unity in the cabinet, Metaxas admitted that some differences had divided the cabinet in the early days of the revolutionary period.

[6] "I do not believe that the king will resign, as some maintain," wrote Piscatory to Guizot, Athens, 16 Sept. 1843 [*Bulletin*], XI, 237. "Those with power in Greece know that, on the person of Otho, peace and order depend," wrote Prokesch-Osten to Archduke John, Athens, 21 Nov. 1834, *Briefwechsel*, ed. Schlossar, p. 175. When two Austrian ships docked at Piraeus in November, after reports in German newspapers that Austria would send such ships so that Otho might embark if he should

The threat of abdication did not, of course, frighten the radicals, who apparently wanted just that. But if Otho remained king, as seemed increasingly likely, he would probably regain enough of his former power to take revenge on his former enemies—enough of a deterrent to be the second reason for his influence. As for the moderates, they knew that successful operation of the constitution would require Otho's cooperation. The domestic situation therefore called for some sort of *modus vivendi* between the desires of the Greek political groups and the requirements of the king.[7]

The International Picture

England, France, and Austria all supported the change from absolutism to constitutional monarchy. England believed the change desirable. France and Austria recognized it as irreversible. By supporting the revolutionary regime, all three powers hoped to prevent the revolution from going any further. All three believed that an important segment of the Napist party, in the interests of Russia, perhaps at its instigation, had hoped to depose Otho and establish an Orthodox (hence pro-Russian) king on the throne. All three feared lest a vacant throne involve Europe in endless disagreement over a successor, plunge Greece into anarchy, and release a wave of Greek irredentism strong enough to disrupt the Ottoman empire and reopen the thorny Eastern question. To avoid an international crisis in the Near East from which Russia might benefit, they sought to bring immediate stability to Greek affairs. They believed Otho essential for that stability.[8]

---

wish to abdicate, Lyons suspected that the Greek court might be behind the reports and the despatch of ships so as to pose the threat of abdication (Lyons to Aberdeen, 16 Nov. 1843, no. 138, Ser. 32, Vol. 123, Archives of the British Foreign Office, Public Record Office, London [hereafter cited as FO 32.123 and so on]).

[7] In his letter to Georgantas for instance (Athens, 9 Sept. 1843*o.s.*, in Georgantas ["Historical Memoirs"], *Parnassos*, v [1881], 845-46), Metaxas talks about the need of mediating between the king and nation.

[8] Concerning English satisfaction with the news, see the statement of Stratford Canning in a letter to Lyons (dated 2 Oct. 1843, as quoted by Stanley Lane-Poole, *Life of Stratford Canning* [London, 1888], II, 119): "It must be allowed there never was a neater revolution or one attended with less popular outrage or of personal suffering. . . . Unfortunately the best of revolutions is a fearful experiment." See also Edouard Driault and Michel Lhéritier, *Histoire Diplomatique de la Grèce de 1821 à nos Jours* (Paris, 1925), II, 248-49, which among other things contains a quotation from Lord Aberdeen, praising the Greek nation "for the manner in which it conducted itself on this important occasion," and which confirms the British interest in keeping the revolution settlement moderate.

Concerning French and Austrian belief in the irreversibility of events and their desire to keep things from going further, see the two following quotations: (1) ". . . there is nothing left to do but attempt to keep the results [of the revolution] within logical limits and guide them wisely" (Guizot to Piscatory, Paris, 29 Sept. 1843, in [*Bulletin*], XI, 252); and (2) "the only advice one can give the king is for him to limit himself so as to salvage from the shipwreck whatever can be salvaged,

Aberdeen, Guizot, and Metternich also agreed that the constitution should be a moderate one which retained wide powers for the monarch. The consensus in this case, as in the common acceptance of the revolution, was not based on political conservatism only but on the realistic consideration that Otho and his father Ludwig would only acquiesce in this kind of constitution.[9]

Ludwig received the news from Greece with indignation. Aside from concern for his son's safety and general political considerations, he feared that the new revolutionary regime might refuse to honor a personal loan he had made to the Greek government in 1836. He protested

---

because a restitution *in integrum* is impossible" (Metternich to Prokesch-Osten, Vienna, 13 Oct. 1843, in *Aus dem Nachlasse des Grafen Prokesch-Osten*, ed. Anton von Prokesch-Osten [the younger] [Vienna, 1881], II, 251, and in Petrakakos [*Parliamentary History*], II, 295).

On the fear of Napist intentions and Russia's involvement, past or future, see the following quotations: (1) "I don't believe that what took place recently [the revolution] was desired, prepared, or sought by Emperor Nicholas or his agents. I repeat what I told Kolettes. The tsar doesn't like crises [troubles]. Whether the event took place by itself or not, it is known that he [the tsar] will pursue and seek opportunites for Russian policy which is essentially as Kolettes describes it [to make Greece a satellite with a half-Russian prince on its throne]" (Guizot to Piscatory, Hotel, 28 Sept. 1843 [*Bulletin*], XI, 258, also 255); (2) "For my part, I am daily more convinced that the real Napists wanted and still want his [Otho's] downfall. In many cases, members of the higher clergy who were not strangers to the revolt have expressed an opinion on this" (Piscatory to Guizot, Athens, 19 Sept. 1843 [*Bulletin*], XI, 249); (3) "The removal of the Bavarian dynasty and the expulsion of the ruling foreigners constitute the real purpose [of this revolt]. . . . I see the revival of the old Russian idea, that of the celebrated Russian memorandum of 9 Jan. 1824, proposing the formation of principalities according to the trans-Danubian system. The Soutsoi [Russian clients] all belong to the conspiracy. Metaxas and Kallerges are merely organs. The King and Queen are completely of the opinion that the conspiracy was known, approved, even consummated by the Russian mission" (Prokesch-Osten to Metternich, Athens, 21 Sept. 1843, in *op.cit.*, ed. A. Prokesch-Osten, II, 240, and in Petrakakos, *op.cit.*, II, 291). See also Lyons (Athens, 27 Sept. 1843, no. 113, FO 32.122), although he is careful not to accuse Catacazy (21 Sept. 1843, no. 112, FO 32.122) presumably because he and Catacazy had, as all knew, been working closely together.

On the fear of the revolt's possible effect on the Eastern question, see the two following quotations: (1) ". . . success is absolutely essential, because the danger is great if we fail in this attempt [to stabilize the situation in Greece]. . . . No one can hope that Europe will [be able to] agree on the election of a new Greek king or arrive at a consensus which will correspond with our interest. And if Europe cannot agree, Greece will vanish in the midst of European disagreement" (Guizot to Piscatory, Hotel, 28 Sept. 1843, in [*Bulletin*], XI, 258); and (2) "The future urgently demands our assistance; otherwise we shall see disorders here, or the murder of the king, and a dreadful uprising throughout Turkey. . . ." (Prokesch-Osten to Metternich, Athens, 21 Sept. 1843, in *op.cit.*, ed. A. Prokesch-Osten, II, 239, and in Petrakakos, *op.cit.*, II, 291). So real was the fear, the Conference of London actually agreed to maintain Greece within her existing territorial limits so as to secure tranquility in the adjacent Turkish provinces (Driault and Lhéritier, *op.cit.*, II, 250).

[9] On Anglo-French accord on a moderate constitution for Greece, see *ibid.*, VII, 149.

privately to the powers and, for a moment, considered publicly denouncing the legations of the three protecting powers in Athens for their role in the events of 15 September. Prussia seems to have encouraged this course as a joint Bavarian-Prussian undertaking. Guizot advised, however, that Ludwig acquiesce in the *fait accompli* and remain satisfied with guarantees for a moderate constitution and preservation of the dynasty.[10]

In the meantime, Ludwig sent Prince Oettingen-Wallerstein on a special mission to the courts of London and Paris. He argued for a joint British-French pronouncement in behalf of a strong monarchical principle in the future Greek constitution. He also urged the despatch of an Anglo-French fleet to the Piraeus to secure Greek compliance. A fleet was not formally sent and the Greek assembly was never officially exhorted to draw up a conservative constitution. As Guizot warned Wallerstein, such direct action would wound Greek national feeling and might intensify any democratic tendencies already existing in Greece. But the British and French courts assured Ludwig that their legations in Athens would quietly work for a moderate constitution. They thus succeeded in winning him over to a recognition of the new situation and hoped that he would persuade Otho to accept the changed circumstances without afterthoughts or reservations.[11]

After a long silence the Russian government issued a circular letter to the chief European courts. Dated 30 October, it disavowed Catacazy for his role in "the deplorable events of September 15" and for counseling Otho to make "degrading concessions." Since the Russian government foresaw only fatal consequences, both for the prosperity of Greece and the tranquility of the Near East, the circular announced, it was withdrawing its minister from Greece until it received proof that a "real" Greek government existed, that "monarchical conditions" would prevail, and that order and stability would be restored. On 23 November Catacazy received notice of his recall and departed immediately. Persiany, secretary of the Russian legation in Athens, remained as an observer but without

[10] *Ibid.*, II, 245. On Ludwig's concern about his loan, see Bourgoing, French Minister in Bavaria, to Guizot, Munich, 5 Oct. 1843, *Gesandtschaftsberichte aus München 1814-1848*, Abt. I. *Die Berichte der französischen Gesandten*, ed. Anton Chroust, v (Munich, 1936), 5-6.

[11] On the Wallerstein mission, Wallerstein's demands, and the Anglo-French response, see Driault and Lhéritier, *Histoire*, II, 245-48. On Ludwig's desire for a naval force, see Bourgoing to Guizot, Munich, 15 Oct. 1843, *Gesandtschaftsberichte*, ed. Chroust, Abt. I, Vol. v, 9. In November 1843, Britain, France, Austria, and Russia all had ships docked at the Piraeus for apparently precautionary purposes, and Lyons did not feel it necessary to increase the British force at that time (Lyons to Aberdeen, Athens, 16 Nov. 1843, no. 138, FO 32.123). According to Lyons (Athens, 10 Nov. 1843, no. 134, FO 32.123), Gasser, Bavarian minister to Greece, informed him that Ludwig approved of Otho's not abdicating and felt that his son's position was more satisfactory then than it had been before.

being officially accredited. Russia had in effect broken off diplomatic ties with Greece.[12]

Russia was refraining from exercising any influence in Greek politics at precisely the time when France and England were intent on playing a very active role. Baron von Bray, Bavarian minister at Petersburg, attributed Russia's behavior first to Tsar Nicholas' abhorrence of constitutions, and second to the tsar's desire to silence prevailing rumors of Russia's "indecent influence" in Greece—a clear reference to Greek and European suspicions that Russia wanted to oust Otho from his throne.[13] Most probably the tsar realized that the close cooperation both between France, Britain, and Austria and between them and Otho stemmed from a common fear of Russian and Napist intentions. He probably believed that any Russian diplomatic influence in Greece at this time, regardless of its professions, would only cement that cooperation.

The Unofficial Cabinet

Actually, the collapse of royal absolutism hardly diffused real power, as one might have expected. Power remained concentrated at the top. But it was not located in the new provisional cabinet, which served only as a shadow government. With the exception of Metaxas, the members of this body were only second echelon leaders of their parties and had to take second place in party activities after the arrival of Kolettes and Mavrokordatos. Moreover, since the cabinet had received its mandate from the revolutionary conspirators, and in fact included some of them, it elicited only antipathy from the king, and hence forfeited the one qualification that European diplomacy required of any new political authority —ability to find a *modus vivendi* with the king. It should not be surprising, therefore, that actual power rested with what I have chosen to call the unofficial cabinet, consisting of the three party leaders (Mavrokordatos, Kolettes, and Metaxas) and the three active ministers in Athens (Lyons, Piscatory, and Prokesch-Osten).[14]

---

[12] Driault and Lhéritier (*Histoire*, II, 244-45) summarize the copy of the circular letter sent by Nesselrode to Kesseleff, Russian ambassador to Paris. On Catacazy's recall, see Lyons to Aberdeen, Athens, 30 Nov. 1843, no. 143, FO 32.123; also Nesselrode to Meyendorff, St. Petersburg, 1 Nov. 1843, *Lettres et papiers du Chancelier ... Nesselrode 1760-1856*, ed. A. Nesselrode (Paris, 1904-12), VIII, 222-24.

[13] Bray to Otho, St. Petersburg, 7/19 Nov. 1843, in *König Ludwig I von Bayern in seinen Briefen an seinen Sohn den könig Otto von Griechenland,* ed. Ludwig Trost (Bamberg, 1891), p. 151, and in Petrakakos [*Parliamentary History*], II, 309, n. 20.

[14] The power of the three ministers lay in their willingness to act in unison, especially the first two, which is attested by Piscatory to Guizot, Athens, 19 Sept. 1843, in [*Bulletin*], XI, 249, and by Eynard to Rev. Jonas King, Geneva, 17 Oct. 1843, a copy of which Lyons enclosed in his despatch of 5 Nov. 1843, no. 132, FO 32.123. As for the role of Prokesch-Osten, see his remark in a previously unpublished letter to Metternich (6 Nov. 1843, in Petrakakos [*Parliamentary History*], II, 350): "The king has the most influential men with him. I want to keep the road clear between these

Since absence from Greece kept them from being involved in the plotting of the revolution, Mavrokordatos and Kolettes were, as publicly acknowledged leaders of their respective parties, the only Greeks of widespread political influence who were not the object of royal resentment. There is reason to believe that, on receiving news of their recall, they deliberately postponed their return so as to escape such involvement. Certainly they knew about the plot. As early as the fall of 1841, Makrygiannes revealed the existence of a plot to Mavrokordatos and swore him to secrecy. On 29 August 1843, Regas Palamides wrote to Kolettes, expressing his "fears" of a general revolution, and urged Kolettes to return to Greece by the end of September. An even more interesting bit of evidence is provided by a curious letter which Kolettes sent to Mavrokordatos. It clearly indicates, through cryptic language, that the two men were discussing the question of radical reform (probably a constitution) and the feasibility of using force to secure it. Obviously they were discussing real possibilities, not just academic hypotheses, which indicates that they knew what was in preparation in Athens. Mavrokordatos had obviously raised the questions, and Kolettes as usual wrote enigmatically so as to avoid a definite stand either way. One of the patients mentioned was obviously the king: the second was anyone's guess:

> Thinking as a doctor, you proposed an excellent therapeutic method, but when the sick man insists in not wanting to be bled, then what should happen? You will say, force him to submit to your treatment, but with whose hands, I ask, can I force him when mine alone are inadequate? With the hands of foreign doctors or foreign men, but those hands you know as well as I do. With the hands of native doctors, or native men? But those hands you know better than anyone else. Besides, the inflammation is not general only but also local, and this being the case, it induced decay in one place of the organism, such decay as to require for rehabilitation I don't know what. Then what should the poor doctor do? My dear brother, the patient is not one but two. The illness is frightful and requires not only mine but your medical knowledge and that of others too. Do you wish to agree and roll up your sleeves. Then I hope something can be done so as to save both. P.S. You perhaps wonder why I'm still here. I'm not the cause. As soon as he [?] learns, he will write and tell you, but from Athens.[15]

men and him." Makrygiannes ([*Memoirs*], ii, 158) cited Mavrokordatos, Lontos, and Kallerges as "the children of foreigners, [the men] who flattered the king."

[15] Paris, 7 Aug. 1843, no. 6806, Vol. 23 [1843], Mavrokordatos Archive, General State Archives, Athens. Concerning Makrygiannes' revelation of the plot to Mavrokordatos, see [*Memoirs*], ii, 120. Regas' letter to Kolettes is quoted in Petrakakos [*Parliamentary History*], ii, 284.

The Greek legations in foreign capitals had been abolished early in the summer of 1843 for ostensible reasons of economy. By the end of June (Kolettes to Mavrokordatos, Paris, 27 June 1840, no. 6760, Vol. 43 [1843], MA), Kolettes had received

Otho recognized the importance of Mavrokordatos and asked Prokesch-Osten, who had already assumed the role of mediator between the king and the Greek political leaders, to assist in erasing whatever bitterness Mavrokordatos might have still felt from the episode of 1841. On his return to Greece, Mavrokordatos replied to Prokesch as follows:

> I told the king two years ago that I am his faithful subject. I repeat that again today. But what was sufficient then is no longer enough. Our duty today is to introduce a prudent and workable constitution with as great a participation of the monarchical factor as possible, to dissolve the Philorthodox and revolutionary plans [presumably for deposing Otho], and to inspire in the nation confidence in the future and in our neighbors trust in us. For each of these aims we must surround the king with respect and veneration. I hope we may succeed. Without King Otho, Greece is lost. That is my belief. At such moments I do not consider past dissatisfaction, which has been forgotten.[16]

Kolettes, who returned on 30 October, also assumed much the same position. For years he had opposed a constitution as premature, and continued to do so, even when others who had previously shared his qualms finally became convinced that a constitution was the only way to save Greece from falling over the precipice. Mavrokordatos had, at some point since the failure of his program in 1841, come out in favor of a constitution, apparently because he saw no other way to make Otho share power. Kolettes wrote to protest:

---

official notice of the decision and instructions to leave. When he wrote Mavrokordatos on 28 July 1843, still from Paris (no. 6795, Vol. 43 [1843], MA, and published in Petrakakos, *op.cit.*, II, 325-28), he felt compelled to explain his continued presence there, admitted his government's instructions to depart at once, and then described an itinerary that was a roundabout way home, rationalized in terms of visiting communities of the Greek diaspora. Then in the letter quoted above, he writes in such a way as to indicate the existence of very *special*, very *secret* reasons why he is taking such a long time to get home. Lyons reveals (Athens, 31 July 1843, no. 86, FO 32.122) that Guizot requested Otho to allow Kolettes to remain in Paris as envoy and that Kolettes himself wished to remain. In a second letter (Athens, 6 Aug. 1843, no. 88, FO 32.122) Lyons reveals that Otho denied the request, complied with Kolettes' request to postpone his return, but discontinued his salary beyond 10 August.

There is no such evidence for Mavrokordatos' deliberate stalling, but the fact is that he got to Greece only after the revolution and that the reasons for stalling were as compelling in his case as they were in Kolettes'.

16 Prokesch to Metternich, Athens, 6 Oct. 1843, in *Aus dem Nachlasse*, ed. A. Prokesch-Osten, II, 247, and in Petrakakos [*Parliamentary History*], II, 294. In the same letter, just prior to quoting Mavrokordatos, Prokesch-Osten wrote: "For the fate of the king, the stance of Mavrokordatos will be decisive. If he comes to terms with the Philorthodox, the king is lost, even before supporting news comes from Europe. The royal couple know this well and they asked me to help dissolve the bitterness which Mavrokordatos probably still nurses."

. . . all those in Athens, thinking they know everything, insist that because you didn't propose a constitution [in 1841], you didn't satisfy the Crown and you *did* displease the nation. And all considered you, as they also think me, a reactionary, one insisting on his old habits, one believing that the only way to do anything is through one's old friends and associates. . . . Now you believe a constitution is the only heroic medicine along with dedication of the king to the Greeks and dismissal of the Bavarians. Can these things be effected against the will of the king and the nation? Do you believe that the grace of the holy spirit enlightened during the period of these two years [since the Mavrokordatos episode] the mind of the king and nation, and prepared them for the acceptance of such a step? Conditions, it is true, have become worse, so much worse now that we have over our heads the London Conference as well, the weight of which makes us often talk nonsense. But do you think that the worsening of circumstances removed the factors which prevented you two years ago from proposing a constitution? How much concerning the ethical corruption of the Athenian Greeks did you not tell me as we ate pilaf together in the Rue d'Anjou? And when you arrived in Athens, you wrote me that you found that corruption even greater than you had imagined. Do you think that now this depravity no longer exists? Do you think that the word Constitution is no longer proposed for self-seeking reasons? Do you think that rank, medals, places, and ministries, etc., don't change the opinions of men, and induce them to call the constitution (*syntagma*) a chaffing (*synkama*) instead? Besides, do you think that a change has taken place in the disposition of the king and that the king is no longer the man you became acquainted with in Athens? If his disposition is the same and the ethical depravity of the others also the same, why do you now make a proposal, which you did not consider adequate and wise to make then? And if those things have changed, don't you see in such a change the fact of a miracle? But such miracles don't occur in our times.

Still thinking a constitution premature, Kolettes was naturally quite willing to make the coming constitution, inevitable as it now was, as conservative as possible. He believed the revolution a Napist-Russian plot to turn Greece into a Russian principality. So anxious was he to thwart any such intention that he was willing to make concessions to the king and collaborate with the powers. His lukewarmness toward the revolution must have constituted a political asset in his relations with the king.[17]

[17] Kolettes to Mavrokordatos, Paris, 28 July 1843, no. 6795, Vol. 43 [1843], Mavrokordatos Archive, published in Petrakakos [*Parliamentary History*], II, 325-28.

In a dialogue with Guizot, which Guizot reports in his *Mémoires pour servir à l'Histoire de mon Temps* ([Paris, n.d.], VII, 281-83) and which he reported to Piscatory (Hotel, 28 Sept. 1843, in [*Bulletin*], XI, 255-57), Kolettes said, "The revolution

Owing to their conservative views, royal favor, and the acknowledged leadership of their parties, Mavrokordatos and Kolettes received the backing of Lyons, Piscatory, and Prokesch-Osten. In order to maintain the concord of the three parties and retain his personal influence, Metaxas joined this combination, but only as a junior partner because he lacked royal favor and the diplomatic support which Russia would probably have given him if it had not pulled out of Greece.[18] In the meantime, Kallerges, a radical who now realized that Otho would probably remain, decided to do the expedient thing. Makrygiannes wrote bitterly:

Kallerges, who was at the head of everything with the help of the ambassadors—he also took some 800,000 drachmas from the government—went over to the foreigners and forgot the 3rd [15th] of September. He, Lontos, and others proved turncoats.[19]

---

is not a spontaneous and national movement. It is a Russian affair. Russia never wanted anything but to make Greece into a state like Wallachia and Moldavia, a principality with a Greek prince who is half-Russian. I saw the beginning of this attempt in 1821. It [Russia] has never stopped since. The philorthodox society is its organ." Lyons reported (Athens, 21 Oct. 1843, no. 125, FO 32.123), "Letters from Paris state Coletti has been in a gloomy state of mind ever since he heard of the Revolution in Greece, and I understand that his own letters, to say the least, betray lukewarmness." Piscatory (Athens, 16 Sept. 1843, in [Bulletin], xi, 241) considered Kolettes' lack of participation in the plot an asset.

On the conservative constitution that Kolettes and Mavrokordatos desired, see a letter from Eynard to Otho, 27 Oct. 1843, in La Restauration Hellénique d'après la correspondance de Jean-Gabriel Eynard, ed. Edouard Chapuisat (Paris & Geneve, 1924), p. 214: "You will see, Your Highness, that Mavrokordatos and Kolettes will be the real supports of your prerogatives and that both will come to some agreement as to how to moderate the ideas of the inexperienced men, who unwisely want a constitution exaggeratedly free."

[18] According to Prokesch-Osten, in a previously unpublished letter to Metternich (7 Dec. 1843, in Petrakakos [Parliamentary History], ii, 340-50), as long as Mavrokordatos and Kolettes were united, Metaxas could not separate himself from them. In a letter to Archduke John (22 Dec. 1843, as quoted in Briefwechsel, ed. Schlossar, pp. 182-85) Prokesch-Osten wrote: "Mavrokordatos is honest but not as strong as he appears on the surface. Kolettes is weaker yet and Metaxas weakest of all. To bind the two and prevent a break is the greatest problem of Mavrokordatos, which he has done with great dexterity. . . ." Prokesch-Osten does not specify what he means by "strong" and "weak" but he may very well mean the strength of each in the assembly.

[19] Makrygiannes [Memoirs], ii, 155. Lyons (Athens, 18 Oct. 1843, no. 119, FO 32.123) comments as follows: "In the meantime Kalergi has dined at Court and Brassier [the Prussian envoy, who was ardently pro-Othonian] and he meet in society on the same terms as before the Revolution. For my part, I thought this attempt to obtain access to the Palace ill-timed, and I expressed my opinion that inconvenience would arise from it, and that it was wholly unnecessary after the solemn assurance which Catacazy, Piscatory, and I had received from Kalergi . . . that the King's Person would be held sacred. A majority of my colleagues, however, was of a different opinion and I considered it right not to separate from them." See also the Kolokotrones Memorandum [Munich], 3 Nov. 1843, in Petrakakos [Parliamentary History], ii, 335.

He made his peace with the court and joined forces with the Mavrokordatos-Kolettes-Metaxas combination. Hence the unofficial cabinet came to control the only significant military force in Athens, where the constituent assembly was scheduled to meet. The objectives of the unofficial cabinet were twofold: (1) to keep the king from acting recklessly, and (2) to persuade the constituent assembly to accept a moderate constitution.

2. POLITICAL DIVISIONS AND RIVALRIES

The Early Form of Alignments

The sources reveal the existence of three distinct camps during the early weeks of the interim period, each corresponding to a different attitude with regard to the revolution.[20] An ostensibly small and discredited group of men, closely associated with the former regime and now threatened with dismissal from office, the *rightists* still favored royal absolutism and disapproved of the revolution. During September, they began to meet at the home of Samourkases, a close associate of Chrestides in the "French" party. Skarlatos Rossetos, a counselor in the ministry of foreign affairs, openly declared that the revolution must be overturned. A Catholic-Armenian doorkeeper of the palace, said to be carrying two pistols on his person, went about threatening to kill Kallerges. Gennaios Kolokotrones, perhaps because his followers had failed to win the assembly elections in his native eparchy of Karytaina, perhaps from misguided loyalty to the king, made no secret of his opposition to the revolutionary change. Indeed, he was in contact with Vasos Mavrovouniotes and other military captains opposed to the revolution (Demodoulias, Tsouras, and Kasomoules among them) who offered to come to Otho's aid with troops. By notifying Otho of such offers to undo the revolution, Kolokotrones was encouraging the king to go back on his promises. But, as Kolokotrones himself asserts, Otho refused to resort to such a device and asked Kolokotrones to restrain the ardor of these counterrevolutionary elements.[21]

[20] Concerning the two extreme positions, see Eynard to Jonas King, Geneva, 17 Oct. 1843 (a copy of which Lyons enclosed in his despatch of 5 Nov. 1843, no. 132, FO 32.123): "that which has ideas too republican and that which would want a reaction in the contrary sense."

[21] Concerning the smallness of this group, yet its potentiality for growth, see Piscatory's letter of 16 Sept. 1843 ([*Bulletin*], XI, 237): "Those who don't want what happened and those who want more are few. . . . Indeed that party [the royal party] does not exist, but it can very easily develop among those whose hopes will be disappointed, and certainly this is a time when everyone has great hopes." Perhaps the segment of public opinion which this group hoped to tap was that which Prokesch-Osten mentioned in a previously unpublished letter to Metternich (7 Dec. 1843, in Petrakakos [*Parliamentary History*], II, 349)—the group which still doubted the readiness of Greece for a constitution, the group which had wanted "a pure monarchy with administrative guarantees." Concerning the activities of the rightists just after the revolution, see Mavrokordatos' letter to his wife, Athens, 1/13 Oct. 1843, in

The *moderates* accepted the revolution and defended Otho so long as he remained willing to rule constitutionally. Their position, it seems, gained the support of most politically articulate Greeks, in part because this alternative promised reform without violence or anarchy, in part because the powers in conjunction with the party leaders declared their support of the king as constitutional monarch. Lyons, the British ambassador, wrote his government that Mavrokordatos was:

convinced that the great majority of the nation, from calculation of the dangers and difficulties of endeavouring to change the dynasty, rather than from any feelings in favour of the present king, is for Otho and the Constitution, provided Otho agree to such a Constitution as will give the ministers the means of carrying on the government, without being thwarted by the indecision, procrastination, and jealousy of interference which has hitherto caused so much evil. In short, they are willing that Otho shall reign with all proper prerogatives and regal appurtenances, but they do not think Him capable of governing.[22]

The *leftists*, the antidynastic group, had miscalculated in believing that the king would abdicate rather than acquiesce in revolutionary demands for a constitution. As Nicholas Dragoumes wrote:

The rest [of the leftist Septembrists] became transfixed when they learned of the king's acceptance because, expecting a sure abdication, they had only provided for a regent chosen from among those in Athens [he does not specify but rumors had it that the man was Michael Soutsos]. They were unprepared for any other possibilities. So much confusion was there over the formation of a new cabinet that Metaxas, the leader of the conspirators, received only a secondary ministry whereas he should have received direction of the interior.

Frightened moderates, who identified them as Napists or Philorthodox and believed them in command of a majority of the Septembrist conspirators, probably exaggerated their numbers and influence. It seems fairly certain that Metaxas at least, and those he controlled, would always have preferred to keep the king if the king would acquiesce in a constitution. Few as they might have been, they were rendered dangerous by the widespread unpopularity of the king which they could always exploit if they chose.[23]

---

ibid., II, 320. Gennaios Kolokotrones, *Apomnemoneumata* (*Cheirographon Deuteron 1821-1862*) [*Memoirs* (*Second Manuscript 1821-1862*)], ed. Emmanuel Protopsaltes (Athens, 1961), 88 (hereafter cited as [*Memoirs II*]).

[22] Lyons to Aberdeen, Athens, 10 Oct. 1843, no. 116, FO 32.123. Or, "It is certain that yesterday [the day of the revolution], if he [the king] was not led to the Piraeus and embarked, it was because of respect for Europe and even more, fear of anarchy," wrote Piscatory to Guizot, Athens, 16 Sept. 1843, in [*Bulletin*], XI, 237.

[23] Nicholas Dragoumes, *Historikai Anamneseis* [*Historical Reminiscences*], 2nd

By itself, neither of the extreme groups could upset the results of the revolution. But a counterrevolutionary attempt by the rightists, though doomed to failure, might give the leftists the excuse they needed to depose the king on grounds of his bad faith. In this connection, the attitude of Otho caused the moderates their greatest worry. His personal ties with the rightists and his obvious bitterness over the revolution aroused suspicions that he might encourage a rightist coup or evoked fears that the public would attribute this design to him.[24]

---

edn. (Athens, 1879), II, 90-97.

On the fewness of their numbers, see Piscatory to Guizot, Athens, 16 Sept. 1843 ([Bulletin], XI, 237) and the quotation in n. 21 above; also his remark in a letter to Guizot, written a few days later (19 Sept. 1843 [Bulletin], XI, 249): "For my part, I am daily more convinced that the actual Napists wanted and still want his [Otho's] expulsion." On the use of the terms "Septembrists" and "Philorthodox" to denote this leftist group, and their alleged desire to overthrow the dynasty, see also Prokesch-Osten to Archduke John, 21 Sept. 1843 ("They wanted more but they did not succeed"), 21 Oct. 1843, and 6 Nov. 1843, all three in Briefwechsel, ed. Schlossar, pp. 164-66, 169-71; also Prokesch-Osten to Metternich, 26 Oct. 1843, in Aus dem Nachlasse, ed. A. Prokesch-Osten, II, 253, and in Petrakakos [Parliamentary History], II, 295.

For evidence that Otho knew about this group and feared it, see Lyons' despatch to Aberdeen, dated 27 Sept. 1843 (no. 113, FO 32.122): "Prokesch-Osten, who has frequent private audiences with King Otho, called on me two days ago and said that the King . . . was alarmed by reports of the existence of a Philorthodox party which intended to dictate to him the choice of being immediately baptized or of abdicating, and that the King was anxious to know whether the British and French missions would discountenance such projects, and in case of need protect him with . . . ships at the Piraeus." As Prokesch-Osten pointed out to his government in a despatch of 21 Sept. 1843 (in op.cit., ed. A. Prokesch-Osten, II, 244, and in Petrakakos, op.cit., II, 294), the queen was without hope that they could last on the Greek throne for more than eight weeks.

[24] Concerning the anxieties of the unofficial cabinet with regard to the attitude and behavior of Otho, see the following remarks:

Piscatory wrote to Guizot on 16 Sept. 1843 (in [Bulletin], XI, 237); "I don't believe, as some do, that he [the King] will abdicate. What one may doubt is whether he will completely submit. Already men whom he thinks he can trust [rightists] have been invited one by one to the palace. A Zenos [Tzenos] whom Lyons justly accused of committing brutalities in Acarnania [as a high official of the gendarmes], was commissioned to exercise his influence over the gendarmerie which, held back by its leaders from participating in the revolution, might be won over to the so-called royal party. . . . The king will delude himself on what may happen and the least blunder may lead to the idea which has become acceptable to everyone [his deposal]."

Lyons wrote Aberdeen on 21 Oct. 1843 (no. 123, FO 32.123): "Mary [Belgian chargé d'affaires] says . . . that it was too evident that He [the King] was acting a part, and this, I am sorry to observe, is the opinion of most persons who have access to Him, and particularly of the Ministers, Councilors of State, and Heads of Departments to whom the King made an address on the 14th instant." See also Lyons to Aberdeen, Athens, 5 Nov. 1843, no. 133, FO 32.123.

Even Prokesch-Osten, who was most sympathetic toward Otho, wrote Metternich on 21 Sept. 1843 (in Aus dem Nachlasse, ed. A. Prokesch-Osten, II, 243, and in

On the evening of 9 October, what looked like an attempt to prepare a rightist coup occurred. The palace received word that civil strife was about to break out in Athens, which was in the midst of elections, and that the military garrison of Athens was planning to intervene.[25] Through D. Mavromichales, Otho sent word to Lontos, Lyons, and Piscatory. In the meantime, he sent Kolokotrones, still his aide-de-camp, to the barracks to urge, in the king's name, obedience and noninvolvement. Kolokotrones arrived to find everything quiet and all sleeping. Instead of withdrawing unnoticed, he awakened the subaltern officers and requested the despatch of two companies to the palace. Just then Kallerges arrived and forced Kolokotrones to withdraw.[26]

Lontos and Kallerges, followed by the public generally, interpreted this incident as evidence, first that Kolokotrones was attempting to win over the Athens garrison for a countercoup, and second that the palace had become the seat of this intrigue. Otho only raised further suspicion about his own involvement by refusing to grant the cabinet its demand for the temporary exile of Kolokotrones. Only after Lyons and Piscatory intervened were the queen and her grand matron able to obtain the acquiescence of the king in what he personally considered an ignoble act against a loyal adherent.[27]

Petrakakos [*Parliamentary History*], II, 293): "If it were someone other than Otho, if his wife were king, I would not worry. But even with him, something can be done."

[25] Prokesch-Osten, in a letter of 21 Oct. 1843 (*Briefwechsel*, ed. Schlossar, pp. 169-71) to Archduke John, represented the event as a deliberate attempt of the leftists to compromise the king and hence realize their objective of ousting him. Gennaios Kolokotrones [*Memoirs II*], p. 89.

[26] Mavrokordatos to his wife, Athens, 1/13 Oct. 1843, and Kolokotrones memorandum [Munich], 3 Nov. 1843, both in Petrakakos [*Parliamentary History*], II, 320 and 335 respectively. Lyons to Stratford Canning, Athens, 13 Oct. 1843, a copy of which was enclosed with despatch no. 118, FO 32.123. Driault and Lhéritier, *Histoire*, II, 245-46. Gennaios Kolokotrones [*Memoirs II*], p. 89.

[27] That the public interpreted the Kolokotrones action as an abortive countercoup in which the king was implicated, see Lyons to Canning, Athens, 13 Oct. 1843 (no. 118, FO 32.123) and the Kolokotrones Memorandum [Munich] (3 Nov. 1843, in Petrakakos [*Parliamentary History*], II, 335), which contains the following interpretation: Lontos and Kallerges "took the occasion to circulate the slander that the King wanted through me to make a revolution . . . which would nullify the results of 15 September. This reached many people who believed it. The cabinet met in extraordinary session and demanded that the king exile me within two hours, otherwise they could not guarantee either his own person or public order; also that otherwise the king would have to abdicate, etc. From this one can infer that either it [the cabinet] was striking against me personally or more likely, that it sought the chief aim of the revolution of 15 September, which failed, namely the removal of the king, a consequence which it had believed certain." Gennaios Kolokotrones ([*Memoirs II*], p. 89) of course denies this interpretation of his action.

Concerning Otho's obstinacy, the intervention of Lyons and Piscatory, and the influence of the queen, see the above-cited letter of Lyons to Canning, along with Driault and Lhéritier, *Histoire*, II, 246, and G. Kolokotrones, *op.cit.*, p. 90.

The provisional government ordered Kolokotrones to leave for Naples that very day (10 October). An angry crowd, from whom he barely escaped, prevented him from embarking at the Piraeus. In the dead of night, he secretly got on board a Greek steamship awaiting him at Phaleron Bay. Kolokotrones violated the government's directives and surprised virtually everyone when he appeared at Munich and received the cordial welcome of Ludwig.[28]

In a memorandum addressed either to King Ludwig or Crown Prince Maximilian, he urged steps for the recall of the ministers who had advised Otho to make concessions on 15 September. He implied that Gasser, the Bavarian minister to Greece, should be replaced and urged that money be sent immediately to Otho. It has been argued that he went much further and urged Ludwig's assistance in staging a royal countercoup. Athens attributed the unfavorable newspaper articles in the *Augsburg Gazette* to Kolokotrones' inspiration and suspected that Otho had secretly ordered Kolokotrones to Munich to round up foreign assistance. Independently of each other, Mavrokordatos and Gasser advised Otho to remove public suspicions by officially dismissing Kolokotrones as a royal aide. Once more Otho resisted until the queen again stepped in. In the meantime, through the intervention of England and France, Ludwig sent Kolokotrones to Naples, his original destination.[29]

Once the danger from the right diminished, the threat from the left decreased accordingly. The strong diplomatic and tripartisan support, which saved Otho from several political blunders, made his abdication increasingly improbable. Abandoned by Kallerges and with no hope of support from Russia, the leftists could only resort to force or, since royal

[28] Kolokotrones Memorandum [Munich], 3 Nov. 1843, and Mavrokordatos to his wife, Athens, 1/13 Oct. 1843, both in Petrakakos [*Parliamentary History*], II, 335-36 and 320 respectively; Gennaios Kolokotrones [*Memoirs II*], p. 90; and Lyons to Canning, Athens, 13 Oct. 1843, no. 118, FO 32.123. So compromised did Mavrokordatos believe the king's position to be that he recommended that the king formally assemble all the high officials of state (cabinet, Council of State, holy synod, etc.) and solemnly proclaim his espousal of the revolution and his belief that any attempt to overthrow the revolution constituted an act of treason. See also an account of the event and the king's speech, which Petrakakos (*op.cit.*, II, 309, n. 20) found in the Vienna archives of the foreign ministry. For reports of the French minister in Bavaria concerning Kolokotrones' activities in Munich, see Bourgoing to Guizot, Munich, 21 Nov. 1843 and 28 Nov. 1843, *Gesandtschaftsberichte*, ed. Chroust, Abt. I, Vol. v, 19-20, 21-22. In the same volume, see excerpts from similar Bourgoing reports of 31 Oct., 4 Nov., and 24 Nov. in footnotes, pp. 12 and 20.

[29] Kolokotrones Memorandum [Munich], 3 Nov. 1843, in Petrakakos [*Parliamentary History*], II, 333-37. The person addressed is not explicitly mentioned in this document, but in the text the vocative "Your Highness" is once used. Petrakakos (*ibid.*, II, 333) states that "King [*sic*] Maximilian II" is being addressed, but it is just as possible that Ludwig is. Concerning further public suspicions about Otho's responsibility for Kolokotrones' presence in Bavaria, and further intervention to secure the dismissal of Kolokotrones from the king's service, see Lyons to Aberdeen, Athens, 5 Nov. 1843, no. 133, 10 Nov. 1843, no. 136, and 21 Nov. 1843, no. 142, all three in FO 32.123; also Driault and Lhéritier, *Histoire*, II, 246.

power was Othonian, try to keep it as limited as possible in the future constitution. Many of them Napists, one-time absolutists, then moderate constitutionalists, they now became exponents of a liberal constitution.

The Later Form of Alignments

By early November, elected representatives to the constituent assembly began to assemble in Athens.[30] No one who had lived through the national assemblies of the Revolutionary period could ignore the possibility that this assembly might follow the old cycle—political schism, the establishment of a rival assembly, then resort to arms. That is why the provisional government showed such vigilance in preventing representatives from bringing armed clienteles with them.[31]

[30] The decree for a national assembly, dated 3 Sept. 1843*o.s.* ([*Government Gazette*], 3 Sept. 1843*o.s.*), specified that the national assembly had to meet within a month of the revolution. The only provision it made for the handling of elections was a vague statement that "the last electoral law published prior to 1833" would apply. According to Petrakakos ([*Parliamentary History*], II, 355, n. 2), most communities followed the electoral law of 1822, supplemented by a law promulgated in 1829 by Kapodistrias for the fourth assembly of Argos, and all elections took place in full freedom. But, as Lyons pointed out (10 Oct. 1843, no. 116, FO 32.123) and Makrygiannes confirmed ([*Memoirs*], II, 148), the redistribution in population (greater concentration in the towns) since the 1820s made these laws somewhat anachronistic. Moreover, there is evidence that the handling of the elections was pretty much a matter of improvisation, that some disorders did occur (Metaxas to Georgantas, Athens, 9 Sept. 1843*o.s.* ["Historical Memoirs"], *Parnassos*, V [1881], 845), and that in some districts each party held its own elections and disputed the validity of others, so that elections were often duplicated or triplicated (Makrygiannes, *op.cit.*, II, 148-49, who blames Kolettes and Palamides for these abuses, and Prokesch-Osten to Archduke John, 6 Nov. 1843, in *Briefwechsel*, ed. Schlossar, pp. 174-77). Because of winter conditions, which delayed the elected delegates in getting to Athens, the cabinet postponed the opening of the national assembly for a week (Lyons to Aberdeen, Athens, 16 Nov. 1843, no. 138, FO 32.123, and Petrakakos, *op.cit.*, II, 356, n. 4).

Writing at the commencement of elections, Piscatory commented as follows (Athens, 16 Sept. 1843, in [*Bulletin*], XI, 248): "They are beginning to be occupied with elections. The battle will be between the Napist and the Constitutionalist parties. Each group appears and declares the same ideas, but each advertises his party label, so that qualified men will probably be eliminated by the elections. The electoral law is still confused and electoral limits unclearly defined, so that no one can predict the probable results. The Constitutionalists think the result assured, but they will do very well to remain energetic. The Napist party is well organized."

Writing after the election returns were in, Lyons commented as follows (Athens, 16 Nov. 1843, no. 138, FO 32.123): "Competent judges in whom I have confidence express themselves satisfied with the result of the elections, and with the prospect of a suitable constitution being agreed to by the Assembly." See also nn. 33 and 35 below for some estimates of the assembly's composition.

[31] For a case of how closely the country came to civil war, see Makrygiannes [*Memoirs*], II, 160-61. On government vigilance, see Metaxas to Georgantas, Athens, 9 Sept. 1843*o.s.* ["Historical Memoirs"], *Parnassos*, V [1881], 845-46; Prokesch-Osten to Archduke John, 6 Nov. 1843, *Briefwechsel*, ed. Schlossar, pp. 174-77; and Lyons to Aberdeen, Athens, 21 Oct. 1843, no. 125, 26 Oct. 1843, no. 126, 16 Nov. 1843, no. 138, all FO 32.123.

The imminence of constitutional deliberations provided a new framework for political alliances. Dissident groups could organize parliamentary blocs instead of resorting to armed conspiracy. Since the proceedings of the constituent assembly would presuppose both a constitutional and an Othonian regime, the existing groups would have to choose different grounds for dissent. In these terms, two basic groupings are discernible. One—roughly equivalent to the moderates but encompassing the rightists who bowed to the inevitable—worked for a constitution which secured a strong monarchy. The other, including mostly Septembrist leftists, favored a more liberal constitution with wide powers for the people and a very restricted monarchy, mostly because of their hostility to Otho and their desire to secure themselves against his future vengeance.[32]

Though legally they had every right to do so, delegates to the assembly did not formulate competing public programs for a constitution or openly organize themselves into voting blocs. But voting blocs there were. At least three can be discerned over a hundred years later—two attested by Makrygiannes and the third discernible by inference. One consisted of thirty delegates, organized by Regas Palamides, Kriezotes, Theodore Grivas, Petsales, and Kalliphronas, all members of the "French" party. Makrygiannes organized the second, in a manner which he himself describes in his memoirs. In December, after periodically collecting delegates at his home for private meetings, he circulated among some sixty-three of them an oath which effected little more than a solemn commitment to collaborate as a group before casting votes in the assembly.[33]

It is reasonable to regard as a third bloc the persistent majorities,

[32] This division is attested to by the Kolokotrones Memorandum [Munich], 3 Nov. 1843, in Petrakakos [*Parliamentary History*], II, 334-35: "In Athens, a division developed for the following reason: The well-thinking and important people agreed secretly that the constitution ought to be a moderate one which would satisfy the honor of the throne and the needs of the country, and that it ought to be voted that the children of the king, though not the king himself, belong to the Orthodox faith, that [in the event of childlessness?] the king ought to adopt a son of Prince Luitpold [Otho's brother] as a successor, in which case the son ought to come to Greece to be raised as a Greek and a member of the Greek faith. . . . The other group opted for a very liberal constitution . . . they deceived the people into thinking that a liberal constitution consists in the reduction of expenses, the distribution of land, promotions, and salary raises. Some from this group were representatives in the national assembly."

In the early part of this interim period, there were apparently some groups which planned to use the assembly as a court to try the king or as a lever to force his conversion to Orthodoxy (see Prokesch-Osten to Metternich, 21 Sept. 1843, in *Aus dem Nachlasse*, ed. A. Prokesch-Osten, II, 240, and in Petrakakos, *op.cit.*, II, 291).

[33] On the first bloc, see Makrygiannes [*Memoirs*], II, 156-58, one section in particular: "Palamides, Kriezotes, Grivas, Petsales, and other smart alecs formed one part. They wanted one chamber, no senate. This was not due to conviction but so that anarchy would result. They commanded *about* thirty votes." On his own bloc of votes in the assembly, see *ibid.*, II, 156, also the text of the oath itself and the editor's note, p. 156. Gennaios Kolokotrones ([*Memoirs II*], p. 90) asserts the existence of another bloc, consisting of all the Peloponnesian representatives and acting according to his instructions (though he himself was not a representative), but this is highly doubtful.

which the Mavrokordatos-Kolettes-Metaxas combination secured, except on specific issues where a minority bloc had the weight of public opinion on its side. But this bloc was a type of coalition between subgroups, just as its leadership was. As the final vote on the senatorial issue reveals, without the support of Metaxas, Mavrokordatos and Kolettes seem to have commanded only a shaky majority or perhaps only the largest minority in the assembly.[34]

This situation reveals that votes in the assembly seldom ran along party lines.[35] The Mavrokordatos-Kolettes-Metaxas combination probably accounts for this because, as we shall see in the next section, when a satisfactory issue or adequate leadership presented itself, "Russian" and "French" groups within the assembly asserted themselves. If this hypothesis is correct, it shows the overriding influence of the individual party leader, although his position did not remain totally unchallenged.

The Program and Strategy of the Unofficial Cabinet

The unofficial cabinet was quick to take the initiative. It had a plan for the sort of constitution it wanted and devised a strategy to secure the support of the constituent assembly.[36] Much of the plan received its for-

[34] See n. 91 below.

[35] Piscatory classified the delegates, according to three-party affiliations, as follows: Napists, 80; "English," 50; "French," 100; and unclassified, 30 (Driault and Lhéritier, Histoire, II, 251). As Driault and Lhéritier were quick to point out, "The distinction was absolutely arbitrary, as the immediate future was to prove"; that is, they were referring to the fact that votes seldom ran along party lines.

There were other lines along which votes might divide and redivide. One is indicated by Petrakakos ([Parliamentary History], II, 364, n. 11): lots of individualists, each with his own following, "about thirty military leaders and as many more political leaders." The other is indicated by both Driault and Lhéritier, op.cit., II, 253, and Petrakakos, op.cit., II, 418, as quoted from Elpis, 12 Feb. 1844o.s.): regional blocs, such as twenty delegates from Mane (greatly overrepresented in terms of population), and some forty heterochthons; that is, representatives of the refugee colonies in Greece or of Greek irredenta in the Ottoman empire (Petrakakos says "thirty-two").

As for the exact total number of delegates in the assembly, Petrakakos (ibid., II, 355, n. 2) states: "Nowhere did we find an exact answer." Those who actually affixed their signatures to the constitutional document were 239, so there were probably at times a few more than this.

[36] As early as 19 Sept. 1843, Piscatory wrote Guizot ([Bulletin], XI, 184) that Lyons and he had spoken and "agreed completely on what the Greek constitution ought to be." The continued agreement between their governments was sufficient to overcome any personal rivalry between them. As regards the agreement among members of the other segment of the unofficial cabinet, Lyons announced in a letter of 16 Nov. 1832 (no. 138, FO 32.123) that the ministers were agreed on the nature of the constitution they would propose to Otho and that there were no divergences between them and the king on points already discussed. In a second letter of 30 Nov. 1843 (no. 145, FO 32.123) he wrote that the king and his ministers had agreed on the following points: (1) the king would have the same prerogatives as secured to the throne by the French constitution, (2) Orthodoxy should be the state religion with full toleration of other faiths, (3) a two-chamber

mulation outside of Greece, through negotiations between the British and French governments on the one hand and Wallerstein on the other, conducted largely in the light of Otho's and Ludwig's demands. By the end of November, they had agreed on a set of provisions.[37]

Six of these are actually reported. Three related to the royal prerogatives of (1) calling or dissolving the legislature, whose assent to all tax and budgetary matters would be required, (2) appointing, transferring, or dismissing all public officials, civil or military, and (3) equal participation with the legislature in initiating and vetoing legislation. Two provisions governed the nature of the legislative body: (4) two-chambered, one chamber elective, the other hereditary or by royal appointment for life, and (5) annual, possibly only biennial, sessions. One provision (6) related to the franchise, which it restricted by a property qualification. Clearly, the program committed the powers to a conservative constitution, with the balance between Crown and nation in favor of the former.[38]

As members of the unofficial cabinet, Mavrokordatos, Kolettes, and Metaxas seem to have acted more like agents of the king and powers than as national spokesmen. To judge from their behavior, they attempted, with a large measure of success, to push through the constituent assembly a general plan negotiated abroad and issuing from the palace. This general impression[39] contains a large measure of truth and is best ex-

---

legislature, the upper house by appointment of the king for life, (4) each legislative branch (King, Senate, Chamber) should enjoy equally the right of initiative and veto, (5) the principle of the independence of the judiciary should be recognized but applied only to the tribunals where the judges were men of tried character (Areopagus), and (6) the law of trial by jury should be amplified.

[37] Driault and Lhéritier, *Histoire*, II, 249.

[38] The six points are persistently mentioned, in part or *in toto* though not always with the same emphasis, in the following correspondence: (1) Aberdeen to Lyons, 29 Nov. 1843, quoted in Petrakakos [*Parliamentary History*], II, 313-14, and paraphrased at greater length by Driault and Lhéritier, *Histoire*, II, 249; (2) Guizot to Piscatory, 28 Oct. 1843, in Guizot, *Mémoires*, VII, 288-305; and (3) Wallerstein to P. Soutsos, 8 Dec. 1843, found by Petrakakos (*op.cit.*, II, 316-17) in the Secret Archive of Otho in Munich and published. See also Alexander Heinze, *Der Hellenische Nationalcongress zu Athen in den Jahren 1843 und 1844* (Leipzig, 1845), pp. 101-107.

[39] This was precisely the basis of press attacks on Mavrokordatos and Kolettes; for instance, *Aiōn*, 5 Dec. 1843o.s. See also nn. 53 and 90 below.

It certainly looks as if the impression is valid when one reads through two extant letters of Philip Ioannou, Otho's adviser, to Mavrokordatos, and a memorandum in Ioannou's handwriting containing instructions for Mavrokordatos, with such statements as "His Majesty commanded me to tell you that he believes it wise for you to take steps so as . . ." (26 Dec. 1843o.s.) or "He [Mavrokordatos] should likewise seek to persuade them [the assembly] that the king be called . . ." (Petrakakos [*Parliamentary History*], II, 388, 391). Yet, such language may simply reflect what Otho or Ioannou think the role of Mavrokordatos should be rather than what it actually was. Also see Piscatory's remark to Archduke John (21 Nov. 1843, *Briefwechsel*, ed. Schlossar, pp. 177-79) that Mavrokordatos and Kolettes were "working together in behalf of the king."

plained by the way in which Mavrokordatos and Kolettes read the existing situation.

These men, it seems, were more anxious to end the revolutionary crisis, with its attendant threats, than to create an ideal constitution. They judged a constitution less by its theoretical imperfections or their own private beliefs than by the extent to which it would command the willing assent of king and nation, those who would have to make it function. Their pragmatic approach therefore determined their task—to mediate between the king and assembly, to get the constitution framed as simply and quickly as possible, and to avoid as many issues as might revive partisan strife.[40]

Such mediation seems to have taken the form of starting with the king's set of demands (program) and modifying them at whatever points the assembly clearly displayed a differing consensus. As mediators they attempted to bring the two sides closer together, but the pattern was one of persistently manipulating the assembly and only sometimes extracting concessions from the king. The reasons are not hard to divine. The king knew what he wanted, was not easily dissuaded, and enjoyed the backing of the powers, whereas a clear-cut consensus among the delegates was far less frequent and there were many among them who would relent to foreign influence. Moreover, the king was surely going to have an important part in implementing the constitution, whereas this particular assembly's task would be finished once it approved a constitution.[41]

Some concrete examples will illustrate how such mediation worked and why it appeared to many Septembrists to be selling out to the king. The king, for instance, regarded the process of constitution-making as negotiation between himself and the nation as represented by the assembly. Consequently, he claimed the right to review and revise the draft constitution before it went before the assembly and the right of representation by a royal appointee at the assembly's deliberations. The opposing view postulated the exclusive right of the nation, as represented by the constituent assembly, to frame a constitution. Royal participation was mere interference. This view was widespread enough to provoke an outburst of opposition, both in the assembly and in the press, if the king's demands were granted.[42]

[40] Prokesch-Osten wrote to Metternich on 26 Dec. 1843 (in *Aus dem Nachlasse,* ed. A. Prokesch-Osten, II, 271, and in Petrakakos [*Parliamentary History*], II, 379): "Mavrokordatos and Kolettes insist on this [following proposals for a constitution by the Westen powers] less from conviction than prudence."

[41] See for instance the three documents by Philip Ioannou, Otho's adviser, two being letters to Mavrokordatos, telling him what the king wanted, the third being a memorandum of instructions for Mavrokordatos to get certain things through the assembly, all published in Petrakakos, *ibid.,* II: (1) letter of 26 Dec. 1843*o.s.* (pp. 386-91); (2) letter of 27 Jan. 1844*o.s.* (p. 392); and (3) memo (p. 391-92).

[42] For the king's demands, see Philip Ioannou to Mavrokordatos, 26 Dec. 1843, in *ibid.,* II, 386-91. According to the Kolokotrones Memorandum [Munich], 3 Nov.

How, then, did the unofficial cabinet prevent open disagreement on this point? The king quietly dropped his demands.[43] But as members of the drafting committee and officers of the assembly (all three vice-presidents) the unofficial cabinet were in the position to act as guardians of the royal interest at every stage of the deliberations. Furthermore, the unofficial cabinet secured an assembly vote to grant the king the right to review and propose changes in the constitution, once completed by the assembly. Hence the cabinet won for the king the essence of his objective by having him forego the means he proposed.

The view which casts Mavrokordatos and Kolettes in the role of agents of the king requires some qualifications. They were agents only after they had negotiated a constitutional program with the king, and Lyons wrote as if the negotiations took place in terms of perfect equality between king and ministers. At some points, indeed, the unofficial cabinet secured concessions from the king by convincing him that the assembly would not budge. It would usually succeed in convincing him by first making every effort to win over the assembly. For instance, they warned the king far in advance that the assembly would insist on discussing the royal succession and accept nothing less than a regulation making profession of the Orthodox faith compulsory for his successor. They promised, at the request of Lyons and Piscatory, to postpone discussion of this issue "to give the Allied Powers an opportunity of expressing their sentiments." In this way, when the king lost on this point, he acquiesced because everything had been tried and had failed.[44]

The unofficial cabinet also devised means to secure a constitution largely in keeping with the king's wishes. In the first place, it captured the machinery of the assembly. Although Notaras was elected chairman, as a token of esteem for his advanced age and for his similar role in previous assemblies, the four vice-chairmen were the ones who really mattered. They were the three members of the official cabinet, plus Lontos. Of these, Mavrokordatos, the parliamentarian, usually presided. He could control the timing of issues for debate so as to round up enough votes or utilize his power of initiative to carry amendments which might water down the consequences of measures he had failed to prevent.[45]

1843 (*ibid.*, ɪɪ, 334-35), one party of Greeks was willing to appoint a committee, apparently representing the king, to draw up a constitution for presentation to the national assembly for consideration, all this in accord with the unfulfilled promise of 1832 by Gise, Bavarian foreign minister, that a committee of a Greek assembly and a committee of the king should negotiate a constitution together. The opposing group, he continued, rejected this method because of the great influence it would give the king over the assembly.

[43] *Ibid.*, ɪɪ, 391, 395.

[44] Lyons to Aberdeen, Athens, 16 Nov. 1843, no. 138, and 30 Nov. 1843, no. 145, FO 32.123.

[45] The election of officers took place on 30 Nov. 1843. Notaras received 216 votes, Mavrokordatos 155, Metaxas 159, Kolettes 147, and Lontos 143 (see *He tes*

Second, they utilized the influence of Lyons and Piscatory, who simply enunciated the official position of their respective governments or employed the custom of banquets to win over hesitating delegates. Makrygiannes described the lobbying activities of Lyons and Piscatory. Even Lyons admitted their existence.[46]

Strategy of the Opposition

The position of the opposition groups—"opposition" in terms of the unofficial cabinet—contrasted markedly. The case of the Makrygiannes group is indicative. The oath that bound the members of his parliamentary bloc committed them to nothing more specific than working for "good laws."[47] Before the revolution, one could argue that this failing stemmed from the dim prospect of ever influencing state policy, but now the imminence of constitutional deliberations urgently invited the formulation of programs by men who cared—and Makrygiannes certainly cared.

Trites Septembriou en Athenais Ethnike Syneleusis, Praktika [*The National Assembly of Third September in Athens. Proceedings*] [Athens, 1843], pp. 16-17 and Petrakakos [*Parliamentary History*], II, 363). According to Makrygiannes ([*Memoirs*], II, 155-57), the whole idea of four vice-presidents was his, intended as a device to maintain party harmony; however that may be, he offers some interesting information on the politics behind the ultimate election, which involved the defeat of Palamides and Th. Grivas. To cite only two examples of how influential the chairman could be, see Makrygiannes (*ibid.*, II, 158), who told how, through a well-timed adjournment, Mavrokordatos prevented the outbreak of a brawl in the assembly chamber, or Prokesch-Osten (to Archduke John, Athens, 22 Dec. 1843, *Briefwechsel*, ed. Schlossar, p. 183), who, with evident respect and admiration, told how Mavrokordatos induced the assembly to forego direct mention of the Third [Fifteenth] of September in the reply to the speech from the throne. For the text of the procedural rules adopted by the assembly, see Heinze, *Nationalcongress*, pp. 45-57.

[46] As early as 19 Sept. 1843, Piscatory wrote his government ([*Bulletin*], XI, 249), concerning the kind of constitution which Lyons and he believed good for Greece: "A salutary influence must be exercised." That he and Lyons followed the proceedings very closely is evidenced by Lyons to Aberdeen, Athens, 31 Dec. 1843, no. 152, FO 32.123. Prokesch-Osten reports to Archduke John (22 Dec. 1843, *Briefwechsel*, ed. Schlossar, pp. 182-85) a Greek captain's saying to him: "The ministers of England and France are so active and speak to all the deputies. Why are you [Prokesch-Osten] so quiet and silent?"

Concerning the banquets, Makrygiannes wrote in one place ([*Memoirs*], II, 147-48), "The banquets which the ambassadors of England and France and others provide, and the daily invitations to the delegates—one leaves them, the other waits for them—those are the banquets that so sweetened our fellow-conspirators, especially Lontos and Kallerges. Palamides was also without character; the scandal extended to all of us." See also *ibid.*, II, 147, 151, 155.

[47] The crucial sentence in this very brief oath reads as follows: "We swear . . . that we will remain united in order to make good and reasonable laws for the fatherland, as many as are beneficial to both fatherland and king, so that the two parts may be united under the constitutional laws of the fatherland." For the full text of the oath, see *ibid.*, II, 230, Appendix.

It was a plain matter of fact that the average politicians, like Makry-giannes, lacked both a set of concrete policy objectives and a parliamentary strategy for realizing them. Limited in education and unfamiliar with the issues and procedures required to run a state of the Western type, they simply could not formulate a program to embody their vague aspirations and their general sense of justice.[48] Without a program they were virtually helpless against men who knew what they wanted, like the more sophisticated Mavrokordatos and Kolettes. Without a strategy they could think of nothing better than conspiratorial activity, resort to arms, or just plain perverseness.[49]

These observations probably apply less to more politically sophisticated men like Palamides, but even his political experience was limited largely to local conditions. The response of more articulate men like him

[48] On 6 Nov. 1843, Prokesch-Osten wrote to the Archduke John of Austria (*Briefwechsel*, ed. Schlossar, pp. 174-77) that virtually none of the Greeks had a clear idea of the constitution which was necessary and desirable. The attitude of Makrygiannes toward the institution of a senate is extremely revealing. Originally he opposed it because he felt the nation too poor to incur the additional expense. Otho defended the idea of a senate before Makrygiannes, and friends whom Makrygiannes consulted and whose judgment he respected argued for the necessity of a senate. Makrygiannes was conscious of his ignorance of the technical aspects of the issue, as he showed when he wrote, "Poor things that we are, we don't understand these things." His particular response to his ignorance was to bow to what he considered the superior judgment of the educated. And so he came out in favor of a senate (see Makrygiannes [*Memoirs*], ɪɪ, 158).

[49] The most noteworthy example of this at the time was the feverish activity of some Rumeliot members of the "French" party, which took the form of organizing military power to serve as the political instrument of their parliamentary bloc. To be sure, men like Palamides and Petsales, who were in collusion with them, looked after the parliamentary strategy of the group, such as it was, and Sophianopoulos, Utopian Socialist and firebrand journalist who wove impracticable schemes of reform, served this group as its publicist, however questionable that reckless service may have been. For the best account of the interesting Sophianopoulos, see Gianni Kordatos, *Historia tes Neoteres Helladas* [*The History of Modern Greece*] (Athens, 1957), ɪɪɪ, 213 and n. But the activity of this group, at least in the early part of the period (October–November 1843) centered about Th. Grivas, who was mobilizing and recruiting an armed following, purchasing gunpowder, and announcing his intention to go to Athens "with sufficient force to protect the king from sinister projects of the National Assembly" (Lyons). Sophianopoulos urged Grivas' wife, who was in Athens at the time, to write her husband and urge him to encamp in Athens with at least 500 men.

A. Georgantas invited Grivas to Livadia, where the former had called an assembly of "all representatives of Sterea Hellas" [Rumely], and Grivas, on 10 Oct. 1843*o.s.*, sent Georgantas a letter of acceptance. Eventually, through the efforts of the provisional government, Grivas went to Athens without his armed following and this group turned to parliamentary tactics through the Palamides bloc in the assembly. For sources on the information in this footnote, see Lyons to Aberdeen, Athens, 21 Oct. 1843, no. 125, 26 Oct. 1843, no. 126, and 16 Nov. 1843, no. 138, FO 32.123; two letters sent Georgantas, one by Metaxas, Athens, 9 Sept. 1843*o.s.* and the other by Th. Grivas, Vostitsa, 10 Oct. 1843*o.s.*, both in ["Historical Memoirs"], *Parnassos*, v (1881), 844-46.

is illuminating. If Mavrokordatos and Kolettes formulated their program largely in response to the pressures of the international situation and the desires of the king, men such as Palamides responded to the wishes of their constituents, in so far as they were intelligible.

In doing so, they raised issues of a special type—not issues that divided specific and well-defined interests within the state, but rather issues on which the bulk of the nation was on one side and foreigners, heterochthons, Westernized Greeks, or the king on the other. The former type of issue was virtually nonexistent, largely because society had simply not developed this degree of articulation. Of the latter type, which we will consider in the next section (autochthonism, the succession), there were very few, and these few stemmed from a diffuse nationalist sentiment which might appeal to all, whether it be the desire to have an Orthodox successor to the present king or the feeling that the nation should be given greater weight in a new constitution than the king. This kind of issue won men like Palamides some victories in the constituent assembly, but it was not sufficient to advance the opposition to power. The opposition betrayed its fundamental weakness in dealing with substantive issues by basing its opposition on a procedural criticism. Its criticism of foreign and royal interference in current Greek affairs opened the first round of political debate and demonstrated that the public would respond much more readily to this line of attack.

The dominant note of the political opposition was sounded from the very beginning when the assembly took up its first real business— replying to the speech from the throne. The first session of the assembly took place on 20 November in the old palace. The king had omitted any direct reference to the revolution. He had represented the work of the assembly as the fulfillment of eleven years of royal policy.[50]

The assembly appointed a seven-man committee to draw up a reply. The first draft of the reply, which Zographos composed, specifically mentioned the revolution. But in the deliberations of the committee, Mavrokordatos insisted on its omission and Kolettes seconded his demand. In order not to offend the king the committee finally decided to water down the reference to a mere phrase—"the fortunate event."[51]

[50] The text of the speech from the throne appears in [Government Gazette], no. 39, 18 Nov. 1843o.s.; [Proceedings], pp. 3-4; Heinze, Nationalcongress, pp. 14-15. For a vivid account of this opening of the assembly, see Prokesch-Osten's letter to Archduke John, 21 Nov. 1843, Briefwechsel, ed. Schlossar, pp. 177-79; and Heinze, op.cit., pp. 13-14.

[51] On the proceedings of the committee, see Elpis, 4 Dec. 1843o.s.; Prokesch-Osten to Archduke John, 22 Dec. 1843, Briefwechsel, ed. Schlossar, p. 183; and Petrakakos [Parliamentary History], II, 385, n. 17. The election of the committee took place on 7 Dec. 1843. [Proceedings], pp. 47-51, lists only six names as members of the committee: Kolettes with 171 votes; A. Mavrokordatos with 161; Perroukas, 117; Zographos, 116; Spyromelios, 91; Anastasios Lontos, 86. Heinze (Nationalcongress, pp. 84-94) lists G. Giones and Rodios, one of whom replaced An. Lontos when the latter resigned.

The draft reply went before the assembly on 17 December, and discussion began the following day and continued for three sessions (18-20 December). A. Petsales, representative from Chalcis and intimate friend of Kriezotes, rose to protest the omission as an insult to the nation. A. Konstakes from Patras went further; approval of the reply, he charged, would constitute abject servility to the king. He went on to condemn Bavaria for sending Wallerstein about Europe "to distort the principle and character of 3 [15] September and to nullify its results." Michael Schinas, a member of the cabinet, announced that a majority of the cabinet had favored some reference to 3 September but had bowed to outside pressure. Metaxas arose to attack a colleague for mentioning the cabinet, "whose policy it was not to become involved in questions facing the assembly." The assembly approved the reply with only a minor amendment after a speech by Trikoupes to justify the omission.[52]

The greater part of the Greek press (Aiōn, Elpis, Philos tou Laou, and Anexartētos) condemned the reply and the assembly's approval of it. According to Philos tou Laou, Makrygiannes threatened that, if the politicians were ashamed to mention the day of the revolution, the army would put the words on its caps. Aiōn revealed the full import of the protest by openly attacking the Mavrokordatos-Kolettes combination as a sinister influence. It accused them of disapproving of the revolution, catering to the king, and collaborating with the foreign legates (an obvious reference to Lyons and Piscatory).[53]

This first political explosion made a number of points clear. The Metaxas-Schinas exchange revealed a breach both within the cabinet and within the Napist party. From the party complexion of both the newspapers and the representatives condemning the reply, it would appear that segments of both the "French" and Napist parties had revolted against their respective leaders (Kolettes and Metaxas).[54] The remarks, both in the assembly and the press, showed a quick reaction against the rise of the unofficial cabinet and its alliance with foreign and royal influence. What started out as a minor question of verbal delicacy turned into a major dispute over an alleged conspiracy against the principles of the revolution and the will of the nation.

[52] Ibid., pp. 87-96; [Proceedings], pp. 66-97; Petrakakos [Parliamentary History], II, 381-82; and Prokesch-Osten to Archduke John, 22 Dec. 1843, Briefwechsel, ed. Schlossar, p. 183. For the text of the reply, see Petrakakos, op.cit., II, 385-86.

[53] Aiōn, 5 Dec.; Philos tou Laou, 9 Dec.; Elpis, 7 Dec.; and Anexartētos, 16 Dec., all 1843o.s. See also Petrakakos [Parliamentary History], II, 382, nn. 14-16.

[54] Levides' "French" newspaper boldly slandered Kolettes in terms usually employed by the "English" and "Russian" parties—as a product of Ali Pasha's court. Piscatory (Athens, 16 Sept. 1843, in [Bulletin], XI, 241) anticipated the problem of rallying "French" support for Kolettes' conservative and royalist program. He wrote, "I will concentrate all my efforts to retain his [Kolettes'] friends toward that end, even if that is difficult."

The First Cabinet Shake-Up, January 1844

From 22 December to 9 January, the constituent assembly recessed while a committee of twenty-one representatives framed a draft constitution. One source estimates that the Napists possessed a plurality of ten on this committee, the "French" four and the "English" seven. Of the cabinet members, only Metaxas and Melas served—further indication of the cabinet's eclipse.[55] Just a few days before the reopening of the assembly, the resignation of Regas Palamides marked the first cabinet shake-up.

Palamides had long taken a course independent of his cabinet colleagues. In October he had held out against the arrest and exile of Sophianopoulos, a "French" extremist who had been encouraging Theodore Grivas to bring military forces to Athens. Indeed, he was suspected of facilitating Sophianopoulos' escape. In November he had surreptitiously inserted a clause in the draft ordinance for a national guard so as to permit the enlistment of "persons of too low a station." In addition, he had been arbitrarily appointing and dismissing personnel throughout the provincial administration in contravention of cabinet policy. It looked as if Palamides had been exploiting his official position to organize a personal following throughout the country, a following made up of the humbler and more turbulent elements in the population. His close contacts with such captains as Theodore Grivas and Kriezotes gave the added impression that he was planning to use military pressure to enhance his influence in the assembly.[56]

[55] The session of 26 Nov./8 Dec. 1843, at which the committee was elected, and the membership of the committee, are reported in [*Proceedings*], pp. 51-55:

A. Mavrokordatos	150	G. Glarakes	106
S. Trikoupes	131	N. Korphiotakes	105
D. Kyriakou	123	J. Kolettes	103
P. Chalikopoulos	118	P. C. Rodios	102
D. Perroukas	118	Geralopoulos	102
A. Metaxas	118	L. Melas	95
Ghikas Giones	115	G. Ainian	90
C. Zographos	115	Pierakos	85
N. Mavrommates	111	G. Grypares	81
B. Theagenes	107	D. Kalliphronas	79

K. I. Damianos, after some uncertainty over the count, finally took his place as the twenty-first member, after barely squeezing Palamides and Monarchides out. The source which catalogued the membership according to the three-party division is Heinze, *Nationalcongress*, p. 83.

[56] Lyons to Aberdeen, Athens, 21 Oct., no. 125, 26 Oct., no. 126, 16 Nov., no. 138, and 31 Dec., no. 152, all 1843, FO 32.123. Paul Karolides (*Synchronos Historia ton Hellenon* . . . [*Contemporary History of the Greeks* . . .] [Athens, 1922-29], I, 532 and n.) attributes Palamides' dismissal to his arbitrary appointments. According to Prokesch-Osten, in a letter to Archduke John, dated 6 Jan. 1844 (*Briefwechsel*, ed. Schlossar, p. 188), Regas was "a most dangerous man," "head of the demagogues." See n. 49 above for an account of the threatening activities of Grivas, with whom Palamides was associated.

As Lyons pointed out during the first sessions of the assembly, Palamides, a member of the government, had become head of a parliamentary opposition. His repudiation by the unofficial cabinet, which commanded a majority in the assembly, became apparent when he failed to get elected to the framing committee or to the vice-presidency of the assembly. On his proposal for voting in the assembly by ballot he secured only 43 votes (against 173) with all his cabinet colleagues voting against his motion. Although resignation represented a political defeat for him, it at least had the merit of freeing him to openly assume the role of opposition leader.[57]

The resignation demonstrated a number of harsh realities—a breach within the "French" party, a popular revolt against Kolettes' leadership, and Kolettes' closer accord with foreign wishes than with those of a large segment of his own party. Piscatory had repudiated Palamides even before the return of Kolettes and now Kolettes did not lift a finger to save him.[58]

The resignation also contributed to the declining influence of Metaxas. Although he clearly wanted the ministry of interior for himself, the king gave it instead to Andrew Lontos, who now directed the two most important ministries—interior and army. If the Lontos appointment constituted a moral defeat for Metaxas, it also meant the growing ascendancy of the "English" party.[59]

3. Controversial Issues and the Breakdown of Tripartisanship

Those issues which aroused controversy in the constituent assembly and became a test of political strength between the unofficial cabinet and the opposition were surprisingly few: (1) the ecclesiastical question, (2) the heterochthon issue, (3) the succession question, and (4) the dispute over a second chamber. In part, the scarcity of issues reflects the public's only dim understanding of constitutional questions and its concern either with broad ideological questions or with specific demands on the state rather than the middle areas of ways and means. In part, it reflects the inability of existing interest groups to utilize parliamentary machinery for the satisfaction of their interests. But it also reflects the

[57] On the proposal sponsored by Palamides, see Heinze, *Nationalcongress*, pp. 40-41, and Lyons to Aberdeen, Athens, 30 Nov. 1843, no. 145, FO 32.123. That Palamides had actually been dismissed by Otho on the advice of the political chiefs [probably Metaxas, Mavrokordatos, and Kolettes], see Prokesch-Osten's letter to Archduke John, 6 Jan. 1844, *Briefwechsel*, ed. Schlossar, p. 188.

[58] Lyons to Aberdeen, Athens, 26 Oct. 1843, no. 126, and 30 Nov. 1843, no. 145, FO 32.123. See also n. 54 above.

[59] There is no notice of either Palamides' "resignation" or Lontos' appointment in the [*Government Gazette*]. Karolides ([*Contemporary History*], I, 532, n. 1) says that the pro-English press interpreted the appointment of Lontos as a moral defeat for Metaxas. Although there may be no causal connection between this set of events and the following observation, Prokesch-Osten reported to Archduke John, in the letter cited in n. 58 above, that there had recently been some tension between Metaxas on the one hand and Mavrokordatos and Kolettes on the other.

skill of the unofficial cabinet in avoiding other possible areas of controversy. When the assembly insisted on discussing such matters as the distribution of state land, claims against the state for Revolutionary services, and pensions for state employees, it was told that such matters were quite out of place in the formulation of a constitution and, by way of compromise, they were relegated to a special category of "supplementary laws" which were to serve as general recommendations for future legislative assemblies to act upon.[60]

The Ecclesiastical Question

The first two articles of the draft constitution dealt with religion and occupied the assembly in three days of controversy (15-17 January). Art. I declared Orthodoxy the official state religion. Although it granted toleration to other recognized faiths, it forbade them the right to engage in proselytizing activity. Art. II confirmed the autocephalous nature of the church in Greece but acknowledged its dogmatic unity with other Orthodox churches. Neither provision was then, or ever had been, in dispute *per se*. Michael Schinas, minister of religion, close personal friend of Constantine Oikonomos, and leader of the Philorthodox position in the assembly, simply felt that the articles did not go far enough in correcting what he considered the "uncanonical" nature of the regency's ecclesiastical settlement of 4 August 1833.[61]

Two pamphlets appeared as the assembly started to consider these first two articles. The first was essentially a defense of the ecclesiastical settlement of 1833 and represented the position of the liberals on the church question. It was written by Misael Apostolides, a liberal cleric, published anonymously, and distributed among all the representatives of the assembly on the night of 14 January 1844. The second—a reply and refutation reflecting the conservative position—was written by Constantine Oikonomos and distributed on 16 January, the second day of debate on Arts. I and II.[62]

[60] For one indication of the public's lack of understanding of constitutional issues, see n. 48 above. On public concern with ideological questions and specific demands, see Conclusion. There were eventually eighteen of these so-called "votes," published in [*Government Gazette*], no. 8, 1 April 1844*o.s.*

[61] The sessions of 3-5/15-18 Jan. 1844 are covered in [*Proceedings*], pp. 107-42, and Heinze, *Nationalcongress*, pp. 135-50. Both the text of the draft articles and Schinas' criticism of them are included.

[62] [Misail Apostolides], *Diatribe autoschedias peri tes arches kai tes exousias ton patriarchon kai peri tes scheseos tes ekklesiastikes arches pros ten politiken exousian* [*Impromptu Treatise concerning the Office and Authority of the Patriarchs and concerning the Relationship between Ecclesiastical and Political Authority*] (Athens, 1843); and [Constantine Oikonomos], *Apantesis eis ten autoschedion diatriben . . .* [*Reply to the Impromptu Treatise . . .*] (Athens, 1843). Reference to both tracts is made by Constantine Oikonomos in *Ta Sozomena ekklesiastika Syngrammata* [*Collected Ecclesiastical Writings*] ed. Sophocles Oikonomos (Athens, 1864), II, 494-95. In a footnote (p. 495, n. 2) the editor attributes authorship of the first tract to Apostolides.

On the first day (15 January), Schinas proposed a series of nine amendments based on ten proposals drawn up during December by members of the holy synod and other bishops temporarily in Athens. The written petition of the bishops reflected the Philorthodox and Napist position on two basic questions: (1) the relations between church and state in Greece, and (2) the relationship between the church of Greece and the church of Constantinople. Of its ten proposed amendments, the first nine dealt with the first question. Provisions three, four, eight, and nine attempted to ensure the autonomy of the church vis-à-vis the secular power. The third invalidated any state decree or law running counter to ecclesiastical law. The fourth recognized the king as "protector and defender [not head] of the church and its rights." In granting his right to govern the church on all external matters, it specified that he should do so within the limits of existing church canons and through the synod, not through his minister of religion. Provision eight called for a strict definition of relations between the secular and ecclesiastical authorities and for clarification of all circumstances under which a cleric could come under the jurisdiction of the secular courts. Provision nine specified that the clergy must not become entangled in politics, vote in elections, or take oaths. In short, by the terms of these amendments, the church would have become a closed corporation, which neither interfered in state affairs nor suffered interference from the state. In any clash between secular and canon law, however, the latter would automatically prevail.[63]

The tenth and last recommendation dealt with the second question of relations with the church of Constantinople. This issue produced one of the most vigorous debates in the assembly (16 January). Schinas insisted that autocephalous status was canonically impossible without prior approval of the mother church. If one agreed with him, then of course the ecclesiastical settlement of 1833 had violated church canons and the church of Greece was schismatic. Trikoupes, one of the authors of this settlement, rose to defend the act of 1833 and oppose the amendment. Then several representatives, even Napists such as Panagiotes Rodios and Andronikos Païkos, made speeches in opposition to the proposed

[63] The petition, dated 23 Dec. 1843o.s., is published in Petrakakos [Parliamentary History], II, 387, n. 18, and in Oikonomos [Collected Writings], II, 492-93. It was signed by Neophytos, Bishop of Euboea, president of the holy synod; Daniel of Cyclades; Jonas, formerly of Elis; Gregory of Achaia; Neophytos of Attica; Gregory, formerly of Mendenitsa; Dionysios of Kynouria; Hierotheos of Acarnania; and Cyril of Samos. On this document, see also Chrysostomos Papadopoulos, Historia tes Ekklesias tes Hellados [History of the Church of Greece] (Athens, 1920), p. 305.

Schinas had received a letter, dated 12 Nov. 1843o.s., from the secretary of the holy synod, and he replied on 15 Nov. with the suggestion that it draw up a list of proposals (see Aiōn, 24 Dec. 1843o.s. and Petrakakos, op.cit., II, 388, n. 18).

For the text of Schinas' proposals to the assembly, see [Proceedings], pp. 114-16, and Heinze, Nationalcongress, pp. 142-45.

amendment. In general, these men argued that all the bishops of Greece had given formal approval to the act of 1833 (an indisputable fact which the Philorthodox explained in terms of the slippery way in which the approval was obtained) and that, since theirs was an assembly elected to draw up a constitution, to tamper with the act of 1833 was beyond their competence. Finally, it was formally proposed that a regular national assembly review the act of 1833. Since this formal motion went counter to the liberal view that the act of 1833 was legal and final, its defeat represented a major victory for the liberal side. But the same question of relations with Constantinople came up indirectly when the assembly addressed itself to the question of church-state relations.[64]

Subsequently, several representatives proposed alternative amendments which, together with those of Schinas, were reviewed in committee and incorporated into two major proposals. It was these on which the assembly debated and voted (17 January), one an amendment to Art. I, the other an amendment to Art. II. The first, which prohibited "all interference with the Established Church" as well as proselytism, was intended to satisfy the Philorthodox without offending the liberals. It was vague enough to be interpreted as a curb on state interference, yet it did not mention the state by name. It gained ready acceptance.[65] The second amendment, as accepted, was again a compromise. Schinas had wanted to add the phrase "and canonically" just after "dogmatically" in the following part of Art. II: "[the church of Greece is] . . . dogmatically united to the church of Constantinople and other Orthodox churches." The reference to the canons in this phrase was intended to insure the church against "anticanonical" practices of the government and to subject the church to the canonical rulings of Constantinople. Opponents of the addition charged that it would invite the interference of the church of Constantinople in the administration of the church of Greece. Instead of this addition, the assembly sanctioned a compromise phrase, which was to be added at the end of the segment of Art. I quoted in the preceding paragraph—"maintaining unchanged like them [the church of Constantinople and other Orthodox churches] the holy apostolic and synodal canons and the holy traditions." Although the rest of the amendment did not incorporate Schinas' specification that all bishops elect a permanent president of the synod (in contrast to the existing practice of having the king appoint the president for a term of one year), it did specify that the synod should be a "synod of bishops." This specification

---

[64] Others making speeches in opposition to Schinas were: C. Axelos, N. Korphiotakes, G. Dokos, and J. Damianos. Among those few who voted in behalf of the motion were Zographos, Palamides, Makrygiannes, Th. Grivas (*ibid.*, pp. 145-48). For Trikoupes' speeches, see [*Proceedings*], pp. 124-32, 136-37. Petrakakos ([*Parliamentary History*], II, 395-99) quotes at length the speeches of Schinas and Trikoupes.

[65] Heinze, *Nationalcongress*, pp. 148-50.

disappointed at least some liberals, who had hoped that members of the lower clergy, such as the liberal Apostolides, Vamvas, and Pharmakides, might eventually receive appointment to the holy synod.[66]

The adopted amendments represented some important concessions to the Napists. For instance, Art. II, as amended, specifically mentioned Jesus Christ as head of the church, as a way of implying that the king was *not* head. It made specific reference to the church of Constantinople, asserted that the canons and traditions must be respected, and implied that the bishops rather than the minister of religion ran the church establishment. Yet, in terms of the original recommendations of the bishops, the amended articles represented a defeat for the Napists.[67]

The Heterochthon Issue

The heterochthon controversy, which preoccupied the constituent assembly for two full weeks,[68] brought to a head ten years of growing tension between the autochthons and the heterochthons. During those ten years this fundamental breach in Greek society lay beneath the surface

[66] On the celebrated and heated debate over the term "canonical," which took place during the second day (4/16 Jan. 1844), see [Proceedings], pp. 123-36, and Petrakakos [Parliamentary History], II, 395, n. 22. On the acceptance of the second amendment, see Heinze, Nationalcongress, pp. 145-48, [Proceedings], pp. 137-42, and Karolides, [Contemporary History], III, 21-23. For a general discussion of the assembly's work on the ecclesiastical issue, see Tryphon Evangelides, Historia tou Othonos, Basileos tes Hellados 1832-1862 [The History of Otho, King of Greece, 1832-1862] (Athens, 1893), pp. 220-67; Papadopoulos [Church], pp. 309ff.; and Charles A. Frazee, "The Orthodox Church of Greece from the Revolution of 1821 to 1852" [unpubl. doct. diss.] (Indiana University, 1965), pp. 278-86.

[67] Art. II of the Constitution of 1844 reads as follows: "The Orthodox Church of Greece, acknowledging for its head our Lord Jesus Christ, is indissolubly united in doctrine with the great church of Constantinople, and with every other church of Christ holding the same doctrines, observing invariably, as they do, the holy apostolic and synodal canons and holy traditions. It is self-governed, exercising its governing rights independent of every other church, and administering them by a holy synod of bishops" (see [Government Gazette], no. 5, 18 Mar. 1844o.s., and [Proceedings], p. 142).

The translated article is George Finlay's in his A History of Greece from its Conquest by the Romans to the Present Time, B.C. 146 to A.D. 1864, ed. H. F. Tozer (Oxford, 1877), VII, 345-46. He has translated and published the constitution of 1864, but Art. II remained the same, except for the addition of another sentence which is not here included.

On the religious aspects of the constitution, see Christos Androutsos, Ekklesia kai Politeia ex apopseos orthodoxou [Church and State from the Orthodox Point of View] (Athens, 1920), pp. 58-64, and Constantine Dyovouniotes, Schesis Ekklesias kai Politeias en te Eleuthera Helladi [Church-State Relations in Independent Greece] (Athens, 1916), pp. 32-36.

[68] 8/20 Jan.–21 Jan./2 Feb. 1844, twelve sessions. See [Proceedings], pp. 142-254; Heinze, Nationalcongress, pp. 150-83; Petrakakos [Parliamentary History], II, 404-16. Also Karolides [Contemporary History], III, 23-32, and Kordatos [History], III, 295-309.

of public consciousness. The objects of press criticism had not been autochthons or heterochthons as such, but smaller groups within these larger divisions, such as kodza-bashis, captains, Phanariots, or Corfiots. But this tension never lay far below the surface. The press was constantly making unfavorable references to a vague category which it called *newcomers (neelydes).*[69]

Moreover, the common aversion toward the Bavarians had tended to eclipse domestic antagonism. The basic charges against the Bavarians— that they had contributed nothing to the Revolution and knew next to nothing about local conditions—applied as well to all the heterochthons who had migrated to Greece after the actual fighting had ceased in 1827. Zaïmes recognized that anti-Bavarian sentiment was merely a special case of a wider antipathy when he warned, just before his death in 1840, "It is easy to expel the Bavarians, but then the Phanariots will be expelled [too] and after them the rest of the heterochthons." The same observation appears in a public petition circulated by antiheterochthons early in 1844:

> It is well-known . . . that the just desperation and aversion of Greeks was not limited merely to Bavarians who occupied a few political and military posts before 3 [15] September, but applied even more against those who came after our holy struggle, and usurped public posts and supplanted in the most unscrupulous manner the combatants [fighters], the sons and relatives of the combatants and of our brothers who fell in behalf of the fatherland.[70]

From the very outbreak of the Revolution, the heterochthons had incurred the hostility of those who resented their semi-Western ways and envied them their generally superior education. But circumstances during the decade of the 1830s gave political and economic dimensions to what originated as localist and cultural prejudice. Both because they outclassed most autochthons in their command of skills required to administer a Western-type state and because the more recent arrivals among them remained free from identification with any of the parties, the Crown by policy had given them preference in staffing the government bureaucracy. To the many impoverished veterans, for whom the state could not adequately provide, all this seemed grossly unfair. If the heterochthons became identified with affluence in the public mind, the well-publicized cases of acknowledged Revolutionary heroes who died

---

[69] For instance, see *Athēna,* 2 May 1836*o.s.* against neelydes and Phanariots.

[70] The original source for Zaïmes' remark is Dragoumes [*Reminiscences*], ɪɪ, 79. See also Karolides [*Contemporary History*], ɪɪ, 374. For the full text of the public petition, from which the quotation in the above text is drawn (entitled ["Concerning the dismissal of new-comers from the public service, To the Greek National Assembly of 3 September"], and dated Athens, 22 Dec. 1843*o.s.*), see Petrakakos [*Parliamentary History*], ɪɪ, 405-406, reprinted by Kordatos [*History*], ɪɪɪ, 296-97.

in indigence (Zaïmes, Mavrommates, and Photelas) became symbols of the plight of the autochthons.[71]

In addition to the exercise of political influence, the heterochthons came to be identified with the possession of relative wealth—wealth obtained at the expense of the autochthons, who constituted the vast majority of the population. With respect to economic privilege, there were two categories of heterochthons—the office-holders and the private merchants. Since the level of public ethics tended to be low, to hold office brought marked economic advantages, such as illicit tax exemption, first option on the purchase of national property, and procurement of tax-free loans from the government. The other group, mostly refugee merchants from Chios and Psara, had salvaged enough of their former wealth to utilize their previous experience in money-making enterprises. They tended to be the usurers who lent privately at interest rates running anywhere from 24 to 36 per cent. In the absence of a national bank until 1842, which would provide long-term interest loans, indigenous elements were at the mercy of these usurers.[72]

The manifold dimensions of autochthon hostility—cultural, political, economic—are vividly reflected in the following tirade of Makrygiannes:

The filth of Constantinople and Europe, with their plethora of carriages, balls, and sumptuousness and luxury, they are our masters and we their slaves. They grabbed the best property, the best places for building homes. In the ministries, [they collected] big salaries. They lend their money at 2-3% a month, they give mortgages. In one year, even less, they foreclose one out of ten. They all become property-owners. They are judges and lords, while the Greeks get beatings wherever they go. Poverty has increased. With the slightest misdemeanor, the veteran is given life-imprisonment or sent to the guillotine.

[71] On their role in the bureaucracy, see pp. 162-63 and 287, above. On the resentment of the impoverished autochthons and the indigence of Revolutionary heroes, see the speech of one of the autochthons during the assembly debate of 13 Jan. 1844o.s.: "Throw one glance at the ministries, the control board, the district attorneyship in the higher courts. Finally who then were the cabinet members? Yesterday and today you heard that Tsamados, because of such a condition [of penury] committed suicide, that Mavrommates and Photelas died in denial of their daily bread and at the end of their life a diploma was given them as a passport to the other life" ([Proceedings], p. 175, quoted in Petrakakos [Parliamentary History], II, 410, and referred to in George K. Aspreas, Politike Historia tes Neoteras Hellados 1821-1921 [Political History of Modern Greece], 2nd edn. [Athens, 1924], I, 172).

[72] On economic perquisites of office, see Athēna's suspicions about Silivergos (11 Nov. 1842o.s.). On merchant usurers and high interest rates, see Makrygiannes [Memoirs], II, 93, or the more specialized works, like A. K. Phrangides, Peri ton Proton Emporon tes Syrou . . . [Concerning the First Merchants of Syros . . .] (Athens, 1902), and D. Zographos, Historia tes Hidryseos tes Ethnikes Trapezes 1833-45 [The History of the Establishment of the National Bank . . .] (Athens, 1925-27), 2 vols.

Such is the benevolence practiced here. The prisons of the state have filled up, and our judges and lawyers have grown rich.[73]

Exponents of the autochthon position in 1844 chose the most direct way of redressing what they considered the imbalance between the two groups—exclusion from citizenship. The objective was not without precedent. In 1825-26 palikars of West Rumely, some of whom were behind the agitation of 1844, organized an autochthon movement to curb the growing influence of the immigrant Souliots.[74]

The occasion for the great debate on the heterochthon issue arose when the constituent assembly considered Art. III of the draft constitution, which defined Greek citizenship. At the first session dealing with this issue (20 January), the assembly heard the formal reading of the several public petitions for exclusion, each with long lists of signatures. The exact number of petitions is unknown, but there were certainly more than the single extant one which carries 2,600 signatures. Since preparation of petitions required planning and time for circulation, their very existence suggests an organized movement in behalf of exclusion.[75]

Seven different formal amendments were presented to the assembly at the opening session. The most extreme required twenty years of residence as a prerequisite for citizenship. But thanks to the parliamentary skill of Mavrokordatos, the presiding officer, the proposal that came up for debate called only for the exclusion of post-1827 heterochthons from office.[76]

The actual organizers of the general movement remain unknown, but certainly Regas Palamides was the leader of the extreme autochthon group in the assembly. He proposed one of the extremist amendments, which the assembly rejected by a vote of 114 to 59. And there is evidence that he used his cabinet office to further the aims of the movement. In protesting against the provisional government's failure to dismiss heterochthons from government service, the extant petition condemned the cabinet's policy of noninterference with existing bureaucratic personnel, the same policy that Palamides had surreptitiously violated while in office. As the assembly was about to resume its deliberations, some 400 armed

[73] Makrygiannes [Memoirs], II, 93.

[74] Concerning the precedent of 1825-26, see for instance the prologue to Panagiotes Soutsos' play entitled "George Karaïskakes," Tria Lyrika Dramata [Three Lyric Dramas] (Athens, 1842), pp. 91-92.

[75] See [Proceedings], pp. 144ff., and Petrakakos ([Parliamentary History], II, 404-405), who points out that details about the content of these petitions are unknown owing to the silence of Heinze and the current newspapers on this matter. See n. 70 above concerning one extant petition.

[76] On the formal amendments see [Proceedings], pp. 142-54, and Heinze, Nationalcongress, pp. 173-76. At the third session (11/23 Jan.), Mavrokordatos, as chairman, proposed that all with proposals get together in committee and combine them into one for discussion, and the assembly voted its agreement ([Proceedings], pp. 159-62).

individuals came to Athens in violation of government orders against such an influx. As minister of the interior, Palamides bore responsibility for what constituted a threat to the peaceful deliberations of the assembly and exposed himself to the suspicion that he had used his office to secure military backing in case of need. This suspicion may have caused the final showdown with his colleagues that led to his resignation.[77]

But Palamides most probably had his own reasons for resigning. Coming as it did shortly before the debate on the heterochthon issue, the resignation of Palamides would invite the public to infer that he resigned, and hence martyred himself politically, because he was more pro-autochthon than his colleagues. It would permit him to dissent openly from the government position in behalf of the autochthons and to assume the leadership of the antiheterochthon parliamentary forces. Both these things he actually did.

Alexander Heinze, the Bavarian artillery officer who published his invaluable personal record of the assembly proceedings, distinguished two main groups with regard to the autochthon-heterochthon issue—those whom he called the "moderates" and those whom he labelled "ultrademocrats." The most important among the former were Mavrokordatos, Kolettes, Metaxas, Trikoupes, Lontos, Constantine Zographos, An. Monarchides, Drosos Mansolas, Andronikos Païkos, Constantine Axelos, Christodoulos Klonares, A. Loidorikes, N. Mavromichales, and Panagiotes Rodios; among the latter, Regas Palamides, Nicholas Poneropoulos, Christos Vlases, Kollinos Kolokotrones, John Makrygiannes, John Velentzas, Nicholas Kriezotes, and Theodore Grivas. Furthermore, Heinze indirectly reveals the size of the latter group by giving the count on the vote concerning Palamides' proposed amendment—fifty-nine. The composition of the first group is heterogeneous, representing all three parties, all sections of Greece, both autochthons and heterochthons. This is understandable, in view of the fact that it was the combined following of the unofficial cabinet. With the exception of Kolokotrones, the youngest son of Theodore, the listed representatives of the second group seem to be drawn largely from two main groups—Peloponnesian primates and Rumeliot captains, both of the "French" party. Obviously, a significant segment of the "French" party, rallying around Palamides, had rebelled against Kolettes' leadership and constituted itself the vanguard of dissident elements in the assembly. This issue had, therefore, precipitated

[77] On Palamides' amendment, see Heinze, *Nationalcongress*, p. 152. See Petrakakos [*Parliamentary History*], II, 405-406 for an account of the criticism in the petition, in conjunction with n. 56 above. Concerning the influx of armed groups into Athens at the time that petitions were circulating and the consequent arrests of some and forced expulsion of others—matters which came up for questioning in the assembly on 11 Jan. 1844 o.s.—see [*Proceedings*], pp. 159-60, and Petrakakos, *op.cit.*, II, 409-10. Kordatos ([*History*], III, 298-99) places Palamides at the head of this movement.

an open revolt within the "French" party against its acknowledged leader.[78]

Although the extremist autochthon group failed to put its amendment through the assembly, the autochthons in general won their point on a more moderate measure. But, though unable to go against the tide, Mavrokordatos used his parliamentary skill to nullify the full force of the measure. He kept the exclusion bill out of the constitution by assigning it to a specially created category of "special legislative measures with the same status as a constitutional provision." Together with Kolettes and Metaxas, he managed to water down the measure with all sorts of exceptions and conditions. The measure defined "autochthon" broadly to include, besides natives of the liberated provinces, anyone who had taken up arms in any part of the Ottoman empire during the Revolution and had established permanent residence by 1827. All others were to be removed from public office, but this did not apply to the army and navy, consular service, or teaching profession. Noncombatants who migrated to Greece between 1827-32 would become eligible for office after two years, those between 1832-37 after three years, and those between 1837-43 after four years.[79]

The Succession Question

The assembly's deliberations on the succession question constituted a bold defiance of European diplomacy and, as an angry Ludwig pointed out, resulted in the unilateral modification of an international agreement by a national parliament. The treaty of 7 May 1832, to which Bavaria and the three protecting powers were signatories, had regulated the succession to the Greek throne by order of primogeniture in the Wittelsbach family. By 1844, it looked as if Otho and Amalia might never have children (as indeed they did not). In that case Otho's younger brother Luitpold or his heirs would assume the throne. Luitpold had already declared his intention to remain a Catholic and to raise his children as Catholics. Art. XL, the constitutional provision making adherence to Orthodoxy compulsory for any future Greek monarch, amounted to the exclusion of Luitpold and hence violated the stated intentions of the treaty of 7 May.[80]

[78] Heinze, *Nationalcongress*, pp. 174-76. See also Petrakakos [*Parliamentary History*], II, 411. It should be noted that of the "moderates" listed, some voted for the moderate exclusion bill, some against; that is, the list includes moderate pro-autochthons as well as pro-heterochthons.

[79] For the text of the exclusion bill, which became law as "Vote II" of the series of eighteen eventually passed as an adjunct to the constitution, see [*Government Gazette*], no. 8, 1 Apr. 1844 o.s. On Mavrokordatos' successful proposals to mitigate the effect of the inevitable exclusion, see [*Proceedings*], pp. 198-204.

[80] Concerning Art. VIII of the treaty of 1832, regulating the succession, see p. 145 above. Art. XL read as follows: "Every successor to the Greek throne must belong to the religion of the Eastern Orthodox Church of Christ" ([*Government*

One of Wallerstein's most urgent demands in Paris and London had concerned protecting the interests of the Bavarian dynasty in Greece. He had succeeded in persuading the Conference of London to sign a protocol ensuring the rights of that dynasty. But when the unlikelihood of deterring the Greeks became apparent, Ludwig sent Count de Rechberg on a special mission to Athens. Lyons and Piscatory, in the meantime, urged Mavrokordatos and Kolettes to use their influence to throw out this provision. Mavrokordatos, as presiding officer of the assembly, hoped to obtain postponement of a decision on the proposed provision for three years. But it was no use. The assembly adopted the measure unanimously and by acclamation, a clear indication that sentiment was too strong even for the powerful moral influence of Kolettes, Mavrokordatos, and the Western ministers to overcome.[81]

On 1 March, Wallerstein was again back in Paris protesting the Greek action. Both England and France sympathized with Ludwig and feared the consequences of unilateral Greek action on a matter defined by an international agreement. But Guizot feared that diplomatic protest would "set Greece on fire" and preferred to see if Otho would sanction the provision. In the meantime, Russia came out of her isolation long enough to urge the Bavarian government that Luitpold, in a necessary concession to the religious sentiments of the Greeks, promise to bring up his second son in the Orthodox faith. This action resulted in the conclusion that Russia had supported the vote of the national assembly.[82]

The passage of this provision, embodied in Art. XL, was certainly a victory for the Napist party, which was and had been the great proponent of Orthodox "interests" in Greece. Undoubtedly their strength in this case they owed to the overwhelming wish of the Greek people for an Orthodox king.[83] Backed also by strong public sentiment, they gained

---

Gazette], no. 5, 18 Mar. 1844o.s.). Concerning Ludwig's complaint, in a letter of 5 Mar. 1844 communicated to the French government, see Driault and Lhéritier, *Histoire*, II, 258-59. For the view that Art. XL meant the virtual exclusion of Luitpold, see a previously unpublished letter from Prokesch-Osten to Metternich, Athens, 6 Jan. 1844, in Petrakakos [*Parliamentary History*], II, 421.

[81] The protocol in question was signed in Nov. 1843. The information in this paragraph is drawn from Driault and Lhéritier, *Histoire,* II, 255-56; the previously unpublished letter from Prokesch-Osten to Metternich, Athens, 6 Jan. 1844, in Petrakakos [*Parliamentary History*], II, 421; and [*Proceedings*], pp. 302-303 (on the session of 28 Jan. 1844o.s. when Arts. XXXIX-XLII were voted *en bloc*). According to Driault and Lhéritier, Mavrokordatos and Kolettes vehemently refused to comply with the Lyons-Piscatory request, and it is Prokesch-Osten who contradicts this statement with his remark about Mavrokordatos' hopes for postponement of the issue.

[82] Driault and Lhéritier, *Histoire*, II, 257, 259-61 (including a quotation from a letter, dated 14 Mar. 1844, by Guizot to St. Aulaire, French minister to London).

[83] According to *ibid.*, II, 260, the passage of Art. XL represented a Philorthodox thrust in the assembly. According to Aberdeen (quoted in *ibid.*, II, 259), the unanimous response of the assembly was due not to religious, but rather to anti-Bavarian sentiment; and "Colettes, Metaxas, and Mavrocordatos did not try to hide it."

a minor victory as well by incorporating in the constitution a provision requiring any future regent, in the event of a vacant throne, to be a Greek citizen of Orthodox faith. Undoubtedly, bitter memories of the Bavarian regency inspired the assembly's support of this measure, but according to an anonymous letter in the private archives of Otho, Metaxas, Zographos, and Michael Soutsos had special reasons—continued hopes that Otho might be expelled in the future. No doubt the writer of the letter still remembered rumors from the past September that the conspirators had intended to make Soutsos regent after the expulsion of Otho. In order to conciliate the royal couple, who objected to the provision, Mavrokordatos used his parliamentary skill to secure a special vote (Vote III) making Amalia automatically regent "in the event of a minority or the absence of a successor as provided by Art. XL."[84] Otho implicitly gave his assent to Art. XL when he accepted the constitution as a whole. As Prokesch-Osten pointed out, he had no choice. "If he had rejected Art. XL, the thirteenth of March would have been his last day in Greece; neither Mavrokordatos, Kallerges, nor the few existing English ships would have been able to help him. . . ."[85]

The Dispute over the Senate

The senate question was the last major issue to engage the assembly. The institution of a senate invited widespread public criticism. It looked like an unnecessary expense, smacked of aristocracy, would tend to conflict with the popularly elected assembly, and might even become an instrument of the Crown.[86]

---

[84] The provision in question is Art. XLV, which reads as follows ([*Government Gazette*], no. 5, 18 Mar. 1844*o.s.*): "If the throne becomes vacant, the Chamber and Senate come together as one body and temporarily elect as regent a Greek citizen of the Eastern faith. . . ." Prokesch-Osten had anticipated the prospect of such a provision in his previously unpublished letter of 6 Jan. 1844 to Metternich, in Petrakakos [*Parliamentary History*], II, 421. For a copy of the anonymous letter, dated 15/27 Feb. 1844, see also Petrakakos, *ibid.*, p. 425.

The special provision concerning Amalia was incorporated as Vote III in the list of votes accompanying the constitution ([*GG*], no. 8, 1 Apr. 1844*o.s.*). This meant that the only case in which Art. XLV would apply was one in which Otho was deposed, otherwise Art. XL would come into effect. Originally, Prokesch-Osten (in the letter to Metternich, dated 6 Jan. 1844, in Petrakakos, *op.cit.*, II, 421) anticipated that this provision would make her regent only in the event that she had a son who became king while still in his minority, but Vote III also applies to a vacancy if there is no successor under the terms of Art. XL. Art. XLIV of the constitution provided for her to automatically become guardian of a son, as distinct from regent, in the event of his being a minor on the death of his father (Heinze, *Nationalcongress*, pp. 196, 371). Zographos proposed that the exception be made (*ibid.*, p. 195).

[85] Previously unpublished letter from Prokesch-Osten to Metternich, 21 Mar. 1844, in Petrakakos [*Parliamentary History*], II, 429-30.

[86] For confirmation of the existence of such objections, see [*Proceedings*], pp. 276, 274, 392, 400 respectively (each page illustrating the cited objections in that order);

The framing committee had accepted the two-chamber provision, but a majority had insisted that the upper chamber be elective. The minority, including the unofficial cabinet, stalled before allowing a vote to be taken, so that Lyons and Piscatory might try to win a majority for life tenure. The majority were "disposed to listen to us," said Lyons, but owing to the strong views of their constituents, they could accept a proposal for life tenure only if it provided a review of the whole matter after ten years of trial.[87]

The nucleus of parliamentary opposition to a second chamber was the Palamides bloc. So doubtful did the assembly's assent to a senate seem that the unofficial cabinet and the king himself exerted strong pressure on the assemblymen. Much later Gregoriades, one who voted against a senate, related the tactics used. During discussion of the senate question, an Aberdeen memorandum in behalf of a hereditary senate was circulated. Otho sent personally for Gregoriades, Georgantas, and Notaras one morning in an effort to win them over. Without question the assembly would not have approved the type of second chamber proposed by the unofficial cabinet but for the skilful manipulation exercised.[88]

The debate on the senate question went through three stages. Long before the two later stages, Art. XIV, establishing a two-chamber legislature, won the easy assent of the assembly by a vote of 159-37. Failing at this first stage, the opposition began to stir up public opinion through the press and hoped to prevent the aristocratic character of the senate by limiting senatorial tenure and making the office elective. Their chance came early in February when Art. LXX, dealing with the method of selecting senators and their length of tenure, came up for consideration. But selection of senators by royal appointment rather than by popular elections won assent by a vote of 119-47, in spite of opposition efforts.[89]

---

also Makrygiannes [*Memoirs*], II, 158; and the monograph by N. D. Levides, *Homiliai kata tes Gerousias kai meta tou symbouliou tes Epikrateias enopion tes pros katartismon schediou Syntagmatos epitropes tes G. en Athenais syntagmatikes Ethnosyneleuseos* [*Speeches against a Senate and with the Council of State before the Committee of the Third Constituent Assembly of Athens for the Formation of a Draft Constitution*] (Athens, 1925).

[87] Lyons to Aberdeen, 31 Dec. 1843, no. 152, FO 32.123.

[88] On the opposition of the Palamides bloc, see Makrygiannes [*Memoirs*] II, 157-58. For an extended account of the maneuverings of the unofficial cabinet, correct in general though mistaken on some details, see Levides [*Speeches*], pp. 115ff. See also the remarks of Gregoriades, made in the session of 17 Nov. 1865*o.s.* of the Greek chamber and quoted by Petrakakos [*Parliamentary History*], II, 418-19 and n.

[89] Art. XV read as follows: "The legislative authority is exercised jointly by the king, assembly, and senate" ([*Government Gazette*], no. 5, 18 Mar. 1844*o.s.*). It was discussed in two sessions (24-25 Jan. 1844*o.s.*), ([*Proceedings*], pp. 273-89; Heinze, *Nationalcongress*, pp. 187-91), and voted without change. Concerning the second issue, the debate and vote on it, which took place in the session of 8 Feb. 1844*o.s.*, see [*Proceedings*], pp. 370-91; Heinze, *op.cit.*, pp. 204-10; also Petrakakos [*Parliamentary History*], II, 416. Concerning the organization of public opinion, see,

The opposition then stepped up its efforts to defeat the motion for life tenure, not only for substantive reasons but also as a gesture of revolt against royal wishes, foreign interference, and the supreme authority of Mavrokordatos and Kolettes. *Elpis* and *Aiōn* both strongly opposed the proposal for life tenure. *Elpis* represented it as a Bavarian attack against Greek freedom and as the product of foreign intrigue. *Aiōn* attacked Mavrokordatos and Kolettes for their collaboration with the foreign ambassadors. These criticisms were reminiscent of those from the previous December concerning the assembly's reply to the speech from the throne.[90]

On the proposal for life tenure as an alternative to ten-year terms, the coalition majority suddenly disappeared. The votes were split 98-98. Metaxas had decided to throw his weight in favor of the opposition, risking for the first time a test of strength between himself on the one hand and his colleagues Mavrokordatos and Kolettes on the other. This made the difference between this vote and the previous two.[91]

Overnight the Mavrokordatos-Kolettes forces rounded up enough representatives, absent on the previous day, to secure a majority for life tenure. The entire next day the assembly debated whether to take a second vote on the same question or accept the tie vote as a rejection of life tenure because it failed to win a majority. A majority of the assembly (111-96) decided to submit the issue to a second vote on the following day. This was tantamount to a victory for the proposal, which became definite by a vote of 112-92.[92] But it was a meagre majority compared to what the unofficial cabinet had usually enjoyed and amounted to a moral defeat. This test of strength also clearly showed that Metaxas did not command a majority in the assembly, even when the existing opposition voted with him.

The Second Cabinet Shake-Up

Shortly after his break with Mavrokordatos and Kolettes, Metaxas resigned from his cabinet post and precipitated the second breach in the

---

for instance, a remark of Prokesch-Osten to Metternich in the letter dated 6 Jan. 1844 (in Petrakakos, *op.cit.*, II, 421): "Throughout Peloponnesos, petitions in favor of one chamber are being circulated."

[90] *Elpis*, 12 Feb. 1844*o.s.*; and *Aiōn*, 13 Feb. 1844, 11 Mar. 1844*o.s.* Also Petrakakos [*Parliamentary History*], II, 418-19 and n., and Karolides [*Contemporary History*], III, 37-38.

[91] [*Proceedings*], pp. 391-407 (session of 9 Feb. 1844*o.s.*); Heinze, *Nationalcongress*, p. 213; Petrakakos [*Parliamentary History*], II, 416-18; and Karolides [*Contemporary History*], III, 38-39. The controlling secretary of the assembly recorded a tie vote of 98-98, while the assembly's stenographer gave a count of 98 in favor of life tenure and 97 for ten-year terms. In view of this discrepancy and the attendant confusion, Mavrokordatos, as president, called for an adjournment after ruling that a recount be taken the following day.

[92] [*Proceedings*], pp. 408-18 (session of 10 Feb. 1844*o.s.*), and pp. 419-22 (session of 11 Feb. 1844*o.s.*); Heinze, *Nationalcongress*, pp. 210-18.

cabinet. He formally announced his resignation to the national assembly on 26 February 1844. In his memoirs, Makrygiannes described the immediate circumstances of Metaxas' resignation, and though he did not state the substance of Metaxas' quarrel with the rest of the unofficial cabinet, it is fairly certain that this quarrel took place when the assembly was debating Art. LXX:

> I took Metaxas and we went [to a private home, after a session of the assembly, where Makrygiannes had arranged to meet with Kolettes and Kountouriotes]. We found upstairs the ministers Lyons, Piscatory, and Prokesch. When they saw me with Metaxas, they wouldn't draw me into the conversation. They all started to talk—Mavrokordatos also came; I didn't understand the language they were speaking [probably French]. I saw poor Metaxas in his conversation very sad and he would get angry. After a while, I asked him: 'What's up?' 'They don't like certain things. They are not to their liking, so I'm going to resign. I can't go on like this any longer.' And he left me and went back and started arguing again. After they all separated, some went into the other room with the ministers and the other half remained and argued.[93]

This little vignette, though tantalizingly vague, leaves little doubt that the previous debate precipitated the decision of Metaxas to resign his cabinet post. In his letter of resignation to the king, he confirmed this by saying that he had lost command of a majority in the assembly. But in his official announcement to the assembly on 26 February 1844, Metaxas denied that the debates or a difference of principles had caused his resignation; rather circumstances, which he could not relate, convinced him that he could no longer be of service to the nation.[94]

The issue of life tenure only gave occasion for the open rupture between Metaxas and the leaders of the other two parties. Latent antagonism had arisen as early as the previous October when, because of the king and diplomats, Metaxas lost his leading position to Kolettes and Mavrokordatos. This left him only two alternatives: either to join the Mavrokordatos-Kolettes coalition as a subordinate member or to place

[93] Makrygiannes [*Memoirs*], II, 161-62. The [*Government Gazette*] carries no notice of Metaxas' resignation, or that of M. Schinas from the ministry of religion-education, who resigned along with him.

[94] For a copy of Metaxas' letter of resignation, see Petrakakos [*Parliamentary History*], II, 419. For the text of his official announcement to the assembly, see [*Proceedings*], pp. 422-24; Heinze, *Nationalcongress*, pp. 220-21; Karolides [*Contemporary History*], III, 39-40, n. 1; and Petrakakos, *op.cit.*, II, 419. Karolides (*op.cit.*, III, 39-40) supports the view that the resignation of Metaxas was the direct result of the vote of February 11/23, but states that his position had been shaken long before. Kolettes attributed the cause of Metaxas' resignation to Mavrokordatos' inability to handle him and hence to the rupture between the two men (Guizot, *Mémoires*, VII, 310-12).

himself openly at the head of a minority opposition. His rejection of the latter alternative was unmistakably clear when he openly criticized the opposition movement organized by Palamides in December. His choice of the former reveals perhaps a hope of being reconciled with the king. But even more, it was neither patriotic nor politically expedient to set forth an opposition movement that might precipitate anarchy or involve him in open conspiracy.[95]

Metaxas was not, however, consistent in abiding by his choice. According to Makrygiannes, he kept one foot in each camp, going nowhere, confusing everyone by his vacillation, losing former adherents to the Kolettes-Mavrokordatos camp without ever winning its support in return. According to Alexander Soutsos, the vitriolic poet, Metaxas betrayed his Septembrist supporters and followed the program of his political rivals, sometimes reluctantly and hysterically like an unwilling woman, sometimes in a manly spirit of conciliation, but without ever regaining the royal favor which he desired.[96]

The previous January, Metaxas had attempted to work his way out of his ineffectual position by proposing to Mavrokordatos a cabinet shake-up with himself as minister of the interior (a post he had wanted when Palamides resigned), Zographos as minister of religion, and Mavrokordatos as minister of economics. He complained that Mavrokordatos had harmed rather than helped him since returning to Greece, even though he himself had generously invited Mavrokordatos and Kolettes back to Greece. Quite obviously, Metaxas was trying to shift the balance of the three-man coalition so that Mavrokordatos and he would be senior partners, and Kolettes rendered ineffectual. Mavrokordatos refused, reaffirming his intention to accept no portfolio in the cabinet until the constituent assembly had finished its work. He must have known quite well that Metaxas' proposals would take from the "English" party the ministry (interior) that could influence the outcome of the elections for the first legislative assembly.[97]

[95] Concerning Metaxas' loss of leadership as a result of the arrival of Mavrokordatos and Kolettes, see n. 18 above; concerning his criticism of the opposition organized by Palamides, see n. 52 above.

[96] Makrygiannes [*Memoirs*], ɪɪ, 161; A. Soutsos, *He Metavole tes Trites Septembriou* [*The Change of the Third of September*] (Athens, 1844), 2nd edn., pp. 166-68.

[97] The information on Metaxas' proposal to Mavrokordatos in January 1844 comes from A. Soutsos [*The Third of September*], pp. 144-46, written in the form of letters, one from Metaxas to Mavrokordatos, the other a reply from Mavrokordatos, both dated Jan. 7/19. It is doubtful that Soutsos has presented direct replicas and even uncertain if these letters were ever written, but there is no reason to doubt the truth of the information or the reality of this occurrence.

Obviously, Metaxas was responding to the shift of the power balance in the cabinet as a result of Palamides' resignation early in January (see n. 59 above). On 6 Jan. 1844 (Petrakakos [*Parliamentary History*], ɪɪ, 421-22), Prokesch-Osten wrote his government about Metaxas' dissatisfaction with the cabinet change. He felt that since Metaxas was helpless with only the support of the "democrats," he would either

This background offers possible motives behind Metaxas' decision to resign. Perhaps, as Soutsos suggests, it was the irrational choice of a frustrated and disillusioned man who simply gave up in the face of an impossible situation. More likely, Metaxas was acting the shrewd politician, anticipating the approaching elections. His affiliation with Mavrokordatos and Kolettes had prevented him from openly courting the opposition support, which was still there for the asking. By resigning over the issue of life tenure, which was being presented by the press as a proposal inspired by foreign influence, Metaxas could become the symbol of opposition to foreign interference and even pose as its victim, a sure way of winning votes.[98]

Royal Acceptance of the Constitution

On 2 March 1844, the assembly accepted the last article (CVII) of the constitution. Five days later a delegation presented the whole document to the king for his approval. The public soon learned that Otho would recommend certain changes. According to some rumors, the king planned to destroy the constitution. Friends from the provinces wrote Makrygiannes offering to send forces to Athens in defense of the constitution. When Makrygiannes denied the rumors, others accused him of having sold out to the king. According to the historian Karolides, the Napists still hoped to get rid of the king and were spreading these rumors to stir up the public.[99]

Momentarily, it looked as if the sustained efforts of the unofficial cabinet would be nullified. Although they had done their utmost to create a constitution acceptable to Otho, they had not entirely succeeded. The opposition, though even less satisfied with the constitution, now came to its defense because the king seemed to oppose it. This time they seemed disposed to resort to force if need be. The parliamentary opposition, some eighty-five in number, threatened to withdraw from the assembly and set up their own rival body in Corinth or Megara if the assembly ac-

---

fall or would become more conservative in his views on the constitution, i.e. agreeing with Kolettes and Mavrokordatos. But the latter possibility Prokesch considered unlikely, and felt personally that it would profit the king to be relieved of him.

In a later letter, this time to Archduke John (6 Mar. 1844, *Briefwechsel*, ed. Schlossar, p. 190), he wrote that Metaxas had tried to extort from the king the ministry of the interior for himself.

[98] A. Soutsos [*The Third of September*], p. 168. The sources show that Kolettes was thinking of the future government at this time (Kolettes to Désages, director of political affairs in the French foreign ministry, Athens, 17/29 Feb. 1844, in Guizot, *Mémoires*, VII, 310-12). There is no reason to believe that Metaxas was any the less concerned. As Kolettes pointed out, the new ministry would find Metaxas a strong opponent, even stronger because Metaxas could easily exploit the public hatred of the Phanariots, who, like the institution of a senate, were associated with aristocracy.

[99] Makrygiannes [*Memoirs*], II, 162-64, and Karolides [*Contemporary History*], III, 50-51.

cepted the king's recommended changes. This suggestion, which amounted to a threat of civil war, induced quick compromise.[100]

On the eleventh of March the assembly began to consider the royal recommendations. On the whole, they consisted of revisions in phraseology intended to enshrine as securely as possible the principle of a strong monarchy. For instance, instead of "The judicial power is exercised by the courts of law," the king wanted the text to read, "The judicial power belongs to the king, who exercises it through his minister." In five days of closed sessions the assembly accepted some of the proposals and rejected others. On 16 March the assembly communicated its decisions to the king. Although he remained unsatisfied, the threat of civil war kept him from holding out for anything more. And so the momentary crisis subsided. Like so much throughout the period of the constituent assembly, this matter too was peaceably settled through compromise.[101]

The Resurgence of the Three Parties

The absence of division along three-party lines during the period of the constituent assembly derived largely from three conditions: (1) the unity of the protecting powers, or more accurately, the unity of England and France and the temporary withdrawal of Russian influence; (2) the close cooperation of the leaders of the three parties almost to the end;

[100] Georgantas ["Historical Memoirs"], *Parnassos*, v (1881), 849-50. He writes that the Septembrists, including Metaxas and Th. Grivas, went to Palamides to consult with him. They decided to let the assembly majority know that some eighty-five of them would leave for Corinth or Megara if Otho's recommendations were adopted. They knew that they could not accomplish this but used it as a threat.

Makrygiannes characteristically gives himself the credit for the king's acquiescence. He became sufficiently aroused to call on the king personally and exhort him to abandon the idea of proposing changes. "If you touch one iota," he warned Otho, "you, the nation, and everyone is in danger." But the king would not relent. Makrygiannes then devised a stratagem. He invited to his home Lampros Nakos, a confidant and a type of intelligence agent of the king, knowing that what Nakos heard would reach the royal ear. Makrygiannes met with his organized following from the assembly and instructed them to express before Nakos their indignation over the proposed changes and to feign astonishment that Makrygiannes himself seemed to acquiesce in this royal move. According to Makrygiannes, his stratagem succeeded. Nakos took the news back to the king, who then privately requested Makrygiannes to retain the public order and promised that no changes would occur ([*Memoirs*], II, 162-64).

[101] For the text of the king's recommendations, see [*Proceedings*], pp. 569-76 (28 Feb. 1844o.s.); Heinze, *Nationalcongress*, pp. 285-95; also Karolides [*Contemporary History*], III, 46-50. The secret sessions were not reported in [*Proceedings*]. For the accepted changes, see *ibid.*, pp. 589f., and Heinze, *op.cit.*, pp. 310-12. Karolides (*op.cit.*, III, 50) said most of the king's recommendations were accepted; Evangelides ([*History*], p. 369) and Georgantas (["Historical Memoirs"], *Parnassos*, v [1881], 850) held the opposite view. For the text of the king's reply, which expressed continued dissatisfaction, see [*Proceedings*], pp. 591-93; Heinze, *op.cit.*, p. 312; Evangelides, *op.cit.*, pp. 269-70; Karolides, *op.cit.*, III, 51-52; and partial copy in Makrygiannes [*Memoirs*], II, 164, n.

and (3) the restraint of the cabinet in exercising patronage, a most potent stimulant of party rivalry. All three conditions resulted from the fear of civil war.

Nevertheless, each party retained its identity. Segments of both the "French" and "Russian" parties refused to follow the conciliatory efforts of their leaders. Although they cooperated with each other, they never merged. Although they curbed the power of the unofficial cabinet by exploiting issues on which there was wide national consensus, each had its pet issues—the "French" had sponsored the heterochthon question and the "Russian" had sponsored the ecclesiastical and succession questions.

The end of the critical period brought an end to the conditions that temporarily halted politics along three-party lines. During the elections for the first legislative assembly, party strife broke out with renewed violence. Metaxas, Mavrokordatos, and Kolettes engaged in a new struggle for political power. The protecting powers again became concerned with the problem of securing the political ascendancy of their respective parties. The constitution offered a new stimulus to office-seeking—assembly seats and senatorial posts. Therefore, even though the problems of the revolution momentarily created new political alignments and erased some of the bases for the old ones, the parties, which had originated during the Revolutionary period and developed during the absolutist period, managed to survive. Indeed, the increased importance of political office under a new constitutional regime meant renewed incentives.[102]

---

[102] "The harmony that prevailed among the party leaders in the National Assembly of 1843 ceased at its dissolution. The old parties under Mavrokordatos, Kolettes, and Metaxas again recommenced their old intrigues and their former struggles for the power of conferring places and salaries on their partisans. The interference of the protecting powers was openly exercised" (Finlay, *History*, vii, 185).

Conclusion

THE eleven years of royal absolutism were hardly enough to cause much noticeable change in the parties, even if they were eleven fluid years. The continuities are more apparent and require as much explanation, particularly because the Crown, ostensibly with public approval, made concerted attempts to extirpate the parties, or, failing that, to undermine them. The most striking feature of party history during this period is the fact of their survival. This fact itself disproved an initial premise of royal policy—that the existence of a party depended on the personality of its leader. It revealed something more positive—that by the absolutist period the parties had become institutionalized.

Because the parties had never developed an organizational set-up exclusively and peculiarly their own, it was easy to assume that they had none at all (or, if it suited one's purposes, to deny their very existence). There was no formal mechanism for the selection or acknowledgement of leaders, no headquarters, no formal body of rules. But in actual fact, the parties grafted themselves onto or grew out of a number of systems intended for other purposes.

The most basic of these derived from the type of society that characterized the Ottoman period, one in which men did not in practice differentiate between spheres of human affairs, such as political, economic, social, or religious. Instead of belonging to a number of groups, each dedicated to a specific function, an individual tended to belong to one group which performed a variety of functions in many fields and served all his needs. As a result, a political associate might very well be a personal friend, a relative by blood or marriage, a professional associate, even an economic dependent or overlord as well. Extended families organized hierarchically into clienteles were political factions as well as economic units or professional organizations (irregular troops). Party associates from different sections of Greece communicated with each other and carried on party business through a traditional mouth-to-mouth communication system conducted sometimes through the wanderings of a monk, the business trip of a merchant, or the social gatherings of landlords and captains. An assemblage at a monastery on the feast-day of its patron saint might, among other things, be a political assembly as well.[1] When we talk about parties on this level, we are simply giving a

---

[1] On the deliberate use of the mouth-to-mouth system to avoid having information fall into the hands of the government, see Anthony Georgantas, "Historikai Apomnemoneumata tes Basileias Othonos" ["Historical Memoirs of the Kingship of Otho"], in *Parnassos*, v (1881), 837. The same writer (pp. 835, 840) writes about the undertaking of ostensible business trips as disguises for, or concurrent with, political meetings and tours. Concerning the use of monks as purveyors of information between political allies (in this case a Larion at Mt. Athos and Makrygiannes), see John Makrygiannes, *Apomnemoneumata [Memoirs]*, ed. John Vlachogiannes, 2nd edn. (Athens, 1947), ii, 110.

501

name to one particular aspect of activity which contemporaries tended to see as one undifferentiated whole.

Another organizational feature of the parties came as a direct legacy from the Philike Hetairia, the secret society which prepared the Greek Revolution. Between its founding in 1814 and the outbreak of the Revolution, it had penetrated virtually all Greek lands under Ottoman rule through a vast network of local units. It developed in men the habit and experience of acting together for a common patriotic purpose. It elaborated the paraphernalia (oaths, ritual, system of emissaries) for giving a vast secret organization some cohesion. It brought forth abiding personal relationships which could later be resumed for other purposes. Whether in imitation of Philike Hetairia or as direct continuations of some segments of it, secret societies, such as those of Makrygiannes and others, appeared during the period of absolutism, supposedly for irredentist purposes but secretly for internal political objectives as well.

The foreign legations of the three protecting powers served the parties as an invaluable organizational prop at the national level. They attracted the factions constituting component parts of their parties. They recruited a group of men who tended to mediate between themselves and party membership. They intervened with the Crown to obtain favors and office for their clients. They articulated for their parties a set of objectives and a strategy for realizing them. They became extremely important to parties in temporary royal disfavor. Once established, this system proved self-sustaining. No power would relax its patronage because of prodding from its Greek clients and fear that rival powers would not relax theirs.[2]

The rather long tenure of Kapodistrias demonstrated that the bureaucracy, instead of serving as a neutral instrument of any government, tended to act as a political group in competition with all outside groups and in time tended to develop into a party. Indeed, the Napist party owed its cohesion, first to the Kapodistrian period when it acquired vested interests in the status quo and exploited the bureaucratic structure for partisan purposes, then to the period of its exclusion from power when it had to close ranks to defend itself against the vengeance of the former political outgroups.

Only once, during the period of the constituent assembly, did the three parties appear in danger of dissolving into something different. The threat of civil war (September 1843–March 1844) evoked some of the conditions for this development—cooperation rather than competition among the powers, unity among the three party leaders, and close cooperation between these two elements and the king. What appeared likely to replace the three parties was a simple division between the indigenous elements on the one hand in behalf of a weak monarchy, with freedom

---

[2] Piscatory to Guizot, Athens, 20 Aug. 1841 [5th report], in "Textes et Documents, La Grèce d'Othon," ed. Jean Poulos, in *L'Hellénisme Contemporain*, 2nd ser., ix (1955), 413.

from foreign interference and autochthon rule, and a foreign-oriented party on the other, working closely with the powers and the king in behalf of a strong monarchy, with close observance of international obligations, and the right of access to public office for all heterochthons.

But so deftly did the combination of Crown, powers, and party leaders handle a dangerous situation that they removed the very condition of crisis on which their cooperation depended. With the promulgation of a constitution acceptable to all sides and the preparation for the first regular elections, the power of political office again became an object of contention between the three leaders and the powers fell once more into dissension as each attempted to dominate Greek politics. Once this kind of struggle recurred, the old loyalties were revived and the three parties reasserted themselves. This fact attests the strength of each party's organizational machinery.

If the parties continued to exist throughout this period, they retained, as their names suggest, their foreign orientation as a defining characteristic. Aside from their use of the legations as an organizational prop, the parties and Greek leaders concentrated more attention on international rather than on provincial politics.[3] There were two basic reasons. In the first place, their leaders realized that, given the international status of Greece and its internal constitution (absolutism), they could influence the Crown and mold the future of Greece much more effectively by catering to the powers than by catering to the home public.[4] As a result, during a showdown over the heterochthon issue in 1843-44, the leaders tended to cooperate with the powers at the expense of letting others stand as spokesmen of popular sentiment. Second, party leaders tended to know more about international politics than about the internal situation, not simply because many of them were heterochthons (like Kolettes or Mavrokordatos) but because existing conditions rendered the positions of the powers much more intelligible than the sentiments of the public.

The existence of a European state system gave international politics

[3] "Hence it comes to pass that the ministers plenipotentiary of the Protecting Powers in the court of Greece occupy a very different position from that which is occupied by the representatives of other powers in other countries . . . ," wrote G. A. Perdicaris, *The Greece of the Greeks* (New York, 1846), II, 68. Nassau Senior (*A Journal kept in Turkey and Greece in the Autumn of 1857, and the beginning of 1858* [London, 1859], pp. 253, 308) reported that in 1843 the Greeks cared little about politics, except foreign politics.

[4] For instance, after his dismissal from office in 1838, Spaniolakes recommended to Lyons the withholding of the remainder of the loan in order to force the hand of the king (Lyons to Palmerston, Athens, 10 May 1838, no. 84, Ser. 32, Vol. 108, Archives of the British Foreign Office, Public Record Office, London, hereafter to be cited as FO 32.108 and so on). However much Mavrokordatos had sought to free Greece from foreign interference, his failure to extract reforms from Otho in 1841 prompted him to urge Lyons to unite with Prokesch-Osten in forcing Otho to grant reforms (Lyons to Palmerston, Athens, 6 Sept. 1841, no. 135, FO 32.107).

an articulation unknown on the domestic scene. National governments formulated policy, which they communicated to the diplomatic corps in their capital and to their own representatives abroad. To know what England was thinking, for instance, a Greek party leader needed only to consult with Lyons or with the Greek minister in London. But to fathom public opinion within the country was difficult in the extreme, both because differentiation of society into a number of specific interest groups had hardly gone very far and because whatever diffuse interests did exist, such as those of regions or élite groups (primates, clergy, captains), lacked the machinery for adumbration to themselves and others. After the first year of the Revolution, the region had no organizational set-up capable of articulating its concerns. Professional organizations, such as chambers of commerce or veterans' associations, did not exist. Indeed, once the state destroyed local and ecclesiastical autonomy, only the parties remained as nongovernmental representatives of interest groups, but there were no subsidiary organizations, apart from that of patronage, capable of conveying the sentiments of the rank and file to the party leaders. And inherent in the notion of patronage was the assumption that the patron bestowed favors as he deemed fitting rather than any idea that he simply acted as the mouthpiece of his clients. In view of this situation it is probably impossible to make any conclusive statement about the extent to which parties represented public sentiment.

In one respect, the parties displayed a change; that is, toward partial identification with a distinct position on some basic issues. To realize the full significance of this development one must remember that the parties originated through a sense of loyalty to a leading personality or a sense of identification with a concrete group rather than because of a commitment to the professed ideals of that group. One must remember too that originally the only clear differentiation of parties on policy matters revolved around the difference of opinion concerning which of the three powers could and would be most useful to Greece, both with respect to foreign policy (commercial treaty with the Ottoman empire, realization of the Great Idea) and internal development (forming the best system of government, securing the remainder of the guaranteed loan, and accumulating foreign capital for establishing a national bank).[5] Thus one has to

[5] Sympathy of each party for its affiliate power was, to a large extent, a product of its estimate of which power would most assist or hinder the realization of the Great Idea. The "Russian" party, of course, believed that if Russia did nothing else, it would eventually provide Greece with an irredentist opportunity by precipitating another war with the Ottoman empire. Since Russia coveted many of the territories to which Greece laid claim, it was necessary to avert an eventual Greco-Russian conflict by proving that an enlarged Greece would be sympathetic toward Russian interests. Some Napists were willing to admit that France might eventually assist Greece in fulfilling her mission, but all abhorred England, not just because that power consistently supported the integrity of the Ottoman empire, but also because

be careful not to exaggerate the extent to which the parties had acquired a fixed ideology by the end of the absolutist period. As a starting point for a discussion of this trend, an anonymous pamphlet published in 1842 and entitled [*The Exhaustion of the Parties*] is instructive.[6]

The pamphlet attempted to define the ideological position of each party. Why were there three parties in Greece, the author asked, no more, no less? Not merely or even essentially because of European diplomatic influence, he answered. Otherwise Austria should also have possessed a party in Greece. Each of the three parties represented a distinct position corresponding to international ideological divisions. However, when the writer proceeded to define the allegedly distinctive position of each party, he ran into difficulty. In the international sphere, he distinguished only two ideological camps—the conservatism of Russia and the liberalism of Western Europe. So he connected the Napists with Russia because

---

the English adamantly refused to abandon their own sovereignty over the Ionian Islands in favor of Greece. Mavrokordatos admitted ("Mavrokordatos Memorandum of 1848," in Nicholas Dragoumes, *Historikai Anamneseis* [*Historical Reminiscences*], 2nd edn. [Athens, 1879], II, 168), and other pro-English and pro-French elements must have recognized, that by backing the Turkish conservative party which opposed progressive Ottoman reforms, Russia was helping to keep the Ottoman empire a tottering state.

Nevertheless, partisans of France and England believed Western support a *sine qua non* for the realization of a greater Greece. They knew that such support would never be forthcoming so long as either power feared the possibility of an enlarged Greece that might become a Russian satellite. Only a pro-Western policy and a pro-Western Greek government would eliminate this suspicion. Alexander Rangabe, for instance (*Apomnemoneumata* [*Memoirs*], [Athens, 1894], II, 89-90), secretly recommended to Otho in 1839 that the incumbent pro-Russian cabinet be dismissed in order to allay any French fears that a boost to Greece was a boon to Russia. Both Mavrokordatos and Kolettes favored an English-French entente in favor of Greece, but the latter complained that English policy, all too affected by the pro Turkish sentiments of the industrial and commercial classes, always wanted to call all the plays. Kolettes firmly believed that France sincerely favored a strong and eventually expanded Greece (Kolettes to Mavrokordatos, Paris, 13 Mar. 1840, quoted in Demetrios A. Petrakakos, *Koinobouleutike Historia tes Hellados* [*Parliamentary History of Greece*] [Athens 1946], II, 260-62; and Paris, 7 June 1841, no. 5932, Vol. 21 [1841], Mavrokordatos Archive, General State Archives, Athens). With the momentary exception of 1839, France never favored an immediate irredentist venture, but such men as Piscatory and Guizot always offered vague encouragement for the future and thus contributed to the reputation of France as sympathetic with the Great Idea.

The "English" party, on the other hand, could hardly argue for the benevolent intentions of England with respect to the Great Idea. Very often the patriotism of English partisans seemed doubtful to the public as they followed England's lead in dampening irredentist enthusiasm. But the "English" party based its policy of friendship to England on the premise that without English support the realization of the Great Idea was impossible. Hence, patience was needed and proof must be offered to that mighty power that the Greeks would do nothing except under its aegis.

[6] [Paul Kalligas], *He Exantlesis ton Kommaton, etoi ta ethika gegonota tes Koinonias mas* [*The Exhaustion of the Parties, or the ethical events of our society*] (Athens, 1842).

of their common adherence to Byzantine tradition and their alleged opposition to change. The "French" and the "English" parties he placed in the liberal camp and distinguished between them merely in terms of class and level of culture. The palikars he identified with France and the educated Greeks with England.

Now, there is much wrong with his analysis, at least in terms of my analysis. In the first place, his assumptions about the class basis of the parties is untenable. Not all palikars were members of the "French" party nor all Westernized educated Greeks members of the "English." Second, on strictly ideological grounds he could not explain why the culturally backward should move toward highly cultivated France and why the culturally advanced, most of whom had not studied in England but rather in France, Italy, and Germany, should revolve around England. Even more, the whole approach of the article was wrong because it attempted to explain the very origins of the parties in terms of adherence to a set of values instead of openly admitting the origin of the parties in terms of nonideological elements and their only later identification with issues.

But the pamphlet also reveals some truths. It shows that people were beginning to identify parties with a set of ideas, even at the expense of distorting the actual facts. More specifically, the "Russian" party was identified with conservatism and Orthodoxy, the "French" party with "palikarism," and the "English" with "educated Westernism." Even more, what seems at first glance to be a shortcoming of the essay (and *is* in terms of its stated purpose) turns out to reveal an essential feature of the parties—differences of cultural orientation or cultural levels, e.g., religio-traditionalist, educated Westernized, and nonintellectual semi-Westernized world views. The author reveals an essential fact about the parties—that they tended to represent different ways of life and conflicting sets of values. After all, cultural differences and different world views are what so strikingly divided Greek society and, insofar as parties reflected differences, they were likely to reflect these.

Before going further, one must enumerate the kinds of issues which the parties did not represent. Issues of public policy were hardly an aspect of politics. During the chaos of the Revolution such issues hardly arose. During the absolutist period some arose, such as the issues of the bank, land distribution, and pensions, but the Crown excluded the parties from any part in policy-making that might have forced them to formulate some form of program. In addition, to have differences of opinion on these subjects required more technical knowledge than most people possessed, and there were no private organizations (what we might call pressure groups or professional organizations) which might articulate the positions of interested parties in such matters.

At the other extreme, however, parties tended not to argue over ultimate objectives. They might espouse incompatible goals or speak one way and act another, but formally at least they all shared a common set of values, such as espousal of the Great Idea, constitutionalism as the ultimate form of government, state dispensation of rewards for Revolutionary services, utilization of all available professional skills in the administration, disavowal of all foreign influence and any form of favoritism toward any of the three powers, acceptance of a church autocephalous with respect to the patriarchate and autonomous with respect to the Greek state. One might say that the basis for this kind of unanimity, whether sincere or merely outward, was nationalist sentiment with its ultimate goal (Great Idea) and the requirements imposed by its institutional expression in the nation-state (national unity). However irresponsibly parties might act in some cases, they all seemed to concur on the necessity of avoiding any issues which might disrupt the fragile unity of the state. This tended to disguise the basic cultural chasm.

And so, between specific policy issues and ultimate questions of values, the parties developed conflicting positions in a middle area: broad questions which involved general means to universally accepted ends. Of these, there were five at the beginning of the period—Bavarianism, constitutionalism, the Great Idea, foreign policy, church-state relations—and six at its end—heterochthonism, the form of the constitution, the Great Idea, foreign policy, church-state relations, and the succession question.

The "Russian" party probably had the most clearly defined ideological position because of its close identification with the defense of church interests. Since the church had a corporate organization and an articulated way of life, this party had in a sense a position ready-made for it to espouse. Hence, it supported reconciliation with the church of Constantinople (within the context of autocephaly), greater powers for the church within the state, and an Orthodox monarchy. On other issues its position tended to be ambiguous or inconsistent. Within the eleven-year period it ran the gamut from support of absolutism to support of the most liberal form of constitutionalism, its position at any one time depending on the favor it enjoyed with the king.

Throughout the earlier years of absolutism the "French" and "English" parties found little they could argue about on principle. Theoretically they both espoused immediate constitutionalism, although in practice their leaders favored temporary postponement. In the absence of any real differences, the contrast of social groups dominating each leader's personal coterie gave each party a particular reputation that it did not entirely merit, the "French" with palikarism and the "English" with educated bureaucrats and professional men.

Although in the period of absolutism only the faintest signs of a fundamental difference on the implementation of the Great Idea arose, by 1848 the reputations of the parties had grown out of a widening breach over the issue of the Great Idea. One camp favored friendly coexistence with the Ottoman empire, the administrative consolidation of the Greek

507

state, and the internal development of wealth-producing resources as the surest means of realizing the Great Idea in the future. Sporadic attempts to instigate uprisings in Turkey, it felt, only antagonized the Ottoman government, subjected Ottoman Greeks to brutal reprisals, and kept Greece in turmoil. The other camp believed Greece's small territory was the cause of administrative inefficiency and economic nonviability. It advocated the utilization of all resources for the clandestine support of armed uprisings wherever and whenever possible. In short, it expected to fulfill the national mission and solve internal problems in one blow. To maintain friendly relations with Turkey was impossible, it argued, and to await a clearly favorable international situation for an attack on the Ottoman empire was as defeatist as such behavior would have been in 1821.[7]

As Dragoumes pointed out in his memoirs, published in the early 1870s, the public identified Mavrokordatos with the former position and Kolettes with the latter. The reputation of each man reached back at least to the Anatolian crisis of 1839-41. During that period, for instance, when Otho momentarily contemplated war against Turkey, it was Kolettes whom he and others considered as the most suitable man to take on such an enterprise. Shortly after, Lyons welcomed Mavrokordatos' assumption of the government as a guarantee against any reckless irredentist ventures.[8]

[7] George Aspreas (*Politike Historia tes Neoteras Hellados 1821-1921* [*Political History of Modern Greece*], 2nd edn. [Athens, 1924], i, 195-96) distinguished two antithetical policies which divided successive generations of party leaders and determined the fluctuating course of the nation's internal-external development. According to him, Mavrokordatos was the formulator of the former policy, subsequently adopted by Charilaos Trikoupes and George Theotokes, and Kolettes the exponent of the latter view, as were Demetrios Voulgares, Epaminondas Delegeorges, Thrasyvoulos Zaïmes, and Th. Delegiannes thereafter.

William Miller (*History of the Greek People 1821-1921* [New York, n.d. but probably 1922], pp. 38-39) made the same observation, when he spoke about two policies before the country in 1844—"the homely policy of the 'English' party under Mavrokordatos, that Greece should first put her own house in order before pursuing the 'Great Idea'. . . . This latter, according to the program of the 'English' party, should by competent internal administration, prudent finance and the maintenance of law and order, make Greece a model of good government throughout the Near East . . ."; and the expansionism of Kolettes, "who led the French party."

Paul Karolides (*Synchronos Historia ton Hellenon . . .* [*The Contemporary History of the Greeks . . .*] [Athens, 1922-29], iii, 337-51) also cited this basic difference in orientation, but in one place he posed this antinomy as the pull between European diplomacy on the one hand and the totality of Greeks on the other, in another as the dilemma facing each Greek political leader in the face of limited resources. He refused to divide Greek leaders along these lines and went to great lengths to prove that Kolettes had never had any practicable plans for the realization of the Great Idea or any monopoly on the nationalist aspirations that embraced the idea.

[8] Dragoumes [*Reminiscences*], ii, 157-59. Concerning public consideration of Kolettes as the man to lead an irredentist venture, see Lyons to Palmerston, Athens, 8

Neither man took the inflexible stand that later commentators attributed to him. Mavrokordatos was quite willing to commit the country to war whenever the international situation permitted, whereas Kolettes acknowledged the need for Greece to put her own house in order before embarking on a foreign venture.[9] But there was a variety of evidence to support the public in its discernment of a difference in orientation between the two men.

In 1834 when the regency was trying to decide on a permanent national capital, Kolettes proposed in writing that the state forego an official capital as a solemn reminder that only Constantinople could serve that lofty purpose, as a sign of Greek faith in the imminence of its acquisition, and as a reminder that until that moment state affairs would remain provisional. While in Paris as Greek minister, he never let slip an opportunity to reiterate Greek irredentist aspirations. In 1844, during the debate on the heterochthon issue, he rose in the constituent assembly to give what became one of the classic expositions of the Great Idea:

Greece, by her geographical location, is the center of Europe; with the East on her right and the West on her left she was destined through her downfall to enlighten the East. Our forefathers executed this task, the second is assigned to us. In the spirit of our oath and this great idea we saw always the delegates of the nation assembling to decide not for the fate of Greece but for the entire Greek race. A nation which, through its own downfall, enlightened so many other nations, is reborn today, not divided into many small states, but consolidated, with one

---

Oct. 1840, no. 113, FO 32.98; 4 Jan. 1841, no. 7, FO 32.103; and 10 Feb. 1841, no. 28, FO 32.104.

Concerning Mavrokordatos as the suitable man to put curbs on an aroused irredentist sentiment, see Lyons to Palmerston, Athens, 31 July 1841, no. 112, and 9 Aug. 1841, no. 113, FO 32.106. On his identification with a policy of internal development as early as 1841, see *Athēna*, 27 Aug. 1841o.s. The reputation of Mavrokordatos as an able administrator bore some relation to his identification with the policy of internal development, even more his assumption of office as an exponent of neutrality after Britain and France intervened to prevent Greece from joining Russia against Turkey during the Crimean War.

[9] "Mavrokordatos Memorandum" in Dragoumes [*Reminiscences*], II, 169. In a letter to Mavrokordatos, dated Paris, 13 Mar. 1840 (as quoted by Petrakakos [*Parliamentary History*], II, 260-62), Kolettes realistically discarded his initial hopes for the acquisition of Crete when he saw that foreign support would not be forthcoming for *enosis*. In 1844 he went as far as to write to Guizot that although he would never be satisfied with the exiguous frontiers of Greece, he was an exponent of the *status quo*: "The time will come when the force of circumstances will bring about what we cannot evoke today without a general conflagration which might even swallow Greece up. I am therefore a partisan of the *status quo*. Since my entry into the cabinet, I have seriously applied myself to curbing the mettle of certain uncircumspect and imprudent individuals who wish to force the government into a dangerous and anti-national path" (M. Guizot, *Mémoires pour servir à l'Histoire de mon Temps* [Paris, n.d.], VII, 324).

government and one religion. . . . What do all the Orthodox Christian peoples in Europe, the East, and elsewhere do? All wait to hear whether we still possess the Greek idea.

On his deathbed in 1847 he expressed regret that he was leaving his mission unaccomplished. Had the king only called him to rule from the very beginning, he implied, the Great Idea might have been realized. Throughout his premiership (1844-47) Kolettes never denied any of the current rumors that he was formulating grandiose irredentist plans, rumors which are in themselves indicative of his growing reputation as an exponent of radical irredentism.[10]

Mavrokordatos actually formulated his ideas in a very important memorandum which he drew up in 1848,[11] a masterful indictment of extreme irredentism and a persuasive presentation of the moderate stand. He first declared his opposition to sporadic border raids and secret societies, which in his opinion thwarted their ostensible objective. Reckless ventures of self-seeking or misguided men, they had to be suppressed. He then enumerated the mistakes of previous Greek governments. Ruptured relations with the patriarchate of Constantinople and the expulsion of heterochthons from Greek government service had alienated many Ottoman Greeks. Failure to negotiate a commercial treaty with Turkey had invited Turkish commercial reprisals, disrupted Greek trade, and hampered normal relations with the Ottoman Greeks. The sad state of Greek internal affairs had left the state totally unequipped to benefit from the Near Eastern crisis of 1839-41. The Greek state had given Ottoman

[10] On Constantinople as the natural capital of Greece, see Dawkins to Palmerston, Nauplion, no. 67, 25 Sept. 1834, FO 32.46; and Karolides [*Contemporary History*], III, 339. On his pressing of Greek irredentist claims in Paris, see his letter to Mavrokordatos, Paris, 13 Mar. 1840, as quoted by Petrakakos [*Parliamentary History*], II, 260-62. The complete text of his speech of 1844 appears in *He tes Trites Septembriou en Athenais Ethnike Syneleusis. Praktika* [*The National Assembly of Third September in Athens. Proceedings*] (Athens, 1843), pp. 190-94 (session of 14 Jan. 1844o.s.), and in Alexander Heinze's *Der Hellenische Nationalcongress zu Athen in den Jahren 1843 und 1844* (Leipzig, 1845), pp. 160-69; part of it, with some mistakes in transcription, in Gianni Kordatos, *Historia tes Neoteres Helladas* [*The History of Modern Greece*] (Athens, 1957), III, 303-306.

On his expressed regrets in 1847, see Guizot, *Mémoires*, VII, 373, and Karolides, *op.cit.*, III, 341; also an excellent sketch of Kolettes as a public figure during his years in office (1844-47) in Miller, *Greek People*, pp. 40-42.

When Kolettes became prime minister in 1844, Guizot became alarmed that, without the moderating influence of Mavrokordatos in the cabinet, Kolettes would adopt an adventurous foreign policy. Guizot felt apprehensive enough to write Kolettes, underlining European opposition to any irredentist ventures and recommending what was essentially Mavrokordatos' policy: "Occupy yourself with the interior of Greece so that it will acquire the consistency of a state well-governed internally and uncontested from without. Today that is the only and the most efficacious mode of action in preparing Greece's future" (Guizot, *op.cit.*, VII, 322-24).

[11] The text of this document is published *in toto* by Dragoumes [*Reminiscences*], II, 165-183.

Greeks no visible proof that Greek rule was any more enlightened or efficient than Turkish or shown Europe that Greek hegemony would provide the Near East with political stability. In the meantime, the Ottoman empire had instituted internal reforms which had restored Turkish self-confidence and persuaded Europe that collapse was not imminent.

His program was, in effect, one for internal development, trade, communications, and education, though it was skilfully presented as clandestine preparation for war. In its emphasis on the growth of trade, the development of a merchant-marine, and the entrusting of explosives to merchants, and in the conspicuous absence of any reference to the irregular captains, while insisting on the need for a new corps of artillerymen, this program implicitly advocated the transfer of responsibility for irredentism from the old military class to the bourgeoisie, and indirectly advanced the economic interests of the latter group. Moreover, the bureaucratic skills that Mavrokordatos cited as prerequisites for the appointees to the central directorate were those for which he and several members of his party were esteemed. In short, Mavrokordatos' policy logically required the leadership of competent bureaucrats and influential merchants, while the opposing orientation stipulated requirements which placed the traditional military class in the direction of irredentist affairs.[12]

The identification of the "French" and "English" parties with opposing irredentist programs is illuminating. First, as a reflection of the way the three parties originated, it shows the continued importance of the personality of the party leader in giving color to his party. Second, it shows the extent to which each party had become identified with a particular social group (the "French" with the palikars and the "English" with bureaucrats and merchants). But one must remember that only on this issue did each party so clearly stand out for the interests of a particular social group. For the rest, on the question of Bavarianism (which later turned into the heterochthon issue) or on the constitutional question of whether to postpone promulgation temporarily, the main division was between the party leaders on the one hand and the rank-and-file on the other.

The above features—survival, international orientation, and the beginnings of ideological articulation—existed *in spite of* rather than because of state action. As the parties bore a close connection to the existing social order and enjoyed the support of the powers, the failings of royal

---

[12] There is a striking similarity between the caution of Mavrokordatos and that of influential Greeks, especially merchants, in their reluctance to assist the Philike Hetairia before the Revolution of 1821. The exponents of the extremist policy accounted for the success of that Revolution in terms of the underground organization and the extremist methods of the Philike Hetairia.

policy need cause no surprise. Even though the Crown formally enjoyed absolute power, the existence of securely established domestic interests, the constant interference of the three powers, and the absence of efficient administrative machinery curbed its effective authority. To destroy the sustaining framework of the parties, the Crown would have had to disrupt the primary institutions on which they were based (family and clientship). It did not have the machinery to engage in such a vast undertaking, and even if it did, it could not have done so without paying the tremendous price of social disintegration. But state action did have some consequences, some unintended. It is these which now need summarizing.

Although the Crown did not succeed in destroying the three parties or in creating a nationwide party of its own, it seems to have prevented their expansion and to have arrested their tendency to assimilate more and more of the still autonomous factions. Without the existence of the Crown as a rival center of attraction and a source of protection to the weak, the three parties might have continued to attract or even swallow up the much weaker family or regional factions. As it was, however, factions such as those of Kountouriotes and Zaïmes, which had jealously resisted complete assimilation into the "French" and "English" parties respectively, found the Crown a ready patron through whom they could preserve their autonomy vis-à-vis the parties.

Without question, the Crown also curbed the ability of the parties to intensify the latent civil strife which always simmered beneath the surface. By preventing any one party from monopolizing power, it allayed some of the bitter animosities of the Revolutionary period. It partially deprived the parties of their military power by dissolving the irregulars and creating a military establishment based on absolute loyalty to the Crown. One must not allow the recurrent criticism of royal policy in the contemporary sources and the limited achievements of the absolutist period to obscure the tremendous improvement over the Revolutionary period in the maintenance of public order and in the behavior of the parties. One must also remember that, after the initial failure of the regency, the Crown learned to be satisfied with much less than it desired.

In other ways, however, the Crown unwittingly contributed to the nullification of its own objectives, often with the irony of producing some unintended consequences. In the first place, the policy of centralization—aimed at weakening the parties by weakening their local instruments and at devising machinery by which the state could displace them as protector and sustainer—backfired. Since all the parties enjoyed some participation in the administration, they all tended to exploit it, as they exploited other kinds of organization (the social organization, the secret societies, the legations) for their own partisan purposes. Since no party monopolized the administration, each was in a sense an opposition group (even when temporarily the favored party), and as opposition groups in competition

512

with a centralized administration the parties had to centralize their activities and hence increase their own internal cohesion.

Second, in refusing to share its policy-making function with either the parties or the powers, the Crown strengthened the parties by limiting them to the traditional functions they performed so well—advancing private interests and obstructing state activity. To gain the acquiescence of the three powers in its refusal to comply with the demands of those powers for policy changes, the Crown selectively appointed Greek clients of the three legations to cabinet office. A legation's reputation for success in obtaining posts for its clientele, by alternately increasing and relaxing pressure for policy changes, tended to expand the membership of each power's client party and to increase the power's hold over the client party. Then, too, by excluding party leaders from any participation in the policy-making function, the Crown encouraged them either to appeal to the legations or to resort to force (revolt or brigandage) in order to influence state policy to some extent. By contributing to close party ties between the parties and the legations, the Crown strengthened an important organizational prop of the parties. By frustrating parties into the use of force, the Crown thwarted its own overriding desire to maintain the public peace.

Third, its policy of balanced representation for all three parties in the administration failed to satisfy any of them, and its policies of Bavarianism and absolutism united them in a common dissatisfaction. This result was unfortunate because it placed the parties in opposition to the king and alienated him from the élite groups which controlled the parties. But the result was fortunate insofar as it caused the parties to bury their past animosities in pursuit of a common objective and to free themselves from the Revolutionary stigma of irresponsible behavior by working toward patriotic goals (overthrow of Bavarianism and absolutism).

In the long-run, the Crown did contribute to the eventual dissolution of foreign-oriented parties and their realignment on other bases. The extent of its contribution to this ultimate result, which began to take place at the end of the 1850s, is difficult to assess. Suffice it to say that, insofar as the Crown contributed to the growth of a new educated group (through the founding of a national university) or the creation of an influential business group (through the establishment of a national bank, the maintenance of public order, and the creation of some public works), it facilitated a process of social regrouping that eventually invited new party alignments.

What sort of significance can one attribute to the parties? This question deserves some brief final comments. I shall concern myself with individuals, élite groups, foreign powers, nation, and state. Without wishing to ignore the unfortunate aspects of party behavior, which are all too obvious to bear further mention, I will attempt here to cite more positive aspects of the parties' role.

In terms of the individual, the role of the party as a protective association is most important. To be sure, a faction or a party often attempted to cheat the government of its legitimate demands and encouraged a person to slough off the responsibilities of citizenship. But it also served as a shield against the all too frequent arbitrary practices of the official. In a time of weak, inefficient, unjust government (in spite of the good intentions of the king), the protection of one's party was undoubtedly regarded a socially indispensable function.

The parties also offered the political means by which segments of social élites (captains, primates, Phanariots, clergy) continued to compete with each other and attempted to preserve their privileged positions against royal inroads. During the Revolution, they had represented the rise of new men (usually captains and Phanariots) to importance. According to Piscatory in 1841, the men of moderate means were becoming more influential in political affairs. There is no evidence to prove his statement. But if he was right, such men probably utilized the party framework to win local elections against the magnate, that is, in cooperation with each other or with other magnates. In any case, the story of the Crown's attempt to undermine the privileged classes is one and the same as its onslaught on the parties, precisely because these groups controlled the leadership of these parties.

The way in which parties and powers exploited each other for mutual advantage, which often conflicted with national interest, accounts for so much of the ill-repute of the three parties then and after. There is nothing very edifying about the way in which the powers attempted to exploit Greek political differences to put pressure on the Crown and to outdo each other. But one must remember that, had it not been for the parties, the powers might have interfered sooner and much more forcefully and directly than they did even in 1843-44.

Perhaps the most significant characteristic of the parties is that they cut across class divisions, regional loyalties, and different ways of life. An awareness of two facts makes this characteristic understandable. First, as protective associations exercising some government functions, the parties depended on a number of skills in order to gain some self-sufficiency. Second, in response to the national framework of politics since the Revolution, parties became nationalized since a party representing all sections of Greece was more effective than a regional one.

This characteristic reveals the peculiar function and significance of parties during these eleven years when the country's greatest problem was national unity and the fusing of dissident elements into a unified nation-state. The parties undoubtedly contributed to the breakdown of localism, to the decline of class warfare, and to the creation of some national cohesion. To be sure, these forces were strong enough to weaken the internal structure of the parties, but the fact remains that men of different camps within the party often cooperated with each other and ignored their differences in the face of external foes. The parties undoubtedly articulated and intensified opposition, but they did so in such a way as to demand cooperation between different regions, classes, and ways of thinking. And parties probably tended to fill the vacuum and relieve the confusion caused by the breakdown of such previous communal organizations as the village, the region, or the church.

In terms of the state and its institutions, the parties were in different ways responsible for both absolutism and subsequent constitutionalism. They indirectly encouraged absolutism because the Crown considered this the only system that could adequately curb the parties and correct the situation which it believed they had created. They were responsible for constitutionalism in a more direct way—by joining together and staging a revolution that imposed constitutionalism on a reluctant king.

The final observation points out an evil that continues to plague Greece even today—overcentralization and the absence of local initiative. This process started with Kapodistrias and continued during the period of absolutism. In order to destroy local abuses, the state also ended local ability to make good changes. To deprive the parties of their ability to exercise widespread influence, the Crown destroyed local autonomy, ecclesiastical freedom, regional privileges, and forbade all manner of meetings and assemblies without prior permission from the government. In so doing, it was disregarding much of what gave Greek life such vitality during the century prior to the Revolution.

Appendices

I: DOCUMENT

"Memoirs concerning the philorthodox society introduced in Greece"[1]

In 1830 a religious society, called Orthodox, was established in Russia under the patronage of the Emperor. Its purpose, I believe, was to counteract the worldwide advance of the English and American bible societies. Inside Russia practically all the nobility, outside Russia practically all the diplomatic officials, are members of that society. To become a member, one must demonstrate, besides [the possession of] other characteristics, the possession of independent wealth. Besides its members, who pay a stipulated annual sum, that society consists of a great number of pensioners [*syntaxiouchoi*] and recipients of aid [*hypotrophoi*], whom it supports with annual grants from the sizeable funds contributed by its members and the government to its treasury. A pensioner is considered anyone who, though not a member of the society ⟨2⟩ knows its purposes and rites [*mysteria*]; a recipient of aid is anyone charged to act by express command.

In Greece, members of that society are Messrs Catacazy and Leles; pensioners Oikonomos, Glarakes, Niketas, Kapodistrias, Perroukas, Paparregopoulos, Ainian, Zokliades, and some others. Finally, the greater part of the higher clergy, the abbots of most monasteries, many political and military figures—that is, as many as have proved themselves fanatical followers of the Russian Party—are recipients of aid.

A few years ago the society, reformed according to the will of the emperor, adopted the aim of uniting the entire eastern church under one leader or Patriarch, on whom would fall the same rights, influence, and authority as those exercised by the Pope of Rome over the clergy of the Western Church.

Aid recipients were therefore sent or introduced to all parts of the East and intensive efforts were made, especially ⟨3⟩ in Greece, where the

The numbers marked ⟨0⟩ indicate the pages of the original document.

[1] To my knowledge, there is only one extant copy of this anonymous, undated document, of which the following is my translation. It is deposited as item no. 5794 in a folder entitled "Undated" in Vol. 21 (1841), Mavrokordatos Archive, General State Archives, Athens (see Chap. VI, nn. 40 and 129, in text).

I have tried in this translation to adhere as closely to the original as possible. Wherever the author has obviously failed to express himself precisely, I have attempted to clarify his remarks with additions, indicated by brackets, but I have attempted to keep these at a bare minimum. Where the English equivalent does not render the exact meaning I have included the original Greek words, also in brackets. I have not tampered with the author's paragraphing or use of capitals, even though each is often arbitrary and without uniformity.

already established independence of the church posed the greatest obstacles.

The Patriarchate of Constantinople, to which they promised this high position, perseveringly promoted and worked for this objective. But in spite of the assertiveness of the aid recipients in Greece, the enterprise was not advancing enough. On the one hand, the diplomatic officials of Russia were unable to take an active part in affairs because of circumstances during the regency period; on the other hand, there was no leader of the Russian Napist Party and hence no center of concerted activity. Feeling this deficiency, the party decided in 1836, after many misgivings, to call Viaro Kapodistrias back to Greece. On the pretext of returning to press inheritance claims,[2] he could assume direction of the interests and ideas of the Russian party.

Salutations had already been sent to Viaro and the necessary steps had been taken, when the appointment from Munich[3] of G. Kolokotrones, as aide-de-camp of His Highness, somewhat ⟨4⟩ interfered with the realization of this plan. The plan subsequently fell through, during the presidency of Rudhart, when Viaro was no longer willing to come to Greece and share with others the authority that the condition of things [now] inspired them to demand.[4]

At the beginning of 1838, because of divisions within the Napist party, it was decided to make new proposals to Viaro. But because he was not interested and gave as a pretext [of his refusal] the aversion of a large segment of the Greek populace toward him, it was decided [to secure] temporarily his brother G.[eorge] Kapodistrias instead of him, not [as was the original intention of Viaro] as leader of the party but as a mere instrument who, because of his name, could be useful in restoring the morale of dispirited adherents [of the party] and in supporting the proposed plans through assurances that such was the intention of the late governor. Consequently, the direction of the political affairs of the party was entrusted to Mr. Glarakes, who was then a cabinet member, and the direction of military affairs to Gennaios Kolokotrones.

G. Kapodistrias, after ⟨5⟩ pretending that he had quarreled and broken off relations with his brothers, arrived in Greece on the pretext of [coming to press] claims of inheritance.

From then on, more active efforts began. After many conferences, it was decided to prepare for the convocation of a national assembly, in which they hoped to have a majority and hence accomplish whatever they desired. The composition of the existing cabinet contributed mar-

---

[2] As heir to John Kapodistrias, his deceased brother.

[3] Otho issued the appointment from Bavaria, where he was visiting during most of 1836.

[4] The writer obviously means that the actual or prospective possession of important public office now gave Kolokotrones and likely candidates for office a firm basis for advancing their own individual claims to party leadership.

velously to this [end] but, wishing to gain control of the Ministry of Economic Affairs also, they worked against Mr. Spaniolakes and, through Mr. Regny, attempted to [secure] the appointment of Mr. George Ainian as Minister. The idea of an assembly had to be justified to the people through the newspapers so that they could get used to what was such a paradoxical [shift of position on this] issue for the Governmentalists. Hence, in May 1839, *Aiōn* took up the constitutional theme. Knowing that that newspaper was considered as his organ, Glarakes pretended to be displeased with its ideas of this sort and to dissociate himself from it. He condemned it and subsequently introduced the newspaper *Hellas*. In the ⟨6⟩ meantime, all [*Aiōn's*] subscribers belonging to their party were instructed not to stop supporting and assisting its [*Aiōn's*] publication. As a result, the number of its subscribers increased rather than decreased.

These are the chief objectives which they attempted to realize:

(1) The introduction of a hereditary senate consisting solely of autochthons.

(2) The exclusion from military and political office of whoever is not an autochthon, or whoever was not [employed] in the Greek public service since the holding of the national assembly of Argos.[5] Only the Heptanesians [Ionian Islanders] whose relatives either fought for, or contributed in behalf of, Greece were to be exempted from [the provisions of] this decree.

(3) The denial of political rights to the Mavromichales' and their heirs as assassins of Governor Kapodistrias, as well as the denial of political rights to all those who were accused of bearing guilt for this act.

(4) The nullification of the law for the independence of the Church and the submission of the Greek Church to the Great Church [Patriarchate] of Constantinople. ⟨7⟩

(5) The pursuit, and expulsion from Greece, without exception, of all the American schools and all the books published by the bible societies.

(6) The erection of a splendid monument for Kapodistrias, the recognition by the government of the claims pressed by his brothers, the satisfaction of these through [the grant of] important national lands, and the appointment of Viaro as president of the Greek Senate.

(7) The obligation of the king to recognize the eastern religion [Orthodoxy] as the religion of the whole State, and [more] especially, as the sole religion of his heirs and Future family. These were the chief aims which they hoped to achieve. As far as internal legislation was concerned, Glarakes had assumed the burden of drawing up such a program, but it had not been completed.

But, to achieve the convocation of an assembly, the consent of the Government was necessary. This was unlikely. So it was decided that Glarakes would skilfully investigate the disposition of the king toward that [prospect]. ⟨8⟩ If he determined that such [royal approval] could

5 1829, when the public administration became predominantly Kapodistrian.

not be obtained, then Kolokotrones, Rangos, and Mamoures should flood Mainland Greece and the Peloponnesos with brigands, and if necessary, brigandage should lead to revolutionary movements. Then began the catechizing of Demarchs, the pursuit of all those whose beliefs conflicted with theirs, tours of various chieftains and politicians to different places, agreements with the Governors, frequently repeated assemblies of demotic authorities, and finally, the persistent demand for the abolition of mobile units [*metavatika*][6] and for the withdrawal of Rumeliot forces from the Peloponnesos. Among such tours, two were the most curious.

The first was that of the elder Kolokotrones, who confined himself to the command that all his followers and acquaintances put their greatest trust in his sons and obey their orders, because he had gotten old and his children had taken his place. The second was that of Colonel Rangos, who by himself traveled over Western Greece [West Rumely] many times, and came to an understanding with various ⟨9⟩ chieftains, among whom were the Gioldases', Pesles, Veres, Tsatsos, E. Chatzopoulos and some others whose names I do not remember. He despatched Nikos Theos and a relative of his outside the country, so that they might reach an understanding with Soter Stratos and the rest [of Stratos' group] as well as with various other Turkish captains.

Among the Governors to whom Glarakes confided his ideas, there are Rados, [J.] Soutsos, Panos, Rangos, Karores, Nengas, Axiotes, Kountoumas, Loidorikes, Oikonomides, Tompakakes, Pakmor, and Anagnostopoulos.

Affairs were in such a condition when the events in Anatolia and the death of the Sultan inspired in them the idea of more direct action and of open attack against the state [*arche*]. Hoping that the Russians would inevitably take Constantinople, they decided to secure through force what they had hoped to achieve through an assembly. Immediately the necessary instructions were given to the Governors and Demarchs, and a large number of important persons [*hypokeimena*] were sent ⟨10⟩ to various provinces to prepare and pave the way for a general disturbance throughout the realm.

Rangos took Western Greece [West Rumely]; Ainian and Loidorikes, Eastern [Greece, East Rumely]; Speliotes, Kalavryta; the Petimezas' and Plapoutas, Elis and Achaia; Gennaios Kolokotrones, Tripolis and Karytaina; Tsokres and Cheliotes, Argolis; Giatrakos, Laconia, etc. Going about various eparchies, these men told some that it was time for us [Greeks] to take action by ourselves in order to instigate a revolt in Rumely [Thessaly], whose liberation the king did not desire. To others [they said] that it was time for us to move so as to throw off the yoke of a government which was tyrannizing us and had deprived us of our rights and individuality in order to give them [the former] to the Bavarians. To others, finally, [they argued] that it was necessary to defend our religion

---

[6] A current device for the suppression of brigandage (see Ch. VI, p. 310, above).

against the threat of westerners, who were supported by their coreligionist our king, and that this was ⟨11⟩ the opportune moment for securing and winning over the most important classes of the people. They were also promising the support of Russia through its awaited navy, [they] were proclaiming that sizeable funds were at their disposal, and that all the Rumeliot chieftains and forces were in league with them, waiting only for the signal to rise up, because this was a national and general movement.

But this method of catechizing posed many difficulties, because everyone was asking about the leader of this movement—who it was that would handle correspondence and give the necessary decrees, when the occasion arose. So it was decided, after a previous conference, to establish a three-man committee, consisting of one military, one political, and one ecclesiastical figure. Ostensibly at least, it would oversee all matters and, more especially, issue diplomas and furnish the agents [*apostoloi*] with the necessary instructions.

At this point the gravest problem occurred, because no one would accept a ⟨12⟩ position which was rendered so dangerous by the possibility that the society might be discovered.

The vanity of Kapodistrias and the levity of Niketas caused them to accept such a dangerous position. But a third, an ecclesiastical, member was needed. In spite of all the exhortations and promises made by Oikonomos and the president of the synod, in spite of all the means which they employed, they were unable to persuade the bishop of Damala to accept that position. For that reason, it was decided that the committee should temporarily consist of only two [members], until either the bishop of Damala was persuaded, or some other bishop was found to accept this difficult task. At the same time, it was decided to disguise the secret purposes of the society by pretending that it sought the insurrection of the Turkish provinces.

In the meantime, Emmanuel Papas had also come. He [had] established connections with Niketas and Kapodistrias, without anyone else's knowing it. Taking a great liking to this young man, as Kapodistrias himself said, and wishing to satisfy ⟨13⟩ his ego, Kapodistrias [had] added some of his [Papas'] ideas to the already prepared plan for the establishment of the philorthodox society. This development caused much trouble and provoked harsh disputes [*exegeseis*] among Messrs Kapodistrias, Niketas, Gennaios [Kolokotrones], Leles, Glarakes, and Valsamakes.

Those quarrels can easily be explained. Appointed a member of that fanciful archpresidency [three-man committee], Kapodistrias believed himself the actual leader of the nation or of a large party. Consequently, not only did he begin to issue diplomas, instructions, and orders, but he also made various promises without having any permission to do so and without the real party leaders' knowing anything about them. As a result, they were forced to accept Emm. Papas and Renieres, but on the condition that Kapodistrias arrange their immediate removal from Greece. They explicitly told Kapodistrias that, in any fatal circumstances, they intended to denounce them [Papas and Renieres] and portray them as men planted to discredit their party. At this point, I must point out that Kapodistrias communicated very little with Emm. Papas and ⟨14⟩ Renieres. They learned most of the society's secrets by flattering and catering to Niketas.

By August 1839, the greatest activity had begun. After inviting a large number of mayors to Karytaina and other places of the Peloponnesos, Gennaios Kolokotrones had announced that everything was ready. After undertaking what were ostensibly tourist jaunts, Ainian announced that Eastern Greece [East Rumely] was ready. Rangos gave assurances that Western Greece [West Rumely] awaited only the signal for revolt and that 2,000 Albanians, under the command of Zervas, Stratos, and Tselios Pitsoures, stood ready to invade. In Athens, a general assembly of the topmost leaders, was immediately convened, in order to decide on a plan of action for the execution of their program.

In the meantime, Kapodistrias sent Renieres off to the Ionian islands, where his mere appearance was intended to serve as a signal that all was ready.

At this point, I should have described what the philorthodox society managed to organize in the Ionian islands, but it was completely impossible for me to learn the party's plans for the Ionian islands ⟨15⟩ and the means it employed for the realization of those [plans]. On this subject, Kapodistrias avoided all my questions. The only things I succeeded in ascertaining were that a company of Albanians were supposed to assemble across from Santa Maura and that the bishops of Zante and Paxos were the leaders of affairs in the Ionian islands. But I am totally ignorant of what they were trying to achieve.

Renieres had received instructions to recall a priest by the name of Velentzas from Aegina to Athens, to then proceed from Poros to Spezza. Glarakes had instructed the Governor of Argolis to send his [Renieres'] passport for the Ionian islands there. As so often happens among those moved by a zeal to serve, Renieres exceeded his instructions. Believing himself engaged in a mission pleasing to God, he began to catechize various individuals in Poros, Aegina, and Spezza and to introduce presidencies in accordance with the practice [of the society].

The report, which Renieres made at my exhortation a few days before his trial, contains practically all that he had, on different occasions, told me, Kleomenes, George Ch. Chrestos, the lawyers Typaldos, Masson, and Stroumpos, and various ⟨16⟩ others. It is the detailed and accurate description of all his activities and of all he knew about the society. For this reason, I feel it unnecessary to repeat these things. I merely point out that the priest Velentzas in Aegina, Sachtoures and Kakogeorges in

Poros, and Kolandroutsos in Spezza not only knew what was actually going on, but had even been informed about the mission of Renieres. So he had no trouble coming to an understanding with them. Indeed, one of them, Kakogeorges, discerned Renieres' great carelessness in trying to catechize whomever he happened to encounter and notified Athens about this. Consequently, Kapodistrias sternly rebuked Renieres, who had by now arrived in Spezza, and commanded him to depart as soon as possible for the Ionian islands.

Not wishing to leave, Emm. Papas still remained in Athens on various pretexts. Sometimes he asked for money, sometimes he played sick, and sometimes he pretended to be awaiting letters from Serres [Thrace]. Such behavior aroused suspicion in the factional leaders and gave cause for clashes with Kapodistrias. Already ill-disposed toward the archpresidency because it had summoned and appointed someone from the ⟨17⟩ Ionian islands [to replace] him [Papas] as general secretary, Emm. Papas openly asked for 1,500 drachmas. When he did not receive [the sum], he quarreled with Kapodistrias, who promised him all sorts of things in an attempt to quiet him. But on the other hand, Niketas and Kapodistrias were trying in every way to deceive Emm. Papas [so as] to secure the diplomas and whatever other documents he possessed.

Realizing this, it seems, not only did he [Papas] not return them, he disclosed them—just how I do not know—to the king through Tzames Karatasos. The letter of Kakogeorges concerning Renieres, the petition from Koloukouvaros to the minister of the army through Colonel Ch. Petros, and finally, the behavior of Papas terrified those directing the society. Thus, at an assembly held in the house of Mr. Leles, it was decided that Glarakes should lull the government to sleep in this way,[7] using for this purpose Schmaltz and all the Bavarians. [It was decided] that the outbreak of the revolutionary movement should take place as soon as possible.

But before I proceed to an analysis of the measures which they [the conspirators] intended to take or the objective ⟨18⟩ which they put forth, I think it necessary to write a few things about the organization of the philorthodox.

Introduced in the month of June [1839], as I mentioned above, that society had as its main objective the acquisition, through arms, of supremacy for the Russian or Napist Party. Besides its known organization, that society had, in addition, a special auxiliary organization known to only a few of its members; that is, as many members as had advanced to the third rank.

There were three ranks of enlistment [*katechesis*]. The first was called

---

[7] The text gives no indication what "this way" was or how the conspirators intended to exploit Schmaltz and the Bavarians. I have no way of knowing whether this was an omission of the copy which I used or an omission in the original document.

the *simple* [*aplous*]. It consisted of those belonging to the Napist party—untried individuals who were enlisted for the first time. The catechism of this first rank envisaged the instigation of revolt in the Turkish provinces.

The second [rank] was called the *grand* [*megas*]. To it especially the clergy belonged. Restoration of the [Orthodox] religion, which had allegedly been persecuted by foreigners, constituted [the objective of] its catechism.

The third [rank] was called the *dread* [*phriktos*]. ⟨19⟩ Those distinguished for their partisan sentiments, the chieftains wielding provincial influence, and the higher clergy belonged to it. Its catechism envisaged the acquisition of rights by means of force and the establishment of an orthodox kingship.

Each of these ranks had its special [recruiting] agents [*apostoloi*] and its own rules. No one, however, could become an agent, if he had not been admitted into the second [rank of] enlistment. Agents did not know who their fellow-agents were and had no relations, one with another. Those of the highest rank, however, were supposed to know the enlistments to the lower ranks and were obliged to introduce the initiate to all the mysteries of initiation into the lower ranks. If one agent, engaged to enlist someone, found him knowledgeable in the catechism of the lower rank, he then had leave to promote the person after a careful examination. Conversely, if the initiate was already initiated into a rank higher than that of the agent, he did not have to explain himself to the agent. He brushed him off in a tactful way, while secretly doing his utmost to assist him in his work.

In this manner ⟨20⟩ the various agents traveled about Greece without knowing one another. It often happened that two came into contact, each trying to enlist the other.

The agents were supposed to receive their diplomas from the archpresidency. Only those enlisted into the third rank had permission to grant diplomas to agents and to appoint such men.

All the initiated took the oath peculiar to their rank, because there were three oaths. The first was administered by the agents on the bible; the second before a clergyman dressed in his vestments; the third in a church before a prelate.

Certificates of oath-taking were drawn up immediately. After being signed by the initiate, the agent, and the priest, then the diploma was granted. For it, the agent had the right to collect a taler [five drachmas], if he wished.

Traveling about in various places, the agents introduced presidencies, consisting, in the large towns, of one president and nine associates [*paredroi*], in the towns of middle category, of one president and five associates, in the ⟨21⟩ small towns, of one president and three associates. The presidents and associates had to belong to the second rank at least. Those presidencies were intended to temporarily replace the existing authorities in case of a revolutionary movement. If, by any chance, there was a member of the philorthodox society, of third rank, in a place, then he had the full right to preside over both the established presidencies and [established] assemblies. In case of an insurrectionary movement, he gave orders to all the presidencies of the eparchy, in which he was located, in conjunction with the leaders in Athens.

It is impossible to estimate the number of diplomas granted by the various agents and the archpresidency. It seems, however, the number [of these] exceeded that of diplomas issued by Kolettes, whom they were trying to imitate.[8]

In Athens, the members of the philorthodox society came together often, and discussed and decided all matters concerning the progress of the society. These assemblies took place, by and large, at the home of Mr. Leles around two in the morning. ⟨22⟩ At these assemblies, only the leaders and the philorthodox of the highest rank gained admittance. Mr. Glarakes presided over these assemblies. Valsamakes was secretary. The registers and other documents were deposited in the home of Mr. Leles, and from it they could absolutely not be taken.

I add here one point that escaped me. Once established, all presidencies had to write two letters, whose format the agents brought with them, the first to the Patriarch of Constantinople, the second to Kapodistrias, begging both to intercede with tsar Nicholas for assistance and protection in their behalf. A large number of such letters had been despatched to the arch-presidency in time.[9]

When, in November, the philorthodox society learned that the Government began to suspect the existence of some society without by any means knowing [the actual] developments, it was decided, as I said above, to hasten the ⟨23⟩ realization of the society's objective. Hence, the opinion of the most important chieftains was solicited with regard to the proper manner and time for launching a movement.

The first and fullest plan, which appeared, proposed [as follows]: in the Peloponnesos, the sudden capture of the fortress of Nauplion, the subsequent movement of various troops from Karytaina, Messenia, Argolis, and Laconia, and the assembling of these at the Gulf of Corinth; in Mainland Greece, the attack on Mesolongi by one body [of troops], the direct movement of other troops against Athens. This plan was not approved because Rodios proved [two points]. On the one hand, [he showed] the impossibility of assaulting the fortress of Nauplion and the great resistance which, in any case, they would encounter from Almeida and Hitz, the head of the artillery, neither of whom could be persuaded to join the society and hence deliver up the fortress or neglect the necessary precautions. On the other hand, [he pointed to] the probability that the campaign against Athens would fail, once the king, informed ⟨24⟩ of

---

[8] A reference, apparently, to Kolettes' Perachora movement of 1831-32.

[9] By "in time" the writer probably means "before the society was exposed."

the movements, ordered the leaders of the Rumeliots in Athens to march against the revolt. Besides, Mamoures, on whom they pinned their hopes, did not agree to effect such a movement. From that time forth, they tried hard to remove the Rumeliot leaders, but because this was impossible and because the execution of such a plan caused endless delay, it was abandoned. Various plans succeeded the first. But because, in the deliberations concerning the execution and adjustment of these [plans], many took part, especially men without the faintest notion about military affairs, nothing had been decided when the King spoke for the first time to Glarakes about the existence of a society and ordered him to investigate.

That same night Glarakes convened an assembly, in which he described the condition of the society's affairs, the difficult position in which they found themselves, and finally, the need to adopt a resolute measure. At that assembly, Kapodistrias proposed that, instead of contemplating ⟨25⟩ distant campaigns, it was better to organize in Athens a body of 600-800 good soldiers, who would by night attack the mint and capture all the public monies. "When we deprive the Government of all its financial means," he said, "then everything can be accomplished." All liked this idea, but because no one dared put it in action, it was decided to convene in Athens at the end of December a general assembly of the top leaders of philorthodoxy, so as to place this plan before them. If it was approved, it should be executed by them. Invitations were therefore issued to all. At the same time, Mamoures and Rangos were instructed to send, on various pretexts, some good soldiers to Athens.

Wanting to gain time, Glarakes told the Government that the investigation did not turn up anything and that probably the allegations stemmed from the intrigue of some party. Finally, the king told Glarakes, in the presence of Païkos and Schmaltz, that he had in his possession documents relating to the society. Schmaltz added that ⟨26⟩ it was a matter of wonder that Mr. Glarakes did not know anything on this occasion, when at other times he had bragged about knowing everything [that went on] and when, on this occasion, persons whom he knew intimately were implicated. The King repeated, "I command you, Gentlemen, to investigate this affair quickly and strictly." As soon as the ministers emerged from the court, Glarakes approached Païkos and told him it was not prudent to make an immediate move before he [Glarakes] took the necessary measures, ordered the Governors and gendarmerie to make a strict investigation and take the necessary steps to prevent it [the plot], if it really existed. The evening of the same day, an assembly was held in which it was decided to either hide or destroy the documents, diplomas, and other papers of the society, to send messengers immediately to all parts [of the kingdom] to inform everyone [all members] about the discovery of the society and urge caution, in their relations and movements, until further orders [were sent]. In this situation, ⟨27⟩ Kapodistrias behaved with exemplary courage. "I know," he said, "that M[anuel] Papas betrayed the society and became a member because of me. Therefore it is only right that I should be the first to suffer the consequences of my error. I think that the remaining documents must be insured. Only the incomplete [description of the] organization, which Renieres copied, should remain among my papers. In the event that they search my house and find it, I will say that those were merely ideas, which I conceived with respect to the Ottoman provinces and which, once I wrote them down in French, M. Papas translated and Renieres copied. Otherwise, having documents in its hands and being unable to track down anything, the Government will probably adopt severe measures and many will suffer, whereas [this way], the matter will be limited to me and possibly to Niketas as well." They accepted this proposal and for this reason only the [description of the] organization remained among Kapodistrias' papers; the seals and the remaining papers disappeared. The letter form addressed to the Patriarch ⟨28⟩ was neglected, as useless, because the contents of that letter had subsequently been revised.

After the lapse of five days, afraid to postpone the investigation any further and learning about the documents which M. Papas had given the King, Païkos ordered a house-to-house search, which Ioannides executed so clumsily that, even though Athens alone had over 1,000 philorthodox [members] holding diplomas, there was no way to expose even one. The most curious thing is that Papadopoulos-Vretos, Vallianos, Panoutsos, or Photopoulos carried the diplomas on their persons while being examined at the inquiry.

Just as soon as the philorthodox society was discovered, Philemon immediately ran to me utterly frightened, and said, "There now, didn't I tell you? You see [what] an intrigue [this is]. It is a desperate attempt to ruin us. I must publish an issue to defend my [party] associates. Try your utmost to obtain the release from prison of my responsible editor, who was recently condemned [in court], so that the newspaper can begin [publication]."[10]

I advised him to speak about this [matter] ⟨29⟩ with Mr. Païkos, whom he claimed as a friend, and with Governor Axiotes. He left immediately. Returning the next day, he said to me, "I accomplished everything. Public Prosecutor Ioannides will close his eyes, because Governor Axiotes is not opposed and therefore there is nothing to fear from the superior [authority] if he [Ioannides] releases my responsible [editor] immediately." Indeed, by these means and through a small bribe, the responsible editor was released on 24 December, even though his sentence specified 8 January 1840. On the 25th, they brought Kapodistrias to jail. On the 26th,

[10] Philemon, of course, was the actual editor of the Napist newspaper *Aiōn*. The reference here is to the ostensible editor, a straw man hired, according to the practice of the day, to bear the trouble of litigation and, if necessary, the penalties of imprisonment entailed by official censorship.

Philemon, who by exception was the only one permitted to enter Medresa[11] during that time, came and begged me to find out from Kapodistrias what they had asked him about the society and what documents
had been found among his papers. I asked him what he thought about
that society. He told me that he did not yet have exact knowledge of
the affair, that he believed it an English intrigue, and that so he intended
to portray it because that was the expedient thing to do. Finally, on the
1st of January 1840, *Aiōn* published its first article on philorthodoxy [the
Philorthodox plot]. To it [this article] ⟨30⟩ Philemon and many of his
like-minded [friends] attributed the hesitation of the king and the ces-
sation of prosecutions and further strict inquiries. Henceforth, Philemon,
whom I continued and continue to frequently see, began to openly support the Governmentalist or Napist Party. During this interval, Philemon
knew in detail what went on. As he said, through Mr. Païkos he learned
the intentions of the Government; through Mr. Velissarios and Valsamakes what transpired during the investigation of Philorthodoxy. Velissarios, the investigator, would come to agreements with him through
Triantaphylles, the previous prosecutor. Learning from Prosecutors Typaldos and Ioannides what transpired, Valsamakes would convey this
[information] to Philemon, through Mr. Panas, a co-worker on the *Aiōn*
[staff] who undersigned articles "the Cosmopolite."

When they brought Kapodistrias to prison, I managed to secure a meeting with him. I asked him what he wanted and he begged me to notify
the English Legation about his imprisonment. From then on, I ⟨31⟩
noticed, both from his remarks and from various letters he would give
me to correct, that he was trying to implicate England in that affair by
behaving as if he had many connections with Mr. Lyons.

During the first months of [his] imprisonment, continuing in the spirit
of *Aiōn*, Kapodistrias would charge me to ask Renieres whence originated
his relations with Pharmakides and Manouses and to learn if they did not
incite and instruct him to introduce Papas to Kapodistrias and to move
him [Papas] to secure a place in the society.

Subsequently, Kapodistrias altered his words. He often told both me
and many of those imprisoned with us that England did not have anything to do with the Philorthodox society. Finally, after the publication of
the decree,[12] when he learned that the Napist Party intended to pin
everything on him and to represent him as the organ of an English
intrigue, Kapodistrias began to despair and often certified that such an
idea was infamous and that the English did not have the slightest notion
of these [things]. ⟨32⟩

N. Renieres often reiterated to me, in the presence of Kapodistrias and

[11] The prison of Athens.
[12] There is nothing to indicate what "decree" is meant; possibly the writer is referring to the formal indictment.

all the other prisoners, that he did not even know Pharmakides and that he had no relations with the anglophiles.

After his release from prison, seeing the Napist intrigue proceeding, Kapodistrias hastened to explain himself to me and to ask my advice and assistance. I did not fail to assist him, as much as I could, in all his tribulations. I had been the first to inform him about the Napist intrigue against him. He made many explanations to his lawyer Mr. Typaldos, as the latter himself acknowledged, and also convinced him that there was nothing English about the Philorthodox society.

These are, in brief, the essentials of what I . . . [unintelligible word] concerning the Philorthodox society from my conversations with Kapodistrias, Valves, Mavrogiannes, and Renieres.

At the beginning of June, the Public Prosecution for the Court of First Instance ordered that the indictment be communicated to the accused. Observing that the court order covered ⟨33⟩ only Kapodistrias and Renieres in its provision for the communication of the indictment, I directed the attention of the former to this circumstance, advised him to dispute it [the indictment], and on the same day myself drew up the protest [anakope] of Renieres. I knew very well that the higher court [epheteion] could not accept the protest of Renieres. Nevertheless, with the intention of gaining time to bring to light the intrigue which I suspected, I advised him to persist.

Pressed by his lawyers, Kapodistrias did not want to submit a protest. Nonetheless he begged me to strengthen the resolve of Renieres [to do so]. It is impossible for me to describe what this unfortunate man [Renieres] suffered [from attempts] to [make him] withdraw his protest —insults, promises, offers of money, threats. They neglected nothing [in their attempts] to achieve their objective. And as if all these means, used by Gianitzes and M. Anagnostakes in order to persuade him, were not enough, the public prosecutor himself had, at the end, to invite him to his office and command him to withdraw his protest, threatening ⟨34⟩ to send him to Medresa. Renieres remained dauntless. Finally, his protest was rejected and they were again summoned to be tried.

In the meantime, here is what I, together with Kapodistrias, discovered. Ramphos and Valsamakes formulated the following plan for the defense. Niketas should solicit P. Paparregopoulos and Kalligas as his lawyers, the former so that he would not receive a place in the formation of the court [as one of the court's judges], the latter so as to cause his uncle Mavrokordatos[13] to be excluded [as judge]. In this way, they believed they would have a majority of the court [the panel of judges on their side]. Niketas should disclaim his signature and consequently allege that the diplomas were forgeries and that his signature had been forged by Papas and Renieres. The public prosecutor should immediately ask

[13] This Mavrokordatos is not to be confused with Alexander Mavrokordatos, who was Greek minister in London at this time.

for the issuance of an order of arrest against Mr. Papas and Renieres for forgery and [petition] for postponement of the trial. The court would accept the first and reject the second, and consequently, after discussion, would decide that no society existed. ⟨35⟩

This plan was liked and they put it into effect. So certain were they of their success that they had already drawn up various articles in order to prove that what they called the misorthodox society was an offspring and nursling of an English intrigue.

Only Kapodistrias opposed this plan, saying that in no way could he deny his signature. His lawyer Typaldos supported his view.

The intrigue became known to everyone. Learning privately that the Napist party intended to portray Kapodistrias as an English organ, I informed him of this immediately. So agitated did he become that he frequently and repeatedly assured me that, if the Kolokotronists did not change their intention, he was determined to appear before the king, sincerely confess all that happened, and [then] beg his mercy.

I did not let Renieres hold aloof [from me?], because I had been informed that M. Anagnostakes would come to the jail, ⟨36⟩ sometimes threaten him, sometimes promise him money, in an attempt to get him [Renieres] to say that he had been planted by Pharmakides, Klonares, Manouses, and Praïdes so that he, together with Emm. Papas would involve Niketas and Kapodistrias in that intrigue.

Having successfully opposed this intrigue through [my] services and advice, I finally persuaded Renieres to confess in the presence of me and his lawyers Stroumpos, Typaldos, and Masson, and I prevailed upon him to draw up a report about [past] events which, having signed, he turned over to his lawyers through me.

The day of the trial arrived. Because neither Kapodistrias nor the advisors of Niketas would give in, the trial was postponed for a few days. It was Monday. That evening Kapodistrias came to me and remained almost to midnight, [all the while] vexed and at a loss over what he should do. Because I advised him to appear before the king and tell the truth, he said, "If they press me any further, I will do so and will tell them [the royal court] ⟨37⟩ where all the documents of the society are deposited, so that the king will know the character of each [conspirator]. I have one more step to take. If I fail, I promise you that I will appear before the king." The next day—Tuesday, that is—I did not see Kapodistrias. Coming to me on Wednesday, he told me that everything was settled, that Consul Paparregopoulos, to whom he had emphatically spoken, persuaded Niketas to acknowledge his signature. "I am certain that we will all be acquitted." And indeed, on Friday, all the philorthodox were acquitted, because the judicial power was able to track down only two [conspirators].[14]

[14] The writer is obviously referring to the legal point on which acquittal was based; namely, that since the court was able to certify the existence of only two

In describing here all that I was able to learn about the purpose of that society during my six-months of cohabitation and uninterrupted contact with the philorthodox [persons], I do not mean to antagonize [burden?] or offend anyone. Isolated as I have been during what is already a year in prison, it was for my own pleasure that I composed ⟨38⟩ judicial chronicles, in which events relating to the philorthodox society occupy an important place. At the appropriate time, I intend to convey these [chronicles] to the Government.

---

conspirators (Kapodistrias and Niketas) and two accomplices (Renieres and Papas), the evidence proved only the existence of the idea of forming a society, not the existence of an actual society with a verifiable membership; that therefore the law which proscribed secret societies did not apply.

II: SELECTED PROSOPOGRAPHY

GUIDE TO THE READING OF PROSOPOGRAPHICAL CHART

THE table below is a list of the major politically active individuals during 1833-44, who turn up in the available sources and receive mention in this book. An attempt is made to identify them in terms of basic categories of information indicated below. Because such data is not readily available, the identifications are often incomplete, many lesser individuals have not been included, and the prosopography is of necessity only a sketchy beginning. Its elaboration and refinement must await, and hopefully will invite, the further investigation of available, scattered, and sometimes obscure sources which may offer such vital statistics and permit the addition of more individuals.

Left Columns

The initials after the names indicate membership in the Council of State (CS) and in the cabinet (CAB) at any time from 1833-43, and membership in the constituent assembly of 1843-44 (CA). The Prosopography, though nowhere else, also includes the *macron* accent in the family names to facilitate pronunciation and to assist those wishing to check such names in Greek reference works.

Party Affiliations

The four main sources for identifying party affiliations are the following: (1) the Lyons correspondence, especially Lyons to Palmerston, Athens, 2 Nov. 1835, no. 2, FO 32.53 (classification of the appointees of the Council of State by parties); (2) Maurer, *Griechische Volk*, ii, passim; (3) Thiersch, *État actuel*, passim; and (4) Piscatory, Athens, 6 Sept. 1841 (7th report), *L'Hellenisme Contemporain*, ix, 427-47 (catalogue of individuals with, among other things, their party affiliation), the last by far the richest source. In some cases, Goudas [*Parallel Lives*] and [*Grand Encyclopedia*] have been useful.

C is used to indicate Constitutionalist, whenever it is impossible to identify absolutely a person more specifically with either the "English" or "French" parties. "Constitutionalist" means, for the purposes of this classification, one who became identified with the Constitutionalist cause during the civil war of 1832.

The second column in this category attempts to classify individuals in terms of the three parties: "English" (Eng), "French" (Fr), or "Russian" (Rus). But in some cases it has been necessary to complicate the classification a bit in order (1) to indicate shifts in party affiliation (for instance, "Eng-Fr" means a shift from the "English" to the "French" party sometime during the absolutist decade); and (2) to indicate major branches of a party (for instance, the Zaïmes faction [Eng-Z], the Kountouriotes faction [Fr-K], the former of the "English" party, the latter of the "French" party).

Regional Identity

The left-hand column of this category divides these men into three simple groups: heterochthons (H) (as of 1821), autochthons (A), and philhellenes (P). The right-hand column refines the classification somewhat. The heterochthon category is broken down into the following subcategories: Bucharest (Buchar); Bulgaria (Bulgar); Cephalonia (Cephal)*; Chios; Constantinople (Const); Corfu*; Crete; Epirus; Ithaca*; Lefkas*; Macedonia (Mac); Montenegro (Monten); Psara; Rhodes; Smyrna; Souli; Thessaly (Thess); Thrace; and Zante*.

The autochthon category is subdivided into the following: Islands, either Spezza (Isl-Sp) or Hydra (Isl-Hy); Rumely, either East (E.Rum) or West (W.Rum); Peloponnesos, either North (Pel-N), Central (Pel-C), or South (Pel-S); or Mane. The philhellenes are divided into English (*Eng*), French (*Fr*), *Italy*, Portuguese (*Portug*), and Scottish (*Scot*).

Social-Occupational Grouping

The left-hand column simply distinguishes between civilian (Civ), military (Mil), naval (Nav) and ecclesiastical (Eccl). In the second column of this category, "civilian" is broken down into the following subcategories: primate (Pr) if his land was essentially landed, (PrM) if an island primate whose wealth was primarily monied; scribal (Sc), referring to a civil servant and/or a member of the liberal professions, such as doctor, lawyer, professor ("ScL" meaning lawyer, "ScD" meaning doctor); and Phanariot (Phan), to which is added "Sc" (PhanSc) if the Phanariot in question is also scribal. The "military," "naval," and "ecclesiastical" categories have not been broken down.

Western Education

The last category is an attempt to identify Western-educated men by an X, followed by an abbreviation to indicate the country or countries where education was received, the various possibilities being: Austria (Aus); Bavaria (Bav); France (Fr); Germany (Ger); Italy, and Russia (Rus). In cases where a man studied in two countries, this will be indicated, as for example "GerAus." In some cases, a blank may not indicate absence of Western education, but simply no evidence for it and X? indicates only that I suspect this is true.

* All Ionian Islands.

NAMES	Party Affiliation "English" C "French" "Russian"	Regional Identity H A Break- P down	Social Grouping Civ Break- Mil down	Western Education
Ainian, George	Rus	A E.Rum	Civ Pr	
Almeïda, K.	Rus	P Portug	Mil	
Anagnostopoulos, Panagiotes	Rus	A Pel	Civ	
Anargyros, Andrew	Eng	A Isl-Sp	Civ PrM	
Androutsos, Anastasios (CA)	Rus	A Isl-Sp	Civ PrM	
Antōniadēs, Emmanuel	Eng	H Crete	Civ Sc	X
Apostolaras	Rus	H Mac	Mil	
Apostolidēs, Misael	Eng	H Crete	Eccl	X Bav
Argyropoulos, Manoles	Eng	H Const	Civ PhanSc	X?
Argyropoulos, Pericles	Eng	H Const	Civ PhanSc	X
Asōpios, Constantine		H Epirus	Civ Sc	X GerFr
Axelos, C. (CA)		H Thess		
Axiōtēs, Alexander	Rus	H Corfu	Civ	
Bastas, Anthony	Eng-Fr	A Pel-S	Civ Pr	
Benakēs, Panagiotes		A Pel-S	Civ Pr	
Botasēs, Nicholas (CS, CAB)	Fr	A Isl-Sp	Civ PrM	
Botsarēs, Kostas (CA)	Eng	H Souli	Mil	
Botsarēs, Notes (CS)	Eng	H Souli	Mil	
Bountourēs, Basil (CS)	Eng	A Isl-Hy	Civ PrM	
Bountourēs, D. (CA)				
Charalampēs, Demetrios		A Pel-N	Civ Pr	
Charalampēs, Soterios	Rus	A Pel-N	Civ Pr	
Chatzēchrēstos, A. (CA)	Fr	H Bulgar	Mil	
Chatzēpetros, Christodoulos	Fr	A E.Rum	Mil	
Chatziskos, Demetrios	Fr	A E.Rum	Civ Pr	
Chrēstidēs, Demetrios (CAB)	Fr	H Const	Civ Sc	X
Christakopoulos, Basil (CA)	Fr	A Pel-C	Civ	
Christenitēs, Lycurgus	Fr		Civ	
Church, Richard (CS, CA)	Eng	P Eng	Mil	
Dariotēs, George (CA)	Eng-Fr	A Pel-S	Civ Pr	
Dariotēs, Panagiotes		A Pel-S	Civ Pr	
Delēgiannēs, Anagnostes (CS)	C	A Pel-C	Civ Pr	
Delēgiannēs, Charalampos	C	A Pel-C	Civ Pr	
Delēgiannēs, John		A Pel-C	Civ Sc	X Fr
Delēgiannēs, Kanellos (CA)	C	A Pel-C	Civ Pr	
Delēgiannēs, Panagiotes	C	A Pel-C	Civ Pr	
Delēgiannēs, Petros	C	A Pel-C	Civ Sc	X Fr
Domnandos, Kyriakos	Rus	H Crete	Civ Sc	X
Doukas, Adam	Fr	A E.Rum	Civ Pr	
Doukas, Constantine	C	H	Civ	
Doumpiōtēs		H Mac	Mil	
Dragoumēs, Nicholas	Eng	H Const	Civ Sc	X
Dyovouniōtēs, G. (CA)		A W.Rum		

NAMES	Party Affiliation "English" C "French" "Russian"	Regional Identity H A Break- P down	Social Grouping Civ Break- Mil down	Western Education
Georgantas, Anthony (CA)	C	A E.Rum	Civ Pr	
Giatrakos, George	Fr	A Mane	Mil	
Glarakes, George (CAB, CA)	Rus	H Chios	Civ Sc	X GerAus
Graillard, Francis		P Fr	Mil-Reg	
Grivas, Gardikiotes	C	A W.Rum	Mil	
Grivas, Phloros	C	A W.Rum	Mil	
Grivas, Stavros	C	A W.Rum	Mil	
Grivas, Theodore (CA)	C	A W.Rum	Mil	
Ierolimos, Manolakes	Fr	A W.Rum	Civ Pr	
Ioannou, Philip		H	Civ Sc	X Bav
Iskos, Andrew (CA)	Eng	A W.Rum	Mil	
Kalamogdartēs, Andrew	Fr	A Pel-N	Civ Pr	
Kalamogdartēs, Anthony (CA)	Fr	A Pel-N	Civ Pr	
Kallephournas (see Kalliphronas)				
Kallergēs, Demetrios (CA)	Rus	H Crete	Mil-Reg	X RusAus
Kalliphronas, Demetrios (CA)	Fr	A E.Rum	Civ Pr	
Kanarēs, Constantine (CA)	Rus	H Psara	Nav	
Kanellopoulos, Kanellos	Fr	A Pel-C	Civ Pr	
Karakatsanēs, Ghikas	Fr	A Isl-Sp	Civ PrM	
Karatasos, Tzames	C	H Mac	Mil	
Karatzas, Constantine (CS)	Fr	H Const	Civ Phan	
Karōrēs, Nicholas	Rus	A E.Rum	Civ Sc	
Katakouzēnos, Alexander		H	Civ Phan	
Kleanthēs, Stamatios		H Thess	Civ Sc	X Ger
Klēmakas, John	Fr	A E.Rum	Mil	
Klōnarēs, Christodoulos (CAB, CA)	Eng	H Epirus	Civ ScL	X Fr
Kolandroutsos, George	Rus	A Isl-Sp	Civ PrM	
Kōlettēs, John (CAB, CA)	Fr	H Epirus	Civ ScD	X Italy
Koliopoulos (see Plapoutas)				
Kolokotrōnēs, Constantine	Rus	A Pel-C	Mil	
Kolokotrōnēs, Gennaios (John)	Rus	A Pel-C	Mil	
Kolokotrōnēs, Theodore (CS)	Rus	A Pel-C	Mil	
Kontogiannēs, Mitsos (CA)	Rus	A E.Rum	Mil	
Kontogiannēs, Evangelos		A E.Rum		
Kontostavlos, Alexander	Eng	H Chios	Civ PrM	
Korphiotakes, N.	Fr			
Kountouriōtēs, George (CS, CA)	Fr-K	A Isl-Hy	Civ PrM	
Kountouriōtēs, Lazaros	Fr-K	A Isl-Hy	Civ PrM	
Kriezēs, Anthony (CAB)	Eng	A Isl-Hy	Nav PrM	
Kriezēs, Demetrios	C	A Isl-Hy	Civ Sc	
Kriezēs, George (CA)				
Kriezōtēs, Nicholas (CA)	Fr	A E.Rum	Mil	
Lassanēs, George L. (CAB)		H Mac	Civ Sc	X Ger
Latrēs, N.	C	H Smyrna	Civ Sc	

NAMES	Party Affiliation "English" C "French" "Russian"	Regional Identity H A Break- P down	Social Grouping Civ Break- Mil down	Western Education
Leventēs, George		A Pel-C	Civ Sc	
Levidēs, Constantine	Fr	H Const	Civ Sc	X Aus
Lidorikēs (see Loidorikes)				
Logothetopoulos, Constantine	Fr	A E.Rum	Civ Pr	
Loidorikēs, Anastasios (CS, CA)	Fr	A E.Rum	Civ Pr	
Loidorikēs, Athanasios (CS)	Eng	A E.Rum	Civ Pr	
Loidorikēs, Panagiotes	Rus	A E.Rum	Civ Pr	
Lontos, Anastasios (CA)	C	A Pel-N	Civ Pr	X
Lontos, Andrew (CAB, CA)	Eng	A Pel-N	Civ Pr-Mil	
Louriōtēs, Andrew	Eng		Civ-PrM	
Makrygiannēs, John (CA)	Fr	A E.Rum	Mil	
Mamoukas, Andrew	Rus	H Chios	Civ Sc	X Ger
Mamourēs, John Gouras	Rus	A E.Rum	Mil	
Manginas, Tatzes (CS)	Eng	A W.Rum	Civ Pr	
Mansolas, Drosos (CS, CAB, CA)	Fr	H Thess	Civ ScD	X Ger
Masson, Edward	Fr	P Scot	Civ ScL	X
Mavrokordatos, Alexander (CAB, CA)	Eng	H Const	Civ PhanSc	X Italy
Mavromichalēs, Katzes	C	A Mane	Mil	
Mavromichalēs, Petros (Petrobey) (CS, CA)	C	A Mane	Mil	
Mavrommatēs, George	Rus	A W.Rum	Civ Pr	
Mavrommatēs, N. (CA)		A W.Rum		
Mavrovouniōtēs, Vasos	Fr	H Monten	Mil	
Melas, Leon (CAB, CA)		H Epirus	Civ ScL	X Italy
Meletēs, Meletes (CA)	Fr	A E.Rum	Civ Pr	
Meletopoulos, Demetrios (CA)	Fr	A Pel-N	Civ Pr	
Meletopoulos, Emmanuel	Fr	A Pel-S	Civ Pr	
Mēlios, Spyros (see Spyromelios)				
Metaxas, Andrew (CS, CAB, CA)	Rus	H Cephal	Civ Pr	
Mexēs, John (CS)	Rus	A Isl-Sp	Civ PrM	
Miaoulēs, Andrew	Eng	A Isl-Hy	Nav PrM	
Monarchidēs, Anagnostes (CS, CA)	Eng	H Psara	Civ PrM	
Moraïtinēs, Aristides	Rus	H Smyrna	Civ ScL	X Fr
Nakos, Lampros	Rus	A E.Rum	Civ Pr	
Nakos, Stamos (CA)		A E.Rum		
Nikētaras Stamatellopoulos, Niketas (CA)	Rus	A Pel-C	Mil	
Niketas (see Niketaras)				
Notaras, George (CA)	C	A Pel-N	Civ Pr	
Notaras, John	C	A Pel-N	Civ Pr	
Notaras, Panagiotes	C	A Pel-N	Civ Pr	
Notaras, Panoutsos (CS, CA)	C	A Pel-N	Civ Pr	
Oikonomos, Constantine	Rus	H Thess	Eccl	

NAMES		Party Affiliation "English" C "French" "Russian"	Regional Identity H A Break- P down	Social Grouping Civ Break- Mil down	Western Education
Oikonomos, John (CA)		Fr	A Megara	Civ	
Orlandos, John		Eng	A Isl-Sp	Civ PrM	
Païkos, Andronikos (CAB, CA)		Rus-Fr-K	H Mac	Civ ScL	X Italy
Palamēdēs (see Palamides)					
Palamidēs, Regas (CS, CAB, CA)		Fr	A Pel-C	Civ Pr	
Palmas, A.		Rus	P Italy	Civ ScL	X
Panas, Daniel			H Cephal	Civ ScL	X Italy
Panas, Elias			H Cephal	Mil	
Panourgias, Nakos (CA)		Fr	A E.Rum	Mil	
Papadopoulos-Vretos, Andrew		Rus	H Ithaca	Civ Sc	
Papakostas	C		A E.Rum	Mil	
Papalexopoulos, Spyridon(?)		Fr		Civ	
Paparrēgopoulos, Constantine		Rus	H Const	Civ Sc	X Rus
Perraivos, Ch. (CA)			H Thess		
Perroukas, Demetrios (CA)		Rus	A Pel-N	Civ PrScL	X
Petimezas, Basil (CA)		Fr	A Pel-N	Mil	
Petimezas, Constantine		Fr	A Pel-N	Mil	
Petimezas, N. (CA)			A Pel-N		
Petrakēs, Anargyros (CA)		Rus	A E.Rum	Civ Pr	
Petrobey (see Mavromichales, Petros)					
Petsalēs, A.			A E.Rum	Civ Pr	
Pharmakidēs, Theokletos		Eng	H Thess	Eccl	X Ger
Philēmon, John		Rus	H Const	Civ Sc	X?
Phōtēlas, Asemakes	C		A Pel-N	Civ Pr	
Pitsipios, C.	C			Civ ScL	
Plapoutas, Demetrios Kolio-poulos (CA)		Rus	A Pel-C	Mil	
Polyzoïdēs, Anastasios (CAB)		Eng	H Mac	Civ Sc	X GerBav
Ponēropoulos, Nicholas (CA)		Fr	A Pel-C	Civ Pr	
Praïdēs, George (CAB)		Eng	A Smyrna	Civ Sc	X GerItaly
Provelengios, Constantine (CAB)		Fr-K	A Isl-Sp	Civ Sc	X Italy
Psyllas, George (CAB)		Eng	A E.Rum	Civ Sc	X Ger
Rados, Constantine		Rus		Civ	X Italy
Rallēs, George (CAB)		Rus	H Const	Civ ScL	X AusFr
Rangos, John		Rus	A W.Rum	Mil	
Rangos, Panos		Rus	A W.Rum	Civ ScD	
Renierēs, Nicholas (CA)			H Crete	Civ ScD	X Italy
Rizos-Neroulos, James (Iakovakes) (CAB)	C	EngFr	H Const	Civ Phan	X
Rodios, Panagiotes (CA)		Rus	H Rhodes	Mil RegD	X ItalyFr
Roma, Dionysios		Rus	H Zante	Civ Pr	
Roukēs, John			A Rum	Mil	
Rouphos, Venizelos		EngFr	A Pel-N	Civ Pr	

NAMES	Party Affiliation "English" C "French" "Russian"	Regional Identity H A Break- P down	Social Grouping Civ Break- Mil down	Western Education
Sachinēs, George		A Isl-Hy	Civ PrM	
Sachtourēs, George	Rus	A Isl-Hy	Civ PrM	
Samourkasēs, John	C	H Const	Civ Sc	
Schinas, Constantine (CAB)	Fr	H Const	Civ Sc	X GerFr
Schinas, Michael (CAB, CA)	Rus	A Pel-S	Civ	
Sikelianos, Michael	Rus	H Lefkas	Civ Pr	
Silivergos, N.		H	Civ	
Simos, Chrysanthos (CA)		A Pel-N		
Simos, Evstathios (CA)	C	H Epirus	Civ	
Sisinēs, George	C Fr(?)	A Pel-N	Civ Pr	
Sisinēs, N. (CA)		A Pel-N		
Skouphos, Nicholas	Fr	H Smyrna	Civ Sc	X?
Skourtaniatēs, Athanasios	Fr	A E.Rum	Mil	
Somachēs	Fr	H Epirus	Civ ScL	
Sophianopoulos, Panagiotes	Fr	A Pel-N	Civ Sc	X
Soutsos, Alexander	C	H Const	Civ PhanSc	X Fr
Soutsos, Charles		H	Civ Phan	
Soutsos, Michael (CS)	Rus	H	Civ Phan	
Soutsos, Panagiotes	Eng	H Const	Civ PhanSc	X Fr
Soutsos, Skarlatos		H Buchar	Mil-Reg	X Bav
Soutsos, Yanko	Rus	H	Civ	
Spaniolakēs, George (CAB)	Eng	H	Civ Sc	X?
Spēliadēs, Nicholas	Rus	A Pel	Civ Sc	
Spyromēlios, Michael (CA)	Rus	H Epirus	Mil	
Staïkopoulos, Staïkos	Eng	A W.Rum	Mil	
Staïkos, John (CA)	Eng	A W.Rum	Mil	
Stamatellopoulos (see Niketaras)				
Stavros, George	Rus	H Epirus	Civ M	X Aus
Stratos, John	Fr	A W.Rum	Mil	
Stratos, Nicholas	Fr	A W.Rum	Mil	
Tertsetēs, George		H Zante	Civ ScL	X Fr
Theocharēs, Nicholas (CAB)	C	H Mac	Civ Sc	X Ger
Theocharopoulos, Soterios (CA)		A Pel-N	Civ Pr	
Theotokēs, John	Fr	H Corfu	Civ Sc	
Tisamenos, George (CAB)	Fr-K	H Epirus	Civ Sc	X?
Tompakakēs	Rus		Civ	
Tompazēs, Iakomakes	Eng	A Isl-Hy	Civ PrM	
Tompazēs, Manuel	Eng	A Isl-Hy	Civ PrM	
Trikoupēs, Spyridon (CS, CAB, CA)	Eng	A W.Rum	Civ Sc	X ItalyFr
Tsamados, Anastasios	Rus	A Isl-Hy	Civ PrM	
Tsamados, M. A. (CA)				
Tsanetakēs (see Tzanetakes)				
Tsavelas (see Tzavelas)				
Tsokrēs, Demetrios	Rus	A Pel-N	Mil	
Tsongas, George	Eng	A W.Rum	Mil	

NAMES	Party Affiliation "English" C "French" "Russian"	Regional Identity H A Break- P down	Social Grouping Civ Break- Mil down	Western Education
Typaldos, John	Rus	H Cephal	Civ ScL	X Italy
Tzanetakēs	Fr	A Mane	Mil	
Tzavelas, Kitsos (CA)	Rus	H Souli	Mil	
Vagias, George		H Epirus	Mil	
Valetas, Spyridon (CAB, CA)	Eng	H Const	Civ Sc	X Fr
Vallianos, Theodore	Rus	H Cephal	Mil-Reg	X?
Valsamakēs, Demetrios	Rus	H Cephal	Civ	X?
Valtinos, George (CS)		H W.Rum	Mil	
Vamvas, Neophytos	Eng	H Chios	Eccl	X Fr
Varnakiōtēs, George	Rus	A W.Rum	Mil	
Velentzas, John (CA)	Fr	A E.Rum	Mil	
Venthylos, John	Fr	H Smyrna	Civ Sc	X Ger
Vlachopoulos, Nicholas (CAB)	Rus	A W.Rum	Mil	
Vlasēs, Christos (CA)	Fr	A Pel-N		
Voulgarēs, Demetrios	Fr-K	A Isl-Hy	Civ PrM	
Voulgarēs, George	Fr-K	A Isl-Hy	Civ PrM	
Xenos, Emmanuel (CS)	Eng			
Zacharitsas, Nicholas	Fr-K	A E.Rum	Civ Pr	
Zaïmēs, Andrew (CS)	Eng	A Pel-N	Civ Pr	
Zaïmēs, John (CA)		A Pel-N	Civ	
Zervas, Nicholas	C	A W.Rum	Mil	
Zographos, Constantine (CAB, CA)	EngRus	A Pel-N	Civ Sc	X Italy
Zotos, Logothetes		A W.Rum	Civ Pr	
Zygomalas, Andrew	Fr	H Chios	Civ ScD	X Fr

Selected Bibliography

THIS IS essentially a bibliography of materials for the period 1833-44 as they relate to the subject and focus of this book. As an attempt to present the reader with a comprehensive picture of the range and type of material available for research on parties and politics during this period, it also covers items which, for reasons of time and location, were not used in the research for this book. Because much of the material is not generally known or has not been evaluated in terms of the subject of this book, the bibliography includes considerable critical comment.

For reasons of time and space, two areas have been left largely outside the range of this bibliography—the period 1821-32 and the full biographical data on important political figures. Works dealing exclusively with the Revolutionary and Kapodistrian periods have been included only when they relate directly and in an indispensable way to the origins of the parties or to conditions fostering them. But much of the included secondary material covering 1833-44 deals with the period 1821-32 as well. There is a crying need for an exhaustive enumeration and evaluation of sources shedding light on domestic politics and political groupings for the period 1821-32—what this book has tried to do for the period 1833-44. What has been done for this earlier period in this book, with largely secondary material of the most obvious relevance, shows, I hope, the value of what such an enterprise might turn up.

The reason for the general exclusion of biographical material is quite simple. The bulk of biographical data on influential Greeks is, in the general absence of full-length biographies, largely in the form of funeral orations, journalistic accounts, and hastily prepared lectures (of which the Gennadius Library, Athens, has the best collection). Such data is therefore diffuse and its enumeration would require too much space. Judging from several samplings, this material concentrates on the Revolutionary career of its subjects, hastily passes over their activities during the absolutist period and, in short, does not sufficiently relate them to their role in the parties to warrant the time and space that enumeration would require. The same can be said of the few scholarly biographies that have appeared. In writing this book, I found sufficient for basic biographical data the two following standard works: Anastasios N. Goudas, *Bioi Paralleloi ton epi tes Anagenneseos tes Hellados Diaprepsanton Andron* [*Parallel Lives of Distinguished Men during the Regeneration of Greece*], 8 vols. (Athens, 1869-76) and *Megale Hellenike Enkyklopaideia* [*Grand Hellenic Encyclopedia*], 24 vols. (Athens, 1926-34). My primary sources (the writings of Finlay, Piscatory, and Lyons especially) are sufficiently illuminating on the basic character of these men and the best guides to their personal roles in the parties. The exceptions of listed biographies, included because of some particular relevance to the subject and focus of the book, are as follows: Lenormant on Metaxas (II D be-

543

low); Bower and Bolitho on Otho (III A); Balanos on Oikonomos and Pharmakides (III B 3); Blancard on Mavrokordatos, Metaxas, and Kolettes; Eardley-Wilmot on Lyons, and Eliopoulos and Georgiou on Kolettes (III c); and the biographies of Abel, Armansperg, Maurer, Rudhart, and Thiersch in III E.

Finally, it should be pointed out that many bibliographical citations— of works on some aspect of 1821-32 or of biographical studies—not listed in this bibliography appear in the footnotes of Part I in the text. Biographies of Otho, Ludwig, and Amalia are also cited in footnotes, as indicated at the beginning of III E below.

I. Unpublished Primary Sources

A. OFFICIAL ARCHIVES BY STATE

AUSTRIA

GEHEIMES HAUS-, HOF-, UND STAATSARCHIV. VIENNA.

Archives of the State Chancery. Greece. Fascicles I, IX, X.

This collection contains more than 1,500 sheets of official unnumbered reports and letters from Prokesch-Osten, Austrian minister in Athens, to Metternich, Austrian chancellor in Vienna. Important items of this correspondence have been published by Anton von Prokesch-Osten (the younger) in a two-volume collection entitled *Briefwechsel . . .* (II A below). Extensive quoted excerpts, sometimes going beyond the two-volume published collection, appear in Petrakakos and Mendelssohn Bartholdy (II A and III A respectively). A single item from this collection, this time by Wallenburg in the temporary absence of Prokesch-Osten, has been published by B. Jelavich in *Balkan Studies* (II A). Extensive use of this material for a study relating to Greece has been made in B. Jelavich's *Russia and the Greek Revolution of 1843* (II A) and in the article of Engel-Janosi (III D).

BAVARIA

BAYERISCHES HAUPTSTAATSARCHIV. MUNICH.

The Secret Archive of Otho. Geheimes Hausarchiv.

This collection, part of the larger private archives of the Wittelsbach family, consists of what is left of the private files of Otho's personal chancery while he was king of Greece. Parts of it were probably withheld before the file was sent to Otho in Bavaria after his deposition in 1862. More substantial parts were destroyed by fire through Allied bombings of Munich during World War II. Before the bombings, the collection consisted of 92 fascicles whose contents are briefly catalogued by Petrakakos in his [*Parliamentary History*], II, 117-19 (II A below). The bulk of the present collection consists of personal correspondence, only some of which relates to Greece: 795 letters from Otho to Ludwig (1821-67), 408 letters from Ludwig to Otho (1821-67), about 100 letters of Amalia to Ludwig, and about 200 from Maximilian II (Otho's elder brother) to Otho.

Select items of the Otho-Ludwig correspondence were published in 1891 in a small volume by Trost, who was then chief archivist of the Geheimes Haus- und Staatsarchiv (II A below). Of the few Greek scholars to work in this archive, Petrakakos and Skandames (II A and III A respectively) have in their works included, in addition to items published in Trost, a few hitherto unpublished items. Occasionally, some of this material has appeared in the Greek popular press—in *Hestia* (1902-1903) and in the 1950s in *Kathēmerinē*. But, by and large, the published portion of this correspondence remains relatively small and does not go much beyond Trost. Happily, however, Dr. Hans Rall, director of the Geheimes Hausarchiv and professor of history at the University of Munich, is currently overseeing the preparation of a complete edition of the Otho-Ludwig correspondence. Pending its completion, the collection has been closed to scholars. As a result, I was unable to utilize this material, though Dr. Rall was kind enough to receive me and tell me about his work.

Although Bower and Bolitho used the collection in preparing their biography of Otho (III A below), neither they nor Petrakakos or Skandames studied it with the parties in mind. But the already published portion of the collection shows that Ludwig and Otho were concerned about the parties and that royal policy was formulated with them in mind. It remains to be seen whether the remainder of the correspondence will turn up further information on the parties as such and on royal policy toward them. It is clear from Petrakakos' catalogue that the Otho Archive originally contained a wealth of material besides personal correspondence —political and financial reports, memoranda on relations with the powers, accounts of various revolts, assemblies, and royal progresses. Such material would be more likely than correspondence to provide this kind of information. But it is unclear how much of this has survived and, if any, when *it* will be published or again be accessible to scholars.

GEHEIMES STAATSARCHIV

Three categories of documents are of special relevance in this varied repository of state papers: (1) in the foreign section, the reports and letters of the Bavarian ministers in Athens to the Bavarian foreign office—Bayerische Gesandtschaftsberichte aus Athen 1832-64, M.A. III:* Griechenland, 1833-64 (Bände 1-35); (2) such items as letters of Armansperg to Ludwig in Politisches Archiv der bayerischen Gesandtschaft Athen, fascs. 1-1000; and (3) Russian documents originating from the Russian legation in Munich before World War I and consisting of both regular reports from Munich to St. Petersburg (in original draft or in

* What the M.A. stands for here is not known. This is the way the citation reads.

notebook) and despatches from the Russian foreign ministry to its representative in Munich.

Two documents from the first category have been published in a separate article by Vakalopoulos (II A below). Materials from the first two categories have been used and cited in the article of Rall (III D). Select items from the third appear in a separate publication by B. Jelavich (II A).

BAYERISCHE STAATSBIBLIOTHEK. MANUSCRIPT SECTION. MUNICH.

Two large collections of special value for Greece, which I was unable to use during research for this book but which I examined during a short visit more recently, are the *Maureriana* and *Thierschiana* collections, the private papers of George Ludwig von Maurer and Friedrich Thiersch respectively.

Maureriana

Materials relating to Greece are found in fascs. 19 and 20. The former, entitled "Denkwürdigkeiten. Die Wittelsbacher in Griechenland," is by far the more important, containing as its most important single item a "history," more properly Maurer's personal memoirs on the formation of the regency and its dissolution in 1834, together with 98 appended documents, intended to supplement Maurer's published three-volume work (II A and B below). This manuscript has been described in an article by Karl Theodor von Heigel, entitled "Denkwürdigkeiten des bayerischen Staatrats Georg Ludwig von Maurer," in *Sitzungsberichte der philos., philol. und der histor. Klasse der Kgl. Bayer. Akademie der Wissenschaften*, IV (Munich, 1903), 471-512. This fascicle also includes a large collection of letters to Maurer on Greece, much of it from Greeks in Greece. Fasc. 20, entitled "Miscellaneous," includes less material on Greece.

Thierschiana

Of this collection, fascs. 119-20 contain manuscript and printed materials on Greece; notes and a journal of his trip to Greece in the early 1830s and his role in affairs there; and a manuscript account of the establishment of the regency, intended to supplement his published two-volume work (II B below). Fascs. 129-31 contain correspondence from him for the years 1798-1858, while fasc. 132 contains the extensive correspondence to him from a vast number of people, among them many Greeks. These letters are arranged alphabetically by correspondent, a separate envelope for each, and fill several boxes.

FRANCE

ARCHIVES DU MINISTÈRE DES AFFAIRES ÉTRANGÈRES. PARIS.

Correspondance Politique, Grèce. Fascs. 8-60 (1830-52)

These fascicles consist of the official correspondence between the

French ministers in Greece and the French foreign ministry. The value of these documents for the diplomatic history of Greece is attested by Driault and Lhéritier (III A below), who used them extensively in writing their diplomatic history. For the domestic developments in Greece, there is no reason to believe that these are any less valuable than the similar despatches in the Archives of the British Foreign Office. Indeed, the small number of Piscatory's despatches from this collection, which have been published by Jean Poulos (II A) would indicate quite the contrary.

GREAT BRITAIN

ARCHIVES OF THE BRITISH FOREIGN OFFICE. PUBLIC RECORD OFFICE. LONDON.

Ser. 9 (Bavaria), vols. 61-145 (1830-60)
Ser. 32 (Greece), vols. 18-287 (1830-62)

This correspondence, from which this book so intensively draws, covers all the significant events of the period and provides information which is not available in newspaper or memoir sources. With more particular reference to the character and operation of the parties, it is valuable in a variety of ways. It helps tackle two elementary yet difficult problems—that of determining the party affiliations of several Greeks (it was Lyons' habit, like that of many others, to categorize politicians in this way), and that of estimating the representation of the three parties in various government bodies, such as the cabinet or Council of State. It reveals the various means that each of the three powers employed to apply pressure on the government and extend their own influence. It provides material from which to infer the general policy of the Crown toward the parties. Finally, it says much about the relations of the ministers of the three powers to each other, and by extension, about the shifting alliances among the three parties. Though intrinsically important because of their richness, these archives are rendered all the more important for my study by the fact that their information has only found its way into two secondary accounts of this period—that of Driault and Lhéritier (III A) and Bower and Bolitho (III A), but even then, only to a limited extent.

GREECE

GENERAL STATE ARCHIVES. ATHENS.

The mass of state documents from the Othonian period, which are now in the possession of these archives, were uncatalogued during my year of research in Greece and were therefore closed. The cataloguers are only now beginning this task and, because of limited personnel, it will be a long while before the documents for this period become available in any quantity. Any definitive study of this book's topic will therefore have to await the completion of this laborious task.

Of the available catalogued material in these archives, the three following collections proved valuable: (1) the Mavrokordatos Archive, (2) the Otho Archive, and (3) the Palamides Archive. Of these three, the first is catalogued separately according to "envelopes" by years and consists largely of correspondence received by Mavrokordatos during his long public career, although it also contains some documents and memoranda which came into his possession as well as a few rough copies of items which he himself composed. Emmanuel Protopsaltes, under the auspices of the Academy of Athens, is currently engaged in publishing the entire archive and, to date, two volumes, from 1803 to the early 1820s, have appeared under the title *Historikon Archeion Alexandrou Mavrokordatou* [*Historical Archive of Alexander Mavrokordatos*], part I (Athens, 1964) and part II (Athens, 1966) as Vol. 5 in the Academy of Athens series called "Mnemeia tes Hellenikes Historias" ["Monuments of Greek History"]. The second and third items belong to a larger collection known as the Historical Archives of John Vlachogiannes because this historian, antiquarian and founder of the General State Archives, privately purchased, collected, and separately catalogued all this material. These Vlachogiannes Archives consist of five parts: (1) Archive of the Revolution, (2) Archive of the Kapodistrian Period, (3) Otho Archive (1833-62), (4) George I Archive, and (5) Private Collections. The second collection cited above is the third part of the Vlachogiannes Archives, consisting of 44 "envelopes" (nos. 131-74), and the third collection is one of the several in the fifth part of the Vlachogiannes Archives, consisting of 3 "envelopes" (nos. 267-69).

Historical Archive of Alexander Mavrokordatos

Out of this mass of correspondence *to* Mavrokordatos during his long public career, five envelopes cover the years 1833-43: vols. 19 (1833-36) —docs. nos. 5200-5380; 20 (1837-40)—nos. 5381-5787; 21 (1841)—nos. 5788-6161; 22 (1842)—nos. 6162-6565; and 23 (1843)—nos. 6566-7065. They contain letters from such important political figures as Kolettes, Metaxas, Zographos, Rizos, Païkos, and from such close personal and political friends as Manoles and Pericles Argyropoulos, Trikoupes, Miaoules, Pharmakides, Monarchides, Kontostavlos, Andrew Lontos, and from a host of humbler political clients. The absence of Mavrokordatos from Greece during most of this period (1833-43) and his eagerness to keep informed about affairs in Greece explain both the large quantity of correspondence and its abundance of information on the Greek internal situation. From these five envelopes, only two letters from Mavrokordatos to his wife, on his arrival in Greece in 1843, and excerpts from some of the many letters of Kolettes have been published—in Petrakakos' second volume (II A below). To my knowledge, the only historical monograph based on research in these archives for this period is that of Pericles Argyropoulos (III D). Even the authors of more recent histories, like

Pipineles, Kordatos, and Skandames (III A) did not use these archives, though they were available. As my footnotes attest, for this book they have been invaluable and essential, even though information on the parties is usually casual, unconscious, and scattered, hence often hidden away in postscripts or in the discussion of other issues and events.

If some letters attest to the presence of parties and the existence of party strife, others prove that, when a government was formed, due consideration had to be given to a proper representation of all three parties. Other letters attest the predominant position of one party in any one tripartisan government and the tendency of politicians to react to it accordingly. Still others, quite in passing, reveal the course of shifting alliances between the parties, as well as intraparty dissensions, so that it is possible to reconstruct, at least in rough fashion, the internal structure of the three parties and their relations to each other. In these letters, one also discerns some of the instruments employed by the parties either to stay in power and increase their freedom of action or to oust another party from power.

The correspondence of course gives ready information on actual events, such as the fusionist "movement," the Philorthodox plot, the Mavrokordatos episode of 1841, and the background of the revolution of 1843. There is also detailed information about the existing administrative paralysis, the restricted powers and inadequate information of even cabinet ministers, resentment of even the most moderate men against the king and the anaktovoulion as early as 1838. In this regard, it is necessary to mention the correspondence of Zographos, while foreign minister, and a series of revealing reports (nos. 5862-5866) drawn up by Pericles Argyropoulos for the benefit of Mavrokordatos, describing the organization and personnel of the various ministries and recommending what he considered the necessary changes.

The Otho Archive

This archive is organized according to ministries and other institutions of government. The bulk of material is largely fiscal. The envelopes of greatest value were those of the ministry of ecclesiastical and educational affairs (no. 132), of the ministry of interior (no. 134), and one marked "Undated 1834—ministry of the economy" (no. 143). No. 132 consists of (1) encyclicals and letters of the holy synod concerning the revolt of Mane (1834) and the Philorthodox plot (1839), showing how the state used the moral authority of the church to win back disaffected elements, and (2) letters to the editors of the newspapers *Ethnikē* and *Sōtēr*, in defense of the "French" party against attacks by the "English" party. No. 134 contains reports of Praïdes, nomarch of Laconia, on the Mane revolt of 1834. No. 143 contains a vast amount of correspondence on both the Mane and Messenian revolts of 1834. Those on the former revolt consist of reports of the eparchs of Gytheon and Itylos to the nomarch of Laconia, and his reports to the minister of interior, and are important primarily for the detail which they provide. The documents on the Messenian revolt, consisting largely of correspondence between the gendarmerie and eparchal officials in Gortynia, the nomarch of Arcadia with the minister of interior, and the minister of interior with the minister of war, provide, in addition to information about the leaders of the revolt and their movements, a very revealing picture of conflicts among the civil and military branches of the provincial administration charged with rounding up the rebels and investigating them, and suggest that the conflicts had their source in the conflicting partisan interests of the officials involved.

The Palamides Archive

The first two envelopes of this archive consist of correspondence which Palamides received largely from personal and political friends—Peloponnesian associates like Christakopoulos, Poneropoulos, and Panagiotes Delegiannes; Peloponnesian clients like Christos Vlases and John Petrokopes; and fellow "French" adherents from other parts of Greece, like Karakatsanes, Chrestides, and Kolettes. The correspondence is extremely valuable because, from it, one can reconstruct to some extent the internal organization of the "French" party and the internal dissensions and rivalries that existed, especially during the period of French preponderance in 1842. One also finds evidence of the eagerness with which men sought public office, its attractiveness as a source of political influence rather than as a direct source of income, the way in which they used party channels to obtain office, and Peloponnesian resentment that the party leaders (Kolettes) seemed to favor the Rumeliot branch of the party for placement. Moreover, the letters of Panagiotes Delegiannes reveal the methods of the opposition party in trying to get an official removed from his post, and those of Christakopoulos reveal the way in which he and Palamides benefited from the official position of their political friend, Karakatsanes, to anticipate the claims of the control board against them, and how they plotted to exonerate themselves by throwing the blame on their political opponent Kolokotrones. The third envelope contains a rough draft of a projected history of events since the outbreak of the Revolution, most notable because of the tremendous antipathy which it displayed toward Mavrokordatos and the Phanariot "aristocratic" element.

ARCHIVES OF THE HISTORICAL AND ETHNOLOGICAL SOCIETY. ATHENS.

Packed away during World War II, this material has been unavailable for general use ever since, although its renewed accessibility is considered imminent.

ARCHIVES OF THE NATIONAL LIBRARY. ATHENS.

The National Library of Greece is also the repository of archives, the most notable of which are the G. Ainian Archive, the John Philemon Collection, and the D. Meletopoulos Archive. These, like the Lontos Archive at the Benaki Museum, are rather thin for the period 1833-43.

THE HISTORICAL ARCHIVES OF THE MINISTRY OF EXTERNAL AFFAIRS. ATHENS.

The archives of the Greek foreign ministry, catalogued and accessible, contain a mass of material which goes far beyond the merely external relations of Greece with other states. For the years 1833-43, for instance, they include folios on such domestic events as the Kolokotrones trial (1834), the trial of the editor of *Sōtēr* (1836), the king's tour of Rumely (1838); on such national institutions as the Council of State; and on military and ecclesiastical national affairs. In the envelopes containing copies of correspondence addressed to the Greek legations in London, Paris, Petersburg, and Constantinople, there are numerous official reports on such events as the regency dispute of 1833-34, the Kolokotrones trial, the Mane and Messenian revolts of 1834, and the Philorthodox plot of 1839. The reason for the prominence of such matters in the archives of the foreign ministry—the necessity to justify Greek government acts, to minimize the dangers of revolts, or to apologize for the criticisms of the powers in the local press—explains why this correspondence is of limited value for this study. Official interpretation tended to slur over embarrassing, although illuminating, facts and was unlikely to deal with domestic party activity which foreign governments did not understand. Nevertheless, these reports do provide much information on the outward unfolding of domestic events. In addition, there are sometimes copies of reports drawn up by Greek provincial officials (usually on revolts) and sometimes letters of a more intimate nature written by the foreign minister to the representatives in foreign capitals, by these representatives to each other, or, less frequently, by the representatives to the home government. Even though these archives reveal a good deal about domestic events in which the parties were involved and much more about the manifold ways in which "protection" of the three powers involved interference in domestic concerns, they tell very little about the parties as such.

ARCHIVES OF THE PARLIAMENT OF THE HELLENES.

Noteworthy items in this archive, which came to my attention too late for use and which would seem to bear great relevance to the topic of this book are listed in Petrakakos' [*Parliamentary History*], II, 115-16 (II A below). They are: "Exposition of the future government of Otho from Munich," "Scholastic article on the [above] report concerning the plan by which the regency and Otho will govern Greece," "Political beliefs of Ludwig I of Bavaria in relation to the governing of Greece by his son Otho," "Rumors concerning a council for guiding Otho after his majority," "The visit to Otho by his father Ludwig," "The illness of Otho," and "Daily memoranda of the doctors Roser, Vitmer, Vitsel [*sic.*]."

STAATSBIBLIOTHEK. OLDENBURG.

This library contains a collection of letters from Queen Amalia to her parents, cited by Skandames (III A below).

PRUSSIA

PREUSSISCHES GEHEIMES STAATSARCHIV. BERLIN-DAHLEM.

The "Bavaria" fascicles of the foreign archives have been selectively published by Chroust (II A below). To my knowledge, Mendelssohn Bartholdy (III A) and Koeppel (III E) are the only historians on Greece during 1833-44 who made use of these.

B. ARCHIVES OF PRIVATE INSTITUTIONS

THE ANDREW LONTOS ARCHIVE. BENAKI MUSEUM. ATHENS.

This large collection of correspondence, addressed to Andrew Lontos during his public career, is richest for the Revolutionary period, and by comparison, rather lean for the years 1833-44. The correspondence of the absolutist period, mostly written during the regency period, came from a vast number of individuals, among them A. Monarchides, A. Zaïmes, Venizelos Rouphos, A. Kalamogdartes, C. Sisines, Adam and Constantine Doukas, D. Zographos, and C. Rangos. It sheds a great deal of light on the local clienteles in Achaia, their conflicts and competition for office, the use of public office to advance one's clients, and the means employed by other political groupings to oust their opponents from power. Some of it deals with the Messenian revolt of 1834 and the role of Zaïmes as the chief investigator of the revolt, and much of it consists of petitions from clients of Lontos, beseeching him to use his influence in the capital to get them placed, promoted, or transferred. In addition, there are two letters from 1843, one addressed to the king by Lontos himself, the other to the minister of interior by five Achaian landowners, asking the state not to press its financial claims against the bankrupt Leon Messenezes, for whom five landowners had promised to provide surety. These letters demonstrate the dire effects of the depression of 1842 on the currant-raisin provinces of northern Peloponnesos and suggest that economic distress may have served as one of the causes of revolt in 1843.

FINLAY PAPERS. BRITISH SCHOOL OF ARCHEOLOGY. ATHENS.

R 8.5   "Journal 1835"
R 8.6   "Journal of a tour to several islands of the Archipelago in August and September 1837"
R 8.7   "Letter Book 1827-36"

R 8.8   "Correspondence 1837-49"
R 8.15   "Miscellaneous. Various Greek Memoranda 1822-43"
S 9.11(b) "Journal" [1833-46]

The above manuscripts constitute only part of the much larger collection of Finlay Papers. There are, in addition to other personal papers on periods outside the range of this book, pamphlets and newspaper clippings which he collected, as well as the manuscripts of his multivolume history of Greece. The writings listed have proved extremely valuable as a supplement to the account of the absolutist period in his history (III A below), which was hastily written and not as thorough as other parts of his history. Their value derives from the inclusion of much detail on the workings of administration and the contents of government policy, in addition to gossip concerning the doings of prominent political figures and the intrigues in which they engaged. Both detail and gossip have an indirect but significant bearing on the character and activity of parties as these affected government policy and practical administration.

"Journal 1835" is an account of the expedition of General Gordon for the investigation and suppression of brigandage in Rumely. Finlay, who accompanied Gordon during most of the expedition, left Athens 11 July 1835 and returned on 6 September of the same year. His observations on Rumeliot administration and general socioeconomic conditions, based on firsthand experience and interviews with several Rumeliots, are supplemented by an account, called "Observations on the state of northern Greece," which enumerates what Finlay considered the causes of brigandage and what he regarded the best measures for eliminating it. His analysis, as well as his journal entries, illuminate the relations between various social groups as well as the political causes and consequences of administrative abuses. The manuscript concludes with some letters from Gordon to Finlay concerning the expedition after Finlay had left it.

Item two, on the islands, is briefer and less penetrating than its counterpart on Rumely, but it enumerates the major grievances of the islanders—the dissolution of the monasteries, the way in which the tenths were collected, and the imposition of the additional pig and stamp taxes.

The correspondence in items three and four is that of Finlay to a great variety of individuals (he kept a copy of all his letters). It deals with his pecuniary affairs, especially his dispute with the Greek government over title to his land, but there is also a great deal on the 1835 negotiations of the Greek government with a representative of British capitalists for the establishment of a bank in Greece. These two items are the least significant for the book.

Of the miscellaneous material in item five, the most important are three letters (published in *Athēna* in 1833) on Finlay's views of the proper policy for governing Greece, a memorandum to Otho urging him to permit the promulgation of a constitution, and a long essay entitled "On Conditions and Prospects of Greece" (with the note, presumably by

Finlay, "I think this was never printed in this form"), in which he describes the patronage exercised by the foreign legations in behalf of their parties, the relations between ruling and ruled classes, the system of referendaries, in which he then goes on to recommend a constitution and the intervention of Britain to secure this constitution from Otho. All these memoranda, of course, involve severe criticism of existing government policy.

Item six was perhaps the most important for my purposes because of its character sketches of the most prominent Bavarians and Greeks, its enumeration of various points of regency and Armansperg policy, and its information on the intrigues of the first three years of the absolutist period. It reveals that Armansperg, by passing remarks in private conversations with Greeks, was attempting to accomplish the same purpose as the medical reports to Munich—prove the king's inability to govern. Most important of all, it brings to light an incident which no other available source, primary or secondary, mentions—the momentary alliance between Kolettes and Lesuire at the end of 1834 and the beginning of 1835. After 1837 the journal has very few entries—a bit on the Mavrokordatos episode of 1841 and nothing on the revolution of 1843. It only really resumes in mid-1844 and extends only through 1846.

C. PRIVATE ARCHIVAL COLLECTIONS

Armansperg, Joseph von. Papers.
    Used by Söltl (II A below).
Gasser, Baroness von. Memoirs.
    Used by Bower and Bolitho (III A).
Hunoltstein, Baron von. Memoirs.
    Used by Bower and Bolitho (III A).
Kobell, Ägid von. Papers.
    Used by Luise von Kobell (II B).
Kolettes, John. Correspondence. Athens.
    Used by Elias Georgiou (II A).
Lyons, Sir Edmond. Correspondence.
    In the possession of his grandson the Duke of Norfolk, as of 1898. Used by Eardley-Wilmot (III C).
Prokesch-Osten, Count Anton von. Private Papers. Gmunden, Upper Austria.
    Preserved in the archives of the Prokesch-Scheinitz family. Used by Engel-Janosi (III D).
Piscatory, Theobald. Correspondence.
    In the possession of Mrs. T. Hermite, his granddaughter. Used by Georgiou (II A).
Psyllas, George. Memoirs.

Cited in *Bulletin Analytique de Bibliographie Hellénique 1961*. Vol. xxii. Athens, 1964.

Zographos, Constantine. Correspondence.
Used by P. Argyropoulos (iii d).

II. Published Primary Sources

A. DOCUMENTS (OFFICIAL AND UNOFFICIAL)

[Albert of Saxe-Coburg-Gotha]. *Letters of the Prince Consort 1831-1861*. Ed. Kurt Jagow and trans. E.T.S. Dugdale. New York, 1938.

Three letters in this collection have relevance for this book, all three written to Frederick William IV of Prussia—the first on the revolution of 1843, the second and third written after the absolutist period and discussing the conduct of Lyons in Greece.

Broglie, Achille C.L.V. de. *Écrits et discours*. 3 vols. Paris, 1863.

The pertinent document is item 10 in Vol. ii, entitled "Discours prononcé à la chambre des députés dans La Discussion du Projet de Loi relatif à la Garantie de l'Emprunt Grec, 18 Mai 1833."

Chapuisat, Edouard, ed. *La Restauration Hellénique d'après la correspondance de Jean-Gabriel Eynard*. Paris and Geneva, 1924.

This personal correspondence, mostly from Eynard to European heads of state as well as to Greek officials and king, but in some cases from them to Eynard, is most important for the light it sheds on the influence of this Swiss financier and philhellene on Greek affairs and his attitude toward Otho, the Greek parties, and Greek administrative chaos. Through his correspondence with Regny, then Lemaître (which figures prominently in the collection), one learns a good deal about the control board as an organ of foreign influence and as an object of Greek and English opposition. The correspondence of 1842-43 reveals Eynard's attempts, before the revolution of 1843, to unite the powers in some effort to pressure Otho into reform, and after the revolution to persuade Otho to rely on Kolettes and Mavrokordatos, in conjunction with Franco-British support. It also sheds light on the financial and political crisis of 1843.

Chroust, Anton, ed. *Gesandtschaftsberichte aus München 1814-1848*. Schriftenreihe zur bayerischen Landesgeschichte herausgegeben von der Kommission für bayerische Landesgeschichte bei der Bayerischen Akademie der Wissenschaften.

Abt. i: *Die Berichte der französischen Gesandten (1816-1848)*. 6 vols. Munich, 1935-37.

Abt. ii: *Die Berichte der österr. Gesandten (1813-1848)*. 4 vols. Munich, 1939-42.

Abt. III: *Die Berichte der Preussen Gesandten (1814-1848).*
5 vols. Munich, 1949-51.

This monumental publication enterprise, sponsored by the Bavarian Academy of Sciences, drawing from the voluminous "Bavaria" series of the French, Austrian, and Prussian foreign archives (I A above) and intended to illuminate Bavarian history through the reports of foreign legates assigned to the Bavarian court, contains much that is pertinent to Greek affairs, as they relate to Ludwig and the Bavarians or as they become a matter of general European concern. Such material, by its very nature and its Bavarian focus of concern, offers little specific and sometimes inaccurate information on the Greek domestic scene. Its chief value in this regard is what it has to say about the influence exercised by Ludwig and other Bavarians on Greece and the various pressures brought to bear on him in his Greek policy by the European powers and by Bavarian domestic politics.

He Dike tou aoidimou Th. Kolokotrone kai D. Plapouta. Skene Politike tou 1833 Etous [*The Trial of Th. Kolokotrones of Blessed Memory and D. Plapoutas. Political Scene of the Year 1833*]. Athens, 1843.

Although it contains the official indictment as well as copies of Franz's petitions and the letter of Nesselrode, this collection consists largely of the testimony given by the witnesses for both the prosecution and the defense. Because of its partisan and contradictory nature, the testimony cannot serve as a reliable guide to what actually happened in 1833, but it does reveal the existence of party alignments and rivalries, as well as the informal channels through which members of each political group normally communicated and cooperated with each other. An anonymous introduction to this collection, written in defense of Kolokotrones and Plapoutas, constitutes a vigorous criticism of all aspects of regency policy and reveals both Napist and more generally Greek grievances against the regency program.

Dakin, Douglas, ed. "British Intelligence of Events in Greece, 1824-27. A Documentary Collection." *Deltion tes Historikes kai Ethnologikes Hetaireias tes Hellados* [*Bulletin of the Historical and Ethnological Society of Greece*], XIII (1959), 33-217.

Although these letters lie outside the immediate chronological scope of this book, they directly relate to the origins of the three parties. Indeed, Dakin utilized this very material in the writing of his own account of the origin of the parties (III C below).

[Eynard, Jean Gabriel]. *Epistolai I. G. Eynardou pros Georg. Stauron, 1841-1843* [*Letters of J. G. Eynard to George Stavros . . .*]. National Bank of Greece Historical Archive. Athens, 1923.

This correspondence with Stavros, head of the newly established bank of Greece, nominee of Eynard for this position and a controversial figure in Greece because of his former identification with Napism, demonstrates the powerful influence of Eynard in the establishment of the bank and the way in which the bank became involved in partisan politics.

France. *Recueil de pièces officielles sur les Affaires d'Orient.* Paris, 1840.

Georgiou, Elias P., ed. and trans. *Th. Piskatores peri Ioannou Kolettou* [*Th. Piscatory concerning John Kolettes*]. Athens, 1952.

This individually published pamphlet consists of a letter written by Piscatory to a friend, Ampère, in August 1855, answering his friend's request for information on Kolettes. Georgiou obtained this document from the Piscatory archive, which remains in the possession of Mrs. T. Hermite, the granddaughter of Piscatory. He based his extensive explanatory footnotes on information obtained during extensive research in the archives of the French foreign ministry.

Great Britain. [Parliamentary Papers] *Convention signed at London, 7th May 1832, appointing H.R.H. Prince Otho of Bavaria King of Greece, with Additional Article, April 1833.* 2 pts.

―――. [Parliamentary Papers] *Correspondence, 1843-44, relative to the Recent Events in Greece.*

―――. [Parliamentary Papers] *Papers, 1835-36, relative to the Third Instalment of the Greek Loan.* 2 pts.

―――. [Parliamentary Papers] *Protocols of Conferences, Nos. 52 to 67, held in London relative to the Affairs of Greece, 1832-1837.*

Greece. *Actes de l'Alliance et de la cour de Bavière relatifs à l'établissement d'un gouvernement constitutionnel en Grèce et aux Bavarois y résident.* Athens, 1843.

―――. *Hai anangaioterai Enkyklioi, Epistolai, Diataxeis, kai Hodegiai tes Hieras Synodou tes Ekklesias tes Hellados 1834-1854* [*The most important Encyclicals, Letters, Decrees and Directives of the Holy Synod of the Church of Greece 1834-1854*]. Athens, 1854.

―――. *Ephemeris tes Kyberneseos, Basileion tes Hellados* [*Government Gazette, Kingdom of Greece*]. Nauplion 16/28 Feb. 1833–5/17 Nov. 1834; Athens, 21 Dec. 1834/2 Jan. 1835―. Until 17/29 May 1835, in German as well as Greek.

These volumes, bound by year, contain all the official acts of the government (laws, decrees, appointments, and treaties) and have been indispensable for the sections of this essay on statecraft and the formal government response to revolts.

―――. *Ephemeris ton Angelion* [*Newspaper of Announcements*]. Athens, Mar. 1835–Dec. 1837; Syros, Aug. 1841–July 1842.

This "newspaper" consists mostly of official judicial decisions throughout the kingdom, concerning criminal, administrative, and economic matters.

―――. *Kanonismos Hyperesias tou Basilikou Somatos Chrophylakes*

[*Regulations for the Service of the Royal Gendarmerie*]. Nauplion, 1834. In German as well as Greek.

――――. *Katastatikon tes Ethnikes Trapezes tes Hellados* . . . [*By-laws of the National Bank of Greece*]. Athens, 1843.

――――. *Recueil des traités, actes et pièces concernant la fondation de la royauté en Grèce et le tracé de ses limites*. Nauplion, 1833.

――――. *He tes Trites Septembriou en Athenais Ethnike Syneleusis. Prak-tika* [*The National Assembly of the Third of September in Athens. Min-utes*]. Athens, 1844.

This official account of the proceedings is indispensable for any study of the constituent assembly of 1843-44—the personnel of the committees, the parliamentary procedure followed, the controversial issues and the various positions taken, the modification of the original draft constitution to incorporate dissident views, the further modifications to secure the formal assent of the king, the tallies of the vote taken on each proposal. It does not, however, identify the author of each recorded speech, or reveal what transpired outside the formal sessions, where so many of the proposed revisions were modified or combined for formal presentation. It must therefore be supplemented by the account of Heinze (II B below).

Jelavich, Barbara. "The Philorthodox Conspiracy of 1839." *Balkan Studies*, VII (1966), 89-102.

This article is the publication, with introduction, of a report of 13 January 1840 to his government by Wallenburg, secretary of the Austrian legation in Athens, containing all that he had yet been able to learn concerning the Philorthodox conspiracy of 1839 and the impact of its discovery on domestic politics in Greece. Although the editor does not cite the location of the document, it is presumably from the Haus-, Hof-, und Staatsarchiv, Vienna (I A above). Similar reports by other legations in Athens are available in the foreign office archives of other European states, but this is the only one that has to date been published.

――――. *Russia and Greece during the Regency of King Otho 1832-1835. Russian Documents on the First Years of Greek Independence*. Institute for Balkan Studies, no. 55. Thessaloniki, 1962.

This small volume consists of 29 documents which the editor found in a larger collection of Russian material located in the Bavarian Geheimes Staatsarchiv (I A above). They are of two varieties—despatches and en-closures sent by Russian legates in Bavaria to the Russian foreign office in St. Petersburg and despatches and enclosures sent by the Bavarian legates in St. Petersburg to the Bavarian government in Munich. Seven of the documents are published separately in the appendix, presumably because (with the exception of one) they date from the period 1821-30. For this study, the most useful documents are some of the enclosures: the in-structions to Catacazy from his government on his appointment as Rus-sian minister to Greece (no. 9), two subsequent despatches of Nesselrode to Catacazy (nos. 15, 20), a report of Catacazy to Nesselrode (no. 16), and a memorandum of the Russian government presented to M. Soutsos, Greek minister in St. Petersburg, for his government in Greece (no. 12). All these are extremely important in revealing Russian policy toward Greece, its short-term aims, its attitude toward regency policy (its complaints and demands), and its manner of pursuing its objectives. The editor has also included a useful introduction which summarizes the contents of the documents and describes Russian policy.

————. *Russia and the Greek Revolution of 1843*. Südosteuropäische Arbeiten, no. 65. Munich, 1966.

Though this work contains a 48 page account of the Greek revolution of 1843, the greater part of it is a collection of diplomatic reports and despatches from the Bavarian Staatsarchiv in Munich. The account, however, is also based on material in the Austrian Haus-, Hof-, und Staatsarchiv in Vienna. This work appeared after the manuscript of this book was completed.

[Kallerges, Demetrios]. *Diaphora Engrapha kai Prokeryxeis tou Stratiotikou tes Proteuouses Dioiketou Dem. Kallerge* [*Various Documents and Proclamations of the Military Commander of the Capital Dem. Kallerges*]. Athens, 1844. See also under Kallerges in II C below.

Klados, J. A. *Epheteris tou Basileiou tes Hellados 1837* [*Year-Book of the Kingdom of Greece*]. Athens, 1837.

Koeppel, Ferdinand. "Ignaz v. Rudhart in Griechenland. Briefe und Schriftsstücke aus seinem Nachlass." *Zeitschrift für bayerische Landesgeschichte*, VII (1934), 221-39.

[Makrygiannes, John]. *Archeion tou Strategou Ioannou Makrygianne* [*Archive of General John Makrygiannes*], Archeia tes Neoteras Hellenikes Historias [Archives of Modern Greek History], no. 2. Ed. John Vlachogiannes. 2 vols. Athens, 1907. Vol. I: "Periechon ta historika engrapha" ["Containing the Historical Documents"]. See also Makrygiannes in II B below.

This first volume of the original edition of Makrygiannes' [*Memoirs*] consists entirely of documents and was omitted from the second edition of 1947. For the period 1833-44, it contains (1) official acts acknowledging his Revolutionary services and announcing his various appointments; (2) several letters which he wrote to newspaper editors for publication; (3) newspaper articles concerning him and his activities; (4) official documents for which he bore some responsibility; (5) a memorandum of John Velentzas, dated 14 December 1841*o.s.*, concerning Velentzas' military career and his irredentist campaign of 1841; and (6) a copy of the first oath, in behalf of the revolution of 1843, which Makrygiannes circulated, and a long list of signatures attached. The oath document is especially important because it helps identify some of the lesser men involved in the revolutionary plot.

Mamoukas, A. Z., ed. *Ta Monasteriaka, etoi hodegiai, nomoi, basilika diatagmata, k.t.l.* [*Monastic Affairs, or Instructions, Laws, Royal Decrees, etc.*]. Athens, 1859.

Maurer, Georg Ludwig von. *Das griechische Volk in öffentlicher, kirchlicher und privatrechtlicher Beziehung vor und nach dem Freiheitskampfe bis zum 31 Juli 1834.* 3 vols. Heidelberg, 1835. Vol. III: "Interessante Neugriechische Urkunden, Gesetze und Verordnungen der früheren und späteren Zeit." See also under Maurer in II B below.

This third volume of Maurer's work, which is not part of the Greek translation, consists entirely of official documents.

Nautes, George A. *Hodegiai pros ton demarchon, eis ekplerosin ton kata tous ischyontas nomous kathekonton autou, kata ten anakrisin ton axiopinon praxeon, kai ten kategorian ton ptaismaton, me pinaka ton peitharchikon parabaseon tou demarchou, hos anakritikou hypallelou* [*Instructions for the Demarch, for the Fulfillment of his Duties according to the Prevailing Laws, with respect to Investigating Punishable Deeds and Charging of Offenses, with a Table of the Disciplinary Transgressions of the Demarch as an Investigating Official*]. 2nd edn. Athens, 1837.

Nesselrode, Alexander de, ed. *Lettres et papiers du Chancelier Comte de Nesselrode 1760-1856. Extraite de ses Archives.* 11 vols. Paris, 1904-12.

Material on Greece is largely confined to a number of letters in Vol. VIII (1840-46), from Nesselrode to Baron von Meyendorff, Russian ambassador to Berlin. These contain references to Catacazy's suspected connection with the Philorthodox plot, and to the tsar's displeasure with him for his role in the revolution of 1843.

Oikonomos, Sophocles, ed. *Ta Sozomena Ekklesiastika Syngrammata Konstantinou . . . tou ex Oikonomon* [*Collected Ecclesiastical Writings of . . . Constantine Oikonomos*]. 2 vols. Athens, 1864-66. See also Oikonomos in II D below.

The first volume is cited in this section of the bibliography because, even though it is a critical and analytical narrative of ecclesiastical events, it consists of more documents than narrative. These documents are official ones, some of them official decrees which appear in [*Government Gazette*], but a large number of them are official correspondence, reports, and minutes, which are published nowhere else and which, because the complete files of the ministry of ecclesiastical affairs are not yet catalogued, are still unavailable elsewhere.

Petrakakos, Demetrios A. *Koinobouleutike Historia tes Hellados* [*The Parliamentary History of Greece*]. 3 vols. Athens, 1935-46.

Only in a strictly formal sense do these volumes, of which a section of the first and the bulk of the second deal with the period 1833-44, constitute a secondary source. A formless collection of official documents and private correspondence loosely held together by intermittent comment of the author, they really constitute what one might call a documentary collection on the constitutional history of Greece.

The work is full of long excerpts from all the most important printed primary sources—Greek newspapers; the memoirs of Dragoumes, Rangabe, and Guizot (Makrygiannes oddly excepted); [*Government Gazette*] and Proceedings of the assembly of 1843-44; Heinze's personal account of these proceedings; the Ludwig-Otho correspondence in Trost; the correspondence of Duke John of Austria and Prokesch-Osten in Schlossar; and the two-volume correspondence between Metternich and Prokesch-Osten (Briefwechsel). With the sole exception of the French foreign archives and the Lontos Archive (Benaki Museum), Petrakakos worked in all the archival collections cited in section I A above. Yet he barely made any use of the British archives, at least for the period in question; and even in the case of the Bavarian and Austrian archives, where he did most of his work, he tended to rely heavily on documents already published in Trost and the two-volume *Briefwechsel.* In the case of the Greek archives, practically the only material which he published was excerpts from the correspondence from Kolettes to Mavrokordatos and a letter from Mavrokordatos to his wife. In short, the work is a gold mine only for someone who reads only Greek and has no access to all the published sources. But in two areas—the bulk of the still unpublished correspondence between Metternich and Prokesch-Osten in the Austrian foreign archives and the Secret Otho Archive—he published some material which is available only in manuscript or which, in the case of the Secret Otho Archive, may no longer exist.

Poulos, Jean, ed. "Textes et Documents, La Grèce d'Othon, Vue en 1841 par l'homme d'État et diplomate François Piscatory." *L'Hellénisme Contemporain*, 2nd ser., IX (Sept.–Oct. 1955), 321-51 (Nov.–Dec. 1955), 408-47.

In two installments, Poulos, editor of the Historical Dictionary of the Academy of Athens, has published eleven important documents from Volumes 33-34 of correspondence on Greece from the archives of the French ministry of foreign affairs (I A above). All were written in 1841 and all but the first document (Guizot's circular letter of March 1841, which is published in Guizot's memoirs), are published for the first and only time. The second document is Guizot's instructions to Lagrené concerning Piscatory's special mission to Greece. The third and fourth are Guizot's instructions to Piscatory. All three, as explanations of the purpose and objectives of the mission, reveal official French policy toward Greece at this time.

Far more important, indeed crucial, for this study are the remaining

561

documents—seven reports, written between 20 June and 6 Sept. 1841, by Piscatory to Guizot during the former's special mission to Greece. Footnote citations of this book will reveal the extent of my indebtedness to them. These reports are important because of the light they shed on the foreign and domestic politics of the Mavrokordatos episode of 1841. They contain accounts of Piscatory's conversations with such important figures as Otho, Lyons, and Mavrokordatos, and describe personal contacts with influential Greeks during Piscatory's tour throughout Greece. They reveal the conflicting objectives and counterstrategies of Otho and Mavrokordatos, the attitude and behavior of the Napist and "French" parties with regard to Mavrokordatos' appointment, and indirectly, the role of Piscatory in transforming the Mavrokordatos episode into a political victory for the "French" party.

These reports are crucial because of the light which they shed on the character of the parties. Piscatory made it a point to describe the internal structure, geographical distribution, and personnel of each party, to describe the operation of the parties at the level of local politics and administration, and to estimate the role of each foreign legation in domestic politics. The seventh or last report is a catalogue of over 100 prominent Greek political figures, and for each there is a short political biography as well as an identification of political affiliation.

In general, the veracity and acuteness of Piscatory's observations is beyond doubt, but his interpretations of these observations is colored by his obvious desire to persuade Guizot that greater French participation in Greek affairs, including greater French patronage of "French" adherents, was necessary.

―――. Ed. and trans. "He Epanastasis tes 3es Septembriou 1843 epi te basei ton gallikon archeion" ["The Revolution of the Third of September 1843 on the Basis of the French Archives"]. *Deltion tes Historikes kai Ethnologikes Hetaireias tes Hellados* [*Bulletin of the Historical and Ethnological Society of Greece*], xi (1956), 223-60.

In this periodical, Poulos has published, in Greek translation, five more documents from the archives of the French foreign ministry, this time from Vol. 40 of correspondence on Greece. Two are Piscatory's reports to Guizot on the revolution of 1843. The first describes the events during the night and early morning of 14-15 September, analyzes the conflicting aims and component parts of the rebel movement, summarizes the political orientation of each member of the new cabinet, and urges the speedy return of Kolettes. The second deals with the immediate aftermath of the revolution (the behavior of the new cabinet, the reaction of the king and Greek antirevolutionaries to the revolution, the situation in the provinces) and reveals the immediate cooperation of Lyons and Piscatory in an attempt to support the moderates, keep Otho on the throne, and influence the character of the new constitution. These are the most important because they clarify the internal political situation. The remaining documents are: (1) the official report of Lyons, Catacazy, and Piscatory to the Conference of London, concerning the revolution; (2) the instructions of Guizot to Piscatory—revealing Guizot's desire for close cooperation with Britain; and (3) Guizot's letter to Piscatory concerning his conversation with Kolettes before the latter departed for Greece— revealing Kolettes' attitude toward and interpretation of the revolution. This last document, though extremely important, had already been published in Guizot's memoirs (II B below).

The Portfolio: or a Collection of State Papers and other Documents and Correspondence, Historical, Diplomatic, and Commercial Illustrative of the History of our Times. 1st ser., 6 vols., London, 1836-37; 2nd ser., 4 vols., London, 1843-44. For a description, see *Portfolio* in II D below.

Prokesch-Osten, Anton [the younger] von, ed. *Aus dem Nachlasse des Grafen Prokesch-Osten. Briefwechsel mit Herrn von Gentz und Fürsten Metternich.* 2 vols. Vienna, 1881.

The letters which pertain to Greece during the absolutist period appear in Vol. II and consist exclusively of correspondence between Prokesch-Osten and Metternich, mostly from the former. It is not until he writes about the revolution of 1843 that Prokesch-Osten actually analyzes the party situation; these letters have been the most valuable for the book. In his earlier letters, which are more valuable for Austrian policy in Greece, there is much background material for this book. The valuable letters of 1835, from which Mendelssohn Bartholdy quotes (III A below) do not appear in this selection. Parts of many of the letters of 1843-44 are quoted by Petrakakos (this section above).

Rados, Constantine N., ed. ["The Revolt of Aetolia-Acarnania in 1836 under Otho"]. *Deltion tes Historikes kai Ethnologikes Hetaireias tes Hellados* [*Bulletin of the Historical and Ethnological Society of Greece*], IX (1926), 539-41.

This item is the publication of a letter, dated 22 February 1836 o.s., by Porphyrios, bishop of Acarnania, who wrote from Mesolongi an account of the Acarnanian revolt describing the movements of the rebels and citing local grievances behind the revolt. It is taken from the Otho Archive of the Vlachogiannes Collection, General State Archives (no. 4367, folder 132, entitled "Ministry of Ecclesiastical and Educational Affairs 1833-62") (I A above).

Ross, Ludwig. *Erinnerungen und Mittheilungen aus Griechenland.* Berlin, 1863.

Though memoirs, this work contains some Ross correspondence, about which see Ross, II B below. For other Ross works, see also II E below.

Schlossar, Anton, ed. *Briefwechsel zwischen Erzherzog Johann Baptist von Österreich und Anton Graf von Prokesch-Osten, nebst Auszügen aus den Tagebuchblättern des Erzherzogs Johann über seinen Aufenhalt in Athen im November 1837. . . .* Stuttgart, 1898.

Although this volume contains summaries of Archduke John's journal on his stay in Greece and letters by him, its chief value for this book stems from the letters of Prokesch-Osten, which are rich with information on the period from 1841 through 1843, especially the Mavrokordatos episode and the revolution of 1843. Though interested in the diplomatic significance of internal events, Prokesch-Osten recognized the important role of the parties and wrote about their activities, but not about their internal structure or membership.

Söltl, J. M. von. *Ludwig I. König von Bayern und Graf von Armansperg.* Nördlingen, 1886.

Formally a secondary account and valuable for its information on the delays in the work of the regency during 1832 while still in Bavaria, this work is primarily a select collection of correspondence, mostly between Ludwig and Armansperg from 1827 to 1837. There are, in addition, letters between Maurer, Abel, and Armansperg; an important letter from Ludwig to Otho, making recommendations concerning royal policy after the royal majority; and Otho's letter of dismissal to Armansperg in 1837. Most of the material is drawn from the private papers of Armansperg, whose wife placed them at the disposal of the editor, a royal privy councilor and professor at the University of Munich.

Spindler, Max, ed. *Briefwechsel zwischen Ludwig I. von Bayern und Eduard von Schenk 1823-1841.* Munich, 1930.

This scholarly edition of correspondence between Ludwig and a high Bavarian official, who was also Ludwig's close personal friend, was published in order to provide "a penetrating insight into one of the most important periods of Bavarian history." There are scattered references in the correspondence to Greek affairs.

Thiersch, Heinrich W. J., ed. *Friedrich Thiersch's Leben.* 2 vols. Leipzig, 1866.

The title gives no such indication, but this work consists of correspondence to and from Thiersch, collected by his son from his father's papers and his father's friends. Vol. ii, covering the period 1830-60, contains a large number of detailed letters on Greek internal conditions, written by Thiersch while in Greece (1831-32). Among them are twelve detailed reports to Ludwig on his attempts to mediate between the warring parties in Greece, and letters to and from the residents of the three protecting powers. Much of the information in these was incorporated in Thiersch's two-volume memoirs (ii b below). The letters on Greece during the absolutist period are far fewer, limited to letters *to* Thiersch from friends there. There is, among others, one unimportant one from Kolettes (1833), but the valuable ones are ten from Rudhart (1837-38) and two from

Prince Maximilian while on a visit to Greece (beginning of 1841). The former show that one of the aims of Rudhart's efforts was the nullification of the parties as a factor in Greek political life, and the latter shed further light on the Mavrokordatos episode.

Thouvenel, L., ed. *La Grèce du roi Otho. Correspondance de M. [Edouard Antoine] Thouvenel avec sa famille et ses amis.* . . . Paris, 1890.

This selection of the correspondence of Piscatory's successor as French minister in Greece deals with the events after 1843, especially the government of Kolettes (1845-47), but it does provide some insight into the nature of the "French" party even before this period and it contains an excellent biographical index identifying the most prominent Greek political figures of the time.

Trost, Ludwig, ed. *König Ludwig I. von Bayern in seinen Briefen an seinen Sohn den könig Otto von Griechenland.* Bamberg, 1891. Partially trans. into Greek in *Hestia* [*Hearth*], 24 Dec. 1902 ff.

This volume, edited by the then custodian of the Bavarian Geheimes Haus- und Staatsarchiv, contains a small but important part of the invaluable Otho-Ludwig correspondence and, with a few exceptions, still constitutes the only portion of that correspondence to appear in print (I A above). The first 85 pages, a running narrative of Otho's reign, contain only quoted excerpts of Ludwig's correspondence *to* Otho and show the freedom with which Ludwig advised Otho on Greek affairs. The most important excerpt for this book is from a letter of 5 April 1835, in which Ludwig lays down the main principles which should govern Greek royal policy after the majority. It, along with other excerpts, proves that the desire to destroy the parties, as damaging to Greek national interests, was one of the objectives of his policy recommendations, especially that of withholding a constitution. The remainder of this volume contains complete documents from Otho's Secret Archive, among them letters from Otho to Ludwig and Metternich, others from Metternich and Archduke John to Otho, and three important memoranda. The first of these memoranda, by Thiersch, advises on royal policy after the royal majority and suggests, by the wholehearted endorsement given it by Ludwig, that the recommendations published in Thiersch's book must have been a major source of royal policy toward the parties, the establishment of the Council of State and the royal phalanx. The second, which is anonymous, concerns events in the royal palace and in the session of the Council of State during the night and early morning of 14-15 September 1843. The third, by Gennaios Kolokotrones, addressed apparently to Ludwig, gives his account of the events leading up to the revolution, relates the subsequent episode which led to his exile from Greece, and recommends moral and financial support for Otho. The second and third memoranda, as well as some of the excerpts, are published by Petrakakos and Skandames (this section above and III A respectively). Bower and Bolitho, in their biography of Otho (III A) are generous in their quotations from Trost.

Tsaousopoulos, Constantine, ed. and trans. ["Letters of a Lady-in-Waiting in Athens to a Friend in Germany (1837-1843)"]. *Deltion tes Historikes kai Ethnologikes Hetaireias tes Hellados* [*Bulletin of the Historical and Ethnological Society of Greece*], VIII (1922), 383-555.

This private correspondence of Julie Nordenphlycht, Amalia's lady-in-waiting, to Countess von Scheele, the grand-lady of the court of Oldenburg, limits itself largely to the details of court life and incidents in the royal progresses throughout the country, but it occasionally gives information which is pertinent to this study. Information, however, is too general to be of great value and serves only to confirm what a variety of other sources reveal.

Vakalopoulos, Apostolos. "Germanika Engrapha apo to Geheimes Archiv tou Monachou schetika me ten Prote Periodo tes Antibasileias sten Hellada (1833-1843)" ["German Documents from the Geheimes Archiv of Munich concerning the First Period of the Regency in Greece"]. *Epistemonike Epeteris Philosophikes Scholes* [*Scholarly Annual of the Philosophical School*], University of Thessaloniki, VIII (1960), 49-97.

This article brings into print for the first time two documents located in the Bavarian Geheimes Staatsarchiv, Munich (I A above): the longer one an apologetic memoir submitted by Maurer and Abel to Ludwig to explain the reasons for friction within the first regency, the second a report of Gasser, Bavarian legate to Greece, to Ludwig, supporting the position of the regency majority. In the course of condemning Armansperg and his wife, both documents touch on the finances and tax system of the state and the role of the English and Russian ministers to Greece, but neither deals with the relation of intraregency friction to domestic politics.

Vellianites, Theodore, ed. and trans. [Letters of Anton von Prokesch-Osten], *Le Messager d'Athènes*, 8-22 July 1929.

This selection of letters from Prokesch-Osten to Archduke John of Austria, taken mostly from the period 1841-42, appeared by installments in successive issues of the newspaper listed above.

Vikelas, D., ed. and trans. "Epistole Goustavou Eichtal" ["Letter of Gustav Eichtal"] [Athens, 1 May 1835]. *Deltion tes Historikes kai Ethnologikes Hetaireias tes Hellados* [*Bulletin of the Historical and Ethnological Society of Greece*], II (May 1877), 515-20.

————. "Epistole Goustavou Eichtal" ["Letter of Gustav Eichtal"] [Nauplion, 5 Aug. 1834]. *Deltion tes Historikes kai Ethnologikes Hetaireias tes Hellados* [*Bulletin of the Historical and Ethnological Society of Greece*], IV (1892), 331-43.

————. "Ho Goustavos Eichtal en Helladi" ["Gustav Eichtal in Greece"].

Hestia [*Hearth*], xxi-xxii (1886), p. 337-42, 353-57, 369-72, 385-89, 401-403, 417-19.

Eichtal, a French philhellene and admirer of Kolettes, served during 1834 and a part of 1835 as an official in the office of political economy, established within the ministry of interior while Kolettes headed it. A journal, kept during Eichtal's stay, and a number of his letters, written to friends and relatives during this time, his son turned over to Vikelas on his death in 1886. Excerpts from the journal and some letters appeared in the weekly *Hestia* by installments. Subsequently, Vikelas published separately and in their entirety two additional letters, as listed above. This material gives an interesting, though not especially revealing, glimpse into the politics of the time, especially the conflict between Armansperg and Kolettes, which resulted in Eichtal's loss of office as well as the fall of Kolettes, his patron. The bias of this material is pro-"French."

Zenopoulos, G. K. and Th. P. Delegiannes, eds. *Hellenike Nomothesia apo tou 1833 mechri tou 1875* [*Greek Legislation from 1833 till 1875*]. 6 vols. Athens, 1875.

B. MEMOIRS AND CONTEMPORARY ACCOUNTS

Abele, J.A.S. *Denkwürdigkeiten und die k. bayerische Expedition nach Hellas.* Mannheim, 1936.

Brandis, Chr. Aug. *Mittheilungen über Griechenland.* 3 vols. Leipzig, 1843.

This ambitious and bulky work, by a Bavarian scholar who served Otho as royal librarian (1837-42), is varied in scope. Vol. i is a travel account, mostly topographical, archeological, and ethnographical, based on trips taken by the author, some of them as a part of royal progresses. Vol. ii is a historical account of the Greek Revolution through the Kapodistrian period, based on written accounts, especially that of Thomas Gordon, or on oral reminiscences, especially those of Gropius, Austrian consul. Vol. iii deals by topic with contemporary conditions in Greece, with major chapters on folk customs, education, literature, the church and the state. The third volume resembles memoirs, but only in a limited sense because the author writes impersonally. Only the last chapter of Vol. iii (on the state) is of direct concern for this book. Its major concern is with statecraft rather than with parties, but Brandis treats statecraft as a response to a particular political situation in which parties played a prominent role. The most convincing apologist, by and large, of regency and royal policy (a defender of the military settlement, the press laws, and absolutism in general), he had a keen sense of the social structure in Greece and the family and clientele basis of the parties. As a result, he was able to appreciate the Crown's wish to liberate the "people" from the influence of the ruling classes (primates and chieftains), to see this as the motive behind the military settlement and the dotation law, to recognize the basis for the staying power of the parties, and to understand the severe limitations which the system of dependency placed on the party leaders' ability to restrain their adherents.

Bronzetti, C. J. *Erinnerungen an Griechenland aus den Jahren 1832-1835.* Würzburg, 1842.

Chursilchen, Michael. *Die bayerische Brigade in Griechenland.* Nürnberg, 1838.

———. *Geschichtliche Erinnerungen an die Expedition nach Hellas.* Amberg, 1855.

Dragoumes, Nicholas. *Historikai Anamneseis* [*Historical Reminiscences*]. 2nd edn. 2 vols. Athens, 1879. 3rd edn., ed. K. Amantos. Athens, 1925. Trans. into French by Jules Blancard under title *Souvenirs historiques.* 1 vol. Paris, 1890.

These memoirs focus largely on major political developments in which the writer played no significant part, rather than on his personal experiences. Although Dragoumes was a Phanariot who held important posts in government ministries during the absolutist period, his work reveals virtually nothing about the doings of the Phanariots as a group and concerns itself only peripherally with the actual workings of the administration. Even though historians have used it extensively as a source of specific information on such events as the Mavrokordatos episode or the revolution of 1843, and even though there is much valuable information on these events, its usefulness in this respect is limited by the fact that Dragoumes was inconsequential as a political figure and hence witnessed these events from the outside or got his information secondhand. Much of the purported information on such subjects as the parties or the statecraft of the regency is merely a set of judgments, treating the parties as largely personal coteries devoid of any ideological basis or regarding regency statecraft as a doctrinaire attempt to transplant Bavarian institutions to Greece regardless of local conditions. For the absolutist period at least, these memoirs are most important because they tell what other Greeks thought about such important matters as Bavarianism and constitutionalism. Dragoumes reveals the range of thought on these two matters and does so by extensively quoting remarks and letters of such prominent men as Mavrokordatos, Trikoupes, Kolettes, Kolokotrones, and Zaïmes.

Georgantas, Anthony. "Historikai Apomnemoneumata tes Basileias Othonos" ["Historical Memoirs of Otho's Kingship]. *Parnassos,* v (1881), 833-51.

This short account, by a "French" Livadiot primate of East Rumely, is an extremely valuable source on the revolution of 1843, its preparation, outbreak, and immediate aftermath. In the course of describing when the idea of this particular conspiracy arose and how it was organized, Georgantas, himself an early conspirator, provides a good bit of detail which shows that the revolutionary organization was largely the already existing network of personal, family, and party ties, infused with a new conspiratorial purpose, and that the normal conduct of business, involving extended trips, served as a major channel of conspiratorial communication. His account of the outbreak of the revolution tells something of what transpired in the meeting of the Council of State during the early morning of 15 September and in the subsequent meetings of the revolutionary cabinet. By quoting a few letters in his own files, from Metaxas, Kanares, T. Grivas, and Makrygiannes (letters otherwise unavailable), this work clarifies the government policy of Metaxas and the provincial activities of parties in response to the revolution.

Guizot, M. *Mémoires pour servir à l'histoire de mon temps.* 9 vols. Paris, 1858-68.

These well-known and long-published memoirs deal in some detail with the Greek internal crisis of 1841 and the Greek revolution of 1843. The pertinent sections of these memoirs include valuable excerpts from official correspondence, such as letters of Guizot to Lagrené and Piscatory, the record of Kolettes' private conversation with Guizot concerning the revolution of 1843, and a letter of Kolettes to Desages, director of the French foreign ministry, concerning his purpose in joining the revolutionary cabinet and the resistance which he encountered, presumably from members of his own party.

Heideck, Karl von. *Die bayerische Philhellenenfahrt 1826-1829.* Darstellungen aus der Bayerischen Kriegs- und Heeresgeschichte, nos. 6-7. 2 vols. Munich, 1897-98.

Included here because the author eventually became one of the three Bavarian regents, the book falls outside the scope of the royal period.

[Heinze, Alexander Clarus]. *Der dritte September 1843 in Athen. Von einem Augenzeugen beschrieben und mit den betroffenden Actenstücken begleitet.* Leipzig, 1843.

Having discovered this title only after leaving Greece and not having been able to locate a copy in this country, I have had to rely on the short excerpts which Petrakakos published in Vol. II of his [*Parliamentary History*] (II A above).

Heinze, Alexander Clarus. *Der hellenische Nationalcongress zu Athen in den Jahren 1843 und 1844. Nach der Originalausgabe der Congressverhandlungen im Auszug bearbeitet und mit geschichtlichen Notizen, Actenstücken u. s. w. begleitet.* Leipzig, 1845.

This private eyewitness account of the proceedings, by a Bavarian officer, is accurate, precise, and thorough, and serves as a valuable supplement to the official account (II A above). It *does* identify the speakers by name and even goes as far as to give a breakdown of the assembly and some of its committees by party affiliation. As a result, for a student of the Greek parties, this account is of greater value than the official one.

Kobell, Luise von. *Unter den vier ersten Königen Bayerns. Nach Briefen und Eigenen Erinnerungen.* 2 vols. Munich, 1894.

The author of these memoirs, granddaughter of Ägid von Kobell, devotes a short chapter to her grandfather's service in Greece (1834-36), first as a member of the second Bavarian regency, then as Bavarian minister to Greece. Since she was a mere child when her grandfather served in Greece and did not accompany him, her brief chapter on Greece is based on the personal papers of her grandfather, to which she later had access and from which she quotes on occasion. Her main objective is to demonstrate her grandfather's success and popularity in Greece. She reports nothing of significance for this book.

Kolokotrones, Gennaios T. *Apomnemoneumata* [*Memoirs*]. Ed. Emmanuel G. Protopsaltes. Athens, 1955.

————. *Apomnemoneumata (Cheirographon Deuteron 1821-1862)* [*Memoirs (Second Manuscript . . .)*]. Ed. Emmanuel G. Protopsaltes. Athens, 1961.

Gennaios Kolokotrones wrote memoirs in two installments, the first (first title above) dealing with the Revolutionary and Kapodistrian periods, the second (second title above) devoted primarily to the entire Othonian period (Parts II-IV) but with a long preliminary section (Part I) of supplementary reminiscences concerning the periods covered in the first installment. The first manuscript, which falls outside the scope of this book's main concern, has long been available. The second is less known.

For the period 1833-44, it is disappointing. Only about one-sixth of it (pp. 73-91) is devoted to the period. There is no information on the internal history of the Napist party or on politics within the court, areas of political life which Gennaios knew intimately. He writes about his visit to the Bavarian court in 1843, but he does not tell why he went or what transpired there. The bulk of his remarks concern the alleged "major" plot, whose existence he denies, the Messenian revolt, which he describes as a mere reaction against the new tax system, the Philorthodox plot, which he represents as nothing more than an irredentist venture, and the revolution of 1843, which he denies having attempted to undo. He writes not about these events as such, but rather about the government's response to them. His obvious intent is to exonerate himself and his party from charges made in connection with all these events, not to tell all that he must have known.

[Kolokotrones, Theodore]. *Diegesis sympanton tes hellenikes phyles apo ta 1770 heos ta 1836* [*Narrative of Events of the Greek Race from 1770 to 1836*]. Ed. with historical introduction by George Tertsetes. Athens, 1846. Reprinted in 2 vols. Athens, 1934. New Greek edn. by Tasos Vournas entitled *Kolokotrone Apomnemoneumata* [*Kolokotrones Memoirs*]. Athens, n.d. Trans. into English by Elizabeth Mayhew Edmonds under title *Kolokotrones, Klepht and Warrior*. London, 1892. Ed.'s introd. to 1st edn. supplied by separately published work entitled *Exakolouthesis ton prolegomenon eis ta hypomnemata tou Kolokotrone* [*Continuation of the Prologue to the Notes of Kolokotrones*]. Ed. George Tertsetes. Athens, 1852.

These memoirs of the elder Kolokotrones hardly get into the royal period. There is only a scanty account of his arrest, trial, and pardon (1833-35). Kolokotrones insists on his innocence and convincingly asserts that his political opponents, even before the regency arrived in Greece, discredited him in the eyes of the regency and the new monarch.

[Makrygiannes, John]. *Archeion tou Strategou Ioannou Makrygianne* [*Archive of General John Makrygiannes*]. Archeia tes Neoteras Hellenikes Historias [Archives of Modern Greek History], no. 2. Ed. John Vlachogiannes. 2 vols. Athens, 1907. Vol. II of 1st edn. reedited in 2 vols. under title *Apomnemoneumata* [*Memoirs*]. Athens, 1947. Trans. into English by H. A. Lidderdale in a one-volume abridgement entitled *Makriyannis. The Memoirs of General Makriyannis 1797-1864*. London, 1966.

This minor masterpiece of demotic prose, which no historian has ever adequately exploited as a source for the Othonian period, has proved invaluable for this study—as a personal manifestation of military class attitudes and popular outlook, as well as a rich repository of detailed information which, if properly used, reveals more than any similar source on the mechanics of politics. In its former function, this work reveals a type of mentality—patriotic, idealistic, self-reliant, suspicious, only partially articulate—which renders understandable the persistent involvement of many Greeks in conspiracy, the chronic dissatisfaction with the performance of any governmental authority, and the general failure to translate vague aspirations into a workable political program. As a source for the mechanics of politics, this work sheds light on important developments which historians have largely ignored, such as the devices employed by Kolettes (1834) to expand his following in the Athens-Piraeus area, the political opposition's use of the Athens municipal council in the campaign against Armansperg (1836), the existence of competing irredentist and conspiratorial organizations between 1836-40, and the alignments and maneuvers constituting a part of the politics of the period of the constituent assembly. Moreover, it has one of the fullest firsthand accounts of the conspiracy which resulted in the revolution of 1843. But the work also has important weaknesses as a source—the tendency of Makrygiannes to exaggerate his own importance in political events, his

frequent failure to locate events chronologically, and his apparent inability to explicate specific political issues.

Maurer, George Ludwig von. *Das griechische Volk in öffentlicher, kirchlicher und privatrechtlicher Beziehung vor und nach dem Freiheitskampfe
bis zum 31 Juli 1834.* 3 vols. Heidelberg, 1835. Trans. into Greek by
Eustathios Karastathes (Vol. i, Athens, 1943) and Christos Pratsikas
(Vol. ii, Athens, 1947) under same title. 2 vols.

Although a partisan work, written as a defense of his record in Greece
by one of the original regents after his dismissal in mid-1834, this work
is the best source for the first year and a half of the Othonian period. It is
a mine of information, especially on those branches of the administration
for which Maurer was responsible—educational, ecclesiastical, and judicial. For this book in particular, the memoirs are important for primarily
three reasons. First, they give a full statement of the formal aims and
intentions behind the first regency's statecraft and policy and reveal that
a vital factor in the formulation and pursuit of these aims was the desire
to allay partisan strife and avoid governing through the parties. Second,
they reveal the political conditions and considerations that affected the
timing and manner of execution of such acts as the dissolution of the
monasteries and the reorganization of the church. Finally, in the process
of discussing the plots of 1833, the Kolokotrones trial, the Mane revolt,
and the regency dispute, they reveal the way in which the "French" party
gained political ascendancy and how the "English" and "Russian" parties
united themselves into a political opposition. This work was not really
intended as a set of memoirs. The work Maurer did write as memoirs
lies unpublished in the Maureriana collection of the Staatsbibliothek in
Munich (i a above).

Neezer, Christopher. *Apomnemoneumata ton proton eton tes hidryseos
tou Hellenikou Basileiou* [*Memoirs concerning the First Years of the
Establishment of the Greek Kingdom*]. Trans. from German and ed. J. C.
Neezer. Constantinople, 1911. Reedited D. Kampouroglou. Athens, 1936.

The author of these memoirs, a Franconian German, served as an army
officer in Greece from 1833-35, then, after a return to Germany, settled
permanently in Greece in 1840. The major part of the memoirs, dealing
with the years 1833-35, does little to illuminate the political picture. There
are only two instances in the entire work when he provides factual information of political consequence, but in each case it is information
important enough to make his memoirs a valuable source for this book.
First, he repeats a conversation which he overheard in Bavaria between
Otho and Maximilian, a conversation which directly confirms that Otho
consciously set out to make the Crown the center of one national Greek
party. Second, he provides one of the best available accounts during the
night and early morning of 14-15 September 1843, dealing with events
inside the palace in response to news that an outbreak would take place,

with the personal confrontation of Otho and Kallerges at a window of the palace within hearing of Neezer, and with the subsequent negotiations which led to royal acquiescence to revolutionary demands. The memoirs, because of Neezer's evaluation of the political situation, derive a secondary value as a plausible though unconfirmed set of statements which were suggestive hypotheses for the research on this book. He asserts that the three parties exploited and encouraged brigandage as a political weapon against the government. He sees the virtual impossibility of keeping the government free from party influence so long as the Crown had to rely on men with party affiliations (the vast majority) to staff official posts. He indirectly suggests that Bavarianism was in part motivated by the regency's desire to undermine the parties and remain free from party influence, but he criticizes this approach (Bavarianism) as dangerous to the Crown and dismisses the attempt to unite all parties into one royal party as impracticable, himself advocating (in 1833) that the regency should unite itself with one of the parties and rule through it. Unfortunately, he never does discuss alternative approaches which the regency, Armansperg, and Otho subsequently adopted with respect to the problem of handling the parties.

Mayer, A. *Auszug aus meiner Tagebuch während meines dreijahrigen Aufenhalts in Griechenland*. Ottobeuren, 1838.

"Lord Nugent's Travels—Greece in 1843-44" (anon. rev.), *The Quarterly Review*, LXVIII (1846), 297-322.

This is much more than a book review. It contains a large number of excerpts from the journal of Lord Nugent, an Englishman (also II E below), who was in Greece during the period of the constituent assembly. That is the reason for its inclusion here. Entries for 14, 16, 18, and 21 December 1843 describe the traveler's attendance at sessions of the constituent assembly and give vivid physical descriptions of some of the most prominent figures (Church, Bountoures, Kolettes, Metaxas, Lontos, Kallerges, Kriezotes, Grivas, and Makrygiannes). The quoted entries for January 1844 describe a tour of the provinces. Very revealing, these show how actively Lyons tried to round up Greek popular support for an upper chamber (he asked the traveler and his party to urge on the provincial the necessity for such an institution) and describe some of the attitudes toward an upper chamber on the part of provincials whom Lord Nugent encountered.

Papadopoulos-Vretos, Andrew. *Historike Ekthesis tes ephemeridos 'Ho Hellenikos-Kathreptes'—Le Compte-Rendu du 'Miroir Grec'*. Athens, 1839.
———. *Politika Symmikta . . . — Mélanges de Politique*. . . . Athens, 1840.
———. *Un Grec très dévoué à la Russie victime du chancelier de cet empire le Prince Gortchacoff*. Paris, 1873.

The author of the three above-listed works was a native of the Ionian

Islands, medical doctor, publicist, and ardent partisan of Russia. He came to Greece in 1831 after expulsion from the Ionian Islands by the British authorities, became deeply involved in Greek politics in 1832 as a personal physician and protégé of Admiral Ricord and editor of *Miroir Grec,* newspaper organ of the Kapodistrian senate rump. He left Greece for Russia in 1833 as a result of the regency's discrimination against the Napist party, and returned to Greece in 1839 in time to witness events connected with the discovery of the Philorthodox plot. Consequently, all three works reflect the extremist views of the Napist party.

The first provides a detailed inside account of one major aspect of the civil war of 1832 (the behavior of Admiral Ricord, the activities of the Kapodistrian senate rump and its newspaper *Miroir Grec*), and a number of documents (such as letters of Ralles, the previous editor of *Miroir Grec*) on which the account is based. The second is a collection of excerpts, largely from Greek and foreign newspapers but also from a few letters of Nesselrode to Augustine Kapodistrias and Baron Rückman. It is still mostly concerned with the events of 1832 and the author's participation in them. The third, a general autobiographical account built around the theme of Russian ingratitude toward one of its most ardent devotees, provides no such detailed account of domestic political events. But it again contains a statement of the Napist "interpretation" of the Philorthodox incident of 1839 as a British intrigue, shows the disjunction between the moderate policy of St. Petersburg and the reckless behavior of its agents on the spot, reveals what Russian patronage might involve (i.e. loans by Admiral Ricord to Perroukas and Ainian) and what a Russian client like Papadopoulos-Vretos might expect from his patron (i.e. appointments and favors), and portrays the system of foreign-oriented parties in Greece as a system of patronage based on the desire for office.

Predl, F. X. M. A. von. *Erinnerungen aus Griechenland 1832-1835.* Würzburg, 1841.

[Prokesch von Osten, Anton]. *Aus den Tagebüchern des Grafen Prokesch von Osten . . . 1830-1834.* Vienna, 1909. See under Prokesch-Osten and Schlossar in II A above.

Pückler-Muskau, H. von. *Briefwechsel und Tagebücher.* Berlin, 1876. See also II E below.

Rangabe, Alexander R. *Apomnemoneumata* [*Memoirs*]. 2 vols. Athens, 1894-95.

These memoirs were written at an advanced age, long after the Othonian period, by a distinguished man of letters who had occupied high administrative posts in Athens during the absolutist period. Although the memoirs cover the major political events of the absolutist period, they are generally not very illuminating and sometimes inaccurate because Rangabe was only a bystander. But in the area of his personal experience

—administrative work and the social life of 'high society'—they are invaluable. There is much information on individual Phanariots who settled in Athens, their precise family ties and marriage alliances, their style of life, and their important administrative role in the government ministries. Because of his close connections with the "French" party, Rangabe provides valuable information on the Perachora movement of Kolettes in 1831-32 and on the behavior of Chrestides at the end of the Mavrokordatos episode and during his subsequent term of office. He also describes incidents which affected or illuminate important political developments, such as the personal incident which precipitated the break between Michael Soutsos and the king or the feverish and stillborn irredentist plans of Rangabe and his young Phanariot friends in response to the Egyptian crisis of 1839-41.

Ross, Ludwig. *Erinnerungen und Mittheilungen aus Griechenland.* Berlin, 1863. See also under Ross in II A above and II E below.

This is a composite work, the bulk of which consists of the two major items included in the title. The "Erinnerungen" was written privately in 1853 for a German museum; the "Mittheilungen" consists of letters written from Greece by Ross to a friend (Funkhänel, director of the gymnasium of Eisenach) between July 1832, when he arrived in Greece, and July 1833. Although the author was an archeologist who served as director of antiquities and a university professor while in Greece, he devotes a good bit of attention to Greek politics. In spite of—perhaps because of —his close association with the court, he is not as informative, detailed, or interpretive on this subject as one might wish, although he covers every important political incident and every important act of statecraft in the 1830s. Most everything he wrote has been incorporated into secondary works or is available in newspaper accounts. But he does, for instance, stress the struggle for power between Armansperg and Kolettes in 1835 more than secondary accounts.

Sander, H. *Erinnerungen eines ehemaligen griechischen Offiziers aus den Jahren 1833-1837.* Darmstadt, 1839.

These memoirs of a German serving in Greece describe the recruitment of volunteers from all parts of Germany for service in Greece, the character of those volunteers, the high death toll among them in Greece (as a result of climate, harsh living conditions, and fighting down revolts), and the gradual return of the survivors to Germany. On Greek conditions, the work reads like a travelogue and is as limited in value as most works of this kind are.

Thiersch, Friedrich. *De l'État actuel de la Grèce.* 2 vols. Leipzig, 1833.

In this account of his mission to Greece in 1831-32, Thiersch does not deal with the royal period. Even though I have restricted this bibliography to material dealing with the period 1833-44, I include this work because much of its information had a direct bearing on the royal period and because it exercised a profound influence on the conception of this book. It suggested two of the hypotheses which I set out to test: first, that the system of clientage, which constituted the main structural element of the parties, was the basic cause for their survival during the absolutist period, and second, that the party situation, by virtue of royal awareness of it and royal determination not to fall victim to it, greatly influenced the character of royal statecraft and the inception of governmental institutions. The first hypothesis was suggested by Thiersch's classic statement of the connection between the system of clientage and the existence of parties. The second was suggested by a list of recommendations intended to serve as the basis of royal policy in Greece and designed to eliminate the parties as an important factor on the political scene. Since Ludwig, Otho, and the regency were certainly aware of them, these recommendations were at least one of the major guides for the actual elaboration of royal policy and one of the sources of the regency's determination, even before its arrival in Greece, to fight down the parties. In addition, this work is one of the few to specify the party affiliations of a large number of individuals who remained on the political scene during the absolutist period. It also provides a very perceptive account of the conditions and legacies with which the Crown had to deal.

C. NEWSPAPERS

The rapid growth of the newspaper press, in spite of restrictive press laws, is a major characteristic of the Othonian period. The following list of newspapers, published between 1833-44, is based primarily on the catalogue of the Library of the Chamber of Deputies, Athens, which contains the most complete collection. The absence of a terminal date in the listing indicates that the newspaper survived into the postabsolutist period. All dates are old-style. Even though non-Greek newspapers noted for their coverage of Greek affairs are not listed below, the two most notable ones bear mention—*Morning Chronicle* (British) and *Augsburg Gazette*.

With the exception of *Hēlios*, edited by the ultraliberal poet Alexander Soutsos, the research for this book was limited largely to semiofficial and acknowledged party newspapers. The semiofficial papers were *Sōtēr* during the period of the first regency, *Ethnikē* during the Armansperg period, *Ho Hellēnikos Tachydromos* thereafter. The reputedly "English" newspaper was *Athēna*, edited by the republican Antoniades and published throughout this period, although *Triptolemos*, a short-lived "Phanariot organ," was more genuinely "English" and representative of the predominantly "English" cabinet of the first half of 1833. The acknowledged Napist newspapers were *Chronos*, *Aiōn*, and *Hellas*. The first two were both edited by the Napist John Philemon, the former financed by

Theodore Kolokotrones and Vlassopoulos and discontinued the same month that Kolokotrones was arrested (September 1833), the latter, started in 1838, really a continuation of the former under a new but related name. The short-lived *Hellas* of 1839, also Napist in orientation though progovernment, in contrast with *Aiōn* which joined the constitutionalist opposition in the spring of 1839, seems to have represented the Michael Soutsos branch of the "Russian" party and seems to reflect a conflict within the "Russian" party. The "French" newspapers were three: *Sōtēr, Elpis,* and *Philos tou Laou. Sōtēr,* edited by the "French" Skouphos, went through a series of changes in its orientation. It began as the organ of Kolettes, enjoying semiofficial status so long as the regency majority prevailed, leading the opposition against Armansperg during the Armansperg-Kolettes conflict (1834-35); it abandoned Kolettes and briefly shifted allegiance to Armansperg, subsequently joined the constitutionalist opposition with the support of Catacazy, then became the great exponent of Othonian absolutism and leader of the fusionist "movement" of 1837-38. *Elpis,* edited by Levides, started its activities in 1836 with the presumed blessing of Kolettes, who is reputed to have sent the press for its operations from Paris.

The object of this particular selection of newspapers was, of course, to discern official policy and each party's response to it, the position of the government and each party on various issues and particular events, as well as the government's attitude toward the parties and the parties' changing attitude toward each other. Since articles appearing in *Ho Hellēnikos Tachydromos* were frequently submitted to the king for approval, this newspaper is obviously a good indication of the royal position. On the other hand, the range of opinion within, and the differences between, the constituent parts of any one party were too great to be represented by any one party organ. For instance, Antoniades, the editor of *Athēna,* was much closer to Lyons' clientele within the "English" party than to Mavrokordatos and his close following. The existence of two Napist newspapers in 1839, *Aiōn* in the ranks of the constitutionalist opposition and *Hellas* progovernment, reflects a split within the Napist party, just as the coexistence of three "French" newspapers, during much of the time, reflects divergent groups within the "French" party. Moreover, the frequent shifts of orientation of *Sōtēr* show the changing tactics of at least one branch of the "French" party. From the subsiding of the usually bitter warfare between *Aiōn* and *Athēna* in 1842, one can discern the existence of the "English"-"Russian" alliance which receives direct documentation elsewhere. Finally, it should be underlined that much of the time individual editors spoke for themselves rather than for a collectively formulated body of opinion.

The news that was reported, however biased the presentation, is also valuable as a source of information as well as party orientation, especially about the numerous revolts, the fusionist "movement," the Philorthodox plot, the Mavrokordatos episode, debates in the Council of State, etc. Letters from the provinces to the editor are a valuable source of information about provincial conditions and developments. Moreover, even rumors, with which newspapers were replete, often reveal actual attempts which never materialized.

Aion [*Age*]. Athens. 25 Sept. 1838—

Aithria [*Serenity*]. Athens. 1-4 Dec. 1843.

Anagennetheisa Hellas [*Regenerated Greece*]. Athens. 10 June 1836–20 Feb. 1837 (in French also).

Anexartetos [*Independent*]. Athens. 21 Nov. 1841–24 Aug. 1844.

Angelos [*Angel*]. Athens. 17 July 1843–7 Sept. 1844.

Athena. Megara. 13 Feb. 1832–18 Mar. 1833.
> Nauplion. 23 Mar.–14 Sept. 1833.
> Athens. 30 May 1834—

Attike Melissa [*Attic Bee*]. Athens. Aug.–Sept. 1841.

Chronos [*Time*]. Nauplion. May–Sept. 1833.

Elpis [*Hope*]. Athens. 7 Oct. 1836–17 Dec. 1837 (in German also); 26 Sept. 1843–28 Dec. 1844.

Ethnike [*National*]. Athens. 1 Oct. 1834–27 June 1835 (in French also).

Helios [*Sun*]. Nauplion. 23 June–24 Nov. 1833.

Hellas. Athens. 28 June 1839–3 Jan. 1840.

Ho Hellenikos Tachydromos [*Greek Courier*]. Athens. June 1836–Dec. 1841 (in French also).

Hermoupolites [*The Hermopolite*]. Syros. Nov. 1839–Mar. 1840.

Hymetike Melissa [*Hymettic Bee*]. Athens. Oct. 1841–Apr. 1842.

Karteria [*Perseverance*]. Patras. Sept. 1842–Aug. 1843.
> Athens. Aug. 1843—

Kyrex Achaïkos [*Achaian Herald*]. Patras. Jan. 1840–June 1841.

Kyrex Proïnos [*Morning Herald*]. Athens. Jan. 1843—

Minos. Patras. Nov. 1841–July 1842 (break, with later resumption).

Misobarbaros [*Semi-Barbarian*]. Syros. 20 Oct. 1837 (only one issue).

Parateretes [*Observer*]. Athens. Nov. 1841—

Pheme [*Fame*]. Athens. Mar. 1837–Dec. 1843.

Philos tou Laou [*Friend of the People*]. Athens. June 1839–July 1842; 9 Dec. 1843—

Radamanthos. Athens. Apr. 1841–Apr. 1842 (break with later resumption).

Sokrates [*Socrates*]. Athens. Dec. 1838–Oct. 1839; June–May 1842 (break with later resumption).

Soter [*Savior*]. Nauplion. Jan.–Dec. 1834 (in French also).
> Athens. Jan. 1835–July 1837; Jan.–Nov. 1838 (break with later resumption).

Telegraphos [*Telegraph*]. Athens. May–Sept. 1843 (break with later resumption).

Terpnos Zephyros [*Delightful Zephyr*]. Athens. Mar.–Apr. 1842.

Triptolemos. Nauplion. 26 July–30 Dec. 1833.

Trite Septembriou [*The Third of September*]. Athens. Sept.–Oct. 1843.
Zephyros [*Zephyr*]. Athens. Mar. 1841–Feb. 1842; Sept. 1843—

D. CONTEMPORARY TRACTS, PAMPHLETS, ACCOUNTS, ETC.

For a virtually exhaustive list of the books published about Greece during the decade 1833-44, see *Hellenike Bibliographia 1800-1863* [*Greek Bibliography 1800-1863*], ed. Demetrios Ghines and Valerios Mexas, 3 vols. (Athens, 1939-41). It reveals that the bulk of printed material was educational (primary and secondary school books, catechisms, and translations of major European works) or official documents (decrees, encyclicals, and programs of official ceremonies). Omitting such works, the following list consists of (1) tracts relating to some of the major questions or issues which influenced the political scene (the religious question, the question of freedom of the press, and the constitutional issue); (2) works on general conditions, usually apologetic or partisan in tone; (3) accounts concerning particular incidents or phenomena; and (4) a few items with special relevance to the parties.

ISSUES

A major category of the pamphlet literature deals with the religious question which figured so prominently during the absolutist period. It reveals the three major issues on which partisan debate focused: (1) the proper nature of the church, argued either in defense or criticism of the autocephalous and caesaropapist ecclesiastical settlement of 1833; (2) the legitimate degree of religious toleration, debated with specific reference to the Protestant missionary enterprise in Greece and the theosophical teachings of Theophilos Kaïres; and (3) the legitimacy of translating Holy Writ into the demotic Greek, a question raised by the publication of such translations under the auspices of the missionary press. It reveals the existence of two basic positions on these issues—the liberal position, articulated by such clerics as Theokletos Pharmakides, Neophytos Vamvas, and Misael Apostolides, and the conservative position, advanced most prominently by Constantine Oikonomos and popularized most successfully by the periodical *Euangelikos Salpinx* [*Evangelical Trumpet*], ed. by Germanos. It demonstrates, finally, the fundamental contrast in cultural orientation between the liberals and conservatives.

The missionary enterprise was the first religious issue to be debated through pamphlet literature. In 1836-37 the conservatives launched their attack with three publications: the empassioned anonymous *Epistole*, the more reasoned tract of Lamprylos, and the patriarchal encyclical of Gregory VI. Apostolides, in *Antapantesis*, and Vamvas, in *Syntomos Apantesis*, came to the defense of the missionaries. Then the debate shifted to the question of the translation of Holy Writ and raised the

579

more fundamental question of the proper nature of the church. As actual translators of Holy Writ, the protagonists in this case were Theokletos Pharmakides and Neophytos Vamvas; Oikonomos and Germanos were the attackers. In 1836, Germanos edited an anonymous pamphlet (*Skepseis*), probably written by Oikonomos, on the Greek church and continued to attack the translation of scriptures in [*Evangelical Trumpet*]. In 1838, Vamvas replied to Germanos in *Apantesis* and to Oikonomos in a tract on the modern Greek church (*Peri tes Neohellenikes Ekklesias*). The following year Oikonomos issued a criticism (*Epikrisis*) of Vamvas' tract on the church, and Vamvas replied with a countercriticism (*Antepikrisis*). To this debate Pharmakides contributed with two pamphlets—*Pseudonymous Germanos* in 1838 and *Apologia* in 1840—the latter coming after his dismissal as secretary of the holy synod and constituting a defense of the ecclesiastical settlement of 1833 in which he had played such a prominent part.

The material on the Kaïres excommunication and banishment (1839), which also involved the issue of religious toleration, appeared in pamphlets devoted exclusively to that incident, the liberal position expressed by Athanasiou in *Ta kata Kaïren*, the conservative view argued by Gregoriades in *Hieros Thriambos*, two consisting of articles concerning the incident by the Napist *Aiōn* and semiofficial *Ho Hellēnikos Tachydromos* respectively, and a final one consisting of a speech by Kaïres himself.

The pamphlet of Panas (*He Baptisis*), published anonymously in 1842, presents the conservative position, but this time in the broader framework of a cultural conflict between East and West.

In this pamphlet controversy, the more basic issue of autocephaly and caesaropapism was subordinated to the missionary and translation issues until the drawing up of a constitution in 1843-44 reopened the question of a proper ecclesiastical settlement. In an attempt to win over the delegates on the eve of their formal consideration of this question, two anonymously published articles appeared: the first by Apostolides (*Diatribe*) in defense of the settlement of 1833, the second by Oikonomos (*Apantesis*) in opposition to it. That same year Edward Masson, the Scottish philhellene, published an English work on the Greek church entitled *An Apology for the Greek Church*.

This issue is the basic concern of the posthumously published two-volume work of Oikonomos, entitled [*Collected Ecclesiastical Writings*] (II A above), which by no means includes all of Oikonomos' ecclesiastical writings. The bulk of this work was written in 1841 and takes the form of a narrative and documentary history of ecclesiastical affairs in Greece from 1821 to 1841, but it is essentially a thoroughgoing and partisan criticism of the ecclesiastical establishment of 1833. In 1852, when attempts were under way to end the schism between the patriarchate of Constantinople and the church of Greece, Oikonomos began to expand the work so as to cover the intervening years and reply to a tract published by Pharmakides during that year. Owing to reasons of health, he never finished the expanded version, but whatever he did add is included in the two-volume publication.

The question of freedom of the press became prominent in the pamphlet literature with the promulgation of a more stringent press law in 1837. In *He Neara peri Exybriseon . . . Nomothesia*, Kalligas, the liberal lawyer, attacked this law and addressed himself to the question in general. Other publications dealing with this issue took the form of accounts of trials against persons accused of violating the law: Athanasiou's account of the trial of *Athēna* (*He dike*), an anonymously published account of the *Elpis* trial (*He dike*), and Alexander Soutsos' own two accounts, the one (*He Proanakrisis*) on the preliminary judicial proceedings against him, the other a general apology (*Apologia*), concerning the subsequent trial and judgment. Other such trials were given widespread publicity in the liberal press.

Throughout the absolutist period, the constitutional question was widely publicized by the liberals in an attempt to exact a constitution from the Crown. The most valuable of such tracts for this essay was a group of dialogues written by Valetas and published under the pseudonym "Sibi" in 1836. By presenting the arguments for and against a constitution for Greece, the essay reveals the existing arguments at the time for supporting and opposing constitutionalism. In the writings of Alexander Soutsos, such as his *Panorama* (1833) and his *Ho Periplanomenos* (1839), he calls for a constitution. *Ai peri Syntagmatos* (listed by title below), consisting of a collection of documents exchanged between Bavaria and the powers in 1832 and published during the crisis which preceded the revolution of 1843, argues that the Crown and the powers have a legal and moral obligation, on the basis of promises made in 1832, to grant the Greeks a constitution.

The revolution of 1843, which made the promulgation of a constitution inevitable, changed the complexion of writings on the constitutional question. Now, it was no longer a question of justifying constitutionalism, but of deciding what kind of a constitution was desirable. In 1841, when anti-Othonian sentiment became pronounced, the American republican constitution had been published by Petsales (*Metaphrasis*). A similar work (*Ta Syntagmata*), edited by Vlassarides with comments by the Utopian socialist Sophianopoulos, consisted of a translation of the Belgian and French constitutions and was clearly intended as propaganda in behalf of the most liberal monarchical constitution possible. A third such work (*Politikon Syntagma*) was the publication by Mamoukas of the constitution voted by the Napist assembly of Argos in 1832. General proposals were embodied in four additional tracts, two anonymous (*Archai, Ho Kometes*), one under the pseudonym Democritos (*Eunomia*), and the fourth by J. Soutsos. There were works dealing with more specific issues, such as that of Athanasiou (*Schedion*), arguing for a one-chamber assembly, and that of Karatsoutsas, a dialogue on the autochthon-heterochthon issues.

GENERAL CONDITIONS

In this category, the only items with a specialized focus are those of Argyropoulos (on local administration), Leconte (on general economic conditions), Soteropoulos (on the land tax), and Strong, whose work bears special mention. Consul in Athens for Bavaria and Hanover, he wrote an authorized account based upon official documents made available to him by the Greek government, whose statistics, though not completely reliable, were the best available. The remaining works, often with an axe to grind, were generally political and international in orientation though they dealt usually with conditions in general: Bertrand, Chrysoberges, [Dialogoi], Faudot, Menas, Petrokokkinos, Raoul-Rochette, and Texier, the last of whom gives a general survey of conditions between 1833-44 to show the value of peace for Greece and to condemn irredentism. Of the four Finlay items listed below, two merit attention here—the earliest (1836-37) is the most scholarly, later revised and incorporated into his multivolume history of Greece; the 1838 article a miscellany on political conditions, recently published foreign works on Greece (Cochrane, Giffard, Hervé, Wordsworth), customs and manners.

EVENTS

The apology of Tertsetes is a pro-Kolokotrones critique of the Kolokotrones trial and a justification of Tertsetes' behavior as one of the dissenting judges. The apology of Louriotes and Orlandos, though dealing primarily with their role in negotiations for British loans during 1824-25, offers information on the activity of the control board in examining Revolutionary financial abuses at the expense of the state, because the work is a reply to the unfavorable decision of the control board in 1835 with respect to their handling of these negotiations.

The two collections of prophecies, one consisting exclusively of those made by the thirteenth-century monk Agathangelos (*Chresmoi*), the other a miscellaneous collection in which Agathangelos figures as only one of the "prophets" (*Sylloge*), are included in this bibliography because they contributed to the expectation that 1840 would be the year in which the Great Idea would be realized, because they demonstrate the religious framework in which irredentism was stimulated among the masses, and because anti-Napists alleged that their publication at this time was a part of the Philorthodox plot discovered in 1839. The anonymous *He Philorthodoxos Hetairia* is a liberal treatment of that event, and the Orphanides essay deals with the trial of some liberal agitators during the celebration of Greek Independence Day 1841. Finlay's 1843 article, written just before the revolution of 1843, is a scathing criticism of the powers and the existing regime and argues that a revolution is inevitable.

The revolution of 1843 and its immediate aftermath produced the largest number of works—the anonymous article ("History") in *British and Foreign Review*, the Finlay article of 1844, those of Duvergier de Hauranne, Karatsoutsas, Kallerges, Keios, Papadopoulos-Vretos, Polymeres, Rangabe, Soliotes, and A. Soutsos, while the work of the constituent assembly is covered by the anonymous review "Lord Nugent's Travels" in *The Quarterly Review* (II B above for special relevance), Polymeres, Sophianopoulos, and A. Soutsos. The Kallerges item, a letter addressed to *Revue des Deux Mondes*, requires special mention because it was written by one of the leaders of the revolution of 1843 in order to dispel the virtually universal belief that an important segment of the conspirators had aimed at the dethronement of Otho, that the purpose of the decrees celebrating the revolution had been to humiliate Otho, that the ministers of some foreign powers had had a hand in the conspiracy. He insisted on his own innocence of such aims and issued these denials in particular reply to the article of Duvergier de Hauranne, which *Revue des Deux Mondes* had previously published.

PARTIES

These works have only a peripheral relationship to the parties as such. For instance, Lenormant's title is misleading. He deals only peripherally with Metaxas' role as party leader and writes what is general biography. In spite of its poetical form and its vituperative character, Soutsos' [*Change of the Third of September*] deals with the role of the most important party figures and relates a number of illuminating though unsubstantiated incidents.

Only one pamphlet during the entire period—Kalligas' [*The Exhaustion of the Parties*]—deals with the parties as such, only to betray his inability to account for the existence of three parties on solely ideological grounds. A speech by Regas Palamides, addressed to the chamber of deputies in 1845 and published separately, reveals a different type of confusion, this time perhaps calculated. He attributes the rise of parties to the baneful influence of heterochthons; yet, on the other hand, acknowledges the existence of factionalism in pre-Revolutionary Greece, the importance of family feuds as a basis for such factionalism, and then, as if unaware of the contradiction, defends the existence of parties as a legitimate expression of the variety of interests and opinions which exist in any state.

Three additional works—*Portfolio*, Parish's *Diplomatic History*, and the anonymously published "Russian Policy in Greece"—require special explanation because they are all three the work of a vocal group in England who were critics of British official policy in Greece, opponents of the Armansperg regime, apologists for the fallen regency majority (especially Maurer), and supporters of Kolettes and his "French" party as the

583

most vigorous anti-Russian group in Greece. Rabid Russophobes, this group aimed at convincing the British public that, as far as Greece was concerned, in supporting the Armansperg regime official British policy was actually advancing Russian expansionist interests in the Near East.

Portfolio was organized and established by King William IV, David Urquhart (the anti-Russian and pro-Turkish publicist), Lord Ponsonby (sometime English ambassador to Constantinople), and others, with the intention of warning the public about the presumed Russian menace and thereby forcing Lord Palmerston to take an even more aggressive stand against Russia. Its sponsorship by the English king explains why Palmerston was forced to tolerate it as a semiofficial English publication, why he even took responsibility for its publication while trying to counteract its detrimental effects, in spite of the fact that its editors used it to wage a violent press campaign against Palmerston's policy in Greece and its executors Dawkins and Lyons.

At least in regard to Greece the subtitle of *Portfolio* is a misnomer. To be sure, the sections on Greece sometimes contain copies of official Greek documents, excerpts from Greek, Bavarian, and English newspapers, and "letters" from correspondents in Greece on conditions there. But all three categories were chosen to subserve the propaganda purposes of the *Portfolio* editors. Moreover, by far the largest portion of the material on Greece is narrative and analysis of a highly prejudiced kind, partially based on Maurer's text. For these reasons, this work has not been included under section II A of this bibliography.

Because of its rabid prejudice, *Portfolio* misrepresented much that went on in Greece between 1832-37, calling this a period of Russian preponderance, when it was largely a period of British ascendancy, regarding Armansperg as the exponent of Russian diplomatic interests, labeling members of the "English" party "Russian" adherents because of their occasional alliance with the "Russian" against the "French" party. Such misrepresentation gives this work only limited value as a source for Greek politics, but these volumes do provide a good bit of information on the civil war of 1832, the Kolokotrones plot of 1833 and Metaxas' connection with it, the Acarnanian revolt of 1836, and the revolution of 1843. And they do reveal important truths lying at the base of the misinterpretation, namely that the "English" and "Russian" parties did ally themselves against Maurer and Kolettes, and that Armansperg did attempt to win the support of some "Russian" adherents.

Parish, secretary of the British legation during the regency dispute of 1833-34, took the side of the regency majority against Dawkins, his own chief, whose recall he actively and underhandedly worked for. Because of such insubordination, Palmerston dismissed him. He therefore had an axe to grind and wrote his book as an *apologia* of his own conduct. Like *Portfolio*, his book is a scathing criticism of British policy in Greece. As a defender of Maurer and Abel, he quoted extensively from the former's work, as well as from that of the pro-"French" Thiersch, but he did not add anything substantial to what was already known. He did, however, make available to one who reads only English a number of important documents (such as Thiersch's reports to Ludwig in 1831-32).

Parish may well have written "Russian Policy in Greece," ostensibly a review of Maurer's work, which appeared in 1835 (II A and II B above). Certainly the views expounded in this article, which is essentially a review of Greek politics since 1832 rather than an actual review of a book, are identical with those of Parish and *Portfolio.*

[Agathangelos]. *Chresmoi . . . [Oracles; or the Prophecy of the Monk Agathangelos, of Blessed Memory, concerning the Singular State of Basil the Great, envisioned in Messine, Sicily, in the Year 1279].* Athens, 1837; Bucharest, 1838.

Apostolides, Misael. *Antapantesis . . . [Counter-Reply to the Reply of the Pseudo-Writer, Plagiarist and Misrepresenter of Foreign Efforts].* Athens, 1837.

————. *Diatribe austoschedias peri tes arches kai tes exousias ton patriarchon kai peri tes scheseos tes ekklesiastikes arches pros ten politiken exousian [Impromptu Treatise concerning the Office and Authority of the Patriarchs and concerning the Relationship between Ecclesiastical and Secular Authority].* Athens, 1843.

[Anon.]. *Archai tes Syntagmatikes Monarchias [Principles of Constitutional Monarchy].* Athens, 1843.

Argyropoulos, Pericles. *Demotike Dioikesis en Helladi [The Demotic Administration in Greece].* 2nd edn. Athens, 1859.

Athanasiou, George. *He dike tou Syntaktou tes Athenas . . . [The Trial of the Editor of 'Athena', accused of Defamation of Character].* Athens, 1837.

————. *Ta kata Kaïren . . . [Acts against Kaïres, or the Declaration of the Truth].* Athens, 1840.

————. *Schedion thesmou ton Hellenon meth' hyperaspiseos tes mias Boules charin ton k. k. Plerexousion [Sketch of a Greek Polity, with a Defense of one Chamber, for the Deputies].* Athens, 1843.

Bertrand, Victor A. *Hellas, politike katastasis autes. Augoustos 1837. Esoterika. [Hellas and her Political Condition. August 1837. Internal Affairs.]* Athens, 1837.

Chrysoverges, Arist. *Diogenes, he enestosa katastasis tes Hellados [Diogenes, the Present Condition of Greece].* Hydra, 1836.

Democritos the Athenian (pseud.). *Eunomia, diatribe autoschedios [Good Government, Impromptu Study].* Athens, 1843.

D. (A). *Dialogoi per ton Hellenikon pragmaton. Ti poieteon dia na apallage to Ethnos apo ten parousan katastasin tou [Dialogues on Greek Affairs. What to do to free the Nation from its Present Condition].* Nauplion, 1837.

He dike tes Elpidos . . . [The Trial of 'Elpis,' containing the Decisions and the Speech of P. Argyropoulos before the Criminal Court]. Athens, 1837.

Duvergier de Hauranne, M. P. "De la situation actuelle de la Grèce et de son Avenir." *Revue des Deux Mondes,* VIII (1844), 193-256.

————. "La Grèce pendant les Trois Derniers Mois." *Revue des Deux Mondes,* new ser., xv (1844), 76-98. See under Kallerges in this section.

[Anon.]. *Epistole . . . [Epistle concerning what is the Hidden Purpose of the Missionaries of the Bible Society (Popularly Known as the Americans), as Revealed by their Acts and Books*]. Paris and Athens, 1836.

Faudot, Ad. *La vérité sur les affaires de la Grèce.* Paris, 1844.

[Finlay, George]. "The Actual Condition of the Greek State." *Blackwood's Edinburgh Magazine,* LV (1844), 785-96.

[————]. "The Bankruptcy of the Greek Kingdom." *Blackwood's Edinburgh Magazine,* LIV (July-Dec. 1843), 345-62.

————. *The Hellenic Kingdom and the Greek Nation.* London, 1836; Boston and New York, 1837.

[————]. "Sketches of Modern Greece." *Blackwood's Edinburgh Magazine,* XLIII (1838), 469-88, 620-30, 816-27.

Gregoriades, Demetrios. *Hieros thriambos tes mias hagias katholikes kai apostolikes tes tou Christou Anatolikes ekklesias. Kata tes ede anaphaneises antitheou planes tou misotheou theosevismou (Theophilou Kaïre) . . . [The holy Triumph of the One, Holy, Catholic, and Apostolic Eastern Church of Christ. Against the already emerged Godless Delusion of Theosophy (Theophilos Kaïres) . . .*]. Constantinople, 1840.

Patriarch Gregory VI. *Enkyklios Ekklesiastike . . . [Ecclesiastical Encyclical Exhorting Orthodox Adherents Everywhere to Avoid the Heterodoxical Teachings Published and Preached . . .*]. Athens, 1837.

"History of the late revolution in Greece" (anon. rev.). *British and Foreign Review,* XVIII (1844), 239-82.

Ta Kaïreia . . . [Concerning the Kaïres Episode, from the Newspaper 'Aion']. Syros, 1839.

Kaïres, Theophilos. *Logos [Speech].* Andros, 1839.

Ta kata ton Th. Kaïren . . . [Acts against Th. Kaïres from Ho 'Hellēnikos Tachydromos']. Athens, [1839].

Kallerges, Demetrios. [Letter of 8/20 Nov. 1844 to editor], in Duvergier de Hauranne, M. P., "La Grèce pendant les Trois Derniers Mois." *Revue des Deux Mondes,* new ser., xv (1844), 82-83.

[Kalligas, Paul]. *He exantlesis ton kommaton, etoi ta ethika gegonota tes koinonias mas [The Exhaustion of the Parties, or the Ethnical Events of our Society*]. Athens, 1842.

————. *He Neara peri Exybriseon en genei kai peri typou Nomothesia [New Legislation on Slander in General and on the Press*]. Athens, 1837.

Karatsoutsas, J. D. *Dialogos . . . [Dialogue . . . concerning Autochthons and Heterochthons]*. Hermoupolis [Syros], 1844.

———. *Ho Evangelismos tes Hellados [The Annunciation of Greece]*. Hermoupolis [Syros], 1843.

Keios, I.G.P. *Ho Agonistes Hellen (kata ten 3 Septembriou 1843) [The Persevering Greek (during the Third of September 1843)]*. Athens, 1843.

A. K. *Ho Kometes. Ta apanta tou Syntagmatos [The Comet. Contents of the Constitution]*. Athens, 1843.

Lamprylos, Kyriakos. *Ho missionarismos kai protestantismos . . . [Missionary Activity and Protestantism in our Parts and in other Parts of the World. And the Relations of Protestantism with the Mother of all Churches and with the Greek Nation]*. Smyrna, 1836; Athens, 1837.

Leconte, Casimir. *Étude économique de la Grèce, de sa position actuelle, de son avenir, suivie de documents sur le commerce de l'Orient, sur l'Égypt, etc.* Paris, 1847.

Lenormant, François. *Le comte André Metaxa et le parti Napiste en Grèce*. Paris, 1861.

Louriotes, Andrew and John Orlandos. *Apologia . . . [Apology . . .]*. Athens, 1839.

Masson, Edward. *An Apology for the Greek Church; or Hints on the Means of Promoting the Religious Improvement of the Greek Nation.* Athens, 1843.

Menas, C. Minoide. *La Grèce constituée et les affaires d'Orient*. Paris, 1836.

"Lord Nugent's Travels—Greece in 1843-4" (anon. rev.). *The Quarterly Review*, LXXVIII (1846), 297-322. See under Nugent in II B above.

[Oikonomos, Constantine]. *Apantesis eis ten autoschedion diatriben peri tes arches kai tes exousias ton patriarchon kai peri tes scheseos tes ekklesiastikes arches pros ten politiken exousian [Reply to the Impromptu Treatise concerning the Office and Authority of the Patriarchs and concerning the Relationship between Ecclesiastical and Secular Authority]*. Athens, 1843.

———. *Epikrisis . . . [Criticism of the Short Reply of . . . Neophytos Vamvas concerning the Neo-Hellenic Church]*. Athens, 1839.

[———]. *Ta Sozomena Ekklesiastika Syngrammata Konstantinou . . . tou ex Oikonomon [Collected Ecclesiastical Writings of . . . Constantine Oikonomos]*. Ed. Sophocles Oikonomos. 2 vols. Athens, 1864-66. See II A above.

Orlandos, John, and Andrew Louriotes. *Apologia . . . [Apology . . .]*. Athens, 1839.

Orphanides, Th. *Ta kata ten heorten tes 25 Martiou (Ta kata ten diken ton heortasanton auton emmetros apologia) [Occurrences during the Holiday of March 25th (Apology in Verse on the Occurrences during the Trial of Those Celebrating it)]*. Athens, 1841.

Palamides, Regas. *Homilia tou Bouleutou Mantineias Rega Palamidou eis apantesin tou logou paraitethentos hypourgou ton Oikonomikon A. Metaxa, en te synedriasei tes Boules te 23 Augoustou 1845* [*Speech of Regas Palamides, Deputy from Mantinea, in Reply to the Speech of A. Metaxas, Retiring Minister of Economic Affairs, at the Chamber Session of 23 August 1845*].

[Panas, Gerasimos]. *He Baptisis tes Kyrias Aikaterines N. Chantzere . . .* [*The Baptism of Mrs. Catherine N. Chantzeres. And Some Historical Thoughts on the Greek and Western Spirit*]. Constantinople, 1841; Hermoupolis [Syros], 1842.

Papadopoulos-Vretos, Andrew. *Notizie storico-biografiche sul colonnello Dem. Callergi etc.* Corfu, 1843.

Parish, Henry Headley. *The Diplomatic History of the Monarchy of Greece from the Year 1830.* London, 1838.

Petrokokkinos, Michael. *Diatribe peri ton sympheronton tes Hellados* [*Essay on the Interests of Greece*]. Marseilles, 1833.

Petsales, A. *Metaphrasis tou Kentrikou Syntagmatos tes Amerikes, meta historikes eisagoges kai hermeneias ton kyrioteron archon autou* [*Translation of the Federal Constitution of America, with Historical Introduction and Interpretation of its Chief Principles*]. Athens, 1841.

Pharmakides, Theokletos. *Apologia* [*Apology*]. 2 vols. Athens, 1840.

———. *Ho Pseudonymos Germanos* [*Pseudonymous Germanos*]. Athens, 1838.

[Anon.]. "He Philorthodoxos Hetairia . . ." ["The Philorthodox Society, or the Fanaticism of the Kapodistrians"] in *He Proodos tou 1840 . . .* [*The Progress of 1840 . . .*]. Athens, 1840.

Politikon Syntagma tes Hellados, kata ten Eth. Syneleusin [*Political Constitution of Greece, during the Fifth National Assembly*]. Ed. A. Z. Mamoukas. Athens, 1843.

Polymeres, G. *Epistole politike pros philon tina en Londino, pragmateuomene peri tes neas ton Hellenon politikes metaboles tes trites Septembriou* [*Political Letter to a Friend in London, written about the New Greek Political Change of the Third of September*]. Hermoupolis [Syros], 1843.

The Portfolio: or a Collection of State Papers and other Documents and Correspondence, Historical, Diplomatic, and Commercial. Illustrative of the History of our Times. 1st ser., 6 vols., London, 1836-37; 2nd ser., 4 vols., London, 1843-44.

Raoul-Rochette, M. "Athènes sous le roi Otho." *Revue des Deux Mondes,* 4th ser., xvi (1838), 179-92.

Rangabe, A. P. *He trite Septembriou* [*The Third of September*]. Athens, [1843].

"Russian Policy in Greece" (anon. rev.), *Foreign Quarterly Review,* xvi (1836), 361-85.

[Anon.]. *Skepseis . . .* [*Thoughts on the Greek Church in Greece, com-*

*posed by a most Wise and Respected Hierarch . . . for the Enlighten-
ment of his Fellow-Believers*]. Ed. Germanos. Athens, 1836.

Soliotes, Niketas. *Ho Demetrios Kallerges, lyrikon drama eis treis praxeis
k.t.l.* [*Demetrios Kallerges, a Lyrical Drama in three Acts etc.*]. Patras,
1844.

Sophianopoulos, Athenodoros and Charilaos. *He Proodos tes Ethnikes ton
Hellenon Syneleuseos tou 1844* [*The Progress of the National Assembly,
of the Greeks, of 1844*]. Athens, 1844.

Soteropoulos, S. *Diatribe peri engeiou Phorologias en Helladi* [*Treatise
concerning the Land Tax in Greece*]. Athens, 1861.

Soutsos, Alexander. *Apologia . . .* [*Apology on the Day of (Court) Judgment*]. Athens, 1839.

———. *He metabole tes trites Septembriou* [*The Change of the Third of
September*]. Athens, 1844.

———. *Panorama tes en Athenais Ethnikes Syneleuseos . . .* [*Panorama of
Greece, or Collection of Various Poems*]. Nauplion, 1833.

———. *Ho Periplanomenos* [*The Wanderer*]. Athens, 1839.

———. *He Proanakrisis . . .* [*The Preliminary Inquiry and my Detention
during 15, 16, and 17 Aug. 1839*]. Athens, 1839.

Soutsos, John A. *Schedion politikou Syntagmatos tes Hellados* [*Plan of a
Political Constitution for Greece*]. Athens, 1843.

Stephanitses, P. D., ed. *Sylloge diaphoron prorreseon* [*Collections of various Predictions*]. Athens, 1838.

Strong, Frederick. *Greece as a kingdom, or a statistical description of that
country from the arrival of K. Otho in 1833 down to the present time.*
London, 1842.

*Ai peri syntagmatos kai peri ton kata ten Hellada Bauaron Praxeis tes
Symmachias kai tes Aules tou Monachou meta semeioseon—Actes de
l'Alliance et de la Cour de Bavière relatifs à l'établissement d'un gouvernement constitutionnel en Grèce et aux Bavarois y résident avec des
notes.* Athens, 1843.

Tertsetes, George. *Apologia* [*Apology*]. Athens, 1835.

Texier, Ed. *La Grèce et ses insurrections.* Paris, 1854.

[Valetas, Spyridon I.] Sibi (pseud.). *Ho Geron Limperes, e dialogoi en
peripato hypthesin echontes ethe kai pragmata Hellenika* [*Old-man
Limperes, or Dialogues during a Walk having as Subject Greek Customs and Things*]. Athens, 1836.

Vamvas, Neophytos. *Antepikrisis eis ten hypo tou presbyterou kai oikonomou Konstantinou tou ex Oikonomon* [*Counter-Criticism against that
of Constantine Oikonomos*]. Athens, 1839.

———. *Apantesis . . .* [*Reply to the Essay of Mr. Germanos against the
Translation of the Scriptures and against the Biblical Society*]. Hermoupolis [Syros], [1834]. Reprinted 1838.

———. *Peri tes neohellenikes Ekklesias . . .* [*Concerning the Neo-
Hellenic Church; What . . . Constantine Oikonomos . . . Conjectures*

about the Translation of Holy Scripture. Short Reply of N. Vamvas].
Athens, 1838.

————. *Syntomos Apantesis* . . . [*Short Reply to the Father* . . . *of the recently Published and Shameless Letter on 'What is the Hidden Goal of the Missionaries of the Biblical Society in Greece'*]. Athens, 1836. Reprinted 1837.

Vlassarides, G., ed. *Ta Syntagmata* . . . [*The Constitutions of France and Troezene, with Instructions for the Election of Representatives, the Decree of the Governor, the Proclamations of the Constitutional Cabinet, the Second Decrees concerning the National Assembly, and some Comments by the Father of Progress (P. Sophianopoulos)*]. Athens, 1843.

E. TRAVEL ACCOUNTS

The travel literature on Othonian Greece is immense. To it the British, Germans, French, and Americans contributed. On the whole, its value for this study is limited. Many of the writers wrote only after a brief visit. Most were barred by the language barrier from direct communication with the Greeks. Most suffered from bias, either of the romantic kind which tended to glorify and excuse everything, or of an ethnocentric and hypercritical kind which condemned as "uncivilized" anything un-Western. By and large, interest was consumed by antiquities, topography, and the quaint aspects of popular customs. Politics commanded far less attention and, in most cases, even less understanding. Although the parties attracted widespread attention, there was considerable confusion about even their number and identity, and a tendency to treat them merely as indicators of the relative prestige of the powers in Greece. The following list is by no means complete; for a more comprehensive listing, the reader is referred to S. H. Weber's *Voyages and Travels in the Near East Made During the Nineteenth Century: Being a Part of a Larger Catalogue of Works on Geography, Cartography, Voyages and Travels in the Gennadius Library in Athens* (Princeton, N.J., 1952).

With the few notable exceptions treated in the next paragraph, each individual work has only limited value; as a collection these works make it possible to appreciate the widespread incidence of certain conditions and attitudes, discernible by virtue of their mention and emphasis in almost all these works—for instance, administrative inefficiency, the large amount of land remaining uncultivated, the strength of xenophobism (especially directed against Bavarians), the intensity of religious sentiment in its conservative form, the cultural contrasts within Greek society and the tensions thereby created. Although less universally mentioned, one might also cite the opposition to the practice of military conscription, initiated in 1838, or the difficulty of the palikars in adjusting to a situation of peace and national (rather than foreign) rule.

The works of About, Baird, and Grénier occupy a special place in this collection of literature because these men supplemented their personal observations with systematic accounts of education, literature, and economy, based upon detailed and statistical information obtained from qualified Greek sources. But the works which individually contributed most to this study are those by Buchon (*La Grèce*), Mure, Perdicaris, Senior, and Slade. A discerning observer, Buchon visited Greece in 1840-41 to collect information on the Frankish period of Greek history. One finds, scattered among descriptions of ruins, terrain, and customs, passing references to the existing system of clientage, to the primates' and chieftains' interest in the new machinery of local government as a means of perpetuating their established influence, to the zeal for education as a path to high public office. Through his frequent descriptions of the demarchs in the various places he visited, one gets a good impression of the semi-Westernized, relatively affluent type of people who generally secured this office. In Mure one finds valuable descriptions of a meeting of a communal assembly (Castri, Rumely), of a local discussion of church affairs (at a khan of Ali Tselepi, Peloponnesos), and of the elaborate organization of brigand activities in Greece. Perdicaris, whose book is only semi-travelogue in character, knew a good bit about parties and understood how some features of royal policy (mixed cabinets, for instance) were a response to them. But even in his case, this kind of awareness was limited. The journal of Senior records a large number of interviews with both Greeks and non-Greeks resident in Greece (unnamed, however). On many points, these recorded indigenous sources deal with contemporary events and issues (1857-58), but in many cases treat more permanent features of Greek society applying to the period of absolutism as well. There is valuable information on brigandage and its connection with the parties, attitudes toward power as a source of personal profit, and various retrospective interpretations of the revolution of 1843. Slade, a discerning naval officer, used his extended stay in the Eastern Mediterranean to become well informed about its affairs. He discerned the limited social honor accorded cultivation of the soil by most Greeks (hence, a major ideological obstacle to the government's plan for the creation of a nation of small landholders), the price that would have to be paid for Westernization, the economic dislocations produced by separation from the Ottoman empire, and the numerous bases for continued attachment to the patriarchate of Constantinople and the tsar of Russia.

About, Edmond. *La Grèce contemporaine.* Paris, 1854.

[Anon.]. *Sketches in Greece and Turkey, with the present condition and future prospects of the Turkish empire.* London, 1833.

Aldenhoven, Ferdinand. *Itinéraire descriptif de l'Attique et du Péloponèse, avec cartes et plans topographiques.* Athens, 1841.

Auldjo, John. *Journal of a Visit to Constantinople, and some of the Greek islands, in the spring and summer of 1833.* London, 1835.

591

Baird, Henry Martyn. *Modern Greece: a narrative of a residence and travels in that country; with observations on its antiquities, literature, language, politics, and religion.* New York, 1856.

Brandis, Chr. Aug. *Mittheilungen über Griechenland.* 3 vols. Leipzig, 1842. See under Brandis in II A above.

Buchon, Jean Alexandre. *La Grèce continentale de la Morée. Voyage, séjour et études historiques en 1840 et 1841.* Paris, 1843.

———. *Voyage dans l'Eubée, Les Iles Ioniennes et Les Cyclades en 1841.* Ed. with bibl. and biog. introd. Jean Longnon. Paris, 1911.

Burgess, Richard. *Greece and the Levant; or, Diary of a summer's excursion in 1834. . . .* 2 vols. London, 1835.

Bremer, Frederika. *Greece and the Greeks. The narrative of a winter residence and summer travel in Greece and its islands.* Trans. Mary Howitt. 2 vols. London, 1863.

Claridge, R. T. *A guide along the Danube, from Vienna to Constantinople, Smyrna, Athens, the Morea, the Ionian Islands, and Venice. From the notes of a journey made in 1836.* London, 1837.

Cochrane, Alexander Baillie. *The Morea; with Some Remarks on the Present State of Greece.* London, 1840.

Cochrane, George. *Wanderings in Greece.* 2 vols. London, 1837.

Cumming, W. F. *Notes of a wanderer in search of health, through Italy, Egypt, Greece, Turkey, up the Danube, and down the Rhine.* 2nd edn. 2 vols. London, 1840.

Damer, [Mrs.] G. L. Dawson. *Diary of a Tour in Greece, Turkey, etc.* 2nd edn. 2 vols. London, 1842.

Fiedler, Karl Gustav. *Reise durch alle theile des königreiches Griechenlands in auftrag der königl. griechischen regierung in den jahren 1834 bis 1837.* 2 vols. Leipzig, 1840-41.

Garston, Edgar. *Greece Revisited and Sketches in Lower Egypt in 1840 with Thirty-Six Hours of a Campaign in Greece in 1825.* 2 vols. London, 1842. Vol. I on Greece.

Giffard, Edward. *A short visit to the Ionian Islands, Athens, and the Morea.* London, 1837.

Grénier, Antoine. *La Grèce en 1863.* Paris, 1863.

Greverus, Johann Paul Ernst. *Reise in Griechenland.* Bremen, 1839.

Herold, Gottfried. *Beiträge zur Kenntniss des griechischen Landes und Volkes in Briefen.* Ansbach, 1839.

Hervé, Francis. *A residence in Greece and Turkey; with notes of the journey through Bulgaria, Servia, Hungary, and the Balkans.* 2 vols. London, 1837.

Hettner, Hermann. *Athens and the Peloponnese, with sketches of northern Greece.* Anon. transl. from German. Edinburgh, 1854.

Howard, George William Frederich (Earl of Carlisle). *Diary in Turkish and Greek Waters.* Boston, 1855.

Klenze, Leo von. *Aphoristische Bemerkungen gesammelt auf seiner Reise nach Griechenland.* Berlin, 1838.

Köppen, A. L. *Sketches of a Traveller from Greece.* . . . Chambersburg, Pa., 1854.

Mure, William. *Journal of a tour in Greece and the Ionian Islands, with remarks on the recent history—present state—and classical antiquities of those countries.* 2 vols. Edinburgh and London, 1842.

Lord Nugent, *Lands, Classical and Sacred.* 2 vols. London, 1845.

Ow, J., Baron von. *Auszeichnungen eines Junkers am Hofe zu Athen.* Pest, Vienna, Leipzig, 1837.

Perdicaris, Gregory A. *The Greece of the Greeks.* 2 vols. New York, 1845.

Pückler-Muskau, H. von. *Südöstlicher Bildersaal.* Stuttgart, 1840-41.

Rey, Étienne. *Voyage pittoresque en Grèce et dans le Levant fait en 1843-1844.* 2 vols. Lyons, 1867.

Ross Ludwig. *Reisen des Königs Otto und der Königin Amalie in Griechenland.* 2 vols. Halle, 1848. See also under Ross in II A and II B above and immediately below.

———. *Wanderungen in Griechenland im Gefolge des Königs Otto und der Königin Amalie, mit besonderer Rücksicht auf Topographie und Geschichte aufgezeichnet.* . . . 2 vols. Halle, 1851.

Senior, Nassau William. *A Journal kept in Turkey and Greece in the autumn of 1857, and the beginning of 1858.* London, 1859.

Skene, Felicia M. F. *Wayfairing sketches among the Greeks and Turks, and on the shores of the Danube. By a seven years' resident in Greece.* 2nd edn. London, 1849.

Slade, Adolphus. *Turkey, Greece, and Malta.* 2 vols. London, 1837.

Spencer, Edmund. *Travels in European Turkey in 1850.* . . . 2 vols. London, 1851.

Stephens, John Lloyd. *Incidents of travel in Greece, Turkey, Russia, and Poland.* 2 vols. New York, 1838. Publ. under title *Incidents of travel in the Russian and Turkish empires.* 2 vols., in London, 1839.

Steub, Ludwig. *Bilder aus Griechenland.* 2 vols. Leipzig, 1841.

Ulrichs, H. S. *Forschungen in Griechenland.* Berlin, 1840.

Zachariä von Lingenthal, [Karl] Eduard. *Reise in den Orient in den Jahren 1837 und 1838 über Vien, Venedig, Florenz, Rom, Neapel, Malta, Sicilien und Griechenland nach Saloniki, dem Berge Athos, Konstantinopel und Trapezunt.* Heidelberg, 1840.

III. Secondary Sources

A. GENERAL HISTORIES

Of the general synthetic works, there are only two dealing exclusively with the entire absolutist period (Voulgares and Pipineles), three if one includes Karolides, who devoted an entire volume of his multivolume work to this period. There are three on the Othonian period as a whole (Bower and Bolitho, Evangelides, and Skandames), six if again one includes works that devote a separate volume to Otho's reign (Driault and Lhéritier, Finlay, and Kordatos). Otherwise, the period gets much shorter treatment. Most of the works in the list below are larger works of broader chronological scope and many reach only into the early part of the absolutist period. Of the non-Greek works, the Germans contributed seven, the English four, and the French one. With regard to this period, then, one can speak only of a German historiographical tradition, in addition to the Greek one.

The German tradition, which started early but came to a quick end by about 1880, had two characteristics of concern here, one unfortunate, the other fortunate. First, its chief focus was on some phase of Greek history prior to 1833, which meant that its treatment of the period starting in 1833 was largely epilogue. Second, there was considerable awareness of the parties as a prominent part of the political scene. Four (Hertzberg, Klüber, Mendelssohn Bartholdy, and Schmeidler) of the seven German historians treat the parties as a serious problem with which the regency and the king had to contend, and they see Crown policy as at least partially a response to this problem.

In the Greek historiographical tradition with respect to this period, the parties are seldom treated as an integral part of the story. Whatever treatment they receive usually takes place in a separate section as if in digression; elsewhere mention of them is all too casual. A second characteristic of Greek historiography, even in more recent times, is the tendency to simply synthesize the findings of previous scholarship and to utilize, at least in an effective way, only published primary sources. This is most clearly demonstrated in the many cases when the historian actually worked in archives. Petrakakos, for instance, performed the valuable service of bringing into print hitherto unpublished documents or excerpts thereof, but he produced a work which was more compilation than history (therefore it is listed in II A above rather than in the list below). Others, who *did* write history, also worked in one or more archives, but their works, with minor exceptions, fail to show it and read as if based almost exclusively on already published and repeatedly utilized sources. Since intensive research on specialized areas has been meager for this period, reliance on the findings of previous research—perfectly legitimate for a historian covering much ground—has meant advancing little beyond the achievements of early research and perpetuating its failings. The achievements of early Greek research had been the careful delineation of the outward course of events and the illumination of institutional and diplomatic aspects of the period. It had largely failed to delineate the inner forces behind those events and had largely ignored the socioeconomic dimensions and the cultural aspects of the period.

594

Aspreas, George K. *Politike Historia tes Neoteras Hellados 1821-1921* [*The Political History of Modern Greece 1821-1921*]. 2nd edn. 3 vols. Athens, 1924. Vol. I: 1821-65.

The work of Aspreas devotes less than 100 pages of the first volume to the period covered by this book. It provides no new information, scarcely documents its numerous assertions, and passes over this period too rapidly to give any sense of change or variation within it. But it is the only Greek history to treat the party situation as a vital factor in the political development of the time or to see Crown policy and behavior as a response to native political conditions. As a result, it suggested a number of hypotheses for the research on this book.

Bower, Leonard, and Gordon Bolitho. *Otho I: King of Greece*. London, 1939.

Though written as a biography of Otho, this important work is virtually a narrative political history of Greece during the Othonian period. Rich in new information on the role of Bavarians in Greek affairs, especially the intrigue against Otho by members of his own court in 1834-36, and on the position of Ludwig and Otho on the constitutional question, this is the best work in English on the Othonian period, impartial and skilful in its treatment of difficult material. Besides all available secondary sources, the authors used valuable archival collections—primarily those of the British foreign office and the Bavarian Haus- und Staatsarchiv (especially the Secret Archive of Otho), but also the English royal archives in the royal library at Windsor Castle and private unpublished collections (Finlay, Baroness von Gasser, and Hunoltstein) (I A, B, and C above).

Driault, Édouard, and Michel Lhéritier. *Histoire Diplomatique de la Grèce de 1821 à nos jours*. 5 vols. Paris, 1925-26. Vol. I: Driault, *L'Insurrection et l'Indépendance (1821-1830)*. Vol. II: Driault, *Le Règne d'Othon. La Grande Idée (1830-1862)*.

The well-known French diplomatic history of Driault and Lhéritier remains a standard and valuable source, both because it has much to say about the domestic situation in Greece and because of the wealth of otherwise unavailable published information drawn from the archives of the major European foreign offices, especially the French. The first two volumes were indispensable for this book because of the close connection between Greek domestic politics and the diplomacy of Europe. But they do not give any substantial information on the workings of the parties or how they influenced government policy. The weaknesses of interpretation are two: (1) the tendency to represent French diplomacy in too favorable a light, as motivated by an overriding concern for the welfare of Greece; and (2) the perpetuation of the typically French myth that the "French" party in Greece was the

595

national party, in the dual sense that it promoted the "true" national interests and represented the bulk of the people.

Evangelides, Tryphon E. *Historia tou Othonos, Basileos tes Hellados 1832-1862* [*The History of Otho, King of Greece 1832-1862*]. Athens, 1893.

This early work is standard and sound as a detailed chronicle but does not provide any detailed analysis of the inner forces behind the outward course of events. It is largely political and institutional history.

Finlay, George. *A History of Greece from its Conquest by the Romans to the Present Time, B.C. 146 to A.D. 1864.* Rev. and ed. H. F. Tozer. 7 vols. Oxford, 1876. Vol. VII: *The Greek Revolution.* Part II: *Establishment of the Greek Kingdom.*

The last volume of Finlay's monumental seven-volume Greek history is still an indispensable source for the Othonian period, but it is uneven in its coverage (passing quickly over the years 1838-42), marred by Finlay's severe criticism of virtually every element that played an influential role in Greek politics, and disappointing for anyone interested in the role of the parties during the period of royal absolutism. Finlay was usually quite justified in his criticism of performance and impartial to the extent that he spared no one and acknowledged limited achievements, but he tended to attribute inadequate performance almost exclusively to moral failings and "lack of statesmanship." He therefore underestimated the role of conditions which would probably have thwarted the most virtuous and statesmanlike of men, even though he was too good a historian to ignore material which shed light on these conditions. As his private unpublished papers show, he knew a great deal more about the parties than he indicated in his history. His insufficient concern with them in his history stems therefore from a failure in conceptualization.

Hertzberg, Gustav F. *Geschichte Griechenlands seit dem Absterben des antiken Lebens bis zur Gegenwart.* 4 vols. Gotha, 1876-79. Vol. IV: *Neueste Geschichte Griechenlands von der Erhebung der Neugriechen gegen die Pforte bis zum Berliner Frieden.*

Based largely on Mendelssohn Bartholdy for the regency period (this section below), this work also makes a point of the Crown's attempt to undermine the parties but fails to pursue the same line of inquiry for the subsequent period which Mendelssohn Bartholdy did not cover. The virtue of Hertzberg's account lies in his recognition of the obstacles to the realization of the Crown's essential task of creating a united and coherent state—the accumulated and conflicting powers of the ruling groups (primates and captains), sectional jealousies, and cultural schism, but he failed to see that the parties were, in part, an expression of these factors and hence a major obstacle. In criticizing regency policy for supposedly being based on a mistaken view of Greece as a *tabula rasa,* Hertzberg was mistaken and revealed how little he appreciated the points he had borrowed from Mendelssohn Bartholdy.

Karolides, Paul. *Synchronos Historia ton Hellenon kai ton loipon Laon tes Anatoles apo 1821 mechri 1921* [*The Contemporary History of the Greeks and other Peoples of the East from 1821 until 1921*]. 7 vols. Athens, 1922-29. Vol. II: 1833-43. Vol. III: 1843-50.

The second volume of the seven-volume study by Karolides, a continuation of the monumental work of Paparregopoulos, deals exclusively with the period 1833-43 and the first part of the third volume gives a detailed coverage of the issues involved in the constitution-making process. In its use of all the then available published documents, foreign as well as Greek, the work is unmatchable in its thoroughness and it is full of long and valuable quotations from such sources as those of Dragoumes and Guizot (II B above). But the work is discursive, poorly organized, and full of moral judgments, especially with respect to the ecclesiastical settlement which the author deplored. And like earlier Greek works of this kind, there is no analysis of underlying trends.

Klüber, Johann Ludwig. *Pragmatische Geschichte der nationalen und politischen Wiedergeburt Griechenlands bis zu dem Regierungsantritt des Königs Otto.* Frankfurt, 1835.

Contemporary with the events he narrated, Klüber stated it as regency policy to do away with the parties and saw the dissolution of the irregular troops as one of the measures taken to implement this policy. But he never showed in detail how else the regency actually handled the parties and indeed he, like Pipineles (this section below) long after him, then demonstrated his failure to appreciate the full significance of the parties (especially their staying power) by overestimating the freedom of action of the regency, simply because it had foreign loans, a German army, a three-power guarantee, and an absolutist system at its disposal.

Kordatos, Gianni K. *Historia tes Neoteres Helladas* [*The History of Modern Greece*]. 3 vols. Athens, 1957. Vol. III: 1833-62.

This work does not go beyond the published sources employed by previous Greek histories on this period. It displays all the weaknesses of the Marxist approach and none of its strengths. The book is marred by antiroyal and anticlerical prejudice. For some unknown reason, there is no attempt to study political developments through class analysis and the work therefore becomes a conventional treatment of already covered material. The work has two more specific failings. First, it treats Otho as a mere puppet of Ludwig and Amalia, hence makes no attempt to understand Otho's behavior as a response to the party situation in Greece. Second, even though Kordatos knew he was writing about a period of royal absolutism, he treated the most prominent member of any one cabinet as if he were a prime minister conceiving and executing policy on his own initiative. As a result, Kordatos minimized even more Otho's great influence in the formulation and execution of policy.

Kremos, G. *Neotate Genike Historia* [*Modern General History*]. Athens, 1890.

This work was written as a continuation of the earlier general history of A. Polyzoïdes, who had stopped short of the Othonian period.

Kyriakides, Epaminondas K. *Historia tou Synchronou Hellenismou apo tes Hidryseos tou Basileiou tes Hellados mechri ton hemeron mas 1832-1892* [*The History of Contemporary Hellenism from the Establishment of the Kingdom of Greece until our own Days*]. 2 vols. Athens, 1892-94.

Like Evangelides and Kremos (this section above), this work is a standard sober work of early Greek scholarship, more descriptive than analytical and largely political and institutional in orientation.

Mayer, A. *Geschichte Griechenlands von der Ankunft König Ottos in Nauplia bis zu seiner Thronbesteigung*. Stuttgart, 1839.

Mendelssohn Bartholdy, Karl. *Geschichte Griechenlands von der Eroberung Konstantinopels durch die Türken im Jahre 1453 bis auf unsere Tage*. 2 vols. Leipzig, 1870-74. Trans. into Greek Angelos Vlachos. 2 vols. Athens, 1873-76. Vol. II: *Von der Verwaltung durch Kapodistrias bis zur Grossjährigkeit des König Otto*.

The author of this excellent work based the section on the regency period on the Austrian and Prussian state archives (I A above), as well as on the private observations of men still surviving from that period. Before finishing his second volume, in which he concluded with the regency period, he published a long article dealing exclusively with that period (cited immediately below). In this article, he quoted from the Prussian archives (the despatches of Count D. Lusi, the Prussian minister to Greece) more extensively than he later did in his two-volume work, but most of the material in this article he did incorporate.

From the correspondence of Prokesch-Osten, of which he made the fullest use and from which he quoted extensively, Mendelssohn Bartholdy described the royal program devised by Otho, Ludwig, and Prokesch-Osten on the eve of the royal majority and showed that it was designed to undermine the parties. Again with the help of Prokesch-Osten, he discerned and described the two contrasting approaches toward the parties—that of the regency majority on the one hand, and that of Armansperg on the other. This work is valuable both because of its basic orientation and for its wealth of detail on the regency period.

———. "Die Regenschaft in Griechenland 1833-1835," *Historische Zeitschrift*, xxvm (1872), 1-60. See comments immediately above.

Miller, William. *The Ottoman Empire and its Successors, 1801-1927*. Rev. edn. Cambridge, Eng., 1936.

A skilful and judicious condensation of more extended treatments, this work consists of only a short chapter on Othonian Greece and is therefore too general to be of much use.

———. *A History of the Greek People 1821-1921*. New York, n.d. but probably 1922.

Paparregopoulos, Constantine. *Historia tou Hellenikou Ethnous apo ton Archaiotaton Chronon mechri tou 1930 meta prosthekon hypo Paulou Karolidou* [*The History of the Greek Nation from the most Ancient Times until 1930, with a supplement by Paul Karolides*]. 8 vols. Athens, 1932.

Since Karolides was the continuator of this monumental and classic work of modern Greek historiography, see under Karolides above.

Phrantzes, Ambrose. *Epitome tes Historias tes Anagennetheises Hellados archomene apo tou etous 1715 kai legousa to 1835* [*Summary of the History of Regenerated Greece from the year 1715 and ending 1835*]. 4 vols. Athens, 1839-41.

This is a pro-Kolokotrones work, written as a corrective to and a refutation of Trikoupes' history of the Greek Revolution. It extends only to the end of the regency period, which it treats summarily as an epilogue to the Greek renaissance and Revolution.

Pipineles, T. N. *He Monarchia en Helladi 1833-43* [*The Monarchy in Greece 1833-43*]. Athens, 1932.

This work is valuable because, in addition to giving a full treatment of the absolutist period, it takes an approach which is novel in terms of Greek works that had gone before it. A monarchist, reflective of the antiparliamentary reaction of the 1930s, Pipineles was revisionist in his attitude toward the first Greek king. At the same time, he applied class analysis to his study of the absolutist period. Considering that period in the light of his own present, he stressed its importance as laying the foundation of later developments. He analyzed the period as an attempted alliance between the Crown and people against a rising middle class in alliance with the traditional agrarian oligarchy, and saw the conflict between Othonian absolutism and growing constitutionalism as a reflection of the power struggle between these two basic groupings. This approach enabled the author to give a fairer appraisal of royal policy than that which was traditional in Greek historiography; that is, to see it as more than a mere doctrinaire attempt to impose Western notions of absolutism and centralized administration without regard for indigenous conditions. He was basically correct in his view that the Crown regarded the parties as the instruments through which the ruling groups abused the people and that the Crown fought the parties out of a sense of obligation to protect the interests of the people. But his belief that the Crown was right in its appraisal of the situation betrays his failure to understand the system of clientage which united various social groups within each party and his inability to appreciate the role of the parties as protectors of their clients. His gravest mistake was his disregard of the tremendous influence wielded by the parties, even without the machinery of constitutional government. As a result, he exaggerated the freedom of action of the Crown during the absolutist period. Finally, even though Pipineles consulted the archives of the French foreign ministry and the Mavrokordatos Archive (I A above) the absence of any new information in his book demonstrates the lack of intensive research in these valuable collections.

Schmeidler, W. F. Carl. *Geschichte des Königreiches Griechenland. Nebst einem Rückblick auf die Vorgeschichte.* Heidelberg, 1877.

A largely derivative work, it repeats, virtually word for word, the same criticisms of regency policy as does the earlier work of Mendelssohn Bartholdy (this section above), but it gives wider coverage than Mendelssohn Bartholdy to the postregency period and it specifically enumerates and describes the parties, though somewhat confusedly and superficially.

Skandames, Andrew S. *Selides Politikes Historias kai Kritikes.* Tomos I: *He Triakontaetia tes Basileias tou Othonos 1832-1862* [*Pages of Political History and Criticism.* Vol. I: *The Thirty-year Period of the Kingship of Otho 1832-1862*]. Athens, 1961.

This massive tome, by the secretary of Prince Peter of Greece, is the most recent work on the Othonian period. It is a comprehensive summation of all previous research and addresses itself to the long-standing issues of Greek historiography, e.g. the merits of a regular army, centralization, an autocephalous church, and constitutionalism. The most valuable portion of the book is a concluding chapter on the Secret Archive of Otho in the Bavarian Geheimes Hausarchiv (I A above)— its history, its contents, research of Greek scholars in it, and progressive attempts to publish its contents. In the tradition of Petrakakos (II A), Skandames brings into print for the first time a few additional items of the Otho-Ludwig correspondence in the Secret Archive, though mostly for the postabsolutist period. The book also contains separate chapters on the parties and revolts and has the merit of appreciating the Crown's attempt to weaken the parties, but it fails to investigate either the parties or royal policy toward the parties in any depth or beyond what had already been done.

Thiersch, Heinrich W. J. *Griechenlands Schicksale vom Anfang des Be-*

freiungs-Krieges bis auf die gegenwärtige Krisis. Frankfurt am Main, 1863.

Written when Thiersch was docent at the University of Marburg, this very brief and sketchy treatment of the absolutist period focuses almost exclusively on the regency period and the revolution of 1843. Largely critical of the regency, especially for its military and ecclesiastical settlement and its failure to grant a constitution, it proposes what became the standard thesis of Greek historiography—that the regents, totally ignorant of Greek conditions and incurably doctrinaire, attempted to impose wholly unsuitable Western institutions in Greece.

Tsivanopoulos, Socrates. *Hellas, He Katastasis tes kata ten Basileian tou Basileos Othonos* [*Greece, Its Condition during the Reign of King Otho*]. Athens, 1864.

Vernardakes, Demetrios. *Kapodistrias kai Othon* [*Kapodistrias and Otho*]. New edn. Athens, 1962. First publ. anon. under title "Epistolimaia Bibliokrisia" ["Epistolary Book Review"] in *Nea Hemera* [*New Day*]. Trieste, 1875.

This long essay, which originated as a book review of Dragoumes' memoirs (II B above), is a minor classic in its depth of insight into the Greek character, in its patriotic national self-critique, and in its moving prose. In essence a sophisticated and well-argued critique of constitutionalism and irredentism, it offers no information or insights bearing directly on the questions raised in this study. Its significance rather lies in its addressing itself to the constitutionalist and irredentist issues which originated in the absolutist period (see Conclusion in the text and II D "Issues" in this bibliography above) and about which debate continued in Vernardakes' time.

Vlachos, Nicholas. *Historia tes Hellados, apo tes Basileias tou Othonos mechri tou Pangosmiou Polemou (1833-1914), kata tas paradoseis tou k. Nik. Vlachou . . .* [*History of Greece, from the Kingship of Otho to the World War, according to the Lectures of Mr. Nich. Vlachos . . .*]. Ed. Michael G. Grammatopoulos. Mimeographed, unbound. N.p., n.d.

In these classroom lectures, Vlachos, professor at the University of Athens, placed a good deal of emphasis on the parties. He pointed out the regency's involvement in party entanglements, but he did not supplement this with the observation that the regency attempted to remain above the parties, nor did he indicate why the regency did get involved. He stressed the royal policy of maintaining the tripartisan composition of successive cabinets and the necessity for this policy, but he failed to indicate the Crown's supplementary policy of successively giving one party preponderance. On the whole, these lectures were too general to be of much value for this study.

———. *Historia tes Hellados* [*History of Greece*]. 2nd edn. Athens, 1951.

Voulgares, N. T. *To Basileion tes Hellados kai he Hellenike Holomeleia (1833-1843)* [*The Kingdom of Greece and the Broader Hellenic Community (1833-1843)*]. Corfu, 1862.

Zinkeisen, J. W. *Geschichte Griechenlands vom Anfange geschichtlicher Kunde bis auf unsere Tage.* 4 vols. Leipzig, 1832-40.

B. TOPICAL STUDIES

The books listed in this section, most of them standard and scholarly, were consulted for background. Those in subsections 1, 3, 6, and some in subsection 4 (on the foundation of the bank and fiscal administration) provided valuable information on the products of statecraft, though only indirectly on statecraft itself. Those in subsection 2 and some in subsection 4 (on foreign loans) are important in describing the foreign influences that had such a direct bearing on the activities of the parties; those in subsections 5 and 7, are important in respectively analyzing the cultural schism and the social divisions to which the parties must be related. The majority of titles in subsection 4 (dealing with the economy) pass over the absolutist period quickly, quite justifiably in the case of those concerned with industry, because there was very little at the time. They were consulted, however, in an attempt to determine the size and political importance of the business elements. There is in these works, which were admittedly written without this question in mind, no evidence that these elements played any role in the parties. A letter from Chrestides to Palamides in the Palamides Archive (Hermoupolis, 9/12 Oct. 1843, folder 258) seems to indicate that the important merchant colony in Syros shied away from involvement in politics, at least at the time of the revolution of 1843. All in all, the chief value of all the works in this section was negative. By their general lack of concern with the parties and with statecraft as such, they point up the need to study the topics with which they deal in the light of party activity.

1. Administrative, Constitutional and Legal

Andreades, Stratis. *La Juridiction Administrative en Grèce.* Paris, 1932.

Chaniotis, C. L. *Le Conseil d'État en Grèce de 1830 à 1930. Comparaison avec le Conseil d'État en France.* Paris, 1930.

Couclelis, Alexandre P. *Les Régimes Gouvernementaux de la Grèce de 1821 à nos Jours.* Paris, 1921.

Kaltchas, Nicholas. *Introduction to the Constitutional History of Modern Greece.* New York, 1940.

Mirasgetzes, Demosthenes. *He Hellenike Poinike Nomothesia kata ta ete 1822-1834* [*Greek Penal Legislation between 1822-1834*]. Athens, 1934.
———. *Ho Protos Poinikos Kodix tes Neoteras Hellados* [*The First Penal Code of Modern Greece*]. Athens, 1940.

602

Paraskevopoulos, G. P. *Hoi Demarchoi ton Athenon, 1835-1907* [*The Mayors of Athens* . . .]. Athens, 1907.

Petrakakos, Demetrios A. *Koinobouleutike Historia tes Hellados* [*The Parliamentary History of Greece*]. 3 vols. Athens, 1935-46. See Petrakakos in II A above.

Somerites, Dionysios. *Ai Boulai tes Hellados* [*The Parliaments of Greece*] (n.p., n.d.).

——. *Peri tes Gerousias en Helladi* . . . [*Concerning the Senate in Greece* . . .]. Athens, 1924.

2. DIPLOMATIC

Andreou, Apostolos. *He Exoterike Politike tes Hellados 1833-1933* . . . [*The Foreign Policy of Greece* . . .]. Athens, 1933.

Driault, Édouard, and Michel Lhéritier. *Histoire Diplomatique de la Grèce de 1821 à nos jours.* 5 vols. Paris, 1925-26. See Driault in III A above.

Lascaris, Stamatios. *Diplomatike Historia tes Hellados, 1821-1914* [*Diplomatic History of Greece* . . .]. Athens, 1947.

Meletopoulos, Charilaos D. *He Europaike Diplomatia en Helladi* [*European Diplomacy in Greece*]. Athens, 1888.

3. ECCLESIASTICAL AND RELIGIOUS

Androutsos, Christos. *Ekklesia kai Politeia ex apopseos orthodoxou* [*Church and State from the Orthodox Point of View*]. Athens, 1920.

Atesis, Basil. *Epitomos Episkopike Historia tes Hellados* [*An Abridged Episcopal History of Greece*]. Athens, 1948.

——. *He Ekklesia ton Athenon apo tou 1833 mechri Semeron* [*The Church of Athens from 1833 to the Present*]. Athens, 1957.

Balanos, D. S. *Politeia kai Ekklesia* [*State and Church*]. Athens, 1920.

——. *Theokletos Pharmakides, 1784-1860* [*Theokletos Pharmakides* . . .]. Athens, 1933.

——. *Hai Threskeutikai Ideai tou Adamantiou Korae* [*The Religious Thought of Adamantios Koraes*]. Athens, 1920.

——. "Konstantinos Oikonomos ho ex Oikonomon" ["Constantine Oikonomos"]. *Ekklesia* [*Church*], XXXIV (1957), 491-98.

Charalampides, Theodore. See under Haralambides below.

Dyovouniotes, Constantine. "He kata to 1834 Dialysis ton Monasterion en te Eleuthera Helladi" ["The 1834 Dissolution of the Monasteries in Independent Greece"]. *Hieros Syndesmos* [*Sacred Association*], XII (1908), no. 84, pp. 1-5, and no. 85, pp. 1-4.

——. *Schesis Ekklesias kai Politeias en te Eleuthera Helladi* [*Church-State Relations in Independent Greece*]. Athens, 1916.

Frazee, Charles A. "The Orthodox Church of Greece from the Revolution of 1821 to 1852." Unpubl. doct. diss. Indiana Univ., 1965.

Haralambides, Theodor. "Die Kirchenpolitik Griechenlands." *Zeitschrift für Kirchengeschichte*, VI (1935), 158-92.

Konidares, Gerasimos. *Ecclesiastike Historia tes Hellados* [*Ecclesiastical History of Greece*]. 2 vols. Athens, 1954-60.

Kostarides, Eugenios. *He Synchronos Hellenike Ekklesia . . . 1821-1921* [*The Contemporary Greek Church . . .*]. Athens, 1921.

Kourilas, Eulogios. *Patriarchike Historia. To Oikoumenikon Patriarcheion . . . To autokephalon tes Hellenikes Ekklesias . . .* [*Patriarchal History. The Ecumenical Patriarchates . . . The Autocephaly of the Greek Church . . .*] Athens, 1951.

Levides, N. D. *Agoreusis enopion tes Syneleuseos peri threskeias* [*Address before the Assembly concerning Religion*]. Athens, 1926.

———. *Ta kata tes Ekklesias tolmethenta* [*Acts attempted against the Church*]. Athens, 1921.

Papadopoulos, Chrysostomos. *Ekklesia Athenon* [*The Church of Athens*]. Athens, 1928.

———. *Historia tes Ekklesias tes Hellados* [*History of the Church of Greece*]. Athens, 1920.

Petrakakos, Demetrios. "Zur rechtlichen Stellung der hellenischen Kirche." In *Festschrift für Emil Friedberg*. Leipzig, 1908. Pp. 269-86.

Saloutos, Theodore. "American Missionaries in Greece: 1820-1869." *Church History*, XXIV (1955) 52-74.

Stephanides, Basil. *Ekklesiastike Historia ap'Arches mechri semeron* [*Ecclesiastical History from the Beginning until Today*]. Athens, 1948.

Vovolines, Constantine. *He Ekklesia eis ton Agona tes Eleutherias* [*The Church in the Struggle for Independence*]. Athens, 1952.

4. ECONOMIC AND FISCAL

Andreades, Andrew M. *Historia ton Ethnikon Daneion* [*History of the National Debts*]. Athens, 1904.

———. *Oeuvres.* Eds. K. Ch. Varvaressos, G. A. Petropoulos, and J. D. Pontos. 3 vols. Athens, 1938-40. In Greek and French.

Anastasopoulos, George. *Historia tes Hellenikes Biomechanias 1840-1940* [*History of Greek Industry . . .*]. 3 vols. Athens, 1947.

Charitakes. *He Hellenike Biomechania* [*Greek Industry*]. Athens, 1927.

Chrestines, D. *Meletai peri tes en Helladi Georgias . . .* [*Studies concerning Agriculture in Greece . . .*]. Athens, 1899.

Dosios, L. *Peri Biomechanias en Helladi* [*Concerning Industry in Greece*]. Athens, 1871.

Evelpides, Christos. *Oikonomike Historia tes Neoteras Hellados* [*Economic History of Modern Greece*]. Phlamma, 1939.

———. *Oikonomike kai Koinonike Historia tes Hellados* [*Economic and Social History of Greece*]. Athens, 1950.

Kampouroglou, Panteleon. *Historia tou Peiraios apo tou 1833-1882 . . .*

[*History of Piraeus from 1833-1842. General Conditions, Commercial, Naval, and Industrial Activity*]. Athens, 1883.

Kirkilitses, Andrew. *Hai Trapezai en Helladi* [*Banks in Greece*]. Athens, 1934.

Kordatos, John. *Eisagoge eis ten Historian tes Hellenikes Kephalaiokratias* [*Introduction to the History of Greek Capitalism*]. Athens, 1930.

Levandes, John A. *The Greek Foreign Debt and the Great Powers, 1821-1898.* New York, 1944.

Liakopoulos, E. *Ethnika Chreoi* [*National Debts*]. Athens, 1893.

Phragides, A. K. *Peri ton Proton Emporon tes Syrou kai tou Emporiou auton* [*Concerning the First Merchants of Syros and their Commerce*]. Athens, 1902.

Pyrsos, George. *Symbole eis ten Historian tes Trapezes tes Hellados* [*Contribution to the History of the Bank of Greece*]. 2 vols. Athens, 1936-46.

Raptarches, K. P. *Historia tes oikonomikes zoes tes Hellados* [*History of the Economic Life of Greece*]. Athens, 1934-36.

Sideres, A. D. *He Georgike Politike tes Hellados . . . 1833-1933* [*The Agricultural Policy of Greece . . .*]. Athens, 1934.

————. *Historia tou Oikonomikou Biou* [*History of Economic Life*]. Athens, 1944.

Soutsos, J. *Ploutologia* [*Plutocracy*]. 2nd edn. 2 vols. Athens, 1882-85.

Speliotakes, S. *Statistike tes Georgias* [*Agricultural Statistics*]. Athens, 1864.

Tompazes, Al. *Ta Paragogika Stoicheia en te Hellenike Georgia* [*The Productive Elements in Greek Agriculture*]. Leipzig, 1871.

Valaorites, P. A. *Ethnike Trapeza tes Hellados 1842-1902* [*The National Bank of Greece*]. Athens, 1902.

Vernadakes, L. *Peri tou en Helladi Emporiou* [*Concerning Commerce in Greece*]. Athens, 1885.

Zographos, Demetrios L. *Historia tes Hellenikes Georgias* [*The History of Greek Agriculture*]. 3 vols. Athens, 1921-24.

————. *Historia tes Hidryseos tes Ethnikes Trapezes 1833-45* [*The History of the Establishment of the National Bank*]. 2 vols. Athens, 1925-27.

5. Intellectual and Cultural

Chaconas, S. G. *Adamantios Korais: A Study in Greek Nationalism.* New York, 1942.

Demaras, Constantine Th. *Historia tes Neohellenikes Logotechnias* [*History of Modern Greek Literature*]. Vol. ɪ: Athens, 1948. 2nd edn.: [Athens], n.d.

————. *Ho Koraes kai he epoche tou* [*Koraes and his Age*]. Athens, 1953.

Parascos, Cleon. "La Grèce et les Influences Intellectuelles Occidentales." *L'Hellénisme Contemporain*, 2nd ser., ɪ (1947), 254-58, ɪɪ (1948), 444-52.

Turczynski, Emanuel. *Die deutsch-griechischen Kulturbeziehungen bis zur Berufung König Ottos.* Südosteuropäische Arbeiten, no. 48. Munich, 1959.

6. MILITARY

Greece, General Staff of the Army, Directorate of the History of the Army. *Historia tes Organoseos tou Hellenikou Stratou 1821-1954* [*History of the Organization of the Greek Army . . .*]. Athens, 1957.

Kteniades, N. *He Hellenike Chorophylake. Historikai Selides.* [*The Greek Gendarmerie. Historical Pages*]. Vol. I. 2nd edn. Athens, 1960.

7. SOCIAL

Argyropoulos, Pericles A. "Les Grecs au service de l'empire ottoman." In *1453-1953: Le cinq-centième anniversaire de la prise de Constantinople.* Athens, 1953.

Bournas, Tasos. *Harmatoloi kai Klephtes* [*Armatoloi and Klephts*]. Athens, 1958.

Giannopoulos, Pyrros Epeirotes. *Hoi phanariotai* [*The Phanariots*]. Athens, 1929.

Gottwald, Joseph. "Phanariotische Studien." *Leipziger Vierteljahresschrift für Südosteuropa,* v (1941), 1-58.

Held, Hans Walter. "Die Phanarioten, ihre allmähliche Entwicklung zur fürstlichen Aristokratie bis zu deren Untergang 1821." Unpubl. diss. Bern, 1920.

Iorga, N. "Le despotisme éclairé dans les pays roumains au XVIIIᵉ siècle." *Bulletin of the International Committee of Historical Sciences,* IX (1937), 100-15. On the Phanariots.

Kandeloros, Takes. *Ho Harmatolismos tes Peloponnesou 1500-1821* [*Armatolism in the Peloponnesos . . .*]. Athens, 1924.

Miller, William. *The Early Years of Modern Athens.* Athens, 1925.

Oikonomopoulos, Elias I. *Harmatoloi kai Klephtai, etoi Tourkokratia en Helladi (1453-1829)* [*Armatoloi and Klephts, or Turkish Rule in Greece*]. Athens, 1902.

Panagiotopoulos, B. P. "Nea Stoicheia peri tou thesmou ton Kapon en Peloponneso" ["New Items about the Institution of Kapoi in the Peloponnesos"]. *Deltion tes Historikes kai Ethnologikes Hetaireias tes Hellados* [*Bulletin of the Historical and Ethnological Society of Greece*], XI (1956), 78-85.

Stamatopoulos, Take A. *Ho Esoterikos Agonas, prin kai kata ten Epanastase tou 1821* [*The Internal Struggle, before and during the Revolution of 1821*]. 2 vols. Athens, 1957-64.

Vlachogiannes, John. *Klephtes tou Moria (1715-1820)* [*Klephts of the Morea . . .*]. Athens, 1935.

Zallony, M. P. *Essai sur les Fanariotes.* Marseilles, 1824.

C. WORKS OF SPECIAL RELEVANCE TO PARTIES

The few titles under this heading reveal the extent to which parties have been neglected as a subject of serious research. The works by Antonakeas and Philaretos are unscholarly and simply have an axe to grind. The Blancard, Eardley-Wilmot, and Eliopoulos studies are general biographies which do not deal in any depth with the relation of their subjects to the parties, although the Eardley-Wilmot biography is based on a private collection of Lyons' correspondence, some of which he quotes (i c above).

The scholarly article of Eleutheropoulos and the equally scholarly book by Daphnes dismiss these early parties as mere personal coteries. The latter work especially is a good example of how one's general frame of reference can limit one's appreciation of raw data and pose an obstacle to serious research. It defines "party" as a group of beings organized in a stable fashion and designed to gain or keep control over the established regime for the advantage of its followers and it acknowledges the existence of those three political groupings with which this book is concerned. And yet, by positing an electoral and parliamentary system of government as an indispensable condition for the formation and functioning of parties, he denies these entities the status of parties, even though they do meet his original definition. He insists that one cannot talk about parties until after the revolution of 1843, which ushered in a constitutional regime.

Only four items, pioneering in their concern for political groupings and in their intensive research, shed light on the parties by dealing with their embryonic antecedents. All four are limited in scope, one (Sakellariou) to the factional divisions in pre-Revolutionary Peloponnesos, the other three (Dakin, Rados, and Vlachos) to the origins of the three foreign-oriented parties between 1824-26. Dakin's revealing account is a by-product of his interest in the influence of philhellenes, but he unearths a great wealth of valuable material from the Public Record Office (both Colonial Office and Foreign Office Records), especially from the correspondence of British officials in the Ionian Islands (see i A and under Dakin in ii A above). Rados also deals only indirectly with the rise of these parties, as a by-product of his reconstruction of the Orleanist attempt, on the basis of an analysis of the extant petitions to, and replies from, the Duke of Orléans, which he publishes in toto. Vlachos is directly concerned with the origins of the parties and bases his account largely on the published papers of Count Dionysios Roma (*Historikon Archeion 1819-1825* [*Historical Archive . . .*], ed. D. Kampouroglou, 2 vols. [Athens, 1901-1906]), an Ionian Greek, who was directly involved in the politics of 1824-26. But Vlachos' monograph is a one-shot affair. One could only wish that he had studied the career of the parties after they had been conceived.

Antonakeas, Nicholas. *Phaulokratia. Politike Historia Hellados, 1821-1950. He Hellas hypo ten dinen ton kommaton* [*Rule by Villany. The Political History of Greece, 1821-1950. Greece in the Whirlpool of Parties*]. 2 vols. Athens, 1950. Vol. I: 1821-1914.

Blancard, Jules. *Études sur la Grèce contemporaine. Alexandre Mavrocordato. Les Métaxas. Coletti.* Montpellier, 1886.

Dakin, Douglas. *British and American Philhellenes during the War of Greek Independence, 1821-1833.* Institute for Balkan Studies, no. 8. Thessaloniki, 1962.

Daphnes, Gregory. *Ta Hellenika Politika Kommata* [*The Greek Political Parties*]. Athens, 1956. Reedited. Athens, 1961.

Eardley-Wilmot, Sydney. *Life of Vice-Admiral Edmund, Lord Lyons.* London, 1898.

Eleutheropoulos, A. "Koinonikai taxeis kai koinonika kommata" ["Social Classes and Social Parties"]. *Archeion ton Oikonomikon kai koinonikon epistemon* [*Archive of Economic and Social Sciences*], I (1921), 3-19.

Eliopoulos, Demetrios. *Ioannes Kolettes* [*John Kolettes*]. Athens, 1890.

Georgiou, Elias P. ed. and trans. *Th. Piskatores peri Ioannou Kolettou* [*Th. Piscatory concerning John Kolettes*]. Athens, 1952. See II A above.

Korisis, Hariton. *Die politischen Parteien Griechenlands. Ein neuer Staat auf dem Weg zur Demokratie 1821-1910.* Hersbruck/Nürnberg, 1966. (Appeared after the manuscript of this book was completed.)

Philaretos, George N. *Xenokratia kai Basileia en Helladi, 1821-1897* [*Foreign Rule and Royalty in Greece*]. Athens, 1897.

Rados, Constantine. "Peri to Stemma tes Hellados. He Apopeira ton Orleanidon (1825-1826)" ["Concerning the Greek Crown. The Orleanist Attempt"]. *Epeteris . . .* [*Annual of the Philological Society 'Parnassos'*)], 2nd per., XIII (1918), 35-116.

Sakellariou, Michael B. *He Peloponnesos kata ten deuteran Tourkokratian (1715-1821)* [*The Peloponnesos during the Second Period of Turkish Rule*]. Texte und Forschungen zur byzantinischen und neugriechischen Philologie, no. 33. Athens, 1939.

Vlachos, Nicholas. "He Genesis tou Anglikou, tou Gallikou, kai tou Rosikou Kommatos en Helladi" ["The Genesis of the English, French, and Russian Parties in Greece"]. *Archeion Oikonomikon kai Koinonikon Epistemon* [*Archive of Economic and Social Sciences*], XIX (1939), 25-44.

D. SPECIALIZED STUDIES ON 1833-43

Very little detailed research has been done on the period 1833-43. The major events still await their historians. Events of the regency period have received most attention. Mendelssohn Bartholdy's study, incorporated in his two-volume work (III A above), served as the basis for Kandeloros' detailed and detached work, which also makes extensive use of newspaper sources. Broadly conceived, it deals with the Messenian revolt and the regency disputes as well as with the trial and preliminary investigation, and thus has become standard, but it is a chronicle rather than an interpretive work. A more recent study of the same event is that of Photiades. The two studies by Kteniades, dealing with the same period, are cited by Kordatos in his history (III A) but came to my attention too late for consultation.

The Argyropoulos monographs are the only detailed treatment of the Mavrokordatos episode. They are based on documents in the Mavrokordatos Archive and in the Zographos Archive (whose location is not stated), and made use of available secondary sources, but are misleading in their portrayal of Mavrokordatos' program as a "constitutional attempt." In a prior lecture, he had made the mistake of representing Mavrokordatos as an advocate of a constitution in the literal sense. In these articles, he retracts that thesis, but only in part, because he still writes about an attempt to place curbs on Otho through some written charter of fundamental laws. Although there is much valuable detail in these articles, there is no attempt to deal with the operations of the parties as such and no awareness of their role in developments during 1841.

The two remaining studies deal with separate aspects of 1833-43 as a part of longer periods. Engel-Janosi's article is an excellent account of Austrian policy toward Greece, both as it was conceived by Metternich in Austria and carried out by Prokesch-Osten in Greece. It also contains valuable information on Ludwig's and Otho's policies and on the interaction of the powers in Greece. Rall's article is a carefully documented study in diplomatic history on the question of the personal religious confession of the Greek monarch as an issue of official European concern and action. The issue, raised by the Catholic faith of Otho as king of an Orthodox people, is treated in terms of Bavarian religio-political divisions and European diplomatic differences and according to its progressive phases up to 1836 (the selection of a monarch for the Greek throne, the consideration of Otho's conversion to Orthodoxy, the question of his choice of a queen and the upbringing of any future offspring). It provides a detailed account of the role of Ludwig in Greek policy and the pressure of Russian diplomacy in Greece during the first three years of the royal period. It also describes the religious settlement of 1833, its origins and immediate consequences, the only part of the article in which the Greek domestic picture comes into view. The excellence of both studies, like those of Dickopf and Koeppel (III E below), derives from both the competence and thoroughness of their authors *and* the use of valuable unpublished source material. Engel-Janosi relied heavily on the private papers of Prokesch-Osten as well as the Austrian and British foreign office archives; and Rall made excellent use of materials in both the Bavarian Haus- und Staatsarchiv (I A).

Argyropoulos, Pericle A. "Ho Alexandros Mavrokordatos kai he Syntagmatike Prospatheia tou 1841" ["Alexander Mavrokordatos and the Constitutional Attempts of 1841"]. *Hellenika*, VIII (1935), 247-67, IX (1936), 85-102.

Engel-Janosi, Friedrich. "Austria and the Beginnings of the Kingdom of Greece." *Journal of Central European Affairs*, I (April, 1941), 28-44, (July, 1941), 208-23. Also publ. in German trans. under title "Österreich und die Anfänge des Königreiches Griechenland" in Friedrich Engel-Janosi, *Geschichte auf dem Ballhausplatz. Essays zur österreichischen Aussenpolitik 1830-1945* (Graz, 1963), pp. 29-64.

Jelavich, Barbara. *Russia and the Greek Revolution of 1843*. Südosteuropäische Arbeiten, no. 65. Munich, 1966. See under Jelavich in II A above.

Kandeloros, Takes. *He Dike tou Kolokotrone kai he Epanastasis tes Peloponnesou* [*The Kolokotrones Trial and the Peloponnesian Revolution*]. Athens, 1906.

Kteniades, N. "He Maniatike Epanastasis" ["The Maniat Revolt"]. *Proia* [*Morning*], 9 May 1936.

———. "He Messeniake Epanastasis" ["The Messenian Revolt"]. *Stratiotike Echo* [*Military Echo*], I (1932).

Photiades, Demetrios. *Kolokotrones. He Dike tou* [*Kolokotrones. His Trial*]. Athens, 1962.

Rall, Hans. "Die Anfänge des Konfessionspolitischen Ringens um den Wittelsbacher Thron in Athen." In *Bayern: Staat und Kirche, Land und Reich, Forschungen zur bayerischen Geschichte vornehmlich im 19. Jahrhundert*. Ed. Wilhelm Winkler. Munich, 1961. Pp. 181-215.

E. STUDIES ON BAVARIANS IN GREECE

The three Bavarians having the greatest impact on Greece were obviously Otho, Ludwig, and Amalia. For a list of biographies on these three, the reader should refer to footnote references in the text (Chap. VI, n. 28, on Otho; Chap. III, n. 87, on Ludwig; and Chap. V, n. 117, on Amalia). The list below enumerates existing biographies of other influential Bavarians: Abel (Gollwitzer), Armansperg (R. Armansperg), Maurer (Dickopf), Rudhart (Koeppel), and Thiersch (Loewe). The Gollwitzer, Armansperg, and Koeppel biographies are dissertations in typescript, to which I have not had access. Dickopf's competent biography of Maurer, which exploits pertinent materials in the Bavarian Geheimes Staatsarchiv and the Maureriana collection in the Bavarian Staatsbibliothek (I A above), is essentially a description and evaluation of Maurer's role as a legist in the context of nineteenth-century German legal scholarship, and it deals only briefly with Maurer's career in Greece and then only in terms of his function as jurist and legislator (*Gezetzgeber*). Although it gives nothing new on Maurer's political involvement as regent, it does offer the same view—vis-à-vis Maurer's laying the foundation of the modern Greek legal system—as this book does in connection with his role in institution-building; namely, that Maurer was no mere doctrinaire theoretician oblivious to existing realities in Greece.

There are two works specifically relating individual Bavarians to their role in Greece: Koeppel on Rudhart and Loewe on Thiersch. The short monograph of Koeppel, an extract from his doctoral dissertation, is based on Bavarian, Austrian, and Prussian archives (I A above), as well as published documents. An account of Rudhart's prime-ministership in Greece, it is the only account of this subject which treats Rudhart's experience as a duel with Otho as well as with Lyons. He recognizes Rudhart's attempt to rally all the parties and hence nullify their influence, he substantiates the contemporary charges about the identification of his and Austria's blueprint for Greece (although it also becomes clear that the blueprint was far more enlightened than contemporary critics believed), he demonstrates the staunch support received by Rudhart from Russia and Austria, and he gives a detailed treatment of Rudhart's attempt to purge the court of Armansperg's friends and establish his own influence there. Indeed, this account coincides remarkably with the one I had previously reconstructed on the basis of Lyons' despatches, showing incidentally the reliability of Lyons' information.

The collective role of Bavarians in Greece from 1833 to 1843 has a limited literature. A recent work deals directly and comprehensively, though not in great depth, with this subject (Seidl). One treats the subject as a part of the phenomenon of Bavarians abroad (Schottenloher). These works deal with the subject from the Bavarian point of view. A study of the subject from the Greek standpoint, dealing with the Bavarian impact on Greece and Greek reaction to the Bavarians, remains to be done.

For published memoirs of numerous Bavarians who served in Greece, the reader should refer to citations in II B above.

Armansperg, R. von. "Joseph Ludwig Graf v. Armansperg." Unpubl. diss. Munich, 1949.

Dickopf, Karl. *Georg Ludwig von Maurer 1790-1872. Eine Biographie.* Münchener historische Studien. Abteilung neuere Geschichte. Ed. Franz Schnabel. Kallmünz, 1960.

Gollwitzer, Heinz. "Karl August von Abel und seine Politik 1837-1847." Unpubl. diss. Munich, 1944.

Koeppel, Ferdinand. *Die griechische Ministerpräsidentschaft J. v. Rudharts unter König Otto. Teildruck aus Ignaz von Rudhart. Eine politische Biographie.* Kallmünz, 1931.

———. "Rudhart, ein Staatsmann des Frühliberalismus." Unpubl. diss. Munich, 1933. See also under Koeppel in II A above.

Loewe, H. *Friedrich Thiersch und die griechische Frage.* Munich, 1913.
————. Friedrich Thiersch. *Ein Humanistenleben im Rahmen der Geistes-
geschichte seiner Zeit.* Munich, Berlin, 1925. See also under Thiersch,
Heinrich, in II A above.

Schottenloher, Karl. *Die Bayern in der Fremde.* Schriftenreihe zur bayer.
Landesgeschichte, no. 44. Munich, 1950.

Seidl, Wolf. *Bayern in Griechenland. Die Geschichte eines Abenteuers.*
Munich, 1965.

Söltl, J. M. von, *Ludwig I König von Bayern und Graf von Armansperg.*
Nördlingen, 1886. See under Söltl in II A above.

Index

Abel, Karl von, 155-57, 171, 211-12, 220-21, 229, 234, 243, 269. *See also* regency, regency majority

Aberdeen, Lord, 430, 458n8, 459, 494. *See also* Britain

absolutism: *monarchical (royal)*, 150, 226, 233, 286; establishment and relation to party situation, 158-61, 374, 515; and Bavarianism, 164; and centralization, 175; and ecclesiastical settlement of 1833, 183; under Armansperg, 255-56; Otho's preference for and party situation, 271; principle of, 272-73; temporary espousal by "Russian" party, 303, 328, 507; and fusionism, 308

    personal (Othonian): 322, 329, 361, 442; as issue in dispute between Otho and Rudhart, 272-73, 276, 278; new system of, 279-84; British criticism of, 321, 367, 388n104; and response of Constitutionalist opposition, 325-26, 427; and Mavrokordatos program (1841), 344, 386-88, 398; continuation in period of "French" ascendancy, 408, 411, 419, 422-23; uniting of parties in opposition to and revolution of 1843, 406-407, 411, 458, 461, 466, 513; impact on parties, 501, 503. *See also* anaktovoulion, monarchy, Otho

Acarnania, 33, 91, 139, 194n99, 262, 360, 384, 468n24, 484n63

Acarnanian revolt, 243, 252, 261-65, 269, 314

Achaia, 64, 132-33, 139, 334, 405n63, 522

Achaia-Elis (nomarchy), 263, 424

Achaikon faction, 64-65, 67

Acheron (river), 32

Acropolis, 75, 137

Adam, Frederick, 98-99

administration, 16 and n25, 21, 41, 90, 94, 168, 198, 238, 282n26, 370-71, 386, 414n12, 430, 431n51, 481, 507-508; paralysis by 1841, 12, 344, 373-78; under Ottoman rule, 20, 24, 26-27, 62-63, 74-75; and relation to parties (dilemma of administrative deterrence), 111, 213, 217, 311, 385, 378-79, 512-13; as basis for Kapodistrian "Russian" party, 112, 131-32, 291-92, 438n66; breakdown in 1832, 147-50;

permanent system of centralization established (1833), 160, 172-75, 183, 189, 385; Bavarians and French employed in, 162, 408, 418-19; checks and balances, 173-74, 373-74, 289n35; fiscal and tax system, 175-80, 317-21; Crown policy of representation for all parties in, 193, 196, 198, 288-90, 300, 512-13; under Armansperg, 243, 250-53, 255, 260; and demands of Britain, France, and Russia, 260, 264, 296-97, 363, 401, 409, 437; Rudhart and Otho's interference with, 273, 275-76; under Otho's personal rule, 285-86, 303-305; "Russian" domination of and Glarakes, 286-87, 303, 305-307, 309-11, 339; and Mavrokordatos program, 392n111, 394n116, 402-40; and "French" ascendancy, 410-11. *See also* bureaucracy, centralization, dilemma of administrative deterrence, finance, taxation

admirals, *see* protecting powers

adoption, 33, 57, 58

Adrianople, 135; treaty of (1829), 47, 200; bishop of, 184

Aegean (sea), 123

Aegean Islands (Archipelago), 26-27, 34, 114, 123, 133, 405. *See also* Islands, Cyclades, Psara, Sporades

Aegina, 115, 133, 248n66, 336, 343, 524; "English" assembly of, 105

Aetolia, 33, 113, 138, 194n99, 262

Agathangelos, 333

agoyates, 36

Agrapha, 33, 72, 138

Aigion, 64, 66, 399n127. *See also* Vostitsa

Ainian, George, 100-101, 128n49, 246, 297, 319, 334, 383, 385, 447, 481n55, 519, 521-22, 524, 536

Aiōn, 8, 311, 313, 341, 421n31, 427, 430, 480; and brigandage, 311; and constitutionalism, 327-28, 334, 521; and Philorthodox plot, 333, 341, 529n10, 530; and abortive Greco-Turkish treaty of commerce, 352, 354; and Mavrokordatos episode, 400; and missionary question, 424-25; truce with *Athēna*, 428; and political opposition, 429 and n48; and senate dispute, 495. *See also* Philemon

Aix-la-Chapelle, congress of, 107

613

and Protestant missionaries, 42, 296, 312-13, 425, 427; and Greek Russophilism, 43, 102; and question of confession of Greek monarch, 52, 147, 198, 284, 346n3, 433, 447, 449 and n92, 458, 472, 476, 479, 491-92, 507; and party divisions in Greece, 131n58; and church in Greece, 181; and religious issue in Greece, 189-91; and "Russian" party, 292, 506; and Philorthodox plot, 331, 334-35, 521, 526; and constitution of 1844, 473n36, 483. *See also* church in Greece; Constantinople, patriarchate of

Otho, king of Greece, 3, 42, 165, 190, 199, 209, 227-28, 249, 256, 259n93, 295, 329, 354n17, 380, 383, 413n11, 427, 430n50 496-97, 503, 504n5, 507-508, 510, 514-15; opposes constitution for Greece, 15, 158-59, 270-71; election and treaty of 7 May 1832, 51-52, 144-45, 147, 149, 161; political responses in Greece to prospective arrival of, 130-31, 133-34, 167; arrival in Greece, 150, 153-54; policy towards parties in Greece, 157, 196, 285-90, 442; and ecclesiastical settlement of 1833, 183-84; Catholicism and question of religious confession of Greek monarch, 191, 198, 284, 315n96; and "major"-"minor" plots, 202; and regency crisis, 206, 212; absence from Greece (1836) and Greek opposition to Armansperg, 218, 264-68; conflict with Armansperg and office of archchancellor, 218, 229-35, 244, 250, 255, 257, 261, 268-69; and Messenian revolt (1834), 221-22; unfavorable reports about health of, 230-32 and n30, 257, 261, 322; accession and statecraft (1835), 235-36, 241n53; trust in Austria, 258; and Acarnanian revolt, 262; marriage to Amalia of Oldenburg and return to Greece, 268; conflict with Rudhart (1837), 270-77; personal absolutism of, 279-82, 325; personal characteristics of, 283-84; Russophil policy, administration of (1838-39), 290-306, 311, 313-15, 317-20; relations with Lyons and Britain, 301-302, 304, 321-22; and fusionism, 307-308; and Philorthodox plot, 330-41, 521, 523, 527-28, 530; and Near Eastern crisis (1839-41), 348, 360-61; and abortive

Greco-Turkish treaty of commerce, 349-50, 352-53, 356; and Greek irredentism (Great Idea), 356, 358, 360-61, 522; relations with Britain (1840-41), 362-70, 402; and administrative paralysis, 376-77; and Mavrokordatos episode, 344, 361, 386-400, 404, 406-407; Francophil policy and continuation of personal absolutism (1841-43), 401-403, 408-10, 415-19; opposition to and tripartisan conspiracy against, 423, 430, 433 and n59; financial crisis and opposition of powers and parties to, 437-38, 440 and n70, 441-42; and revolution of 1843, 443-44, 446-51; during period of constituent assembly, 455, 457-58, 460-61, 463-70, 472, 474-76, 479-80, 482n57; and constitution of 1844, 459, 473-74, 476, 479, 491-94, 498-99. *See also* absolutism, Crown, monarchy, parties

Ottoman empire (Turkey), Osmanlis, and Turks, 5n3, 42, 69, 75, 80, 88, 122, 139, 169, 213, 236, 265n109, 426, 473n35; and Greek irredentism (Great Idea), 12, 23, 52, 200, 331, 334, 344-48, 350-51, 355-59, 361, 458 and n8, 507-508 and n8, 510-11; Greek trade with and abortive Greco-Turkish treaty of commerce, 14, 348-49, 352, 354-56, 364, 504, 511; pre-Revolutionary Greek local autonomy under, 19, 24, 28, 120-21, 173, 175; and Greek Revolution, 19-20, 22, 41, 46, 48, 70, 81, 84-85, 93-95, 113, 115, 118, 147, 156, 176, 180-81, 188, 296, 491; and Greek sectionalism, 19-21; pre-Revolutionary Greek social divisions and administration under, 24-28, 30-35, 38, 51, 71, 73, 180; pre-Revolutionary Greek clienteles and factions under, 29, 53, 55, 61, 64-67; Greek attitudes toward, 37, 39-41; Greek Revolution, European powers, and Eastern Question, 43, 45, 47, 100-101; and Russia, 77, 200, 297, 334; and Near Eastern crisis (1839-41), 344, 348; revolution of 1843 and Eastern Question, 458 and n8. *See also* Porte

otzaks, 32, 109n6

Padua, University of, 107, 114, 117
Païkos, Andronikos, 71, 277, 287, 299-300, 310, 337-38, 340, 354n17, 358,

treaty of 7 May 1832, 48, 144-46, 161, 197, 218, 244, 491
Triantaphylles, 530
Tricoupis, *see* Trikoupes
Trieste, 333
Trikorphois, 79-80
Trikoupes, Charilaos, 508n7
Trikoupes, Spyridon, 118, 127, 131n57, 158, 204, 289n35, 306n76, 363n44, 415; and "English" party, 91, 98, 101-102, 128n49, 129-30, 136, 198, 245; and Hyra revolt (1831), 120-21, 123; and ecclesiastical settlement of 1833, 185n76, 188; as Greek minister to London (1834-38), 195, 206, 279, 308; and constitutionalism, 327; and abortive Greco-Turkish treaty of commerce, 353, 354n17; return to London and Mavrokordatos episode, 365-66, 390-92; and Lyons, 369-70, 372; in constituent assembly, 481n55, 484, 490, 540
Tripolis, 28, 67-68, 76, 117, 139, 202, 214, 224, 227, 334, 375, 381n85, 381n86, 522
Triptolemos, 128
Troezene, constitution of, 49, 110, 131
Troezene, third national assembly of, 48, 105, 110, 118
Troumpianes', 120
Tsamados', 59, 540
Tsamados, Anastasios, 133, 488, 540
Tsamados, M. A., 540
Tsamales, An., 223n13
Tsanetakes, *see* Tzanetakes
tsar of Russia, 44, 97, 102, 190, 201-202, 298, 428, 519. *See also* Alexander I, Nicholas I, Russia
Tsavelas, *see* Tzavelas
Tselios, Demos, 262
Tsimova, 120-21
Tsokres, Demetrios, 134, 224n16, 247, 334, 420, 522, 540
Tsolakoglou's, 72
Tsongas, George, 91-92, 113, 263, 540
Tsouras, 466
Turkey and Turks, *see* Ottoman empire
Typaldos, John, 224n16, 310n87, 340-42, 524, 530-32, 541
Tzanetakes', 32, 69, 120, 140, 210, 541
Tzanetakes, 419, 541
Tzavelas', 32, 59, 116, 541
Tzavelas, Kitsos, 32, 58, 91, 94, 115-16,

126, 132-33, 198, 203, 241, 247n63, 263, 287-88, 300, 332, 541
Tzenos, A., 362, 365, 443n80, 468n24

United States, 424
university, national, 191, 249n69, 315, 332, 378, 513, 278n16
Usiglio incident, 301

Vagias, George, 203n119, 224n16, 541
Valetas, Spyridon, 394-95, 397, 399, 410, 428, 541
Vallianos, Theodore, 114, 117-18, 224n16, 529, 541
Valsamakes, Demetrios, 114, 335, 523, 527, 530-31, 541
Valsamakes, N., 443n80
Valsamakes, P., 224n16
Valtinos, George, 33, 223n11, 246n62, 267-68, 541
Valtos, 113
Valves, Peter, 340, 531
Vamvas, Neophytos, 136, 312, 486, 541
Varnakiotes, George, 33, 91, 113, 541
Vasos, *see* Mavrovouniotes
Vaudreuil, 211
Veïkos, Constantine, 348n6, 447
vekiles, 28, 66-67
Velentzas, John, 94, 138, 359-60, 399n127, 414, 490, 524, 541
Vellisarios, 530
Venice and Venetians, 22, 38, 70, 107
Venizelos-Rouphos', 68
Venthylos, John, 341, 541
Veres, 522
Vervena, 73, 78
veterans, 165, 167, 170-71, 213, 487-88, 504. *See also* irregulars
Vienna, 195, 278n16
Vienna, congress and treaty of (peace of 1815), 22, 36, 107
villages, 27, 31, 119, 139, 148, 227-28, 253-54, 265n109, 286n31, 309n84, 383-84, 515
Villévêque, Laisné, 98, 101
Vitales', 99
Vitales, George, 98, 100, 104
Vitales, Spyros, 98
Vizoulas, John, 319
Vlachopoulos, Alexakes, 408-409, 446
Vlachopoulos, Nicholas, 91, 231n31, 541
Vlachoutses, 428n47
Vlachs, 36, 85-86
Vlases, Christos, 213, 490, 541